RANDOM HOUSE
DICTIONARY OF

AMERICA'S
POPULAR
PROVERBS

and

SAYINGS

Second Edition

RANDOM HOUSE DICTIONARY OF

AMERICA'S POPULAR PROVERBS

and

SAYINGS

Second Edition

GREGORY TITELMAN

Random House Dictionary of America's Popular Proverbs and Sayings, Second Edition

Copyright © 2000 by Gregory Titelman

Library of Congress Cataloging-in-Publication Data is available.

Typeset by Random House Reference & Information Publishing
    and Seaside Press
Printed in the United States of America

Visit the Random House Reference & Information Publishing Web
    site at www.randomwords.com

Second Edition
9 8 7 6 5 4 3 2 1
April 2000
SAP: 10037278
ISBN: 0-375-70584-8

New York   Toronto   London   Sydney   Auckland

CONTENTS

ACKNOWLEDGMENTS

To my children
Elena, Faina and Selig

and, of course,
to my grandchildren.

INTRODUCTION

This new second edition of *The Random House Dictionary of America's Popular Proverbs and Sayings* expands on the well-received first edition, which was published in 1996 under the title *Random House Dictionary of Popular Proverbs and Sayings* and was included on William Safire's *New York Times Magazine* list of best dictionaries for 1997.

This edition features more than 100 new entries along with up-to-the-minute citations taken from a variety of media. The "new arrivals" include recently coined sayings, such as *Pushing the envelope, It takes a village to raise a child, Step up to the plate, the mother of all (battles)*; historical and scientific sayings, such as *Happy is the country which has no history, Fifty million Frenchmen can't be wrong, There are lies, damned lies, and statistics, My lips are sealed*, and *Self-preservation is the first law of nature*; plus dozens of other familiar sayings such as *A house divided against itself cannot stand, All I know is what I read in the papers, No one is above the law, Remember the Alamo!, You ain't seen nothin' yet* and many, many more.

My greatest reward as an author is hearing from readers who use the dictionary of proverbs and sayings for reading, speaking, or teaching their children. As I offer this revised and expanded edition of *The Random House Dictionary of America's Popular Proverbs and Sayings,* I hope readers will continue to use the gems of brevity and wit it contains, quoting them in public and at home. French essayist Michel de Montaigne said, "I do not speak the minds of others except to speak my own mind better" (1580). May you feel empowered by the proverbs and sayings in this dictionary to speak your minds.

GREGORY TITELMAN
New York City
January 15, 2000

INTRODUCTION
TO THE FIRST EDITION

This dictionary contains the best known and most widely recognized proverbs and sayings in America. Proverbs are the collective wisdom of all nations, of all ages, of all times. A proverb typically expresses a commonplace thought in a succinct, often metaphorical way. The same thought can be expressed in several proverbs, and two proverbs can contradict each other. The origin of many proverbs is obscure, but some were popularized in the Bible, Chaucer, Shakespeare, or other literary sources.

Proverbs and popular sayings are often attributed to more that one author. Take the well-known saying *Our country, right or wrong*. Proposing a toast at a dinner in Norfolk, Virginia, in April 1816, American naval officer Stephen Decatur said, "Our country! In her intercourse with foreign nations may she always be in the right; but our country, right or wrong!" John Jordan Crittenden (1787–1863), U.S. senator from Kentucky, said on the Mexican War, "I hope to find my country in the right; however, I will stand by her, right or wrong." Addressing the Anti-Imperialist Conference in Chicago on October 17, 1899, Senator Carl Schurz was quoted as saying, "Our country, right or wrong. When right, to be kept right; when wrong, to be put right." The very issue seemed ludicrous to the British writer G. K. Chesterton (1874–1936), who once commented, "'My country, right or wrong' is like saying, 'My mother, drunk or sober.'" With such a saying, one simply cannot say who coined it; the same idea was expressed by various people. A true proverb, containing a universal sentiment, is even more difficult to trace: the same thought could be found in an ancient Greek source, in the Bible, and in Shakespeare, all expressed differently. When a proverb or saying does come from a well-known source, it often travels widely in its original form: from the Bible, *Judge not, that ye be not judged; There's safety in numbers;* from Shakespeare, *All the world's a stage,* etc.

This dictionary contains scores of proverbs that are currently used in many countries, demonstrating how widespread the sentiment is: *All roads lead to Rome; The dogs bark, but the caravan goes on; A drowning man will catch at a straw; It's a small world; Out of sight, out of mind.*

Many if not most of these proverbs and sayings, while used in America, are of British origin. Often they are first found in collections of proverbs by John Heywood (1546), J. Howell (1659), John Ray (1670), and others: *Every man for himself; Don't cry over spilled milk; What's sauce for the goose is sauce for the gander.* Chaucer, Shakespeare, and other British writers originated or contributed a great deal to the preservation and popularization of some English proverbs used by Americans. Proverbs no longer come mostly from Britain. Born in America, many of them travel to British shores and enrich British English. Some examples are *Actions speak louder than words; Don't swap horses in midstream; The customer is always right; The family that prays together stays together; If you can't stand the heat, get out of the kitchen; Monday morning quarterbacking.*

The popular sayings can generally be subdivided into five categories:

Historical—popular sayings attributed to famous people of the past (for example, Madame de Pompadour, Pyrrhus, Marie Antoinette, Julius Caesar): *After us the deluge; Another such victory, and we are undone; Let them eat cake; I came, I saw, I conquered.*

Scientific—popular sayings attributed to great scientists and philosophers of the past (Archimedes, Galileo, Descartes): *Eureka! (I have found it!); But it does move!; I think, therefore I am.*

Literary—popular sayings associated with famous writers (Dante, Shakespeare, Virgil, Donne): *Abandon all hope, ye who enter here; All the world's a stage; Beware of Greeks bearing gifts; No man is an island.*

Sports—popular sayings attributed to sports figures and journalists (Joe Louis, Knute Rockne, Vince Lombardi): *You can run, but you can't hide; Win this one for the Gipper; Winning isn't everything, it's the only thing.*

Patriotic—popular sayings coined by American political and military leaders (Thomas Jefferson, Patrick Henry, Nathan Hale, Douglas MacArthur): *All men are created equal; Give me liberty or give me death!; I only regret that I have but one life to lose for my country; In war there is no substitute for victory.*

This dictionary differs from others in several ways. First of all, the proverbs and sayings, regardless of their country of origin, are used in America or originated in America. They are modern, having been collected from hundreds of American books and thousands of American journals, magazines, and newspapers published mostly in the 1980's and 1990's. Since proverbs and sayings are usually colorful, they are often used as titles of books and headlines of articles and ads and even as one-liners by politicians and comedians.

All entries in the dictionary are arranged in alphabetical order and are followed by a definition of the proverb or saying and the approximate circumstances of its origin. Asterisks indicate the frequency of usage, from * to *****. Variants of the proverb or usage advice follow, and references to selected other dictionaries of proverbs conclude the introductory part of the entry. Then the reader has a unique opportunity to enter the proverb's or saying's treasury, the laboratory of famous American writers such as Saul Bellow, Truman Capote, William Faulkner, F. Scott Fitzgerald, Robert Frost,

Ernest Hemingway, Arthur Miller, Margaret Mitchell, Upton Sinclair, John Steinbeck, Kurt Vonnegut, Jr., Tennessee Williams, Tom Wolfe, and hundreds of statesmen, politicians, journalists, and ordinary people.

You will notice that standard proverbs and sayings are frequently paraphrased or otherwise altered in the writings of many authors. In general, proverbs and sayings are not set in stone. They tend to vary greatly, depending on the context in which they appear or on the usage of the speaker or writer. Many proverbs are found in jocular contexts that poke fun at the standard senses of the saying, which can often become clichéd.

The dictionary has a number of cross references at the end of entries. They will direct you to a similar or related proverb or saying.

The index will help you find a proverb or saying if you know only part of it or just a single key word.

Wilson Mizner is often quoted as saying, "When you steal from one author, it's plagiarism; if you steal from many, it's research." I too have used the works of many authors, but given the nature of this book I sincerely hope no one will reproach me for it, since I pay due tribute to many of the writers who helped make this book possible. It is the result of fourteen years of painstaking research in the ocean of proverbial wisdom.

It is my belief that this dictionary represents an essential proverbial minimum that every educated person needs to know.

Abandon all hope, ye who enter here. Give up all hope, you that enter Hell. Once you enter, you can never escape. The saying comes from *The Divine Comedy* (1321) by Dante: *Lasciate ogni speranza, voi ch'entrate!* When Dante arrived at the gate of Hell [the Inferno], he could read this inscription upon the gate's lintel. The poet goes through nine circles of Hell, where sinners atone for their earthly sins. The saying has been used in English since about 1820. Often shortened to *abandon all hope.*

> **1321.** ONLY THOSE ELEMENTS TIME CANNOT WEAR
> WERE MADE BEFORE ME, AND BEYOND TIME I
> STAND.
> ABANDON ALL HOPE, YE WHO ENTER HERE.
> —Dante Alighieri, *The Inferno*

1952. Inside the door was a green placard: "Abandon All Hope, Ye Who Don't Wear Green Shirts!" —Kurt Vonnegut, Jr., *Player Piano*

1975. Most of his back was a broad mountainous landscape with a rising sun, and below this, forming an arch above his buttocks, Farragut read, in faded and clumsy Gothic lettering: "Abandon all hope, ye who enter here." —John Cheever, *Falconer*

1991. Bud went down to the newsstand late at night to get the early morning edition of the *Times*. On the front page, a banner read: HOLLYWOOD HI'S AND LOWS, THIS WEEK IN CALENDAR! It was all in red ink. He pulled out the section. There was a large pen-and-ink drawing of the gates of Universal Studios. The caption read: *Abandon hope all ye who enter here.* —*Esquire*

1993. Cathleen Schine says "hopefully" will claim its rightful place in the language someday. I hope not.

A sign over the door of a classroom at the University of North Carolina offers hope for future writers: "Abandon Hopefully All Ye Who Enter Here." —*New York Times Magazine*
See also HOPE FOR THE BEST AND PREPARE FOR THE WORST; HOPE SPRINGS ETERNAL IN THE HUMAN BREAST; WHERE THERE'S LIFE, THERE'S HOPE.

Absence makes the heart grow fonder. Long absence increases friendship and love. The proverb is attributed to Sextus Propertius (about 54 b.c.–a.d. 2): *Semper in absentes felicior aestus amantes.* First cited in the United States in 1755 in *Papers of Benjamin Franklin.* The proverb is found in varying forms: *Absence makes the heart grow harder; Absence makes the heart grow younger; Absence makes the heart grow fonder—distance makes affections wander; No absence makes the heart grow fonder; Distance makes the heart grow fonder*, etc.

1922. Absence makes the heart grow younger. —James Joyce, *Ulysses*

1991. Our Story: Galan has departed. Arn and Maeve are the next to leave, with tiny Ingrid safely tucked in the arms of a nurse. For them it is back to Orr, where Arn must resume his responsibilities as the King's Parker. It has been said that absence makes the heart grow fonder ... —Cartoon by John Cullen Murphy, *"Prince Valiant,"* King Features Syndicate

1991. "I'm not as naive as I used to be, to believe that absence makes the heart grow fonder," she once wrote bitterly to her faraway husband. —*New York Times*

Absolute power corrupts absolutely. *See* POWER CORRUPTS, AND ABSOLUTE POWER CORRUPTS ABSOLUTELY.

Accentuate the positive. Emphasize the posi-

1

tive things in a situation. The proverb originated in the United States, popularized through the song "Accentuate the Positive" (1944), lyrics by Johnny Mercer (1904–76).

1976. You must constantly look at your company's strengths and weaknesses, and as the old song goes, accentuate the positive, eliminate the negative. (This applies to your staff, too.) —Claudia Jessup and Genie Chipps, *The Women's Guide to Starting a Business*

1987. Ted simply had no stomach for that sort of thing. People like praise. Accentuate the positive. —R. Richard Ritti and G. Ray Funkhouser, *The Ropes to Skip & the Ropes to Know*

1988. "Don't tell me about your lack of production experience. That's not important right now. You're playing yourself down. Accentuate the positive." —Henry C. Rogers, *Rogers' Rules for Business Women*

1993. "When Liza Minnelli came to the hospital," Ben said, "I told her I was ashamed for her to see me in my condition. But Liza said, 'Are you kidding? It's miraculous that you're sitting up and actually *moving.*' We started singing, 'Ac-*cen*-tuate the positive, e-*lim*-inate the negative.' It became my theme song." —Claire Carter, "Ac-cent-tuate the Positive," *Parade Magazine*

See also ALWAYS LOOK ON THE BRIGHT SIDE.

Accidents will happen in the best-regulated families. Originally the proverb was used when an unmarried girl or woman got pregnant. This usage is still current in England. The proverb has been traced back to the play *Deuce Is in Him* (1763) by George Colman. First attested in the United States in *Yankey in England* (1815). It is usually used to belittle a minor mishap. The proverb is found in varying forms: *Accidents will happen in the best of families; Accidents will occur in the best of places; Accidents will happen even to the best regulated policemen; Accidents happen in the best-regulated households,* etc. Often shortened to *Accidents (mistakes) will happen.*

1850. Accidents will occur in the best-regulated families. —Charles Dickens, *David Copperfield*

1984. "I myself would not make too much of it," he decided a few seconds after I had finished. "Accidents will happen." —Joseph Heller, *God Knows*

1987. But you go through a period when you start to get on one another's nerves. And then, one day—now, I don't know if his teeth stopped clicking on their own or I just got used to it or what—but it never bothered me another time. You have that kind of thing happen in the best of fami-

lies. —Fannie Flagg, *Fried Green Tomatoes at the Whistle Stop Cafe*

See also THERE'S A BLACK SHEEP IN EVERY FLOCK.

Achilles' heel. One's vulnerable spot. The legend is that Achilles' mother dipped him in the River Styx to make him invulnerable, but his heel remained dry because she was holding it in her hand. Achilles' heel has been used as a metaphor for centuries.

1922. The Boers were the beginning of the end. Brummagem England was toppling already and her downfall would be Ireland, her Achilles heel ... —James Joyce, *Ulysses*

1934. Dick got up to Zurich on less Achilles' heels than would be required to equip a centipede.... —F. Scott Fitzgerald, *Tender Is the Night*

1992. "Among campaign issues, it could be his [Clinton's] Achilles' heel," Ted Koppel said, beginning one of the season's mixed podiatry metaphors. —*New York Times*

1992. For many conservatives, spending, not taxing, is his [George Bush's] Achilles' heel. —William Safire, *New York Times Magazine*

1994. High rates are Con Ed's Achilles' heel and its rate request underscores its predicament. —*Crain's New York Business*

Actions, not words. *See* DEEDS, NOT WORDS.

Actions speak louder than words. Talk is fine but action is better. A person is usually judged less by the way he speaks than by the way he acts. The proverb has been traced back to 1628. First attested in its current form in the United States. In 1856, the proverb was used by Abraham Lincoln.

1856. "Actions speak louder than words" is the maxim; and, if true, the South now distinctly says to the North, "Give us the *measures,* you take the *men.*" —Abraham Lincoln, *Collected Works*, Vol. II

1964. Actions speak louder than words, so I'll sign off. —Bel Kaufman, *Up the Down Staircase*

1975. Actions always spoke louder than words. He [Mike] would give her some action. —Jackie Collins, *The World Is Full of Divorced Women*

1987. Stanley thought for a moment, then delivered his final assessment, "It's true then, Dr. Faust, isn't it—I mean, what they say about actions speaking louder than words?" —R. Richard Ritti and G. Ray Funkhouser, *The Ropes to Skip & the Ropes to Know*

1991. Actions speak louder than words. Perhaps

the first thing parents should consider when their child lies is how prone they are to lying themselves. —*Reader's Digest*

1993. Action is louder than words only when it has not occurred to anyone to use the right words. Nothing in the universe speaks more loudly than the right words. —*Times* (Trenton)

See also DEEDS, NOT WORDS EASIER SAID THAN DONE.

Adversity makes strange bedfellows. *See* MISERY MAKES STRANGE BEDFELLOWS; POLITICS MAKE STRANGE BEDFELLOWS.

After a storm comes a calm. There is always a lull after an upheaval. The proverb dates back to the year 1200. First attested in the United States in *Voyages of Radisson* (c. 1680). The proverbs *The calm before the storm* and *The storm before the calm* are often used too.

1988. In fact, I'm actually starting to view the age of thirty-nine as the storm before the calm. As I hear tell, many women reach a state of grace at forty. —*Ladies' Home Journal*

1991. Mr. Gordon insisted he is not intent on erasing all conflict in the world because debate and disagreement can be inspiring, spun out as a central thread of life.

"I think we've got to accept the storm as well as the calm," he said. —Patti Wieser, "Peace Child Founder Seeks Harmony Through His Music," *Packet/Ledger Extra* (Princeton)

1992. CALM AFTER THE STORM SEEN FOR INSURANCE RATES —Headline of Thomas C. Hayes's article on the toll taken by Hurricane Andrew on many property insurers, *New York Times*

1994. You see the Port-au-Prince bay. It is calm before the storm. —ABC News

After the feast comes the reckoning. You have to pay for excessive pleasures.

1991. "If you're going to feast the night away, remember that after the feast comes the reckoning." —Overheard at the Waldorf-Astoria, New York City

1993. "Don't blame me. I didn't want to buy this fancy raincoat. My father is right saying that after the feast comes the reckoning." —Overheard at Bloomingdale's, New York City.

After us the deluge. It doesn't matter what is going to happen after we are gone. Attributed to Madame de Pompadour, mistress of Louis XV. He allegedly said: *Après nous le déluge.* Some attribute this saying to Louis XV. Either of them could have said it anticipating the French Revolution af-

ter the 1757 defeat of the French and Austrian troops at Rossbach. But neither originated it, for it is an old French proverb, according to *Bartlett's Familiar Quotations*, and it is often used in French too.

1952. "That's almost good enough to carve over your mantel, but I doubt if the deed will let you."

"How about, 'After us the deluge,'" said Paul. —Kurt Vonnegut, Jr., *Player Piano*

1991. AFTER MAO, A MUSICAL DELUGE —Headline of Barry Millington's article about Chinese who are immersed in Western music, *New York Times*

1992. AFTER FIDEL, A DELUGE OF DEALS —Headline of Spencer Reiss and Peter Katel's article on U.S. businesses that are getting ready for a post-Castro Cuba, *Newsweek*

Age before beauty. This is the way some American girls addressed elderly men in the nineteenth and early twentieth centuries. The saying *Beauty before the beast* was also used.

1989. When Ms. Golden reaches the door [of the bus], the driver of the packed vehicle shouts to her, "You'll be the last one on." As Ms. Golden begins to board, the woman behind her pushes her aside. "Age before beauty," she announces as she gets on the bus. —"Metropolitan Diary," *New York Times*

1993. Age before beauty. The "60 Minutes" 25th-anniversary bash was suitably irreverent. Someone said that the Metropolitan Museum of Art (great venue) actually contains some relics older than Mike Wallace. —*New York Post*

Age cannot wither her, nor custom stale her infinite variety. A truly fascinating woman's charms will never wear thin regardless of her age. Coined by Shakespeare in *Antony and Cleopatra* (1606).

1606. *Maecenas:* Now Antony must leave her utterly.
Enobarbus: Never; he will not:
Age cannot wither her, nor custom stale
Her infinite variety.
—Shakespeare, *Antony and Cleopatra*, Act II, Scene II

1922. Age has not withered it. Beauty and peace have not done it away. It is infinite variety everywhere in the world he has created, in *Much Ado about Nothing*, twice in *As You Like It*, in *The Tempest*, in *Hamlet*, in *Measure for Measure*—and in all the other plays which I have not read. —James Joyce, *Ulysses*

An albatross around one's neck. *See* IT'S AN ALBATROSS AROUND ONE'S NECK.

Alcohol (drinking) and driving don't mix. *See* OIL AND WATER DON'T MIX.

All animals are equal, but some animals are more equal than others. Proclaimed equality does not mean true equality. The saying was coined by George Orwell. In his novel *Animal Farm,* pigs control the government, and their proclaimed equality for all is in fact equality for the pigs only.

> **1945.** For once Benjamin consented to break his rule, and he read out to her what was written on the wall. There was nothing there now except a single Commandment. It ran: ALL ANIMALS ARE EQUAL BUT SOME ANIMALS ARE MORE EQUAL THAN OTHERS —George Orwell, *Animal Farm*

> **1985.** Thus, even on the night of such personal triumph, Jason Gilbert was once again reminded that although all Harvard undergraduates are equal, some are more equal than others. —Erich Segal, *The Class*

> **1991.** What's behind the recent rash of plagiarism charges? One explanation is that the initial reports prompted other writers, looking for a new badge of honor, to search for instances in which their words had been lifted. Some plagiarisms, however, are more equal than others (to borrow a phrase). —*U.S. News & World Report*

> **1991.** Here, too, Miss Gordimer [the Nobel Prize-winning novelist] sounded a gentle demurrer. "But the fact is you're all Americans," she said.
> Mr. Dinkins said that was so, but suggested that black Americans still seemed less equal than others. —*New York Times*

> **1993.** In his latest sneaker commercial, Dallas running back Emmitt Smith tells listeners, "All players are created equal, some just work harder in training camp." —*Times* (Trenton)

See also ALL MEN ARE CREATED EQUAL.

All cats are gray in the dark. Things are indistinguishable at night. Used in a variety of contexts. Listed in John Heywood's book of proverbs (1546) as *When all candles be out, all cats be gray.* First cited in the United States in *Papers of Benjamin Franklin* (1745). The proverb is found in varying forms: *All cats are gray at night; All cats look alike in the dark; In the dark, all cats are gray,* etc., and sometimes has a sexual connotation.

> **1648.** Night makes no difference 'twixt the Priest and Clerk;
> Joan as my Lady is as good i' th' dark.
> —Robert Herrick, *Hesperides. No Difference i' th' Dark*

> **1986.** Whoever said all cats are alike in the dark must have been deaf, dumb, and blind. —Jackie Collins, *Hollywood Husbands*

> **1991.** Parking is such sweet sorrow. All cars are gray in the dark. —A. C. McShade, "New York Magazine Competition," *New York*

All chiefs and no Indians. Too many bosses and too few workers to get the job done. Originated in Australia c. 1940 and now used in many English-speaking countries. First attested in the United States in the 1970s. *Too many chiefs and not enough Indians* and *Too many chiefs and not enough braves* are variants of the saying.

> **1984.** Many a business has had its troubles because it was composed of *all chiefs and no Indians,* that is, composed of all (or too many) officers who want to do nothing but give orders to others. —*Business Talk*

> **1987.** First, there are lots of losers in the mobility tournament. There have to be. It is the old "all chiefs, no Indians" dilemma. —R. Richard Ritti and G. Ray Funkhouser, *The Ropes to Skip & the Ropes to Know*

> **1994.** Mr. Dole, while maintaining that "we're not going to be rushed," indicated some disdain of the Gramm approach. "I haven't been advised of that," he told reporters. "There are a lot of chiefs here." —*New York Times*

All for one and one for all. Said of a group of people that supports every one of its members, and every member stands by the whole group. Originally used by Alexandre Dumas in *The Three Musketeers* (1844). In 1993, Walt Disney Pictures released a new film, *The Three Musketeers, All for One and One for All.*

> **1844.** All for one, one for all, that is our motto. —Alexandre Dumas, *The Three Musketeers*

> **1951.** "They don't have real comradeship in the Air Corps, not like you fellows in the Infantry, not the old all-for-one and one-for-all. They're not comrades-in-arms." —James Jones, *From Here to Eternity*

> **1985.** Team Building, or One For All and All For One. —Jacqueline Hornor Plumez with Karla Dougherty, *Divorcing a Corporation*

> **1987.** Sixty-five percent of the department's profits

went to Pierce & Pierce. But 35 percent was split among the eighty bond salesmen and traders themselves. All for one and one for all, and lots for oneself! —Tom Wolfe, *The Bonfire of the Vanities*

1993. The dialogue problem is even more acute with Tim Curry's Cardinal Richelieu. It's a crime to outfit Mr. Curry as such a delectable villain and then leave him little to say beyond "All for one … and more for me!" —*New York Times*

All good things come in threes. People still
believe that good or bad luck may follow someone three times in a row. The word *bad* may substitute for *good*. *Things (death, luck, trouble, misfortune, murders, disasters) come in threes* is a variant of the proverb. First attested in the United States in 1927.

1973. He couldn't believe it. He had been so sure of the picture. Two flops in a row. And now he faced the old show business superstition. Everything bad comes in threes. —Jacqueline Susann, *Once Is Not Enough*

1986. "They say good things come in threes, so…."—Evelyn Marie Adams, two-time milliondollar winner in the New Jersey lottery. —*New York Times*

1993. Things come in threes, they say, and so it was for religious cases during the term of the Supreme Court that just ended. All three cases, in my view, were rightly decided. —James Kilpatrick, syndicated column.

All good things come to those who wait.
Patience will help you achieve your goal. The proverb is of French origin: *Tout vient à celui qui sait attendre* ("All comes to him who knows how to wait"). It has been traced back to about 1530. First attested in the United States in the nineteenth century and popularized by Henry Wadsworth Longfellow in his poem *The Student's Tale*. *Everything comes to (the man, him) those who (can, know how to) wait* is a variant of the proverb.

1863. All things come round to him who will but wait. —Longfellow, *Tales of a Wayside Inn, The Student's Tale.*

1993. "I have sent off dozens of applications. I'm waiting for word," he [Roy] said, testily.

"You don't get anywhere waiting. Your father is proof of that."

"All things come to him who waits," he reminded her. —Garrison Keillor, *The Book of Guys*

1994. Good things come to those who can't wait.

—Commercial for Chrysler Corporation, CBS.

1994. Good things come to those who wait. Better things come to those who wait longer. —*New York Times*

See also IF AT FIRST YOU DON'T SUCCEED, TRY, TRY AGAIN.

All good things must come to an end. There
is an end to everything, to good things as well. The proverb dates back to about 1374 (Chaucer). First attested in the United States around 1680. The word *good* was added much later. *Everything has an end* and *Everything comes to an end* are variants of the proverb.

1984. They say all good things must come to an end, and the Mustang was no exception. —Lee Iacocca with William Novak, *Iacocca*

1991. After Siegel told Gordon he had decided to join Drexel, Gordon's only comment was, "All good things must come to an end." —James B. Stewart, *Den of Thieves*

1992. "It was just wonderful that there was such a place as the Swiss Home," said Adele Bolton, 85, already speaking in the past tense. Ms. Liljegren said, "Everything comes to an end." —*New York Times*

All hell broke loose. Everything went out of
control; wild commotion and confusion ensued. First recorded in 1594 in Robert Greene's play *Friar Bacon and Friar Bungay,* and used by John Milton in 1667 in *Paradise Lost.* The saying may be used in all tenses, but is most common in the simple past. The word *pandemonium* may be used instead of *hell.*

1946. "You better stay out of Europe," I said. "All hell is going to break loose over there and not long either." —Robert Penn Warren, *All the King's Men*

1961. Orr leaped on top of the table after hurling his paddle and came sailing off the other end in a running broad jump with both feet planted squarely in Appleby's face. Pandemonium broke loose. —Joseph Heller, *Catch-22*

1977. For Bellino it was like old times—once again he was going after Nixon. And all hell broke loose. —Victor Lasky, *It Didn't Start With Watergate*

1979. "With the UN decision for the partition and the creation of a Jewish state in Palestine, all hell will break loose." —Howard Fast, *The Establishment*

1984. I had been at Chrysler less than three months when all hell broke loose. —Lee Iacocca with William Novak, *Iacocca*

1988. "Are you blaming me for all that, Jacob?"

"It's related, Samuel. Thrice Caesar refused the crown and all hell broke loose." —Robert Ludlum, *The Icarus Agenda*

1989. "Every time I made one concession, the Kennedys presented a whole new list of demands," said Manchester. "This went on for months. Finally I said, 'no more'—and that's when all hell broke loose." —C. David Heymann, *A Woman Named Jackie*

1991. I didn't notice anything out of the ordinary. But as soon as I closed the door behind me, all hell broke loose: klieg lights lit up the yard, cameras flashed, and dozens of reporters started shouting to me from the fence along the road in front of our house. —Oliver L. North, *Under Fire*

1994. Seeing that some dealers were selling the title [*Jurassic Park*] early and fearing a loss of business, other retailers jumped, too.

"By Friday, all hell had broken loose," Mr. [Jeffrey] Eves said. More than 20 million copies of the tape are in the distribution pipeline. —*New York Times*

All I know is what I read in the papers. I'm just a regular guy who gets information primarily from the newspapers. This American saying was coined by the humorist Will Rogers (1897-1975) in the early 1920s and was used in his letter to President Coolidge dated May 21, 1926. Some 60 years later, Robert Fulghum published *All I Really Need To Know I Learned in Kindergarten*, which has a similar connotation: what people really need to know to be ordinary citizens, they learn since early childhood.

1923. Well, all I know is what I read in the papers. —Will Rogers, *New York Times*

1981. All you have to know about the team, you could find out by looking around Fenway Park yesterday as Joe Rudi led off the bottom of the ninth inning with Milwaukee leading the Red Sox, 6-1, and Rollie Fingers loosening up in the Brewer bullpen. —*Boston Globe*

All in a day's work. *See* IT'S ALL IN A DAY'S WORK.

All in the family. *See* IT'S ALL IN THE FAMILY.

All is for the best in the best of all possible worlds. The saying is of French origin and was originated by Voltaire in 1759, in mocking reference to Leibniz's philosophy, in his most famous book, *Candide: Dans ce meilleur des mondes possibles … tout est au mieux*. In 1911, the saying was used by Bernard Shaw (see quotation below).

Sometimes the words *all* or *possible* are omitted. The saying may be split into two parts and used separately: *All is for the best* or *(in) the best of all possible worlds*.

1911. The administrative departments were consuming miles of red tape in the correctest forms of activity, and everything was for the best in the best of all possible worlds. —Bernard Shaw, *The Shewing-up of Blanco Posnet*

1987. C Company was getting the worst of all possible worlds. —Chris Bunch and Allan Cole, *A Reckoning for Kings*

1992. "In the best of all worlds, everybody would have access to part-time work." —Psychologist Alison Clarke-Stewart, quoted in Erik Eckholm, "Learning if Infants Are Hurt When Mothers Go to Work," *New York Times*

1993. "In the best of all worlds, we would not have to use this type of force because (the threat of allied action) would be made known to the Serbs," McCurry [State Department spokesman] said. —*Times* (Trenton)

1994. Like Buckingham Palace, the Kremlin will officially deny that the monarch has a care in the firmament, or that anything could possibly be wrong in this best of all possible worlds. —*New York Times*

All is grist that comes to the mill. *See* IT'S ALL GRIST FOR THE MILL.

All is not gold that glitters. *See* ALL THAT GLITTERS IS NOT GOLD.

All men are created equal. All human beings are created equal and should enjoy equal rights. The phrase appeared in the *Declaration of Independence* in 1776 and has been used all over the world since.

1776. We hold these truths to be self-evident, that all men are created equal, that they are endowed by their Creator with certain unalienable Rights, that among these are Life, Liberty, and the pursuit of Happiness. —Thomas Jefferson, *Declaration of Independence*

1922. All men are not born equal. Some are born blind, some deaf, some lame, and some are born Jews. —Harry Austryn Wolfson [the first Jew to hold a chair in Judaic studies at Harvard], quoted by Charles E. Silberman in *A Certain People*

1955. Like all the other officers at Group Headquarters except Major Darby, Colonel Cathcart was infused with the democratic spirit: he believed that all men were created equal, and therefore spurned all men outside Group Headquarters with equal fervor. —Joseph Heller, *Catch-22*

1960. "Thomas Jefferson once said that all men are created equal … We know all men are not created equal in the sense some people would have us believe—some people are smarter than others, some people have more opportunity because they're born with it, some men make more money than others, some ladies make better cakes than others—some people are born gifted beyond the normal scope of most men." —Harper Lee, *To Kill a Mockingbird*

1981. The person who said "All men are created equal" never saw my mail. —Abigail Van Buren, *The Best of Dear Abby*

1988. "I believe that every black man in America should get a square deal and a fair deal. As the Constitution says, '*all* men are created equal'." —Erich Segal, *Doctors*

1992. All men are born equal, but some outgrow it. —Morris Mandel, *Jewish Press*

1993. All financial planners are not created equal. —*Modern Maturity*

1993. Far from being a fishing snob, [Herbert] Hoover described fishing as a lesson in democracy, if only because "all men are equal before fish." —*New York Times Magazine*.

See *also* ALL ANIMALS ARE EQUAL, BUT SOME ANIMALS ARE MORE EQUAL THAN OTHERS; THE LAND OF THE FREE AND THE HOME OF THE BRAVE; LIFE, LIBERTY, AND THE PURSUIT OF HAPPINESS.

All or nothing. Completely or not at all. The proverb has been traced back to 1866 and was used by the Norwegian dramatist Henrik Ibsen. First attested in the United States in 1940. Often used as an attribute: an all-or-nothing attitude (choice, demand, game, player, proposition, etc.). *All or none* and *It's all or nothing* are variants of the proverb.

1940. "We should have killed all or none," Pablo nodded his head. "All or none." —Ernest Hemingway, *For Whom the Bell Tolls*

1988. "What do you mean, 'be honest'?"
"This is an all or nothing proposition." —Clifford Irving, *The Campbell Murder Case: Daddy's Girl*

1989. No Bannerman since Cyrus had been willing to play for the goddamn farm.
All or nothing now, he told himself. —Michael Korda, *The Fortune*

1991. I went to Bud [McFarlane] and said, "For God's sake, we can save two of them [hostages]."
But he wouldn't hear of it. "The only authority I have is all or nothing." —Oliver L. North, *Under Fire*

1992. Same with the Palestinians: if they insist on all or nothing on sovereignty, nothing is what they'll get. —William Safire, *New York Times*

1994. It doesn't have to be all or nothing. Men only need to take one risk at a time to achieve some sort of self-expression. —*New York Times Magazine*

1994. Tender Bailey, projecting a teen-idol image somewhere between Jason Priestly and Tom Cruise, has been desperately wooing a girl who's going with someone else. "I said it's all or nothing," Bailey says ruefully, "but the truth is I would have settled for a lot less." —*New York Times*

See *also* YOU CAN'T WIN 'EM ALL; YOU WIN SOME (A FEW), YOU LOSE SOME (A FEW).

All quiet along the Potomac. Everything is calm. The saying is attributed to General George Brinton McClellan (1826–1885). When a lull set in following the Battle of Bull Run during the Civil War (1861–1865), "All quiet along the Potomac" became a watchword for the northerners. The saying caught on thanks to the song *All Quiet Along the Potomac Tonight* published in 1864 with words by Lamar Fontaine and music by John Hill Hewett.**

1947. *Mitch:* Miss Dubois?
Blanche: Oh!
Mitch: All quiet on the Potomac now?
Blanche: She ran downstairs and went back in there with him.
 —Tennessee Williams, *A Streetcar Named Desire*

1966. As McClellan discreetly continued to drill his army without moving it toward Richmond, the derisive Northern watchword became "All Quiet along the Potomac." —Thomas A. Bailey, *The American Pageant.*

1993. All Quiet in New Jersey. —*New York Times*

1994. In Washington, it is not all quiet on the Potomac. —CNN Center in Atlanta anchorman, *The World Today*

See *also* ALL QUIET ON THE WESTERN FRONT.

All quiet on the Western Front. Similar to "All quiet along the Potomac," this saying originated in World War I and was often used in German army communiqués. The saying became especially popular in 1929 when the novel *Im Westen Nichts Neues* (All Quiet on the Western Front) by Erich Maria Remarque was published. The saying was not prompted by "All quiet along the Potomac" but rather by the Russian "All quiet in the Shipka Pass" current in 1915–1916 and by the Russian artist V. V. Vereshchagin's wartime paintings of a Russian soldier frozen to death in the Shipka Pass during the Russo-Turkish War of 1877–1888. Film versions of *All Quiet on the Western Front* in 1930 and 1979 further popularized the saying.***

1974. By morning *Rockaway* was back in service—under the protection of a squad of patrolmen—and La Guardia could tell reporters, with a smile of satisfaction, "All is quiet on the eastern front." —Robert A. Caro, *The Power Broker*

1989. All Is Not Quiet On the West Front. On the West Front of the Capitol framed against the dazzling prospect of the Mall and the Washington Monument, workers were installing the rostrum and the bulletproof shield that will surround it for the swearing-in of the 41st President. —*New York Times*

1993. Everyone agrees that troops in the field would operate in their own languages.
All quiet on the Western Front, right? Wrong. On Monday, Spain announced that it wants to contribute 3,500 soldiers to the force—and added, of course, that Spanish should also be an official language. —Associated Press, "European Language Gets a 3rd Language," *Philadelphia Inquirer*
See also ALL QUIET ALONG THE POTOMAC.

All roads lead to Rome. There are many ways to reach one outcome or destination. During the period of the Roman Empire all roads built in Europe led to the empire's capital city. No matter where you started your journey, Rome was your final destination. *Mille vie ducunt hominem per secula Roman* is medieval Latin for "A thousand roads lead men for ever toward Rome." The proverb was used by Chaucer around 1391. First attested in the United States in *King* (1924) by J. S. Fletcher.

1983. "All roads in our day lead to Moscow." —Lincoln Steffens, quoted in Paul Johnson's *Modern Times*

1990. He [Robert Young] told Medina that as a young man, he felt "in banking all roads led to Rome and to me the Corner was Rome." —Ron Chernow, *The House of Morgan*

1991. "Mrs. Butler, what city would you like to visit? Or do you share Rosemary's conviction that all roads lead to Rome?" —Alexandra Ripley, *Scarlett*

1994. All roads lead to Jericho.
The sleepy town of Jericho has become a new focus of interest for Palestinians who live in the West Bank since it gained self-rule and the Israeli troops left. —*New York Times*

All systems go. Everything is ready! Originally used to report the readiness of the spaceship and its rocket systems to be launched (Cape Canaveral). The phrase may be used when any kind of preparations have been completed and the real activity is about to begin. *All systems are go* is a variant of the phrase.

1986. There's one thing I will do to him—
Because I know he wants it
I get real near—with message clear
I whisper low—all systems go.
—Jackie Collins, *Hollywood Husbands*

1993. All Systems Go. 3d-quarter productivity, annual rate up 3.9%. Late-October sales of cars, built in North America up 10.3%. New home sales in September up 20.8%. —*New York Times*

All that glitters is not gold. The appearance of a thing or person can be deceptive. This proverb is similar to the Latin: *Non omne quod nitet aurum est* ("Not all that shines is gold"). The proverb was used by Chaucer (c. 1374–87), by Cervantes in *Don Quixote* (1605–15), and by Shakespeare in *The Merchant of Venice* in 1596. First attested in the United States in the *Winthrop Papers* (1636). The proverb is found in varying forms: *All is not gold that glitters; All gold ain't what glitters; All is not gilt that glitters,* etc.

1596. *Prince of Morocco* (reads): All that glistens is not gold;
Often have you heard that told.
—William Shakespeare, *The Merchant of Venice,* Act II, Scene VII

1941. To Evelyn Dixon Dillard whose kindness has helped me to keep on believing that while all that glitters is not gold there is after all much real gold still left in the world. —Frances Parkinson Keyes, *All That Glitters*

1991. Of course, given how easy it is for almost anyone to get credit these days, a fool and his money are parted more quickly than ever. And after getting those purchases home, you soon realize that all that glitters is not gold. —*Reader's Digest*
See also APPEARANCES (LOOKS) ARE DECEIVING (DECEPTIVE); DON'T JUDGE A BOOK BY ITS COVER.

All the king's horses, and all the king's men, couldn't put Humpty together again.
The rhyme is often used to mean that what is broken can't be put together again under any circumstances. The phrase first appeared in one of

the widely quoted Mother Goose nursery rhymes (1697). *All the king's men* is often used to indicate loyalty to the boss. Robert Penn Warren's Pulitzer Prize-winning novel *All the King's Men* (1946) helped popularize the phrase.***

1697. Humpty Dumpty sat on a wall,
Humpty Dumpty had a great fall.
All the king's horses,
And all the king's men,
Couldn't put Humpty together again.
—Anonymous, quoted in *The Norton Introduction to Literature*

1956. *Polo:* All the king's men, and all the king's horses … Oh, what's the difference. —Michael Gazzo, *A Hatful of Rain*

1986. "Look where she is now, Doctor. She's in a nut house with scars all over her body, barking at dogs that only she can see. I'm her feckless brother trying to tell you stories that will illuminate her past and make you put Humpty Dumpty back together again." —Pat Conroy, *The Prince of Tides*

1992. Whatever the court decides, the CPSU, as with the Soviet Union itself, is dead. There still are diehard Russians who proudly call themselves communists, but Mr. Yeltsin has moved so swiftly to break up the empire and fragment the party that there is no chance of putting Humpty Dumpty back together again. —*Wall Street Journal*

1992. A paraphrase of an old rhyme, however, comes to mind: All the king's horses and all the king's men will not get George Bush elected again. —*Time*

1994. The original Tara, like Humpty Dumpty, has never been put together again. —"Tara Incognito," *New York Times Magazine*
See also IF IT AIN'T BROKE, DON'T FIX IT.

All the world's a stage. The entire world is nothing but a theater in which people are merely actors. Used by Shakespeare in *As You Like It* (c. 1599). *The world is a stage and all the men and women merely players* is an extended variant of the proverb.

1599. *Jaques:* All the world's a stage,
And all the men and women merely players.
—William Shakespeare, *As You Like It*, Act II, Scene VII

1952. At the beginning and close of each item of business he thought, "To hell with you."
It was to hell with them, to hell with everything. This secret detachment gave him a delightful sense of all the world's being a stage. —Kurt Vonnegut, Jr., *Player Piano*

1994. Jackie [O] never lets down in public. The whole world is a stage and she's its leading lady. —*New York Post*

All things to all men. The fulfillment of everyone's desires. The phrase, St. Paul's, first appeared in the New Testament. It often has a somewhat negative connotation since nobody—even politicians—can be truly impartial no matter how hard they try to prove otherwise. The word *people* is often substituted for *men*.

To the weak became I as weak, that I might gain the weak: I am made all things to all *men*, that I might by all means save some. —I Corinthians 9:22, *Authorized Version*, 1611

1987. Cannes means to be all things to all people. —Vincent Canby, *New York Times*

1989. "Candidates [for New York City mayor] see success as the ability to be all things to all people," said Frank J. Macchiarola, who has the unusual perspective of an academic, a former New York City Schools Chancellor and a losing candidate for city comptroller. —Frank Lynn, *New York Times*

1993. Politicians want to be all things to all people. Real artists don't. —Frank Rich, *New York Times Magazine*
See also YOU CAN FOOL SOME OF THE PEOPLE ALL THE TIME, ALL THE PEOPLE SOME OF THE TIME BUT YOU CANNOT FOOL ALL THE PEOPLE ALL THE TIME.

All work and no play makes Jack a dull boy. In 1659 James Howell included the phrase in his book of English proverbs. Attested in the United States in *Modern Chivalry* (1804) by Hugh Henry Brackenridge (1748–1816), American poet and novelist. The proverb is found in varying forms. Often shortened to *All work and no play*. The proverb may be used in reference to either sex.

1951. "All work and no play," Holmes said, and winked. It was a male wink, implying the turgid weighted pendulum that must be relieved, and it flung a momentary bridge across the gulf of caste that always separated them. "You ought to take a day off yourself," Holmes said. —James Jones, *From Here to Eternity*

1981. All work and no play makes Jack a dull boy—unless, of course, Jack plays around at work. —Abigail Van Buren, *The Best of Dear Abby*

1986. Unfortunately, since her success it was all work, work, work and no time for play. —Jackie Collins, *Hollywood Husbands*

1988. Let it not be said that Harvard Medical School was all work and no play. For to be precise, it was all work and *one* play: the traditional second-year show. —Erich Segal, *Doctors*

1994. Vacation time may be over, but that doesn't necessarily mean it's time for all work and no play. —C. John Zangara, "Putting Off The Grind," *Time Off*

See also BUSINESS BEFORE PLEASURE.

All's fair in love and war. The rules of fair play do not apply in love and war. The proverb is frequently used to justify cheating. The proverb has been traced back to John Lyly's *Euphues* (1578). First attested in the United States in *Horse-Shoe Robinson* (1835). The proverb is found in varying forms.

> **1939.** All is fair in love and golf. —Lewis and Faye Copeland, *10,000 Jokes, Toasts and Stories*

> **1993.** WHAT'S FAIR IN LOVE AND WAR —Headline of Randy Shilts's article on the easing up of antihomosexual rules when the military needs people to fight. *Newsweek*

> **1993.** "You're not miffed because I went behind your back?"
> "All's fair in love and war—whichever it is!" —Cartoon by Alex Kotzky, *Times* (Trenton)

> **1994.** All's Fair: Love, War, and Running for President. —Title of Mary Matalin and James Carville's book on the 1992 presidential campaign, as seen from opposite political sides by this loving couple.

See also THE END JUSTIFIES THE MEANS.

All's well that ends well. If the result of something is positive, any previous difficulties do not matter. Appears in John Heywood's book of proverbs (1546). In 1602, the proverb served as Shakespeare's title for *All's Well that Ends Well*. First attested in the United States in the 1705 *Correspondence Between William Penn and James Logan, 1700–1705*.

> **1602.** Our wagon is prepar'd, and time revives us;
> All's well that ends well; still the fine's the crown;
> Whate'er the course, the end is the renown.
> —William Shakespeare, *All's Well that Ends Well*, Act IV, Scene IV

> **1953.** "... we drove back to the firehouse in beatific silence, all dwindled away to peace." Beatty let Montag's wrist go, let the hand slump limply on the table. "All's well that is well in the end." —Ray Bradbury, *Fahrenheit 451*

> **1979.** "Everyone is going to be all right now," she said to me in the showroom of The American Harp Company. "Something always told me that it

would turn out this way. All's well that ends well," she said. —Kurt Vonnegut, Jr., *Jailbird*

> **1988.** The obstetrician smiled. "All's well that ends well," he remarked, and then turned to his neonatologist and said, "You can take over from here, Laura." —Erich Segal, *Doctors*

> **1991.** All's well that ends well: The stock market panic subsided, President Bush returned to his summer vacation, and the West is switching its attention to other events. —Garry Kasparov, *Wall Street Journal*

> **1993.** Another happy ending—this one for a man writing from California: "Our daughter was estranged from my wife and me for several years.... my wife and I decided to take care of their four-year-old until our daughter has her degree. All's well that ends well." —Malcolm Boyd, *Modern Maturity*

Always look on the bright side. Be optimistic. Don't keep the dark side too close to heart. The proverb has been traced back to 1726. First attested in the United States in 1942. The word *positive* may be substituted for *bright* and the prepositions *at* and *for* for *on*.

> **1985.** "Look on the bright side," Aaron Diamond said on the telephone. "Even Fatty Arbuckle made it back." He paused and coughed. "Under a different name, of course," he added cautiously.
> If there was a bright side, Dawn couldn't find it. —Michael Korda, *Queenie*

> **1986.** "It was dreadful," said Savannah.
> "Oh, c'mon. Look at the bright side. You always dwell on the bad stuff." —Pat Conroy, *The Prince of Tides*

> **1991.** "Ach, Scarlett darling, it can't be as bad as all that," Colum said. "Look at the bright side." —Alexandra Ripley, *Scarlett*

> **1993.** Look at the bright side: no matter how old you are, you're younger than you'll ever be again. —"Current Comedy," *Reader's Digest*

See also ACCENTUATE THE POSITIVE; THERE ARE TWO SIDES TO EVERY STORY.

Always put your best foot forward. Capitalize on your strengths. The proverb has been in common use since about 1495. First attested in the United States in 1744. Often shortened to *Best foot forward*.

> **1979.** "I'm going to try a new approach and claim that the [Fifth] amendment holds in the case, whether invoked or not. You see, Barbara, not only is this the only foot we can put forward, but it

raises a constitutional issue and I want that desperately." —Howard Fast, *The Establishment*

1987. *Job hunter:* It's my resumé ... what I call "putting my best feats forward." —Cartoon by Bob Thaves, *"Frank and Earnest,"* NEA, Inc.

1990. "Put your best foot forward," says Robert Nowaczyk, the human relations executive. "People tend to read what is at the top of the page, so put something great up there—be it education or training or good work experience." —Daniel Moreau, *Take Charge of Your Career*

1994. Put your best foot forward when dealing with older relatives. —Jeane Dixon, "Horoscope," *Times* (Trenton)

Am I my brother's keeper? Am I responsible for my brother's deeds or welfare? According to the Old Testament, Cain murdered his brother Abel and when asked by God where his brother was, said that he was not his brother's keeper. Often changed to *I am not my brother's keeper.*

And the Lord said unto Cain, Where *is* Abel thy brother? And he said, I know not: *Am* I my brother's keeper? —Genesis 4:9, *Authorized Version,* 1611

1952. He was a fine engineer, dull company, and doggedly master of his fate and *not* his brother's keeper. —Kurt Vonnegut, Jr., *Player Piano*

1984. Although our workers took a $2.00-an-hour pay cut, the large number of retirees meant that our labor costs did not go down accordingly. Some of our workers didn't see it this way. Their attitude was: "That's not my problem. I'm not my brother's keeper." —Lee Iacocca with William Novak, *Iacocca*

1988. "Where *are* all those guys?" I asked. "I don't know," the male voice on the other end replied. "I'm not their keeper." —*New York Times*

1992. HIS BROTHER'S KEEPER —Headline of Eleanor Clift's and Michael Meyer's article on Roger Clinton, who credits his brother Bill with saving him, *Newsweek*

1995. Your Brother's Keeper. Not all men are criminals, but almost all criminals are men. By a ratio of 94 to 6, men outnumber women in prison....

Would that strike a responsive or responsible chord? Probably not. Men are not their brother's keepers. —*New York Times*

And that's the way it is. The saying was popularized by CBS anchorman Walter Cronkite and was used as a sign-off sentence for over eighteen years (1962–81) of his TV CBS Evening News

broadcast. The word *but* is often used instead of *and.* The contracted form *that's* is preferred.

1956. *Celia:* I don't love you.
Johnny: And we snap our fingers and that's that?
Celia: That's the way it is.
—Michael Gazzo, *A Hatful of Rain*

1979. "It sounds crazy that a country that's going to be at war and fighting for its existence any day now should be waiting for an air force in this kind of crazy way, but that's the way it is." —Howard Fast, *The Establishment*

1987. "When I say something, I mean it," he [Cuomo] said. "I said I'm going to stay Governor, and that's the way it is." —*New York Times*

1993. "If you have a gun, you have power. That's just the way it is," he [Doug] says. —*Time*

And (yet) it does move! See BUT IT DOES MOVE!

Another day, another dollar. A hard day of work is over, and I have some money to show for it. According to Eric Partridge, this saying originated in the United States about 1910. According to Wolfgang Mieder, first attested in the United States in *Pink Hotel* (1957) by D. Erskine. The saying is found in varying forms: *Another day, another downer; Another day, another dollar and a quarter; Another day, another way,* etc.

1980. As for myself, I was getting paid by the day, so my attitude was, "Another day, another dollar." —Herb Cohen, *You Can Negotiate Anything*

1992. July 19–25. Iraq: Another week, another standoff. —*New York Times*

1993. Another Day, Another Downer. Once again, it was a week of discouraging economic reports. —*Time*

Another such victory, and we are undone. A victory won at great cost. The story goes that Pyrrhus, King (307–272 b.c.) of Epirus, a district in ancient Greece, defeated the Romans at Asculum (279 b.c.) but at great cost to his army. According to Plutarch, when somebody congratulated Pyrrhus on his victory, he would say, "Another such victory over the Romans, and we are undone." This saying is sometimes translated, "One more such victory and we are lost." The word *ruined* may substitute for *undone* or *lost.* ***

1984. On the third assault the British took the hill as the militiamen ran out of gunpowder and retreated. No day of fighting proved more costly to the British than the struggle on Breed's Hill. With more than a thousand redcoats killed or wounded, Gen. Henry Clinton called the battle "a dear bought victory. Another such would have ruined us." —John Anthony Scott, *The Story of America*

1991. Mr. Bush's ostensible "victory," when his veto was sustained in the House [of Representatives], may cause some Republicans to fear, in the words of King Pyrrhus after the battle of Asculum, that 'another such victory and we are undone.' —Tom Wicker, *New York Times*

1992. Fresh from his magnificent victory over Saddam in the Battle of the Agricultural Ministry, George Bush is preparing to declare a similar victory, in the form of Lloyd Bentsen's tax bill. A few more victories like this, and ... —"Another Victory," *Wall Street Journal*

See also PYRRHIC VICTORY.

Any port in a storm. Any assistance is welcome in an emergency. The proverb dates back to 1749 (*Fanny Hill; or Memoirs of a Woman of Pleasure* by J. Cleland). First attested in the United States in the *Warren-Adams Letters* (1775). Originally used by sailors.

1822. As the Scotsman's howl lies right under your lee, why, take any port in a storm. —Walter Scott, *The Pirate*

1912. He would soon be alone with no one to talk to perhaps, and if a sympathetic understanding could be reached with this man now, so much the better. Any port in a storm; any straw to a drowning man. —Theodore Dreiser, *The Financier*

1983. How could you have, Elaine?
    Any cock in a storm!
            —Jackie Collins, *Hollywood Wives*

See also A DROWNING MAN WILL CATCH AT A STRAW; HALF A LOAF IS BETTER THAN NONE.

Anything for (a little) peace and quiet. See ANYTHING FOR A QUIET LIFE.

Anything for a quiet life. One is ready to make concessions, or to change one's conduct in order to preserve peace and calm, even if one is not convinced that it is the right thing to do. Usually used without a verb. The saying first appeared in 1662 as the title of one of the plays of Thomas Middleton (1580–1627). *Anything for (a little) peace and quiet* is a variant of the proverb.

1662. *Anything for a Quiet Life.* —Title of Thomas Middleton's play

1922. —You're not my sister, naughty Tommy said. It's my ball.
    But Cissy Caffrey told baby Boardman to look up, look up at her finger and she snatched the ball quickly and threw it along the sand and Tommy after it in full career, having won the day. —Anything for a quiet life, laughed Ciss. —James Joyce, *Ulysses*

1989. "You're going to bed," she said firmly. *"Now!"*
    "I shall do no such thing."
    " *Now,* Arthur. I mean it."
    "Oh, all right," he conceded. "Anything for peace and quiet." —Michael Korda, *The Fortune*

Anything goes! Anything is allowed. There are no strict standards of conduct. Originated in the United States in the mid-1930s. The phrase was popularized in 1934 through the Broadway musical *Anything Goes* by American composer and songwriter Cole Porter (1893–1964).

1934. In olden days, a glimpse of stocking
    Was looked on as something shocking,
    But now, Heaven knows,
    Anything goes.
            —Cole Porter, *Anything Goes*

1993. "The milieu of the Village has always accepted all kinds of people and their artifacts, from dogs to nipple rings," says Mitchell L. Moss, a Village resident and director of New York University's Urban Research Center. "But the culture of 'Anything goes in Greenwich Village' has stretched the boundaries of civility." —*New York*

1994. They [big health insurance companies] are fighting for their survival, and that's why almost anything goes. —*Adam Smith*, PBS

Anything is possible. Anything may happen.

1992. "In this day and age, anything is possible: rape, murder, drugs, you name it." —Overheard at Columbus Circle station, New York

1994. Does she [Heather Whitestone, Miss America] plan to marry? "Eventually," she says. "But only to a one-woman man. An honest person and also a Christian." Well, that could be tough to find. She nods. "But anything is possible," she says laughing. —*New York Times*

Anything that can go wrong, will go wrong. See IF ANYTHING CAN GO WRONG, IT WILL.

Anything worth doing is worth doing well. If doing something makes sense, do it well. The proverb has been traced back to a Lord Chesterfield letter dated October 9, 1746. First attested in the United States in the *Adams Family Corre-*

spondence (1780). The proverb is found in varying forms: *If a thing's worth doing, it's worth doing well; If a thing's worth doing at all, it's worth doing well; If anything is worth doing, it is worth doing well; If a job's worth doing, it's worth doing well; Anything not worth doing is worth not doing well,* etc.

1943. "I do not maintain, I may say, that the sole, or even the primary object, of football in a college or university is to win games. But I have always thought that anything which was worth doing at all was worth doing well, or at least as well as one is capable of doing it." —Robert Penn Warren, *At Heaven's Gate*

1986. When I opened the bag at home that evening, I found two gifts and a note. In each shoe, a chocolate-chip cookie wrapped in waxed paper. And these words in the note: "Anything not worth doing is worth not doing well." —Robert Fulghum, *All I Really Need to Know I Learned in Kindergarten*

1993. In America, anything worth doing is worth marketing, and anything as valuable as health is sooner or later slated to become expensive. —*Times* (Trenton)

See also IF A THING IS WORTH DOING, IT'S WORTH DOING TWICE.

Appearances (looks) are deceiving (deceptive).

It is wrong to judge by appearances. First illustrated by Aesop (550 B.C.) in his fable "The Fox and the Lion." In 1666, it was included in G. Torriano's collection of Italian proverbs. The proverb appears in *Papers of Benjamin Franklin* (1759).

1987. Many times people say, "Looks are deceiving." This saying comes from the story of Aesop about the wolf who covered himself with the skin of a sheep. In this way he was able to enter the farmyard and kill the sheep. —Robert Dixon, *Complete Course in English*

1991. "I need to know what I'm doing wrong, why I don't look like a lady. I am a lady, Miss Eleanor, I am. You knew my mother, you must know it's so."

"Of course you are, Scarlett, and of course I know. Appearances are so deceiving, it's really not fair." —Alexandra Ripley, *Scarlett*

See also ALL THAT GLITTERS IS NOT GOLD.

An apple a day keeps the doctor away.

Eating fruit regularly keeps one healthy. First found as a Welsh folk proverb (1866): "Eat an apple on going to bed, / And you'll keep the doctor from earning his bread." First attested in the United States in 1913. The proverb is found in varying forms.

1939. "They say that an apple a day will keep the doctor away."

"Why stop there? An onion a day will keep everybody away." —Lewis and Faye Copeland, *10,000 Jokes, Toasts and Stories*

1985. An apple a day keeps the doctor away, the saying goes, but the Environmental Protection Agency has reservations. The worm, in this case, is daminozide, a chemical widely used on apples, which tests on animals have revealed as a possible carcinogen. —*Forbes*

1989. A *joke* a day keeps the doctor away. —Joey Adams, *New York Post*

1991. An apple a day keeps the doctor away. But wait! Has the apple been treated with Alar? —*Washington Post*

1994. Philby betrayed his own wife to woo her away from his friend. The inscription to Melinda [Maclean] reads: "An orgasm a day keeps the doctor away." —*New York Times Magazine*

The apple doesn't fall far from the tree.

Children take after their parents. Nobody knows exactly where the proverb comes from, but there are German and Russian versions as well. The proverb was used in the United States by Ralph Waldo Emerson in 1839.

1955. "You think you're going to get this fellow to marry you, and steady down, and use his talents, and become somebody big. That's what you really think. Listen, it's a very tough job, but it's possible. After all, how far does the apple fall from the tree? Judge Ehrmann is a very big man." —Herman Wouk, *Marjorie Morningstar*

1988. In America, they say, anybody can grow up to be President. They also say that the apple seldom falls far from the tree. In combination, the adages have a currency now because of a little-noticed though historically interesting coincidence: Three of the current crop of candidates for President are sons of United States Senators. —Clifford D. May, *New York Times*

1993. The apple doesn't fall far from the tree. Geographically that's still true in many American families—popular perceptions notwithstanding. A study out of the University at Buffalo (New York) says half the adult children studied live within 25 miles of their parents, and half of those are within five miles. —*Modern Maturity*

See also IT RUNS IN THE FAMILY; LIKE FATHER, LIKE SON; LIKE MOTHER, LIKE DAUGHTER.

April showers bring May flowers. Something good may happen as a result of unpleasant events. The proverb has been traced back to about 1557. First attested in the United States in *Colonial American Poetry* (1671).

> **1557.** Sweet April showers
> Do spring May flowers.
> —Thomas Tusser, *A Hundred Good Points of Husbandry. April Husbandry*

> **1991.** WITH AUTUMN SHOWERS COME, YES, APRIL'S FLOWERS —Headline, Anne Raver's article on the strange weather of 1991, *New York Times*

See also EVERY CLOUD HAS A SILVER LINING; IT'S AN ILL WIND THAT BLOWS NO (NOBODY) GOOD.

An army marches on its stomach. An army must be well fed to fight effectively. The proverb is attributed to both Napoleon Bonaparte and Frederick the Great. It has been traced back to 1904 *(Windsor Magazine)*. The word *travels* may be substituted for *marches*.

> **1929.** "We should go," one of the sergeants said, eating his cheese and drinking a cup of wine.
> "We'll go. Don't worry," Bonello said.
> "An army travels on its stomach," I said. —Ernest Hemingway, *A Farewell to Arms*

> **1986.** While USACAT [U.S. Army Culinary Arts Team] travels the world displaying its culinary achievements, who is minding the kitchen and feeding the fighting Army—the one that must still travel on its stomach? —Chrysler/Plymouth *Spectator*

> **1993.** This food is lousy!
> ... So why are you eating it when it's so lousy?
> I hate fighting on an empty stomach. —Cartoon by Mort Walker, *Times* (Trenton)

> **1994.** "Soup stains ... grease ... spaghetti sauce ... you ever hear of a napkin?"
> "Listen! An army travels on its stomach!" —Cartoon by Chris Browne, King Features Syndicate

See also THE WAY TO A MAN'S HEART IS THROUGH HIS STOMACH.

Art is long, life is short. Originally, life is too short to properly learn art. Now, art outlasts human life; or, art lasts forever, but life is too short to waste. The proverb is of Latin origin: *Ars longa, vita brevis*, though the idea came from the Greek of Hippocrates. The proverb has been traced back to about 1380 (Chaucer) and translated into English as "the life so short, the art so long to learn." First attested in the United States in the eighteenth century.

> **1839.** Art is long, and Time is fleeting,
> And our hearts, though stout and brave,
> Still, like muffled drums, are beating
> Funeral marches to the grave.
> —Henry Wadsworth Longfellow, *A Psalm of Life*

> **1991.** Protect, therefore, your young one's head
> From all such literary swill:
> That Art is Long is often said,
> But Therapy is Longer still.
> —Henry Louis Gates, Jr., *New York Times Book Review*

See also LIFE IS TOO SHORT; LIFE IS SHORT AND SWEET; LIFE IS BUT A DREAM; LIFE IS NO BED OF ROSES; LIFE ISN'T ALL BEER AND SKITTLES; LIFE IS WHAT YOU MAKE IT.

As a dog returns to his vomit, so a fool returns to his folly. See THE DOG ALWAYS RETURNS TO HIS VOMIT.

As go the cities, so goes the nation. See AS MAINE GOES, SO GOES THE NATION.

As Maine goes, so goes the nation. One part of a group can indicate what the rest of the group is likely to do. Originated in the United States as a political maxim around 1888. In Maine, state elections are traditionally held several weeks prior to the national elections, and the result in Maine was regarded as a political weather vane for the mood of the country as a whole. *So goes Maine, so goes the nation* is a variant of the proverb. The word *Maine* may be replaced by another word, and so may the word *nation*.

> **1936.** As Maine goes, so goes Vermont. —James A. Farley, Franklin Delano Roosevelt's campaign manager in the 1936 presidential election in which Roosevelt carried all but two states (Maine and Vermont)

> **1966.** A tremendous landslide overwhelmed Landon, as the demoralized Republicans carried only two states, Maine and Vermont. This dismal showing caused political wisecracks to make the old adage read: "As Maine goes, so goes Vermont." —Thomas A. Bailey, *The American Pageant*

> **1986.** As the family goes, so goes the nation and so goes the whole world in which we live. —Pope John Paul II, quoted in the *Observer* (London)

> **1991.** "I pointed out to him, as go the cities, so goes the country," Mr. Dinkins said, adding that the President did not disagree. But Mr. Dinkins noted that Mr. Bush did not agree either. —*New York Times*

1993. As a street goes, so goes style. —Headline of Amy M. Spindler's article on style, *New York Times*

1994. As Wall Street goes, so goes the New York office market. —*Crain's New York Business*

1995. Ferris is a political genius. For 40 years, ever since Max [Thomas] discovered him, he has been predicting who will be nominated for President, by both the Republicans and the Democrats—and he has never once been wrong. "As Ferris goes, so goes the nation," Max wrote in an early column. Ferris is equal to the whole of Maine. —Noel Perrin, *New York Times Book Review*

As you make your bed, so you must lie in it. *See* YOU'VE MADE YOUR BED, NOW LIE IN IT.

As you sow, so (shall) you reap. People bear responsibility for the results of their actions. The proverb appears in the Bible. First attested in the United States in 1679. The proverb is found in varying forms: *As ye sow, so shall (shalt) ye reap; As one sows so shall he reap; As we sow, we reap; As a man sows, so shall he reap; Whatsoever a man soweth, that shall he also reap; You shall (will) reap what you sow; They reap where they do not sow,* etc.

Be not deceived; God is not mocked: for whatsoever a man soweth, that shall he also reap. —Galatians 6:7, *Authorized Version,* 1611

1928. What a man sows, that shall he and his relations reap. —Quoted by Robert Graves in *The Years with Laura.*

1978. "Brethren, as ye reap so shalt ye sow" ... —Stephen King, *The Stand*

1986. You will continue to read stories of crookedness and corruption—of policemen who lie and steal, doctors who reap where they do not sew, politicians on the take. Don't be misled. They are news because they are exceptions. —Robert Fulghum, *All I Really Need to Know I Learned in Kindergarten*

1987. Whatsoever Ye Soweth, That Shall Ye Also Reap. —R. Richard Ritti and G. Ray Funkhouser, *The Ropes to Skip & the Ropes to Know*

1990. Our son, Rob, loved using the saw and hammer, but never seemed to clean up afterward. One day I was in the garage, stepping over the sawdust, and my hand automatically reached for the broom and dustpan. Suddenly, my brain ordered my body to stand still and appraise the situation. Instead of leaving the work area clean, I propped the broom against the workbench with the following note attached: "As ye saw, so shall ye sweep! Love,

Mom." —Carnita Brandner, *Reader's Digest*

1993. As ye rip, so shall ye sew. —Wise Aldrich, "Real Life Adventure," *Times* (Trenton)

See also WHAT GOES AROUND, COMES AROUND; YOU'VE MADE YOUR BED, NOW LIE IN IT.

Ask, and it shall be given you; seek, and you shall find; knock, and it shall be opened unto you. Be aggressive; go after what you want. The proverb encourages people to be inquisitive and even aggressive. It appears in the Bible. The proverb has been traced back to the fifteenth century. First attested in the United States in Benjamin Franklin's *Poor Richard's Almanac* (1755). It is often used as separate sayings: *Ask, and it shall be given you;* or *Seek, and you shall find;* and *Knock, and it shall be opened unto you.* **

Ask, and it shall be given you; seek, and ye shall find; knock, and it shall be opened unto you. —Matthew 7:7, *Authorized Version,* 1611

1939. "Can you operate a typewriter?"
"Yes, sir, I use the Biblical system."
"I never heard of it."
"Seek and ye shall find."
—Lewis and Faye Copeland, *10,000 Jokes, Toasts and Stories*

1989. Ask, and you will receive; seek, and you will find; knock, and the door will be opened. For everyone who asks receives, he who seeks finds, and to him who knocks, the door will be opened. —Carol S. Pearson, *The Hero Within*

1994. Well, what did he expect?! He said, "Ask and ye shall receive" and then passed a plate of money! —Cartoon by Bob Thaves, NEA, Inc., *Times* (Trenton)

Ask me no questions and I'll tell you no lies. Don't question things and you won't be misled. The proverb was originated by Oliver Goldsmith (1773). In 1906, Kipling wrote in his "A Smuggler's Song," "Them that asks no questions isn't told a lie." First attested usage in the United States in 1775 in the *Warren-Adams Letters* (1917). *Ask no questions and hear no lies* is a variant of the proverb.

1773. *Tony:* Ask me no questions, and I'll tell you no fibs. —Oliver Goldsmith, *She Stoops to Conquer*

1884. I says, "Don't you ask me no questions about it, please. You'll take it—won't you?"
He says:
"Well, I'm puzzled. Is something the matter?"
"Please take it," says I, "and don't ask me noth-

ing—then I won't have to tell no lies." —Mark Twain, *The Adventures of Huckleberry Finn*

1921. "What'd you ask 'em, for instance?"

"Curiosity killed a cat! Ask me no questions and I'll tell you no lies." —Eugene O'Neill, *Diff'rent*

1922. —Did she fall or was she pushed? he asked her.

She answered, slighting:

—Ask no questions and you'll hear no lies. —James Joyce, *Ulysses*

See also CURIOSITY KILLED THE CAT; A FOOL CAN ASK MORE QUESTIONS IN AN HOUR THAN A WISE MAN CAN ANSWER IN SEVEN YEARS.

Ask not what your country can do for you; ask what you can do for your country.

These words by John F. Kennedy are destined to live forever. Few politicians have said so much in so few words. Ralph Keyes questions Kennedy's authorship. He considers that the idea was first expressed by Oliver Wendell Holmes, Jr., in 1884 and again by Warren Harding in 1916.

1961. And so, my fellow Americans: Ask not what your country can do for you—ask what you can do for your country. —John F. Kennedy, *Inaugural Address*

1975. January 20, 1973 ... Nixon was sworn in for the second term by Chief Justice Warren Burger. In his inaugural address, he once more echoed his old rival Kennedy: "Let each of us ask, not just what will Government do for me—but what can I do for myself." —David Wallechinsky and Irving Wallace, *The People's Almanac*

1984. The issue is not what America can do for women, but what women can do for America. —Geraldine A. Ferraro, *New York Times*

1992. Voice from out there: An *election* message from President Bush?

Rabin: Yes.

Rabin (reading): "Ask *not* what your country can do for you ..."

Rabin (reading): "Ask what your country can do for *me.* "

Rabin (reading): "... and before November please?!" —Cartoon by Kirshen, quoted by *Jewish Week* (New York)

1993. Memo to GAO [General Accounting Office]: Ask not what taxpayers can do for you. Ask what you can do for taxpayers. —*New York Newsday*

Attack is the best form of defense. *See* THE BEST DEFENSE IS A GOOD OFFENSE.

B

Back to square one. Start all over again; go back to the beginning. The saying refers to games in which a player begins on the first square of a board and progresses from there. Hence, *square one* is used allusively to mean "a starting point." The saying has been used since the early 1960s.

1987. *60 Minutes* executive producer Don Hewitt said yesterday that commentator Andy Rooney "came in this morning. I said, 'We go back to square one,' and he said, 'Terrific' and that's that"... Translation: Rooney, whose pay was docked for failing to report to work during the Writers Guild of America strike against CBS, will be back on the air starting Sunday, April 29. —*Washington Post*

1993. The opposition delegation at the Angola peace talks said yesterday [April 29] that the ruling Popular Movement for the Liberation of Angola (MPLA) had hardened its stance and the talks were almost "back to square one." —*Christian Science Monitor*

Back to the drawing board. You have to start planing again because something went wrong. This saying has been traced back to a caption of a Peter Arno cartoon published in *the New Yorker* magazine, showing a man with a bunch of blueprints under his arm walking away from an aircraft that has crashed into the ground. "Well, back to the old drawing board," he says.

1987. The story of the W–4 form is not over yet. The Internal Revenue Service is back at the drawing board once again, thinking about yet another redesign of the employee tax withholding form. —*New York Times*

1988. Some teachers began inflating the grades of their best students so that more of them could cash in on the state scholarships, which are worth as much as $10,000 over a college career. So last week it was back to the drawing board —*New York Times*

1989. "I don't know what happens next," said Senator Thomas Daschle, the South Dakota Democrat who is co-chairman of the Senate Democratic Policy Committee. "It's back to the drawing board, I guess." —*New York Times*

1993. State legislatures in the United States are going back to the drawing board in 1993 with more diversity and more new faces—over 30 percent—than during any time in the past decade. —*Christian Science Monitor*

1997. A developer who plans to build a fifty-eight–home subdivision in Macomb Township will have to take his plans back to the drawing board. —*Detroit News*

Bad money drives out good. Things of little value drive good things out. The proverb was first recorded in 1902 in Vincent Stuckey Lean's collection of English and foreign proverbs and comes from the economic principle known as Gresham's law, after Thomas Gresham, founder of the Royal Exchange, who first expressed it. The proverb can be applied to any kind of activity.

1971. When the English financier Sir Thomas Gresham ... expressed the thought that "bad money drives out good," he made no theoretical exposition of the formulation, and not until the latter part of the 19th century did his principle become known as Gresham's law. —*Funk & Wagnalls New Encyclopedia*, Vol. 12

1994. *MM:* Is gossip reported more today than it used to be?
   Smith: Yes, and just like bad money drives out good money, bad gossip drives out good gossip. —*Modern Maturity*

Bad news travels fast. News about people's problems and misfortunes spreads like wildfire, much faster than good news. It was recorded in G. Taverner's collection of proverbs (1539). First attested in the United States in the *History of Plymouth Plantation* (1656) by William Bradford (1590–1657), one of the Pilgrim Fathers and American colonial governor and historian. The proverb is found in varying forms: *Good news travels slowly; bad news travels fast; Bad news travels too fast; Bad news travels quickly; Bad news travels like lightning; Ill news travels fast*, etc.

> **1936.** "I was greatly disturbed to hear of your recent conduct," ran Ellen's letter and Scarlett, who was reading it at the table, scowled. Bad news certainly traveled swiftly. —Margaret Mitchell, *Gone With the Wind*

> **1984.** Bad news travels quickly, even to Joab, and when the first hint of the tidings came to him, he rose and fled for refuge into the tabernacle of the Lord and caught hold on the horns of the altar. —Joseph Heller, *God Knows*

> **1990.** Bad news travels fast. Good news takes the scenic route. —Cartoon by Doug Larson, United Feature Syndicate

A bad penny always turns up. A bad person always shows up, even after an absence. The proverb is usually used in reference to a nasty prodigal person who tends to reappear in the place from which he or she set out. Originated in the United States and has been traced back to the *Adams Family Correspondence* (1766). In 1824 it was used by Walter Scott in his novel *Redgauntlet*. The proverb is found in varying forms: *A bad penny always comes back; A bad penny always returns; A bad nickel, like a bad penny, always turns up*, etc. Often shortened to *a bad penny*, a bad person one cannot get away from.

> **1922.** Turn up like a bad penny. —James Joyce, *Ulysses*

> **1951.** "Well, I'll be damned!" he [Warden] said. "Look who's turned up."
>
> "Bad pennies," Prew said. —James Jones, *From Here to Eternity*

> **1992.** Ross Perot is like a bad penny. He has reappeared. —Sam Donaldson, *"This Week With David Brinkley"*

> **1994.** Pavel M. Aleksandrov and Andrei N. Komogorov ... and novelists like Valentin Katayev, who once defended Mr. Solzhenitsyn ... expressed their deep satisfaction with the timely act of their Government in expelling, like a bad penny, this "slanderer" and "traitor." —*New York Times*

The bad workman always quarrels with his tools. Poor workmen never blame themselves but instead blame their tools. The proverb has been traced back to 1568 and is similar to the late-thirteenth-century French proverb, *Mauvés ovriers ne trovera ja bon hostill* ("A bad workman will never find a good tool"). First attested in the United States in a collection of Chinese proverbs (1875). *Quarrels with* may be replaced by *blames*.

> **1993.** "My husband is not much of a handyman. Whenever he can't fix something he blames his tools." —Overheard at a neighborhood clean-up rally

The ball is in your court. It's your turn to make the next move. Originated in the United States in the mid-twentieth century and refers to the game of tennis. Another word may be substituted for *court*. ****

> **1980.** "Why don't *you* buy the house? And when you buy it, you let me know. You send me a memo, and I'll be happy to move in with you and the children!" I paused, reflected, then continued, "In fact, I don't even know why *I'm* looking at all, because I don't even live at home that much." In other words, I "put the ball in her court"! —Herb Cohen, *You Can Negotiate Anything*

> **1984.** David grinned and said, "I don't need all this prologue, Jack. Let's get to the point."
>
> Osner nodded at Klein. "Mel, the ball's in your court." —Howard Fast, *The Outsider*

> **1991.** "I think there's now a real perception that the ball is in Israel's court and that it will have to come up with a response that shows it's prepared to negotiate if there is a real Arab negotiating partner," said Martin Indyk, director of the Washington Institute for Near East Policy. —Robert S. Greenberger, "Baker's Latest Effort for Mideast Peace Could Trigger Tensions With Israel," *Wall Street Journal*

> **1994.** Perhaps more than anything, the group is eager for flexibility from Federal regulators so states can make their own changes.
>
> "The ball is in our court," said Charlene Rydell, a Democratic State Representative from Maine who is chairwoman of the group's steering committee. —"State Officials Strive to Bring the Health Care Debate Home," *New York Times*

Barking dogs never bite. Don't be afraid of a

dog that barks and a person who yells. Great barkers are no biters. They may be all teeth and no bite. They do not constitute any real danger. The proverb has been used since *Proverbs of Alfred* (c. 1275) and is similar to the thirteenth-century French: *Chascuns chiens qui abaie ne mort pas* ("The dog that barks does not bite"). First attested in the United States in *Alice in the Delighted States* (1929). The proverb is found in varying forms: *A barking dog never bites; Barking dogs do not bite; The loud-barking dog seldom bites; The dog that barks doesn't bite,* etc.

1939. "Come on in, Mike," the genial owner of the estate beckoned to the workman hesitating at the gate.
   "There's a fierce dog ye've got," said Mike dubiously, pointing to an airedale barking furiously just within the place.
   "Don't you know a barking dog never bites?"
   "Sure, an' I know it," said Mike. "What I'm wonderin' is, does thot dog know it?" —Lewis and Faye Copeland, *10,000 Jokes, Toasts and Stories*

1956. Barking dogs never bite. —*New Yorker*

1994. Five weeks ago, Quebec voters elected a new government that wants to pull the province out of Canada. Such a development would normally rattle investors worried about risks in an uncertain political environment....
   "There has been little impact," said Dominik Dlouhy, president of Investments Dlouhy Inc., a Montreal investment house. "The dog barked, but didn't bite." —Clyde Farnsworth, "Quebec Traders Unfazed by Separation," *New York Times*

See also HIS BARK IS WORSE THAN HIS BITE; STILL WATERS RUN DEEP.

Be careful what you wish for. You might get it. See DON'T WISH TOO HARD: YOU MIGHT JUST GET WHAT YOU WISHED FOR.

Be it ever so humble, there's no place like home. See THERE'S NO PLACE LIKE HOME.

Be nice to people on your way up because you'll meet them ('em) on your way down. Never mistreat people in a lower position than yourself, no matter how big you are now, because you may be in their shoes again some day. Originated in the United States. Coined by Wilson Mizner (1876–1933), a Broadway playwright and Hollywood screenwriter. This one-liner is sometimes attributed to Walter Winchell or Jimmy Durante.

1974. The man whose posture is servile in the presence of his superiors and rude or off-hand with his subordinates has forgotten the old chestnut "Be nice to the little man on your way up, you might meet him on your way down." —Milla Alihan, *Corporate Etiquette*

1975. [A senior KGB officer said to an up-and-coming young agent]: "And, as the saying goes, always be nice to people on your way up. You may meet them again on your way down." —John Braine, *The Pious Agent*

Beauty is in the eye of the beholder. Beauty exists in the mind that observes it. Too often people disagree as to whether a person or thing is beautiful. It is truly an individual matter and depends on tastes. Usually said of a person or thing whose beauty does not meet the generally accepted standard. The proverb has been traced back to 1742. The idea was expressed by Shakespeare in *Love's Labour's Lost* (1594–95) and by Charlotte Brontë in *Jane Eyre* (1847). In its current form, it has been used since 1878. Often shortened to *in the eye of the beholder.* Such words as *evil, old age, weeds, fun, a miracle,* etc., are sometimes used instead of *beauty.*

1594–95.
   Princess: Good Lord Boyet, my beauty,
      though but mean,
   Needs not the painted flourish of your praise:
   Beauty is bought by judgment of the eye,
   Not utter'd by base of chapmen's tongues.
      —Shakespeare, *Love's Labours Lost,* Act II,
                                          Scene I

1981. Dear Bill: To recycle an old cliché, old age, like beauty, lies in the mind of the beholder. —Abigail Van Buren, *The Best of Dear Abby*

1986. "Weeds," says I, "are plants growing where people don't want them. In other words," says I, "weeds are in the eye of the beholder. And as far as I am concerned dandelions are not *weeds*—they are *flowers.*" —Robert Fulghum, *All I Really Need to Know I Learned in Kindergarten*

1987. The undemocratic aspects of free sex were compensated for in our harmless and mildly ridiculous way: "Beauty is in the eye of the beholder" was preached more vigorously than formerly ... —Allan Bloom, *The Closing of the American Mind*

1992. A miracle is in the eye of the beholder, thought Hisako. She'd just seen a westbound jet fly nearly across the sky and then, with a sudden turn, fly back to the east. —*New York Times*

1993. [Phil] Caruso wails that sanitation workers

are being paid more than cops. That's unadulterated garbage—a stink bomb he's tossed onto the bargaining table. Dinkins responds by bragging about productivity gains in the sanitation department, which, like beauty, exist almost entirely in the eye of the beholder. —*New York Newsday*

Beauty is only skin-deep. What you don't see is hidden under the skin and it may be more important than physical beauty. The proverb has been traced back to *A Wife* (c.1613) by Thomas Overbury (1581–1613), English poet and essayist. First attested in the United States in 1710. The proverb is found in varying forms: *Beauty is but skin-deep; Beauty is only skin-deep in the eye of the beholder; Beauty isn't always skin-deep; Beauty is only skin-deep, but ugly goes to the bone,* etc.

> **1616.** Beauty's but skin deep. —John Davies, *A Select Second Husband for Sir Thomas Overbury's Wife,* Stanza 13
>
> **1650.** All the beauty of the world, 'tis but skin deep. —Ralph Venning, *Orthodox Paradoxes. The Triumph of Assurance*
>
> **1993.** Beauty may be more than skin deep, but first impressions do make a difference. —Debra Lee Baldwin, "Let's Face It," *Sunday Star-Ledger* (Newark, N.J.)

See also APPEARANCES (LOOKS) ARE DECEIVING (DECEPTIVE).

Beauty is truth, truth beauty. The saying appears in *Ode on a Grecian Urn* (1820) by John Keats (1795–1821). It is, according to W. H. Auden, the Grecian Urn's description of a certain kind of art, the kind from which the evils and problems of this life are deliberately excluded. *Beauty is not always truth, nor truth beauty* is another version of the saying.

> **1820.** When old age shall this generation waste,
> Thou shalt remain, in midst of other woe
> Than ours, a friend to man, to whom thou
> say'st,
> "Beauty is truth, truth beauty,"—that is all
> Ye know on earth, and all ye need to know.
> —John Keats, *Ode on a Grecian Urn,*
> Stanza 5
>
> **1964.** Can you see some posters? Still have leftover yellow on green TRUTH IS BEAUTY, also some black on white LEARNING = EARNING. —Bel Kaufman, *Up the Down Staircase*
>
> **1993.** "Music is music," he tells me. And I'm left pondering whether I've been dismissed or been treated to a grand truth like "beauty is truth, and truth beauty." —*Times* (Trenton)

> **1994.** Want to know what beauty is? Beauty is whatever. —*Times* (Trenton)

Beggars can't be choosers. One should not be picky if one gets something for free. The proverb is similar to the mid-fifteenth-century French: *Qui empruncte ne peult choisir* ("He who borrows cannot choose"). It appears in John Heywood's book of proverbs (1546). First attested in the United States in the *Secret Diary of William Byrd of Westover* (c. 1719). The proverb is found in varying forms: *Paupers can't be fussy; Tramps can't be choosers; Thieves can't be choosers; Beggars shouldn't be choosers,* etc.

> **1936.** Certainly, he's no beauty, she thought coolly, and he's got very bad teeth and his breath smells bad and he's old enough to be my father. Moreover, he's nervous and timid and well meaning, and I don't know of any more damning qualities a man can have. But at least, he's a gentleman and I believe I could stand living with him better than with Rhett. Certainly I could manage him easier. At any rate, beggars can't be choosers. —Margaret Mitchell, *Gone With the Wind*
>
> **1978.** "Want me to check?" Tom asked.
> "Yeah, I guess so. Beggars can't be choosers, can they?" —Stephen King, *The Stand*
>
> **1991.** Instead it is Israel that gets the new barrage of warnings—shape up or starve, or as some fellow put it with such sensitive wit in *The Washington Post,* beggars can't be choosers. —*New York Times*

See also NEVER LOOK A GIFT HORSE IN THE MOUTH.

Behind every great man there is a great woman. Men often owe their success to women. It's women that make them tick. The word *great* may be replaced by *good, successful,* etc.

> **1977.** Behind every broke man there's a woman. —*1001 Insults*
>
> **1981.** "Behind every good man there stands a better woman." In this instance, there were two. I want to acknowledge the help I received from Betty Vaughn and Katie Rawdon, two women who are so thoroughly professional that their careers would have been assured long before the term *women's liberation* was conceived. —Mortimer Levitt, "The Executive Look," *Athenaeum*
>
> **1992.** Behind a lot of successful women, you'll find Marymount College Tarrytown. And today, we're helping women go places in more fields than ever before. —Ad, *New York Times*
>
> **1993.** "First of all, behind every inefficiency and every stupid thing the government does, there's almost always a special interest group that knows

it's stupid, knows it's inefficient, but they're making money off of it," Mr. Sharp said. —*New York Times*

Believe it or not. It sounds strange, but it's true. The phrase originated around 1914. In 1918, American artist Robert LeRoy Ripley made *Believe It or Not* the title of his syndicated newspaper feature. Ripley's cartoons were carried by many American newspapers. Each cartoon was based on an allegedly true story, like the one about the Russian cable PARDON IMPOSSIBLE. TO BE SENT TO SIBERIA and how a man's life had been spared when a Czarist official erroneously placed the period not after the word *impossible* but after the word *pardon*. Believe it or not! Robert Ripley died in 1949 on an island in Long Island Sound that he called Bion, an acronym of Believe It Or Not.

1952. "This play you've just seen was written, believe it or not, by an engineer and manager within the organization." —Kurt Vonnegut, Jr., *Player Piano*

1957. "Moira? Gone to church?"
He [Peter Holmes] grinned. "Believe it or not, that's where she's gone." —Nevil Shute, *On the Beach*

1981. Believe it or not, my husband is a policeman and he is afraid to sleep alone. —Abigail Van Buren, *The Best of Dear Abby*

1988. Judith nodded. "Believe it or not, cooking was once a required course in the Med School." —Erich Segal, *Doctors*

1991. "We first met Mrs. Reagan through Betsy Bloomingdale," recalled Oscar de Lavin, the former Adolfo executive. "That was when she was the governor's wife. She wasn't all that nice then, but she got even worse as she got more powerful. Believe it or not, Leona Helmsley was nicer than Nancy Reagan." —Kitty Kelley, *Nancy Reagan*

1992. A stockbroker catches his wife making love to another man. He yelled out, "What's going on?" She explained, "Believe it or not, John, I've gone public." —Joey Adams, "Strictly for Laughs," *New York Post*

Believe nothing you hear, and only half of what you see. *See* BELIEVE ONLY HALF OF WHAT YOU SEE AND NOTHING YOU HEAR.

Believe only half of what you see and nothing you hear. Question everything, especially rumors. The proverb has been traced back to *Proverbs of Alfred* (c. 1300). First attested in the United States in 1770. In 1845, it was used by the American poet Edgar Allan Poe (1809–49). It is found in varying forms: *Believe nothing you hear, and only half of what you see; Do not (don't) believe anything (everything) you hear nor (and) half of what you read; Never believe anything (everything) you hear; Believe only what they do and nothing of what they say; One must not believe all he hears; You can't believe everything you hear; Don't believe everything you read in the papers,* etc. Usually, they are followed by another old saying: "But I saw it. I saw it with my own two eyes."

1975. "Oh!" Susan sat down deflated. "I mean I heard ..."
"Never believe everything you hear." —Jackie Collins, *The World Is Full of Divorced Women*

1993. As Tim Robbins said, "Question authority, question convention, and question advice —including mine." May I add, "Don't believe everything you read—including this." —Thomas H. Ruddy, *Buzz*

1993. [Wayne] Gretzky earned about $3 million last season from the Kings. The new agreement will not be for $30 million, as reported by some this week, Gretzky said.
"Don't believe everything you read and half of what you hear," Gretzky said about the speculated figure of $30 million over three years. —*New York Times*

1993. Fortunately, there is an antidote for the spin-doctors' poison: Believe only what they do and nothing of what they say. —*New York Times Magazine*

1994. You can believe half of what people tell you. Trouble is, which half? —Joey Adams, *New York Post*

1994. Diplomats arriving in Haiti are told to believe "nothing you hear and only half of what you see." —*New York Times*

1995. In a *New York Times* interview published Nov. 20, Hatfield was consciously dismissive of the election returns, asserting that he was "prepared to work with the White House" and would engage in "bridge-building" with Democrats. When freshman Sen. Fred Thompson asked Hatfield about the *Times* article, Hatfield smiled and said: "Don't believe everything you read in the papers." —*New York Post*

The best defense is a good offense. It is better to attack the enemy head-on than to prepare one's defense and wait for the enemy to attack one. The proverb was first attested in the United States in *Memoirs of the Administration of Wash-*

ington and John Adams (1795) by R. W. Gibbes. In 1799 it was used by George Washington. The proverb is found in varying forms: *Attack is the best defense; Attack is the best form of defense; Offense is the best defense; The best form of defense is attack*, etc.

1967. "My old and very good friend, Jack Dempsey, has a saying which he has proved time and again in the ring. The best defense is a good offense." —Elia Kazan, *The Arrangement*

1977. Melinda slowly arranged the roses in the bowl, gathering her thoughts for the right level of response. "Do you know why you don't have any friends, Hennessy? It's because you're so vulnerable and sensitive and scared. You strike out at people, you think offense is the best defense." —William Safire, *Full Disclosure*

1983. He had learned—at an early age—that the best form of defense was offense. —Jackie Collins, *Hollywood Wives*

1991. When Prof. Anita Hill testified in convincing detail that she had been sexually harassed by Clarence Thomas, the defense was to attack: Destroy Anita Hill. Attack the committee. Charge racism. —*New York Times*

1992. The real lesson is that you need to fight first. The best defense is still a good offense. —*New York Times*

1993. DEMOCRATS TRY OFFENSE AS BEST DEFENSE —Headline of Richard L. Berke's article on the Democrats' sweeping attack on the gun lobby, *New York Times*

See also FORTUNE FAVORS THE BRAVE.

The best is yet to be. Better life is in store for everybody. The saying was coined in 1864 by poet Robert Browning (1812–1889). The proverb is found in varying forms: *The best is yet to come; The worst is yet to come*, etc. *The Best Is Yet to Be* was used by Wayne D. Dosick as the title for his book on renewing American Judaism, and *The Best Is Yet to Come* is the title of Ivana Trump's 1995 book.

1864. Grow old along with me!
　　The best is yet to be,
　　The last of life, for which the first was
　　　made.
　　Our times are in his hand.
　　　　　—Robert Browning, "Rabbi Ben Ezra,"
　　　　　　　　　　　　　　　　Stanza 1

1993. Fox looks at the figures and sees only more deaths as the number of teen-agers continues to grow.

"It is very rare that you find a homicide rate double in half a decade," he says. "It is truly alarming. But the worst is yet to come." —*Times* (Trenton)

1993. "The Look of the Nineties" is a delight and an inspiration. Perhaps, after all, the best *is* yet to be. —*New York Times Magazine*

1994. Hume Cronyn: Well, I can't give a meaningful opinion about aging. I resent it deeply. To hell with all this business of "grow old along with me. The best is yet to be." The best was when I was 30 or 40, and it was pretty damn good! —Connie Goldman, "MM Interview with Hume Cronyn & Jessica Tandy, Ossie Davis & Ruby Dee," *Modern Maturity*

The best of friends must part. Even close friends must part sooner or later. The proverb has been traced back to Chaucer (1385). Used in its current form since the seventeenth century.

1993. "You remember they swore 'for better for worse, for richer for poorer, in sickness and in health, to love and to cherish, till death us do part.' Now, he's filed for divorce."

"Well, even the best of friends sometimes have to part." —Overheard at a Carnegie Hall concert

See also PARTING IS SUCH SWEET SORROW.

The best things come in small packages. Valuable things, like jewelry, are often of small size. May be applied to small people too. The proverb has been traced back to 1659 and is similar to the thirteenth-century French: *Menues parceles ensemble sunt beles* ("Small packages considered together are beautiful"). First attested in the United States in 1931. The word *good* or *precious* can be used instead of *best*. The word *things* can be replaced with other words, such as *diamonds, dynamite, dramas, luck*, etc.

1984. "You know, my dear, the great dramas of life are usually played to small audiences." —Howard Fast, *The Outsider*

1988. Do not be afraid to spend money on yourself. Good luck comes in a small package. —Jeane Dixon, "Horoscope," *Washington Times*

1992. Good things come in Little, Brown packages. —Ad for Little, Brown and Company, *New York Times*

1993. The best things come in small packages ... because small packages often contain jewelry. —*Manhattan Jewish Sentinel*

1994. It is true that good things come in small

packages. —Ad for Miracle-Ear, "Sonya Live," CNN

The best things in life are free. The best things in life such as the moon, the sun, the stars, the flowers in spring and robins that sing are free. Originated in the United States in 1927 and usually attributed to Buddy G. De Silva whose song "The Best Things in Life are Free" became a hit in the Broadway musical *Good News* (music by Ray Henderson).

> **1927.** The moon belongs to ev'ryone,
> The best things in life are free,
> The stars belong to ev'ryone,
> They gleam there for you and me.
> —B. G. De Silva, Lew Brown, and Ray Henderson, "The Best Things in Life Are Free"

> **1992.** Now the best things in life are fat free. —Ad for Kraft General Foods, *People*

> **1993.** The best things in life aren't things. I'm talking about health, love, friendship and, most important, family. —*Reader's Digest*

> **1994.** It seems the best things in life really are free. Stay 3 nights, get a 4th night free. —Ad, *Wall Street Journal*

The best-laid schemes of mice and men often go (gang aft) a-gley. Even the best-laid plans often come to a bad end. Coined by Robert Burns in *Poems* (1785). The word *plan* is often used in place of *schemes*.

> **1785.** The best laid schemes o' mice an' men
> Gang aft a-gley.
> —Robert Burns, "To a Mouse," Stanza 7

> **1946.** The Best-Laid Schemes. —Upton Sinclair, chapter title in *A World to Win*

> **1984.** Alas, it was not to be, for the best laid schemes of mice and men gang aft a-gley. —Joseph Heller, *God Knows*

> **1991.** Dreadful news! There was a mistake in this column on Sept. 7. What the poet Robert Burns really said was that the best-laid "schemes" of mice and men gang aft agley. We had Burns saying "plans" instead of "schemes," and of course we regret the error. —Russell Baker, *New York Times*

Better a big fish in a little pond than a little fish in a big pond. It's better to be an important person in a small community or company than to be an unimportant person in a large community or company. The proverb is found in varying forms: *It is better to be a big fish in a little pond than a little fish in a big pond; Be a big fish in a little pond instead of a minnow in the ocean,* etc. Often shortened to *a big fish in a little pond* or *a little fish in a big pond* or *a big fish* or *a big pond* or *a little fish* or *a little pond.*

> **1984.** The Greenwalds were living the good life in Caracas, where Jerry was a big fish in a little pond. —Lee Iacocca with William Novak, *Iacocca*

> **1985.** "We were a large, competitive bank in small suburbs but relatively small in the city among giants."
> What to do? Easy: Be a big fish in a little pond instead of a minnow in the ocean. —*Forbes*

> **1986.** England was a small pond and she [Silver Anderson] wanted America. —Jackie Collins, *Hollywood Husbands*

> **1992.** "It's like fishing all day and catching a couple of 2-pounders, and all of a sudden you have a 14-pounder on your line. You pull it close to the boat and you put your net in the water, and you suddenly discover your 8-year-old son cut a hole in the net a week ago. It can be very disappointing."
> The Pirates want to net that fish. Now they have one last chance to get into the big pond known as the World Series. —*New York Times*

Better a live dog than a dead lion. *See* A LIVING DOG IS BETTER THAN A DEAD LION.

Better death than dishonor. Better to die fighting than to give up. The proverb originated in the United States and has been traced back to P. Wylie's *Murderer Invisible* (1931). First attested in England in C. Dawes's book *Lawless* (1932). The sentiment is an ancient one. The proverb is found in varying forms: *Death before dishonor; Death is better than disgrace,* etc. *Death Before Dishonor* was used as a title for a 1987 Hollywood film about American commandos fighting Muslim terrorists in a fictitious Middle Eastern country.

> **1931.** Life, contrary to the adage, is usually found to be dearer than honor in a crisis. —P. Wylie, *Murderer Invisible*

> **1932.** Better death than dishonor. —C. Dawes, *Lawless*

> **1989.** *What was the old soldier's code?* Cortez asked himself. *Death before dishonor.* —Tom Clancy, *Clear and Present Danger*

> **1991.** Far from dreading Drexel's demise, they [Milken's loyalists: Ackerman, Kissick, and Fred McCarthy] seemed to welcome it, reasoning that Giuliani would be blamed for the firm's collapse. They believed that the attendant outcry would weaken the government's determination to prose-

cute Milken. This group's motto: "Death Before Dishonor." —James B. Stewart, *Den of Thieves*
See also GIVE ME LIBERTY, OR GIVE ME DEATH; I WOULD RATHER DIE ON MY FEET THAN LIVE ON MY KNEES.

Better late than never. It is better when something is done late, or when something good happens late, than never at all. The proverb has been traced back to about 1200 in English. But it was known to the Roman historian Livy (59 b.c.–a.d. 17). Publilius Syrus (first century b.c.) is quoted as saying, "It is better to learn late than never." It was listed in John Heywood's book of proverbs (1546). First attested in the United States in the *Winthrop Papers* (1630). The proverb is found in varying forms: *Better late than never, but better never late; It's better late than never, but still better never late; Better never than late,* etc.

> **1922.** Better late than never. —James Joyce, *Ulysses*

> **1985.** "I have never trusted people who were born with money. I prefer the *nouveaux riches*—they haven't become bored with money. In any case, better *nouveau* than never." —Michael Korda, *Queenie*

> **1986.** I was pleased that the Swedish Academy of Letters finally recognized Professor Wole Soyinka of Nigeria for his contribution to literature. It is better late than never. —Richard O. Nwachukwu, *Time*

> **1987.** The First Lady was a guest of honor, but, as is her wont, had not announced she would attend in person until nearly the last minute—in this case Thursday afternoon. For Cecile Zilkha, chairwoman of the benefit committee, it was a case of better late than never. —*New York Times*

> **1990.** A citizen of the German Democratic Republic gave new meaning to the age-worn saying "better late than never" when, the day after The Wall was opened, he appeared with books in hand at the American Memorial Library in West Berlin. The man brought back volumes he had borrowed 28 years ago, shortly before The Wall was built, and kept in the hope of some day being able to return them. —*Reader's Digest*

> **1992.** When a fellow rider complained about having to take this mode of transportation [the freight elevator], my boss replied philosophically, "Better freight than never!" —*Reader's Digest*

> **1993.** The real point here, no doubt, is that in the minds of the Swedish Academy some gesture of recognition for black American writing was overdue. And so it may be, and better late than never. —*Times* (Trenton)

See also IT'S NEVER TOO LATE TO LEARN; IT'S NEVER TOO LATE TO MEND.

Better luck next time. May you have luck when you try again. The saying is attributed to Captain Frederick Marryat (1792–1848). Often used as a verbless sentence with a pleasant tone of voice. Sometimes follows such words as *have, hope for* or *wish someone.*

> **1951.** *Nick.* I didn't even want her. Never thought of her that way.
> *Crossman [too sympathetic].* That *is* too bad. Better luck next time. —Lillian Hellman, *The Autumn Garden*

> **1964.** Having Boys in class dis-tracks me from my English. Better luck next time. —Bel Kaufman, *Up the Down Staircase*

> **1980.** "You're pretty good, honey, but I've been at it a lot longer than you. Tell your client I said better luck next time." —Sidney Sheldon, *Rage of Angels*

> **1994.** Ollie North, a normal American, lost, but at least he didn't congratulate Charles Robb, who is not that normal. What was Mr. North supposed to say? "Tough break, normal Americans. Better luck next time. That is, if there is a next time." —Frank Gannon, "Normal Like Me," *New York Times*

Better safe than sorry. It makes sense (and is safer) to take precautionary measures before anything bad happens. The proverb has been traced back to *Rory O'More* (1837) by the Irish novelist Samuel Lover (1797–1868). First attested in the United States in *Murder at the Hunting Club* (1932) by M. Plum. The proverb is found in varying forms: *Better be safe than sorry; It is better to be safe than sorry; Better be sensible than sorry,* etc.

> **1932.** Better be safe than sorry. —M. Plum, *Murder at the Hunting Club*

> **1988.** A gene that controls growth in rainbow trout has been introduced into common carp by scientists, creating a new line of fish that grows faster than its natural relatives.
> "We think this is an entirely appropriate idea," Dr. Powers said. "The ponds have no outlets. They will be covered by a screen. It's overkill but let's be safe than sorry." —*New York Times*

> **1991.** From evolution's standpoint, it is better to be safe than sorry. —*New York Times*

> **1993.** He spoke slowly, "You realize, don't you, that if that's the case, this whole operation will take much longer?"

"I'd rather be safe than sorry." —Victor Sheymov with Roger Jellinek, "The Long-Secret Escape of the K.G.B.'s Cipher Hotshot," *New York Times Magazine*

See also IT IS BETTER TO BE ON THE SAFE SIDE; DISCRETION IS THE BETTER PART OF VALOR.

Better the devil you know than the devil you don't know. It is better to deal with something bad you know than with something new you don't: the new thing might be even worse. The proverb is of Irish origin and has been traced back to the 1539 collection of proverbs by R. Taverner. First attested in the United States in *Dodd Cases* (1934) by K. Livingston. The proverb is found in varying forms: *The devil that you do not know may be worse that the devil you do know; Better the devil we don't know than the one we do; Better the evil I knew than the evil I didn't; The devil I know is better than the devil I don't know,* etc. Often shortened to *better the devil you know.* *The Devil We Knew* (1993) is the title of H. W. Brands' book on the United States' role in the Cold War against the "evil empire."

1977. "Hennessy said to block her out. Who? Absolutely not. Never Marilee, you hear? Let it be Buffie then, better the devil we know." —William Safire, *Full Disclosure*

1980. You've made the ultimatum palatable and have forced the salesman to spend an inordinate amount of time with you. He's doing a cost-benefit analysis of the situation and inwardly groaning, "I've got six hours invested in this meatball! But the devil known is better than the devil unknown. Who knows what else is lurking out there on the street?" —Herb Cohen, *You Can Negotiate Anything*

1985. They [executive search firms] give candidates fantastic job offers. The candidates seem really excited. But at the last moment the candidates change their minds. Filled with worry, they back out. As [Peter] Grimm says, "It's more comfortable sleeping with dragons you know than with ones you don't." —Jacqueline Hornor Plumez with Karla Dougherty, *Divorcing a Corporation*

1988. Lisa asked Alevy, "Why aren't they booting *you?* You're the one who pulled a gun on Burov."

"Well," Alevy replied, "it's the KGB who wants me around, on the theory that it's better to deal with the devil you know." —Nelson DeMille, *The Charm School*

1988. GOP MAY SPURN DEVIL IT KNOWS FOR ONE IT DOESN'T. To regain control of the Senate this November, Republicans will have to win several upsets and strike one Faustian bargain. The bargain is that one of the winners may have to be Lowell P. Weicker. —*Wall Street Journal*

1991. So, your elected officials can hope that voters will think your opponent will be as bad as you and stick with the devil they know. —*New York Times*

1992. Christopher Byron takes one look at Ross Perot and concludes that the devils we know are safer than this new devil. —*New York*

1992. Having admitted that mistakes were made, he [President Bush] is hoping that voters will follow an Irish proverb that is, as it happens, just another way of saying there is no one left to believe: "The devil you know is better than the devil you don't know." —*New York Times*

1994. Even those who said they felt Mr. Cuomo talked a better game than he delivered, and even those who said he had betrayed Mayor Dinkins, seemed nevertheless uninterested in voting for anyone else.

"The devil that you know is better than the devil you don't," said Barbara O'Banyoun West, 60, a retired schoolteacher. —*New York Times*

Better to give than to receive. *See* IT IS MORE BLESSED TO GIVE THAN TO RECEIVE.

Better to light one candle than to curse the darkness. *See* IT IS BETTER TO LIGHT ONE (LITTLE) CANDLE THAN TO CURSE THE DARKNESS.

Between a rock and a hard place. Forced to choose between two unpleasant options. The expression originated in the early twentieth century in the United States. It usually follows *to be caught.* The phrase is found in varying forms: *to be caught between a rock and a hard place: to be caught between a rock and a hard spot; to be caught between a knot and a hard place,* etc.

1984. "I came here with great reluctance. I am between a rock and a hard place. I cannot save the company without some kind of guarantee from the federal government." —Lee Iacocca with William Novak, *Iacocca*

1987. "I'm caught between a rock and a hard place. Veronika refuses to make Christmas for my kids. And Bonnie thinks I should have Christmas for her kids and ignore mine." —*Ladies' Home Journal*

1988. "I'm caught between a rock and a hard place," Mr. Stenholm said. "There's a lot of bitterness and some resolve to vote no on the Democratic plan, but people are all over the lot." —*New York Times*

1991. "This is not something I'm too proud of," he said. "But I [Mr. Rizzo] was caught between a rock and a hard place." —*New York Times*

1992. If new tax laws put you between Little Rock and a hard place, you know who to call. —Ad for Dreyfus Intermediate Municipal Bond Fund, *New York Times*

1994. Con Ed would be even more vulnerable should full-scale competition become a reality.

"They're caught between a rock and a hard place," says one analyst. —Philip Lentz, "Heat Is On: Con Ed Faces New Pressure," *Crain's New York Business*

See also BETWEEN SCYLLA AND CHARYBDIS; BETWEEN THE DEVIL AND THE DEEP BLUE SEA; DON'T JUMP FROM THE FRYING PAN INTO THE FIRE.

Between Scylla and Charybdis. Between two equal dangers. According to an ancient Greek myth, two monsters lived on either side of the narrow strait between Italy and Sicily. Scylla was a six-headed sea monster who lived on a rock on the Italian side of the strait and Charybdis was a whirlpool off the coast of Sicily. When ships tried to avoid Scylla, they drifted into Charybdis. Seeking to avoid one danger, they fell into another. The phrase is often preceded by such verbs as *to be, to sail,* and *to steer.*

1596–97.

Launcelot: Truly then I fear you are damned both by father and mother: thus when I shun Scylla, your father, I fall into Charybdis, your mother: well, you are gone both ways. —Shakespeare, *The Merchant of Venice,* Act III, Scene 5

1984. After weeks of listening to both sides, Mr. Cuomo proposed a compromise that cut the size of the projects from 24 hours to 12. That episode became a symbol of his constant effort to find a middle ground.

"The truth is often found at neither Scylla nor Charybdis," he has often said, "but somewhere near the middle of the straits." —*New York Times*

1993. "You're between Scylla and Charybdis on this," he [Mr. Curiale] said. "You either grant these increases or you risk destroying the only carrier who will insure these people. So what do you do?" —Kevin Sack, "Empire Blue Cross Granted Huge Rise in New York Rates," *New York Times*

See also BETWEEN A ROCK AND A HARD PLACE; BETWEEN THE DEVIL AND THE DEEP BLUE SEA; DON'T JUMP FROM THE FRYING PAN INTO THE FIRE.

Between the devil and the deep blue sea. Between equally dangerous options. The expression is of nautical origin where "the devil" means the seam on a ship's deck nearest its side. Hence, anyone who found himself between the devil and the waterline of a ship or the deep blue sea had a very narrow margin for choice. The verb *to be* is usually used before the phrase. The word *blue* is often omitted.

1922. Between the Saxon smile and yankee yawp. The devil and the deep sea. —James Joyce, *Ulysses*

1993. President Clinton's health-care initiative may still leave people without the health care they need if annual caps for psychological services are so low that they will threaten people with the same "devil or the deep blue sea" choices they face now. —*Times* (Trenton)

See also BETWEEN A ROCK AND A HARD PLACE; BETWEEN SCYLLA AND CHARYBDIS; DON'T JUMP FROM THE FRYING PAN INTO THE FIRE.

Beware of Greeks bearing gifts. Enemies should not be trusted even when they bring you gifts. The saying is attributed to Laocoön, a priest in Troy during the Trojan War, which broke out around 1200 B.C. Laocoön allegedly advised the Trojans not to bring into the city the wooden horse in which the Greeks had secretly hidden their soldiers: *Timeo Danaos et dona ferentes* ("I fear the Greeks, even when they are bringing gifts," from Virgil's *Aeneid*). The proverb has been traced back to 1791 in English. First attested in the United States in *Ethel Opens the Door* (1922). It is found in varying forms: *Beware of the Greek when he comes bearing a horse in his mouth; Beware of the Trojan Horse; I fear the Greeks, even when they are bringing gifts; Fear the Greeks bearing gifts,* etc.

1988. Because Governor Dukakis [Greek by origin] stands 5 feet 8 inches tall, and Vice President Bush is 6 feet 2 inches, cruel Republicans are already playing on the ancient phrase with "Beware of Greeks wearing lifts." —*New York Times Magazine*

1991. BEWARE POSTCARDS BEARING GIFTS AND 900 NUMBERS —Headline of Leonard Sloane's article on telephone fraud, *New York Times*

1992. Perot was a big reason for my change of policy. The poet Virgil said, "Beware the Greeks bearing gifts," which has no bearing here except to introduce my Uncle Charlie, who said, "Beware the millionaire calling for sacrifice." Uncle Charlie flourished back in the Depression before the billionaire was invented, but his wisdom remains just as applicable to Ross Perot as it once was to Rockefellers. —Russell Baker, *New York Times*

1994. BEWARE OF KIN BEARING BIRDS OF PREY —Headline of Janet Maslin's film review of *Greedy, New York Times*

Big Brother is watching you. You're under the watchful eye of the authority in power. The saying was coined by George Orwell in his 1949 classic, *1984*. Originally, Big Brother was the Soviet Union and its intelligence apparatus, the KGB. Now the saying is applied to other countries, companies, and governmental authorities. The main entry is often shortened to *Big Brother*, referring to any authority.

1949. The black-mustachio'd face gazed down from every commanding corner. There was one [poster] on the house front immediately opposite. BIG BROTHER IS WATCHING YOU, the caption said, while the dark eyes looked in Winston's own. —George Orwell, *1984*

1992. Another shopper … an actress from Greenwich Village, said: "That [snooping around shoppers' cars] sure sounds like Big Brother to me. I thought we put something like that all behind us with Russia giving up." —Steven Prokesch, "New York State Crosses the Hudson in Search of Texas," *New York Times*

1993. BIG BROTHER IS WATCHING YOUR TRASH —Headline of Harry Blaze's article on trash recycling, *Times* (Trenton)

1993. Are we so desperate to "streamline" government that we are willing to fatten up "Big Brother" by creating a behemoth police agency where the Drug Enforcement Administration and the Bureau of Alcohol, Tobacco and Firearms are folded into the FBI? —*Sunday Star-Ledger* (N.J.)

1995. "We think that Big Brother is doing more than watching us in this case, and we're very concerned about this," Mr. Cochran said. —*New York Times*

The bigger the better. Bigger things are better.

1986. "Like new parents who weigh the baby several times daily and count each ounce gained as a triumph, they think bigger is better … growth is a cultural value: a company that is not expanding is said to be falling behind. A stigma is associated with the failure to grow." —Judith B. Bardwick, *The Plateauing Trap*

1989. "Well, it's a lot larger than the others."
"Exactly! *Scale!* There's no point in doing some-

thing like this [painting] on a small scale, is there? The bigger, the better, don't you know?" —Michael Korda, *The Fortune*

1993. "Bigger had been better for decades," Sherman writes, "not only because big cars made better profits but because big cars conferred more status. They were synonymous with America. They were a metaphor for G.M. itself." —*New York Times*

1993. We know this is not true of most things, but when it comes to offering you greater selection, value and convenience—our new location proves that bigger is better. —Ad for White Lotus Futon, *New York Times*

The bigger they are, the harder they fall. The more important you are, the more severe the consequences of failure. The proverb has been traced back to *Dives and Pauper* (1493) by H. Parker. In 1670, it was included in John Ray's collection of English proverbs. First attested in the United States in the August 11, 1900, issue of the *Brooklyn Daily Eagle*. In its current form, it is usually attributed to the British-born world heavyweight boxer Bob Fitzsimmons (1858–1917). Some people give credit for this boxing saying to American heavyweight champions John L. Sullivan (1858–1918) or James Corbett (1866–1933). The maxim, however, is of much earlier origin. The proverb is found in varying forms: *The bigger they come, the harder they fall; The wiser they are, the harder they fall; The richer they are, the harder they fall*, etc.

1900. The bigger they are, the further they have to fall. —Robert Fitzsimmons, quoted in the *Brooklyn Daily Eagle*

1984. They say that the bigger you are, the harder you fall. Well, I fell a great distance that week. I instantly identified with every person I had ever fired. —Lee Iacocca with William Novak, *Iacocca*

1984. "You are just a youth," he observed at last, "and he has been a great man of war from his boyhood. Thou art not able to go up against this Philistine to fight with him."
"The bigger they are," I replied, "the harder they fall." —Joseph Heller, *God Knows*

1990. The harder you fall, the higher you bounce. —"Quotable Quotes," *Reader's Digest*

1992. That old chestnut, "The bigger they come, the harder they fall," is well supported by chess. The more aggressive the thrust against the enemy, the more vulnerable another sector of one's own formation becomes. —*New York Times*

1993. "I'm not afraid of a Sumo cat. The bigger

they are, the harder they fall."

WOMP ...

"... Or is it, the harder they fall, the more bones I break?" —Cartoon by Mike Peters, "Mother Goose & Grimm," *Asbury Park* [N.J.] *Press*

1994. The bigger they come, the harder they fall. —Sam Donaldson on O. J. Simpson's alleged crime, "This Week with David Brinkley," ABC News

A bird in the hand is worth two in the bush. It's better to possess something real right now than to count on finding something better in the future. The proverb is similar to the thirteenth-century Latin: *Plus valet in manibus avis unica quam dupla silvis* ("A bird in the hands is worth more than two in the woods"). It has been traced back to the *Life of St. Katharine* (c. 1450) by J. Capgrave. In 1546, it was included in John Heywood's book of proverbs: "Better one bird in hand than ten in the wood." In its present form, it was used by Nathaniel Woodes in his *Conflict of Conscience* (1581) and by Cervantes in *Don Quixote* (1605–15). First attested in the United States in *Poems of Edward Taylor* (c. 1700). The proverb is found in varying forms: *A bird in the hand is worth a dozen in the bush; A bird in the hand is worth a hundred flying*, etc. Often shortened to *A bird in the bush*. Similar proverbs may be found in other languages. Spanish-speaking people, for instance, say: *Más vale pájaro en mano que cien volando* ("A bird in the hand is worth more than a hundred flying"). The Italians would say, *Meglio fringuello in mano che tordo in frasca* ("Better a finch in hand than a thrush on a branch").

1922. A certain whore of an eyepleasing exterior whose name, she said, is Bird-in-the-Hand and she beguiled him wrongways from the true path by her flatteries that she said to him as, Ho, you pretty man, turn aside hither and I will show you a brave place, and she lay at him so flatteringly that she had him in her grot which is named Two-in-the-Bush ... —James Joyce, *Ulysses*

1962. "I happen to be a bird-in-hand man. I don't think you can go wrong taking this. Your story is mature and dramatic, but frankly it's kind of downbeat for films." —Herman Wouk, *Youngblood Hawke*

1993. "First of all, in an age of economic anxiety, a good job in danger of being lost is more potent than a better job not yet visible," Secretary Reich said, calling it "a bird in the hand phenomenon." —*New York Times*

1994. Mr. Jackson suggested a new slogan for the Cuomo campaign. "Pataki," he said, virtually spitting out the name. "Just plain tacky."

He added: "If you vote Republican, or don't vote at all, you aid the bird in the bush and the phantom." —Kevin Sack, "Pataki Courts Black Voters as Jackson Backs Cuomo," *New York Times*

See also A LIVING DOG IS BETTER THAN A DEAD LION.

Birds in their little nests agree. People should live in harmony, especially in small quarters. This nursery proverb may also be used to reprimand children when they fight with each other. Proverbial as far back as 1715 and originated by Isaac Watts (1674–1748), English theologian and writer of hymns. The proverb was popularized by such American writers as F. Scott Fitzgerald, Sinclair Lewis, Margaret Mitchell, and John Steinbeck, to mention but a few.

1715. Birds in their little nests agree;
And 'tis a shameful sight,
When children of one family
Fall out, and chide, and fight.
—Isaac Watts, *Divine Songs for Children*

1934. "Excuse me, Franz," said Kaethe before he could speak. "Excuse me, dear, I had no right to say that. I know my obligations and I am proud of them. But there is a bad feeling between Nicole and me."

"Birds in their little nests agree," Franz thundered. Finding the tone inappropriate to the sentiment he repeated his command in the spaced and considered rhythm with which his old master, Doctor Dohmler, could cast significance on the tritest platitude. "Birds-in-their-nests-agree!" —F. Scott Fitzgerald, *Tender Is the Night*

1961. "Birds in their little nests agree," he said. "So why can't we?" —John Steinbeck, *The Winter of Our Discontent*

Birds of a feather flock together. People who have similar interests and beliefs are usually attracted to each other. The proverb has been traced back to W. Turner's *Rescuing of Romish Fox* (1545), but it was known much earlier. A similar idea can be found in the Bible. In its current form, it has been used since 1660. First attested in the United States in the *Account of Two Voyages to New England* (1674). The proverb is found in varying forms: *Birds of a feather will fly together; Birds of a feather laugh together; Birds of a feather gather no moss; Birds of a feather are drawn together; It is a bird of another feather*, etc. Often shortened to *birds of a feather*.

1922. Birds of a feather laugh together. —James Joyce, *Ulysses*

1962. "Mama, I knew Scotty quite well at the university. He's a decent, responsible fellow."

"That was school. This is business. He's just like the rest of them, and that's why your cousin Eleanor married him, don't fool yourself. They're birds of a feather, that crowd. All money-mad." —Herman Wouk, *Youngblood Hawke*

1982. There were sixteen people in the drawing room, and they had one thing in common: They were wealthy. Nita Ludwig was a firm believer in the "birds of a feather" philosophy. These people felt the same way about the same things; they were comfortable with one another because they spoke the same language. They shared the commonality of the best boarding schools and colleges, luxurious estates, yachts, private jets and tax problems. —Sidney Sheldon, *Master of the Game*

1985. "Who are the guys that mostly get asked to the clubs? Preppies from St. Paul's, Mark's, Groton. It's kind of a common bond. You know, birds of a feather flocking together and so forth." —Erich Segal, *The Class*

1987. In fact, there is a great deal of accounting for taste, and, as social animals, people continually do it. "Birds of a feather flock together" is more collective wisdom and makes the point more directly. —R. Richard Ritti and G. Ray Funkhouser, *The Ropes to Skip & the Ropes to Know*

1993. Gerald R. Roche and Thomas J. Neff could not exactly be called birds of a feather. While Mr. Roche is a registered Democrat, Mr. Neff is a staunch Republican. —*New York Times*

The blacker the berry, the sweeter the juice. Berries are best when they are ripe. The blacker the better. Often used figuratively to indicate that it is easier to deal with people who are mature and experienced. It is also often applied to black women. *The darker the berry, the sweeter the juice* is a variant of the proverb.

1984. "She's a very mature person, the cream of the crop. And as we say in California, the darker the berry, the sweeter the juice." —Overheard in San Francisco

1987. *Want a white woman?*

I never hankered after no white woman! High yellow was as high as I cared to go.

He [Artis O. Peavey] liked them, in fact, big and black ... the blacker the berry, the sweeter the juice. —Fannie Flagg, *Fried Green Tomatoes*

1994. "Have you watched Oprah's latest show about white people of black origin?"

"You bet I have. I was specially impressed by the author of the book *The Sweeter the Juice,* who's white but didn't know that her ancestors were black." —Overheard in a senior citizens club

Blessed are they who expect nothing, for they shall not be disappointed. This proverb was apparently coined by Alexander Pope. In a letter to Fortescue dated September 23, 1725, Pope wrote: "'Blessed is the man who expects nothing, for he shall never be disappointed' was the ninth beatitude." Pope repeated this adage to other correspondents. First attested in the United States in the May 1739 issue of *Poor Richard's Almanac,* by Benjamin Franklin. It is often found in the shortened form *expect nothing.*

1958. I know enough not to expect anything from anyone. That way I'm never disappointed. —L. Bachmann, *Lorelei*

1967. Blessed are they who expect the worst, for they shall get it! —J. Brunner, *Quicksand*

1973. Expect nothing. Live frugally on surprise. —Alice Walker, *Expect Nothing*

1973. "We'll soon see," he said pleasantly. "Expect nothing, then you'll never be disappointed. I dare say some perspicacious Chinaman said that at some time or other." —E. Page, *Fortnight by Sea*

The blind leading the blind. *See* IF THE BLIND LEAD THE BLIND, BOTH SHALL FALL INTO THE DITCH.

Blood is thicker than water. Relationships within the family are stronger than any other kind. The saying was first cited in John Lydgate's *Troy Book* (c. 1412). Appeared in J. Ray's collection of proverbs in 1670. First attested in the United States in *Journal of Athabasca Department* (1821). The proverb is found in varying forms: *Blood is thicker even than floodwater; Blood is always thicker than water; Blood runs thicker than water; Blood may be thicker than water, but money is thicker than blood; Blood is thicker than water, but the paycheck is thicker than blood,* etc.

1961. People who participate in phony deals and shoddy business practices can usually be counted on to betray a friend. And the hackneyed adage that "blood is thicker than water" may be accurate chemically but that's as far as it goes. —Ann Landers, *Since You Ask Me*

1983. "Look," he [Buddy Hudson] said, "I've come back to make peace with you. We both did things we shouldn't have—but what's that old saying—blood is thicker than water. Right?" —Jackie

Collins, *Hollywood Wives*

1984. I had only one card left to play. "What about Bill [Ford] over here?" I said. "I'd like to know what he thinks."

"I've already made the decision," said Henry [Ford].

I was disappointed but not really surprised. Blood is thicker than water, and Bill was part of the dynasty. —Lee Iacocca with William Novak, *Iacocca*

1993. There is a saying that "blood is thicker than water" ... Blood relations are the focus of this Geraldo. —"Geraldo," CBS

1994. George Bush on the Gulf War: "The Middle East is a region where oil is thicker than blood." —*U.S. News & World Report*

1994. Upon being introduced, the President gently tweaked the Governor.

"When Andrew Cuomo, who as you know is a Presidential appointee, wrote his father a note and said, '10 minutes, don't be too long,' and then the Governor came up and embarrassed his son by telling you that, I wrote a note on the note. I said, 'Clinton's Eighth Law: Blood is thicker than water but the paycheck is thicker than blood.'" —*New York Times*

See also CHARITY BEGINS AT HOME.

Blood, toil, tears and sweat. *See* I HAVE NOTHING TO OFFER BUT BLOOD, TOIL, TEARS, AND SWEAT.

Blood will tell. What is inherited cannot be hidden; it will come to the surface sooner or later. The proverb has been traced back to about 1489. First attested in the United States in *The World a Mask* (1850) by G. H. Boker. The word *out* is sometimes used instead of *tell*.

1943. "Pal, you come of a distinguished though impoverished family. Hell, don't you know that a Governor in the family a few generations back when every politician was a Roman statesman and the *res publica* was untainted is enough to make any outfit a distinguished old family. If you play the cards right. Blood will tell." —Robert Penn Warren, *At Heaven's Gate*

1990. She's going to apply for welfare as her mother, grandmother, great-grandmother, and great-great-grandmother did in the past. Blood will tell. —Overheard at the Social Security Office in Manhattan

See also IT RUNS IN THE FAMILY.

Boys will be boys. One cannot expect a boy to behave as a grown man. He will always be mischievous. Applied to men as well when they behave in a childish manner. The proverb has been in common use since the seventeenth century. First attested in the United States in *Charcoal Sketches* (1837). The word *boys* may be replaced by the words *girls, kids, teachers,* etc. *Boys Will Be Boys* is the title of Myriam Miedzian's book (1993) about high school students. It was one of President Reagan's favorite proverbs.

1922. *Corny Kelleher:* What, eh, do you follow me? *Second watch (genially):* Ah, sure we were too.
Corny Kelleher (winking): Boys will be boys. —James Joyce, *Ulysses*

1951. *Crossman:* Boys will be boys and in the South there's no age limit on boyishness. —Lillian Hellman, *The Autumn Garden*

1981. Dear Abby: I know boys will be boys, but my "boy" is seventy-three and he's still chasing women. —Abigail Van Buren, *The Best of Dear Abby*

1989. "People thought there'd be trouble one day. Girls are girls. You can't lock 'em up at home when they're sixteen, seventeen—and if you try, they just do something stupid." —Michael Korda, *The Fortune*

1991. Israeli officials managed over time to acquire photos of ever larger [than 100 miles] areas, and used the KH-11 data in targeting the Iraqi nuclear reactor it raided in 1981. When first told of that raid, President Reagan is quoted as saying, "Boys will be boys." —*New York Times*

1992. What ultimately was successful, in terms of getting usable footage, was the application of a well-known parental dictum: kids will be kids. —*New York Times*

Bread always falls buttered-side down. Of two possibilities, the more damaging one will always occur. The proverb is of British origin, and is first recorded in 1834; in America it dates from the 1860s.

1972. The bread he dropped invariably fell buttered-side downward. —P.D. James, *An Unsuitable Job for a Woman*

1995. Along with the other pressing questions of the age—Why does bread fall buttered-side down? Why do fools fall in love?—we can add this: Why isn't Terrence Trent D'Arby a mega-star? —*Boston Globe*

1998. Drop a piece of toast and it lands buttered-

side down. Put a dozen socks in the clothes dryer, eleven come out. These are among the immutable laws of nature. —Lynn Elber, *Detroit News*
See also IF ANYTHING CAN GO WRONG, IT WILL.

Brevity is the soul of wit. Speakers are better appreciated when they say a lot in a few words. The proverb is first found in Shakespeare's *Hamlet* (1600). It was later used by John Galsworthy, Somerset Maugham, and other writers. First attested in the United States in *Modern Chivalry* (1804) by Hugh Henry Brackenridge (1748–1816).

> **1600.** *Polonius:* Therefore, since brevity is the soul of wit,
>   And tediousness the limbs and outward flourishes,
>   I will be brief ...
>   —Shakespeare, *Hamlet,* Act II, Scene II

1916. Brevity is the soul of lingerie—as the Petticoat said to the Chemise. —Dorothy Parker caption written for *Vogue,* quoted in John Keats's 1970 biography of Parker, *You Might as Well Live*

1977. Levity is the soul of wit. —Melville D. Landon, quoted in *Peter's Quotations*

1993. Meeting tip: Brevity is the soul of wit. —*Modern Maturity*

1994. Brevity is the soul of wit. On second thought, no. Might find a use for that yet. —*Times* (Trenton)

The British are coming. On April 18, 1775, Paul Revere (1735–1818) and two other American patriots made a midnight ride from Boston to Concord to warn people that the British were attacking. The midnight ride of Paul Revere was described by Longfellow in his *Tales of a Wayside Inn* (1863–74). A variant with "Russians" became popular in 1966 when the movie "The Russians Are Coming! The Russians Are Coming!" was released. Other nationalities are also found.

1966. *The Russians Are Coming! The Russians Are Coming!* —Title of a movie starring Carl Reiner, Alan Arkin, and Eva Marie Saint

1976. "Of course, we knew about Paul Revere. Our agents bugged his horse, and when he rode from Lexington to Concord, we got tapes of him shouting, 'The British are coming.'" —Art Buchwald, *Washington Is Leaking*

1987. The acronym STRAC originally stood for Strategic Army Corps—the designation for the Army's standby combat troops that would be the first to save Democracy from itself. By '68, STRAC was used mockingly, with various definitions such as Shit, The Russians Are Coming. —Chris Bunch & Allan Cole, *A Reckoning for Kings*

1993. "The Russians Are Coming! The Russians Are Coming!"
That was the rallying cry of delighted Israeli immigration officials several years ago, when Soviet *aliya* was at its apex and the Israeli government had to scramble to accommodate the huge influx. —*Forward*

1994. The Mongolians are coming, the Mongolians are coming!
The warning that once caused panic in the steppes of Russia now may signal a welcome new addition to Princeton's restaurant scene. J. P. Lee's Original Mongolian Barbecue, a chain of eateries in northern New Jersey, is seeking to open a new franchise at 182 Nassau Street. —*U.S.1* (Princeton)

Brother can you spare a dime? The saying originated in the United States in the 1930s during the Great Depression when millions of Americans became beggars asking for "a dime for a cup of coffee." In 1932 the song "Brother, Can You Spare a Dime?" became an overnight hit (lyrics by Edgar Y. Harburg (1896–1981), music by Jay Gorney, and sung by Harry Richman). In 1975, the British shot a semidocumentary movie of the Great Depression using the same title. *Buddy can you spare a dime?* is a variant of the saying.

> **1932.** Once I built a railroad, made it run,
>   Made it race against time,
>   Once I built a railroad, now it's done,
>   Brother, can you spare a dime?
>   —"Brother, Can You Spare a Dime?" Harms, Inc. Music Publishers Holding Corporation

1991. Because remember, you'll be evoking the wonderful spirit of good old *depression* days when men who had once built railroads actually stood on street corners, believe it or not, saying crazy things like, "Buddy, can you spare a dime?" —Russell Baker, *New York Times*

1993. Buddy, can you spare a buck? Every year when you complete your tax return there's a little box you can check if you want to earmark one dollar of your taxes for the ongoing Presidential Election Campaign Fund. —"Money," *Modern Maturity*

1993. *Panhandler:* Brother, can you spare a dime? —Tom Walker's cartoon, *Sunday Star-Ledger* (N.J.)

1994. Brother, Can You Spare $75,000? So you say you want to make a movie? —*US*

The buck stops here. The saying is used to indicate that the speaker is ready to take full responsibility for his actions. President Harry Truman had a sign saying this on his desk at the White House. This motto was and is used by many politicians. Originally a poker saying (the buck was a marker used to indicate the player who was dealing). *To pass the buck* is an idiomatic expression meaning to shift responsibility to someone else.

1976. In a large corporation there's always someone to pass the buck to. But the buck stops with the owner of a business. —Claudia Jessup and Genie Chipps, *The Women's Guide to Starting a Business*

1987. Quotation of the Day—"It would be better if the President would say, 'The buck stops at my desk. If I didn't know I should have known.'" —Senator Orrin G. Hatch, Republican of Utah, *New York Times*

1987. John M. Poindexter—"You know the buck stops here with me. I made the decision, I—felt that I had the authority to do it; I thought it was a good idea. I was convinced that the President would, in the end, think it was a good idea." (July 15). —"Iran-Contra Hearings," *New York Times*

1987. I was aware the resistance was receiving funds directly from third countries and from private efforts, and I endorsed those endeavors wholeheartedly; but—let me put this in capital letters—I did not know about the diversion of funds. Indeed, I didn't know there were excess funds.

Yet the buck does not stop with Admiral Poindexter, as he stated in his testimony; it stops with me. —"Transcript of Reagan Address on Foreign and Domestic Issues on August 12, 1987," *New York Times*

1988. Q. Mr. President, you didn't know about the divergence of funds you say in the Iran-Contra scandal. Weinberger doesn't know about all of this alleged rampant bribery, fraud. Who's in charge? I mean, where does the buck stop? —"Excerpt from President Reagan's News Conference in Toronto," *New York Times*

1992. "Of all the whoppers George Bush tried to get away with in his speech last night, the biggest one wasn't even about me," Mr. Clinton said. "It came at the end, when this President compared himself to Harry Truman. Harry Truman had a sign on his desk in the Oval Office that said, 'The buck stops here.' If George Bush had a sign on his desk, it would say, 'Don't blame me. I'm just the President.'" —*New York Times*

1993. "I am accountable for that which goes on in my administration," Mr. Dinkins said. "I've said it again and again and again. The buck stops here." —*New York Times*

1993. "Hey, Pop ... Who said, 'The buck stops here'?"

"Ah, you're testing my keen powers of recall from my studies in school ... Elementary! It was the deerslayer in the novel by James Fenimore Cooper." —Cartoon by Art Sansom, "Born Loser," *Times* (Trenton)

Buddy can you spare a dime? *See* BROTHER CAN YOU SPARE A DIME?

A bull in a china shop. A dangerously clumsy person or thing in a delicate situation. Aesop spoke of an "ass in a potter's shop." The current use of the phrase comes from Frederick Marryat's *Jacob Faithful* (1834): "Whatever it is that smashes, Mrs. T. always swears it was the *most valuable* thing in the room. I'm like a bull in a china shop." The metaphor is used in other languages as well.

1983. In the short run, the Jackson candidacy hurts Mondale and helps all the other candidates. In the long run, his presence and get-out-the-vote efforts might help the eventual winner of the nomination. Or Jackson may be like a bull in a china shop, making it more difficult for any Democrat to win in 1984. —*Christian Science Monitor*

1984. They [the Syrians] have been acting like a bull in a china closet for some weeks now. —*New York Times*

1989. Maybe he should enroll Ray Dolley, his director of administrative services, who is known for managing like a bull in a china shop. —*Boston Globe*

1993. Usually soft-spoken, Mr. Seveino admits that he "was a bull in a china shop" earlier in his career. But he claims to have settled down. —*New York Times*

1995. Patrick Wrenn is no bull in a china shop, even though he's quick to admit he holds "five world records for breaking things with my hands." —*Commercial Appeal* (Memphis, Tennessee)

1998. Our economic productivity per person has been magnified even more. Before the industrial revolution, we might have been a mouse in the biosphere's china shop, but by now we have become a full-fledged bull. —*Christian Science Monitor*

A burnt (burned) child fears (dreads) the fire. Experience teaches caution. The proverb has been traced back to the collection of proverbs by Hendyng (1272–1307). In 1546, it was included in

John Heywood's collection of proverbs. In its current form, it has been used since 1580. First attested in the United States in the 1755 *Papers of Sir William Johnson.* The proverb is found in varying forms: *The burnt child fears the fire; A burned child stays away from the fire;* etc.

1913. As a burned child would recoil from fire. —Theodore Dreiser, *A Traveler at Forty*

1984. The burned child fears the fire and when dawn breaks next Tuesday voters may pull the covers over their ringing heads and refuse to get out of bed. —*Newsweek*

See also ONCE BURNED, TWICE SHY.

Business as usual. Despite the difficulty and danger, life goes on. It was a catch phrase of World War I. In a speech in 1914, Winston Churchill said: "The maxim of the British people is 'Business as usual.'" The phrase has been used ever since. During the Nazi air attacks on London in 1940, one could see the "business as usual" and "London can take it" slogans chalked up on the walls of destroyed buildings. *It's business as usual* is often used too.

1988. "We can't be *sure,* and if we're wrong, it's Bollinger and business as usual, and the wolves take over next January." —Robert Ludlum, *The Icarus Agenda*

1991. "Then he should be able to help us. If the answer is yes, we move accordingly. If no, the employee is off the hook and it's business as usual." —John Grisham, *The Firm*

1992. "This is a year when nothing is business as usual," he [Dr. Murphy] said at the time, addressing the impact of layoffs and tax increases. —*New York Times*

1993. Visiting the Rochester Institute of Technology in upstate New York with our son, we saw a poster urging energy conservation. Included was a copy of the institute's utility bill with this message: *What would you do if your utility bill looked like this?*
Underneath someone had scribbled: *Raise tuition and continue business as usual.* —Robert A. Oppenheim, "Campus Comedy," *Reader's Digest*

See also POLITICS AS USUAL.

Business before pleasure. Focus on your duties first and take life's pleasures later. The proverb dates back to *Grobiana's Nuptials* (c. 1640). In 1855, the English novelist William Makepeace Thackeray (1811–63) used the proverb in a slightly changed form, "Business first; pleasure afterwards" (*The Rose and the Ring*). First attested in the United States in the *Diary and Letters of Thomas Hutchinson* (1767). The proverb is found in varying forms: *Business comes before pleasure; Duty before pleasure; Business first, pleasure afterwards,* etc. *Combine business with pleasure* is an expression closely linked with the proverb.

1934. "In any case take your time, take your ease; combine business with pleasure." —F. Scott Fitzgerald, *Tender Is the Night*

1951. "Much as I adore your company, there is still business to attend to. Minerva is opening the door to let someone in, and as Mother Kipfer says, business must come before pleasure." —James Jones, *From Here to Eternity*

1973. "Now my friend up there"—he nodded toward the steps—"he's all business. But me, I like to combine business with pleasure. So you and me is gonna have ourselves a little fuck." —Jacqueline Susann, *Once Is Not Enough*

1992. Mind your own business before pleasure. —Diane Crosby, "Mixed Maxims," *Reader's Digest*

1994. Keep business and pleasure strictly separate this coming week. —Jeane Dixon, "Horoscope," *Times* (Trenton)

See also BUSINESS IS BUSINESS; NEVER MIX BUSINESS WITH PLEASURE.

Business is business. Nothing is more important than business and the profits it brings. There's no justification for not putting it first. The proverb has been traced back to the play *Heir at Law* (1797) by George Colman the Younger (1762–1836). First attested in the United States in *The Confidence Man* (1857) by Herman Melville (1819–91).

1983. He grinned. "Hey—what do you want from me? Business is business. I need an agent, don't I?" —Jackie Collins, *Hollywood Wives*

1986. "Now I have all the respect in the world for our governor—in fact, I was on his campaign committee—but my philosophy is that business is business." —Pat Conroy, *The Prince of Tides*

1989. "Dr. Elliot, if you want to play with the big kids in D.C., Lesson Number One is, Business is Business." —Tom Clancy, *Clear and Present Danger*

1991. Nathan Locke closed his office door and pointed DeVasher in the direction of the small conference table near the window. The two men hated each other and made no attempt to be cordial. But business was business, and they took orders from the same man. —John Grisham, *The Firm*

1992. "I understand that business is business,"

says [book editor Judith] Regan, adding that when she thinks of Madonna now, "I think of her as the Material Girl who can't come up with her own material." —Mitchel Fink, "The Insider," *People*

1993. "This is the first time we've been on the opposite side," Michael Biondi said. "But business is business, and family is family." —*New York Times*

1994. They seem to feel that most newspapers (surely not all) cater to that kind of news and only plant on Page One the most sordid news they can find because business is business and "grim news sells papers." Same for TV. —*Times* (Trenton)

See also BUSINESS BEFORE PLEASURE; NEVER MIX BUSINESS WITH PLEASURE.

The business of America is business. The chief business of Americans is business. The proverb is a slightly changed quotation from U.S. President Calvin Coolidge's speech before the Society of American Newspaper Editors on January 17, 1925.

1925. After all, the chief business of the American people is business. —Calvin Coolidge, quoted by Ralph Keyes in *Nice Guys Finish Seventh*

1961. "The government has no business in business, and I would be the last person in the world to ever try to involve the government in a business of mine. But the business of government *is* business," he remembered alertly, and continued with elation. "Calvin Coolidge said that, and Calvin Coolidge was a President, so it must be true." —Joseph Heller, *Catch-22*

1983. He [Calvin Coolidge] was elected Vice-President under the slogan "Law and Order," and President with the messages "Keep Cool with Coolidge," "Coolidge or Chaos" and "The chief business of the American people is business." —Paul Johnson, *Modern Times*

See also BUSINESS IS BUSINESS.

But it does move! The saying is attributed to Galileo Galilei (1564–1642). In his astronomical observations he confirmed the Copernican theory of the solar system, and came to the revolutionary conclusion that the earth revolves around the sun. At the age of seventy (1632) he was brought before the Inquisition and compelled to retract his views. As one legend has it, Galileo, after publicly denying his scientific discoveries, whispered, *"E pur si muove!"* ("But it does move!"). Variant translations are: *And yet it does move!, And yet it moves!, But still it does move!, Nevertheless, it does move.*

1971. The legend that Galileo whispered "but it does move," as he rose from his knees after the renunciation of his views, is probably apocryphal. —*Funk & Wagnalls New Encyclopedia*, Vol. 10

1984. Despite Italy's antipasto of chronic calamities, *e pur si muove*, as that Renaissance Italian improviser Galileo said, after the Church had compelled him to deny the discovery that the earth moves around the sun: "And yet it moves." —Jeff Davidson, "A Tale of Two Italys," *Reader's Digest*

But that's the way it is. *See* AND THAT'S THE WAY IT IS.

Butter wouldn't melt in his mouth. Said of a person who is not so harmless as he looks. The phrase was first attested in John Palsgrave's book on the French language (1530). In 1546 it was included in John Heywood's book of proverbs: "She looketh as butter would not melt in her mouth." In "Polite Conversation" (1738), Jonathan Swift wrote: "She looks as if butter wouldn't melt in her mouth but, I warrant, cheese won't choke her." As a rule, the saying is used sarcastically. According to William Safire, however, it means "eager to please, oleaginous in an attempt to curry favor," "all sweetness and light." The saying is found in varying forms: *One looks as though butter wouldn't freeze in one's mouth; Sugar wouldn't melt in that one's mouth; Butter wouldn't melt in one's mouth or under one's armpit*, etc.

1936. "I said some terrible things to him that night when he deserted us on the road, but I can make him forget them," she thought contemptuously, still sure of her power to charm. "Butter won't melt in my mouth when I'm around him. I'll make him think I always loved him and was just upset and frightened that night." —Margaret Mitchell, *Gone With the Wind*

1957. Sallow-faced landlady emerged at 2 p.m. "You have a little daughter," says she. Magical transformation! Butter wouldn't melt in mouth. —John Cheever, *The Wapshot Chronicle*

1984. I had a father-in-law who wanted to kill me. Why? Only because I was too good, that's why. Those were the days when butter wouldn't melt in my mouth. —Joseph Heller, *God Knows*

1988. In *The New York Times Magazine* last April, writer James Traub described Francis T. (Mickey) Featherstone, a former gang member, as looking like a cherub: "'If you saw this guy, you'd swear that butter wouldn't melt in his mouth,' says an acquaintance of his. 'But you'd hear the most horrible stories.'" —William Safire, *New York Times Magazine*

Caesar's wife must be above suspicion. Caesar's wife must not only be pure but must not even be suspected of any wrongdoing. "I wished my wife to be not so much as suspected," said Julius Caesar when asked by the prosecutor why he had divorced his wife. The traditional saying was cited in John Lyly's *Euphues and His England* (1580). First attested in the United States in *Newspaper Extracts Relating to New Jersey* (1778). The proverb is found in varying forms: *Caesar's wife ought to be above suspicion; Like Caesar's wife, it must keep its reputation above reproach; Being above reproach, like Caesar's wife, is all very well; A man's grammar, like Caesar's wife, must not only be pure, but above suspicion; Unlike Caesar's wife, no one is above suspicion,* etc. Often shortened to *Caesar's wife.*

1951. "She has to marry a man," Georgette, who knew Alma's plans, explained to Prew, "who is above suspicion and has so much position and prestige that it would be impossible for his wife to have ever been a whore." —James Jones, *From Here to Eternity*

1979. "This is a case of something being purer than Caesar's wife. That damn foundation is sacrosanct." —Howard Fast, *The Establishment*

1981. On the gayer side of the gay controversy: It seems that unlike Caesar's wife, no one is above suspicion—including Damon and Pythias, whose "brotherly" devotion to each other has been the talk of the last two centuries. —Abigail Van Buren, *The Best of Dear Abby*

1987. "Good morning, gentlemen!"
"Uh ... good morning, Mr. Vice President."
"Just thought I'd drop off another urine sample for you boys to test. Caesar's wife and all that." —G. B. Trudeau, *Doonesbury Deluxe*

1989. To their friends' knowledge, John had been a constant husband, one who had never participated in the "summer festival" of affairs and alliances with other women while the wives were staying at their summer homes, and Joyce certainly, like Caesar's wife, seemed above suspicion. —Judith Ramsey Ehrlich and Barry J. Rehfeld, *The New Crowd*

Call a spade a spade. Call things by their proper names and don't try to pretty them up via euphemisms. The phrase has been traced back to Greek and Roman times. The playwright Menander (about 342–292 b.c.) is quoted as saying, "I call a fig a fig, a spade a spade," though some people attribute this saying to Aristophanes (about 450–385 b.c.). Plutarch (a.d. 46–120) considered that "The Macedonians are a rude and clownish people that call a spade a spade." In common use since the sixteenth century. The English clergyman and scholar Robert Burton (1577–1640) wrote: "A loose, plain, rude writer ... I call a spade a spade." His contemporary, the poet John Taylor (1580–1653), said, "I think it good English, without fraud,/To call a spade a spade, a bawd a bawd."

1895. *Cecily:* When I see a spade I call it a spade.
Gwendolen: I am glad to say I have never seen a spade. It is obvious that our social spheres have been widely different. —Oscar Wilde, *The Importance of Being Earnest*

1909. Call a spade a spade, although it may be a shovel. —Mary Roberts Rinehart, *The Man in Lower Ten*

1926. He called a Ford a Ford. —P. G. Wodehouse, *Small Bachelor*

1963. And he took me down to what he called his "den" in order that we might, "... call a spade a

spade, and let the chips fall where they may."
—Kurt Vonnegut, Jr., *Cat's Cradle*

1992. "I am a straight-shooting politician who calls a spade a spade," he [Mr. Zakhem] said. —*New York Times*

1993. When discussing sex, why not call a spade a spade instead of couching it in antiquated euphemisms? —*New York Times Book Review*

1993. "We could've won two games if Drew had made a right decision," Parcells said, with more tolerance than complaint. "But he's a good solid young guy. He calls a spade a spade." —*New York Times*

Call me Ishmael. Call me an outcast, a homeless person, a vagabond, one who is rejected and discarded. According to the Old Testament, Ishmael was the elder son of the Hebrew patriarch Abraham and of Hagar, Egyptian handmaid of Abraham's wife. Ishmael and his mother were driven away into the wilderness. The Arabs consider Ishmael their ancestor. The phrase originated in the United States and was coined by Herman Melville in his novel *Moby Dick* (1851). When a snappy first sentence is needed, *call me ...* or *call it ...* is very much in favor in the nineties.

> **1851.** Call me Ishmael. Some years ago—never mind how long precisely—having little or no money in my purse, and nothing in particular to interest me on shore, I thought I would sail about a little and see the watery part of the world. —Herman Melville, *Moby Dick*

> **1991.** Call me Ishmael if you must, but Norman Mailer's depiction of John Simon as a maniacal Ahab merely marking his time over a long and prestigious (if controversial) career as a film and theater critic and occasional book reviewer ... strikes me as patently absurd. —*New York Times Magazine*

The calm before the storm. *See* AFTER A STORM COMES A CALM.

A can of worms. *See* IT'S LIKE OPENING A CAN OF WORMS.

A car in every garage and a chicken in every pot. *See* A CHICKEN IN EVERY POT.

Carpe diem. *See* SEIZE THE MOMENT.

Carthage must be destroyed. Do it, you've got to do it! Carthage was more prosperous than Rome. In 157 b.c. the Roman military leader and statesman Marcus Porcius Cato (234–149 b.c.) vis-

ited Carthage and realized that its revived prosperity was a constant threat to Rome. He was so jealous of it that for years he used to conclude every speech in the Roman senate, regardless of the subject, by saying, *"Ceterum censeo delenda est Carthago"* ("In my opinion, Carthage must be destroyed"). The saying *Delenda est Carthago* and its English equivalent *Carthage must be destroyed* are used to mean that roadblocks that stand in the way of one's might should be removed at any cost.

> **1967.** Cato, an aristocratic Roman landowner, used to end all his speeches with: "Carthage must be destroyed!" Many Romans lived in mortal fear of another invasion like Hannibal's.... They completely destroyed Carthage and cursed any who might attempt to rebuild it. —Nathaniel Platt, Muriel Jean Drummond, *Our World Through the Ages*

> **1991.** "The Twins must be defeated. I repeat: Minnesota must be destroyed," said an elderly baseball fan. —Overheard at a stadium box office

Cast your bread upon the waters. Be good to others; be a generous giver without expecting immediate reward in return, and you will be rewarded over time. The Old Testament teaches "Cast thy bread upon the waters; for thou shalt find it after many days" (*Ecclesiastes*, 11:1), and many writers employ this proverb in their works. O. Henry (1862–1910) is often quoted as saying, "The bread I had cast upon the waters began to come back in the form of college pudding." Elbert Hubbard wrote in his *Book of Epigrams* (1911), "Cast your bread upon the waters and it will come back to you—buttered."

> **1957.** "Was generous giver myself. On several occasions gave large sums to needy strangers. One-hundred-dollar bill to cab starters at Parker House. Fifty dollars to old lady selling lavender at Park Street Church. Eight dollars to stranger in restaurant who claimed son needed operation. Other donations forgotten, Cast bread upon waters, so to speak." —John Cheever, *The Wapshot Chronicle*

> **1981.** *Bread upon the Waters.* —Title of a novel by Irwin Shaw

> **1983.** Her mother once told Elizabeth N. Metayer, "If you cast your bread upon the water, it will come back as cake." For the 71-year-old grandmother known as "Bibs," the icing on the cake of a life in public service has been five terms as state representative from East Braintree. —*Boston Globe*

> **1997.** Tim and Maria Bonesteel cast their bread upon the waters and got back a flotilla of goodwill. Scores of people came to the aid of the East Wind-

sor couple who run East Windsor Pizza. The Bonesteels' supporters collected about $1,800 to help them pay back taxes and keep their restaurant open. —*Commercial Appeal* (Memphis, Tennessee)

1997. "So many people have called who used to live in the neighborhood, from South Carolina, from Florida, and asked where they could send money [to rebuild the church]," she said. "Charles has cast his bread on the waters and it's come back to him." —Carolina Gonzalez, *New York Daily News*

Cat got your tongue? *See* HAS THE CAT GOT YOUR TONGUE?

A cat has nine lives. Cats have an exceptional power of survival. The proverb is used in reference to people who go through difficult times and survive. "A woman hath nine lives like a cat," said John Heywood in his book of proverbs (1546). First attested in the United States in *New Voyage to Carolina* (1709). The proverb is found in varying forms: *One has more lives than the proverbial cat; A woman hath nine lives like a cat; A woman has nine cat's lives,* etc.

1894. One of the most striking differences between a cat and a lie is that a cat has only nine lives. —Mark Twain, *Pudd'nhead Wilson*

1968. I have died the ninth death of the cat. —Eldridge Cleaver, *Soul on Ice*

1985. A weed is a plant with nine lives. —*Reader's Digest*

1987. "You can't play this way against a team that always seems to have nine lives," said Lowe, referring to the Oilers' demise in the game's final 39 minutes and the Flyers' propensity for constructing stubborn comebacks. —*New York Times*

1988. "A cat has nine lives, Ben," Barney retorted. "You're a very cool cat, so that leaves you with eight more." —Erich Segal, *Doctors*

1991. Creeping over her skin came the blue tinge of death. Moving swiftly, a physician instructed Laneer to shoot a hefty dose of tranquilizer into Angelle. She passed out, suddenly still. All present stood rooted, their hearts in their throats. Slowly, they saw the blue color fade from Angelle's face. Her eyes flickered open; she lapsed into sleep. Laneer thought to herself, *This Girl Has Nine Lives.* —Peter Michelmore, "Young Heroes of St. Jude," *Reader's Digest*

1993. FINALLY, AFTER SEVERAL OF HIS NINE LIVES, ARAFAT IS GOING TO THE WHITE HOUSE —Headline of Youssef M. Ibrahim's article, *New York Times*

1993. You are a bad kitty! I hereby sentence you to life, life, life, life, life, life, life, life, and life. —Cartoon by Bob Thaves, "Frank and Earnest," *Times* (Trenton)

1994. Some computers have nine lives left. Others don't. —Ad by Intel Corporation, *Business Week*

A/The cat in gloves catches no mice. One can't achieve anything if one's too cautious or finicky. The proverb goes back to the fourteenth century and is similar to the French: *Chat engaunté ne surrizera ja bien* ("A gloved cat will never mouse well"). In 1754, it was used by Benjamin Franklin in his *Poor Richard's Almanac.*

1754. Handle your Tools without Mittens; remember that the Cat in Gloves catches no Mice. —Benjamin Franklin, *Poor Richard's Almanac*

See also NOTHING VENTURED, NOTHING GAINED; THERE ARE NO GAINS WITHOUT PAINS.

The cat is out of the bag. Originally the saying meant to reveal a trick following an attempt to sell a cat instead of a pig. Now used to mean that a secret has been revealed. The idiom *let the cat out of the bag* is often used too.

1947. *Stanley:* You know she's been feeding us a pack of lies here?
Stella: No, I don't, and—
Stanley: Well, she has, however. But now the cat's out of the bag! —Tennessee Williams, *A Streetcar Named Desire*

1976. Rumor has it that the CIA plans to give $6,000,000 to the Christian Democrats in Italy to make sure the Communists don't get elected. But there are some people in Washington who feel that now that the cat is out of the bag, the contribution could be counterproductive. —Art Buchwald, *Washington Is Leaking*

1992. He read it [the story in the New Orleans paper] quickly while they watched him. It talked about their friendship, and their strange deaths just six days apart. And it mentioned Darby Shaw, who had disappeared. But no link to the brief.
"I guess the cat's out of the bag," Feldman said. —John Grisham, *The Pelican Brief*

1995. Finally, the cat is out of the bag. Former Defense Secretary Robert McNamara, a main Vietnam War hawk, tearfully admits that the war was a mistake. It took him about 35 years to realize the folly of a war which cost 58,000 American and 3 million Vietnamese lives. —Satya Prasad, "Readers' Forum," "McNamara Sheds Crocodile Tears," *Star-Ledger* (Newark, N.J.)

Catch-22. *See* IT'S A CATCH-22 SITUATION.

C'est la vie. *See* THAT'S LIFE.

A chain is as strong as its weakest link. *See* A CHAIN IS NO STRONGER THAN ITS WEAKEST LINK.

A chain is no stronger than its weakest link. No matter how strong someone or something is, it is always limited by its weakest attribute. The proverb has been traced back to C. Kingsley's letter dated December 1, 1856. First cited in the United States in the early twentieth century. The proverb is found in varying forms: *A chain is as strong as its weakest link; A chain is only as strong as its weakest link; The strength of a chain is its weakest link,* etc.

> **1981.** Chairman Mao never claimed credit for saying, "A chain is as strong as its weakest link." Nevertheless, that principle applies to your complete wardrobe.... —Mortimer Levitt, *The Executive Look*
>
> **1984.** As the weakest link in the chain, Chrysler got hit first. —Lee Iacocca with William Novak, *Iacocca*
>
> **1993.** Our class is the weakest link in a generally strong school chain. And the strength of the chain, as they say, is no greater than its weakest link. —Overhead at a teacher-parent association conference at Princeton Junction, N.J.

Character is destiny. Personality and habitual behavior determine one's destiny. Attributed to the Greek philosopher Heraclitus (about 540–480 b.c.).

> **1984.** "We're Jews, not Greeks. Tell us another flood is coming and we'll learn how to live under water. Character is destiny."
> Friedrich Nietzsche would have understood. If character is destiny, the good are damned. In such wisdom is much grief. —Joseph Heller, *God Knows*
>
> **1992.** Character is destiny, Ms. Sheehy believes, and these profiles of six Presidential candidates and Ronald Reagan try to prove it. —*New York Times*

Charity begins at home. One's own family (or country, etc.) comes before any other responsibilities. The idea of the proverb can be found in the Bible. The proverb dates back to the time of the Roman comic playwright Terence (about 190–159 b.c.). In 1383, John Wycliffe wrote: "Charity should begin at himself." Five hundred years later Dickens said that "Charity begins at home, and justice begins next door." First attested in the United States in the *Winthrop Papers* (1628). The proverb is found in varying forms: *Charity begins and ends at home; Charity begins at home and usually stays there; Delinquency, like charity, begins at home; Brevity, like charity, should start at home; Strength begins at home,* etc.

> But if any widow have children or nephews, let them learn first to shew piety at home, and to requite their parents: for that is good and acceptable before God. —1 Timothy 5:4, *Authorized Version,* 1611
>
> **1643.** But how shall we expect charity towards others, when we are uncharitable to ourselves? Charity begins at home, is the voice of the world; yet is every man his greatest enemy, and, as it were, his own executioner. —Thomas Browne, *Religio Medici,* Part II
>
> **1947.** "They say that charity begins at home, Eugene, but apparently you are not a charitable man." —Irving Stone, *Adversary in the House*
>
> **1981.** Some parents' discoveries don't come in the mail—clarity begins at home. —Abigail Van Buren, *The Best of Dear Abby*
>
> **1986.** Due to a recent disability, I applied for food stamps. I was told to watch a short program on how and where to get them. I was also handed a booklet for the program. It was all in Spanish. When I asked if it would be shown in English, I received a sneer. If you don't speak English, you receive better care. What happened to "charity begins at home"? —Theresa Peters, "To the Editor," *Daily News* (New York)
>
> **1991.** CHARITY BEGINS WITH THE NEW OPPOSITION PARTIES —Headline of Francis X. Clines's article about soup kitchens in Moscow, *New York Times*
>
> **1992.** I know well that the world needs a strong America, but we have learned that strength begins at home. —"Transcript of Speech by Clinton Accepting Democratic Nomination," *New York Times*
>
> **1993.** Finally, the congressman [Payne] discussed the tragedy to our country of not following the old adage: "Charity begins at home." —*Times* (Trenton)

See also BLOOD IS THICKER THAN WATER; EVERY MAN FOR HIMSELF.

The check is in the mail. The saying is used to avoid responsibility, especially for financial debts. Of recent origin.****

> **1984.** "The check is in the mail," he said, putting his hand to his mouth. Read on—and learn to spot the body language of dishonesty. —*Reader's Digest*
>
> **1985.** As a farmer, my brother-in-law often re-

ceives new shipments of young poultry through a farm mail-order service. One Saturday he headed to the post office to pick up a shipment due that day. When he returned empty-handed, my sister asked him what had happened.

"Well," he replied, "it's like they always say—the chick's in the mail." —"All in a Day's Work," *Reader's Digest*

1988. The KGB were strong suspects, and Alevy sent a copy of the repair bill to Lubyanka. Some KGB wag there sent a return note saying, "Check is in the mail." —Nelson DeMille, *The Charm School*

1991. Yesterday Mayor Dinkins put the city's media on notice that he's going to charter a plane for his international trip next month—and anyone who wants to hop a ride has to ante up $6,000—just for transportation.

Says Post editor Jerry Nachman: "We want to go. We don't know yet if we can afford to. I hope the mayor trusts us if we tell him the check is in the mail." —*New York Post*

1992. The card sent to Maggie Anderson by a neighbor [Feb. 8, 1937 and delivered Feb. 8, 1992] redefines "It's in the mail." —"Special Delivery," *People*

1993. That would be welcome news for the local tradesmen, I told him, since his traditional palliative for a temporary shortfall is to answer the phone "The check's in the mail" instead of "Hello." —Calvin Trillin, "Morrissey Threatens to Leave City," *Times* (Trenton)

A chicken in every pot. Prosperity for all the people. In his coronation speech, Henry IV, King of France (1589–1610), promised every peasant "a chicken in his pot on Sunday." The U.S. Republican Party used this phrase as its campaign slogan in 1928, promising not only a chicken in every pot but a car in every garage as well. *A car in every garage and a chicken in every pot* is a variant of the saying.

1589. If God grants me the usual length of life, I hope to make France so prosperous that every peasant will have a chicken in his pot on Sunday. —Henry IV, quoted by Robert Hendrickson in *Business Talk* (1984)

1928. A Chicken in Every Pot. —Republican (Hoover) campaign slogan

1978. He heard George Richardson saying from a great distance: *It's the flu. No more babies because of the flu. Pregnancy is death because of the flu. A chicken in every pot and a wolf in every womb.* —Stephen King, *The Stand*

1992. "Clinton's a showboat," he [a 35-year-old

butcher] said. "He's running around offering a chicken in every pot. When a man makes a lot of promises, you've got to watch him." —*New York Times*

The chickens have come home to roost. One has to face the consequences of one's past actions. In English, the proverb goes back to Chaucer's "Parson's Tale" (c. 1390). It was also well known to Terence (about 190–159 b.c.). First attested in the United States in the *Life of Jefferson S. Batkins* (1871). The proverb is found in varying forms: *Curses, like chickens, come home to roost; Sooner or later all chickens come home to roost; Chickens eventually come home to roost; Your curses will come to roost on your head,* etc.

1922. Husband rolling in drunk, stink of pub off him like a polecat. Have that in your nose in the dark, whiff of stale boose. Then ask in the morning: was I drunk last night? Bad policy however to fault the husband. Chickens come home to roost. —James Joyce, *Ulysses*

1936. It was bad luck to wish that someone were dead, almost as bad luck as to curse someone. Curses came home to roost, Mammy said. —Margaret Mitchell, *Gone With the Wind*

1966. When McGeorge Bundy or another aide would bring an urgent message to his desk, the President would ask, in a voice resigned to bad news and not wholly able to make light of it, "What's happened now?" He liked quoting General MacArthur's reminder to him in late April: "The chickens are coming home to roost, and you happen to have moved into the chicken house." —Theodore C. Sorensen, *Kennedy*

1984. For years, Chrysler had been run by men who didn't really like the car business. And now the chickens were coming home to roost. —Lee Iacocca with William Novak, *Iacocca*

1991. "Chickens come home to roost between now and 1994," he [Salomon's Joseph Bencivenga] says. —Edmund Faltermayer, "The Dead Decade: Verdict on the '80s," *Fortune*

1992. In the wake of the John F. Kennedy assassination, while the entire world was still in shock, Malcolm announced that the white man, by perpetrating a culture of violence against blacks, had set that stage for such a tragedy—that "the chickens were coming home to roost." —Joel Dreyfuss, "Malcolm X," *People*

1993. "You don't understand the repercussions of your own actions until you see them reflected in your children. That's where it comes home to roost." —Jessica Lange, quoted by Nancy Collins in "Full-Tilt Jessica," *Vanity Fair*

1994. And here, argues Ms. Ladd, "the chickens are coming home to roost" in the form of higher state taxes or as deterioration in the quality of popular public services. —*New York Times*

See also AS YOU SOW, SO (SHALL) YOU REAP; WHAT GOES AROUND, COMES AROUND; YOU'VE MADE YOUR BED, NOW LIE IN IT.

The child is father of the man. The character of a person is determined by his or her childhood. The proverb in its present form was used in 1807 by William Wordsworth in the poem, "My Heart Leaps Up." First attested in the United States in *Flush Times of Alabama and Mississippi* (1853). The proverb is found in varying forms: *The child is father to the man; The boy is father of the man; The boy is father to the man; The past is the father of the present,* etc.

1975. "The child is father of the man ..."
   "No, he [Richard Nixon] has always been exactly the same. I never knew a person to change so little.... As you know, most boys go through a mischievous period. Well, none of these things happened to Richard. He was thoughtful and serious" (Hannah Nixon). —David Wallechinsky and Irving Wallace, *The People's Almanac*

1985. "The lady who is my opponent is very charming and very persuasive, but what of her past? What do you know about it? They say the child is the father of the man. Then the past is the father of the present." —Howard Fast, *The Immigrant's Daughter*

1992. THE CHILD IS FARTHER THAN THE MAN —Headline of E. J. Baumeister, Jr.'s article in which he reminisces about his son, *Times* (Trenton)

1992. Mike Wallace goes home again to Brookline High and remembers the boy who was father to the man. —*People*

Choose the lesser of two evils. Choose the less harmful of two bad options. The proverb goes back in English to Chaucer's *Troilus and Criseyde* (c. 1385): "Of harmes two, the lesse is for to chuse." But long before him, the proverb was known to Homer ("The most preferable of evils"), Aristotle ("We must as second best ... take the least of the evils"), and Cicero (*Minima de malis*: "Of two evils, the least should be chosen"). Thomas à Kempis (1380–1471) wrote in his book *The Imitation of Christ*: "Of two evils the less is always to be chosen." *Of two evils, choose the lesser* is a variant of the proverb. First attested in

the United States in the *Winthrop Papers* (1714). The proverb is found in varying forms: *Always take the lesser of two evils; Of two evils choose the lesser; It is a choice of two evils; One has to choose between two evils,* etc.

1936. Mammy sighed resignedly, beholding herself outguessed. Between the two evils, it was better to have Scarlett wear an afternoon dress at a morning barbecue than to have her gobble like a hog. —Margaret Mitchell, *Gone With the Wind*

1992. The newspaper [*The Amsterdam News*] then applied "the lesser of two evils" principle, warning readers against trusting Mr. Abrams and urging them to back the incumbent [Senator D'Amato] but "keep both eyes open all night." —*New York Times*

1993. In an interview with Florio last week, I asked him about a statement by the N.J. Education Association (who refused to endorse either candidate) that appeared to reflect the "lesser of two evils" attitude of many. —*Times* (Trenton)

1994. "If you have two evils, you choose the lesser of the two," Father Belot said. "Right now we feel that the Americans are the lesser." —*New York Times*

A clean bill of health. A document that certifies that someone or something is healthy; by extension, any certification that one is free of any faults. The phrase goes back to the nineteenth century when bills of health were issued to ships' masters to the effect that no infectious diseases had been reported in the port of embarkation. Foul bills of health were given if the ships sailed from infected places. *To be given a clean bill of health* or *to get a clean bill of health* and *to have a clean bill of health* are commonly used idioms.

1990. The Bush administration has given Yasir Arafat and the mainstream of the Palestine Liberation Organization a generally clean bill of health as far as their December 1988 commitments renouncing the use of terror are concerned. —Wolf Blitzer, "PLO Gets Clean Bill of Health in First Administration Update," *Jewish Week* (New York).

1992. The investigations were eventually dropped, and *The Washington Post* said today that it had given Mr. Doder a "clean bill of health." —*New York Times*

1993. "Your heart and lungs sound good. And your reflexes are fine. I'm giving you a clean bill of health."
   "Yes, and it's an expensive one!" —Cartoon by Chic Young and Stan Drake, " *Blondie,* " King Features Syndicate

1995. "I hope President Clinton will get a clean bill of health after years-long Whitewater investigations." —Overheard at Washington Bridge Bus Terminal

Cleanliness is next to godliness. Cleanliness is second in importance only to religious devotion. In *The Advancement of Learning* (1605), Francis Bacon wrote: "Cleanliness of body was ever deemed to proceed from a due reverence to God." British clergyman John Wesley (1703–91) told his congregation that "Cleanliness is, indeed, next to godliness." However, this proverb can be traced to ancient times. According to the fourteenth edition of *Brewer's Dictionary of Phrase and Fable*, it is an old Hebrew proverb used in the late 2nd century by Rabbi Phinehas ben-Yair. First attested in the United States in the *Monthly Anthology and Boston Review* (1806). The proverb is found in varying forms: *Godliness comes next to cleanliness; Cleanliness is furthest from godliness; If we can't have godliness, at least we can have cleanliness*, etc.

1788. Let it be observed, that slovenliness is no part of religion; that neither this, nor any text of Scripture, condemns neatness of apparel. Certainly this is a duty, not a sin. "Cleanliness is, indeed, next to godliness." —John Wesley, Sermon 88, *Sermons on Several Occasions*

1961. From General Peckem's office on the mainland came prolix bulletins each day headed by such cheery homilies as "Procrastination is the Thief of Time" and "Cleanliness is Next to Godliness." —Joseph Heller, *Catch-22*

1986. Cleanliness is next to godliness, we're told, and with these animal-puppet washcloths in their bath, your little ones will be spotless *and* cherubic ($5.95). —*New York*

1993. As we all know, and certainly the Board of Good Burghers here that constitutes representative government knows, tidiness is next to cleanliness. (Whoever said that cleanliness is next to Godliness was probably trying to manipulate some soiled child with a new—and probably fearful—awareness of the Deity. Cleanliness is next to emptiness. But I digress.) —E. J. Baumeister, *Times* (Trenton)

Close but no cigar. Close, but you didn't make it. Close, but not close enough to get a cigar as a prize for hitting a target at a carnival shooting contest. Very few actually got the prize. The saying originated in the early twentieth century and is used as a reply to a very close guess.

1991. Tariq Aziz [recent fortunes] Close, but no cigar. Hope your rent-a-car had unlimited free mileage. —"Conventional Wisdom Watch," *Newsweek*

1992. "Dammit. I knew it was him. It was the kid in the photos, wasn't it?"
"No. Close but no cigar. Keep trying." —John Grisham, *The Pelican Brief*
See also A MISS IS AS GOOD AS A MILE.

Clothes don't make the man. Don't judge a person by the clothing he or she is wearing. The proverb has been traced back to about 1500. First attested in the United States in *Writings of George Washington* (1783). The proverb is found in varying forms: *Clothes do not make the gentleman; Clothes do not unmake the man; It's not just clothes that make the man; Clothes don't make the woman, but they help*, etc.

1983. He opened the closet and selected black slacks, his one and only silk shirt, and a lightweight Yves Saint Laurent jacket. Fortunately, in Buddy's case, clothes did not make the man. —Jackie Collins, *Hollywood Wives*

1993. You are smart enough to understand that clothes don't make the woman, but it sure helps. —Overheard at a Manhattan boutique
See also ALL THAT GLITTERS IS NOT GOLD APPEARANCES (LOOKS) ARE DECEIVING (DECEPTIVE); DON'T JUDGE A BOOK BY ITS COVER.

Clothes make the man. The proverb is of ancient origin. It appears in Babylonian writings. In 1523, it was included in Erasmus's collection of sayings ("Clothes are the man"). Greeks say that "The man is his clothing." Germans say, "Clothes make the man and rag makes lice." The old English proverb says that it takes nine tailors to make a man. First attested in the United States in *Writings of George Washington* (1783). Mark Twain is often quoted as saying, "Clothes make the man. Naked people have little or no influence in society." According to the Sixteenth Edition of Bartlett's *Familiar Quotations*, it is attributed to him. "Tailors," said Steinbeck, "make men in any image they want." Canadian author Steven Leacock (1869–1944) wrote in 1910: "The well-known proverb, 'Clothes make the man,' has its origin in a general recognition of the powerful influence of the habiliments in their reaction upon the wearer." In *Hamlet*, Shakespeare writes, "The apparel oft proclaims the man." The proverb is found in varying forms: *It's clothes, not manners, that makyth man; Fine clothes make the man; Clothes* *do make the woman,* etc. It has its counterparts in other languages too: *Kleider machen Leute* (German, "Clothes make people").

1974. But the first glimpse they will have of you, even before you utter a sound, is how you look and what you are wearing. On the surface this may sound inconsequential, even frivolous, but the cliché that "clothes make the man" still holds good. —Milla Alihan, *Corporate Etiquette*

1989. With his money Ranieri bought five power-boats. "Then I had more boats than suits," he says. Other than that he lived modestly, without flashy cars or new homes. The clothes made the man, and everyone noticed the clothes. —Michael Lewis, *Liar's Poker*

1991. CLOTHES HELP MAKE THE WOMAN —Headline of Eve M. Kahn's article about the outfits for Roma Downey in the role of Jacqueline Bouvier Kennedy Onassis in "A Woman Named Jackie," an NBC miniseries, *New York Times*

1993. On the screen: Eve Southern and Walter Pidgeon in "Clothes Make the Woman." —*Times* (Trenton)

1993. Clothes reflect the man, but if you're smart you can play with it. —Mario Van Peebles, quoted by Eric P. Nash, "Does Fashion Matter?" *New York Times Magazine*

See also CLOTHES DON'T MAKE THE MAN; FINE FEATHERS MAKE FINE BIRDS; MANNERS MAKE THE MAN.

A/The cobbler should stick to his last. One should not interfere in matters in which one is not knowledgeable or informed. The proverb is attributed to the Greek artist Apelles (325 B.C.): *Ne supra crepidam sutor iudicaret* ("The cobbler should not judge beyond his shoe"). Once, a cobbler noticed a fault in a shoe-latchet in a painting by the great artist. When Apelles corrected the fault, the cobbler had the gall to criticize the legs in the painting. "Keep to your trade," Apelles was quoted as saying, "you understand about shoes, but not about anatomy." In 1539, it was included in R. Taverner's collection and in 1721 in J. Kelly's collection of proverbs. First attested in the United States in 1647. The proverb is found in varying forms: *Let the cobbler (shoemaker) stick to his last; It's a wise cobbler that sticks to his last; Every man to his own last; Ne sutor ultra crepidam* (Latin, "Let not the cobbler go beyond his last"), etc. Often shortened to *to stick to one's last.*

1928. I do think that the cobbler should stick to his last. —Aldous L. Huxley, *Point Counter Point*

1964. Shoemaker, stick to your last! And when the dismissal bell rang, they paid me the highest compliment: they groaned! They crowded in the doorway, chirping like agitated sparrows, pecking at the seeds I had strewn ... —Bel Kaufman, *Up the Down Staircase*

1993. "I could never get up enough nerve to run for an office I'm not qualified for. But he *is* running. He forgot that a shoemaker should stick to his last." —Overheard at a Giuliani-for-mayor election rally

A cobbler's child is always the worst shod. *See* THE SHOEMAKER'S KIDS ALWAYS GO BAREFOOT.

Cold hands, warm heart. A reserved, cool exterior may disguise a kind heart. The proverb has been traced back to *Collectanea* (1903) by V. S. Lean. First cited in the United States in *Blue Murder* (1928) by E. Snell. The proverb is found in varying forms: *A cold hand, a warm heart; Cold 'and, warm 'eart,* etc.

1984. "I'm not a cold fish, though my hands are always cold."
   'Cold hands, warm heart,' says the wise proverb. —Overheard in a New Jersey diner

1992. Cold Calls Breed Cold Hearts. —Jeff Herman, *Insider's Guide to Book Editors, Publishers, and Literary Agents*

1993. "I'm freezing, my hands are freezing."
   Well, as my mother used to say, 'Cold hands, warm heart' —Overheard on the Rockefeller Plaza skating rink

Combine business with pleasure. *See* BUSINESS BEFORE PLEASURE.

Comparing apples and oranges. Comparing completely different things. The American proverb is quite recent. The phrase *apples and oranges* is often used allusively to refer to two completely different things.

1983. If, on the one hand, art is seen as exclusively representative of the culture that produced it, then it would no more make sense to compare the art of different cultures than to compare apples and oranges. —*Christian Science Monitor*

1986. He [White House Press Secretary Larry Speakes] said the Mayor [Koch] had "mixed apples and oranges" when he said the Government was spending billions on building Trident submarines but only $20 million on educating people about the evils of drugs. —*New York Times*

1993. [Janet] Reno is unconcerned at how her assertion of BNL-Rome's innocence bolsters the Italian bank's claim against the U.S. for $380 million of the loans to Saddam that James Baker persuaded Agriculture's Clayton Yeutter to guarantee. If the Criminal Division holds that Rome was victimized, shouldn't the United States pay up? "Apples and oranges," [John] Hogan tells me; that's the Civil Division's job. —William Safire, *New York Times*

1993. At one point, the two [Van Cliburn and John Browning] were scheduled to perform the Tchaikovsky concerto a week apart at the Hollywood Bowl; "I'm not saying I came out badly," insisted Mr. Browning. "I'm just saying we both felt uncomfortable—we were apples and oranges." —*New York Times*

1994. Bond insurance for the Buffalo issue was only $157,000, an eighth of what it cost the Dormitory Authority. Defenders of the muni-savers dispute the comparison. "It's like comparing apples and oranges," says Rudolph J. Rinaldi, executive director of the Dormitory Authority." We were trying to reach out to small-time investors and we did that." —*Crain's New York Business*

1997. Bear Stearns analyst Jason Ader said comparing the Millennium group with Mirage is "like comparing apples to oranges. It's just different." —*Detroit News*

1998. Rep. Sheila Jackson Lee (D-TX), Judiciary Committee: "Unfortunately, what I would offer to say is there's been no new thinking in this room, because as I read the provision, "treason and bribery and other high crimes and misdemeanors," I do not hear the claim treason and bribery and unfit morals. So we are discussing actually—apples and oranges for the American people. That confusion causes the divide and the inability for us to come together in a collaborative and bipartisan manner." —*Cable News Network*

1998. "These results are entirely unacceptable," Education Secretary Richard Riley said Tuesday. "They absolutely confirm our need to raise our standards." Education officials blame poor curricula, low expectations of students, and unqualified teachers. But local educators question the weight of a study they say compares "oranges to apples." —*Detroit News*

Comparisons are odious. Don't pass judgment on a person by comparing him with another. People should be judged on their own merits. The proverb dates back to the 14th century and is similar to the French: *Comparaisons sont haÿneuses* ("Comparisons are hateful") or *Toute comparaison est odieuse* ("Comparisons are odious"). John Lyd-

gate (about 1370–about 1450) was probably the first English poet to introduce the proverb to the English people in 1430. It was used by John Fortescue in 1471, John Donne (1572–1631), Cervantes in *Don Quixote* (1605–15), and Jonathan Swift in 1724. The proverb, however, is usually associated with Shakespeare, who used it in a malaproprian fashion in *Much Ado About Nothing*. First attested in the United States in *Dialogue or Third Conference* (1652) by William Bradford (1590–1657), one of the Pilgrim Fathers.

1598–1600.
Dogberry: Comparisons are odorous: palabras, neighbor Verges. —Shakespeare, *Much Ado About Nothing,* Act III, Scene V

1724. A Judge ... checked the Prisoner ... taxing him with "reflecting on the court by such a Comparison, because Comparisons are odious." —Jonathan Swift, *The Drapier's Letters*

1957. Comparisons may be odious, but they are fun. —*New York Times Book Review*

1992. It was in this interview that Mr. Clinton showed just how careful he is treading cultural waters. Asked the defining cultural question of his generation—Who was better, the Beatles or the Stones?—he replied: "Well, they're totally different. To try to compare, as Shakespeare once said, is odious. These are unique people ..." —*New York Times*

Consider the lilies of the field. Words of Jesus, calling upon his followers not to worry about their everyday needs. First appeared in the New Testament.

And why take ye thought for raiment? Consider the lilies of the field, how they grow; they toil not, neither do they spin:
And yet I say unto you, That even Solomon in all his glory was not arrayed like one of these. —Matthew 6:28–29, *Authorized Version,* 1611

1953. Shut up, thought Montag. Consider the lilies of the field.
"Denham's Dentifrice."
They toil not—
"Denham's—"
Consider the lilies of the field, shut up, shut up. —Ray Bradbury, *Fahrenheit 451*

1962. "Consider the lilies, Hub. They toil not, neither do they spin, and yet I say unto you that Solomon in all his glory was not arrayed like one of these."
"Amen, brothers!" —John Updike, *The Music School*

Consistency is the hobgoblin of little minds. *See* A FOOLISH CONSISTENCY IS THE HOBGOBLIN OF LITTLE MINDS.

The course of true love never did run smooth. Problems may crop up even in the most passionate of courtships and the best of marriages. The proverb is found in Shakespeare's *A Midsummer Night's Dream*. First attested in the United States in *Swallow Barn* (1812). The proverb is found in varying forms: *The path of true love never runs smooth; True love never runs smooth,* etc.

> **1595.** *Lysander:* Ay me! for aught that I could ever read,
> Could ever hear by tale or history,
> The course of true love never did run smooth
> —Shakespeare, *A Midsummer Night's Dream,* Act I, Scene I

> **1934.** Ralph's letter was a long, involved, and—in Etta's opinion—priggish document, beginning with another string of apologies, repeating most of what he had said, and going over all their past. Quite a valuable essay on the theme of the course of true love never did run smooth, Etta thought sardonically. —Richard Aldington, *Women Must Work*

A coward dies a thousand deaths. *See* THE COWARD DIES MANY TIMES.

The coward dies a thousand deaths, the brave but one. *See* THE COWARD DIES MANY TIMES.

The coward dies many times. A person who lacks courage is disgraced each time he faces adversity. The proverb has been traced back to *Mortimeriados* (1596). Shakespeare used it in his tragedy *Julius Caesar* (1599). The proverb is found in varying forms: *Cowards die many times before their deaths* (Shakespeare); *A coward dies a thousand deaths; The coward dies a thousand deaths, the brave but one,* etc.

> **1599.** *Caesar:* Cowards die many times before their deaths;
> The valiant never taste of death but once.
> Of all the wonders that I yet have heard,
> It seems to me most strange that men should fear;
> Seeing that death, a necessary end,
> Will come when it will come.
> —Shakespeare, *Julius Caesar,* Act II, Scene II

> **1952.** "In that life, believe me, the thoughtful, the sensitive, those who can recognize the ridiculous, die a thousand deaths." —Kurt Vonnegut, *Player Piano*

> **1986.** I hope he suffered. I hope he died a thousand deaths. —Jackie Collins, *Hollywood Husbands*

Cowards die many times before their death. *See* THE COWARD DIES MANY TIMES.

Cream always comes to the top. The best will always rise to prominence and win recognition. The proverb was first cited in the United States in *Essays* (1841) by Ralph Waldo Emerson (1803–82). The word *rises* may be substituted for *comes.*

> **1964.** Never mind the cream [of the crop]; it will always rise to the top. It's the skim milk that needs good teachers. —Bel Kaufman, *Up the Down Staircase*

> **1989.** "Cream will rise, as they say. Damon just can't handle that it's my cream." —Wayne Care, *Vietnam Spook Show*

> **1993.** "My mother said, 'The cream will rise to the top.' I [Jeff Schwarz] said, "Mom, I've been churning and nothin's rose yet'" —*New York Times*

Crime doesn't pay. Inevitably, sooner or later, criminals will be caught and punished. First attested in the United States in N. Martin's *Mosaic* (1927). The saying was popularized in the 1930s through the radio crime drama "The Shadow." The proverb is found in varying forms: *Crime doesn't pay like it used to; Crime doesn't pay in the end; Who says crime doesn't pay?; Crime does pay after all,* etc.

> **1987.** The man on the radio with the deep voice was saying, *"The weeds of crime bear … bitter fruit … crime does not pay …"* —Fannie Flagg, *Fried Green Tomatoes*

> **1991.** Who says crime doesn't pay? The reader who solves the "Murder Game" mystery gets $10,000.00 in cash! —Ad for Carrol & Graf Publishers, Inc., *New York Times Book Review*

> **1992.** How crime pays…. KLM Productions bought Amy Fisher's rights for $80,000 as part of an intricate bail-financing plan.
> … TriStar Television bought rights from both Mary Jo and Joey Buttafuoco for a reported $300,000. —*People*

> **1993.** With these figures, [Sen. Phil] Gramm set out to prove that unless mandatory minimum sentences are retained, crime will surely pay. Maybe, but political demagoguery already does. —*Times* (Trenton)

> **1994.** Crime, in this country, pays. Go to jail, get

three good meals a day, a free college education, and the best medical care. No wonder prisons are packed. —*Times* (Trenton)

Crossing the Rubicon. Crossing a limiting line after which nothing will be the same. The proverbial expression has been traced back to the early seventeenth century, when it was used to describe undertaking an irrevocable step. The Rubicon River served as the boundary between Julius Caesar's province and Italy itself. In 49 b.c., Caesar crossed the Rubicon and started a nineteen-year civil war. The word *crossing* can be replaced by *passing*. *To cross (to pass) the Rubicon* is often used as a figure of speech. When the word *Rubicon* is used without *crossing* or *passing* it means "a bounding or limiting line."

1992. Estrada took a breath. This was the Rubicon for him: cross this and there was no going back. —Philip Friedman, *Inadmissible Evidence*

1993. "I was convinced a professional theater had something to contribute. But if it was to succeed it must not just cater to a small group of Russian speakers; we had to perform in Hebrew." And indeed, theater critic Giora Manor of *Al Hamishmar* hailed Ayre's decision as "crossing the Rubicon, becoming part of Israeli culture." —*Hadassah Magazine*

1993. Few, if any, of us realized how cathartic that moment would be: we had, in short, crossed the Rubicon of pain. —*New York Times*
See also THE DIE IS CAST.

Cry (yell) uncle. *See* SAY UNCLE.

The cup is either half empty or half full. *See* THE GLASS IS EITHER HALF EMPTY OR HALF FULL.

Curiosity killed the cat. An overly inquisitive person is likely to get hurt. Children are usually warned against curiosity. The proverb was first attested in the United States in 1909. It is found in varying forms: *Curiosity has killed more than cats; Curiosity never killed a cat in spite of all they say; Curiosity killed the cat: satisfaction brought her back,* etc.

1921. "What'd you ask 'em, for instance?".
    "Curiosity killed a cat!" —Eugene O'Neill, *Diff'rent*

1953. *Gypsy:* You know what curiosity did to the tom cat! —Tennessee Williams, *Camino Real*

1975. "Why did you sell your gitfiddle, Chicken?" he asked. "For two cartons of menthols," said Chicken. "But why—why?" "Curiosity killed the cat," said Chicken. —John Cheever, *Falconer*

1993. Americans have always been of two minds about curiosity. On one hand, children were warned against it. Curiosity killed the cat, didn't it? On the other hand, curiosity was also at the heart of all science, therefore to be treasured. —Russell Baker, *New York Times*
See also ASK ME NO QUESTIONS AND I'LL TELL YOU NO LIES A FOOL CAN ASK MORE QUESTIONS IN AN HOUR THAN A WISE MAN CAN ANSWER IN SEVEN YEARS.

Curses, like chickens, come home to roost. *See* THE CHICKENS HAVE COME HOME TO ROOST.

The customer is always right. When a customer is at odds with a salesperson, it is assumed that the customer is always in the right: *Le patron n'a jamais tort.* The proverb has been traced back to *Confessions of Alphonse* (1917) by B. Pain. First attested in the United States in *Good Morning, America* (1928) by the poet Carl Sandburg (1878–1967). Attributed to the American retail merchant John Wanamaker, who used this saying in one of his large-scale advertising campaigns. *Who Said What When* (1991) gives credit for the proverb to H. Gordon Selfridge (1864–1947), a U.S.-born businessman, who adopted this slogan at his stores.

1988. Advertising is a service business. We've all been told the customer is always right, and that we should do everything to make our clients happy and comfortable. —Mary Moore, "Moore, Not Less," *New York Times*

1994. Mr. Sandstrom argued, briefly and tentatively, that her mechanic—not at the Evergreen garage—would probably move the car indoors and the mechanism would thaw by itself. But to no avail. Take it away, she said. Mr. Sandstrom obliged.
    "The customer is always right," he said, climbing into the cab. —*New York Times*

Cut the coat according to the cloth. *See* YOU MUST CUT YOUR COAT ACCORDING TO YOUR CLOTH.

Damn the torpedoes! Full speed ahead!

Damn it, we're going to take the risk! This saying is attributed to Union Admiral David Glasgow Farragut (1801–1870) during the Civil War. On August 5, 1864, at the Battle of Mobile Bay, he refused to consider retreat in spite of the mines (then called torpedoes) ahead and shouted, "Damn the torpedoes! Four bells! Captain Drayton, go ahead! Jouett, full speed!" Often shortened to *Damn the torpedoes!* or *Full speed (ahead)!*

1973. Dean Acheson: "My own view [of the Soviet veto] was not to worry about things that were *not* likely to happen. And therefore, I was in favor of Admiral Farragut's advice, 'Full steam ahead and damn the torpedoes.'" —Merle Miller, *Plain Speaking*

1975. I hesitated a bit before opening the letter from Vincent, but he'd buggered around in my life enough. I was one of the "folks," wasn't I? Damn the torpedoes. —Mark Vonnegut, *The Eden Express*

1977. "The U.S. Attorney came to him last week with the Leigh charge, and our boy Duparquet told them to sic the FBI on Hennessy, damn the torpedoes." —William Safire, *Full Disclosure*

1985. "Damn the torpedoes, full speed ahead," is Navy Secretary John Lehman's maxim toward adversaries foreign and domestic—and he has succeeded splendidly. —Trevor Armbrister, "The Man Who Shaped Up the Navy," *Reader's Digest*

1986. They [the Russians] know we're better at all this fancy technology than they are. Full speed ahead, I say. —*New York Times*

1988. Mr. Stevens is described by associates as a cautious executive. "He does not go the experimental route," one associate said. "He prefers to rely more heavily on the judgment of those around him. But when he made the decision, it's full steam ahead." —*New York Times*

1991. Prosecutors said the death of the witness would not interrupt their case. "Full speed ahead, damn the torpedoes," said Michael P. Sullivan, the prosecutor. —*New York Times*

1993. During Fleet Week in San Francisco, a couple was telling the hotel chauffeur about their Navy son who flies with the Blue Angels. "Last night he got sick on Mexican food," the father said. "But he'll be up there today. I told him, 'Damn the tortillas, full speed ahead!'" —Scott McKellar, quoted by Herb Caen in the San Francisco *Chronicle*

1994. A statesman, [Lord] Bruce said, must learn to disregard unjust criticism "and rely upon his conscience for his peace of mind, and upon his conduct for the respect of his countrymen." As a better and braver admiral once put it, "Damn the torpedoes—full speed ahead!" —Arthur Schlesinger, Jr., "The Bobby Inman Show: Who Is He to Wail?" *New York Times*

1994. A pregnant Israeli woman killed by an Arab terrorist.

Peres holding "Israeli-PLO Peace Process" notice: "Damn the anti-Jewish violence! Full speed ahead!" —Cartoon by Rivi Rosenthal, *Jewish Press* (New York)

See also DON'T FIRE UNTIL YOU SEE THE WHITES OF THEIR EYES; DON'T GIVE UP THE SHIP.

The darker the berry, the sweeter the juice.

See THE BLACKER THE BERRY, THE SWEETER THE JUICE.

The darkest hour is just before dawn. *See* IT'S ALWAYS DARKEST BEFORE DAWN.

Dead in the water. A situation where no action is taken and no progress made; frozen; stalled;

completely helpless. The saying refers to a disabled ship, unable to proceed. It is an Americanism of recent origin.

1980. For Arthur Lane, perennial president of the Boston Shipping Association, the Port of Boston is "lying dead in the water." —*Boston Globe*

1982. Treasury Secretary Donald T. Regan pronounced the national economy "dead in the water" yesterday as the government released figures showing industries down for the seventh month in the past eight. —*Boston Globe*

1990. Memphis State athletic director Charles Cavagnaro said the Metro Conference's proposed 16-team football super conference and 12-team all-sports league is "pretty much dead in the water because I just don't think we can get the schools." —*Commercial Appeal* (Memphis, Tennessee)

1997. "If there really was no way to avoid the implications of the confession, then I probably would be anxious for my client to express remorse he or she may feel," [James] Burdick said. "But only if they were dead in the water and if they were truly remorseful and they wanted to do it, would I let my client speak." —*Detroit News*

1998. Two days after the Senate majority leader, Trent Lott, declared the $516 billion plan "dead in the water," the Senate voted 52–46 for a GOP proposal to use $16 billion of the tobacco money to combat drug abuse. —*Boston Globe*
See also DEAD ON ARRIVAL.

Dead men never bite. Dead people cannot scare or hurt you; there is nothing to be feared from a dead person. The ancient adage has been found in the works of Plutarch and was first recorded in English in the sixteenth century in the form "a dead man doth no harme." The proverb is used in varying forms.

1883. "One more step, Mr. Hands," said I, "and I'll blow your brains out! Dead men don't bite, you know," I added with a chuckle. —R. L. Stevenson, *Treasure Island*

1944. "Buried men bite not" seems to be one of the oldest bits of human prudence. —R. Altrucchi, *Sleuthing*
See also DEAD MEN TELL NO TALES.

Dead men tell no tales. The dead cannot reveal any secrets. The proverb has been traced back to Thomas Becon (c. 1560). First attested in the United States in *Porcupine's Works* (1797). The proverb is found in varying forms: *Dead men can't talk; Dead men do tell tales; Dead men tell no lies,* etc.

1681. Dead men tell no tales. —John Dryden, *The Spanish Friar*, Act IV, Scene II

1931. *Dead Men Do Tell.* —Title of a book by K. Task

1940. *The Dead Men Can Tell.* —Title of a book by H. Reilly

1957. Dead men tell no tales. —*New York Times*

1992. "Whatever made him leave could have kept him from coming back."
  "Dead men don't testify." —Philip Friedman, *Inadmissible Evidence*

Dead on arrival. Completely doomed; without hope of survival or success. The expression was first used literally, in hospital jargon, referring to a body that was dead when it got to the hospital, as opposed to a person who died after getting to the hospital. The phrase is now used figuratively, often in political contexts.

1984. Congressman Cheney, a staunch Reagan supporter, voiced concern that, if the President submits a budget that couples big decreases in domestic spending with significant defense increases—as now seems likely—the Republicans will not be able to get a package approved by the House and the ball will be handed to the Democrats. Such a presidential package, he said, would be "dead on arrival" and could lead to stalemate. —*Christian Science Monitor*

1989. "People have said the President's budgets of recent years have been dead on arrival," said Senator Lloyd Bentsen of Texas, the Democratic Vice Presidential nominee last year, who heads the influential Finance Committee. "But this one is lost in transit. There's much more interest in how President Bush will change this budget than there is in the budget itself." —*New York Times*

1996. President Clinton Monday dressed up his last budget offer to Republicans in a new rhetoric and submitted it as his 1997 proposal to balance the budget. The proposal, required by a legal deadline, gives new meaning to the "dead-on-arrival" budget cliche from the years when Republican presidents submitted doomed proposals to a Democratic Congress. —*Washington Post*

1997. The Michigan Gaming Control Board, appointed by the governor, wants legislation to remove the local preference clause of Proposal E—an idea declared "dead on arrival" by House leaders. —*Detroit News*
See also DEAD IN THE WATER.

Death before dishonor. *See* BETTER DEATH THAN DISHONOR.

Death is a great leveler. Death does not discriminate and makes everyone equal. The proverb has been traced back to the Latin writer Claudian (A.D. 370–408): *Omnia mors aequat* ("Death makes all things equal" or "Death levels all things"). The proverb is often used allusively, with the subject *death* replaced by another noun: *Golf is a great leveler; School uniform is a great leveler,* etc. or shortened to *the great leveler* or *the grand leveler.*

1965. Death is the grand leveller, as my old dad used to say. —A. Acton, *Old Lamos*

1972. Death may be the great leveler—but only in the better world beyond. —E. Lathen, *Murder without Icing*

1992. "There's frustration over the lack of services in publicly funded agencies. There's just so much reluctance to invest in research, to document, to do anything. AIDS is the great leveler." —*Sun-Sentinel* (South Florida)

1994. "The Olympics can be a great leveler," said Roffe-Steinrotter, who scored one of the biggest surprises of the Games when she won the women's super-G last week. —*Sun-Sentinel* (South Florida)

1996. I don't think the Trafalgar Square caper indicates that smoked pigeon on radicchio has replaced bangers and mash in the hearts of the English. The pigeons could be served as anything. As [French chef August] Escoffier, one of them, may have said, "Chopping up is the great leveler." —Calvin Trillin, *Time*

1998. "The Internet has been a great leveler in the mosaic of global commerce, and the world has become a global village in more ways than one," he says. —*Detroit News*

Deeds, not words. Deeds are more important than words. The proverb is of Latin origin: *facta, non verba.* It has been traced back to 1613 and was used by Shakespeare in his play *King Henry the Eighth.* First attested in the United States in the *Winthrop Papers* (1656). *Actions, not words* is a variant of the proverb. Albert Einstein (1879–1955), German-born physicist, in his book *The World As I See It,* wrote: "If you want to find out anything from the theoretical physicists about the methods they use, I advise you to stick closely to one principle: Don't listen to their words, fix your attention on their deeds."

1613. *King Henry:* 'Tis well said again;
And 'tis a kind of good deed to say well:
And yet words are no deeds.

—Shakespeare, *King Henry the Eighth,*
Act III, Scene II

1965. When the Vice-President [Johnson] stopped off at Bonn, the Chancellor [Adenauer] pointed out to him that the only sign in the crowd inscribed "Action, Not Words" was borne by an old woman with whom, he said, he would personally wish neither. —Arthur M. Schlesinger, Jr., *A Thousand Days: John F. Kennedy in the White House*

1986. "The President of the United States has often asked for 'deeds not words' in the quest for control of strategic arms." —Tom Clancy, *Red Storm Rising*

1992. Dear Abby: I have been dating this guy for about four months. I am in my middle 20s and he is in his early 30s. He is a man who believes in actions, not words. —*Times* (Trenton)

1994. Of course words are not deeds, especially in Russia. —*Wall Street Journal*

See also ACTIONS SPEAK LOUDER THAN WORDS.

Defend me from my friends. *See* SAVE US FROM OUR FRIENDS; WITH SUCH FRIENDS, ONE HARDLY NEEDS ENEMIES.

The devil can cite scripture for his purpose. The devil will do whatever it takes, even quote Scripture, to support his position. The proverb is used to indicate that evil people often refer to the Bible or other famous writings to win the trust of good people. The proverb has been traced back to 1573. It was given literary use in Shakespeare's *The Merchant of Venice* (1596–97). First attested in the United States in 1691. The proverb is found in varying forms: *The devil can quote scripture for his own advantage; The devil can quote scripture for his own ends; The devil can cite scripture to his purpose,* etc.

1596–97.
Antonio: Mark you this, Bassanio,
The devil can cite Scripture for his purpose.
—Shakespeare, *The Merchant of Venice,* Act I, Scene III

1966. When the Devil quotes Scriptures, it's not, really, to deceive, but simply that the masses are so ignorant of theology that somebody has to teach them the elementary texts before he can seduce them. —Paul Goodman, *Five Years; Thoughts in a Useless Time*

1984. "Can the Devil cite Scripture for his purpose?"
"I am not the Devil, Absalom. And your sister Tamar is not even betrothed. There is really no law against raping a woman who is not betrothed." —Joseph Heller, *God Knows*

The devil is in the details. *See* GOD IS IN THE DE-
TAILS.

The devil take the hindmost. To hell with the
unfortunate. The proverb is found in print as
early as 1620 in *Philaster* by Francis Beaumont
and John Fletcher. First attested in the United
States in *Colonial Record of Georgia* (1742). It is
part of the proverb *Every man for himself, and the
devil take the hindmost.*

> **1620.** The devil take the hindmost! —Beaumont
> and Fletcher, *Philaster,* Act V, Scene III

> **1936.** "That's your system, isn't it, my green-eyed
> hypocrite? Scarlett, Scarlett! I hoped for more cou-
> rageous conduct from you. I thought the Irish said
> what they thought and the Divvil take the hinder-
> most." —Margaret Mitchell, *Gone With the Wind*

> **1946.** "Yes, I am a student of history, don't you re-
> member? And what we students of history always
> learn is that the human being is a very complicated
> contraption and that they are not good or bad but
> are good and bad and the good comes out of bad
> and the bad out of good, and the devil take the
> hindmost. —Robert Penn Warren, *All the King's
> Men*

> **1984.** Republican economists are also eager to re-
> move the quotas, on the grounds that the market-
> place enforces productivity only if the devil is al-
> lowed to take the hindmost. —William Safire, *New
> York Times*

> **1991.** Too many times when she'd had to curb her
> tongue—she who'd always said what she thought
> and devil take the hindmost. —Alexandra Ripley,
> *Scarlett*

The die is cast. One's mind is made up; the decision has been taken and one is ready to act; there
is no going back. In his book *Life of Caesar*, Plutarch quotes Julius Caesar as saying in Latin,
Jacta alea est or *Alea jacta est* ("The die is cast"),
when he crossed the Rubicon (49 B.C.) to begin
civil war against the Roman government. According to *The Oxford Dictionary of Quotations*, Caesar
originally spoke the words in Greek. Mussolini is
said to have erected a monument at the spot
where Caesar invaded Italy. The saying is often
used by people who enter on a risky and dangerous undertaking. In English, the proverb has been
traced back to *Expedition into Scotland* (1548).
First attested in the United States in the *Letter
Book of John Watts* (1765). The proverb is found
in varying forms: *The die was cast; Alea jacta est;
Jacta alea est; Jacta est alea,* etc. *Die* is the singular of *dice.*

> **1967.** A Boston attorney summed it up this way:
> "The father [Kennedy's] was a tremendous factor
> in the campaign. He remained out of public view.
> He didn't run things, they happened according to
> his plans. He cast the die." —Ralph de Toledano,
> *R.F.K. The Man Who Would Be President*

> **1977.** So the battle lines were fully drawn. At stake
> was not only the fate of the President but the
> power of the press. One or the other would have to
> emerge triumphant. There was no turning back.
> The die was cast. —Victor Lasky, *It Didn't Start
> with Watergate*

> **1987.** In the 70's, he [Robert P. Reus] served as
> chairman of the Telephone Industry Policy Council,
> an industry organization. "I got a feeling early on
> that the die was cast," he said. "So we decided to
> make a very early move." —*New York Times*

> **1994.** "The die was cast," Mr. Peres said today.
> "There is no going back. We won't go back to
> Gaza. Gaza won't come back to us." —*New York
> Times*

See also CROSSING THE RUBICON.

Different strokes for different folks. The approach to different people should be individual-
ized. The proverb also means that different people
have different tastes. Nobody knows exactly
where the saying comes from. Wolfgang Mieder
thinks it originated in the United States and traces
"different strokes" to Southern blacks in the
1950s.

> **1973.** The popular saying around PDAP [Palmer
> Drug Abuse Program] is "different strokes for dif-
> ferent folks," as the basis of the program. —*Hous-
> ton (Texas) Chronicle Magazine*

> **1981.** Different Strokes for Different Folks: Looking
> the Part. —Mortimer Levitt, *The Executive Look*

> **1986.** The whole point, says John Poindexter, Rea-
> gan's national security adviser, is different strokes
> for different folks. "We need different policies to-
> ward Communist dictatorships that repress their
> own people and subvert their neighbors, different
> policies for non-democratic regimes that are slowly
> evolving toward democracy, and different policies
> for non-democratic regimes in which there is no vi-
> able democratic center and the only alternative is
> chaos or a new dictatorship." —Michael Kramer,
> "How Reagan Does It," *New York*

> **1988.** "Lance, it's a fact that poor people get sicker
> and shorter lifespans than rich people. Do you
> think that's fair? That guy was preaching a sort of
> elitist medicine: 'pay now, live later.' I only wish
> I'd had eggs to throw at that bastard."
> Barney smiled at her outburst, while Lance

meekly countered, "Well, Laura, different strokes for different folks."

"No, Lance, the *same* strokes, for the *same* folks." —Erich Segal, *Doctors*

See also EVERY MAN TO HIS OWN TASTE; TASTES DIFFER; THERE'S NO ACCOUNTING FOR TASTES; TO EACH HIS OWN.

Dig the well before you are thirsty. Be prepared before it is too late. The proverb dates back to the Roman comic playwright Plautus (c.254–184 b.c.), who is quoted as saying: *Miserum est opus, igitur demum fodere puteum, ubi sitis fauces tenet* ("It's a wretched business to be digging a well just as thirst is overcoming you"). The verb *get* may be used instead of *are*.

> **1988.** Dig Your Well Before You're Thirsty. —Harvey Mackay, *Swim with the Sharks without Being Eaten Alive*

See also FOREWARNED IS FOREARMED; HOPE FOR THE BEST AND PREPARE FOR THE WORST; NEVER PUT OFF UNTIL TOMORROW WHAT YOU CAN DO TODAY; AN OUNCE OF PREVENTION IS WORTH A POUND OF CURE; TIME AND TIDE WAIT FOR NO MAN.

Discretion is the better part of valor. Exercise caution, don't take unnecessary risks. Proper judgment is better than unwarranted bravery. The proverb has been traced back to Caxton's *Jason* (c.1477) and was popularized by Shakespeare in *King Henry the Fourth, Part I* (1597–98) and by Beaumont and Fletcher in *A King and No King* (1619). First attested in the United States in Benjamin Franklin's *Poor Richard's Almanac* (1747). The proverb is found in varying forms: *The better part of discretion is valor; An ounce of discretion is worth more than a pound of valor; Discretion is better than valor; Discretion is the better part of common sense; Discretion is the better part of married happiness; Silence is the better part of valor,* etc.

> **1597–98.**
> *Falstaff:* The better part of valor is discretion; in the which better part I have saved my life. —Shakespeare, *King Henry the Fourth, Part I,* Act V, Scene IV

> **1963.** Discretion's the better part of valor,
> At least I've often heard you say;
> And he who loves his life, dear mother,
> Won't fight if he can run away.
> —"Farewell, Mother," *Great American Folk Songs*

> **1984.** I sat there in the midst of it all and I said: "Discretion is the better part of valor. Give them what they want. Because if they strike, we'll lose

hundreds of millions of dollars, we'll lose our bonuses, and I'll personally lose half a million dollars in cash." —Lee Iacocca with William Novak, *Iacocca*

> **1987.** "Crist, I wish I were ten or twelve years younger, Kendrick, and I'd whip your tail—I could have done it even at that age. At sixty-three, however, you learn that caution is the better part of valor, or whatever it is." —Robert Ludlum, *The Icarus Agenda*

> **1988.** "What's the real story?"
> "Well, my humble guess is that since the Shysters have now got—in addition to Mack the Truck, who's still only in his second year—two new freshmen who've played in the NBA, Dean Holmes is going the Falstaff route."
> Barney nodded. ' "Discretion is the better part of valor.' And, no doubt, the series will resume as soon as the Truck and his Trucklets graduate." —Erich Segal, *Doctors*

See also BETTER SAFE THAN SORRY; DON'T PUT ALL YOUR EGGS IN ONE BASKET.

Divide and conquer. This ages-old axiom cited by Machiavelli has long been a political weapon used by powers to maintain control over the different nations, classes, parties, and groups they ruled. Originally a Latin saying, *divide et impera* ("divide and rule"), the saying has been in common use since *M. Hurault's Discourse upon Present State of France* (1588) and J. Hall's *Mediations and Voices Divine and Morall* (1605). First attested in the United States in *Narrative of Planting of Massachusetts Colony* (1694). The proverb is found in one more form: *Divide and rule.* It may be used as an attribute of such nouns as *gambit, tactics, theory,* etc.

> **1988.** Ed Koch is far from finished. He is a resilient and flexible politician and a genius at divide-and-conquer tactics. —*New York Times*

> **1988.** This Republican Administration treats us as if we were pieces of a puzzle that can't fit together. They've tried to put us into compartments and separate us from each other. Their political theory is "divide and conquer." —Transcript of the Keynote Address by Ann Richards, the Texas Treasurer, *New York Times*

> **1989.** Obviously, he liked it that way; if he had not, he could have fired either man [Rogers or Kissinger] at any time. Divide and rule. That was Nixon's method. —Stephen E. Ambrose, *Nixon: The Triumph of a Politician, 1962–1972*

> **1992.** Albert Chrobocinski, an Exxon refinery supervisor and the Brick Township Council president,

sees the ward system as nothing but "divide and conquer." —*New York Times*

Divide and rule. *See* DIVIDE AND CONQUER.

Do as I say, not as I do. Act as I tell you, but don't follow my example. The idea of the proverb originally appeared in the New Testament. In English, it has been traced back to the Anglo-Saxon era. In 1546, it was included in the book of proverbs collected by John Heywood. In his book *Table Talk* (1689), the English scholar and jurist John Seldon wrote: "Preachers say, Do as I say, not as I do." First attested in the United States in 1815. *Don't do as I do, but as I say* and *Don't do as I do, but as I say do* are variants of this proverb.

All therefore whatsoever they bid you observe, *that* observe and do; but do not ye after their works: for they say, and do not. —Matthew 23:3, *Authorized Version,* 1611

1983. As my own client I tend to be impatient, to have no objectivity about my work, and to be so easily flattered that someone wants to publish me as to accept terms I would sternly reject if they were offered for one of my authors' properties. So this book is definitely a case of Do What I Say, Not What I Do. —Richard Curtis, *How to Be Your Own Literary Agent*

1989. "Joe Kennedy was the world's greatest hypocrite. His philosophy was quite simple: 'Do as I say, not as I do.'" —C. David Heymann, *A Woman Named Jackie*

1994. "Do as I say, not as I do" doesn't work, she [Diane Tracy] said. "People will do what you do, not what you say." —Frederick J. Egenolf, "Learning to Love Your Career May Mean Breaking the Rules," *The Princeton Packet*

Do as you would be done by. *See* DO UNTO OTHERS AS YOU WOULD HAVE THEM DO UNTO YOU.

Do not go gentle into that good night. Don't give up your principles or your ideas; hold your ground and never say die. Coined by Dylan Thomas (1914–53), Welsh poet and short-story writer.

1952. Do not go gentle into that good night,
Old age should burn and rave at close of day;
Rage, rage against the dying of the light.
—Dylan Thomas, "Do Not Go Gentle into That Good Night"

1987. The aftermath of the Hart story brought forth this lead from T. R. Reid in *The Washington Post:* "Former Presidential candidate Gary Hart is making it clear to his friends and supporters that he will not go gentle into that political night." —*New York Times Magazine*

1991. If that sounds familiar, it is the 1992 version of the Rainbow Coalition rhetoric of 1988. It may not get Mr. Jackson to the finish line, but it almost certainly guarantees him a place at the starting line if he wants it. A former adviser to Mr. Jackson said, "He has no intention of going gently into anyone's good night." —*New York Times*

1991. "This is not going to go gentle into that good night," he [Edmund G. Brown, Jr.] roared at Democrats in Chicago. "This is going to be an explosive ripping apart of the social fabric." —*New York Times*

1991. "It's fairly clear that Darman and Sununu don't understand economic policy," said Representative Dick Armey of Texas, who signed the letter. "Those two have very, very poor political instincts. The nation would be served if Darman and Sununu would go quietly into some good night someplace, and the President would begin listening to Jack Kemp." —*New York Times*
See also NEVER SAY DIE.

Do or die. Succeed or die trying. The proverb has been traced back to about 1577. "This expression," wrote Walter Scott, "is a kind of common property, being the motto, we believe, of a Scottish family." In 1647, it appeared in John Fletcher's writings. In 1794, we see it in Robert Burns's poem, "Scots Wha Hae." In 1854, it was used in a slightly changed form by Alfred, Lord Tennyson in "The Charge of the Light Brigade." First attested in the United States in *The Rebelliad* (1819). The proverb was further popularized in the 1943 Humphrey Bogart/Ingrid Bergman movie *Casablanca* through Herman Hupfeld's lyrics to the song "As Time Goes By."

1794. Lay the proud usurpers low!
Tyrants fall in every foe!
Liberty's in every blow!
Let us do or die!
—Robert Burns, *"Scots Wha Hae"*

1854. Theirs not to make reply,
Theirs not to reason why,
Theirs but to do and die.
—Alfred, Lord Tennyson, "The Charge of the Light Brigade"

1931. It's still the same old story,
A fight for love and glory,

A case of do or die!
The world will always welcome lovers,
As time goes by.
—Herman Hupfeld, lyrics to "As Time Goes
By"

1992. "We were proud when it [the rescue of storm victims] was all over," he [Mr. Russell] said. "We knew that we did it on our own. It was do or die." —*New York Times*

1993. The laboratory must begin to prove it can earn a non-military return for taxpayers, he [Mr. Narath] said. "It's fundamentally do or die." —*New York Times*

1994. In a shootout, physical skill is less important than mental resilience.
"I'm not very good at it, but I love doing it," Ramos said. "All that pressure. Do or die." —*New York Times*

See also MAKE OR BREAK; SINK OR SWIM.

Do unto others as you would have them do unto you. Treat others as you would like to be treated. The Golden Rule set forth by Jesus. First found in English in *Laws of Alfred* (c. 901). First cited in the United States in the *Letter Book of Peleg Sanford* (1668). The proverb is found in varying forms: *Always do unto others what is best for you; Do as you would be done by; Do unto others as you have been done by; Do unto others as others do unto you; Do unto others as you would be done by; Do unto others before they do you,* etc.

And as ye would that men should do to you, do ye also to them likewise. —Luke 6:31, *Authorized Version*, 1611

1961. He turned the other cheek on every occasion and always did unto others exactly as he would have had others do unto him. —Joseph Heller, *Catch-22*

1984. With Joab himself I succumbed willingly to arguments from him that I hoped from the start would prove unanswerable. I was more grateful than I can describe for his realistic universal precept that no laws are legitimate and that, in consequence, there is no such thing as crime. And I could dispute with him no further after he propounded for me the celebrated golden rule upon which the civilized world turns to this day:
"Always do unto others what is best for you." —Joseph Heller, *God Knows*

1985. Bernstein smiled and suggested, "Why not do unto others what you just did unto me?" —Erich Segal, *The Class*

1989. Even villainous behavior may be justified by the Orphan as simply realistic because you must "do unto others before they do unto you." —Carol S. Pearson, *The Hero Within*

1991. "Do unto others what they shouldn't be doing unto you" is how Ace (an enthusiastic participant) sums up the thinking behind the anti-photographer policy. —*New Yorker*

1992. Once the seller of computer equipment had become wealthy, he asked the mentor how he could repay him. "Do unto others as I did unto you," he said. —*New York Times*

1993. Of course if all else fails and you're ridden out of town on a rail, you may be able to ride back in as a director. Then you can do unto others as they did unto you. —*Fortune*

1994. If everyone lived by the Golden Rule, "Do unto others as you would have others do unto you," there would be no bad manners in this world. —Abigail Van Buren, "Dear Abby," *Times* (Trenton)

Do you want the good news or the bad first? *See* THE GOOD NEWS IS ...; THE BAD NEWS IS ...

Doctor Livingstone, I presume? A salutation used to greet a person who has resurfaced after a long absence. In 1870, David Livingstone (1813–1873), a famous doctor and explorer, was presumably lost in the region of Africa west of Lake Tanganyika, a territory inhabited by cannibals. After many privations, he returned to Ujiji on November 10, 1871, and was greeted with the now-famous remark by Henry Morton Stanley, leader of the 200-man strong rescue team dispatched by American newspaper publisher James Gordon Bennett of the New York *Herald.*

1871. On November 10 the people of Ujiji rushed to Livingstone to tell him the exciting news: a white man had arrived! Livingstone, emaciated but erect, stood before his tent, peering in astonishment at the big caravan headed by a tall white man flanked by a porter carrying the Stars and Stripes. The people parted to form a living avenue, down which Stanley stalked to one of the most dramatic meetings of all time.
"Dr. Livingstone, I presume!" —O. K. Armstrong, "He Lighted the Dark Continent," reprinted in *Great Lives, Great Deeds* (1964)

1940. He [Robert Jordan] did not believe there was ever going to be any such thing as a long time any more but if there ever was such a thing he would like to spend it with her [Maria]. We could go into the hotel and register as Doctor and Mrs. Livingstone, I presume, he thought. —Ernest Hemingway, *For Whom the Bell Tolls*

1955. He [Wally] put them [glasses] on and squinted at her [Marjorie]. "Ah. That's better. Dr. Livingstone, I presume?" —Herman Wouk, *Marjorie Morningstar*

1986. I awoke with a rifle barrel against my throat. Then a pencil of light blinded me as I lifted up out of my sleeping bag. Then I heard Luke laughing.
  "Che Guevara, I presume," I said. —Pat Conroy, *The Prince of Tides*

1988. "You do realize that all your patients will rub you with 'Dr. Livingston, I presume?'" —Erich Segal, *Doctors*

1991. Nettled by his silence and his refusal to look at me, I fought down the nervous laughter rising in my throat, and the temptation of a sarcastic "Together at last" or "Mr. Forbes, I presume." —*New Yorker*

The dog always returns to his vomit. A person returns to the scene of his crime. The proverb appears in the Bible. In English, the proverb has been traced back to Chaucer's "Parson's Tale" (c. 1389). First attested in the United States in *Documentary History of State of Maine, Containing Trelawny Papers* (1636). The proverb is found in varying forms: *As a dog returns to his vomit, so a fool returns to his folly; The dog is turned to his own vomit again; The dog has returned to his vomit again; It's a case of the dog returning to his own vomit; Canis revertit suam vomitem* (Latin), etc.

As a dog returneth to his vomit, so a fool returneth to his folly. —Proverbs 26:11, *Authorized Version*, 1611

1961. "The dog is turned to his vomit again." —Bernard Malamud, *The Natural*

1994. "O. J. Simpson is reported to have attended Nicole's funeral."
  "It's a case of the dog returning to his vomit or, to put it bluntly, to the scene of his double murder." —Overheard on the subway

Dog eat dog. The struggle for survival in life or business turns man into an animal. The proverb dates back to the sixteenth century. *Dog doesn't* or *won't eat dog* means that people of the same type do not destroy one another. *Canis caninam non est* is Latin for "A dog does not eat dog's flesh" and *Cane non mangia cane* is Italian for "Dog doesn't eat dog." In 1602, Shakespeare used the same idea in *Troilus and Cressida*. First attested in the United States in *Modern Chivalry* (1792) by Hugh Henry Brackenridge (1748–1816).

Dog eat dog is of much later origin. Often used as an attribute of such nouns as *business, competition, culture, world*, etc., for example, *It's a dog-eat-dog world*. Samuel Goldwyn (1882–1974), the American film producer, is often quoted as saying, "It's a dog-to-dog business and nobody is going to eat me."

1602. *Thersites:* I am a bastard too; I love bastards: I am a bastard begot, bastard instructed, bastard in mind, bastard in valour, in every thing illegitimate. One bear will not bite another, and wherefore should one bastard? —Shakespeare, *Troilus and Cressida*, Act V, Scene VII

1948. He felt a pang of envy as he thought of Whitey Lydon. Everybody was getting ahead of him while he was stuck here. There wasn't anybody you could trust. Dog eat dog. —Norman Mailer, *The Naked and the Dead*

1964. Anyhow I'm quitting at the end of this term and joining the dogs eating dogs eating other dogs in the great big lousy world you're all educating us for. —Bel Kaufman, *Up the Down Staircase*

1981. "The cars would come in off the street and we'd paint 'em and give 'em a tune-up and no manufacturer told us what price to attach, we'd put the price on the windshield in shaving cream and wipe it off and try another if it didn't move inside a week. No import duty, no currency devaluation; it was good clean dog eat dog." —John Updike, *Rabbit Is Rich*

1986. Later, we were always glad that we had been present on the March evening when Savannah made her triumphant debut in that dog-eat-dog subculture of the New York Poetry World. —Pat Conroy, *The Prince of Tides*

1987. "It's clear," Mr. Phillips [a Republican analyst] said, "that we're looking at the growing Republican realization that the social Darwinist state of conservatism—the dog-eat-dog, survival-of-the-fittest economics—has breathed its last." —*New York Times*

1991. But how a city [Atlanta] that is the ultimate example of damn-the-past New South thinking and a book that Mrs. Mitchell envisioned as a portrait of a dog-eat-dog frontier world both came to symbolize a dewy-eyed evocation of Old South gentility and grace is one of life's great ironies, he [Darden Asbury Pyron, author of Margaret Mitchell's biography] said. —*New York Times*

1991. I'm certainly going into this as a dog-eat-dog fight, and I will do what I have to do to be reelected. —George Bush, quoted by William Safire in "Bush's Gamble," *New York Times Magazine*

1994. In the dog-eat-dog deli world of New York,

Mr. [Murray] Klein is a marketing legend, a feisty bull terrier who delights in outhustling and undercutting competitors. —Bryan Miller, "At Zabar's, a Realignment at the Top," *New York Times*

The dog has returned to his vomit again. *See* THE DOG ALWAYS RETURNS TO HIS VOMIT.

A dog is a man's best friend. Commonly used literally. First cited in Great Britain in 1709 and in the United States in *Girl in Black* (1927) by V. Bridges. The proverb is found in varying forms: *Man's best friend is his dog; A dog is the best friend a man can have; A man is the dog's best friend; The dog is man's best friend after his mother,* etc. *Diamonds are a girl's best friend* is a modern variant of the proverb. It is the title of a hit song by Leo Rubin (1900–84), music by Jule Styne (1905–94), first sung in the 1949 Broadway musical *Gentlemen Prefer Blondes,* based on Anita Loos's best-selling novel (1926) of the same name.

1927. I have often heard it said that a dog is the best friend a man can have. —V. Bridges, *Girl in Black*

1935. Truly, the dog was man's best friend. —D. Gardiner, *Translantic Ghost*

1946. "A dog," the Boss said, "is man's best friend. Old Buck, he's the best friend I ever had." —Robert Penn Warren, *All the King's Men*

1959. *Jerry:* Man is a dog's best friend, remember. —Edward Albee, *The Zoo Story*

1978. A few species of domestics had been spared, but as a general rule the plague had taken man and man's best friends. It had taken the dogs but left the wolves, because the wolves were wild and the dogs weren't. —Stephen King, *The Stand*

1987. Browning looked at the dachshund and shook his head. "Sherman McCoy. Friend to man's best friend." —Tom Wolfe, *The Bonfire of the Vanities*

1991. "Amtrak will become the airport's best friend," we wrote down—a summary of several things we learned. —*New Yorker*

1993. ' "A dog is man's best friend' is an old adage which the defendants have either forgotten or decided to ignore." —Judge Charles R. Richey, ordering better treatment of lab animals, *New York Times*

1993. Pockets are a girl's best friend. —*New York Times Magazine*

The dogs bark, but the caravan goes on. Disregard what your enemy is saying, do what you are supposed to do. The proverb is of Asian origin and has been traced back to J. I. Kipling's *Beast & Man in India* (1891). First attested in the United States in the 1930s. The proverb is used in varying forms: *The dogs bark, but the caravan goes on; The dogs bark, but the caravan moves on: Dogs bark while the caravan rolls on,* etc.

1930. After thinking it [situation] over he [an old Moor] murmured: "Dogs bark but the caravan goes on." —*Time*

1936. "Did you ever hear the Oriental proverb: 'The dogs bark but the caravan passes on'? Let them bark, Scarlett. I fear nothing will stop your caravan." —Margaret Mitchell, *Gone With the Wind*

1992. Mort Zuckerman has been an editor and publisher for a dozen years now. Despite that, there is still the feeling among many people in journalism that he is a real-estate developer "meddling" in the affairs of his magazines.

"The dogs may bark," he says, "but the caravan moves on." —*New York*

Doing well by doing good. Being successful as a result of being charitable. The proverb is found in varying forms: *It's a case of doing well by doing good; It's much harder to do good than to do well; He is noted for doing good by doing well,* etc.

1991. "A professional contributions manager puts the company's interest first," he [Paul M. Ostergard, director of corporate contributions for Citibank] said. "It's a classic case of doing well by doing good." —*New York Times*

1991. His [Bob Bass's] motivation for making money? "Doing well in order to do good." —Peter Elkind, "The Breakup of the Bass Brothers," *New York Times Magazine*

1992. There's the altruist and the tycoon;
Their difference is easy to tell,
The former is noted for doing good—
The latter, for doing well.
—G. Sterling Leiby, "Words Apart," *Wall Street Journal*

1993. Laura S. Scher and her company are indeed doing well by doing good. The company, Working Assets Funding Service, is based on the premise that generosity can be painless if it is linked to purchases people are already making and bills they regularly pay. —*New York Times*

1994. Proof that doing well by doing good inspires the poet in everyone. —*New York Times*

1995. *To help an enterprise do well by doing good.* This should be a self-evident obligation of every business and institution. And consumers and private pressure groups are more effective than government at imposing it. —*New York Times Magazine*

Don't add insult to injury. Don't cause additional harm to a person you have already hurt. The proverb has been traced back to *The Foundling* (1748) by Edward Moore (1712–57), English dramatist and miscellaneous writer. First attested in the United States in *Naval Documents* (1775). *To add insult to injury* is used as a figure of speech.

1748. This is adding insult to injury. —Edward Moore, *The Foundling*, Act V, Scene II

1984. I'm so sorry. And now I have to add insult to injury by asking for a ride home. —Howard Fast, *The Outsider*

1986. When it comes to adding insult to injury, the Soviets are past masters. —*New York Post*

1993. Supporters say the idea is simple: "It's nice to see that if a fund doesn't perform, you don't add insult to injury by paying high fees for bad performance," Mr. Phillips said. —*New York Times*

1994. To add insult to injury, Rush [Limbaugh] wrote a book—*The Way Things Ought to Be*—and it sold millions of copies, remaining on the best-seller list for dozens of weeks. —*New York Post*

Don't air your dirty linen in public. One shouldn't make public embarrassing personal matters. The proverb has been traced back to *Pills* (1809) by T. G. Fessenden. In 1867, it was used in *Last Chronicle of Barsetshire* by English novelist Anthony Trollope (1815–82). The proverb is often attributed to Napoleon Bonaparte. In his speech to the Senate in 1814, Napoleon said: "I am the state—I alone am here the representative of the people. Even if I had done wrong you should not have reproached me in public—people wash their dirty linen at home." The proverb is found in varying forms: *Don't wash dirty laundry in public; Some linen is too foul to wash in public; Wash your dirty laundry at home; One doesn't air one's dirty laundry in public*, etc. The proverb has its counterpart in other languages too: *Il faut laver son linge sale en famille* (French, "One should wash one's dirty linen at home"), *Sacar a relucir sus asuntos personales* (Spanish, "To wash one's dirty linen in public").

1936. And no matter which side they took, the relatives heartily deplored the fact that India had taken it upon herself to wash the dirty linen so publicly and involve Ashley in so degrading a scandal. —Margaret Mitchell, *Gone With the Wind*

1981. We never washed our dirty linen in public. —Abigail Van Buren, *The Best of Dear Abby*

1983. Moreover, says Marc Pearl, Washington representative of the American Jewish Congress, for Jews to argue publicly if they think otherwise is a mistake: "We don't hang our dirty laundry out in the public because it's going to be taken the wrong way." —*Newsweek*

1989. He [Robert Bannerman] paused. "What I *do* worry about is a long struggle over The Trust. Airing dirty linen in public is bad politics." —Michael Korda, *The Fortune*

1993. "When I was growing up, there was something discreet and arm's length about monarchy," Mr. Lister said, a bit wistfully. "Now that the royalty has aired its dirty laundry in the press and opened Buckingham Palace to tourists, it doesn't stand for that kind of dignity and prestige." —*New York Times*

1994. "Both sides realize there's nothing to be gained by airing dirty laundry in public." —*Wall Street Journal*

1995. It is always delightful to watch pompous authors and equally pompous reviewers airing their intellectual dirty linen in public. —*New York Times Book Review*

See also IT'S ALL IN THE FAMILY; NEVER TELL TALES OUT OF SCHOOL.

Don't be penny-wise and dollar-foolish. See PENNY-WISE AND POUND-FOOLISH.

Don't believe anything (everything) you hear nor (and) half of what you read. See BELIEVE ONLY HALF OF WHAT YOU SEE AND NOTHING YOU HEAR.

Don't bite off more than you can chew. Don't try to do more than you can realistically handle. Don't overestimate your abilities. The saying originated in the United States and has been traced back, according to lexicographer Charles Earle Funk, some 110 years or even earlier. When an American would say, "Don't bite off more than you can chew," an Italian would say, *Non fare il passo più lungo della gamba* ("Don't take a step longer than your leg").

1948. "You're biting off more than you can take, Stanley." —Norman Mailer, *The Naked and the Dead*

1991. "I have to admire your nerve, Scarlett," said Rhett. "I never questioned whether you could hold your own against General Sherman and his army, but trying to outwit the Roman Catholic Church might be biting off more than you can chew." —Alexandra Ripley, *Scarlett*

1992. Has George Bitten Off More Than He Can Chew? Foreman Vs. Stewart. Live from Las Vegas. Only on HBO. —Ad for Home Box Office, Inc., *Time*

1993. A few months later, sales floundered and Mr. Davies bought the company's maintenance subsidiary.

"I was scared," he said. "I felt like I had bitten off more than I could chew." —*New York Times*

1995. "Last year, we bit off more than we could chew," Mr. Clinton said in a moment of clear-eyed candor. "This year, let's work together, step by step, to get something done." —*New York Times*

Don't bite the hand that feeds you. Don't cause pain to the person or institution that helps or supports you. The proverb is found in the *Spectator* (1711) edited by Joseph Addison (1672– 1719). First attested in the United States in *Winthrop Papers* (1681). Used by Mark Twain in *Pudd'nhead Wilson's Calendar* (1893).

1800. And having looked to Government for bread, on the very first scarcity they will turn and bite the hand that fed them. —Edmund Burke, *Thoughts and Details on Scarcity*

1948. Maybe I don't being as it's a big word, but it seems to me it's easy enough to bite the hand that feeds ya. —Norman Mailer, *The Naked and the Dead*

1951. "Transfer you to da Stockade," Ike growled. "Dat bites de hand dat feeds it dey shoot dogs for." —James Jones, *From Here to Eternity*

1983. "But I do think it best if we don't mention the fact that you're married to Mrs. Jaeger and her friend."

"Sure." Why bite the hand that was draping him in Armani? —Jackie Collins, *Hollywood Wives*

1984. There is much wrong with America, but we are not as bad as the world pictures us. And, when these countries that attack us need help with an insurmountable problem, they know where to go. Unfortunately, it is a fact of life to bite the hand that feeds you. —*U.S. News & World Report*

1987. Principled opposition to this sucker play is muted, because the Heritage Foundation's chief heads the U.S.I.A.'s advisory board and tends not to bite the hand that feeds. —*New York Times*

1991. "Now he's going to tell his story," said Mark Belnick, an attorney for Mr. Milken.... Referring to Drexel's suit against Mr. Milken, Mr. Belnick

added, "This is clearly a case of someone biting the hand that feeds them." —*Wall Street Journal*

1992. Mr. Bush sought to defend his economic record over the last four years, which many polls suggest is at the heart of his political difficulties. Echoing a theme struck here throughout the week, Mr. Bush said the Democrat-controlled Congress had blocked his package to spur economic growth.

"I extended my hand to the Democratic leaders, and they bit it," he said. —*New York Times*

Don't build castles in the air. Be realistic, don't daydream. Usually given as advice to be more pragmatic. The proverb has been traced back to Saint Augustine (354–430), who spoke of "building in the air." English fairy tales are full of castles that vanish in thin air as soon as they are built. The French call them *Châteaux en Espagne* ("Castles in Spain") or *Châteaux en Asie* ("Castles in Asia"). It's worth mentioning that the Spaniards do not "build castles in Spain," nor do the Asians "build castles in Asia." And if they do, they "build them in the air." First attested in the United States in *New England's Prospect* (1634).

13th century.
Thou shalt make castels thanne in Spayne,
And dreme of joye, all but in vayne.
—Jean De Meun, *The Romaunt of the Rose* (about 1277), translated by Chaucer

1991. Scarlett knew she was building castles in the air. —Alexandra Ripley, *Scarlett*

1993. Avoid building castles in the air; down-to-earth choices are essential —Jeane Dixon, "Horoscope," *Times* (Trenton)

Don't burn the (your) candle at both ends. Don't do two different things at the same time, or spend all your energies on any one project, because little time or energy will be left for anything else. You can't go to bed late and get up early without harming yourself. The proverb has been traced back to *Promus* (c. 1594). First attested in the United States in the *Codman Letters* (1798). The proverb is found in varying forms: *Never light your candle at both ends; It doesn't do to burn the candle at both ends; You can't burn the candle at both ends and still live to blow it out*, etc. *To burn the candle at both ends* means to work very hard and is used as a figure of speech.

1920. My candle burns at both ends;
It will not last the night;
But ah, my foes, and oh, my friends—
It gives a lovely light!

—Edna St. Vincent Millay, "First Fig," *A Few Figs from Thistles*

1995. "Please, don't burn your candle at both ends. You're putting in long hours in your offices and have neither time nor energy to play with your kids." —Overheard at a parents' seminar

Don't burn your bridges behind you.

Don't take an irrevocable step without fully considering the consequences. The proverb has been traced back to *Confessions* (1923) by A. Crowley. First attested in the United States in *Om* (1924) by T. Munday. It originally referred to a retreating army that was burning bridges behind itself. *To burn your bridges before you* or *to burn one's boats* are also used. Julius Caesar and other generals allegedly burned their boats when their armies occupied a foreign country to make retreat impossible. The legend has it that when Troy fell, the women stopped the retreat of their husbands by burning their boats. Hernando Cortés (1485–1547), Spanish explorer and conqueror of the Aztec empire of Mexico, destroyed his own fleet to prevent the desertion of some of his troops. The proverb is found in varying forms.

1923. She wouldn't burn her bridges. —A. Crowley, *Confessions*

1977. "The U.S. found itself at the end of August, 1963, without a policy and with most of its bridges burned," a Pentagon official noted. —Victor Lasky, *It Didn't Start with Watergate*

1984. What makes Mr. Karami so often the man of the hour is an ability to be a member of the opposition without burning his bridges with the man at the head of Lebanese authority. —*New York Times*

1988. "What I'm trying to say is that I can understand wanting to burn bridges behind you. But why the hell would anyone want to burn bridges in front of him?" —Erich Segal, *Doctors*

1991. "I am working harder than I've ever had to work in my life, Scarlett. I burned my bridges in Charleston so thoroughly and so publicly that the stench of the destruction is still in the nostrils of everyone in town." —Alexandra Ripley, *Scarlett*

1991. Don't burn bridges. You'll be surprised how many times you have to cross the same river. —*People*

1992. "He [Canseco] pretty clearly burned his bridge when he left here," La Russa said today. "He continues to set fire to it." —*New York Times*

1994. "He [Mr. Wilder] is enormously unpopular with white voters," Mr. Sabato said. "As a governor, his performance was very controversial, and he burned a lot of bridges." —*New York Times*

Don't buy a pig in a poke.

Don't buy anything without carefully examining it. *Poke* (an old Dutch word) means *bag, sack.* The proverb has been traced back to 1546 (the collection of proverbs by John Heywood) and was first attested in the United States in 1732. The proverb is found in varying forms, and has its counterpart in other languages: *Acheter chat en poche* (French, "To buy a cat in a pocket"); *Die Katze im Sack kaufen* (German, "To buy a cat in a sack"); Покупать кота в мешке (Russian, "To buy a cat in a sack"), etc.

1987. CBS sold the team [the Yankees] in 1973 for $10 million after swallowing an operating loss of $11 million.
"The trouble was," Mr. Burke once said, "we didn't go in and feel the goods. We bought a pig in a poke." —*New York Times*

1989. But the problem with cars, as often with people, is that what truly matters lies beneath the surface, and since there were no keys available for any of the autos, their innards had to remain untested. "It is like buying a pig in a poke," admitted Elizabeth Brickfield, the director of enforcement for the Parking Violations Bureau, who dropped by to explain things. —*New York Times*

1992. What did he [President Bush] think about Ross Perot as a candidate for President? There's "too much at stake, as we say here, to buy a pig in a poke." —*New York Times Magazine*

1994. "Of course," added Ms. Moore, who won the licenses on behalf of herself and a small pool of investors, "it could ultimately turn out to be a pig in a poke." —*New York Times*

Don't call us, we'll call you.

Don't have high expectations. Stereotypically used by interviewers at the end of an interview. The saying originated in the United States in the 1960s and was first used by theater directors to get rid of applicants who failed the audition. Often shortened to *Don't call us.*

1980. Don't call me; I'll call you. One Bell System subscriber in 5 has an unlisted phone number. —Mike Feinsilber and William B. Mead, *American Averages*

1981. Two hours later I was back at the *Chronicle* rattling Auk Arnold's cage. This time, however, he was too busy to see me, and a secretary asked me to leave my work (together with my name and phone number). I was given the old "Don't call us—we'll call you" treatment. —Abigail Van Buren, *The Best of Dear Abby*

1984. In any case, it was clear that he wasn't going to hire me. "Don't call us," he said. "We'll call you." —Lee Iacocca with William Novak, *Iacocca*

1986. In the industry, indie prod (independent production, to the uninitiated) equals out on your ass. Canned. Can't cut it. Tough shit. Don't call us we'll call you. —Jackie Collins, *Hollywood Husbands*

1994. Oliver North in the lap of the Virginia's Elephant.

"Thank you. Thank you. Don't call us, we'll call you!"

"Thanks for auditioning, anyway." —Cartoon, *Times* (Trenton)

Don't cast (throw) your pearls before swine. Don't offer anything to people who cannot appreciate its real value. The proverb appeared in the New Testament. It has been traced back to 1340 in English. First attested in the United States in the *Winthrop Papers* (1640). The proverb is found in varying forms: *Don't cast false pearls before real swine; Don't cast priceless pearls before an unappreciative swine; Pearls of wit are too precious to cast before swine; Pearls before swine*, etc. *The casting of false pearls before real swine* is sometimes used as the definition of education.

Give not that which is holy unto the dogs, neither cast ye your pearls before swine, lest they trample them under their feet, and turn again and rend you. —Matthew 7:6, *Authorized Version*, 1611

1947. *Blanche:* I think of myself as a very, very rich woman! But I have been foolish—casting my pearls before swine! —Tennessee Williams, *A Streetcar Named Desire*

1984. I decided to let the matter drop. It was always casting pearls before swine to try to reason from sentiment with the three hard sons of my sister Zeruiah, or with any of the rough six hundred who were with me then. —Joseph Heller, *God Knows*

Don't change horses in midstream. *See* DON'T SWAP HORSES IN MIDSTREAM.

Don't change the rules in the middle of the game. When people have become involved in something on the assumption that certain rules are binding, they will be angered when they are

changed arbitrarily. Often shortened to *don't change the rules*.

1984. Don't change the rules in the middle of the game. —Lee Iacocca with William Novak, *Iacocca*

1992. "I wasn't just mad," he [Mr. Doubleday] added. "I was stunned. I was hurt. If you've ever been a businessman, this is not the way you run a business. I do not believe that you can take a set of rules with a set of guidelines given to the chief officer, the commissioner [Fay Vincent], and change them in midstream because you get mad at him." —Claire Smith, "Doubleday May Sell His Share of the Mets," *New York Times*

1993. "It's really in Sen. Dorsey's hands. Traditionally this is the way it's been handled," he [Senate President Donald DiFrancesco] said. "The majority of the majority feels strongly that you don't change the rules in the middle of the game." —*Times* (Trenton)

1994. "You are going to try and change the rules of the game [of Social Security], especially after people have been paying into it for decades," says William Ritz, the group's public affairs director. "It's not fair, and it's not right." —*Wall Street Journal*

See also DON'T SWAP HORSES IN MIDSTREAM; RULES ARE MADE TO BE BROKEN.

Don't close (bar, lock, shut) the barn (stable) door after the horse runs away (has fled, has been stolen). Take precautions before any damage or loss occurs, not after it has already happened. Originally referring to horse-stealing, but now applied to anything that is done too late rather than too early. The proverb has been traced back to *Douce Ms* (c. 1350) and is similar to the Medieval French: *A tart ferme on l'estabe, quant li chevaux est perduz* ("The stable is shut too late, when the horse is lost"). First attested in the United States in *Kidnapped* (1886) by R. L. Stevenson. The proverb is found in varying forms: *It's no use to close (bar, lock, shut) the barn (stable) door after the horse has been stolen; It is too late to shut the stable door after the horse has bolted; It's a case of locking the door after the horse has been stolen; It's like closing the door after the horse is gone; Don't bolt the door after the horse has gone*, etc.

1987. Asked about the Norwegian effort, a Pentagon official likened the steps to "barring the barn door" after the horses have escaped. —*New York Times*

1992. Industry analysts said the strike authorization was part of the union's continuing resistance to G.M.'s plans to close plants and shift work to outside suppliers. "The union has to act now if it is to affect events," said Harley Shaiken, a former auto worker who is now a professor at the University of California at San Diego.

"If they wait until the national contract expires in September 1993, it will be like closing the barn door after the horse has gotten out," he added. —*New York Times*

1994. "This is like locking the proverbial barn door after the horse has left," said Christopher P. Bruhl, president of the Business Council of Southwestern Connecticut. —*New York Times*

See also IT IS EASY TO BE WISE AFTER THE EVENT.

Don't count your chickens before they are hatched. Don't think that your success, victory, or projected accomplishment is a sure thing until it actually occurs. Used as advice not to be too optimistic. The idea of the proverb comes from Aesop's fable "The Milkmaid and Her Pail" (550 B.C.). In common use since c. 1570 (*New Sonnets* by T. Howell). First attested in the United States in Loomis's collection of proverbs (1821). The proverb is found in varying forms: *Don't count your chickens before the eggs are laid; No good counting the chickens before they're hatched; Don't count your chickens before the cows come home; Never count your chickens before they are hatched,* etc. Often shortened to *Don't count your chickens!* The French equivalent of the English proverb is *Ne vendez pas la peau de l'ours avant de l'avoir tué* ("Don't sell the bearskin before you've killed the bear").

1664. To swallow gudgeons ere they're catched
    And count their chickens ere they're hatched
    —Samuel Butler, *Hudibras*, Part II, Canto III

1949. *Biff, getting away:* Well, all I said was I'm gonna see him, that's all!
    Will, turning away: Ah, you're counting your chickens again. —Arthur Miller, *Death of a Salesman*

1957. "I think it's going to be a boy. That's what it feels like to me. Of course there's no point in counting your chickens before your eggs are hatched but if we do have a baby one of the things I want to buy is a nice chair because I'm going to breast feed this baby ..." —John Cheever, *The Wapshot Chronicle*

1960. I looked down at him. His back was to us, but I could see his broad shoulders and bull-thick neck. He could easily have done it. I thought Jem

was counting his chickens. —Harper Lee, *To Kill a Mockingbird*

1991. No one should count any chickens just yet, but the prospects that Clarence Thomas will get a new job [on the Supreme Court] in the fall are looking up. —*Wall Street Journal*

See also DON'T SHOUT UNTIL YOU ARE OUT OF THE WOODS; THERE'S MANY A SLIP BETWEEN (THE) CUP AND (THE) LIP.

Don't cross the bridge till you come to it.
See LET'S CROSS THAT BRIDGE WHEN WE COME TO IT.

Don't cry over spilled milk. Don't get upset over something that went wrong when there's no remedy for it. The proverb was listed in James Howell's book of proverbs in 1659. First attested in the United States in the *Papers of Henry Laurens* (1757). The proverb is found in varying forms: *It's no use crying over spilled milk; There's no use crying over spilled milk; There is nothing to be gained by crying over spilled milk; No good crying over spilt milk,* etc.

1961. "This morning," she [a high school English teacher] announced, "I'm going to teach you a lesson that has nothing to do with English, but it has a lot to do with life." She picked up the bottle of milk, crushed it against the inside of the stone crock, and it splintered into small pieces. "The lesson," she said, "is don't cry over the spilled milk." —Ann Landers, *Since You Ask Me*

1986. "I made the mistake when I was growing up and in college of not really applying myself to my studies, and I regret that," Quayle says. "Looking back, I should have pursued philosophy and history and economics and things of that sort in college more, but I didn't. But I am not going to cry over spilt milk and that's past me." —*New York Times Magazine*

1993. "A Cat's Little Instruction Book" by Leigh W. Rutledge suggests, from a cat's point of view, what a male or female feline should do in a world dominated by humans. Number 164 "to do" reads: "Don't cry over spilt milk—lap it up instead." —*Times* (Trenton)

See also WHAT'S DONE CANNOT BE UNDONE WHAT'S DONE IS DONE.

Don't cut off your nose to spite your face.
Don't harm yourself just because it might also punish another person. The proverb has been traced back to *Deceit of Women* (c. 1560) and is similar to the French saying that was current in the fourteenth century: *Qui cope son nès, sa face est despechie* ("The man who cuts off his nose

spites his face"). First attested in the United States in *Writings of Christopher Gadsden* (1784). The proverb is found in varying forms: *It's like cutting off your nose to spite your face; It's a case of cutting off your nose to spite your face; You're cutting off your nose to spite your face,* etc. *To cut off one's nose to spite one's face* is almost always used metaphorically.

1936. Oh, how she regretted it all. She had often heard of people cutting off their noses to spite their faces but heretofore it had been only a figure of speech. Now she knew just what it meant. —Margaret Mitchell, *Gone With the Wind*

1951. "There's no sense in losing your head and going off half cocked and cutting off your nose to spite your face. Maybe he didn't even mean any disrespect at all." —James Jones, *From Here to Eternity*

1962. Yousseloff smiled with priestly tolerance, "Artie, I've taken the men off jobs too. I've been through this a hundred times. All they do is come back a day later. If it'll make you feel better I'll send them home, but there's a nine-hundred-dollar payroll under this roof right this minute and they're going to be paid anyway, that's union rules. Don't give way to your emotions. Be mad at me, that's fine, but don't cut off your nose to spite your face." —Herman Wouk, *Youngblood Hawke*

1992. No matter that the Hub provides prenatal care and pediatric services for those who want to have their babies, and contraception for those who don't want to get pregnant in the first place. The motto of the gag rule might well be: Cut off your funds to spite your face. —Anna Quindlen, *New York Times*

Don't do as I do, but as I say. *See* DO AS I SAY, NOT AS I DO.

Don't fire until you see the whites of their eyes. Don't fire until the enemy is close up. Exercise restraint to gain maximum success. Attributed to Colonel William Prescott (1726–95) or General Israel Putnam (1718–90). The famous command was issued to the American soldiers on June 17, 1775, at the battle of Bunker Hill. According to Eric Partridge, the command read: "Men, you are all marksmen—don't one of you fire until you see the whites of their eyes." The attack of the British troops was repulsed. But neither Prescott nor Putnam originated the saying. Pietro Duodo, Venetian Ambassador to France in the seventeenth century, wrote that the horsemen didn't use their pistols or swords "until they could see the whites of their eyes." In 1745, Prince Charles of Prussia said to

his officers, "Silent till you see the whites of their eyes." Twelve years later, during the Prussian attack on the Austrians at Prague (1757), Frederick the Great gave the same order: "By push of bayonets, no firing till you see the whites of their eyes."

1946. If the wind was right, you knew he [Tiny Duffy] was a city-hall slob long before you could see the whites of his eyes. —Robert Penn Warren, *All the King's Men*

1990. Helped by the others, he [Joel] wrapped the ship's line around himself, then clutched the lifesaver to the back of his thighs as he was lowered into the water. "Don't let the sharks see the whites of your feet," Paster warned. —Ron Arias, "Prisoners of the Sea," *Five Against the Sea,* reprinted by *Reader's Digest*

1992. "What you have a tendency to do is try and see the whites of his eyes," said Messier of his team's too-personal approach to Vernon, "instead of just getting back the puck toward the net." —*New York Times*

See also DAMN THE TORPEDOES! FULL SPEED AHEAD!; DON'T GIVE UP THE SHIP.

Don't get mad, get even. Instead of getting angry, repay someone's bad deed. The saying originated in the United States and has been in common use since c. 1965, according to Eric Partridge. It is said to have been one of the favorite proverbs of Joseph Patrick Kennedy (1888–1969), father of John F. Kennedy.

1975. Some of the reasons have their roots in that wonderful law of the Boston Irish political jungle: "Don't get mad; get even." —B. Bradlee, *Conversations with Kennedy*

1977. Kennedy, too, talked about "getting" his enemies. "Don't get mad, get even," was the well-known watchword along the New Frontier. —Victor Lasky, *It Didn't Start with Watergate*

1984. "Don't get mad," Mary reminded me. "Get even." —Lee Iacocca with William Novak, *Iacocca*

1988. Don't Get Mad and Don't Get Even, Either. —Harvey Mackay, *Swim with the Sharks without Being Eaten Alive*

1989. We had a choice, Alexander and I. We could either get mad or get even. —Michael Lewis, *Liar's Poker*

1994. [David Lee] Roth freely admits that he tried to contact his former bandmates—Eddie and Alex Van Halen and Michael Anthony—about a reunion, but they never took his calls.

So, he decided not to get mad, but to get even.

On his coming new solo album "Your Filthy Little Mouth," Roth has employed the talents of one Terry Kilgore, a guitarist with whom Roth wrote his first song when he was 13. —*New York Post*

Don't give up the ship. Don't surrender. Originated in the United States. First attested in 1813 and attributed to Captain James Lawrence (1781–1813), commander of the American frigate *Chesapeake*, who, being fatally wounded in a battle with the British frigate *Shannon* on June 1, 1813, ordered his sailors not to give up their ship. The proverb's earliest appearance in print was in 1814 (*Diary of F. Palmer, Privateersman*) and it has been in common use ever since. "Don't Give Up the Ship" is the motto of the U.S. Navy.

> **1813.** Tell the men to fire faster and not to give up the ship; fight her till she sinks. —James Lawrence's order on board the U.S. frigate *Chesapeake*, quoted by Paul F. Boller, Jr., and John George in *They Never Said It* (1989)

> **1994.** "Every time I want to give up and stop fighting, my dad says, 'Don't give up the ship. Keep on fighting!'" —Overheard at a Columbia University student rally

See also DAMN THE TORPEDOES! FULL SPEED AHEAD!; DON'T FIRE UNTIL YOU SEE THE WHITES OF THEIR EYES; NEVER SAY DIE.

Don't have too many irons in the fire. Don't do more things at the same time than you can handle; don't commit yourself to too many responsibilities. The proverb has been traced back to the 1540s. First attested in the United States in *Papers of Benjamin Franklin* (1753). The proverb is found in varying forms: *Don't put too many irons in the fire; One has a good many irons in the fire*, etc.

> **1936.** "You are well enough, I see. Then, tell me this. Was I the only iron you had in the fire?" —Margaret Mitchell, *Gone With the Wind*

> **1985.** She [Dawn] knew his problems went far beyond those of Empire Pictures. He [Charles] had many other irons in the fire, many of them no doubt hotter—and more important—than this one, which he had grasped mainly because it seemed the right thing to do with her shares. —Michael Korda, *Queenie*

> **1991.** In the scene, Erica, played by Susan Lucci, asks Mr. Buffet, who took over Salomon after a scandal over purchases of treasury notes erupted in August, if he might be interested in buying her company. "I think I have all the irons in the fire that I can handle," he responds. —*New York Times*

> **1993.** He [Abraham Ribicoff] gives President Clinton a mixed grade for his first months in office.
> "He's got good ideas," Ribicoff says. "The one problem that he has is he's got too many irons in the fire, and he hasn't done enough to implement the ideas." —*Times* (Trenton)

See also DON'T BITE OFF MORE THAN YOU CAN CHEW.

Don't hide your light under a bushel. Don't conceal your talent, skills, or good deeds; don't be too modest. The idea of the proverb appeared in the New Testament. The word *bushel* in the proverb and its variants is the vessel originally used as a bushel measure. The proverb has been traced back to Daniel's *Uricrisiarum* (1379). It was attested in the United States in James Fenimore Cooper's novel *The Pathfinder* (1840). The proverb is found in varying forms: *Don't hide your light under a bushel basket; Don't hide your talents under a kitchen bushel; Don't hide your candle under a bushel; Stop hiding your light under a bushel; Never hide your light under a bushel*, etc.

> Neither do men light a candle, and put it under a bushel, but on a candlestick; and it giveth light unto all that are in the house. —Matthew 5:15, *Authorized Version*, 1611

> **1982.** Feldman was dubious about calling it a great motion picture, but Max insisted on inserting the adjective. "We are not hiding lights under any bushels," he [Max Britsky] said. —Howard Fast, *Max*

> **1984.** He [Hal Sperlich] discovered a number of bright young men who had been hidden under bushel baskets. —Lee Iacocca with William Novak, *Iacocca*

> **1994.** I've never been either modest or immodest. I'm open, direct and candid. I'm not going to hide my light in a bushel basket. —Ed Koch, *New York Times*

Don't hit a man when he's down. Don't attack someone who is already hurt. Originally a boxing phrase. According to the boxing rules, you cannot hit another boxer when he is down; you can strike him only when he gets up after the fall. The proverb has been traced back to *Answer to Gairdner* (1551) by Thomas Cranmer (1480–1556). First attested in the United States in *Murder at a Police Station* (1943). The proverb is found in varying forms: *Never hit a man when he's down; Never kick a guy except when he is down; There can be no harm in kicking a man when he's down; Why hit a man when he's down? You can't kick a man when he's down*, etc. The metaphorical phrase *to hit a man when he's down* is also used.

1946. She didn't pack it [the bag] because she was too honorable, or too generous, or too something, to hit him when she thought he was down. Or about to go down. —Robert Penn Warren, *All the King's Men*

1984. Always hit him with more while he's up, and never be too tough on him when he's down. —Lee Iacocca with William Novak, *Iacocca*

1987. "Speaking of acting like a responsible adult, Zonker, when are you going to get a *job* and move out of here?"
"*That's* it—hit me while I'm down!" —G. B. Trudeau, *Doonesbury Deluxe*

1994. Kicking a guy when he's down is frowned upon. It isn't considered sporting. So when Donald Trump and his empire were going under with a massive gurgle, the media treated him fairly kindly. —*Crain's New York Business*

Don't judge a book by its cover. Don't judge things by their appearance only. Originated in the United States. First attested in the journal *American Speech* (1929). Has been used in Britain since 1954 (*Murder in Haste* by H. Gardiner). The proverb is found in varying forms: *Don't ever judge a book by its cover; Never judge a book by its movie; You can't judge a book by its binding; You can never tell a book by its cover; You can't always judge a book by a cover,* etc.

1929. You can't judge a book by its binding. —*American Speech*

1953. *Kilroy:* I still say your suit is clean.
The Baron: Thanks. That's more than I can say about your apparel.
Kilroy: Don't judge a book by the covers. —Tennessee Williams, *Camino Real*

1953. Montag squinted from one face to another as they walked.
"Don't judge a book by its cover," someone said. —Ray Bradbury, *Fahrenheit 451*

1984. Samuel was prepared to settle right off for Eliab, the firstborn. But God was speaking my language when He told Samuel a book must not be judged by its cover or a man by his countenance or height. —Joseph Heller, *God Knows*

1986. When Keith counters that you can't tell a book by a cover, she points out, "Yeah, but you can tell how much it's gonna cost." —*New York Times*

1991. God bless whoever said, "you can't judge a book by its cover," because if he'd judged me by

the way I looked on the day we met I'd be sitting on the shelf with a bunch of sleazy airport romances and self-help books. —Ad for Reebok International Ltd., *People*

1993. As someone who prefers not to judge a book by its cover, or for that matter, by its first 100 pages—the ones that caused this debate—I waited until the entire 631-page tome dropped, like a stone, onto my desk. And I found another reason to wish that "The Last Brother" might be the bombshell that bombs. —Ellen Goodman, *Times* (Trenton)

1994. DON'T EVER JUDGE THIS CONSULTANT BY HER COVER —Headline, *New York Times*
See also APPEARANCES (LOOKS) ARE DECEIVING (DECEPTIVE); STILL WATERS RUN DEEP.

Don't judge a man until you have walked a mile in his boots. Don't criticize another person's work until you've tried to do it yourself; don't judge another person's life until you've been forced to live it. The word *criticize* may be used instead of *judge* and *shoes* instead of *boots*.

1992. Mr. Chechitelli said the forums on diversity and political correctness made him think about things "that never affected me before."
"And it kind of opened my eyes," he said, referring to the discussions, particularly the one on homosexuality. "I think it made me more tolerant. It's like the old cliché: You have to walk a mile in someone else's shoes before you can really see how they live." —*New York Times*

1993. It has been said, my son, that before you criticize a man, you must first walk a mile in his ... —Cartoon by Leigh Rubini, "Rubes," Creators Syndicate, Inc.
See also JUDGE NOT, THAT YE BE NOT JUDGED.

Don't jump from the frying pan into the fire. Don't go from a difficult situation into a worse one. In English, the proverb has been traced back to *Dialogue Concerning Heresies* (1528–30) by Sir Thomas More (1478–1535). First attested in the United States in *James Claypoole's Letter Book* (1681). The proverb is usually attributed to Tertullian (about 160–240 a.d.): *De calcaria in carbonarium* ("Out of the frying pan into the fire"). The same or almost the same sayings can be found in many languages. The proverb is found in varying forms: *Don't leap from the frying pan into the fire; Out of the fire into the frying pan; Out of the frying pan, and into a far worse fire,* etc. The Greek equivalent is "Out of the smoke into the flame." The Russians say Из огня да в полымя ("Out of the fire into the flame"). In

French: *Tomber de la poêle dans le feu* or *Tomber de la poêle dans la braise* ("To leap from the frying pan into the fire").

1922. Out of the frying pan of life into the fire of purgatory. —James Joyce, *Ulysses*

1935. "Sometimes I'm tempted to turn Communist! Funny—me with my fat-headed old Hudson-River-Valley Dutch ancestors!" marveled Julian Falck.

"Fine idea! Out of the frying pan of Windrip and Hitler into the fire of the New York *Daily Worker* and Stalin and automatics!" —Sinclair Lewis, *It Can't Happen Here*

1987. If it is decided that the religious fundamentalism of Iran is a danger to all the nations of the Middle East (including maverick Syria, now Iran's Arab ally) then Israelis will have to ask themselves: Are we jumping from the frying pan into the fire? Are we helping to create an even more dangerous world than we have today? —*New York Times*

1989. Mr. Plaskett said that many foreign airlines had less security than those regulated by the United States. Passengers who shift to foreign airlines, he said, may be moving "out of the frying pan into the fire." —*New York Times*

1991. Seeking safe investments, people drop stocks and buy bonds. Out of the frying pan into the fire. —Jane Bryant Quinn, *Making the Most of Your Money*

1993. Lotus won, with potential damages of $100 million or more. Borland was forced to remove the Lotus conversion feature.

And now, it's out of the frying pan and into the fire. —Peter H. Lewis, "Is Borland Using a Two-Edged Sword in Battling for Sales?" *New York Times*

Don't kill the goose that laid the golden egg. Don't destroy a source of future profits out of greed. The proverb dates back to Aesop (about 550 b.c.). In his fable "The Goose with the Golden Eggs" he tells about a farmer whose goose started laying golden eggs. But he wanted all the gold he could get and he wanted it immediately. Aesop writes: "Thinking to get at once all the gold the goose could give, he killed it and opened it only to find—nothing." The English usage of the proverb has been traced back to the 1480s. First attested in the United States in *Pamphlets of American Revolution* (1764). In 1860, writer Henry David Thoreau (1817–1862) changed the proverb by saying, "Every fowl lays golden eggs for him who can find them." The proverb is found in varying forms: *Kill not the goose that laid the golden eggs; The goose that laid the golden egg shall lay no more for thee*, etc.

1961. It was "Roy Hobbs Day," that had been in the making since two weeks ago, when Max Mercy printed in his column: "Roy Hobbs, El Swatto, has been ixnayed on a pay raise. Trying to kill the bird that lays the golden baseball, Judge?" —Bernard Malamud, *The Natural*

1962. She laughed, sitting up. "Don't eat me, that's killing the goose that lays the golden eggs. I can cook you something." —Herman Wouk, *Youngblood Hawke*

1982. "... we're going to have the mayor and maybe the governor and whoever else Murphy thinks should be there, and after the opening, where we run the picture just once, I'm going to give a party at Rector's for three hundred people. We got a goose that's going to lay golden eggs like nobody ever dreamed about." —Howard Fast, *Max*

1984. In those days [1960–1970] the car industry was like a golden goose. We were making money almost without trying. —Lee Iacocca with William Novak, *Iacocca*

1989. Now, ensconced in the ocher parlor of his town house in Manhattan's East 60's, he [Tom Wolfe] was charting the route from the Bauhaus to his house, expressing concern that developers and officials, in their relentless hunger for golden eggs, were cooking the city's goose. —*New York Times*

1993. THE GOOSE THAT LAID AN EGG IN THE SUBURBS —Headline of Robert Hanley's article on states' permission to hunt flocks, *New York Times*

1994. "The N.H.L. is a great league," said Bartlett, the agent, "but they have to be careful. The I.H.L. and college hockey could compete for their fan base. The golden goose can suddenly stop laying eggs." —*New York Times*

See also DON'T BITE THE HAND THAT FEEDS YOU.

Don't lead with your chin. Don't expose yourself to danger. Originated in boxing. If one fights and doesn't protect one's chin, it ends up in a knockout. First cited in a literal sense in 1922 in Ernest Hemingway's letters. The proverb currently means: Don't be stupid, don't invite your own defeat. *Lead with the (one's) chin* is also used.

1950. You're certainly leading with your chin. —Erle Stanley Gardner, *Musical*

1991. *Senator Rudman:* Mr. Goodman, you accused Gates of suppressing analysts with whom he disagreed on whether or not the Soviets would send MIG aircraft to Nicaragua. And you quoted that "lead with the chin" quote ... I think is unhelpful—unhelpfully leading with our chin to make a prediction when we really don't have anything to go on. —*New York Times*

1993. Debater Ross Led With His Chin. —Garry Wills' commentary on the debate between Ross Perot and Al Gore, *New York Post*

See also DON'T STICK YOUR NECK OUT.

Don't let the fox guard the henhouse. Don't assign a job to someone who will then be in a position to exploit it for his own ends. Said to one who entrusts his money to sharpers. The proverb has been traced back to *Contre-League* (1589) and is similar to the Latin: *Ovem lupo committere* ("To set a wolf to guard the sheep"). First attested in the United States in *Poet's Proverbs* (1924). The proverb is found in varying forms: *Don't put the fox to guard the chicken house; Don't let the fox guard the chicken coop; Don't set a wolf to watch the sheep; It's a case of the proverbial fox guarding the chickens,* etc. The idea is expressed in the old nursery rhyme: "Sleep, my little one, sleep. Thy father guards the sheep."

1984. Naturally, when I brought Doug[las] Fraser [the union president] onto the board [of directors], the business community went wild. They said: "You can't do that! You've putting the fox into the henhouse. You've lost your mind!" —Lee Iacocca with William Novak, *Iacocca*

1987. Throughout the vast space, which had the soaring ceilings of an old-fashioned railroad station, were huddles of dark people, and their voices created a great nervous rumble, and around the edges of the dark people walked white men in cheap suits or sport jackets, watching them like wolves monitoring the sheep. —Tom Wolfe, *The Bonfire of the Vanities*

1989. "It's the fox guarding the chicken house," said Sharon Brown, president of Friends of Beaversprite, who is Mrs. Richards's designated biographer and an animal-rights advocate. "Would you hire a bank robber to run a bank?" —*New York Times*

1991. During last month's summit, when the two presidents were meeting at a *dacha* outside Moscow, U.S. officials got word of a bloody raid on a Lithuanian customs post. But the Soviet side hadn't heard, and it was Sununu who broke the news to Gorbachev. The Soviet leader then put the KGB in charge of investigations, an act one Soviet described as "sending the goat in the garden." In Russian, that means using the fox to guard the chicken coop. But Gorbachev has no other goats to rely on. —*Newsweek*

1992. "I don't think the people of South Carolina are going to put that fox back in the chicken coop," Mr. Hollings said at a Democratic picnic in Rock Hill on Saturday. —*New York Times*

1993. Tough luck, say regulators in New York, Nynex's biggest region. "It would be like giving the fox the keys to the chicken coop," said Richard Stannard, technical staff director for the State Service Commission. —*New York Times*

Don't let the grass grow under your feet. Act promptly; don't delay. The saying dates back to the early seventeenth century. "Let no grass grow under his [hare's] feet," wrote Edward Topsell in his *Foure-Footed Beasts* (1607). The adage was a favorite of Mark Twain: "I didn't wait for breakfast," he wrote in *A Connecticut Yankee in King Arthur's Court* (1889), "No grass grew under my feet." The proverb is found in various forms.

1926. I see you don't let the grass grow under your feet, Mr. Poirot. It will be a pleasure to work with you, I am sure. —Agatha Christie, *The Murder of Roger Ackroyd*

1960. It's no use talking to me about solicitors. I've already provided myself with one. A fine solicitor he is. Not the man to let the grass grow under his feet. —Charles P. Snow, *The Affair*

1986. Never let it be said that Red Sox manager John McNamara came back to California to let the grass grow under his feet. The former Angels manager proved that yesterday, the eve of the third game in the best-of-seven American League Championship Series, when he revealed that Roger Clemens, not Al Nipper, will start Game 4. —*Boston Globe*

1997. The city Parks Department has let some grass grow under its feet—right in Tompkins Square Park. Eighteen lush marijuana plants—some 5 feet tall—have been thriving right under the park office windows. —*New York Daily News*

Don't look a gift horse in the mouth. *See* NEVER LOOK A GIFT HORSE IN THE MOUTH.

Don't make a mountain out of a molehill. Don't make a big fuss over a trifle. The proverb dates back to Lucian (a.d. 125–210). In his "Ode to a Fly" he wrote about "making an elephant of a fly." This Greek proverb was used in Latin: *Arcem ex cloaca facere;* it was picked up by the French: *Faire d'une mouche un éléphant;* and by the Germans: *Aus einer Mücke einen Elefanten machen.* The English proverb has been traced back to Erasmus (1548). First attested in the

United States in the *Winthrop Papers* (1643). The proverb is found in varying forms: *Don't make a mountain out of nothing; Never make a mountain out of a molehill,* etc.

1949. *Willy:* You're my foundation and support, Linda.
Linda: Just try to relax, dear. You make mountains out of molehills. —Arthur Miller, *Death of a Salesman*

1953. "For all you know, you're making—I honestly think you're making a mountain—" —J. D. Salinger, "Pretty Mouth and Green My Eyes," *Nine Stories*

1984. "To me, you're making a mountain out of a molehill," Osner said. —Howard Fast, *The Outsider*

1988. He's a good husband and father, but we argue about this constantly …
Am I making a mountain out of a molehill? —Abigail Van Buren, "Dear Abby," *Newsday*

1989. I think Joe Queenan has made a mountain out of a molehill about the dark side of comic books. —*New York Times Magazine*

Don't make the same mistake twice. Learn from mistakes, so that you don't repeat them. Used literally. The proverb is found in varying forms: *Never make the same mistake twice; Don't make the same mistake over and over again,* etc.

1984. Mistakes are part of life; you can't avoid them. All you can hope is that they won't be too expensive and that you don't make the same mistake twice. —Lee Iacocca with William Novak, *Iacocca*

1994. [Jessica] *Tandy:* Wisdom is learning from all your experience, which means maybe you don't make the same mistakes over and over again. —*Modern Maturity*

1994. Balancing the two appeals is delicate. After taping his ad, Mr. Koch told reporters that the gist of it was: "You made one mistake when you threw me out, so don't make the same mistake twice." —*New York Times*

Don't mix business with pleasure. *See* NEVER MIX BUSINESS WITH PLEASURE.

Don't pass judgment, that you may not be judged. *See* JUDGE NOT, THAT YE BE NOT JUDGED.

Don't play with fire. Don't take unnecessary risks. The proverb has been traced back to *An Heptameron of Civil Discourses* (1582) by George Whetstone (1551?–1587), English author, and "The Garland" in *Silex Scintillans* (1655) by Henry

Vaughan (1622–95), English poet. First attested in the United States in 1928 in Eugene O'Neill's *Strange Interlude*. The proverb is found in varying forms: *If you play with fire, you're apt to get burned; Those who play with fire must expect to get burned; If you play with fire you will burn your finger sooner or later,* etc.

1582. In doing of these things is great daunger … to play with fire; to striue with water; and to blue a woman knowledge of our power. —George Whetstone, *Heptameron*

1655. I played with fire, did counsel spurn … But never thought fire would burn. —Henry Vaughan, *"The Garland"*

1928. "Look here, Nina, we've done all that is necessary, playing with fire is dangerous." —Eugene O'Neill, *Strange Interlude*

1986. Mayor Koch had reacted angrily to Monday's taxi protest and warned drivers that they would be "playing with fire" if they sought to pressure the city into a fare increase by withholding service. —*New York Times*

1988. "I suppose he needs to prove something to himself," she [Maury] replied. "But I think it's playing with fire." —Erich Segal, *Doctors*

1992. They are dreamers, schemers and thrill seekers, people made desperate by the mean walls of the quotidian. They are out of control, playing with fire. —*New York Times Book Review*
See also FIGHT FIRE WITH FIRE.

Don't pour new wine in old bottles. *See* DON'T PUT NEW WINE IN OLD BOTTLES.

Don't put all your eggs in one basket. Spread your risk; don't put all you have into one business or one undertaking. The proverb has been around for centuries. It was used by Cervantes in *Don Quixote.* In 1666, it was included in Giovanni Torriano's collection of Italian proverbs. First attested in the United States in *Letters of John Fairfield* (1838) and used by Mark Twain in *Pudd'nhead Wilson* (1894). The proverb is found in varying forms: *Don't carry all your eggs in one basket; Never lay all your eggs in one basket; One cannot afford to put all one's eggs in one basket,* etc.

1605–15.
'Tis the part of a wise man to keep himself today for tomorrow, and not venture all his eggs in one basket. —Cervantes, *Don Quixote,* Chap. III

1894. Put all your eggs in the one basket

and—WATCH THAT BASKET. —Pudd'nhead Wilson's Calendar. —Mark Twain, *Pudd'nhead Wilson*

1986. Being a workaholic is not simply a matter of the amount of time given to work. It's a state of mind, in which work becomes so important that there are no other major commitments, no other sectors where accomplishments seem significant. For workaholics, all the eggs of self-esteem are in the basket of work. —Judith M. Bardwaick, *The Plateauing Trap*

1987. While acknowledging that the city had to "strengthen" its own management even within the current structure, Mr. Grinker said: "Over the long run we have to have a more balanced system—a better mix of public and private responsibility. You don't put all your eggs in one basket." —*New York Times*

1991. A wise man once said, "If you put all your eggs in one basket, watch that basket." When it comes to stocks, if you put all your eggs in one basket, watch out. —Ad, *Wall Street Journal*

1991. No more than 10% to 15% of conventional job seekers find new positions by answering want ads. The comparable percentage for those making career changes is much lower—1% might be a stretch. So if you career changers plunk all your eggs in the want-ad basket, the chicken will probably never hatch. —*Wall Street Journal's National Business Employment Weekly*

1992. "If we go back to the cold war era, when Israel was perceived as a strategic ally and that was it, it will be a real misunderstanding of the emerging realities," she [Hanan Ashrawi] says. "It means you put all your eggs in one basket, and that one basket is leaky." —*New York Times*

1994. One constant hazard for a fair's budget is nature's bad moods. "Weather is the universal fear in the fair business," Mr. Bjorklund said. "We have a lot of eggs in one 11-day basket." Last summer, in fact, the worst storms in 40 years hit the Indiana State Fair's opening weekend. —*New York Times*

Don't put new wine in old bottles. Don't put something new in an old frame (case, system, etc.). The idea was first expressed in the Bible. It is found in varying forms: *Don't pour new wine in old bottles; You can't put new wine in old bottles,* etc.

Neither do men put new wine into old bottles: else the bottles break, and the wine runneth out, and the bottles perish: but they put new wine into new bottles, and both are preserved. —Matthew 9:17, *Authorized Version,* 1611

1950. I think the British have the distinction above all other nations of being able to put new wine into old bottles without bursting them. —Clement Attlee, *Hansard*

1991. "We didn't want old wine in new bottles," says Tom Furey, who directed the project. —*Fortune*

Don't put off until tomorrow what you can do today. *See* NEVER PUT OFF UNTIL TOMORROW WHAT YOU CAN DO TODAY.

Don't put the cart before the horse. Don't get things in the wrong order. The proverb has been traced back to 1340. In 1546, it was included in John Heywood's book of proverbs. First attested in the United States in *Letters of John Randolph* (1676). The proverb is found in varying forms: *Don't get the cart before the horse; Never put the cart before the horse; It's like putting the cart before the horse; The cart is in front of the horse,* etc. *To put the cart before the horse* means to do things in the wrong order and is commonly used as a figure of speech. Similar phrases were used by the Greeks and the Romans.

1947. "Actually, Mr. Debs, it is a case of which comes first, the cart or the horse." —Irving Stone, *Adversary in the House*

1967. Had Bobby [Kennedy] openly endorsed Nickerson, his candidacy might have constituted a real threat. But as the Washington *Post's* Flora Lewis reported, "the Senator wanted to put his horse at the other end of the cart and join a Nickerson bandwagon after it gathered speed. It never got up to a good roll." —Ralph de Toledano, *R. F. K. The Man Who Would Be President*

1988. Senator Goodman, who had been supportive of the Mayor despite their partisan differences in the past, said yesterday that he was not promoting Mr. Ravitch. "That would be putting the cart before the horse," he said, adding that it was necessary to form the coalition of anti-Koch elements before settling on a candidate. —*New York Times*

1993. Until we address these problems and the many other facets of the medical service industry, we will not have true health care reform. To consider health insurance at this time is putting the cart before the horse. —*Times* (Trenton)
See also WHICH CAME FIRST, THE CHICKEN OR THE EGG?

Don't rock the boat. Don't disturb the status quo; don't upset people and cause problems. The saying alludes to small boats that may be capsized if passengers are clumsy. It has been in common use since the 1920s. The expression was used famously in the song, "Sit Down, You're

Rocking the Boat" from the musical comedy *Guys and Dolls* (1950) by Frank Loesser.

1988. Twenty-six days from today, you and millions of Americans will choose two people to lead us into the future as President and Vice President of the United States. Our opponents say things are okay—don't rock the boat—not to worry. They say we should be satisfied. But I don't think we can be satisfied when we're spending $150 billion a year on interest alone on the national debt—much of it going to foreign banks. —Michael Dukakis, *New York Times*

1989. Political experts are divided about the Bush style. Some believe the President is not building the authority he will need for the tough days ahead. Others, like Henry Graff, a history professor at Columbia University, think Mr. Bush's "small-is-beautiful" style is perfectly suited to the times. "People don't want any rocking of the boat," Mr. Graff said. —*New York Times*

1994. All through the debate about abortion and health care reform, many members of Congress have been talking about the status quo as if it were a peaceable kingdom in the abortion wars. They've described that "state" longingly as utopia where sleeping dogs lie. Where boats don't rock. Where bills pass. —*Boston Globe*

1994. A national referendum on the matter is scheduled, talk shows debate the issue, and Casey Kasem even hosts a "Just say no" TV fund raiser. Meanwhile, the President's sole black adviser (Robert Guillaume) overcomes his don't-rock-the-boat philosophy to rally opposition to his trade.—*Time*

1997. [Bart] Stupak is a boat rocker on Capitol Hill. In 1995, he proposed punishments for "weak-principled opportunists" in Congress who switch parties. —*Detroit News*

1998. "This is a don't-rock-the-boat economy," says Sherry Bebich Jeff, a political scientist at Claremont Graduate University in Southern California. "Incumbents and longtime pols ought to feel pretty good." —*Christian Science Monitor*

1998. Polls show voters have lost faith in Clinton's morals and honesty, but things seem fine, so they figure he's doing a good job and don't want to rock the boat. —

Don't sell America short. *See* NEVER SELL AMERICA SHORT.

Don't set a wolf to watch the sheep. *See* DON'T LET THE FOX GUARD THE HENHOUSE.

Don't shoot the messenger. Don't blame the person who brings bad news. This idea was expressed by Sophocles as far back as 442 b.c. and much later by Shakespeare in *Henry IV, Part II* (1598) and in *Antony and Cleopatra* (1606–07). The word *kill* may be used as a substitute for *shoot.*

c.442 b.c.
Nobody likes the man who brings bad news.
—Sophocles, *Antigone*

1598. Yet the first bringer of unwelcome news
Hath but a losing office, and his tongue
Sounds ever after as a sullen bell,
Remember'd knolling a departing friend.
—Shakespeare, *Henry IV, Part II*, Act I,
Scene I

1606–07.
Come hither, sir.
Though it be honest, it is never good
To bring bad news.
—Shakespeare, *Antony and Cleopatra*,
Act II, Scene V

1992. Instructors tell of the inevitable "midsemester blowup" in which students protest angrily about the one-sidedness of courses. Feminist pedagogues call it the "blame the messenger" reaction, or the "denial" stage. —*New Republic*

1993. The column smacks of a whiny schoolboy who was told by his classmate that his answer to the math problem was the wrong one. Rather than try to find the correct answer, the column attacks the messenger. —*Times* (Trenton)

1993. "I am concerned that if the messenger becomes the focus, the message is lost," said Senator Kassebaum, the ranking Republican on the committee. —*New York Times*

1994. FIRE THE MESSENGERS —Headline, *New York Times*
See also DON'T SHOOT THE PIANO-PLAYER: HE'S DOING THE BEST HE CAN.

Don't shoot the piano-player: he's doing the best he can. Don't hurt innocent people. Originated in the United States in the Wild West, around 1860. During his 1883 tour of the United States, Oscar Wilde (1854–1900) saw this saying on a notice in a Leadville, Colorado, saloon. It is sometimes attributed to Mark Twain, but neither Wilde nor Twain has ever claimed authorship.

1883. Over the piano was printed a notice: Please do not shoot the pianist. He is doing his best. —Oscar Wilde, *Personal Impressions of America (Leadville)*, quoted in *Bartlett's Familiar Quotations*, Sixteenth Edition (1992)

1975. But at the Breymann Redoubt on October 9 [1776], when one of Arnold's men raised his rifle to shoot the Hessian who had wounded his general, Arnold stopped him with, "For God's sake! Don't kill him; he's only doing his duty." —David Wallechinsky and Irving Wallace, *The People's Almanac*

1994. "A smear campaign against President Clinton has gone too far. I really can't comprehend for the life of me why they're shooting the saxophone player who's doing his best as President of this nation." —Overheard at a Manhattan newsstand

See also DON'T SHOOT THE MESSENGER.

Don't shout until you are out of the woods.
Don't feel safe until you are out of danger. The proverb originated in the United States and has been traced back to *Papers of Benjamin Franklin* (1770). It was used by Abigail Adams (1744–1818) in a letter dated November 13, 1800. First attested in England in *Hereward the Wake* (1866) by Charles Kingsley (1819–75). The proverb is found in varying forms: *Don't halloo till you are out of the woods; Don't crow afore you are out of the woods; Don't yell till you're out of the woods; Never halloo until you are out of the woods*, etc. *(Not) to be out of the woods* is a commonly used idiom.

1770. This is Hollowing before you are out of the Wood. —Benjamin Franklin, *Papers of Benjamin Franklin*

1984. Rymer Corp. isn't out of the woods yet: long-term debt of $31 million dwarfs its $4.9 million net worth. —*Forbes*

1987. "Reagan isn't altogether out of the woods, but he's certainly gotten to the firebreak," said Representative Robert Michel of Illinois, the leader of the House Republicans. —*New York Times*

1991. When nothing happened for about a week, I assumed we were out of the woods. —Oliver L. North, *Under Fire*

1993. "I don't think sustained profitability at T. W.A. is anywhere near visible," said Kevin C. Murphy, an airline analyst at Morgan Stanley. "I don't think they're out of the woods." —*New York Times*

1994. "We're not out of the woods yet on inflation," said Lisa Finstrom, currency analyst at Smith Barney Inc. —*New York Times*

1995. "You have two more exams to take, so don't holler till you're out of the woods." —Overheard in the lobby of George Washington High School, New York

See also DON'T COUNT YOUR CHICKENS BEFORE THEY ARE HATCHED; THERE'S MANY A SLIP BETWEEN (THE) CUP AND (THE) LIP.

Don't start anything you can't finish.
Only do what you feel you can complete. The proverb has been traced back to *Dictes and Sayenges of Philosophirs* (1477). First attested in the United States in *Anna Christie* (1921) by Eugene O'Neill (1888–1953). The proverb is found in varying forms: *Don't start what you can't finish; Never start anything you can't finish*, etc.

1994. Memories of maternal advice to their kids: Franz Schubert's mother: "Take my advice, son. Never start anything you can't finish." —Joey Adams, "Strictly for Laughs," *New York Post*

1994. "Oh, well … I learned a long time ago that it's not how you start, it's how you finish." —Cartoon by Charles Schultz, "Peanuts," United Feature Syndicate, Inc.

Don't step on other people's toes.
See DON'T TREAD ON OTHER PEOPLE'S TOES.

Don't stick your neck out.
Don't take unnecessary risks. Originally used in boxing as advice to the fighter to keep his neck and chin drawn in or protected. The proverb originated in the U.S. and has been traced back to *Murder in House with the Blue Eyes* (1939) by J. N. Darby. First attested in England in *Flush As May* (1963) by P. M. Hubbard. The proverb is found in varying forms: *Don't stretch your neck out; It's not a good idea to stick your neck out*, etc.

1939. Don't stick your neck out! —J. N. Darby, *Murder in House with the Blue Eyes*

1940. "Don't you worry. We're doin' somepin, on'y we ain't stickin' our necks out." —John Steinbeck, *The Grapes of Wrath*

1974. On Thursday, 1 July," [Alex] Shipley continued, "I went and had an interview with a friend who had worked for Senator Albert Gore's administrative assistant and asked him what I should do. I told him I wasn't interested, but was wondering if it might help the Democrats if I played along. Or whether I should drop it immediately. He said, 'Don't stick your neck out, but don't say no; see what you can find out.'" —Carl Bernstein and Bob Woodward, *All the President's Men*

1984. They may or may not work out well, but you have to like ten stock pickers [analysts] who are willing to stick their necks out. —*Forbes*

1984. "Charlie, you tell Greer to teach this lad a few lessons—like how a bureaucrat ain't supposed to stick his neck this far out on the block." —Tom Clancy, *The Hunt for Red October*

1988. "Why the hell didn't *you* speak up?"

"I don't know. I guess I was afraid to stick my neck out." —Erich Segal, *Doctors*

1994. "I know that if something goes wrong and I screw up, I'm going to get sued," he [Dr. Hausknecht] said. "But I'm willing to stick my neck out because this is a technique that's got to be made available." —*New York Times*

See also DON'T LEAD WITH YOUR CHIN.

Don't swap horses in midstream. Don't change leaders when they are in the midst of important projects. Probably originated in the United States. Used by Abraham Lincoln in his 1864 presidential campaign. The proverb is found in varying forms: *Don't change horses in the middle of the stream; Don't change horses in the midstream; Don't swap horses while crossing a stream; Don't switch horses in the middle of the river; It never pays to change horses in midstream; It's no use changing horses in midstream; Never change horses in the middle of the stream,* etc. The proverb is often shortened to *swap (change) horses in midstream.*

1864. I do not allow myself to suppose that either the convention or the League have concluded to decide that I am either the greatest or best man in America, but rather they have concluded that it is not best to swap horses while crossing the river, and have further concluded that I am not so poor a horse that they might not make a botch of it in trying to swap. —Abraham Lincoln, "Reply to the National Union League"

1864. I have not permitted myself, gentlemen, to conclude that I am the best man in the country; but I am reminded in this connection of an old Dutch farmer who remarked ... that 'it was not best to swap horses when crossing a stream.' —Abraham Lincoln, *Collected Works* (1953), Vol. VII

1951. "The first thing an Officer has to learn is to be able to switch horses often and in midstream without getting his feet wet," Dynamite smiled. —James Jones, *From Here to Eternity*

1984. In 1944, a major war, the ultimate foreign policy act, was still under way. The argument for Franklin D. Roosevelt was that we should not change leaders in midstream. —*New York Times*

1993. "It is a shame," said Mr. Rutskoi, who was named Acting President by the Parliament two days ago after it voted to oust Mr. Yeltsin. "Who is

changing horses in midstream? We will be the laughing stock of the world." —*New York Times*

See also DON'T CHANGE THE RULES IN THE MIDDLE OF THE GAME.

Don't take any wooden nickels. Don't let yourself be cheated or ripped off. Originated in the United States in the 1920s and 1930s. Money that has no real value is sometimes called *wooden.* It is suggested that in 1825 Yankee peddlers sold wooden objects for a very low price and passed them off as the real thing. Probably stories about wooden nutmegs, wooden hams, and wooden pumpkin seeds contributed to the later use of the phrase *wooden nickels* in America or even to the use of *wooden rubles* in Russia, etc. The proverb is found in varying forms: *Don't take any wooden money; Don't take any rubber quarters,* etc.

1952. The motor stopped, the radio winked off, and the door slammed. "Don't take any wooden nickels," called the car as Paul climbed into his own. "Don't take any wooden nickels, don't take any wooden nickels, don't take any—" —Kurt Vonnegut, Jr., *Player Piano*

1959. An ancient American joke: "Don't take any wooden nickels." —*Bangor Daily News*

Don't take (tear) down a fence (wall) unless you are sure why it was put up. Don't destroy something unless you know why it was built in the first place. Sometimes attributed to Robert Frost (1874–1963).

1965. The loose-leaf notebook of 1945–46 contained propositions from ... Chesterton ("Don't ever take a fence down until you know the reason why it was put up") ... —Arthur Schlesinger, Jr., *A Thousand Days: John F. Kennedy in the White House*

1988. "The commission has some extremely difficult and sensitive decisions to make," the spokesman, Tom Grant, said. "I think my boss subscribes to the old bromide that you don't tear down a wall unless you are sure why it was put up. He believes the commission has some problems, but in general he thinks it works relatively well like it is." —*New York Times*

Don't take the name of the Lord in vain. Don't use the name of God disrespectfully or when it is not necessary. First appeared in the Old Testament.**

Thou shalt not take the name of the Lord thy God in vain; for the Lord will not hold him guiltless that taketh his name in vain. —Exodus 20:7, *Authorized Version*, 1611

1928. *Marsden: (clearing his throat uneasily)* Do I hear my name taken in vain? —Eugene O'Neill, *Strange Interlude*, Act IX

1946. "How in God's name does he use bread crusts in his work and bread crusts slip down his throat?" "Do not take the name of the Lord in vain," he said. And added, "George's work, it's very clever. And artistic." —Robert Penn Warren, *All the King's Men*

1961. He never once took the name of the Lord his God in vain. —Joseph Heller, *Catch-22*

1984. ...I had taken the Lord's name in vain. —Joseph Heller, *God Knows*

Don't tell tales out of school. See NEVER TELL TALES OUT OF SCHOOL.

Don't throw a monkey wrench in the works. Don't spoil what is running smoothly. Originated in the United States. Sometimes attributed to Philander Chase Johnson (1866–1939). The proverb is found in varying forms: *Don't throw a wrench in the works; Don't throw a spanner in the works; Don't throw a spanner into the machinery. Don't throw a spanner in the works*, etc.

1920. Don't throw a monkey-wrench into the machinery. —*Everybody's Magazine*

1952. "Finnerty!" she said. "He's the one who threw a monkey wrench into things." —Kurt Vonnegut, *Player Piano*

1981. "I used to specialize in throwing monkey wrenches into the system; now I am into the politics of building," said Mr. Marks, who recently traveled to Moscow from Washington with 75 Americans to mark the 30th anniversary of Sputnik. —*New York Times*

1992. "This [disclosure] put pressure on North America to save the company's financial performance," said Jack Kirnan, a Solomon Brothers analyst. "It throws a monkey wrench into the near-term outlook." —*New York Times*

1995. A $1 million lottery prize is nothing more than a $1 million annuity, payable over 20 years, with inherent tax liabilities, etc. The money has no volition of its own. However, throw the monkey wrench of human stupidity into the works and anything's possible. —Ralph Castro, "Letters," *New York Times Magazine*

Don't throw caution to the wind. Don't make careless and risky moves. The saying was first attested in the United States in *Great Shakespeare* (1965) by B. Grebanier. *To throw discretion to the wind* is used as a figure of speech.

1984. My initiative weakened. But just in time, up spoke the Devil to rally my faltering spirit and give me the heart I needed to throw at least a little bit of caution to the wind and march to the insistent beat of this different drummer. Let me give the Devil his due. —Joseph Heller, *God Knows*

1992. Bush and Major know well how atrocity stories stimulate their publics to throw caution to the wind. —*Times* (Trenton)

1994. It's not clear at the moment why it took both the CIA and the FBI so long to catch on to Ames. One explanation is that Ames was cautious at first and later, either cocky or unhinged, threw caution to the wind. —*Times* (Trenton)

Don't throw out the baby with the bath water. Don't throw out the essentials while getting rid of the dregs. The proverb has been traced back to *Nigger Question* (1853) by Thomas Carlyle (1795–1881), British essayist and historian. First attested in the United States in *More Changes* (1925) By H. W. Nevinson. The proverb is found in varying forms: *Don't throw the baby out with the bath; Never throw out the baby with the bath water*, etc. *To throw out the baby with the bath water* is always used metaphorically. It has its counterparts in other languages too: *Das Kind mit dem Bade ausschütten* (German, "To throw out the baby with the bath"); выплеснуть Вместе с водой и ребёнка (Russian, "To throw out the baby together with the water"), etc.

1946. "It is because he [Adam Stanton] is a romantic, and he has a picture of the world in his head, and when the world doesn't conform in any respect to the picture, he wants to throw the world away. Even if that means throwing out the baby with the bath." —Robert Penn Warren, *All the King's Men*

1976. "Okay, let's forget about saving money on food," I said. "But surely in this family budget there is some place we can cut waste."

My daughter Jennifer said, "Why don't you give up your season ticket to the Redskins' games?"

"Now, wait a minute," I replied angrily. "Let's not throw out the baby with the bath water." —Art Buchwald, *Washington Is Leaking*

1988. "This is no time to throw the baby out with the bath water." —Robert Ludlum, *The Icarus Agenda*

1991. "We have every right to be irritated with Gorbachev," said a senior administration official.

"He's played the game badly. He's played it disingenuously. But that doesn't mean we throw the baby out with the bath water. We've got a lot of business to do with these people." —*Newsweek*

1994. "Most people recognize that those [NFC East games] are national matchups, and you don't want to throw out the baby with the bath water," [Commissioner Paul] Tagliabue said. —*Washington Post*

1994. *Smith:* What—you can't teach Plato because he was white? Give me a break. It's fine for schools to have Afro-American Studies and Native American Studies to instill pride and teach people what happened, but to throw out the baby with the bath water doesn't make sense. —Lawrence Linderman, "MM Interview with Liz Smith," *Modern Maturity*

Don't tread on me. Respect the sovereignty of the United States. The saying was inscribed on the first official American flag, which was raised on December 3, 1775. The pronoun *me* may be replaced by another pronoun or a noun. In such cases, the saying means "Don't play games with us or else ..." and is used as a firm response. The proverb was used by President Clinton in 1993.

1993. The method, and its execution, seemed to be what the president [Clinton] called it: "A firm and commensurate response" that clearly delivered a message as old as the American Republic: "Don't tread on us." —*Times* (Trenton)

1994. DON'T TREAD ON MY LAB —Headline of Philip Elmer-DeWitt's article on a new era of tighter controls and stingier funding from Washington for researchers, *Time*

1994. He [Bill Clinton] does not want the country to revert to the "don't tread on me" touchiness of the last 12 years, when an attitude on the part of a small country could bring it bombs or invasions. —*Times* (Trenton)

See also DON'T TREAD ON OTHER PEOPLE'S TOES.

Don't tread on other people's toes. Don't offend others by saying or doing something unpleasant to them. The proverb is of American origin and has been traced back to the *Letters of Major J. Downing* (1834). It is found in varying forms: *Don't step on other people's toes; Avoid stepping on anyone's toes; Never tread on anyone's corns,* etc.

1953. "Now let's take up the minorities in our civilization, shall we? Bigger the population, the more minorities. Don't step on the toes of the dog-lovers, the cat-lovers, doctors, lawyers, merchants, chiefs, Mormons, Baptists, Unitarians, second-generation Chinese, Swedes, Italians, Germans, Texans, Brooklynites, Irishmen, people from Oregon or Mexico." —Ray Bradbury, *Fahrenheit 451*

1986. Silver Anderson was hardly hot news. She had been around too long and stepped on too many toes to set the town alight. —Jackie Collins, *Hollywood Husbands*

1987. "He's stepped on a lot of people's toes, but, for him as an individual, that's what he had to do to win the [Nobel] prize," said Dr. Malcolm Gefter, another immunologist at M.I.T. —*New York Times*

1989. A flamboyant maverick with an open dislike for established administrative procedures, he [MacKenzie] stepped on so many toes in his first months in office last year that the town's Legislative Council asked him to resign. —*New York Times*

1994. For years, Thomas H. Lee and Leon Black have acquired one company after another, never hesitating to step on toes or raise the temperature to get their way. —*New York Times*

See also DON'T TREAD ON ME.

Don't try to pull yourself up by your own bootstraps. Don't try to succeed on your own, without other people's help. The origin of the proverb is obscure. It may have derived from a story by the German writer Rudolph Raspe (1737–1794) whose Baron Munchausen managed to save himself by his own bootstraps. The proverb is found in varying forms: *Don't pull yourself up by your own bootstraps; You can pull yourself up by your own bootstraps; It's a case of pulling yourself up by your own bootlaces,* etc. *To pull oneself up by one's own bootstraps* means to be successful by virtue of one's own efforts and is used metaphorically. Martin Luther King, Jr. (1929–1968), is quoted as saying, "It's a cruel jest to tell a man with no shoes to pull himself up by his bootstraps."

1991. I am reminded of a West Coast flight from New York during my Urban League days. My seatmate was a successful white businessman, who, after his first martini, advised me that black people had to pull themselves up by their bootstraps. —Vernon E. Jordan, Jr., "Affirmative Action Works; Thomas Proves It," *Wall Street Journal*

1993. Clarence Thomas picked himself up with other people's bootstraps and went out to prove himself liberated from liberalism. But Ruth Ginsburg picked herself up and started a bootstrap business. —*Times* (Trenton)

1994. There is another, subtler element in General Powell's appeal. His life story—a black man reared in the Bronx, son of Jamaican immigrants, lifted by his own bootstraps—reinforces primal American myths. —*New York Times*

Don't (try to) teach your grandmother (how) to suck eggs. Don't offer advice to people who are more experienced and knowledgeable than you are. The proverb has been traced back to *Quevedo's Comical Works* (1707). First attested in the United States in *Brother Jonathan* (1825) by John Neal (1793–1876). The proverb is found in varying forms: *Don't teach your grandmother to suck eggs; Don't teach your grandmother how to milk ducks; Don't teach your grandmother to steal sheep; Don't try to teach your grandmother,* etc. *To teach one's grandmother to suck eggs* is used as a figure of speech.

> **1988.** "You want a broken puss, buddy?" Laura asked menacingly.
> "Aw, yer mother sucks eggs, girlie." —Erich Segal, *Doctors*
>
> **1992.** "You don't have to bring me into it [the diary] yet. We just want to know if it's there."
> "Don't teach your grandma to suck eggs, Mr. Estrada," she [Mrs. Dodge] said sharply and hung up. —Philip Friedman, *Inadmissible Evidence*

Don't wash your dirty linen in public. *See* DON'T AIR YOUR DIRTY LINEN IN PUBLIC.

Don't wear your heart on your sleeve. Don't let other people know how you're feeling or what you're thinking. The saying dates back to Shakespeare's *Othello* (1604–05). First attested in the United States in *Strephon and Sardon* (1891). The proverb is found in varying forms: *Don't wear your convictions on your sleeve; Don't wear emotions on your sleeve; Don't carry your faith on your sleeve; Don't wear your intelligence on your sleeve,* etc. *To wear one's heart on one's sleeve* is to display openly one's feelings and is used as a figure of speech. Its French equivalent is *Avoir le coeur sur les lèvres* ("To have your heart on your lips").

> **1604–05.**
>> *Iago:* But I will wear my heart upon my sleeve
>> For daws to peck at: I am not what I am.
>> —Shakespeare, *Othello,* Act I, Scene I
>
> **1984.** In a superb magazine piece written before the scientist's exile in Gorky, The Times's Hedrick Smith described him this way: "Private, reticent, soft-spoken and kindly as he is, Sakharov wears his heart on his sleeve." —*New York Times*

> **1989.** Willie is very slight, soft-spoken, almost delicate, a sensitive soul who wears his heart on his sleeve. —*Daily News* (New York)
>
> **1991.** He was known to be a "born-again" Christian—a term I didn't really understand at the time. But he was never one to wear his faith on his sleeve. —Oliver L. North with William Novak, *Under Fire*
>
> **1992.** "It's just that I wear my heart on my sleeve." No doubt she [Suzanne Rhatigan] wouldn't—couldn't—have it any other way. —*New York*
>
> **1993.** Although he [Bob Packwood] may not wear his emotions on his sleeve, he was moved to tears when the 1986 Tax Reform Act passed in committee. —*New York Times Magazine*
>
> **1994.** "As a practicing politician," he [Dan Quayle] told me in the interview, "I never believed in wearing my religious faith on my sleeve." —*Times* (Trenton)

Don't wish too hard: you might just get what you wished for. You may not be happy with the results if your wish is realized. The proverb originated in the period 1830–1860: *Don't you wish you may get it! Be careful what you wish for—you might get it* is a variant that was used by Oscar Wilde (1854–1900).

> **1991.** Oscar Wilde's line that we'd better be careful what we wish for, because we might get it, seems to have gained currency. —*Wall Street Journal*
>
> **1992.** Estrada's week started with the first meeting of his complete prosecution team. He was reminded of the old adage: Be careful what you wish for—you might get it. —Philip Friedman, *Inadmissible Evidence*
>
> **1993.** It is not too much to hope, therefore, that society will shift back again to a more mature, responsible view of appropriate compensation. Such a change could bolster the quality of public education and government, strengthen social morale and cause private enterprise and the leading professions to rise in public esteem. Who knows? It could even help some highly paid professionals and executives. After all, as an old saying goes, "It behooves us to be careful of what we are worshipping, for what we are worshipping, we are becoming." —*New York Times*
>
> **1994.** You have to be careful what you ask for. You might get it. —David Diaz on the January rains in New York, "Channel 2 News at 6," CBS

Don't worry. Be happy. A catchphrase that originated in the United States as the title of a song popularized by the Grammy-award singer Bobby McFerrin. In 1988, George Bush used this "Don't worry. Be happy" theme in his successful presidential campaign.

1991. DON'T WORRY. BE HAPPY. —Headline of William C. Rhoden's article on Charles Barkley, *New York Times*

1993. "I don't quite understand the rationale for holding this meeting since the Republicans have changed their tune about a tax cut this year," said [William] Pascrell. "Four weeks ago, they were singing *Don't Worry, Be Happy* and now they are just whistling 'Dixie.' " —*Times* (Trenton)

1993. Don't Worry, Be Happy. It's hard to screw up Windows applications like "Do you want to save changes to Document 1?" —*U.S. 1* (Princeton)

Double, double toil and trouble; fire burn, and cauldron bubble. The chanting of three witches as they were mixing a potion in Shakespeare's *Macbeth* (c. 1606). Sometimes shortened to *Double, double toil and trouble.* Used in dozens of variations. Often in headlines.

1606. *Three witches:* Double, double toil and
  trouble;
  Fire burn, and cauldron bubble.
    —Shakespeare, *Macbeth*, Act IV, Scene I

1984. Thou shalt not suffer a witch to live, says Exodus, and Saul had endeavored to cut all wizards and witches off from the land. Now he was glad to go underground and felt lucky to find one. He put on other raiment and stole away to the woman by night with two companions he trusted.
  "Double, double, toil, and trouble," the witch at Endor greeted him. She became hysterical when she guessed who he was. —Joseph Heller, *God Knows*

1992. BUBBLE, BUBBLE, LESS SOIL AND TROUBLE —Headline of Robert E. Calem's report on the use of scrubbing bubbles and an advanced computer to get clothes cleaner while economizing on water, *New York Times*

1993. POST–WAR CAULDRON: BUBBLE, TOIL AND TROUBLE —Headline of Carla Anderson's article on New Jersey's place in the world and the country, *Times* (Trenton)

Dr. Jekyll and Mr. Hyde. The two sides of one person: Jekyll (the good side) and Hyde (the evil side). The phrase comes from Robert Louis Stevenson's novel *The Strange Case of Dr. Jekyll and Mr. Hyde* (1886). The saying became more popu-

lar following the release (in 1941) of the movie, *Dr. Jekyll and Mr. Hyde,* starring Spencer Tracy and Ingrid Bergman.

1989. "He's like a Dr. Jekyll and Mr. Hyde personality," Larry Young, who has known Mr. Harrison and his mother for 15 years, said before the police arrested a man they believed to be the suspected double killer last night in Brooklyn. —*New York Times*

1991. "He's almost a Jekyll and Hyde: a fairly tolerant guy, compassionate, open minded on almost any front," said Representative Les AuCoin, Democrat of Oregon. "But suddenly when it comes to choice, it's something else. A look comes in his eye. He almost looks like he's been electrocuted. His eyes bulge and the rhetoric changes." —*New York Times*

1992. Contributing to the public's uncertainty have been George Bush's personal ups and downs, complicated by his peculiar gamble of shifting radically into a "campaign mode"; his quadrennial metamorphosis from compromising Jekyll to partisan Hyde. He is not the candidate of change; he is the candidate who changes. —*New York Times Magazine*

A drowning man will catch at a straw. A desperate person will try anything to save himself, no matter how unlikely. The proverb has been traced back to *Dialogue of Comfort Against Tribulation* (1534) by Thomas More (1478–1535). First cited in the United States in *Colonial Currency* (1720). The proverb is found in varying forms: *A drowning man will clutch at a straw; A drowning man grabs at a straw; A drowning man snatches at straws,* etc.

1948. "You move against my ethics," said the priest.
  "A drowning man clutches at anything," said Nolan, "and ethics may drown with him if *that's* what he grabs instead of a lifeboat." —Ray Bradbury, *I Sing the Body Electric!*

1967. When growing participation in the Republican Presidential stakes made it improper for Henry Cabot Lodge to remain as Ambassador to South Vietnam, Bobby [Kennedy] grasped at a straw. —Ralph de Toledano, *R.F.K. The Man Who Would Be President*

1988. She [Laura] put her hand on his cheek and he grasped it like a drowning man would seize a lifeline. —Erich Segal, *Doctors*

1989. While the strike has begun to cause some economic hardship for the rank and file, striking workers said in interviews that most were deter-

mined to hold out. "We're not going to grasp at straws," Mike Opitz, a first officer who has been with Eastern for 10 years, said recently while he was on the picket line at La Guardia Airport.
—*New York Times*

1992. "I'm like a drowning man grabbing at a straw," said Mr. Morgan, who is 52 years old. "A man at my age looking for a job, with a wife and two kids, a mortgage. I try not to think about it."
—*New York Times*

1993. Richard Van Noy, executive director of the MCIA, said Davies' criticism and suspicions about the meeting are unfounded. "Here it looks like he's losing his battle and he's grasping at straws."
—*Times* (Trenton)

Dwarfs standing on the shoulders of giants.

See IF I HAVE SEEN FURTHER IT IS BY STANDING ON THE SHOULDERS OF GIANTS.

E pluribus unum. Out of many, one; or from many, one. The Latin phrase, taken from a poem, "Moretum," sometimes attributed to Virgil, means: one nation made of many states. On August 10, 1776, it was recommended by John Adams, Benjamin Franklin, and Thomas Jefferson for the Great Seal of the United States and proposed by Swiss artist Pierre Eugène de Simitière. It originally appeared in January 1692 on the title page of the *Gentleman's Journal.* National motto for the United States from 1782 to 1956, when *E pluribus unum* was replaced by *In God We Trust.* **

1973. The motto of Dwayne Hoover's and Kilgore Trout's nation was this, which meant in a language nobody spoke anymore, *Out of Many, One: "E pluribus unum."* —Kurt Vonnegut, Jr., *Breakfast of Champions*

1992. E Pluribus Unum. Our June-July issue celebrated the Fourth of July with an examination of American diversity—which elicited surprisingly diverse responses. —Editor, *Modern Maturity*

1993. "Early immigrants to this country did not want to build a new Sweden, a new Poland, a new Germany—they wanted to become one thing: Americans. *E pluribus unum* is still a good thing: Out of many, one." —*Modern Maturity*

The early bird catches the worm. The person who is active early, or first, succeeds more than others. The proverb has been traced back to *Remains Concerning Britain* (1636) by W. Camden. First attested in the United States in *Sam Slick's Wise Saws* (1853) by Thomas C. Haliburton. The proverb is found in varying forms: *It's the early bird who (that) catches the worm; It's not the early bird that catches the worm, but the smart one; The early bird catches the heavenly worm; The early birds are getting all the worms,*

etc. The idiomatic *early bird* means an early riser, the first customer, train, bus, etc. The Italians say, *Chi dorme, non piglia pesci,* which means "He who sleeps catches no fish."

1909. McNight is always a sympathizer with the early worm. It was late when he appeared. —Mary Roberts Rinehart, *The Man in Lower Ten*

1987. Other projects, the source added, "simply fell by the wayside, when people realized the early birds were getting the best pickings." —*Washington Times*

1988. "He'll be glad to see you tomorrow morning—if eight o'clock isn't too early."
"No, that's absolutely fine. I don't have to tell you what the early bird always catches." —Erich Segal, *Doctors*

1993. The early bird gets the worm and the early and late fisherman or woman who offers the worm in the right way will get more fish. —*Times* (Trenton)

See also FIRST COME, FIRST SERVED.

Early to bed and early to rise, makes a man healthy, wealthy, and wise. A person who lives a life of moderation is sure to succeed. The proverb has been traced back to *Treatise on Fishing with an Angle* (1496). First attested in the United States in *His Book* (1700). Popularized by Benjamin Franklin, who even proposed putting the proverb on an American coin. The proverb is found in varying forms: *Early to bed and early to rise makes Jack a dull boy; Early to bed and early to rise gets the worm,* etc. American humorist and playwright George Ade (1866-1944) once said, "Early to bed and early to rise and you won't meet many prominent people." In 1940, cartoonist and humorist James Thurber (1894-1961) changed the original proverb by saying, *Early to* *rise and early to bed makes a male healthy and wealthy and dead.*

1735. Early to bed and early to rise, makes a man healthy, wealthy, and wise. —Benjamin Franklin, *Poor Richard's Almanac*

1940. Early to rise and early to bed makes a male healthy and wealthy and dead. —James Thurber, "The Shrike and the Chipmunks," *Fables for Our Time*

1984. Early to bed and early to rise is a sure sign you're fed up with TV. —*New York Post*

1986. The people in that house had to be asleep. *Working farmers, early to bed, early to rise—wears you out and dulls the brain,* Edwards thought. —Tom Clancy, *Red Storm Rising*

1992. Dear Sir: In view of our declining economy and our struggling educational system, today's young man can quote, "Early to bed, early to rise, makes a young man healthy, healthy and healthy." —Clair B. Young, "Letters," *Smithsonian*

Easier said than done. It is easier to advise someone to do something than it is to actually do it. The proverb has been traced back to 1546, when it was included in John Heywood's book of proverbs. Often used after the words *it (that)'s a lot (much).* For some people, *It's easier done than said.*

1936. "Now, my advice to you, Miss, is to give him another baby just as quickly as you can."

"*Hah!*" thought Scarlett bitterly, as she left his office. That was easier said than done. —Margaret Mitchell, *Gone With the Wind*

1957. "He's disowned me," Helen began to cry.

"Oh, he has, has he? Well, that's easier said than done." —John Cheever, *The Wapshot Chronicle*

1964. Bester says to "motivate and distribute" books—that is, to get students ready and eager to read. All this is easier said than done. In fact, all this is plain impossible. —Bel Kaufman, *Up the Down Staircase*

1977. "Now it's up to you," Cartwright said, "to get Nikolayev to lift the secrecy and to spring us immediately."

"Easier said than done." —William Safire, *Full Disclosure*

1984. It was up to me to take advantage of all the opportunities they [his parents] never had, so I had to be at the top of my class.

This, however, was easier said than done. —Lee Iacocca with William Novak, *Iacocca*

1991. "It's a lot easier said than done," Byron Scott said. "It will be easy for people who don't know Magic [Johnson] as a person. For us, you could be with the guy for two months and know the kind of person he is." —*New York Times*

See also ACTIONS SPEAK LOUDER THAN WORDS; DEEDS, NOT WORDS.

East is East, and West is West, and never the twain shall meet. People of very different cultures are not ever likely to understand each other fully. The proverb was coined in 1889 by Rudyard Kipling in *The Ballad of East and West.* Often shortened to *East is East, and West is West* or *Never the twain shall meet.* The word *twain* is an archaic form of *two.*

1889. Oh, East is East, and West is West, and
never the twain shall meet,
Till Earth and Sky stand presently at God's
great Judgment Seat;
But there is neither East nor West, Border,
nor Breed, nor Birth,
When two strong men stand face to face,
tho' they come from the ends of the earth!
—Rudyard Kipling, "The Ballad of East and
West"

1945. "You're a city gal, you belong in the center of the fashion belt, don't you? I can't see you living in the big open spaces. The chap who said, 'Oh, East is East, and West is West, and never the twain shall meet,' hit the jackpot as far as you're concerned." —Emilie Loring, *Beyond the Sound of Guns*

1993. East is East, West is West, and when it comes to movie classics AMC is best. —Anchorman, *"American Movie Classics"*

Easy come, easy go. Money acquired without much effort is also spent without much effort. The proverb's idea was first expressed in Chaucer's "Pardoner's Tale" (1386) and was similar to the Medieval French: *Tost acquis tost se despens* ("Soon acquired, soon spent"). In its current form, the English proverb dates back to the early nineteenth century, to *Passages from the Diary of a Late Physician* (1832) by Samuel Warren. First attested in the United States, in different form, in *Works of Anne Bradstreet* (1650). The proverb is found in varying forms: *Light come, light go; Quick come, quick go; It's easy come, but it's easier go,* etc.

1936. "If they kept their money. But I doubt the ability of any of them to keep money more than five years at the rate they're spending. Easy come, easy go." —Margaret Mitchell, *Gone With the Wind*

1960. Funny thing, Atticus Finch might've got him

off scot free, but wait—? Hell no. You know how they are. Easy come, easy go. —Harper Lee, *To Kill a Mockingbird*

1984. I give her up sullenly. She bestows her kiss and goes away. God has let me down again. "Easy come, easy go," is the sardonic philosophy of resignation with which I try to console and amuse myself as I watch her leave. —Joseph Heller, *God Knows*

1992. He got back in seven [minutes] to report that the good doctor's car had been reported stolen on Christmas Day, nice present, huh? Meyer thanked him and hung up.

Easy come, easy go, he thought. —Ed McBain, *Kiss*

1994. Michael Jon Spencer knows all about easy come, easy go.

Mr. Spencer was in desperate need of some fast cash this summer. His not-for-profit company, Hospital Audiences Inc., needed a $200,000 cash infusion after, he says, bureaucratic red tape delayed the receipt of a $260,599 initial advance from a New York City agency.... He got much more than he bargained for: $4,000,000.79. —*Wall Street Journal*

Easy does it. Do everything with care and patience; relax. Used as advice to someone to act patiently. The proverb has been traced back to *The Ticket-of-Leave Man* (1863) by English dramatist Tom Taylor. First attested in the United States in *Climbing Doom* (1908) by L. D. Young. The proverb is found in varying forms: *Careful does it; Gently does it; Quiet does it; Slowly does it; Steady does it; Slow and steady does it*, etc.

1946. "Easy does it, little by little—it's like bringing a big transport down on a landing field!" —Upton Sinclair, *A World to Win*

1960. Countless evenings Atticus would find Jem furious at something Mrs. Dubose had said when we went by.

"Easy does it, son," Atticus would say. "She's an old lady and she's ill. You just hold your head high and be a gentleman. Whatever she says to you, it's your job not to let her make you mad." —Harper Lee, *To Kill a Mockingbird*

1989. Slowly does it, Booker told himself, filled with self-disgust. —Michael Korda, *The Fortune*

1991. Easy does it is the strategy behind a streak of 26 scoreless innings. —*New York Times*

1992. EASY DOES IT —Headline of Elizabeth Gliek's report on how a fictional sleuth helps Walter Mosley find success—and himself. —*People*

1993. The American Yoga Association ... offers such books as "The American Yoga Association Beginner's Manual" and "Easy Does It" (yoga for older people). —*Lear's*

Eat, drink, and be merry, for tomorrow we die. Enjoy life today because we don't know what is going to happen tomorrow. First used in the Old Testament in the books of Ecclesiastes and Isaiah. It was later included in the New Testament in the book of Luke. In America, the proverb has been traced back to the *General History of New England* (c.1700) by Hubbard. The proverb is found in varying, often jocular forms: *Eat, drink, and be merry, for tomorrow the cook leaves; Eat, drink and be merry, for tomorrow we may be starving to death; Eat, drink, be merry, and make love to whom you like; Eat, drink, and be merry, for tomorrow your wife may come home; Eat, drink, and be merry, for tomorrow it will cost more*, etc.

Then I commended mirth, because a man hath no better thing under the sun, than to eat, and to drink, and to be merry. —Ecclesiastes 8:15, *Authorized Version*, 1611

Let us eat and drink; for tomorrow we shall die. —Isaiah 22:13, *Authorized Version*, 1611

1922. Eat drink and be merry ... Love, lie and be handsome for tomorrow we die. —James Joyce, *Ulysses*

1984. Therefore, I began to hate life and came to the conclusion that a man has no better thing to do under the sun than to eat and to drink and to be merry, although that isn't always the easiest thing to do when all you've got is a pastrami. —Joseph Heller, *God Knows*

1991. It's no secret that I wrote the role of Marion Cheever in "Next" for James Coco. I had seen him in many plays Off Broadway and I intuitively knew that just as I "heard" the way I wrote. And I knew him the best way there is to know an actor: through his work. I didn't have to eat, drink and be merry with Jimmy to write for him. It was all up there on stage. —Terrence McNally, *New York Times*

1993. EAT, DRINK AND BE WARY —Headline of Diana Yin's and Carla Anderson's article on a possible change in the tax rules concerning restaurants, *Times* (Trenton)

1994. Eat, drink and be merry—for tomorrow it will cost more. —Joey Adams, "Strictly for Laughs," *New York Post*

See also SEIZE THE MOMENT; GATHER YE ROSEBUDS WHILE YE MAY.

Eat to live; do not live to eat. The proverb is of ancient origin and is attributed to Socrates (469–399 b.c.). It was used by Cicero (106–43 b.c.): *Edere oportet ut vivas, non vivas ut edas* (Latin, "One must eat to live, not live to eat"), and later by Molière (1669) and by Benjamin Franklin (1733). *One should eat to live, not live to eat* is a variant.

5th century b.c.

Bad men live that they may eat and drink, whereas good men eat and drink that they may live. —Socrates, "How a Young Man Ought to Hear Poems"

1669. *Il faut manger pour vivre et non pas vivre pour manger.* ("One must eat to live, and not live to eat.") —Molière, *L'Avare (The Miser)*, Act III, Scene I

1733. Eat to live, and not live to eat. —Benjamin Franklin, *Poor Richard's Almanac*

1982. Until recently the world was divided into those who eat to live and those who live to eat. —*New York Times*

1992. Live to eat. Eat to live. —Ad for Ragu Foods, *Reader's Digest*

Elementary, my dear Watson, elementary! No problem, it's very simple. The saying is attributed to Sherlock Holmes, the English detective invented by Sir Arthur Conan Doyle, who through reason alone could solve any crime, but this famous phrase is not found anywhere in Doyle's books. It is first found in the 1929 movie *The Return of Sherlock Holmes.* Many people, however, still believe that it was Doyle who coined the saying.

1929. In the final scene Dr. Watson is there with his "Amazing, Holmes," and Holmes comes forth with his "Elementary, my dear Watson, elementary." —Review of the film *The Return of Sherlock Holmes, New York Times*

1980. *Elementary, my dear Watson.* Three out of 4 murders and 3 out of 5 assaults result in the arrest of a suspect, the FBI says. —Mike Feinsilber and William B. Mead, *American Averages*

1991. HOW TO PLAY HOLMES? ELEMENTALLY. —Headline, *New York Times*

1993. "Elementary, my dear Watson, the game is afoot."

Sherlock Holmes, the world famous detective created by Sir Arthur Conan Doyle, is honored on a new set of five stamps released by Great Britain. —*Times* (Trenton)

See also IT'S AS SIMPLE AS THAT.

An elephant never forgets. First attested in the United States in *Blue Ridge* (1937) by W. Martyn. The proverb is probably of Greek origin. The Greeks sometimes say, "The camel never forgets an injury," according to Burton Stevenson. *To have a memory like an elephant* is used as a figure of speech.

1937. Like elephants, the Lowes never forget. —W. Martyn, *Blue Ridge*

1987. No one anymore has a memory like an elephant ... —*New York Times*

1991. She [Mis Eleanor] must think I've got a memory like an elephant. So many names, and they all mix up together. They're all looking at me as if I was an elephant, too, or something else in a zoo. —Alexandra Ripley, *Scarlett*

1991. "The Mob never forgets, Tarrance. They're worse than elephants. And they keep secrets better than your side." —John Grisham, *The Firm*

The Emperor has no clothes on. This saying is based on Hans Christian Andersen's fairy tale "The Emperor's New Clothes" (1837). The author tells us about an emperor who spent all his money on elaborate possessions. He hired two weavers, who turned out to be swindlers, to weave the most beautiful fabrics imaginable. They gave him nothing, but claimed that their cloth was so fine it was invisible. People watching the procession with the emperor in this new costume pretended that nothing was amiss until a boy pointed out the obvious: the emperor truly was naked. The saying is often applied to the shallowness of some of the rich and powerful, and to discredited leaders or theories. The word *king* is often substituted for *emperor.*

1837. None of the Emperor's clothes had been so successful before.

"But he has got nothing on," said a little child.

"Oh, listen to the innocent," said its father. And one person whispered to the other what the child had said. "He has nothing on—a child says he has nothing on!"

"But he has nothing on!" at last cried all the people. —Hans Christian Andersen, *Andersen's Fairy Tales* (1945)

1983. J. D. Salinger's "Catcher in the Rye" became a great classic because it described a universal experience—the realization that much of the world around us is phony and that the Emperor has no clothes on —Rudolf Flesch, *Lite English*

1983. Somewhere, we keep hoping, there must be a banker willing to say the emperor has no clothes on, perhaps by declaring an outright default on a country loan. —*Wall Street Journal*

1988. "It's why the king, with all his clothes on or naked, needs a strong prime minister who, in turn, creates his own royal family—from both parties, incidentally." —Robert Ludlum, *The Icarus Agenda*

1993. The more he [Ross Perot] resembles the emperor with no clothes, the more imperious he becomes. —*Times* (Trenton)

1994. You have given me the names of the experts and some justification I can use to defend myself against those who have not yet discovered this long-running version of the emperor's new clothes. There's just nothing there. —*New York Times*

1995. Washington insists it did nothing wrong. This deprives Americans even of the small satisfaction of knowing that the responsible officials and their political masters have learned anything at all from the great U.S.-Mexico combination plate, catch-up with botch-up.

April 3: Senator D'Amato supplies me with his New Yorker's sum-up of American and Mexican behavior: "The king has no suit." —*New York Times*

An empty sack cannot stand upright. It is hard to function when you are in dire need, especially when you are hungry or thirsty. The proverb dates back to the seventeenth century and is also found in Italian sources of that time. First found in the United States in *Poor Richard's Almanac* (1758) by Benjamin Franklin. The proverb is found in many variants.

1758. Poverty often deprives a Man of all Spirit and Virtue; 'Tis hard for an empty bag to stand upright. —Benjamin Franklin, *Poor Richard's Almanac*

1849. You have found it more difficult, I fear, than you imagined, to make the empty sack stand upright. Considering that at least one-third of those born to work cannot find it, why should I? —Edward Bulwer-Lytton, *Caxtons*

1958. We've a long night before us and an empty sack won't stand. —B. Behan, *Borstal Boy*

The end justifies the means. Anything is acceptable if it leads to a successful result. It was known to the Roman poet Ovid (43 b.c.–a.d. 18): *Exitus acta probat* ("The outcome justifies the deeds") and to Saint Jerome (c. 342–420): "The line, often adopted by strong men in controversy, of justifying the means by the end." It has been traced back in English to *Exposition of the Commandments* (1583) by G. Babington. In the seventeenth century, it became the motto of the Society of Jesus: *Cum finis est licitus, etiam media sunt licita* ("Any means are justified if only the end could be achieved"). Matthew Prior wrote in 1700: "The end must justify the means." First attested in the United States in the *Diary* (1657) of Michael Wigglesworth (1631–1705), American clergyman and poet. *The means justify the end* is also used.

1936. Useless for her to argue now that the end justified the means ... —Margaret Mitchell, *Gone With the Wind*

1937. The end cannot justify the means, for the simple and obvious reason that the means employed determine the nature of the ends produced. —Aldous Huxley, *Ends and Means*

1951. "It taught me two things," Malloy grinned. "One, you never could succeed with what I wanted to succeed with by using propaganda; logically, in the end, the end will not only justify the means, it will not even be achieved by them. —James Jones, *From Here to Eternity*

1977. "We felt the ends justified the means. They never do." —Victor Lasky, *It Didn't Start with Watergate*

1986. On the other end of the political spectrum, F. Forrester Church, minister of All Souls Unitarian Church in Manhattan, thinks the decline in ethics is evident in the bombing of Libya—"the ends justify the means"—and in Washington behavior. —*New York*

1988. The audience broke into applause, and Donahue shook his head in distress. "So the means justify the end?"

"In this case," Clyde said cordially—the last word, as it turned out—"*these* means justify *these* ends." —Clifford Irving, *The Campbell Murder: Daddy's Girl*

1991. In the statement, made to a reporter in 1987, he [Judge Thomas] said he did not "think the ends justify the means." —*New York Times*
See also EVERYBODY'S DOIN' IT.

The enemy of my enemy is my friend. Opponents of the same person or thing naturally become allies. It is an ancient Arab proverb.

1985. "In California, I'm an outsider. So is Wolf, so we're natural allies. 'The enemy of my enemy is my friend,' as I believe the Arabs say ..." —Michael Korda, *Queenie*

1987. Up to now, Israel followed the ancient adage of "the enemy of my enemy is my friend." —William Safire, *New York Times*

1991. While the government of Iran had no great sympathy for Communism, they apparently believed that the Sandanistas qualified for that old Middle Eastern proverb: the enemy of my enemy is my friend. —Oliver L. North, *Under Fire*

1994. The proverb "my enemy's enemy is my friend" lends support to the notion that Israel is somehow culpable for the emergence of the militant Hamas movement ... Yasir Arafat attempts to advance this myth, holding Israel responsible for his own problems....

King Hussein of Jordan has chosen to be an enemy of Hamas, which has made him a friend of Israel. In response to Mr. Arafat's indulgence of Hamas, Israeli leaders should ask themselves, What does the proverb say about the friend of my enemy? —*New York Times*

Enough is enough. What one has said or done is already excessive. Usually used as an angry response. The proverb has been traced back to about 1375. In 1546, John Heywood included it in his book of proverbs. First attested in the United States in *The Down-Easters* (1833) by John Neal (1793–1876).

1949. *Will:* I've got a job.
Charley: Without pay? What kind of a job is a job without pay? *He rises.* Now, look, kid, enough is enough. —Arthur Miller, *Death of a Salesman*

1964. When they said good night, he lingered at the door, and seemed, with his inward and foolish—or was it sly?—grin, to be implying that she might let him sleep in the spare berth in her cabin. Enough was enough, and she closed the door in his face. —John Cheever, *The Wapshot Scandal*

1987. "The big question becomes, 'who owns the sunshine?'" she said. "Some day, we'll look out our windows and not be able to see the sky. Somewhere, the people have to say, 'Enough is enough.' Maybe this is the building." —*New York Times*

1991. This is not American. This is Kafkaesque. It has got to stop. It must stop for the benefit of future nominees and our country. Enough is enough....

This is not what America is all about. To ask me to do that would be to ask me to go beyond fundamental fairness.

Yesterday, I called my mother. She was confined to her bed, unable to work, and unable to stop crying. Enough is enough. —"Judge Clarence Thomas: 'My Name Has Been Harmed,'" *New York Times*

1993. Mrs. Clinton made an impassioned plea for "every American to stand up and say to the insurance industry: 'Enough is enough. We want our health care system back.'" —*New York Times*

Et tu, Brute? You also (too), Brutus? So, allegedly, exclaimed Julius Caesar when he recognized his close friend Marcus Brutus among the conspirators who in 44 b.c. stabbed him to death. In *Lives of the Caesars,* Suetonius reports: "Some have written that when Marcus rushed at him, he said in Greek, 'You too, my child.'" The Latin saying is usually used when someone you trust betrays you. It appears in Shakespeare's play *Julius Caesar.* Usually used with another name in place of *Brute.*

1599. [Casca first, then the other Conspirators and Marcus Brutus stab Caesar.]
Caesar: Et tu, *Brute*? Then fall, Caesar. —*Julius Caesar,* Act III, Scene I

1991. *Plotter:* D. Yazov [Soviet Defense Minister].
Conventional wisdom: Et tu, Dmitry? Army's Mr. Potato Head caught his cold too late. —*Newsweek*

1992. Et Tu, Babe. —Title of Mark Leyner's book of *The Times,* reported by *New York Times*

1992. Et tu, Mainers? George Bush may be a summertime neighbor in Kennebunkport, but the final election returns showed that Maine voters awarded the President a sorry third place in November's balloting, with 206,504 votes (30.39%), trailing Ross Perot, who won 206,820 (30.44%) and Bill Clinton, the victor with 263,420 (38.8%). —*Time*

1993. *Et tu,* Bill?
You could almost hear that question being asked by the National Rifle Association as yet another prominent politician, this time Massachusetts' Republican Gov. William Weld, has called for a measure of gun control. —*Times* (Trenton)

1995. It isn't hard enough trying to raise a kid in 1995, we need Rudy Giuliani, a former U.S. Attorney, promoting a 'We'll Kick Your Ass!' campaign? Et tu, Mr. Mayor? —*New York Post*

Eureka! Greek for "I have found it!" The story goes that when the Syracusan philosopher Archimedes (about 287–212 b.c.) was taking a bath, some of the water ran over, and he exclaimed "Eureka!" He concluded that a body must displace its own bulk in water. This method is used to test the purity of gold. The one-word Greek sentence is used as an exclamation of delight when a discovery is made or a triumphant achievement occurs. "Eureka!" is the official motto of the state of California.***

1922. —*Eureka!* Buck Mulligan cried. *Eureka!* —James Joyce, *Ulysses*

1988. "The more I think of it, the more I realize that sex isn't all that much fun—"

"Ah," said the doctor, in the same tone that Archimedes had long ago said *Eureka.* —Erich Segal, *Doctors*

1992. As a record of inquiry into black holes and how they relate to the creation of the cosmos, "Time" is one "Eureka!" episode after another. —*New Yorker*

1992. Eureka! I think I've got it: Michael Bolton—Engelbert of the '90s! —Justin Warner, "Mail," *People*

1993. And as the shift to managed care advances, a far smaller sales force will be needed to sway a few thousand plan benefit providers than is now needed to flog pills to America's 653,000 doctors. Says Vagelos: "I've always thought there would be a better way. This is it. This is eureka." —*Fortune*

1993. As he gathered data over several more weeks, [Russell A.] Hulse realized that something very strange was going on with his measurements.

"My reaction, as those of you who are scientists will understand, was not 'Eureka—A Discovery!' but 'Oh, nuts, what went wrong,'" said Hulse, who got a big laugh from his colleagues in the audience. —*Times* (Trenton)

1994. Mr. [Dean] Hamer saw from the data that most of the gay men in any family were related through the maternal line. "It might sound a little hokey," he writes, "but the only word that came to mind was 'Eureka!'" —*New York Times Book Review*

Even a blind pig occasionally picks up an acorn. Anyone, even a disabled person, can achieve some success. The proverb is found in varying forms: *Even a blind pig finds an acorn once in a while; Even a blind hog picks up an acorn once in a while; Even a blind chicken finds some corn now and then; Even a blind squirrel picks up an acorn once in a while,* etc.

1992. His crusty, cagey deputy is played by oatmeal-loving Wilford Brimley, with his walrus mustache and spurs that jingle-jangle. He's also given to folksy clichés like "Even a blind pig finds an acorn once in a while." —"Tube," *People*

1992. Mr. Miller says, "The figures of speech are not an affection—he really talks that way; he's comfortable with Arkansas slang. When I once beat Governor Clinton at hearts—a rare thing for me—I got him to sign the score sheet, and he

wrote, 'Even a blind hog can find an acorn.'" —William Safire, *New York Times Magazine*

1994. Most of the questions McConnell answered dealt with the basics of baseball—his position, how many home runs he has hit (one this season—"We like to say that even a blind squirrel finds a nut every once in a while," he said) and how much do you get paid (approximately $1,500 per month). —*The Princeton Packet*

Even a worm will turn. Even the most humble will strike back if mistreated and abused beyond a certain point. Originally the proverb ran, "Tread on a worm's tail and it will turn." Listed in John Heywood's book of proverbs (1546). In 1590–91, Shakespeare used it in *Henry VI.* First attested in the United States in *Christographia* (1703). The proverb is found in varying forms: *The worm will turn; Even a mouse will turn; It's a long worm that has no turning; The worm turned and bit the hand that fed it; The worm turned and ate the bird,* etc.

1590–91.
The smallest worm will turn being trodden on. —*Henry VI, Part III,* Act II, Scene II

1990. "Well, all you cretins got your anti-white hate registry law passed, the Jew law, another nail in the coffin of white America," said Tom Metzger in last week's taped message. "Now all you putrid politicians that grovel before the sinister Jew power take notice: one day the worm will turn." —*Jewish Week* (New York)

1994. In fact, the day was one long, sometimes poignant reminder of how the worm has turned for Mr. Cuomo—whose approval ratings now lag Mr. Clinton's in the state by 10 percentage points, 45 to 55 … —*New York Times*

Even Homer sometimes nods. Nobody can be at his best all the time. Even the greatest make a mistake now and then. This Latin saying, *indignor quandoque bonus dormitat Homerus,* goes back to Horace (65–8 b.c.). Homer was the author of the *Iliad* and the *Odyssey* and even in these there are dull passages. The saying is found in varying forms: *Homer occasionally nodded; Even Homer fails to nod at times; Even Jove* [another name of Jupiter] *nods; Famous God Jove nods on occasion,* etc.

65–8 b.c.
Quandoque bonus dormitat Homerus. Sometimes even good old Homer nods. —Horace, *Ars Poetica*

1711. Those oft are stratagems which errors seem,

Nor is it Homer nods, but we that dream.
—Alexander Pope, *An Essay on Criticism*

1994. On this subject, even Homer nods to the point of falling off his chair. —William Safire, "Defuse Those Participles," *New York Times Magazine*

See also DON'T MAKE THE SAME MISTAKE TWICE; HE WHO NEVER MADE A MISTAKE NEVER MADE ANYTHING; TO ERR IS HUMAN, TO FORGIVE DIVINE.

Every cloud has a silver lining. Some good may come out of any gloomy situation. The proverb was found in print as early as 1634 in *Comus* by John Milton (1608–74). First attested in the United States in *Struggle of Petroleum V. Nasby* (1863) by American humorist David Ross Locke (1833–88). The proverb is found in varying forms: *Every bright cloud must have a darker lining; Every stomach has a silver lining; The blackest clouds have silver linings; There is always a silver lining to every cloud; You can't have a silver lining without a cloud*, etc. Often shortened to *a silver lining*, referring to a prospect of hope in a gloomy situation. "So always look for the silver lining/ And try to find the sunny side of life," P. G. Wodehouse said in 1920.

1936. After hard fighting, nearly all of Tennessee was now held by the Union troops. But even with this loss on the top of the others, the South's spirit was not broken. True, grim determination had taken the place of high-hearted hopes, but people could still find a silver lining in the cloud. —Margaret Mitchell, *Gone With the Wind*

1961. Yossarian vomited, and Colonel Korn shot to his feet at the first cough and fled in disgust, so it seemed indeed that there was a silver lining to every cloud, Yossarian reflected, as he drifted back into a suffocating daze. —Joseph Heller, *Catch-22*

1977. The doctor looked at him bleakly. He thought of a cartoon of two men chained to the wall of a dungeon and one saying, "Now here's my plan." Abelson sighed and said, "Okay, Counselor, where's the silver lining?" —William Safire, *Full Disclosure*

1989. The disastrous Alaska oil spill, for which corporate apologies and assurances are poor compensation, is scarcely a cloud with a silver lining. It may provide a new impetus for environmental protection and restoration, but the damage done by the Exxon Valdez and its masters will have been done, and much of it will never be undone. —*New York Times*

1991. WALL ST. FINDS SILVER LINING IN CLOUDY ECONOMIC REPORTS —Headline, *New York Times*

1992. MOST OBVIOUS SIGN THAT EVERY CLOUD HAS A SILVER LINING New York City Opera, beset by budget problems, cut back on the number of productions but increased rehearsal time, making for greatly improved performances. —*New York Times*

1994. The silver lining on the dark cloud was that the 225-stock Nikkei index bounded up 268.26 points yesterday to 20,089.72, its highest close since early September. —*New York Times*

See also IT'S ALWAYS DARKEST BEFORE THE DAWN; IT'S AN ILL WIND THAT BLOWS NO (NOBODY) GOOD; WHERE THERE'S LIFE THERE'S HOPE.

Every dog has his day. Every person will, sooner or later, have a stroke of good fortune and thus a day of joy. The proverb has been traced back to *Erasmus' Adages* (1545) by R. Taverner. In 1562 it was used by John Heywood and later by Shakespeare in *Hamlet* (1600–01). First attested in the United States in the *Life of Elbridge Gerry* (1777). The proverb is found in varying forms: *Every dog deserves his day; Every dog is entitled to his day; Every dog has its day; Every dog shall have his day*, etc. The proverb has its counterpart in other languages too: *Hodie mihi, cras tibi* (Latin, "Today for me, tomorrow for thee"); *Heute mir, morgen dir* (German, "Today I, tomorrow you").

1600–01.

Hamlet: Let Hercules himself do what he may,
The cat will mew, and dog will have his day.

—*Hamlet*, Act V, Scene I

1901. *Caesar:* Every dog has his day; and I have had mine, I cannot complain. —George Bernard Shaw, *Caesar and Cleopatra*, Act III

1939. Every dog has his day. Yes, and those with broken tails have their week ends. —Lewis and Faye Copeland, *10,000 Jokes, Toasts and Stories*

1978. "You know, Harold," Frannie said later that evening, as the party began to break up, "I don't think I've ever seen you feeling so good. What is it?"

He gave her a jolly wink. "Every dog has his day, Fran." —Stephen King, *The Stand*

1982. "We all supported him [Senator Gantling] then, but he's had his day, Mrs. Grant." —James A. Michener, *Space*

1992. Every Dad Has His Day. But What About After? We fly and flurry and make a complete fuss over him for Father's Day. Then it's over, and what's an over-indulged, spoiled-for-the-moment

Dad supposed to do when his devoted family dashes off? —*New York Times*

1994. TV talk-show host John McLaughlin on the return of the Republicans: "Every dogma has its day." —*U.S. News & World Report*

Every employee tends to rise to his level of incompetence. People are promoted until they reach a position they can't cope with. The saying originated in the United States in 1966 and is generally known as the Peter Principle after Lawrence J. Peter (1919–90), who was the first to observe this phenomenon.

1969. In a hierarchy, every employee tends to rise to his level of incompetence. —Lawrence J. Peter with Raymond Hull, *The Peter Principle*

1986. Plateauing is a condition in which many able people will be unable to rise to levels in which they would be competent. The Peter Principle is a condition in which people rise to levels in which they are *in*competent. —Judith M. Bardwick, *The Plateauing Trap*

1987. I have often felt that one of the reasons that the so-called "Peter Principle" is so popular (people are successfully promoted until they reach their level of incompetence) is that, far from being a dismal prediction, it is a completely logical derivation of this most cherished of corporate myths! It is the corporate version of Bentham's "Felicity calculus" applied to the justice of the corporate reward system: each is promoted in exact proportion to ability. —R. Richard Ritti and G. Ray Funkhouser, *The Ropes to Skip & the Ropes to Know*

1992. Lately, other Bush aides prefer to sock it [the blame for their boss's plight] to the Bush-Quayle chairman, Robert M. Teeter, who they contend ran a BarcaLounger campaign when circumstances clamored for a Land Rover. They refer to "the Teeter principle," a snide allusion to the Peter principle, that every talented worker gets promoted, sooner or later, to a job beyond his or her abilities. —*New York Times*

Every little bit helps. This self-explanatory proverb is first recorded in the French of Gabriel Meurier (1530–1601) in his *Deviz Familiers* (1590): "Every little helps, said the ant, pissing into the sea at noon" (*Piu ayde, disçoit le formy, pissant en mer en plein, midy*). Its first appearance in English was in 1602: "The wrenn sayde all helpte when she——in the sea." The proverb was first attested in the United States in E. Hazzard's *Belknap Papers* (1787): "A guinea is a guinea, and every little helps."

1986. Do Clinton's cops make Minnesota any safer? So far, only 186 of 361 promised officers are on the beat. Every little bit helps, most agree, but what happens when the federal pocketbook that pays their way zips shut? —*Star-Tribune* (Minneapolis)

1994. A plastic foam cup for donations hangs on the wall in the Miami Dolphins' locker room, with proceeds going toward a cure for Prime Time fever. "Every little bit helps! Give till it hurts!" reads a note on the cup. —*Arizona Republic*

1997. So though I sometimes disparage technical analysis, I recall the lessons of the Goddess. And even though I favor fundamentals, that doesn't mean I don't have a small piece of my ear attuned to what the chartists are saying. Every little bit helps. —James J. Cramer, *ABC News*

1998. The computer is being tested in Baltimore, Los Angeles, and Miami but is expected to be made widely available soon, Irwin says. As far as police officers, every little bit helps. —Michael J. Martinez, *ABC News*

Every man for himself. Grab whatever you can and don't help or expect help from others. The proverb appeared in Chaucer's "Knight's Tale" (c. 1386). In 1546, John Heywood listed the expanded form of it, *Every man for himself and God for us all,* in his book of proverbs. In 1678, it was included in J. Ray's collection of English proverbs. First attested in the United States in the *Correspondence Between William Penn and James Logan* (1706). The proverb is found in varying forms: *Each man for himself; Every fellow for his own; Every man for himself when there's trouble; It's every man for himself; It's every guy for himself,* etc. The proverb has its counterpart in French: *Sauve qui peut* ("Save him who can." In other words, let each save himself as best he may).

1621–51.
Every man for himself, his own ends, the Devil for all. —Robert Burton, *Anatomy of Melancholy,* Part III, Section 1, Member 3.

1922. Every fellow for his own, tooth and nail. —James Joyce, *Ulysses*

1974. Returning a phone call from the night before, a mid-level White House official described the situation there to Woodward—old loyalties shattered, little work getting done, confusion about who on the staff might be indicted, who ordered what and who ordered whom, who would resign and who would be saved. "It's every man for him-

self—get a lawyer and blame everyone else."
—Carl Bernstein and Bob Woodward, *All the President's Men*

1987. "So what happened with business school, Mike? You must be the first drop-out they've had in years."
"I wouldn't be surprised. You have no idea what those places have become, Mark. First-year students are already talking about 'golden parachutes.' It's just every man for himself!" —G. B. Trudeau, *Doonesbury Deluxe*

1992. Jim Tuller, in his 42nd year of interstate truck driving, "couldn't care less" about who makes it next to the White House. "Lot of new young drivers on the roads nowadays, and they don't stop to help when you're in trouble," he said when asked what is of concern to him. "It's everybody for himself these days." —*New York Times*

1994. The message the departing Mr. Gergen sent was that of an out-to-lunch Administration buffeted by events rather than in charge of them, and of a White House in which every man (and I do mean man) is out for himself. —*New York Times*

See also CHARITY BEGINS AT HOME; THE DEVIL TAKE THE HINDMOST.

Every man for himself, and the devil take the hindmost. *See* THE DEVIL TAKE THE HINDMOST.

Every man is his own worst enemy. One has more to fear from one's own behavior than from the actions of others. The proverb has been traced back to *Religio Medici* (1643) by Sir Thomas Browne (1605–82).

> **1643.** But how shall we expect charity towards others, when we are uncharitable to ourselves? Charity begins at home, is the voice of the world; yet is every man his greatest enemy, and, as it were, his own executioner. —Thomas Browne, *Religio Medici*, Part I, Section 6

> **1994.** *Smith:* Michael [Jackson]'s a great talent; it's too bad he's so weird. He's smart in business, but not in how he comes off. Again, he's his own worst enemy. —Lawrence Linderman, "MM Interview with Liz Smith," *Modern Maturity*

Every man is not born with a silver spoon in his mouth. Not everybody is born to wealth. A silver spoon is a traditional gift given by the godparents when the baby is born; not everybody can afford a silver spoon. The proverb is in Peter Motteux's translation (1712) of Cervantes' *Don Quixote* (1605–15). First attested in the United States in the *Adams Family Correspondence* (1780). The proverb is found in varying forms:

Every man is not born with a silver spoon, let alone a gold one; A lot of people were born with silver spoons in their mouths; He was born with a silver spoon in his mouth, etc. State Treasurer Ann Richards of Texas in a keynote address to the Democratic National Convention in 1988 humorously changed the proverb by suggesting that George Bush was "born with a silver foot in his mouth."

> **1605–15.** Every man was not born with a silver spoon in his mouth. —Miguel de Cervantes, *Don Quixote*

> **1922.** Born with a silver knife in his mouth. That's witty, I think. Or no. Silver means born rich. Born with a knife. But then the allusion is lost. —James Joyce, *Ulysses*

> **1926.** She was born with a silver spoon in her mouth; she thinks she can do what she likes. —John Galsworthy, *The Silver Spoon*

> **1988.** And for eight straight years George Bush hasn't displayed the slightest interest in anything we care about. And now that he's after a job that he can't get appointed to, he's like Columbus discovering America—he's found child care, he's found education.
> Poor George, he can't help it—he was born with a silver foot in his mouth. —"Transcript of the Keynote Address by Ann Richards, The Texas Treasurer," *New York Times*

> **1992.** But Quayle was born not with a mere silver spoon but with a silver ladle in his mouth. —Robert Hughes, *Time*

> **1992.** W. Averell Harriman was born with the proverbial silver spoon in his mouth. His father, E. H. Harriman, "the quintessential railroad baron," was a ruthless, determined and uneducated man who amassed an enormous fortune. —*Wall Street Journal*

> **1993.** "People always think I was born on the back of a horse with a silver spoon in my mouth," says [Diane] English when asked to describe her background. "But I come from this really Felliniesque blue-collar family." —Hilary de Vries, *New York Times Magazine*

> **1994.** Eileen, 34, grew up in the comfortable Boston suburb of Belmont—"with a silver spoon in my mouth," she says. —*Newsweek*

Every man is the architect of his own fortune. Every person is responsible for his or her own future. This proverb is first found in Latin in *The War with Catiline* (c. 40 b.c.): *Sed res docuit id verum esse, quod in carbininbus Appius ait, fa-*

brum esse suae quemque fortune ("Experience has shown that to be true which Appius says in his verse, that every man is the architect of his own fortune"). The later Latin Publilius Syrus expressed the same idea in the form "His own character is the arbiter of everyone's fortune." Cervantes further develops the idea by saying in his *Don Quixote* (1605–15) that "The brave man carves out his fortune, and every man is the son of his own works."

1984. John Z. De Lorean was portrayed by a prosecutor as "the architect of his own destruction" but by a defense lawyer as "a victim of the people whose duty it was to protect him," as the two sides presented closing arguments yesterday at his cocaine conspiracy trial. —*Boston Globe*

1998. Chad Austin, led into the court handcuffed and shackled at the ankles, became the chief architect of his own defense yesterday, imploring a Superior Court jury to believe him when he cast himself as the victim of overzealous police pursuit Feb. 11 in a gun-blazing chase. —*Boston Globe*

1998. Are you the architect of your financial future? —TV commercial by Fidelity Investment, *Cable News Network*

See also GOD HELPS THOSE WHO HELP THEMSELVES; IF YOU WANT SOMETHING DONE RIGHT, DO IT YOURSELF.

Every man makes mistakes. *See* HE WHO NEVER MADE A MISTAKE NEVER MADE ANYTHING.

Every man to his own taste. People's tastes and preferences differ and everyone has his own tastes. The proverb has been traced back to John Lyly's *Euphues and His England* (1580) and is similar to the French: *Chacun à son goût* ("Each to his taste"). First attested in the United States in *Letters of a Loyalist Lady* (1767). The proverb is found in varying forms: *Each to his own poison; Every man to his own humor; Every man to his taste; Everyone (everybody) to his own taste; Every man to his own trade.*

1922. Everyone to his own taste as Morris said when he kissed the cow. —James Joyce, *Ulysses*

1962. "The truth is," Storm said, "I don't like to get shot at."
"Everybody to his own taste," Witt said. —James Jones, *The Thin Red Line*

1983. He [Jason] waddled off on short stumpy legs, and Buddy reflected that he and Gladrags must make a bizarre-looking couple—Gladrags so tall and skinny and black, and Jason so rounded and plump and white. Oh well, everyone to his own kick. —Jackie Collins, *Hollywood Wives*

1993. "The way they are dressed makes me sick."
"Nothing doing. Every man to his taste." —Overheard on Fifth Avenue, New York, during the Gay & Lesbian parade

See also ONE MAN'S MEAT IS ANOTHER MAN'S POISON; ONE MAN'S TRASH IS ANOTHER MAN'S TREASURE; THERE'S NO ACCOUNTING FOR TASTES.

Everybody is wise after the event. *See* IT IS EASY TO BE WISE AFTER THE EVENT.

Everybody talks about the weather, but nobody does anything about it. Everybody complains about a problem, but nothing is done about it. Attributed to Mark Twain (1835–1910) or sometimes to his friend Charles Dudley Warner (1829–1900) and later to Will Rogers (1879–1935). First saw print in a *Hartford* (Connecticut) *Courant* unsigned editorial in 1897.

1981. Dear Abby: Everybody complains about smokers, but nothing is ever done about them. I've had more meals spoiled and more pleasant hours of socializing ruined by people who foul the air with cigarette and cigar smoke. —Abigail Van Buren, *The Best of Dear Abby*

1984. "It's something [anti-Semitism] Jews have lived with a long time," David said. "Like the weather, we can talk about it, but we can't do much to change it." —Howard Fast, *The Outsider*

1989. "Drugs are everywhere," she said. "I see people who are wasted on drugs. Everybody is saying there is a drug problem, but nobody is doing anything about it. —*New York Times*

1992. It's like what Mark Twain said about the weather. Everybody talks about a coherent new U.S. foreign policy, and nobody makes one. Almost nobody. —*New York Times*

1993. Bad academic writing is like bad weather: everybody talks about it, but nobody does anything about it. —*New York Times Book Review*

Everybody's doin' it. The saying originated prior to World War I. The words come from the Irving Berlin song "Everybody's Doin' It Now" (1911). It referred to the turkey trot, a lively dance performed to ragtime music. The phrase was given a new lease on life on October 6, 1992, when *Time* published a cover story "Lying—Everybody's Doin' It (Honest)." Most often used to justify one's misconduct (cheating, lying, etc.).**

1911. Everybody's doin' it, doin' it, everybody's doin' it now. —Irving Berlin, "Everybody's Doin' It Now"

1992. I can think of no better way to encourage ly-

ing than to tell people that "everybody's doin' it."
—*Time*

1993. Milken's lectures have attracted widespread press coverage. Last week, they were featured in Trudeau's Doonesbury cartoon strip.

In one strip, Milken was pictured leading his students in a chant of "Greed Works! Crime Pays! Everybody Does It!" —*New York Post*
See also THE END JUSTIFIES THE MEANS.

Everyone has his fifteen minutes of fame.
The sensation-seeking media can make anyone famous for a short while. Attributed to the American artist and motion-picture producer Andy Warhol (1927–1987). He is often quoted as saying, "In the future everyone will be world-famous for fifteen minutes" (1968). The saying is found in varying forms, most often simply *fifteen minutes of fame,* referring to one's time in the limelight.

1988. The fifteen minutes of fame that the late Andy Warhol promised each of us came to me in the spring of 1984. I was the point man in a nationally publicized effort to outflank Calvin Griffith, the owner of the Minnesota Twins baseball team. —Harvey Mackay, *Swim with the Sharks without Being Eaten Alive*

1992. "But you'll be the star," she said with admiration, not sarcasm.

"Yeah, I'll get my fifteen minutes." —John Grisham, *The Pelican Brief*

1994. [Buz] Male has apologized for the incident and said he was joking when he pointed the pistol at Hanlon as students in his ninth-grade social studies class prepared to leave. Male, who could not be reached for comment yesterday, has said it was "15 seconds of stupidity on my part." —*Washington Post*

1995. It was a habit she picked up back in the '60s. Angela Davis' 15 minutes of fame came when she was revealed as the source of the guns that Jonathan Jackson used in his bloody 1970 assault on the Marin County Courthouse in an effort to free his psychopathic brother (and Davis' "revolutionary lover" George Jackson) from Soledad Prison. —*New York Post*

Everyone to his own taste. See EVERY MAN TO HIS OWN TASTE.

Everyone to whom much is given, of him will much be required. Much is expected where much is given. The proverb first appeared in the New Testament. It has no standard form. Slightly changed variants may be used.

For unto whomsoever much is given, of him shall be much required: and to whom men have committed much, of him they will ask the more. —Luke 12:48, *Authorized Version,* 1611

1961. For of those to whom much is given, much is required. —John F. Kennedy, Speech to the Massachusetts State Legislature

1984. "Every one to whom much is given, of him will much be required." The words of St. Luke have been a motto for Rose Kennedy, the matriarch, and she has been right in grievous ways. Much has been required of the older Kennedys in the way of outward tragedy. As much, perhaps, is being required of the younger Kennedys in inward tragedy, like that of David Kennedy, the third son of Robert and Ethel Kennedy. His episodic life ended yesterday in a Florida hotel room at the age of 28. —*New York Times*

1984. "Listening to a Kennedy talk about money is like listening to a nun talk about sex," Jack Kennedy's college pal, Chuck Spalding, once observed. In this richest of families, the riches are never discussed.

Nonetheless, the 29 younger Kennedys eventually discovered that their grandfather was a very rich man. What they also learned, however, was that they had a social debt. Rose would quote St. Luke to them: "To whom much has been given, much will be required." —*Daily News* (New York)

Everything but the kitchen sink. Absolutely everything that is available, whether it's relevant or not. The saying originated in the early twentieth century and caught on following World War II. The saying is found in varying forms: *Everything and the kitchen sink; Everything except the kitchen sink; Everything but the kitchen stove; Everything including the kitchen stove,* etc.

1987. "My mother was more pragmatic," the Senator [Simon] said in an interview. "My father was the idealist. If it had been up to my father, we would have given away the kitchen sink." —*New York Times*

1988. The attorney for Mr. Dortch, William Diehl, said of the indictment: "It's a rambling document that seems to have everything except the kitchen sink." —*New York Times*

1991. SUNDAY DINNER. SALADS WITH AN EVERYTHING-BUT-THE-KITCHEN-SINK TOUCH. —Headline, *New York Times*

1994. Everything and the kitchen sink: Muscovites hawked their wares in April 1993. —*New York Times*

Everything comes to an end. *See* ALL GOOD THINGS MUST COME TO AN END.

Everything comes to those (the man, him) who (can, know how to) wait. *See* ALL GOOD THINGS COME TO THOSE WHO WAIT.

Everything falls into place. A number of disparate things fit together and get organized. Things are working out. The idiomatic expression *to fall into place* is often used too. The saying is found in varying forms.

1976. When we got back to the United States I asked Walter if I could see his pictures, and he said, "Something happened to my camera, and most of them didn't come out."

The pieces started to fall into place, but I never said anything to anybody about it. —Art Buchwald, *Washington Is Leaking*

1979. "Where are you, Bernie?"

"Barstow. Everything is falling into place. We made the deal for the planes, and the boys have been working on them all day." —Howard Fast, *The Establishment*

1983. His luck was on an up. Everything was falling into place. —Jackie Collins, *Hollywood Wives*

1985. All around her things were falling into place. —Michael Korda, *Queenie*

1986. "I've been able to hire talented assistant coaches. If you win, that brings in money. Money builds facilities. Once you have the talent, everything falls into place," [Johnson said]. —*New York Times*

1992. "There's a lot of deserving guys out there that have the everyday numbers," Eckersley said last night. "Everything fell into place. These things come around once in a lifetime." —*New York Times*

1993. "As I've grown older, I [Mr. Browning] find that if you follow the melodic line as a singer would, then everything else falls into place, the rubati are right." —*New York Times*

Everything has an end. *See* ALL GOOD THINGS MUST COME TO AN END.

Everything is not all peaches and cream. Everything is not easy and simple. The proverb is found in varying forms: *All is not peaches and cream; It isn't all peaches and cream*, etc.

1986. "Naw, you're a girl. Girls are always lovers. I don't want you fighting. I want you all soft and sugary, all peaches and cream for your Daddy." —Pat Conroy, *The Prince of Tides*

1990. Indeed, it seems that one of the greatest challenges of consulting can be knowing when to say "no" to a job offer.

But consulting isn't all peaches and cream. It's a hustle. Like hunting for a job, you're the salesperson and the product. —Daniel Moreau, *Take Charge of Your Career*

1992. After some difficult initial weeks of adjustment to her new home—"she'd throw tantrums; it wasn't all peaches and cream," says Merry—Palani has settled in joyfully. —*People*

1994. All is not peaches and cream for the Bulls. —*N.Y.1.*

See also THERE'S GOOD AND BAD IN EVERYTHING.

Everything old is new again. Things that are well established often find new popularity. The proverb has been traced back to Chaucer (1340–1400), who used to say that every old custom was new again. Chaucer's idea was popularized by Sir Walter Scott (1771–1832) in his collection of ballads and songs *Minstrelsy of the Scottish Border* (1802–03). But the proverb did not really catch on until 1824, which saw the publication of memoirs by the milliner of Marie Antoinette (1755–93). Speaking about the queen's old dress she had made look like new, the milliner said, "Everything old is new again."

1991. Like so many products on the market today, fruit butters prove the adage, "What's old is new again." —*New York Times*

1992. Everything old is new again. They're thinking about putting Penn Station, or something like the old Penn Station, into the 34th Street Post Office. Well, they *had* a Penn Station once. Or we did. —*New York Post*

1993. The phrase "everything old is new again" could well apply to greens appearing in the market today. Greens unfamiliar to most of us—radicchio, kohlrabi, Swiss chard—are the new darlings of the salad set. —*Times* (Trenton)

1994. "What is the 90's?" Mr. Hefner asked, sounding philosophical as he clutched a Jack Daniel's on the rocks. "It's retro: everything that's old is new again. As we approach the millennium, we'll look back and wish we had it back." —*New York Times*

Everything's coming up roses. Life looks great. Originated in the United States in 1957. Title of a popular song from the musical *Gypsy* (1959). The lyrics of the song "Everything's Coming Up Roses" (1957) were written by Stephen Sondheim (1930–) and the music by Jule Styne

(1905–94). It is interesting to note that in 1932 the Democrats launched their presidential campaign promising that "Everything Will Be Rosy with Roosevelt."

1957. Things look swell, things look great,
Gonna have the whole world on a plate.
Starting here, starting now
Honey, everything's coming up roses.
—"Everything's Coming Up Roses"

1974. The Fair Corporation's own publicity was built around [Robert] Moses, of course; the *Time* and *Newsweek* and *Look* cover stories had not only the Unisphere but RM [Robert Moses] on their covers; *Life* 's story was entitled "Everything Coming Up Moses." —Robert A. Caro, *The Power Broker*

1985. "Everything comes up roses when you're someplace where you're unhappy, and you think that anywhere else you could be happy." —Howard Fast, *The Immigrant's Daughter*

1992. Everything's Coming Up Rosie. Rosie Perez never asked to be an actress, not even in a school play. Still, she won raves in *Do the Right Thing*. And now she's taken *White Men Can't Jump,* a movie supposedly about male bonding, and made it her own. —*Newsweek*

1994. Everything's Coming Up Rosie. —Title of a segment on Roseanne, "Hard Copy," CBS
See also HAPPY DAYS ARE HERE AGAIN.

Everything's hunky-dory. Everything is fine. The saying originated in the mid-1880s. Hunkidori was the name of a breath freshener introduced in 1868. First used in the United Kingdom in the 1920s. Some lexicographers think that the freshener may be responsible for the popularity of the hunky-dory saying.

1952. "Hi, there folks," he [Pa] said. "Everything hunky-dory in my little old home, eh?" —Kurt Vonnegut, Jr., *Player Piano*

1963. "Who knows? Maybe everything's gonna be hunky-dory." —J. D. Salinger, *Raise High the Roof Beam, Carpenters*

1992. "There is a lot of talk in the atmosphere today of people saying, 'Well, you know, maybe you don't need to do anything about this economy because the unemployment rate is going down, and housing starts are up, and everything's just hunky-dory,'" Mr. Clinton said at a news conference with Democratic Congressional leaders. —*New York Times*

1993. I will say this. It may have been naive for anyone to seriously assert in the beginning you could go into a situation as politically and militarily charged as that one, give people food, turn around and leave, and expect everything to be hunky-dory. —Bill Clinton, quoted by Thomas L. Friedman in "A Broken Truce: Clinton vs. Bush in Global Policy," *New York Times*

1994. Mr. Jeffords, the only Senate Republican who supported the health care legislation offered by the President, said of his colleagues, "They don't want to end up being considered to have delayed or filibustered." He added, however, "I don't want in any way to lead you to believe it's all going to be hunky-dory." —*New York Times*

Everything's under control. Everything's running smoothly. According to Eric Partridge, the phrase dates back to about 1930. The auxiliary verb *to be* is sometimes omitted. *To get (have) someone or something under control* means to make someone or something manageable and is commonly used as a figure of speech.

1961. "I'm cold," Snowden moaned. "I'm cold."
"You're going to be all right, kid," Yossarian assured him, patting his arm comfortingly. "Everything's under control." —Joseph Heller, *Catch-22*

1992. She [Rosen] led off with the DNA evidence. She seemed to have it all under control. —Philip Friedman, *Inadmissible Evidence*

1993. "Yeltsin seems to have everything under control," said Ezra Zask, president of Ezra Zask Associates, a currency trading fund with $105 million under management that is based in Norfolk, Conn. —*New York Times*
See also EVERYTHING'S HUNKY-DORY.

Evil to him who evil thinks. May he be punished or shamed if he nurtures evil ideas. Often used as a curse against ill-wishers. The proverb has been traced back to about 1348–49. The popular legend is that at a court ball the Countess of Salisbury's garter fell off. Edward III (1312–1377), King of England, noticed that all those present started laughing. He picked up her garter and bound it round his own knee, saying in French, *Honi soit qui mal y pense* ("Evil to him who evil thinks"). About 1348 the Most Noble Order of the Garter was instituted. The proverb was first attested in the United States in the *Lee Papers* (1776). The verb *does* is sometimes used instead of *thinks.*

1349. *Honi soit qui mal y pense.* ("Evil to him who evil thinks"). —Motto of the Order of the Garter

1992. Mr. Zegas accused Dr. Meyerhoff of committing "blackmail" in a letter to prosecutors on July 13 in which he raised his fees from $140 to $200 an hour....

Dr. Meyerhoff said he wrote the letter knowing that the prosecutors had another psychiatrist who was "equally capable."

"Evil to him who evil thinks," he said. —*New York Times*

The exception proves the rule. *See* THERE IS AN EXCEPTION TO EVERY RULE.

Experience is the best teacher. One learns more from experience than from books. The proverb has been traced back to *The Schoolmaster* (1568) by Roger Ascham and comes from the Latin phrase *experientia docet* meaning *experience teaches*. Walter Scott (1854–1900) disagrees with the proverb, saying that "experience is the name every one gives to their mistakes." First attested in the United States in *Addition to Colonial Currency Reprints* (1719). The proverb is found in varying forms: *Experience is a hard master but a good teacher; Experience is the greatest teacher; Experience is the only teacher; Experience teaches us many things*, etc.

1901. Experience is a good teacher, but she sends in terrific bills. —Minna Antrim, *Naked Truth and Veiled Allusions*

1960. Experience is a hard teacher because she gives the test first, the lesson afterwards. —*This Week*

1985. Experience is a good school but is not very strong on vacations. —Quoted in *Changing Times, Kiplinger Magazine*, reprinted by *Reader's Digest*

1991. We're counting on experience to be the best teacher. —Ad for Rockwell International, *Time*

Extremes meet. *See* OPPOSITES ATTRACT.

An eye for an eye, a tooth for a tooth. The punishment should match the crime. The proverb appears in the Old Testament. About 1750 b.c., the Babylonian king Hammurabi included the "eye for an eye, a tooth for a tooth" law into his legal code. First attested in the United States in 1781. Martin Luther King, Jr., considered that the premise of an eye for an eye and a tooth for a tooth would only make us "blind and toothless."

And if *any* mischief follow, then thou shalt give life for life,
Eye for eye, tooth for tooth, hand for hand, foot for foot. —Exodus 21:23–24, *Authorized Version*, 1611

1965. You are a human being with a *free will.* Which puts you above the animal level. But if you live your life without feeling and compassion for your fellowman—you are as an animal—"an eye for an eye, a tooth for a tooth" & happiness & peace of mind is not attained by living thus. —Truman Capote, *In Cold Blood*

1969. "What is your justice?"
"An eye for an eye," Bonasera said. —Mario Puzo, *The Godfather*

1984. "What will it be?" I asked fatalistically. "Breach for breach, I guess. An eye for an eye, and a tooth for a tooth?" —Joseph Heller, *God Knows*

1986. "We clearly are more confrontational," Senator Durenberger said. "We are following a policy of an eye for an eye, a tooth for a tooth." —*New York Times*

1989. "They bury Stump Sisson this morning in Loydsville, and it's time for the eye-for-an-eye, tooth-for-a-tooth routine." —John Grisham, *A Time to Kill*

1993. "If he is in fact the individual, I plan to talk to the jury and ask that they give him the death penalty," he added. "It won't bring my daughter back, but I believe in an eye for an eye." —*New York Times*

The eyes are bigger than the stomach. One desires more than one can handle. The proverb has been traced back to *Euphues and His England* (1580) by John Lyly. In 1651, it appeared in George Herbert's collection of proverbs, *Jacula Prudentum*. The proverb is found in varying forms: *The eyes are bigger than the belly; The eye is bigger than the mouth; One's eyes are bigger than one's tummy*, etc.

1651. The eye is bigger than the belly. —George Herbert, *Jacula Prudentum*

1696. In matters of love men's eyes are always bigger than their bellies. They have violent appetites, 'tis true; but they have soon dined. —John Vanbrugh, *The Relapse*, Act V, Scene 2

1984. "I got the feeling Dick's eyes were bigger than his stomach," Hoffman explains. "He expanded too fast and invested some heavy dollars in new sites that didn't pay off." —*Forbes*

1994. I'm not going to finish this second helping after all ... I can't eat another bite! I guess my eyes are bigger than my stomach! Ha! —Cartoon by Art Sansom, "Born Loser," *Times* (Trenton)
See also DON'T BITE OFF MORE THAN YOU CAN CHEW.

The eyes are the mirror(s) of the soul (mind). A person's thoughts can be ascertained by looking in his or her eyes. The proverb has been traced back in English to *Regiment of Life* (1545). But the proverb was known much earlier. Cicero (106–43 b.c.) is quoted as saying, *Ut imago est animi voltus sic indices oculi* ("The face is a picture of the mind as the eyes are its interpreter"). The Latin proverbs, *Vultus est index animi* or *Oculus animi index,* are usually translated as "The face is the index of the mind." The French say, *Les yeux sont le miroir de l'âme* ("The eyes are the mirror of the soul"). *The eyes are the window of the soul* is a variant form of the proverb.

1781. I did not study the Eye that best index to the mind. —Abigail S. Adams, quoted by I. H. Butterfield et al. in *Adams Family Correspondence* (1973)

1994. The eyes are said to be the mirror of the soul, but with a new special effect used in "The Shadow," the eyes (covered with Mylar contact lenses) can also mirror the lighting, the key grips and the film's director. —*New York Times*

Fact is stranger than fiction. *See* TRUTH IS STRANGER THAN FICTION.

Facts are facts. There is no avoiding the truth. The proverb has been traced back to *Corpse Guard Parade* (1930) by M. Kennedy.

> **1930.** Facts are facts. —M. Kennedy, *Corpse Guard Parade*

> **1991.** When I wrote about the large amount of real estate that Japanese own in Washington, D.C., I got a dozen angry letters from people of Japanese descent, accusing me of encouraging mistrust and making life hard for them. I felt bad about that, but I'm not in the public relations business. Facts are facts. —Andy Rooney, *Times* (Trenton)

> **1993.** "Facts are facts," he [Stallings] said.
> The last fact will be the most exhilarating or the most cruel for an Alabama team that has already exceeded expectations and a Miami group that is still affected by the memories and reality of Hurricane Andrew, which devastated Coach Erickson's home. —*New York Times*

See also FACTS ARE STUBBORN THINGS.

Facts are stubborn things. The truth can't be avoided, even when it's contrary to our expectations. Originally cited in *Liberty and Progress* (1732) by E. Budgell. First attested in the United States in *Essays in Field Husbandry in New England* (1748) by J. Eliot. In 1770 it was used by John Adams, first vice-president and second president of the United States, then a lawyer for several British soldiers charged with the death of five colonists in the Boston Massacre.

> **1770.** Facts are stubborn things; and whatever may be our wishes, our inclinations, or the dictates of our passions, they cannot alter the state of facts and evidence. —John Adams, "Argument in Defense of the [British] Soldiers in the Boston Massacre Trials," quoted by John Bartlett, *Familiar Quotations*, Sixteenth Edition, edited by Justin Kaplan (1992)

> **1988.** "Those are consequences of eight years of borrow and spend, borrow and spend," Mr. Dukakis said. "Facts are stubborn things. These are the facts that we're going to be debating in the course of the next 85 days." —*New York Times*

> **1988.** "Facts are stubborn things," Mr. [Jesse] Jackson says, adapting a refrain from the President's speech Monday night in his own lyrical style. "His anti-drug plan has resulted in more drugs coming this way. Facts are stubborn things. The most indictments of any administration in history. Facts are stubborn things. The biggest deficit and trade deficit in the history of America. Facts are stubborn things." —*New York Times*

See also FACTS ARE FACTS.

Faint heart never won fair lady. You can't be timid in wooing a woman—or anything else. The proverb has been traced back to *Confessio Amantis* (c. 1390) by John Gower. It appears in the English translation of Cervantes' *Don Quixote*. First attested in the United States in the *Correspondence of Samuel Webb* (1777). The proverb is found in varying forms: *Faint heart never saved fair lady; Faint heart never made love to a fair lady; Faint heart never won a lucrative job,* etc.

> **1605–15.**
> Remember the old saying, "Faint heart ne'er won fair lady." —Miguel de Cervantes, *Don Quixote*

> **1800.** Come, Firm Resolve, take thou the van,
> Thou stalk o' carl-hemp in man!
> And let us mind, faint heart ne'er wan
> A lady fair.
> —Robert Burns, "To Dr Blacklock"

1882. Faint heart never won fair lady! —William Gilbert, *Iolanthe*, Act I

1985. Clearly, United's top men [Telecommunications Inc.] have weighed their risks. And they have chosen to go for the opportunity. Faint heart never won fair lady—or success in business, either. —*Forbes*

1991. "Remember the adage, 'Faint heart never won lucrative job'!" —Cartoon by Alex Kotzky, "Apt. 3-G," *Times* (Trenton)

See also FORTUNE FAVORS THE BRAVE; HE WHO HESITATES IS LOST; NOTHING VENTURED, NOTHING GAINED.

Familiarity breeds contempt. When you're too close to someone, you may often become disrespectful or scornful of them. The proverb has a centuries-old history. In his fable "The Fox and the Lion," Aesop (c. 550 b.c.) said that "familiarity breeds contempt." *Parit contemptum nimia familiaritas* is its Latin counterpart, as used by Publilius Syrus in the first century b.c. Much later it was used by Chaucer in his "Tale of Melibee" (1386) and by Cervantes in *Don Quixote*. First attested in the United States in *Voyages of Radisson* (1680). Mark Twain added the words *and children.* The proverb is found in varying forms: *Desperation breeds contempt; Familiarity breeds indifference; Familiarity breeds a variety of contempt; Nothing breeds contempt like unfamiliarity; Unfamiliarity inevitably breeds distrust,* etc.

(undated).
Familiarity breeds contempt—and children. —Mark Twain, *Notebooks* (1935)

1951. They all tried it sooner or later, if they hung around with them long enough. Familiarity bred laxity, like that Hal guy was always saying. —James Jones, *From Here to Eternity*

1986. "Who's she?"
"The hottest *female* agent in town. I was with her once, long ago and far away. And before you ask, she *also* didn't answer my calls when I was desperate."
"Desperation breeds contempt." —Jackie Collins, *Hollywood Husbands*

1988. Often if you stick around the same company—or the same city—too long, you become old hat. You seem stale. People think they know everything about you; they wonder why you haven't moved on. The new way to say it is, "They've seen you in underwear." The old way is, "Familiarity breeds contempt." —*Esquire*

1992. If the intent of [Woody Allen's] *Husbands and Wives* is to demonstrate the wisdom of the old saw "Familiarity breeds contempt," it succeeds,

though with a much narrower application than the movie asks for. —*New Yorker*

1994. Familiarity brings contempt and distance earns respect. —*Times* (Trenton)

See also GOOD FENCES MAKE GOOD NEIGHBORS; NO MAN IS A HERO TO HIS VALET; A PROPHET IS NOT WITHOUT HONOR, SAVE IN HIS OWN COUNTRY.

The family that prays together stays together. Religious families are less likely to disintegrate. Originated by commercial writer Al Scalpone and used as the motto of the Roman Catholic Family Rosary Crusade by Father Patrick Peyton. It first saw print on April 3, 1948, in the *St. Joseph Magazine* (Oregon).

1948. 'More things are wrought by prayer than this world dreams of,' and 'The family that prays together stays together.' —*St. Joseph Magazine* (Oregon)

1961. In a spirit of civic enterprise, he regularly allotted a certain amount of free aerial advertising space to General Peckem for the propagation of such messages in the public interest as NEATNESS COUNTS, HASTE MAKES WASTE, and THE FAMILY THAT PRAYS TOGETHER STAYS TOGETHER. —Joseph Heller, *Catch-22*

1992. Can the family that runs together win together? —*People*

The fat is in the fire. Something that can't be stopped or changed has started, and it is likely to lead to trouble. The proverb first appeared in John Heywood's book of proverbs in 1546. It came into use in the early sixteenth century and is found in varying forms.

1965. He [President Johnson] told me to telephone Bowles and ask him whether he would go to Rio.... When I called him, Chet [Bowles] listened in silence, dismissed the idea of Brazil and finally said, "There's no point in this. I guess the fat's in the fire now." —Arthur M. Schlesinger, Jr., *A Thousand Days*

1988. "But you sure as hell knew there was a lot more fat in the fire than there was smoke in the kitchen." —Robert Ludlum, *The Icarus Agenda*

1992. THE FAT'S IN THE FIRE —Headline of a report on an American sumo wrestler who rocked Japan with charges of racism, *People*

Father knows best. Father is more knowledgeable and experienced. Often used to refer to the popular 1950s TV sitcom of that title, which portrayed an ideal American family. Originated in the United States in 1931. The proverb, *Mother knows* *best* was first used four years earlier as a book title by Edna Ferber. Both sayings may be applied to children as well as adults. The subject *father* may be replaced by any other subject *(the Lord, the government, etc.)*.

1974. Council President Rudolph Halley, a liberal concerned with the social implications of governmental policies, began to question some of Moses' proposals; Moses' attitude—expressed at a lunch at Randall's Island to which Mrs. Halley was also invited—was, she says, "Oh, little boy, sit down. Father knows best." —Robert A. Caro, *The Power Broker*

1978. You see? she lectured herself. The Lord knows best. —Stephen King, *The Stand*

1986. "The government knows best," my mother said, softening. "It needs this plant for national defense."

"Since when does the government know best, Mama?" Luke said in a tired and daunted voice. —Pat Conroy, *The Prince of Tides*

1992. Papa's ideas also presented me with a number of conundrums: Should I, as a child raised not to talk back to adults, try to get my grandfather to see that his world view was clearly ludicrous? Should I pretend that Father—or in this case, Grandfather—knows best, or should I challenge and possibly embarrass him? —*New York Times Magazine*

Fear the Greeks bearing gifts. *See* BEWARE OF GREEKS BEARING GIFTS.

Feather your own nest. Look after your own interests. Based on birds who remove down from their own breasts to make their nests more comfortable for hatching eggs. Used to indicate disapproval of such behavior when done at the expense of others. The proverb has been traced back to *Respublica* (1553). Robert Greene (c. 1560–92) is quoted as saying in 1590, "She sees thou hast fethred thy nest, and hast crowns in thy purse." First attested in the United States in *Wonder Working* (1654).

1553. We will feather our nests ere time may us espy. —*A Merry Interlude Entitled Respublica*

1611. By my faith the fool has feathered his nest well. —Thomas Middleton, *The Roaring Girl*

1922. Feathered his nest well. —James Joyce, *Ulysses*

1989. "We must have a system that is not going to involve members having to vote to increase their own pay and feather their own nest," Mr. Wertheimer said. —*New York Times*

1991. Representative Burton said the group did not tell Mr. Kemp they were sending the letter this weekend, for fear that he would be accused of conspiring to "feather his own nest," as Mr. Burton put it. —*New York Times*

1993. Feather Your Nest at ABC, During Our Pre-Season Down Sale. —Ad for ABC Carpet & Home, *New York Times*

1995. CHICKEN KING TYSON ACCUSED OF FEATHERING HIS NEST —Headline, *New York Post*

Feed a cold; starve a fever. Eat well if you want to recover from a cold but abstain from food to recover from a fever. Also sometimes construed to mean that eating well will allay a fever in cold sufferers. The proverb is found in print as early as 1574 in *Short Dictionary* by J. Withals. First attested in the United States in *The Celebrated Jumping Frog of Calaveras County* (1865) by Mark Twain. The saying is found in varying forms: *Feed a cold and starve a fever; Starve a fever, feed a cold,* etc.

1865. It was policy to "feed a cold and starve a fever." —Mark Twain, *The Celebrated Jumping Frog of Calaveras County*

1991. You starve a fever, feed a cold. —*Wall Street Journal*

1992. A 76-year-old Federal policy of feeding American roads while starving its rails has led to traffic gridlock, highway carnage, air pollution and dependence on foreign oil. —*New York Times*

Fifty million Frenchmen can't be wrong. The saying originated with the American Expeditionary Force soldiers under Gen. Pershing during World War I (1917–18). The U.S. sided with France, and the American troops justified their participation in the war by saying that fifty million Frenchmen could never be wrong. The saying was made famous by the song, "Fifty Million Frenchmen" (1927), written by Billy Rose and Willie Ruskin and popularized by torch singer Sophie Tucker (1884–1966). The phrase is also attributed to American actress Texas Guinan (Mary Louise Cecilia Guinan, 1884–1933). When she and her troupe were refused entry into France in 1931, she was quoted as saying, "It goes to show that fifty million Frenchmen *can* be wrong." Some sources attribute this catchy phrase to Jack Osterman and Mae West. In 1929, Cole Porter's musical *Fifty Million Frenchmen* opened on Broadway; it was his first Broadway hit.

1983. FIFTY MILLION FRENCHMEN. —Headline of an article describing the misfortune of driving French highways in August, *Boston Globe*

1993. Fifty million Frenchmen can't be wrong. So why doesn't the United Nations follow their example and have its own version of the French Foreign Legion? —*Sun-Sentinel* (South Florida)

Fight fire with fire. Respond to harsh or underhanded attacks with similar methods; use tough methods with tough people; fight like with like. The proverb has been traced to Shakespeare's *Coriolanus* (1607–08). First attested in the United States in *Redskins* (1846) by James Fenimore Cooper.

> **1607–08.**
> > *Aufidius:* One fire drives out one fire; one nail, one nail;
> > Rights by rights falter, strengths by strengths do fail.
> > —Shakespeare, *Coriolanus*, Act IV: Scene vii

1952. "Oh, now listen, I'm not going to turn in any bad report on that—"
"It's the way *he* plays. Fight fire with fire."
—Kurt Vonnegut, Jr., *Player Piano*

1987. *Plaques for blacks plaques for blacks plaques for blacks plaques for blacks.* Now the vile phrase was running through his mind. *Plaques for blacks* was a small way of fighting fire with fire. —Tom Wolfe, *The Bonfire of the Vanities*

1993. Mr. Rollins implied that the Republicans were just fighting fire with fire—greasing palms already greased by the Democrats. —*Times* (Trenton)

1994. SENATOR DECIDES TO FIGHT N.R.A.'S FIRE WITH FIRE —Headline, *New York Times*

Figures don't lie. Numbers are indisputable. The proverb has been traced in the United States back to *Colonial Currency* (1739). Charles H. Grosvenor (1833–1917), Congressman of Ohio, was known for his ability to forecast the results of presidential elections. He countered the notion that figures could be interpreted differently by different people with the saying, "Figures won't lie, but liars will figure," and thus became known as "Old Figures." The proverb is found in varying forms: *Facts don't lie; Figures don't lie, but liars can figure; Mathematics cannot lie; Pictures don't lie; Statistics don't lie, people do*, etc.

1993. Figures don't lie, but figures can be selectively interpreted to suit someone's objectives.

—*The Princeton Packet*

1994. Statistics Don't Lie, People Do. Finally, someone said it. Ever since the first economic statistics bubbled forth from that primordial computer, politicians have twisted them, put bows in their hair, buried them or shouted them—always making the facts fit their fancy. —*New York Times*

1995. The facts don't lie. The Big Three want to ban Japanese auto imports while they ignore the Japanese market. —Ad for JAMA, *New York Times*

Finders keepers, losers weepers. The finder of a lost object can keep it; the person who lost it is out of luck. The proverb was first attested in this form in *Glossary of North Country Words* (1825) by J. T. Brockett. Its first use in the United States dates to 1874, in *The Circuit Rider* by E. Eggleston. The shortened versions *Finders keepers* and *Losers weepers* are considered colloquial variants of the earlier proverb *Findings keepings*, which dates back to 1595 (*Country Errors in Harley* by A. Cooke).

1960. "What you reckon we oughta do, Jem?" Finders were keepers unless title was proven. —Harper Lee, *To Kill a Mockingbird*

1980. Finders Weepers. —Title of a book by Miriam Chaikin

1991. IRAN TO IRAQ: MINDERS KEEPERS —Headline, *Time*

1993. "The law of finds applies in international waters, in essence 'finders keepers,'" Hess said. —*Times* (Trenton)

Findings keepings. *See* FINDERS KEEPERS, LOSERS WEEPERS.

Fine feathers make fine birds. Attractive clothes make the person wearing them attractive as well. The proverb has been traced to *Treasury of the French Tongue* (1592) by G. Delamothe. First cited in the United States in *Writings of George Washington* (1783). The proverb is found in varying forms, some negative: *Fair feathers make fair fowl; Fine feathers do not make fine birds; It's not the feather that makes the bird; It takes more than fine feathers to make fine birds*, etc. The French equivalent is *La belle plume fait le bel oiseau*.

1913. Fine feathers make fine birds. —Theodore Dreiser, *A Traveler at Forty*

1987. Sometimes you will hear someone say, "Fine feathers do not make fine birds." This expression comes from the fable of the ugly bird who, coming upon some peacock feathers lying on the ground, put them all together and then tied them to his tail in order to make himself more beautiful. Then he tried to associate with the other peacocks, but the peacocks soon discovered the trick, attacked him, and killed him. —Robert J. Dixson, *Complete Course in English*

1990. "She's all dressed up and nowhere to go." "Nowadays it takes more than fine feathers to make a fine bird." —Overheard at a school recess

See also ALL THAT GLITTERS IS NOT GOLD; APPEARANCES (LOOKS) ARE DECEIVING (DECEPTIVE).

Fingers were made before forks. You can hold food in your hands; you don't need utensils. This proverb is used as an excuse for eating with fingers. It has been traced back to the sixteenth century. We find the proverb in its current form in Swift's *Polite Conversation* (1738): "Fingers were made before forks, and hands before knives." Forks, by the way, came into general use in England following Queen Elizabeth's death in 1603, and Swift regarded the proverb as already a cliché.

1922. Zoe (*tears open the silverfoil*): Fingers were made before forks. (*She breaks off and nibbles a piece to Kitty Ricketts and then turns kittenishly to Lynch*) No objection to French lozenges? (*He nods. She taunts him.*) —James Joyce, *Ulysses*

1934. As they truly used to say to me in my youth… fingers were made before forks—and teeth were used before fingers. —Agatha Christie, *Why Didn't They Ask Evans?*

1957. And she thought that the Gunpowder Plot involved poisoning the Parliament with toadstools because she had learned on a nature walk that fungus was made before Fawkes. —Ogden Nash, *The New Yorker*

Fire in the belly. Energy; drive; passion; potential for accomplishment. The saying originated in the United States in the late twentieth century and gained currency in the 1984 presidential campaign.

1991. *Fire in the Belly (On Being a Man).* —Title of a best-selling book by Sam Keen

1993. Randy Tyree, the Democrats' 1982 nominee for Tennessee governor, has stunned party leaders by saying he intends to run again next year. Tyree, former mayor of Knoxville, told the quarterly convention of Tennessee's Democratic Party Friday night that he remains motivated for another run for office. "The fire's in my belly," he said. —*Commercial Appeal* (Memphis Tennessee)

1995. Exhorted by Sen. Robert Byrd to show "steel in its spine and fire in its belly," the Senate's Democratic minority Thursday blocked Republicans on one of the first major tests of the new Congress. —*New York Times*

1997. Tim Larson, known everywhere in the community, from town hall to the battlefields, announced Wednesday that he intends to run for mayor. "I'm starting to get the fire in my belly," he said. —*Hartford Courant*

1997. McNamara, who is among party leaders miffed at Big Labor's "premature" endorsement, said of a possible Stupak candidacy. "I don't think it's all that far-fetched. He'd probably do very well… If he had fire in the belly." —*Detroit News*

1998. On "[She's] Gone," [Eric] Clapton wrote with lead in his pencil and performs it with grit in his voice and guitar-fire in his belly. —*New York Post*

Fire is a good servant but a bad a master. Fire is helpful when under control but very dangerous when we lose control of it. The proverb dates back to the sixteenth century in the form: "Water is a very good servant, but it is a cruel master." "Why, Fire and Water are good Servants, but they are very bad Masters," noted Jonathan Swift in his *Polite Conversation* (1738). Thomas Carlyle thought that "fire is the best of servants, but what a master!" (*Past and Present*, 1843). He went on to say that "Mammon is like fire: the usefulest of all servants, if the frightfulest of all masters!" The adage was first attested in the United States in the late seventeenth century.

1948. "Fire is a good servant but a bad master." So runs the proverb. I remember hearing it said in the long ago. —H. Beston, *Northern Farm*

1969. Fire and fear, good servants, bad lords. —U. K. Le Guin, *Left Hand of Darkness*

1973. Is not whisky a wonderful thing? But like fire, a good servant but a bad master. —J. Caird, *Murder Remote*

First catch your rabbit and then make your stew. Make any necessary preparations before beginning a project. The proverb is sometimes attributed to Mrs. Hannah Glasse's *Art of Cookery Made Plain and Easy* (1747) or Mrs. Beeton's *Book of Household Management* (1851), but the proverb is found as far back as 1250: "It is commonly said that one must first catch the deer, and afterwards, when he has been caught, skin him." Similar proverbs can be found in many foreign languages.

1863. The great Ulysses—the Yankee generalissimo surnamed Grant—has expressed his intention of dining in Vicksburg on... the Fourth of July... Ulysses must get into the city before he dines in it. The way to cook a rabbit is "first catch the rabbit." —*Daily Citizen* (Vicksburg, Mississippi)

1930. You can't make a Welch rabbit, you know, without first catching your hare. —W. Woodrow, *Moonhill*

1961. "You mean you're going to go on trying?"
   "Strictly speaking," said Miss Marple, "I haven't begun yet. 'First catch your hare' as Mrs. Beeton says in her cooking book." —Agatha Christie, *Miss Marple's Final Cases*
See also DON'T COUNT YOUR CHICKENS BEFORE THEY ARE HATCHED; DON'T SHOUT UNTIL YOU ARE OUT OF THE WOODS; THERE'S MANY A SLIP BETWEEN (THE) CUP AND (THE) LIP.

First come, first served. The first person to arrive, contribute, etc., will be the first person dealt with. The saying has been traced back to about 1219–33: "He who comes first, eats first" (Eike von Repkow) and is similar to the thirteenth-century French: *Qui ainçois vient au molin ainçois doit moldre* ("He who comes first to the mill may grind first"). The phrase appears in Chaucer's *Wife of Bath's Tale* (1390): "He who comes first to the mill, grinds first." First attested in the United States in *Thomas Hutchinson Papers* (1630). The proverb is often used as an attributive in the phrase *on a first-come, first-served basis*. It may be shortened to *it's first come.*

1945. *First Come, First Kill.* —Title of a book by F. Allan

1966. Extending democratic principles to etiquette, Jefferson established the rule of pell-mell at official social functions—that is, first come, first served. —Thomas A. Bailey, *The American Pageant*

1983. Starting today, special benefit tickets for the May 24th celebration are available on a first-come, first-served basis. —*New York Times*

1991. "The firm has a chalet in Vail, a cabin on a lake in Manitoba and two condos on Seven Mile Beach on Grand Cayman Island. They're free, but you need to book early. Partners get priority. After that it's first come." —John Grisham, *The Firm*

1993. In the years before the lottery, spaces were awarded on a first-come, first-served basis, and the night before registration, immigrants would sneak into the church and sleep there, in line. —*New York Times*
See also THE EARLY BIRD CATCHES THE WORM.

First, do no harm. Do not harm the sick person in the course of treatment. Said to have been the first principle of Hippocrates when teaching the physicians of ancient Greece. The saying is often cited in Latin: *Primum non nocere.* Part of the Hippocratic Oath sworn by all physicians.

c.460–377 b.c.
As to diseases make a habit of two things—to help, or at least, to do no harm. —Hippocrates, *Epidemics*

1859. It may seem a strange principle to enunciate as the very first requirement in a Hospital that it should do the sick no harm. —Florence Nightingale, *Notes on Hospitals*

1991. "First, do no harm" is a maxim drilled into would-be doctors by their teachers in medical school. But that adage often fails to get through to the folks who make and sign the laws of the land. —*Times* (Trenton)

1993. The system begs for reform, but any plan must proceed with the same injunction Hippocrates laid down for the physicians of ancient Greece: "First, do no harm." —*Times* (Trenton)

1994. New York City's great teaching hospitals are a national treasure that needs to be protected. First, in the words of the Hippocratic Oath, do no harm. —Daniel Patrick Moynihan, *New York Times*

First impressions are the most lasting. One's immediate reaction to something new is what will endure in the memory. The phrase appeared in William Congreve's play *The Way of the World* (1700). First attested in the United States in *Life of Peter Van Schaack* (1786). The proverb is found in varying forms: *First impressions are lasting; First impressions are important; The first impression is the most lasting,* etc. Often shortened to *first impressions* or *one's first impression.*

1948. But when I first met him he was such a cheerful fellow, a regular Pollyanna, I figured he could get along with anyone. First impressions, it doesn't pay to follow them. Someone like Brown, he's too sure of himself, he goes on first impressions, that's why he has it in for me. —Norman Mailer, *The Naked and the Dead*

1964. *This is room 304. My name is on the board: Miss Barrett. I'll have you for homeroom all term, and I hope to meet some of you in my English classes. Now, someone once said that first impressions—*
   English! No wonder!
   Who needs it?

You give homework?

First impressions, they say, are lasting. —Bel Kaufman, *Up the Down Staircase*

1984. First impressions die slowly, bad impressions take even longer. —Joseph Heller, *God Knows*

1993. If first impressions mean anything, then Rutgers should be just fine this season. —*Times* (Trenton)

1994. As a high-profile lawyer in Los Angeles for clients like Johnny Carson and Jack Nicholson, Mr. Shapiro includes in a biographical brochure a copy of an article he wrote last year. It is titled, "Using the Media to Your Advantage." He wrote, "The first impression the public gets is usually the one that is most important." —*New York Times*

See also ALWAYS PUT YOUR BEST FOOT FORWARD.

First in war, first in peace, first in the hearts of his countrymen. The phrase was first used by General Henry Lee (1756–1818) in a funeral oration for George Washington given in the House of Representatives in December 1799. Lee had served under Washington in the Revolutionary War and was deeply devoted to him. His saying caught on and is used to this day.

1969. We salute Dwight David Eisenhower standing there in our memories—first in war, first in peace and, wherever freedom is cherished, first in the hearts of his fellow men. —Richard Nixon, on the death of Dwight David Eisenhower, quoted by Stephen E. Ambrose, *Nixon*

1974. Washington [Senators], first in war, first in peace, last in the American League. —Quoted in Howard Cosell, *Like It Is*

1993. A popular baseball saying in another era went, "Washington ... first in war, first in peace, last in the American League." ... Now it's "The Mets ... last in the National League, last in intelligence, first in apologies." —Murray Chass, *New York Times*

The first one hundred years are the hardest. Getting started is the most difficult part of any undertaking; it is easier to continue something than to begin. The proverb has been traced in the United States to *Raiders of the Deep* (1928) by L. Thomas. It is found in varying forms: *The first hundred years are the hardest; The first nine months (years) are the hardest; The first year is the worst,* etc. The word *one* may be omitted and the number of years is often changed. The proverb is often used as a consolation in regard to a marriage or a new job. Responding to a reporter's

question on the eve of his fourth inauguration as president on January 19, 1945, Franklin D. Roosevelt said, "The first twelve years are the hardest."

1876–1933.
Life's a tough proposition, and the 1st hundred years are the hardest. —Wilson Mizner, quoted by David Wallechinsky & Irving Wallace, *The People's Almanac*

1971. The First Nine Months Are the Hardest. —Title of a TV special about pregnancy, *People*

1991. Kay reached across the table and gently took Abby's hand. "It'll be okay," she said with a firm smile and a wise look. "The first year is the hardest." —John Grisham, *The Firm*

See also THE FIRST STEP IS THE HARDEST.

The first step is the hardest. The most difficult part of any undertaking is the decision to begin. The proverb has been traced back to *Sir Thomas More* (c.1596) by A. Munday, but it was popularized in the seventeenth century. According to legend, in response to an account by Cardinal de Polignac, of the martyred Saint Denis's miraculous long walk from Montmartre to St. Denis, two miles north of Paris, with his decapitated head in his hands, the Marquise du Deffand (1697–1780) remarked, *"Il n'y a que le premier pas qui coûte"* ("It is only the first step that costs"). In a letter to Madame du Deffand, dated January 24, 1764, Voltaire indicates that she coined the phrase. Hence the French proverb *C'est le premier pas qui coûte.* The Russian version is Только первый шаг труден ("It is only the first step that is difficult"). The English proverb is found in varying forms: *It's the first step that counts; It's the first step that costs; It's the first step that is difficult; The first step is always the hardest; The first mile is always the hardest,* etc.

1992. "Great jobs," his dad cheers. "Let go," he urges his son. "You can do it. The first step is the hardest, the second will be easier." —*Family Circle*

1993. Mr. Leggett said THA is also studying ways, including fencing, to control and limit traffic at the sites. "This is just the first step," Mr. Leggett said. —*Times* (Trenton)

See also THE FIRST ONE HUNDRED YEARS ARE THE HARDEST; A JOURNEY OF A THOUSAND MILES BEGINS WITH ONE STEP.

First things first. A sense of priorities is important; basic things must take precedence. The proverb has been traced to *First Things First* (1844) by G. Jackson. First attested in the United States in

House of Storm (1941) by Mignon G. Eberhart. The word *put* may precede the proverb.

1933. Through this program of action we address ourselves to putting our own national house in order and making income balance outgo. Our international trade relations, though vastly important, are in point of time and necessity secondary to the establishment of a sound national economy. I favor as a practical policy the putting of first things first. —Franklin D. Roosevelt, First Inaugural Address

1957. "Well, first things first. What's your full name?" —Nevil Shute, *On the Beach*

1962. "Well, first things first," Fipps said amiably. "Everybody in the house likes the book. Or at least is impressed." —Herman Wouk, *Youngblood Hawke*

1984. There are 11 weeks between the trials here and the Olympic marathon. Some runners fear that if they run too fast here they will not have enough time to recover sufficiently for the Olympics.... "Who cares?" said Meyer. "If you don't run 2:09 here, you don't run in L.A. First things first, and the rest will take care of itself." —*New York Times*

1988. She hooked her finger under his belt. "First things first. I'd feel awful if I thought I was a one-night stand." —Nelson DeMille, *The Charm School*

1991. No! She had to put first things first. —Alexandra Ripley, *Scarlett*

1993. First things first, he [President Clinton] says, not only to Mr. Yeltsin but to anyone who insists that he has to attend to foreign policy first. —*New York Times*

1994. These days, in addition to her busy professional life, Ms. Nadler finds that she now makes more time for her family. "Now I'm putting first things first." —*Princeton Business Journal*

Fish or cut bait. Make a choice now: either fish or "cut bait" and go home. *Cut bait* means stop fishing. In other words, do your job or let somebody else do it. Originated in the United States in the nineteenth century among fishermen. Later the saying could be heard even in Congress. On August 5, 1876, Joseph Gurney Cannon, Congressman of Illinois, calling on the House to adopt a monetary bill, said, "Now I want you gentlemen on the other side of the House to 'fish or cut bait.'" The saying is found in various forms: *It's fish or cut bait; One has got to fish or cut bait; There is a time to fish and a time to cut bait,* etc.

1977. "So Liddy and Hunt apparently came to see Chuck Colson, and Colson picked up the telephone and called Magruder and said, 'You all either fish or cut bait. This is absurd to have these guys over there and not using them.'" —Victor Lasky, *It Didn't Start with Watergate*

1985. "Vale's not as bad as *that,*" Cantor argued. "With him on the board, we can fight off Corsini easy. If Marty and I had a choice, okay, but we don't have a choice. It's fish or cut bait." —Michael Korda, *Queenie*

1986. Reluctant to give it up, the next year I accepted a position as a visiting professor of business in a university in San Diego, and took a leave of absence from Michigan. In the winter of that second year, Michigan said, "Come home!" What they actually said was, "Fish or cut bait." —Judith M. Bardwick, *The Plateauing Trap*

1993. When it comes to flagging brands, "companies are being forced to fish or cut bait," said Clive Chajet, chairman of Lipponcott & Margulies, a New York marketing and corporate identity company. —*New York Times*

See also HE WHO HESITATES IS LOST; SHIT OR GET OFF THE POT.

A fish out of water. A person who is out of place, in an awkward or noncustomary situation. The phrase dates back to about 1380. Often used after *to be* or *feel like.* It is found in Latin as *Mus in matella* ("A mouse in the pot"), as well as in other languages. In German, the phrase is identical to English: *Wie ein* (or *der*) *Fisch auf dem Trockenen* ("Like a fish out of water").

1679. I am, out of the ladies' company, like a fish out of the water. —Thomas Shadwell, *A True Widow*

1936. "It isn't losing their money, my pet. I tell you it's losing their world—the world they were raised in. They're like fish out of water or cats with wings." —Margaret Mitchell, *Gone With the Wind*

1986. Hirshhorn, I take for granted, would have been a fish out of water on any art acquisition committee. —*Smithsonian*

1994. I felt like a fish out of water. I guess that when I was in the hospital, trying to throw off the effect of a backlash of the brain, I felt an empathy for the way a fish must feel when it has just been lifted into the boat. —*Times* (Trenton)

A fish stinks from the head. The proverb is based on the fact that a fish literally begins to spoil at the head. Once the head begins to rot, the entire body follows. As a figure of speech, it means that any problem in an organization can be traced back to the boss. The proverb is found in

Civil Conversation (1574) by S. Guazzo. First found in the United States in *Account of Voyage to New England* (1674). The proverb is found in varying forms: *A fish rots from the head; A rotten fish stinks from the head; Fish begin to stink from the head; Fish begin to stink from the head, men at the feet; Fish goes rotten from the head; The fish always stinks from the head down(ward),* etc.

1988. Michael Dukakis … tried not to attack President Reagan directly, but he could not resist saying "A fish rots from the head".... —*Washington Times*

1989. "Katyn: Our Shame," read one sign in the Moscow demonstration. It referred to the killings of thousands of Polish officers in a Soviet forest during World War II, a massacre that most historians say was the work of the Russians, and not the Nazis, as the Soviets have asserted.... "Fish begin to stink at the head," read another sign, echoing a protest that early Communists once directed at the Czar. —*New York Times*

Fish where the fish are. Search where you are likely to find what you seek. The proverb is of recent origin.

1980. THE FORD STYLE ON REBATE—WE FISH WHERE THE FISH ARE BITING —Headline, *Boston Globe*

1982. "Marketing 101 says you fish where the fish are," adds Brown. "There are 50 million smokers in the U.S.; just 2 million have some relationship to Camel. With such a huge universe out there, there's no need to take liberties with the law or our own ethics. We're playing according to Hoyle." —*New York Magazine*

1992. Metro-North and its agency, Korey, Kay & Partners in New York, are putting a new twist on the marketing adage to "fish where the fish are." The commuter railroad is sponsoring outdoor advertisements, situated where it believes potential customers—frustrated drivers who might prefer taking the train—are sure to see it: for instance, alongside the Bruckner Expressway, a major artery for commuters from Connecticut and Westchester. —*New York Times*

1997. "The success of some preschool shows in driving licensing and product sales is extraordinary," says Marjorie Kaplan, who oversees children's programming at the Discovery Networks. "When something like Barney comes along, it changes what the world can expect from preschool success. People tend to fish where the fish are." The creators of Barney caught a lot of fish: he has sold 44 million videos, 34 million books, and countless Barney and Baby Bop plush toys.—*Time*
See also GO HUNTING WHERE THE DUCKS ARE.

A fishing expedition. An investigation that has no clearly defined objective and often uses questionable methods in the hope of uncovering incriminating or newsworthy evidence. Such investigation often turns into a political witch-hunt. The saying comes from literal "fishing expeditions" when people fish for anything they can catch. The figurative use of the saying dates back to the early twentieth century.

1980. Under repeated challenges at the April 9 government press conference, spokesmen for the [German] Defense and Interior ministries categorically denied that any blanket investigation of all draftees is planned. They insist that no "fishing expedition" is intended but they must prevent entry into "security-sensitive units and positions" by any soldier with a pre-induction record of "security-endangering efforts and acts." —*Christian Science Monitor*

1980. Sears, Roebuck, Montgomery Ward and K Mart say the FTC has authorized a new hunt of company files even as it was clear that Congress wanted the "fishing expedition" to stop. —*Boston Globe*

1982. In reference to further investigations into the Kennedy assassinations, he [Rep. James C. Wright Jr. (D) of Texas] said: "I think there has to be a demonstration that this is not going to be a broad, freewheeling, headline-grabbing attempt to splurge and send investigators willy-nilly like the headless horseman in all directions, like a fishing expedition costing $6.5 million." —*Christian Science Monitor*

1998. STARR'S FISHING EXPEDITION IN D.C. SHOULD BE DEEP-SIXED. —Headline, *Detroit News*

1998. Representative James H. Maloney was in the minority of the minority yesterday as the Connecticut Democrat voted with 30 other House Democrats and 227 Republicans for a wide-ranging impeachment inquiry of the president. He said he believed the inquiry resolution crafted by Republicans on the Watergate model was too broad and could result in a "fishing expedition."—*Boston Globe*

Flowers leave fragrance in the hand that bestows them. The donor benefits from the gift as much as the recipient. *Flowers leave part of their fragrance in the hand that bestows them* is a variant of the proverb.

1991. As artists find joy in giving beauty to others, so anyone who masters the art of praising will find that it blesses the giver as much as the receiver. There is truth in the saying, "Flowers leave part of their fragrance in the hand that bestows them." —*Reader's Digest*

1993. As I write this letter, my husband of 18 years is living with his girlfriend and her children from a former marriage.... I endured the pain, but chose to be forgiving. In doing so, I was able to smell the fragrance of the violet that clung to the heel of the person who had crushed it. —Abigail Van Buren, "Dear Abby," *Times* (Trenton)

A fool and his money are soon parted. A foolish person will quickly lose, be duped out of, or spend whatever money he gets. The proverb has been traced to *Five Hundreth Pointes of Good Husbandry* by Thomas Tusser (c.1524–80). First cited in the United States in *Boston in 1682 and 1699* (1699). It is found in various forms: *A fool and his money soon part; A fool and his words are soon parted; A fool and his money soon part company; Fools and their money are soon parted,* etc. Often shortened to *a fool and his money.*

1764. A fool and his words are soon parted. —William Shenstone, *Works in Verse and Prose*

1939. A widow and her money are soon married. —Lewis & Faye Copeland, *10,000 Jokes, Toasts and Stories*

1979. Life goes on, yes—and a fool and his self-respect are soon parted, perhaps never to be reunited on Judgment Day. —Kurt Vonnegut, Jr., *Jailbird*

1991. *A Fool and His Money.* —Title of a book by John Rothchild

1991. *At the bank:* "Why is it that a fool and his money never appear when you need a loan?" —Quoted in *Reader's Digest*

1993. A fool and his money are some party. —"New York Magazine Competition," *New York,* quoted in *Reader's Digest*

1994. "How did a fool and his money get together in the first place?" —Joey Adams, "Strictly for Laughs," *New York Post*

A fool can ask more questions in an hour than a wise man can answer in seven years. People with little knowledge should hold their tongues. The proverb has been traced back to *Italian Proverbs* (1666) by G. Torriano. First cited in the United States in *Further Quaeries* (1690). The proverb is found in varying forms: *A fool can ask more questions in a minute than a wise man can answer in an hour; A fool may ask more questions than a wise man cares to answer;*

Fools ask questions that wise men cannot answer, etc.

1738. "Miss, can you tell which is the white Goose?" ... "They say, a Fool will ask more Questions than the wisest body can answer." —Jonathan Swift, *Polite Conversation*

1939. *Professor:* A fool can ask more questions than a wise man can answer.

Student: No wonder so many of us flunk in our exams! —Lewis & Faye Copeland, *10,000 Jokes, Toasts and Stories*

1992. "Is the economy stupid, Mr. Congressman?"

"The answer is no, but you certainly are. You always ask more questions than a wise man can answer." —Overheard at an election rally in New York City

Fool me once, shame on you; fool me twice, shame on me. Anyone who falls for the same deceit twice must accept responsibility for his own gullibility; thus, one should be more watchful the next time around. Originally a child's saying. The same idea can be found in similar proverbs: *If a bee stings you once, it's the bee's fault; if a bee stings you twice, it's your own damn fault; If anyone betrays you once, it's his fault; if he betrays you twice, it's your fault; If people take advantage of you once, shame on them; if they take advantage of you twice, shame on you; Trick me once, shame on you; Trick me twice, shame on me!*

1988. Remember the old child's refrain, "Fool me once, shame on thee. Fool me twice, shame on me." —Robert Packwood, "Are the Arabs Ready to Promise and Deliver Peace for Land?" *Jewish Week* (N.Y.)

1990. Patricia Volk admitted she has had 11 wallets stolen. I had my purse stolen once (I've lived here 14 years) when it was on the back of my chair in a restaurant (my first year in New York City). When I reported it to the police, they ran down a list of "don'ts" concerning purses. What's that old saying, "Fool me once, shame on you; fool me twice, shame on me." Fool me 11 times, come on! —Letters to the Editor, *New York Times Magazine*

1992. I've learned as a boy, "Fool me once, shame on you; fool me twice, shame on me." —Bill Clinton, *World News Now,* ABC

1994. In the old neighborhood in Queens, there's an expression that went something like this: Fool me once, shame on you; fool me twice, shame on me. —Mario Cuomo, referring to his opponent's tax-cut plan, quoted in *New York Times*

See also FOOLS RUSH IN WHERE ANGELS FEAR TO TREAD; YOU CAN FOOL SOME OF THE PEOPLE ALL THE TIME, ALL THE PEOPLE SOME OF THE TIME, BUT YOU CANNOT FOOL ALL THE PEOPLE ALL THE TIME.

A foolish consistency is the hobgoblin of little minds. Only petty and narrow-minded people are inflexible in their judgments. The proverb was coined by Ralph Waldo Emerson in his essay "Self-Reliance" (1841). It can also be found in varying forms: *Consistency is the hobgoblin of little minds; Consistency is the product of small minds,* etc.

> **1841.** A foolish consistency is the hobgoblin of little minds, adored by little statesmen and philosophers and divines. With consistency a great soul has simply nothing to do. —Ralph Waldo Emerson, "Self-Reliance"

> **1988.** "But I'm supposed to be smart, right?"
> "Right."
> "Still, consistency is the product of small minds, isn't that so?"
> "Within reasonable boundaries." —Robert Ludlum, *The Icarus Agenda*

> **1994.** "You can say consistency is the hobgoblin of small minds and accuse me of having a small mind; I'll take it," he [Governor Cuomo] told reporters at a stop in Manhattan, referring to his opposition to capital punishment and his support for tax cuts. "But I have been consistent. Maybe consistently wrong in your book. But consistent. I don't invent positions for campaigns." —*New York Times*

Fools rush in where angels fear to tread. Impetuous people often act unwisely in areas where an expert would exercise reasonable caution. Coined in 1711 by the English poet Alexander Pope. In 1905, the British novelist E. M. Forster (1879–1970) titled his first novel *Where Angels Fear to Tread.* The proverb is first attested in the United States in *Life and Correspondence of James Iredell* (1789). It may take various forms: *Fools rush in where discreet angels fear to tread; Fools poke their noses where angels fear to tread; Fools step in where angels fear to tread; Men walk in where not only angels, but devils fear to tread, One rushes in where others fear to tread,* etc.

> **1711.** ... there they'll talk you dead;
> For Fools rush in where Angels fear to tread.
> Distrustful sense with modest caution
> speaks.
> —Alexander Pope, *An Essay on Criticism*

> **1922.** The horse was just then. And later on at a

propitious opportunity he purposed (Bloom did), without anyway prying into his private affairs on the *fools step in where angels* principle, advising him to sever his connection with a certain budding practitioner.... —James Joyce, *Ulysses*

> **1951.** "You havent changed a bit, have you, Prewitt?" he said sarcastically. "Havent learned a thing. Fools rush in where angels fear to re-enlist, as some great wit once said." —James Jones, *From Here to Eternity*

> **1987.** He [newsman Sam Donaldson] is the inventor of a kind of theater in which he (of course) stars—rushing in where even Dan Rather feared to tread. —*New Republic*

> **1990.** Fools rush in—and get all the best seats. —Quoted in *Reader's Digest*

> **1992.** Billionaire Ross Perot considers rushing in where no angels tread. —*People*

> **1993.** STAKING OUT NEW MARKETS WHERE MANY FEAR TO TREAD. —Headline in *New York Times*

See also FOOL ME ONCE, SHAME ON YOU; FOOL ME TWICE, SHAME ON ME.

Footprints on the sands of time. Great people leave their mark on history. Coined by the American poet Henry Wadsworth Longfellow (1807–82) in "A Psalm of Life" (1839). The saying may take varying forms: *Footprints on the sands of time are not made by sitting down; To leave footprints on the sands of time you must have plenty of sand; You can't put your footprints in the sands of time by sitting down,* etc.

> **1839.** Lives of great men all remind us
> We can make our lives sublime,
> And, departing, leave behind us
> Footprints on the sands of time.
> —Henry Wadsworth Longfellow, "A Psalm of Life"

> **1980.** "Remember: *Plot* is no more than footprints left in the snow *after* your characters have run by on their way to incredible destinations." —Ray Bradbury, "Zen in the Art of Writing," quoted in *New York Times Magazine*

> **1990.** When approached about it, Ford Motor wouldn't comment, saying the information was "legally privileged." And when Henry Ford's close friend Max Fisher was asked, he said, "Frankly, I have never heard of any of this before." It was a Morgan operation in the classic style of Teddy Granfell: it left no footprints behind. —Ron Chernow, *The House of Morgan*

> **1991.** ... environmentalists believe oil drilling at Prudhoe Bay has fatally scarred that area with a vast industrial complex.... "The footprint on the

land," Senator Wirth said, after visiting there, "has all the delicacy of dinosaur tracks." —*New York Times*

For want of a nail the kingdom was lost. In any undertaking, no detail is too small to ignore. The proverb has been traced back to *Confessio Amantis* (c.1390) by John Gower (d.1408). The saying is found in the late fifteenth-century French: *Par ung seul clou perd on ung bon cheval* ("By just one nail one loses a good horse"). In 1651, the saying was included in George Herbert's collection of proverbs: "For want of a nail the shoe is lost, for want of a shoe the horse is lost, for want of a horse the rider is lost." First attested in the United States in *Poor Richard's Almanac* (1757) by Benjamin Franklin. Listed in all major dictionaries of American proverbs.

1757. And again he [Poor Richard] adviseth to Circumspection and Care, even in the smallest Matters, because sometimes *a little Neglect may breed great Mischief;* adding, *For want of a Nail the Shoe was lost; for want of a Shoe the Horse was lost; and for want of a Horse the rider was lost,* being overtaken and slain by the Enemy, all for want of Care about a Horse-shoe Nail. —Benjamin Franklin, *Father Abraham's Speech, or, The Way to Wealth*

1957. Battles that were lost for want of a nail. —*Time*

1984. For want of a nail, believe it or not, a shoe may be lost, for want of the shoe a mule may be lost, for want of the mule a battle may be lost, and for want of the battle, who knows? —Joseph Heller, *God Knows.*

1988. He looked around. All he needed was a lousy two-kopek piece. *For want of a nail...* —Nelson DeMille, *The Charm School*

1991. Recently, reflecting public repugnance, the House voted overwhelmingly to overrule the Department of Health and Human Services. But Bush vetoed the bill and his veto was sustained. So like the horseshoe nail for want of which a kingdom was lost, a patently objectionable public policy originated in cloudy legislative drafting. —*Times* (Trenton)

1993. As human beings acquainted with Murphy's Law (whatever can go wrong usually does) and with the old verses about how a kingdom is lost for want of a horseshoe nail, we know intuitively that those who predict intricate outcomes are often in error. —*Times* (Trenton)

1994. For want of a question, an hour was lost. Only an hour? It could have been more. Because, if you don't ask, you might never know the complete array of resources available to you. —*U.S. 1* (Princeton)

For whom the bell tolls. Because civilization is a collective effort, the loss of the most insignificant life is a loss for all of us; thus, we are all in it together. Coined by John Donne in *Devotions upon Emergent Occasions* (1624). In 1940, it was used by Ernest Hemingway as the title of his novel about the Spanish Civil War.

1624. ...any man's death diminishes *me,* because I am involved in Mankind; And therefore never send to know for whom the bell tolls; It tolls for thee. —John Donne, "Meditation XVII," *Devotions upon Emergent Occasions*

1940. *For Whom the Bell Tolls.* —Title of a book by Ernest Hemingway

1980. *For whom the belle toils.* The average woman with a job outside the home spends 50 per cent less time on housework and child care than full-time housewives do. Nevertheless, she averages 10 hours a week less free time. —Mike Feinsilber & William B. Mead, *American Averages*

1988. "Then there is Ehrlich of the magic bullet aimed at syphilis. Ask not for whom Nobel tolled—it tolled for him in 1908." —Erich Segal, *Doctors*

1990. Ask not for whom the bell tolls; let the answering machine get it. —Quoted in *Reader's Digest*

1994. FOR WHOM THE JOB BELL DOESN'T TOLL —Headline of Robert Lewis's article on age discrimination, *AARP Bulletin*

See also NO MAN IS AN ISLAND.

Forbidden fruit is sweet. What is forbidden always seems to be more attractive and desirable than what is readily available. The saying refers to God's commandment to Adam that he could eat the fruit of every tree in the Garden of Eden except the tree of the knowledge of good and evil. In English, the proverb has been traced back to Chaucer's *Parson's Tale* (c.1386). In 1667, the phrase was used by John Milton in *Paradise Lost.* First attested in the United States in *Pudd'nhead Wilson* (1893) by Mark Twain. The proverb is found in varying forms: *Forbidden fruit is the sweetest; Nothing is so good as forbidden fruit; Stolen fruit is always sweet; Stolen fruits are the sweetest,* etc. Often shortened to *forbidden fruit* or *stolen fruit.*

And the Lord God commanded the man, saying, Of

every tree of the garden thou mayest freely eat; But of the tree of the knowledge of good and evil, thou shalt not eat of it; for on the day that thou eatest thereof thou shalt surely die. —Genesis 2:16, *Authorized Version*, 1611

1667. Of Man's first disobedience, and the fruit
Of that forbidden tree whose mortal taste
Brought death into the world, and all our
   woe,
With loss of Eden.
            —John Milton, *Paradise Lost*

1893. Adam was but human—this explains it all. He did not want the apple for the apple's sake; he wanted it only because it was forbidden. —Mark Twain, *Pudd'nhead Wilson*

1981. If my mail is an accurate barometer, no one is too old to fool around. I hear from men and women in their eighties and nineties who confess sheepishly that they have a taste for "forbidden fruit." —Abigail Van Buren, *The Best of Dear Abby*

1986. "It was not an apple that Eve touched," he said, and he paused. "I think that the forbidden fruit is plutonium." —Pat Conroy, *The Prince of Tides*

See also STOLEN WATERS ARE SWEET.

Forewarned is forearmed. Knowledge of imminent danger can prepare us to overcome it. The Latin version is *Praemonitus, praemunitus.* The proverb has been traced to *Treatises of Fistula* (c. 1425) by J. Arderne. In 1615, it was used by Cervantes in *Don Quixote.* First attested in the United States in *History of New Hampshire* (1685). The proverb is found in a number of forms: *Forewarned, forearmed; Forewarned is quite often forearmed; To be forewarned is to be forearmed,* etc.

1947. *Blanche:* I'm writing a letter to Shep. *[She picks up the letter]* "Darling Shep. I am spending the summer on the wing, making flying visits here and there. And who knows, perhaps I shall take a sudden notion to *swoop* down on *Dallas!* How would you feel about that? Ha-ha! *[She laughs nervously and brightly, touching her throat as if actually talking to Shep]* Forewarned is forearmed, as they say!" —Tennessee Williams, *A Streetcar Named Desire*

1985. To be forewarned is to be forearmed. *Don't* be a has-been. If you've always believed "it's up or out," but you've found yourself in a position a few rungs down, make peace with your life. —Jacqueline Hornor with Karla Dougherty, *Divorcing a Corporation*

1988. "Forewarned, forearmed, Manny. You called. Is everything all right?"
"I should only call in a crisis?"
"You rarely call, period. That privilege is almost exclusively mine." —Robert Ludlum, *The Icarus Agenda*

1994. Dear Mr. Miller [president of the National Fire Protection Association]: I'm pleased to share your holiday safety advice with my readers, forewarned is forearmed. —Abigail Van Buren, "Dear Abby," *Times* (Trenton)

Forgive and forget. Put aside your hard feelings and don't hold grudges for past infractions. The saying dates back to about 1377 (*Piers Plowman* by William Langland). In 1546, it was included in John Heywood's collection of proverbs: "All our great fray ... is forgiven and forgotten between us quite." It appears in Shakespeare's *King Lear* (1605) and Cervantes' *Don Quixote* (1605–15). First attested in the United States in *Apologia of Robert Keane* (1653).

1605. *Lear:* You must bear with me:
Pray you now, forget and forgive: I am old
   and foolish.
        —Shakespeare, *King Lear*, IV, vii

1605–15.
Let us forget and forgive injuries. —Cervantes, *Don Quixote*

1936. Rhett's boats were singularly lucky both in taking out cotton for the Confederacy and bringing in the war materials for which the South was desperate. Yes, the ladies felt they could forgive and forget a great many things for such a brave man. —Margaret Mitchell, *Gone With the Wind*

1960. "Well, I always say forgive and forget, forgive and forget." —Harper Lee, *To Kill a Mockingbird*

1980. During his climb, he has assumed the veneer of a civilized servant of the people; but underneath, he was a gutter fighter, a man who neither forgot nor forgave. —Sidney Sheldon, *Rage of Angels*

1984. "You know how crazy he is," Jonathan tried to explain. "He forgives and forgets."
"And then he forgets he's forgiven," I replied. —Joseph Heller, *God Knows*

1987. "Okay, boil it down for me, Mike [Deaver]. Exactly what message am I now sending to the Jews?"
"Never forget."
"And my message to the Germans?"
"Forgive and forget."
—G. B. Trudeau, *Doonesbury Deluxe*

1989. Brooke forgot nothing and forgave nothing. —Michael Korda, *The Fortune*

Fortune favors the brave. People who act decisively make their own fate. The proverb dates back to the Romans and is found in Ennius (239–169 b.c.), Terence (190–159 b.c.), Virgil (70–19 b.c.), and Pliny the Elder (a.d. 23–79). Chaucer used it in *Troilus and Criseyde* (c.1374). First attested in the United States in *History of Indian Wars in New England* (1677). The phrase takes various forms: *Fortune favors the bold; Fortune favors the audacious; Fortune favors the daring; Fortune favors the brave and the foolish*, etc.

1966. If Jones had lost I doubt whether he could have paid, but fortune even in the twentieth century does sometimes favour the brave. —Graham Greene, *The Comedians*

1984. I was already fully mobilized and searching for new worlds to conquer. Here was tougher game. Fortune favors the brave. —Joseph Heller, *God Knows*

1991. She is always willing to meet new challenges and strongly believes in the old adage that fortune favors the brave. —Overheard at a party in Princeton, N.J.

See also FAINT HEART NEVER WON FAIR LADY; HE WHO HESITATES IS LOST; NOTHING VENTURED, NOTHING GAINED.

Frailty, thy name is woman! Women by nature are weak, hence they are unreliable and may be duplicitous. The phrase first appears in Shakespeare's *Hamlet* (1600–01).

1600–01.
Hamlet: Let me think on't: Frailty, thy name is woman! —Shakespeare, *Hamlet*, I, ii

1922. Bloom *(quickly)* Yes, yes. You mean that I … Sleep reveals the worst side of everyone, children perhaps excepted. I know I fell out of bed or rather was pushed. Steel wine is said to cure snoring. For the rest there is that English invention, pamphlet of which I received some days ago, incorrectly addressed. It claims to afford a noiseless, inoffensive vent. *(he sighs)* 'Twas ever thus. Frailty, thy name is marriage. —James Joyce, *Ulysses*

1992. While "stars" wrestle with such agonizing decisions as whether to undergo liposuction, rhinoplasty or breast-implant surgery, the rest of us must deal with more mundane decisions, such as finding solutions to the recession, poverty, unemployment, crime and homelessness. Why don't these self-indulgent primps face the fact that aging

is a part of life? Vanity, thy name is Hollywood. —Letters to the Editor, *People*

1993. AUDACITY, THY NAME IS LYDIA —Headline of a review of *Lydia, Queen of Palestine*, New York *Times Book Review*

A friend in need is a friend indeed. Real friends stand by and support one another through thick and thin. In time of need or hardship it's easy to see who our real friends are. First recorded by Ennius (239–169 b.c.). Included in the *Durham Proverbs* (1035), the *Proverbs of Alfred* (1275), and William Hazlitt's collection of English proverbs (1821). First attested in the United States in *Winthrop Papers* (1640). Kin Hubbard (1868–1930) put a radical spin on the proverb by saying, *A friend that ain't in need is a friend indeed.* Often shortened to *a friend in need.*

1782. The man that hails you Tom or Jack,
And proves by thumps upon your back
How he esteems your merit,
Is such a friend, that one had need
Be very much his friend indeed
To pardon or to bear it.
        —William Cowper, "Friendship"

1982. "A friend in need is a pest." Fafhrd —Robert Asprin, *Myth Directions*

1986. For six years now, it has been said that President Reagan is good for the Jews and for Israel in particular…. Now, however, our great "friend" in Washington is shooting out wildly in our direction, proving in effect that "a friend in need is a friend indeed," as long as it is his need. —*New York Times*

1991. A FRIEND IN NEED —Headline of a letter to the editor about Joe Papp's support of his actors, *New York Times*

1993. TROUBLE: A FRIEND IN NEED —Headline of an article on a New Orleans technician who switched identities with a critically injured but uninsured coworker, *People*

Friendship is blind. *See* LOVE IS BLIND.

From clogs to clogs is only three generations. *See* FROM SHIRTSLEEVES TO SHIRTSLEEVES IN THREE GENERATIONS.

From each according to his ability, to each according to his needs. This phrase is generally attributed to Karl Marx (1818–83), but many scholars question his authorship. The same idea was expressed earlier by Morelly (1755), the Saint-Simonians (1829), and Louis Blanc (1840).

1755. Nothing in society will belong to anyone, either as a personal possession or as capital goods, except the things for which the person has immediate use, for either his needs, his pleasures, or his daily work. Every citizen will make his particular contribution to the activities of the community according to his capacity, his talent, and his age; it is on this basis that his duties will be determined, in conformity with the distributive laws. —Morelly, *Le code de la nature*

1840. Let each produce according to his aptitudes and his force; let each consume according to his need. —Louis Blanc, *Organization du travail*

1875. From each according to his ability, to each according to his needs. —Karl Marx, *Critique of the Gotha Program*

1988. However, she attaches more authenticity to the origin of another well-known declaration associated with Marx: "From each according to his ability, to each according to his work." That was from the Saint-Simonians, followers of Claude Henri de Rouvroy, Comte de Saint-Simon, in 1829, and Marx changed the last word from *work* to *needs.* —William Safire, *New York Times Magazine*

From little acorns great oaks grow. *See* GREAT OAKS FROM LITTLE ACORNS GROW.

From many, one. *See* E PLURIBUS UNUM.

From shirtsleeves to shirtsleeves in three generations. From poverty (grandparents) to wealth (their children) to poverty (their children's children): grandchildren may lose the fortune made by their parents and grandparents. The word *shirtsleeves* is used as a symbol of hard labor. The proverb originated in the 1880s and is attributed to Andrew Carnegie (1835–1919), who liked to quote the Lancashire proverb, "There's nobbut three generations atween clog and clog." *Three generations from shirtsleeves to shirtsleeves; Shirtsleeves to shirtsleeves in three generations;* and *From clogs to clogs is only three generations* are variants.

1886. Three generations from shirtsleeves to shirtsleeves. —Andrew Carnegie, *Triumphant Democracy*

1979. His name was Redford Alden Wyatt. He never married. According to Sarah, he had not bathed in years.

"Shirtsleeves to shirtsleeves in three generations," as the saying goes.

In case of the Wyatts, actually, it was more like shirtsleeves to shirtsleeves in ten generations. They had been richer than most of their neighbors for at least that long. —Kurt Vonnegut, Jr., *Jailbird*

1988. There's a saying that goes: "It's three generations from shirt-sleeves to shirt-sleeves." What it means is that if your grandparents were poor and your parents become rich and successful, it's common occurrence that you—your generation—will stumble back into the pattern of your grandparents. —Harvey Mackay, *Swim with the Sharks without Being Eaten Alive*

From the mouths of babes come words of wisdom. *See* OUT OF THE MOUTHS OF BABES AND SUCKLINGS COME GREAT TRUTHS.

From the sublime to the ridiculous is but a step. There is often little difference between the great and the pathetic. Great undertakings may end in disaster. The proverb is of French origin: *Du sublime au ridicule il n'y a qu'un pas* ("There is only one step from the sublime to the ridiculous"). Although the saying is often attributed to both Talleyrand and Napoleon, it was used much earlier by Jean François Marmontel (1723–99) and Thomas Paine (1717–1809).

1793. When authors and critics talk of the sublime, they see not how nearly it borders on the ridiculous. —Thomas Paine, *The Age of Reason*

1812. From the sublime to the ridiculous is but a step. —Napoleon Bonaparte, statement on his return from Russia, referring to his defeat at Moscow

1899. Aunt Jane observed, the second time
She tumbled off a bus,
"The step is short from the Sublime
To the Ridiculous."
—Harry Graham, *Ruthless Rhymes for Heartless Homes*

1922. Virag: You intended to devote an entire year to the study of the religious problem and the summer months of 1886 to square the circle and win that million. Pomegranate! From the sublime to the ridiculous is but a step. —James Joyce, *Ulysses*

1994. From the Sometimes Ridiculous (New Line) to the Often Sublime (Fine Line) —*New York Times*

From your lips to God's ears. May the prediction or wish you are making come true. Used to express appreciation for someone's hope that matters will turn out well. Also in the form *from your mouth....* Often shortened to *from your lips.* **

1984. Abigail always made sense. And she was another in the growing roster of those foreseeing that someday soon the Lord would appoint me ruler over Israel.... "From your mouth," I replied with regal courtesy, dipping my head in assent, "to God's ears." —Joseph Heller, *God Knows*

1986. "You'll get a break."
"D'you think so?"
"It happens."
"From your lips ..." —Jackie Collins, *Hollywood Husbands*

1994. "The Contract with America will never gain the full support of the entire nation." "From your lips to God's ears." —Overheard at a Social Security office in New York City

See also IT'S TOO GOOD TO BE TRUE.

Full speed (ahead)! *See* DAMN THE TORPEDOES! FULL SPEED AHEAD!

The further you go, the bigger the fall. *See* THE BIGGER THEY ARE, THE HARDER THEY FALL.

The future ain't what it used to be. The climate of American optimism has waned, so that the past always looks better by comparison. The origin of this saying is obscure. General Norman Schwarzkopf and others have attributed it to Yogi Berra (1925–). But, as with many other Yogi-isms, Yogi Berra never said that. According to one-liner specialist Ralph Keyes, this saying can more reliably be attributed to science fiction author Arthur Clarke (1917–).**

1991. After the Persian Gulf war, when an NBC News interviewer asked Gen. H. Norman Schwarzkopf about his plans, he replied: "Well, as Yogi Berra said, 'The future ain't what it used to be.'" —*New York Times Magazine*

1993. But I am trying to curb my tendency to complain as I grow older that everything has decayed. After all, as the bumper sticker says, ENTROPY IS NOT WHAT IT USED TO BE. —*Times* (Trenton)

1994. "Are you going to run for public office again, four years from now?" ... "The future ain't what it used to be, as the saying goes. But who knows?" —Overheard at a Fourth of July celebration in New York City

The game is not worth the candle. The gain is not worth the effort. The saying dates from the pre-electric era, when candles were used for lighting; thus, continuing a game at night was not worth even the cost of the candles. The proverb is of French origin. Michel de Montaigne (1533–92) is quoted as saying, *Le jeu ne vaut pas la chandelle.* In 1678, it was included in John Ray's collection of proverbs. Although it is usually used in the negative, the affirmative version, *The game is worth the candle,* is also sometimes heard.

1989. Running for President, according to Alsop, was the only game "worth the candle." —C. David Heymann, *A Woman Named Jackie*

1993. "You're wearing yourself out cooking and doing dishes day in and day out. Believe me the game is not worth the candle. Isn't it much better to come here and have some fun?" —Overheard at a New York City restaurant.

Gather ye rosebuds while ye may. Seize the moment; life is short, so enjoy it to the fullest; enjoy life while you are young. Written in this form by the English poet Robert Herrick (1648). The idea, however, is also found in the Bible and Horace. Herrick (1591–1674) was probably influenced by the earlier poetry of Edmund Spenser (1552–99) or by the French poet Pierre de Ronsard (1524–85).

Let us crown ourselves with rosebuds, before they be withered. —*The Apocrypha,* The Book of Solomon, 2:8

1578. *Vivez, si m'en croyez, n'attendez à demain: Cueillez des aujourd'hui les roses de la vie.*

Live now, believe me, wait not till

tomorrow;
Gather the roses of life today
  —Pierre de Ronsard, *Sonnets pour Hélène*

1590. Gather therefore the Rose, whilst yet is prime,
For soon comes age, that will her pride deflower:
Gather the Rose of love, whilst yet is time.
  —Edmund Spenser, *The Faerie Queene*

1648. Gather ye rosebuds while ye may,
Old time is still a-flying;
And this same flower that smiles today
Tomorrow will be dying.
  —Robert Herrick, "To the Virgins, To Make
          Much of Time."

1946. He kissed her, and put his newly-shaven cheek against hers and whispered: "Gather ye rosebuds while ye may, old time is still a-flying." The rhyme was "dying," so he didn't complete the stanza, instead, he told her: "I have found the right woman, and I am going to make her happy." —Upton Sinclair, *A World to Win*
See also EAT, DRINK, AND BE MERRY, FOR TOMORROW WE DIE; SEIZE THE MOMENT.

The genie is out of the bottle. *See* LET THE GENIE OUT OF THE BOTTLE.

A genius is born, not made. *See* POETS ARE BORN, NOT MADE.

Genius is one percent inspiration and ninety-nine percent perspiration. New ideas are necessary to be successful, but hard work is more important. Attributed to the American inventor Thomas Alva Edison (1847–1931), according to lexicographer Wolfgang Mieder. Some authorities attribute this saying to the Comte de Buffon (1707–88); others credit Elbert Hubbard (1856–

1915), an American writer, editor, and printer who allegedly said it as far back as 1914.

1803. *Le génie n'est qu'une plus grande aptitude à la patience.* ("Genius is only a greater aptitude for patience.") —Comte de Buffon, quoted by Hérault de Séchelles, *Voyage à Montbar*

1931. Genius is one percent inspiration and ninety-nine percent perspiration. —Thomas Alva Edison, *Life*

1992. FOR THE GAME, INSPIRATION BEFORE PERSPIRATION —Headline of an article about team preparation before a football game, *New York Times*

Genius is the infinite capacity for taking pains. Intellectual success comes only at the expense of great effort. The proverb dates back to the seventeenth century. Disraeli wrote that "patience is a necessary ingredient of genius" (*The Young Duke*, 1831). Thomas Carlyle wrote in his first volume of *Frederick the Great* (1858) that genius "means transcendent capacity of taking trouble, after all."

1959. Genius is an infinite capacity for taking pains. But we should still foster it, however much of an embarrassment it may be to us. —M. Bradbury, *Eating People Is Wrong*

1974. The modern fashion comes, I suppose, from a literal acceptance of the ridiculous dictum that genius is an infinite capacity for taking pains. —T. Sharpe, *Porterhouse Blue*

See also GENIUS IS ONE PERCENT INSPIRATION AND NINETY-NINE PERCENT PERSPIRATION.

Geniuses, like poets, are born, not taught. *See* POETS ARE BORN, NOT MADE.

Get your act together. Be more effective; start behaving better. The saying dates back to the early 1970s and is ultimately of theatrical origin.

1987. I [former White House chief of staff Donald T. Regan] told the President, when I met with him before Poindexter came in on the... morning of the 21st—that something, sure as hell, was screwy. Because I had asked for a chronology, it had been given to me; they took it back. They couldn't seem to get their act together. —*New York Times*

1988. "Mr. Walesa has to get his act together on the clothes front," she said. The [fashion] designer said Walesa was "a very passive customer." —*Boston Globe*

1994. Harold Ickes is helping the President get his act together and drive a harder bargain on health care. —*Time*

1996. Mr. Clinton and I also support public school choice and charter schools. These give parents more choices and encourage failing schools to get their act together while strengthening America's time-honored tradition of free public education for all children. —*Christian Science Monitor*

1997. "The more CDNow and Music Boulevard make, the more it forces 'traditional retailers' to get their act together," says Keane. —*New York Post*

1998. Last Friday, President Clinton quietly signed a continuing resolution that allows government agencies to go on spending at last year's levels until Oct. 9, when Congress presumably will have its act together. —*Commercial Appeal* (Memphis, Tennessee)

1998. If people could look up health-commission test results on the Internet, it might just prompt the hospitals to get their act together and obey the law. —Editorial, *New York Post*

See also CLEAN UP YOUR ACT!

Girls will be girls. *See* BOYS WILL BE BOYS.

Give a beggar a horse and he will ride it to death. People unaccustomed to wealth or privilege will abuse it when they get it. The proverb is first found in English in G. Pettie's *Petit Palace of Pleasure* (1576): "Set a Beggar on horsebacke, and he wyl neorer alight." Shakespeare immortalized the idea by saying, "It needs not, not it boots thee not, proud queen, Unless the adage must be verified, That beggars mounted run their horses to death" (*King Henry the Sixth*, 1590–91). The proverb is first recorded in America in the seventeenth century. The 1924 Broadway play *Beggar on Horseback*, written by George Simon Kaufman and Mark Connelly, helped popularize the old adage. The proverb is found in many greatly varying forms and is often used allusively as *Set a beggar on horseback* or *A beggar on horseback.*

1923. I should think your early days of forced economy would have taught you not to be quite so extravagant. But there's an old proverb—'Set a beggar on horseback'—and so forth, that jolly well fits you. —C. Wells, *Affair at Flower Acres*

1934. Put a beggar on horseback and he's sure to overstep the mark, or whatever the saying is. —L. O'Flaherty, *Shame the Devil*

1961. He had a good deal of the vulgarity and insolence of the beggar on horseback. —W. H. Lewis, *Scandalous Regent*

See also BEGGARS CAN'T BE CHOOSERS; GIVE A MAN A FISH, AND YOU FEED HIM FOR A DAY; SHOW (TEACH) HIM

HOW TO CATCH FISH, AND YOU FEED HIM FOR A LIFE-
TIME.

Give a man a fish, and you feed him for a day; show (teach) him how to catch fish, and you feed him for a lifetime. The best way to help people is to teach them skills, not offer them handouts. This ancient Chinese proverb is found in varying forms. It was used by Michael Dukakis during his 1988 presidential campaign and by Dan Quayle in his 1992 vice-presidential debate.******

> **1989.** "In Wall Street the old proverb has been reworded: 'Give a man a fish, and you feed him for a day. Teach him how to arbitrage and you feed him forever.' (If, however, he studied at the Ivan Boesky School of Arbitrage, it may be a state institution that supplies his meals)." —*New York Times*
>
> **1992.** The U.S. can give the Russians a fish, as the old proverb goes, and the Russians will have food for a day; the U.S. can show them how to catch fish, and they will have food for years to come. Currently, Russia needs us to do both, but we are doing neither to any significant extent. Not only might the West lose Russia, but Russia might lose Russia as well. —Letters to the Editor, *Time*
>
> **1993.** As they say, give a man a fish and he'll eat for a day. Teach a man to fish and he can afford a good wine to go with it. —Ad for Andersen Consulting, *Fortune*
>
> **1994.** If you give a man a fish, he'll eat for a day; show him how to catch fish, and he will have food for a lifetime. —Van Deward Woods, "Both Sides with Jesse Jackson," CNN

Give credit where credit is due. It's only fair to recognize people for their contributions. The proverb appears in the New Testament and is similar in meaning to the Latin: *Palmam que meruit ferat* ("Let him bear away the palm who has deserved it"). First attested in the United States in Samuel Adams's letter dated October 29, 1777. The phrase may take various forms: *Always give praise where praise is due; Always give thanks where thanks are due; Give credit to whom credit is due; Give honor where honor is due; Give honor to whom honor is due; Praise where praise is due;* etc.

> Render therefore to all their dues: tribute to whom tribute is due; custom to whom custom; fear to whom fear; honor to whom honor. —Romans 13:7, *Authorized Version*, 1611
>
> **1777.** May Honor be given to whom Honor may be due. —Samuel Adams, Letter, October 29

> **1922.** Honour where honour is due. —James Joyce, *Ulysses*
>
> **1982.** "Oh, I wouldn't compare Teddy to Max," Sally said.
> Snider sensed the sarcasm and hostility, but Max, who also had too much to drink, spread his arms and said, "There's a lady respects her husband. But you got to give Teddy credit where credit's due." —Howard Fast, *Max*
>
> **1988.** "Oh, we can't take credit where it isn't due," protested the man from the Mafia, enjoying himself. —Robert Ludlum, *The Icarus Agenda*
>
> **1991.** "It's not gambling," Buckley said. "We play like men. We don't try to disguise when we're in, man. We let you know it. And if you're a good enough player to beat us, we give you credit where credit is due." —*New York Times*
>
> **1994.** Top economic officials are frustrated that the Clinton Administration has not received more credit for recent economic growth.... Nowadays, good news is bad news. The Administration cannot receive credit where credit is due. —Letters to the Editor, *New York Times*

See also PRAISE THE BRIDGE THAT CARRIES YOU OVER.

Give 'em hell, Harry! The phrase *to give someone (merry or holy) hell* has been used by many authors, including John Steinbeck in *The Grapes of Wrath* ("You sure give that fella hell") and Robert Penn Warren in *All the King's Men* ("You were just now giving me hell because I merely offered him the proposition"). On February 23, 1847, President Zachary Taylor (1784–1850) cheered on the Second Kentucky Regiment, whose soldiers were rallying for battle: "Hurrah for Old Kentucky! That's the way to do it. Give 'em hell, damn 'em." But the phrase was widely popularized by the crowds who greeted Harry Truman with the cry. "Give 'em hell, Harry!" during his election campaign for the presidency. The pronoun *them* (*'em*) and the name may be replaced. "Give 'em hell, George!" was used in the 1992 presidential campaign by Bush's Republican supporters.********

> **1945.** In the middle of the speech, some big voice up in the corner hollered out, "Give 'em hell, Harry!" Well, I never gave anybody hell—I just told the truth on these fellows and they thought it was hell. —Harry S. Truman, quoted by David Wallechinsky & Irving Wallace, *The People's Almanac*

1966. Touring the country and showing his "folk-sy" personality to advantage, he [Truman] delivered a series of "give 'em hell" speeches at numerous whistle-stops. —Thomas A. Bailey, *The American Pageant*

1992. Perot's electronic town hall may smack of direct democracy—a horror to congressmen—but would it not be better for pols to hear the people's voice directly than through the filters of their spin doctors? Give 'em hell, Rossy! —Letters to the Editor, *New York*

1992. GIVE 'EM HELL, GEORGE —Slogan at the National Republican Convention, reported on CNN

1992. Well folks, I gotta tell ya. That's the kind of talk that gets yours truly pig-biting mad! And I'm gonna stand up with Dan "Give 'em Hell" Quayle against these sicko liberal actresses like Candice Bergen. —*Weekly World News*

1993. The cloying nostalgist attends the Republican National Convention as a delegate and interrupts the president's address with chants of "Give 'em hell, George!" (And listens to the president respond, in unconvincing Texan argot, "I'm fixin' to!") —*GQ*

1995. Give 'Em Heck, Harry. Oh, those pesky facts, if Merle Miller had used more of them, his 1973 best-selling Harry S. Truman bio, *Plain Speaking,* wouldn't have been such a hit —*Newsweek*

Give him an inch, and he will take a mile. Some people are never pleased with what they are given—they demand more and more. The proverb is first found in English in John Heywood's 1546 book of proverbs. First attested in the United States in *Letters of John Randolph* (1680). The adage is found in a number of forms: *Give him an inch, and he will take an ell; Give him an inch, and he will take a foot; Give him an inch, and he will take a span; Give him an inch and he will take a yard,* etc. Often shortened to *give somebody an inch.*

1984. "When we proposed to buy the church and the parsonage, Soan and Winter fought him tooth and nail, claiming that we were opening the door for the anti-Christ, whatever the hell that is, and give us an inch and we take a foot and before you know it, the whole Ridge will be crawling with kikes." —Howard Fast, *The Outsider*

1992. "If I had won the first set, it would have been a different story," said Navratilova, who instead gave Seles the only window of opportunity she required. "Give her an inch and she blows the doors wide open." —*New York Times*

1993. The liberal government of Premier Robert Bourassa has passed Bill 86, which will allow some outdoor bilingual signs to be posted by some businesses, providing the French lettering is predominant, that is to say, twice the size of the English or Greek or Chinese. But even this is too much for Prof. Léon Dion, an important constitutional expert. In his opinion, give Anglophobes an inch and they will demand a mile. —Mordecai Richler, "On Language," *New York Times Magazine*

Give him enough rope and he'll hang himself. When a person is given enough freedom of action, he may inflict damage on himself. If a guilty person is given some latitude to act, he will reveal his guilt. First cited in *The History of the Holy War* (1639) by English historian Thomas Fuller (1608–61). Recorded in John Ray's collection of English proverbs in 1670. First attested in the United States in *William & Mary College Quarterly* (1698). The word *him* may be replaced by *a man, a thief, a guy, a calf,* etc. Often shortened to *give him enough rope.*

1639. They were suffered to have rope enough till they had haltered themselves. —Thomas Fuller, *The History of the Holy War*

1965. As President Hernan Siles [of Bolivia], who had faithfully carried out the stabilization program in 1956–69, put it, "The United States has given me just enough rope to hang myself." —Arthur M. Schlesinger, Jr., *A Thousand Days*

1989. He believes that Tom Strauss managed to obtain control and that Voute was willing to bide his time, while giving Strauss enough rope to hang himself.... —Michael Lewis, *Liar's Poker*

1992. Miller was giving him the rope, hoping he would loop it around his own neck. Which he was about to do, if he wasn't careful. —Philip Friedman, *Inadmissible Evidence*

Give me a break! That's enough! Stop it! Leave me alone! Give me another chance! The phrase is commonly used by people in all walks of life. The pronoun *me* is sometimes replaced by another pronoun or noun.

1946. "Boss," I said, "I'm going to give Irwin a break. If he can prove to me it isn't true, I won't spill it."
　　"God damn it," he began, "I told you—"
　　"I'm giving Irwin a break," I said. —Robert Penn Warren, *All the King's Men*

1977. "Look, I've got less than four years in which to go down as the greatest President in the history of the United States. Give me a break." —Art Buchwald, *Down the Seine and Up the Potomac*

1983. "Give me a break—I'm out of my head!" —Jackie Collins, *Hollywood Wives.*

1984. Poor people complain that nobody gave them a break, but the rich guy never knows if he's accomplished anything on his own. —Lee Iacocca with William Novak, *Iacocca*

1986. "There were Nazis that used the word *Jew* the same way you're using the word *nigger.* "

"Give me a break, Savannah." —Pat Conroy, *The Prince of Tides*

1988. "Oh, come on, *will* you?" broke in Evan firmly. "Give me a break, friend." —Robert Ludlum, *The Icarus Agenda*

1992. Clemente flipped pages in the notebook. "Said our man Juan went to some big football college in the south. Miami or Texas or Auburn or some other place like that. And he thinks maybe he was Cuban. Period, end of story."

"Give me a break." —Philip Friedman, *Inadmissible Evidence*

1993. "I live in a $400,000 house—give me a break," said Arlene Hauser, one of the neighbors and a real estate agent. "The value of my property is very important to me." —*Princeton Packet* (N.J.)

1994. Give me a break. Isn't it enough that Jay Leno and David Letterman are paid 50 times what they're worth? —Letters to the Editor, *New York Times Magazine*

Give me a place to stand, and I will move the earth. *See* GIVE ME WHERE TO STAND, AND I WILL MOVE THE EARTH.

Give me liberty or give me death! A few weeks before the start of the American Revolution, Patrick Henry (1736–99), called on the American colonies to revolt against England. His battle cry at the Second Virginia Convention on March 23, 1775, "Give me liberty or give me death!," became a slogan for generations of Americans. A similar idea was expressed by Aeschylus (525–456 b.c.): "Death is better, a milder fate than tyranny."

1775. Is life so dear, or peace so sweet, as to be purchased at the price of chains and slavery? Forbid it, Almighty God. I know not what course others may take, but as for me, give me liberty or give me death! —Patrick Henry, Speech at Virginia's Second Revolutionary Convention on March 23, 1775

1965. This was the first nation in the history of the world to be founded with a purpose. The great phrases of that purpose still sound in every American heart, North and South: "All men are created equal"—"government by consent of the governed"—"give me liberty or give me death." —Lyndon B. Johnson, Address on Voting Rights

1987. "General Bermudez, what is your strategy for winning over the peasants?"

"Well, basically, we've been offering the peasants liberty or death." —G. B. Trudeau, *Doonesbury Deluxe*

1993. "Give me liberty or give me a close, comfortable shave."

"George Washington never said that."

"Hey, back off. It's my hallucination!" —Cartoon by Meddick, "Robotman," *Times* (Trenton)

See also I ONLY REGRET THAT I HAVE BUT ONE LIFE TO LOSE FOR MY COUNTRY; I WOULD RATHER DIE ON MY FEET THAN LIVE ON MY KNEES; OUR COUNTRY, RIGHT OR WRONG.

Give me where to stand, and I will move the earth. Statement attributed to Archimedes as an illustration of the principle of the lever. According to Archimedes (287–212 b.c.), he could move the world if he had a lever long enough and a fulcrum strong enough. The words *a place* may be used in place of *where.*

1940. Archimedes also did pioneer work in physics and mechanics, where he discovered the law of floating bodies and established the theoretical principles of the lever and the pulley. "Give me a place to stand," he said, "and I will move the earth." —Hutton Webster, *History of Civilization*

1991. He [Archimedes] showed that great weights could be moved with small effort, provided that the lever was long enough. "Give me a place to stand," he said, "and I will move the world." ... Our world could stand a little shove—especially the world of money.... Our minds need moving, as well as our money.... That's a job for a lever. This book was written to help you find a place to stand. —Jane Bryant Quinn, *Making the Most of Your Money*

Give me your tired, your poor. First line of a poem by Emma Lazarus (1849–1887) inscribed on the base of the Statue of Liberty, which was erected in 1886 in New York Harbor as a gift from the people of France. The poem pays tribute to the United States, as the haven of the oppressed. It was later set to music by Irving Berlin (1888–1989).

1883. Give me your tired, your poor,

Your huddled masses yearning to breathe
free,
The wretched refuse of your teeming shore.
Send these, the homeless, tempest-tossed, to
me:
I lift my lamp beside the golden door.
—Emma Lazarus, "The New Colossus"

1978. "I'm done feeding the inner man," Glen said, getting up. "Give me your poor, your hungry." —Stephen King, *The Stand*

1984. Give me your tired, give me your poor, your huddled masses who learn to breathe free and come November, there will be a change because our time has come. Thank you and God bless you. —Jesse Jackson, *New York Times*

1987. The basic rights are "life, liberty, and pursuit of property and sex." "Give us your poor, your sexually starved...." —Allan Bloom, *The Closing of the American Mind*

1992. The evening opened with a song sung by David King, whose lyrics had even the Statue of Liberty holding her ears: "Give me your huddled masses yearning to be free. Yes, the tired, the proud, the hungry, yes, bring them all to me." —*New York Times*

Give peace a chance! A temporary peace may eventually result in a permanent one. Support any peace initiative. The saying was made on the analogy of *Give someone a chance* and was popularized by the English pop singer and songwriter John Lennon (1940–80). His 1969 song "Give Peace a Chance" has become the anthem of the peace movement in many countries.

1991. Support Croatia in her time of need. Give peace a chance! —Ad for Truth about Croatia, Inc., *New York Times*

1992. All I am saying, to paraphrase John Lennon, is give baseball a chance. —George Vecsey, *New York Times*

1993. Its high point was to repeat a phrase used by Rabin earlier, taking up the slogan of Israel's Peace Now movement, which was based on the 1969 John Lennon song title "Give Peace a Chance"; he strained for emphasis by adding the word *real*: "Our two peoples ... want to give peace a real chance." —William Safire, *New York Times Magazine*

1994. "My decision, our decision in the Government," he [Yitzhak Rabin] said, "is to give peace with Syria a chance—a chance that never existed before." —*New York Times*

Give the devil his due. Give credit to those who deserve it even if you don't like them; be fair even to an unworthy person. First cited in *Pappe with Hatchet* (1589) by John Lyly. Also used by Shakespeare (c.1598) and Cervantes (1605–15). First attested in the United States in *American Broadside Verse* (1769). In *A Connecticut Yankee in King Arthur's Court* (1889), Mark Twain wrote: "We must give even Satan his due." The proverb is found in varying forms: *Even the devil should be given his dues; Give the devil his dues; Give the devil his just dues; You've got to give the devil his dues,* etc.

1598. *Duke of Orleans:* "Ill will never said well."
 Constable: I will cap that proverb
  with—"There is flattery in friendship."
 Duke of Orleans: And I will take up that
  with "Give the devil his due."
   —Shakespeare, *King Henry V,* III, vii

1605–15.
To give the devil his due. —Cervantes, *Don Quixote*

1922. Give the devil his due. —James Joyce, *Ulysses*

1984. My initiative weakened. But just in time, up spoke the Devil to rally my faltering spirit and give me heart. I needed to throw at least a little bit of caution to the wind and march to the insistent beat of this different drummer. Let me give the Devil his due. —Joseph Heller, *God Knows*

1991. "Monday was too easy, it was almost a fluke," Edward Burns, a trader for Chancellor Capital Management, said of the Dow Jones Industrial Average's day-earlier 29-point rebound from Friday's 120-point shellacking. Yesterday, he said, investors were "paying the devil his due." —*Wall Street Journal*

The glass is either half empty or half full. The same situation can be viewed in either a negative or positive way. The saying is found in varying forms: *The optimist's cup is half full, the pessimist's cup is half empty,* etc. Often shortened to *the cup (glass) is half empty* or to *the cup (glass) is half full.*

1985. ... You can say it's like the glass half full or half empty; you can say we're trying to oust the Sandinistas by what we're saying. We're saying we're trying to give those who fought a revolution to escape a dictatorship, to have democracy.... —Ronald Reagan, *New York Times*

1987. "The glass is half full, *not* half empty. So, don't worry about a thing, and nothing needs to be done. Nothing at all." —R. Richard Ritti & G. Ray Funkhouser, *The Ropes to Skip & the Ropes to Know*

1988. Is the wine bottle half full, or is it half empty? That depends on the way you look at it. I suggest that you ignore the precursors of doom. —Henry C. Rogers, *Rogers' Rules for Business-women*

1991. *First NAACP leader (pointing at Justice Thurgood Marshall's shoes on Clarence Thomas):* I say Marshall's shoes are *half EMPTY!*

Second NAACP leader: I say they're *half FULL!* —Cartoon by Summers, *Orlando Sentinel*, reprinted in *U.S. News & World Report*

1993. True, since many of the 287 guild members will not get those jobs, the glass is half empty. But Mr. Murdoch seemed fully prepared to drop the glass on the floor. A broken glass can never again be half full. —Hubert B. Herring, *New York Times*

1994. Although she's job-hopped professionally, Ms. Baker has been married to Gary Baker since she was 19. One reason for that longevity is her sense of humor, she says. Another is that she calls herself "the ultimate the-glass-is-half-full person." —*Crain's New York Business*

Go ahead, make my day. *See* MAKE MY DAY.

Go for it! Give it a try! Just do it! Shoot for the top! Often used to encourage someone to do something. The saying became popular in the 1980s. In 1985, President Reagan used the phrase, "America, go for it!" to promote his tax reform program. Used in everyday speech.

1984. I went home from these meetings and talked things over with Mary. She said. "You won't be happy doing anything except cars. And you're too young to sit around the house. Let's give that bastard Henry [Ford] a shot he'll always remember." She was feisty that way. I also talked it over with my kids. Their attitude was: "If it makes you happy, go for it!" —Lee Iacocca with William Novak, *Iacocca*

1986. "Tower, this is Hunter Leader. We're scrambling. Clear those runways, boy!"

Simon took the microphone. "Roger, Hunter Leader, the runways are yours. Scatter Plan Alpha. Go for it! Out." —Tom Clancy, *Red Storm Rising*

1988. "Go, Hank, go for it! Just stick the damn thing in!" —Erich Segal, *Doctors*

1991. "How much money, Andy?"

Go for it, Andy thought. "Another twenty thousand." —John Grisham, *The Firm*

1994. All of us deserve the best in our lives. But we can't remain prisoners of the past; we need the courage to take a fresh look at life and start over

when necessary.... Go for it! —Malcolm Boyd, *Modern Maturity*

Go hunting where the ducks are. Go where your potential voters or supporters are, to the key area of your activity where much can be accomplished. The proverb is sometimes attributed to Barry Goldwater. *Go hunting where the tigers are* and *If you want to hunt a tiger, you must go where the tiger lives* are variants of the proverb.

1991. Just three weeks after he was elected, William Weld told the Massachusetts Business Roundtable that he approached his task of cutting the state budget by concentrating on the big items. "I'll go hunting where the ducks are, so to speak," he said. —*Boston Globe*

1991. The cold fact of 1988 do suggest that if in 1992 the Democrats—in Barry Goldwater's phrase—are to "go hunting where the ducks are," the most ducks are likely to be found outside of Dixie. —*New York Times*

1991. FOR DEMOS, SOUTH'S NOT WHERE THE DUCKS ARE —Headline of an article about the Democratic Party electoral objectives, *Commercial Appeal* (Memphis, Tennessee)

1992. "If you want to hunt a tiger," she later told prosecutors, "you must go where the tiger lives." —*New York Times*

See also FISH WHERE THE FISH ARE.

Go west, young man. Greater opportunities are available in the American West for pioneering spirits. Although this nineteenth-century saying was often used by, and has been attributed to, the founder and editor of the *New York Tribune*, Horace Greeley (1811–72), the real author was probably John Babsone Lane Soule (1815–91), editor of the *Terre Haute Express* (Ind.), who first offered this advice in 1851. Greeley shared Soule's belief in the West. "Go west, young man," he wrote in a letter to a friend. In an editorial, he later added the phrase, "and grow up with the country." Following Soule's and Greeley's advice, around 254,000 people traveled from the Missouri River to the Pacific between 1840 and 1870.

1851. Go west, young man. —John Babsone Lane Soule, *Terre Haute Express* (Ind.).

1984. When I arrived at the Fort Street Station, a duffel bag on my shoulder and fifty bucks in my pocket, I went outside and asked the first guy I met: "Which way to Dearborn?" ... He said: "Go west, young man—go west about ten miles!" —Lee Iacocca with William Novak, *Iacocca*

1993. GO WEST, YOUNG LADY: CROSSROADS THEATRE OPENS WITH THE STORY OF AFRICAN-AMERICAN HOMESTEADERS —Headline of a theater review, *Time Off* (N.J.)

1994. GO WEST, GRAND AM; BON VOYAGE, OLD BENTLEY —Headline of an article on driving smart, *New York Times*

Go with it. *See* GO WITH THE FLOW.

Go with the flow. Accept things as they are. Take it easy. The saying originated in the 1960s. May be used as an attribute to a noun. *Go with it* is a variant of this slang phrase.

1986. "Relax. Hang loose. Go with the flow." —Jackie Collins, *Hollywood Husbands*

1992. "I'm a Bush supporter, but Clinton looks like he's a shoo-in," Mr. Alger said. "Go with the flow, I guess." —*New York Times*

1994. Go with the flow and you simply can't go wrong. —Patric Walker, "Your Daily Horoscope," *New York Post*

God bless America. Used as an expression of appreciation and gratitude to America and its people for the opportunity to live and work there. Originated by Irving Berlin (1882–1989), whose song "God Bless America" (1938) achieved widespread popularity throughout the world. This patriotic song was originally sung by Kate Smith. The phrase is often used by politicians to end their speeches.

1938. God bless America,
Land that I love,
Stand beside her and guide her
Thru the night with a light from above.
From the mountains to the prairies,
To the oceans white with foam,
God bless America,
My home sweet home!
    —Irving Berlin, "God Bless America"

1984. God bless you and God bless America. —Ronald Reagan, State of the Union Message

1988. The next thing he knew the man was embracing his ankles, sobbing, and howling, "God bless America!" —Erich Segal, *Doctors*

1990. And may God bless this great nation, the United States of America. —George Bush, State of the Union Message

1991. And it's why, when he's finished leading everyone in a rousing chorus of "God Bless America" and the band died down, he [Sam Walton] just can't help adding into the microphone: "Okay everybody, let's hear those cash registers ring." —*Fortune*

1992. My fellow Americans. I end tonight where it all began for me: I still believe in a place called Hope. God bless you, and God bless America. —Bill Clinton, Speech accepting the Democratic nomination for president, *New York Times*

God bless you. I wish you well. Samuel Johnson's (1709–84) last words on his deathbed in 1784 were "God bless you, my dear!" The phrase is also used when someone sneezes, since in many cultures it is believed that the soul leaves the body during a sneeze, and God is called on to protect the sneezer from evil spirits at such a vulnerable time. The word *God* is often omitted.

(undated).
Christmas is coming, the geese are getting fat,
Please to put a penny in the old man's hat;
If you haven't got a penny, a ha'penny will do,
If you haven't got a ha'penny, God bless you!
    —Anonymous beggar's rhyme

1953. "This money will be put to good use. Thanks and God bless you." —Ray Bradbury, *Fahrenheit 451*

1976. "I had to pretend I was a hawk when really I was a dove. I had everyone fooled."
"God bless you," I said. —Art Buchwald, *Washington Is Leaking*

1978. "God bless you," Clair said. "Thank you for coming." —Stephen King, *The Stand*

1989. Thank you and God bless you. —George Bush, State of the Union Message

God helps those who help themselves. No one who has not made a genuine effort to accomplish something can expect God's assistance. It is better to be self-reliant than to pray for divine intervention. Used as advice to lazy people. The proverb dates as far back as Aesop (c.550 b.c.). It is similar to the fifteenth-century French: *Aidez uous, Dieu uos aidera* ("Help yourself, and God will help you"). Erasmus is quoted as saying in 1545, *Dii facientes adiuuant* ("The gods do help the doer"). In 1651, English poet George Herbert expressed the same idea: "Help thyself, and God will help thee." First appeared in its current form in Benjamin Franklin's *Poor Richard's Almanac* (1733). The proverb is found in various forms: *God helps him who helps himself; God helps them that help themselves; Heaven helps those who help* *themselves; Providence helps those who help themselves; The Lord helps those who help themselves,* etc.

1736. "We are taxed twice as much by our *Idleness,* three times as much by our *Pride,* and four times as much by our *Folly,* and from these Taxes the Commissioners cannot ease or deliver by allowing an Abatement. However let us hearken to good Advice, and something may be done for us; *God helps them that help themselves,* as Poor Richard says, in his Almanac of 1733. —Benjamin Franklin, *Father Abraham's Speech, or, The Way to Wealth*

1936. They show you to be a person of energy and determination and a good money risk. It's entertaining, helping people who help themselves. —Margaret Mitchell, *Gone With the Wind*

1946. "This is the truth: you are a hick and nobody ever helped a hick but the hick himself. Up there in town they won't help you. It is up to you and God, and God helps those who help themselves!" —Robert Penn Warren, *All the King's Men*

1961. No one blames you for what you are now, but if you refuse to accept the help that is available, you must bear the responsibility for what you have done to your life and to the lives of those you love. God helps those who help themselves. May God help you. —Ann Landers, *Since You Ask Me*

1984. To fight the specter of high interest rates, we came with a floating rebate plan. We would grant a refund to any customer who bought a car on credit—based on the difference between 13 percent and the prevailing interest rate when the car was purchased.... When I announced the new plan, I said: "The Lord helps those who help themselves." —Lee Iacocca with William Novak, *Iacocca*

1992. Unlike capital gains indexing, the auto insurance initiative is not dead in White House waters. Indeed, it is likely to show up one of these days in a Bush campaign speech. But one of these days is, by any reckoning, very late. If heaven helps only those who help themselves, the President is in deep trouble. —*New York Times*

1995. Like the founders, Andrew Carnegie believed heavily in the transformative power of books. In 1901, Carnegie improved on the founders' gift by financing the branch library system—"to help those who will help themselves," Carnegie said at the time. —*New York Times*

God is always on the side of the big battalions. Fortune favors the strong, the rich, and the famous. The proverb is of French origin: *Le bon Dieu est toujours du côté des gros batail-*lons ("God is always on the side of the big battalions"). The saying can be found in one of Madame de Sévigné's letters (December 22, 1673): *La fortune est toujours, comme disait le pauvre M. de Turenne, pour les gros bataillons* ("Fortune is always, as poor Mr. de Turenne used to say, for the big battalions"). "Poor Mr. Turenne" was none other than Marshal of France Henri de Turenne (1611–75), though he didn't originate the saying. It is often attributed to Napoleon (who is quoted as saying, "Providence is always on the side of the last reserve") and to Frederick the Great (1760) ("God is always with the strongest battalions"). Other possible authors include Roger de Bussy-Rabutin (1677) (*Dieu est d'ordinaire pour les gros escadrons contre les petits;* "God is usually on the side of the big squadrons and against the small ones") and François Voltaire (1735–50) (*Dieu n'est pas pour les gros bataillons, mais pour ceux qui tirent le mieux;* "God is on the side not of the heavy battalions, but of the best shots"). However, the proverb probably originated much earlier. The Roman historian Tacitus (a.d. c.56–c.120) is quoted as saying, *Deos fortioribus adesse* ("The gods are on the side of the stronger").

1776–88.
The winds and waves are always on the side of the ablest navigator. —Edward Gibbon, *The History of the Decline and Fall of the Roman Empire*

1936. "Why, all we have is cotton and slaves and arrogance. They'd lick us in a month."
... "Sir," said Stuart heavily, "what do you mean?"
Rhett looked at him with polite but mocking eyes.
"I mean," he answered, "what Napoleon—perhaps you've heard of him?—remarked once, 'God is on the side of the strongest battalion!'" —Margaret Mitchell, *Gone With the Wind*

1987. There were only two alternatives: either go to ground and attempt to call in a sitrep (which, beyond artillery reach and with no gunships or B-53s, would not do a helluva lot to stop the NVA); or get out, evade contact, and get extraction.... For once, God was on the side of the Shannons. —Chris Bunch & Allan Cole, *A Reckoning for Kings*

1988. In his peroration he [Nixon] recalled the man the Republicans had nominated in Chicago exactly a century earlier: "Abraham Lincoln was asked during the dark days of the tragic War Between the States whether he thought God was on his side. His answer was, 'My concern is not whether God is on our side, but whether we are on God's side.' " —Stephen E. Ambrose, *Nixon*

God is in the details. Whatever one does should be done thoroughly; details are important. The saying is generally attributed to Gustave Flaubert (1821–80), who is often quoted as saying, *Le bon Dieu est dans le détail* ("God is in the details"). Other attributions include Michelangelo, the architect Ludwig Mies van der Rohe, and the art historian Aby Warburg. *The Devil is in the details* is a variant of the proverb, referring to a catch hidden in the details. *Governing is in the details* and *The truth, if it exists, is in the details* are recent variants.

1992. [Mortimer] Zuckerman, moreover, promises attention to the practical matter of editing that the manic Maxwell never found time for. "God is in the details," developer Zuckerman declared last week, quoting the architect's maxim, and then added a typical Zuckermanian zinger: "But so is the Devil." —*New York*

1993. The devil is in the details, and I haven't seen the details yet. —Stephen Wildstrom, "Taxes '93: Ask the Experts," "Prime News," CNN

1994. I don't pretend to know exactly what makes great actors great. But they say that truth lies in the details. And Jessica Tandy, who died last week at 85, was certainly one of the theater's most truthful practioners. —*New York Times*

God moves in a mysterious way. God's plan is unfathomable. Hence, things are not always what they appear to be. Often used to explain or justify an unpleasant event. The proverb has been attributed to the English poet William Cowper (1731–1800). *The Lord* may substitute for *God* and *works* may replace *moves*. *Way* is often used in the plural.

1779. God moves in a mysterious way
His wonders to perform;
He plants his footsteps in the sea
And rides upon the storm
—William Cowper, "Light Shining out of Darkness," *Olney Hymns*

1946. And since the Lord moves in a mysterious way, it should not have surprised Willie that He was using some fat men in striped pants and a big car to work his will. —Robert Penn Warren, *All the King's Men*

1977. *Haldeman:* Ya, it's money ... CIA gets money [*unintelligible*] I mean their money moves in a lot of different ways, too. —Victor Lasky, *It Didn't Start with Watergate*

1978. It was only later on that you might wonder why it had happened that way.... But there was no answering the ways God set about His wonders to perform, and for Abby Freemantle as well as her father, '02 had been a topper. —Stephen King, *The Stand*

1984. He made my baby die. He was working again in one of His mysterious ways. —Joseph Heller, *God Knows*

1989. He didn't like to tell lies, but sometimes Justice required it. He'd learned that much in the federal court system. It was just a practical application of what his minister said: "God moves in mysterious ways, His wonders to perform." —Tom Clancy, *Clear and Present Danger*

1992. "Buddy built the entire offense around Randall. I told Randall that he would pay for what he did, and I don't know if him missing all of last year with the knee injury was it, but God works in mysterious ways." —*New York Times*

1994. "Lord, grant our Church League pitcher speed and accuracy!" BONK.... "The Lord works in mysterious ways!" —Cartoon by Doug Marlette, "Kudzu," Creators Syndicate

God save me from my friends—I can protect myself from my enemies. *See* SAVE US FROM OUR FRIENDS; WITH SUCH FRIENDS, ONE HARDLY NEEDS ENEMIES.

God's in his heaven; all's right with the world. God's benevolence ensures that everything is as it should be. The saying is used to console people in distress and is probably of Biblical origin. It was used by Cervantes in *Don Quixote* (1605–15) and included in John Ray's collection of English proverbs (1678). However, the phrase was made popular by the English poet Robert Browning (1812–89), who used it in *Pippa Passes* (1841).

God *is* in heaven, and thou upon earth: therefore let thy words be few. —Ecclesiastes 5:2, *Authorized Version,* 1611

1841. The year's at the spring
And day's at the morn;
Morning's at seven;
The hillside's dew-pearled;
The lark's on the wing;
The snail's on the thorn:
God's in his heaven—
All's right with the world.
—Robert Browning, *Pippa Passes*

1928. *Nina (immediately gaily mocking):* Oh, very well, old thing! "God's in His heaven, all's right with the world!" —Eugene O'Neill, *Strange Interlude*

1952. "Look at those youngsters over there," Paul heard the Old Man say, "and tell me God isn't in his heaven." —Kurt Vonnegut, Jr., *Player Piano*

1984. "Let's say I put myself in God's hands, and then whatever happened, it was all right. No matter how terrible it was, it was all right—as the poet put it, God's in his heaven, all's right with the world. And then, all of a sudden, the hands were no longer there." —Howard Fast, *The Outsider*

1991. Things were great as far as he was concerned. He would certainly be re-elected because there wasn't anyone around to defeat him.... Herbert Hoover smiled to himself. All was right with the world. —Liz Smith, "A History Lesson for Mr. Bush," *Times* (Trenton)

Gone but not forgotten. Said of a person who has died or left his colleagues or friends but is still remembered. Often used as an inscription on monuments.

1973. Kago said that all he could do was to tell others in the Universe about how wonderful the automobile creatures had been. Here is what he said to all those rusting junkers who were out of gas: "You will be gone, but not forgotten." —Kurt Vonnegut, Jr., *Breakfast of Champions*

1991. Our correspondence might be gone from our screens, but it was hardly forgotten. The computer kept it in its memory. —Oliver L. North, *Under Fire*

1993. *Gone, But Not Forgotten* —Title of a book by Phillip Margolin

1994. Some things that are gone from our lives but not forgotten:
Telephones that ring, watches you have to wind and pants with flies that button.
Heroes who don't have any flaws in their character ...
Weapons like peashooters, water pistols and slingshots. They've been replaced by AK47s.
—Andy Rooney, *Times* (Trenton)

Gone with the wind. Said of something that has been swept away and is no longer here. The saying dates back to the 1890s. In 1896, the English poet Ernest Dowson (1867–1900), used the phrase in his love poem "Cynara." It is also used to invoke the antebellum South, as portrayed in Margaret Mitchell's novel *Gone With the Wind* (1936). In 1939, a motion-picture version of *Gone With the Wind* starring Vivien Leigh, Clark Gable, and

Leslie Howard became the most popular movie of all time.

1896. I have been faithful to thee, Cynara, in my fashion.
I have forgot much, Cynara! gone with the wind,
Flung roses, roses, riotously, with the throng.
—Ernest Dowson, "Cynara"

1936. Was Tara still standing? Or was Tara also gone with the wind which had swept through Georgia? —Margaret Mitchell, *Gone With the Wind*

1981. "Frankly, it's pricey, pretty near five figures, but like I say, it's an investment. That's how people buy cars now, more and more. That old Kleenex mentality of trade it in every two years is gone with the wind." —John Updike, *Rabbit Is Rich*

1992. GONE WITH THE WIND: THE STUFF OF EVERYDAY —Headline of a report on Hurricane Andrew, *New York Times*

Good Americans, when they die, go to Paris. Paris has been a magnet for intellectual Americans since the early days of our history as a nation. The American expatriate community in Paris, mostly writers, poets, and artists, played an active part in the French cultural life, never tearing their ties with their home country. Their love for Paris was expressed in the saying coined by Thomas Gold Appleton (1812–84), a poet and artist, who loved Paris and was an active member of the Paris literary coterie. The saying is sometimes erroneously attributed to Oliver Wendell Holmes (1809–94) who only reported it in his *The Autocrat of the Breakfast-Table* (1858). *Good Americans come to Paris when they die* and *All good Americans, when they die, go to Paris* are variations on the adage.

1858. Good Americans, when they die, go to Paris. —Thomas Gold Appleton, in Oliver Wendell Holmes, *The Autocrat of the Breakfast-Table*

1893. *Mrs. Allonby:* They say, Lady Hunstanton, that when good Americans die they go to Paris.
Lady Hunstanton: Indeed? And when bad Americans die, where do they go?
Lady Illingrowth: Oh, they go to America. —Oscar Wilde, *A Woman of No Importance*

1929. We are those good Americans who go to Paris when they die. —T. Smith, *Topper Takes a Trip*

A good beginning is half the battle. Any endeavor with a good foundation is likely to succeed. The proverb has been traced back to *Middle English Sermons* (c.1415). In 1773, Oliver Goldsmith (1730–74) said, "The first blow is half the battle." Almost always shortened to *half the battle.*

1984. With every new car, public perception is half the battle —Lee Iacocca with William Novak, *Iacocca*

1991. The important thing, as Mr. Williams sees it, is that the center has focused attention on the content of art education and raised the level of discussion and argument in the field. "That's at least half the battle," he said. —Paul Goldberger, *New York Times*

1993. "The single market is only half the battle without a single currency," said Keith Richardson, the secretary general of the European Roundtable, a Brussels-based trade group for some of Europe's largest companies. —*New York Times*

See also THE FIRST STEP IS THE HARDEST.

Good fences make good neighbors. Respect for someone else's property makes a good neighbor. Although the American poet Robert Frost (1874–1963) is often credited with coining this proverb in "Mending Wall" (1914), he did not originate it. It has been traced back to E. Rogers's letter in *Winthrop Papers* (1640). In 1651, English poet George Herbert expressed a similar idea: "Love your neighbor, yet pull not down your hedge." First attested in the United States in *Modern Chivalry* (1815) by American poet and novelist Hugh Henry Brackenridge (1748–1816).

1815. Good fences restrain fencebreaking beasts, and … preserve good neighborhoods. —Hugh Henry Brackenridge, *Modern Chivalry*

1914. There where it is we do not need the wall:
He is all pine and I am apple orchard.
My apple trees will never get across
And eat the cones under his pines, I tell him.
He only says, "Good fences make good neighbors."
　　　　　　　　—Robert Frost, "Mending Wall"

1992. Scott McConnell praises Jerry Brown's use of Robert Frost's line, "Good fences make good neighbors," in opposing the free trade pact…. —Letters to the Editor, *New York Post*

1995. …The fundamental problems in the separation plan could be anticipated even before a truck bomb passed the Gaza checkpoint…. While its advocates cited the phrase that "good fences make good neighbors," in the area of national security what is far more true is that "good neighbors make good fences." —*Manhattan Jewish Sentinel*

See also FAMILIARITY BREEDS CONTEMPT.

A good man is hard to find. It is not easy to find a qualified person (or a decent human being). Commonly used literally. Popularized as a title of a book of short stories by Flannery O'Connor (1955). The subject of the proverb may be changed. *Good men are scarce* is a variant form that dates back to the early 1600's.

1991. "Every time I see a good chef, I just like to have him," Mr. Mehta said. "I put him to work somewhere—in the newsstands, in the jewelry store, anywhere. Because I know that one day I will need him. A good cook is hard to find." —Madhur Jaffrey, *New York Times*

1991. A wood man nowadays is hard to find. Casey as the Bat. —Quoted in "New York Magazine Competition," *New York*

1991. [Jessica] Lange says their relationship is "constantly changing. I keep hoping that it settles into a certain dynamic where there'll be no question Sam [Shepard] and I are best friends, which is hard to come by." —*Vanity Fair*

1995. A GOOD MAN IS HARD TO KEEP: THE CORRESPONDENCE OF FLANNERY O'CONNOR AND S. J. PERELMAN —Headline, *New York Times Book Review*

Good men are scarce. *See* A GOOD MAN IS HARD TO FIND.

A good name is better than precious ointment. Your reputation is your most precious possession. The proverb appeared in the Old Testament. It has been traced back in English to *How Gode Wyfe Taught Her Daughter* (c.1350) and was slightly changed by Francis Bacon in 1625. First attested in the United States in *Colonial Records of Georgia* (1739). The phrase may take varying forms: *A good name is better than great riches; A good name is better than fine jewels; A good name is better than gold; A good name is better than precious stones; A good name is more precious than rubies,* etc.

A good name *is* better than precious ointment; and the day of death than the day of one's birth. —Ecclesiastes 7:1, *Authorized Version,* 1611

1625. A good name is like a precious ointment; it filleth all around about, and will not easily away; for the odors of ointments are more durable than those of flowers. —Francis Bacon, "Of Praise"

1984. Let me tell you something straight from the shoulder: good name in man or woman is the immediate jewel of their soul. A good name is better than precious ointment. —Joseph Heller, *God Knows*

See also A GOOD REPUTATION IS MORE VALUABLE THAN MONEY.

The good news is …; the bad news is …

These phrases are always followed by some pleasant and unpleasant information. People sometimes ask, "Do you want the good news or the bad news first?" to alleviate the distress of someone who is about to receive some bad news. *You'll always get the good news; it's how quickly you get the bad news* is a variant form of the phrase.*****

1984. *Dentist to patient:* The bad news is you've got three cavities. The good news is your gold crowns have tripled in value. —Quoted in *Reader's Digest*

1985. "I have good news and bad news," I told a lecture audience in the fall of 1980, eighteen months into my research on this book. "The good news is that a major revitalization of Jewish religious and cultural life is under way; the bad news is that there may not be enough Jews left to sustain it." —Charles E. Silberman, *A Certain People*

1987. "Anyway, he looks us up and down and says, 'Girls, I got some good news, and I got some bad news. The good news is, if you prove that you're good enough to get through this here course, you ain't got nothin' left to prove as you live.' And he waits for a couple of seconds. 'The bad news is, you gotta prove it to *me!* '" —Tom Clancy, *Patriot Games*

1988. "I've got some good news and some bad news," muttered the CPA. "The good news is your tax return is completed. The bad news is you owe the IRS an extra $2,000." —Charles J. Givens, *Wealth without Risk*

1990. "The good news," said Bryen, "was that we stopped Iraq from buying guns. The bad news was that they almost bought the plant to make those guns." —Judith Miller & Laurie Mylroie, *Saddam Hussein and the Crisis in the Gulf*

1992. Wonder how there can be a bad news followed by a worse news. Does that ever happen in the book? Bad news: you're pushed out of an airplane. Worse news: you don't have a parachute. —*New Yorker*

1994. "The good news is that we were able to pick up Coleman," Giants Coach Dan Reeves said in a statement issued by the club. "The bad news is that we have to let somebody go." —*New York Times*

See also NO NEWS IS GOOD NEWS.

Good news travels slowly; bad news travels fast. See BAD NEWS TRAVELS FAST.

A good reputation is more valuable than money.

The proverb has been traced back to *How Gode Wyfe Taught Her Daughter* (c.1350), but it was known as far back as the first century b.c. First attested in the United States in *Colonial Records of Georgia* (1739). *A good reputation is more precious than fine gold* is a variant.

First century b.c.
A good reputation is more valuable than money. —Publilius Syrus, Maxim 108

1865. It ain't often that a man's reputation outlasts his munny. —Josh Billings, *Josh Billings, His Sayings*

1994. A good reputation is more precious than fine gold, reminds the proverb. In his forthcoming biography of the President, called *Highwire*, John Brummett writes that Clinton "seems to have an almost pathological inability to tell the whole truth." … That is becoming increasingly obvious to more people, even those who script fortune cookies. —*Star-Ledger* (Newark)

See also A GOOD NAME IS BETTER THAN PRECIOUS OINTMENT.

Good riddance to bad rubbish.

Who needs you? I'm glad you're leaving. That thing is worthless: I'm glad I've lost it. The proverb is found in *Dombey and Son* (1848) by Charles Dickens. First attested in the United States in *Assex Gazette* (1771). Often shortened to *good riddance* and used as an exclamation.

1928. All right … good riddance! … I'd have the guts to bump off then, all right! … that'd set her free … come on now! … ask her! … —Eugene O'Neill, *Strange Interlude*

1936. For a moment it was on Scarlett's hot tongue to cry: "Go and good riddance!" but the cool hand of caution stopped her. —Margaret Mitchell, *Gone With the Wind*

1953. *Laura:* I wouldn't worry too much about it. When I'm gone, it will probably be agreed by all that I was an off-horse too, and didn't really belong to the clan, and it's good riddance. —Robert Anderson, *Tea and Sympathy*

1961. "Good riddance to bad rubbish," was Aarfy's unperturbed response.
"Don't say that about her!" Nately protested with passion that was both a plea and a rebuke. "I

want her to stay with me." —Joseph Heller, *Catch-22*

1962. The fan stirred faint eddies of her perfume in the room for a moment, then the scent faded.

"Good riddance to bad rubbish," said Mrs. Hawke. —Herman Wouk, *Youngblood Hawke*

1978. "I imagine he's got the lights on," the Judge said with deceptive idleness. "There's an attraction in that, you know. Obviously this man Impending felt it."

"Good riddance to bad rubbish," Larry said grimly, and the Judge laughed long and heartily. —Stephen King, *The Stand*

1985. "He did a Burton—packed his bags and ran without even asking for his teeth."

"Good riddance to bad rubbish," Vicky said. —Michael Korda, *Queenie*

1988. "You know what, Castellano? I say good riddance to the bastard." —Erich Segal, *Doctors*

1993. And though at the time I certainly felt, "Good riddance," I feel that I might have been a bit hasty. —*New York Times*

1994. As a coach, Mike Keenan deserves to be hailed for having done a good job. As a man, he deserves good riddance. —Dave Anderson, *New York Times*

The good that men do lives after them. People are generally remembered for their good deeds. The proverb has been traced back to *You Can't Be Too Careful* (1942) by H. G. Wells. It however is a reversed version of Shakespeare's phrase in *Julius Caesar* in 1599. The idea of the main entry was well known as far back as Euripides (c.485–406 b.c.).

5th century b.c.
> When good men die their goodness does not
>   perish,
> But lives though they are gone. As for the
>   bad,
> All that was theirs dies and is buried with
>   them.
>   —Euripides, *Temenidae*

1599. Friends, Romans, countrymen, lend me your
>   ears;
> I come to bury Caesar, not to praise him.
> The evil that men do lives after them,
> The good is oft interred with their bones.
>   —Shakespeare, *Julius Caesar*, III, ii

1984. I immortalize him. Why criticize? The good that men do lives after them, while the evil is oft interred with their bones. So let it be with Saul, I decided, and made no mention at all of his killing of the priests, that bloody nut, and his occasional

spells of looniness with the prophets. —Joseph Heller, *God Knows*

1993. She's survived by a daughter and son-in-law, six grandchildren, 11 great-grandchildren, and a niece and several nephews. The good that she did will live after her. —Overheard at church funeral services in Hopewell, N.J.

The good, the bad, and the ugly. Everything or everyone: the good, the bad, and the ugly. The saying originated in 1967 and is associated with the Clint Eastwood movie by that title. The phrase is based on the analogy of *good, bad, or indifferent*, which has been popular since the eighteenth century and is still heard today. The word *ugly* replaced *indifferent*. Other words *(fuzzy, outrageous, ridiculous)* sometimes replace *ugly*. There are dozens of variations, which often appear in headlines.***

1922. The driver never said a word, good, bad or indifferent, but merely watched the two figures … —James Joyce, *Ulysses*

1967. *The Good, the Bad, and the Ugly* —Title of a western directed by Sergio Leone and starring Clint Eastwood and Eli Wallach

1984. The Fords are one of America's last great family dynasties. In any dynasty, the first instinct is self-protection. Anything, *anything* —good, bad, or indifferent—that might affect the dynasty becomes a potential problem in the mind of the man who heads it. —Lee Iacocca with William Novak, *Iacocca*

1988. "Don't worry, Ben, it'll all be there—the good, the bad—and even the ridiculous. But you have to understand—as I keep trying to—that doctors are just frail human beings. And no human being is immune from fear." —Erich Segal, *Doctors*

1991. "I came here to tell you the truth," I told Nields that first morning. "The good, the bad, and the ugly." —Oliver L. North, *Under Fire*

1992. He told her about his witnesses—the good, the bad and the unreliable—about Alexander Blair and the avalanche of paper from Phoenix Enterprises' accountants. —Philip Friedman, *Inadmissible Evidence*

1995. THE GOOD, THE BAD AND THE BARGAINS —Headline of an article on wine, *Time Off* (N.J.)
See also WARTS AND ALL.

Government of the people, by the people, and for the people. Many politicians have tried to define democracy, but Abraham Lincoln's description is the most precise in form and substance. He is usually given credit for the saying, but he was probably not its originator. It is found in Wycliff's Bible in the fourteenth century. On January 26, 1830, in his second speech in the Senate, Daniel Webster said, "The people's Government, made for the people, by the people, and answerable to the people." On May 29, 1850, addressing the New England Anti-Slavery Convention in Boston, Theodore Parker, an American preacher and social reformer, declared: "A democracy—that is a government of all the people, by all the people, for all the people." Parker is probably the source used by Lincoln for his Gettysburg Address.

c. 1330–84.
This Bible is for the government of the people, by the people and for the people. —John Wycliff, quoted by George Seldes, *Great Quotations*

1863. ...We here highly resolve that these dead shall not have died in vain; that this nation, under God, shall have a new birth of freedom; and that government of the people, by the people, and for the people shall not perish from the earth. —Abraham Lincoln, Gettysburg Address

1964. LOST: Poster, printed with Indian ink, saying that *Government of the Students, by the Students, for the Students, shall not perish from Calvin Coolidge.* —Bel Kaufman, *Up the Down Staircase*

1984. Lincoln once said that ours is to be a government of the people, by the people, and for the people. But what we have today is a government of the rich, by the rich, and for the rich and we're going to make a change in November. —Walter Mondale, *New York Times*

1992. If volunteers using petitions can get him on the ballot in all 50 states, he recently announced, he [Ross Perot] would run as a third-party presidential candidate and dedicate himself to a populist overhaul of the American system. "The framers of the Constitution meant for this to be a government by and for the people," he says. —*People*

1994. George Pataki is giving every indication that he will establish a government of D'Amato, for D'Amato, by D'Amato. —Rudolph Giuliani, *New York Times*

The grass is always greener on the other side of the fence. Other people's lives always seem more desirable than our own. We're never satisfied with what we have. The proverb has been traced back to 1545. The original idea can be found in the poetry of Ovid (c.43 b.c.–a.d. c.18): *Fertilior seges est alenis semper in agris* ("The harvest is always more fruitful in another man's fields"). First attested in the United States in the *Bangor Daily News* (Me.) (1959) and The *New York Times* (1959). Variants of this saying include: *The grass is always greener over the next hill; The grass always looks greener on the other side of the hill; The grass is always greener on the other man's lawn; The grass looks greener on the other side of the pastures; The grass is always greener across the street,* etc.

1959. The grass always looks greener on the other side of the fence. —*New York Times*

1984. The grass is always greener when you take care of it. —*Forbes*

1987. "Sometimes, I'm disappointed that recognition didn't happen earlier for me," he said, "but I guess the grass is always greener on the other side. You always want more than you have." —*New York Times*

1993. In truth, luck has been fair to both of us, and we've been true and honest friends long enough to know that the grass is never really greener on the other side but rather, like us, just differently shaded. —*New York Times Magazine*

1994. Says Coopers & Lybrand partner John Rice, "When your company is looking to relocate to another city, you have to look at a whole host of factors—not just the corporate and personal income tax—to see if the grass is really greener." —*Crain's New York Business*

Great minds think alike. People tend to share the same ideas, make the same decisions, act in a similar way. Often used in response to a statement that is exactly or almost the same as one's own. Said in a jocular way. The proverb has been traced back to the early seventeenth century. First cited in the United States in *Winthrop Papers* (1640). The phrase is found in varying forms: *Great minds flow in the same channel; Great minds run in the same gutters (channel); Great minds run in the same channel, and weak ones in the same gutter,* etc.

1988. Alevy said, "Actually, I think we have found two [KGB agents]. Right here. In the embassy, Sam. Right under our noses. Any guesses?"

Hollis thought a moment.... He said to Alevy, "Our nice handyman and housekeeper. The Kellums."

Alevy replied, "Great minds think alike." —Nelson DeMille, *The Charm School*

1993. You're 100 percent right. That's exactly what I was about to say. Great minds think alike. —Overheard on a Trenton-bound train (N.J.)

Great oaks from little acorns grow. Great people begin as small children. Great successes often develop from something very small. The proverb is similar to the Latin: *Parvis e glandibus quercus* ("Tall oaks from little acorns grow"). It appears in Chaucer's *Troilus and Criseyde* (c.1385). First attested in the United States in *Life of Jefferson S. Batkins* (1871). The phrase may take different forms: *Big oaks from little acorns grow; Mighty oaks from tiny acorns grow; Little acorns into great oaks grow; Tall oaks from little acorns grow,* etc.

> **1989.** "Actually, it's gone a little better than I expected, but you always criticize yourself," said Mr. Sununu, sitting in his office only yards from the Oval Office. "You keep learning. You learn to look for the small acorns so you don't have to cut down the oak tree." —*New York Times*
>
> **1993.** FROM LITTLE PACKAGES COME BIG SOUNDS —Headline, "Pop Music," *New York Times*
>
> **1995.** Even basketball superstars start out as schoolkids. Tall oaks from little acorns grow, as the saying goes. —Overheard in Central Park, New York City

A guilty conscience needs no accuser. The internal recognition of one's misdeeds is enough to establish guilt. The proverb has been traced back to Chaucer's *Prologue to Canon's Yeoman's Tale.* First cited in the United States in 1755.

> **1952.** "Why should I think that?" I said, groping for his identity.
> "Because you were thinking about me."
> Then I knew he was speaking of Hinckman's murder and must be the murderer—"a guilty conscience needs no accuser." —*Ellery Queen's Mystery Magazine*
>
> **1957.** See what a guilty conscience he's got. Justifying himself before anyone's accused him of anything. —E. X. Ferrars, *Count the Cost*
>
> **1998.** When I was a kid my mom used to nail me for snatching cookies from the cookie jar. She never saw me take them, but she always knew when I did. When I asked her how she knew, she would respond, "A guilty conscience needs no accuser." —*Arizona Republic*

Guns don't kill people. People do. Slogan used by National Rifle Association supporters. *Guns don't shoot people, people shoot people* and *Guns don't kill people, bullets do* are variants of the catch phrase. Of recent origin.**

> **1993.** Alcohol kills something like 200,000 people per year, cigarettes, 500,000, and guns, 37,000. Oh, sorry. Guns don't kill people. People do. —*New York Times Magazine*
>
> **1994.** Gun controls are silly—after all guns don't kill people, people kill people. —*Princeton Packet* (N.J.)
>
> **1995.** GUNS DON'T KILL, GUN MAKERS DO? —Headline of an article on gun manufacturers, *New York Times*

See also LOCK 'EM UP AND THROW AWAY THE KEY; THREE STRIKES AND YOU'RE OUT.

Hail to the Chief. Title of the official song and anthem of the president of the United States and commander-in-chief of the U.S. Armed Forces. The phrase was originated by Sir Walter Scott in 1810, and the song was written by James Sanderson (1769–1841). It is usually played when the president appears at a ceremony or reception.

1810. Hail to the Chief who in triumph advances! —Walter Scott, *The Lady of the Lake*

1977. The Marine Band played "Ruffles and Flourishes" to announce their arrival, then struck up "Hail to the Chief." —William Safire, *Full Disclosure*

1993. HAIL TO THE CHEF —Headline of an article on healthy eating, *Modern Maturity*

1995. ALL HAIL THE CHIEF. SPEAKING AT TWO LOCAL EVENTS, PRES. CLINTON ANNOUNCES NEW EXECUTIVE ORDER BANNING ALL U.S. INVESTMENT & TRADE WITH IRAN. —Headline, *Manhattan Jewish Sentinel* (N.Y.)

Half a loaf is better than none (no bread). It is better to have something than nothing at all. "Better is half a loaf than no bread," appears in John Heywood's 1546 book of proverbs. First attested in the United States in *Andros Tracts* (1693). The phrase takes varying forms: *Even a crumb is better than no bread; Half a bun is better than no cake; Half a cake is better than none; Half a lie is better than no truth; Half a truth is better than none,* etc. Sometimes shortened to *half a loaf.*

1928. *Darrell:* Nothing left but to accept her terms … I love her … I can help to make her happy … half a loaf is better … to a starving man…. —Eugene O'Neill, *Strange Interlude*

1957. "I suppose that half a loaf is better than no bread, when you're starving." —Nevil Shute, *On the Beach*

1980. Our needs frustrated, we find some solace in reciting old bromides and clichés: "Half a loaf is better than none," or "Give a little, get a little," or "A good negotiation outcome is one where both sides are somewhat dissatisfied." —Herb Cohen, *You Can Negotiate Anything*

1988. The onus remains on the PLO, left all alone by both Jordan and Israel. Jordan having already made its decision and Israel about to, after the election…. It is the PLO which must now decide what to do next, whether half a loaf is better than none. —*Washington Times*

1989. "I've offered him half a loaf, and it's more than he ever expected to get. He'd get the whole loaf from Robert in time, or so he thinks, but now that he's seen me with you, he may have doubts about how soon that's going to happen." —Michael Korda, *The Fortune*

1990. Mikhail Gorbachev … reclaims the initiative by acknowledging that half a loaf is better than none. —*Time*

1992. "Come one," she said. "Half a loaf is better than none."

Carella nodded.

He was thinking that yesterday afternoon Samson Wilbur Cole had walked out of that courtroom a free man, and today Emma Katherine Bowles was walking, too. He was thinking that nowadays if you got anywhere near half a loaf you were lucky. Most of the time, all you got were the crumbs left on the table. —Ed McBain, *Kiss*

1994. Wilbur L. Ross offers a halfway solution to municipal money problems…. Unfortunately, half a bridge is no better than none, except to those who have the construction contracts. —Letters to the Editor, *New York Times*

See also A BIRD IN THE HAND IS WORTH TWO IN THE BUSH; A LIVING DOG IS BETTER THAN A DEAD LION.

Half the battle. See A GOOD BEGINNING IS HALF THE BATTLE.

Handsome (pretty) is as handsome (pretty) does. Good deeds are more important than good looks. The proverb was first recorded by Chaucer in *The Wife of Bath's Tale* (c.1387). In 1766, in his preface to *The Vicar of Wakefield,* Oliver Goldsmith wrote: "Handsome is as handsome does." First attested in the United States in *Journal of a Lady of Quality* (1774). The saying is found in varying forms, including *Beauty is as beauty does.*

> **1922.** Handsome is and handsome does. —James Joyce, *Ulysses*

> **1948.** In *The Howitzer,* when he graduates, they have printed, "The Strategist" under his record, and then to soften it, for it jars with the mellow sentimental glow of yearbooks, they have added a little ambiguously, "Handsome Is as Handsome Does." —Norman Mailer, *The Naked and the Dead*

> **1987.** Oliver North is a slick, perfectly cast (Hollywood-style) Marine as witness, but in his work, out of uniform, he has been a loose cannon camouflaged in the American flag. Handsome is as handsome does. —*Daily News* (N.Y.)

> **1991.** She [Edith Davis] now believed that people could be admitted solely for their looks, their clothes, their possessions, and she raised her daughter accordingly. "Pretty is as pretty does—that's what my mother taught me and that's what I taught Nancy," she said. —Kitty Kelley, *Nancy Reagan*

The handwriting is on the wall. Danger is imminent; the jig is up. In the Old Testament, Belshazzar, the Babylonian king, demands that the Jewish prophet Daniel, interpret a series of words written on the wall: *Mene, mene, tekel, upharsin.* Daniel tells the king that God has numbered the days of his kingdom and it will be divided between the Medes and the Persians. Thereafter, Belshazzar is killed and Darius the Mede seizes the throne.

> In the same hour came forth fingers of a man's hand, and wrote over against the candlestick upon the plaster of the wall of the king's palace; and the king saw the part of the hand that wrote. —Daniel 5:5, *Authorized Version,* 1611

> **1943.** There was so much handwriting on the wall
> That even the wall fell down.
> —Christopher Morley, "Around the Clock"

> **1987.** Not everyone was ready to go as far as Senator Edward M. Kennedy of Massachusetts, who declared that "the handwriting is on the wall that the current installment of U.S. military aid is the last installment." —*New York Times*

> **1988.** He spoke of Berlin, Hitler's rise to power, the Nuremberg Laws of 1935 depriving Jews of civil rights, and how he wished that, like his brother, he had seen the writing on the wall and left. —Erich Segal, *Doctors*

> **1991.** There are, of course, relationships that go on for many years, or lead to a lasting marriage, and once that happens, the handwriting is on the wall and it's merely a matter of time. —*New York Times*

> **1993.** William Lindsey, 50, of Huntington Beach, Calif., wasn't fired. He quit to start his own management-consulting firm. "I saw the handwriting on the wall," he says, "when they began to scale down my group at Hughes Aircraft." —John Ehrlichman, "Who Will Hire Me Now?" *Parade*

Happy days are here again. Title of a 1929 song with lyrics by Jack Yellen (1892–1991) and music by Milton Ager (1893–1979). After being played at the 1931 Democratic presidential convention, it was adopted as Franklin Delano Roosevelt's campaign song.

> **1929.** Happy days are here again,
> The skies above are clear again:
> Let us sing a song of cheer again!
> Happy days are here again!
> —Jack Yellen, "Happy Days Are Here Today"

> **1993.** *Happy Days Were Here Again: Reflections of a Libertarian Journalist* —Title of a book by William F. Buckley, Jr.

> **1994.** A glance at the March 23 *New York Times* could make you think that happy days are here again. Blacks, Jews, organized labor and the Hollywood liberal community took a nearly full-page ad regarding U.S. policy toward Haiti. —*Times* (Trenton)

See also EVERYTHING'S COMING UP ROSES.

Happy is the country which has no history. The history of most countries includes wars, revolutions, assassinations, and other acts of violence. This proverb was first expressed by Benjamin Franklin in his *Poor Richard's Almanac* (1740): "Happy that Nation—fortunate the age, whose history is not diverting." Thomas Jefferson further developed that idea in one of his letters, saying that "blest is that nation whose silent course of happiness furnishes nothing for history to say."

English historian Edward Gibbon wrote in *The History of the Decline and Fall of the Roman Empire* (1766–88): "History... is indeed little more than the register of the crimes, follies, and misfortunes of mankind." George Eliot considered that "the happiest women, like the happiest nations, have no history" (*The Mill on the Floss,* 1860). In reply to Montesquieu's aphorism, "Happy the people whose annals are tiresome," Scottish essayist and historian Thomas Carlyle said, "Happy the people whose annals are blank in history books" (*History of the French Revolution,* 1873).

1957. Quoting the familiar dictum: "Happy is the country which has no history," I remarked that I belonged, like Edward VIII, to a generation which was still on the early side of middle age but had already seen almost more history than any generation could bear. —Vera Mary Brittain, *Testament of Experience*

1998. Yesterday the *London Times,* while urging Blair and Irish Prime Minister Bertie Ahern to battle hard to avert a collapse of the peace process, warned that historical precedents were not encouraging. The prospect of success, the *Times* said, was "vanishingly small." As he leaped into the political breach, the British leader might have been tempted to recall the old proverb, "Happy is the country that has no history." The trouble with Northern Ireland, perhaps, is that it has too much of it. —*Christina Science Monitor*

See also HISTORY IS BUNK; HISTORY REPEATS ITSELF.

Has the cat got your tongue? Why don't you speak? Your silence is suspicious. The saying originated in the mid-nineteenth century and was used when addressing a child who refused to answer a parent's questions after some mischief. Often shortened to *cat got your tongue?*

1982. She met Harch's hateful, frost-gray eyes, and her stomach churned, but she didn't look away.
"Cat got your tongue?"
"I hope not," Quince said. —Dean R. Koontz, *The House of Thunder*

1995. The country wants Colin Powell to run for president. And I want to know if the cat has got his tongue. —Overheard at Washington Square, New York City

Haste makes waste. Hurrying often results in mistakes. It's better to be careful and conscientious than to cut corners. The proverb appeared in Chaucer's *Tale of Melibee* (c.1386) and was listed in the books of proverbs of John Heywood (1546) and John Ray (1678). First attested in the United States in *Poor Richard's Almanac* (1753) by Benjamin Franklin. The saying may be found in varying forms: *Haste not, waste not; Haste makes waste, waste makes want, want makes beggars,* etc.

1961. "Haste makes waste, Purvis. Haste makes waste. If I've told you that once, I must have told you that a hundred times. Haste makes waste." —Joseph Heller, *Catch-22*

1987. Stanley is now racing ahead in the excitement of discovery.... "So he puts them to the test. If they really need something, they'll keep after it. If not, forget it. After all, haste makes waste." —R. Richard Ritti & G. Ray Funkhouser, *The Ropes to Skip & the Ropes to Know*

1992. Haste makes waste. The Saudis were understandably eager to see Hughes people show up with backhoes and screwdrivers. "We asked them to wait," says Currie. "Complex systems get in trouble when your approach is 'Ready ... fire ... aim.' " —*Fortune*

See also EASY DOES IT; MAKE HASTE SLOWLY; SLOW AND STEADY WINS THE RACE.

Haste not, waste not. *See* HASTE MAKES WASTE.

He could sell a drowning man a glass of water. *See* HE COULD SELL ICE TO AN ESKIMO.

He could sell ice to an Eskimo. He is a highly persuasive speaker. He is a slick salesman or con artist. Said of people who are able to talk you into getting something that is absolutely unnecessary. Of recent origin (since 1955). Variants include *He could sell a drowning man a glass of water* and *He could sell sand to the Arabs. He couldn't sell Coke in [the] Sahara,* as used by John Updike, is a negative variant of the proverb.

1981. "I *know* he wants in and I don't *want* him in. He makes me uncomfortable. With that sorehead look of his he couldn't sell.—"
"Coke in Sahara," Charlie finishes for him. —John Updike, *Rabbit Is Rich*

1988. "Imagine: '*A violent and vicious man ... the prime mover in the murders ... and a man, ladies and gentlemen of the jury, who you certainly can't trust.'* And you would probably believe it, as you may now believe that you *can* trust David. —because Rusty Hardin could sell ice to Eskimos." —Clifford Irving, *The Campbell Murder Case*

1989. "Lewie Ranieri could sell ice to an Eskimo," says Scott Brittenham, who accompanied him on many of the sales calls. —Michael Lewis, *Liar's Poker*

1992. This agent was a traveling salesman, and a

very successful one. Man, what a line he had! He could sell sand to the Arabs, and ice to the Eskimos. —Abigail Van Buren, "Dear Abby," *New York Post*

1993. He [Robert Pastorelli] decided to follow his dream. "I felt I had an affinity for acting.... I could sell a drowning man a glass of water." —*Trentonian* (N.J.)

See also HE WOULD TRY TO SELL YOU THE BROOKLYN BRIDGE.

He could sell sand to the Arabs. *See* HE COULD SELL ICE TO AN ESKIMO.

He couldn't sell Coke in [the] Sahara. *See* HE COULD SELL ICE TO AN ESKIMO.

He met his Waterloo. He suffered a decisive defeat; he met his nemesis. In June 1815, Napoleon's army was defeated at Waterloo, Belgium, by British troops led by the Duke of Wellington. Napoleon was exiled to the island of St. Helena, where he died in 1821. The subject can be replaced with another pronoun or noun.**

1922. Bloom: It's a way we gallants have in the navy. Uniform that does it. *(he turns gravely to the first watch)* Still, of course, you do get your Waterloo sometimes. —James Joyce, *Ulysses*

1984. In the past General Haig's battlefields ranged from Vietnam to the Nixon White House during Watergate. But it was not until he became secretary of state under Ronald Reagan that Haig met what he calls "his Waterloo." —Barbara Walters, "20/20," ABC

1991. Fact: Tyson is a fearsome puncher. Myth: Tyson has boxing skills. All punchers meet their Waterloo against a crafty boxer. —*New York Times*

1995. "Where does the common man get a 'citation in the literature' of a play on words?" Robert Brothers of Philadelphia asks.... Will the Independent Counsel cause Bill Clinton to meet his Whitewaterloo? If so, brother Brothers is the acknowledged coiner. —William Safire, "On Language," *New York Times Magazine*

He that is born to be hanged shall never be drowned. If you are destined for one kind of misfortune, a different one is not in store for you. The proverb originated in France in the mid-fourteenth century in the form *Noyer ne peut, cil qui doit pendre* ("He cannot drown who must hang"). First appeared in English in the early sixteenth century. Shakespeare alluded to the saying in different forms: "I have great comfort from this fellow; methinks he hath no drowning mark upon

him; his complexion is perfect gallows" (*The Tempest*, 1611–12); "Go, go; bygone to save your ship from wreck,/Which cannot perish, having thee aboard,/Being destined to a drier death on shore" (*The Two Gentlemen of Verona*, 1594). First attested in the United States in Cook's *History of Col. Nathaniel Bacon's Rebellion* (1731).

1932. Orford might be one of those persons known to proverbial philosophy, who, having been born to be hanged, cannot be killed by any other method. —D. Sharp, *Code-Letter*

1956. There is another picture, and underneath it says... "If you're born to be hanged, then you'll never be drowned." —H. Lewis, *Witch & Priest*

1958. After a narrow escape a fisherman will say: "A man who is being saved to be hanged won't be drowned." —P. D. Westbrook, *Autobiography*

See also ONE MIGHT AS WELL BE HANGED FOR A SHEEP AS FOR A LAMB

He who calls the tune must pay the piper. *See* HE WHO DANCES MUST PAY THE FIDDLER; HE WHO PAYS THE PIPER CALLS THE TUNE.

He who can, does; he who cannot, teaches. *See* THOSE WHO CAN, DO. THOSE WHO CANNOT, TEACH.

He who dances must pay the fiddler. The person who reaps the benefits must foot the bill. Idle pleasures have ruinous consequences. We eventually have to pay for our mistakes. The proverb has been traced back to *Taylor's Feast* (1638) by J. Taylor. Used by William Congreve (1670–1729) in his play *Love for Love* (1695). First cited in the United States in *Jonathan Belcher Papers* (1740). Used by Abraham Lincoln in one of his speeches (1837). The saying is found in varying forms: *If you dance, you must pay the fiddler; Folks that dance must pay the piper; The dancer must pay the fiddler; The dancer must pay the piper; They that dance must pay the fiddler; He who calls the tune must pay the piper,* etc.

1695. I warrant you, if he danced till doomsday, he thought I was to pay the piper. —William Congreve, *Love for Love*

1837. I am decidedly opposed to the people's money being used to pay the fiddler. It is an old maxim and a very sound one, that he that dances should always pay the fiddler. —Abraham Lincoln, *Works*

1988. As Comptroller in 1965, when the city started using capital funds to finance current expenses, I vigorously protested, yet the practice continued and expanded. Not until 1975, when I was Mayor, did we have to pay the piper. —Abraham D. Beame, "Koch Reverts to Poor Finance," *New York Times*

1992. Asked about the fairness of his proposal to raise gasoline taxes by 50 percent a gallon, Mr. Perot said it would not, as the questioner suggested, punish the middle class. "I know it's not popular," Mr. Perot said. He said higher gas taxes are needed because "it's time to pay the fiddler, and if we don't we'll be spending our children's money." —*New York Times*

1993. After the cameras stopped rolling, Burt [Reynolds] turned to Chantal and said, "I've said some angry, bitter things. I'd just as soon never see this air. But if you want to dance, you have to pay the fiddler!" —*Times* (Trenton)

See also HE WHO PAYS THE PIPER CALLS THE TUNE; PAY THE PIPER HIS DUE.

He who does not work, neither should he eat.
One must earn one's keep. Idleness is a sin. Originally used by Paul of Tarsus in his Second Epistle. In 1386, it appeared in Chaucer's *Tale of Melibee*. First attested in the United States in *Works of Thomas Chalkley* (1719). The proverb is found in varying forms: *If you don't work, you shan't eat; Those who will not work shall not eat,* etc. The proverb has equivalents in other languages too: *Qui non laborat, non manducet* (Latin); *Wer nicht arbeitet, soll auch nicht essen* (German).

For even when we were with you, this we commanded you, that if any would not work, neither should he eat. —2 Thessalonians 3:10, *Authorized Version,* 1611

1891. If you won't work you shall not eat. —Rudyard Kipling, "Life's Handicap"

1991. Conservatives like to cite that ancient Puritan teaching: "He who does not work, neither should he eat." But the flip side of that stern motto should be written in the social contract too: "He who *does* work, *does* deserve a decent break." —Barbara Ehrenreich, *Time*

1995. The welfare and food stamp recipients should be told in plain English: you don't work, you don't eat. Period. —Overheard at the Department of Social Services in New York City

He who fights and runs away, may live to fight another day.
It is sometimes wiser to retreat and regroup one's forces than suffer an all-out defeat. The proverb has been traced back to *Tales and Quick Answers* (1532). However, it was current many centuries earlier and was even used by Demosthenes. In 1656, an anonymous author wrote: "He that fights and runs away/May live to fight another day." A century later, the proverb was used by the English playwright and poet Oliver Goldsmith (1728–74). First attested in the United States in *Letters on the American Revolution* (1774). The saying takes varying forms: *He that* (or *who*) *fights and runs away will live* (or *lives*) *to fight another day; The man who fights and runs away lives to fight another day; He who hunts and turns away may live to hunt another day;* etc.

1761. For he that fights and runs away
May live to fight another day;
But he who is in battle slain
Can never rise and fight again.
—Oliver Goldsmith, "The Art of Poetry on a New Plan"

1956. He who hunts and turns away may live to hunt another day. —*New Yorker*

1984. A living dog is better than a dead lion, and he who fights and runs away, may live to fight another day. —Joseph Heller, *God Knows*

1985. He brooded silently for a moment, and then said softly, "He's a sensitive guy, this'll kill him...."
"No," the producer replied. "He's a big boy. He'll live to write another day." —Erich Segal, *The Class*

1989. Even if Koch loses, he will go down fighting his good fight. "I will never run away to fight another day," he told me after the patronage scandal broke. "I want to fight today." Which is why New York's marathon Mayor is running once again. —*New York Times Magazine*

1991. In the 1982 Lebanon war, Yassir Arafat and the PLO were cornered in Beirut. The U.S. and other Western countries intervened to save them. Saved, they later returned to Lebanon to fight another day. —*Sticking Neck Out in Mideast, Daily News* (N.Y.)

1993. Joan Vinson, head of the Perot organization in Maryland, captured the post-Nafta spirit in the message she left on her telephone-answering machine yesterday: "We will live to fight another day.... There's a second vote in '94 and a third in '96." —*Wall Street Journal*

1994. ...In December of 1941 came the war and the Japanese, and in the darkest days of defeat and retreat, Roosevelt ordered MacArthur out, to live and fight another day. —*Crain's New York Business*

See also A LIVING DOG IS BETTER THAN A DEAD LION.

He who has a tiger by the tail dare not let go. One who has taken on a difficult task must see it to completion. The earliest written record of the adage dates back to A. Train's *Adventures* (1930) in the form "one is having a wildcat by the tail." The phrase is used in a variety of forms: *He who has a bear by the tail dare not let go; He who has a lion by the tail dare not let go; I had a bear by the short hairs and I could not let go; It is the old lion by the tail; You've got a bear by the tail and can't let go.* The short form *have a tiger by the tail* is used allusively to refer to a difficult or dangerous situation.

1956. I've got a bear by the tail and don't know how to turn it loose. —*New York Times*

1959. China has a bear by the tail in troubled Tibet. —*Boston Globe*

1972. The Sloan Guaranty Trust... might well have a tiger by the tail. —Emma Lathen, *Murder Without Icing*

1980. Auditors found her multimillion-dollar, patronage-ridden empire so ill-managed that it took months to determine how much money it had tied up in asserts. But if Jean Wallin, a congenial state representative and real estate agent, worries about having a tiger by the tail, she doesn't admit it. —*Associated Press*

1986. Just before the press conference preceeding the ceremony, a longtime friend of the new Teacher of the Year whispered that in choosing [Guy] Doud, the Encyclopedia Britannica selection committee had "caught a tiger by the tail." "He's one of the most involved, dynamic persons I've ever met," he said. —*Christian Science Monitor*

1987. Bork hearings on TV: another tiger by the tail for the Democrats... and danger signal for Biden —Headline, *Boston Globe*

1992. Later, as the reaction to growing Japanese purchases in the U.S. shifted from initial chuckles to increasing concern and both the U.S. and Japan began leveling direct volleys of criticism at one another after President Bush's January visit to Tokyo, the producers realized they had a "tiger by the tail," says Mr. Berkowsky. —*Christian Science Monitor*

1998. Mary, it is so integral to the Republicans moving forward at this juncture. And the problem that they have had so far is that they have focused so much on the impeachment issue, they've basically got a tiger by the tail; they can't let it go and they can't hold on to it either. So, at this point, they're looking for a graceful exit. —*CNN & Company*, Cable News Network

He who hesitates is lost. Swift and resolute action leads to success; self-doubt is a prelude to disaster. The proverb goes back to *Cato* (1713) by English essayist and poet Joseph Addison. First attested in the United States in *The Autocrat of the Breakfast Table* (1858) by Oliver Wendell Holmes.

1985. He who hesitates is last. —Mae West, quoted in *Reader's Digest*

1986. Place your bet somewhere between haste-makes-waste and he-who-hesitates-is-lost. —Robert Fulghum, *All I Really Need to Know I Learned in Kindergarten*

1991. "Attaboy, Mario," the Devil cheered ... "you'll pull even in the polls. Bush is a weenie; he'll crack."
   "Hold it ... I still lose. I can see it in your eyes."
   "It's in your hands," Satan purred. "You want three wishes?"
   "Get lost," Cuomo sneered.
   "He who hesitates," Satan shrugged, "dithers another day." —Joe Klein, "The Temptation of Mario," *New York*

See also FAINT HEART NEVER WON FAIR LADY; FORTUNE FAVORS THE BRAVE; NOTHING VENTURED, NOTHING GAINED.

He who laughs last, laughs best. Minor setbacks don't matter. The real winner is the one who is ahead at the end of the game. The saying has been traced back to John Heywood's 1546 compilation of proverbs. In 1670, John Ray included this version in his book of proverbs: "Better the last smile than the first laughter." The current form has been in common use since 1706 and was used by Sir John Vanbrugh (1664–1726) in his play *The Country House*. First attested in the United States in *Cy Whitaker's Place* (1798). The phrase occurs in various forms: *A last laugh is the best laugh; He who laughs last, laughs longest; He who weeps least, weeps best; It is the last laugh that lasts; It's the last laugh that counts; The last laugh is with me,* etc. The saying has its counterparts in other languages too: *Rira bien qui rira le dernier* (French); *Al reir será el reir* (Spanish); *Wer zuletzt lacht, lacht am besten* (German); Хорошо смеётся тот, кто смеётся последним (Russian).

1977. Bobby [Kennedy] had many "enemies." But none obsessed him more than James Riddle Hoffa, who had often humiliated him in public. There was to be no forgetting. And, inevitably, Bobby was to have the last laugh. —Victor Lasky, *It Didn't Start with Watergate*

1991. Dear Readers: I, not you, owe this mother

and her son an apology. I truly thought her son's letter was just a gag, and I would never poke fun at anyone with a mental illness.... "Paul Roi de France" has the last laugh on me. —Percy Ross, *Daily News* (N.Y.)

1993. As an afterthought, let's say that Donald Trump, for all his hoopla, can't hold a candle to the two females who have dominated his life in recent years. They continue to be spectacular superwomen, and no matter how much he tries to dominate *them* or put them down in ways subtle or obvious, Ivana and Marla keep having the last laugh. —Liz Smith, *Times* (Trenton)

1994. Seventy-seven years ago, Lenin argued that international capitalism would be economically successful but, by growing in a world of competitive states, it would plant the seeds of its own destruction. Although the empire he built is in ruins and his revolution discredited, Vladimir Ilyich may have the last laugh. —*New York Times*

He who lies down with dogs will rise up with fleas. *See* IF YOU LIE DOWN WITH DOGS, YOU'LL GET UP WITH FLEAS.

He who lives by the sword dies by the sword. Those who view war as a solution to a problem will ultimately be destroyed by their own violence. The idea was originally expressed in the New Testament. The proverb has been traced back to *Death of Robert, Earl of Huntington* (1601) by English dramatist and writer Anthony Munday (c.1553–1633). First attested in the United States in *Complete Writings of Roger Williams* (1652). The phrase appears in varying forms: *He that raiseth the sword shall die by the sword; If you draw the sword you will perish by the sword; They that take the sword shall perish by the sword; Those who live by the sword die by the sword; Who takes the sword, shall perish by the sword,* etc.

Then said Jesus unto him, Put up again thy sword into his place: for all they that take the sword shall perish with the sword. —Matthew 26:52, *Authorized Version*, 1611

1952. "If Checker Charley was out to make chumps out of men, he could damn well fix his own connections. Paul looks after his own circuits; let Charley do the same. Those who live by electronics, die by electronics." —Kurt Vonnegut, Jr., *Player Piano*

1978. He had gone to sleep that night sure that he was going to die; no one could be burned as badly as he was and live. A refrain had beaten its way into his head: *Live by the torch, die by the torch. Live by it, die by it.* —Stephen King, *The Stand*

1987. "You live by the sword, you die by it," Senator Simpson said, adding that the discussion in the meeting turned to the current turmoil in the House of Representatives over the leadership of the Armed Services Committee. —*New York Times*

1992. "He who lives by the accusation dies by the accusation," Mr. Cuomo said in an interview. "It's damaging, it's destructive and this will not help any of them defeat Senator D'Amato." —*New York Times*

1993. "I don't know him by sight, but just that he did a lot of abortions," said one member, Vicki Kline. "I certainly wouldn't wish him ill, and in fact I prayed for his conversion for a number of years. But I guess he who lives by the sword perishes by the sword." —*New York Times*

He who never made a mistake never made anything. If you are paralyzed by the fear of making mistakes, you will never achieve your goals. The proverb appeared in *An Outcast of the Islands* (1896) by English novelist Joseph Conrad (1857–1924). On January 24, 1889, it was used by the American diplomat Edward John Phelps (1822–1900) in a speech at the Mansion House in London. The proverb is found in varying forms: *Every man makes mistakes; Everybody makes mistakes; If you don't make mistakes you don't make anything; The man who makes no mistakes usually makes nothing,* etc.

1889. The man who makes no mistakes does not usually make anything. —Edward John Phelps, quoted in *The Oxford Dictionary of Quotations*

1984. "Always remember," he would say, "that everybody makes mistakes." —Lee Iacocca with William Novak, *Iacocca*

1988. "But in my somewhat greater experience I've found that even with the best of intentions, normal people can make mistakes." —Erich Segal, *Doctors*

1993. Your horoscope for today says "If you never make a mistake, you probably are not trying enough new things." Remember that—everybody makes mistakes. —Overheard at a class reunion in Princeton, N.J.

See also DON'T MAKE THE SAME MISTAKE TWICE; TO ERR IS HUMAN, TO FORGIVE DIVINE.

He who pays the piper calls the tune. Decisions are made by those who are in financial control. In the United States, the proverb has been traced back to *Diary of Grace Galloway* (1779). It is found in varying forms: *He who pays the piper* *should call the tune; Whoever pays the piper calls the tune,* etc.

1952. "What a place. I think you're mad, simply mad. But he who pays the piper calls the tune." —Kurt Vonnegut, Jr., *Player Piano*

1985. Israelis must face the realities to which their present leaders seem blind:.... Internally, political freedom is inseparable from economic freedom.... Externally, diplomatic independence is inseparable from economic independence. Israel's enemies sense that weakness in one begets weakness in the other: when Papa pays the piper, Papa calls the tune. —William Safire, *New York Times*

1987. When Pollard reached the sanctuary of the fire stairs, he turned and, furious, said: "Just remember, Sherman. *You* called the tune."

" 'Called the tune.' Terrific. You're a real phrasemaker, Pollard." —Tom Wolfe, *The Bonfire of the Vanities*

1993. HE WHO PAYS THE PIPER ... —Headline of a letter to the editor in suggesting that TV news researchers know what those who pay want, *New York Times*

See also HE WHO DANCES MUST PAY THE FIDDLER; PAY THE PIPER HIS DUE.

He who spares his rod hates his son. *See* SPARE THE ROD AND SPOIL THE CHILD.

He who sups with the devil should have a long spoon. Be extremely cautious if you deal with dangerous people. The proverb has been traced back to Chaucer's *Squire's Tale* (c. 1390): "Therfore bihoverth hire a ful long spoon/ That shal ete with a feend." The proverb was well established by Shakespeare's time: "He must have a long spoon that must eat with the devil" (*The Comedy of Errors*, 1590), "This is a devil, and no monster; I will leave him; I have no long spoon" (*The Tempest*, 1610). The proverb is first attested in the United States in the early nineteenth century in *Papers of Thomas Rufflin* (1834).

1938. They used to say in the old country, "Sup with the devil and you need a long spoon." —James Thomas Farrell, *No Star is Lost*

1941. "We're in British mandated territory, and we can't expect to operate without their protection: so we have to give a slice to some British insiders."

"Who sups with the devil must have a long spoon," quoted the youth sagely. —Upton Sinclair, *Between Two Worlds*

1959. Talk of the devil!... And then go and sup with him. What was that about a long spoon? —Ian Fleming, *Goldfinger*

1970. No spoon on earth is long enough to sup with the devil. —R. Cowper, *Twilight of Briareus*

1979. Hindenburg and the army thought they could use [Hitler].... Who sups with the devil needs a long spoon. —E. Anthony, *Grave of Truth*

1992. His recent speech on foreign policy in Milwaukee, though making Carteresque nods to global democracy and human rights, also made it plain that a defence of American interests sometimes made it necessary to sup with the devil (big devil-supping question, so far unanswered: how tough would Clinton-the-president be with China?). —*Economist* (London)

He would try to sell you the Brooklyn Bridge. Don't trust him—he's dishonest and will try to cheat you. Originated in the United States in the first half of the twentieth century. As a joke, newly arrived European immigrants were asked if they wanted to buy the Brooklyn Bridge.**

1962. "He's sure one high pressure salesman, he'd sell a body the Brooklyn Bridge. I reckon he's sold my son a couple of considerable lemons." —Herman Wouk, *Youngblood Hawke*

1989. "At that moment she [Jackie] could have sold me anything from an Edsel to the Brooklyn Bridge." —C. David Heymann, *A Woman Named Jackie*

1991. In other words, Iran is not a dictatorship. Sure, I thought, and I bet there's a bridge in Brooklyn that you'd like to sell us. —Oliver L. North, *Under Fire*

1992. Sell Los Angeles airport? This glib Bush Administration proposition makes as much sense as the offer once made to greenhorns in New York, to buy the Brooklyn Bridge. —*New York Times*

1994. Forget the Brooklyn Bridge. What investors want now are Brooklyn banks. —*Crain's New York Business*

See also HE COULD SELL ICE TO AN ESKIMO; IF YOU BELIEVE THAT, THERE IS A BRIDGE IN BROOKLYN I'D LIKE TO SELL YOU.

He wouldn't hurt a fly. Said of a very gentle, harmless person who only seems to be confrontational. The expression takes varying forms: *He couldn't* (or *wouldn't*) *hurt a fly; He wouldn't kill* (or *touch*) *a fly; He would never hurt a fly; He would never kill a cockroach,* etc. The saying reaches an ironic apotheosis in the last scene of Alfred Hitchcock's 1960 masterpiece *Psycho*, when Norman Bates (played by Anthony Perkins) attempts to prove that he literally wouldn't hurt a fly by allowing one to alight on his face.

1953. *Kilroy:* I would not hurt a fly unless it had on leather mittens. —Tennessee Williams, *Camino Real*

1963. "I know all about how harmless and gentle and dreamy he was supposed to be, how he'd never hurt a fly...." —Kurt Vonnegut, Jr., *Cat's Cradle*

1987. "They were afraid he and Mrs. Adcock would try to have relations, I guess. I think that's a dream long dead, myself. Geneene said he lost his activities years ago and couldn't possibly harm a fly ... so what would a little hugging and kissing hurt?" —Fannie Flagg, *Fried Green Tomatoes*

1991. "We said, 'That's not the Leroy Strachan we know—he wouldn't hurt a fly,'" says elder Charles Wright. —*Time*

Heads I win, tails you lose. I win in either case: heads or tails. The saying has been in common use since about 1830. Attested in the United States at the end of the nineteenth century. It may be found in varying forms: *Heads you lose, tails you lose; Heads you win, tails I lose; Heads you win, tails you win; It's a heads-I-win-tails-you-lose argument* (or *business;* or *proposition* or *situation*), etc.

1922. I win tails you lose. —James Joyce, *Ulysses*

1958. Heads, you win; tails, Harvard benefits. —*New Yorker*

1965. One could sympathize with Goodman's chagrin but still wonder whether he was not offering a heads-I-win-tails-you-lose proposition. If dissent was punished, terrible; if embraced, worse. —Arthur M. Schlesinger, Jr., *A Thousand Days*

1991. Adjusting the count by a complicated statistical technique that everyone agrees is flawed would feed the resentment of people already suspicious of Government's means and motives. On the other hand, failing to adjust a census that undercounts blacks and Hispanics would alienate minorities.... Heads you lose, tails you lose. —*New York Times*

1993. He generally recommends fixed-rate mortgages for people who expect to remain in their homes five years or more. After all, he says, if rates continue to plunge, you can refinance again later. And if rates go up, "then you've locked in a good rate. It's heads-you-win, tails-you-win." —*Wall Street Journal*

Heads will roll. Some people will be in great trouble. Often used when something has gone ex-

tremely wrong and punishment is imminent. The saying has been attributed to Adolf Hitler (1930).

1993. Republicans control a lot more local governments in New Jersey than Democrats. If the Armacon deals are endemic to the bond industry and government, a lot of political heads are going to roll. —*Times* (Trenton)

1994. HEADS TO ROLL AT STATE [Department] AND THE NSC [National Security Council] —*Time*

1995. "When Aldrich Ames was arrested and sentenced to life for espionage, people thought that heads would roll, but nothing happened." —Overheard on a New York City subway train

Hear no evil, see no evil, speak no evil. *See* SEE NO EVIL, HEAR NO EVIL, SPEAK NO EVIL.

Hell hath no fury like a woman scorned. A woman who has been rejected by her lover is liable to exact a terrible revenge. The adage has been traced back to Beaumont and Fletcher's *Knight of Malta* (1625). Usually attributed to the English dramatist William Congreve (1697); however, it is of much earlier origin and was used by Euripides. First attested in the United States in *Glass Triangle* (1940) by G. H. Coxe. It is found in varying forms: *Hell has no fury like a woman conned; Hell knows no wrath like a woman scorned; Hell knoweth no fury like a woman scorned,* etc. Sometimes shortened to *hell hath no fury* or to *a (the) woman scorned*.

1697. Heav'n has no rage, like love to hatred
    turn'd,
    Nor hell a fury, like a woman scorn'd
      —William Congreve, *The Mourning Bride*

1940. You've heard that one about hell having no fury like a woman scorned? —G. H. Coxe, *Glass Triangle*

1959. Hell hath no fury like a Frenchman scorned. —*New York Times*

1975. Hell hath no fury like a hooker with a press agent. —Frank Sinatra's comment on Judith Exner, quoted by Lois Gould, *New York Times Magazine*

1991. Scarlett laughed harshly. "Poor Colum. You must have heard about the woman scorned, don't be so shocked. Don't fret, I won't frighten you any more." —Alexandra Ripley, *Scarlett*

1993. That old adage about a woman scorned is alive and well. —Cartoon by Wagner, "Grin and Bear It," North America Syndicate

1994. Hell hath no fury like a rock star scorned? ... [David Lee] Roth freely admits that he tried to contact his former bandmates—Eddie and Alex Van

Halen and Michael Anthony—about a reunion, but they never took his calls.... So, he decided not to get mad, but to get even. —*New York Post*

He'll never set the world on fire. He'll never do anything exceptional; he won't amount to much. The name of an important river often replaces *the world*. The Latin saying is: *Tiberum accendere nequaquam potest* ("He'll never set the Tiber on fire"). Germans substitute *the Rhine*, whereas the French refer to *the Seine* and the British use *the Thames*. In the preface to *Pygmalion*, George Bernard Shaw wrote, "With Higgins's physique and temperament Sweet might have set the Thames on fire." Americans usually replace *the Thames* with *the Hudson, the town,* or *the world*.

> **1776.** Matt Minikin won't set fire to the Thames though he lives near the Bridge. —Samuel Foote, *Trip to Calais*
>
> **1957.** She's got the secret that will set the river on fire. —John Cheever, *The Wapshot Chronicle*
>
> **1983.** What to do now? Returning to L.A. with new bride in tow all ready to set the town on fire was one thing. Reality was another. —Jackie Collins, *Hollywood Wives*
>
> **1985.** "Ardabiola" [by Yevgeny Yevtushenko] is curiously humorless for so sprightly a piece of fantasy, but it will pass an hour or two pleasantly enough. No way will it set the Hudson on fire. —*New York Times Book Review*
>
> **1987.** "We've played good enough to win, better than average, but I don't think anybody has exactly set the world on fire." —*New York Times*
>
> **1989.** "Ollie North set the world on fire, and the only thing I could do was keep returning phone calls, keep trying to get our message out," Mr. Morgan said. —*New York Times*
>
> **1992.** "I don't want to set the world on fire," she said. "I just want to do a good, competent job." —*New York Times*

Here goes! Let's stop fooling around and plunge in directly. Used to express one's resolution in beginning a bold or unpleasant action. The phrase has been traced back to 1829.

> **1981.** Dear Abby: I can't quit thinking about what I did today and I've got to tell someone about it, so here goes. —Abigail Van Buren, *The Best of Dear Abby*
>
> **1984.** Given the way fate works, my 1984 predictions will probably be dead wrong. But the tempta-

tion to forecast fearlessly is irresistible. So here goes. —*Forbes*

> **1987.** Mrs. D? Jeremy here. I hope you found the bird-call tribute of some comfort.... I've also written a prose poem I'd like you to hear. I wanted to read it to everyone, but the minister kept looking at his watch.... Ready? Here goes. —G. B. Trudeau, *Doonesbury Deluxe*
>
> **1995.** Here we go.... After weeks of speculation that Ivana [Trump] might be fixing to dump the rock hoisted onto her finger by her Italian beau with that unspellable surname, Ivana is in a marrying mood. —*New York Post*

See also HERE WE GO AGAIN!

Here I stand. I can do no other. This is my position; I must obey my conscience. The saying originated with the German religious reformer Martin Luther (1483–1546), who refused to recant his ideas despite accusations of heresy. The inscription on his monument at Worms reads: *Hier stehe ich, ich kann nicht anders. Gott helfe mir. Amen* ("Here I stand, I cannot do otherwise. So help me God"). In 1992, Bill Clinton not only misquoted Martin Luther ("I'm doing this because I can't do anything else") but also misattributed it to Martin Luther King.

> **1521.** Here I stand; I can do no other. God help me. Amen. —Martin Luther, Speech at the Diet of Worms
>
> **1992.** I believe that Clinton may have intended to refer to King's namesake, Martin Luther, who upon his refusal to acknowledge the error of his ways to the Imperial Diet at Worms, said: "Here I stand; I cannot do otherwise." —Letters to the Editor, *New York Times Magazine*

Here today, gone tomorrow. All things are temporary and fleeting. Also refers to a person who is always on the move. The saying has been traced back to *Life and Conversion of a Christian Man* (1549) by John Calvin (1509–64), the Swiss religious reformer. First attested in the United States in *Attache or Sam Slick in England* (1843) by Thomas Chandler Haliburton. It is found in various forms: *Here today and gone the next; Here today and gone tomorrow; Here today, in hell tomorrow; Here today, here tomorrow,* etc.

> **1686–87.**
> Faith, sir, we are here today, and gone tomorrow. —Aphra Behn, *The Lucky Chance*
>
> **1967.** As a member of a Senate subcommittee investigating conditions in California vineyards, Bobby [Kennedy] advocated strict unionism. Father

Keenan argued that the answer was not that simple. "The problem," he said, "is to know how the Union is to represent people who are here today and gone tomorrow." —Ralph de Toledano, *R.F.K.*

1980. *Gone today, here tomorrow.* Diet experts say that fewer than 10 per cent of the people who lose weight manage to keep most of it off for more than 2 years. —Mike Feinsilber & William B. Mead, *American Averages*

1989. Here today, gone tomorrow—except in cities. What was here in the urban landscape yesterday is very often still here today. —*New York Times*

1993. Here Today, Here Tomorrow —Ad for Barnes & Noble, *New York Times Book Review*

Here we go again. We are going to hear, discuss, or experience the same old thing again. Probably coined by a clown named Harry Paine in the 1870s. He made a somersault and joked, "Here we go again!" "There you go again" was one of Ronald Reagan's favorite expressions. The phrase takes varying forms: *Here you (he, she, they) go again; Here you go; There you (he, she, we, they) go again*, etc.

1936. "There he goes again," thought Scarlett. "Always putting himself in the other fellow's shoes." —Margaret Mitchell, *Gone With the Wind*

1961. Stand back everybody, here they go again. —Bernard Malamud, *The Natural*

1962. "What do you say, Mrs. Hawke? Would you take twenty thousand?"

"Are you offering it?"

"Here we go again," Hawke said. —Herman Wouk, *Youngblood Hawke*

1984. Most people just didn't understand what was going on. They saw the story on television and they thought: "Here we go again. Those guys just got a billion and a half dollars. Why are they going back for more?" —Lee Iacocca with William Novak, *Iacocca*

1987. On Tuesday, for example, Mr. Gorbachev got off a line that stands aside Mr. Reagan's rebuke to President Carter in 1980—"There you go again"—for its crispness. —*New York Times*

1988. Nixon received the wires at the captain's table the evening of December 3. He read one from Stripling aloud. Pat threw up her hands. "Here we go again," she said. —Stephen E. Ambrose, *Nixon*

1992. THERE THEY GO AGAIN: CONJURING UP CAMELOT. CLINTON AND GORE EVOKE KENNEDY AURA, JUST AS HART, KERREY, BIDEN, ETC., DID —Headline, *New York Times*

1993. So, fellow suckers, citizens of the Free World, here we go again. Democratic governments are helping increase the military power of despotism. —A. M. Rosenthal, *New York Times*

1995. We stand now, in linguistic awe, before the mysterious word *there*. It can be an adverb ("There you go again").... —William Safire, "On Language," *New York Times Magazine*

His bark is worse than his bite. He talks tough but he's really harmless. The proverb was included in George Herbert's 1651 collection of proverbs. First attested in the United States in 1841 in the letters of James Fenimore Cooper. The saying occurs in varying forms: *A dog's bark is worse than his bite; His bite is deadlier than his bark; His bite is worse than his bark; The bite is louder than the bark*, etc.

1985. "He hates everybody! He's of the old school—he demands obedience. In Hollywood they nicknamed him 'The Swine.' His bark is worse than his bite, you'll see." —Michael Korda, *Queenie*

1992. Jay Leno's bark won't have as much bite. Johnny [Carson], we really knew ye. —*Newsweek*

1994. "Ruff's bark is just a sound bite." —Cartoon by Hank Ketcham, "Dennis the Menace," *Star-Ledger* (Newark)

See also BARKING DOGS NEVER BITE.

History doesn't repeat itself—historians do.
See HISTORY REPEATS ITSELF.

History is bunk. The work of historians is meaningless and irrelevant. Originated in the United States in the early twentieth century. Attributed to industrialist Henry Ford (1863–1947). On May 25, 1916, in an interview with Charles N. Wheeler of the *Chicago Tribune*, Ford is reported to have said, "History is more or less bunk." However, he later denied that he had used the word *bunk*.

1966. Lean and silent Henry Ford, who was said to have wheels in his head, erected an immense personal empire on the cornerstone of his mechanical genius, though his associates provided much of the organizational talent. Ill-educated, this multimillionaire mechanic was socially and culturally narrow; "History is bunk," he once testified. —Thomas A. Bailey, *The American Pageant*

1984. The day Bunkie was fired there was great rejoicing and much drinking of champagne. Over in public relations, one of our people coined a phrase that soon became famous throughout the company. Henry Ford once said that history is bunk. But today, Bunkie is history." —Lee Iacocca with William Novak, *Iacocca*

History never repeats itself. *See* HISTORY RE-PEATS ITSELF.

History repeats itself. History follows a pattern of events that recur in different eras. Also used to refer to anything that happens more than once. The proverb has been traced back to *Rufus Historie* (1553). It was later used in *Scenes of Clerical Life* (1858) by English novelist George Eliot (1819–80). First attested in the United States in *Marian Rooke* (1865) by H. Sedley. The saying takes various forms: *History always repeats itself; History doesn't repeat itself—historians do; History is repeating itself; History never repeats itself; History never repeats itself exactly,* etc.

> **1920.** History repeats itself. Historians repeat each other. —*Supers and Supermen,* quoted in *Oxford Dictionary of Quotations*
>
> **1922.** ...history repeating itself with a difference.... —James Joyce, *Ulysses*
>
> **1975.** "Monthly Economics Letter," published by First National City Bank in New York City, has been around since 1904. Each issue offers several in-depth articles on world economy. A typical example—"The Great Depression: History Never Repeats Itself," a study of the difference between economic factors of the 1930s and today, showing that present conditions can't be measured by a '30s yardstick. —David Wallechinsky & Irving Wallace, *The People's Almanac*
>
> **1984.** Anyone who says history repeats itself isn't very familiar with history or those who make it. —*Forbes*
>
> **1991.** STOCKS: WILL HISTORY REPEAT ITSELF? —Ad for Merrill Lynch, *New York Times*
>
> **1992.** What happened in L.A. was terrible. History always repeats itself. —Letters to the Editor, *New York Post*
>
> **1993.** The worst thing about history is that every time it repeats itself, the price goes up. —Overheard on the New York University campus

Hitch your wagon to a star. Aim high; be ambitious. Originated in the United States by American essayist and poet Ralph Waldo Emerson (1870).

> **1870.** Hitch your wagon to a star. Let us not fag in paltry works which serve our pot and bag alone. —Ralph Waldo Emerson, "Society and Solitude"
>
> **1964.** You've got to have a dream! They said this in their own words, you understand, startled into discovery. To the young, clichés seem freshly minted. Hitch your wagon to a star! —Bel Kaufman, *Up the Down Staircase*
>
> **1991.** FOR BETTER OR WORSE, CITICORP'S STAR IS HITCHED TO THE ECONOMY —Headline, *New York Times*
>
> **1992.** Taking advantage of his many contacts, he [Averell Harriman] hitched his wagon to the New Deal. —*Wall Street Journal*
>
> **1993.** Be selective. Don't hitch your wagon to the wrong star. —Overheard at a New York City airport

Hobson's choice. No real choice at all. This phrase was coined in 1630 by the English poet Thomas Ward. Tobias (or Thomas) Hobson (1544?–1631) was said to have owned a stable in Cambridge. His horses could be rented by students provided they were willing to take the horse that stood nearest to the stable door. This stipulation deprived his customers of any choice at all. "Every customer was alike well served according to his chance, and every horse ridden with the same justice," wrote Richard Steele in a 1712 essay in the *Spectator.* John Milton (1608–74) immortalized Hobson by making him the subject of two poems.

> **1630.** Where to elect there is but one,
> 'Tis Hobson's choice—take that or none.
> —Thomas Ward, *England's Reformation*
>
> **1987.** Ms. Gorrie called the vote on the program a "Hobson's choice between a weak plan or no plan at all." —*New York Times*
>
> **1989.** Craig nodded to Damon. "But who watches out for the pilots then? It's a Hobson's choice."
> "Maybe it's time we realized that we can't win." —Wayne Care, *Vietnam Spook Show*
>
> **1993.** President Clinton adopted Hobson's style in his Oval Office address the other night. "Now there are only two choices: our plan or no plan." —William Safire, *Times* (Trenton)
>
> **1994.** Faced with a Hobson's choice of boffo ratings or an advertising revenue bonanza, the three major networks have yet to announce whether they'll preempt daytime programming to air the [O.J. Simpson] trial. —*Crain's New York Business*

See also TAKE IT OR LEAVE IT.

Hold your horses. Don't get yourself in a lather; slow down; calm down; be patient. Often used as a warning to think twice before acting hastily. Originated in the United States and was originally used literally. Some 150 years ago, the phrase began to be applied to people as well. The word *just* may precede the phrase.

1951. "Just hold your horses, Corprl [Corporal] Oliver," said the S/Sgt. —James Jones, *From Here to Eternity*

1987. Will you just *hold* your horses? I said I'd be there in a *minute,* for Pete's sake! —G. B. Trudeau, *Doonesbury Deluxe*

1988. Probation? For *murder?* Hey, hold your horses, State of Texas. —Clifford Irving, *The Campbell Murder Case*

1991. As a man with a master's degree in history from Stanford, he [Ray Handley, the Giants' coach] might be aware of the Russian proverb: "The future is his who knows how to wait." Or maybe he just went with the American version: "Hold your horses, will ya?" —*New York Times*

1993. Just Hold Your Horses! Our Crazy Horse Fashion Bash Isn't 'Til Next Saturday —Ad for Macy's department store, *New York Times*

A home away from home. Any temporary place where one feels comfortable. The phrase is found in varying forms: *A home from home; It's like home away from home; It serves one as a home away from home; This little home away from home,* etc.

1969. The Americans were taken to the fifth building inside the gate. It was a one-story cement-block cube with sliding doors in front and back. It had been built as a shelter for pigs about to be butchered. Now it was going to serve as a home away from home for one hundred American prisoners of war. —Kurt Vonnegut, Jr., *Slaughterhouse-Five*

1974. Your private office is your home away from home. —Molla Alihan, *Corporate Etiquette*

1984. Maybe it's because we've [American Express] always put personal service ahead of all other considerations that so many people refer to us as their "home away from home." —*New York Times*

1987. They try to make the hotel your "home away from home.'" —*Jewish Week* (N.Y.)

1988. Most residents were constrained by the demands of their schedule to regard the hospital as their home away from home. —Erich Segal, *Doctors*

1991. "Here we are! Our vacation home away from home!" ... "I love it!" —Cartoon by Mort Walker & Dick Browne, "Hi & Lois," King Features Syndicate, Inc.

1994. AT HOME AWAY FROM HOME —Headline of Andy

Rooney's article on his favorite places in London, *Times* (Trenton)

See also HOME IS WHERE THE HEART IS; HOME, SWEET HOME; THERE'S NO PLACE LIKE HOME.

Home is where the heart is. One prefers one's home to all other places. Home is the place one is most emotionally attached to. Although the proverb has probably been in use since time immemorial, it has been attributed to Pliny the Elder (a.d. 23–79). First attested in the United States in J. J. McCloskey's *Davey Crockett and Other Plays* (1870): "Well, home, they say, is where the heart is." In 1914, the proverb was included in Elbert Hubbard's collection of epigrams. It has hundreds of variants, including *Home is where you are, mother.*

1981. They entertained several times a year, they went out to departmental parties from time to time, but these things did not interest Sulka much. Home was where her heart was, the nest. —Colette Dowling, *The Cinderella Complex*

1983. Home is where the tourists are. —*Forbes*

1988. Cartoonist Jim Morin of the *Miami Herald* shows a homeless man sitting in the street with his belongings and a sign that reads: "Home is where the heart isn't." —*Philadelphia Inquirer*

1989. Home was where Momma was, in Mississippi, although he would never live there again. —John Grisham, *A Time to Kill*

1991. HOME IS WHERE THE SPOUSE IS —Headline, *People*

1993. "Bootsie Bingham the cat lives here. Please don't let her out. Thank you." ... The note on Wilma Bingham's front door says it all: For Bingham, home is where her cat is. —*AARP Bulletin*

1994. But Rosenfield, who denies that his client's marriage is on the skids, does admit that Hamilton or Doherty may not be sleeping at home, adding only, "Home is where your toothbrush is." —*US*

See also A HOME AWAY FROM HOME; HOME, SWEET HOME; THERE'S NO PLACE LIKE HOME.

Home, sweet home. Often said when returning home after a period of absence. The song "Home, Sweet Home," with lyrics by American actor and playwright John Howard Payne (1791–1852), first appeared in the opera *Clari, or the Maid of Milan* at Covent Garden, London, in 1823. The music was probably written by Henry Rowley Bishop (1786–1855). Popularized by divas Adelina Patti (1843–1919), Jenny Lind (1820–87), and Nellie Melba (1859–1931), it became an anthem for millions of exiles pining for home and was especially popular with soldiers during the Civil War.

1823. Home, home, sweet, sweet home! —John Howard Payne, "Home, Sweet Home"

1953. "Where are you now, Arthur?" the gray-haired man asked. "Home?"
"Yeah. Home. Home sweet home. Christ." —J. D. Salinger, *Nine Stories*

1964. He went down the long hall past the seven views of Rome into the library, where he found his old cousin with an open book on her lap. Here was home-sweet-home, the polished brass, the apple-wood fire. —John Cheever, *The Wapshot Scandal*

1984. When it comes to growth, the computer business it's not. But these days, home sweet home is not bad, either. —*Forbes*

1985. Home sweet home: "I love my company. They are the family I turn to when I'm in trouble. They are the people I can confide in. It's hard work, but we have fun." —Production manager of a Fortune 500 company, quoted by Jacqueline Hornor with Karla Dougherty, *Divorcing a Corporation*

1989. "So the Norwegians went home and left their boat here?"
"No, they're still here, poor sods. They're trying to build a plant to freeze the fish, but everybody's lost interest. That's Africa for you.... Here we are. Home, sweet home." —Michael Korda, *The Fortune*

1994. Whatever your dream of Home Sweet Home is, you'll find it listed in the Real Estate section of this newspaper. —*Princeton Packet* (N.J.)

See also A HOME AWAY FROM HOME; HOME IS WHERE THE HEART IS; THERE'S NO PLACE LIKE HOME.

Homer sometimes nods. *See* EVEN HOMER SOMETIMES NODS.

Honesty is the best policy. There are so many pitfalls inherent in deception that it's easier in the long run to tell the truth. This maxim has been traced back to *European Speculum* (1605) by E. Sandys. It appears in Cervantes' *Don Quixote* (1605–15). First attested in the United States in *John Saffin, His Book* (1700). Used by Benjamin Franklin in *Poor Richard's Almanac*. It appears in varying forms, some negative: *Honesty is always the best policy; Honesty is not always the best policy; Honesty is by far the best policy; Honesty is the safest policy; Truth is always the best policy,* etc.

1796. I hold the maxim no less applicable to public than to private affairs, that honesty is always the best policy. —George Washington, Farewell Address

1854. Honesty is the best policy, but he who is governed by that maxim is not an honest man. —Richard Whately, *Thoughts and Apothegms*

1957. He wondered at first if this was a furtive strain of morbidity in himself and if he would damage his chances at a job in the carpet works by speaking frankly. He wondered for only a second. Honesty was best policy. —John Cheever, *The Wapshot Chronicle*

1975. The issue was why people didn't dig Beowulf and what should be done about it. There were hours of half-completed sentences and pregnant pauses. There was talk about how feeling should be in the open. The truth setting you free. Honesty being the best policy. —Mark Vonnegut, *The Eden Express*

1986. Evaluating the truth usually creates feelings of mistrust, and adds to people's long-term uncertainty about their promotion probabilities. Knowledge reduces anxiety. In general, honesty is the best policy. —Judith M. Bardwick, *The Plateauing Trap*

1987. But what is the moral of this story? Take it like it is? Honesty is the best policy? No, not at all. Sooner or later, absolute honesty will be fatal. —R. Richard Ritti & G. Ray Funkhouser, *The Ropes to Skip & the Ropes to Know*

1993. Honesty is the best policy. It's also the most profitable. —Ad for the Better Business Bureau of Metropolitan New York, *New York Times*

1995. Of course the official rule of the market is that honesty is the best policy—or, at least, that any deal mutually beneficial to both buyer and seller requires honesty. And certainly, as every book of salesmanship explains, the appearance of honesty in business is extremely important. —*New York Times Magazine*

Honey catches (attracts) more flies than vinegar. *See* YOU CAN CATCH MORE FLIES WITH HONEY THAN WITH VINEGAR.

Honor thy father and thy mother. Respect your parents. One of the Ten Commandments given to Moses in the Old Testament. The proverb was used in *Civil Conversation* (1570). First attested in the United States in Benjamin Franklin's *Poor Richard's Almanac* (1722).

Honor thy father and thy mother: that thy days may be long upon the land which the Lord thy God giveth thee. —Exodus 20:12, *Authorized Version,* 1611

1955. He was told to honor his father and his mother, and he honored his father and his mother. —Joseph Heller, *Catch-22*

1991. They [parents] insist that we live by all the Ten Commandments, although I seem to recall a special emphasis on number five—"Honor thy father and thy mother." —Oliver L. North, *Under Fire*

See also FATHER KNOWS BEST.

Hope for the best and prepare for the worst. Be optimistic, but prepare for all possibilities. Things will turn out better if your preparations are thorough. The saying has been traced back to *The Tragedie of Gorbuduc* (1561) by Thomas Norton (1532–84) and Thomas Sackville (1536–1608). Used by English clergyman and wit Sydney Smith (1771–1845). First attested in the United States in *Correspondence of John Jay* (1813). The phrase is found in varying forms: *Hope for the best and expect the worst; Hope for the best, and trust in God; Look for the best and expect the worst,* etc. Often shortened to *hope for the best.*

1855. Take short views, hope for the best, and trust in God. —Sydney Smith, *Lady Holland's Memoir*

1961. All he could do was what he had been instructed to do by Colonel Korn and hope for the best. —Joseph Heller, *Catch-22*

1981. It was hopeless. All they could do was believe in justice and hope for the best. —Danielle Steel, *Palomino*

1992. Hope for the best, but prepare for the worst. According to Capt. Fred Crocker of the Hartford, Conn., Fire Department, "People who have prepared for a fire are much more likely to survive than those who haven't." —*Reader's Digest*

1993. The way to send a message is to think first what you want to say, then say it. And hope for the best. —*Times* (Trenton)

See also HOPE SPRINGS ETERNAL IN THE HUMAN BREAST.

Hope springs eternal in the human breast. Even when things look hopeless, people always expect a miracle. It's human nature to always believe the future will be rosier than the present. Originated by English poet Alexander Pope in 1733. Often shortened to *hope springs eternal.*

1733–34.
Hope springs eternal in the human breast:
Man never Is, but always to be blest.
—Alexander Pope, *An Essay on Man*

1946. Hope Springs Eternal —Upton Sinclair, *A World to Win* (chapter title).

1992. One of Mr. [Woody] Allen's lawyers, Harvey I. Sladkus, said it was unlikely that the evening meeting would settle the custody case. But he added: "Hope springs eternal. The judge is a great settler. She takes the ramrod out of the back of you, and sticks in something more flexible." —*New York Times*

1993. "HOPEFULLY" SPRINGS ETERNAL —Headline of an article about acceptable usage of the word "hopefully," *New York Times Magazine*

See also HOPE FOR THE BEST AND PREPARE FOR THE WORST.

A horse of a different color. *See* THAT'S A HORSE OF A DIFFERENT COLOR.

A house divided against itself cannot stand. Any group experiencing internal dissension will be unable to withstand outside pressures; division causes weakness. The proverb appears in the New Testament: "And Jesus knew their thoughts, and said unto them, Every kingdom divided against itself is brought to desolation; and every city or house divided against itself shall not stand" (Matt. 12:25); "If a house be divided against itself, that house cannot stand" (Mark 3:25). In a speech at the Republican state convention in Springfield, Illinois, on June 16, 1858, Abraham Lincoln said, "'A house divided against itself cannot stand.' I believe the government cannot endure permanently half slave and half free. I do not expect the house to fall—but I do expect it will cease to be divided. It will become all one thing, or all the other." "The sister kingdoms of the north—Arabia, Persia, Ferghana, Turkestan—stretched out their hands... and greeted ridiculous Chandrapore, where every street and house was divided against itself, and told her that she was a continent and a unity," wrote E. M. Foster in *A Passage to India* (1924). The proverb is often shortened to the allusive *a house divided.*

1926. It was easy for Claverhouse and his dragoons to keep down a country thus divided against itself, so long as there was no revolution in England. —G. M. Trevelyan, *History of England*

1980. The Democratic Party arrived in New York this week as a house divided. It will leave here that way today. —*Boston Globe*

1988. BAY STATE NEEDS A SPEAKER WHO WILL BRING HARMONY TO A HOUSE DIVIDED —Headline *Christian Science Monitor*

1990. This was a clubhouse divided, with all the

ugly cliques finally exposed. Cardinals were squared away in opposite corners, eyeballing each other with looks, quite frankly, that could kill. —*St. Louis Post-Dispatch*

1991. Jane Dee Hull became Speaker of the House in Arizona when the backlash from the impeachment of Gov. Evan Mecham unseated Joe Lane. She has ruled over a House divided ever since. —*Arizona Republic*

1998. After their frustrating 7–6 loss to the Pittsburgh Steelers Jan. 3 in the AFC playoff semifinals, emotions were running high in the Patriots' locker room. Fingers were pointing all over the place. Players were saying things they would later regret. It seemed like a house divided. —*Boston Globe*
See also UNITED WE STAND, DIVIDED WE FALL.

How do you like them apples? So there! What do you have to say now? What are you going to do about it? Used ironically since the late 1920s.

1961. *Grandma:* They wanted satisfaction; they
    wanted their money back. That's what
    they wanted.
Mrs. Barker: My, my, my.
Grandma: How do you like *them* apples?
Mrs. Barker: My, my, my.
      —Edward Albee, *The American Dream*

1967. "Why, you're welcome, partner. I thought you'd like them apples." —Elia Kazan, *The Arrangement*

1974. For a split second, Ben Bradlee's mouth dropped open with an expression of sheer delight. Then he put one cheek on the desk, eyes closed, and banged the desk repeatedly with his right fist. In a moment he recovered. "How do you like them apples?.…" he said. —Carl Bernstein & Bob Woodward, *All The President's Men*

1994. How do you like them apples, Prime Minister? —Andy Rooney "60 Minutes," CBS.
See also HOW DOES THAT GRAB YOU?

How does that grab you? What do you think of that? Do you like it? Are you impressed? The earliest recorded usage (1915) is *How does dat grab yer?* Popularized by Nancy Sinatra's recording of a song titled "How Does That Grab You, Darling?" in the late 1960s.

1977. "How does a Seeing Eye dog grab you?" —William Safire, *Full Disclosure*

1979. "O.K. Then you're boss. How does that grab you?" —Howard Fast, *The Establishment*

1983. She edged across the front seat. "For a ten-

spot ah'll give you real sweet relief. I'll even share a joint with you. How's that grab you?" —Jackie Collins, *Hollywood Wives*

1986. "How soon will you be ready to go up again?"
    "How does next week grab you?" —Tom Clancy, *Red Storm Rising*

1988. Then she lowered her voice and without apologizing asked, "Now, how does that grab you?" —Erich Segal, *Doctors*
See also HOW DO YOU LIKE THEM APPLES?

Humpty Dumpty sat on a wall. *See* ALL THE KING'S HORSES, AND ALL THE KING'S MEN, COULDN'T PUT HUMPTY TOGETHER AGAIN.

The husband is always the last to find out. Unsavory secrets (such as marital infidelity) are generally known to everyone but the injured party (the spouse); thus, the person most likely to be concerned by a turn of events is the last to be told. The proverb has been traced back to *What You Will* (1604) by English dramatist John Marston (c.1576–1634). First attested in the United States in *Murder of a Fifth Columnist* (1941). The proverb is found in varying forms: *It's generally the husband who's the last to know; The husband's the last to know; The wife is always the last to know; The wife is always the last one to find out,* etc.

1936. "Where—where have you been?"
    "Don't tell me you don't know! I thought surely the whole town knew by now. Perhaps they all do, except you. You know the old adage: 'The wife is always the last one to find out.'" —Margaret Mitchell, *Gone With the Wind*

1957. The Australian was surprised. "Haven't they told you, sir?"
    The American laughed. "Not a thing. I'd say the last person to hear the sailing orders is the captain." —Nevil Shute, *On the Beach*

1975. "He likes to fuck around," Cleo stated blankly, "and I guess everyone knows this, and I guess I'm like a schmucky wife in those TV soap operas who is always the last to find out." —Jackie Collins, *The World Is Full of Divorced Women*

1988. "I learned that your wife, the daughter of a wealthy real estate developer who wanted political influence and literally financed your early campaigns, had a less than enviable reputation."
    "Before and after, Mr. No-name. Only, I was the last to find out." —Robert Ludlum, *The Icarus Agenda*

1991. Brenda, a perky junior, goes first, and her

autobiography ends with the news that she broke up with her boyfriend last night. Mutters another girl in the audience: "I'm always the last to know." —*Time*

1993. [Boris] Becker, when pressed by a tabloid reporter to announce a wedding date, told the questioner that he would be "the last person to know." —*Times* (Trenton)

Hypocrisy is the homage that vice pays to virtue. By pretending to have moral principles, dishonest people are actually showing a kind of respect for their excellence. Said ironically. Originated by the French moralist and epigrammist La Rochefoucauld (1613–80). The word *tribute* or *payment* may substitute for *homage*.

1678. *L'hypocrisie est un hommage que le vice rend à la vertu.* ("Hypocrisy is the homage that vice pays to virtue.") —La Rochefoucauld, *Maxims*

1977. "The people will let me get away with anything as long as I just don't flaunt it."

"That's being a hypocrite."

"Right, Buffie, that's the word—hypocrisy, 'the payment that vice makes to virtue.'" —William Safire, *Full Disclosure*

I am a man; and nothing human is alien to me. I accept that it is human nature to be imperfect; therefore, I am open-minded about other people's behavior. The original Latin phrase is *Homo sum: humani nil a me alienum puto* (as quoted by Cicero in *De Officiis*) or *Nil humani a me alienum est*. It is attributed to the Roman playwright Terence (c.190–159 b.c.) and sometimes to the Greek playwright Menander (343?–291? b.c.). Often shortened to *Nothing human is alien to me.*

1961. Nothing human disgusts me unless it's unkind, violent. —Tennessee Williams, *The Night of the Iguana*

1975. Favorite maxim: *Nihil humani a me alienum puto.* ("I consider that nothing human is alien to me.") —Karl Marx, *Marx's Confession*

1981. And to quote Freud, "Since nothing that is human is alien to me," in an effort to learn more about the transsexual phenomenon, I attended an international weekend seminar at Stanford University. —Abigail Van Buren, *The Best of Dear Abby*

1991. The lasting reaction, besides outrage of one kind or another, may have been a sense of being in the presence of a mystery. "Nothing human is alien to me," Terence said, but this gross offhand brutality, dealt out by guardians of the law, seemed alien enough and disturbing on a fairly deep emotional and moral level. —*Time*

1993. Angelou spoke about her life, how she became a writer, and the U.S. civil rights movement. Quoting a slave, she said, "I am a human. Nothing human can be alien to me." —*Times* (Trenton).

I am not a crook. Statement by Richard Nixon (1913–94) on November 17, 1973, when he was under threat of impeachment for the Watergate burglary, illegal campaign contributions, and other political "dirty tricks." Since then, the phrase has been used ironically.

1973. I made my mistakes, but in all my years of public life, I have never profited, *never* profited from public service. I have earned every cent. And in all of my years in public life I have never obstructed justice. And I think too that I could say that in my years of public life that I welcome this kind of examination because people have got to know whether or not their President is a crook. Well, I am not a crook. —Richard Nixon, *New York Times*

1974. At Disneyworld in Florida, the President told an audience of editors on national TV, "I am not a crook." —Carl Bernstein & Bob Woodward, *All The President's Men*

1993. At an appearance in Kew Gardens, Queens, Mr. Badillo said, "There is no question the Department of Investigation report finds something wrong with the whole loan arrangement. That's why she [Liz Holtzman] refuses to release it. I've never seen a person who was the target of a Department of Investigation say anything but 'I'm not a crook'." —*New York Times*

1994. Player: B. Clinton. Conventional Wisdom: He is not a crook. So what is there to cover up? —*Newsweek*

1994. *Bill Clinton (holding a paper titled "Whitewater"):* I am not a crook. Geez … I'm starting to sound like Nixon. —Cartoon by Toles, *Buffalo News*

I am not my brother's keeper. *See* AM I MY BROTHER'S KEEPER?

I am the state. All political power resides with me. Attributed to Louis XIV, who allegedly told the French parliament in 1651: *L'état c'est moi* ("I am the state"). The same idea has been expressed by Napoleon (1814) and other dictators of various sizes, shapes, and colors. In the 1920s, Frank Hague (1876–1956), the mayor of Jersey City, controlled the entire state of New Jersey. His favorite phrase was "I am the law."

1814. What is the throne?—a bit of wood gilded and covered with velvet. I am the state—I alone am here the representative of the people. —Napoleon Bonaparte, *Address to the Senate*

1937. I am the law. —Frank Hague, *New York Times*

1974. ... Though Mayor Wagner had begun to announce, in his City Hall press conferences, that "I am the Mayor," there is now rather abundant evidence that the statement isn't to be taken as literally as the late Frank Hague's "I am the law." —Robert A. Caro, *The Power Broker*

I am what I am and that's what I am. God's name, meaning "I cause to be what is to be"; my nature is fixed and unchanging. Of Biblical origin. In the Old Testament, God tells Moses, "I AM THAT I AM." The phrase also appears in the New Testament. In the twentieth century, the popular cartoon character Popeye the Sailor declared, "I yam what I yam."

And Moses said unto God, Behold, *when* I come unto the children of Israel, and shall say unto them, The God of your fathers hath sent me unto you; and they shall say to me, What *is* his name? what shall I say unto them? And God said unto Moses, I AM THAT I AM; and he said, Thus shalt thou say unto the children of Israel, I AM hath sent me unto you. —Exodus 3:13, 14, *Authorized Version*, 1611

1968. Do you know what shameless thought just bullied its way into my consciousness? That I deserve you, that I deserve to know you and to communicate with you, that I deserve to have all this happening. What have I done to merit this? I don't believe in the merit system. I Am That I Am. —Eldridge Cleaver, *Soul on Ice*

1985. ... Jews no longer have to suppress or abandon their Jewishness to gain acceptance. "I accomplished all this by my deliberate decision to be myself," Shapiro told me with fierce but quiet pride, "I am what I am, and I can never change." —Charles E. Silberman, *A Certain People*

1987. This is George Will, or, to quote God, "I Am That I Am." —G. B. Trudeau, *Doonesbury Deluxe*

1991. *Be flexible.* "Popeye's 'I am what I am and that's what I am' is no longer appropriate," says Robert Hecht, co-chairman of outplacement firm Lee Hecht Harrison. The more broadly you define

your skills and the more adaptable you make them, the greater your options. —*Fortune*

1993. "I like my character," she said, "and I think she has developed. But it doesn't put any pressure on me. I am what I am." —*Parade*

I came, I saw, I conquered. Reporting to the Roman senate on his military campaign in Asia and his easy victory over Pharnaces II, king of Pontus (47 b.c.), Julius Caesar succinctly said: *Veni, vidi, vici* ("I came, I saw, I conquered"). The saying has been used ever since in both Latin and English. It also occurs frequently in inventive variants.

1984. By combining the skills and efficiencies of their culture with a whole lot of unfair economic advantages, Japan appears capable of looting our markets with impunity.... In Washington this is known as laissez-faire economics, and they love it. In Tokyo they call it *Veni, Vidi, Vici* economics, and believe me, they love it even more. The Japanese have come, they've seen, and they are conquering. —Lee Iacocca with William Novak, *Iacocca*

1987. "What's all this crap about a *house?*" Mannon asked.
"I saw it. I liked it. I rented it." —Jackie Collins, *Hollywood Husbands*

1989. Elsewhere, the subject slumbered, until in 1951 someone told Willem Sandberg, then director of the Stedelijk Museum in Amsterdam, that the collection seen by Barr in 1937 was still in existence in a little town in south Germany. He went. He saw. He marveled. —*New York Times*

1991. Julius Caesar (47 b.c.) said, *Veni, vidi, vici* ("I came, I saw, I conquered"). Sadam's motto is "Iran, Iraq, I ruin." —Letters to the Editor, *Time*

1992. "They came, they saw, they blinked," reported the Los Angeles Times, as if the two men [Bush and Clinton] were about to engage in a hand-to-hand battle, only to suffer at the last minute a mutual loss of nerve. —*New York*

1993. The triumphant shopper returns ... I came ... I saw ... I charged! —Cartoon by Art Sansom, "Born Loser"

1995. BHUTTO CAME, SHE SAW, SHE CONQUERED —Headline of an article about a U.S. visit by Benazir Bhutto, the prime minister of Pakistan, *New York Times*

I cannot tell a lie. A statement used to admit one's wrongdoing. This specious bromide is generally attributed to George Washington. According to legend, young George cut down a cherry tree at the age of six and had the courage to admit it. The saying has been traced back to *The Life of Washington* (1800) by Mason Locke Weems. The word *tell* is sometimes replaced with *live*. * * *

1800. "George," his father said, "do you know who killed that beautiful little cherry tree yonder in the garden?" This was a tough question, and George staggered under it for a moment; but quickly recovered himself; and looking at his father, with the sweet face of youth brightened with the inexpressible charm of all-triumphant truth he bravely cried out, "I can't tell a lie, Pa, you know I can't tell a lie, I did cut it with my little hatchet." —Mason Locke Weems, *The Life of Washington*

1965. A widely mimeographed letter called for contributions to erect a Kennedy statue in Washington. "It was thought unwise to place it beside that of George Washington, who never told a lie, nor beside that of F. D. Roosevelt, who never told the truth, since John cannot tell the difference." —Arthur M. Schlesinger, Jr., *A Thousand Days*

1965. About my typing—First—I cannot tell a lie. I am not a typist. —Truman Capote, *In Cold Blood*

1985. "Were you responsible for that story?"

"I cannot tell a lie. At any rate to *you.* Yes, I was." —Michael Korda, *Queenie*

1992. I cannot tell a lie. His name [Ross Perot's] has come up. —George Bush, "World News Now," ABC.

1993. Hooray for Hollywood—and the jokes that come out of it: They say George Washington never told a lie—he never would have made it as an agent in Hollywood. —Joey Adams, "Strictly for Laughs," *New York Post*

1994. I, uh, cannot, well, tell a lie. "We ... we did, if, the, the, I, I, the stories are just as they have been said. They're outrageous, and they're not so." —Bill Clinton, responding to allegations of sexual misconduct, *Time*

I can't think when I concentrate. Attributed to baseball great Yogi Berra (1925–). As with so many other Yogiisms, he denies ever having said it. But it is so apt that it deserves to be included with such other favorite Yogiisms as "Baseball is ninety percent mental; the other half is physical," "If people don't want to come out to the ballpark, nobody's going to stop them," "Nobody ever goes there anymore; it's too crowded."

1993. ... Sasser has said he has tried yoga and karate, each associated with concentration.... "Yogi (Berra) said, 'I can't think when I concentrate,'" Kirsch said. "That's absolutely true. When you start thinking, that's when you get in trouble." —*Times* (Trenton)

1995. "How hard have you tried?" ... "Not as hard as I could have. I can't think when I concentrate, to borrow a phrase." —Overheard on the Columbia University campus in New York City

I couldn't agree (with you) more. I'm of the same mind; I agree emphatically. The saying has been traced back to the 1930s. First attested in the United States in the late 1950s.

1955. Colonel Cathcart compressed his lips primly and started to rise. "I couldn't agree with you more, sir," he assented briskly in a tone of ostentatious disapproval. —Joseph Heller, *Catch-22*

1963. And Castle nodded sagely. "So this is a picture of the meaninglessness of it all! I couldn't agree more." —Kurt Vonnegut, Jr., *Cat's Cradle*

1975. "Don't want to go into it, it's boring and dull. I just want to have a lovely enjoyable *selfish* evening."

"I couldn't agree with you more." —Jackie Collins, *The World Is Full of Divorced Women*

1982. "My daughter is a rare girl, a rare girl, Mr. Travis."

Jamie nodded. "I couldn't agree with you more, Mr. van der Merwe." —Sidney Sheldon, *The Master of the Game*

1991. Once again—this might be an appropriate time for Barbara and me to thank the President and Mrs. Gorbachev for this fantastic hospitality. And yes, I couldn't agree more about the productive nature of the talks, the enhancement of mutual understanding. This is not diplomatic language, in my view, this is a fact. —George Bush, *New York Times*

I couldn't care less. I don't care at all. Often expresses contempt on the part of the speaker. The saying has been traced back to the 1940s. *I Couldn't Care Less,* an account by Anthony Phelps of the role of the Air Transport Auxiliary in World War II, appeared in 1946. First attested in the United States in the 1950s. *I could care less* is a variant that is often objected to on grounds of logic.

1951. If you're interested, call him up and make an appointment. If you're not, don't. I couldn't care less, frankly. —J. D. Salinger, *The Catcher in the Rye*

1979. "They wanted to know who contributed to the medical fund for the hospital in Toulouse, and when I refused to tell them, they found me in contempt."

"I gave you money for that. Why didn't you tell them? I couldn't care less." —Howard Fast, *The Establishment*

1981. "I Couldn't Care Less What I Look Like." ... This is coverup. The truth is that most men do care, and care deeply, what they look like and what other people think of their appearance. —Mortimer Levitt, *The Executive Look*

1984. "Let's not paint too rosy a picture of the old days," she said. "We always had kids who couldn't care less. We always had rotten teachers." —*New York Times*

See also MY DEAR, I DON'T GIVE A DAMN.

I disapprove of what you say, but I will defend to the death your right to say it. This pithy expression of the principle of free speech was used for many years as the motto of an American newspaper. It is commonly attributed to François Voltaire (1694–1778). According to Norbert Guterman, the source is Voltaire's letter to M. le Riche (February 6, 1770), but S. G. Tallentyre (pen name of Evelyn Beatrice Hall) claims in her book *The Friends of Voltaire* (1907) that it is a paraphrase of a line from the "Essay on Tolerance."

1770. *Monsieur l'abbé, je déteste ce que vous écrivez, mais je donnerais ma vie pour que puissiez continuer à écrire.* ("Father l'abbé, I detest what you write, but I would give my life to make it possible for you to continue to write.") —François Voltaire, quoted by Norbert Guterman, *The Anchor Book of French Quotations*

1994. There was a time when liberals would say, "I don't agree with what you say, but I will defend to the death your right to say it." For Sayen and other right-bashers, that time is over. For them, the Bill of Rights guarantees freedom of speech and religion only for the Left; no conservatives need apply for protection. —Letters to the Editor, *Times* (Trenton)

1995. Beilin said forcefully, but with a touch of irony: "It drives me crazy to see Jews are coming to convince Congress not to send troops to the Golan Heights.... But if Mort Klein wants to go and say, 'We have to save Yossi Beilin from himself,' I will fight for his right to do that...." —*Manhattan Jewish Sentinel* (N.Y.)

I don't give a damn. See MY DEAR, I DON'T GIVE A DAMN.

I fear the Greeks, even when they are bearing gifts. See BEWARE OF GREEKS BEARING GIFTS.

I have a dream. I believe in a utopian future; I have faith. On August 28, 1963, Martin Luther King, Jr. (1929–68), the leader of the American civil rights movement, delivered his famous "I Have a Dream" speech before a quarter million of his followers who had gathered in Washington, D.C., in a massive protest demonstration. It has been used ever since to refer to utopian idealism and high hopes for the future.

1963. I have a dream. It is a dream deeply rooted in the American dream. I have a dream that one day this nation will rise up and live out the true meaning of its creed: "We hold these truths to be self-evident: that all men are created equal." —Martin Luther King, Jr., "I Have a Dream"

1980. "I have a dream ..." I have a dream that Rabbi Hertzberg has devoted his considerable talents and his inexhaustible energy plus the $5 million to establishing a FREE Jewish school ... I have a dream. It's too bad I have to wake up." —Letters to the Editor, *Present Tense*

1988. "Don't be frightened, you're in a Red Cross tent. What's the last thing you remember?"
"Dr. King ... 'I have a dream' ... What happened after that?" she asked.
"Well," Bennett said, smiling, "I guess you had a dream, too." —Erich Segal, *Doctors*

1992. "I have a dream that some day I'll be a business executive and I'll invite kids in to learn business skills," she says. —*New York Times Magazine*

1994. "Like poor Martin Luther King," he [Kim Philby] said, in one K.G.B. lecture, "I have a dream." —*New York Times*

I have news for you! Things are not as you say. Let me bring you up to date. Often used to disagree with someone's point of view or statement. Originated in the late 1940s. *I've got news for you* is a variant.

1960. "Hey, I got news for you, as they say." —Edward Albee, *The Zoo Story*

1993. I've got some news for you, Harry. I recall some guy named Agnew making exactly the same argument a few years ago. Surely, you recall the speech about the "unelected elite from New York to Washington" who decided what people should see and hear on the nightly newscasts? —*Times* (Trenton)

1994. I fail to see why Bela Liptak finds the Environmental Protection Agency's dioxin draft reassessment good news.... If he thinks it vindicates his position on recycling, then I have some bad news for him. —Letters to the Editor, *New York Times*

1995. "Kitty Carlisle is a lovely lady, and I have news for you: No way will she ever marry him. —*Modern Maturity*

I have not yet begun to fight. Reply of American naval hero John Paul Jones (1747–92) to a demand to surrender his sinking ship, the *Bonhomme Richard,* to the English in 1779. As his ship sank, Jones boarded his opponent's vessel to achieve a spectacular victory. The saying has been used ever since to indicate that one can rebound from the direst of setbacks.

1779. Sir, I have not yet begun to fight —John Paul Jones, quoted by David Wallechinsky & Irving Wallace, *The People's Almanac*

1950. Great steps, he [President Roosevelt] repeated, had been taken toward that goal. But, he added, the New Deal still had a long hard road to follow. "We have only just begun to fight," he promised. —Lewis Paul Todd & Merle Curti, *The Rise of the American Nation*

1991. But in writing this book, I looked through some of the letters I sent home to my parents from Vietnam in 1968 and 1969, and a few of the lines jumped out at me: ... "Don't worry. I have not yet begun to write." —Oliver L. North, *Under Fire*

1992. The TCI disclosures on Capitol Hill came as Clark Clifford and his law partner Robert Altman met with reporters here to reassert their innocence in the face of federal and New York state charges, filed this week, that they accepted bribes to help BCCI secretly acquire and control U.S. financial institutions.... "I have not yet begun to fight," proclaimed the frail, 85-year-old Mr. Clifford, an adviser to Democratic presidents since the Truman administration. —*Wall Street Journal*

1993. WE HAVE ONLY BEGUN TO FIGHT —Headline of an interview with Al Gore, *Fortune*

1994. For his part, Mr. Cuomo recalled his impoverished roots in South Jamaica, Queens, then said young people there now do not have the chances or support he did, and worried that "we have to do a little bit more.".... "We haven't begun to fight," he vowed. —*New York Times*

I have nothing to offer but blood, toil, tears, and sweat. Hard work and sacrifice are the most important ingredients for success. Winston Churchill coined the expression in a speech to the House of Commons after his election as prime minister of Great Britain in 1940. John

Donne (1611), Lord Byron (1823), and Jack London also used similar phrases.

1611. Mollify it with thy tears, or sweat, or blood. —John Donne, *An Anatomy of the World*

1823. Year after year they voted cent per cent,
  Blood, sweat, and tear-wrung
    millions—why? for rent!
      —George Gordon, Lord Byron, *The Age of Bronze*

1940. I would say to the House, as I have joined this Government, I have nothing to offer but blood, toil, tears and sweat. —Winston Churchill, Speech before the House of Commons.

1975. Jack London contributed a manifesto calling on the socialist movement in New York to rally to the novel [*The Jungle* by Upton Sinclair], which he termed "an Uncle Tom's Cabin of wage slavery. It is alive and warm. It is brutal with life. It is written of sweat and blood, and groans and tears." —David Wallechinsky & Irving Wallace, *The People's Almanac*

1987. The images still live: Winston Churchill promising blood, sweat, and tears: Martin Luther King promising that we shall overcome. —R. Richard Ritti & G. Ray Funkhouser, *The Ropes to Skip & the Ropes to Know*

1993. Kerry Kennedy owns a small furniture store that employs seven people in Titusville, Fla. Like most small business owners, he's poured his heart and soul, his sweat and blood into that business for years. —Bill Clinton, Address to Congress on Health Care, *New York Times*

1994. BLOOD, SWEAT AND GEARS: TOURING FRANCE ON A BIKE —Headline, *New York Times*

I have promises to keep, and miles to go before I sleep. My life is not my own; I have higher duties that will require a lifetime to achieve. These evocative lines are from American poet Robert Frost's "Stopping by Woods on a Snowy Evening" (1923). Either phrase may be used separately, with a slightly different meaning.

1923. The woods are lovely, dark and deep.
  But I have promises to keep,
  And miles to go before I sleep,
  And miles to go before I sleep.
    —Robert Frost, "Stopping by Woods on a Snowy Evening"

1973. Things were going to be done and it was going to be great fun; the challenge awaited and these men did not doubt their capacity to answer that challenge. Even the campaign quote of Jack Kennedy seemed to keynote it. He had used it again and again, moving swiftly through small towns in the New Hampshire winter, closing each speech with the quote from Robert Frost: "… But I have promises to keep,/And miles to go before I sleep,/And miles to go before I sleep." History summoned them, it summoned us: there was little time to lose. —David Halberstam, *The Best and the Brightest*

1988. It made Barney realize yet again that what *he* had achieved—or not achieved—was so unsubstantial, superficial by comparison…. Yeah, he told himself, in Robert Frost's words, I've got "miles to go before I sleep." —Erich Segal, *Doctors*

1991. Kennedy and Sorensen kept a humor file for speech openings and a collection of appropriate endings Jack knew by heart. A favorite closing quotation was a paraphrase of a Robert Frost poem:

> Iowa City is lovely, dark and deep
> But I have promises to keep
> And miles to go before I sleep.
> —Thomas C. Reeves, *A Question of Character*

1993. Robert Frost wrote: "The woods are lovely, dark and deep. But I have miles to go before I sleep and promises to keep." … If he had been talking about fishing in August he might have written: "The waters are lovely, as a crystal dish. But I would make a simple wish. For one late summer largemouthed fish." —*Times* (Trenton)

I have seen the future, and it works. Communism is a superior system of government and its hegemony is inevitable. The saying was coined by American leftist journalist Lincoln Steffens (1866–1936) in a letter to Marie Howe (April 3, 1919) after his visit to revolutionary Russia, where he was received by Lenin. Now often parodied.

1919. I have seen the future, and it works. —Lincoln Steffens, quoted in *Who Said What When*

1931. "So you've been over into Russia?" said Bernard Baruch, and I answered very literally, "I have been over into the future, and it works." —Lincoln Steffens, *Autobiography*

1989. THEY'VE SEEN THE FUTURE, AND IT DOESN'T WORK —Headline of an article on the downfall of Communism, *New York Times*

1992. Three hours later, he [a plastic surgeon] has drawn a gentle portrait of the woman I will someday meet in the mirror…. I have seen the future. And I don't like it at all. —*Health*

1994. BALTIMORE HAS SEEN THE FUTURE, AND IT IS BIO-TECHNOLOGY —Headline, *New York Times*

I need that like I need a hole in my head. I don't need that at all. Of Yiddish origin. Originated in the United States in the late 1940s.**

1984. Unfortunately, the government's new attitude seems to be starting with a marriage between Toyota and General Motors, the two giants of the industry. We need that like a hole in the head. —Lee Iacocca with William Novak, *Iacocca*

1987. To Voicer William von Bargen re your smug, ignorant derogatory remarks concerning blacks: I am sure you might be totally unaware of the thousands of intelligent, self-respecting and yes! law-abiding blacks who need your fogey-ish advice like a hole in the head! —Letters to the Editor, *Daily News* (N.Y.)

1992. When I heard the news that the Goodwill Games were coming here, my first thought was: New York needs another sports event like it needs another hole in the street. —*New York Times*

I never met a man I didn't like. This often parodied bromide originated with the popular American humorist Will Rogers (1879–1935) whose epitaph reads: "I joked about every prominent man in my lifetime, but I never met one I didn't like." The word *man* in the main entry may be replaced by other nouns. *I never bet a man I didn't like* and *I rarely met a contra I didn't like*, coined by Sheldon B. Akers and Oliver North, respectively, are recent versions.

1989. "They feel the P.S.C. has never seen a rate interest that it didn't like." —*New York Times*

1991. *Will Rogers' Cat:* I never met a mouse I didn't like. —Cartoon by Sam Gross, *New Yorker*

1992. Collecting antique radios is practically an addiction, Belanger says…. Joe Koester knows what he means. A 50-year-old Defense Department manager from Laurel, Md., he says dryly: "I never met an antique radio I didn't like," paraphrasing Will Rogers' view of people. —*AARP Bulletin*

1993. Bill Clinton has no position on this issue other than supine; could it be he never met a tax he didn't like? —William Safire, *Times* (Trenton).

1994. Far from quoting Mr. Kissinger as praising Stalin and Mao to establish that he "never met a dictator [he] did not like," the review stresses his new insistence that political leaders must respect values as well as power. —Letters to the Editor, *New York Times Book Review*

I only regret that I have but one life to lose for my country. Last words of American patriot Nathan Hale (1755–76) before being hanged by the British as a spy. If Hale actually did use those words, he was probably influenced by English writer Joseph Addison (1672–1719).

> **1713.** What pity is it
> That we can die but once to serve our
>   country!
> —Joseph Addison, *Cato*

1939. My only regret is that I have but one wife to send to the country. —Lewis & Faye Copeland, *10,000 Jokes, Toasts and Stories*

1984. There's even a story going around the country these days about a third-grade history class where the teacher is giving a little quiz: ... "Now, class," says the teacher, "who said, 'I only regret that I have but one life to give for my country'?" ... A little Japanese girl in the first row stands up and replies: "Nathan Hale, 1776." —Lee Iacocca with William Novak, *Iacocca*

See also GIVE ME LIBERTY OR GIVE ME DEATH; I WOULD RATHER DIE ON MY FEET THAN LIVE ON MY KNEES.

I shall return. Defiant parting shot of General Douglas MacArthur in March 1942 when he was ordered to leave the Philippines by President Franklin Roosevelt. MacArthur did indeed return to the Philippines in 1944.

1966. Before the inevitable American surrender, General MacArthur was ordered by Washington to depart secretly for Australia, there to head resistance against the Japanese. Leaving by motorboat and airplane, he proclaimed, "I shall return." —Thomas A. Bailey, *The American Pageant*

1988. "Mr. President," he said, "I feel terrible at having let you down."
  "How so?"
  "As Supreme Commander U.S. Army of the Pacific I should have held on to Okinawa. But believe me, sir, I shall return."
  "I am sure you will, General MacArthur," Barney replied. —Erich Segal, *Doctors*

1991. It took them several months to come back after the Korean war began and half a year to recover when Iraq swallowed Kuwait. But like Douglas MacArthur, the Dow does return. —*Fortune*

1992. BOSS TELLS THE POST: " I SHALL RETURN. " GEORGE [Steinbrenner] SAYS N.Y. WANTS HIM BACK —Headline, *New York Post*

1993. Veteran Flyers broadcaster Gene Hart, exiled to radio-only duties the past five seasons, will return to the TV booth next season.... "What, you think (General) MacArthur was the only one who returned?" said Hart with a chuckle when contacted at his Cherry Hill home. —*Times* (Trenton)

I think that I shall never see a poem lovely as a tree. First line of a maudlin verse by American poet (Alfred) Joyce Kilmer (1886–1918), whose slender reputation rests on this single poem. Generations of schoolchildren were forced to memorize it and have taken their revenge in scores of parodies over the years.

> **1913.** I think that I shall never see
> A poem lovely as a tree.
> —Joyce Kilmer, "Trees"

> **1933.** I think that I shall never see
> A billboard lovely as a tree.
> Indeed, unless the billboards fall
> I'll never see a tree at all.
> —Ogden Nash, "Song of the Open Road,"
>   *Happy Days*

> **1939.** I think that I shall never see
> A hazard rougher than a tree—
> A tree o'er which my ball must fly
> If on the green it is to lie.
> —Anonymous, quoted by Lewis & Faye
> Copeland, *10,000 Jokes, Toasts and Stories*

I think, therefore I am. Originated in 1637 by the French philosopher and mathematician René Descartes (1596–1650) as a philosophical proof of the reality of the self. The saying often appears in Latin: *Cogito, ergo sum.*

1940. The first modern philosopher was the mathematically-minded Descartes (1596–1650), a Frenchman by birth but a Hollander by residence for much of his life. In his *Discourse on Method* he begins with the axiom, "I think therefore I am," that is, with self-consciousness as a fundamental principle, from which he concludes that whatever things we conceive very clearly and distinctly must be true. —Hutton Webster, *History of Civilization*

1986. *Graffiti:* Cogito ergo spud. I think, therefore, I yam. —Herb Caen, quoted in *Reader's Digest*

1988. The syllogism runs along the lines of Descartes's "I think, therefore I am." But in medicine the formula is, "I have a degree, therefore I am a doctor." —Erich Segal, *Doctors*

1993. I SHOP, THEREFORE I DROP —Headline, *New York Times*

1994. WE THINK, THEREFORE WE MUST RETHINK —Headline of an article on the social sciences, *New York Times*

I told you so. I warned you, but you acted otherwise. This smug phrase, which has been traced back to Byron in 1823, is often used when an earlier prediction or advice was disregarded. The expression was used by Harry Truman on the morning after his stunning election upset victory in 1948. More recently, Rush Limbaugh titled his 1993 book *See, I Told You So.*

1823. Of all the horrid, hideous notes of woe,
   Sadder than owl songs or the midnight blast,
   Is that portentous phrase, "I told you so."
      —George Gordon, Lord Byron, *Don Juan*

1945. If she consulted Shep he would say, "I told you so." —Emilie Loring, *Beyond the Sound of Guns*

1967. They would question Bobby [Kennedy], read their material into the record, and abstain from voting either pro or con on his appointment. Then, if he acquitted himself badly, they could say, "I told you so" and make what capital they could do it. —Ralph de Toledano, *R.F.K.*

1977. "I told you the first thing he'd say is 'I told you so.'" —William Safire, *Full Disclosure*

1989. When his eyes met Jake's, he frowned and shook his head as if to say "I told you so." —John Grisham, *A Time to Kill*

1991. "I want you to take these letters to America for me, please, Colum. This one's to my Aunt Pauline. I want her to know I got her letter so she'll get all the pleasure possible out of her love for telling people 'I told you so.'" —Alexandra Ripley, *Scarlett*

1993. Polls showed her candidacy in big trouble. Editorial endorsements (including ours) piled up against her. Nevertheless, her calm, her poise and her outward confidence never wavered. And, like Harry Truman on the morning after in 1948, she now can say: "I told you so." —*Times* (Trenton)

I, too, shall pass. See THIS, TOO, WILL (SHALL) PASS.

I was not born yesterday. I'm not naive. I am knowledgeable and experienced. I'm no longer young. I'm not new here. The saying has been traced back to 1837. Attested in the United States much later.

1946. "You weren't born yesterday," I said, and was suddenly angry with him. "You weren't deaf and dumb all the time you had the job in the courthouse in Mason City." —Robert Penn Warren, *All the King's Men*

1950. *Born Yesterday* —Title of a movie written by Garson Kanin and starring Judy Holliday

1953. As security-minded as the next one, I replied I was visiting Devonshire for my health.
   "Really," she said, "I wasn't quite born yesterday, you know."—J. D. Salinger, "For Ésme —with Love and Squalor," *Nine Stories*

1984. "Let me live in here with you. Make me your queen. You won't be sorry. I'll do such things to you—I know not what they are. They'll make you hum, they'll make you sing songs."
   "Take her back," I directed. "I sing songs now."
   I wasn't born yesterday. —Joseph Heller, *God Knows*

1993. Dear Bea: Where did you get the idea that older women are invisible? A few years ago, Frances (formerly "Mrs. Norman") Lear launched Lear's magazine with the catchy subtitle, "For the Woman Who Wasn't Born Yesterday." —Abigail Van Buren, "Dear Abby," *Times* (Trenton)

1994. Having reached something of a zenith with the O.J. Simpson trial, the media event, it should be remembered, was not born yesterday. —*New York Times*

I won't take no for an answer. I insist. I'm determined to get my way. Often used as a polite way of urging an unwilling or uncertain person to do something. *Wouldn't* can replace *won't.*

1974. Marching down to the front desk, she ordered a new chandelier, told the clerk it must be installed by the following day at 10 a.m., cut off his protestations with a curt "I won't take 'no' for an answer!" and swept out the door without waiting for a reply. —Robert A. Caro, *The Power Broker*

1977. The settlement of the steel strike was another feather in the cap of President "I Won't Take No for an Answer" Johnson. —Art Buchwald, *Down the Seine and Up the Potomac*

1979. "Look, I can do this. I'll call our New York office, and I'll tell them it's double-A-one priority. If it's humanly possible, I won't take no for an answer." —Howard Fast, *The Establishment*

1984. "Mr. Reagan, don't take 'nyet' for an answer," Mr. Mondale said in a speech before the American Society of Newspaper Editors here. —*New York Times*

1989. "You must let me drop you off. I won't take no for an answer." —Michael Korda, *The Fortune*

1991. Starting in college, Mr. Lampert aggressively courted the rich and famous—and their sons. He refused to take no for an answer from the powerful investors he admired. —*Wall Street Journal*

1993. "These are tough, hard-driving businessmen who have achieved what they have by not taking 'no' for an answer." —*New York Times*

I would rather die on my feet than live on my knees. Resistance at any cost is preferable to slavery; it's better to die in battle than capitulate. The same idea was expressed by the Roman historian Tacitus (a.d. c.55–a.d. c.117) and attributed to the Mexican revolutionary Emiliano Zapata (1877?–1919). The axiom was popularized by Spanish political leader Dolores Ibarruri. *It is better to die on your feet than live on your knees* and *We would rather die on our feet than live on our knees* are variants. The latter version was used by Presidents Franklin Roosevelt and Gerald Ford.

1936–39.
It is better to die on your feet than live on your knees! They shall not pass. —Dolores Ibarruri, quoted by Edward Vernoff & Rima Shore, *The International Dictionary of 20th Century Biography*

1941. We, too, born to freedom, and believing in freedom, are willing to fight to maintain freedom. We, and all others who believe as deeply as we do, would rather die on our feet than live on our knees. —Franklin Roosevelt, Speech on receiving an honorary degree from Oxford University

1961. "Why don't you use some sense and try to be more like me? ..."
"Because it's better to die on one's feet than to live on one's knees," Nately retorted with triumphant and lofty conviction. "I guess you've heard that saying before."
"Yes, I certainly have," mused the treacherous old man, smiling again. "But I'm afraid you have it backward. It is better to *live* on one's feet than die on one's knees. *That* is the way the saying goes." —Joseph Heller, *Catch-22*

1987. "When we find a people who would rather fight on their feet than live on their knees," said Representative Hunter, a conservative Republican from California, "the argument is that they're mercenaries." —*New York Times*

I wouldn't give him the time of day. That person is not important to me; I regard him with contempt. I won't give him a chance. The saying originated in the mid-twentieth century. The subject can be replaced by another noun or pronoun.

1960. Mr. Ewell seemed determined not to give the defense the time of day. —Harper Lee, *To Kill a Mockingbird*

1974. As for the *News,* it was to fulfill its responsibility to the public by exposing "Communists" in the Housing Authority; says Orton, "If you came in with any information that might be derogatory to [Robert] Moses, the *News* wouldn't give you the time of day." —Robert A. Caro, *The Power Broker*

1984. A great nation, God promised, whose hand would always be against every man.... To me He would not give the time of day. —Joseph Heller, *God Knows*

1986. He knew for a fact that if he wasn't Mr. Silver Anderson they [rich people] wouldn't give him the time of day. —Jackie Collins, *Hollywood Husbands*

1987. Jim Moss, a PTL executive vice president until he was fired in 1979 during one of many purges at PTL, recalls that each day after the Bakker television show "little old women wanted just to touch his hand, people who had given him their life savings. But he wouldn't give them the time of day." —*Time*

1989. *Chicago Sun-Times* Washington correspondent Peter Lisagor heard Kennedy speak to a group of journalists at Harvard and was astonished when Jack said of labor leaders George Meany and Walter Reuther, "I wouldn't give them the time of day, but in politics you simply have to." —Stephen E. Ambrose, *Nixon*

1993. The first time the two actually spoke was Valentine's Day 1989. "But she wouldn't give me the time of day so I didn't think she was interested," Dan remembers. —*Times* (Trenton)

I wouldn't like to meet him in the dark. That person is sinister and untrustworthy. The saying originated in the twentieth century and was first used among women. The word *like* may be replaced with *want.*

1987. "Seymore Pinto. He was a famous murderer!"
"Oh ... no, well, I guess he was before my time."
"Well, you're lucky, because he was a mean somebody. I think he was half Indian, or maybe he was Eye-talian, but whatever he was, you wouldn't want to meet with him on a dark night, I can tell you that." —Fannie Flagg, *Fried Green Tomatoes*

1991. He spoke with some disdain about Soviet officials who "weren't heard from for a couple of days"—an apparent reference to Foreign Minister Aleksandr A. Bessmertnykh—and criticized Mr. Gorbachev's decision to retain Gen. Mikhail A. Moiseyev as Minister of Defense.... "I wouldn't want that guy behind me in a dark hall now," the official said. —*New York Times*

I wouldn't touch it (him) with a ten-foot pole. I won't have anything to do with it. The "pole" refers to the long poles formerly used to propel barges. The saying has been traced back to about 1758. It is found in varying forms: *I*

wouldn't touch it with a barge pole; I wouldn't stir it with a barge pole. The subject and object may vary, as may the length of the pole.

1959. As American-born son would say—"Would not touch with ten-foot pole." —*Bangor Herald* (Me.)

1981. Dear Abby: Let me say that I was married for four years and I never had any complaints from my wife, but if Indians are better lovers than white men I would like to find out why … Ed in East Illinois.

Dear Ed: I wouldn't touch your request with a ten-foot totem pole. Try the Bureau of Indian Affairs or the American Indian Movement. —Abigail Van Buren, *The Best of Dear Abby*

1983. He thought of the old joke … *I wouldn't go near you with a ten-foot pole. … Show me a pole with ten feet and who needs you.* —Jackie Collins, *Hollywood Wives*

1989. He trusted me, I think, even though we had known each other for only four months. And here I was, selling him something I probably wouldn't touch with a barge pole if there hadn't been such glory in it for me. —Michael Lewis, *Liar's Poker*

1994. I wouldn't touch her [Madonna] with a ten-foot pole. —Bob Grant, "The Best of Bob Grant," WABC

I wouldn't want to be in his shoes (place). I wouldn't want to be in that situation. Also used to refer to seeing things through someone else's eyes. *To put oneself in someone else's shoes (place)* is frequently encountered.

1928. *Darrell (Resentfully):* I can't agree with you. I find her quite charming. It seems to me if I were in Gordon's shoes I'd do exactly what he has done. *(In confusion—thinking bitterly)* … In Gordon's shoes! … I always was in Gordon Shaw's shoes! —Eugene O'Neill, *Strange Interlude*

1936. "Yes, yes, I know we've been insulted and lied to—but if we'd been in the Yankees' shoes and they were trying to leave the Union, how would we have acted? Pretty much the same. We wouldn't have liked it."

"There he goes again," thought Scarlett. "Always putting himself in the other fellow's shoes." —Margaret Mitchell, *Gone With the Wind*

1953. "What would *you* do if you were in my shoes?" Sandra asked abruptly. —J. D. Salinger, "Down at the Dinghy," *Nine Stories*

1956. I wouldn't have been in that man's shoes for a million dollars. —*New Yorker*

1960. Atticus was right. One time he said you never really know a man until you stand in his shoes and walk around in them. —Harper Lee, *To Kill a Mockingbird*

1976. As a matter of fact, I wouldn't have wanted to have been in Rocky's shoes the night he came home and broke the news to Happy. —Art Buchwald, *Washington Is Leaking*

1980. "You've heard the song 'Backstabbers,' haven't you?" she asked, sitting on their floor. "Well, backstabbers wouldn't be in my shoes if you paid them." —Norman Mailer, *The Executioner's Song*

1984. Firings are never pleasant, so you have to handle them with as much compassion as you can muster. You have to put yourself in the other guy's shoes and recognize that no matter how you dress it up, it's a pretty bad day in anyone's life. —Lee Iacocca with William Novak, *Iacocca*

1987. Mr. Wilson says Rose was not inspired by anyone specific in his own life. "She's not my mother, and I didn't model her after anyone I know," he said. "I just tried to understand her and to place myself in her shoes." —*New York Times*

1989. "I can appreciate the pressure you're both under. I've been in your shoes many times myself, and I know what you're going through." —John Grisham, *A Time to Kill*

1991. "They wanted to see how we were going to pay the money off," says the source. "Frankly, if I had been in their shoes, I would have done the same thing." —*New York*

Idle hands are the devil's tools. Idleness is the root of mischief. This maxim has been traced back to Chaucer's *Tale of Melibee* (c.1386). First attested in the United States in *Collections* (1808). The proverb is found in varying forms: *Satan has some mischief for idle hands to do; The devil finds work* (or *mischief*) *for idle hands to do; The devil finds work for idle fingers,* etc.

1715. For Satan finds some mischief still
For idle hands to do.
—Isaac Watts, *Divine Songs for Children: Against Idleness and Mischief*

1952. "How could Finnerty get to be a problem nationwide or even Iliumwise? He's only been here a few days."

"Idle hands do the Devil's work, Paul." —Kurt Vonnegut, Jr., *Player Piano*

If a bee stings you once, it's the bee's fault; if a bee stings you twice, it's your own damn fault. *See* FOOL ME ONCE, SHAME ON YOU; FOOL ME TWICE, SHAME ON ME.

If a frog had wings, he wouldn't bump his backside every time he jumps. *See* IF FROGS HAD WINGS, THEY WOULDN'T BUMP THEIR TAILS ON ROCKS.

If a pig had wings, it could fly. What you say is just wishful thinking: it can never happen. The saying has been traced back to *Proverbs of Scotland* (1862). The Walrus in *Alice's Adventures in Wonderland* (1865) by Lewis Carroll questioned "whether pigs had wings." First attested in the United States in *Green Thicket World* (1934) by H. Vines. The adage is found in varying forms: *If a pig (pigs) had wings, one could fly; If that happens, then pigs can fly; When pigs fly, that's when,* etc. It may be reversed: *Pigs could fly if they had wings.* As a rejoinder to the suggestion that something impossible may happen, it is usually abbreviated to *when pigs fly* or *if bunny rabbits grow wings.*

1984. "So, except for the crew, we'd keep her [the Russian submarine]...."
"Yes, if we could hide her. And if a pig had wings, it could fly." —Tom Clancy, *The Hunt for Red October*

1987. If bunny rabbits grow wings and we get that wonderful reduction [in nuclear arms], the West will be required to spend more, far more, to offset the East bloc's gargantuan superiority in tanks and artillery, motorized infantry, and tactical power, if, that is, the West wishes to remain free. —*Washington Times*

1988. "What's so funny, Castellano?"
"Your libido will wane when pigs fly, Dr. Livingston." —Erich Segal, *Doctors*

1991. Rosemary stared, unabashedly curious. "What if Scarlett changed? She might grow up."
Rhett grinned. "To quote the lady herself—'when pigs fly.' " —Alexandra Ripley, *Scarlett*
See also IF FROGS HAD WINGS, THEY WOULDN'T BUMP THEIR TAILS ON ROCKS; IF WISHES WERE HORSES, BEGGARS WOULD RIDE.

If a thing is worth doing, it's worth doing twice. There's no point to making a commitment to do something unless you intend to do it wholeheartedly. The maxim has been traced back to a letter dated October 9, 1746, from Lord Chesterfield to his son. First attested in the United States in *Adams Family Correspondence* (1780). The proverb is found in varying forms: *If a job's worth doing, it's worth doing well; Anything worth doing is worth doing well; If a task is worth doing, it's worth doing well,* etc.

1746. Whatever is worth doing at all is worth doing well. —Philip Dormer Stanhope, Earl of Chesterfield, *Letters to His Son*

1910. The prime truth of woman, the universal mother ... that if a thing is worth doing, it is worth doing badly. —G. K. Chesterton, *What's Wrong with the World*

1989. You know those old saws: If you liked the book, you'll love the movie. If a thing is worth doing, it's worth doing twice. Well, consider if you will, the case of Beaujolais, the only wine that comes not once, but twice in a year. —Frank J. Prial, *New York Times*

1991. An age-old ideal of leisure lingered well into this century, perhaps best summed up by legendary quaffer G. K. Chesterton: "If a thing is worth doing," he wrote, "it is worth doing badly." Mr. Rybczynski adds: "If a sport was undertaken, it was for the love of playing, not of winning, not even of playing well." —*Wall Street Journal*
See also ANYTHING WORTH DOING IS WORTH DOING WELL.

If anyone betrays you once, it's his fault; if he betrays you twice, it's your fault. *See* FOOL ME ONCE, SHAME ON YOU; FOOL ME TWICE, SHAME ON ME.

If anything can go wrong, it will. A jocular way of saying that no matter how carefully you lay your plans, some minor contingency will be overlooked and the plan will fail utterly. Sometimes attributed to George Nichols, an American aerospace executive who in 1949 expanded a remark by Captain E. Murphey of the Wright Field Aircraft Laboratory into the maxim that has become famous as *Murphy's Law.* The word "Law" is ironic, since the saying itself implies that no so-called law is infallible. The 1992 sixteenth edition of Bartlett's *Familiar Quotations,* edited by Justin Kaplan, lists it as an anonymous saying. *Anything that can go wrong, will* and *What can go wrong will go wrong* are variants.

1976. If the media covers an event that is poorly organized and doesn't quite come off, they are going to think twice about coming out next time. Again, remember Murphy's Law: what can go wrong will go wrong. Arrange for backup alternatives, including rain dates. —Claudia Jessup & Genie Chipps, *The Women's Guide to Starting a Business*

1978. *Sue:* "My God, Nicky, what's that? The thought for the day?"
Larry: "Yeah, it's ugly, but he's right. There's an old saying, Navy, I think, that goes, 'Whatever *can*

go wrong *will* go wrong.'" —Stephen King, *The Stand*

1986. In a scene known for wild, volatile groups, Murphy's Law ("Anything that can go wrong will go wrong") has a reputation for being one of the most extreme. —*New York*

1988. Somehow, defying laws of chance but obeying Murphy's Law, viewers missed three goals Monday night in the game between the United States and Czechoslovakia, which was won by the Czechoslovaks, 7–5. —*New York Times*

1991. "Everything that could go wrong did ... except for Pitney Bowes. They kept us in touch with our clients." —Ad for Pitney Bowes, *Fortune*

1993. How did the system get its reputation? Maybe because it was ruled by Murphy's Law. For example, one could dial Tel Aviv and be put through to Jerusalem. —*Hadassah Magazine*

1994. A tragic blunder in the skies over Iraq is a reminder that the first law of war is Murphy's. —*U.S. News & World Report*

If at first you don't succeed, try, try again.

Don't give up too easily; persistence pays off in the end. The proverb has been traced back to *Teacher's Manual* (1840) by American educator Thomas H. Palmer and *The Children of the New Forest* (1847) by English novelist Frederick Marryat (1792–1848). Originally a maxim used to encourage American schoolchildren to do their homework. Palmer (1782–1861) wrote in his *Teacher's Manual:* "'Tis a lesson you should heed, try, try again. If at first you don't succeed, try, try again." The saying was popularized by Edward Hickson (1803–70) in his "Moral Song" (1857) and is now applicable to any kind of activity.

1922. If you fail try again, Edy Boardman said. —James Joyce, *Ulysses*

1949. *Bernard:* Yeah, I'm going. *He takes the bottle.* Thanks, Pop. *He picks up his rackets and bag.* Good-by, Will, and don't worry about it. You know, "If at first you don't succeed ..." —Arthur Miller, *Death of a Salesman*

1984. If at first you don't succeed, forget it. —*Forbes*

1991. They [the Russians] believe that if at first you don't succeed, try, try again: *Pervy blinn komom* ("The first pancake is always a flop"). —*Newsweek*

1993. Money and career matters should be on an upward curve. If a first attempt did not succeed, try again. —Jeane Dixon, "Horoscope," *Times* (Trenton)

If frogs had wings, they wouldn't bump their tails on rocks.

You're just indulging in wishful thinking. Originated in the United States in the mid-twentieth century. The word *frogs* is sometimes used in the singular. The word *rocks* may be replaced by *the ground,* and the word *tails* by *behind* or *asses.* The variant *If a frog had wings, he wouldn't bump his backside every time he jumps* was listed in the 1942 *Dictionary of Quotations* by H. L. Mencken. The saying was popularized by President Bush in 1992. According to William Safire, the proverb is an American variant of the English "If my aunt had been a man, she'd have been my uncle" and the German "If my aunt had wheels, she would be an omnibus."

1992. President Bush went to New Hampshire the other day to tell voters that he cares about their economic distress. But when asked whether he would agree to further extend last year's extension of unemployment insurance benefits, he dismissed the question curtly: "If a frog had wings, he wouldn't hit his tail on the ground—too hypothetical." —*New York Times*

1992. F.D.R. rejected what he called "iffy questions"; he saw them as reportorial traps. President Bush, too, dismisses hypothetical questions; asked about extending unemployment benefits if the economy sinks again, he replied, "If a frog had wings, he wouldn't hit his tail on the ground." —William Safire, *New York Times Magazine*

See also IF A PIG HAD WINGS, IT COULD FLY; IF WISHES WERE HORSES, BEGGARS WOULD RIDE.

If I have seen further it is by standing on the shoulders of giants.

Whatever I have accomplished would have been impossible without the discoveries of my predecessors. Though this adage is often attributed to Isaac Newton (1675–76), he was not the first to say it. As early as 1126 Bernard of Chartres said that "we stand like dwarfs on the shoulders of giants," referring to the ancients. The saying is seldom quoted in its entirety. It is most often seen as: *dwarfs standing on the shoulders of giants* or *on the shoulders of giants,* etc. In 1993, Supreme Court justice Ruth Bader Ginsburg said: "I surely would not be in this room today without the determined efforts of men and women who kept dreams of equal citizenship alive in days when few would listen. People like Susan B. Anthony, Elizabeth Cady Stanton, and Harriet Tubman come to mind. I stand on the shoulders of those brave people."

1675–76.
If I have seen further [than you and Descartes] it is

by standing on the shoulders of giants. —Isaac Newton, Letter to physicist Robert Hook

1965. *On the Shoulders of Giants* —Title of a book by Robert K. Merton on the history of the saying

1970. If I have any wisdom in this field, at all, it is because I am a dwarf standing on the shoulders of giants. —Richard Nelson Bolles, *What Color Is Your Parachute?*

1993. For Mitchell, the opportunity to be a mentor is of prime value. *Goodbye, Mr. Chips* was one of his favorite books. "The end of the story," he recounts, "is that the professor in an English school, who didn't have any children, says, 'Every student I ever taught was my child and my role was to be the shoulders on which everyone could stand so that they could see further than I could ever see.' " —*U.S. 1* (Princeton)

If in doubt, do nothing. *See* WHEN IN DOUBT, DO NOTHING.

If it ain't broke, don't fix it. Any attempt to improve on a system that already works is pointless and may even be detrimental. Originated in the United States in the twentieth century. Government official Bert Lance (1931–) was quoted in the May 1977 issue of *Nation's Business* as saying, "If it ain't broke, don't fix it." Lance's advice, according to William Safire, "has become a source of inspiration to anti-activists." Since then, many variants have been coined, including, *Fix it before it's broke; Fix it before it breaks; If it ain't broke, break it; Even if it ain't broke, fix it; If I can't fix it, it ain't broke; If it ain't broke, why fix it?*

1987. Consequently, if we already possess routines which experience has shown to function smoothly in everyday situations, well ... if it ain't broke, why fix it? —R. Richard Ritti & G. Ray Funkhouser, *The Ropes to Skip & the Ropes to Know*

1988. Your boss might think that you're doing fine without his extra input, and he's reluctant to tamper with excellence—the old, "If it ain't broke, don't fix it" philosophy. —Henry C. Rogers, *Rogers' Rules for Businesswomen*

1991. If it ain't broke, fix it. Because the best time to fix something is before it's broken. —Ad in *Wall Street Journal*

1992. Several critics of your redesign have said, "If it ain't broke, don't fix it." Presumably these are the same people who don't reshingle their roofs or use fluoride on their teeth. I'd like to see their motto replaced with, "If you want it, need it or love it, take care of it." —Letters to the Editor, *Time*

1994. HEALTH CARE: DON'T FIX IT IF IT AIN'T BROKE —Headline, *New York Post*

1995. High up on any list of ain't-broke, don't-fix-'em institutions is America's huge web of universities. —Frank Rich, *New York Times*
See also LEAVE WELL ENOUGH ALONE; LET SLEEPING DOGS LIE.

If it looks like a duck, walks like a duck, and quacks like a duck, it's a duck. The outward appearance and behavior of a person provide such obvious evidence of his nature that it's silly to inquire any further. Originated in the United States in the 1950s. The saying has been attributed to Senator Joseph R. McCarthy (1908–57), as well as to labor leader Walter Reuther (1907–70), who suggested it as a surefire way to identify communists. "Explaining how to tell a communist," wrote William Safire in the *New York Times Magazine* in 1992, "he [Walter Reuther] said, 'If it quacks like a duck, and waddles like a duck, then it just may be a duck.' "

1982. "A boy looks at me, right away I'm a tramp. That's all you ever got to say to me, I'm a tramp. Beautiful words!"
"You act like a tramp, you dress like a tramp, you're a tramp!" Sarah stated. —Howard Fast, *Max*

1988. "If it walks like a duck and talks like a duck and looks like a duck, it's usually a duck. But not the pair of Bally shoes; he wasn't a duck, he was a slap-tailored weasel whose name was stricken from our *list* of ducks." —Robert Ludlum, *The Icarus Agenda*

1991. Will the real candidate please stand up? Douglas Wilder. Looks, walks and quacks like a candidate—is he? —*Time*

1992. A mechanical duck waddles across the TV screen. Then, the toy dissolves ... into a video of Bill Clinton jogging. The voice-over explains that Clinton claims he's not like one of those Democrats in Congress who "tax and spend." Sound of duck quacking. Voice-over: "If it talks like a duck, walks like a duck, it must be a Democrat." —*New York*

1993. " THE CAVE" WALKS, BUT DOESN'T QUACK, LIKE AN OPERA —Headline of a review of the opera *The Cave, New York Times*

If I've told you once, I've told you a thousand times. You're not paying attention to me! I mean what I say! Stop ignoring me! Often used to scold a child. The word *thousand* can be replaced by any other number.

1986. "You's not eating, Howie," Poppy complained. "The lobster is delicious."

"If I've told you once I've told you fifteen times. I *am not* hungry, so stop shoving food at me. Just back off." —Jackie Collins, *Hollywood Husbands*

1991. *Physician to patient:* "If I've told you once, I've told you a hundred times—I do *not* treat amnesia cases!" —Quoted in *Reader's Digest*

If not us, who? If not now, when? We must act and we must act now. The saying is credited to the great Jewish scholar Hillel (c. 60 b.c.–c.a.d. 10). In 1992, it cropped up in several ads. "Quietly ask yourself 'If not now, when?'" read the ad for Omega watches in the *New York Observer*. MCI appealed to "60 Minutes" viewers, "If not us, who? If not now, when?" The Salvation Army, pleading for donations, asked *New York Times* readers, "If not now... When?"

60 b.c.–a.d. 10.
If I am not for myself, who is for me? and if I am only for myself, what am I? and if not now, when? —Hillel, *The Wisdom of the Fathers*

1987. It would be tragic if Congress passed up this opportunity to do the best it can for disadvantaged children. Before opting for half a policy, it should ponder Hillel's challenge "If not now, when? If not us, who?" —*New York Times*

1990. They died for the right of ordinary people to live a decent and honest life and not to be humiliated and kicked around by idiots who take their God from a printed book.... Those are the aspirations to which we should be dedicated today. If not us, whom? If not now, when? —*Forward* (N.Y.)

1991. And come to think of it—the whole country, knowing now how close Iraq came to the bomb, knowing now that the death trade goes on and on, why isn't it screaming, in pain and anger, for action? And if not now, when? —A. M. Rosenthal, *New York Times*

1995. Moving the [U.S.] embassy for the sake of peace. If not now, when? —*Manhattan Jewish Sentinel* (N.Y.)

If the blind lead the blind, both shall fall into the ditch. Ignorant leaders can only bring their followers to ruin. The idea was first expressed in the New Testament. Saint Jerome (c.342–420) explicitly extended the proverb to encompass the idea of leadership: "An unstable pilot steers a leaking ship, and the blind is leading the blind straight to the pit. The ruler is like the ruled." The parable is illustrated in a painting by the Flemish master Brueghel the Elder (c.1525–69). First attested in the United States in *Writings of Samuel Johnson, President of King's College* (1733). Often shortened to *the blind leading the blind* and used after *it is a case of*. A frequent parody substitutes *bland* for *blind*.

Let them alone: they be blind leaders of the blind. And if the blind lead the blind, both shall fall into the ditch. —Matthew, 15:14, *Authorized Version*, 1611

1947. *Blanche:* Which way do we go now, Stella—this way?

Stella: No, this way. *(She leads Blanche away.)*

Blanche (laughing): The blind are leading the blind! —Tennessee Williams, *A Streetcar Named Desire*

1966. Eisenhower had clearly grown during his momentous eight years as President, despite political inexperience, advancing years, three major illnesses, and often lackadaisical leadership—"the bland leading the bland." —Thomas A. Bailey, *The American Pageant*

1977. "Not going to look good," Henry warned, feeling safe enough to argue against his own interest, "the lame leading the blind." —William Safire, *Full Disclosure*

1989. "What television does is take off all the highs, take off all the lows, and squeeze them into a little box. That's where *The Tonight Show* shines. It's the bland leading the bland." —Laurence Leamer, *King of the Night: The Biography of Johnny Carson*

1993. Mr. Dinkins has been so vilified by the Patrolmen's Benevolent Association—a newspaper advertisement by the union last week carried a picture of Mr. Dinkins and President Clinton above the headline. "The Blind Leading the Blind"—that he is hardly the candidate most associated in the public mind with the police. —*New York Times*

If the mountain will not come to Mohammed, Mohammed will go to the mountain. If one cannot get one's own way, one must adjust to the inevitable. The legend goes that when the founder of Islam was asked to give proofs of his teaching, he ordered Mount Safa to come to him. When the mountain did not comply, Mohammed raised his hands toward heaven and said, "God is merciful. Had it obeyed my words, it would have fallen on us to our destruction. I will therefore go to the mountain and thank God that He has had mercy on a stiff-necked generation." The saying has been traced back in English to *Essays* (1625) by English philosopher Francis Bacon (1561–

1626). It was included in John Ray's book of English proverbs in 1678. First attested in the United States in *Jonathan Belcher Papers* (1733). In German, the phrase translates as *Wenn der Berg nicht zum Propheten kommt, muß der Prophet zum Berg kommen.*

1625. Mahomet made the people believe that he would call a hill to him, and from the top of it offer up his prayers for the observers of his law. The people assembled: Mahomet called the hill to come to him again and again: and when the hill stood still, he was never a whit abashed, but said, 'If the hill will not come to Mahomet, Mahomet will go to the hill.' —Francis Bacon, "Of Boldness"

1962. Hawke shot him a sly look. "Well, the fact is the mountain's going to go to Mohammed instead, and don't ask me to unriddle that dark saying till we've had some chow." —Herman Wouk, *Youngblood Hawke*

1979. Now she tossed the script aside, rose, and kissed him lightly. "Dear Alex—what brings the mountain to Mahomet?"

"So now you're Mahomet? A small mountain I have always been. I'm here because you don't answer your telephone." —Howard Fast, *The Establishment*

1987. Okay. If these people do not have the guts to face battle, then we'll fight on their terms. I have enough firepower to make sure if the mountain doesn't come to me, I can remove the mountain. —Craig Bunch & Allan Cole, *A Reckoning for Kings*

1988. "Well, hello, old friends," he said, sarcastically. "What brings the mountain to Mohammed?" —Erich Segal, *Doctors*

If the shoe fits, wear it. If my assessment is correct, you must accept it, even if it is unflattering. The original phrasing, *If the cap fits, wear it,* is rarely used in the United States. The U.S. variant first appeared on May 17, 1773 in the *New York Gazette & Weekly Mercury:* "Why should Mr. Vanderbeck apply a general comparison to himself? Let those whom the shoe fits wear it." *If the shoe fits, put it on* is also used. Recent spins on this proverb include *If the shoe fits, you're lucky* (Malcolm Forbes) and *If the shoe fits, it isn't on sale.*

1951. "Hey," Bloom said. "You mean me? Are you callin me a son of a bitch?"

"If the shoe fits, friend, you wear it," Maggio said. —James Jones, *From Here to Eternity*

1961. "What kind of malice is in you?" said Father Herzog, angry.

"I have nothing against Mikhail. He never harmed me," Zipporah said. "But he was a brother who gave, so I am a sister who doesn't give."

"No one said it," Father Herzog said. "But if the shoe fits, you can wear it." —Saul Bellow, *Herzog*

1985. Anyway, it's clear to see through the thick clouds of his verbosity that he's trying to disguise a life of quiet desperation. He concludes with the philosophical observation, "If the shoe fits, you've got to wear it." —Erich Segal, *The Class*

1990. In a broad rebuttal to recent Congressional criticism, Mr. Cheney complained in his address that lawmakers were offering "complaints instead of solutions."... Mr. Cheney noted that his speech was prepared before Mr. Nunn spoke. "But obviously, if the shoe fits, wear it, Sam," Mr. Cheney added. —*New York Times*

1993. If the shoe doesn't fit, you simply don't have to wear it. —Wendy Wasserstein, *Lear's*

1994. "The word 'storm,'" he explains, "brings out visions of forceful winds, significant snows, a nor'easter. A more technical term would be a 'low pressure system.' That sounds cumbersome.... For want of a better word, 'snow event' just seems to be it. If the boot fits, wear it." If you catch the drift. —*Times* (Trenton)

If there were no God, it would be necessary to invent Him. Generally attributed to French philosopher Voltaire (1769), who wrote in one of his letters, *Si Dieu n'existait pas, il faudrait l'inventer* ("If God did not exist, it would be necessary to invent Him"). However, a similar idea was expressed by the Roman poet Ovid (43 b.c.– a.d. 17): *Expedit esse deos, et, ut expedit, esse putemus* ("It is convenient that there be gods, and, as it is convenient, let us believe that there are"). John Tillotson (1630–94) wrote: "If God were not a necessary Being of Himself, He might almost seem to be made for the use and benefit of men." The subject is often altered to accommodate other "necessities."

1991. "If Gorbachev didn't have a Yeltsin, he would have to invent him," Yeltsin wrote wryly in his 1990 autobiography, *Against the Grain.* —Time

1992. "If Groundhog Day hadn't existed, we would have had to invent it," said Elaine Light, a local booster. —*Reader's Digest*

If we don't hang together, we will hang separately. *See* WE MUST INDEED ALL HANG TOGETHER, OR, MOST ASSUREDLY, WE SHALL ALL HANG SEPARATELY.

If wishes were horses, beggars would ride.

It is useless to indulge in wishful thinking. The aphorism has been traced back to *Proverbs in Scots* (c.1628) by J. Carmichael. It was included in John Ray's 1670 collection of English proverbs and in J. Kelly's 1721 collection of Scottish proverbs. First attested in the United States in *Ra-ta-plan!* (1930) by D. Ogburn. The saying is found in varying forms: *If wishes were horses, think how cheap horses would be; If wishes were horses, beggars could ride,* (or *might*) etc.

1844. If wishes were horses, beggars would ride; If turnips were watches, I would wear one by my side. —James Orchard Halliwell, *Nursery Rhymes of England*

1930. If wishes were horses, beggars would ride. —D. Ogburn, *Ra-ta-plan!*

1973. "They even had a saying about the futility of ideas: "If wishes were horses, beggars would ride!" —Kurt Vonnegut, Jr., *Breakfast of Champions*

1991. If wishes were horses, beggars might hide. Hunts down bums and kills them dead. —Quoted in "New York Magazine Competition," *New York*

1992. Don't you wish to coin one [proverb]? (As they said in the 17th century, "If wishes were horses, beggars would ride.") —William Safire, "On Language," *New York Times Magazine*

See also IF A PIG HAD WINGS, IT COULD FLY; IF FROGS HAD WINGS, THEY WOULDN'T BUMP THEIR TAILS ON ROCKS.

If you believe that, there is a bridge in Brooklyn I'd like to sell you. Don't be so gullible: that's an obvious lie. Originated in the United States in the 20th century.***

1984. He knew the story that they were searching for a lost sub, but Eaton believed that as much as if they'd explained that they had a bridge they wanted to sell. —Tom Clancy, *The Hunt for Red October*

1991. Criticizing a remark of Mr. Kennedy's, Orrin Hatch said, "Anybody who believes that, I know a bridge up in Massachusetts and I'll be happy to sell it to them." Later Senator Hatch apologized, saying he meant a bridge in Brooklyn.... And if you believe that, there is a bridge in Brooklyn I'd like to sell. —Anna Quindlen, *New York Times*

1992. The head of the Justice Department's fraud section, Lawrence Urgenson, today strongly denied that he urged a C.I.A. lawyer, George Jameson, to provide misleading information to prosecutors.... "If anybody swallows the notion that the general counsel for the C.I.A. was intimidated into signing this letter, I have a bridge in Brooklyn I want to sell him. That is absurd, just plain absurd." —*New York Times*

1993. Advocates of the North American Free Trade Agreement, known to all as NAFTA, are touting the pact as a way of stemming the flood of Mexican migrants weighing down California's weak economy.... Well, if you buy that argument there's a nice bridge in Brooklyn I'd like to sell you. —*Times* (Trenton)

See also HE WOULD TRY TO SELL YOU THE BROOKLYN BRIDGE.

If you can make it here, you can make it anywhere. If you can achieve success in this town, you can succeed anywhere. Usually refers to New York City. Originated in the United States. The saying is a slight variation on a line from the song "New York, New York" (1977), written by Fred Ebb (lyrics) and John Kander (music). It was first sung by Liza Minnelli (1977) in the movie of the same title and later popularized by Frank Sinatra (1980). The word *here* may be replaced by a geographic name (*If you can do it at Kay Graham's, you can do it everywhere; If you can do that in Harlem, you can do it in the world*). **

1977. If I can make it there, I'd make it anywhere —Fred Ebb, "New York, New York"

1985. "Are you suggesting that London, Amsterdam, and Paris are 'try-out towns'?"
"I am indeed," Hurok said without blinking. "For New York, every other city on earth is New Haven. When you make it *here* you've really made it." —Erich Segal, *The Class*

1992. "If you can make it here, you can make it anywhere," said Edward Reuter, 64, chairman of Daimler-Benz, paraphrasing Frank Sinatra while in New York. Reuter, who has agreed to remain as head of the company for two years beyond the mandatory retirement age of 65, should have reversed the line. Daimler is making it everywhere around the world *except* New York—or the rest of the U.S. —*Fortune*

1993. The level of incivility, always on the rise, has lately reached a fever pitch. Diehard New Yorkers still pretend to find it charming, a test of strength in the shopworn "if you can make it here" or "only in New York" manner. —Letters to the Editor, *New York Times*

1994. If you can make it in New York, why not Washington? ... That's what the policy wonks at The Manhattan Institute are asking themselves while shutting down their D.C. satellite office this month after two years. "Washington's different," says President William Hammett. "It just didn't work out." —*Crain's New York Business*

If you can't beat (lick) 'em, join 'em. Once you realize there's no hope of besting your rivals, make peace so you can gain an edge by the alliance. Originated in the United States in 1941. "There is an old political adage which says, 'If you can't lick 'em, jine [join] 'em,'" wrote Quentin Reynolds in *The Wounded Don't Cry* (1941). The saying is current in all English-speaking countries, but *lick* is used only in America. Some of the most common variants are: *If you can't beat 'em, starve 'em; If you can't lick 'em, buy 'em; If you can't kill 'em, join 'em; If you can't enjoin them, lick them; If you can't fight 'em, debate 'em.*

1948. "You see, at that school I was from the wrong side of the tracks—funny in a way but perfectly true. He was of them, from them, with them, and part of them. That was something I never could be, coming from where I came. He was the first kid I ever envied.... "Well, as the old saying goes, 'If you can't lick 'em, jine 'em.' That's what I did." —Harold Robbins, *Never Love a Stranger*

1962. We're in an if-you-cannot-lick-'em-join-'em age.
A slovenliness-provides-its-own-excuse age.
—Ogden Nash, *"Everyone But Thee and Me."*

1964. Addressing the Inter-American Press Association, the President began as follows: "I'm very proud to be here tonight. I'm particularly interested in the fact that two of our distinguished guests are former Prime Ministers of Peru and are now publishers of newspapers. It does suggest to those who hold office that when the time comes that if—as they say in the United States—if you can't beat them, join them." —Booton Herndon, *The Humor of JFK*

1966. President Johnson, waving both the stick and the carrot, delivered a nationally televised speech, on April 7, 1965, at the Johns Hopkins University in Baltimore. On the one hand, he pledged himself to defend South Vietnam to the end; on the other, he proposed a billion-dollar program to aid economic development of Southeast Asia, including North Vietnam. He also offered to negotiate a peaceful settlement without prior conditions. These proposals were warmly applauded in America, although some Republican critics sneered, "If you can't lick 'em, buy 'em." —Thomas A. Bailey, *The American Pageant*

1976. "One of the heads of the families said, 'We have a saying in the Costa Nostra: If you can't kill 'em, join 'em.'" —Art Buchwald, *Washington Is Leaking*

1981. But Charlie sees the problem after all; he expresses it: "Look. You're the son-in-law, you can't be touched. But me, the old lady is my connection here, and it's sentimental at that, she likes me because I remind her of Fred, of the old days. Sentiment doesn't beat out blood. I'm in no position to hang tough. If you can't beat 'em, join 'em." —John Updike, *Rabbit Is Rich*

1993. Discounters, led by Medco, were revolutionizing its market and undermining margins. Roy Vagelos, CEO of the undisputed champ of the pharmaceutical industry, concluded: If you can't beat 'em, buy 'em. —*Fortune*

1994. Confronted with the foretaste of daunting competition, it appears postal authorities are bowing to the old adage, "If you can't beat 'em, join 'em." —*Wall Street Journal*

If you can't run with the big dogs, stay under the porch. Know your limitations; don't try to compete with stronger and more experienced players. *If you're gonna run with the big dogs, you can't pee like a puppy* is one variant. The expression was popularized by George Bush.

1988. Game-show host Bob Eubanks calls himself a weekend cowboy and doesn't wax romantic about the way of life. But he relishes cowboy humor and cites a favorite saying: "If you're gonna run with the big dogs, you can't pee like a puppy." —*US*

1992. Signaling that he was primed for battle, Mr. Bush closed with these words: "So you tell Governor Clinton and that Congress, 'If you can't run with the big dogs, stay under the porch.'" —*New York Times*

1994. "Grampa, can you tell me your outlook on life?" ... "Sugar catches flies, but if you've swallowed a camel and you can't run with the big dogs, don't bite off more than you can shake a stick at." —Cartoon by Brian Crane, "Pickles," *Times* (Trenton)

See also IF YOU CAN'T STAND THE HEAT, GET OUT OF THE KITCHEN.

If you can't stand the heat, get out of the kitchen. If the pressures are too great for you, leave it to those of us who can handle it without complaining. Originated in the United States. Generally attributed to Harry S. Truman, though he credited his friend General Harry H. Vaughan. George Bush used the expression in his 1988 presidential debate with Michael Dukakis. In 1992, President Bush added a new twist to the old saying: "As regarding Mr. Perot, I take back something I said about him. I once said in a frivolous moment when he got out of the race, if you can't stand the heat buy an air-conditioning company. And I take it back." According to Russell Baker, in his 1992 debate with President Bush, Bill Clinton declared that there was only one thing the voters needed to know about him: "I am not Bush." This prompted the following outburst from Bush: "Neither am I. I'm Harry Truman. If you can't stand the kitchen get in out of the heat." The words *can't stand* may be replaced by *don't like* and the word *get* by *stay*.

1974. Dean Acheson wrote that Harry Truman was totally without what he called "that most enfeebling of emotions, regret." ... *Regret* was self-indulgent, as bad as, maybe worse than, telling people how you *felt*. No time for it. "If you can't stand the heat, stay out of the kitchen." —Merle Miller, *Plain Speaking*

1988. "No, no, no, sir," Barney argued back somnolently, "even if you ignore our state of health, what about the unlucky patient who is seen by a doctor who can barely stay awake? Is it in *his* best interests that he be treated by a zombie? Tired people make mistakes."

The doctor looked at Barney scornfully. "Livingston, this is part of your education and you know what they say: If you don't like the heat, get out of the kitchen." —Erich Segal, *Doctors*

1989. "These guys are a bunch of little babies," he [Steinbrenner] said. "We've got guys earning $2 million a year, and they don't want criticism. Try telling that to the cab driver, policeman or fireman in New York, and see what he thinks. If they don't like it, it's too bad. They're in the oven; if they can't stand the heat, then it's time to get out and get into something else." —*New York Times*

1990. If you can't stand the heat, get out of the kitchen. That's what tough-talking politicians say, making it sound as though only a wimp would head for the exit. —*Washington Post*

1992. I said to him, "Mr. Baker, do you ever get writer's block?" He just showed his famous white teeth, tousled my hair and said, "The day I can't stand the heat, I'll get out of the kitchen." —Art Buchwald, *New York Times*

1994. Animadversion about people in politics is among our most sacred traditions, and those who can't stand the heat don't belong in the kitchen. —Arthur Schlesinger, Jr., *New York Times*

See also IF YOU CAN'T RUN WITH THE BIG DOGS, STAY UNDER THE PORCH.

If you don't like it, you can lump it. Too bad! You'll have to put up with it whether you like it or not. The saying has been traced back to *Our Mutual Friend* (1864) by Charles Dickens. First attested in the United States in the mid-nineteenth century. The word *lump* is of American origin. *If you don't like it, you can stick it up your ass* is a vulgar variant. "If you do not like them ... /Stick them up your —," wrote Ernest Hemingway in *Poems* (1929). Often shortened to *like it or lump it*.

1864. "I'm going to call you Boffin, for short.... If you don't like it, it's open to you to lump it." —Charles Dickens, *Our Mutual Friend*

1985. This "like it or lump it" choice faced President Reagan last October when Congress dropped a $458-billion appropriations bill on his desk, the largest appropriations package in American history. —*Reader's Digest*

1988. "What about your patients?" she asked in a semi-chiding tone.

"Hey, kiddo, don't you even know what day it is? Tomorrow's Saturday. The couch doesn't work weekends. So like it or lump it, I'm on my way." —Erich Segal, *Doctors*

1991. [Bill] Gates is the Henry Ford of our generation, and if you don't like it, go build a Honda. —*New York Times Magazine*

See also TAKE IT OR LEAVE IT.

If you don't make mistakes you don't make anything. *See* HE WHO NEVER MADE A MISTAKE NEVER MADE ANYTHING.

If you know what I mean. Often used ironically following a vague and unclear statement. The catch phrase originated in the twentieth century and has been used by F. Scott Fitzgerald, Margaret Mitchell, Arthur Miller, and John Cheever, to mention only a few. *You know what I mean?; Do you know what I mean?; Do you know what I'm saying?; You know what I'm saying?* are variants of the saying.

1925. "I like your dress," remarked Mrs. McKee, "I think it's adorable."

"... It's just a crazy old thing," she said. "I just slip it on sometimes when I don't care what I look like."

"But it looks wonderful on you, if you know what I mean," pursued Mrs. McKee. —F. Scott Fitzgerald, *The Great Gatsby*

1936. "Every day my accursed shrinking from realities makes it harder for me to face the new realities. Do you know what I mean?" —Margaret Mitchell, *Gone With the Wind*

1949. *Happy:* My brother is—I think he pulled off a big deal today. I think we're going into business together.
Stanley: Great! That's the best for you. Because a family business, you know what I mean?—that's the best.
—Arthur Miller, *Death of a Salesman*

1957. "In New York I had lots of friends. Of course I was mistaken, once. I was mistaken in my friends. You know what I mean?" —John Cheever, *The Wapshot Chronicle*

1962. "Nancy, when I got off the plane in Lexington and heard the accents and *smelled* Kentucky, if you know what I mean—the air here has a smell, you know, a nice smell, you could bring a tank of it to New York and let it loose in my room and I'd tell you what it was—I tell you my heart went down in the bottom of my shoes." —Herman Wouk, *Youngblood Hawke*

1984. "It was kind of nice being a P.F.C.," he reminisced yearningly. "I had status—you know what I mean?—and I used to travel in best circles." —Joseph Heller, *Catch-22*

1986. "It's hot water, sir, full of sulfur. Just as soon not drink that shit, if you know what I mean." —Tom Clancy, *Red Storm Rising*

1990. Years later, Morgan partner and then chairman George Whiney would say: "I always find that I have to guard myself because of a fear that I will sound soft and foolish, but he was a great gentleman, a cultured gentleman, if you know what I mean...." —Ron Chernow, *The House of Morgan*

If you lie down with dogs, you'll get up with fleas. People who associate with disreputable characters are inevitably harmed by the connection. The proverb has been traced back to J. Sanford's *Garden of Pleasure* (1573). It is similar to the Latin: *Qui cum canibus concumbunt cum pulicibus surgent* ("They who lie with dogs will rise with fleas"). The saying appeared in 1651, in George Herbert's collection of proverbs ("He that lies with the dogs, riseth with fleas") and in 1721 in J. Kelly's Scottish proverbs ("He that sleeps with dogs must rise with fleas"). First attested in the United States in *Poor Richard's Almanac* (1733) by Benjamin Franklin. The aphorism is found in varying forms.

1953. Sleep with dogs and rise with fleas. —Saul Bellow, *The Adventures of Augie March*

1991. One of the violinists spat accurately into a potted palm. "Too late, I say. Lie down with dogs, get up with fleas." —Alexandra Ripley, *Scarlett*

1993. Furlong depicted Hill as a follower who was unaware his cohorts were robbing the restaurants.... "I told the jury, when you lie down with dogs, you get up with fleas," Furlong said. —*Times* (Trenton)

See also A MAN IS KNOWN (JUDGED) BY THE COMPANY HE KEEPS.

If you play both ends against the middle, the middle will soon fold up. If you set two sides against each other for your own gain, you may get into trouble with both sides. The proverb originated in the United States and was first cited in Reuben Maury's *Wars of the Godly* (1928). It is found in varying forms. *To play both ends against the middle* is a common figure of speech.

1928. Bennett played both ends of the religious fight against the middle. —Reuben Maury, *Wars of the Godly*

1965. Dao will be part of the junta, of course; but from our point of view he's the part we need least. He's playing both ends against the middle. Don't forget he's still Assistant Chief of Staff to Cung. —Morris West, *The Ambassador*

1977. She's playing both ends against the middle, doing something for him, keeping a secret for us, so she comes out on top no matter who wins. —William Safire, *Full Disclosure*

1987. "You're dealing with two highly controversial people. Why do you have to play both ends against the middle?" —Overheard at the offices of the *Daily News* (N.Y.)

If you want peace, prepare for war. The best way for a nation to avert war is to intimidate potential aggressors by its military readiness. The proverb has been traced back in English to *Chronicle of Edward IV* (1548) by E. Hall. First attested in the United States in *Colonial Records of South Carolina* (1755). The Latin saying *Si vis pacem, para bellum* ("If you want peace, prepare for war") is attributed to the Roman historian Cornelius Nepos (c.94–24 b.c.) and used by the Roman military strategist Vegetius (a.d. 379–95). *Wish* or *desire* may substitute for *want*.

a.d. 379–95.
Qui desiderat pacem, praeparet bellum. ("Let him who desires peace, prepare for war.") —Vegetius, *Epitoma Institutionum Rei Militaris*

1621. Happy is that city which in time of peace thinks of war. —Anonymous inscription found in the armory of Venice, quoted by Robert Burton, *The Anatomy of Melancholy*

1790. To be prepared for war is one of the most effectual means of preserving peace. —George Washington, First Annual Address

1986. The ancient Romans held to a similar dictum: "If you want peace, prepare for war." —*New York Newsday*

If you want something done right, do it yourself. No one can fulfill your intentions as well as you can yourself. The proverb has been traced back to *Christian State of Matrimony* (1541) by Swiss reformer Heinrich Bullinger (1504–75). First cited in the United States in *Poems* (1858) by Henry Wadsworth Longfellow (1807–82). The phrase may take varying forms: *If you want a thing well done, do it yourself; If you want a thing to be well done, you must do it yourself*, etc.

1858. That's what I always say; if you want a
  thing to be well done,
  You must do it yourself.
      —Henry Wadsworth Longfellow, *Poems*

1992. If You Want Something Done Right, Do It Yourself —Ad for Kraft General Foods, *Reader's Digest*

1993. If you really want something done today, you had better do it yourself. —Jeane Dixon, "Horoscope," *Times* (Trenton)

1994. I've heard more than once that "the best way to get something done is to do it yourself." I didn't believe it. Now I have to pay for it. —Overheard at a school conference in New York City

If you're gonna run with the big dogs, you can't pee like a puppy. *See* IF YOU CAN'T RUN WITH THE BIG DOGS, STAY UNDER THE PORCH.

If you're not part of the solution, you're part of the problem. Anyone who doesn't take direct action to make things better is just an obstacle to changing the status quo. The saying originated in the United States in the 1960s. The American activist Eldridge Cleaver is generally credited with its coinage (1968). However, according to Ralph Keyes, it was used earlier by City College (N.Y.) president Buell Gallagher (1964). Either part can be used separately in the affirmative or the negative: *part of the solution* or *part of the problem. You are (you're) either part of the solution or you're part of the problem* is Cleaver's

version.***

1968. What we're saying today is that you're either part of the solution or you're part of the problem. —Eldridge Cleaver, *Newsweek*

1988. "Matter of fact," the speaker continued, looking at Bennett, "we want you to teach a first aid class, since you're a surgeon, train a medical corps to treat bullet wounds. Now, are you with us, brother?"
  Bennett was taken aback.
  Jamal-Jack prodded him. "Come on, man, you know what Eldridge says—'If you ain't part of the solution you're part of the problem.'" —Erich Segal, *Doctors*

1989. "That crowd around Dinkins—they are part of the problem, not part of the solution," Mr. Giuliani said. —*New York Times*

1990. WE ARE PART OF THE SOLUTION —Sign on a Chicago apartment building for low-income families

1992. Mr. Nader asserts that Mr. Aspin has lost the fervor he demonstrated in the early 1970's for investigating waste, fraud and abuse. Mr. Aspin, he says, is now part of the problem. —*New York Times*

1994. When the other side in a lawsuit loses, then demands money to prevent an appeal (as happened to Culbertson), you tell them to jump in the lake, not write them a check for nearly half a million dollars. Culbertson's writing a check makes her part of the problem, not part of the solution. —Letters to the Editor, *Newsweek*

If you've got it, flaunt it. Wealthy or otherwise well-endowed people have a right to be ostentatious. The saying appeared in the movie *The Producers* (1968), written and directed by Mel Brooks (1926–   ). In 1969, it was picked up as an advertising motto by Braniff airlines. *When you got it, flaunt it* is also common. The word *have* is sometimes substituted for *got. If you've got it, hide it* is a recent jocular variant.***

1968. That's it, baby. If you've got it, flaunt it. —Mel Brooks, *The Producers*

1982. It was, he supposed, the difference between new money and old money. Old money's motto was, *If you have it, hide it.* New money's motto was, *If you have it, flaunt it.* —Sidney Sheldon, *The Master of the Game*

1983. "It has to have set old Adam back at least two grand. If you got it, Bibi, flaunt it." —Jackie Collins, *Hollywood Wives*

1988. We all know people from modest circumstances who have made it big. And flaunt it.

—Harvey Mackay, *Swim with the Sharks without Being Eaten Alive*

1991. "I grew up in Chicago, and I was always interested in cars. But the late 40's and early 50's were a particularly good time. We were just coming out of World War II, and for the manufacturers, it was kind of like, 'If you got it, flaunt it.'" —*New York Times*

1993. IF YOU'VE GOT IT, HIDE IT —Headline of a review of a book about drug dealing, *New York Times Book Review*

1994. For both Fat Roy and Forgotten Woman, the look says, "Yo! If you've got it, flaunt it—and God bless the elasticized waistband." —*New York Times Magazine*

If you've seen one, you've seen 'em all.
They all look alike, there's no real difference, so it's enough to see one to have an idea of all the others. Construed to indicate a jaded or pseudo-sophisticated view of things. Originated in the twentieth century. When vice-presidential candidate Spiro T. Agnew (1918–) used the phrase to refer to a city slum, he was widely criticized. Sometimes used by men of women and vice versa to mean that if you've seen one sexual organ, you've seen them all. *Quand on en a vu un, on les a vu tous* is a French equivalent. *One* and *'em* may be replaced by other words.

1968. To some extent, if you've seen one city slum you've seen them all. —Spiro T. Agnew, Speech in Detroit, *New York Times*

1980. "I'm not much of a sightseer. My theory is that if you've seen one church, you've seen them all." —Sidney Sheldon, *Rage of Angels*

1993. There is no mention of President Reagan in the article. Is it possible that Reagan might have the same thing to say about trees: "If you've seen one, you've seen them all"? —Letters to the Editor, *New York Times Magazine*

1995. Politicians talk of "reinventing government" (never mind that the whole idea of reinventing anything is antilogical): Can one reinvent the romance of work, so that you can see one, see 'em all, and see one again, as if for the first time, too? —Roger Rosenblatt, *Modern Maturity*

Ignorance is bliss. In dangerous or difficult circumstances, it's often a blessing not to fully understand the situation. Naïve people are often happier than knowledgeable ones. It's easier to do something if you don't know how hard it is. Sometimes used ironically. The adage was origi-

nated by the English poet Thomas Gray (1761–71) in 1742. First attested in the United States in *Clovernook* (1852). The saying takes varying forms: *If (where) ignorance is bliss, 'tis folly to be wise; If ignorance is bliss, we must be a deliriously happy lot; Ignorance is bliss, and we're in seventh heaven,* etc. A famous ironic use is in George Orwell's *1984* (1949), where it is used with such statements as "War is Peace."

1742. Yet ah! why should they know their fate,
Since sorrow never comes too late,
And happiness too swiftly flies?
Thought would destroy their paradise.
No more; where ignorance is bliss,
'Tis folly to be wise.
— Thomas Gray, "On a Distant Prospect of Eton College"

1922. ... this remark passed obviously in the spirit of *where ignorance is bliss....* —James Joyce, *Ulysses*

1986. "It's all crap," says he. "All lies. Your senses lie to you, the president lies to you, the more you search the less you find, the more you try, the worse it gets. Ignorance is bliss." —Robert Fulghum, *All I Really Need to Know I Learned in Kindergarten*

1989. "I did it in ignorance," Mr. Feld said of founding his first [ballet] company, nursing a cup of coffee at his large neat kitchen table one recent morning. "You know the saying that ignorance is bliss? I confirm the validity of that adage." —*New York Times*

1991. "Ignorance may be bliss, but apathy is *paradise!* " —*Wall Street Journal*

1993. What the Boss failed to mention was that things had changed in Jersey City. The mayor was, curse the word, a Republican.... Ignorance is bliss and the recently interred had a glorious day. At dusk, they were re-interred. —*Times* (Trenton)

1994. If ignorance is bliss, why aren't more people happy? —*Jewish Press* (N.Y.)

1995. Americans who willingly swim in a sea of ignorance can blame themselves when the quality of their lives deteriorates. An example: As the crucial Senate vote on the balanced-budget amendment approached, were most Americans—whatever their political persuasion—aware of the vast implications of this latest attempt to change the Constitution? No.... If ignorance is bliss, we must be a deliriously happy lot. —Bob Herbert, *New York Times*
See also WHAT YOU DON'T KNOW CAN'T HURT YOU.

Ignorance of the law is no excuse. A person who commits a crime is considered guilty even if he was unaware that his act was illegal. The saying is of Latin origin: *Ignorantia juris neminem excusat* ("Ignorance of the law excuses no one"). It has been traced back to *Dialogues in English* (1530) by St. German. First cited in the United States in *Almanacs* (1755). The maxim is found in varying forms: *Ignorance of the laws is no excuse for breaking them: Ignorance of the law excuses no man; (nobody),* etc.

1689. Ignorance of the law excuses no man; not that all men know the law, but because 'tis an excuse every man will plead, and no man can tell how to refute him. —John Selden, *Table Talk*

1973. "Yes, ignorance of the law is no excuse!" Sadoff said. —Joyce Carol Oates, *Do with Me What You Will*

1994. I hereby confess that I, deliberately and with forethought, purchased a quantity of rat poison and wantonly placed it where it would be devoured by innocent, unsuspecting rodents whose only sin was eating my baby ducklings. Like the mean Mr. Balun, I am a law-breaking senior citizen. The fact that I was unaware that it is illegal to kill rats makes absolutely no difference. Ignorance of the law is no excuse. I am clearly culpable. —*Star-Ledger* (Newark, N.J.)

I'm from Missouri; you've got to show me.

I don't believe you; prove it to me. I'm not so easy to fool. The saying is generally attributed to Colonel Willard Duncan Vandiver (1854–1932) of Columbia, Missouri, who used it in a speech before The Five O'Clock Club of Philadelphia in 1899. John A. T. Hall, Congressman of Iowa, criticized him for being the only guest not in evening clothes. Vandiver retorted that Hall must have stolen his own suit, because it was so ill-fitting, adding: "I'm from Missouri; you've got to show me [that the suit is yours]." Vandiver never claimed to have originated the phrase. General Emmett Newton, on the other hand, claimed to have coined it in 1892 when he was a small boy as a response to another boy who bragged that his collection of badges was better than Newton's. According to some sources, the saying was current as far back as the Civil War. The expression was popularized by the song, "I'm from Missouri and You've Got to Show Me" (lyrics by Lee Raney and music by Ned Wayburn).

1899. I come from a state that raises corn and cotton and cockleburs and Democrats, and frothy eloquence neither convinces nor satisfies me. I'm from Missouri. You have got to show me. —Willard Duncan Vandiver, Speech at a naval banquet in Philadelphia

1961. … In social dealings with foreigners, the Englishman is *from Missouri,* he has got to be shown. —D. W. Brogan, quoted in the 1981 *Webster's Third New International Dictionary of the English Language*

1994. I'm not from Missouri, but you'll still have to show me why Clinton's health plan is better. —Overheard at an Empire Blue Cross and Blue Shield public meeting

Imitation is the sincerest form of flattery.

Usually said ironically when someone tries to gain attention by copying someone else's original ideas. Coined by Charles Caleb Colton in 1820 in his *Lacon.* First attested in the United States in *Malice* (1940) by E. Cameron. The adage is found in varying forms: *Imitation is the highest form of flattery; Imitation may be the sincerest form of flattery,* etc.

1940. Imitation may be the sincerest form of flattery. —E. Cameron, *Malice*

1985. Then Miss Levin turned her attention to Danny Rossi. Or rather her guns. In her opinion, the music, though ambitious and energetic, was, to say the least, derivative. Imitation may be the sincerest form of flattery, but Stravinsky and Aaron Copland could justifiably ask Rossi to pay royalties. —Erich Segal, *The Class*

1987. Q.: Thanks, Mr. President. I'm afraid I've caught your laryngitis.
A: Imitation is a sincere form of flattery. —President's news conference on foreign and domestic issues, *New York Times*

1992. Clinton campaign officials said today that the President's proposals were a poor attempt to mimic Mr. Clinton's record on job training without explaining how he would pay for it…. "They say that imitation is the sincerest form of flattery," said George Stephanopoulos, the campaign's communications director. —*New York Times*

1994. Imitation may be the sincerest form of flattery, but Italian designer Gianni Versace takes no pleasure in all the compliments he has been receiving…. One of the standouts of his 1994 fall collection—a $1,232 rubberized-silk mini-dress was barely off the runway in Milan when Macy's and other U.S. retailers began ordering a look-alike vinyl version that would sell for just $170. —*Wall Street Journal*

In for a penny, in for a pound. Once you start something, you might as well go all the way with it. The proverb has been traced back to *Canterbury Guests* (1695) by Edward Ravenscroft. First attested in the United States in *Writings of George Washington* (1785). It is found in varying forms: *In for a dime, in for a dollar; In for a penny, in for the whole bankroll,* etc.

1695. Well, then o'er shoes, o'er boots. And in for a Penny, in for a Pound. —Edward Ravenscroft, *The Canterbury Guests: Or, A Bargain Broken*

1882. In for a penny, in for a pound. —W. S. Gilbert, *Iolanthe*

1978. His life! Had he not himself offered it again and again?
But your soul ... did you offer your soul as well?
In for a penny, in for a pound, the Trashcan Man thought, and gently put one hand around the gold chain and the other around the dark Stone. —Stephen King, *The Stand*

1993. Rentz, the lawyer for Craddock, termed the government's strategy "a mistake." "If their theory is 'in for a penny, in for a pound,' then they should have indicted everyone who was in the [Waco] compound," he said. —*Times* (Trenton)
See also PUT YOUR MONEY WHERE YOUR MOUTH IS.

In God we trust. Official motto of the United States since 1956. The phrase was first used in the U.S. national anthem, "The Star-Spangled Banner," written by Francis Scott Key in 1814. In 1864, "In God We Trust" was engraved on the two-cent coin.

1814. Then conquer we must, when our cause it is just,
And this be our motto: "In God is our trust!"
—Francis Scott Key, "The Star-Spangled Banner"

1906. It always sounds well—In God We Trust. I don't believe it would sound any better if it were true. —Mark Twain, quoted by Justin Kaplan, *New York Times*

1991. The Federal appeals court in New Orleans upheld the practice, finding that the student-led prayers posed no greater constitutional threat than the legend "In God We Trust" on United States currency.... —*New York Times*

1993. IN GOD WE TRUST. ALL OTHERS PAY CASH. —Sign at a store in Trenton, N.J.

1994. At Hodge's, the best-selling item is a $3 bill labeled a "queer reserve note," with Mr. Clinton's picture on the front and, on the back, the words "In Bill We Trust. NOT!" —*New York Times*

In the beginning was the word. The saying is of Biblical origin and refers to the creation of the universe. The New Testament phrase is often echoed in accounts of other beginnings.

In the beginning was the Word, and the Word was with God, and the Word was God. —John, 1:1, *Authorized Version*, 1611

1920. Polyphiloprogenitive
The sapient sutlers of the Lord
Drift across the window-panes.
In the beginning was the Word.
—T. S. Eliot, "Mr. Eliot's Sunday Morning Service"

1983. In the beginning are the words: fifty thousand, seventy thousand, a hundred thousand or more. —Richard Curtis, *How to Be Your Own Literary Agent*

1991. In the Beginning There Was Vermouth —Ad in *New York Times Magazine*

1993. In the beginning, there was chicken à la king and divinity fudge. —*Modern Maturity*

1994. In the beginning, of course, there was the Word. Sometime later came the Dinner Party. And now, from Vice President Al Gore, the Metaphor. —*Wall Street Journal*

In the country of the blind, the one-eyed man is king. Among incompetents, even mediocrity passes for brilliance. The proverb has been traced back to about *Why Come Ye Nat to Courte?* (c.1522) by English poet John Skelton (c.1460–1529). Erasmus (c.1469–1536) wrote in *Adagia: In regione caecorum rex est luscus* ("In the country of the blind, the one-eyed man is king"). The French philosopher Jean-Jacques Rousseau (1712–78) explained the meaning of the aphorism in his *Confessions* (1781–88): "In the country of the blind the one-eyed man is king; I passed for a good teacher, because the rest in town were bad." The saying takes varying forms. The words, *kingdom* or *land* may substitute for *country.*

1911. In the Country of the Blind the One-eyed Man is King. —H. G. Wells, "The Country of the Blind"

1952. "Almost nobody's competent, Paul. It's enough to make you cry to see how bad most people are at their jobs. If you can do a half-assed job of anything you're a one-eyed man in the kingdom of the blind." —Kurt Vonnegut, Jr., *Player Piano*

1970. "I see you trying to observe what is behind these tented glasses. No, no, that's quite all right. One eye is functioning. Like the old saying about the one-eyed being King in the Country of the Blind." —Saul Bellow, *Mr. Sammler's Planet*

1989. When asked the key to his success, he said, "In the land of the blind the one-eyed man is king." —Michael Lewis, *Liar's Poker*

1991. Referring to the process by which advertising is scrutinized by agencies before being released, he added, "Testing is a crutch the one-eyed use to beat up the blind." —*New York Times*

1993. Whatever happens come supper, President Clinton will have a good time. The popularity ratings of the other G-7 members are scraping the seabed, and in the land of the single-digit popularity ratings, the double-digit man is king. —*Times* (Trenton)

See also IF THE BLIND LEAD THE BLIND, BOTH SHALL FALL INTO THE DITCH.

In the spring a young man's fancy lightly turns to thoughts of love. Spring is the season of new growth between winter and summer, so, naturally, it is also the season for love. Coined in 1842 by the English poet Alfred Tennyson (1809–1914). It is found in varying forms: *In the spring a young man's fancy lightly turns to what he's been thinking about all winter; In the spring a young man's thoughts turn to love,* etc.

1842. In the Spring a livelier iris changes on the burnish'd dove;
In the Spring a young man's fancy lightly turns to thoughts of love.
—Alfred, Lord Tennyson, "Locksley Hall"

1994. Spring, and a young person's fancy turns to love. —*New York Post*

In this world nothing is certain but death and taxes. *See* NOTHING IS CERTAIN BUT DEATH AND TAXES.

In unity there is strength. People who band together as a group can accomplish more than they can if they act as individuals. The proverb has been traced back to Aesop (c.550 b.c.). It appears in *Dicta Sapientum* (1526) by Erasmus. The idea of unity was expressed earlier in the Bible. First attested in the United States in *Complete Writings of Roger Williams* (1654). *Union* may substitute for *unity*. Listed in all major dictionaries of American proverbs.

c.550 b.c.
Union is strength. —Aesop, "The Bundle of Sticks"

Behold, how good and how pleasant *it is* for brethren to dwell together in unity! —Psalms, 133, *Authorized Version,* 1611

1855. All your strength is in your union.
All your danger is in discord;
Therefore be at peace henceforward,
And as brothers live together.
—Henry Wadsworth Longfellow, *The Song of Hiawatha*

1993. The old adage that in unity there is strength is applicable now as never before. —Overheard at the offices of the *New York Post*

See also THERE'S SAFETY IN NUMBERS; UNITED WE STAND, DIVIDED WE FALL; WE MUST INDEED ALL HANG TOGETHER, OR, MOST ASSUREDLY, WE SHALL ALL HANG SEPARATELY.

In victory: magnanimity. Be unselfish, gracious, great-hearted, even in victory. Part of the epigraph used by Winston Churchill (1874–1965) for his multivolume history of World War II. Though it did not appear in print until 1948, the saying first occurred to Churchill in the aftermath of World War I.

1948. In War: Resolution. In Defeat: Defiance. In Victory: Magnanimity. In Peace: Good Will. —Winston Churchill, *The Gathering Storm*

1977. Cartwright cautioned: "Remember Churchill's words—'in defeat, defiance; in victory, magnanimity....'" —William Safire, *Full Disclosure*

1992. "In victory, magnanimity." So Winston Churchill advised. But for Bill Clinton it will have to be watchful magnaminity. —Anthony Lewis, *New York Times*

In war there is no substitute for victory. Diplomatic half-measures can only prolong the conflict; the enemy must be totally vanquished. The saying probably originated during World War II. It is usually attributed to General Douglas MacArthur, who used it in his address to a joint meeting of Congress on April 19, 1951. The saying, however, was used by General Dwight D. Eisenhower seven years earlier. *In war* is often omitted.

1944. In war there is no substitute for victory. —Dwight D. Eisenhower, *Letters to Mamie*

1951. In war there is no substitute for victory. —Douglas MacArthur, Address to a Joint Meeting of Congress

1956. Actually, of course, my letter of January 13 had made it clear that Communism was capable of attacking not only in Asia but also in Europe and that this was one reason why we could not afford to extend the conflict in Korea. But then MacArthur added a belittling comment about our diplomatic efforts and reached his climax with the pronouncement that "there is no substitute for victory." —Harry S. Truman, *Memoirs*

1991. One of his [Alan Dale Fliers, Jr.] first acts was to assemble the [Central America] task force's 75 employees for a recital of Gen. Douglas MacArthur's famed 1962 speech at West Point. It is an address that resounds with calls to "the sure knowledge that in war there is no substitute to victory; that if you lose, the Nation will be destroyed; that the very obsession of your public service must be, Duty! Honor! Country!" —*New York Times*
See also IF YOU WANT PEACE, PREPARE FOR WAR.

In wine there's truth. Those who are drunk often speak the truth. This ancient proverb has Greek and Roman sources and is often cited in its Latin form, *In vino veritas*. It is first found in English in the mid-sixteenth century. There is a related proverb, "When wine is in, wit is out," that dates back to Chaucer's *Pardoner's Tale* (c. 1386). Charles Dickens skillfully merged it with the main entry and came up with "Wine is it, truth is out." In his *Nicholas Nickleby* (1838–39), we can read: "'We have been—we have been—toasting your lovely daughter, Mrs. Nickleby,' whispered Sir Mulberry, sitting down behind her. 'Oh, ho!' thought that knowing lady: 'wine in, truth out.'" The proverb is found in a number of languages.

1934. The man who made the proverb "There's truth in wine" must have been pretty well soaked when he made it. —R. Graves, *Claudius the God*

1950. I have found in life that all the old proverbs are true, discovering it as one comes across them one by one; and none truer than that which the wisdom of Rome discovered, *in vino veritas.* —Lord Dunsany, *Strange Journeys of Colonel Polders*

1958. There's an old saying, *"In vino veritas,"* meaning, as I see it, that a man sees things plainer when he's drunk. —E.C. R. Lorac, *People Will Talk*

1998. THE NANNY CASE: IN VINO VERITAS —Headline, *New York Post*

Innocent until proven guilty. *See* ONE IS INNOCENT UNTIL PROVEN GUILTY.

It ain't a fit night out for man or beast. The weather is abominable. The saying is generally attributed to the American humorist W. C. Fields (1880–1946). He used it several times in the movie *The Fatal Glass of Beer* but denied having coined the phrase.

1920s.
It ain't a fit night out for man or beast. —W. C. Fields, *The Fatal Glass of Beer*

1993. "It's getting dark and cold out there. Let's go now!" ... "I'm not sure I want to go. It ain't fit night out for man or beast." —Overheard in the lobby of an apartment building in New Jersey

It ain't over till it's over. *See* IT'S NOT OVER TILL IT'S OVER.

It ain't over till the fat lady sings. *See* THE OPERA AIN'T OVER TILL THE FAT LADY SINGS.

It all depends on whose ox is gored. Your view of the justness of the outcome of a dispute depends on which side you are on and the degree of personal loss you have suffered ("ox is gored"). The proverb was used by Martin Luther (1483–1546). First attested in the United States in Richardson's *Beyond the Mississippi* (1867). *It's all right when it's your ox that's being gored but not mine* is a variant of the saying.

1854. It makes a difference whose ox is gored. —Martin Luther, *Works*

1960. The enduring moral of Noah Webster's fable No. 8 "... It depends on whose ox is gored." —*New York Times*

1984. "Where were you when loan guarantees were made available for steel companies, shipbuilders, and airlines? Why didn't you speak up about trigger prices on foreign steel? I guess it depends on whose ox is being gored!" —Lee Iacocca with William Novak, *Iacocca*

1993. But doing what is right has its penalties. With every cut in the budget, with every new promulgation or law, and with every new appointment, Clinton gores someone's ox—millions in some cases. —*Times* (Trenton)

1994. John Leo, less celebrated, is a very smart guy and a wonderful writer who, somewhat unfashionably, gores the wrong ox, the "wrong" depending on your point of view. —*Crain's New York Business*

1995. DOES AMERICA'S POLICY DEPEND ON WHOSE WHALE IS GORED? —Headline, *New York Times*

It comes with the territory. There are certain duties or hardships entailed by one's position. The saying was coined in 1949 by American playwright Arthur Miller in *Death of a Salesman*. In 1984, when the younger daughter of President

Lyndon Johnson was asked how she reacted to criticism of her father, she said, "It comes with the territory of public life. If you don't recognize that, it is inevitable you will end up with ulcers." *Goes* may substitute for *comes,* and *turf, job, office,* etc., may be used in place of *territory.*

1949. *Charley (to Biff):* A salesman is got to dream, boy. It comes with the territory. —Arthur Miller, *Death of a Salesman*

1984. "Her husband's in the dress business. She told me she realizes how hard it will be for us to get along on what they pay you, so I must feel free to go down there with her and pick up some dresses, on the house."

David sighed. "I suppose it comes with the territory." —Howard Fast, *The Outsider*

1986. "I shrimp for a living," my father said, and his voice was tired. "The smell comes with the territory." —Pat Conroy, *The Prince of Tides*

1987. There had been a lot said. But I guess that goes with the turf…. —Donald T. Regan, *New York Times*

1988. "I must say, all you Brooklynites certainly are ambitious."

"Well, it goes with the territory," Barney responded with as much levity as he could muster. —Erich Segal, *Doctors*

1991. Sam Keen, a writer and philosopher, says in his best-selling book on men, *Fire in the Belly* …, "Only men understand the secret fears that go with the territory of masculinity." —*New York Times*

1992. He [Michael Milken] was just another finagler, after all. The financial world abounds in finaglers, always has, always will. They go with the territory, as fixed wheels, stacked decks and loaded dice go with casino sports. —Russell Baker, *New York Times*

1993. Mayors and Presidents, too, understand who their real audience is. They face the media because it comes with the territory. —*New York Times*

1994. "It goes with the territory," commented the talk-radio impresario. He has stirred repeated, often race-related notoriety over his 25 years in New York…. —Francis X. Clines, *New York Times*

It doesn't grow on trees. *See* MONEY DOESN'T GROW ON TREES.

It figures. It makes sense. It all adds up. It's exactly as one would have expected. Used as a somewhat ironic response. First cited in the mid-1940s.

1976. "The few times we've shown erotic films to pandas they started throwing orange peels at each other." … "It figures," I said. —Art Buchwald, *Washington Is Leaking*

1986. "How did you know what I was thinking?"

"It figures." —Jackie Collins, *Hollywood Husbands*

1988. "Don't believe him, Barn," Laura chided. "He was at Oxford on a Rhodes scholarship."

"It figures," Barney said. —Erich Segal, *Doctors*

It goes against the grain. It is contrary to the natural, expected, or regular order of things. The allusion is to wood, which is difficult to plane against the grain. The saying appears in Shakespeare's *Coriolanus* (1607). First attested in the United States in *Winthrop Papers* (1675).

1607. *Sicinius:* Your minds,
Pre-occupied with what you rather must do
Than what you should, made against the grain
To voice him consul.
—Shakespeare, *Coriolanus,* II, iii

1965. "All hell broke loose from her dad until he learned she was pregnant. But still he never wished me good luck and that has always gone against the grain." —Truman Capote, *In Cold Blood*

1988. "As I read you, I'm 'counterproductive' because I've made some noise about several things I feel pretty strongly about and what you've heard goes against your grain." —Robert Ludlum, *The Icarus Agenda*

1989. That's one of the things that goes against the grain of being brought up that you should be modest, you should be humble. —Johnny Carson, quoted by Laurence Leamer, *King of the Night: The Biography of Johnny Carson*

1991. "This approach is antiquated," said Martin Rosenthal, managing attorney of Harvard Law School's Criminal Justice Institute, speaking of the Massachusetts approach. "It goes against the grain of one or two decades of increasing openness in the judicial system." —*New York Times*

1994. I think every elected official should have a few issues on which he or she feels so strongly that he is willing to go against the grain and stand on principle. —Congressman Dick Zimmer, *Princeton Packet* (N.J.)

It goes in one ear and out the other. It makes no impression; it is forgotten as soon as it is heard. Said of someone who hears but disregards a piece of news or a warning. The proverbial saying has been traced back to Chaucer (c. 1385). The expression is also found in other languages: *Geht zum einen Ohr herein und zum anderen wieder hinaus* (German); В одно ухо входит, а в другое выходит (Russian) *It goes in at one ear and out at the other* is a variant.

> **1936.** And when Scarlett took the trouble to listen to them at all, most of what they said went in one ear and out the other. —Margaret Mitchell, *Gone With the Wind*
>
> **1984.** "Too many people learn by rote. It goes in one ear and out the other," says Yasuo Motahashi, principal of the Kanrish Yosei Gakko. —*Forbes*
>
> **1993.** "I don't listen to the fans," Aguiar said. "I listen to what Al and Bruce tell me to do. Every week I hear the fans yelling at me. It goes in one ear and out the other." —*New York Times*
>
> **1994.** ... Sons of former Paterno players have heard the same observations. At first, words usually pass in one ear and out the other: *You get better, or you get worse.* —*New York Times*

It goes with the territory. *See* IT COMES WITH THE TERRITORY.

It is a long road that has no turning. Bad times cannot last forever; things will eventually change for the better. The proverb has been traced back to the seventeenth century. First attested in the United States in Paine's *American Crisis* (1778). The proverb is found in varying forms.

> **1845.** It's a long lane that knows no turnings. —Robert Browning, *The Flight of the Dutchess*
>
> **1910.** 'Twas a long lane that had no turning. —E. Phillpotts, *Tales*
>
> **1930.** You have reason when you say that a road does not lengthen without a turning at its end. —R. King, *Murder*
>
> **1965.** It's a long worm that has no turning. —Earl Stanley Gardner, *Case of the Beautiful Beggar*

It is better to be a big fish in a little pond than a little fish in a big pond. *See* BETTER A BIG FISH IN A LITTLE POND THAN A LITTLE FISH IN A BIG POND.

It is better to be happy than wise. Wisdom is worthless if you are not happy. The proverb has been traced to John Heywood's book of proverbs (1546). Often shortened to *better happy than wise.*

> **1980.** What the heck are you saying, "smart, intelligent"? It's out of style. Better—I repeat, *better* —happy than wise! —Overheard at a fund-raising party
>
> **1991.** "Give him a video game, and he's happy as a lark." ... "Surprised? They say it is better to be happy than wise." —Overheard at a New York City day care center
>
> **1993.** Guard against quarreling with loved one tonight. Sometimes it is better to be happy than right! —Jeane Dixon, "Your Horoscope," *Times* (Trenton)

See also IGNORANCE IS BLISS.

It is better to be on the safe side. A wise person exercises extreme caution to eliminate any risk at all. The saying goes back to 1668. First cited in the United States in 1932. The phrase takes varying forms: *It is best to be on the safe side; Nothin' like bein' on the safe side*, etc. Often altered to *just to be on the safe side* meaning "just to be cautious."

> **1984.** "I don't expect it to come to that. Just to be on the safe side, give me a number where I can reach you during the afternoon." —Saul Bellow, *Him with His Foot in His Mouth and Other Stories*
>
> **1988.** "Don't ask me how I know this," he cautioned, "but from what I hear, this man is extremely careful. He even prescribes post-operative antibiotics just to be on the safe side." —Erich Segal, *Doctors*
>
> **1989.** "My sixty-fifth birthday is less than a year away. That gives me time to make all my arrangements for The Trust. Oh, I may draw up a temporary document between now and then, just to be on the safe side." —Michael Korda, *The Fortune*
>
> **1992.** To be on the safe side, I ordered two wigs from my hairdresser the day after I had been diagnosed. —*People*
>
> **1993.** To be on the safe side, they [the Bairds] notified the Immigration and Naturalization Service that they had hired the couple and wanted to sponsor them for resident status. —Letters to the Editor, *Newsweek*

See also BETTER SAFE THAN SORRY.

It is better to be safe than sorry. *See* BETTER SAFE THAN SORRY.

It is better to die on your feet than live on your knees. *See* I WOULD RATHER DIE ON MY FEET THAN LIVE ON MY KNEES.

It is better to give than to receive. *See* IT IS MORE BLESSED TO GIVE THAN TO RECEIVE.

It is better to have loved and lost, than never to have loved at all. The pleasures of love are still greater than the pain of its loss. The saying was first used in this form by the English poet Alfred Tennyson (1850), but has a precursor in a play (1700) by William Congreve.

1700. Say what you will, 'tis better to be left than never to have been loved. —William Congreve, *The Way of the World*

1850. 'Tis better to have loved and lost,
Than never to have loved at all.
        —Alfred, Lord Tennyson, *In Memoriam*

1940. It is better to have loafed and lost than never to have loafed at all. —James Thurber, "The Courtship of Arthur and Al," *Fables for Our Time*

1989. "Hugh [Auchincloss] liked me and I think felt badly that it hadn't worked out. He said as much in his letter and closed by quoting that famous line from Tennyson, 'Tis better to have loved and lost than never to have loved at all,' then added, 'P.S. And I ought to know.' And I think he did because he'd been married twice himself before he married Jackie's mother." —C. David Heymann, *A Woman Named Jackie*

1994. It is better to have loved and lost providing no alimony is involved. —Joey Adams, "Strictly for Laughs," *New York Post*

It is better to light one (little) candle than to curse the darkness. Taking some positive action, however small, can help to dispel one's despair at the evils and injustice of this world. The proverb is probably of Chinese origin. The Christophers, an American religious organization, use it as their motto: "Better to light one candle than curse the darkness." Also the title of a popular inspirational song. Eulogizing Eleanor Roosevelt on November 7, 1962, Adlai Stevenson said: "She would rather light candles than curse the darkness, and her glow has warmed the world."

1984. "I sit here with this silly candle, and then I think about the song, it is better to light just one little candle than to sit and curse the dark." —Howard Fast, *The Outsider*

1990. For 41 years Christopher Awards have recognized the creative writers, producers and directors who have achieved artistic excellence in films, books, and television specials affirming the highest values of the human spirit. Inscription on the Award: "Better to light one candle than curse the darkness." —*New York Times*

1993. During her lunch break, Sister Piper chats with the prison administrators.... "If she makes one person think a little more and repent for their sins then she's done her job," says Warden Robert Sanders. "Better to light one candle than curse the darkness." —*Princeton Packet* (N.J.)

It is better to lose the battle and win the war. On June 14, 1940, for the third time in the last century, German troops marched into Paris. France fell. Four days later, De Gaulle went on the air from London to tell the world, *La France a perdu une bataille! Mais la France n'a pas perdu la guerre!* ("France has lost a battle. But France has not lost the war!") Among the variants of the proverb are *You can win the battle and lose the war; You can win all the wars and lose all diplomatic battles; You win the battle, but the war goes on;* and *One loses the battle, but keeps the spoils.*

1988. Five years ago, people who loved Boston feared their city was threatened by a mob of monolithic office towers that, left unchecked, would crush the city's historic charm and livability. So opponents fought specific projects, and they fought the general idea that a growing city should proclaim the fact with soaring towers. They lost some battles, but won the war. —*Boston Globe*

1993. [Johnny] Oates got out of the game, without using Mark Williamson, who threw 62 pitches Saturday night, and Jim Poole, who had worked in four of the previous six games. As Oates said, "It's better to lose the battle and win the war." After all, it was only the last week in June and a wise [Baltimore] manager weighs every option. And sometimes sacrifices one game for the greater good. —*Times* (Trenton)

1993. "There'll be Olympics, after all, Grandmother. We won the argument with the women. They're out." "You won the battle, Leonardo. Will you win the war?" —Cartoon by Lee Falk and Sy Barry, *The Phantom* (King Features Syndicate)

1994. Joe Camel may have won a battle, but the war goes on. —*New York Times*

1998. CNN LOSES BATTLE, BUT KEEPS SPOILS —Headline, *Boston Globe*
See also IN WAR THERE IS NO SUBSTITUTE FOR VICTORY.

It is better to travel hopefully than to arrive. True contentment derives from the doing of something, not its end point. Anticipation is often more exciting than the event itself. The saying was coined in 1881 by the Scottish novelist, essayist, and poet Robert Louis Stevenson (1850–

94).

1881. To travel hopefully is a better thing than to arrive, and the true success is to labor. —Robert Louis Stevenson, "El Dorado," *Virginibus Puerisque*

1975. As much as it was better to travel hopefully than to arrive, as much as I believed that and had lived by it, once you've arrived, you've arrived, and there's not much to be done about it. —Mark Vonnegut, *The Eden Express*

1991. With the 1991 *Mobil Travel Guide,* you will not only travel hopefully, you can be sure to enjoy yourself once you've arrived. —Ad for Mobil guidebooks, *New York Times*

It is easier for a camel to go (pass) through the eye of a needle than it is for a rich man to enter the kingdom of heaven. Of Biblical origin. In the New Testament, Jesus advises his disciples to share all their possessions with the poor, because it is impossible to be both rich and worthy of salvation. The proverb can also be found in the Koran. It has been traced back in English to *Treatise on Dying Well* (1534). First attested in the United States in *Works of William Smith* (1754). A variant form is *Talk about getting a camel through the eye of a needle.*

And again I say unto you, It is easier for a camel to go through the eye of a needle, than for a rich man to enter into the kingdom of God. —Matthew 19:24, *Authorized Version,* 1611

1936. "Oh, Rhett, how you run on! If you've got the money, people always like you."
"Not Southerners. It's harder for speculators' money to get into the best parlors than for the camel to go through the needle's eye." —Margaret Mitchell, *Gone With the Wind*

1983. It may still be true that it is as easy for a rich man to get into heaven as for a camel to wriggle through the eye of a needle, but you would never know it from the way the rich in general distribute their wealth. —*Forbes*

1989. "It is easier for a camel to pass through the eye of a needle than for a rich man to enter the Kingdom of Heaven," Emmett DeWitt intoned in his reedy voice. "I thought that might set an appropriate tone to the service." —Michael Korda, *The Fortune*

It is easy to be wise after the event. Hindsight is 20/20: once the outcome is known, our critics may feel smug about telling us where we went wrong. The proverb has been traced back to 1590. The word *fact* may substitute for *event.* Often shortened to *wise after the event.* **

1987. Back at the hotel, Nixon received a handwritten letter from Tom Dewey. "In another 12 hours," Dewey said, "you will be elected to the most awesome responsibility in the World or you will be liberated. If elected, you.... will have earned it in heart-ache and labor far above and beyond the call of duty.... If you are defeated, pay no attention to the Monday morning quarterbacks. Everybody knows how to conduct a campaign better after the event." —Stephen E. Ambrose, *Nixon*

1994. "He [President Clinton] should have reshuffled his staff much earlier." ... "It is easy to be wise after the event." —Overheard at a public library in Princeton, N.J.

See also DON'T CLOSE (BAR, LOCK, SHUT) THE BARN (STABLE) DOOR AFTER THE HORSE RUNS AWAY (HAS FLED, BEEN STOLEN); MONDAY MORNING QUARTERBACKING.

It is more blessed to give than to receive. By sharing with others, a charitable person gains more than is given, because the spiritual benefits of unselfishness vastly outweigh the value of mere material possessions. First used in the New Testament by Paul of Tarsus, quoting a central teaching of Jesus. The proverb has been traced back to *Confession Amantis* (c.1390) by John Gower. First seen in the United States in *Simple Cobler of Agaawam in America* (1647). The proverb is found in varying forms: *It is better to give than to receive; It is more divine to give than to receive,* etc.

It is more blessed to give than to receive. —Acts 20:35, *Authorized Version,* 1611

1985. Loyalty given is loyalty repaid. Employees once created a papier-mache dummy and named it Chairman Pat. The idea was to have the boss [Patrick McGovern] around even when he wasn't.... Says McGovern, "As you give, so shall you receive." —*Forbes*

1991. "Nancy, I think, is one of those people who find it more divine to receive than to give," said Peter McCoy. —Kitty Kelley, *Nancy Reagan*

1993. It may be more blessed to give than to receive, but nobody ever said you couldn't have it both ways. —*Modern Maturity*

It never rains but it pours. One stroke of good (or ill) fortune is often followed by many other instances of luck (or misfortune) when you least expect them. The proverb dates back to the eighteenth century. In 1726, English physician John Arbuthnot (1667–1735) published a book entitled *It Cannot Rain But It Pours.* Jonathan Swift (1667–1745) and Alexander Pope (1688–1744) collaborated on an essay entitled "It Cannot Rain But It Pours." The saying has been in use ever since. First cited in the United States in 1755 in the *Papers of Benjamin Franklin. When it rains, it pours* was used as a motto for Morton's salt.

1848. It never rains but it pours, and one cannot fall in with a new fact or a new acquaintance but next day twenty fresh things shall spring up as if by magic. —Charles Kingsley, *Yeast*

1957. It never rains but it pours. After saying good-bye to Moses, Leander and Sarah came home to find this letter from Coverly on the hall table. —John Cheever, *The Wapshot Chronicle*

1979. Barbara told Joe about Bernie and then about the subpoena.
"It never rains but it pours. You poor kid." —Howard Fast, *The Establishment*

1984. When it rains, it pours, and for me it rained pretty hard in 1956. —Lee Iacocca with William Novak, *Iacocca*

1991. Imus began on-the-air taunting of his rival disc-jockey John Gambling of WOR. "Gambling/ Your rambling/Days are through," Imus chanted. "When it's raining, it's pouring/Here's Imus in the morning...." —*New York*

It runs in the family. Said of characteristics that are common among members of the same family or group. The saying is found in Richard Brinsley Sheridan's play *The School for Scandal* (1777).

1777. Learning that had run in the family like an heir-loom. —Richard Brinsley Sheridan, *The School for Scandal*

1893. *Mrs. Warren:* Don't you go taking any silly ideas into your head about me. Do you hear?
Frank (gallantly wooing her with his voice): Can't help it, my dear Mrs. Warren: it runs in the family.
—George Bernard Shaw, *Mrs. Warren's Profession*

1957. "The Hammers were in some financial difficulty so I bought this piano from them and now Mrs. Hammer comes and gives a lesson twice a week. It's very easy."
"Perhaps it runs in the family," Leander said. —John Cheever, *The Wapshot Scandal*

1960. Jem was the product of their first year of marriage; four years later I was born, and two years later our mother died from a sudden heart attack. They said it ran in the family. —Harper Lee, *To Kill a Mockingbird*

1987. My other half is about to drive me insane. I

might send him out to the dogs. Even one of his old hounds snores, just like he does. I told him the other day, it must run in the family. Ha. Ha. —Fannie Flagg, *Fried Green Tomatoes*

1989. "What credentials do you bring with you?"
"Genius runs in my family. I finished *summa cum laude* at BC, and I'm second in my law class." —John Grisham, *A Time to Kill*

1994. Adventure runs in the family. McKenna. —Ad for ABC, *New York Times*
See also IT'S IN THE BLOOD; LIKE FATHER, LIKE SON; LIKE MOTHER, LIKE DAUGHTER.

It takes a heap of living to make (a house) a home. A house is only a home if we associate it with happy times and have made it a warm, cozy, inviting place by living there. This sentimental bromide was coined in 1916 by American poet Edgar Guest (1881–1959). Ogden Nash (1902–71) later added that it "takes a heap o' payin'" too.

1916. It takes a heap o' livin' in a house t' make it home,
A heap o' sun an' shadder, an' ye sometimes have t' roam
Afore ye really 'preciate the things ye lef' behind,
An' hunger fer 'em somehow, with 'em allus on yer mind.
—Edgar Guest, "Home"

1992. So what is Martha doing to her house in East Hampton, L.I.? "I'm *renovating* the inside and *restoring* the outside," she says, "while working on a new book about homekeeping." ... *Homekeeping?* "It's not just *housekeeping.* Once your house becomes your home, you have more at stake." (It takes a heap of livin' to make a housekeeper a homekeeper.) —William Safire, *New York Times Magazine*
See also A MAN'S HOME IS HIS CASTLE; HOME, SWEET HOME; HOME IS WHERE THE HEART IS; THERE'S NO PLACE LIKE HOME.

It takes a thief to catch a thief. The most qualified person to catch a thief is another thief, because they both think the same way. Used both literally and as a figure of speech, usually with some irony. The proverb has been traced back to *Pleasant Notes upon Don Quixote* (1654) by E. Gayton. First attested in the United States in *Voyage to South America in 1817 and 1818* (1819) by American poet and novelist Hugh Henry Brackenridge (1748–1816). The proverb is found in varying forms: *Get a thief to catch a thief; It takes a crook to catch a crook; It takes a crow to catch a* crow; It takes a rogue to catch a rogue; It takes a thief to spot a thief; Set a fox to catch a fox; Set a thief to catch a thief, etc.

1957. There's an old expression: "It takes a rogue to catch a rogue." —Bangor Herald (Me.)

1991. "Why was he hired as our doorman? He's got a criminal record." ... "So what? It takes a thief to catch a thief. It is as simple as that." —Overheard in the lobby of an apartment building in New York City

1993. IT TAKES A THIEF —Headline of an article about the effect of stolen bases on the World Series —New York Times

1994. In the city where gangster rap reigns, the Los Angeles rapper Coolio rhymes instead about imaginary greener pastures on his debut album, It Takes a Thief. Consider him an escape artist. —New York Times

See also IT TAKES ONE TO KNOW ONE.

It takes a village to raise a child. Raising a child well is a communal effort. The proverb originated in Africa and is found in the 1950's in collections of Swahili proverbs. In America it became a household phrase thanks to Hillary Clinton's 1995 book, It Takes a Village and Other Lessons Children Teach Us (1995). The saying is often shortened to It takes a village.

1996. We have learned that to raise a happy, healthy, and hopeful child, it takes a family, it takes teachers, it takes clergy, it takes business people, it takes community leaders, it takes those who protect our health and safety, it takes all of us. Yes, it takes a village. —Hillary Clinton, Speech at the Democratic National Convention in Chicago

1996. What's the argument between Hillary Clinton and Bob Dole? She says it takes a village to raise a child. He says it takes a family. —Arkansas Democrat Gazette (Little Rock)

1997. It takes a village to raise a fair. On 176 acres of Midtown this week, that village has risen—a village with its own police force, bank, church, beer hall, eateries, fire station, medical center, and housing. —Commercial Appeal (Memphis, Tennessee)

1997. We frequently quote the African proverb, "It takes an entire village to educate a child." Effective role models always make the difference in the lives of our students. —Detroit News

It takes all kinds of people to make a world. We have to be tolerant of people who are different from us. Usually said in reference to people who are regarded as eccentric or socially unacceptable. The saying has been traced back to Cervantes' Don Quixote (1605–15). First appeared in the United States in Nature and Human Nature (1855) by Thomas Chandler Haliburton. It takes all sorts to make a world is a variant. Often shortened to It takes all kinds (sorts, types). The short form originated earlier and is found in The Book of Common Prayer (1548).

1605–15.
"Look, my friend," said Don Quixote, "not all knights can be courtiers, nor can all courtiers be, nor should they be, knights-errant. There have to be all kinds in this world, and even though we may all be knights, there is a great deal of difference between us." —Cervantes, Don Quixote

1973. He told Trout about people he'd heard of in the area who grabbed live copperheads and rattlesnakes during church services, to show how much they believed that Jesus would protect them.
"Takes all kinds of people to make up a world," said Trout. —Kurt Vonnegut, Jr., Breakfast of Champions

1984. Yet I could not kill Saul when I had the chance. It takes all kinds to make a world, doesn't it? —Joseph Heller, God Knows

1992. "You think the letter's for real, then?"
McMorris shrugged, a gesture that involved most of his massive upper body. "It takes all kinds. The letters from crazies, mostly you can tell, you know?" —Philip Friedman, Inadmissible Evidence

1994. When Marina's children play, he arrives unannounced and shouts to high heaven. When Marina tells him "Please, Mr. Carter, control yourself," he unfailingly says, "Call me Arthur." Oh well, it takes all types. —New York Post

It takes one to know one. Only a person with identical character traits would be able to recognize those traits in someone else. Often used as a curt rejoinder to deflect an accusation: you're only saying that about me because it's true of you. Originated in the late nineteenth or early twentieth century.

1981. I told him he was a liar and a cheat. He said it took one to know one. —Abigail Van Buren, The Best of Dear Abby

1984. Years later, I could see when I'd been had by the layout editors of the country's most prestigious newspapers and magazines. It takes one to know one! —Lee Iacocca with William Novak, Iacocca

1985. "It takes one to know one!" Style traits are easiest to recognize in others if I personally understand those characteristics. —Pat Burke Guild & Stephen Garger, *Marching to Different Drummers*

1986. It's too late for justice.
Really, Howard. Is that what you think?
Believe me, Clarissa Browning is a grade A cunt.
Thank you, Whitney. It takes one to know one.
—Jackie Collins, *Hollywood Husbands*

1988. It had been a professional confidence. So he concluded by saying, "I'll get you a good name, Laura."
"Fine. Be sure he's blond. It takes one to understand one." —Erich Segal, *Doctors*
See also IT TAKES A THIEF TO CATCH A THIEF.

It takes two to make a quarrel. In any dispute or altercation, both parties are equally guilty—provocation never necessitates retaliation. The proverb has been traced back to the 1706 *Spanish and English Dictionary*. First cited in the United States in the 1845 *New Weekly Post Boy*, in *Newspaper Extracts*. The word *quarrel* may be replaced by other words: *accident, argument, bargain, fuss, peace,* etc.

1925. "You're a rotten driver," I protested. "Either you ought to be more careful, or you oughtn't to drive at all."
"I am careful."
"No, you're not."
"Well, other people are," she said lightly.
"What's that got to do with it?"
"They'll keep out of my way," she insisted. "It takes two to make an accident." —F. Scott Fitzgerald, *The Great Gatsby*

1939. It takes two to make a quarrel, and the same number to get married. —Lewis & Faye Copeland, *10,000 Jokes, Toasts and Stories*

1989. Nixon said, "We too want peace, but it takes two to make peace." The veteran replied, "Yes, and the two are North Vietnam and South Vietnam." —Stephen E. Ambrose, *Nixon*
See also IT TAKES TWO TO TANGO.

It takes two to tango. Certain activities require mutual *cooperation* to achieve a common goal. Originated in the United States in the 1920s. Popularized by Pearl Bailey's recording of the 1952 song "Takes Two to Tango" by Al Hoffman and Dick Manning. General Ed Rowny titled his memoirs *It Takes One to Tango.*

1952. There are lots of things you can do alone!
But it takes two to tango.

—Al Hoffman & Dick Manning, "Takes Two to Tango"

1982. Tandem is founded on a well-ordered set of management beliefs and practices. The philosophy of the company emphasizes the importance of people: "That's Tandem's greatest resource—its people, creative action, and fun." This ethic is widely shared and exemplified by slogans that everyone knows and believes in: ... "It's so nice, it's so nice, we do it twice." ... "It takes two to Tandem." —Terrence E. Deal & Allan A. Kennedy, *Corporate Cultures*

1989. "She showed up on David's doorstep in late May. David took her in. Then she wanted to go back to her parents, but he said, 'No, you should kill them, like I once told you.'
"They talked each other into it. That's how such things happen. It takes two to tango." —Clifford Irving, *The Campbell Murder Case*

1991. Mrs. Garcia, whose clothes and shoes match just a bit too perfectly and whose malapropos ("It takes two to tangle, you know") are an embarrassment, is a good enough mother for indulged and overprotected island girls, but to emancipated New York teen-agers she's "a terrible girlfriend parent, a real failure of a Mom." —*New York Times Book Review*

1992. It takes two to bingo. Trend watch: Will bingo become the next craze in Hollywood theme parties? The game was at the center of the surprise 38th-birthday bash tossed by Geena Davis for her boyfriend, Hollywood security guru Gavin de Becker. —*People*

1993. In boxing, it takes two to tango. —Marc Steven, "Eyewitness News," ABC
See also IT TAKES TWO TO MAKE A QUARREL; IT TAKES TWO WINGS TO FLY.

It takes two wings to fly. Balance and cooperation are necessary to accomplish something important. The proverb was included in J. Kelly's collection of *Scottish Proverbs* (1721): "You can't fly with one wing." It was used by the Democrats in the presidential election of 1992.

1992. But the wisdom of Mr. Clinton's choice was immediately questioned by the Rev. Jesse Jackson, who has twice unsuccessfully sought the Democratic nomination for President and has on several occasions offered himself as a Vice-Presidential running mate. "I have deep concerns about the ticket. It takes two wings to fly and here you have two of the same wing." —*New York Times*
See also IT TAKES TWO TO TANGO.

It was the best of times, it was the worst of times. Opening line of Charles Dickens' classic novel of the French Revolution, *A Tale of Two Cities* (1859). The phrase is still used to describe any historical period of social upheaval and intoxicating excitement, or anything that is simultaneously excellent and awful. Often shortened to *(it was) the best of times* or *(it was) the worst of times,* or *it was the best of …, it was the worst of ….*

> **1859.** It was the best of times, it was the worst of times, it was the age of wisdom, it was the age of foolishness, it was the epoch of belief, it was the epoch of incredulity, it was the season of Light, it was the season of Darkness…. —Charles Dickens, *A Tale of Two Cities*
>
> **1984.** How was he able to mount so large a rebellion so swiftly and fiercely? Why did he want to?
> It was not the best of times, I'll admit, but was it the worst? —Joseph Heller, *God Knows*
>
> **1991.** The big rally in small caps is just one part of the schizophrenic financial markets of 1991. It is hard to remember a time when the beginning of *A Tale of Two Cities* was more applicable. —*New York Times*
>
> **1993.** It is the best of songs, it is the worst of songs. With this spin on Dickens' classic line, critic Dave Marsh begins his expedition to plumb the depths of the "Louie Louie" phenomenon, "Louie Louie," of course, being a rock-and-roll song so nonsensical and dumb, not to mention infectious and riotous, that it has become a staple of Americana. —*Washington Post*

It will all come out in the wash. Everything will work out all right; everything will come to a satisfactory conclusion. The allusion is to restoring the original appearance of clothing by laundering it. Originated in the late nineteenth century. However, the saying can be found in Cervante's *Don Quixote* as early as 1605.

> **1881.** It all goes into the laundry, but it never comes out in the wash. —Rudyard Kipling, "Stellenbosh"
>
> **1993.** Kathleen Norris's well-written love affair with laundry (Hers: "It All Comes Out in the Wash," Aug. 22) conjures up a single, clear message: this woman has entirely too much time on her hands. —Letters to the Editor, *New York Times Magazine*

It will play in Peoria. This will be acceptable to average Americans who live in towns far from Washington and New York. Now used in a political context, but probably of theatrical origin.

> **1970.** It will play in Peoria. —John D. Ehrlichman
>
> **1993.** May I share it [a nighttime prayer] with you
> for your approval?
> Now I lay me down to sleep,
> I pray the Lord my soul to keep.
> In the morning when I wake,
> I pray the Lord my hand to take.
> Abby, isn't that a happier message to go to sleep on? We think so. Janice Todd.
> Dear Janice: It is indeed a "happier message," but as we old-timers would say, "I don't think it will play in Peoria." —Abigail Van Buren, "Dear Abby," *Times* (Trenton)
>
> **1994.** BUT WILL IT PLAY IN PEORIA? —Headline of an article on the Fed's increase in interest rates, *Business Week*

It won't wash. That story, idea, theory, explanation, etc., does not stand up to scrutiny. The origin is uncertain, but the phrase may allude to shoddy merchandise that falls apart in the wash.

> **1946.** "It won't wash," he said in a perfectly amiable fashion. —Robert Penn Warren, *All the King's Men*
>
> **1974.** "The thing was terrible," McGoldrick was to say later. "Those savage attacks on Lehman, personal stuff, just wouldn't wash." —Robert A. Caro, *The Power Broker*
>
> **1979.** Smiling, Montego handed Bently the bill of sale Bernie had just signed. Bently glanced at it, handed it to his associates, and said sourly "It won't wash, Feinstein. We know damn well what those planes are intended for, and it just won't wash." —Howard Fast, *The Establishment*
>
> **1987.** Administration explanations about why the Geneva talks don't go anywhere simply won't wash —*New York Times*
>
> **1989.** Rep. Ed Roybal says Elvis is a bad influence on youth. That doesn't wash. They said that in the '50s and we turned out OK. I receive many letters from today's youth telling me how much they admire Elvis and hate the music of the '80s. —Priscilla Parker, *USA Today*
>
> **1993.** And then there's Roper, who never develops beyond a simply evil man, a caricature, a cartoon…. I'm afraid it doesn't wash. —*Times* (Trenton)

It's a blessing in disguise. A catastrophic event has brought with it some unexpected benefit. The phrase dates back to the eighteenth century. *It* may be replaced with other subjects.

1963. Mrs. Silsburn cleared her throat. "It sounds to me," she said, "like a blessing in disguise that everything's turned—... Goodness. I don't know what to say, really. It just sounds to me like a blessing in disguise that every—" —J. D. Salinger, *Raise High the Roof Beam, Carpenters*

1984. ... people sometimes bite off more than they can chew. In some cases that's a blessing in disguise, because it indicates that the guy is stretching, and for him, even a partial success may be worth a great deal. —Lee Iacocca with William Novak, *Iacocca*

1987. I believe there is now the growing sense that we can accomplish more by cooperating. And in the end, this may be the eventual blessing in disguise to come out of the Iran-contra mess. —Ronald Reagan, Address on foreign and domestic issues, *New York Times*

1993. "Maybe it's a blessing in disguise that we have the extra time." —*New York Times*

1994. "It would be a blessing in disguise of sorts, with all the injuries and Mess and Ricky not under contract," said Olczyk. —*New York Times*

See also EVERY CLOUD HAS A SILVER LINING.

It's a Catch-22 situation. It's a no-win situation: no matter what you do, you lose—specifically, because the qualification or criterion for what you want simultaneously disqualifies you for consideration. The saying was coined by Joseph Heller in his novel of World War II, *Catch-22* (1961). Yossarian, Heller's protaganist, is determined to avoid being killed. The best way to achieve that goal, he reasons, is to be grounded by reason of insanity. But according to Catch-22, anyone who wants to get out of combat duty can't be really crazy.

1961. There was only one catch and that was Catch-22, which specified that a concern for one's own safety in the face of dangers that were real and immediate was the process of a rational mind. Orr was crazy and could be grounded. All he had to do was ask; and as soon as he did, he would no longer be crazy and would have to fly more missions.... If he flew them he was crazy and didn't have to; but if he didn't want to he was sane and had to. —Joseph Heller, *Catch-22*

1984. It's the old Catch-22. Want a loan? Show us that you don't need it, and then we'll give it to you. If you're rich, if there's money in the bank, there's always plenty of credit. But if you don't have the cash, then you can't get any. —Lee Iacocca with William Novak, *Iacocca*

1987. Head coaches are the personal choices of team owners. Obviously what made Mr. Campbell "the very best man" for the Atlanta job was not his record, but the confidence he inspired in Mr. Smith. For blacks, that's a familiar Catch-22: Lack the credentials and credentials are all-important; possess the credentials and it's "intangibles" that are decisive. —*New York Times*

1994. Cece Morrell, manager of corporate communications for USA Networks, which runs both the widely listed USA Network and the harder-to-find Sci-Fi Channel, said: "It's a Catch-22. You can't get listed if you don't get ratings. And you can't get ratings if you can't get listed." —*New York Times*

1995. "The denial of marriage rights puts gay people in an excruciating Catch-22," Wolfson said. "In all sorts of situations—government benefits, parenting rights, immigration, health care—gay people are told you can't have this right or this benefit unless you're married. Then they're told you can't get married." —*Star-Ledger* (Newark, N.J.)

It's a close call. It's a near miss: a narrow escape from danger, injury, failure, etc.; a decision that could go either way. The phrase originated in the United States in the late nineteenth century. It is probably of baseball origin, referring to plays where an umpire could have made the call either way. Mark Twain used the expression in his fiction. *It's a close shave,* a synonymous saying, originated in the United States in the early nineteenth century, probably among barbers.

1961. "He has to be crazy to keep flying combat missions after all the close calls he has had." —Joseph Heller, *Catch-22*

1973. Someone had made a sudden turn off the road, into a driveway; but nothing happened, no accident, he was safe. He checked Elene and saw she had not hurt herself. "My God, what a close call." —Joyce Carol Oates, *Do with Me What You Will*

1986. "Fighting Terrorism" ... is a primer on high-level strategy. The world does not go to war, but it seems to be a close call. —*New York Times*

1988. ... When you're facing death, it's probably a close call. —Richard Nixon, *Washington Times*

1991. With the Smith case, local lawyers are saying that for the first time in a career of victories Mrs. Lasch has met her match.... Of the noteworthy cases she has tried, "this is the only one where it's a close call," said Anthony Natale, a defense lawyer in West Palm Beach. —*New York Times*

1993. Saxton said that when James Boatright, dep-

uty assistant secretary of the Air Force for installations, called the choice between Plattsburgh and its competitors "a close call," he made it easier for the commissioner to question the Pentagon's recommendation. —*Times* (Trenton)
See also THAT'S TOO CLOSE FOR COMFORT.

It's a date which will live in infamy. Following Japan's surprise aerial bombardment of Pearl Harbor on December 7, 1941, President Franklin Roosevelt used this phrase in his address to Congress. The memorable phrase is thus inextricably linked to that moment in history.

> **1941.** To the Congress of the United States: Yesterday, Dec. 7, 1941—a date which will live in infamy—the United States of America was suddenly and deliberately attacked by naval and air forces of the Empire of Japan. —Franklin Delano Roosevelt, *War Message to Congress*

> **1991.** Mr. Bush had set a difficult task for himself today. He wanted to give proper due to "the day of infamy," as he called it, paraphrasing President Franklin D. Roosevelt's memorable phrase. —Maureen Dowd, *New York Times*

> **1992.** Today the crowd erupted in laughter as Mr. Bush said: "Four years ago, I met with you as Vice President: Sept. 7—a day that will live in infamy. O.K., I wanted to say it before you did. What does it take to live something down with this crowd?" —*New York Times*

It's a different (new) ball game (ballpark). Things have changed radically; the new situation is nothing at all like what we're used to. Originally, the saying meant literally a ball game different from baseball, such as basketball, football, etc. It has been common since the 1930s and is now used figuratively. Often used with the word *whole* before *different* or *new*.

> **1979.** Judge Meadows has sat on five contempt cases, the most recent one in forty. In every case, he suspended sentence and leveled a fine. Now, it's a whole new game. —Howard Fast, *The Establishment*

> **1984.** "That new sports car will take us from being a £15 million company to a £50 million company, which is a whole different ball game." —*Forbes*

> **1986.** "Listen," Sadie said. "You know I never try to influence you in any way, but I've read the script, and it's not bad at all." She paused and signaled the waiter to get her another vodka. "Plus this is going to raise your price to new heights. I'm not saying we'll always get this kind of money, but

we're in a whole new ballpark." —Jackie Collins, *Hollywood Husbands*

> **1988.** Nelson Algren once observed in conversation that "no matter how many novels you write, it sure as hell doesn't get any easier. Each new book is a whole new ball game." —*New York Times Book Review*

> **1992.** *A Whole Different Ball Game* —Title of a book on baseball by Marvin Miller, *New York Times*

> **1994.** "It's a whole new ball game," says Ed Walloga, director of communications at Greater Talent Network Inc. in New York. "Since the election, we've seen heightened interest in speakers with a real message about overcoming obstacles." —*Crain's New York Business*

It's a dream come true. One has achieved one's greatest wish. An event beyond one's wildest expectations has occurred. *It* may be replaced by other nouns or phrases.

> **1980.** Is a dream a lie if it don't come true,
>   Or is it something worse?
>   —Bruce Springsteen, "The River"

> **1983.** Hollywood. A magic place Angel had only read about. Hollywood. A dream come true! —Jackie Collins, *Hollywood Wives*

> **1991.** For himself, he said, the joy is in tracking the lost treasure. "Each one was fun and different," he explained. "Each one, you had to do something else to make the thing happen. I've been successful and I'm lucky. It really is a dream come true." —*New York Times*

> **1994.** The magazine and TV show are aimed at Hispanic mothers and provide news-you-can-use on a range of subjects, from health and nutrition to parenting and money.... "It's a dream come true, and a natural evolution for me too," she says. —*Crain's New York Business*

It's a drop in the bucket. An insignificant quantity. The phrase first appears in the Old Testament. Such words as *just, only, no more than* may precede *a drop.* Other variants include *a mere (single, small, tiny) drop. It's a drop in the ocean* is a synonymous expression.

> Behold, the nations *are* as a drop of a bucket, and are counted as the small dust of the balance. —Isaiah 40:15, *Authorized Version,* 1611

> **1936.** "... he made his money out of the block-

ade—"

"Of course, he did, honey, some of it. But that's not a drop in the bucket to what that man has really got." —Margaret Mitchell, *Gone With the Wind*

1977. "The guy has all the money in the world," she said, munching noisily, "and he means to use it to do good things. Like start magazines. Or buy book publishers. His family already owns the biggest movie-tape distribution outfits, and that's just a drop in the bucket." —William Safire, *Full Disclosure*

1984. "If I had it to do over again, I wouldn't," King explains. "We raised $853,000, a drop in the bucket, and we tarnished our image as tough and efficient tax enforcers." —*Forbes*

1986. That empire is said to be worth $1.6 billion, which makes even a $45,000 cup a very small drop in a very big bucket. —*New York Times*

1991. Senator Wirth pointed out that that's a drop in the bucket, a tiny portion of the 660 billion barrels of oil in the Middle Eastern reserves, not much of an addition to the 26.5 billion barrels already in U.S. reserves, and only about 200 days of oil consumption at this country's gluttonous rate. —Tom Wicker, *New York Times*

1993. With the city facing a $2 billion deficit, the aide suggested, why not let the borough [Staten Island] secede? ... "That would have been a very, very large drop in the bucket," said First Deputy Mayor Norman Steisel, who recalled the budget discussions. —*New York Times*

It's a labor of love. It's work done not for profit or from necessity, but for the satisfaction of accomplishment. In the New Testament, the expression refers to the faithful who do God's work literally as a labor of love.

Remembering without ceasing your work of faith, and labor of love. —1 Thessalonians 1:3, *Authorized Version*, 1611

1968. Dear George [Bush]: ... I have your good note about the considerations about the vice-presidency and want you to know that it was a labor of love.... —Thomas Dewey, *New Yorker*

1993. "Nothing makes me happier than crafting a terrific complaint, or a good brief," Mr. Lerach said. "To me, doing what I'm doing is like a painter, or a sculptor sculpting: it's work, but it's a labor of love." —*New York Times*

1994. "It's a lot of work, but it's a labor of love," said Ms. De Santis, one of the team's founders, who began skating 20 years ago with her children on weekends when her husband worked. —*New York Times*

It's a piece of cake. It's very easy to do. First used in the mid-twentieth century. During World War II, British soldiers used the expression to describe a mission that was extremely easy to accomplish. Sometimes shortened to *piece of cake*. Often used in the negative: *no piece of cake; not a piece of cake.*

1987. Senator Jake Garn of Utah, chairman of the Laxalt committee, said after the news conference that raising $2 million "is not a piece of cake, but I believe the support is there—I think the money will be there." —*New York Times*

1989. In a two-hour stay at Walter Reed Army Medical Center in Washington, the 63-year-old First Lady sipped a colorless solution of a radioactive form of iodine through a straw.... "She's just fine, piece of cake, never broke her stride," said Mrs. Bush's press secretary, Anna Perez, after Mrs. Bush returned to the White House. —*New York Times*

1991. He knew that McDeere had talked to Tarrance half a dozen times now and that tomorrow, Tuesday, McDeere would become a millionaire. Piece of cake. —John Grisham, *The Firm*

1993. "How's that diet that mom put you on, dad?" ... "Piece of cake." —Cartoon by Brian Crane, "Pickles," *Times* (Trenton)

1994. When Ray, my mentor in these matters, suggested that I next try Katahdin, whose Baxter Peak is but 5,267 feet above sea level, my reaction was, "Piece of cake." —*Wall Street Journal*

See also IT'S LIKE TAKING CANDY FROM A BABY.

It's a sign of the times. It's a characteristic feature of the present; it's a trend. The saying first appeared in the New Testament and has been used ever since.

When it is evening, ye say, *It will be* fair weather, for the sky is red. And in the morning, *It will be* foul weather to day, for the sky is red and lowering. O ye hypocrites, ye can discern the face of the sky; but can ye not *discern* the signs of the times? —Matthew 16:2, 3, *Authorized Version*, 1611

1956. *Celia:* I'm sorry I did that.

Polo: It's a sign of the times ... a sign of the times.

—Michael Gazzo, *A Hatful of Rain*

1991. The Playbill lists Mr. Arcenas's assignment as "New York City, the present day," and surely it's a sorry sign of the times that the only color the designer can muster is gray. —*New York Times*

1992. I don't go to libraries—I get my education from reading signs. The time of the signs: On a diaper service truck: "Pick a dry baby." ... On a plumber's truck: "A flush is better than a full house." —Joey Adams, "Strictly for Laughs," *New York Post*

1993. It's a flashing sign of the times. Fashion designers are seeing red this fall. —*Sunday Star-Ledger.* (Newark, N.J.)

It's a small world. This may seem like a big place, but you run into people you know surprisingly often. The expression is also used by a person who meets an acquaintance in an unexpected place. The saying has been traced back to 1886. First attested in the United States in 1905. Often shortened to *small world*.

1951. "And so you're from Baltimore," he said pleasantly. "I cant get over it. Its sure a small world." —James Jones, *From Here to Eternity*

1963. "And you're a Breed?"
"The fourth generation in this location."
"Any relation to Dr. Asa Breed, the director of the Research Laboratory?"
"His brother." He said his name was Marvin Breed.
"It's a small world," I observed. —Kurt Vonnegut, Jr., *Cat's Cradle*

1981. "It's a small world," says Steven Wright, "but I wouldn't want to paint it." —*Times* (Trenton)

1985. "I know a lot of people, it's true," he said, as if it was a cross he had to bear. "That's the trouble with London. It's a big city, but a small world." —Michael Korda, *Queenie*

1988. "Higher education is really a small world, a close-knit network of people who make it a habit to know what's going on," said H. Gerald Quigg, vice president for university relations at the University of Richmond. —*New York Times*

1992. "We both got relatives from near Krakow. Small world." —Philip Friedman, *Inadmissible Evidence*

1994. Networking is All. Los Angeles is, in the end, a small world. —*New York Times Magazine*

It's all grist for the mill. It's something of limited value that can be used for one's profit or advantage. The allusion is to producing flour out of whole grains. This metaphoric expression has been traced back to *Church-History of Britain* (1655) by English divine and historian Thomas Fuller (1608–61). First attested in the United States in *New English Canaan of Thomas Morton* (1637). The idiom takes varying forms: *All is grist that comes to the mill; All's grist that goes to his mill*, etc. It is sometimes shortened to *grist for one's mill*.

1936. "No, there is no Klan now. We decided that it did more harm than good because it just kept the Yankees stirred up and furnished more grist for the slander mill of his excellency, Governor Bullock." —Margaret Mitchell, *Gone With the Wind*

1978. Poetry, novels, technical books, the encyclopedia, comic books, magazines—everything was grist for her mill. —Howard Fast, *Second Generation*

1984. Kremlinologists get a wealth of grist for their mills as the candidates began election meetings. —*New York Times*

1988. "I hope you didn't see that ugly little rumor in the columns about myself and Jessica Forbes. I just happened to be sitting next to her at dinner. But I guess everything a Senator's daughter does is grist for the gossip mills." —Erich Segal, *Doctors*

1994. "From all those audits and investigations, and from hundreds of pages of testimony under oath, the government has plucked a tiny handful of questions and answers to use as grist for its perjury mill," Mr. Loughlin said. —*New York Times*

It's all in a day's work. It's not pleasant, but it's normal. The anonymous saying has been current since the eighteenth century. Often shortened to *all in a day's work*. Popularized by *Reader's Digest* magazine, which has long published a column called "All in a Day's Work" (featuring humor on the job).

1957. "I don't know that we found out very much, and one of the ship's company developed measles. Still, that's all in the day's work." —Nevil Shute, *On the Beach*

1991. When I arrived at his home here, he responded appropriately, handing over a poem he'd written about my visit.... I chuckled, he smiled. "All in a day's work," he said, then hastily corrected himself. "Actually, that was a quicky—it only took about 15 minutes to write. The good ones take longer. Maybe 20 minutes." —*Wall Street Journal*

1992. Crime is all in a day's work for Schwartzman, 30, and Poiner, 31, who report the city's seamier side for the *Post* and the *Daily News*, respectively. —*People*

It's all in the family. Close-knit families share everything and often close ranks against outsiders. It's only safe to discuss certain issues within one's family. Often shortened to *all in the family*, which was used as the title of a popular sit-com written by Norman Lear and starring Carroll O'Connor and Jean Stapleton as Archie and Edith Bunker. *Keep it (all) in the family* is a variant.

1962. "Excuse me. You are going to discuss the lawsuit against the Hawke Brothers Coal Company. I will go out for a walk and smoke a cigar."

Hawke's sister said, "Oh, don't be ridiculous, John, it's all in the family." —Herman Wouk, *Youngblood Hawke*

1986. "I've always hoped Luke or Tom would take over after I'm gone. That's what I pray to the good Lord for. "It'd be nice to keep it in the family, don't you think?" —Pat Conroy, *The Prince of Tides*

1989. "Would you agree that there's some benefit to keeping all this in the family, and out of the papers for the time being?" —Michael Korda, *The Fortune*

1992. All in the families: Who's who in organized crime. A generation of mob family leaders is on the way out—albeit with no sign of a decline in organized crime itself. —*New York Post*

See also DON'T AIR YOUR DIRTY LINEN IN PUBLIC.

It's all over and done with. The matter is closed; forget it; let's put it behind us. An informal saying often used in conversation. The phrase is found in varying forms: *It's over and done; It's done with; It's over, it's done with; Over and done with,* etc.

1922. Bad times those were. Well, well. Over and done with. —James Joyce, *Ulysses*

1936. "I won't think about it any more," she decided. "It's over and done with and I'd have been a ninny not to kill him." —Margaret Mitchell, *Gone With the Wind*

1983. He just wanted the whole scene over and done with. —Jackie Collins, *Hollywood Wives*

1984. "Does he have to go to prison for not being an informer?"

"He'll hack it," David said. "Then it's over and done with." —Howard Fast, *The Outsider*

1986. "I'll have the party," she agreed. "And when it's over and done with I want my entire house recarpeted.'" —Jackie Collins, *Hollywood Husbands*

1989. "Well," he said, "all that is your business, not mine. Grandmother wants a settlement," he added quietly. "She wants it all over and done with, as quietly and quickly as possible." —Michael Korda, *The Fortune*

1991. "It's history, it's over, it's done with," Mer-

rill said. —*New York Times*

1994. Hank Brown said he really thinks "the war is over and done with." —Mary McGrory, *Times* (Trenton)

See also IT'S ALL OVER BUT THE SHOUTING.

It's all over but the shouting. The hard part is over—now let's celebrate. Originated in the mid-nineteenth century. Often used in sports and political contexts. *It's all over bar the shouting* is a variant.

1945. "Do you, like the others I have met since I came home, think that the European war is over but for the shouting?" —Emilie Loring, *Beyond the Sound of Guns*

1984. Goliath lay where he had fallen, staining the sandy earth brown. There was not even a twitch. My joy was immense.... It was all over but the shouting, and God knows there was plenty of that. —Joseph Heller, *God Knows*

1988. Sometimes he would get as little as four hours sleep. But this was his last term, the home stretch. In a few weeks, they would hear from the colleges and it would be all over but the shouting. —Erich Segal, *Doctors*

1991. BRAVES MAKE SURE THE SHOUTING ISN'T OVER —Headline of an article about an Atlanta Braves game, *New York Times*

See also IT'S ALL OVER AND DONE WITH.

It's all smoke and mirrors. It's an illusion achieved by deliberate and calculated deception. Said of any attempt to conceal one's real motives from opponents or the public at large. The allusion is to the cloud of smoke and the mirrors used by conjurers to conceal their tricks. The saying is often used in a political context. It is found in various short forms: *smoke and mirrors; all smoke and mirrors; more smoke and mirrors,* etc.

1991. Asserting that President Bush lacks "backbone," Mr. Pinkus charges: "He caved in on the passage of a civil-rights bill that will create a lot of litigation, not jobs for minorities, and he caved in on controlling spending. It was all smoke and mirrors." —*Wall Street Journal*

1993. Remember the Bill Clinton campaign promise to reduce the national debt by 50 percent in four years? ... Well, the administration now has approximately 39 months to reduce the debt approximately 53 percent. Cutting it by 53 percent will get the debt to 50 percent of the Jan. 20, 1993, amount. Looks to me like the time to do it is going down and the percentage is going up. More smoke and mirrors. —*Trentonian* (N.J.)

1994. ... It seemed that of this entire generation of artists, he was the most likely to prove indestructible.... "Indestructible?" he said recently in the elegant living room of his Upper West Side apartment. "That's very flattering. It should be an ideal. It just seems that way. It's all mirrors." —*New York Times*

It's all systems go. *See* ALL SYSTEMS GO.

It's always darkest before the dawn. Be patient: things are not as hopeless as they seem. Alludes to the fact that the coldest (and therefore bleakest) time of day is immediately before sunrise. This inspirational bromide dates to *A Pisgah-Sight of Palestine* (1650) by English divine and historian Thomas Fuller (1608–61). It has been current since the seventeenth century. First attested in the United States in *Letters of R. L. Stevenson* (1889). The adage is found in varying forms: *It's always dark before the sun shines; The darkest hour is just before the dawn; The darkest hour proves to be that just before the dawn*, etc.

> **1946.** "I sometimes wonder if Bess is not planning to break it up, Lanny. She has been so impatient of late. We made a bargain, but she can't stick to it."
> "You know the old saying, that the darkest hour is just before dawn; and I've an idea this may apply to your case. Go to your study and fiddle, and leave Bess to me for a while." —Upton Sinclair, *A World to Win*

> **1982.** It's always darkest before ... daylight savings time. —Judith Frost Stark, *Don't Cross Your Bridge Before ... You Pay the Toll*

> **1985.** "Fairbanks and I were going to make a film together a few years ago. What was it called? *Darkest Before Dawn*, I think...." —Michael Korda, *Queenie*

> **1991.** They do say it's always darkest before the dawn, she thought. I reckon this is proof of it. —Alexandra Ripley, *Scarlett*

> **1992.** "It's always darkest before you go blind," reads Ms. Knesevitch. This particular contribution, she says, is headed for the pessimism category. —*Princeton Packet* (N.J.)

It's an 800-pound gorilla. It's an overwhelming or dominating force that cannot be controlled and therefore may cause great difficulties. Originated in the early 1970s as a popular riddle. *Question:* "Where does a 500-pound gorilla sleep?" *Answer:* "Anywhere he wants to." The subject *it* may be replaced by other pronouns or nouns. The number may be changed too. Governor Cuomo was called "an 800-pound gorilla" by Ed Koch and "a 900-pound gorilla" by the *New Republic*.

> **1989.** "He was the 2,000-pound gorilla," one lawyer said of the beefy Shapiro. "He was overbearing, impossible, outrageous." —*New York Newsday*

> **1991.** The merger outlook for Citicorp, which has dominated consumer banking in the region for more than a decade, is murky. Its size and deep portfolio of problem loans would probably scare off any potential partner. "It's an 800-pound gorilla," Mr. Litan says. —*Wall Street Journal*

> **1992.** Ross Perot is an 800-pound gorilla that will go anywhere they want it to go with television. —*"MacNeil/Lehrer News Hour,"* PBS

> **1993.** Lewis calls health-care reform "the 800-pound gorilla of this administration." —*Times* (Trenton)

> **1994.** What happens when an 800-pound gorilla turns into a 1,000 pound gorilla? The gorilla is more dangerous. But it's too big to move. —*Crain's New York Business*

It's an albatross around one's neck. Said of a heavy burden or a curse one can't get rid of. The metaphor derives from Samuel Taylor Coleridge's poem *The Rime of the Ancient Mariner* (1798), which tells the story of a sailor who kills a large white seabird said to be a good omen. As punishment for the bad luck that ensues, his shipmates hang the dead albatross around his neck to represent his guilt.

> **1798.** Ah! well a-day! what evil looks
> Had I from old and young!
> Instead of the cross, the Albatross
> About my neck was hung.
> —Samuel Taylor Coleridge, *The Rime of the Ancient Mariner*

> **1986.** She was definitely considering Zeppo White's advice. "Get rid of him, kiddo. He's an albatross around your neck. Dump the putz." —Jackie Collins, *Hollywood Husbands*

> **1987.** The citizens of Austria, whose freedom to vote is based solely on American power, are now stuck with the albatross they chose [Kurt Waldheim]. —William Safire, *New York Times*

> **1988.** "The delay, ironically, has turned out to be an asset," the chairman of the cable commission, William B. Finneran, said in a telephone interview. "Had New York been expeditiously wired, we would now be stuck with inadequate technology. We'd have an albatross all over the city." —*New York Times*

1992. "They raise taxes on residents or they take the town to a point of bankruptcy," said Steven A. Romalewski, the Long Island coordinator for the New York Public Interest Research Group. "It's an albatross around their neck." —*New York Times*

1993. Georgie believed her husband had much to give. But privately she told him she couldn't support him unless he quit drinking. He [Senator Bob Packwood] flew into a rage. "You don't want me to be President!" she recalls him shouting. "You're just an albatross around my neck. If you're going to make me stop drinking, I'll leave you." —*New York Times Magazine*

It's an ill wind that blows no (nobody) good. Someone is likely to capitalize on any given unwelcome or disastrous situation; one person's misfortune may turn out to be another's good luck. This naval proverb is used to explain one's good luck at the expense of someone's misfortune. Listed in John Heywood's 1546 book of proverbs: "An ill wind that bloweth no man to good." Used by Shakespeare in his play *Henry VI, Part Three* (1591). The proverb has been in common use ever since. First attested in the United States in *Letters of James Murray, Loyalist* (1739). The phrase may be found in varying forms: *An ill wind blows no good; It's an ill wind that blows nobody any good; It's an ill wind that blows nobody good luck; It's an ill wind that blows no one good,* etc. Often shortened to *an ill wind.*

> **1591.** *Son:* Ill blows the wind that profits nobody. —Shakespeare, *3 Henry VI,* II, v

> **1987.** It's an ill wind that blows no good.... Mariette Hartley spent all year trying to breathe life into CBS's ill-fated "Morning Program," but about a month ago, she said, she was informed it was going off the air (its last day is next Friday) and advised to look for other work.... But almost before anything could happen, Ms. Hartley received a call from her manager, Arlen Dayton, passing along an offer to make a movie. —*New York Times*

> **1991.** After 15 years as a high school history teacher in Washington, Erich Martel was unnerved by what he considered an ill wind of inaccuracies and wishful thinking blowing into the curriculum.... That ill wind, Mr. Martel said, was Afrocentricity. —*New York Times*

See also EVERY CLOUD HAS A SILVER LINING.

It's as simple as that. That's all there is to it; it's a straightforward issue that's easy to understand; no additional information or explanation is needed. Used in informal conversation. The say-ing has appeared in works by Margaret Mitchell and Ernest Hemingway, among others and is commonly used at present.****

> **1936.** But since that day two years ago when Ashley, newly home from his three years' Grand Tour in Europe, had called to pay his respects, she had loved him. It was as simple as that. —Margaret Mitchell, *Gone With the Wind*

> **1940.** The next time you came that way you heard that they had been shot. It was as simple as that. —Ernest Hemingway, *For Whom the Bell Tolls*

> **1945.** "I passed the information along to the secretary. He got in touch with Cal. It was as simple as that." —Emilie Loring, *Beyond the Sound of Guns*

> **1978.** "I want you to live. It's as simple as that." —Howard Fast, *Second Generation*

> **1986.** On screen she was magic. It was as simple as that. —Jackie Collins, *Hollywood Husbands*

> **1988.** "Then we must be extraordinarily careful and make certain Evan Kendrick never learns about us. It's as simple as that." —Robert Ludlum, *The Icarus Agenda*

> **1992.** Years spent coping with family violence have convinced her, she said, that people need to stop trying to control others and concentrate on controlling themselves: "People have to learn to live together, it's as simple as that." —*New York Times*

> **1994.** "These are experts who should be celebrated, not punished," Mrs. O'Leary said in an interview on Friday. "We want to bring them back into the fold. We want an environment where employees feel safe to voice their concerns. We have zero tolerance for reprisals. It's as simple as that." —*New York Times*

It's business as usual. *See* BUSINESS AS USUAL.

It's déjà vu all over again. In French, *déjà vu* means "already seen." In 1979, the phrase was included among 6,000 important vocabulary words, compiled by Craig & Peter Norback as *The Must Words.* Even high school students were often unfamiliar with it, but it became very popular when the phrase *all over again* was added to it. The saying is generally attributed to baseball great Yogi Berra (1925–), but as with so many Yogiisms, he denies coining it.****

> **1991.** The President took a brief political detour from his four-week vacation in Kennebunkport, Me., this morning to fly to Pittsburgh, with Mr. Thornburgh in tow, to speak to the National Fra-

ternal Order of Police convention. As Mr. Bush liked to say in the 1988 Presidential campaign, quoting the New York Yankees catcher Yogi Berra, it was "déjà vu all over again." —Maureen Dowd, *New York Times*

1992. In yesterday's game, Oakland's Dave Stewart needed a lot of talent and luck to work out of a seventh-inning jam, one that ended when Toronto's hottest hitter, Roberto Alomar, lined into a double play.... "Without that snare it could have been déjà vu, here we come, again," Winfield said. —*New York Times*

1993. Well, as Yogi Berra might say, it's *déjà vu* all over again. A group of new Russian immigrants has started the Gesher Theater, and in less than two years it has become a cultural force. —*Hadassah Magazine*

1994. Next week's superbowl, as Yogi Berra said, will be déjà vu all over again. —Morton Dean, "Good Morning America," ABC

See also I CAN'T THINK WHEN I CONCENTRATE; IT'S NOT OVER TILL IT'S OVER.

It's getting out of hand. The situation is unruly, disorderly, excessive, hard to control. The subject may be replaced by other nouns.

1992. "Your sisters were a riot too. You guys get out of hand when you get together, don't you?" —Danielle Steel, *Mixed Blessings*

1993. It's getting out of hand, but is anyone really surprised? First streakers, then pitchers getting harassed and now a drop-in skydiver. Sports, like any other cultural phenomenon, is a microcosm of the world and now is accruing the ills of its role model. —*New York Times*

1994. Dr. Dunnan, the headmaster, put it this way: "It got out of hand, which is when we began to think it's time to dissemble the protective shell around the Fisher Landau program and let it continue as a part of the school." —*New York Times*
See also IT'S OUT OF ONE'S HANDS.

It's Greek to me. It's unintelligible. The saying appeared in Shakespeare's *Julius Caesar* (1599) and has been in common use ever since. An English speaker who doesn't know or understand something says, "It's all Greek to me." A French speaker might say either, *C'est du Grec pour moi* ("It's Greek to me") or *C'est du Chinois pour moi* ("It's Chinese to me"). Both Spanish speakers and Russians opt for the Chinese alternative (*Eso es chino para mi; Китайская грамота*).

1599. *Casca:* Nay, an I tell you that, I'll ne'er look you i' the face again; but those who understood

him smiled at one another and shook their heads; but, for my own part, it was Greek to me. —Shakespeare, *Julius Caesar,* I, ii

1964. She received her B.A. degree with Phi Beta Kappa and Magna Cum Laude (It's Greek to us!) and her M.A. (Miss America?) with highest honors. (Boy! What a record!) ... Listed among her favorites are Chaucer the poet (That's Greek to us too!) and reading books. —Bel Kaufman, *Up the Down Staircase*

1984. He was especially interested in splitting atoms, which at that point seemed still in the realm of scientific fiction. It all sounded like Greek to me.... —Lee Iacocca with William Novak, *Iacocca*

1988. "I still have radio traffic, but it's still Greek to me." —Nelson DeMille, *The Charm School*

It's in the blood. It is typical of the whole family. It's inborn. Usually said of a characteristic feature that one shares with one's parents or relatives.

1922. —It's in the blood, Mr Bloom acceded at once. —James Joyce, *Ulysses*

1952. "My mother got fat, and my grandmother got fat, and I guess it's in the blood; but somebody needed them, they were still some good." —Kurt Vonnegut, Jr., *Player Piano*

1989. "I wanted to be an explorer, you know. I saw myself leading expeditions all over the world, naming mountains and rivers after myself...."
"Why an explorer, of all things."
"Why not? Perhaps it's in the blood. Cyrus was a kind of explorer—an adventurer, anyway." —Michael Korda, *The Fortune*

1994. After his acquittal, Lauria said he only wanted to be a cop again.... "I was born a cop. It's in my blood. I will always be a cop." —*New York Post*
See also IT RUNS IN THE FAMILY; LIKE FATHER, LIKE SON; LIKE MOTHER, LIKE DAUGHTER.

It's in the lap of the gods. It's beyond human control: nobody knows what may fall from the lap of the gods. The saying was coined by Homer (eighth century b.c.). It is found in varying forms: *All is in the lap of the gods; It's on the lap of the gods; That's (all) on the knees of the gods,* etc.

Eighth century b.c.
It lies in the lap of the gods. —Homer, *Iliad,* 17, 1, 514

1992. "I want to go down with Tess Dodge, if I can find her. And that's all there is. It's in the laps of the gods, as they say." —Philip Friedman, *Inadmissible Evidence*

1993. His chances for reelection are in the lap of the gods. —Overheard at a public library in Princeton, N.J.

See also IT'S OUT OF ONE'S HANDS.

It's just what the doctor ordered.
It is exactly what one needs or want. Often shortened to *just what the doctor ordered.*

1971. Roosevelt wheeled himself briskly across the gray-painted wooden ramps.... "Ah! Doesn't this feel swell! Warm sun and ocean air. Just what the doctor ordered." —Herman Wouk, *The Winds of War*

1981. It was a ground-floor apartment with a small sunny garden, and it was going to be perfect for Samantha because it had no stairs, an easy access, and a doorman. It was just exactly what the doctor ordered. —Danielle Steel, *Palomino*

1986. Sen. Ernest F. Hollings (D-S.C.), discounting recent criticism of Fletcher's earlier performance in the job, praised his experience and judgment, saying, "I think the fella is really just exactly what the doctor ordered." —*Washington Post*

1988. To them, Cuomo's Jackson-stroking was just what the scenarist ordered, because most Mario Scenarios now give Jackson a key supporting role. —*Newsweek*

1991. But the Gingrich plan isn't what the economic doctor would order. It would reinstate, permanently, tax subsidies for retirement accounts of upper-income families and cut taxes on other types of savings. —*New York Times*

1992. According to data provided by Y. & R. New York, awareness of the Dr Pepper theme, "Just what the Dr ordered," rose in the second quarter to a record 89 percent, compared with 71.3 percent when it was introduced in 1987. —*New York Times*

1993. "The Clinton plan is just what the doctor ordered," says Gary J. Spirgel, president of Health Force. —*Wall Street Journal*

It's like looking for a needle in a haystack.
Said of a lost thing that is nearly impossible to find. Not only is the needle tiny, it also resembles the pieces of straw among which it is hidden. *Looking for a needle in a bottle of hay* is the original form. The French say *Chercher une aiguille dans une botte de foin* ("To look for a needle in a bundle of hay"). The idea was expressed in Shakespeare's *Midsummer Night's Dream* (1595–96) and Cervantes' *Don Quixote* (1605–15). Find-ing or *searching for* can replace *looking for.* Often shortened to *a needle in a bottle (bundle) of hay* or *a needle in a haystack.* In the United States, however, the latter is usually used.

1615. As well look for a needle in a bottle of hay. —Cervantes, *Don Quixote*

1904. *Larry:* ... It's such a big place that looking for a man there is like looking for a needle in a bundle of hay. —George Bernard Shaw, *John Bull's Other Island*

1916. "Where's our army?" asked Letty suddenly. "Lost somewhere in France," said Teddy. "Like a needle in a bottle of hay." —H. G. Wells, *Mr. Britling Sees It Through*

1980. ... [It] would have been like searching the white man's proverbial haystack for a dangerous needle. —*People*

1986. Finding the right piece of DNA is an almost unimaginably complicated task. Scientists have likened it not simply to finding a needle in a haystack but to finding a particular strand of hay. —*New York*

1991. FINDING IRAQI NUKES: NEEDLES IN A HAYSTACK —Headline, *Newsweek*

It's like opening a can of worms.
This is a highly problematical situation or complex problem. Broaching it may lead to utter chaos. The saying originated in the United States in the midtwentieth century and refers to the live bait kept in jars or other containers by fishermen. This figure of speech also occurs as *a whole new can of worms.*

1972. President: Oh well, this is a can of worms, as you know, a lot of this stuff that went on.... But the way you have handled all this seems to me has been very skillful, putting your fingers in the leaks that have sprung up here and spring there.... —Victor Lasky, *It Didn't Start with Watergate*

1975. If you want to open this can of worms, that's O.K. with me. You'll lose more than you can gain. —Overheard in the lobby of a New York apartment building

1993. Catanzaro and John Call, John Allen's attorney, had argued that the statements should have been thrown out because Seelig had demanded to speak with the brothers.... "I think this opens a whole new can of worms for the prosecution," Catanzaro said. "If this comes back, they can't use the statements." —*Times* (Trenton)

See also PANDORA'S BOX.

It's like taking candy from a baby.
It's almost

too easy, because one's opponent is not a worthy rival.

1951. "But I hate to take candy away from babies," Fatso grinned. —James Jones, *From Here to Eternity*

1991. Competitors are following suit, after having initially ignored Windows in favor of OS/2. Some, in fact, say Microsoft misled them into supporting OS/2, a charge Microsoft denies.... In any case, Microsoft has had the market for applications that work with Windows nearly to itself. "It's almost like taking candy from a baby," said Scott Oki, senior vice president of sales, marketing and services for Microsoft. —*New York Times*

1993. Applause and laughter from the gallery, then he turns to his long-time caddy, Fanny Sunesson, and says softly with cocky coolness: "It's like taking candy from a baby." —*Times* (Trenton)

See also IT'S A PIECE OF CAKE.

It's love that makes the world go round. See LOVE MAKES THE WORLD GO ROUND.

It's music to my ears. That's wonderful news. I'm happy to hear it. *It* can be replaced by *that* or another subject. Similarly, *my* can be replaced by another pronoun or noun. Often shortened to *music to my ears.*

1990. It's music to your ears, "I'll put in a good word for you." —Daniel Moreau, *Take Charge of Your Career*

1992. Dudley Clendinen's account of his journey toward gay identity in "The Gay Vote: Music to My Ears" (Op-Ed, Aug.1) contains a curious omission. He makes no mention of how his wife reacted. Was his coming out music to her ears—or to the children's? Does it matter? —Letters to the Editor, *New York Times*

1994. MEA CULPAS ARE MUSIC TO REPUBLICAN EARS —Headline of an article on the Whitewater hearings, *Times* (Trenton)

It's never too late to learn. Older people can continue to renew themselves by learning new things. The proverb has been traced back to about 1530: "Never too old to learn" (Barclay). The *too late* form dates back to 1678. Either form is currently used. First attested in the United States in *Journal of John Penrose, Seaman* (1783).

1986. It's *never* too late to fly! —Robert Fulghum, *All I Really Need to Know I Learned in Kindergarten*

1991. Learning is a lifelong process. It's never too late to learn what you need to succeed. —*Wall Street Journal's National Business Employment Weekly*

1992. It's never too late to learn something old. —*New Yorker*

See also LIVE AND LEARN.

It's never too late to mend. It's always possible to change for the better or improve morally. The adage was coined by English playwright Robert Greene (1558–92) in 1590. First cited in the United States in *Public Papers of George Clinton, First Governor of New York* (1778).

1590. *Never Too Late to Mend* —Title of a pamphlet by Robert Greene

1980. "Sorry for smoking." ... "It's never too late to mend, as the proverb says." —Overheard at a movie theater in New York City

See also IT'S NEVER TOO LATE TO LEARN; LEAST SAID, SOONEST MENDED.

It's no skin off my nose. That problem is not my concern. That task is not difficult for me. The saying originated in the early twentieth century and is of boxing origin. The pronoun *my* may be replaced with another pronoun or noun. *Nose* is often replaced by *behind* or *ass.* Often shortened to *no skin off my nose.*

1946. "I don't care whether he ever gets there," she said. "It won't be skin off my nose." —Robert Penn Warren, *All the King's Men*

1955. "What's going to happen to their morale? Now, men, it's no skin off my behind." —Joseph Heller, *Catch-22*

1977. "... if they don't eat breakfast, it's no skin off the adults' bones." —Art Buchwald, *Down the Seine and Up the Potomac*

1983. "You'd better come in. Ain't no skin off my ass if you rob the place." —Jackie Collins, *Hollywood Wives*

1993. "My escort will be here shortly! I would prefer you stayed out of sight, Max!"

"It's no skin off my nose, but Benny will be offended!" —Cartoon by Alex Kotzky, "Apartment 3-G," North America Syndicates

1994. If you'd settled for peanuts—an advance of, say, fifteen or twenty thousand simoleons—the publisher could have said, "If you don't want to get out there and sell your own book it's no skin off my nose, J.P." —Russell Baker, *New York Times*

See also I COULDN'T CARE LESS.

It's no use to close (bar, lock, shut) the

barn (stable) door after the horse has been stolen. *See* DON'T CLOSE (BAR, LOCK, SHUT) THE BARN (STABLE) DOOR AFTER THE HORSE RUNS AWAY (HAS FLED, HAS BEEN STOLEN).

It's none of your business. Don't be so nosy! It's a private matter that doesn't concern you. Used in informal speech as an impolite rejoinder to a question. Often shortened to *none of your business.*

1975. "What did they pay you to do that film?"
"None of your business." —Jackie Collins, *The World is Full of Divorced Women*

1981. Of course I didn't expect an answer, but be-hold—73 said yes, 21 said they would if they thought they could get away with it, and 9 told me it was none of my business. —Abigail Van Buren, *The Best of Dear Abby*

1984. Frankly, if asked on leaving the polling place how I had voted, I'd say, "None of your damned business." —Gerald Ford, *U.S. News & World Report*

1986. "Don't ask so many questions. It's none of your business." —Pat Conroy, *The Prince of Tides*

1991. "Well, uh, we just need that information."
"It's none of your business." —John Grisham, *The Firm*

It's not my cup of tea. I don't like it. It's not to my taste. I would prefer something else. It doesn't interest me. The saying is of British origin and was used in the affirmative sense in the mid-eighteenth century. The negative form has been current since the 1920s.

1979. "If this is not your cup of tea," he wrote, "we'll find something that is." —Kurt Vonnegut, Jr., *Jailbird*

1988. Lord knows Jesse [Jackson]'s not my cup of tea. —Patrick J. Buchanan, *New York Post*

1992. "It's really not particularly sexual," he added. "My interest in sex is purely intellectual, at this point. I'm like Mimi. It's not my cup of tea." —*New York Times Magazine*

1993. Gregory Pavlik is not my cup of tea. The 21-year-old former columnist for the University of Pennsylvania's student newspaper is a mighty conservative young man. —*Times* (Trenton)

1994. Last year's problem-plagued *Saturday Night Live* wasn't everybody's cup of coffee.... Linda Richman, with her New Yawk squawk and Yiddish yakking, kept the Saturday night series perking with her *Coffee Talk,* spilling beans on celebrities

and roasting neighbors with whom she didn't see "oy-to-oy." —*MetroWest Jewish News* (N.Y.)

It's not over till it's over. Never give up hope until the outcome is final: in life, as in baseball, miracles can and often do, happen. Attributed to Yogi Berra (1925–) in 1973, when he was managing the ragtag New York Mets. Probably the most famous of all Yogiisms. *It ain't over till it's over* and *It's never over till it's over* are variations. George Bush is usually given credit for saying, "Politics is like baseball. It isn't over till the last batter swings" (1992).

1973. It ain't over till it's over. —Yogi Berra on the game of baseball

1980. It's not over until it's over (Yogi Berra). —Quoted by Herb Cohen, *You Can Negotiate Anything*

1988. Asked why he had not done well in recent primaries, Mr. Jackson said that "the pundits and the press" had "given a certain tilt to the campaign," reinforcing the perception that Mr. Dukakis was the obvious Democratic nominee.... "It's not over till it's over," Mr. Jackson said. "I'm going to run till it's over." —*New York Times*

1989. "You can't quit, Jake. Your client needs you."
"To hell with my client. He tried to fire me today."
"He needs you. This thing ain't over till it's over." —John Grisham, *A Time to Kill*

1991. Although he has made progress in shrinking debt, Beré won't say whether the company is better off than if it had never done the LBO. Nor will he declare that the company's problems are behind it: "It isn't over until it's over." —*Fortune*

1992. "I'm not dating. I don't know if she is," he says of Pfeiffer. "Nothing's over till it's over." —*People*

1994. During a discussion of change (as in "changing world," not as in "pocket change"), the chief executive officer of Allied Signal noted that Yogi Berra was wrong when he said, "It ain't over till it's over." Why? Because it's never over. Change never stops, making it a good idea not only to remain aware of change but also to realize that we all see change from different perspectives. —*Car and Driver*

See also THE OPERA AIN'T OVER TILL THE FAT LADY SINGS.

It's not the early bird that catches the worm, but the smart one. *See* THE EARLY BIRD CATCHES THE WORM.

It's not the end of the world. It may be bad, but it's not *that* terrible. Used to reassure someone that nothing much happened and eventually everything will be all right. The saying has been current since the late nineteenth century. The word *earth* may be substituted for *world*.

1979. "Do cheer up, Harvey. It's not the end of the world, not by any means." —Howard Fast, *The Establishment*

1983. "You see, I told you it wasn't the end of the world." —Jackie Collins, *Hollywood Wives*

1986. "Tom," he said, catching me staring at him. "Go in and tell your mother to quit boo-hooing. It's not the end of the world." —Pat Conroy, *The Prince of Tides*

1988. I was not out there when that stock market dropped, wringing my hands and saying this was the end of the world as some political leaders were. Because it isn't the end of the world. —George Bush, Second debate between Bush and Dukakis, *New York Times*

1989. "You hate to lose a player as valuable as Keith," said Davey Johnson, "but it's not the end of the world. We've got a lot of guys who can play first base." —*New York Times*

1992. It's not the end of the world, he told himself. This wasn't a definitive statement. —Philip Friedman, *Inadmissible Evidence*

1993. In 1985, he [David Henry Hwang] wrote *Rich Relations*, his first play with non-Asian actors, a farce about family life and reincarnation. The reviews were poor, and Hwang himself concedes the play is "problematical." But the failure freed him. "I realized, it's okay. I'm still alive. It's not the end of the world." —*New York*

1994. Growing up among the paramilitaries and bombs in the Protestant neighborhood of Tiger's Bay has given the small-framed blonde an edge. "So much has happened," she says. "I've seen girls who have broken up with their boyfriends and think it's the end of the world. I know that things can be a lot worse." —*Wall Street Journal*

It's not what you know, but who you know. It is more important to have good contacts than to have knowledge. This cynical aphorism has been used since about 1945. *It's not who you know or what you know, it's what you know on whom* is a variant.

1984. While nobodies like Obadiah, Nehemiah, Zephaniah, Habakkuk, and Zechariah do. Believe me, it's not *what* you know, but who you know. —Joseph Heller, *God Knows*

1988. "It's Not Only Who You Know, But How You Get to Know Them" —Harvey Mackay, *Swim with the Sharks without Being Eaten Alive*

1991. Even fellow corporate lobbyists concede—often with a dollop of envy—that the granting of such a plum assignment gives the chosen lobbyist, such as Mr. Duberstein, a huge edge in attracting high-paying clients.... "Access is the name of the game. It's not what you know, it's who you know." —*Wall Street Journal*

1992. It's often said: "It's not what you know—it's who you know." But that's only half true—at least in the book-publishing industry. This book gives you names you need to know to get published. And having the contacts is an invaluable advantage.... —Jeff Herman, *Insider's Guide to Book Editors, Publishers, and Literary Agents*

1993. "I'm rehabilitated, myself, and ready to put my potentials back outside in the street," said Ms. Hurd, 31, who was convicted of second-degree murder at the age of 19. "But I'm afraid it's not what you know, it's who you know and I don't know nobody." —*New York Times*

It's not what you say, but how you say it. Style is often more revealing than the actual content of the message. *You are what you say and how you say it* is the original form.

1991. Redneck, gay, Ms., honey, boy, Mario, Alan: you are what you say and how you say it. There's been a lot of palaver about the oversensitivity of feminists to the language, and I must admit that I don't find it necessary to call women womyn. —Anna Quindlen, *New York Times*

1992. As one Bush researcher explains: "It's not just what they say, it's how they say it. When people talk about 'change,' what words do they use?" —*New York Times Magazine*

1993. WATCH WHAT THEY PAY, NOT WHAT THEY SAY —Headline of an article on the effect of TV reporting on stock prices, *New York Times*

It's not whether you win or lose but how you play the game. Earnest effort and good sportsmanship are more important than winning or losing. Coined by American sportswriter Grantland Rice (1880–1954).

1954. For when the One Great Scorer comes
 To write against your name,
 He marks—not that you won or lost—
 But how you played the game.
  —Grantland Rice, "Alumnus Football," *The Tumult and the Shouting*

1975. "How you play the game" is for college

boys. When you're playing for money, winning is the only thing that matters. —Leo Durocher, *Nice Guys Finish Last*

1991. Exactly what is sportsmanship these days? Is it the age-old admonishment that "It's not whether you win or lose but how you play the game?" Or is it Vince Lombardi's rubric that winning isn't everything, it's the only thing? —*New York Times*

1992. The underlying premise of these Olympics is clear: it isn't how you play the game. It's whether you win. —Anna Quindlen, *New York Times*

See also WINNING ISN'T EVERYTHING, IT'S THE ONLY THING.

It's not worth the paper it is written on. It is worthless. Usually applied to IOUs, checks, promises, etc., that are not worth considering. In 1861, Johann Bernhard, Graf von Rechberg (1806–99), in a dispatch concerning the recognition of Italy, wrote: "Guarantees which are not worth the paper they are written on." *Printed* is often substituted for *written.*

1922. —Then our friend's writ is not worth the paper it's printed on, Ben Dollard said. —James Joyce, *Ulysses*

1988. The Vice President made that pledge [to hold the line on taxes]. He's broken it three times in the past year, already, so it isn't worth the paper it's printed on. —Michael Dukakis, Second debate between Bush and Dukakis, *New York Times*

1989. It now appears that the dispute over the proposed U.S.-Japanese joint venture to build the FSX fighter plane will be settled by an exchange of secret side letters.... There is one major problem with this approach: Side letters aren't worth the paper they're printed on. —*New York Times*

1992. Any so-called biography that tries to take our parents from us, that gets this basic fact about our family wrong, is not worth the paper it is printed on. —Jean Kennedy Smith et al., *New York Times*

1994. "We all know that tabloid accounts are not worth the paper they're written on," she said in Judge Ito's chambers earlier this week. "In fact, I heard one celebrity once say he wouldn't allow his dog to urinate on them." —*New York Times*

It's out of one's hands. The matter is out of or beyond one's control.

1991. "I want the decisions to be made by third parties," he said. "I want to be able to say to politicians, 'Hey, it's out of my hands. All our contri-

butions are handled by the PAC.'" —*New York Times*

1992. "I won't bother asking you how you let it get out. Just bring this thing to a close."

"It's out of my hands. The judge has the diary and a request for a protective order." —Philip Friedman, *Inadmissible Evidence*

1994. "We want to start the season on Saturday," said Brodeur, "but it's out of our hands." —*New York Times*

See also IT'S GETTING OUT OF HAND; IT'S IN THE LAP OF THE GODS.

It's out of this world. Said of something that is out of the ordinary, excellent, extremely beautiful. The phrase originated in the twentieth century.

1951. "You guys aint seen it like I have. Its out of this world, thats all." —James Jones, *From Here to Eternity*

1977. Her cooking's out of this world. —J. D. Salinger, *Raise High the Roof Beam, Carpenters*

1988. The good professor did not disappoint them. Though the first question dealt with the pioneering work on metabolism of recent Nobel Prize winner Sir Hans Krebs, it was nonetheless out of this world. —Erich Segal, *Doctors*

It's politics as usual. *See* POLITICS AS USUAL.

It's six of one and half a dozen of the other. *See* SIX OF ONE AND HALF A DOZEN OF THE OTHER.

It's survival of the fittest. Only the strongest ones survive or succeed. The saying originated in the latter half of the nineteenth century. In *Principles of Biology* (1867), English philosopher Herbert Spencer described Darwin's theory of natural selection as "survival of the fittest." Later, this biological principle of evolutionary progress was applied to any form of struggle for survival or success.

1859. The expression often used by Mr. Herbert Spencer, of the Survival of the Fittest, is more accurate, and is sometimes equally convenient. —Charles Darwin, *On the Origin of Species*

1889. While the law [of competition] may be sometimes hard for the individual, it is best for the race, because it insures the survival of the fittest in every department. —Andrew Carnegie, "Wealth," *North American Review*

1902. The growth of a large business is merely a survival of the fittest. —John D. Rockefeller, quoted by W. J. Ghent, *Our Benevolent Feudalism*

1984. I probably would have said to Chrysler: "Leave the government out of this. I believe in survival of the fittest. Let the marginal guy go broke." —Lee Iacocca with William Novak, *Iacocca*

1991. "Let's be realistic," she said. "Many of those kids have zero self-esteem, and they often have so little guidance in their homes that a life, even their own, seems to have little meaning or value. Those are the kids that'll kill you for a dime. It's survival of the fittest out there." —*New York Times*

1993. His money depleted and no job in sight, he rode the subways at night rather than check into a city shelter. "It looked like prison again, like survival of the fittest," he said. —*New York Times*

1994. E-mail conversation is a battle of wits. If you've got the brains, you can crush your opponent; if you play dumb and become submissive, don't think it won't be noticed. Think of it as survival of the fittest. —Letters to the Editor, *Newsweek*

See also EVERY MAN FOR HIMSELF.

It's the early bird that catches the worm.
See THE EARLY BIRD CATCHES THE WORM.

It's the economy, Stupid! Economy is the key issue. The catch phrase originated in the 1992 presidential election campaign. A sign in the Little Rock headquarters of James Carville, political adviser to Bill Clinton, read IT'S THE ECONOMY, STUPID! He posted it as a constant reminder that the main emphasis of the campaign should be on the economy. This motto was widely used during the campaign and is credited with helping Clinton win the election. The word *economy* is now often replaced with other nouns. Some of the variations include "It's the *Deficit*, Stupid!" (in a financial newsletter); "The *Mideast*, Stupid!" (in the *Forward*); "It's the Health-Care Crisis, Stupid!"; and "It's Florio, Stupid." William Safire suggested that James Carville change his motto to "It's the taxation, stupid," while another political pundit advised changing, "It's the Economy, Stupid" to "It's California, stupid."*****

1993. As James Carville would put it, "It's the election, stupid." —*Washington Post*

1994. In the 1992 Presidential campaign, a sign in the Clinton campaign office read IT'S THE ECONOMY, STUPID. That was good politics but poor statesmanship. There is a world of difference between campaigning and governing. We cannot have a strong domestic policy unless we have a strong foreign policy. —Richard Nixon, *Time*

It's the exception that proves the rule. *See* THERE IS AN EXCEPTION TO EVERY RULE.

It's the first step that costs. *See* THE FIRST STEP IS THE HARDEST.

It's the fox guarding the chicken house. *See* DON'T LET THE FOX GUARD THE HENHOUSE.

It's the greatest thing since sliced bread. What a brilliant idea! What a fine thing! Said of any innovation more important than a bread slicer. Often used sarcastically. The expression originated in the mid-twentieth century. *Chinese checkers, chopped liver, packaged bread, swinging doors, chewing gum, the hula hoop,* or *the hamburger* may replace *sliced bread.* The word *best* can substitute for *greatest.*

1974. "Once, during the Florida primary, Howard [Hunt] had some fliers printed saying that Mayor Lindsay, of New York, was having a meeting and there would be free beer. Howard handed these fliers out in the black areas, and of course there was no meeting or beer, so the blacks would come for their beer and leave hating Lindsay. Howard thought this was the greatest thing since Chinese checkers." —Carl Bernstein & Bob Woodward, *All the President's Men*

1981. Dear Abby: I'll never forget the first night of my honeymoon. My darling fell fast asleep at midnight while I was awake until seven o'clock the next morning just listening to him snore.... Then a friend introduced me to the greatest invention since sliced bread. Ear plugs! They have saved my marriage, and I am not kidding. —Abigail Van Buren, *The Best of Dear Abby*

1991. This innovation [televised press conferences] had been Pierre Salinger's idea, and while some advisers and newsmen had raised objections (James Reston called it "the goofiest idea since the hula hoop"), Jack was confident that the publicity was worth the risk of a slip of the tongue. —Thomas C. Reeves, *A Question of Character: A Life of John F. Kennedy*

1992. Should her self-image tilt this way or that, Jones's family is there to keep things in perspective. "My mom thinks I'm the best thing since swinging doors," she says. —*People*

1994. Everyone, it seems, is registering an opinion or making a prediction about the Internet. Some people say it's a snare and a delusion. Others think the Internet is the greatest thing since packaged bread. —*U.S. 1* (Princeton)

It's the last straw that breaks the camel's

back. Said of something that finally causes disaster in an already bad situation. Alludes to weighing articles where the last pinch turns the scale. The proverb dates back to 1655: "It is the last feather may be said to break the horse's back" (John Barnhall). In 1670 John Ray included it in his collection of proverbs. First attested in the United States in *Bill Arp, So Called* (1866). The proverb is found in varying forms: *It's the last straw that breaks the horse's back; The last straw breaks* (or *broke* or *will break*) *the camel's back; The last straw breaks the horse's back*, etc. Often shortened to *the last straw*.

1914. This was the last straw. He was throwing up her lawless girlhood love to her as an offence. —Theodore Dreiser, *The Titan*

1936. Careless of the disapproval of Aunt Pitty's friends, she behaved as she had behaved before her marriage, went to parties, danced, went riding with soldiers, flirted, did everything she had done as a girl, except stop wearing mourning. This she knew would be a straw that would break the backs of Pittypat and Melanie. —Margaret Mitchell, *Gone With the Wind*

1954. *The Last Straw* —Title of a book by D. M. Disney.

1969. "What a cow, what a stupid cow! Ain't that the last straw!" —Joyce Carol Oates, *Them*

1975. Details of the crime vary—it was never reported in the newspapers—but the neighborhood believes that a man with a knife forced her away from her class, took her to a deserted area of the park and raped her. If there was a last straw, that was it. —Robert A. Caro, *The Power Broker*

1984. Of course, this minor transgression was merely the last straw in a relationship that had never been very good to begin with. —Lee Iacocca with William Novak, *Iacocca*

1986. "Reykjavik was the last straw in showing the Europeans the penalties of overdependence on American leadership," explains Adm. James Eberle, director of the Royal Institute of International Affairs in London. —*U.S. News & World Report*

1987. Throughout the campaign, Nixon had demanded that [Helen Gahagan] Douglas state her position on the question of the admission of Red China to the United Nations, but she refused to answer. "This is the last straw," Nixon declared. —Stephen E. Ambrose, *Nixon*

1990. The last straw came when Ford Motor, dismayed by Guaranty's handling of its pension fund, switched the fund to Morgan. —Ron Chernow, *The House of Morgan*

1992. "Roberto really wanted me out of there. He threatened me, and I think that was some kind of last straw for Moriah." —Philip Friedman, *Inadmissible Evidence*

1994. But industry analysts said the new F.C.C. rules were a factor in the failure of the merger.... "It's the straw that broke the camel's back," said John Reidy, a media analyst for Smith Barney Shearson. —*New York Times*

It's the only game in town. It's the only available option. According to Eric Partridge, the catch phrase dates from 1900 or earlier. The full version is: *I know it's crooked, but it's the only game in town.* In *Hollywood Husbands* (1986), Jackie Collins revamped the old saying, adding to it something very familiar and likable: "It's the only ballgame in the park." Often shortened to *the only game in town*.

1980. "I can appreciate your desire to play the political game. It's the best game in town for a man who doesn't grow up, but I refuse to think of you as a small boy." —Howard Fast, *The Establishment*

1984. I think *The Wall Street Journal* is living in the last century. Unfortunately, it's the only game in town. The *Journal* is a monopoly and it's become arrogant, like General Motors. —Lee Iacocca with William Novak, *Iacocca*

1986. Countries like Jordan, Morocco and Saudi Arabia seek American goods, know-how and implicit promises of protection not only because America is the best game in town but because America is the only game in town. —*New York Times*

1991. Privately, Truman complained about "this immature boy" and credited "Kennedy's Pa" for the convention victory. Jack soon smirked to Judith Campbell, "That old bastard has no other option. I'm the only game in town. I think he'd support the devil before he would Nixon." —Thomas C. Reeves, *A Question of Character: A Life of John F. Kennedy*

It's the real McCoy. It is the genuine thing, not an imitation. Originated in the United States in the late 1890s. One theory of the phrase's origin traces it to boxer Kid McCoy (1873–1940). In an attempt to cash in on the fame of the legendary McCoy, many other fighters assumed the same name, much to the public's confusion. On March 25, 1899, the *San Francisco Examiner* informed its readers that *the real McCoy* had pulverized his opponent. The phrase has been in common usage ever since. According to another theory, the phrase derives from the name of the A. & M. Mac-Kay company, the Glasgow manufacturer of a Scotch whisky known as "the real MacKay (McCoy)." Hence, *the real McCoy* sometimes refers to drugs or alcohol. The subject *it* can be replaced by other pronouns or nouns. The word *real* may be omitted, but the definite article *the* should always be used.

1986. "I like the Barnum and Bailey Circus. The goddamn real McCoy." —Pat Conroy, *The Prince of Tides*

1987. Mr. Haig, asked to criticize Mr. Dole, characterized the Senator as "watered down pineapple juice" and urged voters to remember that "Haig & Haig is the real McCoy." —*New York Times*

1991. Emanuel tells of Garrett Morgan, a Clevelander who created the first traffic light and gas mask. Makila Sands did her report on Elijah McCoy, possibly the namesake for "the real McCoy," she says, because his automatic machine lubricator was much copied but never replicated. —*Wall Street Journal*

1993. Sports fans everywhere deserve to know that a genuine America's Team is thriving in Manhattan, Kan. This moniker is not some hyped marketing play, a la the Dallas Cowboys, but the real McCoy, à la the 1960 United States Olympic hockey team. —Letters to the Editor, *New York Times*
See also IT's THE REAL THING.

It's the real thing. It is the genuine thing, not an imitation. This common expression has been popularized as a slogan for Coca-Cola. "Can't beat the real thing." The subject *it* can be replaced by other pronouns or nouns. *The real thing* is gradually replacing *the real McCoy*. ****

1934. So when she had seen approval of Dick Diver in her mother's face it meant that he was "the real thing"; it meant permission to go as far as she could. —F. Scott Fitzgerald, *Tender Is the Night*

1948. "Julie let Frank out by the servants' entrance, and at the door he kissed her. Ruth, watching, knew it wasn't any kid stuff. This was the real thing." —Harold Robbins, *Never Love a Stranger*

1963. "A year later young Lewis chanced to hear Jimmy Yancey play the piano. 'This,' as Lewis recalls, 'was the real thing.'" —Kurt Vonnegut, Jr., *Cat's Cradle*

1975. Coca-Cola. It used to be "the real thing" when pharmacist John Styth Pemberton brewed it up in his backyard before the days of drug paranoia. —David Wallechinsky & Irving Wallace, *The People's Almanac*

1992. Prestige comes with a price. Small boxes went for as little as $2, but the asking price for a suede necklace box was a whooping $25. "That's real suede, ma'am." But *is* it the real thing? —*New York*

1993. The rule laid down by President Harry Truman: ... If the American people have to choose between a real conservative and an imitation conservative, they will always choose the real thing. —John Kenneth Galbraith, *Modern Maturity*

1994. One day I traveled to the bomber base where Jimmy Stewart was stationed as a B-24 pilot, to do a story about his being given the Distinguished Flying Cross. Jimmy Stewart was no Hollywood hero. He was the real thing. —Andy Rooney, *Times* (Trenton).
See also IT's THE REAL MCCOY.

It's the tip of the iceberg. What you've seen so far barely suggests the enormity of the problem or situation. Originated in the mid-twentieth century. The metaphor alludes to the fact that an iceberg's mass floats unseen under the water, exposing only the tip. The words *only* and *just* are often used before *the tip*. It can be replaced by any other subject.

1969. "I believe that Broke's been made the victim of an elaborate frame-up. I think, to employ a well-known metaphor, that all we can see is the tip of the iceberg, and that there is depth beyond depth below it." —Michael Gilbert, *The Etruscan Net*

1974. *World-Telegram* rewriteman Fred J. Cook recalls the reporter saying: "This [Robert Moses] is the most powerful SOB in the city. If this is so bad at the tip of the iceberg, there must be more." —Robert A. Caro, *The Power Broker*

1984. What happened to us, as I explained again and again, represented only the tip of the iceberg when it came to the problems facing American industry. —Lee Iacocca with William Novak, *Iacocca*

1991. The "slide show" and the two documents were only the tip of the unfairness iceberg. —Oliver L. North, *Under Fire*

1994. "What you see in *The New Yorker* is the tippy tippy top of the iceberg," said Mr. Mankoff, an animated man with long, graying brown hair. "We are the iceberg." —*New York Times*

It's too good to be true. It's unbelievable; there must be some hidden faults or drawbacks. The saying has been common since the sixteenth century. In 1580, the expression appeared in the title of a book by Thomas Lupton, *A Dream of the*

Deuill and Diues Siuquila: Too Good to Be True. Some 350 years later, George Bernard Shaw put a new spin on the phrase in the title of his play *Too True to Be Good* (1932). In 1992, Ross Perot declared: "Five of my kids are too good to be true, thanks to their mother." Some versions begin with *it looks, it seems, it sounds,* or *it turns out.*

1884. "It's too good for true, honey, it's too good for true." —Mark Twain, *The Adventures of Huckleberry Finn*

1928. *Evans:* Sometimes I feel it's too good to be true ... don't deserve it ... and now ... if that'd happen ... then I'd feel sure ... it'd be there ... half Nina, half me ... living proof! —Eugene O'Neill, *Strange Interlude*

1936. He tried to think of something to say and couldn't, and silently he blessed her because she kept up a steady chatter which relieved him of any necessity for conversation. It was too good to be true. —Margaret Mitchell, *Gone With the Wind*

1962. Here was any old soldier's dream of a perfect piece of thievery. It was too good to be true. —James Jones, *The Thin Red Line*

1975. "A year-round stream running through the property. Old fruit trees are still bearing." And the asking price—$12,000. I caught myself just before the drool came over my lip. Would I be interested in having a look? It sounded too good to be true. —Mark Vonnegut, *The Eden Express*

1979. Sally put her arms around him and kissed him. "I like you. You're absolutely an angel, you're too good to be true." —Howard Fast, *The Establishment*

1983. Does Streisand sing? This was turning out to be too good to be true. Where was the catch? —Jackie Collins, *Hollywood Wives*

1988. It seemed too good to be true. Last week the Soviet state tourism monopoly, Intourist, announced it was organizing trips to six Soviet cities for foreign reporters covering the [Moscow Summit] meeting. —*New York Times*

1991. Simplesse, the touted fake fat from Nutra-Sweet, was supposed to ensure the company's success and usher in an era of guiltfree gluttony for American calorie counters and cholesterol watchers, or so NutraSweet executives predicted. It promised all the taste of real fat, without being fattening. ... It seemed too good to be true. And it was. —*Wall Street Journal*

1994. Scores too good to be true.... A team of stu-dents from Steinmetz High School were the surprise victors earlier this month in the Illinois academic decathlon. Their secret, it turned out: They cheated. —*New York Times*

See also IT'S TOO MUCH OF A GOOD THING.

It's too little, too late. Said of any action that is neither adequate or timely enough to be effective. Often used in political contexts. The saying originated in the United States in 1935 and is attributed to American historian Allan Nevins (1890–1971). In the May 1935 issue of *Current History,* Nevins argued that the rise of Nazism was a result of the West having offered Germany too little aid for reconstruction, "and that too late." Following World War II, President Truman warned that a "too-little-too-late" policy should not be repeated. English statesman David Lloyd George (1863–1945) has been quoted as saying, "It is always too late, or too little, or both. And that is the road to disaster." Often shortened to *too little, too late.*

1935. The former allies have blundered in the past by offering Germany too little, and offering even that too late, until finally Nazi Germany had become a menace to all mankind. —Allan Nevins, in *Current History*

1956. Free men in Europe and in Asia, eager to resist aggression, could not wait for the future delivery of arms, which might come too late. Indeed, the main purpose of this aid proposal was to make sure that we did not have another tragic instance of "too little and too late"—the kind of thing that had helped Hitler subjugate Europe. —Harry S. Truman, *Memoirs*

1984. Near the end of the meeting, Bill [Ford] made an honest effort to change his brother's mind. But it was too little, too late. —Lee Iacocca with William Novak, *Iacocca*

1989. For good measure, Saab will also criticize German and Japanese competitors in a series of ads that will appear next month.... All of these moves might be too little, too late. —*New York Times*

1994. "Congress has done something and that's a very positive step," he said. "It's not too little and it's not too late in helping aid this process." —*New York Times*

It's too much of a good thing. In excess, even desirable things become burdensome; moderation is preferable in all things. The phrase appears as early as 1599, in Shakespeare's *As You Like It.* However, the same idea was expressed by Chaucer in his *Canterbury Tales* (1387): "That that is overdoon, it wol nat preeve Aright, as clerkes seyn; it is a vice." Often shortened to *too much of a good thing.*

1599. *Rosalind:* Are you not good?
Orlando: I hope so.
Rosalind: Why, then, can one desire too
    much of a good thing?
                —Shakespeare, *As You Like It,* IV, i

1981. Now here's a lady with a problem that some women would love to have: too much of a good thing. —Abigail Van Buren, *The Best of Dear Abby*

1988. In my lectures on exercise, I often take your title ["Body and Mind: 'Too Much of a Good Thing'"] one step further, quoting the so-called Mae West rule: "Too much of a good thing … is wonderful." —*New York Times Magazine*

1989. "The lighting made them [the streets] safer, and everyone thought it was good. But now we've got too much of a good thing, and we're beginning to appreciate darkness again." —*New York Times*

It's your funeral. You're bound to fail, but go ahead; it won't affect me. Said ironically to someone who is about to make a bad decision or do something risky. Originated in the United States in about 1850. The earliest recorded appearance in print in the United States was in 1906: "T'wan't none of my funeral" (J. C. Lincoln).

1913. "Flodie nodded, with a hard look in her eyes. 'All right,' she said slowly, and gulped something down. 'It's *your* funeral.'" —Gelett Burgess, "Love in a Hurry"

1951. "Quit stalling me," Stark said. "I aint going to coax you. Either you want it or you dont want it."

"I'd sure like to," Prew said slowly. "But I cant," he said, finally getting it out finally.

"Okay," Stark said. "Its your funeral." —James Jones, *From Here to Eternity*

1961. "Better throw a couple of warm-ups."

"My arm is loose," said Roy.

"It's your funeral." —Bernard Malamud, *The Natural*

1965. "That'll cost you plenty," the artist said. "You don't want all those little blocks though, just the outline and some better features."

"Just like it is," Parker said, "just like it is or nothing."

"It's your funeral," the artist said, "but I don't do that kind of work for nothing." —Flannery O'Connor, "Parker's Back"

1993. "Why don't we just get you to the U.S. right now?"

"Out of the question."

"O.K., it's your neck." —Victor Sheymov with Roger Jellinek, *New York Times Magazine*

See also IT'S NO SKIN OFF MY NOSE.

Jack of all trades and master of none. Said of someone who has a basic familiarity with many things but isn't an expert at anything. In 1612, appeared in *Essays and Characters of a Prison* by Geffray Mynshul. The phrase has been in use in the United States since 1721. Often shortened to *jack of all trades,* which originated earlier than the full saying. Similar proverbs occur in other languages: *Tout savoir est ne rien savoir* ("To know everything is to know nothing") (French); *Aprendiz de todo, oficial de nada* (Spanish).

1965. "I'm a jack of all trades, so to speak, a master of few and so is Perry." —Truman Capote, *In Cold Blood*

1986. "To me, acting is a business," he says with a slow smile. "You have to be a jack of all trades: a salesman, because you're not pitching yourself as the product; a marketing manager" —*Weekend Woman* (Trenton)

1988. He clarified: he'd worked on tugboats, done die casting, been a fork lift operator, a septic tank installer, a line installer for grease traps—"just an all-around jack of all trades and a master of none." —Clifford Irving, *The Campbell Murder Case*

1989. The low pay of engineers—150 rubles a month against 250 for a skilled factory worker—has turned many into high-class jacks-of-all-trades, if the price is right. —*U.S. News & World Report*

1992. You can accuse Bragg of being a politically correct lefty or a musical jack-of-all-styles. —*People*

A jackass can kick a barn door down, but it takes a carpenter to build one. Incompetents can destroy the careful work of more experienced people. Used in political contexts. The saying was coined in 1953 by Speaker of the House Sam Rayburn (1882–1961). "It takes longer to build," he said, "than it does to kick one down."

1953. A jackass can kick a barn down, but it takes a carpenter to build one. —Sam Rayburn

1994. Former House Speaker Sam Rayburn used to say that "any jackass can kick a barn door down, but it takes a carpenter to build one." Maybe the only sure answer to this sort of irresponsibility, and the impact it is having on the formation of talented, cohesive administrations, is for those who run the media to insure that there are more carpenters among today's political commentators. —*New York Times*

Jekyll and Hyde. *See* DR. JEKYLL AND MR. HYDE.

A journey of a thousand miles begins with one step. Don't be overwhelmed by the difficulty of the project: just get started. Any goal can be achieved through determination and persistence. Even a small step in the right direction is better than doing nothing at all. Sometimes used to urge someone to stop procrastinating. The proverb is attributed to Chinese philosopher Lao-tzu (c.604–531 b.c.). *A journey of a thousand miles must begin with a single step* is a common variant.

1965. He [President Kennedy] did not exaggerate the significance of the agreement. It was not the millennium: it would not resolve all conflicts, reduce nuclear stockpiles, check the production of nuclear weapons or restrict their use in case of war. But it was "an important first step—a step toward peace—a step toward reason—a step away from war." He concluded with the Chinese proverb he had put to Khrushchev two years before in Vienna: "A journey of a thousand miles must begin with a single step." —Arthur M. Schlesinger, Jr., *A Thousand Days*

1985. If we can recall the traditional Chinese axiom, that the longest journey begins with the first step, we can begin to solve some of our problems, instead of waiting around for the "big solution" to materialize out of thin air. —*Forbes*

1993. There is a saying, "A journey of a thousand miles starts with a single step." —Richard Riordan, newly elected mayor of Los Angeles, on his plans to rebuild the city, "Good Morning America," ABC

See also THE FIRST STEP IS THE HARDEST; GREAT OAKS FROM LITTLE ACORNS GROW.

Judge not according to appearances. Don't make snap judgments without further examination; look beneath the surface of things. The proverb is used by Jesus in the New Testament to answer his critics. It can be found in William Tyndale's translation (1526). First attested in the United States in *Poor Richard's Almanac* (1751) by Benjamin Franklin. The saying is found in varying forms: *Don't judge according to appearance; Never judge from appearances; You must not judge by appearances*, etc. The word *looks* is sometimes substituted for *appearances*.

Judge not according to the appearance, but judge righteous judgment. —John 7:24, *Authorized Version*, 1611

1985. "You can't judge by appearances," he said. —Michael Korda, *Queenie*

1994. You know what they say—you should never judge from appearances. —Overheard on a Washington-bound train

See also APPEARANCES (LOOKS) ARE DECEIVING (DECEPTIVE); DON'T JUDGE A BOOK BY ITS COVER.

Judge not, that ye be not judged. Don't be judgmental, because the same scrutiny might be applied to you and you might be guilty of the same offense. Appears in the New Testament as part of the Sermon on the Mount. The maxim has been traced back to 1481. In 1865, it was used by Abraham Lincoln in his Second Inaugural Address.

Judge not, that ye be not judged. For with what judgement ye judge, ye shall be judged; and with what measure ye mete, it shall be measured to you again. —Matthew 7:1, *Authorized Version*, 1611

1865. Both read the same Bible, and pray to the same God; and each invokes His aid against the other. It may seem strange that any men should dare to ask a just God's assistance in wringing their bread from the sweat of other men's faces; but let us judge not that we be not judged. —Abraham Lincoln, Second Inaugural Address

1989. Although I'm not very religious there is a lot to be said for maxims like "Judge not, lest ye be judged," and "Let he who is without sin throw the first stone." —Clifford Irving, *The Campbell Murder Case*

See also IT TAKES ONE TO KNOW ONE; LET HIM WHO IS WITHOUT SIN CAST (THROW) THE FIRST STONE.

Justice is blind. True justice is impartial. Justice is often personified as a blindfolded woman holding aloft a pair of scales in which she weighs the claims of opposing parties. The saying has been traced back to 1663. First attested in the United States in 1782. *When love is blind, so is justice* is a recent variant.

1991. Justice is supposed to be blind; the color of a person's skin should not determine their guilt or innocence. —Oliver L. North, *Under Fire*

1992. How could four L.A.P.D. members be found not guilty of brutality witnessed by everyone in the world who owns a television set? The phrase "justice is blind" has taken on a sad new meaning. —Letters to the Editor, *Time*

1994. Justice is blind, you know, and they wouldn't take death for an answer. —*Times* (Trenton)

See also LOVE IS BLIND.

Keep a stiff upper lip. Be self-reliant. In adversity, remain calm and cool and face difficulties and danger with fortitude. Alludes to the trembling lip of a person undergoing emotional stress. The proverb originated in the United States and has been traced back to 1815. First attested in England in *Brother Jonathan* (1825).

1849. And though hard be the task,
"Keep a stiff upper lip."
—Phoebe Cary, "Keep a Stiff Upper Lip"

1912. "I'm going over there with Harper Steger when he comes. If he won't change I'll send out notice to my creditors, and notify the secretary of the exchange. I want you to keep a stiff upper lip, whatever happens." —Theodore Dreiser, *The Financier*

1977. In order to be a good candidate's wife, she must show a stiff upper lip and stick with the standard clichés about her husband, her home, and her children. —Art Buchwald, *Down the Seine and Up the Potomac*

1993. "We are trying to keep a stiff upper lip about leaving, but it's hard after so many years here," said Rick Jensen, Litton's director of real estate and construction. —*New York Times*

1995. America's games once embodied the ideal of masculinity: guts, loyalty and stiff upper lips. But when manly became macho, sport lost its purpose, and way. —Robert Lipsyte, *New York Times Magazine*

See also KEEP YOUR CHIN UP.

Keep your chin up. Don't get upset. Always remain cheerful in the face of adversity. Originated in the United States in the 1940s. Sometimes shortened to *chin up*.

1982. "Do more than try. Keep your chin up. That's doctor's orders." —Dean R. Koontz, *The House of Thunder*

1985. She felt like a sailor drowning at sea, reaching out for the lifebuoy that represented the last, slim chance for survival.
"Chin up!" he told her, patting her arm, but she merely drew farther away from him into her corner of the taxi and stared out the rain-washed window at the lights. —Michael Korda, *Queenie*

1991. YOU'RE DOING WONDERFULLY. CHIN UP. KISS YOUR WIFE, CHILDREN. PET YOUR DOG. I'M 81. FRIENDS HERE BELIEVE YOU. —Oliver L. North, *Under Fire*

1992. They were churchgoers, teetotalers. The First Ladies were real ladies, they kept their chin up. —*Life*

1994. The eyes of Assistant United States Attorney Bill Johnston, who lives in Waco, brimmed with tears as he said, "These agents did not die in vain, and I want to encourage law-enforcement officers all across the country, and especially the A.T.F., to keep their chin up." —*New York Times*

See also KEEP A STIFF UPPER LIP.

Keep your eyes open and your mouth shut.
See KEEP YOUR MOUTH SHUT AND YOUR EYES OPEN.

Keep your eyes wide open before marriage, half shut afterwards. Be careful not to marry the wrong person; but once you've made a commitment, be tolerant of your spouse's shortcomings. The proverb originated in the United States and was popularized by Benjamin Franklin in 1738 in his *Poor Richard's Almanac*.

1993. "Another drink! Sometimes I wonder why I married you!"
"There's an old proverb.... 'Enter into marriage with both eyes open. After you marry, shut one.'"
—Cartoon by Mort Walker, "Beetle Bailey," King Features Syndicate

1994. "There's no question in my mind that the president cheated on his wife." ... "Then why didn't she do something about it?" ... "You remember the old adage, 'Keep your eyes wide open before marriage, half shut afterwards.' She acted like a First Lady even then." —Overheard at a senior citizens center in New Jersey

See also DISCRETION IS THE BETTER PART OF VALOR; LOOK BEFORE YOU LEAP; MARRIAGES ARE MADE IN HEAVEN; MARRY IN HASTE, REPENT AT LEISURE.

Keep your feet on the ground. Establish a strong position. Don't get carried away. Be realistic. The saying is used both literally and figuratively. The proverb is first attested in the United States in 1931. The word *get* or *have* may substitute for *keep*.

> **1940.** Tom grinned. "Keep all four feet on the groun'," he said. "I didn' mean nothin'. Jus' take her easy over this ditch." —John Steinbeck, *The Grapes of Wrath*

> **1992.** "I'm trying to keep both feet on the ground," Mr. Hastings said this morning of his victory after several unsuccessful attempts to win elected office. —*New York Times*

> **1993.** Oprah Winfrey's lawyer remarks of his old friend: "She grew up poor and she maintains a perspective about the value of money. We have a joke between us: she still has both feet on the ground, she just wears better shoes." —Liz Smith, *Times* (Trenton)

See also STAND ON YOUR OWN TWO FEET.

Keep your fingers crossed. Hope for success. The saying derives from the superstition that bad luck may be averted by making the sign of the cross. Originated in the 1920s.

> **1957.** "There's nothing much that you can do with them [engines] at sea if they do. Just keep your fingers crossed and hope they'll keep on spinning around." —Nevil Shute, *On the Beach*

> **1984.** People are keeping their fingers crossed these days in the $300 billion mutual fund industry. —*Forbes*

> **1991.** "They [the Iranians] realize hostages are an obstacle to any productive relationship with us. They want to remove the obstacle.... If this comes off, may ask you to do the second round after the hostages are back. Keep your fingers crossed." —Oliver L. North, *Under Fire*

> **1993.** These measures, in turn, will never be passed until we throw the liberals out of Congress. We can do that next year. Until then, keep your fingers crossed and pray that it isn't already too late to salvage our economy. —Letters to the Editor, *Princeton Packet* (N.J.)

> **1994.** "My fingers are still crossed, but I think rates will continue to rise and eventually choke this vigorous housing activity," said David Lereah, the chief economist with the Mortgage Bankers Association. —*Wall Street Journal*

Keep your mouth shut and your eyes open. If you want to succeed, pay close attention to what's going on around you and don't speak idly. The saying has been traced back to 1581. First attested in the United States in 1930. *Keep your eyes open and your mouth shut* is a variant.

> **1987.** "This is a real chance for you to learn about The Company and how it does business. So listen to them and learn." ... And then as a parting word, the summation of a lifetime's wisdom.... "Remember, keep your eyes open and your mouth shut!" —R. Richard Ritti & G. Ray Funkhouser, *The Ropes to Skip & the Ropes to Know*

> **1992.** "Keep your mouth shut and your eyes and ears open, and you'll learn something!" —Overheard in the elevator of a New York City apartment building

Keep your nose clean. Stay out of trouble. Maintain the appearance of good behavior. The proverb has been traced back to *Tragedy in E Flat* by L. R. Gribble (1938). First attested in the United States in *The Grapes of Wrath* (1940) by John Steinbeck.

> **1940.** "Homicide," he said quickly. "That's a big word—means I killed a guy. Seven years. I'm sprung in four for keepin' my nose clean." —John Steinbeck, *The Grapes of Wrath*

> **1943.** "Keep your nose clean and you'll keep out of trouble." —Manning Long, *False Alarm*

> **1951.** "All you got to do is keep your nose clean and show you're a better man than Preem." —James Jones, *From Here to Eternity*

> **1974.** "Stay in touch and keep your noses clean," he warned. The Judge could be very unpredictable. —Carl Bernstein & Bob Woodward, *All the President's Men*

Keep your nose to the grindstone. Work hard. Persevere and be diligent in your work so you can get ahead. A grindstone is used to sharpen tools to make them more efficient. The proverb has been traced back to John Heywood's book of proverbs (1546). First cited in the United States in *Simple Cobler of Aggawam in America* (1647). *Get, have,* or *put* may substitute for *keep*.

1928. *Darrell:* He's pretty sure there's an opening—*(With a condescension he can't help)*—but you'll have to get your nose on the grindstone to make good with him. —Eugene O'Neill, *Strange Interlude*

1984. Don't just stand there, make something happen. It isn't easy, but if you keep your nose to the grindstone and work at it, it's amazing how in a free society you can become as great as you want to be. —Lee Iacocca with William Novak, *Iacocca*

1987. The masses are getting the nose-to-the-grindstone pep talk while the intelligentsia and Western audiences are thrown the bone of freer expression and a few freed dissidents. —*New York Times*

1993. "A person keeps their nose to the grindstone, works hard, pays their bills on time," Mrs. Patten said in a letter to Hillary Rodham Clinton. "Then when your health goes bad they kick you into the corner." —*New York Times*

Keep your powder dry. *See* PUT YOUR TRUST IN GOD, AND KEEP YOUR POWDER DRY.

Keeping up with the Joneses. Attempting to match one's neighbors' social and living standards. The precise origin of this saying is unknown, but in 1913 Arthur R. ("Pop") Momand adopted it as the title for a series of cartoons published in the New York *Globe* and other papers. Since Momand lived in an exclusive New York suburb, the title may have been prompted by his personal experience of trying to emulate his neighbors' elegant life style. Momand is largely forgotten now, but the phrase has become an irreplaceable American idiom.

1966. If we were going to "keep up with the Joneses," we would have to acquire overseas real estate, as other powers were doing. —Thomas A. Bailey, *The American Pageant*

1968. Keeping up with the Joneses was a full-time job with my mother and father. —Quentin Crisp, *The Naked Civil Servant*

1973. "I ended up in the joint because I wanted to keep up with the Joneses." —Jamey McDonald, quoted by Erickson, Crow, Zurcher, & Connett, *Paroled But Not Free*

1991. While Subaru "was never something to keep up with the Joneses with," Mr. Wackman said, referring to previous campaigns focusing on practicality and value, Wieden "went one step farther, and it was kind of gutsy on their part." —*New York Times*

1992. Demons named Jones set standards for the keeping-up competition. Since they usually lived next door, you rarely had a day off from the consumption stakes. When the Joneses bought a third TV set and a second car everybody else was expected to shell out pronto at the same rate. This was called "keeping up with Joneses." —Russell Baker, *New York Times*

1993. "There was a time when I wondered what I was going to do," Lindsey admits. "What we did was tighten our belts. We don't eat out much anymore, and we haven't bought a new car in more than five years, and for sure we don't try to keep up with the Joneses." —John Ehrlichman, *Parade*

Kids will be kids. *See* BOYS WILL BE BOYS.

Kill the goose that laid the golden egg. *See* DON'T KILL THE GOOSE THAT LAID THE GOLDEN EGG.

Kilroy was here. Anonymous graffito used especially during World War II by ordinary soldiers to mean "I was here." Nobody knows who the original Kilroy was. One theory has it that a shipyard inspector at Quincy, Massachusetts, named Kilroy used the tag to mark the cargo he had inspected. The saying probably originated around 1940 and was widely used by American and British troops all over the world. It was chalked on walls, sidewalks, windows, fences, and billboards wherever the troops were stationed. Russian soldiers had a similar tag: "Ivanov was here." Such graffiti were found on the walls of the German Reichstag in 1955. "Kilroy was here" reappeared during the Vietnam War.

1959. Really the writer doesn't want success.... He knows he has a short span of life, that the day will come when he must pass through the wall of oblivion, and he wants to leave a scratch on the wall—Kilroy was here—that somebody a hundred, or a thousand years later will see. —William Faulkner, quoted by John Bartlett, *Familiar Quotations*, Sixteenth Edition edited by Justin Kaplan

1993. Kilroy was here! That's right! Kilroy, the elusive G. I. Joe of WWII, was last seen at the Express Press picking up new letterheads and envelopes. In the 45–46 years since the war ended, Kilroy has been around here living quietly in this neck of the woods. —Ad for the Express Press, *Princeton Packet* (N.J.)

1995. The best-known single sentence to come out of America's part of World War II is not from a general's dispatch or a politician's speech. It is three words from a common soldier whose name stood for every soldier: "Kilroy was here." Nobody knows for sure if there was a Kilroy, but it doesn't matter; he was the universal American soldier, and the *here* where he declared himself to have been was any place where Americans fought, or waited to fight. —Samuel Hynes, *New York Times Book Review*

The king can do no wrong. In its primary sense, the proverb meant that the king is not subject to the same rule of law as his subjects; his pronouncements and behavior cannot be questioned. When *the king* is replaced by other words, such as *the boss* or a proper noun, it can mean that person is infallible, or incapable of wrongdoing, or above criticism. The Latin version of the legal principle's *Rex non potest peccare* ("The king can do no wrong"). The saying has been traced back to *England in the Reign of Henry VIII* (1538) by T. Starkey. First cited in the United States in *Winthrop Papers* (1647). "That the king can do no wrong is a necessary and fundamental principle of the English constitution," wrote Sir William Blackstone (1723–80) in his *Commentaries on the Laws of England* (1765–69).

> **1985.** Dear, sweet man—yet always he faced her with the attitude that Barbara Lavette could do no wrong, which was perhaps the main reason she had never married him. —Howard Fast, *The Immigrant's Daughter*

> **1989.** Like the other Salomon executives, Massey was flying high in 1985 on the back of a series of record earning quarters. These were not merely records for Salomon Brothers but records for all of Wall Street. He could do no wrong. From his description the firm could do no wrong. —Michael Lewis, *Liar's Poker*

> **1989.** Through most of 1988 Mr. Cisneros's love affair with Linda Medlar, a former political fundraiser, produced constant gossip here.... But Mr. McDermott offered a warning: "Henry's popularity is still enormous, and the worst thing that could happen is for him to start thinking that the king can do no wrong." —*New York Times*

> **1991.** "He's your husband, it's your duty to warn him. Eleanor Butler thinks he can do no wrong...." —Alexandra Ripley, *Scarlett*

> **1993.** The old "China lobby," which in the 1950s owned Congress in the name of Chiang Kai-shek and forbade American contact with the mainland, has been supplanted by the "China can do no wrong" lobby. Equally conservative and Republican, but just as pathologically committed in the other direction. —*Times* (Trenton)

The king has no clothes on. *See* THE EMPEROR HAS NO CLOTHES ON.

The king is dead—long live the king. According to Sir William Blackstone (1723–80), "The king never dies." In this spirit, the traditional English announcement of the death of a king includes the announcement of his heir's advent to the throne. The sentence is sometimes adapted to describe similar changes: *King Coffee is dead—long live King Coffee* (James Brooke, 1993), *Tonality Is Dead: Long Live Tonality* (Michael Beckerman, 1994).**

> **1993.** Booted bosses, ornery owners, and beefed-up boards reflect a shift in corporate power. The imperial CEO has had his day—long live the shareholders. —*Fortune*

> **1994.** SMALLPOX IS DEAD. LONG LIVE SMALLPOX. —Headline of an article on the dangers of preserving the smallpox virus, *New York Times Magazine*

Knock, and it shall be opened unto you. *See* ASK, AND IT SHALL BE GIVEN YOU; SEEK AND YOU SHALL FIND; KNOCK, AND IT SHALL BE OPENED UNTO YOU.

Knowledge is power. Knowledge is a tool that can be used to control and change the world. The idea is found in the Old Testament. Many authorities attribute this aphorism to British philosopher Francis Bacon (1597): *Nam et ipsa scientia potestas est.* However, a similar phrase was used by Shakespeare in *Henry VI* (1591). First attested in the United States in 1806. The proverb takes varying forms: *Knowledge brings power; Knowledge gives a man power; Knowledge itself is power; Knowledge is power, and power is success*, etc. *Knowledge is power, if you know it about the right person* and *When dealing with warranty repairs, knowledge is power* are recent humorous variants.

> A man of knowledge increaseth strength. —Proverbs 24:5, *Authorized Version*, 1611

> **1876.** Of a truth, Knowledge is power, but it is a power reined by scruple, having a conscience of what must be and what may be.... —George Eliot, *Daniel Deronda*

> **1943.** "Bacon wrote: Knowledge is power. Bacon was thinking of knowledge of the mechanisms of the external world. Shakespeare wrote: Self-knowledge is power. Shakespeare was thinking of the mechanisms of the spirit, to which the mechanisms of the external world, including other persons, are instruments." —Robert Penn Warren, *At Heaven's Gate*

> **1953.** "And I said, patting your hand, 'What if I

give you trench mouth?' and you shrieked, 'Knowledge is Power!' " —Ray Bradbury, *Fahrenheit 451*

1987. Knowledge is not in itself power, and though it is not in itself vulnerable to power, those who seek it and possess it most certainly are. —Allan Bloom, *The Closing of the American Mind*

1990. Knowledge is the most democratic source of power. —Alvin Toffler, *Powershift: Knowledge, Wealth, and Violence at the Edge of the 21st Century*

1992. Knowledge is power, but clandestine knowledge is power squared. —Letty Cottin Pogrebin, *New York Times Magazine*

1993. "Knowledge is power," she says, insisting that women need to learn more about breast cancer and its treatment in order to decide, along with their doctors, how to treat their own cases should they be diagnosed with the disease. —*AARP Bulletin*

See also IT'S NOT WHAT YOU KNOW, BUT WHO YOU KNOW; A LITTLE KNOWLEDGE (LEARNING) IS A DANGEROUS THING; MONEY IS POWER.

Lafayette, we are here. We are repaying our debt. Despite the official neutrality of the French government, the Marquis de Lafayette fought side by side with Washington's troops in the American Revolution. Nearly 150 years later, American troops under the command of General John Joseph Pershing (1860–1948) landed in France to defend their European allies against the Germans in World War I. On July 4, 1917, Colonel Charles E. Stanton (1859–1933), Pershing's delegate, said at the tomb of Lafayette in Paris: *Lafayette, nous voila!* These words are sometimes attributed to Pershing himself, but he denied having said "anything so splendid." In World War II, American soldiers in France recycled the phrase as "Lafayette, we are here again."

1917. Lafayette, we are here. —Colonel Charles E. Stanton, *New York Tribune*

1966. The Allied forces rolled irresistibly toward Germany, and many of the Americans encountered places, like Château-Thierry, familiar to their fathers in 1918. "Lafayette, we are here again," proclaimed some of the American soldiers jocosely. —Thomas A. Bailey, *The American Pageant*
See also ONE GOOD TURN DESERVES ANOTHER.

The land of the free and the home of the brave. Epithet of the United States. The line is taken from "The Star-Spangled Banner," written by American lawyer and poet Francis Scott Key and first published in the *Baltimore Patriot* on September 20, 1814. National anthem of the United States since March 3, 1931. In 1992, a sign protesting the presence of nearly 200 FBI agents and police officers who had surrounded the Idaho cabin of white separatist Randy Weaver: LAND OF THE FREE????HOME OF THE BRAVE 800 ARMED GOV'T "SOLDIERS" AGAINST ONE AMERICAN FAM-

ILY. A 1993 ad for British Airways offered: "See the land of the free for free. Fly British Airways from the USA to any country we serve, and we'll fly you for free on a holiday in the USA." R. J. Reynolds protested anti-smoking legislation with a 1994 ad that asked: "Where Exactly *Is* the Land of the Free?"

1814. And the star-spangled banner in triumph shall wave
O'er the land of the free and the home of the brave!
—Francis Scott Key, "The Star-Spangled Banner"

1922. Well now, look at that. And America they say is the land of the free. —James Joyce, *Ulysses*

1966. We must remember that America was founded and built by generations of nonconformists. We must not permit truth and thought to become captives in the Land of the Free. —Thomas Bailey, *The American Pageant*

1988. "Hey, Castellano. Welcome back to the land of the free and the home of the brave." —Erich Segal, *Doctors*

1922. ... they [the native-born sons and daughters of immigrants] would never be *true* Americans here in this land of the free and home of the brave, they would forever and merely remain wops, polacks, spics, micks, or niggers. —Ed McBain, *Kiss*

1993. America is the land of the free, the home of the brave, the golden opportunity, the chicken in every pot—all of those things. —*Lear's*

1995. AGAIN, BOMBS IN THE LAND OF THE FREE —Headline of an article about the Oklahoma City bombing, *New York Times*

The land was ours before we were the land's. Even before the American Revolution, the land belonged to the colonists, not England. The saying was coined by poet Robert Frost (1874–1963) in 1942.**

1942. The land was ours before we were the
land's;
She was our land more than a hundred
years
Before we were her people.
—Robert Frost, "The Gift Outright"

1965. ... from memory he [Robert Frost] recited
The Gift Outright —"The land was ours before we
were the land's"—changing the last line:

Such as we were we gave ourselves outright
(The deed of gift was many deeds of war)
The land vaguely realizing westward,
But still unstoried, artless, unenhanced,
Such as she was, such as she *will* become.
—Arthur M. Schlesinger, Jr., *A Thousand
Days*

The last drop makes the cup run over. One
can only tolerate so much before the situation becomes unbearable. The proverb has been traced
back to *The Church History of Britain* (1655) by
English clergyman and historian Thomas Fuller
(1608–61). In its current form, it has been attested
in H. G. Bohr's *Handbook of Proverbs* (1855). The
adage is found in varying forms: *The last drop
makes the cup turn over; The last drop wobbles,
the cup flows over; The last drop makes the bucket
overflow,* etc. It has counterparts in other languages: *C'est la goutte d'eau qui fait déborder le
vase* (French); *La última gota es la que hace rebo-
sar el vaso* (Spanish); *Der letzte Tropfen, der den
Krug* (or *Eimer*) *überfließen läßt* (German); Посл-
едняя капля, переполнившая чашу (Russian).

1992. If you mention Perot's name again, I'll go
ballistic. My cup is filling and will soon run over.
—Overheard at a Philadelphia mall

1994. NY's cup running over; Stanley's the least of
it —*Crain's New York Business*
See also IT'S THE LAST STRAW THAT BREAKS THE
CAMEL'S BACK.

The last of the Mohicans. The last surviving
representative of a group; the last of anything. Title of a novel by James Fenimore Cooper (1826).
Refers to the novel's main character, the Indian
chief Uncas.

1985. "I am the last of the Mohicans in my family," says a businessman who was running a mid-
western machinery company. With no one to pass
the reins to, he sold the company's operating

assets a decade ago for more than $100 million.
—*Forbes*

1988. Now seeking a fourth Senate term at age 57,
he [Lowell Weicker] is again running as the last
Mohican of GOP liberalism. —*Wall Street Journal*

1991. "I'm sort of one of the last of the Mohicans,"
she [Claudette Colbert] said. —*New York Times*

1994. "We're the last of the Mohicans," says flag-
man Randy Heald as he climbs aboard a bright orange caboose. Most railroads have retired their ca-
booses, but union contracts still require them on
25% of Central Vermont trains. —*Wall Street Journal*

The last straw will break the camel's back.
See IT'S THE LAST STRAW THAT BREAKS THE CAMEL'S
BACK.

**Laugh and the world laughs with you;
weep and you weep alone.** Put on a happy
face: people are attracted by laughter but repelled
by tears. Coined by the popular American poet
Ella Wheeler Wilcox (1850–1919) in "Solitude"
(1883) and later set to music by Louis Gottschalk
(1829–69). However, a similar idea was expressed
by the Roman poet Horace (65–8 b.c.): *Ut ridenti-
bus arrident, ita flentibus adsunt humani voltus*
("Human faces laugh seeing those who laugh, and
correspondingly weep seeing those who weep").
The word *cry* can substitute for *weep*.

1883. Laugh and the world laughs with you;
Weep, and you weep alone;
For the sad old earth must borrow its mirth,
But has trouble enough of its own.
—Ella Wheeler Wilcox, "Solitude," *New York
Sun*

1907. Laugh, and the world laughs with you;
weep, and they give you the laugh. —O. Henry,
"The Trimmed Lamp"

1957. "Regret handkerchief tone of letter: Laugh
and the world laughs with you. Weep and you
weep alone." —John Cheever, *The Wapshot Chronicle*

1992. Street Tip. Laugh and the world laughs with
you. Cry and you get a federal bailout. —*Wall
Street Journal*

Laughter is the best medicine. Humor can
provide a temporary respite from one's ills. In recent years, the proverb has been shown to be literally true—laughter stimulates the release of
healing chemicals in the brain. One cancer patient
claimed to have overcome his disease by taking liberal doses of "I Love Lucy."

"Laughter, the Best Medicine" —Title of a regular feature in the *Reader's Digest*

1994. If laughter was really the best medicine, doctors would have found a way of charging for it. —Joey Adams, "Strictly for Laughs," *New York Post*

Lead with one's chin. *See* DON'T LEAD WITH YOUR CHIN.

Learn from the mistakes of others. Other people's errors can serve as a model of what not to do and help you foresee the same pitfall. The proverb was used by Chaucer around 1374. *Others* may be replaced by different words.

1982. Learn from the mistakes of others —you can never live long enough to make them all yourself. —*Bits & Pieces*

1986. He never learned a single thing from his mistakes. —Pat Conroy, *The Prince of Tides*

1991. Learn from the mistakes of others. You won't live long enough to make them all yourself. —Jane Bryant Quinn, *Making the Most of Your Money*

1993. A good day to evaluate your goals and methods. Learn from past mistakes. —Jeane Dixon, "Horoscope," *Times* (Trenton)

See also DON'T MAKE THE SAME MISTAKE TWICE.

Least said, soonest mended. Apologies are useless and any discussion will only make things worse. The proverb has been traced back to *Remains of Early Poetry* (c.1460). Used by Cervantes in *Don Quixote* (1605–15). First cited in the United States in *William & Mary College Quarterly* (1698). The saying takes varying forms: *Least said, sooner mended; The least said, the easier mended; The less said, the sooner mended*, etc.

1605–15.
Little said is soon amended. —Cervantes, *Don Quixote*

1993. "The heart of a heartless world
is what's at stake." "Least said,
soonest mended."
—Elizabeth Macklin, *"Given the Questions,"*
New Yorker

1994. "What's that supposed to mean? You haven't uttered a word all night." ... "Less said, soonest mended." —Overheard at a Red Lobster restaurant in New Jersey

See also ACTIONS SPEAK LOUDER THAN WORDS; DEEDS, NOT WORDS.

Leave no stone unturned. Spare no effort to achieve your objective. According to Greek legend, a Persian general defeated at the battle of Plataea (477 b.c.) had hidden a great store of treasure in his tent. Polycrates the Theban searched everywhere in the tent to no avail. The oracle of Delphi told him "to leave no stone unturned." Thus he did, and thus the treasure was found. The saying can be found in *Heracleidae* (c. 428 b.c.) by Euripides (c.485–406 b.c.).

1914. If you are willing to let the matter drop I will make handsome provision for you both; if, instead, you choose to make trouble, to force this matter into the daylight, I shall leave no stone unturned to protect myself, to put as good a face on this matter as I can. —Theodore Dreiser, *The Titan*

1936. Religion forbade fornication on pain of hell fire but if the Church thought she was going to leave one stone unturned in saving Tara and saving the family from starving—well, let the Church bother about that. She wouldn't —Margaret Mitchell, *Gone With the Wind*

1989. "There is a genuine desire among many people who are strong supporters of Israel to make sure that we leave no stone unturned in the pursuit of peace," he continued. —*New York Times*

1993. "We are involved in a very, very in-depth investigation," country Prosecutor Harris Y. Cotton said at a morning news conference. "No stone will be left unturned." —*Times* (Trenton)

Leave well enough alone. Don't try to fix what is already adequate. Don't meddle in others' affairs. The maxim has been traced back to Chaucer's "Envoy to Burton" (c.1396). The idea, however, was expressed in ancient times by Aesop. "Why not let it alone?" was the favorite saying of the British prime minister Lord Melbourne (1779–1842). First cited in the United States in *Correspondence of Andrew Jackson* (1833). The proverb is found in varying forms: *Better let well enough alone; Leave well alone; Let well alone; Let well or ill alone*, etc. *Leave bad enough alone* is a humorous twist on the old saw.

1934. "I'm going to him," Nicole got to her knees. "No, you're not," said Tommy, pulling her down firmly. "Let well enough alone." —F. Scott Fitzgerald, *Tender Is the Night*

1936. Scarlett held her peace, for it was easier to let well enough alone, and life went on smoothly enough, on the surface. —Margaret Mitchell, *Gone With the Wind*

1960. I knew I had annoyed Miss Caroline, so I let

well enough alone and stared out the window until recess when Jem cut me from the covey of first-graders in the schoolyard. —Harper Lee, *To Kill a Mockingbird*

1962. Tall said no more, and so neither did Stein. He was willing enough to let well enough alone. —James Jones, *The Thin Red Line*

1984. "Let's leave well enough alone," she said. She covered it up. She didn't want any scandals. —Lee Iacocca with William Novak, *Iacocca*

1987. Not only does an SS officer drag a woman by her hair on the way to her fate worse than death but he also pauses to light a cigarette. Mr. Klimov can't leave bad enough alone. —*New York Times*

1991. "When you came to Charleston, you were backing me into a corner. Crowding me. You're doing it now. You can't leave well enough alone." —Alexandra Ripley, *Scarlett*

See also LET SLEEPING DOGS SLEEP; IF IT AIN'T BROKE DON'T FIX IT.

The leopard can't change its spots. Human nature is as fixed and unchanging as the spots on a leopard's skin. The phrase goes back to the Old Testament. It has been traced back in English to *First Examination of Anne Askewe* (1546) by English clergyman and author John Bale (1495–1563). First attested in the United States in *Complete Writings of Roger Williams* (1652). The saying is found in varying forms: *A leopard doesn't change his spots; A leopard never changes its spots; You can't change a leopard's spots*, etc.

Can the Ethiopian change his skin, or the leopard his spots? —Jeremiah, 13:23, *Authorized Version*, 1611

1936. He went about his campaign slowly, subtly, not arousing the suspicions of Atlanta by the spectacle of a leopard trying to change his spots overnight. —Margaret Mitchell, *Gone With the Wind*

1984. Today Charles F. Wittenstein, southern counsel and civil rights director for the Anti-Defamation League of B'Nai B'rith, here to observe the election, said in an interview, "We don't think the leopard [David Duke, former Ku Klux Grand Wizard] has changed his spots." —*New York Times*

1985. Friedman admits that it's often difficult to get the leopard to change its spots. But he believes that, for Type A people, modifying behavior is a key to avoiding heart attacks. —*Reader's Digest*

1988. "I couldn't change those any more than a zebra could change his stripes, but there may be mitigating circumstances why they should remain privately held beliefs rather than publicly ex-

pressed ones." —Robert Ludlum, *The Icarus Agenda*

1990. "As for our dictators, Hitler and Mussolini," Lamont wrote Lady Astor in 1937, "they don't seem to have changed their spots very much, but I seem to think that raging at them will do no good, and if there is a possibility of methods of appeasement, these are our only chance." —Ron Chernow, *The House of Morgan*

1991. Each time I was promoted, I had taken an oath to support and defend the Constitution of the United States. I meant those words, and I obeyed them. This tiger didn't change his stripes. —Oliver L. North, *Under Fire*

1992. "I'm not asking you to change your spots. I'm just asking you to take out the garbage." —Cartoon by Al Ross, *New Yorker*

1994. 'An elderly leopard' changes its spots by creating an alliance to expand into brand consulting. —*New York Times*

See also YOU CAN'T MAKE A SILK PURSE OUT OF A SOW'S EAR.

Less is more. Everything is more elegant, meaningful, and effective when reduced to its most essential form. The proverb was coined by English poet Robert Browning (1812–89) in 1855. Often attributed to Bauhaus architect Ludwig Mies van der Rohe (1886–1969), who pioneered the streamlined style. However, the idea was well known in ancient times. Hesiod (c.700 b.c.) is quoted as saying, "Fools, they do not even know how much more is the half than the whole."

1855. Well, less is more, Lucrezia: I am judged. —Robert Browning, *Andrea del Sarto*

1992. Decoration was banished: the bronze, travertine and glass spoke for themselves: "Less is more." —*Modern Maturity*

1993. For years, I used Warhol's illustrations from the Sunday Times, in my classes in drawing, commercial art and design, to show how, as the Bauhaus had proclaimed, Less is more. —Letters to the Editor, *New York Times Magazine*

1994. Less is more. Your coverage of Fashion Week was excellent. I enjoyed it immensely. The photo of beautiful Ivana Trump in her miniskirt made my day. —Letters to the Editor, *New York Post*

Let bygones be bygones. Forget the past and don't hold a grudge. The saying has been traced back to Robert Pitscottie's *Chronicles of Scotland* (1577): "Byganes to be byganes." In 1648, Sir Frances Nethersole used the "Let bygans be bygans" form, which is still current today. First cited in the United States in *Diary of Cotton Mather* (1710).

1889. Well, then, what are they waiting for? Why don't they leave? Nobody's hindering. Good land, I'm willing to let bygones be bygones, I'm sure. —Mark Twain, *A Connecticut Yankee in King Arthur's Court*

1922. … the aggrieved husband would overlook the matter and let bygones be bygones with tears in her eyes…. —James Joyce, *Ulysses*

1956. *Polo:* The old man's down in Garrity's. He wants to buy you a drink.
Johnny: Is he sore?
Polo: He says he wants bygones to be bygones.
—Michael Gazzo, *A Hatful of Rain*

1957. "Into every real friendship a little rain must fall. Let's pretend it was that, honey, shall we, let's pretend it was just a little rain. Let's go and get the men and drink a friendship cup and let bygones be bygones. Let's pretend it was just a little rain." —John Cheever, *The Wapshot Chronicle*

1970. "The Holocaust" was published in the summer of 1965. It had taken me all my life to become an overnight success. Now that I had spilled my blood in writing the book the vultures and parasites swarmed in to get their cut. Most notable was Lou Pepper, who was willing to let bygones be bygones. —Leon Uris, *QB VII*

1984. His [Henry Ford's] second alternative was to come over and say a few words. We could shake hands, and he could put his arm round me. This would be letting bygones be bygones. —Lee Iacocca with William Novak, *Iacocca*

1991. When Bhagwan Shree Rajneesh was arrested for some wrongdoing, the *Washington Post* editorialist Meg Greenfield was heard to murmur, "Let Bhagwans be Bhagwans," a play on *bygones* from Sir Francis Nethersole's 1648 "Let bygans be bygans." —William Safire, "On Language," *New York Times Magazine*

1992. All I am saying, to paraphrase John Lennon, is give baseball a chance. That's right. Bygones be bygones. It's a whole season. —George Vecsey, *New York Times*

1994. By creating a threat, Saddam makes possible his grand concession: If we will let bygones be bygones, he will not make war. —William Safire, *New York Times*

See also FORGIVE AND FORGET; LET THE DEAD BURY THE DEAD.

Let him stew in his own juice. He created the

problem, so let him suffer for it. The proverb has been traced back to about 1300. First attested in the United States in *Jonathan Belcher Papers* (1733). After the end of World War I, a great number of American soldiers were left behind in Europe. They were anxious to go home, and their common cry was, "Let Europe stew in her own juice." The same saying occurs in other languages: *mariner dans son jus* (French); *freir en su aceite* or *cocer en su propia salsa* (Spanish); *im eigenen Saft schmoren* (German); and вариться в собственном соку (Russian). *Brew, gravy, grease, piss, soup, kettle, anger,* etc., may be used instead of *juice.*

1966. As early as 1934 a spiteful Congress had passed the Johnson Debt Default Act, which prevented debt-dodging nations from borrowing further in the United States. If attacked again by aggressors, they could "stew in their own juice." —Thomas A. Bailey, *The American Pageant*

1975. She knew that Mike would be phoning her as soon as she arrived at the Connaught. This would give him another night of stewing.
Let him stew. —Jackie Collins, *The World Is Full of Divorced Women*

1984. But I was so enraged by what had happened that it's a good thing I found myself a new job right away. Otherwise, I might have burned myself out, just stewing in my own anger. —Lee Iacocca with William Novak, *Iacocca*

1988. Let the Kremlin leaders stew in the juices of an arms overhead four times the percentage of ours. —William Safire, *New York Times*

1993. "Banks have stewed in their own juices," said Mel Blake, a top strategist at Bank of Boston Corp. —*Washington Post*

Let him twist slowly, slowly in the wind. String him up, then leave him dangling helplessly. The allusion is to a lynching. This unpleasantly vivid figure of speech was originated by John Ehrlichman, one of President Nixon's closest advisers, in a telephone conversation with John Dean in March 1973.

1973. I think we ought to let him [Patrick Gray] hang there. Let him twist slowly, slowly in the wind. —John Ehrlichman, quoted by John Bartlett. *Familiar Quotations*

1992. Don't try forgetting your Social Security number though, or officious drones will clean your clock. Or is "hang you out to dry" the idiom I'm looking for? "Pump you up," maybe? Or could it be "leave you twisting slowly in the wind"? —Russell Baker, *New York Times*

1993. Washington is still gabbling: Was Bob Kerrey taking malicious pleasure in making Bill Clinton twist slowly, slowly, for two days, or was he that rarest of birds in Washington, a man with a conscience who had no price? —Mary McGrory, *Times* (Trenton)

Let him who is without sin cast (throw) the first stone. No one is perfect, we have no right to condemn others. According to the New Testament story, an adulteress was brought to Jesus for judgment. When he commanded that the first stone be cast by a sinless person, the crowd dispersed in shame.

So when they continued asking him, he lifted up himself, and said unto them, He that is without sin among you, let him first cast a stone at her. —John, 8:7, *Authorized Version,* 1611

1922. J. J. O'Molloy: My client, an innately bashful man, would be the last man in the world to do anything ungentlemanly which injured modesty could object to or cast a stone at a girl who took the wrong turning when some dastard, responsible for her condition, had worked his own sweet will on her. —James Joyce, *Ulysses*

1987. I am appalled at the arrogant and blatant disrespect with which the American media so unashamedly attack President Reagan.... So the president made a mistake. He has admitted his error. Are we going to dwell on it? Drag him through mud? What will that accomplish? To all those reporters craving for a story, I say: "Let him that is without sin among you cast the first stone." —Letters to the Editor, *Washington Times*

1989. In contrast to both Rockefeller and Trump, Milken had to work to get his riches rather than inheriting them. That doesn't mean he did it all legally, or that he deserved $550 million a year. But please: let he who is without massive material acquisition cast the first stone. —*New Republic*

1991. Only John McCain can be said to be clearly less culpable than Mr. Cranston. But considering the numerous free trips Senator McCain, the lone Republican to be investigated, and his family took at Mr. Keating's expense, it is doubtful that he is eager to cast the first stone at his colleague. —*New York Times*

1994. Casting the first stone, Oliver? ... Spice your history with a grain of salt, filmmaker Oliver Stone ("JFK") urged the graduating class at the University of California at Berkeley.... "Every night you see Dan Rather and his clones, trying to sell their version of events, repeated through channels A, B, C, D, E," he said. "I sometimes think the media has dreamed our history up. Please study the event in more depth and with more skepticism." —*New York Post*

See also JUDGE NOT, THAT YE BE NOT JUDGED; NOBODY IS INFALLIBLE; NOBODY IS PERFECT.

Let my people go. Deliver my people from slavery or harsh treatment. The phrase is from the Bible, when Moses told Pharaoh of God's command, "Let my people go." Pharaoh refused and God sent the plagues to afflict Egyptians. Only then did Pharaoh let the Jews out. It was Moses who led them out of Egypt on a journey that became known as Exodus. The saying is used in many circumstances in which people are being held against their will by an oppressive government.

And afterward Moses and Aaron went in, and told Pharaoh, Thus saith the Lord God of Israel, Let my people go, that they may hold a feast unto me in the wilderness. —Exod. 5:1, *Authorized Version,* 1611

1981. About 500 protesters including natives of Haiti chanting in Creole, "Let my people go," gathered yesterday in a peaceful protest outside a refugee detention center here. —*Boston Globe*

1987. WITH CRIES OF 'LET MY PEOPLE GO,' 200,000 RALLY FOR SOVIET JEWRY —Headline, *Boston Globe*

Let nature take its course. Don't try to change what seems logical and inevitable; it's folly to meddle with the laws of the universe. Used both literally and figuratively. The proverb has been traced back to *Beryn* (c.1400). First attested in the United States in *Margaret* (1845). *Nature will have its course* is a variant.

1580. Let us permit nature to have her way; she understands her business better than we do. —Montaigne, *Essays*

1991. I'm not going to abort my pregnancy. Let nature take its course. —Overheard at a HIP clinic in New Jersey

1993. "Any time one comes up with a structural response to a problem, there are those who say there's a natural response, that nature should take its course." —*Times* (Trenton)

Let not your left hand know what your right hand does. *See* NEVER LET YOUR LEFT HAND KNOW WHAT YOUR RIGHT HAND IS DOING.

Let sleeping dogs lie. Don't ask for trouble by stirring up a potential source of grief. The proverb has been traced back to Chaucer's *Troilus and*

Criseyde (c.1374): "It is nought good a slepyng hound to wake." The French version of that era was: *N'esvellez pas lou chien qui dort* ("Don't wake a sleeping dog"). In 1546, it was included in John Heywood's book of proverbs. English Prime Minister Robert Walpole (1676-1745) preferred the Latin: *Quieta non movere* ("Don't disturb the peace"). First attested in the United States in *Mystery of the 13th Floor* (1919) by L. Thayer. *It is best to let a sleeping dog sleep* is a variant.

1849. Let sleeping dogs lie—who wants to rouse 'em? —Charles Dickens, *David Copperfield*

1936. He never mentioned Ashley and her love for him or made any coarse and ill-bred remarks about "coveting her." She thought it best to let sleeping dogs lie, so she did not ask for an explanation of their frequent meetings. —Margaret Mitchell, *Gone With the Wind*

1956. I deduced that Messrs. Truman and Chinigo had decided to let sleeping dogs lie. —*New Yorker*

1978. Joseph was very quiet. This must have been one of his difficult days. It was just as well; she wouldn't have to make conversation. If only sleeping dogs were allowed to lie! She had been feeling, for the last year or two, a welcome lightening of care—the natural result of Iris' good fortune—and in consequence she had been able to go for more than a week sometimes without even thinking of certain things. And now the sleeping dogs had been awakened. —Belva Plain, *Evergreen*

1993. LISTEN, DOCTOR, LET SLEEPING COUCH POTATOES LIE —Headline, Letters to the Editor, *New York Times*

1994. All through the debate about abortion and health care reform, many members of Congress have been talking about the status quo as if it were a peaceable kingdom in the abortion wars. They've described that "state" longingly as a utopia where sleeping dogs lie. Where boats don't rock. —Ellen Goodman, *The Star-Ledger* (Newark, N.J.)

See also LEAVE WELL ENOUGH ALONE; IF IT AIN'T BROKE, DON'T FIX IT.

Let the buyer beware. A legal principle stipulating that the seller of a product cannot be held liable for its quality after the deal has been struck. The onus is placed on the buyer to examine the product thoroughly beforehand. The maxim is often used in its Latin form: *Caveat emptor.* However, the principle was accepted as far back as the Code of Hammurabi (fl. 1792-1750 b.c.). The proverb has been traced back to *Book of Hus-*

bandry (1523) by J. Fitzherbert. First attested in the United States in *Essays on Field Husbandry in New England* (1758).

1966. The Hundred Days Congress passed the "Truth in Securities Act" (Federal Securities Act), which required promoters to transmit to the investors the fullest sworn information regarding the soundness of their stock and bonds. The New Dealers thus reversed the old adage to read: "Let the seller beware." —Thomas A. Bailey, *The American Pageant*

1989. The law of the bond market is: Caveat emptor. That's Latin for "buyer beware." —Michael Lewis, *Liar's Poker*

1991. "Let the buyer beware" is certainly the watchword when a sweepstakes postcard arrives bearing a 900 number. —*New York Times*

1992. In art, as on 14th Street, caveat emptor. —Letters to the Editor, *New York Times Magazine*

1993. CAVEAT EMPTOR —Headline of a Mobil ad about the dismal future of electric cars, *New York Times*

1994. Outlet stores, which sell name-brand merchandise at discounted prices, and off-pricers, such as T.J. Maxx and Marshalls, which feature irregular and closeout merchandise, are cashing in on bargain-conscious consumers. But, buyer beware: The prices at some outlets mimic the retailers. —*Princeton Living*

See also THE CUSTOMER IS ALWAYS RIGHT.

Let the cat out of the bag. *See* THE CAT IS OUT OF THE BAG.

Let the chips fall where they may. Disregard the consequences. Indicates that the speaker will go on with his actions despite someone's displeasure. The allusion is to the lumber industry: the woodcutter continues to hew and ignores any small chips that fly around as a result. The proverb was used by Senator Roscoe Conkling (1829-88) of New York in a speech supporting the nomination of Ulysses S. Grant for a third presidential term.

1880. He will hew to the line of right, let the chips fly where they may. —Roscoe Conkling, speech before the Republican National Convention

1946. I was a very thorough and well-trained research student. And truth was what I sought, without fear or favor. And let the chips fly. —Robert Penn Warren, *All the King's Men*

1963. And he took me down to what he called his "den" in order that he might "... call a spade a spade, and let the chips fall where they may." —Kurt Vonnegut, Jr., *Cat's Cradle*

1965. The incident provoked her into doing what she had never done before—abandon her duties. Let the mail fall where it may, this was news that Myrt must hear at once. —Truman Capote, *In Cold Blood*

1984. "I can't say that people at ABC might not be a little upset," Mr. Powell said. "But I thought you just have to say what you think needs to be said and let the chips fall." —*New York Times*

1986. I'd like to say something about my own role in all of this. I was aware of our Iran initiative and I support the President's decision. And I was not aware of and I oppose any diversion of funds, any ransom payments or any circumvention of the will of the Congress or the law of the United States of America.... And as the various investigations proceed, I have this to say: let the chips fall where they may. —George Bush, *New York Times*

1987. This is one area where Mr. Jacoby admits to a certain reckless disregard for practical consequences, saying that he has, perhaps foolishly, "let the chips fall where they may." —*New York Times*

1991. People who say "Let the chips fall where they may" usually figure they will not be hit by a chip. —Quoted in *Reader's Digest*
See also WHAT WILL BE, WILL BE.

Let the cobbler (shoemaker) stick to his last. See THE COBBLER SHOULD STICK TO HIS LAST.

Let the dead bury the dead. Look to the future and put the past behind you. Of Biblical origin. In the United States, it has been traced to *History of Cosmopolite* (1815) by L. Dow. First attested in England in *What Dare I Think?* (1931) by J. S. Huxley.

Follow me; and let the dead bury their dead. —Matthew, 8:22, *Authorized Version,* 1611

1960. "There's a black boy dead for no reason, and the man responsible for it's dead. Let the dead bury the dead this time, Mr. Finch. Let the dead bury the dead." —Harper Lee, *To Kill a Mockingbird*

1989. "Let the dead bury the dead," Burton Grimm had said, like so many people finding in the Bible a justification for what he wanted to do—and certainly it was a lot easier for the dead to bear guilt than for the living, so perhaps he wasn't wrong. —Michael Korda, *The Fortune*
See also LET BYGONES BE BYGONES.

Let the genie out of the bottle. To release an evil spirit or a new force; to invite the unexpected. Probably from *The Arabian Nights' Entertainments.* According to legend, King Solomon sealed *jinn* in bottles and threw them into the sea. A fisherman who found one of the bottles released the *jinni,* but then was unable to put it back in the bottle. Thus, *to put the genie back into the bottle* means to do the impossible, such as putting the toothpaste back into the tube.***

1950. But let me tell you, that to approach the stranger
Is to invite the unexpected, release a new force,
Or let the genie out of the bottle.
—T. S. Eliot, *The Cocktail Party*

1987. It has proved so easy and so convenient to lay the blame on Israel—to claim that "the Israelis made us do it"—instead of taking responsibility ourselves. This genie, once let out of the bottle, doesn't climb back in that easily. —*New York Times*

1989. Mr. Brzezinski believes that the death of Communism is now inevitable. The West can spur along the process of disintegration by promoting the cause of human rights, he suggests. And now that the genie of freedom has been released from the bottle of Communist totalitarianism, he says, it can't ever be forced back in. —*New York Times*

1991. "Rosemary thinks it's because he was gone for so long, then came back like a genie from a bottle and bought me everything in this house, bought her the pretty frocks she'd been longing for." —Alexandra Ripley, *Scarlett*

1993. "It is incredibly favorable," Majure said. Selling even a portion of a state-run company to the public, he said, forces the firm to operate more efficiently and in the public eye.... "It lets the genie out of its bottle," Majure said. —*Washington Post*

1994. We had sullied the future of generations to come, we had introduced into the equation something we could never control and put back into the bottle again. —Ossie Davis, quoted in *Modern Maturity*

Let them eat cake. Said to show contempt for the plight of those less fortunate than the speaker. Often attributed to Marie Antoinette (1755–93). According to legend, when the notoriously extravagant queen of France was told that her subjects had no bread to eat, she replied: *Qu'ils mangent de la brioche* ("Let them eat cake"). However, Rousseau (1712–78) used the same phrase two or three years earlier. Marie Thérèse of Austria (1638–83), the wife of Louis XIV, and John Peckham, the archbishop of Canterbury (thirteenth century), are also sometimes credited with its coinage. But the lineage of this expression appears to be even longer. Zhu Muzhi traces it to an ancient Chinese emperor who, being told that his subjects didn't have enough rice to eat, replied, "Why don't they eat meat?"

1781–88. At length I recollected the thoughtless saying of a great prince, who, on being informed that the country people had no bread, replied, "Let them eat cake." —Rousseau, *Confessions*

1980. *Let 'em eat wrappers.* Thirteen cents of the average food dollar go for packaging. Three cents go for advertising and promotion. —Mike Feinsilber & William B. Mead, *American Averages*

1984. "What will be done with the people who lack bread for themselves?"
"Let them eat cake," he said calmly. "Man does not live by bread alone." —Joseph Heller, *God Knows*

1988. WEDDING ROYALE: LET 'EM EAT CAKES. —Headline, *Women's Wear Daily*

1991. LET 'EM EAT BAIT —Ad for Raid roach bait, *People*

1992. "What about the poor guy who runs for President and hasn't got a nickel?" his conscience persisted. "It's like you're saying to the people 'let 'em eat cake.' " —Campaign ad for Edward Patterson, *New York Observer*

1994. What does she care about an increase in property taxes? She cares nothing at all since she is eligible for Farm Tax Assessment! ... And just what is Gov. Whitman's response to all of these educational concerns? She says to cut the fat out of the school's budgets.... This is the equivalent of Marie Antoinette's "Let them eat cake!" response. —Letters to the Editor, *Times* (Trenton)

Let there be light. The saying first appeared in the Old Testament to refer to God's creation of the universe out of the void.

And God said, Let there be light: and there was light. —Genesis, 1:3, *Authorized Version*, 1611

1977. In the beginning God created Man, which, according to all the latest birth control statistics, was a big mistake.... And Man said, "Let there be light," and there was light.... —Art Buchwald, *Down the Seine and Up the Potomac*

1993. Let there be light! Mari-Lou Nania said "Let's light a landmark" in 1992. And today, lights shine from the facade and steeple of the historic 131-year-old Trinity Episcopal Church in Southport, Conn. —*Daily Times* (White Plains, N.Y.)

Let well enough alone. *See* LEAVE WELL ENOUGH ALONE.

Let's all hang together or we shall surely hang separately. *See* WE MUST INDEED ALL HANG TOGETHER, OR, MOST ASSUREDLY, WE SHALL ALL HANG SEPARATELY.

Let's cross that bridge when we come to it. Don't get ahead of yourself; deal with each problem as it arises. The proverb has been traced back to American poet Henry Wadsworth Longfellow (1850). First attested in England in *Household Tales* (1895) by S. D. Addy. It can be found in varying forms: *Don't cross the bridge before you reach it; Don't cross the bridge till you come to it; Never cross the bridge until you find it,* etc.

1850. Don't cross the bridge till you come to it,
Is a proverb old, and of excellent wit.
—Henry Wadsworth Longfellow, "The School of Salerno," *The Golden Legend*

1936. Just what the loser would do, should Scarlett accept either one of them, the twins did not ask. They would cross that bridge when they came to it. —Margaret Mitchell, *Gone With the Wind*

1939. *Father:* Then where will you get the twenty-five dollars to pay that poor girl for her whistling?
Vinnie: Now, Clare, let's not cross that bridge until we come to it.
—Howard Lindsay & Russel Crouse, *Life with Father*

1981. "I want to be able to be proud of what we have, not afraid of who might find out."
"We'll cross that bridge later." —Danielle Steel, *Palomino*

1982. *Don't Cross Your Bridge Before ... You Pay the Toll* —Title of a book by Judith Frost Stark

1989. "We believe the show, based on its artistic merits, seems to be just right," he said, "and our feeling was that if President Nixon were to sue, we'd cross that bridge if we came to it." —*New York Times*

1992. Asked what Mr. Ferrer would do if Ms. Segarra did not resign, Mr. Roswell said, "We'll cross the bridge when we get to it." —*New York Times*

1994. When pressed about how he would respond if the Rangers did not sign him in the upcoming week, Messier had little to say.... "I guess I'll have to cross that bridge when I come to it," he said....

—*New York Times*
See also ONE DAY AT A TIME; ONE THING AT A TIME.

Let's face it. Let's be brutally honest now. Often said before stating some truth one would prefer not to acknowledge. Used by American composer and lyricist Cole Porter (1891–1964) as the title of a Broadway musical (1941). The phrase has been in common usage since the 1970s. Sometimes shortened to *face it.*

1973. "Yes! Right! Leftovers from that [Peace Corps], and God knows what else, and social workers and teachers and even some ministers, and even some priests, and let's face it, Marvin, some loud-mouthed members of your own profession—who did *not* graduate from Harvard Law—and, to come right close to home, not to spare anyone at all, let's face it, the sons of certain prominent men who should know better—and I do mean your neighbor Jackson Dawe—" —Joyce Carol Oates, *Do with Me What You Will*

1982. Face it, most people are too timid to speak up and renounce the rascal who fouls the air. —Abigail Van Buren, *The Best of Dear Abby*

1984. "Let's face it," I said. "The subway is just a showpiece for the capital." —Lee Iacocca with William Novak, *Iacocca*

1987. Evelyn leaned out her window and calmly said, "Let's face it, honey, I'm older than you are and have more insurance than you do" and drove away. —Fannie Flagg, *Fried Green Tomatoes*

1992. "If one has to get in, let it be Clinton," came the voice of a retiree, Patricia Eisner, who until Thursday was a Perot supporter. "I want to believe what Clinton says because it sounds great. But face it, none of them would say what you wouldn't want to hear. They'd be a fool." —*New York Times*

1994. "They tried to make a glamour girl out of me," the brown-haired, blue-eyed actress [Martha Raye] complained. "Let's face it, I'm not a glamour girl. I'm a clown." —*New York Times*

Let's get America moving again. Let's work together to improve the lot of all Americans. Coined by President John F. Kennedy in 1960. The saying has been used ever since.***

1966. Kennedy's "get America moving" theme, with its call to action and sacrifice, struck a rather depressing note of self-disparagement. —Thomas A. Bailey, *The American Pageant*

1992. Bill Clinton and I want to get our country moving forward again, put our people back to work and create a bright future for the United States of America. —Al Gore, Debate among Quayle, Gore, and Stockdale, *New York Times*

Let's get it off the ground. Let's get it (a plan, idea, program, project, etc.) started. *To get something off the ground* and *to get off the ground* are both used as figures of speech.

1984. Maybe the one thing you need to get off the ground is the Touchscreen Personal Computer. —*Forbes*

1988. I've had a wonderful life and have been awarded many times over by meeting parents whose children have been helped through research. The most gratifying experience is getting this community foundation off the ground. —George Hitchings, co-winner of the Nobel Prize for medicine, *Philadelphia Inquirer*

1989. If the mortgage department were forced to work with the government department, he [Bill Simon] said, "the mortgage market would never get off the ground; it would be subjugated." —Michael Lewis, *Liar's Poker*
See also LET'S GET THE SHOW ON THE ROAD.

Let's get the show on the road. Let's get moving. Let's put our plan, idea, program, project, etc., into effect. Originally used by American theater company owners to urge actors to prepare for a tour. This show business phrase dates to 1910 and has been in common use since 1930.

1951. "Come on, come on," Prew said. "Whats holding things up? Lets get this show on the road." —James Jones, *From Here to Eternity*

1981. "Work up some storyboards with Charlie and let's see if we can get this show on the road." —Danielle Steel, *Palomino*

1985. "What the hell kept you? I've been waiting for hours."
"Hey, I'm right on time. I had a class till noon. What's the matter with you? C'mon, let's get the show on the road." —Erich Segal, *The Class*

1986. Barnes spotted the interpreter squatting, talking to a gaggle of kids, and shouted to get the show on the road. —Dale A. Dye, *Platoon*

1988. For one thing, it [the Shultz plan] provides that issues not resolved in the face-to-face talks be referred back to the conference. And while Shultz insists the conference will have no adjudicatory role, that's far easier said than done once the show is on the road. —*New York Post*

1992. During the fourth bow, the conductor leaned over to the pizza-box virtuoso and whispered:

"We've got a hit. Let's take this thing on the road." —*New York Times*

See also LET'S GET IT OFF THE GROUND.

Let's get to the bottom of it. Let's find the whole truth of what has happened. The word *bottom* has meant "ultimate cause" of something since the sixteenth century and was used in this sense by Shakespeare. "Then let's get to the bottom of this," says Margaret Mitchell in her *Gone with the Wind* (1936). *To get to the bottom of it* has become one of the most frequently used idiomatic expressions in the late twentieth century.

1983. Physicist Paul Davies of the University of Newcastle-upon-Tyne, England, has summed up the situation by saying, "It's all very scary, and one wishes the theorists would do a better job in getting to the bottom of it." —*Christian Science Monitor*

1986. "Much in this case is hard to understand, and all Americans are entitled to have their questions answered," the President [Reagan] said. "That's why I am determined to get to the bottom of this matter and to get all of the facts out." —*New York Times*

1988. Barbara Potter's underwear is getting more attention than her overheads. When you get down to the bottom of things, there was nothing to see but her game. —*Arizona Republic*

1988. It has been clear for some time that the jury will not be able to get to the bottom of the Brawley case. —*New York Times*

1998. Attorney General Janet Reno, mired in arcane election-law legalese, seems perpetually reluctant to appoint a special counsel to get to the bottom of questionable White House and congressional fund-raising. —*Christian Science Monitor*

1998. "We haven't had a prosecution in this state in the last years of Mr. Engler's administration of anybody with their hand in the till. Now, it is inconceivable to me that we have no graft, that nobody has their hand in the till in this state. And I [Geoffrey Fieger] am determined to get to the bottom of it." —*Detroit News*

Let's kill all the lawyers. The first step to a perfect society is to get rid of lawyers. The line comes from Shakespeare's *Henry VI, Part II,* and is uttered by one of the followers of Jack Cade, an ignorant lower-class demagogue who leads an insurrection against the king. Though it was not Shakespeare's intention, the line is usually quoted sympathetically.

1590–91.
Dick: The first thing we do, let's kill all the lawyers. —Shakespeare, *Henry VI, Part II,* IV, ii

1988. Nocturnal joggers on Avenue Louis Pasteur at the moment were startled to hear several lusty male voices bellowing from a third-floor window in Vanderbilt Hall, "Kill the lawyers!" —Erich Segal, *Doctors*

1991. In the spirit of Shakespeare's "The first thing that we do, Let's kill all the lawyers," I have this bit of advice for George Bush: First, fire Jack Kemp. —*Times* (Trenton)

1992. "Every one of us has had more than one of Shakespeare's lines thrown at us at some point," says Ms. Krummenacher, who keeps a plaque with the words "Let's kill all the lawyers," from "Henry VI, Part II," on her office wall. —*Wall Street Journal*

1994. DON'T KILL THE LAWYERS, JUST CUT THEIR BIG BILLS —Headline, *Crain's New York Business*

A liar is not believed when he tells (speaks) the truth. Once your credibility is lost, you can never regain it. The idea was expressed in ancient times by Aristotle (384–322 b.c.). The English proverb has been traced back to *Dictes and Sayings of Philosophers* (1477). The adage is found in varying forms: *If a liar tells the truth, he is also not believed; No one believes a liar when he tells (speaks) the truth; You can't believe a liar when he tells (speaks) the truth,* etc.

384–322 b.c.
Liars when they speak the truth are not believed. —Aristotle, quoted by Diogenes Laertius, *Lives of Eminent Philosophers*

1994. Wisdom is not often found in a fortune cookie, but after lunch in a Chinese restaurant, my fortune said, "A liar is not believed even though he tells the truth." ... Of course, I thought immediately of President Clinton. —*Star-Ledger* (Newark, N.J.)

See also HONESTY IS THE BEST POLICY; ONE LIE LEADS TO ANOTHER.

A liar should have a good memory. A liar must be able to keep track of the lies he has told, so he can keep his stories straight. The proverb is of Latin origin, *Mendacem memorem esse oportet* ("It is fitting that a liar should be a man of good memory") and was first recorded in this form by Quintilian (A.D. c. 35–c. 100). "He who has not a good memory," says Montaigne in his *Essays* (1580–95), "should never take upon him the trade of lying." First attested in the United States in Cotton Mather's *Magnalia Christi Americana: or the Ecclesiastical History of New England from its First Planting* (1702).

1922. Wonderful liar. But want a good memory. —James Joyce, *Ulysses*

1933. I'm not a good liar... but I have a good memory. —E.C. R. Lorac, *Murder*

1977. Don't tell any more lies than you've got to. They're a great strain on the memory. —E. X. Ferrars, *Blood Flies Upwards*

1990. They say a liar has to have a good memory. In that case, Mr. Reagan's testimony is proof of his honesty. —*Washington Times*

See also A LIAR IS NOT BELIEVED WHEN HE TELLS (SPEAKS) THE TRUTH; A LIE CAN GO AROUND THE WORLD AND BACK WHILE THE TRUTH IS LACING ITS BOOTS; ONE LIE LEADS TO ANOTHER.

A lie can go around the world and back while the truth is lacing up its boots. A lie spreads like wildfire, whereas the truth is revealed very slowly. In 1859, the English nonconformist preacher C. H. Spurgeon (1834–92) indicated that it was already "an old proverb." The phrase *lace up* is sometimes replaced with *pull up, put up*, or *tie up. A lie can travel round the world while the truth is tying up its shoestrings* is a variant form.

1859. If you want truth to go round the world you must hire an express train to pull it; but if you want a lie to go round the world, it will fly: it is as light as a feather, and a breath will carry it. It is well said in the old proverb, "a lie will go round the world while truth is pulling its boots on." —C. H. Spurgeon, *Germs from Spurgeon*

1993. Despite these facts, as Chief Seattle biographer David Buerge likes to say, "It was a case of the lie going a thousand miles while the truth was just putting on its boots." —*Reader's Digest*

1994. O. J. Simpson and his 'dream team' of lawyers are generating one lie after another while poor Marcia Clark is still lacing up her shoes. —Overheard at a public library in New Jersey

Lie down with dogs, get up with flies. See IF YOU LIE DOWN WITH DOGS, YOU'LL GET UP WITH FLEAS.

Life begins at forty. Middle age marks the start of a welcome new stage of life. Maturity is the best time of life. Generally attributed to American writer W. B. Pitkin (1878–1953).

1932. *Life Begins at Forty* —Title of a book by W. B. Pitkin

1937. "Life Begins at Forty" —Title of a song by Jack Yellen & Ted Shapiro, sung by Sophie Tucker

1990. Life may begin at 40, but so too does age discrimination, at least according to the law. —Daniel Moreau, *Take Charge of Your Career*

1991. All our age benchmarks, which used to seem solid as rocks, have turned into shifting sands. *Life Begins at 40?* More like *60. —New York Times*

1993. Life begins at 40, they used to say, but the average young person thinks 30 is over the hill. —Liz Smith, *Times* (Trenton)

1994. The final curtain would be looked upon not as an end, but as a bridge to a whole new life. After all, doesn't life begin at 40? —*Times* (Trenton)

Life is but a dream. Life is fleeting and evanescent. The proverb is found in print as early as 1874 in a poem written by English poet James Thomson (1834–82). The idea is also frequently expressed in the works of Shakespeare.

1874. For life is but a dream whose shapes return,
Some frequently, some seldom, some by night
And some by day.
    —James Thomson, "The City of Dreadful Night"

1911. Perhaps life is just that ... a dream and a fear. —Joseph Conrad, *Under Western Eyes*

1993. Zachary pauses, raises a fork over his diced cantaloupe and, clear as a bell, breaks into a tuneless song, "Merriree, merriree, merriree, merriree, life is but a dream." —*New York Times Magazine*

See also LIFE IS JUST A BOWL OF CHERRIES; LIFE IS NO BED OF ROSES; LIFE IS SHORT AND SWEET; LIFE IS TOO SHORT.

Life is hard by the yard, but by the inch life's a cinch. Take things one at a time or you'll be overwhelmed by life's difficulties. Move slowly but surely and you'll succeed.

1992. "Inch by inch, life's a cinch; yard by yard, life is hard," is another well-liked observation. —*Princeton Packet* (N.J.)

See also ONE DAY AT A TIME; ONE THING AT A TIME; SLOW AND STEADY WINS THE RACE.

Life is just a bowl of cherries. Life is sweet and easy, so don't take it too seriously. The saying originated in the United States in 1931 and was first heard in the Broadway show *George White's Scandals*. The lyrics of the song by that title were written by Lew Brown (1893–1958), with music by Ray Henderson (1896–1970), and it was introduced by Ethel Merman (1909–84). The word *but* may be used in place of *just*. The saying is often used with heavy irony. *If Life Is Just a Bowl of Cherries, What Am I Doing in the Pits* is the title of a book by Erma Bombeck (1978).

1978. Then she'd turn around and smile and never miss a note; and move into another song. Before you knew it, she'd be playing *Stars Fell on Alabama* or *Life Is Just a Bowl of Cherries,* and her tiny little feet would just fly over those pedals like butterflies! —Fannie Flagg, *Fried Green Tomatoes*

1990. When he was young and still wet behind the ears, he thought that life was just a bowl of cherries. Well, they're sour now. —Overheard on a Washington-bound train

Life is no bed of roses. Life is not always ease, pleasure, and happiness. The proverb was first cited in the United States in *Correspondence of the American Revolution* (1780). Attested in England in *The Corpse with the Grimy Glove* (1938) by R. A. J. Walling.

1966. The laboring man himself had no bed of roses. —Thomas A. Bailey, *The American Pageant*

1979. "Did it ever occur to you that my life has been no bed of roses, that I've messed it up as much as one human being can mess things up?" —Howard Fast, *The Establishment*

1984. But don't ever get the idea He made things easy for me. Life as one of God's chosen has never been a bed of roses. —Joseph Heller, *God Knows*

1994. Of course, life with the emotionally scarred queen of television [Rosanne] is probably no bed of rosey—er, roses. —Liz Smith, *Times* (Trenton)
See also LIFE ISN'T ALL BEER AND SKITTLES.

Life is short and sweet. The brevity of life makes its pleasures all the more intense. Originated in the United States in *Port Folio* (1802). First attested in England in *Fortune Speaking* (1931) by H. C. Bailey. *Life is sweet* is a variant.

1981. Charlie's approach to life was always so damn practical.
"It's not that simple."
"Why not? Look, Sam, life is very short and can be very sweet if you let it." —Danielle Steel, *Palomino*

1991. Life is short. So make it sweet. Treat yourself to the grandeur of a transatlantic voyage on the QE2. —Ad for Cunard, *New York Times*
See also ART IS LONG, LIFE IS SHORT; LIFE IS TOO SHORT; LIFE IS WHAT YOU MAKE IT.

Life is short, art is long. *See* ART IS LONG, LIFE IS SHORT.

Life is too short. Make the most of your time before it's too late. Don't let opportunities to enjoy life pass you by. The proverb has analogues in the Bible. *Life is too short to be little; Life is too short to fool with dishonest people;* and *Life is too short to waste time on trifles* are variants.

1976. It's hard work but it's fun. I say to people who work for me, I want to make some money and I want you to make some money, but let's have fun too. Life is too short not to. —Claudia Jessup and Genie Chipps, *The Woman's Guide to Starting a Business*

1979. "Gibbs," asked Gilmore, "have you ever heard of Ralph Waldo Emerson?"
"No."
"He was a writer, and he made a statement you and me live by. Emerson said, 'Life is not so short that there is not always time for courtesy.'" —Norman Mailer, *The Executioner's Song*

1987. She was sitting next to the end of the left side in the second row, and so it was a little awkward, perhaps even a little obvious. But life is short! —Tom Wolfe, *The Bonfire of the Vanities*

1991. "Sometimes I put my hands out like a scale," he says. "I ask myself: How much does this problem matter? I think of a friend of mine who was killed in a plane crash. 'Life is too short,' I can hear her say." —*Fortune*

1992. Mickey Rooney, the 5-foot-3-inch actor, who titled his autobiography "Life Is Too Short," said, "Mickey Rooney is supporting Perot." —*New York Times*
See also ART IS LONG, LIFE IS SHORT; EAT, DRINK, AND BE MERRY, FOR TOMORROW WE DIE; GATHER YE ROSEBUDS WHILE YE MAY. LIFE IS BUT A DREAM; LIFE IS WHAT YOU MAKE IT; SEIZE THE MOMENT.

Life is what you make it. We are all the architects of our own lives. The proverb has been traced back to William James (1842–1910), who wrote in 1897: "Life is worth living, we can say, since it is what we make it, from the moral point of view." First attested in the United States in *Trap for Bellamy* (1941).

1988. "Life here is what you make it. Like in the West." —Nelson DeMille, *The Charm School*

1992. I like these words a Florida reader found on a community bulletin board: "Life is not what you make it, but what you make out of what it brings to you." —Malcolm Boyd, *Modern Maturity*

See also LIFE IS HARD BY THE YARD, BUT BY THE INCH LIFE'S A CINCH.

Life isn't all beer and skittles. Life is not all play; one also has to work. *Skittles* is a British game similar to bowling. Thus, the phrase *beer and skittles* suggests the leisure-time activities of working men. The proverb has been traced back to Dickens', *Pickwick Papers* (1836). It has been current in its present form since 1857 when it was used in *Tom Brown's Schooldays* by Thomas Hughs. First attested in the United States in *Nature and Human Nature* (1855) by Thomas Chandler Haliburton. The word *wholly* may substitute for *all.*

> **1836.** *They* don't mind it; it's a regular holiday to them—all porter and skittles. —Charles Dickens, *Pickwick Papers*

> **1857.** Life isn't all beer and skittles, but beer and skittles, or something better of the same sort, must form a good part of every Englishman's education. —Thomas Hughs, *Tom Brown's Schooldays*

> **1872.** Life is with such all beer and skittles;
> They are not difficult to please
> About their victuals.
>   —Charles Stuart Calverley, "Contentment"

> **1894.** Life ain't all beer and skittles, and more's the pity. —George du Maurier, *Trilby*

> **1993.** I'm trying to teach my husband that life is not all beer, skittles, and football. —Overheard at a barbecue in Princeton Junction, N. J.

See also LIFE IS NO BED OF ROSES.

Life, liberty, and the pursuit of happiness. The three most important rights enjoyed by Americans. The phrase was coined by Thomas Jefferson in the Declaration of Independence.

> **1776.** We hold these truths to be self-evident, that all men are created equal, that they are endowed by their Creator with certain unalienable rights, that among these are life, liberty, and the pursuit of happiness. —Thomas Jefferson, Declaration of Independence

> **1951.** "Every man's supposed to have certain rights."
> "Certain inalienable rights," Starks said, "to liberty, equality, and the pursuit of happiness. I learnt it in school, as a kid." —James Jones, *From Here to Eternity*

> **1986.** "Let us shout the words of Thomas Jefferson in the Declaration of Independence. Let us shout those words as they come to our doors: 'Whenever any form of government becomes destructive of these ends—life, liberty, and the pursuit of happiness—it is the right of the people to alter or abolish it, and to institute new government.'" —Pat Conroy, *The Prince of Tides*

> **1988.** Hollis said to them, "Do you understand that you have no more rights to life, liberty, and the pursuit of happiness than any prisoner here?" —Nelson DeMille, *The Charm School*

> **1992.** Ms. Clinton has already advanced women's rights. Her presence will remind us that the Founding Fathers guaranteed Americans more than life and liberty. They promised us the pursuit of happiness, too. —Susan Faludi, *New York Times*

> **1994.** IT'S TIME FOR LIFE, LIBERTY, THE PURSUIT OF RETIREMENT —Headline, *Philadelphia Inquirer*

See also ALL MEN ARE CREATED EQUAL.

Lift yourself up by your own bootstraps. *See* DON'T TRY TO PULL YOURSELF UP BY YOUR OWN BOOTSTRAPS.

The light at the end of the tunnel. *See* THERE'S ALWAYS A LIGHT AT THE END OF THE TUNNEL.

Lightning never strikes twice in the same place. An unusual event never occurs twice under the same circumstances or to the same person. The proverb has been traced back to P. H. Myers (1857). First attested in the United States in *The Man in Lower Ten* (1909) by American writer Mary Roberts Rinehart (1876–1958). *Lightning never strikes twice in the same place except it forgets where it struck last* is a variant. The word *seldom* or *rarely* may substitute for *never.*

> **1857.** Lightning never strikes twice in the same place, nor cannon balls either, I presume. —P. H. Myers, *Thrilling Adventures of the Prisoner of the Border*

> **1909.** Ghosts are like lightning; they never strike twice in the same night. —Mary Roberts Rinehart, *The Man in Lower Ten*

> **1991.** "How similar to the original will the sequel be? "I think lightning strikes twice in the same place very rarely," Mr. Zast said. "But we're not going to let them dictate the way our commercial appears." —*New York Times*

Like attracts like. Similar people and things are easily drawn to one another. The proverb has been traced back to *Scottish Legends* (1375). First cited in the United States in *Ladies Monitor* (1818). The word *attracts* may be replaced by *marries* or *mates.*

> **1936.** Someone else had said: "Like must marry

like or there'll be no happiness." —Margaret Mitchell, *Gone With the Wind*

1994. Do you recall the pleasure you had when you played with a magnet? As a youngster the magnet was magic. It drew to itself nails, needles and other pieces of steel. Yet, when you held it over a piece of wood or glass, it created no response. This teaches a lesson: "Like attracts like." —*Jewish Press* (N.Y.)

1995. They say that like attracts like. Small wonder that Hollywood's attracted so much trash. —Overheard at a New Brunswick, N.J., movie theater

See also BIRDS OF A FEATHER FLOCK TOGETHER.

Like begets like. *See* LIKE BREEDS LIKE.

Like breeds like. Offspring are often like their parents. Similar people have similar manners. The proverb has been traced back to *Sermons* (1557) by R. Edgeworth. First attested in the United States in *Chainbearer* (1845) by James Fenimore Cooper. The article *the* is sometimes inserted before *like* and *breed* is often replaced with *begets*.

> **1842.** Like men, like manners: Like breeds like, they say. —Alfred, Lord Tennyson, *Poems*

> **1994.** "Her Mother never sent thank-you notes either. I guess like breeds like." —Overheard at a Manhattan restaurant

See also IT'S IN THE BLOOD; LIKE FATHER, LIKE SON; LIKE MOTHER, LIKE DAUGHTER.

Like cures like. Desperate sicknesses must have desperate cures: poison is an antidote for poison. The Latin equivalent is *Similia similibus curantur.* Motto of homeopathic medicine, which was founded by the German physician C. F. S. Hahnemann (1755–1843).

> **1992.** They [pregnant women who were nauseated] were given ipecac (which is commonly used to cause vomiting), but told it was something that would cure their nausea. It did by both subjective and objective measures. Their belief was enough to override the known physical effect of ipecac. (This is not "like cures like"; the dose was not homeopathic.) —*New York Times Magazine*

Like father, like son. A son often resembles or takes after his father. In Latin: *Qualis pater talis filius* ("As is the father, so is the son"). The proverb has been traced back to *Psalter* (c.1340). First attested in the United States in *Almanacs* (1774). *Like Father, Like Son* is the title of a 1987 film starring Dudley Moore and Kirk Cameron. Af-

ter the bodies and personalities of the two are temporarily switched, they arrive at a greater understanding of their similarities and resolve their conflicts.

> **1980.** *Like Gatsby, like son.* On average, the higher your social class, the more you drink. So says the United States Government. —Mike Feinsilber & William B. Mead, *American Averages*

> **1985.** Interest in Roz, I well realized, meant marriage and nothing else. Well, I sometimes thought, okay, so be it, *a rabbi's a daughter.* Like father, like son. —Herman Wouk, *Inside, Outside*

> **1987.** In retirement in Florida, Abe keeps close watch on the son's activities and, predictably, returns to action. The conflict is multigenerational, having begun with Abe's father, who founded the firm, and presumably extending to Abe's grandson—like father like son like son. —*New York Times*

> **1991.** The television evangelist Jimmy Swaggart declared the performance "an abomination," but the Reagans applauded Ron's performance. "Like father, like son," said the President after someone explained the spoof to him. —Kitty Kelley, *Nancy Reagan*

> **1992.** LIKE FATHER, LIKE SONS —Headline of an article about a father-son team charged with conspiracy, *Newsweek*

See also THE APPLE DOESN'T FALL FAR FROM THE TREE; IT'S IN THE BLOOD; LIKE BREEDS LIKE; LIKE MOTHER, LIKE DAUGHTER.

Like marries like. *See* LIKE ATTRACTS LIKE.

Like mates like. *See* LIKE ATTRACTS LIKE.

Like mother, like daughter. Daughters tend to share their mother's physical and moral traits. The proverb has been traced back to about 1300. First cited in the United States in 1644.

> **1985.** "She takes her mother's side, which just goes to show how wrong Freud was about fathers and daughters. It's a case of like mother, like daughter—they're not the kind of women who forgive and forget, I'll tell you that." —Michael Korda, *Queenie*

> **1993.** LIKE MOTHER, LIKE DAUGHTER —Headline, *New York Times*

See also THE APPLE DOESN'T FALL FAR FROM THE TREE; IT'S IN THE BLOOD; LIKE BREEDS LIKE; LIKE FATHER, LIKE SON.

The lion shall lie down with the lamb. The powerful and dangerous will be tolerant of the poor and weak. The idea of the proverb is derived from the Old Testament: "The wolf also shall dwell with the lamb, and the leopard shall lie down with the kid; and the calf and the young lions and the fatling together; and a little child shall lead them" (Isa. 11:7). Since life does not provide us with a great number of examples of such idealistic human tranquility and friendship, the proverb is often used in the negative: *The lion does not lie down with the lamb.*

1989. Soviet President Mikhail Gorbachev, head of the world's oldest officially atheist state, will enter the historic center of Christianity on Friday and shake hands with Polish-born John Paul II, the century's most-outspoken, anti-communist pontiff. "The lion is lying down with the lamb..." —*Sun-Sentinel* (South Florida)

1994. The lion doesn't lie down with the lamb—probably because the lamb got swallowed by the boa constrictor—but there is an element of Eden in South America's rain forests. Plants from the region already treat some human ills, and the search goes on for exotic roots, stems, and berries that some say could restore mankind to a state of healthful bliss. —*Commercial Appeal* (Memphis, Tennessee)

1998. Only in Scripture does the lion lie down with the lamb. But how in my life? Can I dwell gently among God's creatures, particularly when I like to eat them? —*Sun-Sentinel* (South Florida)

See also EVERY CLOUD HAS A SILVER LINING; IT'S ALWAYS DARKEST BEFORE THE DAWN; IT'S AN ILL WIND THAT BLOWS NO (NOBODY) GOOD; WHERE THERE'S LIFE THERE'S HOPE.

A little bird told (whispered to) me. I won't name the source of my information. Usually used as an evasive answer to the question of how one learned something secret. The idea is of Biblical origin. The earliest form of the saying was included in John Heywood's collection of proverbs (1546). In 1583, Brian Melbancke wrote in *Philotimus:* "I had a little bird, that brought me newes of it." In 1711, in "Letter to Stella," Jonathan Swift came close to the current version: "I heard a little bird say so."

Curse not the king, no not in thy thought; and curse not the rich in thy bedchamber: for a bird of the air shall carry the voice, and that which hath wings shall tell the matter. —Ecclesiastes, 10:20, *Authorized Version,* 1611

1937. "Who told you, Michael?"

"A little bird," he said archly. —W. Somerset Maugham, *Theatre*

1943. "He had it bought for him, but a little bird told me. You know, a little bird with a cigar in his mouth and a derby on the side of his head." —Robert Penn Warren, *At Heaven's Gate*

1982. "Tell me what the surprise is."

"Well, a little bird told me it's your birthday," George said, "and I want to take you to lunch today." —Sidney Sheldon, *The Master of the Game*

A little knowledge (learning) is a dangerous thing. Incomplete knowledge of a subject is often worse than no knowledge at all. The idea was expressed as far back as the first century b.c. by Publilius Syrus: "Better be ignorant of a matter than half know it." The proverb is attributed to Alexander Pope (1688–1744), who used it in *An Essay on Criticism* (1711). In *Science & Culture* (1881), T. H. Huxley (1825–95) wrote: "If little knowledge is dangerous, where is the man as to be out of danger?"

1711. A little learning is a dang'rous thing;
Drink deep, or taste not the Pierian spring:
There shallow draughts intoxicate the brain,
And drinking largely sobers us again.
　　　　　—Alexander Pope, *An Essay on Criticism*

1939. A little woman is a dangerous thing. —Lewis & Faye Copeland, *10,000 Jokes, Toasts and Stories*

1953. "A little learning is a dangerous thing." —Ray Bradbury, *Fahrenheit 451*

1981. For some of our elders a little money is a dangerous thing. —Abigail Van Buren, *The Best of Dear Abby*

1985. My professor asked if I knew the phrase, "A little knowledge is a dangerous thing." ... When I told him I did, he added ... "Well, my dear, at this point in your career, you are a potential threat to mankind." —Quoted in *Reader's Digest*

1993. The Op-Ed piece by Diana Edensword and Gary Milhollin ... is an example of the old adage that a little knowledge is a dangerous thing. —Letters to the Editor, *New York Times*

See also KNOWLEDGE IS POWER; LIVE AND LEARN.

Little strokes fell great oaks. If you are persistent, you will achieve great results. The saying has been traced back to Chaucer's *Roman of the Rose* (c.1370). John Lyly (c.1554–1606) wrote in 1579: "Many strokes overthrow the tallest oaks." The proverb was used by Shakespeare in *Henry VI, Part III* (1591). First attested in the United States in *Poor Richard's Almanac* (1750) by Benjamin Franklin. *Small* may be used instead of *little* and *big* instead of *great.*

1591. *Messenger:* And many strokes, though with a little axe,

Hews down and fells the hardest-timber'd oak.

—Shakespeare, *Henry VI, Part III,* II, i

1750. 'Tis true there is much to be done, and perhaps you are weak handed, but stick to it steadily, and you will see great Effects, for *constant Dropping wears away Stones,* and by *Diligence and Patience the Mouse ate in two the Cable;* and *little Strokes fell great Oaks,* as Poor Richard says in his Almanac, the Year I cannot just now remember. —Benjamin Franklin, *Father Abraham's Speech, or, The Way to Wealth*

1957. Little strokes fell big oaks. —*Time*

Live and learn. We profit by our experience. Often said after making a mistake. The proverb has been traced back to *The Glasse of Government* (1575) by English poet George Gascoigne (c.1525–77). Included in James Howell's collection of English proverbs in 1659. First cited in the United States in *Belknap Papers* (1784). The proverb is found in varying forms: *Live and learn; One must live and learn; We live and learn; Who lives may learn,* etc.

1961. I tossed the gun into the drawer. "Live and learn!" I said. —John Steinbeck, *The Winter of Our Discontent*

1979. That is what they think the teacups are.

Live and learn! —Kurt Vonnegut, Jr., *Jailbird*

1993. "I thought they were going to commit to me for a couple of years and it was my understanding that they didn't have the money to go get somebody like that. I guess you live and learn, though." —*Times* (Trenton)

See also EXPERIENCE IS THE BEST TEACHER; A LITTLE KNOWLEDGE (LEARNING) IS A DANGEROUS THING.

Live and let live. Be tolerant of others and let them run their own lives. The proverb is of Dutch origin and has been traced back to *Ancient Law-Merchant* (1622) by G. De Malynes. Included in John Ray's collection of English proverbs in 1678. First attested in the United States in the works of John Adams (1785). *Live and let live as long as all is quiet* is a new variant coined by novelist John Grisham.

1955. "Dear me," Vera said to Marjorie with a grin, "have I stepped on your toes? I'm sorry, I'm sure."

"Live and let live," Sandy said. —Herman Wouk, *Marjorie Morningstar*

1965. "I taught my children the Golden Rule. Live & let live and in many cases my children would tell on each other when doing wrong and the guilty one would always admit, and come forward, willing for a spanking. —Truman Capote, *In Cold Blood*

1976. "All he's doing is stalling. Doesn't it make you furious?"

"Live and let live, I always say." —Art Buchwald, *Washington Is Leaking*

1978. "I want to be ready. And that's why I don't say anything about Mr. Dunaway and Vesta Adcock. We have to live and let live." —Fannie Flagg, *Fried Green Tomatoes*

1984. If "pragmatism" and "pluralism" meant a new openness and tolerance, a willingness, in common parlance, "to live and let live," an erosion of dogmatism, and a decline in religious and racial prejudices, they also meant an often bewildering absence of certitude, a sense of confusion and even abandonment. —Page Smith, *The Rise of Industrial America*

1988. I am not an absolutist on this. Live and let live is my philosophy. —Russell Baker, *New York Times*

1990. "In my view, it was much more prudent, much more professional, and much more willing to look at each situation on a case-by-case basis. Maybe this goes with the live-and-let-live attitude of New York, the original melting-pot city." —David Burnham, *A Law unto Itself*

1993. If you are willing to live and let live, you will experience a greater sense of freedom and a rare feeling of confidence, contentment and optimism. —Patric Walker, "Your Daily Horoscope," *New York Post*

Live every day as though it were your last. Live every day to the fullest. Make the most out of life.

1987. "I don't know how long the good Lord is going to let me live, but I'm in the jumping-off years, you know that. That's why I live every day like it could be my last." —Fannie Flagg, *Fried Green Tomatoes*

1989. "He [Jack Kennedy] enjoyed variety. He loved adventure. 'Live each day as if it's your last'—that became his philosophy." —C. David Heymann, *A Woman Named Jackie*

1991. "They were never in the house. They were always out fishing, or playing tennis, or merely going for walks. They were one of those couples who acted as if every day could be their last." —*Vanity Fair*

See also EAT, DRINK, AND BE MERRY, FOR TOMORROW WE DIE; LIFE IS TOO SHORT; LIFE IS WHAT YOU MAKE IT; SEIZE THE MOMENT.

A living dog is better than a dead lion. It is better to live modestly than to die valiantly. There's always hope for the living but death is as final for the great as it is for less important people. The proverb appears in the Old Testament. It has been traced back to *Minor Poems of Vernon MS* (c.1390). First cited in the United States in 1677 in the *History of Indian Wars in New England* (1677). The word *live* may substitute for *living*, and the words *ass, donkey, horse, jackass,* or *mouse* for *dog. Better live dog than dead lion* is a common variant.

> For to him that is joined to all the living there is hope; for a living dog is better than a dead lion. For the living know that they shall die; but the dead know not any thing, neither have they any more a reward; for the memory of them is forgotten. —Ecclesiastes, 9:4, 5, *Authorized Version,* 1611

1930. They always prefer a live mouse to a dead lion. —W. Somerset Maugham, *Cakes and Ale*

1984. I decided from the bottom of mine, and determined on the spot that there was nothing better for me to do than to escape speedily into the land of the Philistines if I did not wish to perish one day by the hand of Saul. A living dog is better than a dead lion, and he who fights and runs away, may live to fight another day. —Joseph Heller, *God Knows*

See also HE WHO FIGHTS AND RUNS AWAY, MAY LIVE TO FIGHT ANOTHER DAY.

Lock 'em up and throw away the key. Put criminals in jail with no hope of ever being released.

1989. "He's practically a recluse now," she continued. "Drinks like a fish, I've been told. If he bought one of *these* horrors, they ought to lock him up in one of those funny farms in Connecticut and throw away the key." —Michael Korda, *The Fortune*

1993. So for the next two years we are going to hear promises of no taxes and no crime. We can't get there from here. The no-crime, "put them in jail and throw away the key" politicians know that jails cost money and keeping people in jail costs lots of money and money means taxes. —*Times* (Trenton)

1994. LOCK 'EM UP AND THROW AWAY THE KEY. —Headline, *Time*
See also THREE STRIKES AND YOU'RE OUT.

Look before you leap. Think carefully before you plunge into any serious decision. Don't act rashly. The maxim has been traced back to the *Douce MS* (c.1350). Included in John Heywood's collection of proverbs in 1546. First cited in the United States in the *Life and Writings of Francis Makemie* (1694). The phrase takes varying forms: *Leap before you look; Look before you leap and think before you speak; Look twice before you leap; Think twice before you leap; You had better look before you leap,* etc.

1605. Thou shouldst have looked before thou hadst leapt. —Ben Jonson, George Chapman, & John Marston, *Eastward Ho!*

1664. As the ancients
    Say wisely, have a care o' th' main chance,
    And look before you ere you leap.
                    —Samuel Butler, *Hudibras*

1957. Q. Then how am I to decide where to invest my money? A. *Look before you leap.* —*New Yorker*

1961. He was polite to his elders, who disliked him. Whatever his leaders told him to do, he did. They told him to look before he leaped, and he always looked before he leaped. —Joseph Heller, *Catch-22*

1970. Applying the steps in this chapter to any other path you want to follow will likewise help you immediately. That includes volunteer work, internships, temporary work (which agency should you sign up with), etc. It's just detailed common sense application of the old refrain, "Look before you leap." —Richard Nelson Bolles, *What Color Is Your Parachute?*

1994. Look before leaping into business deals. —Jeane Dixon, "Horoscope," *Times* (Trenton)
See also DISCRETION IS THE BETTER PART OF VALOR; MARRY IN HASTE, REPENT AT LEISURE; SLOW AND STEADY WINS THE RACE.

Look on the bright side. *See* ALWAYS LOOK ON THE BRIGHT SIDE.

Loose lips sink ships. People who don't watch their tongues may inadvertently reveal sensitive information that gets themselves or others into trouble. This World War II catch phrase pertained especially to defense plant workers and soldiers. Often shortened to *loose lips. A slip of the lip can sink a ship* is a variant.

1975. "A slip of the lip can sink a ship!" yelled Dwayne. —Kurt Vonnegut, Jr., *Breakfast of Champions*

1987. Mr. Hopkins, who said he was "appalled" when Mr. Aspin left the hearing Tuesday and talked at length with reporters waiting outside, was particularly harsh in his criticism today. "It makes us bring back the old saying, perhaps—loose lips sink ships," Mr. Hopkins said. —*New York Times*

1989. "I'm telling you that it's not a good move to hang around with them, whatever you call them. There are more spies and creeps here than anywhere in Asia."

"They're friends and they aren't spies."

"Fraternization looks bad on the old report card. Loose lips sink ships." —Wayne Care, *Vietnam Spook Show*

1990. Don't talk to people at work about your plans, or how you're doing. Loose lips sink more than ships. —Daniel Moreau, *Take Charge of Your Career*

1991. " 'Loose tongues lose lawsuits.' That was Mr. Bendini's motto, and he applied it to everything." —John Grisham, *The Firm*

The Lord gives and the Lord takes away. We cannot question the will of God. Said to console someone for a terrible and inexplicable loss of property or a loved one. In the Old Testament, Job speaks these words in prayer after learning of the decimation of his wealth and the sudden death of his children. Cited in the United States in 1771: "The Lord who gave can take away." The archaic forms *giveth* and *taketh* are often seen, and the proverb is often parodied.

And said, Naked came I out of my mother's womb, and naked shall I return thither: The Lord gave, and the Lord hath taken away; blessed be the name of the Lord. —Job, 1:21, *Authorized Version,* 1611

1948. "The Lord giveth and the Highway Commissioner taketh away," said Hank, drily. —Ray Bradbury, *I Sing the Body Electric!*

1952. "Why did it have to happen?" It was one more hollow echo to the question humanity had been asking for millenniums, the question men were seemingly born to ask.

"The Lord giveth, and the Lord taketh away," said Finnerty. —Kurt Vonnegut, Jr., *Player Piano*

1978. They wanted to hear about how she ate beeswax, or stayed away from fried pork, or how she kept her legs up when she slept. But she did none of those things, and was she to lie? God gives

life and He takes it away when He wants. —Stephen King, *The Stand*

1984. "You look lovely tonight," he said seriously. "Off to the Osners' to pay our deep respects to money and power. The Lord giveth and the Lord taketh away, and it all balances out." —Howard Fast, *The Outsider*

1985. His friend, after having heard the entire story [of the hurricane's devastation], replied, "Henry, the Lord giveth, and the Lord taketh away." The first man thought for a few minutes and replied slowly and without rancor, "You're right, Fred. I just wish he would have taken it back the way he gave it to me—a little at a time." —Quoted in *Reader's Digest*

1989. "The Navy giveth, and the Navy taketh away." —Tom Clancy, *Clear and Present Danger*

1990. "The Courts Giveth and the Courts Taketh Away" —David Burnham, *A Law unto Itself*

1992. Cynthia and Melinda, Angela's daughters, born on the twenty-eighth of July last year, eleven days after his father's murder; what the Lord taketh away, the Lord giveth back. —Ed McBain, *Kiss*

1994. Health insurance spokesmen on the Clinton administration's health care program: "The big print giveth and the fine print taketh away." —*U.S. News & World Report*

The Lord helps those who help themselves. *See* GOD HELPS THOSE WHO HELP THEMSELVES.

The Lord moves in a mysterious way. *See* GOD MOVES IN A MYSTERIOUS WAY.

Losers weepers. *See* FINDERS KEEPERS, LOSERS WEEPERS.

Love conquers all. People who love each other can overcome any obstacle. Love is more powerful than anything else. The adage has been traced back to Virgil (37 b.c.): *Omnia vincit amor.* It appears in Chaucer (c.1387) as *Amor vincit omnia.* First cited in the United States in *Phantom* (1929) by S. Quinn.

37 b.c.
Omnia vincit Amor: et nos cedamus Amori. ("Love conquers all things: let us too give in to Love.") —Virgil, *Eclogues*

1929. *Amor omnia vincit*—love conquers all. —S. Quinn, *Phantom*

1991. Yet, in her third novel, *Temples of Delight,* the South African–born Barbara Trapido, who's lived in England since 1963 and deftly appropriated the polished style of sophisticated British social comedy, applies her sharp sense of social nuances and her dry wit to advance the old-fashioned proposition that love conquers all. —*Wall Street Journal*

1992. Toward the end of *Fear*, Mr. Rybakov leaves the impression that Sasha and Varya will soon be reunited. Even in Stalin's universal gulag, love may yet conquer all. —Herbert Mitgang, *New York Times*

1993. The idea that you're going to find somebody who's absolutely perfect, or the idea that you find someone who completes you, is such a crock of shit. Where that started is really dangerous, dangerous history. It comes from fairy tales. It comes from the way we were conditioned. Well, love does not conquer all. —Susan Sarandon, quoted in *GQ*

See also LOVE IS BLIND; LOVE MAKES THE WORLD GO ROUND.

Love is blind. When we are in love with someone, we cannot see any faults in that person. The proverb appears in Plato (c.427–347 b.c.), Chaucer (1390), and Shakespeare (1591). First cited in the United States in 1646 in *Thomas Hutchinson Papers* (1865). The adage is found in varying forms: *Friendship is blind; Love is blind; Friendship closes its eyes; Love is blind and makes its victims blind; Love is deaf as well as blind,* etc. It has counterparts in other languages: *L'amour est aveugle* (French); *Liebe macht blind* (German); Любовь слепа (Russian).

1591. *Valentine:* I have loved her ever since I saw her, and still I see her beautiful.
  Speed: If you love her you cannot see her.
  Valentine: Why?
  Speed: Because Love is blind.
      —Shakespeare, *The Two Gentlemen of Verona,* II, i

1596–97.
  Jessica: Here, catch this casket; it is worth the pains.
  I am glad 'tis night, you do not look on me,
  For I am much asham'd of my exchange;
  But love is blind, and lovers cannot see
  The pretty follies that themselves commit.
      —Shakespeare, *The Merchant of Venice,* II, vi

1966. "Love is blind," Grandma said in an unyielding voice. "But I am not blind. I'll open your eyes for you." —Molly Picon, *So Laugh a Little*

1987. "I know," Jack laughed quietly. "Your eyes are always closed. Maybe your love is blind, but mine isn't." —Tom Clancy, *Patriot Games*

1992. WHEN LOVE IS BLIND, BUT SO IS JUSTICE. —Headline of an article on legal aspects of marriage, *New York Times*

1993. Once more we proved what we all know—friendship is blind. —Erma Bombeck, *Times* (Trenton)

1994. The pseudonymous Walter Scott writes in *Parade* of "the cliché about love being blind," which should be "love's being blind." —William Safire, "On Language," *New York Times Magazine*

See also BEAUTY IS IN THE EYE OF THE BEHOLDER.

Love makes the world go round. The major motivation for all human activity is the search for love. The words are found in an anonymous French song, *C'est l'amour, l'amour, l'amour, Que fait le monde A la ronde.* First cited in *David* (1656). Recorded in Lewis Carroll's *Alice's Adventures in Wonderland* (1865). In 1882, it was included in William Gilbert's collection of proverbs. First attested in the United States by O. Henry in *Brandur Magazine* (1902) and later in *Ruler of Men* (1906). The song "Money Makes the World Go Around" from the muscial *Cabaret* (1966) parodied the old saw.

1865. "'Oh, 'tis love, 'tis love that makes the world go round!'"
  "Somebody said," Alice whispered, "that it's done by everybody minding their own business." —Lewis Carroll, *Alice's Adventures in Wonderland*

1902. It's said that love makes the world go round. The announcement lacks verification. It's the wind from the dinner horn that does it. —O. Henry, *Brandur Magazine*

1961. "What difference does it make to anyone if I'm in the plane or not?"
  "No difference."
  "Sure, that's what I mean," Doc Daneeka said. "A little grease *is* what makes this world go round." —Joseph Heller, *Catch-22*

1962. Captain Bosche's eyes had narrowed to slits, and with them he stared at Bell. "Well, there are all sorts of attitudes and opinions, I guess," he said profoundly. "That's what makes the world go round." —James Jones, *The Thin Red Line*

1992. Now I know that physical attractiveness is important, but it doesn't make the world go round. Family and friends do. —*People*

1994. Love doesn't make the world go 'round—but it sure makes the ride worth while. —Joey Adams, "Strictly for Laughs," *New York Post*

Love me, love my dog. If you love someone, you also have to love everything that person loves. The Latin equivalent is *Qui me amant, amat et canem meam.* The proverb has been traced back to *Early English Miscellanies* (c.1485). It was included in John Heywood's book of proverbs in 1546. First attested in the United States in *Warren-Adams Letters* (1775). Similar proverbs occur in other languages: *Qui m'aime aime mon chien* (French); *Quien bien quiere a Beltrán, bien quiere a su can* (Spanish).

1936. And Melanie, with a fierce "love-me-love-my-dog" look on her face, made converse with astounded hostesses. —Margaret Mitchell, *Gone With the Wind*

1992. Love me, love my horse, says one candidate for Governor. —*People*

1993. I suspect David Updike's problems have little to do with changing attitudes in the United States and a lot to do with his "love me, love my kids" whining. —Letters to the Editor, *New York Times Magazine*

See also YOU HAVE TO TAKE THE BAD WITH THE GOOD; YOU HAVE TO TAKE THE BITTER WITH THE SWEET.

The love of money is the root of all evil. *See* MONEY IS THE ROOT OF ALL EVIL.

Love your neighbor as yourself. This dictum of fairness and social justice is of Biblical origin and was first expressed in the Old Testament. The proverb has been traced back to *First Fruits* (1578) by Giovanni Florio (1553?–1625). The archaic *thy … thyself* is often seen. Extended variants include: *Love your neighbor, but do not pull down the fence; Love your neighbor, but leave his wife alone,* etc.

Thou shalt not avenge, nor bear any grudge against the children of thy people, but thou shalt love thy neighbor as thyself: I *am* the Lord. —Leviticus, 19:18, *Authorized Version,* 1611

1939. *Dr. Lloyd:* "What is thy duty toward thy neighbor?"

Whitney: "Whew!" *(He pulls himself together and makes a brave start.)* "My duty toward my neighbor is to love him as myself, and to do to all men as I would they should do unto me." —Howard Lindsay & Russel Crouse, *Life with Father*

1961. In fact, he loved his neighbor and never even bore false witness against him. —Joseph Heller, *Catch-22*

1988. "After all, the Old Testament commands us to 'love thy neighbor as thyself.'" —Erich Segal, *Doctors*

1989. Christ said to "love your neighbor as yourself." Sacrifice, however, has been misinterpreted as loving your neighbor *instead* of yourself. —Carol S. Pearson, *The Hero Within*

1994. "This Book says we should love our neighbors …" "Obviously, you haven't met my neighbors." —Cartoon by Browne, "Hagar the Horrible," *Times* (Trenton)

Luck is the residue of design. A good leader leaves nothing to chance. Good planning is the foundation of success. Attributed to baseball executive Branch Rickey (1881–1965), who revolutionized the game by inventing the farm system.**

1960s.

Luck is the residue of design. —Branch Rickey, quoted by Howard Cosell, *Like It Is*

1989. And, thus, in one of the strangest twists in modern Soviet politics, Mr. Mikhail Gorbachev is being helped by a man he fired, who was his friend and who is now the Soviet Union's No. 1 maverick. Just plain lucky, one supposes. Or, as the baseball executive Branch Rickey, once said, luck is the residue of design. —*New York Times*

See also GOD HELPS THOSE WHO HELP THEMSELVES.

Make a virtue of necessity. When faced with a bad situation, one should try to turn it to one's advantage. The proverb has been traced back to Chaucer's *Troilus and Criseyde* (c.1374) and is similar to the French: *Faire de nécessité vertu* and to the Latin: *Facere de necessitate virtutem.* First attested in the United States in *Collected Letters of Cotton Mather* (1678).

> **1932.** Here was the fellow publicly confessing his disgrace! An old dodge, that—taking the sting out of criticism! Making a virtue of necessity! —John Galsworthy, *Flowering Wilderness*

> **1957.** "You can't fine them or send them to jail because there won't be time to bring the case on. May as well give a reasonable date, and make a virtue of necessity." —Nevil Shute, *On the Beach*

> **1991.** In other words, President Reagan could have tried to make a virtue out of a necessity. —Oliver L. North, *Under Fire*

> **1994.** By the time the future comes, it may be abundantly clear that the current challenge to high consumption is the leading edge of a transition, in the form of an old social process called making a virtue out of necessity. —*New York Times*

Make haste slowly. Move quickly but also methodically. If you must act swiftly, proceed with caution. Sometimes quoted in Latin: *Festina lente.* It was the favorite maxim of both Augustus and Erasmus. The saying has been traced back in English to Chaucer's *Troilus and Criseyde* (c.1374). First cited in the United States in *Jonathan Belcher Papers* (1734).

> **63 b.c.–a.d. 14.**
> *Festina lente.* ("Make haste slowly.") —Augustus, quoted by Suetonius, *Lives of the Caesars*

> **1374.** He hasteth well that wisely can abide. —Chaucer, *Troilus and Criseyde*

> **1744.** Make haste slowly. —Benjamin Franklin, *Poor Richard's Almanac*

> **1948.** Roosevelt, at this point, believed in the policy of making haste slowly. —Robert E. Sherwood, *Roosevelt and Hopkins*

> **1984.** You're always in a rush. Believe me, you'd be better off if you made haste slowly. —Overheard at a corporate meeting in Queens, N.Y.

See also EASY DOES IT; HASTE MAKES WASTE; ONE THING AT A TIME; SLOW AND STEADY WINS THE RACE.

Make hay while the sun shines. Take full advantage of any favorable condition or opportunity before it passes. The allusion is to drying grass for fodder by spreading it out in the sunshine. The proverb appeared in Alexander Barclay's satire, *Ship of Fools* in 1509 and in John Heywood's book of proverbs in 1546. First attested in the United States in the *New English Canaan of Thomas Morton* (1637). Sometimes shortened to *make hay.*

> **1546.** When the sun shineth, make hay. —John Heywood, *Proverbs*

> **1984.** Meanwhile, the IMF makes loans to Poland at 6 percent while we ask Polish Americans to buy houses at 14 percent. If the Democrats can't make hay out of that, they *deserve* to lose. —Lee Iacocca with William Novak, *Iacocca*

> **1986.** It should be noted now, also more in sorrow than in anger, that on "Nightline" the ordinarily precise Ted Koppel asked Senator Patrick J. Leahy a very imprecise question. "Do you have," he said, "the foggiest notion of what's going on?" ... Mr. Leahy, a Vermont Democrat, leaped at that one. He said, of course, that he didn't. This was hard to

believe; Mr. Leahy sounded like a politician making hay. —*New York Times*

1989. "I wouldn't overestimate his attention span." "I don't. That's why I'd like to make hay while the sun shines." —Michael Korda, *The Fortune*

1994. These Princeton-area summer people make hay while the sun shines, and when the flurries begin to fly as well. —*Princeton Packet* (N.J.)
See also STRIKE WHILE THE IRON IS HOT.

Make it or break it. *See* MAKE OR BREAK.

Make my day. If you proceed with your threat, I'll destroy you and enjoy doing it. Originated in the United States. The original sense, associated with some pleasant event that cheers one up, was radically revised when "Dirty Harry," a disaffected cop played by actor Clint Eastwood, used it as a warning before blowing out the brains of a punk who dared to reach for his own gun. The phrase was later adopted by Ronald Reagan.

1983. Go ahead, make my day. —Clint Eastwood, *Sudden Impact*

1985. I have only one thing to say to the tax increasers: "Go ahead and make my day." —Ronald Reagan

1986. Travis made him a cup of overly strong black coffee served in a mug with MAKE MY DAY OH PLEASE MR. EASTWOOD! emblazoned on the side. —Jackie Collins, *Hollywood Husbands*

1987. [*In a subway car*] "*Shoot him!* For God's sake, somebody *shoot him!*"
"Let's show this creep a little street justice!"
"*Me?* What about that guy over *there?* He's got a *screwdriver!*"
"A screwdriver! *Everyone down!*"
"Hey, man, I'm an electrician!"
"*Make my day! Make my day!*"
—G. B. Trudeau, *Doonesbury Deluxe*

1987. *Q.* President Reagan, the revolutionary Government of Iran has caused a lot of pain for your Administration over the last few years.
A. Yes.
Q. And I just wonder if you're going into the gulf, looking, positively seeking a chance to punch them in the nose, saying as you once did to terrorists, "Go ahead, make my day"? —*New York Times*

Make or break. Succeed or fail, often used to refer to a crucial situation. The phrase has been traced back to the fifteenth century. In 1840, it was used by Charles Dickens in *Barnaby Rudge*. *Make it or break it* is the full form.

1951. The fact that it was Blues Berry whom they heard screaming proved they were serious, that this time the Major and Fatso were out to make it or break it, showdown or else. —James Jones, *From Here to Eternity*

1984. Hart's immediate problem is paying off his 4-million-dollar debt. That is a make-or-break issue that could haunt the Colorado senator for years. —*U.S. News & World Report*

1987. Influenced by concessions from Moscow, by his wife's concern for his place in history, perhaps even by a sense of his own mortality prompted by an assassin's bullets and by serious illnesses, Mr. Reagan approaches the end of his second term, in the certain belief that "what he does with Gorbachev will make or break him." —*New York Times*

1991. A stockbroker can make you or—quite literally—break you. The less you know about investing, the more breakable you are. —Jane Bryant Quinn, *Making the Most of Your Money*

1992. "I don't think this will make or break us," Mattingly said. "We just have to hold our own and put some wins together." —*New York Post*

1994. Your attitude will make or break a business deal. Get with it! —Jeane Dixon, "Horoscope," *Times* (Trenton)
See also SINK OR SWIM.

A man can't be in two places at once. *See* ONE CAN'T BE IN TWO PLACES AT ONCE.

Man does not live by bread alone. People have spiritual as well as physical needs. The idea was first expressed by Moses in the Old Testament. Now often used literally to refer to other material objects. Ralph Waldo Emerson (1803–82) quoted the proverb in the *North American Review* in 1875. The saying is found in varying forms: *Man cannot live by bread alone; No man can live by bread alone,* etc. It has counterparts in other languages: *Der Mensch lebt nicht vom Brot allein* (German).

And he humbled thee, and suffered thee to hunger, and fed thee with manna, which thou knewest not, neither did thy fathers know; that he might make thee know that man doth not live by bread only, but by every *word* that proceedeth out of the mouth of the Lord doth man live. —Deuteronomy, 8:3, *Authorized Version,* 1611

1875. Man does not live by bread alone, but by faith, by admiration, by sympathy. —Ralph Waldo Emerson, *North American Review*

1881. Man is a creature who lives not upon bread

alone, but principally by catchwords. —Robert Louis Stevenson, *Virginibus Puerisque*

1935. Such corporations as a means of overcoming union influence and democratization frequently grant their employees more in wages and comforts than the union standard demands. But "man can not live by bread alone." Men must have industrial liberty as well as good wages. —Louis D. Brandeis, *The Curse of Bigness*

1987. "She kept a bottle in her apron, and Momma would say, 'Idgie, you're just encouraging people into bad habits.' But Aunt Idgie, who liked to drink herself, would say, 'Ruth, man does not live by bread alone.'" —Fannie Flagg, *Fried Green Tomatoes*

1991. One theology major was doing particularly well, but decided to sell everything and invest it all in a bakery. He had heard that it was a takeover target, which would cause the stock to rise. This failed to happen, however, and the price dropped, almost wiping him out.... The professor [of economics] asked if he had learned anything from the exercise.... "Man does not live by bread alone," said the theology student. —Quoted in *Reader's Digest*

1994. NOT BY BREAD ALONE —Headline of an article on volunteers who feed and house the homeless, *Taste of the Nation* (N.J.)

A man is as old as he feels. Youthfulness is a matter of attitude, not chronological age. An old person may feel young, and a young one may feel old. The earliest appearance of the proverb in print was in *Thames Journal* (1871). First attested in the United States in *Green Ink* (1926) by J. S. Fletcher. The saying takes varying forms: *A man is as old as he feels; A man is no older than he feels; You're as young as you feel; You're as old as you think you are*, etc. *A man is as old as he feels, a woman as old as she feels like admitting* is a jocular variant.

1947. I always say ... that a person is as old as they feel. —J. D. Carr, *Sleeping Sphinx*

1976. Have you ever thought about buying a Harley-Davidson 30 XL motorcycle? You're only as young as you feel, and once you roar off on one of our 1976 models, you will know the thrill of.... —Art Buchwald, *Washington Is Leaking*

1989. "A man is as young as the woman he feels." —Vance Packard, *The Ultra Rich: How Much Is Too Much*

A man is known (judged) by the company he keeps. Choose your friends wisely: your rep-

utation can be either harmed or enhanced by association. The proverb has been traced back to *Preparations to Marriage* (1591). Cervantes quoted it in *Don Quixote* (1605–15), which was first translated into English in 1612. First cited in the United States in *Journal of Proceedings in Georgia* (1737). *A man is often known by the friends he knows;* and *Sometimes a man is known by the friends he hasn't* are variants. Another jocular version is *A man is known by the company he keeps and a woman is known by the company she is kept by.*

1605–15.
That is certainly the case if there's any truth in the old saying, "Tell me what company you keep and I'll tell you who you are." —Cervantes, *Don Quixote*

1948. We're all on to you, Jimmy Andrews, and the voters of Ward 9 don't want a bigot. So watch out for the Company YOU KEEP. —Norman Mailer, *The Naked and the Dead*

1953. *Herb:* Now when you came here, I told you to make friends slowly. I told you to make sure they were the right kinds of friends. You're known by the company you keep. —Robert Anderson, *Tea and Sympathy*

1991. You can tell her by the company she keeps. Donna Karan. Bob Mackie. Perri Ellis. Claude Montana. HBA. —Ad for Birger Christensen, *New York Times Magazine*

1992. You can tell a lobbyist in Washington by the company that keeps him. —*Wall Street Journal*

1994. Warner ... was once secretary of the Navy and is often defined in terms of the company he keeps. He is the good right hand of Sen. Sam Nunn, D-Ga., chairman of the Senate Armed Services Committee—too good, some Republicans complain. He was married to Elizabeth Taylor and now dates Barbara Walters. —Mary McGrory, *Times* (Trenton)

See also IF YOU LIE DOWN WITH DOGS, YOU'LL GET UP WITH FLEAS.

Man proposes, God disposes. Things do not always work out according to plan. People can make plans, but in the final analysis we are all in the hands of God. The saying has been traced back to the fourteenth century and is similar to the French proverb of the time: *L'homme propose et Dieu dispose* or *Car se li homme mal propose, Diex ... les dispose* ("If man proposes evil, God ... disposes of it"). The Latin version—*Homo proponit, sed Deus disponit* ("Man proposes but God disposes")—can be found in the *Imitation of*

Christ (1420) by Thomas à Kempis (1380–1471) and *Piers Plowman* (1550 edition) by William Langland (1330–1400). First attested in the United States in *Wonder Working Providence of Sions Savior* (1654). The adage is found in varying forms: *Man proposes and circumstance disposes; Man proposes and luck interposes*, etc. Humorous variants include *Man proposes and woman accepts;* and *Man proposes, wife disposes.*

1605–15.
Man appoints, and God disappoints. —Cervantes, *Don Quixote*

1978. "Well, we could get up a search party. She can't have gone far."
Nick double-circled the phrase *Man proposes, God disposes.* Below it he wrote, "If you found her, how would you bring her back? Chains?" —Stephen King, *The Stand*

1986. Reagan is not a dictator, and he must cope with a media and a Congress, both of which have difficulty chewing gum and crossing the street at the same time. Reagan proposes and Congress, with media help, disposes. —*New York City Tribune*

1989. The obstacle to this goal has been the Communist Party. Mr. Gorbachev proposes, but the party disposed. —*New York Times*

1994. The transfer is only temporary, of course. One of these days, a President will offer a competing vision of public support for personal freedom. Could even be Clinton; but for now, the Congress proposes and the Congress disposes. —William Safire, *New York Times*
See also IT'S IN THE LAP OF THE GODS.

A man who is his own lawyer has a fool for a client. One cannot be objective about one's own concerns. The earliest appearance of the proverb in the United States was in *Port Folio* (1809). It was also used by English poet and critic Leigh Hunt (1784–1859) in his *Autobiography* (1850). The saying is found in varying forms: *A man who acts as his own lawyer has a fool for a client; A man who is his own advocate has a fool for a client; He who doctors himself has a fool for a doctor; He who is his own lawyer (attorney, counselor) has a fool for a client; He who is his own doctor (physician) has a fool for a client*, etc.

1809. He who is always his own counselor will often have a fool for his client. —*Port Folio*

1956. "A man who is his own advocate has a fool for a client," says one of the favorite aphorisms of the legal profession. —*New York Post*

1959. He who doctors himself has a fool for a physician. —*New York Times*

1983. The famous proverb of the legal profession, that the lawyer who represents himself has a fool for a client, may be apt for the writing profession. As my own client I tend to be impatient, to have no objectivity about my work.... —Richard Curtis, *How to Be Your Own Literary Agent*

1994. You need someone with experience to tell you what needs to be included [in a living trust]. When you do it yourself, you don't even know if you're using up-to-date information. As the saying goes, if you act as your own attorney you have a fool for a client. —*Princeton Business Journal*

1995. A FOOL FOR A CLIENT —Headline of an article about the trial of L.I.R.R. killer Colin Ferguson, who acted as his own attorney in court, *Time*

A man who makes no mistakes usually does not make anything. *See* HE WHO NEVER MADE A MISTAKE NEVER MADE ANYTHING.

Manners make the man. People are judged by their manners and conduct. The proverb has been traced back to *Douce MS* (c.1350). First cited in the United States in *Poor Richard's Almanac* (1742) by Benjamin Franklin. Motto of Winchester College and New College, Oxford, both founded by William of Wykeham (1324–1404).

1899. A breach of faith may be condoned, but a breach of decorum can not. "Manners maketh man." —Thorstein Veblen, *The Theory of the Leisure Class*

1959. Unfortunately mannerisms do not make the man. —*Time*

1961. "Remember the old boy who said, 'Manners maketh man'? Well, that's changed now. Tailors make men to any image they want." —John Steinbeck, *The Winter of Our Discontent*

1992. "From the time kids learn to walk and talk, we tell them that manners make the man. But when they grow up, they see that manners don't make the man, money does." —Overheard at a New York City bank
See also CLOTHES MAKE THE MAN; FINE FEATHERS MAKE FINE BIRDS.

Man's best friend is his dog. *See* A DOG IS A MAN'S BEST FRIEND.

A man's got to do what a man's got to do. One must follow the dictates of conscience, whatever the consequences. One must do whatever is necessary to achieve the desired result. One has no choice in the matter. Originated in the United States. Usually associated with actor John Wayne (1907–79), who used it in the 1939 John Ford western *Stagecoach.* ***

1989. Crowell smiled and continued, "I admire him for what he did. It took guts. I'd hope I'd have the courage to do what he did, 'cause Lord knows I'd want to. Sometimes a man's just gotta do what he's gotta do." —John Grisham, *A Time to Kill*

1992. "Andrew [Stein] wants to be mayor, and he's gotta do what he's gotta do, but he's lost support among African-Americans because of this," says the Reverend Calvin Butts of the Abyssinian Baptist Church, who until last week was Stein's key ally in the black community. —*New York*

1993. "Don't you see the $100 sign?" ... "Well, a dog's got to do what a dog's got to do." —Overheard in Central Park, New York City

A man's home is his castle. You are the boss in your own house and nobody can tell you what to do there. No one can enter your home without your permission. The proverb has been traced back to *Stage of Popish Toys* (1581). In 1644, English jurist Sir Edward Coke (1552–1634) was quoted as saying, "For a man's house is his castle, *et domus sua cuique tutissimum refugium*" ("One's home is the safest refuge for all"). First attested in the United States in *Will and Doom* (1692). In England, the word *Englishman* often replaces *man.*

1922. True to the maxim that every little Irishman's house is his castle. —James Joyce, *Ulysses*

1961. "I said King's X, Miss Hothouse Rhubarb, and I meant King's X." I slammed the door and shouted, "A man's bathroom is his castle." —John Steinbeck, *The Winter of Our Discontent*

1968. "A man's home is his castle" is a saying not meant for Negroes; a Negro's castle exists only in his mind. —Eldridge Cleaver, *Soul on Ice*

1976. "Car pooling is a drag," Allan told me. "Who wants to talk to four guys every morning? I think a man's automobile is his castle, and there is no reason he should share it with anybody else." —Art Buchwald, *Washington Is Leaking*

1977. Governor George C. Wallace is a reasonable man. When he makes a point for segregation, he never attacks the Negro head on. He always resorts to using another type of illustration. He will say when arguing against the civil rights bill, "You may want to sell your house to someone with blue eyes and green teeth and that's all right. I don't object. But you should not be forced to do it. A man's home is his castle." —Art Buchwald, *Down the Seine and Up the Potomac*

1988. This was Texas. A man's home is his castle—he can defend it with bazookas and machine guns if he knows where to get them. —Clifford Irving, *The Campbell Murder Case*

1992. An Englishman's home may or may not be his castle; these days it could also be his (or her) mock-Tudor cottage, his Laura Ashley boudoir, or his Conran's modernist machine for living. But whatever else it may be, an Englishman's home is above all a perfect opportunity to redecorate. —*New York Times*

1994. A man's home is his castle, but his apartment lobby belongs equally to that tasteless boob down the hall. —*New York Times Magazine*

A man's word is as good as his bond. Verbal promises are binding and must be honored. The proverb has been traced back to Chaucer's *Book of the Duchess* (c.1400). Cervantes quoted it in *Don Quixote* (1605). First cited in the United States in *The Diary of Col. Landon Carter of Sabine Hall* (1777). The adage takes varying forms: *An Englishman's word is his bond; A gentleman's word is as good as his oath; A gentleman's word is his bond; A man's word is as good as gold; A Quaker's word is as good as his bond,* etc.

1922. To cut a long story short Bloom, grasping the situation, was the first to rise from his seat so as not to outstay their welcome having first and foremost, being as good as his word that he would foot the bill for the occasion.... —James Joyce, *Ulysses*

1960. If the judge released Arthur, Mr. Radley would see to it that Arthur gave no further trouble. Knowing that Mr. Radley's word was his bond, the judge was glad to do so. —Harper Lee, *To Kill a Mockingbird*

1973. "Harry Truman grew up in a society in which a man's word was his bond. If a man's word could be trusted there was no place he couldn't go. Nobody here ever doubted Harry Truman's word." —Merle Miller, *Plain Speaking*

1989. The bond markets lapse into Latin after a couple of drinks. *Meum dictum pactum* was another Latin phrase I used to hear, but that was just a joke. It means "My word is my bond." —Michael Lewis, *Liar's Poker*

1990. Speaking to "Institutional Investor," Greenhill and Dick Fisher said the firm had neither a verbal nor a written agreement with Olinkraft that enforced confidentiality. For the House of Morgan—the historic custodian of the "my word is my bond" approach to business—this defense seemed a betrayal of the Morgan tradition. —Ron Chernow, *The House of Morgan*

1992. "His word [Trump's] is gold," says Greenberg, smiling. "His word is his bond, but sometimes his memory is bad." —*New York*

1993. "We're tough negotiators and Brian is a tough negotiator, but a deal is a deal," Wallace said. "We shook hands on a deal. If you can't stand by your word, then what good is it. A man's word is his bond." —*Times* (Trenton)

Many are called, but few are chosen. Everyone is welcome to apply, but only the most qualified people are accepted. Originally appeared in the New Testament as the moral of one of Jesus' parables. First attested in the United States in *Diary of William Bentley* (1791).

And when the king came in to see the guests, he saw there a man which had not on a wedding garment: And he saith unto him, Friend, how camest thou in hither not having a wedding garment? And he was speechless. Then said the king to the servants, Bind him hand and foot, and take him away, and cast *him* into outer darkness; there shall be weeping and gnashing of teeth. For many are called, but few are chosen. —Matthew, 22:11–14, *Authorized Version,* 1611

1988. "You'd be doing the subcommittee a disservice based on a misplaced appraisal of my credentials. Do yourself a favor. Call one of the others."

"The beautiful book, that most holy of books, has so many answers, doesn't it?" asked the Speaker aimlessly, his eyes once again straying. "Many might be called, but few are chosen, isn't that right?" —Robert Ludlum, *The Icarus Agenda*

1992. Please be realistic—for every writer who gets published, there are probably several thousand waiting in line. "Many are called, few are chosen." —Jeff Herman, *Insider's Guide to Book Editors, Publishers, and Literary Agents*

March comes in like a lion and goes out like a lamb. March usually begins with wild weather and ends fair, mild and pleasant. The proverb has been traced back to the early seventeenth century. "I would chuse March, for I would come in like a Lion," J. Fletcher wrote in *Wife for a Month* (1625), "But you'd go out like a Lamb when you went hanging." The adage is listed in J. Ray's collection of *English Proverbs* (1670). First attested in the United States in Ames's *Almanacs* (1740). The proverb is found in a variety of forms and is used with descriptions of weather, but is often used figuratively in reference to general behavior.

1956. The Christmas season could be described as the proverbial month of March in reverse: In like a lamb, out like a lion. —*New York Times*

1982. As March was going out like a lion, 25 sawmills in nine Western states suddenly roared to life and 10,500 laid-off workers were called back. —*Christian Science Monitor*

1992. March may not have come in like a lion by northern standards, but the first day of the month gave Floridians a chilly roar Saturday, with a cold growl yet to come tonight. —*Sun-Sentinel* (South Florida)

1991. If today's forecast holds up, Memphians can expect March to come roaring in like a lion. Forecasters predict rain and severe thunderstorms today along with winds gusting up to 30 mph. —*Commercial Appeal* (Memphis, Tennessee)

1993. True to his name, March came in like a lion and let the party roar. Tony March celebrated the opening of Tony March Buick-GMC and his new Saturn of Hartford dealerships in the city's North Meadows section Wednesday night. —*Hartford Courant*

1994. We're pretty sick of this... We're hoping that if March is coming in like a lion, it'll go out like a lamb. —*Associated Press*

1995. April took over March's traditional role, pounding like a lion last week on Manchester. —*Hartford Courant*

1996. The 104th Congress came in like a lion two years ago, roaring about the revolutionary things it was going to do, but went out like a lamb last week, meekly following President Clinton wherever he wished to lead. —*Commercial Appeal* (Memphis Tennessee)

1998. They say that March comes in like a lion and goes out like a lamb, which in fact does happen enough that the hackneyed adage holds some truth. But what in the name of Old Man Winter can we say about the so-called February from which we've just emerged? —*Boston Globe*
See also NOT WITH A BANG BUT A WHIMPER.

Marching to a different drummer. Living and behaving in an individualistic manner. The saying originated in the second half of the nineteenth century, but became current in the mid-twentieth century. It is an allusion to Henry David Thoreau's *Walden* (1854): "If a man does not keep pace with his companions, perhaps it is because he hears a different drummer. Let him step to the music which he hears, however measured or far away."

1991. NORTHEASTERN SAUDI ARABIA—The sounds of war may be music to some ears. But others, even here amid the tanks with their gun barrels aimed north toward a hostile border, prefer the beat of a different drummer. —*Boston Globe*

1992. Today's CDs (Christmas discs) move to the beat of some very different drummer boy, boasting an ethnic diversity undreamt of by certain governors of Mississippi. —*Commercial Appeal* (Memphis, Tennessee)

1995. The rest of the 49 states look to us, squint and say, "Wasn't Massachusetts the state that voted for Marx or McGovern or one of them? Aren't they the state that still keeps refusing to execute people?" Yep, and here we are in musicland marching to different drummers again. —*Boston Globe*

1996. The safer approach is to stick to conventional housing styles, [Dorcas] Helfant says. "This is not the time of your life you want to march to a different drummer," she says. —*Detroit News*

1997. Just two and a half years ago, Zajedno's troika of leaders pranced to very different drummers. The best-known of them, novelist Vuk Draskovic, was negotiating with Milosevic about joining the strongman's Socialists in a coalition government. —*Time*

1998. [Larry] Stefanki, who had worked with John McEnroe, hooked up with [Marcelo] Rios in 1995 after Rios's agent came up to him and said, "This guy walks to a different drummer." —*Detroit News*

Marriages are made in heaven. Ideal alliances are foreordained. Marriage is an ideal state. Sometimes used ironically. The proverb has been traced back to *The Palace of Pleasure* (1566) by William Paynter (c.1540–94). First attested in the United States in *Letters from New England* (1696). The saying takes varying forms: *All marriages are made in heaven; Happy marriages are made in heaven; Matches are made in heaven,* etc. Often shortened to *a marriage made in heaven.* It has counterparts in other languages: *Les mariages sont écrits dans le ciel* (French); *Ehen werden im Himmel geschlossen* (German).

1978. "Marriage is probably the most difficult, delicate undertaking any human being attempts, and we don't have an iota of preparation or training, only the idiotic presumption that marriages are made in heaven and that one lives happily ever after." —Howard Fast, *Second Generation*

1984. There were some obvious advantages to the plan [of a merger between Chrysler and Volkswagen]. Our dealer network would increase dramatically. Our purchasing power would be much greater. We could spread our fixed costs over a much larger volume of cars. It really was a marriage made in heaven. —Lee Iacocca with William Novak, *Iacocca*

1985. He then patiently explained that when he was a boy the best marriages were not made in heaven, but over lunch at the club. Pity that sort of thing was going out of style. —Erich Segal, *The Class*

1992. "He had an idea about raising money in Europe and Japan, and he was looking for something to hang it on. He read about me and my dream." Morales looked at Estrada. "A marriage made in heaven." —Philip Friedman, *Inadmissible Evidence*

1993. *A Marriage Made in Heaven or Too Tired for an Affair* —Title of a book by Erma Bombeck

1994. "The carillon bell contains a minor third, and Hebrew modes go very well on these bells," he said. "With this minor sound and the ancient modes, it's a marriage made in heaven." —*New York Times*

Marry in haste, repent at leisure. If you marry someone you don't know very well, you will regret it all your life. The proverb has been traced back to *Duties of Marriage* (1566). Witty variants appear in Shakespeare, Congreve, and Byron. First attested in the United States in *New English Canaan of Thomas Morton* (1637). The adage can be found in varying forms: *Better stay chaste than marry in haste; Don't get angry in haste to repent at leisure; Marry in Lent and you'll live to repent; Marry in May and repent in December,* etc.

1593–94.
> *Kate:* No shame but mine: I must, forsooth,
> be forc'd
> To give my hand oppos'd against my heart
> Unto a mad-brain rudesby, full of spleen;
> Who woo'd in haste and means to wed at
> leisure.
> —Shakespeare, *The Taming of the Shrew*,
> III, ii

1693. *Sharper:* Thus grief still treads upon the
> heels of pleasure;
> Married in haste, we may repent at leisure.
> *Setter:* Some by experience find those words
> mis-placed:
> At leisure married, they repent in haste.
> —William Congreve, *The Old Bachelor*

1819–24.
Now hatred is by far the longest pleasure;
Men love in haste, but they detest at leisure
—George Gordon, Lord Byron, *Don Juan*

1922. Marry in May and repent in December. —James Joyce, *Ulysses*

1961. Don't marry on the spur of the moment. If love is real, it will last. The tired line "marry in haste, repent in leisure" may be cliché, but it still makes good sense. —Ann Landers, *Since You Ask Me*

1992. MARRYING IN HASTE —Headline of an article about two runners who wed halfway wed through a marathon, *People*

See also LOOK BEFORE YOU LEAP.

The means justify the end. *See* THE END JUSTIFIES THE MEANS.

The meek shall inherit the earth. Humble people will triumph in the end. The proverb originated in the New Testament as part of the Sermon on the Mount.

Blessed are the meek: for they shall inherit the earth. —Matthew, 5:5, *Authorized Version*, 1611

1978. ... His favorite [proverb], spoken not in humility but in grim expectation: "The meek shall inherit the earth." —Stephen King, *The Stand*

1980. The meek shall inherit the earth—but not its mineral rights. (J. Paul Getty) —Herb Cohen, *You Can Negotiate Anything*

1986. We were Americans, we were southerners, and, God help us, we were heroically and irrevocably stupid and compliant. The meek may yet inherit the earth, but they will not inherit Colleton. —Pat Conroy, *The Prince of Tides*

1990. Comedian Mel Brooks, who appeared in *The Muppet Movie*, once said that the basic message of *The Muppet Show* was that "The meek shall inherit the earth." —*Reader's Digest*

1992. Meek [Carrie Meek], and ready to inherit her place in Congress. —*People*

1993. A sign at the very beginning of the exhibit, on a wall just to the right of the entrance, advises: "Insects won't inherit the earth—they own it now." —*New York Times*

A merry heart makes a cheerful countenance. Your state of mind is reflected in your appearance. The proverb appears in the Old Testament. It has been traced back in English to *Garden of Pleasure* (1573). First attested in the United States in *Travels Through U.S., 1806–1811* (1812).

A merry heart maketh a cheerful countenance; but by sorrow of heart the spirit is broken. —Proverbs, 15:13, *Authorized Version*, 1611

1960. The driver of the wagon slowed down his mules, and a shrill-voiced woman called out: "He that cometh in vanity departeth in darkness!"
    Miss Maudie answered: "A merry heart maketh a cheerful countenance!" —Harper Lee, *To Kill a Mockingbird*

Might makes right. By imposing their will on weaker people, those in power make the rules. Force overcomes right. The motto has been traced back to *Political Songs* (c. 1330). In 1546, it was included in John Heywood's collection of proverbs. First cited in the United States in *General History of New England* (1700). In 1860, Lincoln reversed the order to *Right makes might*. In the twentieth century, the slogan is often associated with fascist ideology. *Might is right* and *Might overcomes right* are variants.

1860. Let us have faith that right makes might, and in that faith let us to the end dare to do our duty as we understand it. —Abraham Lincoln, Address at Cooper Union

1957. Might was still right. —*Time*

1984. Some people don't want to admit that Israel was hurt by the policy of might makes right. —Anthony Lewis, *New York Times*

1993. "When parents hit a child, they are teaching the following: Might makes right." —Abigail Van Buren, "Dear Abby," *Times* (Trenton)

See also IT'S SURVIVAL OF THE FITTEST.

Miles to go before I sleep. *See* I HAVE PROMISES TO KEEP, AND MILES TO GO BEFORE I SLEEP.

The mills of the gods grind slowly, but they grind exceedingly fine. Justice is often a slow process, but it is inevitable. The proverb has been traced back to the third-century Greek philosopher Sextus Empiricus: "The mills of the gods grind slowly, but they grind small." The maxim appears in George Herbert's book of proverbs (1640). In 1870, American poet Henry Wadsworth Longfellow, translating a work entitled "Retribution" (1654) by German poet Friedrich von Logau (1604–55), wrote: "Though the mills of God grind slowly, yet they grind exceeding small."

1979. He paused and studied her again. "You're an

odd one. Nothing to do with this history, but may I ask what you're in here for?"

"Since it appears to be a common question that pervades this place, I don't mind. I'm almost used to it. Contempt of Congress."

"Oh? Wait a minute, Barbara Cohen. I remember. But that was ages ago."

"Like the mills of the gods, the mills of justice grind slowly, but they grind exceedingly fine." —Howard Fast, *The Establishment*

1984. "I'm tired of waiting. I live like a bum."

"What's the big rush? It's the mills of the gods."

"What about them?"

"The mills of the gods grind slowly," he told me, "yet they grind exceedingly fine." —Joseph Heller, *God Knows*

See also CRIME DOESN'T PAY; MURDER WILL OUT; TRUTH WILL (COME) OUT.

A mind is a terrible thing to waste. Slogan of the United Negro College Fund since 1972. In 1989, Dan Quayle was widely ridiculed for his bungling misquotation of the line at a Fund luncheon.

1984. We will launch a renaissance in education, in science and learning. A mind is a terrible thing to waste. —Walter Mondale, *New York Times*

1989. In preparation for a luncheon for the United Negro College Fund, Quayle's aides had put the group's slogan, "A mind is a terrible thing to waste," in the Vice President's talking points. But he rambled off-course: "And you take the U.N.C.F. model that what a waste it is to lose one's mind or not to have a mind is being very wasteful. How true that is." —*New York Times Magazine*

1993. A waist is a terrible thing to mind. —Cartoon by Art Sansom, "Born Loser," *Times* (Trenton)

1994. Minds of businesspeople, especially, are terrible things to waste. —*U.S. 1* (Princeton)

Mind your p's and q's. Watch your step. Be on your best behavior. The origin of this saying is unknown. It has been suggested that *p* stands for "please" and *q* for "thank you" and that children were once admonished for not using these words. According to another theory, *p* meant a *p*int of alcohol and *q* a *q*uart. E. D. Hirsch, Jr., argues that it derives from a teacher's request that students keep their handwriting legible and not confuse the letters *p* and *q*. The maxim has been current since the seventeenth century.

1979. "You're one of a kind, Mrs. Cohen. This is not Alcatraz, but neither is it the Fairmont. Just mind your P's and Q's. —Howard Fast, *The Establishment*

1985. Here there were no demands on her to "sit up straight," or to "behave like a lady," or to "mind your Ps and Qs." —Michael Korda, *Queenie*

1987. The more they drank, of course, the drunker they became, until it was likely that the next day, when the vessel was to sail, they would be unable to work. It therefore fell to the quartermaster to insure that the seamen were sober enough to serve on the vessel. So, as they left the vessel for an evening of revelry, he would admonish them to "mind your p's and q's"—don't drink too much. —Douglas Starr, "On Language," *New York Times Magazine*

1993. Queen will expect Buckingham Palace tourists to mind their P's and queues. —*Times* (Trenton)

Misery loves company. Unhappy people find comfort in sharing their woes with others who have suffered similar pains and setbacks. The idea was expressed in the first century by Publilius Syrus. The saying has been traced back in English to *Meditations on Passion* (c.1349) and is similar to a mid-fourteenth century Latin aphorism: *Gaudium est miseris socios habuisse penarum.* In 1670, it was included in John Ray's collection of English proverbs. First attested in the United States in 1775.

1775. All my Letters are intersepted by those Rebels who want Every one to be kept in Dark like themselves. (Misery Loves Company). —T. Gilbert, quoted by W. B. Clark et al., *Naval Documents of the American Revolution*

1981. It's reassuring to know that others suffer from the same feeling of anger, jealously, hostility, insecurity, and guilt that plague them. Misery does love company. —Abigail Van Buren, *The Best of Dear Abby*

1990. Misery loves company, but guilt loves it even more. —*Washington Post*

1992. Still, most Democrats have been wandering in the wilderness for the better part of 12 years, reduced to chicken-in-the-pot lunches at Duke Zeibert's and misery-loves-company suppers with fellow also-rans. —*New York Times*

See also MISERY MAKES STRANGE BEDFELLOWS.

Misery makes strange bedfellows. Misfortune may force us to befriend people we would otherwise avoid. The phrase first appears in Shakespeare's *Tempest* (1611). First cited in the United States in *Writings of John Quincy Adams* (1813). *Adversity makes strange bedfellows* is a variant.

1611. *Trinculo:* Alas! the storm is come again! my best way is to creep under his gaberdine; there is no other shelter hereabout; misery acquaints a man with strange bedfellows. —Shakespeare, *The Tempest*, II, ii

1984. I had Abishai transfer him far away from me to the front of our pathetic column, well out of earshot and closer to Bathsheba, whom he'd vilified as a harlot, and with whom he is now in league. Misery makes strange bedfellows. —Joseph Heller, *God Knows*

1985. "There's nothing more dangerous than the doctrine of necessity. Far from making good bedfellows, it usually makes the worst kind." —Michael Korda, *Queenie*

1991. But adversity makes for strange bedfellows, and the fact is, as Will and I sauntered out into the sun with our ghosts at peace, I was thinking of Sister George's music and not Sister Immaculata's fury. —*New York Times Magazine*

See also POLITICS MAKES STRANGE BEDFELLOWS.

A miss is as good as a mile. If you miss a mark, it's irrelevant how close you come: the outcome is the same. The proverb has been traced back to *Remains Concerning Britain* (1614) by English historian William Camden (1551–1623). It has been common in the United States since 1788.

1825. He was very near being a poet—but a miss is as good as a mile, and he always fell short of the mark. —Sir Walter Scott, *Journal*

1894. *Man:* A narrow shave; but a miss is as good as a mile. —George Bernard Shaw, *Arms and the Man*

1957. A Miss was better than a mile tonight as Winifred Ann Zebley won her case in traffic court. —*Bangor Daily News* (Me.)

1959. A miff was as good as a smile. —*Time*

1982. A miss is as good as a ... Mr.! —Judith Frost Stark, *Don't Cross Your Bridge Before ... You Pay the Toll*

See also CLOSE, BUT NO CIGAR.

Monday morning quarterbacking. Second-guessing. Criticism after the fact. Football games are traditionally played on Sunday, so Monday was often devoted to analyzing the errors made by the quarterbacks and postulating what they should have done. The phrase first appeared in

Barry Wood's *What Price Football* (1932). *Monday morning quarterback* is a common form.

1983. As any Monday-morning quarterback can tell you, when your friend said she was sure you wouldn't want to attend because the party was set for couples and you were single, you should have told her you would either bring an escort or come alone and take your chances. —Abigail Van Buren, "Dear Abby," *New York Post*

1984. Political Monday-morning quarterbacking is a popular pursuit in this city, and it appears that this year's election prognosticating and lint-picking will by no means be confined to watering holes or to the outcome of domestic contests. —*New York Times*

1987. "Criminals can be very hard to subdue. There's always the Monday morning quarterback, but a lot of times, people don't realize what went on. A white cop with a black person, a black cop with a white person—it's always more complicated than what people think." —*New York Times*

1993. "If they believe they weren't liable, they should have litigated," Ms. Lieberman said. "It's the equivalent of Monday morning quarterbacking: They wanted to have the case settled and behind them, and now they want to claim they didn't do anything wrong." —*New York Times*

See also DON'T CLOSE (BAR, LOCK, SHUT) THE BARN (STABLE) DOOR AFTER THE HORSE RUNS AWAY (HAS FLED, BEEN STOLEN); IT IS EASY TO BE WISE AFTER THE EVENT.

Money begets money. Those who already have money find it easy to make more. The rich tend to get richer. The adage has been traced back to *Discourse upon Usury* (1572). In 1670, it was included in John Ray's collection of proverbs. First used in the United States in 1748 by Benjamin Franklin. Variants include: *Money attracts (breeds) (comes to) (draws) (gets) (goes to) (makes) money;* and *Money loves company.*

1748. Remember that money is of prolific generating nature. Money can beget money, and its offspring can beget more. —Benjamin Franklin, "Letter to My Friend A. B."

1936. Money breeds money.
     Money rules the world.
          —Carl Sandburg, *The People, Yes*

1961. "Wish I knew something about business."
     "I can tell you all I know in one sentence. Money gets money." —John Steinbeck, *The Winter of Our Discontent*

1980. The old saying is still valid: "Money goes to

money." —Herb Cohen, *You Can Negotiate Anything*

1992. "Emily's List [a political action committee that supports liberal women candidates] makes a difference because money begets money," says New York Senate hopeful Geraldine Ferraro.... —*People*

Money burns a hole in his pocket. The very fact of having money makes a person eager to spend it. The proverb has been traced back to Thomas More (c.1530). First cited in the United States in *Tim Bunker Papers* (1868). *To have money to burn* is a similar figure of speech. Other pronouns (*my, your, her,* etc.) are often used.

c.1530.
A little wanton money, which burned out the bottom of his purse. —Thomas More, *Works*

1976. There is only one agency in Washington that has money to burn and it doesn't have to answer to anybody. —Art Buchwald, *Washington Is Leaking*

1985. He will soon have $1 billion burning a hole in his pocket. —*Forbes*

1992. Shorin wants another leg to his business and last year launched *Topps Magazine* for card collectors of all ages. He's also contemplating another special dividend, or a stock buyback, or just sitting tight. Says he: "The money won't burn a hole in my pocket." —*Fortune*

1995. No matter how selfish or manipulative it may seem, you must extricate yourself from an extravagant joint endeavor. You don't have money to waste, but what you have seems to be burning a hole in someone else's pocket. —Patric Walker, "Your Daily Horoscope," *New York Post*

Money can't buy happiness. Money can buy material things, but real happiness must be truly earned. Now often used ironically. Rousseau (1712–78) wrote in 1750: "Money buys everything, except morality and citizens." The proverb first appeared in the United States in *William & Mary College Quarterly* (1792). It is found in varying forms: *Money can't buy everything; Money can't buy friends; Money can't buy love,* etc.

1936. "You do talk scandalous!"
"Scandalously and truly. Always providing you have enough courage—or money—you can do without a reputation."
"Money can't buy everything." —Margaret Mitchell, *Gone With the Wind*

1963. Money couldn't buy friends, but you get a better class of enemy. —Spike Milligan, *Puckoon*

1964. I don't care too much for money,
    Money can't buy me love.
        —John Lennon & Paul McCartney, "Can't Buy Me Love"

1977. "If he's so rich, why is he"—Jonathan had in mind to say "sucking hind teat" but he instantly changed that to—"playing second fiddle in politics. Money can buy happiness, but it can't buy power." —William Safire, *Full Disclosure*

1982. Let the rest of the world believe that money could not buy everything. These people knew better. Money bought them beauty and love and luxury and a place in heaven. —Sidney Sheldon, *Master of the Game*

1988. As a former starving vacuum-cleaner salesperson, she's learned the true value of a buck and looks forward to a rosy future: "They say money can't buy you happiness, but I don't care. When I get enough money I'll just pay people to tell me I'm happy and, because I'll be so shallow at that point, I'll believe them." —*US*

1989. In December 1986 the third Mrs. Carson walked into a Manhattan store and bought needlepoint pillows that read ANYONE WHO SAYS MONEY DOESN'T BUY HAPPINESS DOESN'T KNOW WHERE TO SHOP. —Laurence Leamer, *King of the Night: The Biography of Johnny Carson*

1992. Even if Mark Harris did marry Martha [Raye] for her money, that should be their business. Who says money can't buy happiness? —Letters to the Editor, *People*

1993. Always remember, my son, "money can't buy happiness." However, in some cases, it *can* be used as a down payment. —Cartoon by Browne, "Hagar the Horrible," *Times* (Trenton)
See also MONEY ISN'T EVERYTHING.

Money doesn't grow on trees. It is not easy to earn money. Often said to someone, especially a child, who spends money frivolously as an admonition to be more frugal. The proverb has been traced in the United States as far back as about 1750. The word *money* may be replaced by other subjects: *happiness, experience, good jobs, real professionals,* etc.

1951. "I can always tell a good man when I see one. Stark'll make me one damn fine cook."
"Yes, Sir," Warden said. "I think he will."
"You do?" Holmes said, surprised. "Well. Well, it's like I say, real soldiers don't grow on trees, and you have to look hard before you find one." —James Jones, *From Here to Eternity*

1969. And then the newspaper girl held up her hand. "Mr. Trout—" she said, "if I win [a free trip], can I take my sister, too?"

"Hell no," said Kilgore Trout. You think money grows on trees?" —Kurt Vonnegut, Jr., *Slaughter-house-Five*

1980. True, I had inherited the depression-type mentality which forever leaves a still small voice in the victim's spirit to whisper: "Jobs don't grow on trees." —Norman Podhoretz, *Making It*

1985. A lot of homeowners have discovered that trees grow on money. —Quoted in *Reader's Digest*

1990. Kids used to think money grew on trees. Now they know better: it comes out of cash machines. —*Ladies Home Journal*

1991. The archconservative newspaper publisher William Loeb wrote a front-page editorial in the *Manchester Union-Leader* saying that while the President cuts federal programs and asks Americans to sacrifice, Nancy must not live as if "money grows on trees." —Kitty Kelley, *Nancy Reagan*

1993. "Money doesn't grow on trees," she would often say, using the ancient cliché, then add: "In fact, it doesn't grow anywhere unless you plant it, water it and cultivate it. You have to pay attention. All the time." —*Times* (Trenton)

Money doesn't stink. *See* MONEY HAS NO SMELL.

Money gets money. *See* MONEY BEGETS MONEY.

Money goes to money. *See* MONEY BEGETS MONEY.

Money has no smell. It doesn't make any difference how money is obtained. Attributed to the Roman emperor Vespasian (a.d. 9–79). According to legend, Vespasian's son criticized him for levying a tax on all public rest rooms. Holding a coin from the first payment under his son's nose, Vespasian asked him if it smelled. The son said no. *Atque e lotio est* ("And yet it comes from urine"), replied Vespasian, *Pecunia non olet* ("Money doesn't stink"). The proverb is often quoted in Latin. It also occurs in German as *Geld stinkt nicht*; the word *stink* may also be used in English in place of *smell*.

1946. Perhaps I was a fool to feel that way about my little inheritance. Perhaps it was no different from any other inheritance anybody had. Perhaps the Emperor Vespasian was right when, jingling in his jeans the money which had been derived from a tax on urinals, he wittily remarked: *"Pecunia non olet."* —Robert Penn Warren, *All the King's Men*

1984. "Even Vespasian when he collected his toilet tax had to justify himself: *Pecunia non olet.* But we've come to a point where it's *only* money that doesn't stink. —Saul Bellow, *Him with His Foot in His Mouth and Other Stories*

Money is no object. The price is not important. Said by someone who can afford any price.

1934. "It was possible for me to arrange that, by a stroke of luck. And, may I add," he smiled apologetically, "that as they say: money is no object." —F. Scott Fitzgerald, *Tender Is the Night*

1991. When the man found the car needed a quart [of gas], he asked, "What kind do you use?"

"I just want the finest," Mary said. "Money's no object." —*Reader's Digest*

1992. "Money is no object, and these voices tell us he'll spend whatever it takes to snuff this thing out." —John Grisham, *The Pelican Brief*

1993. Money is the object. Like F. Scott Fitzgerald and Charles Dickens, Edith Wharton died (in 1937) before completing her last novel. Now Marion Mainwaring (*Murder in Pastiche*) has finished *The Buccaneers* ..., Wharton's saga of five young American nouveaux riches. —*Modern Maturity*

Money is power. Those who have money also have influence. In a letter to Douglas Kinnaird, Byron (1788–1824) wrote: "They say knowledge is power. I used to think so, but now know that they meant money." Attested in the United States in *Almanacs* (1741).

1922. —Because you don't save, Mr Deasy said, pointing his finger. You don't know yet what money is. Money is power. —James Joyce, *Ulysses*

1936. Money is power, freedom, a cushion, the root of all evil, the sum of blessings. —Carl Sandburg, *The People, Yes*

1946. "Money is power," Lanny said. "Money commands respect and obedience from other people, and not everybody has the strength of character to carry such a responsibility." —Upton Sinclair, *A World to Win*

1955. "Yes. Shut up, please. I thought of all the clichés. 'It's not money, but what you can buy with it. Money is power. Money is security. Money is freedom.' And so forth." —Herman Wouk, *Marjorie Morningstar*

1992. She is always handing out money and presents, and they treat her like she is some kind of queen.... I have nothing to give, so I am ignored. I am not homeless yet, and God forbid I ever should be, because I'd be dumped into a state home and forgotten. Money is power. —Abigail Van Buren, "Dear Abby," *Times* (Trenton)

1994. In our capitalist society, money is power and freedom—and a sense of security. —*Princeton Living*

See also KNOWLEDGE IS POWER; MONEY IS THE ROOT OF ALL EVIL; MONEY MAKES THE MARE TO GO; MONEY TALKS.

Money is the root of all evil. Money perverts moral values. Crimes and other evil deeds often result from greed. First appeared in the New Testament. It has been traced back in English to *Homilies* (c.1000). First attested in the United States in *History of Indian Wars in New England* (1677). The adage has often been turned on its head as: *The lack of money is the root of all evil. Money is the root of all evil in politics* is a recent variant coined in 1992 by an unsuccessful candidate for public office.

For the love of money is the root of all evil. —Timothy, 6:10, *Authorized Version,* 1611

1872. The want of money is the root of all evil. —Samuel Butler, *Erehwon*

1903. Lack of money is the root of all evil. —George Bernard Shaw, *Man and Superman*

1957. Moral of whole career appeared to be: Make money. Hell hath no fire that burns like need. Poverty is the root of all evil. —John Cheever, *The Wapshot Chronicle*

1961. ' "The love of money is the root of all evil," ' intoned the Judge.
    "I do not love it, Judge. I have not been near enough to it to build up any affection to speak of." —Bernard Malamud, *The Natural*

1990. When Lamont said money was the root of all evil, Jack shyly interrupted: "The Bible doesn't say 'money,' " he grinned. "It says, 'The *love* of money is the root of all evil.' " —Ron Chernow, *The House of Morgan*

1991. MONEY IS THE ROOT OF ALL MUSICALS —Headline, *New York Times*

1994. Money. At turns, it's been deemed the root of all evil, what makes the world go round, revealed not to grow on trees. Our attitude towards it says more about ourselves than most anything could. —*Princeton Living*

1995. Money is, apparently, the root of all evil, and the methods by which our political candidates are selected is, as Jack Kemp said, "revolting." —Letters to the Editor, *New York Times Magazine*

Money isn't everything. Money may be important, but other factors weigh equally heavily. The idea was expressed by American humorist Charles Farrar Browne (1834–67) in *Artemus Ward: His Book* (1842): "My friends, money is not all. It is not money that will mend a broken heart or reassemble the fragments of a dream." The aphorism was first used in its current form in 1928 by Eugene O'Neill in *Marco Millions:* "Money isn't everything, not always." American journalist and wit Franklin Pierce Adams (F.P.A.) (1881–1960) added: "Money isn't everything, but lack of money isn't anything."

1965. Soon Ball became Under Secretary of State for Economic Affairs; on entering his impressive new office in the State Department, he is said to have gaily remarked, "Monnet isn't everything." —Arthur M. Schlesinger, Jr., *A Thousand Days*

1967. "Before it's too late, learn. Money is everything." —Elia Kazan, *The Arrangement*

1991. "You'll be paid."
    "Man, money ain't everything." —John Grisham, *The Firm*

1992. For our customers, money isn't everything. It's everywhere. —Ad for Chase Manhattan bank, *Wall Street Journal*

1994. Money isn't everything, but with prices today it's nothing. —Joey Adams, "Strictly for Laughs," *New York Post*

See also MONEY CAN'T BUY HAPPINESS.

Money loves company. See MONEY BEGETS MONEY.

Money makes money. See MONEY BEGETS MONEY.

Money makes the mare to go. Money makes things happen. Those who can pay well get what they want. The adage has been traced back to *Early English Carols* (c.1500). In 1670, it was included in John Ray's collection of English proverbs. First cited in the United States in *Papers of Sir William Johnson* (1771).

(undated).
    "Will you lend me your mare to go a mile?"
    "No, she is lame leaping over a stile."
    "But if you will her to me spare,
    You shall have money for your mare."
    "Oh, ho! say you so?
    Money will make the mare to go."
            —*Old Glees and Catches*

1936. M-G-M [Metro Goldwyn Mayer] … forces us to revise an old adage: Mayer makes the money go. —*New Yorker*

1946. They had a roll of money, and "money will make the mare to go," and likewise all her Chinese substitutes. —Upton Sinclair, *A World to Win*

1946. "I understand some things," Adam said grimly, and the jaw set.

"And some you don't, just like I don't, but one thing I understand and you don't is what makes the mare go. I can make the mare go." —Robert Penn Warren, *All the King's Men*

1957. The old saying, "Money makes the mare go," could very well be transposed to read, "Money makes the horses pull." —*Bangor Daily News* (Me.)

See also MONEY IS POWER; MONEY TALKS.

Money talks. An offer of money is often the most persuasive argument in getting someone to do what you want. The saying has been traced back to G. Torriano's *Italian Proverbs* (1666). Aphra Behn (1640–89) wrote in *The Rover* (1680): "Money speaks sense in a language all nations understand." First attested in the United States in the *Saturday Evening Post* (September 3, 1903). *Money talks and big business money talks loudest* is a recent variant (1991). Another common modern variant is *money talks, bullshit walks.*

1903. When money talks it often merely remarks "Good-by." —*Saturday Evening Post*

1951. In New York, boy, money really talks—I'm not kidding. —J. D. Salinger, *The Catcher in the Rye*

1951. "Balls!" Maggio said. "You seen them four clubs up before you bet. Put the blame on Mame."

"I call," Andy said.

"Money talks," Maggio said. —James Jones, *From Here to Eternity*

1965. Money doesn't talk, it swears. —Bob Dylan, "It's Alright, Ma (I'm Only Bleeding)"

1980. Money talks … but does it tell the truth? —Herb Cohen, *You Can Negotiate Anything*

1984. America is different from Europe. Here auto workers are as capitalistic as management. And no wonder. When it comes to hourly workers, the UAW members *are* the elite of the world. And when money talks, ideology walks. —Lee Iacocca with William Novak, *Iacocca*

1986. "Don't get too excited. Mannon's a lot pickier than everyone seems to think."

"Money talks."

"To some people."

"To everyone." —Jackie Collins, *Hollywood Hus-*

bands

1991. She'd pay the man a king's ransom if need be. American, the official said. Good. Money talks in America. —Alexandra Ripley, *Scarlett*

1992. "If money talks, there will be plenty of California alumni saying 'no' when Rowan College calls for donations," Ms. Weydt said, drawing applause and cheers. —*New York Times*

1993. I hate to say it but money talks. Axles get greased, wheels move and red tape is severed when major bucks are involved. —Erma Bombeck, *Times* (Trenton)

1994. If money talks, then the local currency here says it all. —*New York Times*

See also MONEY IS POWER; MONEY MAKES THE MARE TO GO.

Monkey see, monkey do. Refers to the thoughtless imitation of another's actions. It may be used as a criticism or admonition of people (often children) for imitating others. The phrase originated in America in the 1920s and reached Britain in the 1950s.

1983. Supporters of the MX who are honest enough to acknowledge its purpose as a nuclear war–fighting weapon argue that there is no reason to make Soviet targets safe from U.S. ICBMs when comparable targets in this country are at risk from Soviet ICBMs. This argument, however, substitutes monkey-see-monkey-do logic for a well-reasoned de-escalation of nuclear competition. —*Christian Science Monitor*

1986. If parents are tube addicts, chances are their kids will be, too. The proverbial monkey-see, monkey-do pattern is never more true than where TV is concerned. [Nicholas P.] Criscuolo would rather have kids see their parents reading than tubing. —*Christian Science Monitor*

1992. Maybe it was monkey see, monkey do, when a mob protested at a Brooklyn courthouse to show its displeasure over the conviction of crime boss John Gotti. —*Commercial Appeal* (Memphis, Tennessee)

1997. Monkey see, monkey do. Baby boomers fondly remember the antics of Curious George, the mischievous fictional monkey created by H. A. Rey and his wife, Margaret. Nowadays, baby boom parents are rereading the adventure of George to their children. They are buying up Curious George memorabilia, too. —*Detroit News*

The more the merrier. Everyone's welcome to join in: the more people who get involved, the better it will be. The saying appears in *Early Eng-*

lish *Alliterative Poems* (c.1380). In 1546, it was included in John Heywood's collection of proverbs. First attested in the United States in the *Papers of Thomas Jefferson* (1786).

1962. "I mean there's room for both of us, I trust." "Lord, yes," Hawke said. "The more the merrier." —Herman Wouk, *Youngblood Hawke*

1975. I was glad to see him. He was supposed to know something about engines, but I was so happy about the way things were turning out that I would have joyously welcomed anyone. The more the merrier. —Mark Vonnegut, *The Eden Express*

1979. "Be my guest," I said. "The more the merrier." —Kurt Vonnegut, Jr., *Jailbird*

1987. Mr. Fennimore, who is white, and Joseph Price, a black, said before going on patrol last night that they both have patrolled with Hasidic Jews in the past and would welcome more.... "The more the merrier," Mr. Fennimore said. "The more eyes in the street, the better it is." —*New York Times*

1991. "Let them in," commanded the driver of an M16 bus on Lexington Avenue. "The more, the merrier." —*New York Times*

1993. "The land on their reservations isn't good for much, but it's fine for buffalo," McFarlane says. "The idea would be to get them going as producers. The more the merrier, I say." —*New York Times Magazine*

1994. The more the merrier. —Bob Dole commenting on candidates for the 1996 presidential race, "Meet the Press," NBC

The more things change, the more they stay the same. Nothing changes too much. The proverb is of French origin and was used by the French novelist Alphonse Karr (1808–90). It also appears in George Bernard Shaw's *Revolutionist's Handbook* (1903).

1849. *Plus ça change, plus c'est la même chose.* ("The more things change, the more they remain the same.") —Alphonse Karr, *Les Guêpes*

1977. According to the Senate Intelligence Committee, "More than 175 reports overheard on the wiretap, which continued until 1948, were delivered to the Truman White House." ... As the French say: The more things change, the more they remain the same. —Victor Lasky, *It Didn't Start with Watergate*

1986. A brief verbal confrontation with the Mongols, then a musing about which danger to Russian integrity was greater, the German or the Mongol.

"Jesus, you know they *still* think that way?" Toland chuckled.

"The more things change ..." —Tom Clancy, *Red Storm Rising*

1992. She [Hillary Rodham Clinton] noted that even before Mrs. Roosevelt moved into the White House, she was assailed for speaking out too much. "So the more times change," she said, "the less times change, apparently." —*New York Times*

1993. It's no longer true that the more things change, the more they remain the same. Nowadays, they just get worse. —*Times* (Trenton)

See also HISTORY REPEATS ITSELF.

A mother can take care of ten children, but sometimes ten children can't take care of one mother. A mother may devote her life to her children, only to be forgotten and neglected in her old age. The saying is of Jewish origin.**

1991. While reading my mail, I am often reminded of that old saying, "A mother can take care of ten children, but sometimes ten children can't take care of one mother." —Abigail Van Buren, *The Best of Dear Abby*

1992. "Why did they put you in a nursing home?" ... "You asked why?! The old cliché that a mother can take care of ten kids—seven in my case—but the kids can't take care of their mother is still valid, I'm sorry to say." —Overheard in a Jewish nursing home

See also FATHER KNOWS BEST; HONOR YOUR FATHER AND YOUR MOTHER.

The mother of all.... The most striking or impressive example of. The phrase is an overliteral translation of an Arabic idiom used by President Saddam Hussein at the beginning of the Gulf War in January 1991. The saying quickly caught on and became popular in all English-speaking countries.

1991. Three days before the first direct US-Iraq talks on resolving the Persian Gulf crisis and nine days before the UN deadline for the withdrawal of Iraqi forces from Kuwait, Saddam Hussein yesterday delivered a fiery speech urging his country's military to prepare to fight "the mother of all battles... against the foolish, tyrant American administration." —*Boston Globe*

1991. All other measures of distinction pale in comparison to the mode and style of travel of a true monarch, which is why I can state without fear of contradiction that Queen Elizabeth II is peerlessly regal, the true article, the mother of all queens. —*Boston Globe*

1998. On Wednesday the Rev. Ian Paisley, firebrand leader of the radical Democratic Unionist Party (DUP), launched a "no" campaign and promised to hold rallies throughout Northern Ireland. Dr. Paisley calls the peace pact "the mother of all treachery" and insist a Clinton visit would be "interference." —*Christian Science Monitor*

1998. Greenspan closed his eyes to the speculative games those hedge funds were playing as long as they made money for U.S. institutions. I hope he will start setting tough lending rules for the U.S. banks to hedge funds. Greenspan's bailout of one hedge fund was the Mother of All Interventions. —*Time*

The mountain labored and brought forth a mouse. A mighty effort (the mountain in labor) yielded a very small effect (a mouse). Said when high expectations are disappointed, when people wishing too much end up with nothing or when people promise a lot, but deliver very little. The Roman poet Horace (65–8 b.c.) used the phrase to satirize the work of bad poets: *Parturient montes, nascetur ridiculus mus* ("The mountains will be in labor, and a ridiculous mouse will be brought forth"). A similar idea was expressed by Aesop: "A huge gap appeared in the side of the mountain. At last a tiny mouse came forth." ("The Mountain in Labor"). The proverb has been traced back to *Confessio Amantis* (c.1390) by English poet John Gower (?1330–1408). First attested in the United States in *Hinckley Papers* (1685).

1962. Most of the review had attacked the extravagant boasts on the jacket. The book itself Gebble had dismissed as "a laboring mountain that never even brings forth its mouse." —Herman Wouk, *Youngblood Hawke*

1967. "There were thirteen, as a total, who could be said to be law breakers who were at the time we filed this report still members of the Teamsters and holding office.... It seems to me that in a three-year investigation as widespread as it was, that to be able to come up with only thirteen violators was a case of the mountain having labored and brought forth a mouse." —Ralph de Toledano, *R.F.K.*

1991. "It will be illuminating to hear from competent and knowledgeable witnesses familiar with the details of how the committee conducted the long, arduous and expensive Keating Five investigation," Mr. Helms said. "Such a public investigation may disclose that the committee labored and brought forth a mouse." —*New York Times*

Much ado about nothing. A great deal of talk or fuss and little or no substance. The expression was current in Shakespeare's time and was used as the title of one his comedies (c.1599). *To make much ado about something* is also heard.

1976. "Advertising and Publicity: Much Ado About Something." —Claudia Jessup & Genie Chipps, *The Woman's Guide to Starting a Business*

1981. Sex is much ado about nothing. I say, "If you want something done right—do it yourself." Alone and Happy. —Abigail Van Buren, *The Best of Dear Abby*

1986. G. Gordon Liddy, who calls the whole Iran uproar "much ado about nothing," suggests that the President might have "said something to the effect of 'Who shall rid me of this troublesome priest?'" —*New York Times*

1989. Mr. Mumford concluded, "Architecturally, in short, Rockefeller Center is much ado about nothing." —*New York Times*

1991. "I consider it an honor to give the First Lady clothes," Adolfo told reporters.... "I think anything she does is valid, and what she's doing for fashion is wonderful," said David Hayes.... "All this fuss is much ado about nothing," said Oscar de la Renta. —Kitty Kelley, *Nancy Reagan*

1992. To some people, the dispute over Mr. Aspin's pork barrel activities is much ado about very little. —*New York Times*

1994. SPY CASE IS MUCH ADO ABOUT TRULY LITTLE —Headline of an article about media coverage of spy Aldrich Ames, *New York Newsday*

Mum's the word! Keep it quiet. Don't say a word. Said as a request not to disclose a secret. The saying was popular in Shakespeare's time and is found in *Henry VI, Part II*. In its current form, the phrase has been used since about 1700. *The word is mum* is a variant.

1590–91.
Hume: Seal up your lips, and give no words but mum. —Shakespeare, *Henry VI, Part II*, I, ii

1987. Dear Case: You will get no green light from me. The word from here is to keep your thoughts to yourself. It just might be that this woman can help your son be a better person in every way. I wouldn't bet the rent, but don't count it out. Meanwhile, mum's the word, mom. —Ann Landers, *New York Newsday*

1988. Mom's the word. Her career has been spent playing wives and mothers.... —*US*

1992. MUM'S THE WORD IF SEEKING POST FROM CLINTON —Headline, *New York Times*

1993. For Bulls, mum's the word —*Times* (Trenton)

1995. MOM'S THE WORD —Headline of an article on mothers' fashion advice, *New York Times Magazine*

Murder will out. Murder is bound to be discovered sooner or later. The proverb has been traced back to *Cursor Mundi* (c.1300). It was used by Chaucer in *The Canterbury Tales* (c.1390) and was a common Shakespearean theme, driving the plots of *Titus Andronicus* (1593–94), *The Merchant of Venice* (1596–97), and *Hamlet* (1600–1601). The current form, *Murder will out,* appears in Cervantes' *Don Quixote* (1605). First cited in the United States in *Modest Reply to Mr. Blair's Answer* (1705).

1593–94.
> *Tamora:* What! are they in this pit? O
>   wondrous thing!
> How easily murder is discovered!
> > —Shakespeare, *Titus Andronicus,* II, iii

1596–97.
Launcelot: Truth will come to light; murder cannot be hid long. —Shakespeare, *The Merchant of Venice,* II, ii

1600–01.
> *Hamlet:* For murder, though it have no
>   tongue, will speak
> With most miraculous organ.
> > —Shakespeare, *Hamlet,* II, ii

1853. Sir Leicester's cousins, in the remotest degree, are so many murders, in the respect that they "will out." —Charles Dickens, *Bleak House*

1957. The adage of "murder will out" is a fallacy. —*Bangor Herald* (Me.)

1975. Murder will out? Not always. On March 23, 1857, Emile l'Angelier—vomiting and violently ill with stomach cramps—staggered home before dawn to his shabby lodgings in Glasgow, Scotland. His landlady called a doctor, who prescribed laudanum, but a few hours later Emile was dead. —David Wallechinsky & Irving Wallace, *The People's Almanac*

See also CRIME DOESN'T PAY; THE MILLS OF THE GODS GRIND SLOWLY, BUT THEY GRIND EXCEEDINGLY FINE; TRUTH WILL (COME) OUT.

Murphy's law. *See* IF ANYTHING CAN GO WRONG, IT WILL.

Music hath charms to soothe the savage breast. Music can soften even very violent people. The proverb is attributed to English playwright William Congreve (1697), but a similar idea was expressed by Shakespeare a century earlier. Often misquoted as ... *beast.*

1604. *Duke:* 'Tis good; though music oft hath such
>   a charm
> To make bad good, and good provoke to
>   harm.
> > —Shakespeare, *Measure for Measure,* IV, i

1697. Music has charms to soothe a savage breast,
> To soften rocks, or bend a knotted oak.
> > —William Congreve, *The Mourning Bride*

1922. Too poetical that about the sad. Music did that. Music hath charms. Shakespeare said. —James Joyce, *Ulysses*

1978. When the silence hit again, Nadine laughed and clapped her hands. Joe threw his stick away and jumped up and down on the sand, making fierce hooting sounds of joy. Larry couldn't believe the change in the kid, and had to caution himself not to make too much of it. To do so would be to risk disappointment.
Music hath charms to soothe the savage breast. —Stephen King, *The Stand*

1984. "Are you going to play for me?" he inquired distantly, and paused for some answer from me with his mouth hanging open, like a man with a stroke.
"I am going to play and sing for you."
"They tell me," he mused inquiringly, "that music hath charms to soothe the savage breast." —Joseph Heller, *God Knows*

1994. The lyrics of *Tom Dooley* are accompanied by a melancholic and plaintive melody that is quite different from the pounding, mechanical rhythm of much rap. As Shakespeare put this point: "Music hath such a charm to make bad good, and good provoke to harm." —Letters to the Editor, *New York Times Magazine*

My country, right or wrong. *See* OUR COUNTRY, RIGHT OR WRONG.

My dear, I don't give a damn. Parting words of Rhett Butler to Scarlett O'Hara in *Gone With the Wind. I don't give a damn (a good God damn, a goddamn, a twopenny damn, a tinker's damn, a tinker's hoot, a darn)* is a centuries-old expression that was given a new lease on life by Margaret Mitchell. The use of *damn* was considered shocking when the movie came out (1939). The main entry is one of the ten most frequently heard quotations, according to a 1992 survey by *Time* magazine.

1936. "I wish I cared what you do or where you go but I can't.... My dear, I don't give a damn." —Margaret Mitchell, *Gone With the Wind*

1939. Frankly, my dear, I don't give a damn. —Sidney Howard, *Gone With the Wind* (screenplay)

1951. "Think they'll make ya pay for 'em?" he said.

"I don't know, and I don't give a damn." —J. D. Salinger, *The Catcher in the Rye*

1961. He wished again that he was where Aarfy was, making obscene, brutal, cheerful love with a juicy drunken tart who didn't give a tinker's dam about him and would never think of him again. —Joseph Heller, *Catch-22*

1969. Sonny came over and embraced him. "I don't give a damn what your reasons are, just as long as you're with us." —Mario Puzo, *The Godfather*

1977. Pressured by Kissinger to do something about the "madman's" activities, the President called in Colson and Haldeman and said: "I don't give a damn how it is done, do whatever has to be done to stop these leaks and prevent unauthorized disclosures; I don't want to be told why it can't be done." —Victor Lasky, *It Didn't Start with Watergate*

1984. "I don't give two damns if you stop being a rabbi." —Howard Fast, *The Outsider*

1989. The Syrians are foreign aggressors, Arabs killing Arabs in an Arab land. The world does not give one damn. —A. M. Rosenthal, *New York Times*

1991. "You don't give a damn what happens to my mother as long as the party invitations keep arriving, and we both know it." —Alexandra Ripley, *Scarlett*

1993. These new photographers were beyond smiling. They didn't give a tinker's hoot how the customer felt about them. —Russell Baker, *New York Times*

1994. Does Rhett frankly, as he insisted in one of the most famous movie lines ever, not give a damn? —*New York Times*
See also I COULDN'T CARE LESS.

My hands are tied. I am not free to act. The saying dates back to the second half of the seventeenth century and was first recorded in Thomas Fuller's *The Holy State and the Profane State* (1642). In this book, the English preacher and his-

torian wrote that "when God intends a Nation shall be beaten, He ties their hands behind them." The pronoun *my* may be replaced with another pronoun or adjective.

1981. Federal officials said yesterday that their "hands are tied" until town-meeting members vote on a bylaw that would allow local licensing of tank cars storing vinyl chloride in the Consolidated Rail Corp. (Conrail) yards here. —*Boston Globe*

1987. U.S. Trade Representatives Charlene Barshevsky is stewing over South Korea's treatment of the Big Three automakers and other U.S. exports, but her hands are tied. —*Detroit News*

1994. While [Mayor] Menino remains sympathetic to the cause, his chief of staff, Alyce Lee, said the mayor lacks the authority to reconsider the case. "His hands are tied," she said. —*Boston Globe*

1995. Saying "my hands are tied" by a century-old law, Interior Secretary Bruce Babbitt reluctantly approved the sale of 110 acres of federal land in Idaho yesterday for $275. It may contain $1 billion worth of minerals. —*Boston Globe*

1997. [Defense lawyer Roy] Black also predicted that his first-time offender client "wouldn't serve one day of jail time." Black said "his hands were tied" in the case because under Virginia law, the defense has been barred fro introducing evidence that might have helped [Marv] Albert. —*New York Post*

1998. "I don't want to release these men if I don't have to, but my hands are tied. I have to follow the law," Judge Thomas said Wednesday. —*Detroit News*

1998. "It's the very system I've been against for 10 years—the parole system that let him out," Giuliani said. But the mayor added the protesters would be better served marching on the State Assembly. In this case, the mayor said, the Parole Board did all it could—but its hands are tied by state law. —*New York Post*
See also MY LIPS ARE SEALED.

My lips are sealed. I cannot or will not speak or reveal something private. The saying has been traced back to 1782, when Fanny Burney used it in her *Cecilia:* "I make it quite a principle to seal my lips from the moment I perceive him." It is also used with other nons in place of "my."

1981. There's a heroine in this Cape Cod town, an elementary school teacher, but nobody will reveal her name. The school superintendent won't say, the principal of the Simpkins school won't tell you, and the fire chief's lips are sealed. —*Boston Globe*

1992. Among prominent playwrights whose talents have been nurtured at the ATL [Actors Theatre of Louisville, Ky.], Martin is known as "America's best-known unknown playwright." She's never been photographed or interviewed. If anyone knows her identity, his lips are sealed. —*Commercial Appeal* (Memphis, Tennessee)

1996. Ninety percent of buyers know why the seller is moving before they venture an offer on a home, [Gloria C.] Arneberg estimates. Even if the listing agent's lips stay sealed, clues about seller motivation abound, she says. —*Detroit News*

1998. So how does Ewing think he's progressing? Asked directly how the session went, that wonderful Ewing smile surfaced and he used his right hand to make a zipper-like motion across his lips. Then he said, "My lips are sealed." —*New York Post*

1998. Forever the good company man, he will not spill any beans on L'Affaire Fraschilla. "My lips are sealed," Camesecca said, "because of the legalities involved." —*New York Post*

See also MY HANDS ARE TIED; MUM'S THE WORD!

Nature abhors a vacuum. No space stays vacant for long. The Latin equivalent of the ancient principle is *Natura abhorret vacuum.* The English proverb has been traced back to *Answer to Gardiner* (1551) by Thomas Cranmer (1489–1556), archbishop of Canterbury. In 1534, Rabelais (c.1483–1553) quoted the Latin version, as did Spinoza (1632–77) in 1677. First attested in the United States in *Almanacs* (1766). Variants may substitute other words for *nature* or *vacuum.*

> **1922.** Nature abhors a vacuum. —James Joyce, *Ulysses*
>
> **1984.** "Nature abhors the weak," Brooks Adams wrote in a cynical variation on the more familiar aphorism. So, indeed, it seems in this era. —Page Smith, *The Rise of Industrial America*
>
> **1986.** "Nature abhors a vacuum, but it abhors perfect happiness even more," I said. —Pat Conroy, *The Prince of Tides*
>
> **1992.** The Clinton foreign-policy consensus is creating a vacuum, and politics abhors a vacuum. —William Safire, *New York Times*
>
> **1994.** Mother Nature, the axiom states, hates a vacuum. So what happened when Broadway producers couldn't find any musical product except revivals? Disney stepped in and filled the gap with a $2 million epic production of "Beauty and the Beast." —Liz Smith, *Times* (Trenton)

See also LET NATURE TAKE ITS COURSE.

Nature will take its course. See LET NATURE TAKE ITS COURSE.

Necessity is the mother of invention. Dire situations inspire ingenious solutions. If worse comes to worst, people will apply all their imagination and skill to deal with the problem. In Latin: *Mater artium necessitas.* The adage has been traced back to *Vulgaria* (1519). In 1658, Richard Franck wrote in his *Northern Memoirs:* "Art imitates Nature, and Necessity is the Mother of Invention." The proverb was first attested in the United States in *William Fitzhugh and His Chesapeake World* (1681). It can be found in other languages: *La nécessité est la mère de l'invention* (French); *Not macht erfinderisch* (German). The guitarist Frank Zappa called his band The Mothers of Invention.

> **1976.** "Mothers of Invention: The Birth of a Business" —Claudia Jessup & Genie Chipps, *The Woman's Guide to Starting a Business*
>
> **1984.** In 1981, as the roof was caving in, it seemed a merger might be the only way out. They say that necessity is the mother of invention. —Lee Iacocca with William Novak, *Iacocca*
>
> **1988.** Necessity may be the mother of invention, it can also inspire extraordinary deceit. —Tobias Wolff, "This Boy's Life," *Esquire*
>
> **1992.** So what does this survivor of 40 years of fashion wars think of this latest battle? "Fashion magazines are the mother of invention," he [Richard Avedon] says. "May the best mother win." —*New York*
>
> **1995.** Another [tale] introduces us to three buddies in the house painting business who cook up an ingeniously naughty scheme to show a snooty loft tenant what kind of guys she's really hired. "Necessity may be the mother of invention," writes Mr. [John] Yau, "but it's also the uncle of hilarity." —*New York Times Book Review*

See also NECESSITY KNOWS NO LAWS.

Necessity knows no laws. In an emergency, the law may be disregarded. Sometimes quoted in Latin: *Necessitas non habet legem* ("Necessity has no law"). The proverb has been traced back to

Piers Plowman (c.1377) by English poet William Langland (c.1332–c.1400). First cited in the United States in *Winthrop Papers, 1498–1649* (1674).

1654. Necessity hath no law. —Oliver Cromwell, Speech to Parliament

1930. Jim [Ferguson of Texas] kept on talking about Necessity Grigg.... "You know the old proverb 'Necessity knows no law.' Judge Grigg knows so little about law that you could properly say he doesn't know any".... The name has stuck ever since. —*American Mercury*

1993. "You should never take the law into your own hands" ... "Necessity knows no laws, man." —Overheard at a New York City police precinct
See also NECESSITY IS THE MOTHER OF INVENTION.

Neither give nor take offense. Maintain your equanimity: avoid either antagonizing your opponent or taking umbrage at his imagined slights, since in both cases, the quarrel will be your fault. *Neither take offense nor make offense* is a variant. *No offense (taken)* is often used.

1653. There are offenses given and offenses not given but taken.—Izaak Walton, *The Compleat Angler* 1839–57.No man lives without jostling and being jostled; in all ways he has to elbow himself through the world, giving and receiving offense. —Thomas Carlyle, *"Sir Walter Scott," Critical and Miscellaneous Essays*

1922. —Is he a jew or a gentile or a holy Roman or a swaddler or what the hell is he? says Ned. Or who is he? No offense, Crofton. —James Joyce, *Ulysses*

1988. "Laura, please don't take offense if I tell you Dr. Lemaistre is a skilled man—and a good man." —Erich Segal, *Doctors*

1991. "No offense, Will, but a man can't go very far without an education."
"No offense taken. And none given, but I figure you're wrong." —Alexandra Ripley, *Scarlett*
See also IT TAKES TWO TO MAKE A QUARREL.

Nero fiddled while Rome burned. Said to refer to heedless and irresponsible behavior in the midst of a crisis. Legend has it that in a.d. 64 the emperor Nero (a.d. 37–a.d. 68), last of the Caesars, set fire to Rome to see "how Troy would look when it was in flames" and to serve as a suitable background for a recitation of his poetry while accompanying himself on the lyre. *Nero* may be replaced by another subject.

1924. It was time he got back to Elderson, and what was to be done, and left this fiddling while

Rome burned. —John Galsworthy, *The White Monkey*

1933. He [Calvin Coolidge] slept more than any other President, whether by day or by night. Nero fiddled, but Coolidge only snored. —H. L. Mencken, *American Mercury*

1978. *The firestorm,* he thought.
They were all dead in Las Vegas. Someone had fiddled when he should have faddled, and a nuclear weapon had gone off.... —Stephen King, *The Stand*

1984. Despite the problems that entangle public life, Italians survive and thrive privately, and no people seem to have so much fun while in such deep trouble. How do they manage to fiddle away so productively while Rome burns? —*Reader's Digest*

1985. It's sometimes smart to leave; no one wants to fiddle while a career burns or sing a sad song along with Peggy Lee. —Jacqueline Hornor Plumez with Karla Dougherty, *Divorcing a Corporation*

1987. At Parish-Hadley on the East Side a client suggested to Gary Hager: "Let's be slightly careful while Rome is burning. Don't show me anything too expensive." —*New York Times*

1989. "The law we would have used was the conspiracy statute, but the constitutional issues were so murky that the investigation died a natural death, much to everyone's relief."
"Same thing here, isn't it? Except while we fiddle ..." —Tom Clancy, *Clear and Present Danger*

1991. "You've heard the thing about Nero fiddling while Rome burned. Well, President Bush is fiddling while he's going to vacate the White House. The fact that he is surrounded by advisers who think the economy is in recovery is incredible." —*Wall Street Journal*

Never believe everything you hear. *See* BELIEVE ONLY HALF OF WHAT YOU SEE AND NOTHING YOU HEAR.

Never cry wolf. Don't try to deceive others about the possibility of disaster lest they abandon you when you most need them. Liars are always caught in the traps they set for themselves. In English, the proverb has been traced back to a translation of *Aesop's Fables* (1629). The original fable dates to about the sixth century b.c. It tells the story of a rural shepherd boy who twice cried "Wolf!" to summon the villagers when in fact his flock was in no danger at all. The disgruntled villagers therefore ignored his cries for help when a real wolf attacked, killing the boy as well as his sheep.

1983. *Never Cry Wolf* —Title of a movie, written and directed by Carroll Ballard, about a Canadian biologist studying wolves in the wild

1984. He knew what would happen to his people if Chrysler failed. And he knew we weren't crying wolf. —Lee Iacocca with William Novak, *Iacocca*

1986. Democrats have been crying wolf about the economy for years, screeching that recession was just round the corner. —Ralph de Toledano, *New York City Tribune*

1992. You've no doubt heard the tale of the boy who cried wolf. Well, here's the tale of the critic who cried genius. —*People*

1993. "We've proven it can be done," said Haytaian. "At the time, Jim Florio and editorial writers predicted the sky would fall. But it didn't. And now he's crying wolf again." —*Times* (Trenton)

See also HONESTY IS THE BEST POLICY; A LIAR IS NOT BELIEVED WHEN HE TELLS (SPEAKS) THE TRUTH.

Never give a sucker an even break. Put your own interests first. Use other people's gullibility to your own advantage. This cynical aphorism originated in the United States in the 1920s. According to Bartlett's *Familiar Quotations,* it was coined by Edward Francis Albee (1857–1930). It has also been attributed to Wilson Mizner (1876–1933). But it is most often associated with W. C. Fields (1880–1946), who first used it in the play *Poppy* (1923) and later made it famous through his screen characterization of a bungling con artist.

> **1928.** Since we have coined a slogan, Never give
> the sucker an even break and the Old
> Army Game goes—Let the dance go on....
> —Carl Sandburg, *Good Morning, America*

1930. "Do you get the idea?"
"Sure I get the idea. It's the old army game: first, pass the buck; second, never give a sucker an even break...." —Theodore Fredenburgh, *Soldiers March*

1941. *Never Give a Sucker an Even Break* —Title of a movie starring W. C. Fields

See also IT AIN'T A FIT NIGHT OUT FOR MAN OR BEAST; ON THE WHOLE, I'D RATHER BE IN PHILADELPHIA.

Never had it so good. *See* YOU NEVER HAD IT SO GOOD.

Never judge a book by its cover. *See* DON'T JUDGE A BOOK BY ITS COVER.

Never let your left hand know what your right hand is doing. Keep things secret. Tell no one. Of Biblical origin. The proverb was first cited in the United States in *Extracts from the Itineraries of Ezra Stiles* (1766). *Let not your left hand know what your right hand does* is an older variant. A more recent sense is that communication is poor between two parties who should be acting in concert.

> But when thou doest alms, let not thy left hand know what thy right hand doeth. —Matthew, 6:3, *Authorized Version,* 1611

1961. When he gave to charity, his left hand never knew what his right hand was doing. —Joseph Heller, *Catch-22*

1991. "The right hand doesn't always know what the left hand is doing," said one Soviet official. —*Newsweek*

Never look a gift horse in the mouth. It's pointless to find fault with something you get for free. Alludes to checking a horse's teeth to determine its age and value. The longer the teeth, the older the horse. In Latin: *Equi donati dentes non inspiciuntur* or *Noli dentes equi inspicere donati.* The proverb has been traced back to *Vulgaria* (c. 1510). In 1546, it was included in John Heywood's collection of proverbs. First cited in the United States in *Sam Slick's Wise Saws* (1853) by Thomas Chandler Haliburton. *Einem geschenkten Gaul nicht ins Maul sehen* (German); and Дарёному коню в зубы не смотрят (Russian) both translate as "Don't look at a gift horse's teeth." *Don't look a gift horse in the mouth* is a variant.

1951. "I know quite a few people in Washington," Karen offered. "Maybe I can give you some addresses before you leave ship."
"Would you really?"
"Surely. Of course, they're not any of them Senators or presidents of anything, and none of them know Evelyn Walsh McLean."
"Never look a gift horse in the mouth," the young Lt/Col said. —James Jones, *From Here to Eternity*

1977. Though it seemed strange that Fensterwald would be doing this for someone he hardly knew, Alch said, "I was not about to look a gift horse in the mouth." —Victor Lasky, *It Didn't Start with Watergate*

1983. Charities are usually not so picky about donors and they don't look gift horses in the mouth. —*Forbes*

1984. "Why am I looking a gift rabbi in the mouth or eyes or whatever? We've known each other a long time, David. There can't be too many surprises." —Howard Fast, *The Outsider*

1989. Instead, he placed a call to one of his fellow Harvard Oversees and was immediately offered Morgan Guaranty's Gulfstream. "Not as nice as mine," he said, "but one can't look a gift horse in the mouth." —Michael Korda, *The Fortune*

1991. The winner was Lauri Kay, the writer. She is well past the point of looking any gift horse in the mouth. "I have something to wear to my next job interview," she said appreciatively. —*New York Times*

1994. Here is one gift horse President Clinton has to look in the mouth: a 3½-foot-tall, woven wicker and reed horse given by Peter Kravchenko, the Byelorussian minister of foreign affairs.... Mr. Clinton, like other federal employees, can't accept gifts for personal use, though he can take them on behalf of the government. —*Wall Street Journal*
See also BEGGARS CAN'T BE CHOOSERS.

Never mix business with pleasure. Keep your work separate from more frivolous activities, or your work will suffer. Don't do business with your friends. The proverb has been traced back to 1913. First attested in the United States in 1931. *You can't mix (combine) business with pleasure* is also used, and the meaning is also reversed to suggest that mixing business with pleasure is the ideal situation.

1934. "In any case take your time, take your ease; combine business with pleasure." —F. Scott Fitzgerald, *Tender Is the Night*

1951. "But as I said, as long as I do not mix business with pleasure, these horrible missionaries' descendants dont bother me." —James Jones, *From Here to Eternity*

1973. "Now my friend up there"—he nodded toward the steps—"he's all business. But me, I like to combine business with pleasure." —Jacqueline Susann, *Once Is Not Enough*

1983. "I wanna come with you," Rocky had griped. "I wanna meet the great Sadie La Salle."
"Another time," Ferdie replied firmly.
Another time. Another century. Never mix pleasure with business. A cliché. But a true one. —Jackie Collins, *Hollywood Wives*

1985. "It's absolutely foolish to get emotionally involved in any company unless you own it. I keep a part of myself separate: I never mix business with pleasure. Family with business." —Jacqueline Honor Plumez with Karla Dougherty, *Divorcing a Corporation*

1988. The man certainly knew how to mix business with pleasure. —Nelson DeMille, *The Charm*
School

1994. Mid-month favors romantic and financial affairs: quietly, you contemplate changes on the job front. Later, business and pleasure are a good mix. —"Your Monthly Stars," *Princeton Living*
See also BUSINESS BEFORE PLEASURE.

Never put off until tomorrow what you can do today. Don't procrastinate: do what you are supposed to do as soon as you can. The maxim has been traced back to Chaucer's *Tale of Melibee* (c.1386). First attested in the United States in *Winthrop Papers* (1690). *Don't put off until tomorrow what you can do today* is a variant. Jocular versions include *Always put off till tomorrow what needs to be done today;* and *Never do today what you can put off till tomorrow.*

1749. No idleness, no laziness, no procrastination; never put off till tomorrow what you can do today. —Earl of Chesterfield, *Letters to his Son*

1757. Have you somewhat to do To-morrow, do it To-day. —Benjamin Franklin, *Father Abraham's Speech, or, The Way to Wealth*

1922. Never put on you tomorrow what you can wear today. —James Joyce, *Ulysses*

1961. They told him never to put off until the next day what he could do the day before, and he never did. —Joseph Heller, *Catch-22*

1984. Don't put off until tomorrow what can be put off today. —*Forbes*

1987. Good executives never put off until tomorrow what they can get someone else to do today. —*Bits & Pieces*

1989. Alexa had been taught "never to put off to tomorrow what you can do today"—virtually the household motto, as it was for every farm family—but she had learned a lot since coming to New York, and putting off things when you could get away with it was one of them. —Michael Korda, *The Fortune*

1991. One Americanism Strauss can't translate: never put off until tomorrow what you can do today. The Russian proverb about work is *Rabota ne volk, v les ne ubezhit.* It means, "Work isn't a wolf, it won't run into the woods." Or: put it off, if you possibly can. —*Newsweek*

Never say die. Keep fighting. Never surrender. Never give up hope no matter what. Used to encourage someone at a difficult time. Used by Charles Dickens in *The Pickwick Papers* (1837). First cited in the United States in 1814 in the *Di-*

ary of Benjamin F. Palmer, Privateersman, 1813–1815. The 1939 movie *Never Say Die* helped to popularize the saying.

1939. *Never Say Die.* —Title of a movie starring Martha Raye and Bob Hope

1977. "The Boss will go along," Melinda said. "He has no other choice. Never say die. And maybe it's better to have previous blindness out in the open, where we can fight it out once and for all." —William Safire, *Full Disclosure*

1987. The first lesson in environmental protection is this: When there's a chance to make serious money out of real estate speculation or development, the speculators and developers never say die. Neither do the politicians who support and are supported by them. —John B. Oakes, *New York Times*

1988. To Herb Klein, Nixon complained that "our so-called 'liberal' friends never say die." —Stephen E. Ambrose, *Nixon*

1993. The never-say-die *New York Post* staggered back to life yesterday after unions agreed to $602 million in reduced operating costs "to stop the bleeding" at the nation's oldest continuously published daily. —*Times* (Trenton)

See also DON'T GIVE UP THE SHIP; DO NOT GO GENTLE INTO THAT GOOD NIGHT; I HAVE NOT YET BEGUN TO FIGHT; NEVER SAY NEVER; WHERE THERE'S LIFE, THERE'S HOPE.

Never say never. Think positively. Life is full of surprises and even things that seem impossible may indeed happen. The expression can be found in Charles Dickens' *Pickwick Papers* (1837).

1977. "No chance for him becoming jockey number four, you think." Fowler made it a statement.

Leigh agreed: "That would mean he'd have to change inside, and then change outside. Never happen. Well, never say never, but not soon. Not in this term." —William Safire, *Full Disclosure*

1983. *Never Say Never Again* —Title of a James Bond movie, starring Sean Connery and Klaus Maria Brandauer

1991. That was "rock bottom," Mr. Taylor says. "I felt like getting the hell out. But being of Scottish heritage, one never says never." —*Wall Street Journal*

1992. As a child, I was told "never say never." Perhaps this adage should be extended to "never say always." —Letters to the Editor, *New York Times*

1995. At 46, thinner, richer, blonder and prettier than ever, Ivana [Trump] is—are you sitting down?—thinking about having more kids…. "I never say never!" Ivana tells me, laughing coquettishly and nearly making me fall out of my office swivel chair. —*New York Post*

See also IT'S NOT OVER TILL IT'S OVER; NEVER SAY DIE; THE OPERA AIN'T OVER TILL THE FAT LADY SINGS.

Never sell America short. Don't underestimate America's future. Originated in the United States in the mid-nineteenth century. *Don't sell America short* is a variant. In financial markets, *to sell a stock short* means to gamble that a stock will decrease in value rather than increasing. Generalized to people, *to sell someone short* is to assume that person will not amount to much in the world, or will be unable to meet a challenge.

1966. Speculation ran wild, and an orgy of boom-or-bust trading pushed the bull markets up to dizzy peaks. "Never sell America short" and "Be a bull on America" were favorite catchwords, as Wall Street sharks gouged one another and fleeced greedy lambs. —Thomas A. Bailey, *The American Pageant*

1984. She felt sorry for him and all the hundreds of other young actors just like him. "Look," she said patiently, "don't sell yourself short." —Jackie Collins, *Hollywood Wives*

1986. She took my hand and squeezed it. "You sold yourself short. You could've been more than a teacher and a coach." —Pat Conroy, *The Prince of Tides*

1988. Senator D'Amato was also not ready to predict the Mayor's demise. "Don't sell the Mayor short," he said in a telephone interview. —*New York Times*

1994. "Don't sell it short" is a gentle way of suggesting that something is not a stinker. —*New York Times*

Never speak ill of the dead. Show respect for the dead by ceasing to pass judgment on them; since the dead can no longer harm anyone, it's time to recall their good deeds and forgive their evil ones. Attributed to Chilon of Sparta (6th century b.c.. The Latin version is *de mortuis nil nisi bonum* ("of the dead say nothing but good"). The proverb has been traced back to *Flores Sententiarum* (c.1540) by Erasmus. First attested in the United States in *Will and Doom* (1692). The aphorism is found in varying forms: *Concerning the dead speak no evil; Don't speak ill of the dead; Of the dead all things are good; Speak well of the dead*, etc.

1952. And there would be one or two lonely

drunks with nothing to lose anyway, men who had fallen into disfavor one way or another, who knew they had received their last invitation. And what the hell, the liquor was free. *De mortuis nil nisi bonum.* —Kurt Vonnegut, Jr., *Player Piano*

1979. "They say one doesn't speak ill of the dead," she once said to Tom. "I don't know why. I think it's much more damaging to speak ill of the living. My husband is dead, but there is nothing good I care to say about him. He was an animal." —Howard Fast, *The Establishment*

1991. But Justice Marshall has also been uncommonly direct in his negative comments about political figures. He once told an interviewer for The Washington Post, "I wouldn't do the job of dogcatcher for Ronald Reagan." ... And he had this to say about President Bush: "It's said that if you can't say something good about a dead person, don't say it. Well, I consider him dead." —*New York Times*

Never speak of rope in the house of a man who has been hanged. Be tactful. Be considerate of other people's feelings. Don't stir up bad memories. Avoid sensitive topics. The proverb has been traced back to J. Minsheu's *Dictionary in Spanish and English* (1599). First cited in the United States in *Nature and Human Nature* (1855) by Thomas Chandler Haliburton.

1605–15.
'Tis ill talking of halters in the house of a man that was hanged. —Cervantes, *Don Quixote*

1933. There is an old and somewhat lugubrious adage that says, "Never speak of rope in the house of a man who has been hanged." —Franklin D. Roosevelt's reply to criticism that he prolonged the Depression, quoted by William Safire, "On Language," *New York Times Magazine*

Never tell tales out of school. Certain secret information must not be revealed to outsiders. Originally, the maxim was directed at children, to discourage them from gossiping about teachers and other students. It has been traced back to *Practice of Prelates* (1530) by William Tyndale (c.1492–1536). In 1546, it was included in John Heywood's collection of proverbs. First attested in the United States in *Anarchaid* (1786). *Don't tell tales out of school* is a variant.

1992. *Tales Out of School.* —Title of a book by Joseph A. Fernandez, written while he was still New York City Schools chancellor

1993. I hope this isn't telling tales out of school, but the male offspring, who lives in a city far from

here under what he hopes is an assumed name (since our first names are different, he's *sure* we won't be connected), has had his first scrape with the law. —*Times* (Trenton)

1994. Dear Abby: Your advice to "Peggy" to tell her boyfriend that she had slept with his brother was the dumbest advice you could ever give to someone.... Why in the world would she ruin a good relationship with "George," plus ruin the brothers' relationship with each other by telling tales out of school? —Abigail Van Buren, "Dear Abby," *Times* (Trenton)

See also DON'T AIR YOUR DIRTY LINEN IN PUBLIC; THE CAT IS OUT OF THE BAG.

A new broom sweeps clean. A new boss often makes radical changes immediately after taking control of an organization. The proverb has been traced back to the mid-sixteenth century. In 1546, it was included in John Heywood's book of proverbs. First cited in the United States in *Letters and Papers of Cadwallader Colden* (1752). Sometimes shortened to *a new broom.* Witty extensions of the adage include: *A new broom sweeps clean, but an old one knows where the dirt lies;* and *A new broom sweeps clean, but an old one scrapes better.*

1956. A new broom sweeps clean but it takes the old one to know where the dirt lies. —*Bangor Daily News* (Me.)

1992. New broom at the NEA. On Tuesday, Anne-Imelda Radice provided evidence that there really is a new spirit at the National Endowment for the Arts: The acting NEA chairwoman overruled NEA advisory panels and refused to give grants to two artistic projects containing explicit sexual material. —*New York Post*

1993. GIANTS HOPING THEY CAN BORROW THAT OLD 1986 BROOM —Headline, *New York Times*

Nice guys finish last. If you really want to win, fight tooth and nail to the very end, disregarding the rules of fair play and decency if need be. Originated by Leo Durocher (1905–91), manager of the Brooklyn Dodgers in 1951–54.

1975. *Nice Guys Finish Last* —Title of a book by Leo Durocher

1988. "He was a nice guy," Barney said sternly.
"Wasn't it Hemingway who said 'nice guys finish last'?"
"No, it was Leo Durocher, formerly of the Brooklyn Dodgers." —Erich Segal, *Doctors*

1988. Remember the bathtub test? I learned it early in life—after toilet training but before I learned that "nice guys finish last." The bathtub test goes like this: "Fill a bathtub with water. Put your fist in the water and then pull it out. The size of the hole you leave is how important you are." —Paul Terhorst, *Cashing In on the American Dream*

1993. The fact is, nice guys don't always finish last. And as the polls show, this is advice many politicians would be wise to follow. —Letters to the Editor, *Washington Post*

1994. Campbell Theron Montgomery, the amiable stagehand shot dead on a Rockefeller Center sidewalk on Aug. 31, is getting a memorial. His fellows in the Broadway Bowling League have named a trophy after him. Starting next week, bowlers will vote on which opponent was the most fun. In the end, nice guys finish first. —*New York Times*

See also IT'S NOT WHETHER YOU WIN OR LOSE BUT HOW YOU PLAY THE GAME; IT'S SURVIVAL OF THE FITTEST; MIGHT MAKES RIGHT; NEVER GIVE A SUCKER AN EVEN BREAK.

No dice. Nothing doing; absolutely not; definitely not. Said when one refuses to do what is requested or when someone fails to do something. Alludes to a failure to throw a winning number with the dice. This slang expression originated in the United States in the early twentieth century.

1977. "What did he say?" the Mayor wanted to know.
"No dice." —Art Buchwald, *Down the Seine and Up the Potomac*

1984. Finally, on July 13, the very same day we were paying the loans, we offered $250 million for the warrants.
"No dice," said the Loan Board. "We're selling them to the highest bidder." —Lee Iacocca with William Novak, *Iacocca*

1985. "Ina Blaze was just about to kiss me, but I told her 'No dice.' I heard she has a cold. You can't be too careful about germs." —Michael Korda, *Queenie*

1986. Nancy Reagan reportedly shares their view [about ousting Donald Regan]. But the President is adamant. "I tried, but no dice," Mr. Deaver told a friend with a shrug. —*New York Times*

1988. "You're right—she's flat as a boy! But no dice—she's still wearing a shirt." —Erich Segal, *Doctors*

1993. "Look, maybe the baby isn't musical," I suggested. Nice try, but no dice. —*New York Times Magazine*

See also NO WAY, JOSÉ.

No good deed goes unpunished. Life is so un-fair that one is more likely to get into some sort of trouble than be rewarded if one attempts to do a good deed. It was attributed to American financier John P. Grier, banker Andrew W. Mellon, and writer Clare Boothe Luce, but its ultimate origin is unknown.

1989. "I know the truth, and he can't forgive me for knowing it. Or perhaps it's as Oscar Wilde said, 'No good deed goes unpunished.'" —Michael Korda, *The Fortune*

1991. Art Moreau died of a heart attack the following year without ever being recognized for the enormous contribution he had made to the fight against terrorism.... As the old saying has it, no good deed goes unpunished. —Oliver L. North, *Under Fire*

1992. Jay Hershenson, a spokesman for Chancellor W. Ann Reynolds, said the restructuring was intended to give the institute "academic" status by turning it into a major research center that would be used to build a new doctoral program in Italian studies. "This is a situation in which no good deed goes unpunished," Mr. Hershenson said. —*New York Times*

1994. Spin-doctoring into the storm of criticism, George [Stephanopoulos] tried to point out that Clinton ethics rules were more stringent than ever before, and that reporters were holding this Administration to higher standards. "This is proof of the old adage," he insisted, "that no good deed goes unpunished." —William Safire, "On Language," *New York Times Magazine*

No ifs, ands or buts. Do exactly as I say, with no questions and no objections. Originally *ifs and ans* (*ans* is an archaic form of *ands*, which in this case also meant "if"). *No ifs, ands or buts about it; No ifs; No buts;* and *But me no buts* are variants of the phrase.

1947. *Stanley:* I don't want no ifs, ands or buts! —Tennessee Williams, *A Streetcar Named Desire*

1987. I have had issued a directive prohibiting the N.S.C. [National Security Council] itself from undergoing covert operations—no if's, and's or but's. —Ronald Reagan, *New York Times*

1988. It's the law. No ifs, ands, or butts.... On April 6th, the new no-smoking law takes effect. —*New York Times*

1994. "There's no ifs, ands, or buts that he's the favorite for the Conservative endorsement," Mr. Long said of Mr. London. —*New York Times*

1995. I hope you provide more space for this sort of thing. Indeed, why not start a special section, perhaps entitled "Ifs, Ands and Rebuts"? —Letters to the Editor, *New York Times Book Review*

No man can serve two masters. *See* YOU CAN'T SERVE GOD AND MAMMON.

No man is a hero to his valet. Great reputations are essentially hollow praise: those who know us best can see our frailties and foibles only too well. The idea goes back to ancient times. Antigonus (c. 382–301 b.c.), who was described by Herodotus as "Son of the Sun," said, "My valet is not aware of this." The aphorism has been traced back to the first English translation of Montaigne's *Essays* (1580–95) in 1603. "Few men have been admired by their own households," said Montaigne. The saying however, is sometimes attributed to Madame Cornuel (1605–94): *Il n'y avoit pas de héros pour les valets de chambre.* First attested in the United States in *Papers of John Steele* (1801). The word *valet* may be replaced with *wife and butler, saddle horse,* or *hometown.*

1985. "What will Quayle think when he sees we haven't finished breakfast?" she asked as Charles closed the bedroom door behind them.
  "The obvious, I suppose. Never mind. No man is a hero to his valet. Or a saint!" —Michael Korda, *Queenie*

1992. "Honesty requires one to say that no one's a hero to his valet, and one would have qualms about anyone, I think," Mr. Kristol said. "But I'm totally confident that he [Dan Quayle] is capable of being President." —*New York Times*

1994. If it is true that no man is a hero to his valet, then it is also true that incessant publicity has made valets of us all. Jacqueline Kennedy knew that—which is why we never really knew her. —*Times* (Trenton)

See also FAMILIARITY BREEDS CONTEMPT; A PROPHET IS NOT WITHOUT HONOR, SAVE IN HIS OWN COUNTRY.

No man is an island. No one is entirely independent of others. Coined by English poet John Donne in *Devotions upon Emergent Occasions* (1624). Ernest Hemingway used Donne's line as an epigraph to *For Whom the Bell Tolls* (1940).

1624. No man is an island, entire of itself; every man is a piece of the continent, a part of the main. —John Donne, *Devotions upon Emergent Occasions*

1964. Dear Syl—Don't try. There's no communication; no one really listens. Every man is an island. Give him a container of coffee instead. Bea. —Bel Kaufman, *Up the Down Staircase*

1965. … It was not in the least a diary but, rather,

a form of anthology consisting of obscure facts ("Every fifteen years Mars gets closer. 1958 is a close year"), poems and literary quotations ("No man is an island, Entire of itself"), and passages from newspapers and books paraphrased or quoted. —Truman Capote, *In Cold Blood*

1980. Theoretically, we may know that "no man is an island," but faced with the pressures of daily living, we tend to forget this interdependence. —Herb Cohen, *You Can Negotiate Anything*

1991. ONE MAN IS AN ISLAND —Headline of an article about the isolation of Fidel Castro in the post-Soviet world, *Newsweek*

1992. "No man is an island, entire of itself," John Donne wrote. Surprisingly, the same is now turning out to be true even for bacteria, the simplest of organisms. These single-celled creatures, long viewed as independent and self-sufficient, nonetheless are endowed to lead a rich social life. They rarely live alone. —*New York Times*

1994. No woman is an island. We're little U-hauls full of the men we used to go out with. —Cartoon by Cathy Guisewite, "Cathy," *New York Newsday*

No news is good news. If one hears nothing from or about another person, then everything must be O.K. and nothing bad has occurred. A lack of knowledge is better than knowing something is definitely bad. In 1616, James I wrote: "No news is better than evil news." The current form was used by James Howell in 1640: "I am of the Italians' mind that said, 'Nulla nuova, buona nuova' [no news, good news]." First cited in the United States in *Writings of Samuel Johnson, President of King's College* (1754). The verb *is* can be omitted.

1936. Everywhere, women gathered in knots, huddled in groups on front porches, on sidewalks, even in the middle of the streets, telling each other that no news is good news, trying to comfort each other, trying to present a brave appearance. —Margaret Mitchell, *Gone With the Wind*

1982. No news is … impossible. —Judith Frost Stark, *Don't Cross Your Bridge Before … You Pay the Toll*

1989. No news was good news in the bunker…. The news that dribbled in was bad: the embassy in Saigon had been breached by sappers, Hue was under a state of siege, Da Nang was surrounded and the noose tightened by the hours. —Wayne Care, *Vietnam Spook Show*

1992. MORE NEWS ALSO GOOD NEWS FOR BUSH: HE SURGES ON TV —Headline, *New York Times*

1993. No nudes, good news. Director Mark Rydell

rang to tell me that his new film for Paramount—"Intersection"—is indeed intensely intimate.... Rydell insists there will not be any *blatant nudity*.... —Liz Smith, *Times* (Trenton)

No one ever went broke underestimating the intelligence of the American people.

Crazy ideas, shoddy goods, and gimmicks of various types are highly profitable. Americans can be easily manipulated. Often said to explain the success of something considered inferior by the speaker. The cynical saying, in slightly altered form, was coined by H. L. Mencken (1880–1950). *Nobody (no one) ever went broke underestimating the taste of the American public* is a variant form.

1926. No one in this world, so far as I know ... has ever lost money by underestimating the intelligence of the great masses of the plain people. —H. L. Mencken, *Chicago Tribune*

1992. Is it any wonder Time Warner has prospered by marketing the oeuvres of racists, trollops and paranoiacs? It shouldn't be to anyone who merely remembers the dictum "Nobody ever went broke underestimating the taste of the American public." That is something Time Warner understands and understands well. —Letters to the Editor, *New York Times*

1994. Listen, no one ever went broke underestimating the taste of the American public. [Howard] Stern and Rush Limbaugh have been number one in nonfiction. *The Bridges of Madison County*, which is an idiotic book, was the bestselling novel in the country. I don't want to sound like an old fogey, but I don't know what the world's coming to. —Liz Smith, quoted in *Modern Maturity*

No one is above the law.

The law should be applied equally to all citizens. The saying is of American origin and dates back to President Theodore Roosevelt. In his Third Annual Message to Congress on December 7, 1903, the President said, "No man is above the law and no man is below it; nor do we ask any man's permission when we require him to obey it." The lessons of Watergate, the Iran-Contra hearings, and President Clinton's impeachment by the House of Representatives were that "no man is above the law and no man is below it."

1985. Declaring that "no one is above the law," a federal prosecutor yesterday urged that former Pentagon official Paul Thayer be put behind bars for his part in a $3 million illegal stock trading scheme. —*Boston Globe*

1987. When he was appointed to Florida's Su-

preme Court, Stephen Grimes learned the hard way that justices aren't above the law. Grimes and wife, Fay, drove here to be on hand when Gov. Bob Martinez announced his appointment. They left their car in what they thought was a public parking lot. When they returned, the car had been towed. —*Sun-Sentinel* (South Florida)

1989. The trial of Oliver L. North began yesterday with the prosecutor painting the former White House aide as a man who "placed himself above the law" and North's defense lawyer describing him as a patriot who was only following orders and is now being "abandoned by his government." —*Boston Globe*

1990. "Mr. Campeau" [Canadian billionaire], said US magistrate Robert Collins, "I want to make it clear to you that no matter how important a man you are, in this country no man is above the law." —*Boston Globe*

1997. The old platitudes on courthouses around the country have new, relevant life today in light of the Supreme Court's unanimous opinion in the matter of Paula Corbin Jones vs. William Jefferson Clinton. Equal justice under law. This is a government of law, and not of men. No man is above the law. Justice delayed is justice denied. —*Commercial Apeal* (Memphis, Tennessee)

1997. Was he a hood? Sure. Does he deserve to be in jail in this wonderful state of dementia until he dies? No way. No man is above the law, but no law is above justice. —*New York Post*

1997. "Paula has always felt that the courts would find that no man is above the law," said Cindy Hayes, head of a fund set up to pay Jones's legal expenses. —*Detroit News*

No one is perfect. See NOBODY IS PERFECT.

No pain, no gain. See THERE ARE NO GAINS WITHOUT PAINS.

No person is indispensable.

Even the most experienced people can be replaced. No one has total job security. The proverb comes from the French: *Il n'y a point d'homme nécessaire*. In his election campaign of 1912, "There is no indispensable man," Woodrow Wilson declared. In 1932, Franklin Delano Roosevelt used the same words to refer to Herbert Hoover. THERE'S NO INDISPENSABLE MAN became Wendell Willkie's slogan in 1940, this time meaning F.D.R. *Nobody is indispensable* and *There is no indispensable man* are variants.

1977. "Many well-meaning and wise men and women pointed out to me that no person is indispensable." —William Safire, *Full Disclosure*

1985. Here's one dictum that's hard to believe but true: no one is indispensable. Remember the words of the manipulating Mighty Oz who tells his employees that he *needs* them, that they can't possibly leave him now. As an executive recruiter told me, "It's great for the ego to think the company will fall apart without you." But the plain fact is, it won't. —Jacqueline Hornor Plumez with Karla Dougherty, *Divorcing a Company*

1988. Anyone who thinks he or she is indispensable should stick a finger into a bowl of water and notice the hole it leaves when it's pulled out. —Harvey Mackay, *Swim with the Sharks without Being Eaten Alive*

1994. "No one is indispensable," Mr. Nethercutt said in an interview. "The cemetery is full of people who were indispensable." —*New York Times*

No problem. O.K. Easily done. Often used as a response to a request. The phrase originated in the United States in the mid-twentieth century and is used all over the world even by people who don't speak English.

1979. "Could you call him and ask whether he'll see me now? As a favor, please."
"No problem." —Howard Fast, *The Establishment*

1983. "Money up front," he said.
"No problem." —Jackie Collins, *Hollywood Husbands*

1991. Kendall Mahan added a new twist. He wanted to meet Saturday mornings. Early, say seven-thirty.
"No problem," Mitch said as he took the notebook and placed it next to the others. —John Grisham, *The Firm*

1992. "Ms. Miller, if you have any motions on this subject, or any renewals of motions you've already made, I'd like to have them before we start tomorrow. Say, eight-thirty, if you can."
"No problem, your honor." —Philip Friedman, *Inadmissible Evidence*

1995. You're losing your house? No problem. Just sell that jackpot. —*New York Times Magazine*
See also NO SWEAT.

No smoke without fire. See WHERE THERE'S SMOKE, THERE'S FIRE.

No sweat. Don't worry, it's easy. The phrase has been used, according to lexicographer Eric Partridge, since 1935. It is considered slang.

1975. "Excuse me," Marty was inquiring, "can you tell me how one goes about getting married?"
"Well?" Mufflin asked excitedly when he hung up.
"No sweat," responded Marty happily. —Jackie Collins, *The World Is Full of Divorced Women*

1984. "I attended a higher naval school. Like your Annapolis. I would like to get a proper degree in electronics," Bugayev said, voicing his own dream.
"No sweat. I can help you out." —Tom Clancy, *The Hunt for Red October*

1985. "We can claim mental and physical cruelty. You should get a landmark settlement." He rubbed his hands together. "No sweat." —Michael Korda, *Queenie*

1988. "Mama says men think ambition in a woman is unattractive."
"No sweat, Laura. Nothing about you could ever be unattractive." —Erich Segal, *Doctors*

1993. "Bull, I wanted to apologize for taking a swing at you at the reunion!"
"Hey, don't sweat it ... I punched you out enough in high school." —Cartoon by Balton, "Funky Winkerbean," *Times* (Trenton)
See also NO PROBLEM.

No way, José. Definitely no (not). The rhyming word *José* can be omitted. Originated in the United States in the 1970s.

1984. We quickly retreated from our position. As a compromise, we offered the loan board $120 million for the warrants. No way. —Lee Iacocca with William Novak, *Iacocca*

1986. *Shit,* Howard thought. *He thinks he's Harry Cohn and this is the 1950s. No way, José.* —Jackie Collins, *Hollywood Husbands*

1987. "Sweetheart, let me button your sweater. It's a little chilly."
"No way, José," said Campbell. —Tom Wolfe, *The Bonfire of the Vanities*

1988. "Hey, come on!" protested Ahmat. "I know you and Bobbie go back a long time but that doesn't give you the right to order me to endanger your life! No way, José." —Robert Ludlum, *The Icarus Agenda*

Nobody is indispensable. See NO PERSON IS INDISPENSABLE.

Nobody is infallible. Everybody can make a mistake. The saying has been traced back to 1880. *No one is infallible* is a variant.

1961. "Nobody is infallible," Colonel Cathcart said sharply, and then continued vaguely, with an afterthought: "Nobody is indispensable, either." —Joseph Heller, *Catch-22*

1991. All right, so I'm not infallible when it comes to the demise of shows. —*People*

1993. "We Baptists don't believe in the infallibility of the umpires!" —Cartoon by Doug Marlett, "Kudzu," *Times* (Trenton)

See also NOBODY IS PERFECT.

Nobody is perfect. Even the best people have some shortcomings. Often said to counter a critical remark about someone. In the United States, the proverb has been traced back to *Diary of the French Revolution* (1803). The phrase appears in a play by Oscar Wilde (1854–1900) in 1895.

1895. Charity, dear Miss Prism, charity! None of us are perfect. I myself am peculiarly susceptible to draughts. —Oscar Wilde, *The Importance of Being Earnest*

1931. We ain't none of us perfect that I knows of. —L. Hollingworth, *Death Leaves Us Naked*

1975. "Nobody's perfect."
"I'm not looking for perfection, I'm looking for truth, and frankly, Mike, I don't think you're the man who can give it to me." —Jackie Collins, *The World Is Full of Divorced Women*

1977. The computer seemed very annoyed when I fed it the question. It replied on the tape, "Nobody's perfect." —Art Buchwald, *Down the Seine and Up the Potomac*

1983. What a pity that a man possessed of such immense and unique talents as Jefferson should have so completely misunderstood the loving and forgiving God of the Jews. Oh, well, no one's perfect. —Letters to the Editor, *Smithsonian*

1985. *He:* I suppose you think I'm a perfect idiot.
She: Oh, no, nobody's perfect. —Herman Wouk, *Inside, Outside*

1990. As questions of possible conflicts of interest in merger work surfaced, Bob Baldwin would quote Jack Morgan's dictum of doing first-class business in a first-class way: "Nobody's perfect, but we think we have the highest ethical standards in the industry." —Ron Chernow, *The House of Morgan*

1991. "I think good grooming is important," the executive explained. "But this guy was so perfect, he was scary. His clothes were perfect. His hair was perfect. His fingernails were perfect. Even his teeth were perfect. He was plastic, and I don't trust that. Nobody is perfect." —*Reader's Digest*

1993. "It's hard to live by the church," said Dwight Richards, 20, a trumpeter in the church band. "I sin, nobody is perfect." —*Times* (Trenton)

1994. I have never been as outraged as I was while reading Claude Lewis' column April 27 on the "undeserved" honors bestowed on former President Richard M. Nixon. The article was a disgrace and tremendously tasteless in the wake of President Nixon's death.... It is obvious to *most* that no one is perfect. Everyone makes mistakes. —Letters to the Editor, *Philadelphia Inquirer*

See also LET HIM WHO IS WITHOUT SIN CAST THE FIRST STONE; NOBODY IS INFALLIBLE.

None so blind as those who refuse to see.
See THERE ARE NONE SO BLIND AS THOSE WHO WILL NOT SEE.

None so deaf as those who will not hear.
See THERE ARE NONE SO BLIND AS THOSE WHO WILL NOT SEE.

Not to know someone from Adam. Not to recognize someone. The idiom has been widely used since the nineteenth century. "He called to see my Governor this morning, and beyond that I don't know him from Adam," wrote Charles Dickens in *The Old Curiosity Shop* (1841). The saying is found in a variety of forms: *I couldn't make you from Adam; I don't know her from Adam; I don't know you from Adam's off ox; I didn't know him from Adam's house cat.*

1988. Take my progress in French, for instance. At 15, I was first out of 27 boys and earned the teacher's comment: "Very good work and progress." The headmaster, who didn't know me from Adam, latched onto this success and observed in his final summing-up: "He appears to have the makings of a real linguist." —*Christian Science Monitor*

1997. In 1991, while Smith was watching film of an upcoming opponent, he took notice of the other team on the tape—Eastern Michigan. He was so impressed, he dropped Braun a note to tell him. "I seldom do that," Smith said. "I didn't know him from Adam." —*Detroit News*

Not with a bang but a whimper. With a muted finish rather than a spectacular conclusion. The phrase was coined by T. S. Eliot in his poem *The Hollow Men* (1925): "This is the way the world ends/Not with a bang but a whimper." Congressional Republicans impeached President Clinton in 1998 "not with a bang," as they had expected, "but with a whimper." The saying is used in a wide variety of forms.

1986. The Glorious Fourth without fireworks? As unthinkable as the Statue of Liberty without the torch or the 1812 Overture ending in a whimper. —*Boston Globe*

1988. After 7 years, one of President Reagan's most cherished policies is ending not with a bang but a whimper. The policy is the one of aiding the Nicaraguan contra rebels, who have been locked in an inconclusive civil war with the country's ruling Sandinistas throughout the Reagan era. —*Christian Science Monitor*

1993. If, as it appears, this is Kevin McHale's last season, the career of one of the greatest players of all-time is ending with a whimper, not a bang. —*Boston Globe*

1996. The first economic statistics of 1996 suggest the economy entered the year with a whimper, rather than a bang. —*Boston Globe*

1997. The grand experiment has failed. A decade of dreams for a South Florida theater went up in smoke during the past year or so, in wisps extending from one end of the Gold Coast to the other. Some companies went out with a bang, others with a whimper. —*Sun-Sentinel* (South Florida)

1998. Kenneth W. Starr's investigation into the Whitewater land venture, the possible abuse of FBI files, and the dismissal of the White House travel office staff appear to be ending with neither a bang nor a whimper, but rather a silence. —*Boston Globe*

Nothing could be further from the truth. It is patently false. It is an outright lie. Said as an emphatic denial of a preceding statement.***

1957. He seemed to feel that he lived in a small town where everyone would know who he was. Nothing, of course, could be further from the truth. —John Cheever, *The Wapshot Chronicle*

1979. General Douglas MacArthur broke his silence and said, in an address to the Congress of the United States, "It has been said, in effect, that I am a warmonger. Nothing could be further from the truth." —Howard Fast, *The Establishment*

1986. "You think the man hates me," Leonard said of Hagler. Leonard shook his head to indicate that nothing could be further from the truth. —*New York Times*

1988. There have been press reports to the effect that I thought Kennedy was the easiest to beat. Nothing could be further from the truth. —Richard Nixon, quoted by Stephen E. Ambrose, *Nixon*

1989. Many say Elvis shouldn't be honored because of his lifestyle. Some say he died from alcohol and drug abuse. Nothing could be further from the truth. —Priscilla A. Parker, *USA Today*

1991. The first point that I want to address with you is the idea that this is somehow a political ploy that I am involved in.... Nothing could be further from the truth. —Anita Hill, *New York Times*

1993. Malcolm blessed black rage, while King preached the virtues of Christian love. True.... Most forcefully, Malcolm spoke the uncompromising truth about black America while King, in Malcolm's words, was a "20th-century Uncle Tom"—the "best weapon the white man" has ever had. Nothing could be further from the truth. —*New York Times*

1995. Mr. Knox says that Mr. Fukuyama's announcement of the end of history meant "the end of full-scale wars between powers." Nothing could be further from the truth. —Letters to the Editor, *New York Times Book Review*

Nothing human is alien to me. *See* I AM A MAN; AND NOTHING HUMAN IS ALIEN TO ME.

Nothing hurts like the truth. *See* THE TRUTH (ALWAYS, OFTEN) HURTS.

Nothing is certain but death and taxes. Death and taxes are two unavoidable evils while nothing else in life can be guaranteed. The joke is in the equation of death with taxes. The proverb has been traced back to Daniel Defoe's *Political History of the Devil* (1726). Defoe's version was "Things are certain as Death and Taxes." First attested in the United States in *Writings of Benjamin Franklin* (1789). In a letter to Jean-Baptiste Leroy dated November 13, 1789, Franklin wrote: "In this world nothing can be said to be certain, except death and taxes."

1936. "Death and taxes and childbirth! There's never any convenient time for any of them!" —Margaret Mitchell, *Gone With the Wind*

1987. There is, of course, no final solution. Like death and taxes, lateness and absenteeism will always be with us. —*Bits & Pieces*

1988. "I said to myself, 'Please, God, no more Afghanistans, no KAL airliners, no Nick Daniloffs this time.'"

"That's like praying for an end to death and taxes." —Nelson DeMille, *The Charm School*

1991. "This market is so steady, so solid, so consistent. It's like death and taxes, only much more fun," said William Bondlow, the publisher of Globe Communications's Bridal Guide. —*New York Times*

1993. "In this world nothing is certain but death and taxes," Ben Franklin said back in 1789, and few today would argue with that proposition. But most Presidents—while accepting the inevitability of death—have been unable to avoid the temptation to tinker with the tax code. —*Modern Maturity*

1994. "But if the Yankees lose the series, will Buck Showalter be back as manager?"
"You know Steinbrenner. All he keeps saying is, 'Nothing's a sure thing but death and taxes.'"
—*New York Times*

Nothing new under the sun. *See* THERE'S NOTHING NEW UNDER THE SUN.

Nothing succeeds like success. One success often leads to another. The appearance of success is a great competitive advantage. The proverb is of French origin: *Rien ne réussit comme le succès* and was used by Alexander Dumas the Elder (1802–71) in *Ange Pitou* (1854). First attested in the United States in A. D. Richardson's *Beyond the Mississippi* (1867). *Nothing succeeds like excess* is a jocular variant.

1965. "It is a better rule that nothing succeeds like successors." —Arthur M. Schlesinger, Jr., *A Thousand Days*

1971. Nothing recedes like success. —*Observer* (London)

1984. Who would have believed that a time might come when a man like me would regard the day of his death as better than the day of his birth?... Nothing fails like success. —Joseph Heller, *God Knows*

1988. The first woman to manage a major presidential campaign, Estrich, 35, is a shrewd strategist who's also a Harvard Law school professor. "Nothing succeeds like success," she says. "The fact that I'm running an effective campaign is more important than my gender." —*Ladies' Home Journal*

1992. Nothing succeeds like excess. —*Atlantic*

1993. As Christopher Lasch states in his book *The Culture of Narcissism:* "Nothing succeeds like the appearance of success." —*Reader's Digest*

1994. FOR KAY BOYLE, NOTHING SUCCEEDED LIKE EXCESS —*New York Times Book Review*
See also SUCCESS BREEDS SUCCESS.

Nothing to write home about. It's ordinary, mediocre. Nothing special or exciting. The expression in its current form dates back to the late nineteenth century.

1928. He was ... bleeding a bit, but nothing to write home about. —G. D. H. Cole, *The Man from the River*

1945. "I don't wonder. In this outfit of what the current stylists call 'courageous colors,' I'm something to write home about." —Emilie Loring, *Beyond the Sound of Guns*

1978. Then I was promoted to corporal and machine guns, and then I made sergeant, which is what runs the British army, because when it comes to brains, their officers are nothing to write home about. —Howard Fast, *Second Generation*

1986. *Q.:* I am a fan of the beautiful Victoria Principal of TV's *Dallas.* What were her other acting credits before that show came along?
A.: Not much to write home about. —*Daily News Magazine* (N.Y.)

1992. Picture postcard theater, for all its blandishments, is not something to write home about. —*New York Times*

Nothing ventured, nothing gained. You can't get anywhere unless you're willing to take a risk. The saying dates back to Chaucer (c.1374) and is similar to the late fourteenth century French proverb: *Qui onques rien n'enprist riens n'achieva* ("He who never undertook anything never achieved anything"). The proverb was included in John Heywood's collection of proverbs in 1546. First cited in the United States in *Letters and Papers of Cadwallader Colden* (1748). It takes varying forms: *Nothing ventured, nothing lost; Nothing ventured, nothing won,* etc. A variant used by Dickens and Agatha Christie is *Nothing ventured, nothing have.*

1984. "If they allow us to go up," he had whispered to his armor bearer, "we will go up. I will take my spear and hope that the Lord hath delivered them into our hand. If they don't, they don't. We'll go back to the camp. Nothing ventured, nothing gained." —Joseph Heller, *God Knows*

1989. "Let me be perfectly frank—I see no point in false modesty—I *am* the right man for the job."
"I'm the last person he'd ask," she said.
"Well, nothing ventured, nothing gained, eh?" —Michael Korda, *The Fortune*

1992. Your letter is further testimony to the wisdom of keeping all one's old telephone numbers and addresses. Nothing ventured, nothing gained. —Abigail Van Buren, "Dear Abby," *Times* (Trenton)

1993. NOTHING VENTURED —Headline, *Modern Maturity*

See also FAINT HEART NEVER WON FAIR LADY; FORTUNE

FAVORS THE BRAVE; HE WHO HESITATES IS LOST; HE WHO NEVER MADE A MISTAKE NEVER MADE ANYTHING.

Nothing will come of nothing. Do nothing and nothing is what you get. Everything must come from something. In Latin: *Ex nihilo nihil fit* was originally a scientific statement. The proverb has been traced back to Chaucer's *Boece* (c.1380) The phrase appears in Shakespeare's *Lear* (1606). First attested in the United States in *Writings of Samuel Johnson, President of King's College* (1716). Variant forms include: *From nothing, nothing is made; Nothing comes from (out of) nothing,* etc.

> **1606.** *Lear:* What can you say to draw
> A third more opulent than your sisters?
>   Speak.
> *Cordelia:* Nothing, my lord.
> *Lear:* Nothing!
> *Cordelia:* Nothing.
> *Lear:* Nothing will come of nothing.
> —Shakespeare, *Lear,* I, i

1987. "Was there any part of the curriculum he was particularly good—or, let me say, adept at, anything he did better than anything else?"
"Not particularly."
"No?"
"It's difficult to explain, Mr. Fallow. As the saying goes, '*Ex nihilo nihil fit.*'" —Tom Wolfe, *The Bonfire of the Vanities*

1987. Mrs. Whitehead was asked during a recess if she thought it fair to take Mr. Stern's only child while she had two children of her own.... With an icy edge in her voice, she replied: "Nothing comes from nothing." —*New York Times*

1993. The universe itself, or that part of it that I can see from here, hangs from one fact: EX NIHILO NIHIL FIT. Nothing comes from nothing. —*Times* (Trenton)

See also YOU DON'T GET SOMETHING FOR NOTHING; YOU CAN'T GET BLOOD FROM A STONE.

Now is the time for all good men to come to the aid of their country. At first glance, this line appears to be a call to patriots to help their country in time of need. However, it actually originated in the United States in 1867 as a practice exercise for aspiring typists in Weller's *Typing Test.* Often echoed in the phrase *now is the time,* used as a call to action.

1952. "I suppose now *is* the time," said von Neu-mann matter-of-factly. —Kurt Vonnegut, Jr., *Player Piano*

1987. Okay, we're *now* in the final hour of the "Save the Gown" telethon! If you want to help stabilize Mrs. Reagan's inaugural gown, *now* 's the time! —G. B. Trudeau, *Doonesbury Deluxe*

1991. Now's the time for all good men to
Get recession off our backs.
Show the nation your intent to
Live as credit cardiacs.
—Felicia Lamport, *New York Times*

1992. NY92. Now is the time for all good Democrats, Republicans, Independents and other interested parties to come to the aid of their psyches in The Restaurant at Windows On The World, where the most unconventionally lavish $19.92 Prix Fixe Grand Buffet Luncheon in town will be delectably electable between 12:00 noon and 2:30 p.m. every Monday to Saturday through Election Day. May the best appetites win. —Ad for Windows On The World, *New York Times*

Now you see it, now you don't. Said of something that suddenly disappears. The saying originated among magicians and conjurers, who performed their sleight of hand between the first phrase and the second, pausing slightly for effect.

1961. People bled to death like gentlemen in an operating room or expired without comment in an oxygen tent. There was none of that tricky now-you-see-me-now-you-don't business so much in vogue outside the hospital, none of that now-I-am-and-now-I-ain't. —Joseph Heller, *Catch-22*

1982. "Now you see it, now you don't."—H. Shadowspawn —Robert Asprin, *Myth Directions*

1989. Five days later, Whitney Young, executive director of the National Urban League, called the record of the Nixon Administration uneven, indecisive, and flabby. "It's sort of like Jell-O," said Young. "You can't really get hold of it, you know. It's what I call white magic, now you see it, now you don't." —Stephen E. Ambrose, *Nixon*

1993. REFORM IN MEXICO: NOW YOU SEE IT ... —Headline, *New York Times*

1994. A young Princeton firm has cooked up a way for sports teams to make more money with relative ease. The invention—real time video insertion. Now you see it (viewing at home), now you don't (at the ballpark). —*U.S. 1* (Princeton)

O Romeo, Romeo! wherefore art thou Romeo? Although this line from the balcony scene of Shakespeare's *Romeo and Juliet* is often misconstrued as a request to know the whereabouts of the beloved, it should actually be understood as "Why must you be *named* Romeo—and thus be the son of my father's enemy?" *Wherefore* does not mean "where," it is an archaic word meaning "why."

1594–96.
> *Juliet:* O Romeo, Romeo! wherefore art thou Romeo?
> Deny thy father, and refuse thy name.
> —Shakespeare, *Romeo and Juliet,* II, ii

1991. Enter Romeo, bedraggled and weary after a long day at the office. He squints at the candles and flips on the overhead lights. "Why's it so dark in here, honey? I can't see a thing." He shuffles off to get his beer, then remembers with a jolt that tonight is the play-offs and rushes upstairs to the television. "Men are creeps," sighs Juliet, as she thinks back to the days of passion, romance, the balcony in Verona. "O Romeo, Romeo! wherefore art thou Romeo?" —*McCall's*

1992. *Question:* O Romeo, Romeo! Wherefore art thou, Romeo?
> *Answer:* Living in a modest four-room Victorian row house in Camden Town, a slightly seedy district of London. For Leonard Whiting, now 41, playing Romeo at 17 was the bright spot in a film career that quickly faded.
> —*People*

Of two evils choose the lesser. *See* CHOOSE THE LESSER OF TWO EVILS.

Off with his (her) head! Get rid of the offender immediately! Literally, chop off his or her head.

Now used to suggest the dictatorial nature of the speaker or the enormity of the offense. Spoken by Gloucester in Shakespeare's *Richard III* (1592–93) and the Queen of Hearts in Lewis Carroll's *Alice's Adventures in Wonderland.*

1592–93.
> *Gloucester:* Talk'st thou to me of ifs? Thou art a traitor;
> Off with his head!
> —Shakespeare, *Richard III,* III, iv

1865. The Queen turned crimson with fury, and, after glaring at her for a moment like a wild beast, began screaming, "Off with her head! Off—" —Lewis Carroll, *Alice's Adventures in Wonderland*

1961. The fog shot forth a snaky finger and Roy carefully searched under it for the ball but it was already in the catcher's mitt.
"Strike two."
"Off with his head," Otto shrieked. —Bernard Malamud, *The Natural*

1984. Each time Henry [Ford] walked into a meeting, the atmosphere changed abruptly. He held power of life and death over all of us. He could suddenly say "off with his head"—and he often did. —Lee Iacocca with William Novak, *Iacocca*

1991. IN FORMER EAST BERLIN, IT'S OFF WITH LENIN'S HEAD —Headline of an article on the dismantling of Lenin's statue, *New York Times*

1992. OFF WITH THEIR WIGS? —Headline of an article on perukes worn by British barristers, *New York Times*

1993. You say, "off with her head," but what I'm hearing is, "I feel neglected." —Caption of a drawing, *Modern Maturity*

1994. OFF WITH THE HEADS OF THE CIGARETTE KINGS —Headline of an article on new regulations for the tobacco industry, *Times* (Trenton)

Offense is the best defense. *See* THE BEST DEFENSE IS A GOOD OFFENSE.

Oil and water don't mix. Said of things with such different natures that they cannot be combined. Often used to explain conflicts between incompatible people. Originated in the United States in 1783. Attributed to Joseph Jones of Virginia. There are several similar sayings: *Alcohol (drinking) and driving don't mix; Smoking and sports don't mix,* etc.

1990. "The breaking point. You've had enough!" said one advertising art director in his late forties who quit over an "oil and water" personality clash with his boss. —Carole Hyatt, *Shifting Gears*

1991. RECESSION AND RE-ELECTION DON'T MIX —Headline of an article about George Bush's chances for re-election, *New York Times*

1991. "They were like oil and water—they just didn't mix," said one ex-clerk who sorted mail on the overnight shift and asked to remain anonymous. —*New York Times*

1993. Mustaches and diving masks, I discover, don't mix. —*Modern Maturity*

1993. Dante and Amanda "had father-daughter friction at first—sometimes they're like oil and water." —*Lear's*

1994. "The two would never get along! They're like oil and water." —Cartoon by Alex Kotzky, "Apt. 3-G," *Times* (Trenton)

Old habits die hard. People tend to be slow to give up traditional ways of doing things and accept change. This aphorism has been traced back to 1450. First cited in the United States in an article by Benjamin Franklin printed in *London Chronicle* on December 26–28, 1758. The word *customs* may substitute for *habits*. The word *old* is sometimes omitted. The noun *die-hard,* meaning a person who vigorously resists change or progress, is based on this proverb.

1987. Old habits die hard—if you don't bring the camera back, kid, you better still have the strap—and Tarpy found himself in the unfortunate position of only being able to take wonderful black-and-white photos of people trying to kill him. —Chris Bunch & Allan Cole, *A Reckoning for Kings*

1989. "Habits die hard," he told her, "and the older you are, the harder." —Michael Korda, *The Fortune*

1991. Sometimes it tells you old habits die hard. Maybe Senator Simpson would call my colleagues Tony or Tom in a letter to the editor, but somehow

I doubt it. Somehow I suspect they would be Mr. Lewis and Mr. Wicker. —Anna Quindlen, *New York Times*

1992. Old habits die hard. I remember how the mother of one playmate tied leftover slivers of soap together with a rubber band. When the slivers stuck together on their own, making something like a bar of soap, she stored the rubber band for next time. —*New York Times Magazine*

1993. I acknowledge that the practice is usual and customary, but I don't see it as a put-down for women. (I almost said "the weaker sex"; Old habits die hard.) —Abigail Van Buren, "Dear Abby," *Times* (Trenton)

1994. A few [subway riders] even said they had never considered abandoning their daily ritual of buying tokens. Old habits die hard, they said. —*New York Times*

Old soldiers never die; they just fade away. This line is taken from "Old Soldiers Never Die," copyrighted by British songwriter J. Foley (1905–70) in 1920. Bartlett's *Familiar Quotations* lists it as an anonymous British army song (c.1915). The song gained renewed popularity after General Douglas MacArthur used it in a speech on his dismissal by Truman in 1951. *Simply* may substitute for *just.* The word *soldiers* is often replaced by other nouns, especially in punning takeoffs on the original chestnut.

1920. Old soldiers never die,
   Never die,
   Never die,
   Old soldiers never die,
   They simply fade away.
      —J. Foley, "Old Soldiers Never Die"

1951. I still remember the refrain of one of the most popular barracks ballads of that day, which proclaimed most proudly that old soldiers never die; they just fade away. I now close my military career and just fade away. —Douglas MacArthur, Address to a Joint Meeting of Congress

1951. They said old soldiers never died. No, they went to live in cottages on Kahala Avenue at the foot of Diamond Head. —James Jones, *From Here to Eternity*

1957. Clearly, old soldiers never die; they simply keep on arguing. —*New Yorker*

1982. "Old heroes never die; they reappear in sequels." [M. Moorcock] —Robert Asprin, *Myth Directions*

1986. Old bankers never die; they just yield to maturity.

Old lecturers never die; they know they'll see dais.

Old dictators never die; they just fly the coup.

Old politicians never die; they just harangue in there.

—Quoted in *Reader's Digest*

1990. Old fishermen never die; they just wade away.

Old welders never die; they just pass the torch.

Old truckers never die; they just semiretire.

Old philosophers never die; they Kant.

Old plagiarists never die; they just steal away.

Old insurance agents never die; it's against their policy.

—Quoted in *Reader's Digest*

1991. For the computer to become a major American institution, we will need to fill highways with slogans such as, "Old programmers never die, they just eternally loop," and "Old computer operators never die, they just remain on downtime." —*Computerworld*

1993. "Old fishermen never die, they just smell that way!" —Cartoon by Art & Chip Sansom, "Born Loser," *Times* (Trenton)

1993. "True innovators never die," the ad concludes. "They just reinvent themselves." —*Wall Street Journal*

1994. Old weapons systems never die—even after the mission they were designed for vanishes and the service that wanted them changes its mind. —*New York Times*

On a wing and a prayer. Under the most tenuous and hazardous circumstances. The metaphor comes from the image of a damaged airplane trying to land. The phrase first appeared as the title of a song, *Comin' In on a Wing and a Prayer* (1943): "Tho' there's one motor gone, we can still carry on/Comin' in on a wing and a pray'r." The song was written by Harold Adamson (1906–80) with music by Jimmy McHugh. The 1944 movie *Wing and a Prayer,* directed by Henry Hathaway, about brave pilots aboard an aircraft carrier during World War II, made its title a household saying.

1985. When I was a child, a relative often used the phrase "on a wing and a prayer." When he used this expression, he was talking about luck—barely making it under the most tenuous circumstances. Sometimes our sense of prayer is along this line—that it's a rather uncertain form of help that may or may not work. —*Christian Science Monitor*

1986. A survey for the American Association of State Colleges and Universities found 27 percent of the presidents have a formal contract, 12 percent have an oral agreement, and 39 percent only a letter from their board describing their job duties. That's why, says Newman, college presidents are cautious. "If anything goes wrong, they're the point man for the heat," he says. "They're out there on a wing and a prayer by themselves." —*USA Today*

1986. The initial can-do spirit that swept the embassy after the Russian service employees left has given way to irritation and anger about the increased workload and lack of relief from the United States. "It is just so difficult," one American said. Another commented, "We are operating on a wing and a prayer." —*New York Times*

1994. The campaign to put the Memphis Belle on a postage stamp is taking off on more than a wing and a prayer. —*Commercial Appeal* (Memphis, Tennessee)

1996. FAMILY SURVIVES CRASH ON A WING AND A PRAYER; LINCOLN PARK COUPLE, DAUGHTER WALK AWAY AFTER SMALL PLANE CRASH-LANDS ON HIGHWAY —Headline, *Detroit News*

On the shoulders of giants. *See* IF I HAVE SEEN FURTHER IT IS BY STANDING ON THE SHOULDERS OF GIANTS.

On the whole, I'd rather be in Philadelphia. The raffish American comedian W. C. Fields (1879–1946) is said to have requested that this epitaph be inscribed on his gravestone. The implied joke is that Philadelphia, known for its blue laws, is a dull town, but even that place is better than this one (death).

Undated.
On the whole, I'd rather be in Philadelphia. —W. C. Fields, epitaph

1993. Ruth once asked Fields how he got into the theatre. "I was fifteen, and hungry," he said.... And now it's Letterman at the Gothic-domed theatre.... On the whole, I'd rather be in Philadelphia. —*New Yorker*

1994. The legendary comedian W. C. Fields asked that his epitaph read: "On the whole, I'd rather be in Philadelphia." If he were a business owner today, he might have second thoughts. —*Crain's New York Business*

See also IT AIN'T FIT NIGHT OUT FOR MAN OR BEAST; NEVER GIVE A SUCKER AN EVEN BREAK.

Once a thief, always a thief. People never change. You can rely on them to behave as they did before. When said of a person with a history of wrongdoing, it means he or she can never be trusted. The proverb has been traced back to J. Stevens's *New Spanish and English Dictionary* (1706). The word *thief* may be replaced by *crook, drunkard, Englishman, fighter, knave, liar, preacher, whore,* etc.

1939. Grampa waved his hand back and forth. "Once a fella's a preacher, he's always a preacher. That's somepin you can't get shut of." —John Steinbeck, *The Grapes of Wrath*

1966. British deserters, conniving with ingenious Americans, would often secure fraudulent naturalization papers. But His Majesty's press gangs laughed aside such documents, whether genuine or not, holding to the principle "Once an Englishman, always an Englishman." —Thomas A. Bailey, *The American Pageant*

1983. Confusion and anger mixed with the fury that welled up inside him. He took his knife from the side of his boot and ripped at the offending poster. Joey had done this.
Once a whore always a whore. —Jackie Collins, *Hollywood Wives*

1992. He [General Secord] plans to vote for George Bush and to sue special prosecutor Lawrence Walsh "on a host of issues." After all, once a fighter, always a fighter. —*People*

1994. General Powell also talks with his successor as Chairman of the Joint Chiefs, Gen. John Shalikashvili, although he is reportedly extremely careful not to seem to trespass on General Shalikashvili's turf.... "There's no resentment at all that I've heard," a senior Pentagon official said. "But that's just the way it is—once a general, always a general, retired or not, especially if you're a major star like Colin Powell." —*New York Times*
See also I AM WHAT I AM AND THAT'S WHAT I AM; THE LEOPARD CAN'T CHANGE ITS SPOTS; A LIAR IS NOT BELIEVED WHEN HE TELLS (SPEAKS) THE TRUTH.

Once bitten, twice shy. *See* ONCE BURNED, TWICE SHY.

Once burned, twice shy. One who had an unpleasant experience is especially cautious. The proverb has been traced back to *Sponge's Sporting Tour* (1853) by English novelist Robert Smith Surtees (1803–64). First attested in the United States in *Dead Sure* (1949) by S. Sterling. The form *burnt* is sometimes seen. *Once bitten, twice shy* is a variant.

1985. It's worth pointing out that the phrase "Once burned, twice shy" applies to no group more accurately than to investors. —*Forbes*

1987. No, he'll never be President, and the chances are that he'll never be Vice-President. But he keeps thinking he will. And partly because of this, he does what he's told these days, no more and no less. Once bitten, twice shy, as they say. —R. Richard Ritti & G. Ray Funkhouser, *The Ropes to Skip & the Ropes to Know*

1988. "You can win one and then lose one, young man. Once successful, twice burned. Those people play hardball." —Robert Ludlum, *The Icarus Agenda*

1991. "Once burned, twice bitten," he sagely began. "Therefore, everything that follows is based on the hypothesis that Cuomo won't run. Or, I should say, again won't run." —Tom Wicker, *New York Times*

Once more unto the breach, dear friends. This famous exhortation to the troops in Shakespeare's *Henry V* also suggests that the battle will be cruel and bloody. Hence, it usually refers to arduous and unpleasant undertakings. Because the line includes the words "once more," it may also be used to suggest the repetition or recollection of such an event, rather than being invoked as a call to arms.

1598. *King Henry:* Once more unto the breach, dear friends, once more. —Shakespeare, *Henry V*, III, i

1982. "Once more into the breach ..."—Zarna, the Human Cannonball —Robert Asprin, *Myth Directions*

1992. ONCE MORE UNTO THE GRAVE —Headline of Russell Baker's article on the Vietnam War and the 1992 presidential election, *New York Times*

1992. ONCE MORE UNTO THE BRINK: CUBAN CRISIS RELIVED —Headline of an article on the thirtieth anniversary of the 1962 Cuban missile crisis, *New York Times*

One can't be in two places at once. Literally, one cannot be expected to be in attendance at two distant places or events at the same time. Figuratively, one must decide between two conflicting ideologies, positions, jobs, etc. In either case, the expression implies some frustration at having to make a difficult choice. The aphorism has been traced back to *The Ship of Fools* (1509) by English poet Alexander Barclay (c.1476–1552). Attested in the United States in 1936. Variants include *A man can't be in two places at once;* and *You can't be in* *two places at the same time.* Similar to the Yiddish proverb *You can't dance at two weddings at the same time.*

1936. She couldn't be in two places at once and the good Lord knew she was doing her best for them all in Atlanta. —Margaret Mitchell, *Gone With the Wind*

1978. Members cannot be in two places at once.... Years ago, House members returned home for months at a time.... Today, they race home for a day, a weekend, a week.... The quality of their contact has suffered. "It is like a one-night stand in a singles bar." —Richard F. Fenno, *Home Style: House Members in Their Districts*

1992. "Who says you can't be in two places at once?" Lipton asks. —*Time*

1993. FOOTBALL MAGICIAN WHO WAS IN TWO PLACES AT ONE TIME —Headline of an article on Pop Warner, who coached two football teams in 1895, *New York Times*

1995. "The Speaker's crown jewel will be gone," exulted Senator Russell D. Feingold, Democrat of Wisconsin. His party's main argument of the day, that promising a balanced budget and a tax cut in the same electioneering breath is a charade, drew the Yiddish proverb, in straight English, from Senator Paul Wellstone, Democrat of Minnesota. "You can't dance at two weddings at the same time," he quoted.... —Francis X. Clines, *New York Times*

One day at a time. Do it gradually. Concentrate on short-term goals. Don't get ahead of yourself. Take satisfaction from small accomplishments. Limit your focus to what you must do in the immediate present to achieve your long-term goal, lest you become so overwhelmed by the size of the project that you give up hope and do nothing at all. Motto of Alcoholics Anonymous, a self-help organization founded in 1934 that encourages members to stay sober one day at a time rather than taking an inviolable pledge never to drink again. Also, title of a 1970s TV sit-com portraying the lives of working mothers. *Take* or *take it* often precedes the phrase.***

1976. I look around this office, which is located in the heart of downtown Chicago, and I think, my god. We've got fifteen hundred square feet, we've got three computers, we've got three printers, we got a good amount of money in furniture, and five years ago we had an empty cabinet in my house. You do a business one day at a time. And it happens. —Claudia Jessup & Genie Chipps, *The Woman's Guide to Starting a Business*

1987. If business is running smoothly it's very tempting to adopt a "take each day as it comes" policy. —Ad for NatWest, *New York Times*

1992. "They're together now," says a friend. "Hey, it's one day at a time." —*People*

1992. "I'm taking one day at a time," said Ms. Neff, who took out a loan to cover the $5,400 she lost in state aid. —*New York Times*

1993. I'm proud to say that I have been sober for a year now, and the fun is just beginning. As they say in A.A. [Alcoholics Anonymous], "One day at a time"; things do get better. Wised Up in Yakima, Wash. —Abigail Van Buren, "Dear Abby," *Times* (Trenton)

1994. "Do you dream to be President?" ... Gore laughed nervously.... "Would you believe me if I told you that since I was a young child I dreamed of becoming *Vice* President of the United States?" he asked.... After the translation, the crowd roared. But that response would not do and Gore tried another nonanswer: "I take one year at a time." —*New York Times Magazine*

See also ONE STEP AT A TIME; ONE THING AT A TIME.

One for all and all for one. *See* ALL FOR ONE AND ONE FOR ALL.

One good turn deserves another. Said when repaying a favor. Also used ironically to mean that turnabout is fair play. The adage has been traced back to *Latin MS* (c.1400). First attested in the United States in *Vindication* (1717).

1983. "Why are you so good to me, Karen?" he asked quizzically.

She grinned. "'Cause one good turn deserves another—and baby, your turns are gooood!" —Jackie Collins, *Hollywood Wives*

1991. Throughout the time they were here, the surveillance was maintained—just as the Iranians had undoubtedly done for *our* visit to Tehran. One good turn deserves another. —Oliver L. North, *Under Fire*

1992. One good heart deserves another. —Ad for Van den Bergh, Inc., *Reader's Digest*

1992. One good reform deserves another, yet New York resists changing the crazy names it gives its courts. —*New York Times*

See also ONE HAND WASHES THE OTHER; YOU SCRATCH MY BACK, I'LL SCRATCH YOURS.

One hand washes the other. Favors must be reciprocated. If you expect me to help you, you must first help me. The allusion is to the interdependence of the hands in the act of washing: neither can be cleaned without the aid of the other. The proverb has been traced back to *Garden of Pleasure* (1573). First attested in the United States in *Diary of Philip Hone* (1836).

1961. "What difference does it make to anyone if I'm in the plane or not?"

"No difference."

"Sure, that's what I mean," Doc Daneeka said. "A little grease is what makes this world go round. One hand washes the other." —Joseph Heller, *Catch-22*

1980. If our attitude is embodied in the saying "Give a little, get a little," or "One hand washes the other," we would make a counter-offer increasing the initial lowball offer. —Herb Cohen, *You Can Negotiate Anything*

1985. "Perhaps I should explain," he went on, "that Lucien does a little talent scouting for me. Nothing formal, you understand, Miss Kelley. We're old friends, Lucien and I. One hand washes the other." —Michael Korda, *Queenie*

1989. "So I say we report what happens, and this jerk from NSA says, you could do better. I know that he means that we could lie, and I explain my position on integrity of intelligence and he said, one hand washes the other, and forty-five minutes later I left." —Wayne Care, *Vietnam Spook Show*

1990. "Panama is a funny country," Harari said. "It's not really a country. It's more like a business. I know the right people or—to put it another way—the storekeeper. One hand washes the other in Panama." —Victor Ostrovsky & Claire Hoy, *By Way of Deception*

1993. How could Ed Dennis not be grateful? His judgment about the Waco fiasco: "There is no place in the evaluation for blame, and I find no fault...." One hand whitewashes the other. —William Safire, *The Times* (Trenton)

1994. From the appreciative crowd, Sam Stern, a longtime resident of this Rockland County village, observed: "Of course, we will support him [Mario Cuomo]. One hand washes the other." —*New York Times*

See also ONE GOOD TURN DESERVES ANOTHER; YOU SCRATCH MY BACK, I'LL SCRATCH YOURS.

One is innocent until proven guilty.

At a trial, the burden of proof rests with the prosecution, not with the defendant. The saying expresses one of America's fundamental legal principles, but it may be used in everyday situations as well. Often shortened to *innocent until proven guilty*. ***

1978. "Legally, we couldn't keep him at all, at least according to the Constitution we adopted at our meeting last night, because under that document a man's innocent until proven guilty in a court of law." —Stephen King, *The Stand*

1984. I also respect very much something that is very typically American, and that is you are innocent until proven guilty. —Ronald Reagan, *New York Times*

1988. "Innocent until proven guilty" is an uphill battle for the mind. —Clifford Irving, *The Campbell Murder Case*

1989. "Do you feel your 'no comment' will be translated as saying you're guilty?"

"To my knowledge," he [Pete Rose] said, "you're innocent until proven guilty." —*New York Times*

1991. "Aren't I innocent until proven guilty? Isn't this a free country?" Milken asked aggressively. —James B. Stewart, *Den of Thieves*

1991. "Roy represents people who can afford him. You're basically innocent until proven broke." Miami prosecutor Michael Band, on Willie Smith's high-priced defense attorney, Roy Black. —*Newsweek*

1992. As for the fuss over Mr. Jordan, he says it is overblown. "I have to assume that Vernon Jordan is an honorable man, until he's proven otherwise," Mr. Nofziger said. "If he is not honorable, then put him in jail." —*New York Times*

1993. "Roscow! Are *you* the one who chewed up my book?"

"I'm innocent until proven guilty." —Cartoon by Brian Crane, "Pickles," *Times* (Trenton)

One lie leads to another.

Once you tell one lie, you will find yourself forced into devising more lies to cover up your own dishonesty. A person who believes he's gotten away with one lie finds it increasingly easier (and more necessary) to be deceitful. The proverb has been traced back to *Floures for Latine Speaking* (1534). *One lie begets another* is a variant.

1962. One lie draws ten after it. —*Bangor Daily News* (Me.)

1993. "You had to bring up the lunches, didn't you, Sophie?"

"You know what grandpa used to say ... 'One lie leads to another'!" —Cartoon by Doux & Wilson, "Judge Parker," *Times* (Trenton)

See also HONESTY IS THE BEST POLICY; A LIAR IS NOT BELIEVED WHEN HE SPEAKS (TELLS) THE TRUTH.

One man's gravy is another man's poison.

See ONE MAN'S MEAT IS ANOTHER MAN'S POISON.

One man's loss is another man's gain. Said when something exchanges hands or one person profits by the misfortune of another. The proverb has been traced back to *Correspondence of Swift* (1733). First attested in the United States in *Circus* (1927) by J. Tully. Variant forms include: *His loss is my gain; One man's adversity is another man's opportunity; One man's gain is another man's loss,* etc.

1984. Many unknown people wrote to us, saying in a hundred different ways that they were with us, that Henry Ford's loss was Chrysler's gain. —Lee Iacocca with William Novak, *Iacocca*

1985. After I gave it [a dress] to her, she [the daughter] thanked me.
"Oh, you're welcome, honey," I said. "My loss is your gain."
"No, Mom," she said, grinning. "Your *gain* is my gain." —Quoted in *Reader's Digest*

1988. A special advisory board has unanimously recommended that Mayor Koch appoint Dr. Charles S. Hirsch, the Suffolk County Medical Examiner, to be the New York City Chief Medical Examiner, city officials said last night.... However, an associate interviewed at the county medical examiner's office in Hauppague, L.I., said, "Our loss is going to be New York City's gain." —*New York Times*

1991. "... so I says to myself, 'Bill, one man's panic is another man's profit, and I know which one of those men old Bill's going to be.' " —Alexandra Ripley, *Scarlett*

1993. Surveying the situation, the Flyers' loss is about to be the Devils' gain in a big way. —*Times* (Trenton)

1994. Like so many Democrats of his generation, he [President Clinton] and his policy advisers are not comfortable wielding military power; the big stick just does not rest easy in their palms. Perhaps it is because the use of force is a zero-sum game: one side's gains are the other side's losses. —*New York Times*

See also FINDERS KEEPERS, LOSERS WEEPERS; IT'S AN ILL WIND THAT BLOWS NO (NOBODY) GOOD.

One man's meat is another man's poison. Values are relative. What one person likes may be loathsome to another. Originated in ancient times. The adage has been traced back in English to T. Whythorne's *Autobiography* (c.1576). In 1647, Beaumont and Fletcher wrote in *Love's Cure:* "What's one man's poison, signor,/Is another's meat or drink." In 1709, Oswald Dykes included the current version in his collection of *English Proverbs*. First attested in the United States in *Adams Family Correspondence* (1776). The proverb is found in varying forms: *One man's gravy is another man's poison; One man's poison is another man's meat; What's one man's meat is another man's poison,* etc.

1939. Restaurant Version: One man's meat is another man's croquette. —Lewis & Faye Copeland, *10,000 Jokes, Toasts and Stories*

1984. "We are so confused about good and evil that one man's saint is another man's monster." —Howard Fast, *The Outsider*

1984. One man's meat is a cow's death. —*Forbes*

1987. One can only speculate why American writers resist acknowledging the legitimacy of the Soviet system among Russians, but a probable cause is that Americans believe that the Soviet system is illegitimate and that to say otherwise is to be a dupe or a traitor. But, as your article suggests, one people's bread is another people's poison. —Letters to the Editor, *New York Times*

1989. American philosophers tell us that truth is relative and morality a matter of taste, no different really from preferring asparagus over beets. Judges, following close behind, instruct democratically elected legislatures that in making public policy they may not choose between competing conceptions of the good. After all, one person's decency is another's perversion. —Letters to the Editor, *New York Times*

1994. Use money, use entrapment, find their vulnerabilities. Again, it's as old as Babylon. One side's patriotism is another's perfidy. —Sydney A. Schanberg, *New York Newsday*

1995. One man's sacred cow is another's Big Mac. —Ad for Global Guardian Trust, *New York Times*

See also DIFFERENT STROKES FOR DIFFERENT FOLKS; EVERY MAN TO HIS OWN TASTE; ONE MAN'S TRASH IS ANOTHER MAN'S TREASURE; THERE'S NO ACCOUNTING FOR TASTES.

One man's trash is another man's treasure. Items that appear worthless to one person may have enormous value to someone else. Often heard at flea markets, yard sales, thrift shops, recycling areas, etc. Of recent origin. Variants include *One man's garbage is another man's gold mine; One man's treasure is another man's trash,* etc.

1992. ONE MAN'S PROP IS ANOTHER MAN'S TREASURE —Headline, *New York Times*

1993. Understand that one person's trash is another's treasure. You can offer the person who buys a whole group of things in a lot a few dollars for the items you want. —*Modern Maturity*

1993. "These are warts, these are clearly warts,'" on the agreement, he said.... But American businesses, many of which advocate unrestricted free trade in all but their own industries, said they were pleased. "One man's wart is another man's beauty mark," said Timothy Regan, a trade official at Corning Inc., a glass manufacturer based in Corning, N.Y. —*New York Times*

1994. ... When W.B.C. stripped [Riddick] Bowe of the title and awarded it to Lewis, Bowe at a news conference and in front of Lewis, threw the W.B.C. championship belt in a garbage can.... Lewis plucked it out, and had it on display in the gym at the Concord. "One man's garbage," said Lewis, "is another man's gold mine." —*New York Times*

See also DIFFERENT STROKES FOR DIFFERENT FOLKS; EVERY MAN TO HIS OWN TASTE; ONE MAN'S LOSS IS ANOTHER MAN'S GAIN; ONE MAN'S MEAT IS ANOTHER MAN'S POISON; THERE'S NO ACCOUNTING FOR TASTES.

One might as well be hanged for a sheep as for a lamb. If the punishment for a serious transgression is similar to that for a less serious one, you might as well commit the serious one. The proverb, alluding to death penalty by hanging for sheep-stealing, was included in John Ray's collection of *English Proverbs* (1678): "As good be hang'd for an old sheep as a young lamb." The proverb appears in *Clarisa; or the History of a Young Lady,* the novel that won Samuel Richardson European fame in 1747–48: "So in for the lamb, as the saying is, in for the sheep." First attested in the United States in *Diary and Autobiography of John Adams* (1787).

1912. If you are wise, George, you'll go to your office and write me your check for three hundred thousand dollars... You can't be hung any more for a sheep than you can for a lamb. —Theodore Dreiser, *The Financier*

1923. *The Archbishop:* I prophesy now that you will be hanged... If you do not learn when to laugh and when to pray.
Bluebeard: My lord: I stand rebuked. I am sorry: I can say no more. But if you prophesy that I shall be hanged, I shall never be able to resist temptation because I shall always be telling myself that I may as well be hanged for a sheep as a lamb.
—George Bernard Shaw, *Saint Joan*

1965. William Henry would as soon have been hanged for robbing a bank as for stealing a loaf. —B. Grebanier, *Great Shakespeare*

1977. She might as well be hung for a sheep as a lamb and make the most of her meal. —B. Pym, *Quarter in Autumn*

See also HE THAT IS BORN TO BE HANGED SHALL NEVER BE DROWNED; THE COWARD DIES MANY TIMES.

One more such victory and we are lost. See ANOTHER SUCH VICTORY, AND WE ARE UNDONE.

One must crawl before he walks. See YOU HAVE TO LEARN TO CRAWL BEFORE YOU CAN WALK.

One nation under God, indivisible, with liberty and justice for all. Part of the Pledge of Allegiance to the Flag of the United States, first used on October 12, 1892 and subsequently amended in 1924, when the words *the flag of the United States* were substituted for *my flag.* The words *under God* were added in 1954. Often used as a patriotic bromide by politicians, especially those running for office.

1892. I pledge allegiance to my flag and to the republic for which it stands: one nation, indivisible, with liberty and justice for all. —The Pledge of Allegiance to the Flag of the United States

1924. I pledge allegiance to the flag of the United States of America and to the republic for which it stands: one nation under God, indivisible, with liberty and justice for all. —The Pledge of Allegiance to the Flag

1977. The important thing now is to heal the wounds and go forward together as one people, one nation under God with liberty and justice for all. —Art Buchwald, *Down the Seine and Up the Potomac*

1988. On a campaign swing through Springfield, Mo., Oct. 27 Mr. Reagan said the Democratic Party had been taken over by liberals. He added: "Harry Truman's party believed in working Americans and in keeping America's defenses strong, and yes, in 'one nation under God.' And today the party that believes in that is stronger than ever. It's called the Republican Party." —*New York Times*

1992. And that's why I want to say just a few things about my visit, to speak to you about what I've seen in the city, and most importantly, as I said at a marvelous ecumenical church service yesterday at Mount Zion, we are one people; we are one family; we are one nation under God. —George Bush, *New York Times*

1992. But this is America. There is no them; there's only us. One nation, under God, indivisible, with liberty, and justice, for all. ... That's what the New Covenant is all about. —Bill Clinton, *New York Times*

1994. "One nation, under God, indivisible, with liberty and justice for all." Echoes from childhood, words we like to believe express the reality of our nation in this post-civil rights era. —*Times* (Trenton)

One picture is worth a thousand words. Visual images have a greater impact than words. The proverb was originated in 1927 by Fred R. Barnard, according to lexicographer Christine Ammer, as a slight alteration of his earlier *One look is worth a thousand words (1921). A picture is worth a thousand words* is a variant.

1988. The ability to draw is not important. What *is* important is that your pictures help you to remember to tell us about yourself (your background, family, interests, hobbies, future goals). Your teacher and classmates want to get to know you. Remember, "A picture is worth a thousand words." —Paulette Dale & James C. Wolf, *Speech Communication for International Students*

1989. The result of the Texas statute is obviously to deny one in Johnson's frame of mind one of many means of "symbolic speech." Far from being a case of "one picture being worth a thousand words," flag burning is the equivalent of an inarticulate grunt or roar that, it seems to say, is most likely to be indulged in not to express any particular idea, but to antagonize others.... —Chief Justice William Rehnquist, *New York Times*

1993. "The old adage: 'A picture is worth a thousand words,' is true here," said Maureen Siegel, chief of criminal operations in the Los Angeles City Attorney's office. —*The Times* (Trenton)

1994. If a picture is worth a thousand words, how many spreadsheets is a map worth? —*New York Times*

One rotten apple spoils the barrel. See THE ROTTEN APPLE SPOILS THE BARREL.

One step at a time. Cautiously, slowly, gradually, step by step. Often preceded by the verb *take.* ***

1901. It's beyond me. We can only walk one step at a time in this world. —Rudyard Kipling, *Kim*

1977. "I'll alert Fowler, too," Hennessy said, delighted that the President had decided to take the matter in hand.

"No, we'll only take one step at a time, and each one if we have to." —William Safire, *Full Disclosure*

1979. "I can't make those years up."

"Well," she told him, "maybe you can't, but you have to put it behind you. If you take one step at a time, you'll find yourself a woman, and some kids. You can still have it all." —Norman Mailer, *The Executioner's Song*

1985. "It's a new technique. It requires time, and great delicacy. There is a certain danger of infection. We go one small step at a time, therefore it is not a big dramatic procedure." —Michael Korda, *Queenie*

1986. "Run through it," the pilot said quietly. "Analyze it one step at a time." —Tom Clancy, *Red Storm Rising*

1988. "Let's take one step at a time," she replied and bent down over him to pull off his loafers. —Erich Segal, *Doctors*

1992. The question was so casual Estrada did not pump his answer. "Slowly. One step at a time. We're trying hard." —Philip Friedman, *Inadmissible Evidence*

1993. "People ask me how do you do a marathon. I answer one mile at a time," he said. —*New York Times*

See also ONE DAY AT A TIME; ONE THING AT A TIME.

One swallow does not make a summer. Don't draw conclusions prematurely based on a single fact. Alludes to the fact that the migratory patterns of swallows herald a change of season, as in the popular song "When the Swallows Come Back to Capistrano." Attributed to Aristotle. The adage has been traced back to *Proverbs of Erasmus* (1539). John Heywood included it in his collection of proverbs in 1546. First attested in the United States in *Complete Writings of Roger Williams* (1652). It is found in varying forms: *One swallow does not make a spring; One swallow makes not a summer, nor even two swallows,* etc.

1844. One foul wind no more makes a winter, than one swallow makes a summer. —Charles Dickens, *Martin Chuzzlewit*

1939. "Always remember that one swallow does not make a spring."

"No, but the swallows the size that you take would make one fall all right." —Lewis & Faye Copeland, *10,000 Jokes, Toasts and Stories*

1956. How many swallows make a summer? —*New Yorker*

1995. "Two Big Macs, please. After all, one swallow does not make a spring lunch." —Overheard at McDonald's, New York City

One thing at a time. Address each problem separately as it arises. Be patient. The proverb has been traced in the United States back to *Correspondence Between William Penn and James Logan* (1702). First attested in England in the *Letters* (1772) of English divine John Wesley (1703–91). Other forms include: *One thing at a time and do it well; One thing at a time, and that done well, is a very good thing, as many (or any) can tell.*

1981. "What's he so hostile for?" Harry beseeches the women. "All I've said was I don't see why we should fire Charlie so the kid can peddle convertibles. In time sure. In 1980, even. Take over, young America. Eat me up. But one thing at a time, Jesus. There's tons of time." —John Updike, *Rabbit Is Rich*

1982. Take up each problem as you get to it. As Casey Stengel used to tell his baseball players when they began to tighten up in the homestretch: "We play 'em one at a time." —Quoted in *Bits & Pieces*

1986. He decided it didn't have to make sense. *One thing at a time,* he told himself. —Tom Clancy, *Red Storm Rising*

1989. "Getting back might be kinda exciting, PJ," Mantaigne observed darkly.

"One thing at a time, Francie. And we do have that alternate place to land." —Tom Clancy, *Clear and Present Danger*

1991. "I'm so sure you'll make the Bishop change his mind."

Colum smiled. "One thing at a time, Cousin." —Alexandra Ripley, *Scarlett*

See also ONE DAY AT A TIME; ONE STEP AT A TIME.

The only thing we have to fear is fear itself.

Be optimistic about the future: we can accomplish anything if we face our problems squarely instead of being undermined by doubt. Although the proverb has been traced back to Francis Bacon (1605), it is often attributed to Franklin Delano Roosevelt, who used it in his first Inaugural Address in 1933. *We have nothing to fear but fear itself* is a variant.

1933. The great Nation will endure as it has endured, will revive and will prosper. So, first of all, let me assert my firm belief that the only thing we have to fear is fear itself—nameless, unreasoning, unjustified terror which paralyzes needed efforts to convert retreat into advance. —Franklin D. Roosevelt, First Inaugural Address

1960. But it was a time of vague optimism for some of the people: Maycomb County had recently been told that it had nothing to fear but fear itself. —Harper Lee, *To Kill a Mockingbird*

1992. To capture the mood of present-day Americans, Roosevelt's first Inaugural would have to be revised to read, "The only thing we have to fear is absolutely everything." —Russell Baker, *New York Times*

1994. I should like to assure the Democrats that they have nothing to fear but fear-of-Newt itself, but that would mislead them. A party that doesn't stand for much has plenty to fear from one that stands for plenty, even when, as now, it looks like plenty of nothing. —Russell Baker, *New York Times*

The opera ain't over till the fat lady sings.

The outcome of any contest isn't known until the final results are in. Thus, don't make premature judgments or give up too soon. Often associated with Wagnerian opera, specifically Brunhilde's "Fire Song," in *Die Walküre,* and the fact that Wagner may seem interminable to nonaficionados. Thus, one's impatience would be relieved when "the fat lady sings." Originated in the United States in the 1970s. Bartlett's *Familiar Quotations* attributes the coinage to San Antonio TV sports commentator Dan Cook. Ralph Graves claims in the August 1991 issue of *Smithsonian* that it has its roots in Southern proverbial lore: "Church ain't out till the fat lady sings." There are still other attributions, but nobody really knows who coined this popular saying. *The fat lady has sung* is a variant meaning "it's finally over."

1978. One day three years ago, Ralph Carpenter, who was then Texas Tech's sports information director, declared to the press box contingent in Austin, "The rodeo ain't over till the bull riders ride." Stirred to top that deep insight, San Antonio sports editor Dan Cook countered with, "The opera ain't over till the fat lady sings." —*Washington Post*

1987. Not bad for a rookie, he thought. Then he put away his notebook, because as far as he was concerned, this press conference was over. For Tarpy, the fat lady had finally sung her song. —Chris Bunch & Allan Cole, *A Reckoning for Kings*

1988. "Do you like the ballet?"

"Only at the end when the fat lady sings." —Nelson DeMille, *The Charm School*

1989. Our spooks report that one-third of the Red Army is becoming Christian—what greater proof that "godless Communism" is past? ... Yes; true; you bet. Then why are you so crabby, Safire, about Mr. Gorbachev and suspicious of his goals? The cold war is over—why can't you hear the fat lady singing? —William Safire, *New York Times*

1992. "They can't run it, Smith. They may have a

few more facts than *The Times-Picayune,* but they can't name Mattiece. Look, we'll verify before anyone. And when it's nailed down, I'll write the story with everyone's name along with that cute little picture of Mattiece and his friend in the White House, and the fat lady will sing." —John Grisham, *The Pelican Brief*

1994. THE FAT LADY HAS SUNG —Sign held aloft at a basketball game, "Eyewitness News," ABC

1994. Both Yankee and Rebel teams employed spies to figure what the other was planning. One of the best was the Rebs' Belle (La Belle Rebelle) Boyd.... Rebel Coach Joe (Yogi) Johnson said of Belle: "The battle ain't over till the shady lady whispers." —*New York Times*

See also IT'S NOT OVER TILL IT'S OVER.

The operation was successful—but the patient died. Used when a technical success nonetheless results in an overall failure. Said ironically.**

1988. "How do you feel, Ben?" Herschel asked anxiously.

"Hi, Dad," he answered, still half comatose. "I don't feel anything yet. What happened?"

"To change the old chestnut, Landsman," Barney said, "the operation was successful—but the doctor died!" —Erich Segal, *Doctors*

1992. It is important to know the path, the process, through which the present is made. Inducing cultural amnesia runs the risk of reproducing the medical scenario of "the operation was a success but the patient died." —Gayle Pemberton, *The Hottest Water in Chicago*

1994. The operation was a success, but the client died. —Barry Dunsmore on the Bosnian Serbs' victories in Bosnia, "Good Morning America," ABC

Opportunity knocks but once. When you see an opportunity to improve your lot, act quickly and resolutely—you may never get another chance. The proverb dates to ancient times (a.d. c.8). The early fifteenth-century French *Il n'est chance qui ne retourne* ("There is no opportunity which comes back again") is very similar in meaning. It has been traced back to *Bandello* (1567) by English writer and politician Geoffrey Fenton (c.1539–1608). First attested in the United States in *Port Folio* (1809). Variants include: *Opportunity knocks, at least, at every man's door; Opportunity never knocks twice at any man's door; Opportunity seldom knocks twice,* etc. *Opportunity knocks* is used to advise somebody that

now is the time to act.

1961. "Opportunity only knocks once in this world," he would say. Major Major's father repeated this good joke at every opportunity. —Joseph Heller, *Catch-22*

1990. *Opportunity Knocks* —Title of a film starring Dana Carvey

1991. You've heard it said that "Opportunity only knocks once." Don't believe it. Opportunity is knocking all the time. The problem is that it often knocks too soon. —*Reader's Digest*

1992. Does opportunity knock in Brooklyn & The Bronx? ... When you're in Cable TV sales, it does more than knock. It opens new doors to great growth and the high earnings potential of Cablevision! ... Make opportunity knock for you! No resume necessary. —Ad for Cablevision of New York City, *New York Times*

1995. WHEN OPPORTUNITY KNOCKS, MLICKI GETS JOB DONE FOR METS —Headline, *New York Times*

Opposites attract. People with opposing qualities and traits are often drawn together by their complementarity. The proverb has been traced back in the United States to *Mystery of the Downs* (1918) by J. Watson and A. J. Rees. First attested in England in *Vane Mystery* (1930) by A. B. Cox. It may be found in varying forms: *Extremes meet; It's a case of the attraction of opposites; Opposites are attracted to each other; Opposites attract each other,* etc.

1922. Woman's reason. Jewgreek is greekjew. Extremes meet. Death is the highest form of life. —James Joyce, *Ulysses*

1988. Andrew Davies claims: "They say opposites attract—That's why I married a girl with money." —Joey Adams, "Strictly for Laughs," *New York Post*

1992. We all know that "opposites attract," but once they're living together, they often begin to feel mismatched. Even partners who seem well suited in terms of background, education, tastes and goals usually have some opposing traits that create problems. —*Family Circle*

1993. "Why did you marry your husband?" asked the neighborhood gossip. "You don't seem to have much in common."

"It was the old story of opposites attracting each other," explained the wife. "I was pregnant and he wasn't." —Quoted in *Reader's Digest*

See also LIKE ATTRACTS LIKE.

An ostrich with its head in the sand. It was once erroneously believed that an ostrich would bury its head in the sand to avoid predators, using the logic that if you can't see the enemy it can't see you. Hence, any person who closes his eyes to reality is compared to an ostrich with its head in the sand. The phrase is often invoked in political contexts, especially in reference to foreign policy. Countering the mood of American isolationism prior to World War I, in a speech at Des Moines on February 1, 1916, Woodrow Wilson said, "America cannot be an ostrich with its head in the sand."***

1992. "She knew that during the 1930's she [Simone de Beauvoir] had closed her eyes to the entire world of politics, national and international," Ms. Crosland writes. "She had barely read the newspapers, she had on her own admission behaved like the ostrich, she had buried her head in the sand." —*New York Times Magazine*

1993. Doing nothing is a crime, but sending troops to the Horn of Africa while neighboring nations stick their head in the sand is even worse. —Letters to the Editor, *Time*

1994. "We can't even get any information to tell our clients," says one broker in the Southeast. "Everybody knows it's a bad situation, but we've got our heads in the sand, hoping it'll go away." —*Business Week*

An ounce of prevention is worth a pound of cure. It's more prudent to head off a disaster beforehand than to deal with it after it occurs. The proverb has been traced back to *De Legibus* (c.1240) by English jurist Henry De Bracton (d. 1268). First attested in the United States in *Documentary History of Maine Containing Baxter Manuscripts* (1772). Addressing a joint session of Congress on the health-care issue on September 22, 1993, President Clinton said, "You know how all of our mothers told us that an ounce of prevention was worth a pound of cure? Our mothers were right." The adage is found in varying forms: *Prevention is better than cure; Prevention is cheaper than treatment,* etc.

1975. Minute Metric Movies. 28 grams of prevention is worth 450 grams of cure. —David Wallechinsky & Irving Wallace, *The People's Almanac*

1985. An ounce of don't-say-it is worth a pound of didn't-mean-it. —Quoted in *Reader's Digest*

1990. An ounce of prevention is worth a pound of cure, particularly when it comes to hangovers. —Quoted in *Reader's Digest*

1993. What we need to know is what can be done before the violence against others takes place. We need to try to intervene before it is too late. An ounce of prevention is worth a pound of cure. And in this case, it was probably worth a ton of lives. —*Times* (Trenton)

1993. *Patient:* I don't need an ounce of prevention or a pound of cure, I need a ton of sympathy! —Cartoon by Bob Thaves, "Frank and Ernest," *Times* (Trenton)

1994. PREVENTION MAY BE COSTLIER THAN A CURE —Headline of an article on the relative costs of heart transplant and curbing carcinogenic pollution, *Wall Street Journal*

See also A STITCH IN TIME SAVES NINE.

Our country, right or wrong. A true patriot supports his country even when it is wrong. Of American origin. Attributed to Stephen Decatur (1779–1820), a U.S. naval officer. In April 1816, he offered this toast at a dinner held in Norfolk, Virginia: "Our country! In her intercourse with foreign nations may she always be in the right; but our country, right or wrong." In a letter to John Adams dated August 1, 1816, John Quincy Adams (1767–1848), wrote: "My toast would be, may our country be always successful, but whether successful or otherwise, always right." Other authorities credit the German-born American legislator Carl Schurz. Speaking at an Anti-Imperialist Conference on October 17, 1899, he tempered the slogan somewhat: "Our country, right or wrong. When right, to be kept right; when wrong, to be put right." *My country, right or wrong* is also often seen.**

1989. I agree wholeheartedly with that great German American patriot Carl Schurz, who said over 100 years ago, "My country right or wrong. When in the right, to be kept in the right. When in the wrong, to be put in the right." —*Forward* (N.Y.)

1992. Young Bill Clinton was too bright to blindly accept the old maxim "My country, right or wrong." He questioned our involvement, as did millions of Americans, and asked what our country was doing there [in Vietnam]. —*Newsweek*

1994. Regrettably, the presidency of a former Hollywood actor with a well-polished script and a home-spun flair for patriotism mesmerized many of us.... No longer was it that canard about "my country right or wrong." It now became a "them-against-us" mentality wrought by Reagan's Social Darwinists and compliant members of Congress. —*Star-Ledger* (Newark)

Out of many, one. *See* E PLURIBUS UNUM.

Out of sight, out of mind. If one doesn't see

someone or something for some period of time, one tends to forget that person or thing. The adage has been traced back to the late thirteenth-century *Proverbs of Alfred*. It appears in Thomas à Kempis's *Imitation of Christ* (1420). In its current form, it was used by Barnabe Googe (1540–94) in *Eglogs* in 1563. First attested in the United States in *Winthrop Papers* (1629). The expression also occurs in other languages: *Ojos que no ven, corazón que no siente* (Spanish); *Aus den Augen aus dem Sinn* (German); С глаз долой—из сердца вон, all of which can be translated as "Far from eye, far from mind (or heart)."

1952. *Proctor (pushing his arm away):* You'll leave her out of sight and out of mind, Mister. —Arthur Miller, *The Crucible*

1957. Out of sight, but not quite out of mind. —*New Yorker*

1985. "There's so much litigation around Konig's estate that Braverman's got to figure it may take years before it's sorted out, and in the meantime this stock can't be voted against him. Out of sight is out of mind." —Michael Korda, *Queenie*

1988. To counter the criticism, and to lessen the drag on the Republican ticket, Mr. Bush's aides have employed a simple strategy throughout the campaign: act as if Mr. Quayle did not exist.... Jeff Fishel, a government professor at the American University here, said the Republicans' motives are quite obvious: "Out of sight, out of mind is the hope." —*New York Times*

1989. "It is frightening how little we know about board and care homes," said John Heinz of Pennsylvania, the ranking Republican on the Senate Special Committee on Aging. "This is an industry out of sight, out of mind and out of control." —*New York Times*

1991. As anyone in promotion knows, "out of sight out of mind" where public relations is concerned. —*New York Times*

1992. Out of sight but not out of mind: The other day, a reader called to ask if the Joffrey Ballet, which has been on tour, would ever perform in New York City again. The answer at this point is yes. —*New York Times*

1993. "I was glad for Jean [Harris]," Mrs. Caris said in a soft voice. "But I was wondering when is it going to be my turn. Jean had an awful lot of publicity behind her, but the rest of us—we're out of sight, out of mind." —*New York Times*

Out of the frying pan into the fire. See DON'T JUMP FROM THE FRYING PAN INTO THE FIRE.

Out of the mouths of babes and sucklings come great truths. Children often speak more clearly, wisely, truly, and directly than their elders. Of Biblical origin. *From the mouths of babes come words of wisdom* is a variant. It is sometimes shortened to *from (out of) the mouths of babes.*

Out of the mouth of babes and sucklings hast thou ordained strength because of thine enemies, that thou mightest still the enemy and the avenger. —Psalms, 8:2, *Authorized Version,* 1611

1984. "Out of the mouths of very babes and sucklings comes ordained strength in true words of wisdom," I observe. —Joseph Heller, *God Knows*

1985. "No," she said firmly. "It wouldn't work, David, You can't frighten Vale. You'd either have to buy him off or do something that destroys him."

"From the mouth of babes," Konig said, beaming. —Michael Korda, *Queenie*

1991. Colum laughed. "Cat O'Hara, did you know your godfather was a grumpy?"

"Today yes," said Cat.

This time Colum's laugh wasn't forced. "Out of the mouths of babes," he said. —Alexandra Ripley, *Scarlett*

1992. He [a 14-year-old boy] told the New York Times: "You always got to be bad here, or you just don't make it. We're supposed to go to school and make something of ourselves. Look around. What do they expect us to be? Lawyers?" ... Out of the mouths of babes. —Ed Koch, *New York Post*

1995. OUT OF THE CRAYONS OF BABES —Headline of Garry Trudeau's article on the connection between great artists and their children's art, *New York Times Magazine*

1995. The other day I was playing the computer game "Where in the U.S.A. Is Carmen Sandiego?" with my 9-year-old daughter, Orly.... But instead of giving my daughter the answer, I wanted to see if she could figure it out herself, so I asked her: "Where are cars made?" And without missing a beat she answered: "Japan." ... From the mouths of babes. —*New York Times*

Over my dead body. I'll do all I can to prevent it. The saying has been traced back to the early nineteenth century. It is almost always used in the first person singular, even in reported speech.

1983. U.S. Marine Capt. Charles Johnson was determined to defend his position. When an Israeli tank headed straight toward him he took his .45 caliber automatic out of his holster, loaded it, and told the Israeli officer facing him that the tank

could come through "only over my dead body."
—*Christian Science Monitor*

1989. The official rhetoric from the business community toward any tax increase continues to be an over-my-dead-body "no." —*Boston Globe*

1990. He [Jerry Falwell] is clearly not enjoying himself. In fact, the photograph suggests that he is doing this over his own dead body. —*The New Yorker*

1994. Gov. Weld yesterday declared that the New England Patriots will leave Massachusetts "over my dead body," but it appears the price of keeping them here and building a Boston convention center and football stadium is going to be high. —*Boston Globe*

1997. "She saved our lives, and there is no way we are going to let them take her away," said Rodriguez, 43, wiping away tears... "They'll have to go over my dead body to take away the dog. If it weren't for the dog, me, my husband, and two of my children would have certainly died in the fire. —*New York Post*

1998. If somebody had stopped me when I was 21 and wiping the effects of tear gas from my eyes after a political brush with college authorities and told me that some day I'd be a member of a garden club, I would have said, "Over my dead body."—*Hartford Courant*

1998. Folks differ on what exactly happened when she confronted the Army Corps of Engineers three decades ago, but they agree the message was clear: You'll take this farm over my dead body.—*Detroit News*

Paddle your own canoe. Don't expect other people to help you; depend only on yourself. First attested in the United States in *History of Cosmopolite or Lorenzo Dow's Journal* (1802). The proverb was used by Frederick Marryat (1792–1848), a British novelist and seaman. Sarah Bolton's poem in *Harper's Magazine,* cited below, popularized the proverb.

> **1844.** I think it much better that ... every man paddle his own canoe. —Frederick Marryat, *Settlers in Canada*

> **1854.** Voyage upon life's sea,
> To yourself be true,
> And, whatever your lot may be,
> Paddle your own canoe.
> —Sarah Bolton, *Harper's Magazine*

> **1924.** "The really big people don't talk ... they paddle their own canoes in what seem backwaters." —John Galsworthy, *The White Monkey*

> **1992.** Slavery, a painful topic for blacks, is a sensitive area in Mount Greenwood too. It comes up in conversation often as whites say that past and even current discrimination is irrelevant. "It's up to them [blacks] to paddle their own canoe," said Catherine Nielsen, a long-time resident. "Don't always think about the fact that they were slaves." —*New York Times*

See also PULL YOURSELF UP BY YOUR OWN BOOTSTRAPS.

Pandemonium broke loose. *See* ALL HELL BROKE LOOSE.

A Pandora's box. A subject or situation that might be best to leave alone, especially if you aren't fully informed of what you're getting yourself (and others) into. According to classical mythology, when Pandora got married she brought with her a large vase (Pandora's box). When she opened it all the ills of humanity flew forth, and only Hope remained in the box, while the ills spread far and wide and continue to afflict humanity. *To open (a) Pandora's box* is to introduce a lot of problems.

> **1975.** If you open that Pandora's box, you never know what Trojan 'orses will jump out. —Ernest Bevin, quoted by Sir Roderick Barclay, *Ernest Bevin and the Foreign Office*

> **1984.** "I ain't gonna remain quiet for them or for anybody else," he said. "They opened Pandora's box. They picked on my family. Now, I want to see what they're going to do when I start coming back." —*New York Times*

> **1986.** Lucy [Mercer] is troubled by their affair: "We've opened a Pandora's box." But Franklin assures her, "I've never felt this way about anyone before." —*New York Times*

> **1987.** Meanwhile, students in Paula Kavett's sixth-grade class at Barnum Wood are emptying a "Pandora's Box" of words on nuclear energy and debating whether the concepts are a benefit or detriment to society. —*New York Times*

> **1992.** Josephine Rohr, the attorney representing a Supercuts franchisee in its dispute with Hispanic employees, said bilingual incentive pay "would open a Pandora's box" if required in the private sector, forcing employers, for instance, to assess language skills. —*New York Times*

> **1993.** The return of professional figure skaters to Olympic competition has exposed a Pandora's box of problems that the sport's antiquated system of categorizing and judging skaters cannot handle. —*New York Times*

> **1994.** I hope that other men and women who served in Nam will read it and close their personal Pandora's box of guilt and nightmares. —*New York*

266

Times Magazine
See also BEWARE OF GREEKS BEARING GIFTS.

Paper bleeds little. You can accomplish anything on paper because it is two-dimensional and fails to account for human factors and situational variables. The proverb originated in the United States. The earliest appearance in print was in Ernest Hemingway's *For Whom the Bell Tolls* (1940).

1940. "That they should let us do something on paper," El Sordo said. "That we should conceive and execute something on paper." ... ' "Paper bleeds little,' " Robert Jordan quoted the proverb. —Ernest Hemingway, *For Whom The Bell Tolls*

1985. He [Goldner] reached into his drawer and pulled out the bulky contract. "It's all perfectly legal," he said, placing it on the desk.... Vale pushed it off the desk with the tip of his cane. "Paper!" he said with a sniff. "Paper doesn't bruise or bleed." —Michael Korda, *Queenie*

Parting is such sweet sorrow. Parting is both sweet and sad. The saying was coined by Shakespeare in 1594 in *Romeo and Juliet*.

1594. *Juliet:* Good night, good night! parting is
   such sweet sorrow,
   That I shall say good night till it be morrow.
      —Shakespeare, *Romeo and Juliet*, Act II,
      Scene II

1984. "Run somewhere else and leave me alone. I know trouble when I see it. Goodbye, goodbye, parting is such sweet sorrow, but not from you." —Joseph Heller, *God Knows*

1989. Many members of the Reagan staff have already packed their belongings in preparation for their departure from the White House, and the President, contemplating his own imminent return to Southern California, chose Juliet's words to express his emotions: "Parting is such sweet sorrow." —*New York Times*

1989. People ask how I feel about leaving, and the fact is parting is "such sweet sorrow." The sweet part is California, and the ranch and freedom. The sorrow? The goodbyes, of course, and leaving this beautiful place. —Ronald Reagan. "Farewell Address to American People." *The New York Times*

1994. PARTIES ARE SUCH SWEET SORROW —Headline, *New York Times Book Review*

The party's over! Your carefree life is over; now it's time to get down to business. This saying implies an earlier, ongoing period of good times or beneficial events and indicates that the speaker believes those good times have ended.

1974. Bounding up the front steps of City Hall early on the morning of his Inauguration Day, he [La Guardia] had stopped, a roly-poly figure in a ridiculous black hat and a rumpled black suit, and had shaken his little fist at its Georgian elegance and shouted, *"E finita la cuccagna!"* ("No more free lunch!"), a phrase which, a friend explained, the Mayor was using to promise "The party is over! No more graft!" —Robert A. Caro, *The Power Broker*

1983. ' "Street People' is canceled," Oliver said bluntly. "Over. Finished. Kaput.... The party's over." —Jackie Collins, *Hollywood Wives*

1991. With his victory, Mr. Carey [president of the International Brotherhood of Teamsters] proclaimed: "To those who think the Mafia is still in charge, let me be clear. The party's over." —*New York Times*

1992. Quoting Gary Dunning, McKenzie says: "If we don't get through the next 12 to 18 months and get through them right and get rid of the debt, the party's over." Some party. —*New York Times Magazine*

1993. My skeptical side kept shouting, "Look at the ticket sales this year for your shows ... Down! How many movie offers this year? Face it, Yakov, the party's over." —*Parade Magazine*

Patience is a virtue. The ability to wait for something without excessive frustration is a valuable character trait. The proverb has been traced back to *Piers Plowman* (1377) by William Langland and is similar to the Latin, *Maxima enim ... patientia virtus* ("Patience is the greatest virtue") and the French, *Patience est une grant vertu* ("Patience is a great value"). Some ten years after Langland, Chaucer wrote in *The Canterbury Tales* (1386) that "Patience is a high virtue." Sometimes followed by the wry rejoinder *but virtue can hurt you.*

1594. Patience is a virtue, but pinching is worse than any vice! —John Lyly, *Mother Bombie*, Act V, Scene III

1632. Patience, the beggar's virtue,
   Shall find no harbour here.
      —Philip Massinger, *A New Way to Pay Old
      Debts*, Act V, Scene I

1798. There is a point when patience ceases to be a virtue. —Thomas Morton, *Speed the Plow*, Act IV, Scene III

1977. On second thought, patience may be a virtue, but it will never help a rooster lay an egg. —Dr. Laurence J. Peter. *Peter's Quotations. Ideas For Our Times*

1993. Patience is a cardinal virtue now. —Jeane Dixon, "Horoscope"

See also IF AT FIRST YOU DON'T SUCCEED, TRY, TRY AGAIN; SLOW AND STEADY WINS THE RACE.

Pay as you go. Pay for something gradually as you use it. Originated in the United States in 1820, and, according to William Safire, used by Thomas Jefferson (1743–1826). In 1855, it was included in the collection of proverbs of Henry George Bohn (1796–1884). Often used as an attribute, *pay-as-you-go,* of such words as *basis, budget, plan, principle, senator,* etc. *Pay-as-you-go* withholding tax was conceived by Beardsley Ruml, a banker and an economist of New York, to help finance the war effort in World War II. In politics, "pay-as-you-go economics" means a balanced budget. In the early nineteenth century John Randolph, a lawmaker from Virginia, told the U.S. Senate: "Mr. President! I have found the philosophers' stone! It is contained in four words: Pay as you go."

1820. It is incumbent on every generation to pay its own debts as it goes—a principle which, if acted upon, would save one-half the wars of the world. —Thomas Jefferson, quoted in *Safire's Political Dictionary*

1956. My chief obstacle was getting the Congress to vote for tax levies to finance the total government program on a pay-as-you-go basis. —*Memoirs by Harry S. Truman,* vol. 2

1984. To the Congress, my message is: We must cut spending and pay as we go. —Mario Cuomo, *New York Times*

1987. "Paul [Simon], you're not a pay-as-you-go Democrat," Representative Richard A. Gephardt declared last week in a nationally televised debate among 12 Presidential candidates. —*New York Times*

1992. "You need more than a pay-as-you-go mentality," says T. W. Kang, a Tokyo management consultant. "It takes a lot of up-front work" and financial investment to build credibility in Japan. —*Wall Street Journal*

1994. Stark, who favors government-run health care, surprised colleagues last week by joining forces with Representatives Sander Levin of Michigan and Ben Cardin of Maryland on a pay-as-you-go plan that would phase in benefits to workers as companies helped states meet voluntary spending targets. —*Time*

Pay the piper his due. You have to pay a price for what you receive. The proverb has been traced back to *Taylor's Feast* (1638) by John Taylor. In 1695, William Congreve wrote in *Love for Love:* "I warrant you, if he danced till doomsday, he thought I was to pay the piper." First attested in the U.S. in *Diary of Grace Galloway* (1799). *You must pay the piper* is a variant of the proverb. Often shortened to *pay the piper.* Over the years, the meaning of the proverb has been broadened. It is often used now to mean that one has to face the consequences of one's actions.

1988. Listen to Murray Weidenbaum, former head of President Reagan's own Council of Economic Advisers, in his new book, *Rendezvous with Reality:* "We are consuming more than we are saving, and spending more than we are earning. We are rapidly approaching the time when we will have to pay the piper." —*Philadelphia Inquirer*

1992. We consume too much and invest too little. We've got to pay the piper for past excesses. —*New York Times*

1993. These greedy seniors who moan and groan over having to pay the piper after benefiting all these years from the government's excesses must not have any children and grandchildren. —*AARP Bulletin*

1994. "Serious charges are being leveled against these officers," said Officer Kieran Breen, a patrol officer at the precinct for seven years. "I'd like to believe they're not true, but if they are, they have to pay the piper." —*New York Times*

See also HE WHO DANCES MUST PAY THE FIDDLER; HE WHO PAYS THE PIPER CALLS THE TUNE.

The pen is mightier than the sword. The written word is more powerful than any physical weapon. The proverb has been traced back to *Institution of Christian Prince* (1571) and *Heptameron of Civil Discourses* (1582). "No more sword to be feared than the learned pen," was the form of proverb at that time. Robert Burton (1577–1640) said that "the pen is worse than the sword" (1621), and it was Edward Bulwer-Lytton (1803–73) who was the first to coin the current form (1839). This adage was first used in the United States in *Clouded Moon* (1938) by M. Salt-marsh. The word *pen* may be replaced by another word or words.

1621. *Hinc quam sit calamus saevior ense patet.* (From this it is clear how much the pen is worse than the sword.) —Robert Burton, *The Anatomy of Melancholy*

1839. Beneath the rule of men entirely great,
The pen is mightier than the sword.
—Edward George Bulwer-Lytton, *Richelieu*,
Act II, Scene 2

1992. For Eva Twardokens [a pilot], the ski is mightier than the sky. —*People*

1993. "It has long been recognized that the pen is mightier than the sword," said Randall L. Tobias, vice chairman of the American Telephone and Telegraph Company. "The modern version of that is: the fax machine is mightier than the rifle." —*New York Times*

A penny for your thoughts. Tell me what you are thinking about. The saying has been traced back to John Heywood's collection of proverbs (1546) and is used when addressing a person who seems to be daydreaming or deep in thought.

1922. And she [Edy Boardman] said to Gerty:—A penny for your thoughts. —James Joyce, *Ulysses*

1961. "If you care to offer me a penny for my thoughts, I think that's why she's coming." —John Steinbeck, *The Winter of Our Discontent*

1978. "Penny for your thoughts," Lucy said to Larry, and put her hand on his arm. —Stephen King, *The Stand*

1985. The young Scottish couple was sitting on a park bench, gazing pensively into the distance. After a long silence, the lassie turned to her laddie and whispered, "A penny for your thoughts, Angus."
"I was just thinkin'," he replied, "how nice it'd be if ye gave me a wee bit of a kiss."
Blushing, she kissed him. After a little while, she again asked, "'Nother penny for your thoughts, Angus."
—Quoted in *Reader's Digest*

1993. PENNY FOR HIS THOUGHTS. —Headline, *Time Off*

A penny saved is a penny earned. Money not wasted can be used in the future. A responsible person saves even small amounts of money. Every cent that is saved will add up. The proverb has been traced back to Herbert's *Outlandish Proverbs* (1640) and is first attested in the United States in *William & Mary College Quarterly* (1699). For sev-

eral centuries people said, "A penny saved is a penny got." In the twentieth century, the word *earned* is used more often than *got*.

1963. "He [Dr. Felix Hoenirker] loved ten-cent stores," said Miss Faust.
"I can see he did."
"Some of his most famous experiments were performed with equipment that cost less than a dollar."
"A penny saved is a penny earned."
—Kurt Vonnegut, Jr., *Cat's Cradle*

1990. Thrift used to be a basic part of the American ethic. Before we were a nation, Ben Franklin exhorted us: "A penny saved is two pence clear." All of us would benefit by returning to that thinking. —Quoted in *Reader's Digest*

1991. Lately I've begun to think that many of my favorite sayings are simply out of date. That realization hit home while I was stooping to retrieve a coin. "A penny saved is a penny earned," I said. My teen-age daughter frowned. "What does *that* mean? You can't buy *anything* with a penny," she stated in a matter-of-fact way. —Quoted in *Reader's Digest*

1994. "You know what they say about a penny saved."
"A penny saved is a penny earned?"
"No. A penny saved is a congressional oversight." —Brian Crane, "Pickles," *Times* (Trenton)
See also PENNY-WISE AND POUND-FOOLISH.

Penny-wise and pound-foolish. Said of a person who is stingy about spending small amounts of money but spends recklessly on expensive items. The proverb has been traced back to *The Anatomy of Melancholy* (1621) by Robert Burton (1577–1640), English writer and clergyman. In 1747, it was used by Benjamin Franklin in his *Poor Richard's Almanac*. The pound is the main unit of currency in Great Britain; *don't be penny-wise and dollar-foolish* is the rarely used American variant of the saying.

1987. "The problem in any police agency is that training assumes lower priority than putting people out on the street. In a lot of ways that's penny wise and pound foolish." —*New York Times*

1990. "Western Europe is drifting toward catastrophe. Penny-wise and pound-foolish, we dribble out little loans and grants, too little and too late, meeting a crisis here and there ... while we neglect to deal constructively on a great scale with the problem of the reconstruction of Western Europe." —Ron Chernow, *The House of Morgan*

1991. Elimination of the penny might afford some

slight physical convenience, but the total social cost exceeds what a liberal democracy ought to countenance. It would be nothing less, one might say, than penny-wise and pound-foolish. —Quoted in *Reader's Digest*

1992. While he criticized Pennsylvania's direct aid program as ill-conceived, Professor Zumeta said it was "penny wise and pound foolish" for the state to eliminate the subsidy program rather than to restructure it along the lines of those in states like New York. —*New York Times*

1993. The razor-thin vote to restore courtesy busing could easily be undone next year if we continue to elect board members who are so incredibly "penny-wise-and-pound foolish." —*Times* (Trenton)

See also A PENNY SAVED IS A PENNY EARNED.

People who live in glass houses shouldn't throw stones.
Those who are vulnerable should not attack others. The proverb has been traced back to Geoffrey Chaucer's *Troilus and Criseyde* (1385). George Herbert wrote in 1651: "Whose house is of glass, must not throw stones at another." This saying is first cited in the United States in *William & Mary College Quarterly* (1710). Twenty-six years later Benjamin Franklin wrote, "Don't throw stones at your neighbors', if your own windows are glass." *To live in a glass house* is used as a figure of speech referring to vulnerability.

1946. ... So the Boss bought himself a big wad of radio time and aired his views of Congressman Petit and treated the nation to a detailed biography, in several installments, of Congressman Petit, who, it developed from the work of the Boss's research department, had thrown a grenade in a glass house. —Robert Penn Warren, *All the King's Men*

1984. People who live in glass houses shouldn't throw stones—and, considering the average U.S. citizen's knowledge of world history and geography, we are living in one made of the most fragile glass. —*Newsweek*

1988. Anyway, he rationalized, Peter's not got everything. I mean, there's no mention of a wife or kids.... But then Barney's superego challenged *him*. Who are you to throw stones, Dr. Livingston? Where are the wife and kiddies waiting in *your* glass house? To which his ego responded, give me time, I've got to finish this residency, start up practice. Besides, I'm almost married. —Erich Segal, *Doctors*

1990. He-who-lives-in-a-glass-house should never invite over he-who-is-without-sin. —Quoted in *Reader's Digest*

1991. People who live in glass houses should not throw stones—even if it was rather a pathetic, underhanded job. —*Connoisseur*

1993. At the other network news divisions, however, several journalists accused Mr. Rather of throwing stones while living in a rather luxurious glass house. —*New York Times*

See also THE POT CALLING THE KETTLE BLACK.

The Peter Principle. *See* EVERY EMPLOYEE TENDS TO RISE TO HIS LEVEL OF INCOMPETENCE.

The Phoenix is rising again.
Out of complete destruction new life has started. The Greek legend goes that an Arabian bird called the phoenix burns itself to ashes at the end of its life and is then reborn to live again. It rises up every five hundred years, according to the myth. *To rise like a/the Phoenix from the ashes* or *to rise from the ashes* are used as figures of speech.

1613. *Cranmer:* Nor shall this peace sleep with her; but as when
The bird of wonder dies, the maiden phoenix,
Her ashes new-create another heir
As great in admiration as herself.
—Shakespeare, *King Henry the Eighth*, Act V, Scene V

1948. "It was then, Charlie, I got my inspiration. Build Grynwood again. A gray jigsaw puzzle put back together! Phoenix reborn from the sootbin." —Ray Bradbury, *I Sing the Body Electric!*

1978. "I don't believe that man arising from the ashes of the superflu is going to be anything like man arising from the cradle of the Nile with a bone in his nose and a woman by the hair. That's one of the theories." —Stephen King, *The Stand*

1984. With determination, with luck, and with help from lots of good people, I was able to rise up from the ashes. —Lee Iacocca with William Novak, *Iacocca*

1985. Edgar Waldorf rose like a phoenix from his sofa of despair. —Erich Segal, *The Class*

1988. There is no graduation day in psychoanalysis, for in a sense it never ends. Indeed, the most significant part of the therapy begins only when the patient rises phoenixlike from the ashes of his inhibitions, stands vertical, and walks out into the labyrinth of daily life, his psyche now a compass that will—hopefully—lead him to the right decisions. —Erich Segal, *Doctors*

1991. "The Phoenix is rising again," said the city's ebullient Mayor [of Secaucus], Sharpe James. But if the Phoenix is rising, its flight has not reached the neighborhoods of this 325-year-old city, which lost 52,000 residents, a decrease of 16 percent, between 1980 and 1990. —*New York Times*

1993. Beirut is rising from the ashes. —"International Hour," CNN

Physician, heal thyself. Before you try to fix other people's problems take care of your own. The proverb is of Biblical origin. It has been traced in English to *De Regimine Principum* (c. 1400). First attested in the United States in *Christographia* (1703). It is one of the most popular proverbs of the health care reform era (the early 1990s). *Patient treat (heal) thyself* is a recent jocular variant of the proverb.

And he said unto them, Ye will surely say unto me this proverb, Physician, heal thyself. —Luke 4:23, *Authorized Version*, 1611

1992. Hooray for Barbra Streisand's healthy response to critics of her movie *The Prince of Tides* ("Physicians, Heal Thyselves," My Turn, June 29)! —*Newsweek*

1993. Under our proposal there would be one standard insurance form, not hundreds of them. We will simplify also—and we must—the government's rules and regulations, because they are a big part of this problem.... This is one of those cases where the physician should heal thyself. —Bill Clinton, *New York Times*

1993. PATIENT, TREAT THYSELF —Headline of Al Cole's article on over-the-counter medications, *Modern Maturity*

1994. Journalists, heal thyselves! —"60 Minutes" *See also* PRACTICE WHAT YOU PREACH.

A picture is worth a thousand words. *See* ONE PICTURE IS WORTH A THOUSAND WORDS.

Pie in the sky. *See* WORK AND PRAY, LIVE ON HAY, YOU'LL GET PIE IN THE SKY WHEN YOU DIE.

A pig is a pig. *See* PIGS ARE PIGS.

Pigs are pigs. A bad person is a bad person no matter where he comes from. The proverb has been traced back to 1822. *Pigs is pigs* and *A pig is a pig* are variants of the proverb.

1992. "It's not pork," said Mr. Edwards, "if you're bringing jobs that will be created anyway and you have them in Oklahoma rather than West Virgin-

ia." In response, Mr. Istook shot back. "A pig is a pig no matter whose pigpen it happens to be in." —*New York Times*

1993. "A pig is a pig even if she's wearing an executive suit." —Overheard at a restaurant

Pigs could fly if they had wings. *See* IF A PIG HAD WINGS, IT COULD FLY.

Pigs is pigs. *See* PIGS ARE PIGS.

Piss or get off the pot! *See* SHIT OR GET OFF THE POT!

A place for everything and everything in its place. One's things should be kept in order. The proverb is first found in print in George Herbert's collection of proverbs (1640). It was later recorded in Frederick Marryat's (1842) and in Isabella Beeton's (1861) work. First attested in the United States in Thomas Chandler Haliburton's *Nature and Human Nature* (1855).

1855. There was a place for everything, and everything was in its place. —T. C. Haliburton, *Nature and Human Nature*

1861. A place for everything and everything in its place. —Isabella Mary Beeton, *The Book of Household Management*

1875. A place for everything, and everything in its place. —Samuel Smiles, *Thrift*

1956. "A place for everything," his father used to say, "and everything in its place." —*New Yorker*

1957. A place for everyone—everyone in his place. —*New York Times*

A plague on both your houses. A curse on both of you. The phrase comes from Shakespeare's *Romeo and Juliet* (1595). The saying was used by Franklin Delano Roosevelt regarding labor and management.

1595. *Mercutio:* A plague o' both your houses! They have made worms' meat of me.
　　　　—Shakespeare, *Romeo and Juliet*, Act III, Scene I

1992. He glanced over the verses again. "Also, Ms. Miller has made the temptations of Juan Alvaro as pivotal a part of this trial as the lust of Roberto Morales. So I think, in fairness, that if these verses say anything to us they say 'a plague on both your houses.' No juror would be swayed in either direction by them, but rather, if anything, confirmed in the opinion he or she already held." —Philip Friedman, *Inadmissible Evidence*

1993. John L. Lewis, a giant of the labor movement, was enraged that Franklin Delano Roosevelt had forced an end to the coal miners' strike by seizing the mines. He was most offended that F. D.R. said of labor as well as management, "A plague on both your houses." —*New York Times*

1994. "Memory tells me that the Croats and the Bosnians were the most willing collaborators of the killing squads of Nazi Germany," Mr. [Miles] Lerman said. "So it would be logical for me to say, a plague on both your houses. But morality dictates to me that we are 50 years away from the Holocaust and it does not give the Serbs of today the license to kill and maim women and children." —*New York Times*

Poets are born, not made. The ability to write poetry is a God-given skill; it can't be taught. Lucius Annaeus Florus (c.125) is quoted as saying, "Each year new consuls and proconsuls are made; but not every year is a king or a poet born." From this derived the Latin proverb, *Poeta nascitur, non fit* ("The poet is born, not made"). The proverb was well known in the Renaissance era ("The poet is born, the orator made") and it has been traced back to 1581. In 1605-15 it was used by Cervantes in *Don Quixote*. First attested in the United States in 1812. The proverb is found in varying forms: *A genius is born, not made; Geniuses, like poets, are born, not taught*, etc. A humorous variation is Wilson Mizner's *"Poets are born, not paid."*

1605–15.
There is an opinion, and a true one, to the effect that 'the poet is born,' that is to say, it is as a poet that he comes forth from his mother's womb ... —Cervantes, *Don Quixote*

1623. For a good poet's made, as well as born. —Ben Jonson, *To the Memory of My Beloved, the Author, Mr. William Shakespeare*

1941. "Oh, she's really a lady—the kind that is born, not made," Lisa Fendall informed him briefly. —Frances Parkinson Keyes, *All That Glitters*

1984. Some people think that good salesmen are born, not made. —Lee Iacocca with William Novak, *Iacocca*

1988. "I have just come from the embassy in Masqat. What I saw there wasn't pretty—Arab-pretty."
    "Nor to us. However, may I quote an American congressman who said on the floor of the House of Representatives that 'a terrorist isn't born, he's made!'" —Robert Ludlum, *The Icarus Agenda*

1992. Banks Are Born, Not Made. —Ad for Banco Provincia, *New York Times*

1993. THE CONSTITUTION WAS MADE, NOT BORN. —*New York Times Book Review*

Politics as usual. Politicians always act in the same deceitful way. The expression is derived from *business as usual* and is used to criticize the political party in power.

1992. Aware of how much was wrong with "politics as usual," we thought that people like [Tim] Wirth and [Kent] Conrad would work for change from the best place to achieve it: the floor of the Senate. —*New York Times Magazine*

1994. "When Republicans named George [Pataki] say read my lips, it's politics as usual all over again." —Ad by Mario Cuomo Campaign, quoted by Kevin Sack, *New York Times*
See also BUSINESS AS USUAL.

Politics makes strange bedfellows. In politics, one has to form alliances with all kinds of people, even with those one doesn't like. The proverb originated in the United States and was first found in print in the 1839 *Diary of Philip Hone, 1828–1851* (1927) by Philip Hone (1780–1865). In its current form the proverb was used by Charles Dudley Warner (1829–1900) in his little essay *My Summer in a Garden* (1870). It is actually a recycled old proverb, *Misery makes strange bedfellows*, used by Shakespeare in *The Tempest* (1611). Shakespeare's proverb was further paraphrased by American radio host Goodman Ace (1899–1982): "Politics make estranged bedfellows."

1870. Politics makes strange bedfellows. —Charles D. Warner, *My Summer in a Garden*

1936. "Ashley Wilkes and I are mainly responsible."
    "Ashley—and you?"
    "Yes, platitudinously but truly, politics make strange bedfellows." —Margaret Mitchell, *Gone With the Wind*

1977. For, if anything [Matthew] Troy [the Queens Democratic leader] represented the earthy patriotism of New York's hard-hat voters, a fact which, according to Mankiewicz, "made him a special hero to us." Politics do indeed make strange bedfellows. —Victor Lasky, *It Didn't Start with Watergate*

1989. What united this odd collection of "strange bedfellows," Nixon explained to the reporters, was that "they are all unhappy about something, all protesting against centralized government, and all calling for greater individual freedom." —Stephen E. Ambrose, *Nixon*

1993. "If that man becomes President, I'll never

have to work again."—Campaign boast attributed to Gennifer Flowers, self-proclaimed mistress of President-elect Clinton, 1992

This was the moment when bedfellows made the usual strange politics, lived to tattle the tale and won America. —*New York Times Magazine*

1994. BEDFELLOWS MAKE STRANGE POLITICS —Headline, *New York Times Book Review*

See also MISERY MAKES STRANGE BEDFELLOWS.

Possession is nine points of the law. One who actually possesses something has a stronger legal position than one who claims to be the owner of the thing. There is no law that says so, but centuries-old legal practice has recognized that notion. The proverb has been traced back to *Edward III* (1595). The current version of the proverb is found in T. Draxe's *Bibliotheca Scholastica* (1616): "Possession is nine points of the Law." In 1709, it was included in O. Dykes's collection, *English Proverbs*. First cited in the United States in *History of New England* (c.1700). According to Christine Ammer, the nine points referred to in the proverb are: (1) a good purse; (2) a lot of patience; (3) a good case; (4) a good lawyer; (5) good counsel; (6) good witnesses; (7) a good jury; (8) a good judge; and (9) good luck. The proverb is found in varying forms: *Possession is nine parts of the law; Possession is nine-tenths of the law; Possession is 90 percent of the law; Possession is eleven points of the law*, etc.

1697. Possession is eleven points in the law. —Colley Cibber, *Woman's Wit*, Act I

1738. *Colonel:* Miss, you have got my handkerchief; pray, let me have it.
Lady Smart: No, keep it, Miss; for they say Possession is Eleven Points of the Law.
—Jonathan Swift, *Polite Conversation, Dialogue I*

1920. And looking up at the houses he thought: "After all, we're the backbone of the country. They won't upset us easily. Possession's nine points of the law." —John Galsworthy, *In Chancery*

1993. "Why has he grabbed all the money from their joint bank account?"
"Possession is nine-tenths of the law, as they say." —Overheard at Princeton Junction

1994. Granted, it was long common practice for conquerors to plunder art, and light-fingered American soldiers have grabbed their share. But rules have changed; the Yeltsin Government itself seeks the restitution of czarist properties elsewhere. It is hard to reconcile this with Russia's dreadful example of looting masses of art, hiding it and then claiming that possession is 90 percent of the law. —*New York Times*

The pot calling the kettle black. Said of people who accuse others of sins similar to their own. The proverb has been traced back to *Don Quixote* (1605–15) by Cervantes. First attested in the United States in *Works of Washington Irving* (1807). It is used in response to criticism by someone who has no right to do it.

1936. "My goodness, I didn't start this war and I don't see any reason why I should be worked to death and—"
"A traitor to Our Glorious Cause!"
"The pot's calling the kettle black." —Margaret Mitchell, *Gone With the Wind*

1979. Finally Eloise said, "Oh, you're wicked, Jean. You are so wicked."
"Ha!" Jean exclaimed. "I am wicked? If ever there was a case of the pot calling the kettle black!" —Howard Fast, *The Establishment*

1988. He [Nixon] was especially eager to force Kennedy to vote, because "he is pretending to be more conservative than Hubert. It is not true—it's a case of the pot calling the kettle black." —Stephen E. Ambrose, *Nixon*

1991. This week's episode, "Calling the Kettle Black," showed Martin finding a joint of marijuana in his son's bedroom. —*New York Times*

1994. [Tonya] Harding, who has not been convicted of any crime, may not have done the right thing, but that's no excuse for the pot to call the kettle black. —*Newsweek*

See also PEOPLE WHO LIVE IN GLASS HOUSES SHOULDN'T THROW STONES.

Poverty is no sin. It is not a shameful thing to be poor. Used to tell people who are poor that poverty is not something to be ashamed of, or, by someone poor, as a response to people who treat the poor as though they ought to be ashamed. The proverb has been traced back to *Second Fruits* (1591) and in 1651 it was included in George Herbert's collection of proverbs. It is found in varying forms: *Poverty is no sin, but it is terribly inconvenient; Poverty is no crime; Poverty is no disgrace.*

1889. It is easy enough to say that poverty is no crime. No; if it were men wouldn't be ashamed of it. It is blunder, though, and is punished as such. A poor man is despised the whole world over. —Jerome K. Jerome, *Idle Thoughts of an Idle Fellow*

1915. It's no disgrace t' be poor, but it might as well be. —"Kin" Hubbard, quoted in Bartlett,

Familiar Quotations, sixteenth edition, edited by Justin Kaplan

1969. To quote the American humorist Kin Hubbard, "It ain't no disgrace to be poor, but it might as well be." —Kurt Vonnegut, Jr., *Slaughterhouse-Five*

1990. Poverty is no disgrace to a man, but it is confoundedly inconvenient. —Sydney Smith, quoted by Potter Briscoe, *Sydney Smith: His Wit and Wisdom*

1993. "I know that poverty is no sin, but neither is it an American dream." —Overheard at the welfare office in Washington Heights

See also GIVE ME YOUR TIRED, YOUR POOR.

Power corrupts, and absolute power corrupts absolutely. People in power are often corrupt, and the more power they possess, the more corrupt they are. William Pitt (1708–78), British conservative politician, in a speech on January 9, 1770, said: "Unlimited power is apt to corrupt the minds of those who possess it." "Power tends to corrupt," said Lord Acton in 1887, in what has become the familiar form of the proverb, "and absolute power corrupts absolutely. Great men are almost always bad men." The proverb is found in varying forms: *Power does not corrupt men; but fools, if they get into a position of power, corrupt power* (Bernard Shaw); *Power does not corrupt. Fear corrupts, perhaps the fear of a loss of power* (John Steinbeck); and *Power corrupts, but lack of power corrupts absolutely* (Adlai Stevenson). The expression is often shortened to *power corrupts.*

1977. "Power corrupts," Jonathan quoted back.
"Power tends to corrupt," said Cartwright, correcting the quote, "but there is no guarantee that it corrupts. Sometimes men corrupt power." —William Safire, *Full Disclosure*

1984. "Power corrupts, I've noticed," he observed, and averted his eyes as though in shamefaced confession. "And absolute power corrupts absolutely." —Joseph Heller, *God Knows*

1993. Nothing should be presumptively classified. No document should be exempt from the balancing test, not even the specifications of weapons systems or the identities of intelligence assets. Obviously some secrets must be kept, but to paraphrase Lord Acton, absolute secrets corrupt absolutely. —*Times* (Trenton)

1994. BIG MONEY CORRUPTS POLITICS, ABSOLUTELY. —Headline, *New York Times*

Practice makes perfect. The more you practice, the better your skills are. The proverb has been traced back to the 1550s–1560s, when its form was *Use makes perfect.* The Latin version is: *Uses promptos facit.* First attested in the United States in *Diary and Autobiography of John Adams* (1761).

1967. "Oh, Daddy, you're so clever. Well, I guess practice makes perfect?" —Elia Kazan, *The Arrangement*

1985. Coach didn't believe that practice makes perfect. Only *perfect* practice makes perfect. —Quoted in *Reader's Digest*

1988. It isn't Practice That Makes Perfect; You Have to Add One Word: It's Perfect Practice That Makes Perfect. —Harvey Mackay, *Swim With the Sharks Without Being Eaten Alive*

1992. It is not news that when Nature was dishing up rhetorical gifts, Bush did not hold out his plate. But by the verve of his delivery here he proved, again, that practice makes adequate. —*Times* (Trenton)

1993. Power Means Brutality; Practice Makes Perfect. —*New York Times*

1994. Words to live by (or not), as some prominent figures might have said them: ... Ralph Nader on term limits: "Congressmen are living proof that practice doesn't make perfect." —*U.S. News & World Report*

Practice what you preach. Behave the same way you tell others to. The proverb has been traced as far back as 254–184 b.c. (Plautus) and to about a.d. 342–420 (Saint Jerome), and is first attested in the United States in 1702 in *Magnalia Christi Americana* (1833). Lincoln Steffens (1866–1936), American journalist-reformer, used to say: "Never practice what you preach. If you're going to practice it, why preach it?" "Gov. Willie Stark practices what Machiavelli preached," wrote Paul Burka (1992).

254–184 b.c.
Practice yourself what you preach. —Titus Maccius Plautus, *Asinaria*, Act III, Scene III

342–420.
Do not let your deeds belie your words, lest when you speak in church someone may say to himself, "Why do you not practice what you preach?" —Saint Jerome

1931. That we should practise what we preach is generally admitted; but anyone who preaches what he and his bearers practise must incur the gravest moral disapprobation. —Logan Pearsall Smith, *Afterthoughts*

1983. As a literary lion, [Theodore] Roosevelt preached what he practiced. —Edmund Morris, *Smithsonian*

1986. Practice what you preach, Donahue, or else remember what they say about people who live in glass houses. —*New York Post*

1989. In May 1968, when Ritter, then a Manhattan theology professor, was delivering a homily, a student challenged him to "practice what you preach." —*Daily News* (N.Y.)

1992. Rep. Newt Gingrich is bent on overthrowing the Democratic establishment in Congress, Capitol Hill niceties be damned. But the Republican whip doesn't always practice what he preaches. —*New York Times Magazine*

1994. Remember that Paul Hill, convicted murderer of Dr. John Bayard Britton and James Barrett in Pensacola, Fla., spouted his hateful rhetoric on *Donahue* and *Nightline* only months before practicing what he preached. —*New York Times Magazine*

Praise the bridge that carries you over. Give credit to everything that helps you. The proverb has been traced back to the seventeenth century. In 1678, it was included in John Ray's collection of English proverbs, and is first cited in the United States in *Journals of John Montresor* (1769). The proverb is found in varying forms: *Cherish the bridge that brought you across; Everyone speaks well of the bridge that carries him over; Speak well of a bridge that has carried you safely over,* etc.

1984. "Why are you so bitter about the company that has made out of you a top-notch engineer? You got to stick to the bridge that carries you across." —Overheard at a hotel

1994. "This is home. Our home. He [Steve] said he would like to build me a new house here, and that is fine, but I'll still keep this one, fix it up and let others in the family use it. None of us will change. Money won't change love. I firmly believe what I have taught Steve and all my boys—cherish the bridge that brought you across." —*New York Times*

Praise the Lord and pass the ammunition. God is helpful, but not as much as a strong fighting force. To win in battle, we must rely on both divine aid and our fighting skills. The saying is attributed to Captain William Maguire (1890–1953), U.S. Navy Chaplain. It was popularized in 1942 when American composer and lyricist Frank Henry Loesser (1910–1969) put it to music.

1941. Praise the Lord and pass the ammunition. —William Maguire, quoted by Paul F. Boller, Jr. & John George, *They Never Said It*

1942. "Praise the Lord and Pass the Ammunition." —Popular song, music and lyrics by Frank Loesser

1987. "And what is the proper attitude toward the Soviets as we pursue progress?" he [George Bush] said. "Praise God, and keep your guard up." —*New York Times*

1991. I gave Betsy the same answer I had given to so many Marines who had wondered the very same thing: "Trust in the Lord and use good equipment." —Oliver L. North with William Novak, *Under Fire*

1993. TRUST IN GOD, BUT LOCK YOUR CAR —Headline, quoted in *Reader's Digest*

1993. Could it be possible that money, not principle, is the driving force? Perish the suspicion—and pass the ammunition. —*New York Times*

See also GOD HELPS THOSE WHO HELP THEMSELVES; PUT YOUR TRUST IN GOD, AND KEEP YOUR POWDER DRY.

Pretty is as pretty does. See HANDSOME (PRETTY) IS AS HANDSOME (PRETTY) DOES.

Prevention is better than cure. See AN OUNCE OF PREVENTION IS WORTH A POUND OF CURE.

Prevention is cheaper than treatment. See AN OUNCE OF PREVENTION IS WORTH A POUND OF CURE.

Pride goes before a fall. If you allow yourself to become full of pride, you will soon find yourself humiliated. Be modest. The proverb comes from the Old Testament. It has been traced back in English to *Douce MS* (c.1350) and *Confessio amantis* (c.1390). In 1546, it was included in John Heywood's collection of proverbs. First attested in the United States in *Poetical Meditations* (1725). The proverb is found in varying forms: *Pride comes before a fall; Pride goes before destruction; Empty pride usually takes a fall; Pride goes before, and shame comes behind,* etc.

Pride *goeth* before destruction, and an haughty spirit before a fall. —Prov. 16:18, *Authorized Version,* 1611

1984. It was just before we ventured to Keilah that I talked to God for the first time. And He answered. He helped me decide. Back then, He always answered me, and I had no need for a Samuel or a Nathan. I could speak for myself. I was on even better terms with my God, back then, than they ever were. No wonder I grew proud. I had to learn that pride goeth before destruction, and a haughty spirit before a fall. —Joseph Heller, *God Knows*

1989. *Pride goeth before the fall,* Captain Jackson told himself fifteen minutes later. —Tom Clancy, *Clear and Present Danger*

Procrastination is the thief of time. Needless delay is a waste of valuable time. The proverb has been traced back to *Night Thoughts* (1742) by Edward Young (1683-1765), English poet. It is first attested in the United States in *Papers of Alexander Hamilton* (1784).

> **1742.** Procrastination is the thief of time. —Edward Young, *Night Thoughts,* quoted in *Who Said What When* (1991)
>
> **1891.** Punctuality is the thief of time. —Oscar Wilde, *The Picture of Dorian Gray*
>
> **1922.** Procrastination is the Thief of Time. —James Joyce, *Ulysses*
>
> **1935.** Far from being the thief of Time, procrastination is the king of it. —Ogden Nash, *The Primrose Path*
>
> **1961.** From General Peckem's office on the mainland came prolix bulletins each day headed by such cheery homilies as "Procrastination is the Thief of Time" and "Cleanliness is Next to Godliness." —Joseph Heller, *Catch-22*

See also NEVER PUT OFF UNTIL TOMORROW WHAT YOU CAN DO TODAY; TIME AND TIDE WAIT FOR NO MAN.

The proletarians have nothing to lose but their chains. One of the most famous sentences written by Marx and Engels in their *Communist Manifesto.* The origin of the saying is still murky. It may have been used earlier by Jean Paul Marat (1743-93), the French revolutionist. *To have nothing to lose and a lot (everything) to gain* and *to have everything to gain and nothing to lose* are the usual modern forms and often used as figures of speech.

> **1848.** Let the ruling classes tremble at a communist revolution. The proletarians have nothing to lose but their chains. They have a world to win. —Karl Marx and Friedrich Engels, *The Communist Manifesto*
>
> **1986.** "I've got everything to lose and nothing to gain," she protested feebly. —Jackie Collins, *Hollywood Husbands*
>
> **1989.** He was magnificently persuasive. But he was risking nothing by laying his job on the line; he had nothing to lose and everything to gain ... —Michael Lewis, *Liar's Poker*
>
> **1991.** I believe President Bush has nothing to gain

and much to lose from a veto, even if it is sustained. —*New York Times*

> **1993.** The families of the 1843 expedition had been recruited in Independence, Mo., earlier that year. The United States was in the midst of a severe economic depression and many had been persuaded by the argument: "You have everything to gain and little to lose by moving to the new frontier." —Quoted in *Reader's Digest*
>
> **1994.** Mr. Sudoplatov was hardly in a position of power when he made his claims [of spying by America's scientists for Russia] in 1982. He had nothing to gain by lying and everything to lose. —*Wall Street Journal*

See also WORKERS OF THE WORLD, UNITE!

A promise is a promise. Once a promise is made, it is expected to be kept.

> **1985.** Dawn took the pen. It felt cold in her fingers. She did not recall having ever signed anything that made her happy or was to her advantage. When a man presented you with something to sign, it was usually bad news.... Still, a promise was a promise. She thought. —Michael Korda, *Queenie*
>
> **1989.** It was even more irrational to conceal the secret of their marriage once he was dead. A promise was a promise, and she [Alexa] would never have broken her word to Arthur, but death surely released her from that obligation—made it, in fact, impossible to keep. —Michael Korda, *The Fortune*
>
> **1991.** "Stay for the party. It's only the beginning."
> "I wish I could," said Scarlett fervently. "It's the best party I've ever been to in my life. But I promised I'd be back."
> "Ah, well, then. A promise is a promise." —Alexandra Ripley, *Scarlett*
>
> **1992.** When is a promise not a promise? when it is made by the State of New York. Or more precisely, when it is made by the State of New York in times of fiscal distress. —*New York Times*

See also PROMISES, PROMISES!; PROMISES ARE LIKE PIECRUST: THEY ARE MADE TO BE BROKEN.

Promises are like piecrust: they are made to be broken. Promises are not reliable and shouldn't be trusted. The proverb has been traced back to *Heraclitus Ridens* (1681), and was popularized by Jonathan Swift in 1738. First attested in the United States in *American Museum* (1789). The proverb is found in varying forms: *Promises are like piecrust: easy made and easy broken; Some promises are like good piecrust: short and* *easy to break*, etc. The expression is often shortened to *Promises are made to be broken.*

> **1738.** *Lady Smart:* ... Miss Caper is to be married to Sir Peter Giball; one thing is certain, that she hath promis'd to have him.
> *Lord Sparkish:* Why, Madam, you know promises are either broken or kept.
> *Lady A:* I beg your pardon, my Lords, promises and pie-crust are made to be broken.
> —Jonathan Swift, *Polite Conversation*

> **1871.** "Promises like that are mere piecrust," said Ralph. —Anthony Trollope, *Ralph the Heir*

> **1989.** "I'll write when I get settled." ... "Me, too," Corey said, scuffing a toe into the floor.... Promises made, and promises broken, Craig thought. —Wayne Care, *Vietnam Spook Show*

> **1991.** "You promised last night that you'd send the money to Uncle Henry today," she [Scarlett] said automatically. She wished he'd be quiet for a minute. She needed to think. Was it really "a futile attempt"? She refused to believe it.
> "Promises are made to be broken," Rhett said calmly. —Alexandra Ripley, *Scarlett*

See also A PROMISE IS A PROMISE; PROMISES, PROMISES!

Promises, promises! It is easy to make promises you aren't likely to keep. The saying is often used sarcastically or jokingly.

> **1992.** "Just a few more questions," Carella said. "You promised me ..." "Promises, promises," Meyer said. —Ed McBain, *Kiss*

> **1992.** Promises, Promises. The promise of youth, so long ingrained in the American character, keeps on taking a beating. —*New York Times Magazine*

> **1992.** Now, by way of expiation, he [President Bush] seems to offer a tax *cut*, and seems intent on clamping a firm lid on Federal expenditures for entitlements. Evidently, he hopes somehow to save $300 billion a year. It is impossible to see how he could do so without wholly eliminating Federal medical insurance for the elderly and the poor. That's just one reason his plan, without extensive elaboration, sounds like promises, promises. —Editorial, "What the President Deserves," *New York Times*

See also A PROMISE IS A PROMISE; PROMISES ARE LIKE PIECRUST: THEY ARE MADE TO BE BROKEN.

The proof of the pudding is in the eating. No matter how highly something is praised, believe nothing until you've tried it yourself. Judge everything by the results; test everything in action. The proverb has been traced back to about 1300, and it was popularized by Cervantes in *Don Quixote* (1605), and Jonathan Swift in *Polite Conversation* (1738). Later used by John Galsworthy in *White Monkey* (1924). First attested in the United States in the 1769 *Papers of Lloyd Family of Lloyd's Neck*. The proverb is found in varying forms: *The proof is in the pudding; The proof of the pudding is the chewing of the bag*, etc.

> **1605.** The proof of the pudding is in the eating. —Miguel de Cervantes, *Don Quixote*

> **1988.** At a press conference, Shultz said that the Soviets still must spell out exactly how they plan to withdraw from Afghanistan. He said that he anticipates this will occur in the UN talks between the Soviet-installed Afghan government and Pakistan, a U.S. ally. "The proof of the pudding will be in the eating," he said. —*Newsday* (N.Y.)

> **1991.** "The proof is in the pudding," Rolf Ekeus, chairman of the United Nations special commission for the elimination of weapons of mass destruction, told reporters after talks with Iraqi Foreign Ministry officials. "We will wait until we see it." —*New York Times*

> **1993.** "The proof will be in the pudding," he [Sen. Pete V. Domenici] said. "If it [the economy] doesn't work, it's not going to be much of a victory." —*Times* (Trenton)

See also ACTIONS SPEAK LOUDER THAN WORDS; SEEING IS BELIEVING.

A prophet is not without honor, save in his own country. Prophets are not appreciated in the places where they live. The proverb appears in the Bible. It has been traced back to 1485. First cited in the United States in 1632. This biblical proverb is used in other languages too.

> "A prophet is not without honor, save in his own country, and in his own house." —Matt., 13:57, *Authorized Version*, 1611

> **1946.** In Florence the signory thought him an amusing fellow and his letters often made them laugh, but they had no great confidence in his judgment and never followed his advice. "A prophet is not without honor save in his own country," he sighed. —W. Somerset Maugham, *Then & Now*

> **1959.** [George Kennan] was a prophet without honor in his own country or any other Western country. —*Christian Science Monitor*

> **1985.** "I have a very good reputation in New York. A prophet is always without honor in his own place, and I realize you can't afford a Sunday sec-

tion like that." —Howard Fast, *The Immigrant's Daughter*

1989. The phenomenon of "Gorby-mania" has been amply documented, and opinion polls indicate it continues unabated. A poll commissioned in West Germany and in the Soviet Union by *Stern* magazine showed that Mr. Gorbachev was more popular in West Germany than at home, prompting one Soviet official to recall the biblical wisdom (which he passed as a Russian proverb) that "a prophet is not without honor, save in his own country." —*New York Times*

1991. For years, Friederich von Hayek was a prophet little honored in this land. In a 1944 best seller, "The Road to Serfdom," the Austrian-born economist warned the West that socialism—whether German Nazism, Soviet Communism or the "gentler and kinder" British brand—would inevitably lead to poverty and loss of liberty. —*New York Times*

Prosperity is just around the corner. Better times are coming soon. The saying originated after the 1929 stock market crash. This political slogan was widely used by President Herbert Hoover's supporters, though it was not a coinage of Hoover himself.**

1966. Grim-faced Herbert Hoover remained at his desk in the White House, conscientiously battling the depression through short lunch hours and long working days and nights. Out on the firing line his supporters halfheartedly cried, "The Worst Is Past," "It Might Have Been Worse," "Prosperity is Just around the Corner." —Thomas A. Bailey, *The American Pageant*

1991. During the evening you will be honored by a surprise caller: President Herbert Hoover. He will make a brief speech declaring, "Prosperity is just around the corner." —Russell Baker, *New York Times*

Providence is always on the side of the big battalions. *See* GOD IS ALWAYS ON THE SIDE OF THE BIG BATTALIONS.

Pull yourself up by your own bootstraps. *See* DON'T TRY TO PULL YOURSELF UP BY YOUR OWN BOOTSTRAPS.

Punctuality is the politeness of kings. Important people do not need to be on time, so it is an act of courtesy for them to do so. The proverb is attributed to Louis XVIII (1755–1824). He is quoted in *Souvenirs de J. Lafitte* (1844) as saying, *L'exactitude est la politesse des rois* ("Punctuality

is the politeness of kings"). In 1834, Anglo-Irish novelist Maria Edgeworth (1768–1849) said that "Politeness is the virtue of princes." *Punctuality is the politeness of princes* is a variant.

1929. *Boanerges:* Oh, good morning to you. They say that politeness is the punctuality of kings.
    Sempronius: The other way about, Mr. Boanerges. Punctuality is the politeness of kings, and King Magnus is a model in that respect.
        —Bernard Shaw, *The Apple Cart,* Act I

1962. Punctuality is the virtue of the bored. —Evelyn Waugh, *The Diaries of Evelyn Waugh*

1984. "Why did the doc say, 'Punctuality is the politeness of kings'?"
    "Because the gentleman that came ten minutes late is never on time." —Overheard in a doctor's office

Pushing the envelope. Pushing any type of boundary; advancing and pioneering. The saying dates back to the early 1980s and is a figurative use of a phrase in aeronautical engineering, where the *envelope* refers to the safe performance limits of an aircraft, taken from a mathematical sense where the envelope is a boundary of a group of curves. The aeronautical sense was popularized in Tom Wolfe's *The Right Stuff.*

1983. To be sure, each race I kept and still keep "pushing the envelope"—challenging my limitations—but without distracting visions of someday vaulting to the top. —*Christian Science Monitor*

1988. Back from the competitive dead is West Springfield gymnast Tim Daggett, who was up on the apparati only four months after snapping both bones in his left leg at last year's world championships. "You could say that I'm pushing the envelope," says Daggett, who'll be competing in next weekend's USA-USSR challenge at Phoenix. —*Boston Globe*

1997. "Dr. Kervorkian has always shown a desire to push the envelope if he doesn't get the proper media attention. I think he wants to perform organ transplants, but I think he realizes this is a useless gesture." —*Detroit News*

1998. Pushing the envelope on abortion rights and risking the wrath of voters, the three candidates for the Democratic nomination for governor said yesterday they would lower the age requiring parental consent for an abortion from 18 to 16. —*Boston Globe*

1998. Never a daredevil himself, Ed Long watched and admired those who pushed the envelope:

Amelia Earhart, Charles Lindbergh, and, recently, John Glenn. Another man who wasn't about to let age stop him from doing what he loved. —*Cable News Network*

1998. Split lip? Separated shoulder? Busted ribs? Get right back in the game. Pushing the envelope of agony has always been an essential part of ice hockey's stoic ethos. —*Time*

See also THE SKY'S THE LIMIT.

Put first things first. See FIRST THINGS FIRST.

Put on the back burner. Put in a position of low priority. The saying alludes to the image of a cooking stove, where a dish getting attention must be close at hand, on the front burners, but something less important can be pushed to the back of the stove. The American expression dates from the early 1960s.

1968. Truce talks, once more, have been temporarily pushed on the back burner. —*U.S. News & World Report*

1989. Mr. Maloney would not say whether any corruption inquiry had been destroyed by Mr. Hatcher's slaying. Another senior official said the inquiry had been "placed on a back burner." —*New York Times*

1994. Clinton's personal cause—healthcare—is on the back burner. —*Time*

1997. After they marry on July 27, Cara Gallagher and Stephen Bianchi will return to their own home in New York City with a growing retirement nest egg and a keen awareness of their financial needs. Not bad for a couple at an age—20-something—when money issues are often put on a back burner. —*New York Times*

1998. After years of simmering on the back burner, French cuisine has become red hot. Note the popularity of recently opened restaurants, from Pastis in Los Angeles and Brasserie Ji in Chicago to Balthazar in New York and Truc and Zinc in Boston. —*Boston Globe*

See also PUT ON THE FRONT BURNER.

Put on the front burner. Put in a position of high priority. The natural antonym to PUT ON THE BACK BURNER, q.v.

1984. Boston School Superintendent Robert Spillane, after a meeting at the White House between President Ronald Reagan and education leaders yesterday, praised Reagan for keeping the issue of discipline in public schools "on the front burner." —*Boston Globe*

1987. Presidential aspirant Jesse Jackson led a giant rally in New York City last Thursday and put on the front burner the plight of some 80,000 home health care workers who he said are paid less than a living wage by the Koch Administration. —*Amsterdam News* (New York City)

1993. "It hasn't been forgotten [the shooting death of a 9-year-old boy]," said one law enforcement source familiar with the investigation. "It hasn't come off the burner. It is still on the front burner." —*Boston Globe*

1994. Lawmakers on Capitol Hill almost always suffer a bout of nervousness as elections approach. This year, with health care on the front burner, it's an epidemic. —*Boston Globe*

1998. The study of heat shock proteins and tumors began as a sidelight for Pramod Srivastava. But it's definitely on the front burner at the University of Connecticut Health Center in Farmington. —*Hartford Courant*

See also PUT ON THE BACK BURNER.

Put that in your pipe and smoke it. It's final (even if you don't like it or disagree with it). The proverb has been traced back to 1824; it is also found in *The Pickwick Papers* by Charles Dickens. Usually an imperative or infinitive form is used after *can*.

1931. His voice rose gloatingly, almost to hysteria. "Put that in your pipe and smoke it, you gurly big bully!" he yelled. "Smoke it till it sickens ye." —Archibald Joseph Cronin, *Hatter's Castle*

1946. "He married money. Cousin Mathilde says so, and she knows everything. He was broke but he married money. Now, smarty, put that in your pipe and smoke it!" —Robert Penn Warren, *All the King's Men*

1978. Another fellow stated that he had seen lights in the sky the night before Mother Abigail's disappearance and that the Prophet Isaiah had confirmed the existence of flying saucers ... so they'd better put that in their collective pipe and smoke it, hadn't they? —Stephen King, *The Stand*

1981. "Dear Smoker: Because your nervous habit pollutes their air, that's why. Now put that in your pipe and smoke it!" —Abigail Van Buren, *The Best of Dear Abby*

Put up or shut up. Either back up your statement or don't say anything to begin with. Originated in the United States in the nineteenth century and comes from poker. The saying has been traced back to 1887 and was found in the Louisville *Courier Journal.* In 1889 Mark Twain used it in *A Connecticut Yankee in King Arthur's Court.*

1951. "You'd have a better chance there than you would out on the Range."

"Do you want to bet? or dont you?" Stark demanded. "Put up or shut up." —James Jones, *From Here to Eternity*

1965. When someone proposes something which seems tough, hard, put-up-or-shut-up, it is difficult to oppose it without seeming soft, idealistic, mushy, etc. —Arthur M. Schlesinger, Jr., *A Thousand Days*

1967. "That's really why we threw this party, to draw a line. Anything you say from now on you have to mean. Put up or shut up." —Elia Kazan, *The Arrangement*

1987. Senator Helms, standing in a lobby of the Capitol shortly after the vote, said: "[Richard G.] Lugar has been actively campaigning for this. He's been calling and writing. I haven't made one single call. I haven't asked one senator to vote for me.... I'm simply saying it's put-up or shut-up time about the seniority system," Mr. Helms added. —*New York Times*

1988. "I got a C-note says I can swallow that roast beef whole. Put up or shut up." —Erich Segal, *Doctors*

1993. How many of our generation would want to be starting out today? It's time our generation shut up and put up. —*AARP Bulletin*

1994. The Clinton Administration may at last stop waffling. If this debacle doesn't focus the President's mind, nothing will.... It's put-up-or-shut-up time. I don't know about you, but I've got my TV Guide clip-and-save copy of Newt Gingrich's "Contract With America" handy. —*New York Times*

See also PUT YOUR MONEY WHERE YOUR MOUTH IS.

Put your money where your mouth is. Back up your bragging with justification. Don't make empty boasts. This adage originated in the United States in the 1930s and comes from gambling. The proverb is found in jocular forms with variants in place of *mouth.*

1967. She [Gwen] said I should for once in my life live what I talked. "Put your money," she said, "where your mouth is." —Elia Kazan, *The Arrangement*

1973. "I don't want a cent. But from now on—cut all this talk how you love January and how concerned you are about her future. Put your money where your mouth is!" —Jacqueline Susann, *Once Is Not Enough*

1979. May I say, further, that on this very day

Emil Larkin puts his money where his mouth is. —Kurt Vonnegut, Jr., *Jailbird*

1984. "By appearing in these ads, you're putting your money where your mouth is." —Lee Iacocca with William Novak, *Iacocca*

1986. "The only way we'll be able to do it is to put our money where the money is." —"The People," CBS

1987. "We're not spending money freely," said the Mayor, who characterized his proposed spending plan as prudent.... "What we are doing is that we are targeting our spending," he said. "We're putting our money where our philosophy is." —*New York Times*

1991. "This is very much a case of putting your money where your mouth is," said David Johnson, a lawyer representing BCCI's controlling shareholders in Abu Dhabi. "We wouldn't be here at all if there weren't a serious intention to develop a rescue scheme." —*Wall Street Journal*

1994. They [Ford, AT&T, General Electric] believe in the future. And they put their money where their belief is. —Ad by Digital Equipment Corporation

See also PUT UP OR SHUT UP.

Put your trust in God, and keep your powder dry. Trust in God but be sure you can function without God's aid if necessary. Advice allegedly given by Oliver Cromwell to his soldiers when they were about to cross a river (*powder* is gunpowder). The proverb has been traced back to 1834. It is first attested in the United States in 1945, and often shortened to *Keep your powder dry.*

1834. Put your trust in God, my boys, and keep your powder dry! —Valentine Blacker, "Oliver's Advice, An Orange Ballad," quoted by Edward Hayes in *Ballads of Ireland* (1856)

1945. "Do you mean that? Then, why haven't you told the Carters that my announcement that night at Mountain Lodge was a joke?" ...

"I'm keeping my powder dry." —Emilie Loring, *Beyond the Sound of Guns*

1988. Stepping down, Henry Maier [Milwaukee Mayor] keeps his powder and wit dry. —*New York Times*

1994. "We're asking them to keep their powder dry. That's it." —*New York Times*

See also GOD HELPS THOSE WHO HELP THEMSELVES; PRAISE THE LORD AND PASS THE AMMUNITION.

Pyrrhic victory. A victory or goal achieved at too great a cost. In 279 b.c. Pyrrhus, King of Epirus, defeated the Romans at Asculum but lost his best officers and many soldiers.

1934. "I'm sharing the fate of the women of my time who challenged men to battle."

"To your vast surprise it was just like all battles," he answered, adopting her formal diction.

"Just like all battles." She thought it over. "You pick a set-up, or else win a Pyrrhic victory, or you're wrecked and ruined—you're a ghostly echo from a broken wall." —F. Scott Fitzgerald, *Tender Is the Night*

1988. Hollis said, "Tolstoy gives an accurate description of a French Pyrrhic victory, yet there are some Russians who think that it was a Russian victory." —Nelson DeMille, *The Charm School*

1989. When he [John Tower] speaks to the National Press Club this week, this articulate conservative should challenge his successor and chief tormentor [Sam Nunn] to extended televised debate. In the subsequent voting, the best that Senate Democrats could achieve is another Pyrrhic victory. —*New York Times*

1991. Environmentalists won a great victory in the Clean Air Act of 1990. It may prove Pyrrhic, however, if the price of regulating away pollution proves to be more than Americans can afford. —*New York Times*

1992. The publishers won a Pyrrhic victory. There is a ceiling now on Berlusconi's share of the market, but he could lift it himself with a new ad agency set up under somebody else's name. —*The New Yorker*

See also ANOTHER SUCH VICTORY, AND WE ARE UNDONE.

Quid pro quo. To exchange something for something else; tit for tat. This expression is Latin, and its literal translation is "something for something." The earliest written record of the saying in English is Shakespeare's *Henry the Sixth* (1589–90). When the Earl of Suffolk asked Margaret, "Lady, wherefore talk you so?", the latter responded, "I cry you mercy, 'tis but *quid* for *quo*." The expression is among the most common Latin phrases used in English.

1989. Blackmail is a fact of life in politics. Call it a power play or a quid pro quo arrangement or whatever; it is used to block bills, pass bills, and influence appropriations and appointments. —*Sun-Sentinel* (South Florida)

1996. Each plan, whether put forth by the tobacco industry or the "No Ifs, Ands, or Butts" campaign by convenience store owners, seeks some type of quid pro quo to get government off their backs. —*Christian Science Monitor*

1997. Harvard Pilgrim Health Care agreed to add New England Medical Center to its list of health care providers. Though it denied there was any quid pro quo arrangements, Harvard OK'd the deal. —*Boston Globe*

1998. But the question of whether the president lied under oath and also may have persuaded someone else to lie under oath—with the promise of a good job as a quo pro quo—is not a small one. A private citizen would face time in prison. —*Christian Science Monitor*

1998. The [Justice] department quietly informed Senate Democratic leader Tom Daschle of South Dakota on Aug. 17 that it would examine whether the industry and Senate Republicans engaged in an illegal quid pro quo: political advertising in exchange for votes. —*Hartford Courant*

See also ONE GOOD TURN DESERVES ANOTHER; ONE GOOD HAND WASHES THE OTHER; YOU SCRATCH MY BACK, I'LL SCRATCH YOURS.

Rats desert a sinking ship. Everyone gives up when facing too great a crisis. Rats are said to be the first ones to smell gas in a mine or to leave a falling house or a sinking ship. The proverb has been traced back to 1579. In about 1610, it was used by Shakespeare in his play *The Tempest*, but the same idea was expressed as early as the first century (Pliny the Elder). The expression is first attested in the United States in 1755 in *Papers of Benjamin Franklin*. The proverb and its variants are used in reference to people who display disloyalty in difficult times.

a.d. 77.
When a building is about to fall down, all the mice desert it. —Pliny the Elder, *Natural History*

1610. *Prospero:* In few, they hurried us aboard a bark,
    Bore us some leagues to sea; where they prepar'd
    A rotten carcass of a boat, not rigg'd,
    Nor tackle, sail, nor mast; the very rats
    Instinctively had quit it.
        —Shakespeare, *The Tempest*, Act I, Scene II

1985. Dawn sipped her tea. "I can't think why you should, Kraus. As soon as David was in trouble, you ran off like a rat leaving ..."
    "The sinking boat." —Michael Korda, *Queenie*

1992. Meanwhile, Carville, exulting in victory, seemed agitated to friends who speculated he was worrying about Mary [Matalin]. "She's hurting," he said in Little Rock. "Who wouldn't be? There are a lot of rats over there [the Bush campaign] who left the ship. She wasn't one of them. I'm real proud of her." —*People*

Read my lips. I assure you I speak the truth. I am being totally honest here. The saying is used to mean that one should listen closely to what the speaker says. The saying has been traced back to 1978. Popularized by President Bush in his nomination speech on August 19, 1988. *Watch my lips* is a variant of the saying.

1987. "That's *Dr.* Sinatra, you little Bimbo!"
    "Yes, sir, Dr. Sinatra. Would you like another card?"
    "Whadda ya mean *gotta* shuffle? *Deal*, sister!"
    "I'm sorry, Dr. Sinatra, those are the house rules."
    "Read my lips, honey! I said, *deal* the cards!"
—G. B. Trudeau, *Doonesbury Deluxe*

1988. The Congress will push me to raise taxes, and I'll say no, and they'll push, and I'll say no, and they'll push again. And all I can say to them is read my lips: No New Taxes. —George Bush, *Acceptance Speech at the Republican National Convention in New Orleans*

1989. "What's this?"
    "Read my lips, forty-four minutes of GDRS [General Directorate Rear Services]." —Wayne Care, *Vietnam Spook Show*

1990. When it comes to taking forceful, timely measures in such critical areas as education, the environment, crime and drugs, George Bush's "vision thing" can be summed up in four words: Read my lip service. —*New York Times Magazine*

1993. "Just be truthful," Bethea said. "Be honest. Don't be like George Bush. Don't say 'Read my lips.'" —*Times* (Trenton)

1994. "You know, George I said, 'Read my lips,'" Mr. Lundine said, referring to former President Bush. "Well, Pataki has been on this side and that side of abortion and assault weapons and basic issues. I think George II should say, 'Read my flips.'" —*New York Times*

Remember the Alamo! Refers to the heroic defense of Texas volunteers of the Alamo fort from February 24 to March 6, 1836, against Mexican General A. del Santa Anna's thousand-man army. On March 6, five days after Texas declared its independence from Mexico, Santa Anna attacked the Alamo and the last of the 189 Americans were slain, including Davy Crockett and J. Bowie. But they were not forgotten. Forty-six days later, on April 21, 1836, with the battle cry *Remember the Alamo!* 750 Texans headed by Gen. Sam Houston routed the Mexican army and captured Santa Anna. The catchy slogan came from Sidney Sherman (1805–73), who was a colonel in Houston's army. His regiment, according to Gen. Houston, attacked the enemy, "singing the war cry, Remember the Alamo."

1987. "The presidential press conference is now open for questions. You may begin, gentlemen."

"About your memory, Mr. President. How is it possible that you can't remember whether or not you approved that first shipment of arms to Iran?"

"Oh, I remember the Alamo." —*Sun-Sentinel* (South Florida)

1991. State employees: Rush the Barricades!!! Remember the Alamo!! —*Boston Globe*

1995. Remember the Alamo? Remember Desert Storm? Remember Betsy Ross, the Battle of Gettysburg, the words to America the Beautiful? The kids at Alamo Elementary School remember what the Alamo was about, and much more. —*Commercial Appeal* (Memphis, Tennessee)

1997. Remember the Alamo? Absolutely—but don't forget the rest of this colorful Texas city. The Alamo is an American shrine and a stirring sight but hardly the only attraction in the area. —*Boston Globe*

1997. Remember the Alamo. Mexican siege cannons couldn't level the Alamo, but the historic mission in San Diego is slowly crumbling under the long assault of nature. —*Commercial Appeal* (Memphis, Tennessee)

Render unto Caesar the things which are Caesar's and unto God the things that are God's. Keep politics separate from religion. The saying appears in the New Testament. The proverb has been traced back in English to *Sermon at Paul's Cross* (1601), and is first attested in the United States in *Letters of John Randolph* (1680). Often shortened to *Render unto Caesar the things which are Caesar's.*

Show me the tribute money. And they brought unto him a penny.

And he saith unto them, Whose *is* this image and superscription?

They say unto him, Caesar's. Then saith he unto them, Render therefore unto Caesar the things which are Caesar's; and unto God the things that are God's. —Matt. 22:19, 20, 21, *Authorized Version*, 1611

1963. There was a quotation from *The Books of Bokonon* on the page before me. Those words leapt from the page and into my mind, and they were welcomed there.

The words were a paraphrase of the suggestion by Jesus: "Render therefore unto Caesar the things which are Caesar's."

Bokonon's paraphrase was this:

"Pay no attention to Caesar. Caesar doesn't have the slightest idea what's *really* going on." —Kurt Vonnegut, Jr., *Cat's Cradle*

1987. But his hands were not tied at this moment. He began twisting them as if trying to open a jar of pickled peaches, as he attempted to explain to the Major the structure of the Episcopal Church and the theology underlying the structure and the theology of the theology and what could and could not be rendered unto Caesar. —Tom Wolfe, *The Bonfire of the Vanities*

1992. The only role for government is to assure that each woman—regardless of race, class, or economic status—has the right and the liberty to make her own decision. "Render unto Caesar those things which are Caesar's and render unto God those things which are God's." Caesar has no business in a woman's bedroom or a woman's heart. —*Princeton Packet*

1995. RENDER UNTO CAESAR, PAY THE PIPER OR JUST GET THAT CHECK IN THE MAIL —Headline, *Tax Notes*, quoted in *New York Times*

The reports of my death are greatly exaggerated. Written by "Mark Twain" (Samuel L. Clemens), after a newspaper mistakenly published his obituary. The form is now often used to refer to any exaggeration.

1897. The report of my death was an exaggeration. —Mark Twain's note, *New York Journal*

1947. "Gene, there's been a report that you are dying."

"As Mark Twain said, the report is exaggerated." —Irving Stone, *Adversary in the House*

1985. Like the report of Mark Twain's death, Herberg's obituary for ethnicity was greatly exaggerated; less than a decade later Nathan Glazer and Daniel P. Moynihan surveyed the field and announced that the ethnicity was alive and well and flourishing in New York. "The point about the melting pot," they wrote, with only partial exaggeration, "is that it did not happen." —Charles E. Silberman, *A Certain People*

1988. Vice President Bush soundly defeated Senator Bob Dole in the New Hampshire Republican primary today, keeping his Presidential candidacy alive after one of the most difficult weeks in his political life.... "Tonight, I somehow feel that I have a lot in common with Mark Twain," Mr. Bush told his cheering supporters. "Reports of my death were greatly exaggerated." —*New York Times*

1991. JAPANESE REPORTS OF POLITICAL DEMISE OF [PRIME MINISTER TOSHIKI] KAIFU MAY BE GREATLY EXAGGERATED —Headline, *Wall Street Journal*

1992. Dee Dee Myers, the campaign press secretary, said today that reports of divisions within the campaign have been "grossly exaggerated." —*New York Times*

1993. Yes, there is rapid change in computer technology, but rumors of the mainframe's death are exaggerated. —Ad for IBM, *New York Times*

1994. "Reports of my death have been greatly exaggerated," Mark Twain once said. New York City's tobacco business would be justified in sending a similar message to *Crain's* after reading "NY cigarette trade going up in smoke." —*Crain's New York Business*

1995. "The No. 1 lesson," Mr. Clinton declared, "is not to be cynical, not to give up, not to turn back, but to bear down and go forward and do what is right for the American people. It will come out all right in the end." ... Taking some license with Mark Twain's famous quote, the President said, "The reports of our demise are premature." —*New York Times*

The rest is history. The result is a natural reaction to what came before, and the end of the story is well known to everybody.

1993. But Carville's strategy petered out. In the face of tax hikes and a listing economy, the assault weapons issue was a slim reed that eventually bent, then snapped in two. Whitman squeezed by with less than a 1 percent margin.

The rest is history: Rollins self-destructed, Carville got married, and the Garden State—and all of us residents who don't leave at the end of a political campaign—are left to wrestle with the frightening reality of handguns. —*Times* (Trenton)

1994. "I was looking for a way to supplement my income, and found that the cleaning business was lucrative and flexible, in terms of hours. I started picking up additional cleaning assignments, and then, hiring additional people to help me. Finally I left my full time job with Westminster [Choir College], and began concentrating on this full time. And the rest," he says, "is history." —*U.S.1* (Princeton)

Revenge is sweet. Retaliation brings satisfaction. The proverb has been traced back to the sixteenth century. It appeared in print in *The Palace of Pleasure* (1566) written by English author William Paynter (1540–94). The proverb was used by Shakespeare and Byron. First attested in the United States in 1656; the idea of the proverb was expressed as early as the eighth century b.c. (Homer, *Iliad*). *Vengeance is sweet* is a variant of the proverb and was first used by William Paynter.

1607–08.
> *Coriolanus:* "Forgive our Romans." O! a kiss
> Long as my exile, sweet as my revenge!
> —Shakespeare, *Coriolanus*, Act V, Scene 3

1818. Sweet is revenge—especially to women. —George Gordon Byron, *Don Juan*

1993. "Youth crime impacts on every one of us every day. We've got to find a way to stop it. I am thrilled by the challenge." ... Revenge, it seems, is not always sweet. —*New York Post*

1994. HOW H-P [Hewlett-Packard Co.] USED TACTICS OF THE JAPANESE TO BEAT THEM AT THEIR GAME. IT HOGGED PATENTS, CUT COSTS AND PARED PRICES TO GRAB MARKET IN INKJET PRINTERS. TESTED ON TORTILLAS AND SOCKS
It was such sweet revenge. —*Wall Street Journal*

The rich get richer and the poor get poorer. People who already have money can earn more money easily, while poor people can never rise out of poverty. The saying first appeared in the late nineteenth century. The proverb was popularized in the song *Ain't We Got Fun* (1921) written by American songwriters Gus Gerson Kahn (1886–1941) and Raymond B. Egan (1890–1952). *The rich get rich and the poor get children* is a humorous variant of the saying and was used in the above-mentioned song. *The rich get richer* and *the poor get poorer* may be used separately.

1921. There's nothing surer,
> The rich get richer and the poor get poorer,
> In the meantime, in between time,
> Ain't we got fun.
> —Gus Kahn and Raymond B. Egan, "Ain't We Got Fun"

1925. "One thing's sure and nothing's surer
> The rich get richer and the poor

get—children."
—F. Scott Fitzgerald, *The Great Gatsby*

1984. It seems that in the United States the one thing you can count on is that even during a depression, the rich get richer. —Lee Iacocca with William Novak, *Iacocca*

1991. Hats off to Liz Taylor for her decision to marry a blue-collar man, the construction worker Larry Fortensky. Other stars talk about grave social problems…. The social problem in question is the one that goes by such ungainly terms as "class polarization" or the "shrinking middle class"—the insidious economic trend that is making the rich richer, the poor poorer and the middle class exceedingly nervous. —*New York Times*

1992. "Since the middle of Reagan's term, and especially since Bush, the rich have gotten richer," he [Robert R. Pyle] goes on. "The poor have gotten children, and the middle class, like me, have gotten poor." —*New York Times Magazine*

1994. Q. Mr. President, to go back to domestic matters for a moment, you mentioned looking at the record, I want to ask you about one part of the record that does not look so good. The Census Bureau reported that through the first year of your term, through the end of 1993, median income has gone down; the rich have continued to get richer; the poor have continued to get poorer … —*New York Times*

A rising tide will lift all boats. An improvement in one area of society will improve quality in every other sphere. This saying originated in the United States in the 1960s and was popularized by the Kennedy family. The phrase is mostly used by economists and politicians.**

1963. As they say on my own Cape Cod, a rising tide lifts all the boats. And a partnership, by definition, serves both partners, without domination or unfair advantage. —John F. Kennedy, quoted in *Public Papers of Presidents of U.S.*

1988. The theory used to be that all Americans had a stake in prosperity. The comforting notion was that the rising tide would lift all boats. Now, however, the theory and some of the boats have holes in them. —*Washington Post*

1990. The country was in a sharp economic expansion coming out of '82. This made everybody look smart—you know, the rising tide lifts all boats. —*Washington Times*

1991. Under the "virtuous" leadership of the Republicans, more money has been leeched from the middle class than from the wealthy in this country. This money has gone not into welfare but into defense spending, S & L bailouts, and the national deficit. David Stockman's philosophy that "a rising tide will lift all boats" lifted the yachts and sank the life rafts. —*New York*

1992. GM's market value fell by over $1 billion, dropping it another notch to No. 16 by that measure. The market is one rising tide that can't lift all boats. —*Fortune*

1994. The rising tide is lifting all boats. —"Good Morning America," ABC News

1995. Our businesses are more productive and here we have worked to bring the deficit down, to expand trade, to put more police on our streets, to give our citizens more of the tools they need to get an education and to rebuild their own communities. But the rising tide is not lifting all the boats. —Bill Clinton, "State of the Union Address," *New York Times*

The road to hell is paved with good intentions. All of us have good intentions, but we rarely act on them. All the good intentions we failed to act on will, joined together, lead us into hell. The proverb has been traced back to 1574. Originally, "Hell is full of good intentions or desires" is attributed to Saint Bernard (1091–1153), while there are other variations: "Hell is full of good meanings and wishes" (George Herbert, 1651); "Hell is paved with good intentions" (John Ray, 1670). "The road to" was added later and was included in Henry George Bohn's collection of proverbs in 1855. First attested in the United States in 1890 in the *Principles of Psychology* by William James.

1903. Hell is paved with good intentions, not with bad ones. —George Bernard Shaw, *Man and Superman*

1984. Acting on reflex, and with only the most pietistic intentions, poor Uzzah put forth his hand to take hold of the ark when it shook on the wagon after one of the oxen stumbled. And the anger of God was kindled against Uzzah for this misjudgment and God smote him there, and there he died by the ark of God, right there on the spot. The road to hell, I've written, is paved with good intentions. —Joseph Heller, *God Knows*

1992. THE ROAD TO HELL IS PAVED WITH YELLOW BRICKS —Headline, *New York Times Book Review*

1993. He [Steve Kalafer] said that at a recent meeting he attended, a state official, hearing that a businessman had promised to alter a parking lot in the future, said "The road to hell is paved with good intentions." … The businessman hit back with: "Yes, but the road to heaven is paved with common sense." —*Times* (Trenton)

1994. "The only thing that rings some bells is that Kuchma said he would like to restructure some of the structures that deal with religion," said [Chief Rabbi of Ukraine] Bleich.... "We'll have to see how this will affect the Jews. He's said he wants to change the freedom-of-religion law to make it more democratic," he said, but added: "The road to hell can be paved with good intentions." —*MetroWest Jewish News*

Rob Peter to pay Paul. Take money that should rightfully go to one person or institution and give it to another that's virtually the same as the first. The origin of the proverb is unknown. The proverb is first attested about 1380. In 1546, it was included in John Heywood's collection of proverbs: "To rob Peter and pay Paul." George Herbert listed it in his collection (1640) as "Give not Saint Peter so much, to leave Saint Paul nothing." First attested in the United States in *Thomas Hutchinson Papers* (1657). The proverb has its counterpart in other languages: *Découvrir saint Pierre pour couvrir saint Paul* (French, "Strip Peter to clothe Paul"); *Desnudar a uno santo para vestir a otro* (Spanish, "To undress one saint to dress another"); *Dem Peter nehmen und dem Paul geben* (German, "To take from Peter and give to Paul").

> **1380.** How should God approve that you rob Peter, and give this robbery to Paul in the name of Christ. —John Wyclif, *Select Works*, Vol. III
>
> **1578.** He robbeth Peter to pay Paul. —John Florio, *Firste Fruites*
>
> **1912.** It is obvious that this was a case of robbing Peter to pay Paul. There was no real clearing up of the outstanding debt. —Theodore Dreiser, *The Financier*
>
> **1922.** So anyhow when I got back they were at it dingdong, John Wyse saying it was Bloom gave the ideas for Sinn Fein to Griffith to put in his paper all kinds of jerrymandering, packed juries and swindling the taxes off of the government and appointing consuls all over the world to walk about selling Irish industries. Robbing Peter to pay Paul. —James Joyce, *Ulysses*
>
> **1944.** A government which robs Peter to pay Paul can always depend on the support of Paul. —George Bernard Shaw, *Everybody's Political What's What*
>
> **1991.** Republican Senator Christopher Bond of Mis-

souri denounced the plan as pitting "one city's babies against another city's babies." Florida Governor Lawton Chiles, who chairs the National Committee to Prevent Infant Mortality, said it amounted to "robbing Peter to pay Paul." —*Time*

> **1992.** "Our government's tax policy is a case of robbing Peter to pay Paul." —Overheard at a newspaper stand in Manhattan
>
> **1993.** The Republican leader in the Texas House of Representatives, Tom Craddick, of Midland, was harsher: "There's a lot of smoke and mirrors, shifts, robbing Peter to pay Paul," he said. —*New York Times*

A rolling stone gathers no moss. A person who never stays long in one place will never be encumbered by responsibilities. Conversely, the person who is on the move all the time will never accomplish much either. The proverb is based on the Latin: *Saxum volutum non obducitur musco*. It has been traced back to about the first century b.c. (Publilius Syrus). In 1546, it was included in John Heywood's book of proverbs. First cited in the United States in 1721 in *A Word of Comfort to a Melancholy Country* by John Wise (1652–1725). The proverb is sometimes shortened to *a rolling stone*. "The Rolling Stones" is the name of a popular rock band started in the 1960s.

> **1929.** "A rolling stone gathers no moss," he said, "but a sitting hen loses feathers." —Katharine Susannah Prichard, *Coonardoo*
>
> **1965.** "Like a Rolling Stone" —Title of a song by Bob Dylan
>
> **1992.** Poor Jerry Hall!?? You'd think a gal from Texas would have had more horse sense. At least get married legally! Didn't her mama ever tell her that Rolling Stones gather no moss? —*People*
>
> **1994.** A rolling Moss gathers no stones. —George Wayne, "Kiss Me, Kate [Moss]," *Vanity Fair*

Rome was not built in a day. Radical changes cannot happen overnight; it takes time to accomplish grand undertakings. The saying has been traced back to 1545 and is a translation of the medieval French, *Rome ne fut pas faite toute en un jour* ("Rome was not made in one day"). In 1546, it was included in John Heywood's collection of proverbs. First attested in the United States in 1646 in *Thomas Hutchinson Papers*. The word *Rome* may be replaced by any other name. The proverb has its counterpart in other languages: *Rom wurde nicht in einem Tage erbaut* (German, "Rome was not built in one day"); *No se ganó Za-*

mora en una hora (Spanish, "Zamora [an impregnable fortress] was not won in an hour"); Москва не сразу строилась (Russian, "Moscow was not built in a day"), etc.

1963. "It wasn't easy, and it wasn't done over night, either."
"Rome wasn't built in a day." —Kurt Vonnegut, Jr., *Cat's Cradle*

1978. "Right now he's probably still concentrating on getting the power back on, re-establishing communications ... maybe he's even had to indulge in a purge of the fainthearted. Rome wasn't built in a day, and he'll know that." —Stephen King, *The Stand*

1984. "You'll be king, you'll be king," Samuel muttered without conviction. "Why worry, what's your hurry? Bide your time. Rome wasn't built in a day." —Joseph Heller, *God Knows*

1984. "I'm making mistakes," Koch said. "But Rome wasn't built in a day, and New York City can't be changed in five months." —Edward I. Koch, *Mayor*

1986. "In my own quiet way, I contribute to this town as much as any of them. But Rome wasn't built in a day." —Pat Conroy, *The Prince of Tides*

1991. *Question:* Why wasn't Rome built in a day?
Answer: Because it was a government job.
—Glenn E. Spradlin, quoted in *Reader's Digest*

1992. "Are you saying you've already *given* us this information?" Carella asked.
"No, Rome wasn't built in a day," the I.S. detective said. —Ed McBain, *Kiss*

1994. What if Mr. Katzenberg, the exile from Disney, says yes to too many live-action movies like *Cabin Boy* and *Angie* while waiting the years it takes to create an animated cash cow like *The Lion King*? What if Mr. Spielberg makes another *Always*? Metro Goldwyn Mayer, like Rome, wasn't built in a day. —*New York Times*

A rose by any other name would smell as sweet. The name of something doesn't affect its character. The saying first appeared in 1594 in Shakespeare's *Romeo and Juliet*.

1594. *Juliet:* What's in a name? that which we call a rose
By any other name would smell as sweet.
—Shakespeare, *Romeo and Juliet,* Act II, Scene II

1992. BY ANY OTHER NAME: JUNK MAIL —Headline, *New York Times*

1993. You look familiar, Rose—Do you ever go by any other name? —Thaves, *Frank and Ernest*

1994. Sweetness, it seems, by any other name is just as sweet. —*Philadelphia Inquirer*

1994. A rose by any other name may smell as sweet, but Forest City Ratner Cos. is hoping that different rules apply to shopping malls. A year ago, the big developer rechristened the Albee Square Mall in downtown Brooklyn in a radical attempt to change the mall's image. —*Crain's New York Business*

See also A ROSE IS A ROSE IS A ROSE IS A ROSE.

A rose is a rose is a rose is a rose. The inherent qualities of a rose remain the same no matter what you call it. This phrase was originated by the American writer Gertrude Stein (1874–1946). According to Stein, it is not easy to describe the defining characteristics of objects. As Judith M. Mardwick put it, "A janitor is still a janitor even when the title is Custodial Engineer." Stein's *rose* was the English artist Sir Frederick *Rose,* and she was a great admirer of his paintings. Alterations of the saying are used in varying jocular contexts: *A pope is a pope is a pope* (Harry Reasoner); *A flop is a flop is a flop is a flop* (Bill Carter), etc.

1913. Rose is a rose is a rose is a rose. —Gertrude Stein, "Sacred Emily"

1983. But as Oliver Easterne constantly said in his highly unoriginal way, "A star is a star is a star." —Jackie Collins, *Hollywood Wives*

1985. Like Gertrude Stein's rose, "a good department head is a good department head" ad infinitum. —Jacqueline Hornor Plumez with Karla Dougherty, *Divorcing a Corporation*

1989. "A rose is a rose is a rose," said Jerome M. Becker, a former New York Criminal Court judge now in private practice. "He committed the murder under the influence of cocaine and to me that's simple: It's murder and his conduct was depraved." —*New York Times*

1991. Roses may deserve all the pampering. They are the most loved flower, according to the American Rose Society. Nobody ever said "Marigold is a marigold is a marigold," the society argued in lobbying successfully for the rose as the national flower in 1986. The rose had no *true* competition, says Don Ballin, who was president of the society. —*Wall Street Journal*

1995. A bigot is a bigot is a bigot, whether it's a black Louis Farrakhan or a white Pat Buchanan. —*Manhattan Jewish Sentinel*

See also A ROSE BY ANOTHER NAME WOULD SMELL AS SWEET.

The rotten apple spoils the barrel. One bad person can make everyone he's associated with look bad. The proverb has been traced back to 1340 and is similar to the Latin: *Pomum compunctum cito corrumpit sibi junctum* ("A rotten apple quickly infects its neighbor"). In 1855, it was included in Henry George Bohn's collection of proverbs. Benjamin Franklin used it in 1736 in *Poor Richard's Almanac*: "The rotten apple spoils his companion." The proverb is found in varying forms. The word *bad* is often used in place of *rotten*, the words *box, bushel, its companions (neighbors), his companion (neighbor, fellow)* are used in place of *barrel*, the words *destroys* and *injures* are used in place of *spoils*. The saying is often shortened to *a bad apple* or *bad apples*.

1961. "Don't worry about the men. They'll be easy enough to discipline and control when you've gone. It's only while you're still here that they may prove troublesome. You know, one good apple can spoil the rest." —Joseph Heller, *Catch-22*

1974. "... Gordon Liddy got up and made a speech about how this one bad apple, McCord, shouldn't be allowed to spoil the whole barrel." —Carl Bernstein & Bob Woodward, *All The President's Men*

1983. Now is as good a time as any to say that most photographers are hard-working, decent men and women who do their job and go on their way. It's just the two or three rotten apples who spoil the barrel and make it hard on the others, jostling, demanding more and more shots, making life miserable for famous people who visit the city. —*Daily News* (N.Y.)

1987. The rotten apple in the barrel is Nicaragua. —George Shultz, "Meet the Press"

1990. Corruption, they inevitably argue, is the product of the ubiquitous "rotten apple in the barrel." —David Burnham, *A Law Unto Itself*

1992. Some of the police protesters blocked traffic on the Brooklyn Bridge. They jumped on parked cars, harassed passers-by and left City Hall Park littered with beer cans ... Police brass are poring over videotapes to find the bad apples in blue. —*New York Times*

1993. Evan's reluctance to report the positive side to a full-service broker illustrates a point he should have made: every profession or business has its bad apples, so be careful and know the entire story. —GQ

1994. Politicians in general have fallen into disrepute. There are a few good apples in the barrel. —*Times* (Trenton)

A Rube Goldberg machine. An exceptionally complicated machine (or design) that performs very simple tasks. The name comes from American cartoonist Ruben Lucius Goldberg (1883–1970) whose cartoons featured such machines. The phrase is now firmly entrenched in the English language.**

1993. "A lot of these computers have a Rube Goldberg flavor." —Overheard at a store

1994. "A Rube Goldberg machine"—that's how one disgusted lobbyist described the so-called Mainstream Coalition proposal for health-care reform that surfaced last week. He probably meant the proposal is an outlandish contraption that is likely to break down on the road. But it's worse than that; it's not even headed in the right direction. And that may be true of any other health-care proposal coming from this Congress. —*New York Times*

Rules are made to be broken. The existence of rules makes it likely that people will break them, sometimes for the better. The proverb has been traced back to 1953 and is found in *Expedition to Earth* by Arthur C. Clarke. First cited in the United States in 1960.

1953. Rules are made to be broken. —Arthur C. Clarke, *Expedition to Earth*

1994. Rules are made to be broken. —"Good Morning America," ABC News

Safety first. Attend to matters that insure your safety before doing anything else. The proverb has been traced back to 1915. Originally a motto of the Industrial Council for Industrial Safety. It was first used in the United States in 1937 in *Dangerous Dowager* by Erle Stanley Gardner (1889–1970).

1937. After all, you know, safety first. —Erle Stanley Gardner, *Dangerous Dowager*

1993. N.F.L. EXPANSION FOLLOWS SIMPLE PHILOSOPHY: SAFETY FIRST —Headline, *New York Times*

1994. Safety first: study the habits and habitat of this wily American species, the stockbroker. —*Newsweek*

See also BETTER SAFE THAN SORRY.

Save for a rainy day. Always put aside a little money so you'll have some when the need arises. The saying has been traced back to about 1566. First attested in the United States in 1753 in the *Papers of Benjamin Franklin.* The proverb is found in varying forms: *Save your pennies for a rainy day; Save for a rainy day, 'cause there are clouds in the sky,* etc. The word *save* may be followed by *it* or *your money* or *your pennies.* The word *save* may be replaced by *put aside (away).*

1953. I gave away a lulu of a Picasso story that had just reached me, one that I might have put aside for a rainy day. —J. D. Salinger, *Nine Stories*

1957. None of your damned putting by against a rainy day. —*New Yorker*

1976. "The price of oil is made in the marketplace. When the Arabs shut off their spigots, we had two choices: sell oil at the fixed prices the government laid down or make a few bucks for a rainy day." —Art Buchwald, *Washington Is Leaking*

1987. A deposit in the Favor Bank is not *quid pro quo.* It's saving for a rainy day. —Tom Wolfe, *The Bonfire of the Vanities*

1991. "They was working harder than any nigger ever did and putting by every nickel they earned for the next rainy day." —Alexandra Ripley, *Scarlett*

1993. One wonders what other little nest eggs are tucked away in its books for a rainy day. —*New York Times*

Save us from our friends. False friends are worse than open enemies. The saying has been traced back to 1477. Queen Elizabeth I (1533–1603) is quoted as saying in 1585, "There is an Italian proverb which saith, From my enemy let me defend myself; but from a pretensed friend Lord deliver me." In 1821, it was used by the British statesman George Canning (1770–1827). One variant, *Defend me from my friends; I can defend myself from my enemies,* is attributed to Claude Louis Hector, Duc de Villars (1653–1734). There are several other variants of the proverb: *Defend me from my friends; God save me from my friends—I can protect myself from my enemies,* etc.

1821. Give me the avowed, erect and manly foe;
Firm I can meet, perhaps return the blow;
But of all plagues, good Heaven, thy wrath can send,
Save me, oh, save me, from the candid friend.

—George Canning, *New Morality*

1946. Defend Me from My Friends! —Upton Sinclair, *A World to Win*

1964. … Voltaire entertained his guests with the best table talk in Europe. People came to stay three days, remained three months. "God protect me from my friends!" Voltaire sighed. "I will take care

290

of my enemies myself." —Quoted in *Great Lives, Great Deeds*

1985. According to William Allen White (not a wholly reliable witness), [Warren G.] Harding told him, "I can take care of my enemies all right. But my damn friends, my God-damn friends, White, they're the ones that keep me walking the floors nights." —Paul Johnson, *Modern Times*

See also WITH SUCH FRIENDS, ONE HARDLY NEEDS ENEMIES.

Say uncle. Surrender! This expression originated in the United States in about 1900. Lexicographer Charles Earle Funk thinks that the phrase may have some Latin connection. When a Roman boy was in trouble, he cried, *Patrue mi Patruissime* ("Uncle, my best of uncles"). *Cry (holler, yell) uncle* is a variant of the saying, which is always used figuratively.

1961. The middle-aged big shots would not let Nately's whore leave until they made her say uncle. —Joseph Heller, *Catch-22*

1979. He said, "Okay, my friend, anytime you want to say uncle, just quit." —Norman Mailer, *The Executioner's Song*

1981. Once eager to spring out of the house and into the world, women are beginning to cry "Uncle!" *The problem is that they have sprung out into the world, but they have not really left the house.* —Colette Dowling, *The Cinderella Complex*

1985. Later, pressed again to say whether this did not mean he [President Reagan] was seeking to overthrow the Sandinista Government, he replied, "not if the present Government would turn around and say" to the Nicaraguan rebels, "all right, if they'd say, 'uncle,' or 'all right and come back into the revolutionary Government and let's straighten this out and institute the goals.'" —*New York Times*

1989. Mr. Wright was in trouble even before he cried "uncle" on the floor of the House [of Representatives] and agreed to a straight up-or-down vote on the raise, a vote he and everyone else presumes will be overwhelmingly negative. —*New York Times*

1992. "He [President Bush] didn't yell uncle; he screamed it," said James Carville, a top strategist to Mr. Clinton. —*New York Times*

1994. Uncle Sam's tax assisters had me crying uncle. —*New York Post*

Scrambled eggs can't be unscrambled. *See* YOU CAN'T UNSCRAMBLE EGGS.

Scratch a Russian and you find a Tartar. A person may claim to be one thing but turn out to be quite different once you look below the surface. The proverb is attributed to Napoleon: *Grattez le Russe et vous trouverez le Tartare* ("Scratch the Russian and you will find the Tartar"). It is sometimes considered offensive. The proverb was first attested in the United States in the 1823 *Diary of James Gallatin, 1813–1827*. The form is flexible; nouns *Russian* and *Tartar* may be replaced with other nouns in variants. An example is "Scratch a Democrat and You Will Find a Rebel," a slogan used by the Republicans in their presidential campaign against the Democrats who were torn by factions as far back as 1868.

1823. Very true the saying is, "Scratch the Russian and find the Tartar." —*The Diary of James Gallatin*

1966. It [a prominent feature of a presidential campaign] found expression in such slogans as "Vote As You Shot" and "Scratch a Democrat and You Will Find a Rebel." —Thomas A. Bailey, *The American Pageant*

1993. Scratch any politician and in his or her shadow you will see a well-heeled special-interest lobbyist. —*Times* (Trenton)

1994. "Scratch Vladimir Zhirinovsky and you find a Russian Hitler." —Overheard in a Russian restaurant

Scratch my back and I'll scratch yours. *See* YOU SCRATCH MY BACK, I'LL SCRATCH YOURS.

See no evil, hear no evil, speak no evil. Said of people who don't want to be involved. The origin of the proverb is unknown. The proverb is often represented by three monkeys covering their eyes, ears, and mouth respectively with their hands. The seventeenth century legend related to the *Three Wise Monkeys* is said to have read: *Hear no evil, see no evil, speak no evil.* The saying was carved over the door of Sacred Stable, Nikko, Japan.

1939. "Hear no evil, see no evil, speak no evil," and you'll never be a success at a tea party. —Lewis & Faye Copeland, *10,000 Jokes, Toasts and Stories*

1984. *The Eye Rub.* "See no evil," says the wise monkey.
   The Ear Rub. This is an attempt by the listener to "hear no evil." —Allan Pease, "How to Tell If Someone Is Lying," quoted in *Reader's Digest*

1988. See-No-Evil, Speak-No-Evil, and Hear-No-

Evil left the room, programmed robots reacting to a familiar marching tune. —Robert Ludlum, *The Icarus Agenda*

1992. Hear No Bar, Speak No Bar ... When the Monkey Bar abruptly closed June 1, New York lost another landmark of the night. —*New York Times*

1993. SEE NO EVIL —Headline of an editorial on a New Jersey child rape and murder, *Times* (Trenton)

See also EVIL TO HIM WHO EVIL THINKS.

Seeing is believing. People believe that what they see is real. The proverb has been traced back to 1609 and it was cited in an unpublished manuscript in the library of Trinity College, Cambridge. First attested in the United States in the 1732 *Jonathan Belcher Papers*.

1956. Seeing is deceiving. It's eating that's believing. —*New Yorker*

1987. If seeing is believing, then Sir Richard Attenborough will believe his movie *Cry Freedom* will be seen in South Africa when South Africans start seeing it. —*New York Times*

1991. SEEING IS BELIEVING —Headline, *Scientific American*

1994. CRAFTSMEN: SEEING IS BELIEVING. —Headline of an article on Blue Mountain craftsmen, *New York Post*

See also THE PROOF OF THE PUDDING IS IN THE EATING; WHAT YOU SEE IS WHAT YOU GET; YOU HAVE TO SEE IT TO BELIEVE IT.

Seek and ye shall find. *See* ASK, AND IT SHALL BE GIVEN YOU; SEEK, AND YOU SHALL FIND; KNOCK, AND IT SHALL BE OPENED UNTO YOU.

Seize the day. *See* SEIZE THE MOMENT.

Seize the moment. Live for today. Enjoy your life now since nobody knows what the future holds. Coined by the Roman poet Horace (65 b.c.–8 b.c.) who wrote in his *Odes: Carpe diem, quam minimum credula postero* ("Seize the day, put no trust in the morrow"). Often found in its Latin form, *carpe diem*. Now often used in the sense "take charge," especially in political contexts.

1956. *Seize the Day.* —Title of a novel by Saul Bellow

1977. The rose, used often in *carpe diem* poems as a symbol of the transitoriness of feminine beauty, sometimes symbolizes other things as well. —Carl E. Bain, Jerome Beaty, & J. Paul Hunter, in *The Norton Introduction to Literature*

1989. He [the national director of the NAACP] seized the moment and spouted national statistics on crime and arrests and convictions and inmate population and summed it all up by declaring that the criminal justice system was controlled by white people who unfairly persecuted black people. —John Grisham, *A Time to Kill*

1991. Mr. Bush seized the moment, after the Persian Gulf war, for a new effort at Arab-Israeli peace. —*New York Times*

1992. Indeed, what is most striking about Mr. Nixon's charge to seize the moment, nearly all of which is sensible and sound, is the continuity of his counsel. —*New York Times Book Review*

1993. For the first time in this century leaders of both political parties have joined together around the principle of providing universal, comprehensive health care. It is a magic moment, and we must seize it. —Bill Clinton, *New York Times*

See also EAT, DRINK, AND BE MERRY, FOR TOMORROW WE DIE; GATHER YE ROSEBUDS WHILE YE MAY; MAKE HAY WHILE THE SUN SHINES; STRIKE WHILE THE IRON IS HOT.

Self-preservation is the first law of nature. One's own survival or the survival of those dear to one is the most important natural instinct. The proverb is of Latin origin, *Primamque ex natura hanc habere appetitionem* ("By nature our first impulse is to preserve ourselves"), and dates back to Cicero (106–43 B.C.). "It is onely upon this reason, that selfe-preservation is of Natural law," wrote John Donne in his *Biathanatos*. The adage was first attested in America in the late seventeenth century. In a letter to John Holmes dated April 22, 1820, Thomas Jefferson describes slavery as follows: "We have the wolf by the ears; and we can neither hold him, nor safely let him go. Justice is in one scale, and self-preservation in the other." American economist Thorstein Veblen in his book *The Theory of the Leisure Class* (1899) wrote: "With the exception of the instinct of self-preservation, the propensity for emulation is probably the strongest and most alert and persistent of the economic motives proper."

1926. The first law of nature urged him to safety. —Edgar Wallace, *The Ringer*

1941. Self-preservation is the first instinct of a sane man. —J. McClure, *Caterpillar Cop*

1972. Since when has guilt been stronger than self-preservation? —J. McClure, *Caterpillar Cop*

1975. What it amounted to was that he'd do a great deal for dear Maggie but that self-preservation was the first law of nature. —P. D. James, *Black Tower*

See also CHARITY BEGINS AT HOME; EVERY MAN FOR HIMSELF.

Sell down the river. To betray someone. The saying originated in the southern states of the United States and was used in connection with the illegal slave trade after 1808. The South and Southwest cotton and sugar businesses were booming, and slaves from the upper South were bought, transported down the Mississippi River and sold at the markets of Natchez or New Orleans. The phrase is firmly entrenched in the language, but its meaning has broadened and is used for any example of a betrayal.

1852. Now, here, it seems to me, you're running an awful risk. You can't hope to carry it out. If you're taken, it will be worse with you than ever; they'll only abuse you ... and sell you down river. —Harriet Beecher Stowe, *Uncle Tom's Cabin*

1958. The Weimar Republic was sold down the river. —*New York Times Magazine*

1979. At lunch, Boyd Kimmelman wept without tears. "Oh, I am something," he said. "The boy genius, all ready to inscribe a page in the history books, the brilliant California lawyer who destroyed the House committee. Brilliant—I am an idiot, an unredeemed idiot! And I sold you down the river, Barbara." —Howard Fast, *The Establishment*

1986. The U.S.I.A. [U.S. Information Agency] man went back to turn his boss around, programming the director to insist he was agreeing only to medium-wave swaps, not an offer of jamming; Radio Free Europe/Radio Liberty agreed not to complain publicly about being sold down the river. —*New York Times*

1991. "I think Reagan sold us down the river," said actor Gary Merrill.... "And I felt that Reagan kind of sold the idea to the union. I felt we should have held out for residuals of some kind on the sale of movies to TV." —Kitty Kelley, *Nancy Reagan*

1992. In that word—"maintained"—you can see a media guy struggling with the problem of how to report what politicians say without selling the public down the river. —Russell Baker, *New York Times*

1995. In a political diatribe about the United Nations abandonment of Bosnia, I zapped the British

general in charge, Sir Michael Rose, as the reincarnation of the British Prime Minister Neville Chamberlain, who sold another small country down the river in Munich in 1938. —William Safire, *New York Times Magazine*

Separate the men from the boys. Identify the competent and brave. The saying has been traced back to the 1930s.

1962. Then Gaff crawled out in front of them and looked back. "Well, fellows, this is where we separate the men from the boys," he told them, "the sheep from the goats. Let's crawl." —James Jones, *The Thin Red Line*

1991. Gov. Ned McWherter said Monday that legislators will need to slash another $120 million out of a proposed state budget for the next fiscal year on top of $255 million in already planned cuts. "This will separate some of the men from the boys," McWherter told reporters.—*News-Sentinel* (Knoxville, Tennessee)

1996. You have to be able to take a punch in politics. This separates the men from the boys and the women from the girls. —*Christian Science Monitor*

1997. It was a race that didn't separate the men from the boys—not by much anyway. Ben Thomas of Boone, N.C., won the first Tennessee Road Mile in 4 minutes, 10 seconds on Saturday. Jasmin Keller of Knoxville was not far behind at 4:36 to take the women's overall. —*News-Sentinel* (Knoxville, Tennessee)

See also SEPARATE THE SHEEP FROM THE GOATS; SEPARATE THE WHEAT FROM THE CHAFF.

Separate the sheep from the goats. To sort out the good from the bad, the useful from the useless. The saying is of Biblical origin: "And all nations will be gathered before Him. And He will separate them from one another as a shepherd parts the sheep from the goats" (*Matt.* 25:32). P. G. Wodehouse writes in his *Uncle Fred in the Springtime:* "'I wish I had a brain like yours,' said Lord Ickenham. 'What an amazing thing, I suppose you could walk down a line of people, giving each of them a quick glance, and separate the sheep from the goats.'" The verbs *tell* and *sort (out)* may substitute for *separate.*

1985. "You've got to throw a lot of these pigmies out of Congress," he says. To that end, he applauds the vote this week... "The more votes we can get, the better—because it helps separate the sheep from the goats." —*Christian Science Monitor*

1987. And now that Republicans are no longer even partially responsible for congressional policy, the conservatives feel free to push the agenda without fear of coming into conflict with friends on Capitol Hill. Says Howard Phillips: "We need to start having roll-call votes again to separate the sheep from the goats." —*U.S. News & World Report*

1993. You had to be either totally cool or totally uncool to appreciate it at the times, but disco was the hippest popular music in the '70s (well, some disco, at least). For the rest of us, the next best thing was Steely Dan. Indeed, to separate the sheep from the goats in college dorms all you had to do was head for the LP collections. —*Boston Globe*

1994. The conditions in the camps once again test the resolve of UN members. UN troops are urgently needed to separate the sheep from the wolves—to disarm the Hutu soldiers and move them to separate camps farther away from the Rwandan border. —Editorial, *Christian Science Monitor*

1998. Sithe [Energies Corp.] is targeting its efforts to the Northeast, hoping to maximize profits, using sophisticated arbitrage to minimize fuel costs and to get the best price for its power. The ability to juggle those elements "is what's going to separate the sheep from the goats," said Wellford. "It's going to be a fast race." —*Washington Post*

See also SEPARATE THE MEN FROM THE BOYS; SEPARATE THE WHEAT FROM THE CHAFF.

Separate the wheat from the chaff.

To separate the valuable from the worthless. The saying alludes to the ancient process of winnowing grain to remove the worthless outer covering, chaff, from the valuable grain.

1989. He once worked for the phone company, he said, so he was able to run strange numbers through the computer. With a list of phone numbers and his telephone on the alert, he is able to separate the wheat form the chaff, so to speak. —*New York Times*

1993. She also provides a thoughtful discussion of Mrs. Lindbergh's considerable literary output, separating the wheat from the chaff. —*Christian Science Monitor*

1998. [James] McGaugh said emotional arousal affects memory routinely, not just during extremely emotional events. Day to day, it's a way to help the brain separate the wheat from the chaff of life. —*Associated Press*

1998. Pro: Dorothy Beardmore, state Board of Edu-

cation member from Rochester: "The primary benefit is to establish what the child has learned. Interestingly enough, and you have to separate the wheat form the chaff, it never entered our minds that people would object to it." —*Detroit News*

1998. They [the Red Wings] outshot and outskated the Caps, and our goal was not about to derail them. Federov was brilliant for the second straight game, and when the season ends, he will be one of the major differences separating the champs from the chaff. —*Detroit News*

1998. The Philadelphia-born Calder was a fluent and effusively industrious artist who made thousands of works, and [curator Marla] Prather has done a fine job of winnowing the wheat from the chaff, of which, truth to tell, there is a great deal. —Robert Hughes, *Time*

See also SEPARATE THE MEN FROM THE BOYS; SEPARATE THE SHEEP FROM THE GOATS.

Set a thief to catch a thief. *See* IT TAKES A THIEF TO CATCH A THIEF.

Ships that pass in the night.

People who meet each other once and never meet again. In spite of their closeness, there is no lasting contact. The saying comes from Henry Wadsworth Longfellow's poem "Elizabeth" (1863–1874).

1863–74.

> Ships that pass in the night, and speak each other in passing;
> Only a signal shown and a distant voice in the darkness;
> So on the ocean of life we pass and speak one another,
> Only a look and a voice; then darkness again and a silence.
> —Henry Wadsworth Longfellow, *Tales of a Wayside Inn*, "The Theologian's Tale: Elizabeth"

1993. "Francine dumped me. She said we were two ships passing in the night, and then my cargo shifted." —Thaves, *Frank and Ernest*

The shit hits the fan.

A nasty angry reaction when some deed, action, or situation becomes known to people from whom it's been kept secret. The saying originated in the United States in the 1930s. It is often used in time clauses beginning with *when* and *then*. The word *shit* may be replaced with *crap*.

1951. O'Hayer took a turn around the small space, looking at the piles of equipment, turning some things over, straightening a pile or two. "Those things are going to have to be separated for size," he said.... "They already been separated," Warden said, without looking up. "Where were you when the shit hit the fan?" —James Jones, *From Here to Eternity*

1974. When the reporters engulfed him, he [Fiorello La Guardia] did not admit that he had agreed to dismiss [Robert] Moses. Instead, when he was asked, "What are you going to do?" he replied, "I'll think it over." And he decided that night to postpone writing Ickes the letter he had promised.... That proved to be a wise move. For the next day, as one of his advisers was to put it, "the shit hit the fan." The public, that most fickle of lovers, embraced Robert Moses in January as fervently as it had pushed him away in November. —Robert A. Caro, *The Power Broker*

1975. Hitching to Swarthmore was a bore. Being stopped by the cops and searched again and again was a bore.... At Swarthmore, talk talk talk talk talk. The shit is on the fan or very close. —Mark Vonnegut, *The Eden Express*

1977. "You can't walk around feeling guilty, and be a chief executive. He was wrong about the previous blindness. He should have said so, and gotten on with it."

"That's what he tried," Andy said, "then the shit hit the fan." —William Safire, *Full Disclosure*

1979. He couldn't pretend, he said, not to be concerned by Gary's reaction. The shit, Schiller assured them, would certainly hit the fan if Gary found out. —Norman Mailer, *The Executioner's Song*

1984. The office of the deputy chief of naval operations for submarine warfare had administrative control of all aspects of submarine operations. "Keeping you busy?"

"You know it! The crap's really hit the fan." —Tom Clancy, *The Hunt for Red October*

1987. "Because any minute now, you're gonna be interrupted. The shit is about to hit a very big fan." —Chris Bunch & Allan Cole, *A Reckoning for Kings*

1989. Craig, suddenly sullen, said, "What's up? Nobody's been hit, have they? The planes all made it back?"

"The shit hit the proverbial fan while you were gone." —Wayne Care, *Spook Show*

Shit or get off the pot. Take action or let someone else have a chance. Originated in the United States in the mid-twentieth century. Sometimes attributed to Richard Nixon (Vice President at the time) who allegedly made the remark to President Eisenhower when the latter did not show enthusi-

asm for his assistant in 1952. *Shit-or-get-off-the-pot* may be used as an attribute to a noun. *Piss or get off the pot* is a variant.

1986. No one is going to help Gator ... and no one is going to help me! It's time, Chris screamed at himself urging his leg muscles into action. Soldier or stay home! Shit or get off the pot! The time for rational observation and academic distancing is gone. —Dale A. Dye, *Platoon*

1988. "He's taking us into a new era. We're standing *tall* again and it's about time. We're telling the crumbs of this world to shit or get off the pot!" —Robert Ludlum, *The Icarus Agenda*

1991. He [Tom Schopf] told me that he had already assigned these topics and that I had better "proceed" (euphemism) with speciation "or get off the pot." —Stephen Jay Gould, "Opus 20," *Natural History*

See also FISH OR CUT BAIT.

The shoe is on the other foot. The situation has completely reversed. The saying has been traced back to the nineteenth century. Until then, shoes had been made different in size, but not in form and people could put the same shoe on either foot.

1990. During the height of the Holocaust there were tens of thousands of cases of Jews who assumed identity as Christians in order to escape the fate that Hitler had ordained for them. Today in Israel the shoe is on the other foot. —*Jewish Week* (N.Y.)

1993. Today, the shoe is on the other foot. Yitzhak Rabin, whose resignation as Prime Minister in 1977 precipitated Begin's election, was returned to office as a self-declared peacemaker. —*New York Times*

The shoemaker's kids always go barefoot. Whatever a person's skills or talent, those closest to her or him rarely benefit. The proverb appeared in John Heywood's book of proverbs in 1546. It was used by Robert Burton (1577–1640) in *The Anatomy of Melancholy* (1621–51). *The shoemaker's son always goes barefoot* and *The cobbler's children go barefoot* are variants of the proverb. The word *kids* may be replaced by *children* or *child*.

1621–51.
Him that makes shoes go barefoot himself. —Robert Burton, *The Anatomy of Melancholy*

1981. Dear Abby: A doctor's wife said: "The shoemaker's kids always go barefoot." I know what she means. —Abigail Van Buren, *The Best of Dear Abby*

1991. The household is spare, surprisingly short of electronic gadgets for a computer technician's dwelling. The Garbers have a pair of TV sets, though only one works, and a stereo rig that Ed bought from a pawnshop for $229, but no compact disk player, VCR, or PC. "The shoemaker's children go barefoot," Nancy notes good-naturedly. —Lee Smith, *How the Average American Gets By*

1994. "It was like the cobbler's children who have no shoes," said Ron M. Green, a labor and employment lawyer at Epstein, Becker & Green in New York. —*New York Times*

Shoot first and ask questions afterwards. When in doubt, assume the worst: Attack and be reasonable later. "Shoot first and inquire afterwards, and if you make mistakes, I will protect you," Herman Goering was quoted as saying in 1933 when instructing the Prussian police. The word *later* is often used in place of *afterwards*.

> **1936.** It would take a brave man to break such news to Rhett, for Rhett had the reputation for shooting first and asking questions afterwards. —Margaret Mitchell, *Gone With the Wind*

> **1992.** And if you see one of those officials, shoot first and ask questions later. —*New Yorker*

> **1994.** Shoot Kids First Ask Questions Later Eh! Mr. Mayor.—Notice on the building in the Gowanus Houses where 13-year-old Nicholas Heyward, Jr., was fatally wounded by a police officer on September 27, 1994. —*New York Times*

A shot in the arm. A boost that puts new life into someone or something, alluding to the benefits of a shot administered by a doctor or nurse, or to an injection of a drug by an addict. It originated in the United States in the early twentieth century and is widely used all over the world. In 1993, "rescuing" the King's English, BBC started purging its broadcasts of Americanisms, and "a shot in the arm" was its first victim.

> **1987.** The increase in the city's bond rating, to A-, from BBB+, "is a real shot in the arm that polishes the city's image" and will help the city sell its bonds at lower interest rates, said William F. McCarthy, a managing director at Merrill Lynch & Company. —*New York Times*

> **1989.** "Even after all these years, New York still gives me a shot in the arm," she [Ann Marie Cunningham] said. —*New York Times*

1993. *Kelly:* "We're going to get planes, people and new buildings, and old buildings will be rehabilitated. It's going to be a tremendous shot in the arm for the country's economy." —*Times* (Trenton)

1994. Outriders and other personnel in the United States already are allowed to wear corporate logos on their clothing. Jockeys in England also can wear corporate logos.... The measure was proposed to provide a "shot in the arm for the racing industry in New York," said a spokeswoman for the Lexington, Ky.–based Jockeys' Guild. —*Crain's New York Business*

The show must go on. No matter how adverse conditions are, whatever has been planned must be carried out. Originally a saying of entertainers. It was first included in the *Dictionary of Americanisms* in 1867.

> **1946.** "The show must go on, Governor! And for you there is no 'stand-in'—as they call it in Hollywood." —Upton Sinclair, *A World to Win*

> **1983.** "Well, Gina," he [Oliver] began. "Business is business, and as bad as I feel about Neil's ... er ... unfortunate illness, the show must go on, as someone once said. —Jackie Collins, *Hollywood Wives*

> **1986.** "Caesar [a Bengal tiger] mauled our former animal trainer outside of Aiken, South Carolina, and I have been forced to step in because, as you know, ladies and gentlemen, the show must go on." —Pat Conroy, *The Prince of Tides*

> **1992.** "It would be horrible to open with Julie in the hospital," said Carole Rothman, the artistic director of Second Stage. "You want these openings to be happy occasions, they're so fraught with anxiety, anyway. So we postponed. This isn't a case of 'the show must go on.' " —*New York Times*

> **1994.** A woman was attacked by a spooked elephant in a Manhattan TV studio moments before it appeared on "Live With Regis and Kathie Lee."
> But the show must go on and, minutes after the stomping—even while Yelena Aleynikova was being rushed to the hospital—the perturbed pachyderm successfully made its TV debut. —*New York Post*

Silence is golden. It is best not to speak. Now also used in the sense that quiet is a priceless gift. The proverb has been traced back to 1865, and was first attested in the United States in *Changes* (1923) by H. W. Nevinson.

> **1969.** Silence is golden. What a cliché! —Archibald Joseph Cronin, *A Pocketful of Rye*

> **1988.** Cindy said, in a pleading manner, "Remem-

ber how she locked me in the closet ... when she slapped me and said, 'Silence is golden.'" —Clifford Irving, *The Campbell Murder Case*

1993. SILENCE IS NOT GOLDEN —Headline, *New York*

1993. Silence is golden when your nerves have been jangled by everyone talking at once. —Clarence Brown, *Right Words Beat Silence*, *Times* (Trenton)
See also SPEECH IS SILVER; SILENCE IS GOLDEN.

Sink or swim. Fail or do something to succeed. The proverb has been traced back to about 1368 (Chaucer). In 1596–97, Shakespeare used it in *King Henry the Fourth, Part I*. The proverb was first attested in the United States in the 1652 *Complete Writings of Roger Williams*. Commemorating John Adams (1767–1848) and Thomas Jefferson (1743–1826), two former U.S. presidents, Daniel Webster (1782–1852) said on August 2, 1826: "Sink or swim, live or die, survive or perish, I give my hand and my heart to this vote."

1596–97.
Hotspur: If he fall in, good night! or sink or swim. —Shakespeare, *Henry the Fourth, Part I*, Act I, iii.

1965. If Diem felt this backing to be anything less than wholehearted, the policy would not work. This became known, in the phrase of Homer Bigart of the *New York Times*, as the period of "sink or swim with Ngo Dinh Diem." —Arthur M. Schlesinger, Jr., *A Thousand Days*

1969. Little Billy was terrified, because his father said Billy was going to learn by the method of sink-or-swim. —Kurt Vonnegut, Jr., *Slaughterhouse-Five*

1985. "It's not me who's brutal, Dan, it's the business. Broadway is strictly sink or swim, either one night or ten years! It's a goddamn war between the artists and *The New York Times*!" —Erich Segal, *The Class*

1986. As for his conducting activities, which are apparently to increase in the future, it may be too early to make definitive pronouncements. In any case, Domingo's *Romeo* is probably a sink-or-swim situation—with limited rehearsal time, no Met revival is likely to reveal much about the man on the podium, even one in the unique position of having once performed the leading tenor role in the same production. —*New York*

1987. Susan Sussman, 45, of Evanston, Ill., the author of the children's book *There's No Such Thing as a Hanukkah Bush, Sandy Goldstein,* said that when she was a child, "most parents had a 'sink or swim' approach to child rearing." —*New York Times*

1992. While the decision of Sears, Roebuck to detach its financial services businesses is what shareholders, analysts and consultants have demanded with increasing insistence for years, it will leave the battered retail business to sink or swim. —*New York Times*
See also DO OR DIE; MAKE OR BREAK.

Six of one and half a dozen of the other. It makes no difference how you approach it, it's all one and the same. The saying has been traced back to 1836, when it first appeared in *The Pirate and the Three Cutters,* a novel by Frederick Marryat (1792–1842). The saying has its counterpart in other languages: *C'est chou vert et vert chou* (French, "It's cabbage green and green cabbage"); *Lo mismo da* (Spanish, "It's the same thing"); Что в лоб, что по лбу (Russian, "It's in the forehead or over the forehead"), etc.

1836. "I knows the women, but I never knows the children. It's just six of one and half-a-dozen of the other, ain't it, Bill?"—Frederick Marryat, *The Pirate and the Six Cutters* 1852–53."Mostly they come for skill—or idleness. Six of one, and half-a-dozen of the other. —Charles Dickens, *Bleak House*

1951. "Ah, whats the difference? They all the ferkin same. Five cents of one, a nickel of the other." —James Jones, *From Here to Eternity*

1970. "You wouldn't upset him. He thinks the same thoughts whether you talk to him or not. Six of one, half a dozen of the other. He's brooding about this anyway." —Saul Bellow, *Mr. Sammler's Planet*

1985. Ambivalence: six of one, half doesn't of the other. —Shelby Friedman, *Toward More Picturesque Speech*

The sky is not going to fall. No matter what you think, nothing catastrophic is going to happen. This saying is often used to keep people from panicking when their fears are unfounded. Taken from the children's story about Chicken Little. One day, while Chicken Little was going about her business, a nut hit her on the head. But Chicken Little thought a piece of sky had fallen and hit her head, so she ran around the barnyard yelling, "The sky is falling! The sky is falling!" to warn the other animals. The moral of the story is "Don't assume that a small thing is a major catastrophe. Check your facts before you alarm everyone else." Hence the negative form of the saying. *The sky is not falling* is a variant of the saying.***

1987. The law banned discrimination on the basis of sexual orientation in housing, employment and public accommodations. ... After passage, Mayor Koch said: "The sky is not going to fall. There isn't going to be any dramatic change in the life of this city." —*New York Times*

1992. They [pessimists] warned about an avalanche of bank failures, concealed by regulators and set off by new rules that take effect on Dec. 19 and require tougher and swifter action against the weakest banks. ... But the deluge is turning out to be more of a trickle. ... "The sky is not falling," said Andrew C. Hove Jr., chairman of the Federal Deposit Insurance Corporation. —*New York Times*

1993. "The big news is that there is no crisis, the sky is not falling," she [Karen Ferguson] said. —*Times* (Trenton)

1994. The sky is not falling, except maybe on the president's head. Mr. Clinton isn't helping whatever slim chance he has of a second term with his neo-Malthusian cant. Ask Jimmy Carter. —*Wall Street Journal*

See also IT'S NOT THE END OF THE WORLD.

The sky's the limit. There is no limit to what one can achieve or to how much may be done or spent to what one can achieve. The saying is often used to motivate people. In his book *Don Quixote* (1605), Cervantes wrote: "No limits but the sky."

1937. Aside from that, the sky's the limit. —Erle Stanley Gardner, *Dangerous Dowager*

1946. "I have a secret fund, and there is nothing I'd rather use it for. As you Americans say, the sky is the limit!" —Upton Sinclair, *A World to Win*

1949. *Willy:* Without a penny to his name, three great universities are begging for him, and from there the sky's the limit, because it's not what you do, Ben. It's who you know and the smile on your face. It's contacts, Ben, contacts! —Arthur Miller, *Death of a Salesman*

1951. "There'll be women everywhere. All of them out on the loose. With the sky the limit." —James Jones, *From Here to Eternity*

1983. "How much?"
   "Enough to pay Elaine off, for a start. And when Daddy goes, the sky's the limit!" —Jackie Collins, *Hollywood Wives*

1984. "I invest conservatively and always hoard as much as I can. But with the wealth of nations, the sky is the limit to what I could spend." —Joseph Heller, *God Knows*

1987. "It shows that all of the dreams we have had can come true," said Arthur J. Freeman, a theorist at Northwestern University who has followed the recent developments. "The sky is the limit." —*New York Times*

1988. He [Felix Rohatyn] laid much of the blame on his own profession: "In the field of takeovers and mergers, the sky is the limit." —Judith Ramsey Ehrlich & Barry J. Rehfeld, *The New Crowd*

1991. "Work on it whenever you can. In fact, if the name Koker-Hanks crosses your mind while you're driving home, stick it for an hour. The sky's the limit on this one." —John Grisham, *The Firm*

1992. "These young people have to know that the sky's the limit for them," Granville says. —Quoted in *Reader's Digest*

1993. Wall Street. THE SKY'S NO LIMIT Buy low, sell high. —*New York Times*

1994. Mr. Allman, too, sees a generation gap. "For everyone under 45, the sky's the limit," he notes. "Everyone over 65 or 70 is scared to death." —*New York Times*

A slip of the lip can sink a ship. *See* LOOSE LIPS SINK SHIPS.

Slow and steady wins the race. Keep on doing something steadily and you'll succeed. The proverb has been traced back to Samuel Smile's book, *Self-Help* (1859). First cited in the United States in R. G. Dean's book, *What Gentleman Strangles a Lady?* (1936). Lexicographers usually refer this saying to Aesop's fable "The Hare and the Tortoise." The Hare, confident that it could beat the slower Tortoise, fell asleep after having run very fast at the beginning of the race, while the Tortoise slowly and steadily continued, reached the finish line, and won the race. Also found in the variant: *Slow and easy wins the race.*

c.550 b.c.
Slow and steady wins the race. —Aesop, "The Hare and the Tortoise"

1978. Stu woke up when Tom eased him down.
   "Sorry," Tom said apologetically. "I had to rest my arms." He first twirled, then flexed them.
   "You rest all you want," Stu said. "Slow and easy wins the race." —Stephen King, *The Stand*

1992. "I think's she [Ms. Holtzman] is on her way up," Mrs. Straus said. "Will she rise fast enough? I think slow and steady might win it." —*New York Times*

See also HASTE MAKES WASTE; MARRY IN HASTE, REPENT AT LEISURE; SLOW BUT SURE.

Slow but sure. The best way to do a job well is to proceed with care and close attention to details. The proverb has been traced back to Legh's book,

Accidence of Armoury (1562), and is first attested in the United States in the *Dedham Historical Register* (1759). *Slow but sure wins the race* and *Slowly but surely* are variants of the proverb.

1993. Slowly but certainly, as more of us become convinced by facts and necessity, we are breaking our bad energy habits and making our planet more habitable and more sustainable. —*Times* (Trenton)

1993. "Slowly but surely, it's been banned by a lot of places," Mr. Stern said yesterday on his show, which originated at WXRK-FM and is fed live by satellite to stations in more than a dozen other radio markets. "I thought that the cool thing about putting out a book was that you at least had the right to say anything you wanted to say without fear." —*New York Times*

See also HASTE MAKES WASTE; MARRY IN HASTE, REPENT AT LEISURE; SLOW AND STEADY WINS THE RACE.

Small world. *See* IT'S A SMALL WORLD.

Smoking and sports don't mix. *See* OIL AND WATER DON'T MIX.

Smoking gun. Hard evidence of guilt. The allusion is to a gun just fired with smoke still coming out of it; the smoke indicates that it was just fired, and whoever is holding it must have pulled the trigger. Now DNA seems to be the indisputable evidence of guilt. The metaphor is a recent Americanism.

1986. "There is probably no smoking gun here," said a man who served in the White House during the Watergate years. —*New York Times*

1987. President Reagan declared yesterday that there was "no smoking gun" that could prove he knew of or approved the diversion of profits from Iranian arms sales to the Nicaraguan rebels. —*Boston Globe*

1987. "Sure, it was complicated fraud," Mr. Merola said. "Our basic problem was that we could not convey that to the jury. In the Bronx, you need a smoking gun or a knife to convince a jury a crime has been committed." —*New York Times*

1988. Scores of memorandums released yesterday by the Dukakis administration do not contain any "smoking gun" evidence to support contentions of a sweetheart deal in the selection of a New Braintree site for a planned prison. —*Boston Globe*

1991. Researchers said Thursday they have identified a gene that is a "smoking gun" link to an early stage of colon cancer.—*Associated Press*

1998. After eight months there's no smoking gun, no smoking anything, just a simmering stew of subdivided Ozark property without sewer lines and endless minutiae about closing costs and mortgage points. —*Time*

1998. Everybody looks for a smoking gun in cases like these. There may not be a smoking gun in those memos, but will it help Republicans fortify their case on this matter? —*Cable News Network*

Snug as a bug in a rug. Very comfortable. The rhyming simile alludes to a clothes-moth hidden in a rolled-up rug and is usually attributed to Benjamin Franklin who used it in a 1772 letter to Miss Georgiana Shipley. In this letter, he offered an epitaph for her dead pet squirrel called Skugg: "Here Skugg lies snug/As a bug in a rug." But the phrase appeared slightly earlier in an anonymous work, *Stratford Jubilee* (1769): "If she [a rich widow] has the mopus's money/I'll have her, as snug as a bug in a rug." The phrase appeared even earlier in various non-rhyming versions. "He sits as snug as a Bee in a Box," wrote Edward Ward in *The Wooden World Dissected* (1706). "Let us sleep as snug as pigs in pease-straw," declares one of the characters of Thomas Heywood's play *A Woman Killed with Kindness* (1603).

1992. Last fall, prior to the arrival of winter, we secured the storm windows, hoping to be "snug as a bug in a rug," as the saying goes.—*Christian Science Monitor*

1998. Well, the furnace went on this month without disaster, the house is well insulated (you did it last month, of course) and everyone is as snug as a bug in a rug. —*Boston Globe*

So far, so good. Everything is fine up to this point. The saying is of Scottish origin and dates from 1721.

1946. Irwin had had the stock, and had sold it to Messrs. Satterfield and Cantor. So far, so good. —Robert Penn Warren, *All the King's Men*

1982. "So far, so good," Aahz murmured, scanning the backs in front of us to be sure we were unobserved. —Robert Asprin, *Myth Directions*

1984. Remember the joke about the guy who jumps off the 50th floor without a parachute and when he passed the 30th floor, somebody shouts, "How is it going?" and he answers, "So far, so good." —*New York Times*

1986. "So far, so good, Captain. Nothing big has come loose yet." —Tom Clancy, *Red Storm Rising*

1989. Wanda Womack, a young woman with a sympathetic glow about her, looked at Jake and smiled ever so slightly. It was the first positive signal he received from the jury since the trial started…. "So far so good," Carl Lee whispered. —John Grisham, *A Time to Kill*

1991. "How's your crop?"

"So far, so good. If we don't get a real rain." —Alexandra Ripley, *Scarlett*

1993. "So far so good," said one mother watching as her daughter took a book, "Pat the Bunny," from a rack. —*New York Times*

1994. The [Channel] tunnel trip, a 35-minute journey on a specially designed train, hurtling through darkness at about 90 miles an hour, is unnervingly smooth and uneventful. That is just what Eurotunnel, the outfit that operates the trains, wants it to be.

"So far, so good," said Judy Campbell, cautiously. She was half-way along the 31-mile trip on an exploratory test run. —*New York Times*

So goes Maine, so goes the nation. *See* AS MAINE GOES, SO GOES THE NATION.

So help me God. I swear I'm telling the truth. Often used at the end of an oath or solemn statement: "Do you solemnly swear to tell the truth, the whole truth and nothing but the truth, so help you God?"

1946. "I will do those things. So help me God." —Robert Penn Warren, *All the King's Men*

1960. When he [Robert E. Lee Ewell] turned around to take the oath, we saw that his face was as red as his neck …

"—so help me God," he crowed. —Harper Lee, *To Kill a Mockingbird*

1977. "George Washington added 'So help me God' to the end of the oath." —William Safire, *Full Disclosure*

1979. She pulled open the drawer in the night table next to her and took out a gun and pointed it at him. "I'm counting to thirty. I want you out of here and downstairs and out of my house, or so help me God, I'll commit justifiable homicide." —Howard Fast, *The Establishment*

1986. "Yet she also knows you have a strong sense of family and duty. My job was to balance these two counterweights. If I could have done this without you, so help me God, I would have." —Pat Conroy, *The Prince of Tides*

1988. "Did you ever let anyone know that?"

"I've tried, Congressman, so help me God, I've tried." —Robert Ludlum, *The Icarus Agenda*

1991. Mrs. Fitzpatrick stepped in front of the woman. "I have six children," she said. "Get out of

here. Colum, get this butcher out of this house before she kills Mrs. O'Hara and I kill her. So help me God, that's what will happen." —Alexandra Ripley, *Scarlett*

A soft answer turns away wrath. When someone is angry with you, responding with kindness will deflect his or her anger. Of Biblical origin. It is first attested in the United States in the 1642 *Trelawny Papers* in the *Documentary History of the State of Maine* (1884).

A soft answer turneth away wrath: but grievous words stir up anger. —Prov. 15:1, *Authorized Version*, 1611

1974. A pleasant voice, a clear mind, and an outgoing personality always come through. Speak briefly and to the point, and even if the call is a disagreeable one, follow the proverb that "A soft answer turneth away wrath." —Milla Alihan, *Corporate Etiquette*

1978. John Freemantle pretended not to hear these things, and at home he would quote from the Bible—"A soft answer turneth away wrath" … —Stephen King, *The Stand*

Something is rotten in the state of Denmark. I suspect that something is very wrong. The saying first appeared in Shakespeare's *Hamlet* (about 1601). *The state of Denmark* may be replaced by names of places characterized by wrongdoing, corruption, and bribery.

1601. *Marcellus:* Something is rotten in the state of Denmark.

Horatio: Heaven will direct it.

Marcellus: Nay, let's follow him.
—Shakespeare, *Hamlet,* Act I, Scene IV

1974. "Sometimes I don't know whether to laugh or cry. I'm an accountant. I'm apolitical. I didn't do anything wrong. But in some way, something is rotten in Denmark and I'm part of it." —Carl Bernstein & Bob Woodward, *All The President's Men*

1984. Although the press was mostly unaware of these squabbles, our dealers were getting the distinct impression that something was rotten in Denmark. —Lee Iacocca with William Novak, *Iacocca*

1992. Something is rotten over at ABC's divorce drama, *Civil Wars: Love is in the air.* Stars Peter Onorati and Margaux Hemingway have been moving rapidly toward romance in the past few weeks. —*People*

Sometimes one can't see the wood for the trees. Focusing on small details or the most obvious features of a situation prevents one from seeing the bigger picture. The proverb has been traced back to 1546 (John Heywood's book of proverbs), and is first attested in the United States in the 1813 *Adams–Jefferson Letters* (1959). *One can't see the forest for the trees* is a variant form.

1958. We are still in the thick of all these trees, and the shape of the wood is hard to make out. —*New York Times Book Review*

1976. You have to persuade your financial sources that you are a good risk. Bowl them over with your confidence and enthusiasm, your ability to see both the forest and the trees. —Claudia Jessup & Genie Chipps, *The Woman's Guide to Starting a Business*

1986. Some of [Henry] Adam's judgments seem unduly small-scale. Sometimes the piquancy of a tree makes him lose sight of the wood ... —*New York Times*

1991. "We see the banking industry emerging toward normalcy, which should be achievable within the 1992–1993 time frame," Mr. Crowley said. "However, the process will be pockmarked by various unexpected and unnerving events, and investors must be prepared not to let such 'trees' get in the way of the forest," he added. —*Wall Street Journal*

1994. SEE THE FOREST? THE WORLD BANK CAN'T EVEN SEE THE TREES. —*New York Times*

The sooner the better. This saying has been traced back to about 1475, and is first recorded in the United States in the 1640 *Winthrop Papers*.

1936. "When may I speak to your father?"
"The sooner the better," she said. —Margaret Mitchell, *Gone With the Wind*

1946. "He'll be like a baby. And the skin will be inclined to break down. He will get infections easily. The respiratory control will be impaired, too. Pneumonia will be likely. That's what usually knocks off cases like this sooner or later."
"It sounds to me the sooner the better," I said, ... —Robert Penn Warren, *All the King's Men*

1969. She thought of that man hanging over her, his weight on her, all that love pushed into her and released as if it had been just too much for him and he had to get rid of it, the sooner the better. —Joyce Carol Oates, *Them*

1984. "When does he want them?"
"The sooner the better, I should think," Abner decided, "from everyone's point of view." —Joseph Heller, *God Knows*

1988. "I tried to call you."

"That's okay," he replied. "We'll just make it another time, that's all."
"The sooner, the better," Grete replied enticingly. —Erich Segal, *Doctors*

1989. "You'd better get over here," Simon said. She noticed his reluctance had vanished completely. "The sooner the better." —Michael Korda, *The Fortune*

1991. Giuliani remained calm. "Here's what our thinking is," he began. "You've got a problem. The sooner you resolve it, the better." —James B. Stewart, *Den of Thieves*

See also PROCRASTINATION IS THE THIEF OF TIME.

Sow your wild oats. To indulge in wild and stupid things in one's youth. The phrase has been traced back to 1542 (Thomas Becon) and was first used in the United States in the 1650 *Works of Anne Bradstreet* (1932). The phrase has a male sexual connotation.

1922. Father is a wellknown highly respected citizen. Just a little wild oats, you understand. —James Joyce, *Ulysses*

1936. "There was nothing really wrong with the boys—boys must sow their wild oats." —Margaret Mitchell, *Gone With the Wind*

1992. I can only imagine the pain Magic's wife, Cookie, must have endured during their 14-year relationship while he pursued his basketball career and sowed his wild oats. —*People*

1993. "It was there that I started to try to write songs, but I usually threw the result out the window," he [Mr. Shindell] said. And he wanted to "sow my wild oats." So he left the seminary, and took off "to bum around Europe for awhile." —*Time Off*

Spare the rod and spoil the child. A child who is never punished will grow up to be rude and inconsiderate. "The man who has never been flogged," says Menander (about 342–292 b.c.), "has never been taught." The proverb appears in the Old Testament. It has been traced back to about 1000 b.c. and was first attested in the United States in *Letters* by William Byrd (1674–1744). *He who spares his rod hates his son* and *He who spares the rod spoils the child* are variants of the proverb.

He that spareth his rod hateth his son: but he that loveth him chasteneth him betimes. —Prov. 13:24, *Authorized Version*, 1611

1664. Love is a boy by poets styled;

Then spare the rod, and spoil the child.
—Samuel Butler, *Hudibras*

1984. So he concocted his unconscionable plot to rape her, and I went for the fiction of his illness hook, line, and sinker. By sparing the rod, I had spoiled this child; by sparing him again, I set the stage for much worse. —Joseph Heller, *God Knows*

1989. "This isn't New York. Farm people expect kids to pull their own weight. 'Spare the rod and spoil the child' is still the local recipe for child-rearing." —Michael Korda, *The Fortune*

1993. The thousands of good Christians who gather to hear James Dobson talk of his Focus on the Family Crusade may think: "Wow, that's the greatest, and every American should hear and heed: Discipline our kids, don't spare the rod and spoil the child." —*New York Times*

1994. DISCIPLINE: SPARE THE ROD—BUT CRACK DOWN —*Newsweek*

Speak softly and carry a big stick. Don't be openly aggressive, but have the ability to use great force if necessary. This old saying was popularized by President Theodore Roosevelt (1858–1919) in 1901.

1901. There is a homely old adage which runs: "Speak softly and carry a big stick; you will go far." If the American nation will speak softly and yet build and keep a pitch of the highest training a thoroughly efficient navy, the Monroe Doctrine will go far. —Theodore Roosevelt, *Speech at the Minnesota State Fair*

1967. Robert D. Novak, then a reporter for the *Wall Street Journal* though himself politically left of center, wrote that as Attorney General Bobby [Kennedy] might well be an "unqualified disaster," not only because of the implications of nepotism or the brotherly link with the President but for his "aggressive, sometimes abrasive personality" and his "policy of speaking loudly and carrying a big stick." —Ralph de Toledano, *R.F.K.*

1986. It is probably fair to conclude that in modern times no one has used the "bully pulpit" more dramatically than Ronald Reagan. But Reagan has actually reversed Teddy Roosevelt's injunction to "speak softly and carry a big stick"—and who can argue with speaking loudly, if mere rhetoric gets the job done without having to use the stick? —*New York*

1989. "I'll tell you one thing," Nixon continued. "I played a little poker when I was in the Navy ... I learned this—when a guy didn't have the card, he talked awfully big. But when he had the cards, he just sat there—had that cold look in his eyes. Now,

we've got the cards ... What we've got to do is walk softly and carry a big stick." —Stephen E. Ambrose, *Nixon*

1991. SPEAK SOFTLY AND CARRY A BIG HATCHET —Headline of article dealing with New York City fiscal crisis, *Time*

1994. "He is using the courtroom as a bully pulpit, even when he doesn't necessarily have the authority to make good on the threats ... You might say Judge Ito has talked loudly but carried a little stick." —*New York Times*

Speak well of the dead. *See* NEVER SPEAK ILL OF THE DEAD.

Speech is silver, silence is golden. Speech is good but silence is better. The proverb appeared in the book, *Sartor Resartus* (1834) by Thomas Carlyle (1795–1881). First cited in the United States in *Biglow Papers* (1848) by James Russell Lowell (1819–91).

1834. As the Swiss inscription says: *Sprechen ist silbern, Schweigen ist golden* —"Speech is silvern, Silence is golden"; or, as I might rather express it, speech is of time, silence is of eternity. —Thomas Carlyle, *Sartor Resartus*

1986. "When my wife speaks it's like sterling silver, but, when she stops, it's like 24-karat gold." —Overheard at a barber shop
See also SILENCE IS GOLDEN.

The spirit is willing but the flesh is weak. Even though one's spirit might be willing to resist temptation, one's body may be unable to resist. The proverb appears in the Bible and it has been traced back to 1608. It was first cited in the United States in the 1816 *Life of Elias Smith.*

Watch and pray, that ye enter not into temptation: the spirit indeed *is* willing, but the flesh *is* weak. —Matt. 26:41, *Authorized Version*, 1611

1579. The delights of your flesh are preferred before the holiness of the spirit. —John Lyly, *Euphues*

1938. Since then I have written many other books; and though ceasing my methodical study of the old masters (for though the spirit is willing, the flesh is weak), I have continued with increasing assiduity to try to write better. —W. Somerset Maugham, *The Summing Up*

1994. The spirit is willing, but the spinal column is still weak. —*New York Times*

A/The squeaky wheel gets all the grease. *See*

THE WHEEL THAT DOES THE SQUEAKING IS THE ONE THAT GETS THE GREASE.

Stand on your own two feet. Be independent. The proverb has been traced back to 1582, and is first attested in the United States in 1791 (used by Thomas Jefferson and quoted in the *Works of John Adams*).

1936. "I want to stand on my own feet for what I'm worth...."
"But I'm offering you a half-interest in the mill, Ashley! You would be standing on your own feet because—you see, it would be your own business." —Margaret Mitchell, *Gone With the Wind*

1992. I love my mother too, but the most she wants for me is to be able to stand on my own two feet. —*People*

1993. Today's children are self-disciplined, kind and efficient. Even as tots, they will want to stand on their own two feet. —Jeane Dixon, "Horoscope"

1994. Voices have recently been heard in our political arena saying we should do away with the organizations raising money in the Diaspora for Israel.... "Who needs it?" they say. "We can and should stand on our own two feet." —*MetroWest Jewish News*

Stand up and be counted. Make one's position publicly known. This saying originated in the United States at the turn of the twentieth century and has been widely used since the 1920s.

1980. I'm not a weak man. I've never been a punk, I've never been a rat, I've always fought—I ain't the toughest son of a bitch around but I've always stood up and been counted among the men. —Norman Mailer, *The Executioner's Song*

1988. For every black who voted for him [Jesse Jackson], three whites were willing to stand up publicly and be counted in his support. —*New York Times*

1988. Israel today is a nation under siege—by Palestinian Arabs, by a hostile press, by hypocrite governments.... It is time for American friends of the Jewish state to stand up and be counted, to assert proudly our identification with her government and her cause.... —*New York Times*

1991. Daniel C. Bachmann, a lawyer who has known Judge Kelly for nearly 40 years, said, "Pat is something of a maverick." ... "He's a man who's willing to stand up and be counted," Mr. Bachmann said. —*New York Times*

1993. Your love of research and good books comes in handy today. A passive approach will no longer

do where family matters are concerned. Stand up and be counted. —Jeane Dixon, "Horoscope"

Stay tuned. Wait for further events or information. The saying originated on radio and TV and was used only before commercials. Now often used figuratively.***

1992. 'YES' TO ONE CANADA? IF JAYS WIN THE SERIES, STAY TUNED. —Headline, *New York Times*

1993. The city of Los Angeles (population 3,433,600) recently outlawed smoking in public restaurants, but the restaurateurs were able to overturn that ruling.... Stay tuned—the battle is not over yet. —Abigail Van Buren, "Dear Abby," *Times* (Trenton)

1994. All in all, the drama over whether the question will go to the voters in May turned out to be much more compelling than the substance of the charter. And perhaps that was part of the problem.... So stay tuned. And prepare to study the charter all summer long. —*Philadelphia Inquirer*
See also IT'S NOT OVER TILL IT'S OVER.

Step on a crack, break your mother's back. Stepping on a crack in the sidewalk will bring bad luck.

1992. "Watch your step, sweetie. Remember the old adage, 'Step on a crack, break your mother's back.'" —Overheard on Broadway

1993. Avoid stepping on a crack for fear of breaking my mother's back. —*Times* (Trenton)

Step up to the plate. Face a task or responsibility with courage. This American phrase is of recent origin and comes from baseball. It alludes to home plate, where a batter stands to face the pitcher.

1995. The events in Russia and Israel, the Bosnia negotiations, a potential "train wreck" with Congress over the budget, and the electoral season starting in the US prove that now, more than ever, the president needs a commanding secretary of state. It is time for Secretary of State Warren Christopher to step up to the plate. —*Christian Science Monitor*

1997. The man who's running the funny-money hearings yesterday challenged President Clinton to "step up to the plate" and explain a pattern of White House stonewalling. —*New York Post*

1997. In every instance, I served only because I cared enough to step up to the plate and accept responsibility. My only goal was to contribute to the well-being of my community and the betterment thereof. —*Sun-Sentinel* (South Florida)

1998. Peter says some women are still having problems balancing work and family. For them the problem is twofold. "Men don't step up to the plate and take over child-care issues, and women are reluctant to pass on the power." —*Detroit News*

1998. I want to know why Saudi Arabia has taken the position of not allowing our planes to take off from bases in their kingdom in possible actions again Saddam. Kudos to the tiny nation of Bahrain for stepping up to the plate. —*New York Daily News*

See also GET YOUR ACT TOGETHER.

Stick to your guns. Hold to your convictions and rights. The proverb has been traced back to the *Life of Samuel Johnson* by James Boswell (1740–95). It was first attested in the United States in *Seven Keys to Baldpate* (1913) by Earl Derr Biggers (1884–1933).

1769–91.
Mrs. Thrale stood to her gun with great courage in defense of amorous ditties. —James Boswell, *Life of Samuel Johnson*

1913. Stick to your guns. —Earl Derr Biggers, *Seven Keys to Baldpate*

1922. He, B, enjoyed the distinction of being close to Erin's uncrowned king in the flesh when the thing occurred on the historic fracas when the fallen leader's, who notoriously stuck to his guns to the last drop … —James Joyce, *Ulysses*

1986. "At one point in history," Mr. Mathews said, "this guy [Jim Wright] had the nerve to go for it, and he won. He took on the big guys. And the essence of leadership is courage, the ability to stick to your guns." —*New York Times*

1988. Dear Puzzled: I would stick to my guns and not be maneuvered into calling the ex-husband and asking him to return the table. —Abigail Van Buren, "Dear Abby"

1991. Mr. Whipple, now head of an association of former intelligence officers, said that several times he asked Mr. Gates for advice on how to deal with the situation, and was told "Stick to your guns." —*New York Times*

1993. Since the U.S. Senate is considered safe for the pro-NAFTA folks the lower chamber's decision is key. I predicted a NAFTA win two months back—I'll stick to my guns. —*Times* (Trenton)

1994. MAYOR STICKS TO GUNS ON TAXES, PRIVATIZATION —*Crain's New York Business*

Sticks and stones may break my bones, but words (names) will never hurt me. Although a physical attack may harm me, I am not bothered by cruel words or name-calling. I don't care what you're saying. This children's taunt was first listed in *Folk Phrases of Four Counties* (1894) by G. F. Northall, and is first attested in the United States in *Miss Linsey* (1936) by S. G. Gibbons. The proverb is found in varying forms: *Sticks and stones may break my bones, but hard words cannot hurt me; Sticks and stones may break my bones, but words can never hurt me; Sticks and stones will break my bones, but lies will never hurt me,* etc.

1894. Sticks and stones will break my bones, but names will never hurt me! Said by one youngster to another calling names. —G. F. Northall, *Folk Phrases in Four Counties*

1936. Sticks and stones may break my bones, but hard words cannot hurt me. —S. G. Gibbons, *Miss Linsey*

1987. "So he curses," Richard Calloway said. "Kids curse, too. My grandmother had a saying: 'Sticks and stones may break my bones, but names will never hurt me.'" —*New York Times*

1988. The old children's taunt goes, "Sticks and stones may break my bones, but words can never hurt me." It applies to Israel, the other way around. It has been the words, and the pictures, of young Palestinians defying the Israeli Army after 20 years of occupation, with no end in sight, that are bringing the region to a new sense of urgent crisis. —*New York Times*

1989. We don't mind name-calling. They [Iran] keep calling us the great Satan, and that doesn't bother us. Sticks and stones—remember the old adage—will hurt our bones…. But performance is what we're looking for. And I don't see so far any sign of change. —*USA Today*

1992. My mother used to tell me, "Sticks and stones may break your bones, but names will never hurt you." —"ABC Talk Show"

1993. A rule as old as childhood has been amended: "Sticks and stones will break my bones, but names will never harm me." Maybe not. But nowadays it can break the back of the person who used the name. —*Times* (Trenton)

Still waters run deep. Don't be fooled by appearances. Quiet people are likely to be passionate or complex, even though they don't show it. The proverb has been traced back to *Cato's Morals* (about 1400) in *Cursor Mundi* (1873). In 1721, it was included in James Kelly's collection of proverbs. It was first cited in the United States in the 1768 *Works of William Smith* (1803). *Smooth waters run deep* is a variant. The proverb has counterparts in other languages: *L'eau qui dort est pire que celle qui court* (French), *Del agua mansa me libre Dios, que de la brava me libro yo* (Spanish); *Stille Wasser sind tief* (German), etc.

1590–91.
> *Suffolk:* Smooth runs the water where the brook is deep,
> And in his simple show he harbours treason.
> The fox barks not when he would steal the lamb;
> No, no, my sov'reign; Gloucester is a man
> Unsounded yet, and full of deep deceit.
> —Shakespeare, *King Henry the Sixth, Part II*, Act III, Scene I

1982. Within an hour, everyone in Klipdrift had heard the news. How Ian Travis was really Jamie McGregor, and how he had gotten Van der Merwe's daughter pregnant. Margaret Van der Merwe had fooled the whole town.
"She doesn't look like the kind, does she?"
"Still waters run deep, they say." —Sidney Sheldon, *Master of the Game*

1992. Walt [Kramarz] is a member of Holy Cross of Trenton. He is a grad of the long-gone Trenton Catholic High School. Just the mention of that drew one of Walt's rare laughs and broad smiles. He is the quiet river that runs deep. —*Times* (Trenton)
See also BARKING DOGS NEVER BITE.

A stitch in time saves nine. If you deal with problems immediately, when they first appear, you will save yourself a lot of money and trouble later. This adage is listed in the 1732 Thomas Fuller's book of proverbs, and was first cited in the United States in the 1797 *Journal of Tour of North America in 1796–1791* by Francis Baily (1774–1844). The word *nine* was probably introduced for assonance.

1980. Though despondent, my wife continued the futile search for two months. Throughout her ordeal [house-hunting] I remained cheerful—since *I* was not looking. During the weekends, to raise her spirits, I said such things as, "Keep up the good work! All of your efforts will eventually pay off," and "A stitch in time saves nine!" —Herb Cohen, *You Can Negotiate Anything*

1989. "They're my friends and they aren't spies."
"Fraternization looks bad on the old report card. Loose lips sink ships."
"And a stitch in time saves nine," Craig answered. —Wayne Care, *Vietnam Spook Show*

1993. A STITCH IN TIME —Headline of an article about a large quilt that was raffled off to raise funds for protection of the Amazon rain forest, *Times* (Trenton)

1993. Preventive medicine, said Ted Kennedy, "is the stitch in time that can save billions." —*The New York Times*
See also AN OUNCE OF PREVENTION IS WORTH A POUND OF CURE.

Stolen waters are sweet. What is forbidden is always the best. Of Biblical origin. The proverb has been traced back in English to 1548. In 1721, it was included in James Kelly's collection of proverbs, and is first attested in the United States in about 1700 (*General History of New England* by Hubbard).

> Stolen waters are sweet, and bread *eaten* in secret is pleasant. —Prov. 9:17, *Authorized Version*, 1611

1984. She was dead right about premarital studio, though, as a love nest for our secret, immoral meetings. Stolen waters are sweet, and bread eaten in secret is pleasant, as I frequently remarked to her. —Joseph Heller, *God Knows*
See also FORBIDDEN FRUIT IS SWEET.

Stone walls do not a prison make. Although our bodies may be imprisoned, our spirits and minds cannot be contained by walls. The line is from Richard Lovelace (1618–58) in his famous 1649 poem, "To Althea, from Prison." William Wordsworth (1770–1850) said that "stone walls a prisoner make, but not a slave."

1649.
> Stone walls do not a prison make,
> Nor iron bars a cage;
> Minds innocent and quiet take
> That for an hermitage.
> —Richard Lovelace, "To Althea, from Prison"

1989. "The Berlin wall has crumbled down. The Kremlin walls are next on the line. Remember the saying that stone walls do not a prison make, nor iron bars a cage?" —Overheard at a newspaper stand

The storm before the calm. *See* AFTER A STORM COMES A CALM.

Strike while the iron is hot. Don't delay; act

immediately when the time is right. The proverb has been traced back in English to about 1386 in Chaucer's *Tale of Melibee*, but the idea was expressed as early as the first century b.c. Publilius Syrus's maxim 262 read: "You should hammer your iron when it is glowing hot." Rabelais wrote in *Gargantua and Pantagruel* (1534): "Strike while the iron is hot." In 1546, John Heywood included it in his collection of proverbs, and it is first attested in the United States in the 1682 *James Claypoole's Letter Book* (1967). The proverb has its counterpart in other languages: *Il faut battre le fer pendant qu'il est chaud* (French); *Batir el bierro cuando está al rojo* (Spanish, "Strike while the iron is red"); *Das Eisen schmieden, so lange es heiß ist* (German); Куй железо, пока горячо (Russian), etc.

> **1984.** There was no time to lose. Europe was wide open. Asia too. Now that we had iron, he argued, we should strike while it was hot. —Joseph Heller, *God Knows*
>
> **1987.** The idea wasn't to strike while the iron was hot to coin a cliché. It just happened that the playwright August Wilson and the director Lloyd Richards, two of the men responsible for the current Broadway hit "Fences," had another one in the wings. —*New York Times*
>
> **1988.** "I figured I should strike while the iron is hot," he said. "I just wrote a book, and I'd like to write another." —*New York Times*
>
> **1994.** A short trip lifts your spirits or romantic hopes. Business matters progress smoothly. Strike while the iron is hot. —Jeane Dixon, "Horoscope"
> *See also* MAKE HAY WHILE THE SUN SHINES.

Success breeds success. People who are successful find it easy to repeat their success. The proverb originated in the United States in the 1927 book, *Mosaic*, by N. Martin, and is found in varying forms: *Success begets success; Success creates success; Success makes success as money makes money*, etc.

> **1927.** Success begets success. —N. Martin, *Mosaic*
>
> **1967.** It has always been evident that success creates success. —J. Richardson, *Courtesans*
>
> **1993.** "Success generally breeds success, and this is really helping the South," Mr. Schwab said. —*New York Times*
> *See also* NOTHING SUCCEEDS LIKE SUCCESS; SUCCESS IS NEVER FINAL; VICTORY HAS A HUNDRED FATHERS AND DEFEAT IS AN ORPHAN.

Success has many parents. *See* VICTORY HAS A HUNDRED FATHERS AND DEFEAT IS AN ORPHAN.

Success is never final. Success must be followed by hard work. You can't give up once you've made it. The proverb originated in the United States. The complete variant of the proverb is *Success is never final and failure is never fatal*.

> **1990.** She has an aphorism she keeps on her desk: "Success is never final and failure is never fatal." It's something she believes in: "Success is an ongoing thing. I know I'm in a volatile business. If I go broke, I'll do it elegantly and go into something else. If I fail, it's okay. I can live with it. I can always find other places to put my energy. I'm comfortable with who I am." —Carole Hyatt, *Shifting Gears*
>
> **1993.** "People often judge other people by success. They forget that success is never final." —Overheard at a conference
> *See also* IF AT FIRST YOU DON'T SUCCEED, TRY, TRY AGAIN; NOTHING SUCCEEDS LIKE SUCCESS; VICTORY HAS A HUNDRED FATHERS AND DEFEAT IS AN ORPHAN.

The sun never sets on the British Empire. The British Empire spans such a large area that the sun will always be shining on some part of it. The idea of this proverb was expressed in the seventeenth century, in varying forms.

> **1631.** Why should the brave Spanish soldier brag the sun never sets in the Spanish dominions, but ever shineth on one part or other we have conquered for our king? —John Smith, *Advertisements for the Unexperienced*
>
> **1648.** It may be said of them [the Hollanders] as of the Spaniards, that the sun never sets on their dominions. —Thomas Gage, *New Survey of the West Indies*
>
> **1786.** The richest monarch in the Christian world;
> The sun in my own dominions never sets.
> —Johann von Schiller, *Don Carlos*, Act I, Scene I
>
> **1827.** The sun never sets on the immense empire of Charles V. —Walter Scott, *Life of Napoleon*
>
> **1829.** His Majesty's dominions, on which the sun never sets. —John Wilson, *Noctes Ambrosianae*
>
> **1993.** Notably missing from these pages is any serious discussion of Disraeli's role in foreign policy, though these are the years when the sun never set on the British empire. —*Wall Street Journal*
>
> **1993.** COULD THE SUN EVER SET ON THE BBC? —Headline, *New York Times*

A swan song. The final performance of an actor, singer, composer, poet, etc. According to folklore, swans sing most beautifully before they die. The phrase is of ancient origin and is found in the works of Plato, Aristotle, Euripides, Cicero, etc. It was used by Shakespeare in several plays.

1604–05.
> *Emilia:* What did thy song bode, lady?
> Hark, canst thou hear me? I will play the swan,
> And die in music.
> —Shakespeare, *Othello,* Act V, Scene II

1712. Thus on Meander's flowery margin lies
Th' expiring swan, and as he sings he dies.
—Alexander Pope, *The Rape of the Lock*

1909. I know that it is my swan song. I am almighty proud of it. —Jack London, *Martin Eden*

1922. Explain the swan-song too wherein he has commended her to posterity. —James Joyce, *Ulysses*

1991. He [Gorbachev] bitterly attacked the idea of a commonwealth, and, in what sounded suspiciously like a swan song, sought to defend his record. —*Wall Street Journal*

1994. The building is not exactly a fitting swan song for Sir James, whose masterpiece with Mr. Wilford was the sinuous Neue Staatsgalerie in Stuttgart; the caliber of workmanship at the Irvine library is not high enough. —*Wall Street Journal*

The sword of Damocles hanging over one. This expression is used when one has a foreboding that some disaster is impending. According to a Greek legend, Damocles, a nobleman, often expressed his admiration of the grandeur and happiness of the king. The king decided to put an end to his flattery and invited Damocles to a banquet. Damocles enjoyed the delights of the table until he saw a sword hanging over his head suspended by a single hair. The sword was supposed to show Damocles that kingship is not all riches and pleasures but impending danger as well.

1984. These [14.4 million] warrants were a sword hanging over our head. —Lee Iacocca with William Novak, *Iacocca*

1988. "Everything would be great if I didn't have to take organic chemistry but I want to get the damn thing out of the way so it won't hang over me like the Sword of Damocles." —Erich Segal, *Doctors*

1992. I just celebrated my sixty-ninth birthday and my husband will be 72 in July. We think of cancer as a sword of Damocles hanging over us. —*New York*

1994. Worst of all, the possibility of their own job being eliminated hangs over the office like the sword of Damocles. —*Princeton Business Journal*

The tail cannot shake the dog. This adage asserts the rightness of social hierarchies: the minority can't take control of the majority; the subordinate can't boss the boss around. The positive variant, *The tail is wagging the dog,* is often found. English poet Rudyard Kipling (1865–1936) used a variant in *The Conundrum of the Workshops* (1892). First cited in the United States in the 1959 mystery book, *Murder of Estelle Cantor* by C. F. Gregg.

> **1892.** We know that the tail must wag the dog, for
> the horse is drawn by the cart;
> But the Devil whoops, as he whooped of
> old: 'It's clever, but is it Art?'
> —Rudyard Kipling, *The Conundrum of the
> Workshops*

1936. The tail was beginning to wag the dog. —C. F. Gregg, *Murder of Estelle Cantor*

1959. The wags were tailing the top dog. —*Time*

1991. Gone also are most of the old, odd power relationships. No longer will tails wag dogs. —*New York Times Magazine*

1994. Although the merger has the blessing of federal antitrust officials, smaller local travel agencies already fear that an engorged AmEx will be able to hammer out deals with airlines, hotels and rental car companies that no small agency can match.... When you get that big, the tail is wagging the dog," says Harold Stevens, owner of Stevens Travel Management in Manhattan. —*Crain's New York Business*

See also DON'T (TRY TO) TEACH YOUR GRANDMOTHER (HOW) TO SUCK EGGS.

Take it easy. Relax, calm down. Goodbye and be careful. Often used as a simple farewell. A very frequent phrase in America, it originated in the United States in the years following the 1929 Great Depression.

1962. "So long, Peale."
"Take it easy, Peale."
"Good luck, Peale." —James Jones, *The Thin Red Line*

1963. "Take it easy, honey, take it easy," the Lieutenant suggested, rather nervously. —J. D. Salinger, *Raise High the Roof Beam, Carpenters*

1975. "Take it easy. Calm down," Russell Hayes said. "I know she's a wonderful girl, but if it's not to be, it's not to be." —Jackie Collins, *The World Is Full of Divorced Women*

1988. "Livingston, is that you?" he asked in a tone that sounded as if each syllable was painful.
"Yeah, yeah, just take it easy, Maury. You're gonna be all right." —Erich Segal, *Doctors*

1991. "Take it easy," Mr. Tracy said as photographers swarmed toward him when he appeared in the Syrian Foreign Ministry, the bright lights and flashes of their cameras appearing to throw him off balance. —*New York Times*

1992. "I promised secrecy. If I'm not sure I can deliver, I'm calling the whole thing off."
"Hey, take it easy." —Philip Friedman, *Inadmissible Evidence*

1993. "Take it easy, O'Brian," [Officer] Keenan said. "I'm not here to arrest you." —*New York Times Book Review*

See also EASY DOES IT.

Take it from me. Trust me when I tell you this. Believe what I am saying. The saying originated in the United States and dates back to the seventeenth century. It has been used in Britain since 1910. In *The Unprofitable Servant,* O. Henry (1862–1910) wrote: "Take it from me—he's got the goods."

1951. "You're a woman," Warden said, looking at her in the thin kimono. "All woman. Take it from me." —James Jones, *From Here to Eternity*

1978. "You're not responsible for Harold Lauder's actions, keed." He took her hand in both of his and held it tightly. He looked at her. "Take it from me, the original dipstick, ostrich, and drippy dick. You can't hold it against yourself." —Stephen King, *The Stand*

1981. "Maybe I can help you. You gotta approach Stateside with a lot of clout. You gotta come in with balls. Know what I mean?"

"Well, when they see Muffin ..."

"Not enough, take it from me, I should know." —Jackie Collins, *The World Is Full of Divorced Women*

1985. "Age stinks. Take it from me." —Michael Korda, *Queenie*

1988. "Can you help me?"

"Only if you feel genuinely strong enough to survive rejection, Laura. Take it from me, it's maddening to see the boy who sat next to you in Chem or Bio—whom you practically tutored so he could scrape by with *a B*—get accepted by the Med School, while you and *your A* still aren't deemed good enough to go there at all." —Erich Segal, *Doctors*

See also TAKE MY WORD FOR IT; I CANNOT TELL A LIE.

Take it or leave it. I've made you the best offer I can. You can accept it as is or forget the whole deal. The saying has been traced back to 1576. It was typically used by salesmen when buyers did not accept their best prices. *Take-it-or-leave-it* is sometimes used in a sentence as an attributive.

1939. We got to get a tire, but, Jesus, they want a lot for a ol'tire. They look a fella over. They know he got to go on. They know he can't wait. And the price goes up.

Take it or leave it. I ain't in business for my health. —John Steinbeck, *The Grapes of Wrath*

1951. *Nick:* This is your day, Nina. But pass up the chance to play it too hard, will you? Take me or leave me now but don't—. —Lillian Hellman, *The Autumn Garden*

1953. *Kilroy:* Yep, I'm a sucker that won the golden gloves!

Loan Shark: Congratulations. My final offer is a piece of green paper with Alexander Hamilton's picture on it. Take it or leave it. —Tennessee Williams, *Camino Real*

1961. "You'll agree to it because it will send you home safe and sound in two weeks, and because

you have no choice. It's that or a court-martial. Take it or leave it." —Joseph Heller, *Catch-22*

1979. "We need three thousand dollars to cover us. I'll give you a hundred and seven thousand dollars, take it or leave it." —Howard Fast, *The Establishment*

1983. "Take it or leave it," Oliver had said, enjoying every minute. "But remember—if you take it I don't expect any trouble from you. I'm in charge—the asshole rules. Okay?" —Jackie Collins, *Hollywood Wives*

1987. "Um. Mr. Dupis, my client would like to talk to you personally."

"Dupis? Harris here! This isn't an Arab bazaar, mon ami! All I've got is $17 mil cash! Take it or leave it!" —G. B. Trudeau, *Doonesbury Deluxe*

1989. He sighed, "I'll take the $100,000 you offered me before Gino came round."

She refused. Sixty thousand, take it or leave it. —Clifford Irving, *The Campbell Murder Case*

1991. Bill Coats, an Atlanta real-estate developer, complains that Delta's service has become more mechanical, less personal. "Perhaps it was my perception," he says, "but there's a 'take it or leave it' [attitude]. Delta didn't used to be that way. —*Wall Street Journal*

1992. When he [Ross Perot] announced his willingness to serve, on the cable television program "Larry King Live," five months ago, that was all he offered to voters—himself—in a take-it-or-leave-it shot: "If voters in all 50 states put me on the ballot—not 48 or 49 states, but all 50—I will agree to run." —*New York Times*

1993. "We're willing to pay $700,000 ... for some guy to come in and be a backup to Randall. That's it. 'Take it, or leave it.' " —*Times* (Trenton)

1994. "For the first time, if the tenant says, 'Here's my last offer, take it or leave it,' we often leave it. We're passing on deals." —*Crain's New York Business*

Take my wife—please! Take my dearest possession—Really, I'd be delighted to be rid of her! This expression originated in the United States and is associated with the American comedian Henny Youngman (1906–). The joke is that *take* initially seems to mean "consider." Variants can substitute other words for *wife*.

1984. Murray was also a great storyteller. He got most of his material from his brother-in-law, who happened to be Henny Youngman. One time he brought Henny down from New York to address a sales rally at the Broadwood Hotel in Philadelphia. Henny warmed up the crowd, and then I introduced the new cars. It was the first time I ever heard those famous words: "Take my wife—please!" —Lee Iacocca with William Novak, *Iacocca*

1987. Henny Youngman was another of the entertainers. "I just arrived from Bloomingdale's," Mr. Youngman told the crowd. "I visit my wife there twice a week. Take my wife, please." —*New York Times*

1992. [Woody] Allen's gags and situations no longer betray even a trace of delight at the absurdities of human behavior; his bemused vision of romantic folly has turned, over the years, into a bilious take-my-wife-please routine. —*New Yorker*

1993. Take Jesse Helms; as Henny Youngman would say, "Please." —*Times* (Trenton)

1994. TAKE MY BUSINESS, PLEASE. —Headline, *U.S.1* (Princeton)

Take my word for it. You don't need to check to find out whether what I say is true. You can trust me. Accept my word as a guarantee of truth. *You take my word for it* is also used.

1953. "Houses have *always* been fireproof, take my word for it." —Ray Bradbury, *Fahrenheit 451*

1961. The chaplain's smile was embarrassed. "I'm afraid I couldn't say. I don't think I know him that well."

"You can take my word for it," Yossarian said. "He's as goofy as they come." —Joseph Heller, *Catch-22*

1962. "You take my word for it. That's a money review." —Herman Wouk, *Youngblood Hawke*

1974. "LaRue, Porter and Magruder. They all knew about the bugging, or at least lied to the grand jury about what they knew. And Mitchell. But Mitchell is mostly speculation. Take my word on the other three. I know." —Carl Bernstein & Bob Woodward, *All the President's Men*

1979. "This is the arrest order," he said, offering her a folded document.

"I'll take your word for it." —Howard Fast, *The Establishment*

1984. *Mr. Iacocca:* "Congressman, I couldn't convince you. You will have to take my word for it." —Lee Iacocca with William Novak, *Iacocca*

1988. Surrounded by her children, Columba Bush [President Bush's daughter-in-law] says this election may be the most important ever for Hispanic voters "to elect a President who cares about strong family values. But don't take my word for it," she says. "Ask my father-in-law." —*New York Times*

1989. "If you don't mind, however, pick a pew at the rear of the church. There's no point in pushing Grandmother too far. Take my word for it." —Michael Korda, *The Fortune*

1993. "We permanently raised the standards for policy analysis," he claims. "Before McNamara, people could argue on the basis of the loosest generalities and use the method of authority: 'I fought World War II—take my word for it.'" —*New York Times Magazine*

See also I CANNOT TELL A LIE; TAKE IT FROM ME.

Take the bitter with the sweet. *See* YOU HAVE TO TAKE THE BITTER WITH THE SWEET.

Take the good with the bad. *See* YOU HAVE TO TAKE THE GOOD WITH THE BAD.

Talk is cheap. You can talk all you want to. It's what you *do* that matters. This adage was first used in the United States in 1843–44 in *The Attaché, or Sam Slick in England* by Thomas Chandler Haliburton (1796–1865). *Talk is cheap, but it takes money to buy land (liquor, whiskey)* is an extended variant.

1948. Talk is pretty cheap. —Norman Mailer, *The Naked and the Dead*

1978. Life is cheap, abortion makes it cheaper. —Stephen King, *The Stand*

1989. "There are rumbles on The Hill that somebody ought to do something about the Cartel, that the attack on Jacobs was a direct attack on—"

"I watch C-SPAN, too, Bob. Talk is cheap." —Tom Clancy, *Clear and Present Danger*

1992. Talk is cheap? For some immigrants, it's priceless. —*Jewish Week* (N.Y.)

1993. Because Dallas is young and talented and hungry and knows that talk is cheap but fun—especially after you win. —*New York Times*

Talk of the devil, and he is bound to appear. The person who has been talked about secretly is likely to show up unexpectedly. The earliest appearances of the proverb in print were in *Adagia* (1500) by Erasmus (1466–1536) and in *Endimion* (1591) by John Lyly (about 1554–1606). In 1666, it appeared in G. Torriano's collection of Italian proverbs and in 1721 in James Kelly's collection of Scottish proverbs. It is first attested in the United States in 1728 in *The History of the Dividing Line Betwixt Virginia and North Carolina* by William Byrd (1674–1744). The word *speak* may substitute for *talk*. *Talk (speak) of the devil and he's sure to appear* is a variant of the proverb. *Speak of the devil!* is a shortened variant used when someone being discussed shows up unexpectedly.

1952. "I planned to keep my big mouth shut about it," said Paul.

Shepherd looked up with seeming pleasure and surprise. "Well, speak of the Devil." —Kurt Vonnegut, Jr., *Player Piano*

1962. Scott Hoag was sitting on the desk top when Hawke and his mother came in. He jumped down and strode toward them. "Hey, Art! Talk of the devil. We just been arguing whether you would really make the trip down from New York for this." —Herman Wouk, *Youngblood Hawke*

1977. "And speak of the devil, here's our chief of staff now, looking a little the worse for wear." —William Safire, *Full Disclosure*

A task that's worth doing at all is worth doing well. See ANYTHING WORTH DOING IS WORTH DOING WELL; IF A THING IS WORTH DOING, IT'S WORTH DOING TWICE.

Tastes differ. See THERE'S NO ACCOUNTING FOR TASTES.

Tell that (it) to the marines. I don't believe you. Said of a far-fetched story that lacks credibility. This saying originated as *That will do for the marines, but the sailors won't believe it.* It has been traced back to the 1800s, when marines were considered by sailors as second-rate, inexperienced men: tell the story to them and they would believe it. When Charles II was told that an officer of the Maritime Regiment of Foot had seen a flying fish, the king allegedly said, "Whenever we cast doubts upon a tale that lacks likelihood we will first 'Tell it to the Marines.'" The saying was used by Lord Byron (1823) and Sir Walter Scott (1824). The words *horse marines* may substitute for *marines (Go and tell that to the horse marines!).*

1823. "Right," quoth Ben, "that will do for marines." —George Byron, *The Island*

1824. Tell that to the marines—the sailors won't believe it. —Walter Scott, *Redgauntlet*

1977. Harry shook his head. "I was in the Navy when I was a kid, I was never in the Marines."

Hennessy's head snapped toward him: "'Tell it to the Marines.'" —William Safire, *Full Disclosure*

Tell the truth and shame the devil. Be truthful even when you have good reasons not to do so. The proverb has been traced back to 1548 (*Ex-*

pedition into Scotland by W. Patten), and Shakespeare used it in *King Henry the Fourth, Part 1* (1597–98). It was first cited in the United States in the *Diary of Elihu Hubbard Smith, 1771–1789.* The word *speak* may be used in place of *tell.*

1597–98.
> Glendower: Why, I can teach thee, cousin,
>   To commandthe devil.
> *Hotspur:* And I can teach thee, coz, to
>   shame the devil
> By telling truth: tell truth and shame the
>   devil.
> —Shakespeare, *King Henry the Fourth, Part I*, Act III, Scene I

1958. Tell the truth and shame the Devil. —*New Yorker*

1986. "Tell the truth and shame the devil," my mom used to say, but she forgot to tell me that sometimes you can't shame Mr. Splitfoot sober. —Stephen King, *It*

A tempest in a teapot. A great fuss about a trivial thing. The proverb dates back to Cicero (106–43 b.c.): *Excitabat enim fluctus in simpulo* and has been in use ever since. The proverb has its counterpart (as *A storm in a glass of water*) in other languages: *C'est la tempête dans un verre d'eau* (French); *Es una tempestad en un vaso de agua* (Spanish); Буря в стакане воды (Russian), etc.

1936. "I consider the whole affair a tempest in a teapot," said Scarlett coldly ... —Margaret Mitchell, *Gone With the Wind*

1987. One official, who said the espionage case was potentially one of the most damaging in history, cautioned: "This could all turn out to be a tempest in a teapot." —*New York Times*

1990. The Arabs' hysterical reaction to the flow of Soviet Jewish immigration to Israel, and especially their charges that the new immigrants are being settled in Judea and Samaria, is a political tempest in a teapot. —*Jewish Week* (N.Y.)

1991. FOR TRUE SAN FRANCISCANS, IT WAS MORE THAN A TEMPEST IN A TEAPOT —Headline, *Wall Street Journal*

1992. The furor over Mr. Fordice's comments was "a tempest in a teapot," said David Beckwith, a spokesman for Vice President Dan Quayle. —*New York Times*

1993. Despite a conclave yesterday between counsel for Regent and the departed dean, Mr. Titus, who remains on the payroll, could still sue.... "Though it's a tempest in a teapot, it's a mighty big teapot," said his lawyer, Donald Lemons of Richmond. —*New York Times*

1994. Public men frequently give themselves away in small things and Ramon Cortines is no different. When he arrived in New York as the new schools chancellor he announced that the Rainbow Curriculum was merely a "tempest in a teacup." —*New York Post*

See also MUCH ADO ABOUT NOTHING.

TGIF. *See* THANK GOD IT'S FRIDAY.

Thank God It's Friday. I've survived another work week. It's almost over. Typically said by working people on Friday afternoon before the weekend begins. This saying is often abbreviated to TGIF, and each letter is pronounced separately.

1970. There is a vast world of work out there in this country, where at least 111 million people are employed in this country alone—*many of whom* are bored out of their minds. All day long. Not for nothing is their motto TGIF—"Thank God It's Friday." They *live* for the weekends, when they can go do what they really want to do. —Richard Nelson Bolles, *What Color Is Your Parachute?*

1978. *Thank God It's Friday* —Movie title

1989. "Today is Friday," Grimm continued. "TGIF, right?" —Michael Korda, *The Fortune*

1994. Thank God It's Thursday. At many restaurants and clubs, especially in New York, Thursday night has become the big social night of the week. —*New York Times*

Thanks, but no thanks. I'm not interested, but thank you anyway. This expression is used as a refusal, often with an ironic connotation. It originated in the United States in the 1950s.

1988. Senator Alfonse M. D'Amato said yesterday that he would not be part of any Republican effort to form a fusion coalition against Mayor Koch.... "Thanks, but no thanks," said the Senator, who questioned the appropriateness of his involvement in such political maneuvering. —*New York Times*

1993. Nike, Thanks but No Thanks. While dozens of the nation's top high school basketball players may have compromised their eligibility by playing in an all-star tournament in Oregon this month, it appears that the three players from New York City may not suffer serious consequences if they return a gift they received. —*New York Times*

1994. In both cases, however, executives of the two firms found the deals highly resistible and both replied with a firm, "Thanks but no thanks." —*Manhattan Jewish Sentinel*

That doesn't ring a bell. That doesn't sound familiar. The metaphor originated at the beginning of the twentieth century and alludes to a school bell that reminds students that the break is over and it's time to go to class. The phrase is used in a variety of forms, including the positive *to ring a bell,* meaning "to sound familiar."

1977. "I'd like to see Mr. Luciano," I said. "How do I get in touch with him?"

"Luciano? Luciano?" said Mr. Raimondo. "The name rings a bell. Now where would I have heard it before?" —Art Buchwald, *Down the Seine and up the Potomac with Art Buchwald*

1985. Mr. Adams was asked about Decree 50, a Salvadoran order that suspends Constitutional guarantees. Anyone who cares about human rights in that country knows about Decree 50, and Mr. Abrams used to be Assistant Secretary for Human Rights. He answered: "It doesn't ring a bell." —*New York Times*

1992. If John Doyle's name doesn't ring a bell with a lot of Memphians, his voice probably will. For more than 20 years, Doyle has worked part-time as an announcer for the Audichron time and temperature service. —*Commercial Appeal* (Memphis, Tennessee)

That government is best which governs least. This saying is one of the basic tenets of the Republican Party. It originated in the mid–1840s and is usually attributed to our third president, Thomas Jefferson (1743–1826), although its original author, according to Ralph Keyes, was probably John Louis O'Sullivan, diplomat and editor of *The United States Magazine and Democratic Review.*

1987. It was Thomas Jefferson who said that the government is best which governs least.... —William F. Buckley, Jr. *Daily News* (N.Y.)

1992. [Arthur] Friedman, a former town chairman and congressional hopeful, resigned from the party after the convention last summer endorsed planks on issues like abortion that mandated government intrusion into private decisions: "To me, that's not Republicanism. To me, Republicanism was, 'Government is best that governs least.'" —*U.S. News & World Report*

1993. Do the American people really disapprove of big government? Rhetorically, yes; we are all theoretical Jeffersonians—"that government is best which governs least." —*The Times* (Trenton)

See also GOVERNMENT OF THE PEOPLE, BY THE PEOPLE, AND FOR THE PEOPLE.

That's a horse of a different color. That's quite a different matter. The saying appears in Shakespeare's *Twelfth-Night* (1601–02). *It's* can be used instead of *that's* and *another* in place of *different*.

1601–1602.
Maria: My purpose is, indeed, a horse of that color. —Shakespeare, *Twelfth-Night; Or, What You Will*, Act II, Scene III

1867. "What did you think of his wife: That's a horse of another color altogether." —Anthony Trollope, *Last Chronicles of Barset*

1922. ... It's a horse of quite another colour to say you believe in the existence of a supernatural God. —James Joyce, *Ulysses*

1991. The American League West teams are on a much shorter track now, and, to their lessening surprise, they are chasing a horse of a different color. —*New York Times*

That's all there is to it. That's final; there is nothing more to say. This American phrase has been traced back to 1904: "That's all there is, there isn't any more." This "signature curtain line" was added by Ethel Barrymore (1879–1959), famous American actress, to Thomas Raceward's play, *Sunday* (1904). *That's all there is—there is no more* and *That's all there is* are variants of the saying.

1934. "That is useless. Nicole and I love each other, that's all there is to it." —F. Scott Fitzgerald, *Tender Is the Night*

1953. "I don't talk *things*, sir," said Faber. "I talk the *meaning* of things. I sit here and *know* I'm alive."

That was all there was to it, really. —Ray Bradbury, *Fahrenheit 451*

1993. Topping out is the day you look in the mirror and say to yourself, "This is all there is." The promotions have stopped. You're not going to get a better job. —*Newsweek*

1994. Somebody once asked Art Buchwald whether it was hard to keep coming up with great ideas for his humor columns. Why, not at all, he said, not in a country that sends a cake to Ayatollah Khomeini.... That's all there is to it. —*New York Times*

See also THAT'S THAT.

That's an albatross around one's neck. See IT'S AN ALBATROSS AROUND ONE'S NECK.

That's life. Life isn't fair, what happened to you isn't fair, but you need to accept it and go on. It is used to soften one's disappointment. It comes from the French *C'est la vie*, which is often used, too. *Such is life* is a variant.

1979. Clara—are you still alive? She hated me. Some people did and do. That's life. —Kurt Vonnegut, Jr., *Jailbird*

1987. "I don't pay you enough, Endicott."
"That's life. C'est la vie." —G. B. Trudeau, *Doonesbury Deluxe*

1991. On the scrubby lawns that separate the strips of apartments in the East End, children continued over the weekend to ride their bikes, chase one another and sit on stoops and talk.... "It's weird," said Ms. Butler. "They're still their friends. But this is life." —*New York Times*

1992. Some creditors have since settled for less than 100 cents on the dollar, but among those still owed is the ad agency. Says its boss, George Lois, of the $42,267 he's out: "Hey, that's life." —*Fortune*

1993. What about the lack of offensive support? ... "That's life," he [Frank Tanana] said. "You deal with it." —*Times* (Trenton)

See also THAT'S SHOW BUSINESS; THAT'S THE WAY THE COOKIE CRUMBLES.

That's music to my ears. See IT'S MUSIC TO MY EARS.

That's no skin off my nose. See IT'S NO SKIN OFF MY NOSE.

That's one small step for [a] man, one giant leap for mankind. The words of American astronaut Neil A. Armstrong making his first steps on the moon on July 20, 1969. The "a" before "man" was probably lost in transmission.

1969. That's one small step for [a] man, one giant leap for mankind. —Neil Armstrong, *New York Times*

1973. The manager reminded Trout of what the first man to set foot on the Moon had said: "One small step for man, one great leap for mankind." —Kurt Vonnegut, Jr., *Breakfast of Champions*

1993. Unconditional love is the high road of love: not easily accessible. Putting aside rigid agendas, deprogramming our critical selves, accepting our powerlessness to change anyone but ourselves, is a steep climb. Not so far as the moon, perhaps, but one great leap for womankind. —Frances Lear, *Lear's*

1994. One small step for Dow Jones, one big leap

into the on-line information age. At least so it seems. —*U.S.1* (Princeton)

That's show business. That's the way life is: unpredictable. The saying originated in show business, but is applicable to any activity. The phrase *show business* may be shortened to *show biz* or even simply *biz*.

1983. Karen always got what she wanted; it had been that way since she was a little girl. And if someone got hurt along the way, well, that's show biz—as Daddy always said. —Jackie Collins, *Hollywood Wives*

1986. This is not an insurance company, this is not a law office. This is *show-business* ... —Stephen King, *It*

1990. A cabby pulled up and yelled, "Hey, J.R., get in! I got room just for you." [Larry] Hagman hopped in and, as the cab screeched off, shouted to his mother, "That's show business!" —Quoted in *Reader's Digest*

1992. That's Show Biz? ... Some angry actors think New Line Cinema is out of line. The horrified thespians say that while the film company was shooting *Who's the Man?* in Harlem last Monday, the production crew corralled what appeared to be junkies and homeless people from the street and used them as extras, treating them "like dogs." —*New York*

1993. The cheering throngs think they're witnessing an epic battle between good and evil, while the handlers/promoters know that it's all show biz, with the news media providing the color commentary. —*New York Times Magazine*

1994. Poor baby! David Letterman should not have been shocked when Madonna socked it to him and used four-letter words on his late-night talk show [*People*, April 11].... But don't worry, Dave, it's not Karma, just show biz. —*Time*

See also THAT'S LIFE; THAT'S THE WAY THE COOKIE CRUMBLES.

That's that. That's all; that's the end of the matter. The phrase has been in common use since the early twentieth century. *And that's that* and *Well, that's that* are variants of the saying.

1936. "He's going to marry Sue and that's that." —Margaret Mitchell, *Gone With the Wind*

1943. *Mabel:* ... When I read you were getting married I thought, well, that's that. He'll just fade quietly away and I won't ever see him again. —Terence Rattigan, *While the Sun Shines*

1962. *George:* I'll hold your hand when it's dark

and you're afraid of the bogey man ... but I will not light your cigarette. And that, as they say, is that. —Edward Albee, *Who's Afraid of Virginia Woolf?*

1984. Remember what breakfast used to be like? You didn't have much of a choice. You simply ate some bacon and eggs and toast with cereal on the side, and that was pretty much that. —*Metropolitan Home*

See also THAT'S ALL THERE IS TO IT.

That's the $64,000 question. That's the most difficult question. The saying originated in the United States in the 1940s. In 1941, a contestant on the CBS *Take It or Leave It* TV quiz show who answered a question could take a small prize, or leave it to bet double-or-nothing on another question. $64,000 was the top prize for the most difficult question. "In the 1950s," wrote *The New York Times Magazine*, "$64,000 was an incredibly generous prize for a TV game show, and 'The $64,000 Question' became a national phenomenon. Audiences loved watching ordinary people answering question to win huge sums." Dr. Joyce Brothers, psychologist and media personality, won the top prize in 1957.

1992. Why did Milken do it? The first book to answer the billion dollar question. —Ad for *Highly Confident* by Jesse Kornbluth, *New York Times Book Review*

1993. The contention that the federal mechanism would be self-funded also bears close scrutiny, according to Synder.... "That's the $64 question," he said. "All these things always look good on paper." —*Times* (Trenton)

1994. The $64 question is whether the Israeli-Jordanian love-fest on the White House lawn, and subsequent developments between Rabin and Hussein, will tempt the lion of Damascus out of his lair, or whether he will feel wounded and retreat still further into dangerous isolation ... —*Metro-West Jewish News*

1995. THE $135,000 QUESTION —Headline of article on Ron Brown's finances that may cost him his job, *Time*

That's the name of the game. That's the most essential point of something, what it's all about. This saying originated in the United States in the early 1960s, and has been in common use since about 1965. It was popularized through the movie, *Fame is the Name of the Game* (1966) and the TV series, *The Name of the Game* (1968–71).

1962. Multiplication, that's the name of the game,

And each generation does it just the same. —Bobby Darin, "Multiplication"

1977. "Getting" Nixon was the name of the game. —Victor Lasky, *It Didn't Start with Watergate*

1979. "How are we doing?"
"We're making money."
"That's the name of the game, isn't it?" —Howard Fast, *The Establishment*

1984. While I have no reason to believe he [Henry Ford] was breaking the [income tax] law, as far as he was concerned, the name of the game was: take the government for all you can. —Lee Iacocca with William Novak, *Iacocca*

1988. "Deep down, I'm still afraid, but at least I can deal with it—which is the name of the game, as I learned from Dr. Cunningham." —Erich Segal, *Doctors*

1992. And the way baseball is now, Powell can still formulate strategy, conclude that the world is in danger, lead the best and the brightest and their lovers, and tell us that the name of the game is winning. —*New York Times*

1993. Teti said the project will ensure a place for recreation after other areas have been commercially developed.... "It's about improving the quality of life," she said. "That's really the name of the game." —*Times* (Trenton)

1994. IN THE ON-LINE MARKET, THE NAME OF THE GAME IS INTERNET —*New York Times*

That's the way it is. See AND THAT'S THE WAY IT IS.

That's the way the ball bounces. See THAT'S THE WAY THE COOKIE CRUMBLES.

That's the way the cookie crumbles. That's life and there's little one can do about it. One has to accept one's fate. The phrase has been in common use since 1954. The saying is found in varying forms: *That's the way the ball bounces* and *That's the way the mop flops.*

1959. *Jerry:* The way you cross your legs, perhaps; something in the voice. Or maybe I'm just guessing. Is it your wife?
Peter [furious]: That's none of your business! [*A silence.*] Do you understand? [*Jerry nods. Peter is quiet now.*] Well, you're right. We'll have no more children.
Jerry [softly]: That *is* the way the cookie crumbles. —Edward Albee, *The Zoo Story*

1972. "I have no pals."
"You poor bastard. Life's treated you pretty bad, huh?"

"That's how the cookie crumbles." —Morris Farhi, *The Pleasure of Your Death*
See also THAT'S LIFE; THAT'S SHOW BUSINESS.

That's too close for comfort. We narrowly escaped what would have been a nasty encounter. The phrase is a modern cliché, according to Christine Ammer.**

1993. "They found evidence of extreme stress on the heart," Margaret says. "His doctor said, 'I wouldn't say you had a heart attack. You had an episode.'" ... Whatever it was, it was too close for comfort. —*Lear's*

1993. When I wish them for Maria, it sometimes feels a little too close for comfort to the cult of the nice girl, who puts the needs of others before her own. —*The New York Times*
See also IT'S A CLOSE CALL.

That's water under the bridge (over the dam). That happened in the past, cannot be undone, and can no longer be a consideration. The proverb comes from the saying: *A lot of water has flowed (passed, gone) over the dam (under the bridge). Under the bridge* is British and is the oldest part of the proverb. *Over the dam* is its American variant.

1952. "Long time ago, wasn't it, Doctor? Seems like a hundred years."
"Like yesterday."
"Ha ha. Lot of water under the dam since those days, eh?" ...
"*Over* the dam," said Buck Young, filling the grim void in the conversation. "Or under the *bridge.*" —Kurt Vonnegut, Jr., *Player Piano*

1953. "She was as rational as you and I, more so perhaps, and we burned her."
"That's water under the bridge." —Ray Bradbury, *Fahrenheit 451*

1956. *Father:* When your brother comes in, don't say anything to him, Johnny. It's all water under the bridge. —Michael Gazzo, *A Hatful of Rain*

1961. "You see, sir, if I invested Mary's money, I might lose it, the way I lost my own, the way my father lost the pot."
"Water under the bridge, Ethan—water under the bridge." —John Steinbeck, *The Winter of Our Discontent*

1974. [Arthur Hays] Sulzberger [The New York Times publisher] apologized, and shortly thereafter invited Moses, as he did every summer, to visit Iphigene and himself at their country home. "A lot of water has gone under the bridge ...," the publisher wrote, "but I hope it hasn't washed the bridge away." —Robert A. Caro, *The Power Broker*

1979. On the defensive now, Drake again stressed that he had not known Barbara's identity.

"Of course," Tom said. "That's water under the bridge." —Howard Fast, *The Establishment*

1982. "Gentlemen, please!" Aahz called, holding up his hands for order. "All that is water under the draw-bridge, as well as being totally beside the point. Remember, neither of you currently have the Trophy. *We* do." —Robert Asprin, *Myth Directions*

1984. What a lot of water, I reminisced dejectedly, had gone under the bridge since I first had blazed forth as a star from little Bethlehem. —Joseph Heller, *God Knows*

1989. "Water under the bridge," Robert boomed. "The first lesson of politics is to forget what happened yesterday." —Michael Korda, *The Fortune*

1993. The change was made, some time ago, and perhaps I ought to consider it water under the bridge, but I don't. —*Times* (Trenton)

See also IT'S ALL OVER AND DONE WITH.

That's where the money is. Response of famous bank robber Willie Sutton (1901–80), when asked why he robbed banks. The saying is found in varying forms.***

1969. Every employee is required to own a pair of safety glasses, and to wear them in areas where manufacturing is going on. GF & F [General Forge and Foundry Company] has sixty-eight thousand employees in Ilium. That calls for a lot of lenses and a lot of frames.

Frames are where the money is. —Kurt Vonnegut, Jr., *Slaughterhouse-Five*

1993. AS SUTTON SAID, IT'S WHERE THE MONEY IS. In an overly warm New York conference room last week, Trevor Manuel was trying to persuade investors to put money into South Africa. —*New York Times*

1994. In this novel [*Pretty Boy Floyd* by Larry McMurtry & Diana Ossana] Charley Floyd is too nice to go where the real money is. —*New York Times Book Review*

Their name is legion. They are numerous or extensive. The saying first appeared in the New Testament and has been in common use ever since.

What *is* thy name?" And he [the spirit] answered, saying, My name *is* Legion: for we are many. —Mark 5:9, *Authorized Version*, 1611

1962. Fife's own experience with women had not, of course, been legion. —James Jones, *The Thin Red Line*

1978. "He doesn't know himself. He has the name of a thousand demons. Jesus knocked him into a herd of pigs once. His name is Legion." —Stephen King, *The Stand*

1988. The number of people who blessed him [Hank Dwyer], remembered him in their prayers, named their children after him, were legion. —Erich Segal, *Doctors*

1991. Mr. Yeltsin's supporters—and they are still legion … —*New York Times*

There are lies, damned lies, and statistics. Statistics are the worst sort of misleading statements. In his *Autobiography*, Mark Twain attributes the saying to British politician and novelist Benjamin Disraeli (1804–81): "There are three kinds of lies: lies, damned lies, and statistics." The expression has not been found in Disraeli's writings, however. Nevertheless, it is often quoted as being a real Disraeli coinage.

1984. In 1975 he [Michael Wheeler] wrote a biting critique of the polls titled with Benjamin Disraeli's phrase "Lies, damned lies, and statistics." "The press is often preoccupied with small blips, which could be merely statistical accidents," he asserts. —*Christian Science Monitor*

1992. British Prime Minister Benjamin Disraeli once supposedly declared that there are three kinds of lies: "Lies, damned lies, and statistics." To which New Hampshire voters might add: Throw in political polls, which can be just as befuddling. —*Boston Globe*

1997. Jeff Jacoby's op-ed Dec. 4 column, 'For charity, look to the South, not New England,' reminds me of something Benjamin Disraeli said: "There are lies, damned lies, and statistics." —*Boston Globe*

See also FIGURES DON'T LIE.

There are more ways to kill a cat besides (without) choking (skinning) him to death. *See* THERE'S MORE THAN ONE WAY TO SKIN A CAT.

There are no gains without pains. Nothing can be achieved without hard work. The proverb has been traced back to the 1577 *Works of Young Wit* by Nicholas Breton, and is first attested in the United States in Benjamin Franklin's 1745 issue of *Poor Richard's Almanac*. The proverb is found in varying forms, now especially: *No pain(s), no gain(s).*

1745. So what signifies *wishing* and *hoping* for better Times. We may make these Times better if we bestir ourselves. *Industry need not wish*, as Poor

Richard says, and *He that lives upon Hope will die fasting. There are no Gains, without Pains.* —Benjamin Franklin, "Father Abraham's Speech, or, The Way to Wealth"

1987. Now, remember, people, no *pain*, no *gain!* I want you out on the volleyball court in full sweats *every* day at 9:00! To make time, I'm canceling Dr. North's immunology course! —G. B. Trudeau, *Doonesbury Deluxe*

1988. "Let's face it—let's talk sense to the American people.

"Let's tell them the truth, that there are no gains without pains ..." —Adlai Stevenson, quoted in *New York Times*

1989. As Adlai Stevenson once remarked, however, there are no gains without pains. —*New York Times*

1991. For Marion, the decision was agonizing. She didn't want to put Craig through any more pain. Ultimately, she and Ernie decided to let Craig make the decision.

"Mum," he said, "no pain, no gain." —Quoted in *Reader's Digest*

1992. LESS PAIN, MORE GAIN —Headline, *Time*

1993. One year ago, the Republicans struggled to stay together as they defied Florio's claims that their budget and tax cuts would create havoc in state services and put 6,000 state workers on the unemployment lines.

They expected pain then but argued, "No pain, no gain."

This time around, the slogan was "All gain, no pain," especially for GOP legislators seeking reelection. —*Times* (Trenton)

See also NOTHING VENTURED, NOTHING GAINED; YOU CAN'T MAKE AN OMELETTE (OMELET) WITHOUT BREAKING EGGS.

There are none so blind as those who will not see. The most deluded people are those who choose to ignore what they already know. The proverb has been traced back in English to 1546 (John Heywood), and resembles the Biblical verse quoted below. In 1738, it was used by Jonathan Swift in his *Polite Conversation*, and it is first attested in the United States in the 1713 *Works of Thomas Chalkley*. The proverb is found in varying forms: *None (are) so blind as those who refuse to see; None so deaf as those who will not hear,* etc.

Hear now this, O foolish people, and without understanding; which have eyes, and see not; which have ears, and hear not. —Jer. 5:21, *Authorized Version*, 1611

1922. There's no-one as blind as the fellow that won't see, if you know what that means. —James Joyce, *Ulysses*

1962. "There are none so blind as those who won't see. She didn't want to see it and I didn't want her to." —Herman Wouk, *Youngblood Hawke*

1977. "Fowler wasn't even born blind," Duparquet said, "he only went blind a few years ago. You say he could be President?"

"Goddamn!" Bannerman exploded, slamming his open palm on the Cabinet table, as Duparquet had hoped he would. But the Treasury Secretary quickly capped his anger: "General, there are none so blind as those who will not see, as the saying goes." —William Safire, *Full Disclosure*

There are none so deaf as those who will not hear. *See* THERE ARE NONE SO BLIND AS THOSE WHO WILL NOT SEE.

There are other fish in the sea. There are even better ones out there. Don't be upset over what you've lost. This proverb is often used as a consolation for losing a girlfriend or a boyfriend, and has been traced back to about 1573. First attested in the United States in *Keziah* (1909) by J. C. Lincoln, the proverb is found in varying forms: *There are plenty more fish in the sea; There are more fish in the sea than ever came out of it; The sea is full of other fish; There's more than one fish in the sea,* etc.

1976. Hsing-Hsing honestly believes Ling-Ling is the only fish in the sea. —Art Buchwald, *Washington Is Leaking*

1989. The store manager assures a jilted lover that "there are other fish in the sea" and that, furthermore, "time heals all wounds." —*New York Newsday*

1991. "They're still welcome," he said of Sony, "but they're not the only fish in the ocean." —*New York Times*

1992. The President shifted and recrossed his legs at the knees. "Come on, Denton, you know what I'm saying. There are bigger fish in the pond." —John Grisham, *The Pelican Brief*

There are two sides to every story. There's always a different point of view, which is entitled to be heard. The proverb has been traced back in English to 1742, and is first attested in the United States in the 1802 *Diary and Autobiography of John Adams* and in an 1817 letter of Thomas Jefferson. The proverb was first expressed in ancient times, as far back as 485–410 b.c. Protagoras said that "there are two sides to every question." In about 428 b.c., Euripides said, "In a case of dissension, never dare to judge till you've heard the other side." The word *argument, coin, everything, question* or *quarrel* may replace *(every) story*.

1945. From his trousers pocket he drew a package of cigarettes and offered it. She shook her head.

"No thanks."

"Won't accept one from me because you've been alerted against me? There are two sides to every story, remember." —Emilie Loring, *Beyond the Sound of Guns*

1985. "Barbara darling, I'm in no condition to go philosophic. They told us one side of the story. There's another side." —Howard Fast, *The Immigrant's Daughter*

1987. As if anticipating that objection, Vogel said: "Now, there's two sides to this thing, and both of them have to do with what happens to a good kid like this if he has the misfortune of being black and growing up in the Bronx." —Tom Wolfe, *The Bonfire of the Vanities*

1991. It should come as no surprise that many women are easily seduced by fame. Just ask any male rock star (if you can fight your way through the readily available female fans). Remember: There are two sides to every story. —*New York Times*

1993. "There's two sides to every story," Ms. Bratman said. While the decision to leave came as a surprise, Ms. Bratman said it would be easy to find another tenant. —*Princeton Packet*

1994. In our opinion, secondhand smoke is not the same as the smoke a smoker inhales.... What we are saying is that there are always two sides to every argument. Both sides need to be heard and evaluated in order to make an informed decision. —Ad for R. J. Reynolds Tobacco Co., *New York Times*

There is an exception to every rule. There is no rule that covers every circumstance. The proverb has been traced back to the 1579 book, *Newes from the North,* and is first attested in the United States in the 1691 book, *Fitzhugh and His Chesapeake World, 1676–1701.* The proverb is found in varying forms: *It's the exception that proves the rule; The exception proves the rule; There is (there's) no rule without an exception,* etc. The proverb has its counterpart in other languages: *Nulla regula sine exceptione* (Latin, "No rule without an exception"); *Faire exception à la règle* (French, "It's an exception to the rule"); *Keine Regel ohne Ausnahme* (German, "No rule without an exception"); Нет правила без исклю-

чения (Russian, "No rule without an exception"), etc.

1952. Dentists are holding up pretty good, though. They're the exception that proves the rule, I say. —Kurt Vonnegut, Jr., *Player Piano*

1981. So serious was the president about his new image that he actually telephoned Efron two days after the broadcast to ask, "How did I look? Do you have any further suggestions?"

Unfortunately, President Johnson was the proverbial exception to the rule. —Mortimer Levitt, *The Executive Look*

1985. True enough, the three best-known political pundits of the prewar period—Walter Lippmann, David Lawrence, and Arthur Krock—were Jews, and so were the flamboyant and influential reporter and editor Herbert Bayard Swope, brother of Gerald Swope of General Electric, and reporters such as Ben Hecht and A. J. Liebling. But these men were exceptions to the rule. —Charles E. Silberman, *A Certain People*

1989. "All men are boys—they never grow up."

"What about Great-grandfather?"

"Cyrus was the exception to the rule." —Michael Korda, *The Fortune*

1991. "I'm not perfect. Some of them are, believe me. They're machines, robots. They live, eat and sleep for Bendini, Lambert & Locke. I like to have a little fun."

"So you're the exception—"

"Rather than the rule, yes. And I don't apologize for it." —John Grisham, *The Firm*

1992. "The veracity of other people is well within the exceptions to that rule," Miller argued. —Philip Friedman, *Inadmissible Evidence*

1994. I've had it on unimpeachable (though secondhand) authority that when the composer Ben Weber met Virgil Thomson, Thomson asked (without really asking), "I hear you are homosexual." Weber agreed that he was. Thomson: "I hear you're a 12-tone composer." Again, Weber agreed. "Well," said Thomson, "you can't be both. Now which is it?" ... Perhaps Weber was one of those exceptions that prove the rule. But the mystery behind the "rule" remains. —*New York Times*

There is honor (even) among thieves. Even criminals, who live by betraying other people, do not betray each other. The proverb has been traced back to about 1630, and is first attested in the United States in the 1799 *Life of Late Gen. William Eaton* (1813).

1990. "The defendant refused to name names."

"There is honor even among thieves, says the

old saw." —Overheard in the lobby of the Brooklyn courthouse

There isn't a (specific) bone in one's body.
There is not a (particular) characteristic, attitude, etc. in someone's character. The earliest written record of this expression dates back to the early twentieth century. Margaret Mitchell wrote in her novel *Gone with the Wind* (1936): "This was difficult, for Scarlett had not a subtle bone in her body." The metaphoric expression is usually used in negative constructions and may be found in a variety of forms.

1986. Hatch said, "I know Ronald Reagan very well and he doesn't have a racist bone in his body." —*City Tribune* (New York City)

1986. Says Houston Oilers general manager Ladd Herzeg: "I don't' believe there's a phony bone in his body. He's a man of character. I'm not sure I've met many people who are as sincere as he is." —*Christian Science Monitor*

1988. "He just doesn't have a false bone in his body, and the camera reads that honesty. He's incapable of telling a lie, which I think is the mark of a great actor." —*Christian Science Monitor*

1990. Mr. Shultz had no such intention [to seek the presidency]. He didn't have a political bone in his body. —*Christian Science Monitor*

1993. "I just find it absolutely devastating for all of us," said Mr. Kemp, adding that it was Mr. Rollins's idea to have him campaign for Mrs. Whitman in Newark, Camden, and Trenton. "There's not a racist bone in Ed Rollins's body." —*New York Times*

1998. He [Gov. Pete Wilson] called [Sonny] Bono, who once considered running for the governorship, "California's gift to Congress and the country... He didn't have a mean bone in his body." —*Detroit News*

1998. While he loved kicking the ball up and down the field, he would not defend or try to steal it. "I might hurt somebody," he explained. Hmmmm. Didn't look as if he had a competitive bone in his body. —*Christian Science Monitor*

There lies the rub. *See* THERE'S THE RUB.

There must be a first time for everything.
Whatever it is, everything has to have a starting point. The proverb has been traced back to Chaucer's *Prologue* to the *Clerk's Tale* (about 1390), and was first cited in the United States in the 1792 *Papers of Alexander Hamilton* (1961).

There's always a first time (for everything) is a variant of the proverb.

1948. "What's the matter, baby?" I asked, pulling her close and kissing her.
"I'm afraid," she said. "I never did this before."
...
"There's always got to be a first time, baby," I said, "and I won't hurt you." —Harold Robbins, *Never Love a Stranger*

1973. "It's the first time I ever got a turn-down. But like they say—there's always a first ..." —Jacqueline Susann, *Once Is Not Enough*

1975. "Hey—I hear you turned Ramo down. He's destroyed. It's the first time a lady has gotten a look at superrock in the buff and said no thanks."
"There's always a first time." —Jackie Collins, *The World Is Full of Divorced Women*

There'll be hell to pay. There'll be a lot of trouble; there'll be serious consequences. The saying originated about 1800 and has been traced to Lord Paget's letter of 1807: "There has been hell to pay between the Dukes of York and Cumberland." *There'll be the Old Harry to pay*, and *Hell and Tommy to pay*, are variants of the saying. THERE'LL BE THE DEVIL TO PAY is a synonymous expression.

1987. "As long as they [CIA] treat me right, I am going to be their greatest advocate," says Sen. David Boren. "But the first time they don't tell me something that they should have, when they have reason to trust me, then there'll be hell to pay," he said. —*Sun-Sentinel* (South Florida)

1989. "We've got a building fire. If it jumps the 300 (U.S. Forest Service) road and goes one-quarter mile northeast, there is going to be hell to pay," said Herkenhoff, a division supervisor in the Tonto National Forest. —*Arizona Republic*

1996. Christmas Eve. A time to light the logs in the fireplace and share the warmth of the season with loved ones. Sip a little eggnog. Read from Dickens. Wrap the last of the... Yikes! You forgot to buy a present for your beloved wife/husband/lover/child! There'll be hell to pay on this heavenly holiday if he/she/they have nothing to open tomorrow morning. —*Arizona Republic*

1997. And if we got beat by the [*Detroit*] *Times*, the Hearst paper that was the other afternoon daily on Detroit, there would be hell to pay in our circulation department—and sometimes even in editorial, if there had been a delay in closing some pages. —*Detroit News*

1998. We're in the middle of the game now and have to figure out a way to win. We really can't afford to walk away. But there will be hell to pay if

these "riverview casinos" end up crowding the river, our soothing, shining treasure, with a gang of fat, flashy upstarts who scar the skyline and smash our hearts. —*Detroit News*
See also THERE'LL BE THE DEVIL TO PAY.

There'll be the devil to pay. There will be a great deal of trouble. The metaphor alludes to striking a bargain with the devil and paying a price. Jonathan Swift in his *Journal to Stella* (1711) speaks about the Earl of Strafford's plan to go to Holland and "then there will be the devil and all to pay." In 1821, Walter Scott employs a longer version of the phrase in *The Pirate:* "If they hurt but one hair of Cleveland's head, there will be the devil to pay and no pitch hot."

1988. In "Spellbinder," as in "Fatal Attraction," quick sex leaves you with the devil to pay—loose women represent fatality, they are Lucifer's minions. —*Los Angeles Times*

1989. "Don't tighten 'em down too much, now," he said as I left. "Be the devil to pay next time you gotta change 'em." —*Christina Science Monitor*

1997. This is the year for changing a campaign finance system awash in special-interest money and skyrocketing costs. There ought to be the devil to pay for inaction. —*Hartford Courant*
See also THERE'LL BE HELL TO PAY.

There's a black sheep in every flock. There is one bad person in every group of people. The proverb was first attested in the United States in 1779, and in Britain, it was cited in Sir Walter Scott's 1816 book *Old Mortality*. Black sheep are generally regarded as inferior in quality to white sheep since their wool resists dying. The word *flock* can be replaced with *family* or *fold*. The adage is often shortened to *a/the black sheep,* a person who brings disgrace on the family, group, or community.

1936. "Mrs. Whiting's cousin, Mrs. Coleman, whose husband came from Charleston, told me about him. He's the black sheep of a lovely family—oh, how could any of the Butlers ever turn out anything like him?" —Margaret Mitchell, *Gone With the Wind*

1941. "I shouldn't suppose you'd want a black sheep like me in your flock." —Frances Parkinson Keyes, *All That Glitters*

1952. "Any relation to the big cheese across the river?"
    "My half-brother."
    "You the black sheep, honey?" —Kurt Vonnegut, Jr., *Player Piano*

1977. "I came to America in my mother's arms. My father was a pioneer. Maybe I *was* the black sheep of my family." —*Down the Seine and Up the Potomac with Art Buchwald*

1982. "No one knows this, but you'll keep it to yourself, won't you? George is the black sheep of the family." —Sidney Sheldon, *Master of the Game*

1989. He was the black sheep of a family that otherwise had produced a steady succession of sharp, flint-eyed Yankee traders and farmers, with an unlovable talent for buying up their less fortunate neighbors' properties at rock-bottom prices. —Michael Korda, *The Fortune*

1991. "Nancy is a dreadful woman without a thought in her head," she [Professor Robinson] said years later. "A frozen face. Every family has a black sheep; mine just happens to be famous." —Kitty Kelley, *Nancy Reagan*

1993. "I'm the black sheep of my family," says Joseph, a trucker with "mom" tattooed on his arm. —*Princeton Packet*

There's a pot of gold at the end of the rainbow. The legend goes that if you reach the point where a rainbow meets the earth, you will find a pot of gold. Used to refer to chasing after imaginary or unrealistic things.

1943. A pot of gold at the end of the rainbow. —E. W. Teale, *Dune Boy*

1963. Minton and his wife exchanged another of those pitying *duprass* glances. Then Milton said to me, "Yes. The pot of gold at the end of the rainbow is ours." —Kurt Vonnegut, Jr., *Cat's Cradle*

1991. As lottomania sweeps the nation, thousands of Americans are becoming sudden millionaires—but pots of gold don't seem to go to their head. —*Time*

1992. "Labor, minorities, environmentalists, blacks, Hispanics, women, retired people, you name it, all see the pot of gold at the end of the rainbow," a top Clinton aide said. —*New York Times*

1994. A Goldman partnership, says Samuel Hayes 3d, a finance professor at the Harvard Business School, is "the epitome of professional recognition on Wall Street." And financially, he adds, it is "the pot of gold at the end of the rainbow." —*New York Times*

There's a season and a time for every purpose under the heaven. Everything has its proper time. The proverb appears in the Old Testament. It has been traced back in English to about 1390 and is first attested in the United

States in 1682. *There's a season for all things; There's a time to be born and a time to die* are variants of the entry proverb.

> To every *thing there is* a season and a time to every purpose under the heaven:
> A time to be born, and a time to die; a time to plant, and a time to pluck up *that which is* planted;
> A time to kill, and a time to heal; a time to break down, and a time to build up;
> A time to weep, and a time to laugh; a time to mourn, and a time to dance.
> —Eccles. 3:1-4, *Authorized Version*, 1611

1953. To everything there is a season. Yes. A time to break down, and a time to build up. Yes. A time to keep silence, and a time to speak. Yes, all that. But what else. What else? Something, something ... —Ray Bradbury, *Fahrenheit 451*

1968. All things have their season. —Michael K. Joseph, *The Hole in the Zero*

1977. "I'm no home wrecker," she said lightly, pulling one of her long black hairs off his jacket. "And I don't want to lose you."

"There's a time to build, and a time to wreck," he told her, not so lightly. —William Safire, *Full Disclosure*

1986. Ecclesiastes tells us that "to every thing there is a season," including a "time to be born, and a time to die." And, pursuing a rather less speculative response to the question Why death? some scientists have theorized that our cells have a maximum life span, that human beings are genetically programmed to die. —Judith Viorst, *Necessary Losses*

1988. I think we have to remember that there's a season for everything in our lives. And if we have young children and we don't want to leave them with a baby-sitter, we should stay at home and get by the best we can. —*Ladies' Home Journal*

1989. Mayor Biagio DiLieto, a former police chief who has driven New Haven's powerful Democratic Party machine for the last decade, shocked supporters and critics today when he announced that he would not seek a sixth two-year term in office this fall ... "There is a time to come and a time to go," Mr. DiLieto said. —*New York Times*

1991. A TIME TO KILL, AND A TIME TO HEAL —Headline of article dealing with a brutal murder-suicide in a prominent family, *Time*

1993. "There's a time to stay and a time to go and a time to fold 'em, and we only wish our new president all the best." —George Bush, *Newsweek*

1994. A TIME FOR WAR, AND A TIME FOR PLAY. —Cap-

tion, *New York Times*
See also THERE'S A TIME AND PLACE FOR EVERYTHING.

There's a season for all things. *See* THERE'S A SEASON AND A TIME FOR EVERY PURPOSE UNDER THE HEAVEN.

There's a skeleton in every closet. Everyone however well they keep up appearances, has a well-hidden secret. Often in the shortened form *skeleton in the closet,* meaning any embarrassing or damaging secret. The proverb has been traced back to *Punch in the East* (1845) and *The Newcomes* (1854) by William Thackeray (1811–63). The proverb was first cited in the United States in 1876.

1854. And it is from these that we shall arrive at some particulars regarding the Newcome family, which will show us that they have a skeleton or two in their closets, as well as their neighbors. —William Thackeray, *The Newcomes*

1922. Wife locked up at home, skeleton in the cupboard. —James Joyce, *Ulysses*

1981. There was a close rapport between these patients [bisexual] and their families for years until circumstances forced the skeletons out of the closet. —Abigail Van Buren, *The Best of Dear Abby*

1984. Prior to each interview, Mondale's staff researches the background of the invited candidate [for a Democratic running mate] and makes dozens of phone calls to see if there are any skeletons in the closet. —*U.S. News & World Report*

1987. NO SKELETONS IN MY CLOSET
Asked by a member of the audience about his own morals, Mr. [Jesse] Jackson responded, "I have no skeletons in my closet." —*New York Times*

1988. The question Vice President Bush's campaign is raising about Senator Bob Dole's finances seems too contrived and nitpicking—even in this year of The Skeleton in the Closet—to divert inquiry from Mr. Bush's own involvement in the Reagan Administration's Iran-Contra scandal. —*New York Times*

1992. "They're both no angels," said Michael De-Vito, a retired bus mechanic for the Transit Authority, describing Mr. Abrams and Senator D'Amato, who will oppose each other in next month's Senate election. "Abrams has a lot of skeletons in his closet, too—they're advertising it on TV," added Mr. DeVito. —*New York Times*

1994. "I not only have no skeletons, I have no closet." Oliver North denying he covered up medical information, including possible treatment for depression, that could potentially damage his Senate bid in Virginia. —*Newsweek*

1995. Dr. [Kary B.] Mullis is unrepentant.... "If everybody likes you then something is really wrong," he said. "My past is full. If you want to look for skeletons in a closet, come look in some of my closets. I've got eight dead penguins back in there, but they're all plastic." —*New York Times*

See also ACCIDENTS WILL HAPPEN IN THE BEST-REGULATED FAMILIES; THERE'S A BLACK SHEEP IN EVERY FLOCK.

There's a sucker born every minute. There are many naive or stupid people who can become easy victims of cheating and ripoffs. This adage originated in the United States in the 1850s, and is often attributed to circus showman Phineas Taylor Barnum (1810–1891). According to Linda A. Altshuler, Executive Director of The Barnum Museum, after 10 years' research, the historian Arthur Saxon conclusively determined that this saying has been erroneously ascribed to Barnum. The proverb is found in varying forms: *A sucker is born every minute; A sucker is born every minute, and two to take him; In the West a sucker is born every minute, but in New York they appear in chunks of roe*, etc.

1975. The lessons of childhood linger. If for no other reason, that is the objective and motive of the pitchman. In spite of new math, we do old math. In spite of Mali and Upper Volta, we call it French Equatorial Africa. In spite of reason, we buy Kellogg's Rice Krispies. Yes, even we rational and intelligent adults prove P. T. Barnum's axiom—"There's a sucker born every minute"—daily. —Quoted in *The People's Almanac*

1992. Americans want something definite—not generalized statements such as, "people would be paying less in other health expenses ... their out-of-pocket costs, and *probably* their premiums, would be lower as a result." "Probably"—that's what Americans are getting tired of hearing. "Probably" means "there's a sucker born every minute." —*AARP Bulletin*

1994. "There's a sucker born every minute,"
P. T. Barnum declared
(And a con man is born every hour)
To make sure no sucker is spared.
                              —*Wall Street Journal*

There's a tide in the affairs of men. There is a rhythm to our lives, and one should not miss the opportunity in the flow of events. The proverb was coined by Shakespeare in 1599 in his play

Julius Caesar. It was first attested in the United States in the 1784 *Diary of Chief Justice William Smith, 1784–1793*.

1599. *Brutus:* There is a tide in the affairs of men,
    Which, taken at the flood, leads on to
        fortune;
    Omitted, all the voyage of their life
    Is bound in shallows and in miseries.
        —Shakespeare, *Julius Caesar*, Act IV, Scene III

1946. A TIDE IN THE AFFAIRS OF MEN —Chapter title in Upton Sinclair's *A World to Win*

1993. "There is a tide in the affairs of men/which taken at the flood leads on to fortune." That tide is with us now, but the "affairs" have extended from white men to include a far larger group of us, some of whom, unlike James Atlas, were not until very recently allowed to read the great works of Western civilization in the Harvard library. —*New York Times*

There's a time and place for everything. Everything has its proper time and place. The proverb has been traced back in English to Chaucer's *Prologue* to the *Clerk's Tale* (1390), and is first cited in the United States in the 1623 book, *Three Visitors to Early Plymouth*. The proverb is found in varying forms: *There's a time for all things; There's a time for everything*, etc.

1951. "Holden ... One short, faintly stuffy, pedagogical question. Don't you think there's a time and place for everything?" —J. D. Salinger, *The Catcher in the Rye*

1991. "Well, I'm not leaving this minute, Scarlett darling. There's time for everything." —Alexandra Ripley, *Scarlett*

1992. A time for everything sign in an Athens, Greece, hotel: "Visitors are expected to complain at the office between the hours of 9 and 11 A.M." —*Modern Maturity*

1993. "There is a time for everything, it's important to remain well balanced in all things," [Andrew] Eisen said. —*Times* (Trenton)

See also THERE'S A SEASON AND A TIME FOR EVERY PURPOSE UNDER THE HEAVEN.

There's a time for all things. See THERE'S A TIME AND PLACE FOR EVERYTHING.

There's a time for everything. See THERE'S A TIME AND PLACE FOR EVERYTHING.

There's a time to be born and a time to die.

See THERE'S A SEASON AND A TIME FOR EVERY PURPOSE UNDER THE HEAVEN.

There's always a first time for everything.
See THERE MUST BE A FIRST TIME FOR EVERYTHING.

There's always a light at the end of the tunnel.
Remain hopeful: there's always something good and useful after a long period of hardship and despair. The proverb, which has been traced back to about 1922, was popularized by John F. Kennedy in 1962. *To see a/the light at the end of the tunnel* has become a favorite American expression and is now used in other countries as well.

1962. We don't see the end of the tunnel, but I must say I don't think it is darker than it was a year ago, and in some ways lighter. —John F. Kennedy on the Vietnam War, *New York Times*

1977. We feel the machine slipping from our
      hands
    As if someone else were steering;
    If we see a light at the end of the tunnel,
    It's the light of an oncoming train.
               —Robert Lowell, *Since 1939*

1978. *Rowe's Rule:* the odds are five to six that the light at the end of the tunnel is the headlight of an oncoming train. —*Washingtonian*

1991. The final year at Annapolis is normally the best. Not only can you finally see the light at the end of the tunnel, but you get to pick the service you're going into, and the location and the date for reporting to your new command. —Oliver L. North, *Under Fire*

1992. Thirty years ago in London I was pronounced dead—I've read my own obituary. I had a terrible case of pneumonia, and I stopped breathing for five minutes. And while I was dead I went on and on through a long tunnel until I saw a light at the end of it. The light was wonderful and I wanted to go into it. But Mike Todd was standing at the end of the tunnel, and said, "You have to go back, you can't come over yet, you have to fight to go back." So I did. —Elizabeth Taylor, quoted in *Life*

1993. A sign in the English department at the University of Oklahoma in Norman read: "Due to budget cuts, we regret to inform you the light at the end of the tunnel is being turned off. Effective immediately." —Quoted in *Reader's Digest*

1994. Gerstner appeared with the top management of the company, a rare turnout. His chief financial officer, Jerome York, said the company's recent financial performance—it managed a small profit last quarter—was "at least a few photons, if not light at the end of the tunnel." —*Washington Post*
See also EVERY CLOUD HAS A SILVER LINING; IT'S A BLESSING IN DISGUISE; IT'S AN ILL WIND THAT BLOWS NO (NOBODY) GOOD; THERE IS A POT OF GOLD AT THE END OF THE RAINBOW; WHERE THERE'S LIFE, THERE'S HOPE.

There's always (a) tomorrow.
Cheer up, it's not the end of the world. You'll get another chance.

1992. Jordan mused that he wished he had known that little statistic. He might have done something about it. There is always tonight. —*New York Times*

1992. Gary Jr. collapses in his dad's arms, "I can't [walk]," he cries. Gary hugs him.
    "Don't worry," he says cheerfully. "There's always tomorrow." —Donna E. Boetig, "Father Love," *Family Circle*

1992. "Things will never be the same, the only sure thing is change," she sang, "but there's always tomorrow." —*People*
See also IT'S NOT THE END OF THE WORLD; TOMORROW IS ANOTHER DAY.

There's always room at the top.
You can succeed if you try hard. The earliest appearance of the proverb in print in England is the 1914 book, *Price of Love* by Arnold Bennett (1867–1931). It was coined by the American statesman and orator Daniel Webster (1782–1852) who used it as far back as 1801. Popularized through the best-selling book, *Room at the Top* (1957) by John Braine (1922–86).

1801. There is always room at the top. —Daniel Webster's response to advice that he stay out of the crowded legal profession.

1914. The Imperial had set out to be the most gorgeous cinema in the Five Towns; and it simply was. Its advertisement read: "There is always room at the top." —Arnold Bennett, *Price of Love*

1951. *Q.* I have submitted my short stories to all the leading magazines, but I still haven't been able to get one published. I'm beginning to be discouraged. What should I do?
    A. There's always room for one more good writer at the top, and the best way to get there is to start at the bottom. —Erskine Caldwell, *Call It Experience*

1966. Although [Horatio] Alger's own bachelor life was criticized, he implanted morality and the conviction that there is always room at the top (especially if one marries the boss's daughter). —Thomas A. Bailey, *American Pageant*

1988. People think that at the top there isn't much room. They tend to think of it as an Everest. My message is that there is tons of rooms at the top. —Margaret Thatcher, *Daily Telegraph*

1994. Dr. Swain is undaunted by difficulties. "The world is very competitive, but there's always room at the top," she said. —*New York Times*

There's good and bad in everything. Every person or thing has both good and bad qualities.

1987. "It took three men to hold Onzell when Willie Boy was buried. She went crazy and tried to jump in the grave with him. I don't ever want to go to another one of those for as long as I live."

"I know there's good and bad in everything," Evelyn said, "but I still can't help but envy them, somehow. I just wish I could be free and open like they are." —Fannie Flagg, *Fried Green Tomatoes*

1990. "I make $600 a week, but I'm putting in 45 hours."

"There's good and bad in everything, as they say." —Overheard at a restaurant

See also YOU HAVE TO TAKE THE BITTER WITH THE SWEET.

There's many a slip between (the) cup and (the) lip. Nothing is certain until the action is finished. The proverb is similar to several classical variants by Cato the Elder and Palladas; it has been traced back in English to the 1539 *Proverbs of Erasmus* by R. Taverner. It is first attested in the United States in the 1758 *Writings of George Washington*. The old form *twixt* or *betwixt* (between) is still used.

1621–51.
Many things happen between the cup and the lip. —Robert Burton, *The Anatomy of Melancholy*

1848. There's many a slip between the cup and the lip! Who knows what may happen. —William Thackeray, *Pendennis*

1985. These are ambitious plans, and any entrepreneur could tell Reichartz that there will be many a slip between cup and lip. —*Forbes*

See also DON'T COUNT YOUR CHICKENS BEFORE THEY ARE HATCHED; DON'T SHOUT UNTIL YOU ARE OUT OF THE WOODS.

There's more than one way to skin a cat. There are many ways to do something. The proverb appeared in John Ray's collection of English proverbs in 1678, and is first attested in the United States in *John Smith's Letters* (1839). *There are more ways to kill a cat besides choking him to death* is a variant of the saying. The words *with butter* or *on cream* may replace the words *to death* in the latter version.

1936. "There's more ways of killing a cat than choking him to death with butter," giggled Melanie when the whiskered old man had thumped down the stairs. —Margaret Mitchell, *Gone With the Wind*

1948. "Every man has his price, there's more ways than one to skin a cat." —Norman Mailer, *The Naked and the Dead*

1953. There is more than one way to burn a book. And the world is full of people running about with lit matches. —Ray Bradbury, *Fahrenheit 451*

1988. However, there's more than one way to skin a shareholder, and Kravits and Johnson fell out over technique. —*New Republic*

1989. Mr. Bush himself has argued that Federal money is not the only answer to domestic problems. At a recent news conference he said: "You don't show your determination to solve a problem by simply increasing Federal spending. There are other ways to skin a cat." —*New York Times*

1991. If an actress has reservations about biting, smacking, or kicking a fellow actor in the groin, she needn't despair. She can always grab, push, shove or struggle instead. "There are 100 million ways to skin a cat," says Mr. Turner, who choreographs fights for "Guiding Light" and "Loving," among other TV series. —*New York Times*

There's more to it than meets the eye. The situation is more complicated than what one sees on the surface. The saying originated in the nineteenth century and was coined on the analogy of "more … than meets the ear" (1631) by John Milton (1608–74). *There's less to it than meets the eye* is a variant.

1894. *Petkoff:* Your photograph, with the inscription "Raina, to her chocolate Cream-Soldier: a Souvenir." Now you know there's something in this more than meets the eye; and I'm going to find it out. —Bernard Shaw, *Arms and the Man*, Act III

1906. "There's more here, sir, however," he [the Inspector] said, "than meets the eye. I don't believe in suicide, nor in pure accident, myself." —John Galsworthy, *The Man of Property*

1922. There is less in this than meets the eye. —Tallulah Bankhead, quoted in Bartlett's *Familiar Quotations*, sixteenth edition, edited by Justin Kaplan

1983. "Not to give is dumb economically," notes Charlotte Curtis, associate editor of *The New York Times* and a keen observer of the very rich. But there is more to it than that. —*Forbes*

1984. Our [American Express] employees are discovering there's more to these new commercials than meets the eye. —*New York Times*

1989. "Being unoffensive builds no credit," said Fred I. Greenstein, chairman of the political science department at Princeton University. "A sense begins to develop that there is less there than meets the eye. If Bush makes things too small, when he really wants something, people won't have any reason to pay attention." —*New York Times*

1994. Think about it: would Mayor Rudolph W. Giuliani want to ban Albert Einstein, Edward R. Murrow, Leonard Bernstein, Franklin Roosevelt and E. B. White, to name a few, from smoke-free Gracie Mansion? The average life span of those personalities was rather respectable, by the way. There is much more to this than meets the eye. —*New York Times*

There's no accounting for tastes. People's tastes differ and there's no logic to it. The proverb is derived from the Latin *De gustibus non est disputandum* ("There is no disputing about taste") and it has been traced back in English to 1599. It is first cited in the United States in the 1808 book *Tears and Smiles.*

> **1936.** "There's no accounting for tastes and I've always heard the Irish were partial to pig—kept them under their beds, in fact." —Margaret Mitchell, *Gone With the Wind*
>
> **1992.** There's just no accounting for destiny. Andrew Morton, the author of "Diana: Her True Story," the best seller that's been called the longest divorce petition in British history, had plans to discuss his new-found fame at the Princess of Wales's favorite London restaurant, San Lorenzo, in chic Beauchamp Place. —*New York Times*
>
> **1993.** Nadia's sex appeal would crank up a notch. And Joe—that wacky Joe!—well, there's no accounting for taste, but his oddness is part of his charm, no? —*New York Times Book Review*
>
> **1994.** The Old Guy was left talking to himself. *De gustibus,* he muttered. *Chacun à son goût.* To each his own. He didn't believe a word of it. —*New York Times*

See also EVERY MAN TO HIS OWN TASTE; TO EACH HIS OWN.

There's no business like show business. Entertainment is the best profession and nothing comes even close. This saying was coined by Irving Berlin (1888–1989), who made it the title of a famous song in the 1946 musical *Annie Get Your Gun.*

> **1946.** There's no business like show business
> Like no business I know.
> —Irving Berlin, "There's No Business Like Show Business"
>
> **1985.** Harry Goldhandler sat way over on the side of the fifteenth row, while the jokes I heard him dictate in Florida rocked the Winter Garden, and his ingenious variation of "Dr. Cutballs" brought down the house.
> There's no business like show business. —Herman Wouk, *Inside, Outside*
>
> **1985.** Later this fall Hurwitt introduces, with an extensive ad campaign, his first new product: Horizon cereal, aimed at active adults.... It's a big risk. Hurwitt will know within six months whether the risk pays off. There's no business like show business. —*Forbes*

See also THAT'S SHOW BUSINESS.

There's no fool like an old fool. One doesn't necessarily get smarter with age. Old people can be especially foolish. The proverb has been traced back to John Heywood's book of proverbs (1546). It was first cited in the United States in *Tom Sawyer* (1876) by Mark Twain (1835–1910). The proverb is found in varying forms: *An old fool is worse than a young fool; No fool like an old (a young) fool; There's no fool like a learned fool,* etc.

> **1546.** There is no fool to the old fool. —John Heywood, *Proverbs*
>
> **1920.** You're an old woman, Emily, and there's no fool like an old fool. The man's twenty years younger than you, and don't fool yourself as to what he married you for. Money! —Agatha Christie, *The Mysterious Affair at Styles*
>
> **1983.** He lay back in the chair and waited.
> There's no fool like an old fool ... a young fool ... a middle-aged fool ... —Jackie Collins, *Hollywood Wives*
>
> **1991.** It is true, as Rembar suggests, that old and wise are often juxtaposed, but he overlooks the equally common dictum that "there is no fool like an old fool." —*New York Times Magazine*

There's no honor among thieves. *See* THERE IS HONOR (EVEN) AMONG THIEVES.

There's no indispensable man. *See* NO PERSON IS INDISPENSABLE.

There's no joy in Mudville. After all the hopes and expectations, defeat is hard to bear. The proverb was coined by American balladeer Ernest Lawrence Thayer (1863–1940), whose poem and song, "Casey at the Bat," published on June 3, 1888, in the *San Francisco Examiner*, became an overnight hit. The Mudville fans expected their baseball team to win, but they were badly disappointed when their beloved Casey lost the game. The saying is often used in variants with other place names.

> **1888.** Oh, somewhere in this favored land the sun is shining bright;
> The band is playing somewhere, and somewhere hearts are light;
> And somewhere men are laughing, and somewhere children shout,
> But there is no joy in Mudville—mighty Casey has struck out.
> —Ernest Lawrence Thayer, "Casey at the Bat, A Ballad of the Republic, Sung in the Year 1888"

1986. "There's no joy in Mudville, Mighty Casey has struck out," said Peggy Noonan, the former Presidential speechwriter, who said her friends in the White House were "feeling real bad." They were saddened, she said, by the way the chief of staff, Donald T. Regan, and his aides "let the strongest guy in America turn into a guy squirming on TV." —*New York Times*

1991. *Q:* Suppose that Mighty Casey, instead of striking out to end the game, had smote a towering home run over the outfield fence. But alas, while strutting around the bases, he tripped, fell, broke a leg and was unable to reach home plate. Would there have been any joy in Mudville? —*New York Times*

> **1993.** Happy Birthday, Gene Paluzzi, who I hear has got the gout ...
> But there is no joy in Mudville—mighty Casey has struck out.
> —Frank Cammuso & Hart Seely, "Scooter at the Mike," *New York Times*

There's no place like home. Home is the place where we feel most comfortable. The idea of the proverb was originally expressed by Thomas Tusser (1524–80) in *A Hundredth Good Pointes of Husbandry* (1570), but it was popularized by the song, "Home, Sweet Home," (1923) written by John Howard Payne (1791–1852), an American actor and playwright. *Be it ever so humble, there is (there's) no place like home* is a line from the song and is also a variant of this proverb. It is first cited in the United States in *Three Brides, Love in a Cottage, and Other Tales* (1856).

> **1823.** 'Mid pleasures and palaces tho we may roam,
> Be it ever so humble, there's no place like home;
> A charm from the sky seems to hallow us there,
> Which, seek through the world, is ne'er met with elsewhere.
> Home, home, sweet home!
> There's no place like home! there's no place like home!
> —John Howard Payne, "Home, Sweet Home," in the opera *Clari, the Maid of Milan*

1985. BE IT EVER SO CORPORATE, THERE'S NO PLACE LIKE HOME —Jacqueline Hornor Plumez with Karla Dougherty, *Divorcing a Corporation*

1988. Today Michael held a breakfast meeting in the boardroom, faxed the winning proposal to New York, had his dry cleaning picked up and his orchestra tickets delivered, attempted 30 laps in the pool (did 29), went to a great restaurant with Doris for a midnight snack, and never left home.

There's no place like home. There's no place like The Rittenhouse. —Ad, *Philadelphia Inquirer*

1991. THERE'S NO PLACE LIKE JAIL —Headline, *Time*

1993. FOR FAIR, THERE'S NO PLACE LIKE HOME —Headline, *Times* (Trenton)

1994. FOR SOME RUSSIAN JEWS, THERE'S NO PLACE LIKE HOME —Headline, *Manhattan Jewish Sentinel*

See also HOME, SWEET HOME.

There's no royal road to learning. There's no easy way to learn something new. Royal roads were built smooth, straighter and better and using them required no big effort. The story goes that when King Ptolemy I asked Euclid (about 325 b.c.) if there were not some easier ways of mastering geometry than learning, Euclid said, "Sire, there is no royal short cut to geometry." The proverb has been traced back in English to the 1824 *Journals of Ralph Waldo Emerson* (1961). *There's no royal road to success* is a variant of the proverb.

1824. There is no royal road to Learning. —Ralph Waldo Emerson, *Journals*

1857. There is no royal road to learning; no short cut to the requirement of any valuable art. —Anthony Trollope, *Barchester Towers*

1987. "What are you going to study at the university?"

"Computer science."

"You'll have to work hard."

"'There's no royal road to learning and to success,' my father used to say." —Overheard at Columbia University

See also THERE ARE NO GAINS WITHOUT PAINS.

There's no rule without an exception. See THERE'S AN EXCEPTION TO EVERY RULE.

There's no substitute for victory. See IN WAR THERE IS NO SUBSTITUTE FOR VICTORY.

There's no such thing as a free lunch. Nothing in life is free; you can't get something for nothing. The proverb has been traced back to around 1950, and appears in Robert A. Heinlein's science-fiction book *The Moon Is a Harsh Mistress* (1967). It is often attributed to Nobel Prize winner Milton Friedman (1912–) who popularized but did not coin it.

1967. "Oh, 'tanstaafl.' Means 'There ain't no such thing as a free lunch.' And isn't," I added, pointing to a FREE LUNCH sign across the room, "or these drinks would cost half as much." —Robert A. Heinlein, *The Moon Is a Harsh Mistress*

1975. *There's No Such Thing as a Free Lunch* —Title of a book by Milton Friedman

1984. Largely because of Massachusetts' success and O'Neill's high-level support, the House Ways & Means Committee is now studying federal tax amnesty. Other states are considering similar programs. But, sadly, there is still no such thing as a free lunch—even for the government. —*Forbes*

1985. "Life has taught me many things," Konig said. "One of them is that there's no such thing as a woman's instinct. It's just a woman's way of not telling how she found something out." —Michael Korda, *Queenie*

1986. There's no such thing as a free lunch. Nothing in life is free. Especially from a bank. —Ad, *New York Times*

1989. But in diplomacy, as in economics, there is no free lunch. The Soviets can hardly be expected to show flexibility in America's backyard as long as Washington shows no flexibility on Moscow's doorstep. —*New York Times*

1991. But a week before President Mikhail Gorbachev visits London for talks with leaders of the seven major industrial nations, the debate has taken on a sense of realism. As one national newspaper remarked, borrowing a Western phrase, "there is no such thing as a free lunch." —*Wall Street Journal*

1991. Says New York University's Edward Altman, who subscribed to this argument and wrote a book in the mid-Eighties supporting it: "There was a free lunch until 1988. But the people got greedy." —*Fortune*

1994. Says Peter Peterson, author of *Facing Up*, a new book on deficit cutting: "There never was a free lunch, and there certainly isn't one today." —*U.S. News & World Report*

1995. It used to be said—and widely accepted—that "there's no such thing as a free lunch." The notion reflected an understanding that there's a price to be paid for everything. —*New York Post*

See also THE BEST THINGS IN LIFE ARE FREE; THE PARTY'S OVER!; THERE'S NO SUCH THING AS A FREE RIDE; YOU DON'T GET SOMETHING FOR NOTHING.

There's no such thing as a free ride. Nothing in life is free. If it appears to be "free," somebody is paying for it. The proverb was originated on the analogy of "There's no such thing as a free lunch."***

1977. "Five to one, the nays have it," said Vice-President Nichols. "Mr. Attorney General, is it possible for me to cast a vote for the record?"

"No," said Duparquet; no free rides. —William Safire, *Full Disclosure*

1984. "But let me tell you something, if those clowns figure they're getting a free ride right down the line, they're mistaken." —Howard Fast, *The Outsider*

1991. There is such a thing as a free ride. Buy two tickets, get one free with MasterCard. —Ad for MasterCard

1993. Oh, there are some progressive features left. Fairness is advanced by finally making well-off earners buy tickets for the free ride they got in the '80s. —*Times* (Trenton)

See also THE BEST THINGS IN LIFE ARE FREE; THE PARTY'S OVER!; THERE'S NO SUCH THING AS A FREE LUNCH; YOU DON'T GET SOMETHING FOR NOTHING.

There's no time like the present. Act now; don't delay. The proverb has been traced back to G. Legh's *Accidence of Armoury* (1562): "Mary [to be sure] sir no time better then euen now." Mary de la Rivière Manley's *The Lost Lover* (1696) brings the proverb to its current form, "No time like the present." First cited in the United States in the late eighteenth century.

1993. If you're anticipating a wedding or baby shower this summer, there's no time like the present to begin planning. —*Los Angeles Daily News*

1993. There's no time like the present to think about doing something about your house, you know, peeling paint, broken wall shingles, split clapboards, and other horrible things that happen to houses. —*Boston Globe*

1998. We grow up hearing the worn adages: *Time flies; time is of the essence; there's no time like the present.* Words of wisdom that we commit to memory and never completely grasp. The truth of these phrases was never drummed into our brains as it should have been. We never took it seriously, not really. —*Newsweek*

See also MAKE HAY WHILE THE SUN SHINES; NEVER PUT OFF UNTIL TOMORROW WHAT YOU CAN DO TODAY; PROCRASTINATION IS THE THIEF OF TIME; STRIKE WHILE THE IRON IS HOT; TIME AND TIDE WAIT FOR NO MAN; TIME FLIES; TIME IS OF THE ESSENCE.

There's no use crying over spilled (spilt) milk. See DON'T CRY OVER SPILLED (SPILT) MILK.

There's nothing good or bad but thinking makes it so. Whether something seems to be good or bad depends on one's point of view. Shakespeare coined the phrase in *Hamlet* (1600–01). *Nothing is evil but thinking makes it so* is a variant.

1600–01.
>   *Hamlet:* Denmark's a prison.
>   *Rosencrantz:* Then is the world one.
>   *Hamlet:* A goodly one; in which there are
>   many confines, wards, and dungeons,
>   Denmark being one o' the worst.
>   *Rosencrantz:* We think not so, my lord.
>   *Hamlet:* Why, then, 'tis none to you; for
>   there's nothing either good or bad, but
>   thinking makes it so: to me it is a prison.
>   —Shakespeare, *Hamlet*, Act II, Scene II

1994. "You guys forget that O. J. is America's icon, the top of the football cream. He couldn't have done it."

"You're entitled to your opinion. 'Nothing is good or bad,' as the old saw goes, 'but thinking makes it so.'" —Overheard at a McDonald's

There's nothing new under the sun. What seems to be new is not new at all. Everything has existed before. The proverb appears in the Old Testament, and was first used in English by Chaucer in the *Knight's Tale* (1386). It is first attested in the United States in the *Works of Anne Brad-*

street (1650). The proverb was used by Thomas Jefferson in 1801.

> That thing that hath been, it *is that* which shall be; and that which is done *is that* which shall be done; and *there is* no new *thing* under the sun. —Eccles. 1:9, *Authorized Version*, 1611

1650. There is no new thing under the sun. —*Works of Anne Bradstreet*, 1932

1801. We can no longer say there is nothing new under the sun. —Thomas Jefferson, *Writings*

1922. Nothing new under the sun. —James Joyce, *Ulysses*

1984. Don't try telling me there is ever anything new under the sun. —Joseph Heller, *God Knows*

1991. Sports heroes long have been lionized, of course, but the adulation has grown to a point where it seems to me to be something new under the sun. —*Wall Street Journal*

1992. "The Bible says Roman soldiers cast lots for Jesus' garments," he said, as passers-by headed toward Le Paree Orgy, a topless bar. "Lots are nothing but dice. There's nothing new under the sun." —*New York Times*

1993. Further proof that there is nothing new under the sun—or the bust: ... The picture of Gwendolyn Fisher wearing a cocktail dress "with cutouts resembling champagne glasses" on the bodice below the bustline sent me scurrying to my ephemeral file. —*New York Times*

1994. There is nothing new under the sun. America's hip culture looks strangely like the one that led to the fall of the Roman Empire. —*Time*

1995. A skeptic might wonder what the notion of a meme adds to the paradigm of cultural revolution. Perhaps there is nothing new under the sun. *Plus ça change, plus c'est la meme chose.* —*New York Times Magazine*

See also THE MORE THINGS CHANGE, THE MORE THEY STAY THE SAME.

There's safety in numbers. One always feels safer behaving the same way as other people do; one feels more secure in a group of people. The proverb appears in the Old Testament. It has been traced back to the seventeenth century, and is first cited in the United States in Theodore Dreiser's novel *Titan* (1914). The proverb is found in varying forms: *There's strength in numbers; There's comfort in numbers,* etc.

> Where no counsel *is*, the people fall: but in the multitude of counsellors *there is* safety. —Prov. 11:14, *Authorized Version*, 1611

1914. After seeing him she thought at first that she would question him, but later decided that she would wait and watch more closely. Perhaps he was beginning to run around with other women. There was safety in numbers—that she knew. —Theodore Dreiser, *Titan*

1988. To put it more bluntly, in times of crisis doctors believe there is safety in numbers. —Erich Segal, *Doctors*

1989. Forty percent of the thirteen hundred members of Yale's graduating class of 1986 applied to one investment bank, First Boston, alone. There was, I think, a sense of safety in the numbers. —Michael Lewis, *Liar's Poker*

1991. What gay men and lesbians miss most when they move to suburbia is the sense of community that comes from living amid people like themselves.

"There's a lot of comfort in numbers," Mr. Nolan said. "That's a level of security we don't have here." —*New York Times*

1992. "All right," Martinez said. "I warned you. If you think there's safety in numbers, you're wrong." —Philip Friedman, *Inadmissible Evidence*

1993. There's usually safety in numbers. In boxing, there's a chance of corruption in numbers. —*New York Times*

1994. "There's little safety in these numbers," said anchorwoman Paula Zahn prior to releasing FBI 1993 crime statistics. —"CBS This Morning"

See also THE MORE THE MERRIER; UNITED WE STAND, DIVIDED WE FALL.

There's the rub. That's the difficulty. The saying comes from the ancient game of bowls, a precursor of bowling, where *rub* meant something that hindered the movement of the ball. The saying was first used by Shakespeare in Hamlet's famous soliloquy, "To be, or not to be." *There lies the rub* is a variant of the saying.

1600–01.
    Hamlet: To die, to sleep;
    To sleep; perchance to dream: ay, there's
        the rub;
    For in that sleep of death what dreams may
        come ...
            —Shakespeare, *Hamlet*, Act III, Scene I

1922. ... He was quite sanguine of success, providing puffs in the local papers could be managed by some fellow with a bit of bounce who could pull the indispensable wires and thus combine business with pleasure. But who? That was the rub. —James Joyce, *Ulysses*

1976. FBI Director Clarence M. Kelley has said in a

speech that collecting information about private citizens is not a serious threat unless data are misused. What guarantees are there that the raw files will not be misused? And there, as Hamlet's masseur would say, is the rub. —Art Buchwald, *Washington Is Leaking*

1994. "There's the rub, here lies my zhlub, I married a schlemiel," sings the title character's wife, Tryna Rytza (Rosalie Gerut), about her arranged marriage to Schlemiel, a lazy simpleton (Larry Block) whom she loves in spite of his faults. —*New York Times*

See also THAT'S THE WAY THE COOKIE CRUMBLES.

They never miss an opportunity to miss an opportunity. Some people always miss opportunities to do something important. The saying was coined by Israel's former foreign minister Abba Eban (1915–). The subject *they* may be replaced by another subject. A similar idea is attributed to George Bernard Shaw (1856–1950).**

(undated).
A man who never missed an occasion to let slip an opportunity. —George Bernard Shaw on Lord Archibald Rosebery (1847–1929), quoted in the *Macmillan Dictionary of Quotations*

1991. It is misjudgments like these that provoked the memorable rebuke from Israel's former Foreign Minister Abba Eban that the Palestinians have never missed an opportunity to miss an opportunity. —*New York Times*

1992. Congress virtually never reacts to economic downturns in time to make them go away sooner, and never exploits good times to make real progress on the deficit. In short, Washington never misses an opportunity to miss an opportunity. —*New York Times*

See also LIGHTNING NEVER STRIKES IN THE SAME PLACE TWICE; OPPORTUNITY KNOCKS BUT ONCE.

They that sow the wind shall reap the whirlwind. Those who start wrong or violent actions will suffer the more violent consequences of their actions. The proverb appears in the Old Testament. It has been traced back in English to 1583, and is first attested in the United States in *Potiphar Papers* (1853) by George William Curtis (1824–92). The proverb is found in varying forms: *If you sow the wind you reap the whirlwind; Sow the wind and reap the whirlwind*, etc. It is often shortened to *sow the wind* or *reap the whirlwind*.

For they have sown the wind, and they shall reap the whirlwind. —Hos. 8:7, *Authorized Version*, 1611

1984. I knew that Absalom would come after me, and I knew he would die. He had sown the wind. He would reap the whirlwind. —Joseph Heller, *God Knows*

1987. It was the children [after the Hiroshima bombing], more than anything else, who reaped the "whirlwind of insanity," he said. —*New York Times*

1990. In early 1929, when Leffingwell heard reports that Monty was getting "panicky" about the frothy conditions on Wall Street, he impatiently told Lamont, "Monty and Ben sowed the wind. I expect we shall all have to reap the whirlwind.... I think we are going to have a world crisis." —Ron Chernow, *The House of Morgan*

See also HE WHO LIVES BY THE SWORD DIES BY THE SWORD.

A thing of beauty is a joy for ever. Something beautiful brings us pleasure for a long time. The saying was originated by John Keats (1795–1821). Often shortened to *A thing of beauty.*

> **1818.** A thing of beauty is a joy for ever:
> Its loveliness increases; it will never
> Pass into nothingness ...
> —John Keats, "Endymion"

> **1939.** A thing of beauty is a joy until it goes in
> bathing.
> What the girls say—A thing of beauty is a
> boy forever.
> —Lewis & Faye Copeland, *10,000 Jokes,*
> *Toasts and Stories*

1991. A CATCH ON THE SURFACE IS A THING OF BEAUTY. —Headline, *New York Times*

1994. "Well, what do you think? He swears that it's a thing of beauty but doesn't guarantee that it'll be a joy forever." —Cartoon, *Modern Maturity*

A thing worth doing is worth doing well.
See IF A THING IS WORTH DOING, IT'S WORTH DOING TWICE.

Things come in threes. *See* ALL GOOD THINGS COME IN THREES.

Think before you speak. Before you say something, think it over carefully. The proverb dates back to R. Edgeworth's *Sermons* (1557), calling on his parishioners to "thinke well and thou shalt speak well." When W. Painter wrote his book in 1623, *Chaucer New Painted,* he modified slightly the old saw, "Think twise, then speak, the old Prouerbe doth say, Yet Fooles their bolts will quickly shoot away."

1990. The June newsletter from Massport is required reading for Gov. Dukakis, who was recently scolded for making a joke about a fictional bomb in White House aide Ron Kaufman's luggage at Logan Airport. A long article on airport-security tips for passengers ends with the advice: "Think before you speak. Casual joking remarks may not be viewed as such by secret agents." —*Boston Globe*

1993. An open letter to Charles Barkley: Although you are one of the greatest basketball players in the world, you owe it to yourself, nobody else, the following: 1) a good dose of humility, and 2) the self-control to think before you speak and act. —*Arizona Republic*

1997. I'd like to warn those who are lucky enough to be on TV or quoted in the newspapers to please stop and think before you speak. You are representing not only yourself but thousands of other teens who don't want to be remembered as the screwed-up crazy and stupid Class of 2000. —*Sun-Sentinel* (South Florida)

1997. Think before you speak. Plan ahead. Try to see the other guy's point of view. Tell the truth. If you can't say anything nice, don't say anything. Moderation in all things. To thine own self be true. —*Time*

1998. Tommy John, WPIX-TV's Yankees' voice, should consider thinking before he speaks. —*New York Daily News*

See also BETTER SAFE THAN SORRY; I THINK THEREFORE AM; LOOSE LIPS SINK SHIPS; WORDS ONCE SPOKEN YOU CAN NEVER RECALL.

The third time is the charm. It takes three tries to get something done right. The proverb has been traced back to John Kelly's collection of Scottish proverbs, and is first attested in the United States in 1832.

1922. Third time is the charm. —James Joyce, *Ulysses*

1993. "This was a show that I could do and still continue my recovery," he [Gregory Hines] said. "I still have a ways to go. But when I hit the stage, I'm a walking, talking neon sign for God. I'm a work in progress. I can't move or sing as well as I used to—but *I will.* The healing process has been an incredible celebration of will and faith. So this is a third chance at life. As they say, the third time is the charm." —*Parade Magazine*

See also ALL GOOD THINGS COME IN THREES.

Thirty pieces of silver. A bribe for betrayal. Anyone can be bought. According to the Bible, Judas Iscariot received 30 pieces of silver for selling out

Jesus. The phrase is used for any kind of bribery and betrayal.***

Then one of the twelve, called Judas Iscariot, went unto the chief priests,

And said *unto them,* What will ye give me, and I will deliver him unto you? And they covenanted with him for thirty pieces of silver. —Matt. 26:14–15, *Authorized Version,* 1611

1946. "Oh, not for Gummy. The only difference between him and Judas Iscariot is that Gummy would have got some boot with that thirty pieces of silver. Oh, Gummy would sell out anything." —Robert Penn Warren, *All the King's Men*

1986. "It is not evil in any way that I can judge evil. Its only fault that I can see is that it produced people who didn't love her enough, people who would sell her to strangers for thirty pieces of silver." —Pat Conroy, *The Prince of Tides*

1991. "Judas sold out for just 30 pieces of silver," wrote Joan Vennochi, beginning one of her columns in *The Boston Globe.* —Quoted in the *New York Times*

1992. "… he peddles that story for his thirty pieces of silver and walks away free." —Philip Friedman, *Inadmissible Evidence*

1994. Mr. Farrakhan's spokesman also assailed African-American artists and intellectuals, including Alice Walker, August Wilson, Bayard Rustin, Henry Louis Gates and Cornel West. The film maker Spike Lee he labeled "Spook Lee" and accused him of being a Judas who took 30 pieces of silver—$30 million—from white financiers to falsify the life of Malcolm X. —*New York Times*

This land is your land. The saying is the title of a song written and performed in 1956 by Woody Guthrie (1912–67), a folk singer and guitarist. The saying is often used in headlines of articles and titles of books.

1956. This land is your land, this land is my land,
From California to the New York island,
From the redwood forest to the Gulf Stream waters,
This land was made for you and me.
—Woody Guthrie, "This Land Is Your Land"

1992. THIS ELAND IS YOUR ELAND —Headline article on tours to Kenya, *New York*

1993. *Bosnian Serb* (singing): This land is my land, yes, it's all my land, from Banja Luka to Mljet Island. I'll just take over wherever I land, this land was made for me to seeeeize.
Muslim: Boy, do I hate Serbian folk songs. —Quoted in the *New York Times*

1994. *This Land Is My Land.* —"CNN World Report"
See also THE LAND OF THE FREE AND THE HOME OF THE BRAVE; THE LAND WAS OURS BEFORE WE WERE THE LAND'S.

This, too, will (shall) pass. Don't worry: tough times will eventually come to an end. This proverb has been traced back to the 1852 collection of aphorisms, *Polonius,* by Edward Fitzgerald (1809–83), and was first used in the United States in 1859 by Abraham Lincoln. The proverb is attributed to King Solomon. A sultan asked Solomon to develop a sentence which would be visible at any time, and which would be true and appropriate in both adverse and prosperous times. And Solomon came up with the following sentence: "And this, too, shall pass away." *Solemn words and these are they: Even this shall pass away* is a variant of the proverb. *It* is often used instead of *they.*

1859. It is said an Eastern monarch once charged the wise man to invent him a sentence, to be ever in view, and which should be true and appropriate in all times and situations. They presented him the words: "And this, too, shall pass away." How much it expresses! How chastening in the hour of pride! How consoling in the depth of affliction! —Abraham Lincoln "Address to the Wisconsin State Agricultural Society"

1984. He [my father] never let any of us surrender to despair, and I confess there was more than one moment in 1981 when I felt ready to throw in the towel. I kept my sanity in those days by recalling his favorite saying: "It looks bad right now, but remember, this too shall pass." —Lee Iacocca with William Novak, *Iacocca*

1986. "Look, Doc, relax. I've had nosebleeds before. This too will pass." —Pat Conroy, *The Prince of Tides*

1991. "I'm sorry for your family," Boesky said. "I'm worried about your mental health. Remember [Levine], all things will pass." —James B. Stewart, *Den of Thieves*

1993. Down the cobbled street ignore the stares from under canopies of bars: umbrella envy—it, too, shall pass. —*New Yorker*

1994. The parody title is a breath of fresh air. Or a bucket of cold water. The world does go on, it says. A play is only a play, and it, too, shall pass. —*New York Times*

Those who can, do. Those who can't, teach.

Those who are able to do something do it; those who cannot do something teach it. The proverb was coined by George Bernard Shaw in 1903, and is found in varying forms: *He who can, does; he who cannot, teaches; Those who can, do. Those who can't, criticize; Those who can, do; those who can't, attend conferences,* etc.

1903. He who can, does. He who cannot, teaches. —George Bernard Shaw, *Man and Superman*

1964. "Those who can, do; those who can't, teach." Like most sayings, this is only half true. Those who can, teach; those who can't—the bitter, the misguided, the failures from other fields—find in the school system an excuse or a refuge. —Bel Kaufman, *Up the Down Staircase*

1974. He [Robert Moses] tried to roar back at his critics. "Those who can, build. Those who can't, criticize," he said. —Robert A. Caro, *The Power Broker*

1977. Those who can, do; those who can't, teach (George Bernard Shaw). And those who can't, teach, teach teachers. —Dr. Laurence J. Peter, *Peter's Quotations*

1988. It has always seemed an addled adage: "Those who can, do. Those who cannot, teach." Some of the doers, it now seems, have long yearned to educate. Lawyers, nurses, millwrights, accountants and executives—people of experience—in growing numbers are leaving their professions, earning teaching certificates and heading for the classroom. —*New York Times*

1990. Don't take too seriously the axiom that—"Those who can't do, teach." ... For you, teaching may be the time you need to recharge batteries and set a new course in your career—or discover you thrive in a classroom. —Daniel Moreau, *Take Charge of Your Career*

Those who cannot remember the past are condemned to repeat it. One should study history to avoid mistakes of the past. The saying was coined by George Santayana (1863–1952) in his book, *The Life of Reason.* The idea, though, was expressed by Euripides (c. 485–406 b.c.).

About 407 b.c.
> Whoso neglects learning in his youth,
> Loses the past and is dead for the future.
> —Euripides, *Phrixus*

1905–06.
Those who cannot remember the past are condemned to repeat it. —George Santayana, *The Life of Reason*

1994. It brings back memories of World War II, when many were slow to acknowledge the senseless slaughter of millions of Jews and others.... An oft-quoted passage admonishes us not to forget the past, lest we be condemned to repeat it. As we think about D-day, perhaps we ought to apply its lessons to the slaughter going on right now. —*Time*

Those who know don't speak; those who speak don't know. Knowledgeable people don't feel that they need to talk all the time; those who are ignorant always offer their opinions on every subject. The proverb is of Chinese origin and was recorded by Lao-tzu (c.604–c.531 b.c.). The proverb is found in varying forms: *He who knows does not speak. He who speaks does not know; Those who say don't know, and those who know don't say,* etc.

About 604–about 531 b.c.
> He who knows does not speak.
> He who speaks does not know.
> —Lao-tzu, *The Way of Lao-tzu, 56*

1989. Best of all, he gave us a rule of thumb about information in the markets that I later found useful: "Those who say don't know, and those who know don't say." —Michael Lewis, *Liar's Poker*

1992. Those who know don't talk and those who talk don't know. —Joseph A. Califano, "Good Morning America"

Those who live in glass houses shouldn't throw stones. *See* PEOPLE WHO LIVE IN GLASS HOUSES SHOULDN'T THROW STONES.

Those who say don't know, and those who know don't say. *See* THOSE WHO KNOW DON'T SPEAK; THOSE WHO SPEAK DON'T KNOW.

Three strikes and you're out. You get three tries; if you don't succeed on your third attempt, you'll get no additional tries. The saying is derived from baseball: batters are allowed two strikes at the ball and if they miss the ball the third time, they are out. In the 1990s some states passed laws stipulating that criminals convicted of a third felony offense would be imprisoned for life without parole. Both sayings may be used in reference to any kind of activity: three gross violations and you're finished.***

1992. "If you want to be blunt about it, Stacey has two strikes against her, and she rises above it all," Martin says. —*New York Times Magazine*

1993. Governor-elect Christine Todd Whitman, who was unfairly accused by Gov. Florio of being soft on crime, has endorsed a similar measure for

New Jersey. "Three strikes and you're in—for life without parole," she has said. —*Times* (Trenton)

1993. Three strikes, you're out?... Christine M. Niedermeir, a Fairfield, Conn., Democrat who seemed just a few years ago to be the party's great young hope in a section of the state dominated by Republicans, has now lost three elections in a row—most recently a race for top local official of her own hometown. While giving her high marks for effort, party leaders are suggesting that perhaps her future is in party work beyond the ballot box. —*New York Times*

1994. "Three strikes and you're out" or "three strikes and you're in" has become the popularly echoed proposal of diverse leading officials across the nation—from Governor Mario Cuomo and Pete Wilson to President Bill Clinton—as they struggle to address the public's outrage and growing intolerance of the justice system's seeming inability to protect the public from repeat and violent predatory criminals. —*Jewish Press* (N.Y.)

1995. California's habitual-offender law is off to a shaky start. The law, dubbed "Three Strikes and You're Out," requires anyone convicted of three felonies, including one violent crime, to serve 25 years to life in prison. —*New York Times*

See also LOCK 'EM UP AND THROW AWAY THE KEY; GUNS DON'T KILL PEOPLE. PEOPLE DO.

Till death us do part. Until one of us dies. Taken from the wedding ceremony of the *Book of Common Prayer* (1661), which includes "till death us do part." The order is often reversed to "death do us part." Sometimes this saying is used not in reference to marriage but to an unattainable goal. According to Eric Partridge, the saying has been current in the United States as a figure of speech since about 1965. The saying was popularized through the 1992 movie, *Till Death Us Do Part,* starring Arliss Howard and Treat Williams.

1985. Divorce is extreme, and it is smart to try to work things out before you make that final break. But you *don't* have to stay in the wrong corporate family 'till death do you part. —Jacqueline Hornor Plumez with Karla Dougherty, *Divorcing a Corporation*

1988. All he [Barney] wanted was to be with Shari till death did them part. —Erich Segal, *Doctors*

1992. "Couples are becoming more sober about the 'Until death do us part,'" said Dr. William J. Doherty, a therapist and the director of graduate studies at the University of Minnesota. —*New York Times*

1993. One or the other must leave,
One or the other must stay,
One or the other must grieve,
That is forever the way.
That is the vow that was sworn,
Faithful 'til death do us part.
Braving what had to be borne,
Hiding the ache in the heart.
　　　—Anonymous, quoted in "Dear Abby," by
　　　　　　　　　　　　　Abigail Van Buren

Till hell freezes over. This anonymous saying has been traced back to the 1910s–1920s. P. G. Wodehouse (1881–1975) was among the first to use the saying. F. Scott Fitzgerald (1896–1940) used to end his letters with "Yours till hell freezes over." *Until* may substitute for *till.*

1939. "I'll be aroun'," I says. "I'll be aroun' till hell freezes over!" —John Steinbeck, *The Grapes of Wrath*

1966. The outraged Democrats in Congress, reading the handwriting on the wall, undertook to launch a filibuster "until hell froze over." —Thomas A. Bailey, *The American Pageant*

1969. I never ask them for anything—they can wait till hell freezes over before I ask them for a dime, them with all their money. —Joyce Carol Oates, *Them*

1987. Sidney Sheldon turned down $14.5 million for his Holmby Hills, California estate. (Holmby Hills is very like Beverly Hills only more so.) With Sidney's novels about love and lust selling the way they do, he can hold out till Holmby Hills freezes over. —*New York Post*

1991. "I can disappear in the middle of the night, vanish into the air. If that happens, you and the Moroltos can fight each other till hell freezes over, and I'll be playing dominoes in the Caribbean." —John Grisham, *The Firm*

1994. "If I don't have answers by Oct. 1, I will have an oversight hearing every two weeks," Mr. Robles said. "I'll sound like Adlai Stevenson when I say, 'I'll do it till hell freezes over or I get answers.'" —*New York Times*

Time and tide wait for no man. Don't put anything off until a later time; time passes and the opportunity will be lost. *Tide* is an archaic word equivalent to *time.* The proverb has been traced back in English to about 1386 Chaucer's *Prologue* to the *Clerk's Tale.* In 1546, John Heywood included it in his collection of proverbs ("The tide tarrieth no man"). In 1592, Robert Green added the word *time* ("Time nor tide tarrieth no man"). It is first attested in the United States in the 1656 *History of Plymouth Plantation,* written by William Bradford (1590–1657) and published for the first time in 1856. *Time waits for no man* is a variant of the proverb.

1791. Nae man can tether time or tide. —Robert Burns, *Tam o'Shanter*

1963. Now that was a favorite saying of Jake Beam's, who used to be stationmaster at the old Bertha Furnace station, before they discontinued the passenger station. "Time and tide," he would say so solemn, "and the Alton railroad wait for no man." —John Updike, *The Centaur*

1985. Your corporate life and your personal life do not have to be at war. Time waits for no man, but no man—or woman—need wait for time. You can do everything you want (or at least 80 percent) right now. —Jacqueline Hornor Plumez with Karla Dougherty, *Divorcing a Corporation*

1991. "You skinnied down and up that thing like greased lightning," she [Scarlett] said with honest admiration when Rhett was beside her again.

"Or a monkey," he corrected. "Come on, my dear, time and tide wait for no man, not even a woman." —Alexandra Ripley, *Scarlett*

1992. Time waits for no man, but true love waits forever. —Ad for movie, *Forever Young, New York Times*

See also PROCRASTINATION IS THE THIEF OF TIME; SEIZE THE MOMENT; STRIKE WHILE THE IRON IS HOT; TIME FLIES; TIME IS MONEY.

Time flies. While we dawdle, our lives pass swiftly. The proverb has been traced back in English to 1386 in Chaucer's *Prologue* to the *Clerk's Tale.* The earliest American appearance in print is 1710 in *Mayflower Descendant.* The idea was first expressed by Virgil (70–19 b.c.), who wrote in the *Aeneid: Fugit inreparabile tempus* ("Time is flying never to return"). The proverb is found in varying forms: *How time flies!; Time flies like the wind;* and in Latin as *tempus fugit* etc.

1922. How time flies! —James Joyce, *Ulysses*

1973. He said to Elena, "Your mother says you're doing well in school, going to graduate in a few months! Time flies!" —Joyce Carol Oates, *Do With Me What You Will*

1984. He [David] had once asked Martin, "How often do you see your kids?"

His son, Joe, was established in Canada and a Canadian citizen now. "Eight months ago was the last time," Martin had said. "How time flies!" —Howard Fast, *The Outsider*

1989. It would be the work of the moment—and easily forgotten as the years went by. Time flies. —Kurt Vonnegut, Jr., *Jailbird*

1992. WHY TIME FLIES … AND HOW TO SLOW IT DOWN —Headline, quoted in *Reader's Digest*

1993. "I can't believe this is it for this group," said senior Miami linebacker Michael Barrow. "This class has been through a lot. You look back and you say, 'Wow, how time flies.'" —*New York Times*

1994. "Time flies," Pat Riley said earlier in the day, before the Knicks played the first major league sports event on the New York subway line since the baseball players went on strike on Aug. 11 and the lords of hockey self-destructed in October. —*New York Times*

See also PROCRASTINATION IS THE THIEF OF TIME; STRIKE WHILE THE IRON IS HOT; TIME AND TIDE WAIT FOR NO MAN; TIME IS MONEY.

Time heals all wounds. Pain, grief, and hatred—any intense emotion—fade as time goes by. The proverb has been traced back to about 1374 (*Troilus and Criseyde* by Chaucer). It's first attested in the United States in 1830 (*Correspondence of Andrew Jackson*). The proverb is found in varying forms: *Time is a great healer; Time heals; Time will heal,* etc.

1957. "Time cures all things," he would say or, "The poor man goes before the thief." —John Cheever, *The Wapshot Chronicle*

1967. "Congratulations, this is all going to work out."

"Of course it will," I said.

"I always said your heart was in the right place."

"And now you're sure," I said.

"Time heals," he said.
        —Elia Kazan, *The Arrangement*

1977. "You developed an attachment with a woman half your age, Sven," Hennessy said quietly, no longer the chief of staff or even the official intimate adviser, but the old friend and former divorce attorney. "It happens to a lot of guys. And you're right, you eat your heart out after a while, you pay in blood. But there comes a time you finish paying. Something new comes up. Time wounds all heels." —William Safire, *Full Disclosure*

1979. Time, which is said to heal most sorrows, left her memory undulled … —Howard Fast, *The Establishment*

1987. "People are capable of change," Mrs. Abraham said. "Time heals." —*New York Times*

1993. "I personally don't think that time will heal this wound," said Dan Radford, secretary–treasurer of the Cincinnati AFL–CIO Labor Council. "If I sound bitter, it's because I am." —*Times* (Trenton)

1995. My friends and family tried to tell me that time would heal the hurt, anger, and all that went with it. At that time, it was hard for me to understand.

Continue with your therapy and the divorce recovery group—they both helped me.

Giving yourself time to heal is the key. —Abigail Van Buren, "Dear Abby"

Time is money. Every minute you waste is money lost. The proverb's earliest appearance in print was 1572 (*Discourse upon Usury* by T. Wilson). It is first cited in the United States in Benjamin Franklin's *Advice to a Young Tradesman* (1748).

1748. Remember that time is money. —Benjamin Franklin, *Advice to a Young Tradesman*

1862. Take away *time is money*, and what is left of England? Take away *cotton is king*, and what is left of America? —Victor Hugo, *Les Misérables*

1974. Most European countries are quite aware of the American slogan, "Time is money." —Milla Alihan, *Corporate Etiquette*

1977. "Tell Vasily time is money." —William Safire, *Full Disclosure*

1984. "Remember that time is money," Ben Franklin wrote in *Advice to a Young Tradesman.* —*Forbes*

1987. "Boopsie! We're waiting!"

"It's a small, intimate film about growing up, Zonker. It's called 'Chugalug.'"

"*Boopsie!* Time is money, sweetheart!" —G. B. Trudeau, *Doonesbury Deluxe*

1989. "Hey, pal, time is money," he said, moving on to a woman in a mink coat. A short while later, arms loaded with lox, herring and whitefish, she was on her way. I continued to wait, pretending I was still on California time. —*New York Times*

1991. SINCE TIME IS MONEY, AN AIRLINE SHOULD HELP YOU MAKE THE MOST OF YOUR INVESTMENT —Ad, *New Yorker*

1992. "We look at ourselves as the U-boat," he [Rick Hawkins] continued, "that can move in and out very quickly. We understand the time-is-money concept." —*New York Times*

1993. You've heard the old expression, "Time is money"? Most folks don't realize it, but they could save thousands of dollars by changing the present loans. —*Times* (Trenton)

See also PROCRASTINATION IS THE THIEF OF TIME; TIME AND TIDE WAIT FOR NO MAN.

Time is of the essence. Time is absolutely essential; it is important that time is not wasted and things are done promptly. This anonymous saying has been in use since the nineteenth century.

1980. "To make things move quickly is our concern," says M. Chib. Adds Mr. Mirdna: "Time is the essence of the whole thing. If we start at the earliest, the damage [to the 350-year-old Taj Mahal] could be minimized." —*Christian Science Monitor*

1984. When the Lynn City Council voted to turn over 70 acres of prime waterfront land to a local attorney who promised to develop it into a marine-related industrial park, the contract contained a clause stating "time is of the essence." —*Boston Globe*

1997. Irvin's attorney, State Sen. Royce West, said he isn't worried by police plans to analyze the tape. "I understand the investigation is going to be timely, but believe it should be done with all deliberate speed. Time is of the essence." —*Detroit News*

1998. Time is of the essence for a 46-year-old Canton music teacher diagnosed with leukemia in February, as her husband calls for bone marrow donors to come forward to provide a successful match for his wife. —*Boston Globe*

1998. Could a person in that state survive? "Sure," says [Dr. John] Ochsner, "depending on the size of the rent, or tear. If it wasn't too big, they could put the patient on a heart-lung machine and just go in and do [the repair] effectively. It's pretty obvious with that lesion, if you can get them in a hospital and on a heart-lung machine early enough, you can save them. But time is of the essence. It took about an hour and 45 minutes from the time of the accident to the time the Princess [Diana] entered the operating room." —Thomas Sancton & Scott McLeod, *Death of a Princess: the Investigation*

See also TIME IS MONEY.

A time to be born and a time to die. *See* THERE'S A SEASON AND A TIME FOR EVERY PURPOSE UNDER THE HEAVEN.

Time waits for no man. *See* TIME AND TIDE WAIT FOR NO MAN.

Time will tell. Whether something is true or false, good or bad, real or fake can only be known in the future. The proverb has been traced back to 1530, and is first attested in the United States in 1609. The proverb is found in varying forms: *Only time will tell; Time (will) tell(s) all tales,* etc.

1978. I could see he was just spoiling for an argument—one of the things that makes Harold hard to like is how eager he is to show off how much he knows (and he sure does know a lot, I can't take that away from him Harold is superbright)—but all Glen said was, "Time will tell, won't it?" —Stephen King, *The Stand*

1988. "That might well be the case, young fella," broke in the old Irishman, nodding his head. "Only time will tell, won't it?" —Robert Ludlum, *The Icarus Agenda*

1991. "There are always many things that complicate the issue," says [Vincent] Schaefer, his shock of white hair lending the statement a certain oracular quality. Time will tell, [Daniel] Smiley might have added. Time will tell. —*The Sciences*

1992. Mr. Goldhaber said he had long talks with Apple and IBM to ensure that Kaleida would enjoy entrepreneurial autonomy. "Time will tell, but I'm extremely optimistic—or I can assure you I wouldn't have done this," he said. —*Wall Street Journal*

1993. If U.S. Attorney General Janet Reno were to send lawyers to New Jersey without opening a parallel probe in New York City, her partisan colors would truly be showing. Will she do it? Time will tell. —*New York Post*

1994. Only time will tell whether the competitive providers have the historic dependability—and prowess—not only to endure, but to thrive in New York. —*Crain's New York Business*

Times change. *See* TIMES CHANGE AND WE WITH TIME.

Times change and we with time. Circumstances, conditions and values change all the time and they affect our lives. The proverb has been traced back in English to John Lyly's *Euphues, Anatomy of Wit* (1579). The anonymous Latin proverb, *Tempora mutantur nos et mutamur in illis* ("Times change, and we change with them"), was recorded in 1579. *Omnia mutantur nos et mutamur in illis* ("All things change, and we change with them") is attributed to the Emperor Lothair (795–855). It is first cited in the United States in the 1934 book, *Murder of Honest Broker* by W. Sharp. The proverb is often shortened to

Times change. The word *times* is sometimes replaced with another subject.

1973. He experienced a sort of bittersweet happiness as he told himself, "Times change. Times change." —Kurt Vonnegut, Jr., *Breakfast of Champions*

1979. I don't think a black or Hispanic would have been allowed to join [the union] back in the good old days. Times change. —Kurt Vonnegut, Jr., *Jailbird*

1982. "As I recall, our profit was pretty good before I left. I thought we agreed we wouldn't get involved in manufacturing war supplies." Kate felt an anger rising in her. "You agreed. I didn't." She fought to control it. "Times change, David. We have to change with them." —Sidney Sheldon, *Master of the Game*

1988. I wouldn't have done that when *Parachute* first came out in 1970. But times do change! —Richard Nelson Bolles, *What Color Is Your Parachute?*

1989. "I can't imagine how he got on the estate without being seen. We've never had guards, not since Cyrus's death. Well, the world is changing. We may have to change with it." —Michael Korda, *The Fortune*

1993. "Times change and I change with them," she said. "I acknowledge the past and pass it on." —*New York Times*

1994. Named chairman of the Assembly's Codes Committee in 1987, Silver moved that traditionally left-leaning body decidedly to the right—particularly in matters relating to the fight against crime.... But times change, sad to say. —*New York Post*

Timing is everything. The selection of the right moment for doing something is extremely important. The idea of the proverb was well-known to the ancients and was used by Hesiod about 700 b.c. The proverb has varying forms: *In life, timing is everything; In politics, timing is everything,* etc.**

About 700 b.c.
Observe due measure, for right timing is in all things the most important factor. —Hesiod, *Works and Days*

1993. Timing is everything.... After lunch, Representative Anthony Beilenson (D-California) reaps a harvest of goodwill simply by showing up. Thanks to his quick scheduling change, the Californians at last meet with a real-live Congressman. Beilenson has likely never faced a friendlier crowd. —*Modern Maturity*

1994. ... In politics, as in so much else, timing can be everything. —*New York Times*

See also THERE'S A SEASON AND A TIME FOR EVERY PURPOSE UNDER THE HEAVEN; THERE'S A TIME AND PLACE FOR EVERYTHING.

The tip of the iceberg. See IT'S THE TIP OF THE ICEBERG.

To be forewarned is to be forearmed. See FOREWARNED IS FOREARMED.

To be left holding the bag. To be forced to take responsibility for wrongdoings committed by others. The saying has been used in the United States since 1783, when Thomas Jefferson wrote "She will leave Spain the bag to hold" (1783).

1981. A grocery store "horse race" apparently went haywire, and a New England supermarket chain may be left holding the bag. —*Boston Globe*

1984. With the defection of over half of New England's Division I women's basketball teams to various conferences, Northeastern, Boston University, New Hampshire, Maine, and Vermont were left holding the bag. —*Boston Globe*

1989. If you are having trouble seeing these bank executives as real criminals, consider that the Mafia has been doing the same thing for years. Once gangsters gain a foothold in a legitimate business, they try to milk it dry by siphoning off cash, building up large credit lines from suppliers, and then liquidating inventories. When they pull out, all that remains is a shell of a company with creditors holding the bag. —*Christian Science Monitor*

1992. Whoever engineered the theft of more than $120,000 worth of toy trains earlier this month didn't want to get caught holding the bag. —*Hartford Courant*

1996. [Winston] Bryant's TV commercials are being backed up with ads aired by the Arkansas Democratic Party. One spot features a federal worker who was laid off during the last year's government shutdown. The worker says on camera, "Tim Hutchinson had the gall to shut down the government with Newt Gingrich and then announce he needed his paycheck, leaving the rest of Arkansas holding the bag." —*Cable News Network*

1998. One ominous sign is that during the recent turbulence, the market was apparently sustained by smaller investors, while some bigger players got out of stocks. The big players are more likely to have done the arithmetic described above, meaning small investors could be left holding the bag in the event of a sustained downturn. —*Christian Science Monitor*

To be, or not to be: that is the question. I don't know whether I should act or not. The saying was coined by Shakespeare in *Hamlet* (1600–01). The expression is often used by a speaker who is of two minds about something. It was originally used by Hamlet while contemplating suicide.

1600–01.
Hamlet: To be, or not to be; that is the question. —Shakespeare, *Hamlet*, Act III, Scene I

1922. *Stephen:* To have or not to have that is the question. —James Joyce, *Ulysses*

1961. Only a fraction of his countrymen would give up their lives to win it, and it was not his ambition to be among them. To die or not to die, that was the question, and Clevinger grew limp trying to answer it. —Joseph Heller, *Catch–22*

1987. Some problems take care of themselves, and some are too risky to handle. Notice that even Hamlet considered this alternative ... "to be or not to be." The main thing is to avoid confusing a decision not to act with not being able to decide to act. —R. Richard Ritti & G. Ray Funkhouser, *The Ropes to Skip & the Ropes to Know*

1990. Boarding a plane, I handed the flight attendant my ticket. "I see you got the Shakespeare seat," she said.
"Why is it called that?" I asked.
"Because," she replied, "it's 2B, and the other seats are not 2B." —Quoted in *Reader's Digest*

1991. "To be or not to be, that is the question. Next question?" —Cartoon by Al Ross, *New Yorker*

1991. *Cuomo variations for horn blowers on a cartoon by Doug Marlette:*
To run for President or not to run for President. That is the question with which Geraldo Rivera wrestles day and night. —Russell Baker, *New York Times*

To bite the bullet. To force oneself to do an unpleasant or difficult job or brace oneself against a dangerous situation. The saying dates back to the times when wounded soldiers were treated without anesthesia, and they literally bit on a bullet to ease the pain. "Bite on the bullet, old man," says Rudyard Kipling in *The Light That Failed* (1891), "and don't let them think you're afraid." Anesthesia replaced bullet biting, and the saying got a new lease on life. P. G. Wodehouse was the first to use the saying figuratively. In *The Inimitable*

Jeeves (1924), we read "Brace up and bite the bullet. I'm afraid I have bad news for you."

1984. "In 1981 we bit the bullet and started liquidating the stores," Comey says. It was the best move he ever made. —*Forbes*

1987. MAYOR KOCH BITES A HARD BULLET —Headline of an article about mayor's decision to impose a hiring freeze, *New York Times*

1987. "I thought he [President Reagan] bit the bullet as he should have," said George Aldridge, 62 years old, a retired Army colonel who sells insurance, "but I think he still has a lot of bridges to mend." —*New York Times*

1992. Normally in Italy, debate on such important questions might go on for years, but today's situation leaves leaders with no alternative but to bite a bullet. —*Christian Science Monitor*

1997. First Selectman Roland Dowd thinks it's time for the town "to bite the bullet" and get rid of its $26 million in long-term debt. —*Hartford Courant*

1998. Mr. Yeltsin has staked his reputation on a stable currency and low inflation. Amid signs he is considering a third run for office in 2000, Yeltsin cannot afford to back down. Nevertheless, "the government may be better off to bite the bullet and devalue rather than taking on another loan," says Mr. Dolan. —*Christian Science Monitor*

To die with one's boots on. To die violently or while being active. The analogy comes from soldiers dying in combat with their boots on. Stephen Vincent Benét declared in *A Ballad of William Sycamore, 1790–1880* (1923): "And I died in my boots like a pioneer/With the whole wide sky above me." The expression has been expanded to refer to anyone who keeps on working or intends to work to the end. *To die in one's boots* and *To die with one's shoes on* are variants of the saying.

1989. The next morning he was back at work, just like the four other times he has been mugged. "I'm going to die with my shoes on," he declared yesterday. "I have no intention of giving up. As long as my people need me, I'll be here." —*New York Times*

1989. He was a communist revolutionary, and he died with his boots on. —*Sun-Sentinel* (South Florida)

1991. "It used to be if you became a general manager or a club president you'd have it for life if you wanted; you'd die with your boots on," said Green. —*New York Times*

1994. "I hope to do 50 [seasons] more," [Harry] Caray said between innings of a recent Cubs exhibition game. The 70-something announcer says he would like to die with his boots on, if his health is good, "and I was still going pretty good as of last night." —*Commercial Appeal* (Memphis, Tennessee)

1996. Q. Did the famous western bandit Doc Holliday die with his boots on? L. J. Boston. A. No. According to historian Dale Pierce, Dr. John Henry Holliday, the Georgia dentist who left his home state for the Wild West, died in 1887 in a tuberculosis sanatorium. —*Boston Globe*

1998. He didn't die with his boots on the day a horse rolled over on him, but it sure hurt Barry Corbin to think that some darned sawbones might hack up his best footwear just to set the doctor's busted leg. —*Fort Worth Star-Telegram*

See also OLD SOLDIERS NEVER DIE; THEY JUST FADE AWAY.

To each his own. Each person has her or his own unique inclinations or idiosyncrasies. This saying originated in the United States. The earliest appearance in print was 1713 in John Wise's *Churches Quarrel Espoused.*

1985. "My wife is on the steering committee of the Southern California right-to-life organization. She does her thing. I do mine."

"You Devrons are a remarkable family, each unto his own." —Howard Fast, *The Immigrant's Daughter*

1987. I wonder why they cover sports other than baseball. To each his own, I guess. —G. B. Trudeau, *Doonesbury Deluxe*

1991. Q: Does the idea of secluded public beaches for nude swimmers in New Jersey offend you?

Faith Loftin: No. To each his own. I wouldn't go myself, but if there was one down the street, it wouldn't bother me. —*Times* (Trenton)

1992. "He hits his head on the wall and then he shakes the head around a little, and he's ready to go. Personally, I think it's a little crazy. But to each his own." —*New York Times*

1993. To each his own. And only a pet lover can understand the sense of putting away a beloved pet in such extravagant style. —Abigail Van Buren, "Dear Abby"

See also EVERY MAN TO HIS OWN TASTE; THERE'S NO ACCOUNTING FOR TASTES.

To err is human, to forgive divine. People make mistakes, but only something greater than we are can forgive us. The proverb is based on the Latin: *Humanum est errare.* It has been traced back in English to Chaucer's *Knight's Tale* (1386) and J. I. Vives' *Introduction to Wisdom* (1539). The proverb is found in varying forms: *To err is human, to keep it up is folly; To err is human, to persist in it, beastly,* etc. It is often shortened to *To err is human.*

1635. I presume you're mortal, and may err. —James Shirley, *The Lady of Pleasure*

1711. To err is human, to forgive divine. —Alexander Pope, *An Essay on Criticism*

1966. Worst of all, he [Truman] permitted designing old associates of the "Missouri gang" to gather around him, and, like Grant, was stubbornly loyal to them when they were caught with the cream on their whiskers. "To err is Truman" was a cynical explanation. —Thomas A. Bailey, *The American Pageant*

1978. To err is human but to really foul things up requires a computer. —*Farmers' Almanac*

1980. At the outset of a negotiation you should always come on like velvet, not coarse sandpaper. State your case moderately, scratch your head, and admit you might even be in error. Remember, "To err is human; to forgive, divine." —Herb Cohen, *You Can Negotiate Anything*

1987. "TO ERR IS HUMAN ... TO FORGIVE, DIVINE ..."
"Yes sir." —Fannie Flagg, *Fried Green Tomatoes*

1988. "We're human beings," an ICU nurse once dared to remind her. "To err is human—"
"No," Laura had retorted. "To err is fatal." —Erich Segal, *Doctors*

1991. Then she slammed the phone down, repeating what the manager had just said— "Unfortunately, Madam, we are only human and we erred." —*New Yorker*

1993. To err is human. To guarantee, divine. —Ad, *New York Times Magazine*

To the victor belong the spoils. In a war or other contest, the winner gets the booty. The proverb originated in the United States and was first used in 1832 by Senator William Learned Marcy (1786–1857) of New York. *The victor gets the spoils* and *To the victor go the spoils* are variants of the proverb.

1832. They [Democrats] see nothing wrong in the rule that to the victor belong the spoils of the enemy. —William L. Marcy

1922. The victor belongs to the spoils. —F. Scott Fitzgerald, *The Beautiful and the Damned*

1951. "Winning this year is not enough. We must plan on winning next year. In this world it is the winner who gets spoils." —James Jones, *From Here to Eternity*

1984. From Betah to Berothia, two cities of Hadadezer, I took exceeding much brass, for to the victor belong the spoils. —Joseph Heller, *God Knows*

1987. Incumbents have traditionally campaigned for office on the public's time. But when they distort the process, when they transform the mechanisms of government into a taxpayer-supported machine for self-perpetuation, then the victors belong to the spoils. —*New York Times*

1988. Ukrainian nationalism is real; it's much more than the feeling the proudest Texans have for their state. The Soviets are tied to their conquests of empire by the need to set an example in their most troubling region; in F. Scott Fitzgerald's phrase, "the victor belongs to the spoils." —*New York Times*

1993. TO THE RUTHLESS BELONG THE SPOILS —Headline, *New York Times Book Review*

1994. TO THE LOSER GO THE SPOILS —Headline, *Time Off*

Tomorrow, and tomorrow, and tomorrow. Slowly, the future continues to become, from one day to the next, forever. The line is from Shakespeare's *Macbeth* (about 1606).

1606. *Macbeth:* To-morrow, and to-morrow, and
   to-morrow,
   Creeps in this petty pace from day to day,
   To the last syllable of recorded time;
   And all our yesterdays have lighted fools
   The way to dusty death.
      —Shakespeare, *Macbeth,* Act V, Scene V

1952. *Tomorrow and Tomorrow and Tomorrow and Other Essays* —Title of Aldous Huxley's collection of essays

1991. For the first time in years, rich people were thought to be shrewd as well as lucky. This is where we are now, and it is probably all good—at least for the economy. Tomorrow and tomorrow and tomorrow. —*Esquire*

1992. Mr. Brown told a crowd of cheering supporters in Manhattan last night that he was in for the long haul. "I'll see you all over this country tomorrow, tomorrow and tomorrow," he said. —*New York Times*

Tomorrow is another day. Today didn't go so well, but we'll have another chance tomorrow. The proverb has been traced back to about 1520 (*Calisto & Meliboea* by J. Rastell), and is first attested in the United States in Earl Derr Biggers's book, *Seven Keys to Baldpate* (1913). The proverb was popularized through Margaret Mitchell's *Gone With the Wind* (1936) and the 1939 movie based on it. The proverb is found in varying forms: *Tomorrow is a new day; Tomorrow is also a day.*

1913. Tomorrow is another day. —Earl D. Biggers, *Seven Keys to Baldpate*

1922. *Bloom:* I wanted then to have now concluded. Nightdress was never. Hence this. But tomorrow is a new day will be. —James Joyce, *Ulysses*

1936. "Tomorrow I'll think of some way to get him back. After all, tomorrow is another day." —Margaret Mitchell, *Gone With the Wind*

1973. "Tomorrow's another day. You send her a few flowers and everything will be as good as new." —Jacqueline Susann, *Once Is Not Enough*

1975. It was harder and harder to concentrate. That was OK. Attendance wasn't required. Everyone seemed to be drifting in and out of it. Eventually we'd all drift off to sleep. Tomorrow was another day. —Mark Vonnegut, *The Eden Express*

1990. "We've talked and worked together and shared, and now it has all soaked in," Haskins said. "I kept telling my kids about tomorrow, about tomorrow being a brighter day. Well, tomorrow is here." —*New York Times*

1991. "Books," she sermonized, "have become products like cereal or perfume or deodorant … And writers have to fight tooth and nail to hold onto as much as possible of the work they've done." After all, tomorrow is another payday. —*New York Times*

1992. But if Scarlett O'Hara had it right—if "tomorrow is another day"—then can we expect a better four years ahead if Bush is returned to office? —*New York Times Magazine*

1993. Hillary [Clinton] works tirelessly to counteract Bill's belief that tomorrow is at least another day away. —*Time*

1994. "I shut my eyes tight. Tomorrow is another day, but I want to sleep for a hundred years. Then, when I wake up, my father will be back. There'll be paper chains in the room and we'll be eating cake. 'In the camp,' he'll say, 'I had bread made out of sawdust.' He'll smile. He will never leave us again." —*New York Times*
See also THERE'S ALWAYS (A) TOMORROW.

Too little, too late. See IT'S TOO LITTLE, TOO LATE.

Too many chiefs and not enough Indians.
See ALL CHIEFS AND NO INDIANS.

Too many cooks spoil the broth. If too many people work on the same project, the job won't be done properly. This proverb has been traced back to 1575, and is first cited in the United States in about 1700 in the *General History of New England* (1865). It is found in varying forms: *Too many cooks spoil the stew* (*the pie* or *the brew*).

1987. At a conference in Miami last month, a Brazilian official, Luiz Barboza, said the problems that debtor countries have with the Treasury involve not Mr. Baker but "all the little Bakers"—the assistant secretaries and deputy assistant secretaries who ply Latin America seeking to help them cope with their debts in return for their adoption of Reagan economic policies. "Too many Bakers spoil the dough," Mr. Barboza said. —*New York Times*

1991. "Too many cooks may spoil the broth"
Is often a stated view,
But it is my experience
That one cook can do it, too.
　　　　　　　　　—*Wall Street Journal*

1994. TOO MANY COOKS CAN SPOIL THE FUND —Headline, *New York Times*

1995. The old adage "too many cooks spoil the sauce," will be tested when the chefs participating in Taste of the Nation, a food-and-wine tasting benefit taking place in Forsgate Country Club in Jamesburg May 1, gather in the club's kitchen the afternoon of the party. —*Time Off*
See also ALL CHIEFS AND NO INDIANS; IF YOU WANT SOMETHING DONE RIGHT, DO IT YOURSELF.

Toot your own horn lest the same be never tooted. Praise yourself; others may never do it. This saying originated in the United States in about 1776. It is often shortened to *toot your own horn* and means the same thing as *blow your own horn* or *blow your own trumpet*. The saying was popularized through Neil Simon's Broadway play, *Come Blow Your Horn* (1961).

1986. The 46-year-old Robb, instead of tooting his own horn, deferentially used his after-coffee remarks to praise Georgia senator Sam Nunn. —*New York*

1987. "We just don't believe in tooting our own horns as much as people in other parts of the country," Mr. Kaercher [editor of *Midwest Living*] said. —*New York Times*

1988. The same "experts" who bamboozled us about the innocence of marijuana and the safety of moderate use of "nonaddicting" cocaine are again blowing their trumpets and beating their drums to influence well-meaning but gullible politicians to abandon all reason and consider legalization of drugs as the answer. —*New York Times*

1990. While you are tooting the horn about your accomplishments you will also be touting your skills. —Daniel Moreau, *Take Charge of Your Career*

1992. With apologies to his mother, who taught him never to toot his own horn, President Bush was bragging the other day, sort of. —*New York Times*

1993. "Really? I never told you I was Harry Truman in a previous life?"

"Never! Gosh, I don't know. I toot my own horn ..." —G. B. Trudeau, "Doonesbury"

1994. "In this business, if you don't blow your own horn, there's no music," Governor Cuomo said at a breakfast meeting at the New York Hilton in midtown Manhattan. —*New York Times*

A tooth for a tooth. *See* AN EYE FOR AN EYE, A TOOTH FOR A TOOTH.

The torch has been passed to a new generation. This expression is a line taken from John Kennedy's Inaugural Address on January 20, 1961. The idea, though, originated in ancient times and was used by Lucretius (99–55 b.c.).

99–55 b.c.
Thus the sum of things is ever being renewed, and mortals live dependent one upon another. Some nations increase, others diminish, and in a short space the generations of living creatures are changed and like runners pass on the torch of life. —Lucretius, *On the Nature of Things*

1961. Let the word go forth from this time and place, to friend and foe alike, that the torch has been passed to a new generation of Americans, born in this century, tempered by war, disciplined by a hard and bitter peace, proud of our ancient heritage, and unwilling to witness or permit the slow undoing of those human rights to which this nation has always been committed, and to which we are committed today at home and around the world. —John Kennedy, *Inaugural Address*

The Tower of Babel. A confusion of many people talking without understanding each other. The story is from the Old Testament: the descendants of Noah built a city and a tower at Babel, and tried to build the tower so high that it would reach up to heaven. God interrupted the construction of the tower, causing confusion among the builders by confounding their tongues, and scat-

tered them all over the earth speaking different languages. Often reduced to *Babel*, meaning simply confusion.

Therefore is the name of it called Babel; because the Lord did there confound the language of all the earth: and from thence did the Lord scatter them abroad upon the face of all the earth. —Gen. 11:9, *Authorized Version,* 1611

1892. In street and alley, what strange tongues are loud,
Accents of menace alien to our air,
Voices that once the Tower of Babel knew!
O Liberty, white Goddess! Is it well
To leave the gates unguarded?
—Thomas Bailey Aldrich, *The Unguarded Gates*

1953. "You've been locked up here for years with a regular damned Tower of Babel." —Ray Bradbury, *Fahrenheit 451*

1973. "Louder, please, there's a tower of Babel going on in this place," her mother says. —Joyce Carol Oates, *Do With Me What You Will*

1986. One Administration official said Mr. Meese had been deeply troubled by an "Unseemly public display" being conducted by quarreling officials involved in the Iran deal.... "There was a Tower of Babel on this subject," the official said. —*New York Times*

1992. "The Tower of Babel in food labels has come down, and American consumers are the winners," Dr. Louis W. Sullivan, the Secretary of Health and Human Services, said at a news conference today. —*New York Times*

1993. If a homeland, a country with defined boundaries, were given to every ethnic group on our planet, then we'd have more than a thousand countries. Would the United Nations, which now has only a hundred-plus member countries, then be similar to the Tower of Babel, plagued with chaos, as some politicians? —*Times* (Trenton)

1994. The language spoken at most sessions of the recent International Conference on Population and Development in Cairo was English. But the participants were unknowingly speaking three different languages, said William F. Vendley, executive director of the World Conference on Religion and Peace, who was an official nongovernmental representative at the meeting.... The result, he contends, was sometimes a broadening of perspectives and sometimes sheer Babel. —*New York Times*

A tree is known by its fruit. People should be judged by the character of their children. The proverb appears in the Bible, and has been traced back in English to Chaucer's *Parson's Tale* (c. 1389). Shakespeare used it in *King Henry the Fourth, Part I* (1597–98). In 1670, it was included in James Ray's collection of English proverbs. It is first attested in the United States in *New-England's Prospects* (1865).

> Either make the tree good, and his fruit good; or else make the tree corrupt, and his fruit corrupt: for the tree is known by *his* fruit. —Matt. 12:33, *Authorized Version*, 1611

1597–98.
Falstaff: If that man should be lewdly given, he deceiveth me; for, Harry, I see virtue in his looks. If then the tree may be known by the fruit, as the fruit by the tree, then, peremptorily I speak it, there is virtue in that Falstaff. —Shakespeare, *King Henry the Fourth, Part I*, Act II, Scene IV

1928. "No, there's something wrong with the mental life, radically. It's rooted in spite and envy, envy and spite. Ye shall know the tree by its fruit." —D. H. Lawrence, *Lady Chatterley's Lover*

1986. Mr. Jackson, who disavowed remarks by Mr. Farrakhan in 1984 as "reprehensible" and distanced himself from the Farrakhan views after growing protests, says he believes the minister should be at least given the benefit of the doubt.... "It is true that you judge a tree by the fruit and not by the bark it wears," said Mr. Jackson. —*New York Times*

See also HANDSOME (PRETTY) IS AS HANDSOME (PRETTY) DOES; A MAN IS KNOWN (JUDGED) BY THE COMPANY HE KEEPS.

A Trojan horse. A hidden danger that is presented as a gift. According to Homer's *Odyssey,* a huge hollow wooden horse full of soldiers was given as a gift to the Trojans by the attacking Greeks. At night, when the Trojans were asleep, the Greeks got out of the horse, opened the gates, and stormed the city, thus ending the Trojan War.

1940s–1950s.
If you open that Pandora's Box, you never know what Trojan 'orses will jump out. —Ernest Bevin, quoted by Roderick Barclay in *Ernest Bevin and the Foreign Office*

1986. "Our students are there for an education," said Ray C. Hillam, a university spokesman, as he watched the protesters. "They think we're a Trojan horse, but we're not." —*New York Times*

1992. Somebody had to have leaned on her awfully hard to get her to come aboard in the second seat, Estrada was sure. The result was likely to be a gift horse full of angry Greeks. —Philip Friedman, *Inadmissible Evidence*

1993. NAFTA'S TROJAN HORSE —Headline, *New York Times*

1994. The extravagance on the South Lawn of the White House on that fateful day in September, was all President Clinton with "Peace Now" in the chorus and President Carter behind the stage. The *New York Times* called the agreement "A Gift" (to President Clinton). *We* knew that it would be a "Trojan Horse." —*Jewish Press* (N.Y.)

See also BEWARE OF GREEKS BEARING GIFTS; (A) PANDORA'S BOX.

Trust everyone, but cut the cards. It's OK to trust everyone, but always take precautions to protect yourself just in case. The proverb comes from the game of cards where players cut the cards to prevent cheating. It was used by Finley Peter Dunne (1867–1936) in *Mr. Dooley's Opinions* (1900). The proverb is an American variant of the Russian Доверяй, но проверяй ("Trust, but verify") and was popularized by President Reagan.

1900. Thrust ivrybody, but cut th' ca-ards. —Finley P. Dunne, *Mr. Dooley's Opinions*

1986. Always trust your fellow man. And always cut the cards. —Robert Fulghum, *All I Really Need to Know I Learned in Kindergarten*

1987. "We have listened to the wisdom in an old Russian maxim," Mr. Reagan said. "Though my pronunciation may give you difficulty, the maxim is, 'Doveryai no proveryai,' 'Trust but verify.'" —*New York Times*

1988. "I know there've been some people that have worried a little about Gorbachev and me in these summit meetings, and they think maybe I'm kind of—well, I've gotten a little easier here," he [Reagan] said in Mesquite. "But I just want you to know, I made it plain to him from the very beginning with an old American saying: Trust everyone, but cut the cards." —*New York Times*

Trust in the Lord and use good equipment.
See PRAISE THE LORD AND PASS THE AMMUNITION.

The truth (always, often) hurts. Knowing the truth can hurt. Living with a falsehood can often be more comforting. The proverb has been traced back to 1872, when it was used by Robert Browning (1812–89) in *Fifine at the Fair*. Its earliest appearance in the United States was in 1956, as recorded by Bartlett Jere Whiting. The proverb is found in varying forms: *If the truth hurts, so be it; It's the truth that hurts; The truth never hurts any-*

one; Truth harms no man; Truth never hurts the teller, etc.

1872. So absolutely good is truth, truth never hurts the teller. —Robert Browning, *Fifine at the Fair*

1934. The truth never harmed no man. —C. Bush, *Dead Shepherd*

1956. It's the truth that hurts. —S. W. Taylor, *I Have*

1986. We want the truth. The President wants it. I want it. And the American people have a fundamental right to it. And if the truth hurts, so be it. We gotta take our lumps and move ahead. —Vice President George Bush, *New York Times*

1992. "I don't know what I'd think. I'm afraid I might believe him. Sorry."

"No need. We can't afford to fool ourselves, even if the truth hurts." —Philip Friedman, *Inadmissible Evidence*

1993. After reading your cover story, I had the pleasure of seeing Robbins's *Bob Roberts.* The movie was hilarious and sad at the same time, because the truth hurts. —*Buzz*

Truth is beauty. *See* BEAUTY IS TRUTH, TRUTH BEAUTY.

Truth is stranger than fiction. What happens in real life can be harder to believe than made-up stories. Edmund Burke (1729–97), as early as 1775, compared *fiction* and *truth,* but the proverb was first used in this form by Lord Byron in *Don Juan* (1823). The saying is first attested in the United States in 1845, and in 1897 the proverb was used by Mark Twain. It is found in varying forms: *Truth is greater than fiction; Truth is stronger than fiction; Truth is more plausible than fiction; Truth is stranger than fiction, but not so popular; Fact is stranger than fiction; Life is stranger than fiction,* etc.

1775. When we speak of the commerce with our colonies, fiction lags after truth; invention is unfruitful, and imagination cold and barren. —Edmund Burke, *On Conciliation with America*

1823. 'Tis strange—but true; for truth is always strange;
Stranger than fiction.
—George Gordon, Lord Byron, *Don Juan*

1897. Truth is stranger than Fiction, but it is because Fiction is obliged to stick to possibilities; Truth isn't. —Mark Twain, *Pudd'nhead Wilson's New Calendar*

1984. "I don't expect much. 'Why people have taken to saying that truth is stranger'—or did I say

'stronger'?—than fiction." —Saul Bellow, *Him with His Foot in His Mouth and Other Stories*

1992. STRANGER THAN FICTION —Headline, *New Yorker*

1993. Big flops: *X, Hoffa,* and *Chaplin* all struggled at the box office. The truth is stranger, but not more profitable, than fiction. —*Entertainment Weekly*

Truth is truth to the end of reckoning. Truth never changes. The proverb has been traced back to about 1566. In 1604, it was used by Shakespeare in *Measure for Measure.*

1604. *Isabella:* It is not truer he is Angelo
Than this is all as true as it is strange;
Nay, it is ten times true; for truth is truth
To the end of reckoning.
—Shakespeare, *Measure for Measure,* Act V, Scene I

1953. "Truth is truth, to the end of reckoning, we've cried." —Ray Bradbury, *Fahrenheit 451*

1994. "Fearful in Florida" wanted to know whether to tell the truth in a sexual harassment case a former co-worker had filed. Your advice was to see a lawyer before blowing any more whistles. Why. The truth is the truth—and I fear that many will read your advice as a suggestion that they should conveniently "forget" what they saw. —Abigail Van Buren, "Dear Abby"

See also HONESTY IS THE BEST POLICY; TELL THE TRUTH AND SHAME THE DEVIL; THE TRUTH SHALL MAKE YOU FREE.

Truth lies at the bottom of a well. The truth is often hard to find. The ancient proverb has been attributed to Democritus (c. 460–c. 370) who allegedly said, "In truth we know nothing, for truth lies in the depth." English novelist Laurence Sterne (1713–68) invokes the proverb in his *Tristram Shandy* (1759–67): "Whilst the unlearned... were all busied in getting down to the bottom of the well, where Truth keeps her little court." First attested in the Unites States in the late eighteenth century. For Edgar Allan Poe (1809–49), "truth is not always in a well. In fact, as regards the whole important knowledge, I do believe that she is inavariably superficial."

1973. He was picking up a stone, which he now tossed into the well... "I wonder what's at the bottom of it. Truth—could it conceivably be?"

"Truth at the bottom of the well?" There was a trace of impatience in Dr. Howard's voice. A foolish proverb—but most proverbs are thoroughly foolish. Folk wisdom is almost always fatuous. One doesn't come at truth—or at any truth worth finding—by peering down into dark places. —M. Innes, *Appleby's Answer*

1998. He [Pablo Picasso] simply couldn't stop at half measures. "Are you happy with what you did?", he was asked during the filming of some of his works. "Yes, yes," he replied, "but it's still too external.... I have to get to the bottom..., risk everything. Show all the paintings that could be behind a painting." And later, "You have to risk adventure to surprise truth at the bottom of the well." —*Christian Science Monitor*

The truth shall make you free. Knowing what is true will free you from the bonds of deceit. The proverb appears in the Bible, and is first found in English in William Cowper's *The Task* (about 1784). It takes varying forms: *Know the truth and the truth shall set you free; The truth will set you free,* etc.

And ye shall know the truth, and the truth shall make you free. —John 8:32, *Authorized Version,* 1611

1946. I had found the truth, I had dug the truth up out of the ash pile, the garbage heap, the kitchen midden, the bone yard, and had sent that little piece of truth to Adam Stanton. I couldn't cut the truth to match his ideas. Well, he'd have to make his ideas match the truth. That is what all of us historical researchers believe. The truth shall make you free. —Robert Penn Warren, *All the King's Men*

1975. He [Luke] wasn't perfect. He tripped over his own rhetoric from time to time. "The truth will set you free," and then a little lie. —Mark Vonnegut, *The Eden Express*

1982. As the chief financial officer of a fast-growing computer company said to his managers after taking them through their first budgeting exercise, "Trust the budget; the budget will make you free." —Terrence E. Deal & Allan A. Kennedy, *Corporate Cultures*

1984. The path Jack Ryan had chosen was in the CIA. The agency's official motto was, The truth shall make you free. —Tom Clancy, *The Hunt for Red October*

1984. The U.S. is not the U.S.S.R. The truth is not an inconvenience to be shaded, manipulated and molded to fit the needs of statecraft. "The truth shall make you free" is not an empty piety. In times of crisis, we expect Moscow to lie and we expect Washington to tell the truth, and that difference has been blurred in February of 1984. —William Safire, *The New York Times*

1993. ... The message from Washington seems to be: Don't ask and certainly don't pursue the truth, for the truth shall make ye free. —Todd Gitlin, *Times* (Trenton)

1994. Like so much writing that looks simple—"The truth will set you free," "To thine own self be true," and so forth—"Rob the rich" has power to lead the mind down labyrinthine corridors until it winds up trapped at uncertainty. —Russell Baker, *New York Times*

See also HONESTY IS THE BEST POLICY; TELL THE TRUTH AND SHAME THE DEVIL; TRUTH IS TRUTH TO THE END OF RECKONING.

Truth will (come) out. The truth cannot be hidden forever. Sooner or later it will be revealed. The proverb has been traced back to John Lydgate's book *Life of St. Alban,* written in 1439. It was used by Shakespeare in *The Merchant of Venice* in 1596. It is first attested in the United States in the *Letters of Rev. William Gordon, Historian of the American Revolution* in 1780. The proverb is found in varying forms: *The truth will out; The truth will come to light,* etc.

1596. *Launcelot:* Well, old man, I will tell you news of your son. Give me your blessing; truth will come to light; murder cannot be hid long; a man's son may, but, in the end, truth will out.
—Shakespeare, *The Merchant of Venice,* Act II, Scene II

1936. "The Yankees might easily have thought him a member of the Klan if the whole truth had come out!" —Margaret Mitchell, *Gone With the Wind*

1961. "It will let them know that we're not the least bit afraid to have the whole truth about you come out." —Joseph Heller, *Catch–22*

1962. The truth had at last come out. —James Jones, *The Thin Red Line*

1974. "It'll never come out, the whole truth. You'll never get the truth." —Carl Bernstein & Bob Woodward, *All the President's Men*

1977. "Nobody has suggested lying," Cartwright said with as much sincerity as he could muster. "What we are obliged to do is make sure the truth comes out, not some exaggeration that would distort the truth." —William Safire, *Full Disclosure*

1990. "If the truth came out," he [Pierpont] conceded regarding the staggering price, "I might be considered a candidate for the lunatic asylum." —Ron Chernow, *The House of Morgan*

1991. If there was even a grain of truth to these

stories [of a drug connection], it surely would have come out. —Oliver L. North, *Under Fire*

1994. "Officer Thompson has no political agenda, no racial agenda," said Mr. Agulnick. "He wants the truth to come out." —*New York Times*

See also MURDER WILL OUT.

Turn the rascals out. This common political phrase was coined by Charles Anderson Dana (1819–97), American writer and editor of the New York *Sun*. In collaboration with George Ripley (1802–80) he opposed the extension of slavery to new territories. "Turn the rascals out!" became the major slogan of the Liberal Republican Party (Greeley) campaign in 1872. The saying may have originated on the analogy of Shakespeare's "lash the rascals naked." It is found in varying forms: *Throw the rascals out; Throw the bums out,* etc.

1604. *Emilia:* O heaven! that such companions thou'dst unfold,
And put in every honest hand a whip
To lash the rascals naked through the world.
—Shakespeare, *Othello,* Act IV, Scene II

1966. Reform-minded citizens gradually banded together to organize the Liberal Republican Party. Voicing the slogan "Turn the Rascals Out," the reformers urged purification of the Grant administration and amnesty for the South. —Thomas A. Bailey, *The American Pageant*

1994. As for our midterm elections, many players in Washington will retire or be retired by a throw-the-bums-out mood. —*New York Times*

Turnabout is fair play. Reversing a situation or relations is only fair. The proverb has been traced back to 1755 in the *Life of Captain Dudley Bradstreet,* and was given literary use by the Scottish novelist Robert Louis Stevenson (1850–94) and American writer Lloyd Osborne (1868–1947) in their novel, *The Wrecker* (1892). It is first attested in the United States in the 1777 *Documentary History of the American Revolution.*

1892. You had your chance then; seems to me it's mine now. Turn about's fair play. —Robert Louis Stevenson & Lloyd Osborne, *The Wrecker*

1966. The New Democracy also trumpeted the ideal of "rotation in office"—or "a turn about is fair play." —Thomas A. Bailey, *The American Pageant*

1988. Turnabout, the adage has it, is fair play. But sometimes turnabout produces a delicious irony, if not a red face or two. —Ad, *New York Times*

1992. Turnabout is fair play: in 1956, Clare Boothe

Luce led the Republicans in denouncing Democrats as *troubadours of trouble* and *crooners of catastrophe.* As Democrats expressed their dissatisfaction with the lingering war and slow economic growth in 1970, a Republican wordsmith, recalling Mrs. Luce's alliterative ripostes, fed Vice President Spiro Agnew a nice bit of alliteration with which to castigate the castigators: he called them the *nattering nabobs of negativism.* (I was that wordsmith; that year, I was big on *n's.*) —William Safire, *New York Times Magazine*

1993. ... Mr. Stephanopoulos acknowledged that Mr. Clinton had used the Haiti issue against Mr. Bush in the Presidential campaign, saying: "I guess in their minds turnabout is fair play." —*New York Times*

Two heads are better than one. The help and advice of another person is always welcome. The proverb has been traced back to about 1390. In 1546, it was included in John Heywood's collection of proverbs, and it is first attested in the United States in the 1743 *Boston Evening Post.* The main entry is listed in all major dictionaries of American proverbs.

1957. Two heads are better than one, of course. —*Christian Science Monitor*

1980. *Two paychecks are better than one.* In 1978, 1 American family in 5 had income totaling more than $25,000, and in two thirds of those families, at least 2 members worked. —Mike Feinsilber & William B. Mead, *American Averages*

1984. Two heads are better than one—except in a head-on collision. —*New York Post*

1992. Two heads are better than one. —Carol Martin [on two-headed turtles], "Channel 2 News This Morning"

1993. Long-range plans require quick thinking or action today. Two heads work better than one, so do two hearts that beat as one! —Jeane Dixon, "Horoscope"

Two is company, three is a crowd. A third person is unwelcome when two people want to be alone. The proverb was included in the 1706 *New Spanish and English Dictionary* by J. Stevens, and in 1860, it was listed in W. C. Hazlitt's collection of English proverbs. It is first attested in the United States in the *Season Ticket* (1860) by Thomas C. Haliburton. The proverb is found in varying forms: *One is company, two is a crowd, three is too many, four's not allowed; Two's company, three's a crowd, four on a sidewalk is not* *allowed*, etc.

1860. Three is a very inconvenient imitation, constituting, according to the old adage, "no company." —Thomas C. Haliburton, *Season Ticket*

1922. Under the mistletoe. Two is company. —James Joyce, *Ulysses*

1965. "Do you want to go to the jazz concert?"
"Sure. But three's a crowd."
"I'm sick, Liz. Do me a favor. Go with him in my place." —George P. Elliot, *In the World*

1991. "Two's company," the old rhyme starts, and never more so than for people who live alone and need some help. —*Daily News* (N.Y.)

Two strikes against someone (something).
See THREE STRIKES AND YOU'RE OUT.

Two wrongs don't make a right. Avenging yourself against someone who has wronged you will not right the wrong. This saying is first cited in the United States in B. Bush's *Letters* (1783), and is found in varying forms: *Two wrongs don't make one right; Two wrongs won't right a wrong,* etc.

1781. Three wrongs will not make one right. —B. Bush, *Letters*

1922. What retribution, if any?
Assassination, never, as two wrongs did not make one right. —James Joyce, *Ulysses*

1961. "Why didn't you just hit him over the head and take the bedsheet away from him?" Yossarian asked.
Pressing his lips together with dignity, Milo shook his head. "That would have been unjust," he scolded firmly. "Force is wrong, and two wrongs never make a right." —Joseph Heller, *Catch-22*

1973. Two wrongs don't make a right, but they make a good excuse. —Thomas Szasz, *The Second Sin*

1974. "... There can be no whitewash at the White House ... Two wrongs do not make a right ..." —President Nixon, quoted in *All the President's Men*

1989. When the Sawyer campaign was criticized for airing political commercials making fun of Mr. Daley, showing him fumbling with note cards which, among other things, reminded him of his name, Mr. Sawyer pulled them off the air.... His own advisers sometimes grind their teeth with frustration: "I'll say to him, 'Your Honor, you have got to hit back, you got to get together,' and he'll just shake his head and say, 'Two wrongs don't make a right.'" —*New York Times*

1991. "Just because the House has done something that may not be right, that doesn't mean we should do it," said Sen. Charles Grassley (R., Iowa). "Two wrongs don't make a right." —*Wall Street Journal*

1993. But just as two wrongs do not make a right, two falsehoods do not justify your providing important and limited space to an anti-Semitic and anti-astronaut kook. —Alan M. Dershowitz, *New York Times Book Review*

1994. Is capital punishment inhumane?... Yes. Two wrongs do not make a right. —*Times* (Trenton)

Uneasy lies the head that wears the crown.
Those who have power over the lives of others cannot sleep soundly because of their great responsibility, or because their subjects may be plotting against them. The proverb was first used by Shakespeare in *King Henry the Fourth, Part II,* (1597). The saying is found in varying forms: *Heavy is the head that wears the crown; Uneasy is the head that wears the crown,* etc.

> **1597.** *King Henry:* Deny it to a king? Then, happy low, lie down!
> Uneasy lies the head that wears a crown.
> —Shakespeare, *Henry the Fourth, Part II,*
> Act III, Scene I

> **1984.** "David, my son, I have a thing I must reveal to you," he began hoarsely as we walked in starlight that balmy evening. "Uneasy lies the head that wears a crown. Believe me, I know." —Joseph Heller, *God Knows*

United we stand, divided we fall. If we don't stick together, we will fail in our struggle for a better future. This saying originated in the United States in 1768. The saying comes from "The Liberty Song" composed by John Dickinson, an army officer and member of the First Continental Congress; it was first published in the *Boston Gazette* on July 18, 1768. *By uniting we stand, by dividing we fall* is the original version of the saying.

> **1768.** Then join hand in hand, brave Americans all,
> By uniting we stand, by dividing we fall;
> In so righteous a cause let us hope to succeed,
> For Heaven approves of each generous deed.
> —John Dickinson, in *Great American Folk Songs,* collected and edited by Jim Morse

> **1987.** See that man ... over there ...
> He's my ... brother!
> Hands across America ...
> Hands across ...
> ... This land I love!...
> ... Divided we fall ...
> ... United we stand ...
> ... Hands across ... I'm just a Gigolooo!
> —G. B. Trudeau, *Doonesbury Deluxe*

> **1992.** His [Ross Perot's] book, *United We Stand,* went on sale yesterday. The book describes itself as a "plan for the 21st century" and provides specific recommendations to solve many of this country's most nettlesome economic and social problems. —*New York Times*

> **1993.** POLITICAL PARTNERSHIP: UNITED THEY STAND. Bill and Hillary turned their marriage into a joint adventure. —*Time*

See also THE MORE THE MERRIER.; THERE'S SAFETY IN NUMBERS.

Vanity of vanities; all is vanity. Everything is worthless, futile, and of no real value. The saying appears in the Old Testament.

> Vanity of vanities, saith the Preacher, vanity of vanities; all *is* vanity. —Eccles. 1:2, *Authorized Version*, 1611

1940. Vanity, vanity, all is vanity
   That's any fun at all for humanity.
                              —Ogden Nash, *Ha! Original Sin!*

1965. "All that there," the woman said, pointing to his arm, "is no better than what a fool Indian would do. It's a heap of vanity." She seemed to have found the word she wanted. "Vanity of vanities," she said. —Flannery O'Connor, "Parker's Back"

1984. One time even before that, in an access of pride during a lull between conquests, I decided to construct a spectacular edifice to myself and call it a temple of the Lord; but God said no. God knew my inward reason. Vanity of vanities, said the Preacher, all is vanity. God had no need for Ecclesiastes to acquaint Him with vanity. —Joseph Heller, *God Knows*

Vanity, vanity, all is vanity. *See* VANITY OF VANITIES; ALL IS VANITY.

Variety is the spice of life. Different activities enrich one's life and make it enjoyable and not boring. The proverb has been traced back in this form to William Cowper's (1731–1800) *The Task* (1785), but its idea was expressed centuries earlier by Publilius Syrus (first century b.c.) and by Samuel Johnson (1709–84). The earliest appearance in print in the United States was in the 1778 *Heath Papers.*

First century b.c.
No pleasure endures unseasoned by variety. —Publilius Syrus, *Maxim 406*

The joy of life is variety; the tenderest love requires to be rekindled by intervals of absence. —Samuel Johnson, *The Idler*

1785. Variety's the very spice of life,
   That gives it all its flavour.
                              —William Cowper, *The Task*

1985. Jocks from Alabama find themselves applying to a house along with pre-med types, philosophers, and would-be novelists. And when it does work, this setup really can enrich a person's life as much as any academic course.

But this is far less true where preppies are concerned. Variety is not the spice of our lives. —Erich Segal, *The Class*

1991. Variety is the spice of life. Dine in world class restaurants, then dance the night away. Or take a chance in our European casino … The choice of activities is endless on the only 24-hour city to cross the Atlantic. —Ad, *New York Times*

1992. Spice is the variety of life. —Ad, for Grey Poupon Mustard, *New York Times Magazine*

1993. CARIBBEAN: VARIETY IS THE SPICE. —Headline, *Modern Maturity*

Vengeance is sweet. *See* REVENGE IS SWEET.

Veni, vidi, vici. *See* I CAME, I SAW, I CONQUERED.

The victor gets the spoils. *See* TO THE VICTOR BELONG THE SPOILS.

Victory has a hundred fathers and defeat is an orphan. A lot of people claim to be responsible for victory, but nobody takes responsibility for defeat. This proverb was popularized by President

348

John F. Kennedy (1961), but it was coined by the Italian diplomat, and son-in-law of Mussolini, Count Galeazzo Ciano (1903–44). The proverb may be found in varying forms: *Success has many parents; Victory has a hundred memories but defeat has amnesia* (W. E. I. Gates).

1942. *La victoria trova cento padri, e nessuno vuole riconoscere l'insuccesso.*
Victory has a hundred fathers, but defeat is an orphan. —*The Ciano Diaries 1939–1943*, Vol. 2

1965. We dispersed to engage in a morning of counterbriefing while the President left for his press conference in the State Department auditorium. Here he dismissed the inside stories: "There's an old saying that victory has a hundred fathers and defeat is an orphan." (I later asked him where he had come upon this felicitous observation. He looked surprised and said vaguely, "Oh, I don't know; it's just an old saying.") —Arthur M. Schlesinger, Jr., *A Thousand Days*

1991. I've been sitting here reading all the well-deserved raves for "The Adams Family" movie, which surprised the heck out of the world box office at its smash hit opening and caused Paramount Picture executives to do a veritable jig of joy. Chairman Brandon Tartikoff even talked to *The New York Times* to say how "stunned" he was. And, of course, everybody is taking bow after bow because, as they say, success has many parents. —*Times* (Trenton)

1992. Since defeat is an orphan and victory has many fathers, it is virtually impossible to discern parentage of a lousy idea. —*Time*

Virtue is its own reward. Those who are virtuous need no special incentives. The proverb has been traced back to the 1509 *Ship of Fools* by Alexander Barclay (c.1476–1552) and translates the Latin *Ipsa sui pretium virtus sibi* ("Virtue is its own reward").

a.d. c.25–99.
Virtue herself is her own fairest reward. —Silius Italicus, *Punica*

c.200.
Virtue was sufficient of herself for happiness. —Diogenes Laërtius, *Lives of Eminent Philosophers*

1643. That virtue is her own reward, is but a cold principle. —Thomas Browne, *Religio Medici*

1969. Not once had Woltz uttered a threat against Don Corleone himself. Genius had its rewards. —Mario Puzo, *The Godfather*

1985. "Then you can have the essence of true education, Andrew. I'll arrange for you to have tutorial with me, and we'll go through the Eliot diaries together. Grades won't enter into it. Just reading them will be their own reward." —Erich Segal, *The Class*

See also A GOOD NAME IS BETTER THAN PRECIOUS OINTMENT; HONESTY IS THE BEST POLICY.

The voice of the people is the voice of God. The will of the people cannot be denied. The saying is of Latin origin, *Vox populi vox Dei*, and dates back to Alcuin's *Letter to Charlemagne* (A.D. 800). Alexander Pope disagreed with Alcuin's definition, saying, "The people's voice is odd,/It is, and it is not, the voice of God" (*Imitations of Horace*, 1738). The proverb was first attested in the United States in the early eighteenth century. The adage is often shortened to *The voice of the people*.

1987. Sen. Daniel K. Inouye, who has a voice like the Voice of God in these hearings, if God were a Japanese-American from Hawaii, is a certified hero, as the Distinguished Service Cross in his lapel makes subtly clear. —*Boston Globe*

1989. I imagine they are fine citizens. After all, we elected them and the voice of the people is the voice of God, remember that. —*Washington Post*

1991. Talk radio today is the voice of the people. It has its screamers and its soothsayers—on both sides of the microphone. —*Christian Science Monitor*

1994. Much as I hate to say it, "majority rule" and "the voice of the people" are extremely overrated. —*Sun-Sentinel* (South Florida)

1997. The biggest story in American government this past week comes from California, where a federal appeals court heard the voice of the people. Seven years ago, Californians approved Proposition 140, a state term-limits referendum. —*New York Post*

Walls have ears. Be careful what you say; you never know who may be listening. The proverb has been traced back in English to Chaucer's *Knight's Tale* (1387): ("Fields have eyes and woods have ears"). "That feeld hath eyen, and the wode hath eres" echoes the Latin *Campus habet lumen, et habet nemus auris acumen* ("The field has sight, and the wood a sharp ear"). In 1546, it was included in John Heywood's collection of proverbs. It was used by Cervantes in *Don Quixote* (1615) and by Sir Walter Scott in *The Fortunes of Nigel* (1822), and is first attested in the United States in *Universal Asylum* (1791). In World War II, the proverb was used as a security slogan to warn people of enemy agents. The proverb is found in varying forms: *The wall has ears and the plain has eyes; Fields have eyes, and woods have ears; If walls have ears the woods have eyes,* etc. The proverb has its counterpart in other languages: *Les murailles ont des aureilles* (French); *Las paredes oyen* (Spanish); *Die Wände haben Ohren* (German); У стен есть уши (Russian), etc.

1546. Fields have eyes and woods have ears. —John Heywood, *Proverbs*

1615. Walls have ears. —Cervantes, *Don Quixote*

1727. Walls have tongues, and hedges ears. —Jonathan Swift, *A Pastoral Dialogue between Richmond Lodge and Marble Hill*

1885. Woods have tongues
As walls have ears.
　　—Alfred, Lord Tennyson, *Idylls of the King, Balin and Balan*

1922. *Mrs Breen:* Mr Bloom! You down here in the haunts of sin! I caught you nicely! Scamp!
Bloom (hurriedly): Not so loud my name. Whatever do you think of me? Don't give me away.

Walls have ears. —James Joyce, *Ulysses*

1961. "Mr. Baker gave me hell for letting you spend a thousand dollars."
　"Why, that old goat!"
　"Mary—Mary! The walls have ears." —John Steinbeck, *The Winter of Our Discontent*

1980. "I won't go to a hotel. Moretti's got ears everywhere." —Sidney Sheldon, *Rage of Angels*

1990. "What I want to tell you is that walls have ears." —Victor Ostrovsky and Claire Hoy, *By Way of Deception*

1992. WALLS HAS EARS.
Jeannette Walls's November 16 column about the "Styles of the *Times*" section ["Hot Type: 'Styles' Victims"] quoted me as saying that the New York *Times* was "doing something right" to alienate its older white male readers. This is not true, as Walls was repeatedly told. —Arthur Sulzberger, Jr., *New York*

War is hell. War is an experience full of horror. The saying has been traced back to 1591, when Shakespeare used it in *King Henry the Sixth, Part II* (1591). The saying is attributed to United States General Sherman (1820–91).

1880. There is many a boy here today who looks on war as all glory, but, boys, it is all hell. You can bear this warning voice to generations yet to come. I look upon war with horror. —Gen. William T. Sherman

1982. "War may be Hell ... but it's good for business!" —Robert Asprin, *Myth Directions*

1988. It has often been said that war is hell. Yet it is rarely admitted that for the privileged few war can be a hell of a good time. —Erich Segal, *Doctors*

1989. War is hell, thought Carl Lee. He listened in-

350

tently. Now, Vietnam was bad. He'd been shot. He'd lost friends. He'd killed people, many people. —John Grisham, *A Time to Kill*

1991. President Bush: "War is hell, and it's a terrible thing." —Quoted in *New York Times*

1993. If war is hell, can peace lead to the Apocalypse? —*Times* (Trenton)

1994. Let's not regard the Germans as enemies. War is never black or white: war is hell for all involved. —*Time*

War is too important to be left to the generals. The phrase is of French origin: *La guerre! C'est une chose trop grave pour la confier à des militaires* ("War is much too serious a matter to be entrusted to the military"). It is attributed to Talleyrand (1754–1838) and Clemenceau (1841–1929).**

(undated).
War is too serious a matter to entrust to military men. —Attributed to Georges Clemenceau in Hampden Jackson, *Clemenceau and The Third Republic*

(undated).
War is much too serious a matter to be entrusted to the military. —Attributed to Charles Maurice de Talleyrand, quoted by Briand to Lloyd George during World War I

(undated).
"Somebody, I forgot who, said war is too important to be left to the generals, and that's true ... we ought to try to devise a way to keep them out of politics altogether." —Harry S. Truman, quoted by Merle Miller, *Plain Speaking*

1987. Shannon wondered why the fuck he'd ever taken John F. Kennedy seriously. If his father had taught him the old saw that wars are too important to be fought by generals, Shannon had learned that politicians could make it even worse. —Chris Bunch and Allan Cole, *A Reckoning for Kings*

1993. Thought for Today: "Government is too big and important to be left to the politicians." —Chester Bowles, American diplomat, businessman, author—and politician (1901–1986). —*Times* (Trenton)

1994. Peace is too precious a commodity to leave it solely to diplomats and politicians. —*Times* (Trenton)

Warts and all. Including all defects. The saying is attributed to Oliver Cromwell (1599–1658) who, the story goes, asked an artist, Sir Peter Lely (1618–80), to paint his portrait exactly as he saw him with all his blemishes.

1762–71.
Mr. Lely, I desire you would use all your skill to paint my picture truly like me, and not flatter me at all; but remark all these roughnesses, pimples, warts, and everything as you see me, otherwise I will never pay a farthing for it. —Oliver Cromwell, in Horace Walpole, *Anecdotes of Painting in England*

1992. "That's basically how I operate," said Mr. Funk. "I paint what I see. Sometimes people don't like it because they want to have a favorable spin on things. And sometimes people I paint don't like it. But nevertheless, I paint what I see. What we have, we report, good, bad, indifferent, warts and all." —*New York Times*

1993. A first printing of 50,000 has been upped to 125,000. This is a "warts and all" bio of the famous conservative TV and radio talk king. Colford says he has info that will shock and surprise [Rush] Limbaugh's thousands of devoted fans and listeners. —*Times* (Trenton)

1994. In recounting Hand's life, Mr. Gunther's greatest worry was that biography could become hagiography. "I began despite the fear that my admiration might preclude an absolutely unprejudiced portrayal," he writes in his preface. "I end hoping I have pictured him fully, warts and all. He remains my idol still." —*New York Times*

Waste not, want not. The less we waste, the less we lack in the future. The proverb has been traced back to 1772, and is first cited in the United States in the 1932 *Topper Takes a Trip* by T. Smith.

1989. Bannerman ate rapidly and methodically, without any sign of enjoyment, like a child who had been told not to leave anything on his plate. Had he been taught to "waste not, want not" by some governess or nanny sixty years ago? —Michael Korda, *The Fortune*

1990. DENMARK: WASTE NOT, WANT NOT —Quoted in *Reader's Digest*

1991. Ours is often a wasteful society. In recent years, however, society increasingly—and justifiably—has been brought to task for being so. Companies, too, occasionally need to be reminded that "wasting not" can be both good for the environment, and good for the bottom line, as well. —Ad, *New York Times*

1993. The eleventh commandment, according to Patricia Gallagher, should be, "Thou shalt never pay full price for anything." ... Why should you? asks Gallagher, a mother of four young children, who lives by such age-old proverbs as "A penny saved is a penny earned; waste not, want not; and little things make a difference." —*Times* (Trenton)

1994. WASTE NOT, WANT NOT: MGM'S OUTTAKES ARE A MOVIE. —Headline, *New York Times*

See also YOU MUST CUT YOUR COAT ACCORDING TO YOUR CLOTH.

Watch my lips. *See* READ MY LIPS.

Watch what we do, not what we say. One should be judged by one's actions, not by one's words. The proverb is of recent origin (1969) and is attributed to John N. Mitchell, Nixon's Attorney General. The pronoun *we* may be changed to other pronouns or nouns.**

1992. Sometime between going to work for President Nixon and going to prison, Attorney General John N. Mitchell made a statement that all sleuths, professional and amateur, should have heeded.... "Watch what we do, not what we say," Mitchell said, in 1969. —*New York Times*

1992. Ms. [Carolyn M.] Scott cautions against overreliance on indexes of consumer confidence, which now receive much attention, because they measure opinion that could prove fleeting: "Watch what they do, not what they say," she urged. —*New York Times*

1993. "The key word is say what you do and do what you say," says Len Newton, who works with John Keane and Associates to market software that helps firms with ISO [the International Organization for Standardization] registration. "You have to say what you do to represent the quality to your buyers. You have to say it at every step in the process. And document it." —*U.S.1*

See also ACTIONS SPEAK LOUDER THAN WORDS; DO AS I SAY, NOT AS I DO.

A watched pot never boils. If you hang around, waiting for something to happen, it never will. The proverb has been traced back to Elizabeth Gaskell's *Mary Barton* (1848), and is first cited in the United States in *Puzzle of the Pepper Tree* (1933) by S. Palmer.

1848. "Come now," said Mrs. Sturgis, "my master told me to see you to bed ... What's the use of watching? A watched pot never boils, and I see you are after watching that weather-cock." —Elizabeth Gaskell, *Mary Barton*

1933. The watched pot was beginning to boil. —S. Palmer, *Puzzle of the Pepper Tree*

1958. If he was a watched pot, he would never boil. —*New Yorker*

1994. It began simmering late last year. And while it is true that a watched pot never boils, it is clear that the complex cauldron that makes up the domestic advertising market has now heated to a strong and steady perk. —*Crain's New York Business*

Water seeks its own level. People tend to rise or sink to their level of competence; we usually find ourselves among people who are much like us. The proverb was first attested in the United States in the 1778 *Papers of George Clinton, First Governor of New York*. Found in varying forms: *Water finds its own level; Water will find its own level*, etc.

1941. No Tammany man can rise above the local machine. Governor Smith achieved that destination, but Albany is a long way from the Bowery.... A return to the city of Tammany would be a counsel of despair. People elsewhere would say that water cannot rise above its own level and that the level in New York is contemptibly and irretrievably low. —Robert Moses, quoted by Robert A. Caro in *The Power Broker*

1984. The aphorisms started flowing like water as all the old clichés got dusted off. Ours is a profit-and-loss system.... Water seeks its own level. Survival of the fittest. —Lee Iacocca with William Novak, *Iacocca*

1993. "My wife wants to live in Soho, and I don't blame her. The old saw still holds true, 'Water seeks its own level.' The only problem (is) I can't afford it." —Overheard at a neighborhood clean-up rally

See also EVERY EMPLOYEE TENDS TO RISE TO HIS LEVEL OF INCOMPETENCE.

Water, water everywhere, nor any drop to drink. Despite being surrounded by something, you still can't benefit from it. The saying was coined by the English poet Samuel Taylor Coleridge (1772–1834). The saying is sometimes misquoted as "... and not a drop to drink." Often in variants with another noun replacing *water*.

1798. Water, water, everywhere,
　　Nor any drop to drink.
　　　　—Samuel T. Coleridge, *The Rime of the Ancient Mariner*

1987. [American in a third-world country jail] "Water ... water ... Oh, right, and where the hell are you when I need *you*?" —G. B. Trudeau, *Doonesbury Deluxe*

1991. Lawyers, lawyers, everywhere. There were probably more lawyers per square inch on the 50th floor of the Equitable Building on Wednesday evening—some 450 of them—than at any recent social gathering. —*New York Times*

1992. Water, Water ... Well, Not Everywhere: Conflicts in the Making? —George J. Demko, *Why in the World*

1993. WATER, WATER EVERYWHERE —Headline of the story on the 1993 Midwest Floods, "McNeil/Lehrer News Hour," PBS

1994. Money, money everywhere, but not a cent to spend. Buck stops with Arafat—but his pockets have holes. —*Manhattan Jewish Sentinel*

The way to a man's heart is through his stomach. The easiest way to win a man is to feed him well. The proverb was first cited in the United States in John Adams's letter dated April 15, 1814, and in *Fern Leaves* (1853) by Fanny Fern (1811–72). It appeared in England in R. Ford's *Handbook for Travellers in Spain* (1845), and is listed in all major dictionaries of American proverbs. It is found in varying forms: *The quickest way to a man's heart is through his stomach; The best way to reach a man's heart is through his stomach; The way to a man's heart is through his belly,* etc.

1814. The shortest road to men's hearts is down their throats. —John Adams, *Works*

1853. The way to a man's heart is through his stomach. —Fanny Fern, *Fern Leaves*

1983. "If you're really serious," David said, "then I'll tell you the secret to a man's heart."
"Tell me!" Kate said eagerly.
"Through his stomach." —Sidney Sheldon, *Master of the Game*

1994. FRANCINE'S CAFE.
"Francine knows that the way to my heart is through my stomach. It's too bad she keeps making my mouth pay the toll!" —Bob Thaves, *Frank and Ernest*

See also AN ARMY MARCHES ON ITS STOMACH.

Way to go! Well done! According to Eric Partridge, the saying has been used since about 1950, originally by coaches to encourage athletes. It was popularized through the TV series *Rowan and Martin's Laugh-in* (1960s).

1988. He [Barney] took careful aim ... and sank it [the ball]: his first Varsity point!
Laura cupped her hands and cheered, "Way to go, Barney!" —Erich Segal, *Doctors*

1991. Stuart and I would usually end up sitting around and waiting for the girls, and he'd use the

opportunity to tease me: "Way to go, Dad." —Oliver L. North, *Under Fire*

1993. "Way to go! I didn't know you had it in you, you old smoothie!" —Batiuk, "Funky Winkerbean"

1994. As Mr. Giuliani shopped in the Chelsea section of Manhattan, passers-by stopped to thank him for supporting Mr. Cuomo. "Way to go, Rudy!" a man shouted from across the street while another grabbed Mr. Giuliani's hand and told him, "You're a man of great principle." —*New York Times*

We have met the enemy, and they are ours. We have engaged the enemy and defeated them. This saying is sometimes attributed to Lieut. Oliver Hazard Perry (1785–1819) who, in his dispatch to Gen. William Henry Harrison (1773–1841), announced his victory at the battle of Lake Erie on September 10, 1813. Over 150 years later, in 1970, the American artist Walt Kelly (1913–73) used a slightly changed variant, *We have met the enemy, and he is us,* in the *Pogo* cartoon, which changed its meaning: We have encountered the enemy, and we are our own enemy.

1813. We have met the enemy, and they are ours. —Gen. Oliver Hazard Perry, quoted by David Wallechinsky & Irving Wallace, *The People's Almanac*

1970. We have met the enemy and he is us. —Walt Kelly, "Pogo"

1991. We have met the enemy and they are furs. A mink is a terrible thing to waste. —*New York*

1993. IN MANY WAYS, THE ENEMY IS US —Headline of an editorial on health-care costs in America, *Times* (Trenton)

1994. In *A Map of the World* [by Jane Hamilton], it's not so much, as Walt Kelly put it in *Pogo,* that "we have met the enemy and he is us." It's that Alice, in a move that could either save or destroy her, has decided not to believe in enemies at all. —*New York Times Book Review*

We have nothing to fear but fear itself. See THE ONLY THING WE HAVE TO FEAR IS FEAR ITSELF.

We must indeed all hang together, or, most assuredly, we shall all hang separately. If we don't cooperate, we will be doomed. Benjamin Franklin (1706–90) said this to John Hancock (1739–1793) at the signing of the Declaration of Independence on July 4, 1776. *Stick together or get stuck separately* is a variant of the proverb used since 1942.

1776. We must indeed all hang together, or, most

assuredly, we shall all hang separately. —Benjamin Franklin

1990. "The game you are stepping into is dangerous. There is much to learn. It's not a simple game. And life is not always the ultimate in this game. Always remember that in this [intelligence] business we have to hang on to each other—or we may hang *next* to each other." —Victor Ostrovsky & Claire Hoy, *By Way of Deception*

1993. A MATTER OF TIME: PUNTERS HANG ALONE AND HANG TOGETHER. —Headline, *New York Times*
See also UNITED WE STAND, DIVIDED WE FALL.

We shall overcome. We will eventually win our struggle. The saying is the title of the civil rights movement's popular song (adapted in the 1960s) originating from before the Civil War days, and revived c.1900 by C. Albert Tindley as a Baptist hymn called *I'll Overcome Some Day*. It was sung in 1946 by black tobacco workers at Charleston, South Carolina.

1965. The crowd, joining hands, rocking back and forth, cried, almost ecstatically, "Dream some more." Then in the dusk the vast assemblage quietly dispersed. Snatches of the poignant old Baptist hymn which the movement had made its own hung in the air:

> We shall overcome, we shall overcome,
> We shall overcome some day.
> Oh deep in my heart I do believe,
> We shall overcome some day.
> —Arthur M. Schlesinger, Jr., *A Thousand Days*

1967. On one side trip, he [Robert Kennedy] entertained peasant farmers with "We Shall Overcome" and "The Marine Corps Hymn" in his off-pitch voice. —Ralph de Toledano, *R.F.K: The Man Who Would Be President*

1991. Dr. Hooks compared Mr. Bush with the only President who has called Texas home, Lyndon B. Johnson, and said, "We have moved from a President who said of civil rights, 'We shall overcome,' to a President who vetoes civil rights bills and says, 'You can't override.'" —*New York Times*

Wealth makes many friends. If you have a lot of money, there will always be people who'll call you friend. The proverb appears in the Old Testament and is first used in English in Chaucer's *Tale of Melibee* (1386). It is first attested in the United States in the 1804 *Modern Chivalry* by Hugh Henry Brackenridge (1748–1816).

Wealth maketh many friends; but the poor is sepa-

rated from his neighbor. —Prov. 19:4, *Authorized Version*, 1611

1977. "They say, 'wealth makes friends.' But what about the poor?"
"And the poor make children." —Overheard at N.Y. Association for New Americans

1984. Wealth makes many friends, of course, but the poor is separated from his neighbor, and if all the brethren of the poor do hate him, how much more do his friends go far from him? —Joseph Heller, *God Knows*
See also THE RICH GET RICHER, AND THE POOR GET POORER.

What a tangled web we weave when first we practice to deceive. People who tell a lie soon find themselves enmeshed in increasingly complicated lies. One lie will lead to more lies than you can keep track of. The proverb was coined by Sir Walter Scott (1771–1832) in *Marmion* (1808).

1808. Oh, what a tangled web we weave,
When first we practice to deceive!
—Walter Scott, *Marmion*

1994. That oft-quoted line "Oh, what a tangled web we weave when first we practice to deceive" is right on. The news must be edited for style, clarity, grammar, libel, countless other things. But the juice of it, the impact of it, cannot, and should not, be diluted with premeditation. —*Times* (Trenton)

What are you driving at? Tell me what you're implying. This saying is used when someone's hint or implication is not clear.

1928. *Darrell (puzzled and irritated—thinking confusedly):* What's he driving at? ... why doesn't he get the hell out and leave us alone?... —Eugene O'Neill, *Strange Interlude*, Act VI

1977. "No big deal," Hennessy assured her. "I think I know what he's driving at." —William Safire, *Full Disclosure*

1979. "You do understand what I'm driving at?"
"You don't have to convince me. That stupid display in Washington caused me enough grief." —Howard Fast, *The Establishment*

1985. Yakushkin replied simply. "It doesn't work that way."
"What the hell are you driving at?" —Erich Segal, *The Class*

1987. "... through sickness and health."
"What do you mean? What are you driving at?" —G. B. Trudeau, *Doonesbury Deluxe*

What can go wrong, will go wrong. *See* IF ANYTHING CAN GO WRONG, IT WILL.

What can't be cured must be endured. If it can't be helped, you must put up with it. The proverb has been traced back to about 1377, and is first cited in the United States in the 1698 *Diary of Samuel Sewall.*

> **1936.** Gradually, Scarlett drew courage from the brave faces of her friends and from the merciful adjustment which nature makes when what cannot be cured must be endured. —Margaret Mitchell, *Gone With the Wind*

> **1946.** What can't be cured must be endured. —Bergen Evans, *The Natural History of Nonsense*

> **1987.** What can't be cured must be obscured. —R. Richard Ritti & G. Ray Funkhouser, *The Ropes to Skip & the Ropes to Know*

See also DON'T CRY OVER SPILLED MILK; WHAT'S DONE CANNOT BE UNDONE.

What did the President know, and when did he know it? Republican Senator of Tennessee Howard H. Baker, Jr., vice chairman of the Watergate Committee, first posed this question, which Watergate conspirators were repeatedly asked during the hearings in 1973. The question is often used when discussing political scandals. "President" may be replaced with other words.***

> **1977.** Probably the most intriguing area of investigation conducted by Thompson under the aegis of Senator Howard Baker, vice chairman of the Watergate Committee, had to do with exactly what the CIA knew—and when. —Victor Lasky, *It Didn't Start with Watergate*

> **1987.** Richard M. Nixon and Howard H. Baker, Jr. also came to national prominence through Congressional committee hearings—Mr. Nixon through his participation in 1948 in the House Un-American Activities Committee's investigation of Alger Hiss and Mr. Baker 25 years later at the start of the Senate Watergate Committee hearings on President Nixon in 1973, with his constantly repeated question: "What did the President know, and when did he know it?" —*New York Times*

> **1989.** What did they know and when did they know it? This question about an official "cover-up" of illegal acts, familiar to America's Watergate fans, is now being asked by a belatedly aroused free press in West Germany. —*New York Times*

> **1991.** WHAT DID THEY KNOW, AND WHEN DID THEY KNOW IT? —Headline, *Time*

> **1992.** What did George Bush know about the Iran-contra affair and when did he know it? The answers turn out to be: a lot, and early. —*New York Times*

> **1993.** "If Florio did not know what was going on around him then he is incompetent. Ask Jim Florio 'What did you know and when did you know it?'" —Roger Stone, quoted by Richard Reeves in *New York Times Magazine*

> **1994.** In closing arguments earlier this week, Ms. Weeks's lawyer, Philip E. Kay, asked a version of the question that entered the jargon with Watergate: "What did Baker know, when did they know it, and what did they do?" —*New York Times*

What goes around, comes around. What you do or say today will come back to you in the future. The proverb originated in the United States in the 1970s. The earliest appearance in print was 1974 in Eddie Stone's book, *Donald Writes No More.*

> **1974.** No one can say why Donald Goines and Shirley Sailor were murdered. The ghetto philosophy, "what goes around comes around," is the only answer most people can give. —Eddie Stone, *Donald Writes No More*

> **1985.** "What goes around comes around," a gay man said, and people at City Hall spoke of "poetic justice," or retribution long deserved. —*Washington Post*

> **1986.** It should have been Ben with you, he thought drowsily. I think that was the way it was really supposed to be. Why wasn't it Ben?
> Because it was you then and it's you now, that's all. Because what goes around always comes around. I think Bob Dylan said that ... or maybe it was Ronald Reagan. —Stephen King, *It*

> **1987.** "You have to make good on contracts."
> "You have to? Why?"
> "Because everybody in the courthouse believes in a saying: 'What goes around comes around.' That means if you don't take care a me today, I won't take care a you tomorrow." —Tom Wolfe, *The Bonfire of the Vanities*

> **1989.** No sooner had the royal accusers sent Louis XVI and his queen to the guillotine, than they themselves were being hoist onto the tumbrels by men whose own heads would later drop into the basket. What goes around comes around. —*Washington Times*

> **1991.** When networking to make a career change, understand that the primary point is to maximize your exposure to a lot of people who may hear neat bits of information you wouldn't hear on your own. It's relatively unlikely that any networking

lead will offer The Big Plum during your meeting. It's hard not to get impatient but remember the Second Great Truth of the Job Market: *What goes around, comes around.* —*Wall Street Journal's National Business Employment Weekly*

1992. If you focus on what you want, you will be living in a perpetual state of need. On the other hand, if you focus on what you have to offer, you will live in a perpetual state of generosity. They say, "What goes around, comes around." —*Time Off*

1994. Hillary Rodham and Bernie Nussbaum worked together 20 years ago probing Watergate. This ain't Watergate. But hey, what goes around comes around. —*Newsweek*

See also AS YOU SOW, SO (SHALL) YOU REAP; THE CHICKENS HAVE COME HOME TO ROOST; ONE GOOD TURN DESERVES ANOTHER; WHAT GOES UP MUST COME DOWN; WHAT WILL BE, WILL BE.

What goes up must come down. No matter how high you go, you'll fall to earth sooner or later. The proverb probably originated in the 1870s, according to Eric Partridge, and is commonly associated with the Newtonian law of gravitation. The earliest appearance in print was 1929 (*The Stretchers* by F. A. Pottle), and it is first cited in the United States in Norman Mailer's *The Naked and the Dead* (1948).

1948. In the larger meanings of the curve, gravity would occupy the place of mortality (what goes up must come down) and wind resistance would be the resistance of the medium. —Norman Mailer, *The Naked and the Dead*

1993. WHAT IS DOWN MUST COME UP? —Headline, *New York Times*

1994. What goes up must come down. And this is just what happened at the stock market. —"Bob Grant Talk Show," WABC

See also THE BIGGER THEY ARE, THE HARDER THEY FALL; WHAT GOES AROUND, COMES AROUND; WHAT WILL BE, WILL BE.

What has happened once can happen again. If something is possible, it is possible for it to recur.

1992. "We're vulnerable to something along the line of the 1918–1919 influenza pandemic that killed 20 million people worldwide," said Dr. Robert E. Shope, co-chairman of the report committee and a virologist at Yale University. "It's happened once; it can happen again," he said at a news conference at the academy's headquarters. —*New York Times*

1993. It happened once again. It has happened 41 times since I joined the Police Department in 1971. —*Philadelphia Inquirer*

What makes someone tick? What motivates someone? The saying is derived from a question about clocks: A person's character is compared to the workings of a clock.

1962. Property, in some form or other, was, in the end, what always made the watch tick. —James Jones, *The Thin Red Line*

1984. He [Henry Ford] was there every day to throw his weight around, but he never knew what made the place tick. —Lee Iacocca with William Novak, *Iacocca*

1986. "We've never had a coach at this table or a southerner, and it's natural for us to want to know what makes you tick." —Pat Conroy, *The Prince of Tides*

1988. "Let me tell you something," George Bush said to a high school student's query not long ago. "The latest thing in politics is to stretch you out on some kind of psychoanalytical couch to figure out what makes you tick." —*New York Times Magazine*

1989. "I don't understand you, Row Ark. You don't like fried dill pickles, you're attractive, very bright, you could go to work with any blue-chip law firm in the country for megabucks, yet you want to spend your career losing sleep over cutthroat murderers who are on death row and about to get their just rewards. What makes you tick, Row Ark?" —John Grisham, *A Time to Kill*

1994. BROKERS: WHAT MAKES THEM TICK? —Headline, *Newsweek*

What must be, must be. *See* WHAT WILL BE, WILL BE.

What the eye doesn't see the heart doesn't grieve for. If a person is unaware of something unpleasant or dangerous, he or she cannot be concerned about it. Often used to justify keeping something secret. The proverb is of Latin origin, *Quod non videt oculus, cor non dolet* ("What the eye sees not, the heart rues not"). Its first English use is in the sixteenth century, and it is recorded in America by the seventeenth. The adage may take varying forms.

1922. *Bloom:* You know how difficult it is. I needn't tell you.
    Zoe (flattered): What the eye can't see the heart can't grieve for. —James Joyce, *Ulysses*

1928. Connie guessed, however, that her father

had said something, and that something was in Clifford's mind. She knew that he didn't mind whether demi-vierge or demi-monde, so long as he didn't absolutely know, and wasn't made to see. What the eye doesn't see and the mind doesn't know, doesn't exist. —D. H. Lawrence, *Lady Chatterley's Lover*

1956. Like the fella says, "What the ears don't hear the heart doesn't grieve." —H. Cahill, *Shadow of my Hand*

1961. Granted that what the eye didn't see the heart couldn't grieve, he realized he was nevertheless doing the dirty of the rottenest sort on Pauline. —Allan Sillitoe, *Key to the Door*

1979. "The Norrises don't know about it yet."
"There you are, 'What the eye does not see'—" He broke off. —M. Barson, *So Soon Done For*
See also IGNORANCE IS BLISS; OUT OF SIGHT, OUT OF MIND.

What this country needs is a good five-cent cigar. The country would be better off if it had excellent products at affordable prices. The saying was coined by Vice President Thomas Riley Marshall (1854–1925) in the 1910s–1920s and has a humorous connotation. Franklin P. Adams (1881–1960) is quoted by Robert E. Drennan as saying, "There are plenty of good five-cent cigars in the country. The trouble is they cost a quarter. What this country needs is a good five-cent nickel."

c.1920.
What this country needs is a really good 5-cent cigar. —Thomas R. Marshall, *Tribune* (N.Y.)

1946. "My friends—" she [Sadie Burke] twisted her mouth in a nasty, simpering mimicry—"my friends, what this state needs is a good five-cent cigar. Oh, my God!" —Robert Penn Warren, *All the King's Men*

1977. Sam Zophar liked to show off his grasp of history, Smitty said to himself, noticing how the op-ed page editor had picked up the idea and ran pictures of Mrs. Wilson [Woodrow Wilson's wife] —who had run the country from her husband's bedside—and Thomas Riley Marshall, the Hoosier Vice-President who never got the chance to step up, and was only remembered for his "What this country needs is a good five-cent cigar" remark made during a dreary Senate debate. —William Safire, *Full Disclosure*

1993. What this country needs is a new cabinet post! —Doug Marlette, "Kudzu"

What will be, will be. Whatever the future holds is what will happen. The proverb is often found in the Italian version, *che serà serà*, popularized in a song. The proverb has been traced back in English to Chaucer's *Knight's Tale* (1390), and in 1546, it was included in John Heywood's collection of proverbs. It is first attested in the United States in V. Williams' book, *Crouching* (1928). The proverb is found in varying forms: *What must be, must be; What would be, would be*, etc.

1975. "Jesus, Russell, what is it with you? Anyone would think you were happy about what's going on."
"What will be will be ..." Russell repeated sagely. —Jackie Collins, *The World Is Full of Divorced Women*

1979. "Please don't worry. Whatever will be will be." —Howard Fast, *The Establishment*

1983. She refused to live a well-guarded life. What would be would be. —Jackie Collins, *Hollywood Wives*

1991. Scarlett giggled. Charlotte stopped. What would be, would be. —Alexandra Ripley, *Scarlett*

1993. The well-to-do will now find the top tax brackets are in the neighborhood of 40 percent. Ms. Corcoran figures her disposable income will drop 10 percent. "What will be, will be," she said. —*New York Times*

What you don't know can't hurt you. Often, it is less painful to remain ignorant than to have all the facts. This expression is usually used as an excuse for not telling someone about something. The proverb has been tracked back to *Petite Palace of Pleasure* (1576) by G. Pattie, and is first attested in the United States in E. Walter's book, *The Easiest Way* (1908). It is found in varying forms: *What one doesn't know won't hurt him; What a fellow doesn't know won't hurt him; What a man doesn't know can't hurt him; What you don't know can hurt you*, etc.

1908. What a fellow doesn't know doesn't hurt him, and he'll love you just the same. —E. Walter, *The Easiest Way*

1931. What they don't know caint hurt them. —William Faulkner, *Sanctuary*

1946. I owed my success in life to that principle. It had put me where I was. What you don't know don't hurt you, for it ain't real. —Robert Penn Warren, *All the King's Men*

1958. What she don't know won't hurt her. —*New Yorker*

1989. "Your father and the Walden girl were

married here."

"Because she *comes* from Illinois, Cordy."

"Let me remind you that Eleanor told you to keep out of this, Robert!"

"What she doesn't know won't hurt her." —Michael Korda, *The Fortune*

1994. What kids don't know can definitely hurt them. —Joan Lunden, "Good Morning America"

See also LITTLE KNOWLEDGE (LEARNING) IS A DANGEROUS THING.

What you see is what you get. This expression was originally used by salesmen to assure customers of the quality of their products. The saying was given a new lease on life by Walter Mondale during his 1984 Presidential campaign. WYSIWYG is a common computer-users' acronym.

1984. "When he [Mr. Hart] is in the Northeast, he says one thing. When he's here, he says something else. Well, that's the difference. What you see is what you get." —Walter Mondale, *New York Times*

1987. "My wife says I'm the most uncomplicated man in the world," Dukakis admits. "I guess I am." Even his 83-year-old mother says of him, "What you see is what you get." —*Time*

1989. "Felix and Liz [Rohatyn] have the only genuine salon in New York," said Kati Marton, author of a biography of Raoul Wallenberg and wife of Peter Jennings, the anchorman for the ABC evening news. "Both Felix and Elizabeth are so down to earth. There are no airs about them. What you see is what you get." —Judith Ramsey Ehrlich & Barry J. Rehfeld, *The New Crowd*

1990. The lenders who would lend to anyone who said "real estate" aren't lending now. So we aren't going to build any more product. What you see is what you get. —*Washington Post*

1991. "We both deal with our businesses very intently, and both want to be the best we can be," Mr. Smith said. "But we keep a sense of humor and an ease of communication, speaking clearly and listening very well. That's what makes it work." ... Mr. Rosenberg responded with a laugh, a shrug and a nod. "What you see is what you get," he said. —*New York Times*

1992. "What you see is what you get," says his wife, Ruth, a tough-minded and well-liked lawyer at the influential Washington firm Akin, Gump, Hauer & Feld. —*New York Times Magazine*

1993. "I'm not a flamboyant personality like Andre," said [Peter] Sampras. "What you see is what you get." —*Times* (Trenton)

1994. WHAT YOU DON'T SEE IS WHAT YOU GET —Headline, "Relaxation Techniques," *New York Times Magazine*

What's done cannot be undone. Once you've done or said something, you cannot undo it if you change your mind. The proverb was included in John Heywood's book of proverbs (1546), and in 1605–06 it was used by Shakespeare in *Macbeth*. It is first attested in the United States in the *Diary and Autobiography of John Adams* (1782).

1605–06.

> *Lady Macbeth:* Come, come, come, come, give me your hand. What's done cannot be undone.
>
> —Shakespeare, *Macbeth,* Act V, Scene I

1974. "The bridge is pretty damn rickety, what with the flood of abuse and bilge we have been subjected to, but we shall drop in," [Robert] Moses replied. For some weeks thereafter, the *Time* 's Title I play, while substantial, appeared considerably toned down.... But what he [Sulzberger] had done could no longer be undone. —Robert A. Caro, *The Power Broker*

1978. "Well," Starkey said, passing a hand over his face. "It's done. Can't be undone." —Stephen King, *The Stand*

1990. Rebuked by Fed governor Roy A. Young in Washington, Harrison courageously replied that the world was "on fire" and that his actions were "done and can't be undone." —Ron Chernow, *The House of Morgan*

1991. "What's done can be undone, Scarlett." —Alexandra Ripley, *Scarlett*

See also DON'T CRY OVER SPILLED MILK; WHAT'S DONE IS DONE.

What's done is done. Once something is finished it can't be changed. This proverb is listed in John's Heywood's book of proverbs (1546). In 1605–06, Shakespeare used it in *Macbeth*. It was first used in the United States in the *Diary and Autobiography of John Adams* (1782).

1605–06.

> *Lady Macbeth:* Things without all remedy Should be without regard: what's done is done.
>
> —Shakespeare, *Macbeth,* Act III, Scene II

1969. "Don't do anything rash until you've heard what he has to say. You can only cause a lot of trouble. What's done is done." —Mario Puzo, *The Godfather*

1979. It was almost eight o'clock. Enough of this,

Barbara decided. What was done was done. —Howard Fast, *The Establishment*

1985. "Well, what's done is done—I think you've made a mistake." —Michael Korda, *Queenie*

1991. "What's done is done," a Salomon spokesman said yesterday of the latest dismissals. "We don't anticipate further cuts." —*Wall Street Journal*

1994. "What is done is done," Dowd said about his success in the playoffs last spring. —*New York Times*

See also DON'T CRY OVER SPILLED MILK; WHAT'S DONE CANNOT BE UNDONE.

What's good for General Motors is good for America. What is good for big business is good for America as a whole. The saying originated in the United States and is generally attributed to President of General Motors Charles Erwin Wilson (1890–1961), testifying before the Senate Committee on Armed Services on January 15, 1953, about his nomination as Secretary of Defense. The idea, though, had been expressed many years earlier. *General Motors* and *America* are often replaced with other nouns.

1939. "And remember this: What's good for the bank is good for the country." —In the movie "Stagecoach"

1946. "The Boss sure thought a lot of him, and what was good enough for the Boss is good enough for old Tiny." —Robert Penn Warren, *All the King's Men*

1953. For years I thought what was good for our country was good for General Motors, and vice versa. The difference didn't exist. —Charles Erwin Wilson, *New York Times*

1961. "They all belong to the syndicate," Milo said. "And they know that what's good for the syndicate is good for the country, because that's what makes Sammy run." —Joseph Heller, *Catch-22*

1965. "You will never hear from me," he [Luther Hodges, Secretary of Commerce] said early on, "that this country should do this or that simply because business wants it. What is good for General Motors may, or may not, be good for the country." —Arthur M. Schlesinger, Jr., *A Thousand Days*

1983. Forbes decided to try provoking the volatile Chrysler chairman: Why shouldn't Americans buy Japanese if they are willing to sell to us at bargain prices? Iacocca shrugs. "I'm not going to worry about it. Let the government worry about it. I'll be retired. Let GM do what they want to do. If you're saying what's good for GM is good for the country, print it." —*Forbes*

1984. After all, what's good for Chrysler is good for the dealers, and vice versa. —Lee Iacocca with William Novak, *Iacocca*

1991. WHAT'S GOOD FOR JAPAN ISN'T NECESSARILY GOOD FOR THE U.S. —Headline, *Business Week*

1992. "To have the sport expand and grow in size with Disney will be unbelievable for hockey," Mr. Moore said. "And anything that's good for hockey is good for the Kings." —*New York Times*

1993. "As far as we're concerned, what is good for Mercer County and its citizens is good for New Jersey National Bank," he [Wallace] said. —*Times* (Trenton)

What's good for the goose is good for the gander. See WHAT'S SAUCE FOR THE GOOSE IS SAUCE FOR THE GANDER.

What's in a name? A name has no substance to it. It means nothing. Shakespeare used the phrase in about 1595 in *Romeo and Juliet*. Three hundred years later Helen F. More wrote a poem about William Dawes, the American patriot, which she titled "What's in a Name?"

1595. *Juliet:* What's in a name? that which we call a rose
By any other name would smell as sweet.
—Shakespeare, *Romeo and Juliet*, Act II, Scene II

1922. You will say those names were already in the chronicles from which he took the stuff of his plays. Why did he take them rather than others? Richard, a whoreson crookback, misbegotten, makes love to a widowed Ann (what's in a name?), woos and wins her, a whoreson merry widow. —James Joyce, *Ulysses*

1940. "What were the big ones with the low wings?"
"Heinkel one elevens."
"By any name they are as bad," Joaquin said.
—Ernest Hemingway, *For Whom the Bell Tolls*

1981. What's in a name? Plenty, I have learned. —Abigail Van Buren, *The Best of Dear Abby*

1989. In Verona, we stood in the courtyard under Juliet's balcony, and Ned, with a bit of motherly prompting, recited Juliet's famous soliloquy. Did the other tourists, who smiled in amazement at him, know that this was a handicapped boy? That he was *scempio*? (*What's in a name? ... a rose / By any other name would smell as sweet*). —William & Barbara Christopher, *Mixed Blessings*

1991. *A killer bee by any other name ...* may not be so bad, as a Missouri apiarist discovers in

Guatemala, where the "bravo" bee is a real honey. —*Smithsonian*

1992. Since none of [Newark-based] KIWI's 208 current staffers hail from New Zealand, what's in the name? —*New York*

1992. What's in a name? A lot, if you're a political unknown. —*People*

1993. What's in a name? Sometimes it's better not to ask. —Abigail Van Buren, *Times* (Trenton)

1993. Kareem Abdul-Jabbar was the name Lew Alcindor chose for himself in 1971. Kareem means generous. Abdul means servant of God. Jabbar means powerful.
But what's in a name? —*New York Post*

1994. What's in a name? Nothing, if you're TV's Roseanne Arnold or rock music's former Prince. —*Times* (Trenton)

What's past is prologue. What has already happened is just the beginning. The line comes from Shakespeare's *The Tempest* (1611–12).

1611–12.
> *Sebastian:* We all were sea-swallow'd,
>   though some cast again,
> And by that destiny to perform an act
> Whereof what's past is prologue, what to
>   come
> In yours and my discharge.
> —Shakespeare, *The Tempest*, Act II, Scene I

1991. On October 4, Mobil celebrates its 125th birthday. A century and a quarter. A long time for any commercial entity, and something to take pride in. And we do, while bearing in mind that "what's past is prologue." It's the *next* 125 years that really count. —*New York Times*

1993. What's Passed Is Prologue. So you're going to watch the 27th Super Bowl on Sunday? No, you're not. You're going to watch the 208th. Really. —*Entertainment Weekly*

See also THE BEST IS YET TO BE; LET BYGONES BE BYGONES; LIFE BEGINS AT FORTY; THAT'S WATER UNDER THE BRIDGE (OVER THE DAM).

What's sauce for the goose is sauce for the gander. What applies for one person should equally be applied to another. The proverb appeared in John Ray's collection of English proverbs in 1670, and is first attested in the United States in the 1757 *Colonial Virginia Satirist*. The proverb is found in varying forms: *What's good for the goose is good for the gander; Sauce for the goose is sauce for the gander; Sauce for the gander is sauce for the goose,* etc.

1922. *Bello:* How many women had you, eh, following them up dark streets, flatfoot, exciting them by your smothered grunts, what, you male prostitute? Blameless dames with parcels of groceries. Turn abut. Sauce for the goose, my gander O. —James Joyce, *Ulysses*

1982. It's important too for the person who supervises others to practice promptness and regularity as well as preach them. Regular hours set a good example for everyone. Employees feel better about complying when they know that what's sauce for the goose is sauce for the gander, too. —*Bits & Pieces*

1988. "I got very mad. I figured, what's good for the goose is good for the gander, so I took hold of her dress and I tore it down to her waist." —Clifford Irving, *The Campbell Murder Case*

1989. "Something we can exploit?"
"It would seem so. Emil's treating it as codeword material."
"Sauce for the goose," Ritter observed with a smile. —Tom Clancy, *Clear and Present Danger*

1992. I found it ironic that in the same issue you reported on Senator Goldwater's plans to marry a woman 32 years younger and quoted his granddaughter as saying, "If you find someone at that age who turns you on, that's great." I agree—for both the goose and the gander. —*People*

1993. What's good for the geese may be bad for anyone who feeds them if Clinton officials approve an ordinance intended to thin the birds' ranks. —*Sunday Star-Ledger*

The wheel comes full circle. The situation has reverted to one similar to the way it started. Often used to mean that one is going to be punished for his actions. The saying first appears in Shakespeare's *King Lear* (1605). It is often shortened to *come full circle* meaning events bring us back to where we began. *The wheel turns full circle* is a variant form.

1605. *Edmund:* Thou hast spoken right, 'tis true;
> The wheel is come full circle.
> —Shakespeare, *King Lear*, Act V, Scene III

1942. Now the wheel has turned, and here I am myself. —E. S. Holding, *Kill Joy*

1974. The secret fund had brought the reporters full circle—first the bugging, and now the cover-up. —Carl Bernstein & Bob Woodward, *All the President's Men*

1984. And now the Knudsen-Ford relationship had come full circle. —Lee Iacocca with William Novak, *Iacocca*

1989. With Poland's accusation that it was Soviet forces that massacred Polish officers—not the Nazis, as Stalin had claimed—the Katyn Forest tragedy is coming full circle. —*New York Times*

1991. "I still love him [Mikhail Baryshnikov] so much. I think of him as such a great friend. We've come full circle." —Jessica Lange, quoted in *Vanity Fair*

1992. Cordero has come full circle. As a young boy growing up on the rough streets of New York City, deserted by his father and living with his Puerto Rican-born mother, Carmen, busy working two jobs, he looked on the old folks in the neighborhood as his surrogate family. —*People*

1993. Then came the computer, access its electronic memory, all you had to remember was which key to press. Now this evolution has come full circle with a story-on-a-disk that destroys itself as you read it, leaving nothing but the memory of words glimpsed briefly on a computer screen. —*New York Times Book Review*

1994. Mario Andretti's racing career, which started here [Nazareth, Pa.] in 1959, has come full circle. Well, sort of. —*Times* (Trenton)

See also IT'S DÉJÀ VU ALL OVER AGAIN.

The wheel that does the squeaking is the one that gets the grease. Whoever makes the biggest fuss gets all the attention. The proverb has been traced back to *Josh Billings: His Sayings* (1865) by Henry Wheeler Shaw (1818–85), American humorist. In 1937, it was included in Bartlett's *Familiar Quotations* and in 1948 in the *Macmillan (Home) Book of Proverbs, Maxims and Familiar Phrases* by Burton Stevenson. The proverb is found in varying forms: *The wheel that squeaks the loudest is the one that gets the grease; The squeaky wheel gets all the grease; 'Tis the squeaky hinge that gets the oil,* etc.

1865. The wheel that squeaks the loudest
　　Is the one that gets the grease.
　　　　　　　　　—Josh Billings, *The Kicker*

1952. 'Tis the squeaky hinge that gets the oil. —R. Marshall, *Jane Hadden*

1986. "Hello, children," he [Grandpa Wingo] said, smiling when he saw us. "I can't quite get the squeak out of this wheel." —Pat Conroy, *The Prince of Tides*

1989. [Harry] Dent [Nixon's political adviser] said that Wallace was exploring widely shared sentiments in the South. The view from Dixie was that "the administration is heading left in an effort" to get liberal votes. There is a feeling down there that

"the squeaky wheel gets the grease." —Stephen E. Ambrose, *Nixon*

1990. Do as others have done—put heat on your state legislature and urge your friends to do the same. The wheel that squeaks gets the oil. —*Washington Post*

1992. "You know what?" she [Congresswoman Maxine Waters] says. "All the government systems work the same: The squeaky wheel gets the oil." —*People*

1993. Americans won't be reconvinced of the virtues of public action unless they see that public action delivers the goods. And this can happen only if squeaky wheels squeak from the left. —*Times* (Trenton)

When a dog bites a man, that is not news; but when a man bites a dog, that is news. The more outrageous the story is the more likely it will get media attention. This saying originated in the United States in about 1880. Some scholars attribute it to Charles A. Dana, editor of *The Sun* (N.Y.), but it was probably first used by the city editor of *The Sun* John B. Bogart (1845–1921).

1989. When she [Jackie Kennedy] was photographed toppling off her mount during a horse show, she telephoned Jack long distance and asked him to have the photo "killed." He refused ("Jackie," he said, "when the First Lady falls on her ass, it's news ..."). —C. David Heymann, *A Woman Named Jackie*

1991. What causes newspapers and television to pay so much attention to David Duke is that he is sensational—a certified extremist who claims to have moved to the mainstream, a celebrated night rider who insists he's going straight at last, a racist bigot who confounds history by pleading he is not and never has been. He gets space and time because he's a man biting a dog; and because he gets space and time he keeps biting the dog, which brings him more space and time—hence contributions. —*New York Times*

1993. ... The man-bites-dog journalistic possibility of watching Columbia win its third straight game was enough to make a native New Yorker—that is to say, me—shuttle up to Boston for the day. And I quickly discovered I was not alone. —*New York Times*

1994. After four games the Giants are ranked dead last in total offense in the entire league. That's right. Last in the entire league. It's unusual, man biting dog, and it can basically be attributed to one thing: Rodney Hampton. —*New York Times*

When a lady says no, she means perhaps; when she says perhaps, she means yes; when she says yes, she is no lady. No woman saying no means no. The proverb is used by men to justify sexual aggression. It has been traced back to Shakespeare's play *The Two Gentlemen of Verona* (1594). *A lady says no, meaning maybe, and maybe, meaning yes; but when she says yes, she isn't a lady* is a variant of the proverb.

> **1594.** *Julia:* Since maids, in modesty, say 'No' to that
> Which they would have the profferer construe
> 'Ay' [yes].
> —Shakespeare, *The Two Gentlemen of Verona*, Act I, Scene II

1982. When a diplomat says yes, he means perhaps. When he says perhaps he means no. When he says no, he is not a diplomat. When a lady says no, she means perhaps. When she says perhaps, she means yes. But when she says yes, she is no lady. —Lord Denning

1992. It seems that Holly [Dunn] had just pulled the plug on a record of hers—asking radio stations everywhere to stop playing it even though it was careering toward the top of the country charts. Her problem: The lyrics featured the highly retrograde sentiment, "When I say no, I mean maybe, or maybe I mean yes." —*Fortune*

When Adam delved and Eve span, who was then the gentleman? When the world was populated by two people only, Adam and Eve, social hierarchies were irrelevant. The proverb dates back to Richard Rolle (c. 1340), who is quoted by G. G. Perry's *Religious Pieces* as saying, "When Adam dalfe and Eue spane/Go spire if thou may spede,/Where was than the pride of man/That now merres his mdede?" In his *Historia Anglicana*, Thomas Walsingham cites John Ball's famous speech at Blackheath to the men in Wat Tyler's Rebellion of 1381 in which he invoked Rolle's quotation, "When Adam delved and Eve span, who was then the gentleman?" The adage was first recorded in the United States in Thacher's *Sentiments* (1764).

1918. It is not only the humanising influence of the garden, it is the democratising influence too. When Adam delved and Eve span, Where was then the gentleman? —A. G. Gardiner, *Leave in the Wind*

1939. While Adam toiled, Eve spun. —T. Scudder, *Jane Welsh Carlyle*

1955. She's not only doing the spinning for Eve's part but the delving for Adam's as well. —L. Bromfield, *Passion*

When I hear the word culture, I reach for my gun. The saying is of German origin: *Wenn ich Kultur höre ... entsichere ich meinen Browning!* ("Whenever I hear the word culture ... I release the safety-catch of my Browning!"). It was used by German novelist and playwright Hanns Johst (1890–1978), although it is often attributed to Herman Goering (1893–1946). The saying is found in varying forms: *When I hear anyone talk of Culture, I reach for my revolver; Whenever I hear the word culture, I reach for my pistol*, etc.

1933. When I hear the word "culture" ... I reach for my pistol! —Hanns Johst, *Schlageter*, Act I, Scene I

1992. "Whenever I hear the word 'expectations' I reach for my gun," said Robert Solow, the Nobel Prize-winning economist from M.I.T. —*New York Times*

See also SHOOT FIRST AND ASK QUESTIONS AFTERWARDS.

When in doubt, do nothing. Don't do anything if you're not 100 percent sure. This saying is first attested in *Uncle John* (1874) by G. J. Whyte-Melville. Ten years later it was used by G. Weatherly in *Little Folks Proverb Painting Book* (1884), and in 1894 it was used by Mark Twain. The proverb is found in many widely varying forms. The French equivalent is *En cas de doute, on s'abstient* ("In case of doubt, do nothing") or *Dans le doute, abstiens-toi* ("When in doubt, don't do anything").

> **1884.** Err ever on the side that's safe,
> And when in doubt, abstain.
> —G. Weatherly, *Little Folks Proverb Painting Book*

1894. As to the Adjective: when in doubt, strike out. —Mark Twain, *Pudd'nhead Wilson*

1970. Personnel or Human Resource people tend to live by the motto: "*When in doubt, screen them* [applicants] *out*"—which means that *you can get screened out by them even if you were absolutely right for the job.* —Richard Nelson Bolles, *What Color Is Your Parachute?*

1974. On more than one occasion, he [Howard Simmons, the managing editor] told Bernstein and Woodward to consider delaying a story or, if necessary, to pull it at the last minute if they had any doubts. "I don't care if it's a word, a phrase, a sentence, a paragraph, a whole story or an entire series of stories," he said. "When in doubt, leave it out." —Carl Bernstein & Bob Woodward, *All the President's Men*

1977. "What I mean is, we all of us look at this through our own eyes, and we're all 'right'—we're sure as hell we know the right thing to do, even when we come out on opposite sides of this. But I say, when you don't know what to do—do nothing." —William Safire, *Full Disclosure*

1991. Seasoned Wall Streeters like Maurits Edersheim, 73, deputy chairman of Smith Barney International and an investor since 1939, didn't flinch a bit. Says he: "With events like this, I recall the French proverb, *En cas de doute, on s'abstient* —'In case of doubt, do nothing.' So I did nothing." —*Fortune*

1992. Never, never, never give your checking account number in response to a solicitation from someone you don't know. If someone you know asks for this information, be sure you know why he/she needs it. When in doubt, don't give it out. —*Modern Maturity*

1993. When in doubt, doubt. —*Times* (Trenton)

1994. In Hollywood, the big-bang theory works like this: When in doubt, blow it up. If doubts persist, blow it up again, only bigger. —*The New York Times*

1995. His motto, whenever he's caught in a tough spot, is "When in doubt it's vitally important to *keep moving*. Velocity is important. Kinetic energy frees the brain and confuses the enemy." —*New York Times Book Review*

When in Rome, do as the Romans do. Don't set your own rules when you are someone's guest. The proverb has been traced back to the 1530 *Commonplace Book* and it is first cited in the United States in about the 1680 *Voyages of Radisson* (1885). The proverb is often attributed to Saint Ambrose (c.340–397), whose advice to Saint Augustine read: *Si fueris Romae, Romano vivito more; si fueris alibi, vivito sicut ibi* ("When you are at Rome live in the Roman style; when you are elsewhere live as they live elsewhere"). English divine Jeremy Taylor (1613–67) also used the proverb. The proverb is found in varying forms: *When in Rome, do as the Romans; When you are at Rome, do as Rome does; When in Rome, do as Rome does; When you go to Rome, do as Rome does*, etc, and *Rome* may be replaced by any other place-name.

1957. When in San Francisco do as natives do. —*New Yorker*

1985. Konig seated Dawn, threw up his hands as if he were overjoyed to see Winchell, made a motion to indicate that he would talk to him later, then sat down and ordered a dry martini.
"In America," he said, "I do as the Americans do." —Michael Korda, *Queenie*

1988. "Hell of a fucked-up country, isn't it?"
Hollis replied, "When in the third Rome, do as they tell you." —Nelson DeMille, *The Charm School*

1992. To raise money in America, do as the Americans do. —*New York Times*

1993. When in Rome.... In markets overseas, companies must respect cultural differences. —*New York Times*

See also A MAN'S HOME IS HIS CASTLE.

When it rains, it pours. *See* IT NEVER RAINS BUT IT POURS.

When one door closes, another one opens. When one opportunity is missed, there is always another one out there. First listed in the collection of proverb by S. Palmer (1710). Sean O'Casey wrote in *Juno & Paycock* (1925): "Ah, God never shut wan door but he opened another." The adage gained wide U.S. currency only in the late nineteenth century.

1994. PROPERTY LAW OPENS ONE DOOR, CLOSES ANOTHER —Headline of Mark Klein and Mike Holt's article about the Omnibus Budget Reconciliation Act of 1993, *Arizona Business Gazette*

1996. Like many employees of the fallen Whittle Communications empire, Tom Russell found that the adage about one door closing and another opening is true. He has opened a home-based business, Russell Design Group, at 511 Taylor Road in South Knoxville. —*News-Sentinel* (Knoxville, Tennessee)

1997. "The key is to give it your all and never be afraid to fail. You learn from failures," she [Uwa Osimiri] says. "If one door closes, try to open another." —*Detroit News*

1997. "My mom always told me when one door closes another one opens," Joanna, 12, said while preparing for the play running through July 20. "I want to keep reaching for that big star." —*Detroit News*

1998. St. Andrew's Church choir Director Colleen Puscus always believed that when one door closes, another opens. So when her choir arrived in Rome to sing before Pope John II, and members were told the Vatican would be closed to the public on the day they were to sing, she kept the faith. —*Hartford Courant*

When the cat's away, the mice will play.

When someone in charge is away, subordinates will take advantage of it. The proverb is similar to the Latin: *Dum felis dormit, mus gaudet et exsilit antro* ("When the cat falls asleep, the mouse rejoices and leaps from his hole") and to the early fourteenth century French: *Ou chat na rat regne* ("Where there is no cat the rat is king"). The proverb has been traced back in English to about 1470, and was used by Shakespeare in *Henry the Fifth* in 1599. It is first attested in the United States in *Port Folio* (1802).

> **1599.** *Westmoreland:* For once the eagle England
> being in prey,
> To her unguarded nest the weasel Scot
> Comes sneaking and so sucks her princely
> eggs,
> Playing the mouse in absence of the cat.
> —Shakespeare, *Henry the Fifth,* Act I,
> Scene II

1922. Wristwatches are always going wrong. Wonder is there any magnetic influence between the person because that was about the time he. Yes, suppose, at once. Cat's away the mice will play. —James Joyce, *Ulysses*

1991. Sure, when the cat's away, the mice will play. But not Norman Steisel.... Mr. Steisel, New York's City's Deputy Mayor, has filled in as the boss while Mayor David N. Dinkins spends a week in South Africa, and he has had his hands full. —*New York Times*

1993. It is well-established in custom and precedent that when the cat's away, the mice may play. While President Clinton was off summiteering last week, Washington was trying to divert itself from a withering heat wave by playing speculation games about its No. 1 critic, Ross Perot, and his millions of followers. —*Times* (Trenton)

When the going gets tough, the tough get going.

When the situation gets critical, those who aren't weak-willed work harder and never give up. The proverb is attributed to Joseph P. Kennedy (1888–1969), the father of President John F. Kennedy. It was recently popularized by Billy Ocean's song "When the Going Gets Tough the Tough Get Going" (1986). The saying is found in varying forms: *When times are tough, the tough see opportunities; When the going gets going, the tough get tough; When the going gets rough, he (she) may want to leave; When the going got tough, he (she) decided it was time to go,* etc. *When the going gets tough (rough)* may be used separately.

1956. "I don't intend to take over military command of the situation in Korea—I leave that up to the generals—but I want to make it perfectly plain that we cannot desert our friends when the going gets rough." —*Memoirs by Harry S. Truman*

1961. "The old man [John F. Kennedy's father] really made 'em stay on their toes," a family friend says. "He used the needle. He'd prod those kids, make 'em think fast on their feet. He'd bear down on 'em and tell 'em, 'When the goin' gets tough, the tough get goin',' and they listened and learned." —Rowland Evans, Jr., *The Saturday Evening Post*

1970. Baron Marcel Bich, the millionaire French pen magnate probably spoke for them all last month when he said, "When the going gets tough, the tough get going!" (*Quand le chemin devient dur, les durs se cheminent!*). —*New Yorker*

1981. "I don't think there's anything you couldn't pull through. Remember that, kiddo, if the going ever gets too rough." —Danielle Steel, *Palomino*

1984. You can be friends with someone for decades. You can share all the good times and bad with him. You can try to protect him when the going gets rough. And then you have some rough luck yourself and you never hear from the guy again. —Lee Iacocca with William Novak, *Iacocca*

1986. The flip side is the Middle East. There, Reagan's rhetoric was at its height, but the president cut and ran when the going got tough. —*New York*

1989. "Tomorrow's going to be tough."
"And the tough get going." —Wayne Care, *Vietnam Spook Show*

1991. Employees were given pins with the message, JUNK BONDS KEEP AMERICA FIT. One of the videos featured [Frederick H.] Joseph and firm chairman Robert Linton lip-synching the lyrics, "When the going gets tough, Drexel gets going." —James B. Stewart, *Den of Thieves*

1992. L.A.P.D. [Los Angeles Police Department]. When the going gets tough, these cops get going. The other way. —*Entertainment Weekly*

1993. Even when the going gets steep, Anchor House riders keep going. —*Times* (Trenton)

1994. "The going is getting tough," says a former Kroll employee who left a month ago. —*Crain's New York Business*

When X speaks, Y listens.

X's prestige is high, so Y has no other choice but to listen when X speaks. The word *speak* may be replaced with *talk.* Popularized by a television commercial for E. F. Hutton: "When E. F. Hutton talks, people listen."***

1986. "I'm told there's a radically different atmosphere on the board of directors these days," says a CBS executive who asked not to be identified. "When Larry Tisch talks, CBS listens." —*New York*

1989. When producer James L. Brooks (the director of *Broadcast News* and *Terms of Endearment* and the creator of TV's *Taxi*) speaks, Hollywood listens. —*New York Newsday*

1991. When the venerable historian John Hope Franklin speaks, I listen. —*Newsweek*

1993. WHEN ANNIE TALKS, PEOPLE LISTEN —Headline, article on the opening night of *Annie Warbucks*, *New York Times*

1994. Yes, flashy jewelry. Yes, purple hair. But when she speaks, clients listen. —*New York Times*

When you come to a fork in the road, take it. When you have to make a choice, do it. This favorite American saying is usually attributed to Yogi Berra (1925), though he denies ever saying it or others like it: "If the people don't want to come to the park, nobody's going to stop 'em"; "You can observe a lot just by watching," etc.

1925. When you come to a fork in the road, take it. —Attributed to Yogi Berra

1994. *MM:* If you had to do it over again, would you still choose physics?
  Lederman: Yeah, but I'd try to find a better track. Maybe I should have been a theorist rather than an experimenter. Then I wouldn't have had to work so hard. As Yogi Berra has been quoted as saying, "If you come to a fork, take it." —*Modern Maturity*

1994. My philosophy in life is—when you come to a fork in the road, take it. —Larry King, *Larry King Weekend*

See also IT'S NOT OVER TILL IT'S OVER; IT'S DÉJÀ VU ALL OVER AGAIN.

When you got it, flaunt it. *See* IF YOU'VE GOT IT, FLAUNT IT.

When you lie down with dogs, you get up with fleas. *See* IF YOU LIE DOWN WITH DOGS, YOU'LL GET UP WITH FLEAS.

Where are the snows of yesteryear? Why doesn't anything last? The proverb was originated by French poet François Villon (1431–c.1463) in his *Ballade des dames du temps jadis* (1461). Sometimes found in its French form. In 1870, English poet Dante Gabriel Rossetti (1828–82) translated the ballad after Villon. Bartlett Jere Whiting dates the earliest appearance of this nos-

talgic proverb in print in the United States to 1935 and lists it in his 1989 collection of *Modern Proverbs and Proverbial Sayings*.

1461. *Mais où sont les neiges d'antan?* (But where are the snows of yesteryear?)
  —François Villon, "Le Grand Testament, Ballade des dames du temps jadis"

1870. Tell me now in what hidden way is
  Lady Flora the lovely Roman?
  Where's Hipparchia, and where is Thais,
  Neither of them the fairer woman.
  Where is Echo, beheld of no man
  Only heard on river and mere—
  She whose beauty was more than human?...
  But where are the snows of yesteryear?
  —Dante Gabriel Rossetti, "The Ballad of Dead Ladies"

1961. "Where are the Snowdens of yesteryear?"
  The question upset them, because Snowden had been killed over Avignon when Dobbs went crazy in mid-air and seized the controls away from Huple.
  The corporal played it dumb. "What?" he asked.
  "Where are the Snowdens of yesteryear?... *Où sont les Neigedens d'antant?*" Yossarian said to make it easier for him. —Joseph Heller, *Catch-22*

1964. Her tyranny was now with the snows of yesteryear. —Compton Mackenzie, *My Life and Times*
See also GONE WITH THE WIND.

Where do we go from here? What is our next move? Nobody knows for sure who coined this catch phrase. It originated in the United States in the late 1910s, and was popularized through the song "Where Do We Go From Here?" (1917) with lyrics by Percy Wenrich (1887–1952) and music by Howard Johnson (1887–1941). The saying is often used in a political context.

1917. When Pat would see a pretty girl, he'd whisper in her ear
  Oh joy! Oh boy! where do we go from here?
  —Percy Wenrich, "Where Do We Go From Here?"

1932. *Gilda:* Last year was bad enough. This is going to be far worse.
  Leo: Why be scared?
  Gilda: Where do we go from here? That's what I want to know.
  —Noel Coward, *Design for Living*, Act I, Scene I

1950. On November 30 [1950] I received a message from British Prime Minister Clement Attlee asking if he might come to Washington and discuss, on a person-to-person basis, what meaning we should give to the Korean events and where we might go from there. —*Memoirs by Harry S. Truman*, Vol. Two

1953. *Montag* walked to the kitchen and threw the book down. *"Montag,"* he said, *"you're really stupid. Where do we go from here?"* —Ray Bradbury, *Fahrenheit 451*

1974. Mrs. Hattie Arnez of Astoria Boulevard played the accordion and they all sang the plaintive "Where Do We Go from Here?" —Robert A. Caro, *The Power Broker*

1977. "Look, Sam," Smitty said, seeming to capitulate, "why don't you just tell us as much of the story as you're going to, and then we'll see where we go from there." —William Safire, *Full Disclosure*

1979. "I suppose we own a very substantial part of the world. The question is, where do I go from here?" —Howard Fast, *The Establishment*

1981. Two doctors have told us they cannot help us because they can't find anything "wrong" with her. So where do we go from here? —Abigail Van Buren, *The Best of Dear Abby*

1984. "In the ten years you've known me, Martin, how many petitions for civil rights have we signed, how many antiwar demonstrations, how many peace vigils?"

"Quite a few. Where do you go from there?" —Howard Fast, *Outsider*

1986. "What about us, Tom?" she [Sallie] said. "Where do we go from here?" —Pat Conroy, *The Prince of Tides*

1987. Where does Mr. Reagan go from here? Senator Laxalt has this answer. "He's going to have to address himself to the fact that in all these years he's been blessed by top staff, and he's been able to really delegate freely." —*New York Times*

1988. Evan returned to the table and sat down, a man exhausted, beaten. "Where do we go from here?" —Robert Ludlum, *The Icarus Agenda*

1989. "I don't think I should discuss that," Alexa said. "I mean, where we go from here, legally, that's something I have to talk to Mr. Stern about." —Michael Korda, *The Fortune*

1991. Where we go from here. At *Fortune's* Education Summit, executives, politicians, and educators agreed on how to fix America's schools—from developing a curriculum that teaches the skills industry needs to more preschool education. Now to do it. —Fortune

1994. "Where do we go from here?" asked Lions safety Bennie Blades. "We go out and keep playing football." —*New York Times*

1995. WHERE DO WE GO FROM HERE? —Headline, *Time*

Where there's a will, there's a way. If one is determined, anything can be achieved. The proverb has been traced back to George Herbert's *Outlandish Proverbs* (1640), and is first attested in the United States in *The Honest Man* (1838). The proverb is found in varying forms: *Where there's a will, there's an estate; Where there's a will, there's a contestation; Where there's a will, there's a lawsuit; Where there's a will, there's relatives; Where there's a will, there are relatives—and murder*, etc. It is often shortened to *Where there's a will.*

1922. *Daisy:* George didn't come in till late, I suppose?

Sylvia: Oh, no, he got away in fairly decent time. Where there's a will, there's a way, you know, even at official functions. —W. S. Maugham, *East of Suez*

1977. "Look around for me, Harry. I'm a little hung up emotionally on Buffie, and that's not good—I need an escape hatch. Nothing complicated. Know what I mean? You do know what I mean, because Herb tells me your life is not affected by the paralysis in your legs. I worried about that for you."

"It's going to be tricky, but where there's a will." —William Safire, *Full Disclosure*

1984. "You're playing politics and you don't know how. And I will not be alive to save you when you fail. There is just no way, no way in the world, you can succeed in making Solomon King."

For only one moment does she appear to be sobered. And then the spell is over. "There is always a way," she responds, as though thinking aloud, "where there is a will." —Joseph Heller, *God Knows*

1991. Where there's a will, there's a way. Sail to or from Europe for $1,480 to $9,640. Or take advantage of our low standby fares.... Take your pick. —Ad, *New York Times*

1992. The saying "Where there's a will, there's a way" is not the whole truth. Given the will, you still have to anticipate obstacles and plan how to deal with them. —Quoted in *Reader's Digest*

1993. WITH RICHES, WHERE THERE'S A WILL, THERE'S A CONTESTATION —Headline, *Times* (Trenton)

Where there's life there's hope. As long as there are signs of life, don't give up hope. A translation of several Latin originals: Terence (c.190–159 b.c.) said, *Modo liceat vivere, est spes* ("While there's life, there's hope") and the Roman orator and statesman Cicero (106–43 b.c.

is quoted as saying: *Dum anima est, spes esse dicitur.* This Latin saying was translated into English and included in R. Taverner's collection of proverbs in 1539 and in J. Ray's collection in 1670. It is first attested in the United States in 1893 in the *Correspondence of Samuel B. Webb.* The proverb is found in varying forms: *As long as there's life there's hope; While there's life there's hope; While there's life, there's soap; While the man lives he will hope; While the sick man has life, there is hope; Where there's hope there's life; Where there's laughter, there's hope,* etc.

1764. To the last moment of his breath
  On hope the wretch relies;
And e'en the pang preceding death
  Bids expectation rise.
          —Oliver Goldsmith, *The Captivity*

1979. "I'm dying, Walter," she said. "That's enough to know."
  "Where there's life there's hope," I said, and I prepared to run upstairs. —Kurt Vonnegut, Jr., *Jailbird*

1984. In a burst of good intention she tried to help me. "At any rate, the worst hasn't happened yet. While there's life there's hope." —Archibald J. Cronin, *Shannon's Way*

1992. WHERE THERE'S LAUGHTER, THERE'S HOPE —Ad, *People*
See also HOPE FOR THE BEST AND PREPARE FOR THE WORST; HOPE SPRINGS ETERNAL IN THE HUMAN BREAST; IT'S NOT OVER TILL IT'S OVER; NEVER SAY DIE.

Where there's no vision, the people perish.

People suffer if they have no plans for or dreams of a better future. The proverb appears in the Old Testament.

Where *there* is no vision, the people perish: but he that keepeth the law, happy *is* he. —Prov. 29:18, *Authorized Version,* 1611

1984. I am David the king. Though ancient and decrepit, I am nonetheless her prince. I am her legend. She has no vision, she says, of ever being with anyone else.
  "Where there is no vision," Bathsheba observes dully, "the people perish." —Joseph Heller, *God Knows*

1992. I hope no one ever tries to raise a child without a vision. I hope nobody ever starts a business or plants a crop in the ground without a vision. For where there is no vision, the people perish.
  One of the reasons we have so many children and so much trouble in so many places in this nation is because they have seen so little opportunity, so little responsibility, so little loving, caring community that they literally cannot imagine the life we are calling them to lead. And so I say again: Where there is no vision, America will perish.
—Bill Clinton, *New York Times*

Where there's smoke, there's fire. If there is a rumor, there is something going on. The proverb has been traced back to *Bruce* (1375) by J. Barbour, and in 1546, it was included in John Heywood's collection of proverbs. In 1579, John Lyly (c. 1554–1606) used the proverb in his *Euphues.* It is first cited in the United States in the 1773 *Papers of James Madison.* The proverb is found in varying forms: *No smoke without fire; There's no fire without smoke; Where there is so much smoke there must be some fire; There was smoke, but no fire; A great deal of smoke and very little fire; No fire without smoke,* etc.

1951. "Quiet guys like that are bad. The ones that get drunk by themselves. They awys flip their lid."
  "You think so?" Warden said, suddenly narrowly, that other part of his mind turning in and clocking up the platitude, and reminding him that where theres smoke theres fire and where theres platitude theres liar. "Some of them dont." —James Jones, *From Here to Eternity*

1971. "There's another lie," the President said, turning off the radio with a disgusted gesture. "Those Nazis are the most outrageous liars, really. The Red Cross can't get in there [German-held parts of the Soviet Union] at all. I think, and I certainly hope, those stories are terribly exaggerated. Our intelligence says they are. Still, where there's smoke—" —Herman Wouk, *The Winds of War*

1976. The computer seemed to ignore my message and came back with, "There's a liberal actor in *The Towering Inferno* who sneaked off for a weekend to Lake Tahoe with a right-wing married actress from the same picture."
  "Do you have proof of this?"
  "No," the computer replied, "but where there's smoke there's fire." —Art Buchwald, *Washington Is Leaking*

1990. America's reaction to such charges is the opposite: where there's smoke, there's fire." —William Safire, *New York Times*

1991. His client, Mr. Nuric said, is still looking for a job in the brokerage industry. "There was so much smoke created, and no fire, that it created a real difficulty for him," he said. —*New York Times*

1992. Where there's smoke ... —*New York*

1993. WHERE THERE'S SMOKE, THERE'S A CAMPAIGN. —Headline, *Times* (Trenton)

1994. Where There's Smoke, There's Safire. —*Newsweek*

Where's the beef? When do we get to the heart of the matter? The phrase was originated by Donna Weinheim of the BBDO advertising firm and was used in the early-1980s commercials to advertise Wendy's hamburgers. In 1984, Walter Mondale picked it up during his presidential bid implying lack of substance in his opponents' promises.

1984. Mr. Mondale charged Mr. Hart that there was no substance to his "new ideas." At one point in the debate, the former Vice President turned to Mr. Hart and said, "When I hear your new ideas, I'm reminded of that ad, 'Where's the beef?'" —*New York Times*

1987. In 1984, he [Gary Hart] proclaimed a campaign of new ideas but couldn't shake Walter Mondale's taunt, "Where's the beef?" —*New York Times*

1991. As a history teacher for more than 15 years, who has followed the debate over history teaching in New York State, I can only roll my eyes and ask, "Where's the beef?" —*New York Times*

1992. Meantime, Mr. Perot is waking up American politics and the parties will never be quite the same. Is that bad? Where's the beef is a good question. So is what's the beef. —*New York Times*

1993. For anxious, angry and cynical citizens in New Jersey, it is never too soon for a candidate [Christine Whitman] who postures as an agent of change to answer that proverbial political question: "Where's the beef?" —*Times* (Trenton)

1994. HERE'S THE BEEF: HILLARY BENT RULES IN CATTLE DEAL. —Headline, *New York Post*

Which came first, the chicken or the egg? This query is the ultimate rhetorical question, used as a reply to an unanswerable question between there's no way of knowing which comes first. *Chicken-and-egg* is sometimes used in a sentence as an attributive.***

1926. We unwrapped the little parcels of lunch. "Chicken."
"There's hard-boiled eggs."
"Find any salt?"
"First the egg," said Bill. "Then the chicken.... I reverse the order ... First the chicken; then the egg." —Ernest Hemingway, *The Sun Also Rises*

1950. The old question, "Which came first, the chicken or the egg?" is a good one to keep in mind when thinking about the Industrial Revolution. For example, did improvements in transportation and

communication come first, and then the big factories and mass production? Or was it the other way around? —Lewis Faul Todd & Merle Curti, *Rise of the American Nation*

1982. However, the more she thought about it, the more she came to feel that the love had been there first. Or at the very least, the love and the desperate need for McGee's strength had come to her simultaneously.
Which came first, she thought, the chicken or the egg? And does it matter anyway? What matters is how I feel about him—and I really want him. —Dean R. Koontz, *The House of Thunder*

1987. The increase in the number of independents, said president of the Association of Independent Television Stations, Preston R. Padden, "is a chicken and egg sort of thing." —*New York Times*

1991. WHICH CAME FIRST: THE BALL OR THE HOLE? —Headline, golf's saga in the land of its origin, Advertising Supplement, *New York Times Magazine*

1992. If anything, there is more mystery in the biographical sections than in the cosmic stuff, which Morris treats almost whimsically. A hen appears against a field of stars as Hawking asks, "Which came first, the chicken or the egg?" —*People*

1993. Ricci said the team wants to make sure the stadium is set before it commits to the agreement, and the county wants to see a team before it goes ahead with construction.... "It's like the chicken and the egg," Ricci said. "Which comes first?" —*Times* (Trenton)

See also THAT'S THE $64,000 QUESTION.

While there's life there is (there's) hope. *See* WHERE THERE'S LIFE THERE'S HOPE.

Whom the gods would destroy, they first make mad. Deities drive people crazy before they destroy them. The proverb has been traced back in English to George Herbert's collection of proverbs (1640) and is based on Euripides (c.485–406 b.c.), who said, "Those whom God wishes to destroy, he first makes mad." Publilius Syrus (first century b.c.) is quoted as saying, "Whom Fortune wishes to destroy she first makes mad." It was first cited in the United States in 1704 in *Correspondence between William Penn and James Logan, 1700–1705*. The proverb is found in varying forms: *Whom the gods wish to render harmless they afflict with sanity; Those whom the gods wish to destroy they first make bored,* etc.

1687. For those whom God to ruin has designed, He fits for fate, and first destroys their mind.— —John Dryden, *The Hind and the Panther*

1875. Whom the Gods would destroy they first make mad. —Henry Wadsworth Longfellow, *The Masque of Pandora*

1970. *Whom the Gods Would Destroy.* —Title of R. Powell's book

1984. "Saul is mad."

"You're telling me? Whom the gods would destroy they first make mad." —Joseph Heller, *God Knows*

1985. Those whom the gods would destroy they first make blind with greed. —*Forbes*

1991. As the most political of diplomats, Baker shares Irving Kristol's observation: "Those whom the Gods would destroy they first tempt to resolve the Arab–Israeli conflict." —*Time*

Who's counting? No one cares, so go ahead and do as you please. *But* often precedes the saying.**

1988. "The target will be reached in six minutes, thirty-four seconds unless we encounter unexpected head winds over the mountains which will extend our time to six minutes, forty-eight seconds or perhaps fifty-five seconds, but then who's counting?" —Robert Ludlum, *The Icarus Agenda*

1992. "That's three questions," said Mr. Clinton.... "I know," the old man called after him. "But who's counting?" —*New York Times*

Who's minding the store? Who is in charge? This query was originally used by customers when no salesman was present to help them. Now the saying is often used in a political context, sometimes meaning, who is minding the country. The saying was popularized in the 1963 movie *Who's Minding the Store?* starring Jerry Lewis. The verb *mind* is sometimes replaced by *run* or *watch*, the word *store* by *shop*.

1961. Yossarian smiled feebly at McWatt, feeling ill, and asked, "Who's minding the store?" —Joseph Heller, *Catch–22*

1988. Ossie's off working in TV's "Stryker" with Burt Reynolds, but it has been a long time between plays for her: How come? "I kept saying 'No, No, No, No,' for years, to anything I was offered. Ossie [Davis] worked, so when the kids were growing up, someone had to mind the store. Me!" —*Daily News* (N.Y.)

1991. "As he went into surgery, he [Ronald Reagan] looked around at the doctors and said, 'I hope you people are all Republicans.' One surgeon assured him, 'Today, we're all Republicans, Mr. President.'" When he saw Mike Deaver, Ed Meese, and Jim Baker, who went in to talk with him be-

forehand, he said, 'Who's minding the store?'" —Kitty Kelley, *Nancy Reagan*

1992. "He [President Bush] goes on vacation too much," Mr. Jeffrey said. "Every time you look around he's at Kennebunkport or something. Who's running the shop?" —*New York Times*

1993. You link the childcare issue with the "Year of the Woman" (which, you suggest, may become "The Year of Who's-Minding-Her-Kids"). —*Newsweek*

1994. WHO'LL MIND THE STORE? —Headline, article on private management and schools, *New York Times*

Whose bread I eat, his song I sing. I am loyal to whoever feeds me.

1946. Life on board the *Oriole* exemplified the old-time saying: "Whose bread I eat, his song I sing" or, at any rate, his song I hear! —Upton Sinclair, *A World to Win*

1992. "Why does he always quote his boss?"

"What's wrong with that? Whose bread he eats, his song he sings." —Overheard at a restaurant

See also DON'T BITE THE HAND THAT FEEDS YOU; HE WHO PAYS THE PIPER CALLS THE TUNE.

Win this one for the Gipper. If you need a reason to win, do it for someone who inspires you. The proverb originated in the United States in the 1920s and is attributed to Knute Rockne, then-coach of the Notre Dame football team. One of his best players, George Gipp (the Gipper), died at the age of twenty-five. Before he died, he told Knute Rockne: "Rock, someday when things look real tough for Notre Dame, ask the boys to go out and win for me." The coach honored his deathbed request and Notre Dame defeated Army by an unprecedented score of 12–6. In 1940, *Knute Rockne—All-American,* a motion picture based on the life of George Gipp, was released, and Ronald Reagan played the Gipper. "Win this one for the Gipper" became one of the major political slogans of Ronald Reagan.

1940. Some day, when things are tough, maybe you can ask the boys to go in there and win just one for the Gipper! —Robert Buckner, *Knute Rockne—All-American,* spoken by Ronald Reagan

1977. "Don't lose Curtice," Ericson said, "and remember that Bannerman put a lot of heat on Reed. Preston might not have liked that." Those tactical tips were not the sort of historic advice Duparquet had in mind. He shrugged and turned to leave.

"Win it for the Gipper," said Hennessy. —William Safire, *Full Disclosure*

1991. What can you say to a 7–7 team that, miraculously, is still assured of a playoff berth if it wins its last two games?... Can you urge the players to win one for the Gipper or warn them about how tough it's going to be to play a loosey-goosey fast-closing New England team this Sunday at Giants Stadium? —*New York Times*

1992. In 1986, Ronald Reagan crisscrossed the country imploring his followers to "cast one last vote for the Gipper" by re-electing the Republicans they sent to the Senate on his coattails in 1980. —*New York Times*

1994. Columnist Garry Wills is trying to revise history in saying Jimmy Carter's contributions helped win the Cold War.... The fact is, it was Ronald Reagan's "Peace Through Strength" policy, the buildup of the military, SDI and his telling Mikhail Gorbachev to "tear down the Berlin Wall" that won the Cold War.... This is one for the "Gipper," Mr. Wills. —*New York Post*

A winner never quits, and a quitter never wins.

If you want to win, you can't quit. *A quitter never wins, and a winner never quits* is a variant of the proverb.

> **1990.** "I keep telling him that a quitter never wins, and a winner never quits, but I'm not sure he's going to quit smoking." —Overheard in a New Jersey diner

> **1992.** A WINNER NEVER QUITS—AND A QUITTER NEVER WINS.
> It was Bill Clinton's big day, and he ended up getting a dramatic boost in the polls, but Ross Perot stole the headlines with his sudden decision to bow out. —*Newsweek*

See also FINDERS KEEPERS, LOSERS WEEPERS; WINNING ISN'T EVERYTHING, IT'S THE ONLY THING.

Winning isn't everything, it's the only thing.

Nothing matters but winning. This adage originated in the United States in 1953, and it is often attributed to Vanderbilt University coach Red Sanders. In a 1962 interview, Vince Lombardi (1913–1970), football coach of the Green Bay Packers, said, "Winning isn't everything, but wanting to win is."

> **1982.** "Winning isn't the most important thing, it's the only thing!"—J. Caesar. —Robert Asprin, *Myth Directions*

> **1988.** One of America's best-loved coaches, Vince Lombardi of the Green Bay Packers, said with well-placed hyperbole, "Winning isn't everything—it's the *only* thing." Lombardi was talking about football; he could have been coaching American life.... Kevin O'Connell [a lawyer] had concluded, "If winning is the only thing, then if you lose, you lose everything." —Carole Hyatt & Linda Gottlieb, *When Smart People Fail*

> **1991.** Governor Cuomo is not a man of the 1950's, but a different man of the 1990's, when winning is widely regarded not only as the main thing but the only thing. —James Reston, *New York Times*

> **1993.** Vince Lombardi had it wrong: Winning is not the only thing—not if in the process you lose what you stand for. —*Times* (Trenton)

> **1994.** Many parents think that winning isn't everything; it's the only thing. —"American Journal," CBS

See also IT'S NOT WHETHER YOU WIN OR LOSE BUT HOW YOU PLAY THE GAME; A WINNER QUITS, AND A QUITTER NEVER WINS.

The winter of our discontent.

A time of dissatisfaction. The phrase was the opening line of Shakespeare's *Richard the Third* (1592–93). In 1961, John Steinbeck (1902–68) published his novel *The Winter of Our Discontent*. It is often used in a political context to describe people's unrest or dissatisfaction.

> **1592–93.**
> > *Gloucester:* Now is the winter of our
> > discontent
> > Made glorious summer by this sun of York.
> > —Shakespeare, *Richard the Third*, Act I,
> > Scene I

> **1961.** *The Winter of Our Discontent.* —Novel by John Steinbeck

> **1988.** They took some consolation in the fact that this would be the last winter of their discontent. —Erich Segal, *Doctors*

> **1989.** That evening he [Johnny Carson] once again came out late. "Welcome to the winter of my discontent," he said. —Laurence Leamer, *King of the Night: The Biography of Johnny Carson*

> **1991.** Though another winter of discontent is months away, there is already renewed speculation about Mr. Gorbachev's future. Indeed, if he were an American politician one of the many confident commentators on the Washington talk-show circuit would get a big laugh with a line like: "Stick a fork in him. He's done." —*New York Times*

> **1992.** "The Winter of Discontent." —*Time*

> **1993.** THE WINTER OF OUR DISCOUNTS —Headline of article on flea-market shopping mentality, *New York*

Wisdom is better than rubies. It is more important to be wise than rich. The proverb has been traced back to *Never Too Late* (1590) by Robert Greene (1558–92), and is first attested in the United States in *Christographia* (1702). The word *rubies* may be replaced with *riches* or *wealth*.

1982. "If wisdom is better than riches, grandpa, does that mean that rich people can buy wisdom, too?" —Overheard in a playground

1984. "Solomon, my boy," I say, "let me give you some wisdom. Wisdom is better than rubies, you know, and maybe even better than peacocks and apes." —Joseph Heller, *God Knows*

See also THE WISDOM OF SOLOMON.

The wisdom of Solomon. King Solomon was famous for his wisdom. The proverbial phrase was first mentioned in the Old Testament, and is found in varying forms: *As wise as Solomon*, etc.

And there came of all people to hear the wisdom of Solomon, from all kings of the earth, which had heard of his wisdom. —Kings 4:34, *Authorized Version*, 1611

1961. Giving advice is an imposing responsibility and I am aware of the faith and trust placed in me by millions of readers. Had I been blessed with the wisdom of Solomon, I could not pull out of my hat the answers to all the questions put to me in a single day. —Ann Landers, *Since You Ask Me*

1993. No disrespect intended, but the case that gave Solomon his reputation for judicial wisdom was a piece of cake. All he had to figure out was which of the two women before him was lying, a task greatly facilitated by the fact that the liar was also unbelievably stupid. How else can you explain her cheery "OK!" when Solomon proposed that the baby each woman claimed was her own be chopped in two, each claimant getting an equal share? —*Times* (Trenton)

With malice toward none, with charity for all. With ill will toward no one and kindness for everyone. The saying is part of Abraham Lincoln's 75-word sentence, the concluding paragraph of his Second Inaugural Address delivered on March 4, 1865. A similar idea was expressed in 1838 by John Quincy Adams (1767–1848) in his letter to A. Bronson.

1838. In charity to all mankind, bearing no malice or ill will to any human being, and even compassionating those who hold in bondage their fellow men, not knowing what they do. —John Quincy Adams, "Letter to A. Bronson"

1865. With malice toward none, with charity for all, with firmness in the right as God gives us to see the right, let us strive on to finish the work we are in, to bind up the nation's wounds, to care for him who shall have borne the battle and for his widow and his orphan, to do all which may achieve and cherish a just and lasting peace among ourselves and with all nations. —Abraham Lincoln, *Second Inaugural Address*

1992. MALICE TOWARD SOME —Headline, *New Yorker*

With such friends, one hardly needs enemies. People who have untrustworthy friends don't need enemies. The proverb has been used in the United States since c.1920, according to Eric Partridge. It is found in varying forms: *With friends like that, who needs enemies; If you have the government for an ally, you don't need any enemies; With colleagues like that, you don't need enemies; With you as a partner I don't need enemies;* etc.

1977. President Kennedy was reported to be shocked and dismayed by the murders. But Madame Nhu, still in the United States, accused him of having incited the coup. Said the Tiger Lady: "If you have the Kennedy administration for an ally, you don't need any enemy." —Victor Lasky, *It Didn't Start with Watergate*

1987. Walking to the meeting where the faculty capitulated to the students ..., I heard a professor of biology loudly asking, perhaps for our benefit, "Do these social scientists really believe there is any danger?" My friend looked at me sadly and said, "With colleagues like that, you don't need enemies." —Allan Bloom, *The Closing of the American Mind*

1988. As Alexander Haig put it in an interminable Republican "debate" in Iowa the other night: "If you can't answer your friends, what in heaven's name is going to happen next November if you are our standard-bearer and these Democrats get after you on the subject?" ... With such friends, Mr. Bush hardly needs enemies. —*New York Times*

1989. "Somebody has to pick up the slack for your bad playing."

"With you as a partner I don't need enemies, right?" —Wayne Care, *Vietnam Spook Show*

1991. WITH RAND M C NALLY, WHO NEEDS THE CIA? —Headline, *Business Week*

1993. With friends like that, Mr. Yeltsin needs no enemies. —*New York Times*

1994. As Reeves stammered his thanks, [Tom] Hanks loudly replied: "Thank *you,* Mister Gay Entertainment Television!" With plugs like that, who needs sponsors? —*Newsweek*

See also SAVE US FROM OUR FRIENDS.

A/The wolf in sheep's clothing. A description of someone dangerous who pretends to be a friend. The phrase is taken from Aesop's fable "The Wolf in Sheep's Clothing." The same idea can be found in the Bible. The phrase is used in varying forms: *A snake in sheep's clothing; A wolf in lamb's clothing; To see the wolf behind the sheep's clothing; The sheep in the clothes of the wolf; A sheep in a wolf's clothing*, etc.

> Beware of false prophets, which come to you in sheep's clothing, but inwardly they are ravening wolves. —Matt. 7:15, *Authorized Version*, 1611

c.550 b.c.
The lamb ... began to follow the wolf in sheep's clothing. —Aesop, "The Wolf in Sheep's Clothing"

1922. Charity to the neighbor, says Martin. But where is he? We can't wait.
 —A wolf in sheep's clothing, says the citizen. That's what he is.
 —James Joyce, *Ulysses*

1991. The Senecas say that residents are merely trying to continue a tradition of taking advantage of the Indians. "This is just a sheep in wolf's clothing," said Clavin John, the Seneca President. —*New York Times*

1991. "It's the proverbial wolf in sheep's clothing," says a Greenpeace USA spokesman. "For a tiny step of environmental penance, they can buy years of time for environmental abuses." —*Wall Street Journal*

1993. BEWARE OF WOLVES IN SHEEP'S CLOTHING —Ad, *U.S.1* (Princeton)

The wolf is at the door. The danger is imminent. This proverb has been traced back in English to John Skelton (c.1460–1529), and *to keep the wolf from the door* was included in John Heywood's collection of proverbs in 1546. It is first cited in the United States in 1702 in *Magnalia Christi Americana* (1833–55). The proverb is found in varying forms: *There is a wolf at the door; There's no wolf at the door*, etc.

1893. There's a whining at the threshold—
 There's a scratching at the floor—
 To work! To work! In Heaven's name!
 The wolf is at the door!
 —Charlotte Perkins Gilman, "In This Our World: The Wolf at the Door"

1936. "Didn't you get the money for the taxes?

Don't tell me the wolf is still at the door of Tara." —Margaret Mitchell, *Gone With the Wind*

1947. ... the man is a sword cutting daisies, that not privation but luxury is the wolf at the door and that the fangs of this wolf are all the little vanities and conceits and laxities that Success is heir to ... —Tennessee Williams, *A Streetcar Named Desire*

1957. One way to keep the wolf from the door is to act like one. —*Time*

1984. While all these ideological arguments were raging, the nation's tenth-largest corporation was falling apart. Obviously, that's not the time to talk ideology. When the wolf is at the door, you get pragmatic in a big hurry. —Lee Iacocca with William Novak, *Iacocca*

1985. "Did Carla tell you that I now pay her four hundred a week in alimony?"
 "No, she didn't."
 "It's no fortune, but it keeps the wolf away from the door." —Howard Fast, *The Immigrant's Daughter*

1987. "We're always just a step ahead of the wolf at the door," Dr. Lobach said. —*New York Times*

1991. The wolf is gone from the door, thanks to sales of big jets. —*New York Times*

1993. "The whole health care sector is the biggest wolf crier you have ever seen. But every so often there is really a wolf at their door." —*New York Times*

A woman's place is in the home. Women should stay home to cook, raise children, and do household chores. The proverb is considered prejudicial, old-fashioned, and offensive to women. It dates back to John Stephen's *High Life in New York* (1844), in which he asserted that "a woman's place is in her own house, a taking care of the children."

1943. I go up in arms against the silly old-fashioned prejudice that women's place is always at home. —Agatha Christie, *Moving Finger*

1997. For a few blustery days in late October, they gathered here from across the United States to show that a woman's place is in the home—as long as it can be parallel-parked. —*Los Angeles Times*

1997. Coming of age in the 1970s, I cringed whenever I heard the exhausted adage " A woman's place is in the home." While the concepts of marriage and motherhood appealed to me, cleaning up after myself and other people did not. —*Christian Science Monitor*

1998. Using the battle cry, "This woman's place is

in the House—the House of Representatives," [Bella] Abzug beat Rep. Leonard Farbstein, a seven-term Democrat, in the 1970 primary for an Upper West Side seat. —*New York Post*
See also HOME IS WHERE THE HEART IS; THERE'S NO PLACE LIKE HOME; A WOMAN'S WORK IS NEVER DONE.

A woman's work is never done. There is always something for a woman to do around the house. The proverb is now often used to celebrate the wider achievements of women. It is traced back to T. Tusser's *Five Hundred Points of Husbandry* (1570). Benjamin Franklin lists the adage in his *Poor Richard's Almanac* (1722), and Americans found out that "if you go among the Women, you will learn... that a Woman's Work is never done."

1983. Work was something men did, usually to make money. And whatever it was that women did had a different name—woman's work, as in the maxim "Woman's work is never done." —*Christian Science Monitor*

1997. It is often said a woman's work is never done. For now, that axiom is more than true for Patricia O'Brien, the incoming dean of the Simmons College Graduate School of Management. —*Boston Globe*

1998. Their current collaboration, called "A Woman's Work Is Never Done," which opened last week and runs through June 21 at Hudson Square, honors the vast, silent, and too often overlooked world of women's handwork. —*New York Post*
See also A WOMAN'S PLACE IS IN THE HOME.

A word to the wise is sufficient. Intelligent people don't need to be told something twice. The proverb has been traced back to 1275. In 1546, it was included in John Heywood's book of proverbs, and is first attested in the United States in 1645 in *John Wheelwright*. It was popularized by Benjamin Franklin in 1757. The proverb is found in varying forms: *A word is enough to the wise; A word to the wise is enough,* etc. Often shortened to *a word to the wise* and used as a warning. The saying is sometimes quoted in Latin: *Verbum sat sapienti* ("A word is sufficient to a wise man").

1757. Father Abraham stood up, and reply'd, If you have my Advice, I'll give it you in short, for a *Word to the Wise is enough,* and *many Words won't fill a Bushel,* as *Poor Richard says.* —Benjamin Franklin, "Father Abraham's Speech, or, The Way to Wealth," quoted in *An American Primer,* edited by Daniel J. Boorstin

1956. A word to the wise is not sufficient if it doesn't make any sense. —*New Yorker*

1961. The Judge then hissed, "You may lose Miss Paris to someone else if you are not careful."
Roy bolted up. "To who for instance?"
"A better provider."
"You mean Gus Sands?"
The Judge did not directly reply. "A word to the wise—" —Bernard Malamud, *The Natural*

1989. "I hear the Museum of Modern Art decided to acquire a Baldur."
Bannerman chuckled. "Saw the light, did they?"
"I thought you might have had something to do with it."
"A word to the wise. Nothing more." —Michael Korda, *The Fortune*

1991. Quanex. The company that made steel products. Then, made better steel products. Then, made titanium products. Then, made even better titanium and steel products. Then, made aluminum products. Then, made the best aluminum, titanium, and steel products. Then, made the Fortune 500. A word to the wise ... Quanex. —Ad, *Wall Street Journal*

1992. "A word to the wise, Mr. Estrada: Find this Johnny, and find him soon." —Philip Friedman, *Inadmissible Evidence*

1993. My suggestion would be to refer these beggars to a mission, or offer them some real work—and see what happens.—Mrs. F. E. Altaras.
Dear Mrs. Altaras: Yours is an excellent suggestion. A word to the (street) wise should be sufficient. —Abigail Van Buren, "Dear Abby"

Words once spoken you can never recall. Be careful what you say because you can't take back something you've said. This proverb dates to back to Chaucer's *The Maunciple's Tale* (c.1386), and was first attested in the United States in the 1792 *Universal Asylum.*

1989. Stern had warned her not to get into any substantive discussion without him. "Words can't be withdrawn," he had told her, his expression severe—not that it was anything she didn't already know. "You can bite your tongue all you like, but you can't call them back." —Michael Korda, *The Fortune*

1993. "Think twice before you say something. Remember that words once uttered can never be retrieved." —Overheard on a subway train
See also LOOSE LIPS SINK SHIPS; KEEP YOUR MOUTH SHUT AND YOUR EYES OPEN; SILENCE IS GOLDEN; SPEECH IS SILVER, SILENCE IS GOLDEN.

Work and pray, live on hay, you'll get pie in the sky when you die. The rich promise us a better life when we die. The lines come from the poem *The Preacher and the Slave* (1911) by Joe Hill (1879–1915). It is often shortened to *pie in the sky* to refer to something unrealistic. It may be used as an attribute, *pie-in-the-sky,* of nouns.

> **1911.** You will eat, bye and bye,
>   In that glorious land above the sky;
>   Work and pray, live on hay,
>   You'll get pie in the sky when you die.
>   —Industrial Workers of the World, "Songs
>   of the Workers"

1983. "You're offering me pie in the sky." —Jackie Collins, *Hollywood Wives*

1989. If elected, she [Laura] could promise them no miracles, no pie in the sky, no convertibles for every garage (laughter). —Erich Segal, *Doctors*

1993. Who says there are no more free lunches? Whitman's pie-in-the-sky tax cut proposal sounds like one of those diets where they tell you that you "eat whatever you want and never gain a pound." —*Times* (Trenton)

See also PROMISES ARE LIKE PIECRUST: THEY ARE MADE TO BE BROKEN; PROMISES, PROMISES!

Work never hurt anybody. If you think you're too delicate to work for a living, you're wrong. The proverb has been traced back to *Young Mrs. Jardine* (1879), and is first attested in the United States in *Icebound* (1923). The proverb is found in varying forms: *Hard work never hurt anyone; Hard work never killed anybody yet; Honest work never hurt any man; Work will never kill any man,* etc.

1939. *Father: (Sitting.)* What kind of work is this you're planning to do?
Clarence: Sort of salesman, the ad said.
Father: Um-hum. Well, work never hurt anybody. —Howard Lindsay & Russell Crouse, *Life with Father*

1957. Hard work never hurt anyone. —Pelham O. Wodehouse, *Over Seventy*

1993. "Have you ever heard that work never hurt any man?"
"But what about women, ma'am?" —Overheard at a clean-up rally

Workers of the world, unite! One of the most famous quotes of Marx and Engels. *Workers* can be replaced by other subjects.

1848. Working men of all countries, unite! —Karl Marx & Friedrich Engels, *The Communist Manifesto*

1988. Gang of the world, unite! You have nothing to lose but your postage. —*New York Times Magazine*

1991. The recent tongue-in-the cheek headline in a *Izvestia* should serve as a warning: "Special Services of All Countries, Unite!" —*New York Times*

1993. Grocery shoppers of the world, unite! Supermarkets know everything about you. It's time you learned something about them. —*New York Times*

1994. WORKERS OF THE WORLD, MAKE FRIENDS! —Headline, *New York Times Book Review*

1995. Hypocrites of the world unite! —*New York Times*

See also THE PROLETARIANS HAVE NOTHING TO LOSE BUT THEIR CHAINS.

The world is a stage and all the men and women merely players. *See* ALL THE WORLD'S A STAGE.

The world is an (one's) oyster. If you have a lot of money, you can have anything you want. The proverb first appears in Shakespeare's play *The Merry Wives of Windsor* (1600).

1600. *Falstaff:* I will not lend thee a penny.
Pistol: Why, then, the world's mine oyster,
   Which I with sword will open.
   —Shakespeare, *The Merry Wives of Windsor,*
   Act II, Scene II

1949. *Willy:* You guys! There was a man started with the clothes on his back and ended up with diamond mines!
Happy: Boy, someday I'd like to know how he did it.
Willy: What's the mystery? The man knew what he wanted and went out and got it! Walked into a jungle, and comes out, the age of twenty-one, and he's rich! The world is an oyster, but you don't crack it open on a mattress! —Arthur Miller, *Death of a Salesman*

1962. When an interviewer asked him, "Doesn't it trouble you to know that all your books hereafter will be compared to *Chain of Command?* " Hawke blurted innocently, "But they won't. Ah can raht better than that. Ah'm rahtin' betta raht now." It was an unlucky answer, picked up by a national magazine and run as a caption under a revolting picture of Hawke eating an oyster, so: The World His Oyster—"Ah'm rahtin' betta raht now." —Herman Wouk, *Youngblood Hawke*

1973. "The hero won the gunfight, and ten years ago if I had a twenty-year-old daughter who was dating a David, I'd have said, 'What's your rush?

The world is your oyster. And I'll give it to you.'"
—Jacqueline Susann, *Once Is Not Enough*

1987. He [Hugh Ford] begins [his book "Four Lives in Paris"] with Antheil, the brash, cocky, world-is-my-oyster American abroad. —*New York Times Book Review*

1989. "If these two companies are together, the world, in every shape and form, will truly be our oyster," Mr. Ross said. —*New York Times*

The worm turns. *See* EVEN A WORM WILL TURN.

The worst is yet to come. *See* THE BEST IS YET TO COME.

Would you buy a used car from this man?
Do you trust this man? The saying originated in the United States and is attributed to the American comedian Mort Sahl, according to *The Penguin Dictionary of Modern Quotations*. The saying was often used with regard to Richard Nixon and is now applicable to anyone whose honesty is in doubt.

1986. Mr. Nixon, after all, was dogged by a reputation as a man from whom one should never buy a used car. —*New York Times*

1989. Indeed, from Chappaquiddick on, Nixon and his supporters could answer the question, often asked of Nixon, "Would you buy a used car from this man?" with a question of their own, "Would you go for a ride with this man?" —Stephen E. Ambrose, *Nixon*

1991. B. Yeltsin.
Conventional Wisdom: Americans still wouldn't buy a used car from him. But he's in the driver's seat. —*Newsweek*

1994. He [Richard Nixon] was demonized on the left and lionized on the right. "Nixon's the One," supporters chanted; "Would you buy a used car from this man?" detractors sneered. —*New York Times*

See also I AM NOT A CROOK.

Yes, Virginia, there is a Santa Claus. The saying was originated by Francis Pharcellus Church (1839–1906), editor of the *New York Sun,* in 1897. Virginia was a New York girl who wanted to know whether Santa Claus was a myth. "I am 8 years old," she wrote to the *New York Sun.* "Some of my little friends say there is no Santa Claus. Papa says, 'If you see it in the *Sun,* it's so.' Please tell me the truth, is there a Santa Claus? Virginia O'Hanlon." Francis P. Church responded on the editorial page of the *New York Sun* on September 21, 1897. Often shortened to *yes, Virginia,* to affirm any unlikely thing or event.

1897. Yes, Virginia, there is a Santa Claus ... Thank God! he lives, and lives forever. A thousand years from now, Virginia, nay ten times ten thousand years from now, he will continue to make glad the heart of childhood. —Francis P. Church

1970. One final word about registers: the very term "register" can be misleading. The vision: one central place where you can go, and find listed every vacancy in a particular field of endeavor. *But, sorry, Virginia; there ain't no such animal.* All you'll find by going to any of these places is A Selected List of some of the vacancies. A smorgasbord, if you will. —Richard Nelson Bolles, *What Color Is Your Parachute?*

1985. Yes, Virginia, there *is* such thing as Cafe Society!—and all of it gathered to ooh and aah the glamorous DAWN AVALON, and star of *Flames of Passion,* the hit of the year.... —Michael Korda, *Queenie*

1991. "There is no Santa Claus, Virginia ...," Rooney said he would have written in response to the famous letter to *The New York Sun* in 1897. —*Times* (Trenton)

1992. Dear Virginia: No, kid. There is no Santa Claus. There's no Easter Bunny, nor are there any of the tooth fairies you've no doubt been told about. But it is Christmas Eve, it is getting late, and there is Jack Daniel's ... —*New York*

1994. Yes, Virginia, there is a Hollywood, but it does not happen to be well represented at Cannes this year, even if both the opening and closing selections are American. —*New York Times*

You ain't seen nothin' yet. The most remarkable thing is yet to come. The saying was popularized by Al Jolson (1886–1950) when he proclaimed, "You ain't heard nothin' yet, folks," in the introduction to the first "all talking, all singing, all dancing" motion picture—*The Jazz Singer,"* released by the Warner Brothers. Jolson was promoting his own song "You Ain't Heard Nothin' Yet," written by Gus Kahn and Buddy de Sylva in 1919.

1983. The boom years of this economy were made when there were attempts to involve the black community. For those people who think they've seen a renaissance in Boston—what's the old Hollywood accent?—"You ain't seen nothin' yet." —*Christian Science Monitor*

1984. "You know, so many people act as if this election means the end of something," Mr. Reagan concluded in an indirect reference to the fact that this was the last election night of his career. "To each one of you I say, it's the beginning of everything," Mr. Reagan said. Then he stirred full-throated cheers by repeating an informal slogan of his campaign, "You ain't seen nothin' yet." —*New York Times*

1987. If you thought you saw a lot of Tip O'Neill when he was Speaker of the House, you ain't seen nothin' yet. —*Boston Globe*

1995. Gov. Don Sundquist took care to praise lawmakers, the state's prosecutors, and his lobbying team at a ceremonial signing of his 20-bill crime package Thursday, but promised "You ain't seen nothin' yet." —*Commercial Appeal* (Memphis, Tennessee)

1998. THINK LAST YEAR WAS AMAZIN'? YOU AIN'T SEEN NOTHIN' YET —Headline, *New York Post*

1998. Well, well. And you thought that your son was a chip off the old block. That your daughter was a gal just like the gal that married her dear old dad. You ain't seen nothin' yet. —*Boston Globe*

See also THE BEST IS YET TO BE.

You are what you eat. Your health, looks, and well-being result from the kinds of food you consume. The proverb has been used in the United States since 1941.

1991. "I need stuff that's fast, cheap and easy."

"You'd better be careful," I said without thinking. "You know, you are what you eat."

"Mom!" she exclaimed. "I'm not *that* kind of girl!" —Quoted in *Reader's Digest*

1992. If you are what you eat, the survivor of tonight's world heavyweight championship fight will have been nourished either by sandwiches or seaweed. —*New York Times*

1993. "The old saying is true—you are what you eat," Pierson concludes. "And you have to make that choice every day." —Quoted in *Reader's Digest*

1993–94. According to a survey done for the Pfaltzgraff (dinnerware) Company, you are how you eat. —Susan Champlin Taylor, "I Can't Hear You, I've Got Food in My Mouth," *Modern Maturity*

1994. Call it the ultimate Power Diet.

The Army is taking the adage "You Are What You Eat" to new heights, researching not the perfect weapon, but the perfect food to build a Super Soldier. —*The Philadelphia Inquirer*

1994. CANNIBALISTIC CULTURE: YOU ARE WHAT YOU EAT —*Wall Street Journal*

See also EAT TO LIVE; DO NOT LIVE TO EAT.

You better believe it. Yes, absolutely. The saying originated in America in the mid-1880s. *You'd better believe it* is a variant.

1953. *Kilroy:* I'm a free man with equal rights in this world! You better believe it because that's news for you and you had better believe it! —Tennessee Williams, *Camino Real*

1976. "If the publisher doesn't advertise a book, the writers scream like mad."

"You mean people are going to scream at Jackie?"

"You better believe it. I've never known a writer who didn't scream at his editor." —Art Buchwald, *Washington Is Leaking*

1981. "Would you believe after twenty-five years of marriage my husband still sets the alarm for 6 a.m. so he can have sex before? You'd better believe I am also tired!" —Abigail Van Buren, *The Best of Dear Abby*

1986. Jack laughed. "According to you *no* movie is any good unless it comes from your studio."

Howard licked his lips and rolled his eyes. "You'd better believe it." —Jackie Collins, *Hollywood Husbands*

1987. "Morning, everybody! Big day today!"

"Is that right?"

"You better believe it! It's *election* day!" —G. B. Trudeau, *Doonesbury Deluxe*

1992. "What do we do," Baldini said, "there are thieves in the Police Department. I guess you know that. Plenty of them."

"You better believe it," Di Luca said. —Ed McBain, *Kiss*

1993. "All the game needs," he [Rick Dell] says, "is for the Yankees to be in the World Series." Spoken like a lifelong Yankees' fan? "You better believe it," says the Trenton State College coach. —*Times* (Trenton)

1994. Sergeant Deleno said he planned to buy a ticket for tonight's $70 million Lotto jackpot. "You'd better believe it," he said. "I won't have to deal with this if I hit." —*New York Times*

See also TAKE IT FROM ME.

You can catch more flies with honey than with vinegar. People respond better to politeness than they do to rudeness or meanness. The proverb has been traced back to G. Torriano's *Common Place of Italian Proverbs* (1666). It first appeared in the United States in Benjamin Franklin's *Poor Richard's Almanac* in 1744, and is found in varying forms: *A spoonful of honey will catch more flies than a gallon of vinegar; More flies are caught with honey than vinegar; Honey catches more flies than vinegar; Honey attracts more flies than vinegar; It's easier to catch flies with honey than with vinegar; You catch more flies with molasses than with vinegar; You can catch more flies with sugar than vinegar; You can't catch flies with vinegar, etc.

1744. Tart Words make no Friends: spoonful of honey will catch more flies than Gallon of Vinegar. —Benjamin Franklin, *Poor Richard's Almanac*

1922. One tablespoon of honey will attract friend

Bruin more than half a dozen barrels of first choice malt vinegar. —James Joyce, *Ulysses*

1984. Mr. Solarz concedes that the letter to Mr. Ortega took a distinctly sympathetic tone. But he said, "You catch more flies with honey than with vinegar." —*New York Times*

1991. "Walk them [horses] out in the light where I can see them," she said.

Owner and dealer and people nearby all protested furiously. "Takes all the sport out," said a small man in riding breeches and a sweater.

Scarlett insisted, but very sweetly. Catch more flies with honey, she reminded herself. —Alexandra Ripley, *Scarlett*

1992. "Generally speaking, you're going to catch a lot more flies with honey than with vinegar, as the saying goes." —Philip Friedman, *Inadmissible Evidence*

You can fool some of the people all the time, all the people some of the time, but you cannot fool all the people all the time. One can't fool people all the time. The saying is attributed to Abraham Lincoln, though it is not found in any of his works: the only available source is Alexander K. McClure's book, *Abe Lincoln's Yarns and Stories,* published in 1904, which quotes Lincoln using the saying in a conversation with a caller at the White House.

1856. If you once forfeit the confidence of your fellow citizens, you can never regain their respect and esteem. It is true that you may fool all the people some of the time; you can even fool some of the people all the time; but you can't fool all of the people all the time. —Abraham Lincoln, quoted by Alexander K. McClure in *Abe Lincoln's Yarns and Stories*

1945. "Why should he and I talk about her? I'm through. 'You may fool all of the people some of the time'—you know the rest." —Emilie Loring, *Beyond the Sound of Guns*

1985. *You Can Fool All of the People All of the Time.* —Title of Art Buchwald's book

1988. I trusted that the common man would always sooner or later, stand up for right rather than wrong, and vote for the general welfare rather than the narrow interests of a special group. My favorite President was Abraham Lincoln who I respected for his wise words, "You can fool some of the people all of the time, and all of the people some of the time but you can't fool all of the people all of the time." —*New York Times*

1989. TRYING TO FOOL ALL OF THE PEOPLE ALL OF THE TIME —Headline, *New York Times*

1991. You, Mr. President, and all you members of Congress might just be facing a popular revolt in November 1992. It's easy to fool most of the people, distracted and bewildered as they are, most of the time. But after 5 or 10 years, enough people actually get the joke. —*New York Times*

1992. Today is the birthday of George Bush. The greatest president of them all. That's not my opinion—it's his as well ... George says. "You can't fool all the people all the time—once every four years is enough." —Joey Adams, *New York Post*

1993. You can fool some of the people some of the time, but not all of the people all of the time. That's basically how it went with the Flyers deciding not to renew Mike Emrick's play-by-play contract. —*Times* (Trenton)

1994. I mention anarchy only because of my Congressman. Came in here the other day, said, "Friend, you can fool some of the people all of the time, and I can tell from looking at you that you're part of that sweet-smelling, ever-loving, eternally foolable some." —Russell Baker, *New York Times*

See also FOOL ME ONCE, SHAME ON YOU; FOOL ME TWICE, SHAME ON ME.

You can get a boy out of the country, but you cannot get the country out of the boy. *See* YOU CAN TAKE A BOY OUT OF THE COUNTRY, BUT YOU CAN'T TAKE THE COUNTRY OUT OF THE BOY.

You can lead a horse to water, but you cannot make him drink. You cannot force people to do what you think is good for them. The proverb has been traced back to c.1175 (*Old English Homilies*). In 1546, it was included in the book of proverbs by John Heywood, and is first attested in the United States in the 1692 *Will and Doom.* The proverb is found in varying forms.

1915. If he is very strongly set against the work, perhaps it is better that he should take the opportunity there is now to break his articles. I am naturally very disappointed, but as you know you can take a horse to the water, but you can't make him drink. —W. Somerset Maugham, *Of Human Bondage*

1985. You can lead a horse to water, but if you can get him to float on his back you have something. —*News-Times* (Danbury, Connecticut)

1992. "If you asked me today, I'd say that the jury is still out," says Mr. Price, who managed an adult-fitness club for 10 years before opening his Kidsports. "You can lead a horse to water, but the question is, can you make it drink? Once you get the adults in, can you keep them interested?" —*Wall Street Journal*

1993. Sister Mary Ann Walsh, communications director for World Youth Day, denied there was a water shortage. "There was plenty of water, but you can lead a person to water, and you can't make them drink," she said. —*Times* (Trenton)

1994. You can lead your son to college but you can't make him think. —*Jewish Press* (N.Y.)

1995. As a former publisher of *The Times*, Arthur Hays Sulzberger, once remarked, "Along with responsible newspapers we must have responsible readers" because "the fountain serves no useful purpose if the horse refuses to drink." Just don't turn off the water. —*New York Times Magazine*

You can never step into the same river twice. *See* YOU CAN'T STEP TWICE INTO THE SAME RIVER.

You can run, but you can't hide. You can try to escape from what you fear, but eventually you will have to face it. The saying originated in the United States in the 1940s, and is attributed to the American boxer Joe Louis (1914–81), who was quoted thus on the eve of his fight with the light heavyweight champion Billy Conn. It is often used in a political context.

1987. Joe Louis once said about somebody who was to face him in the ring: He can run but he can't hide. Mario Cuomo can run from running, but Gary Hart has made sure the Governor can't hide. —*New York Times*

1988. "Well, I'd say it was my country and I ran it, not the Americans. I wouldn't be pressured by Americans or the Kremlin to run and hide somewhere else." —Nelson DeMille, *The Charm School*

1989. Although Mr. Dinkins is hardly in seclusion, Mr. Giuliani's campaign said he was disproving the adage that you can run, but you can't hide. —*New York Times*

1991. "We need a great headline," Niles [Latham, an editor at the *New York Post*] said. "We'd like to use 'YOU CAN RUN BUT YOU CAN'T HIDE.' If you can get the President to use it, we'll put the whole line in quotes." —Oliver L. North, *Under Fire*

1992. "If you know and I know, how long till Ellis knows?"

"Too late for him. Maybe he can run, but he can't hide." —Philip Friedman, *Inadmissable Evidence*

1993. He can sun, but he can't hide. —*Modern Maturity*

1994. "They [Republicans] can run, but they can't hide the fact that they have to pay for a trillion dollars in promises," said Gene Sperling, a senior aide to the President. —*New York Times*

See also MURDER WILL OUT; TRUTH WILL (COME) OUT.

You can say that again. You are absolutely right; I agree with you. The saying originated in the late 1920s. The word *that* is stressed.

1948. "It was beautiful there. You know you can't beat America for beautiful country."

"You can say that again, brother," Gallagher snorted suddenly. —Norman Mailer, *The Naked and the Dead*

1952. "Holy cow!" said a recruit.

"You can say that again," said the sergeant. —Kurt Vonnegut, Jr., *Player Piano*

1976. "My territory was Georgia, from Savannah to Stone Mountain."

"That's a lot of territory to cover."

"You can say that again. I was really dragging at the end of a week." —Art Buchwald, *Washington Is Leaking*

1977. "That's shocking. A man of your rank being made second secretary."

"You can say that again." —Art Buchwald, *Down the Seine and Up the Potomac*

1978. "She is a very unusual child."

"You can say that again." —Howard Fast, *Second Generation*

1983. "Montana Gray," she announced, noting his confusion. "I look a little different out of working hours."

He whistled softly, relieved that Frances hadn't tracked him down, and delighted to see Montana. "You can say that again." —Jackie Collins, *Hollywood Wives*

1992. You can say this again! Three rules of life given me some years ago. I pass them on, for I have found them practical. The first is *"go,"* the second is *"keep going,"* and the third is, *"help someone else to go."* —*Jewish Press* (N.Y.)

See also YOU SAID IT.

You can take a boy out of the country, but you can't take the country out of the boy. Changing a person's place or position does not change his or her character or personality. The proverb originated in the United States. Its earliest appearance in print was in 1938. The proverb is found in varying forms especially by substituting a specific place name for country.

1938. You can take a boy out of the country but you can't take the country out of the boy. —Caption, B. Baer, "Hollywood"

1942. You can take a boy out of Brooklyn, but you can never get Brooklyn out of the boy. —Willis Todhunter Ballard, *Say Yes to Murder*

1982. "Like the old saying goes, 'you can take the boy out of thieving' ... Heck! Most demons are thieves. It's the only way to get something if you don't have any native coinage." —Robert Asprin, *Myth Directions*

1986. "Yeah. You can take a kid out of Colorado—"

"But you can never take Colorado out of the kid!" Jack finished Mannon's sentence ... —Jackie Collins, *Hollywood Husbands*

1987. Back in the good old days, when eager young rubes were descending upon the great metropolises in search of fame and fortune, it used to be said that you can take the boy out of the country but you can't take the country out of the boy. —*Washington Post*

1989. When he [Richard Nixon] addressed the employees of the U.S. Embassy in Bangkok he hauled out a baseball cap and announced that while you can take American boys out of the United States, "you can never take baseball out of an American boy." —Stephen E. Ambrose, *Nixon*

1993. You can take a Haitian out of Haiti but you can't take Haiti out of Haitians. —Harry Tubman, "Headline News," CNN

You can't argue with success. Success justifies everything. *It's hard to argue with success* is a variant of the saying.**

1980. It's easy to lock yourself in—or to get locked in by others—because one aspect of the power of precedent is based on a "Don't make waves," "You can't argue with success," and "We've always done it this way" outlook. —Herb Cohen, *You Can Negotiate Anything*

1993. That has led some skeptics to say Intel is not innovating, but is merely protecting an I.B.M.-bestowed monopoly.... It's hard to quibble with success.... Today there are more than 104 million computers around the world that use Intel chips. And all indications are that by next year Pentium will be a success, too. —*New York Times*
See also NOTHING SUCCEEDS LIKE SUCCESS.

You can't be in two places at once. See ONE CAN'T BE IN TWO PLACES AT ONCE.

You can't beat a man at his own game. You can't surpass people in their own environment or if they're more qualified. The proverb has been traced back to the 1756 *Papers of Henry Laurens*. The proverb is found in varying forms: *Anyone*

can be fooled at the other man's game; You can beat the bastards at their own game; You can't beat the rich at their own game; You can beat the IRS at their own game, etc.

1985. "No, no, I'll come back, you'll see ... I'll beat the bastards at their own game!" he [Konig] added, with a ferocity that startled Queenie. —Michael Korda, *Queenie*

1992. "You said you were going to beat Jadwin at his own game. How?" —Philip Friedman, *Inadmissible Evidence*

1993. First, advertisers sold products. Then, using images with a depth charge of desire, they sold fantasy—and beat editors at their own game. —*New York Times Magazine*

1994. HOW I BEAT THE IRS AT ITS OWN GAME —Headline, *New York Post*
See also YOU CAN'T WIN 'EM ALL.

You can't beat somebody with nobody. You cannot defeat your opponents if you have no supporters. This saying is usually used in a political context.

1967. The preparations were necessary and would have been made even if Jack Kennedy had been pledged all the convention votes. The Kennedy forces, in fact, sometimes acted as if that were the case. "You can't beat somebody with nobody," they said, quoting the old political adage. —Ralph de Toledano, *R.F.K.: The Man Who Would Be President*

1993. "The new tenant of City Hall is going to be the candidate with more diverse ethnic support. As they say, you can't beat somebody with nobody." —Overheard in New York
See also IF YOU CAN'T BEAT (LICK) 'EM, JOIN 'EM.

You can't burn your candle at both ends. See DON'T BURN THE (YOUR) CANDLE AT BOTH ENDS.

You can't change a leopard's spots. See THE LEOPARD CAN'T CHANGE ITS SPOTS.

You can't eat your cake and have it too. See YOU CAN'T HAVE YOUR CAKE AND EAT IT TOO.

You can't fight City Hall. It's hard for ordinary people to overcome bureaucracy and red tape. This saying is usually used as advice not to get involved in battles you can't win. The proverb originated in the United States in the late seventeenth century. The word *beat* or *lick* is sometimes used instead of *fight*.

1967. "The office, with its long wooden desks and rows of benches, its walls marked with posters and slogans, looked like the campaign headquarters of some lesser political candidate who knows he couldn't lick city hall." —Ralph de Toledano, *R.F.K.: The Man Who Would Be President*

1974. "The feeling among people was, what's the use," explains Arthur Katz. "You can't lick City Hall. And even if you could, you certainly can't lick Robert Moses." —Robert A. Caro, *The Power Broker*

1983. Many of my colleagues are as deeply concerned about these matters as I am. Others, however, don't study royalty statements as carefully as they should, or take a You Can't Beat City Hall attitude ... —Richard Curtis, *How to Be Your Own Literary Agent*

1989. ... even though the saying goes that you can't fight City Hall, you can be sure someone will always be trying. And that's the way it should be. —Ed Koch, *New York Times Magazine*

1992. "You *can* beat City Hall," he [Hunter S. Thompson] said in a telephone interview from his home in Woody Creek, Colo., where he is still obviously high (emotionally) over Bill Clinton's defeat of George Bush in the Presidential election. —*New York Times*

1993. "It's so secretive, it's like working through the CIA," Donahue said. "You can't fight the Diocese of Trenton. They're the boss." —*Times* (Trenton)

1994. The people working in the community say it smells terrible. And the odor can come or go in a matter of hours.
"It makes you very angry," Ms. DeSapio said. "It's like the old adage, you can't fight City Hall. You get so frustrated you really can't fight City Hall." —*New York Times*

You can't fit a round peg in a square hole.
A person shouldn't be given a job he or she is not qualified for. The proverb has been traced back to Sydney Smith's lecture in *Sketches of Moral Philosophy* (1804). It was used by Mark Twain in his *Following Equator* (1897). The proverb is found in varying forms: *You can't drive a square peg into a round hole; You can't put square pegs in round holes; You can't fit a round (square) peg in a round (square) hole*, etc. Often found as *a round (square) peg in a square (round) hole*, meaning someone or something totally unsuitable.

1921. His presence suddenly brings out the fact that they are unhappy men, ill at ease, square pegs in round holes. —George Bernard Shaw, *Back to Methuselah*, Part II

1936. "All the men of that description, barring the badly maimed ones, have already got something to do. They may be round pegs in square holes but they've all got something to do." —Margaret Mitchell, *Gone With the Wind*

1957. Why put a square egg in a round roll? —*New York Times*

1958. A hip peg in a square world. —*Time*

1984. Nobody was doing anything right. The vice-presidents were all square pegs in round holes. —Lee Iacocca with William Novak, *Iacocca*

1985. You're bored. Frustrated. Going to work is a chore. Instead of thinking that maybe this corporation isn't for you, you try to fit the square peg in the round hole. And you don't dare talk about your feelings with anyone ... —Jacqueline Hornor Plumez with Karla Dougherty, *Divorcing a Corporation*

You can't fly with one wing. *See* IT TAKES TWO WINGS TO FLY.

You can't get a quart into a pint pot. One can't do the impossible. The earliest appearance of the proverb in print dates from 1896. The proverb is found in varying forms: *You can't put a quart into a pint pot; You can't get a quart out of a thimble; It is impossible to place a gallon within a pint pot*, etc.

1896. They had been too ambitious. They had attempted what he might describe in homely phrase as putting a quart into a pint pot. —*Daily News*

(undated.)
However, one cannot put a quart in a pint cup. —Charlotte Perkins Gilman, *The Living of Charlotte Perkins Gilman*, quoted in *The Macmillan Dictionary of Quotations*

1934. He whistled thoughtfully. "You can't get a quart into a pint pot—is that it?" asked the South African officer, quick to see the reason. —C. F. Gregg, *Execution of Diamond Deutsch*

1978. You can't put a quart into a pint pot. —P. McGinley, *Bogmail*
See also YOU CAN'T FIT A ROUND PEG IN A SQUARE HOLE; YOU CAN'T GET BLOOD FROM A STONE.

You can't get blood from a stone. You can't get something from someone who doesn't have it. The proverb has been traced back to G. Torriano's *Common Place of Italian Proverbs* (1666). First attested in the United States in the *Letters from William Cobbett to Edward Thornton* (1800). The proverb is found in varying forms: *You cannot get blood out of a stone; You can't get blood from a rock; You can't squeeze blood from a stone; You can't get blood out of a turnip,* etc.

1949. *Willy:* If I had forty dollars a week—that's all I'd need. Forty dollars, Howard.
   Howard: Kid, I can't take blood from a stone. —Arthur Miller, *Death of a Salesman*

1955. "Greech wouldn't pay him anything more, I know. Blood from a turnip and all that." —Herman Wouk, *Marjorie Morningstar*

1979. "Now, do we have a deal for a hundred and seven thousand?"
   "Boy, you'd squeeze blood from a stone." He nodded. "We have a deal, boy. You squeezed me, and I caved in. We do have a deal." —Howard Fast, *The Establishment*

See also YOU CAN'T GET A QUART INTO A PINT POT.

You can't get something for nothing. *See* YOU DON'T GET SOMETHING FOR NOTHING.

You can't go home again. If you try to return to a past you remember, it won't be the same as your memories of it. Thomas Wolfe (1900–38) coined the saying in his classic novel *You Can't Go Home Again* (1940). The saying is found in varying forms: *You can go home when you can't go anywhere else; You can't come back to a home unless it was a home you left; Who says you can't go home again; You can go home again.*

1950. *Edward:* And so will you send me to the sanatorium?
   I can't go home again.
                     —T. S. Eliot, *The Cocktail Party*

1987. All I said, sir, was that you can never go home, that you can't look back, that tomorrow is another day, live and let live, time will tell, and life goes on. —G. B. Trudeau, *Doonesbury Deluxe*

1991. The São Paulo program is an example of an unusual situation in which developed countries in the Northern Hemisphere are learning from the mostly developing countries in the Southern Hemisphere.... Dr. Perlman quoted an Australian aboriginal woman who said: "If you've come to help me, you can go home again. But if you see my struggle as part of your own, perhaps we can work together." —*New York Times*

1992. "Who says you can't go home again? The hell you can't!" declared [Mike] Wallace outside one of his youthful residences. —*People*

1993. Anyone who went to college and took a course in American literature knows the theory behind Thomas Wolfe's classic novel, *You Can't Go Home Again*. But if you fish you *can* go home again, any time you want, as long as you have a pond or lake nearby. —*New York Times*

1994. The idea consultants can succeed with their own restaurants is catching. Witness Clark Wolf and The Markham, and Roger Martin's launch last week of Roger's in Bridgehampton. The Martin story is fascinating proof you can go home again—in his case, to the restaurant he operated 20 years ago. —*Crain's New York Business*

You can't have it both ways. You must decide. You can't have two different things at once if one choice negates the other possibility. The proverb has been traced back to 1927, and its earliest appearance in print in the United States was in *Broken Vase* (1941) by Rex Stout (1886–1975).

1941. One cannot have it both ways. —Rex Stout, *Broken Vase*

1957. "You men can't have it both ways," he told them. —Nevil Shute, *On the Beach*

1984. For a while he had thought he would have it both ways, but at Sweets I had made it clear he couldn't any longer. —Edward I. Koch, *Mayor*

1986. I admit to being well disposed to profits. It is far better to succeed than not, and I've had it both ways. —*New York*

1989. Some selectively praise the document while simultaneously condemning it. They can't have it both ways. —*New York Times*

1992. "Look, you can't have this both ways," Andrew said, his voice rising. "Either you trust me or ..." —Ed McBain, *Kiss*

1993. Steinbrenner cannot have it both ways. He signed a record cable contract and still expects fans to pay twice to see the Yankees. —*New York Times*

1994. The Minneapolis TV station is now, er, uh, how to put it, "massaging" the news so it is more palatable to family viewers, especially the kids.... Sorry, but you can't have it both ways. The news is the news is the news ... No cosmetics. No powder and paint. —*Times* (Trenton)

See also YOU CAN'T HAVE YOUR CAKE AND EAT IT TOO.

You can't have your cake and eat it too. One can't use something up and still have it to enjoy. This proverb was recorded in the book of proverbs by John Heywood in 1546, and is first attested in the United States in the 1742 *Colonial Records of Georgia* in *Original Papers, 1735–1752*. The adage is found in varying forms: *You can't*

*eat your cake and have it too; You can't have eve-
rything and eat it too; Eat your cake and have the
crumbs in bed with you,* etc.

1922. You cannot eat your cake and have it.
—James Joyce, *Ulysses*

1987. In philosophy and morals the hardest and
most essential rule is "You can't eat your cake and
have it too," but dialectic overcomes this rule.
—Allan Bloom, *The Closing of the American Mind*

1989. ... Mr. [Robert F.] McDermott said in an interview, "I've told Henry, and I make no secret
about it, divorce is acceptable, ending the affair is
acceptable, but it is not politically acceptable to tell
the world you want to have your cake and eat it
too." —*New York Times*

1991. The expression, "Having your cake and eating it too," has become an urgent battle cry for the
food industry. —*New York Times*

1992. "It's a case of having your cake and eating
it, too," Mr. Blass said. "A woman has the ease
and comfort of a loose caftan, and a little skin
showing to make it interesting." —*New York Times*

1993. Fact: It's possible to have your cake and eat
healthy too. —Ad, *Modern Maturity*

1994. You can have your torte and eat healthfully,
too. —*New York Times*

See also YOU CAN'T HAVE IT BOTH WAYS.

You can't judge a book by its cover. *See*
DON'T JUDGE A BOOK BY ITS COVER.

**You can't live with men; neither can you
live without them.** Whichever alternative one
chooses, neither is comfortable. The proverb has
been traced back to 1711, often shortened to *can't
live with 'em, can't live without 'em.*

1987. My other half has no fashion sense. I came
home the other afternoon looking so smart in my
new snood that I got over at Opal's beauty shop,
and he said my snood looked like a goat's udder
with a fly net on it.... Then, on our anniversary,
he carries me over to Birmingham to a spaghetti
restaurant, when he knows I'm on a diet.... Men!
Can't live with them, and can't live without them.
—Fannie Flagg, *Fried Green Tomatoes*

1993. Can't Live With 'em, Can't Live ...
I suppose that a few people have noticed that all
the gimmicky equipment intended to facilitate
communicating among human beings has resulted
in a general boggle in which it's well nigh impossible to reach anyone who knows anything. The
computer can't think. —*New York Times*

You can't lose what you never had. Something you've never possessed is not a loss. The
proverb has been traced back to Christopher Mar-
lowe's *Hero and Leander* (1593), and is first attested in the United States in Eugene O'Neill's
Strange Interlude (1928). The proverb is found in
varying forms: *What you never had, you can never
lose; What one never had, one can never miss;
You cannot lose what you haven't got; You never
miss what you never had,* etc.

1928. *Marsden:* Why? ... for her sake ... my own,
too ... when she has a child I know I can entirely
accept ... forget I have lost her ... lost her? ... silly
ass! ... how can you lose what you never possessed? ... except in dreams! ... —*Strange Interlude,* Act III, in *Three Plays of Eugene O'Neill*

1936. You dinna miss what you dinna ken. —J. J.
Farjeon, *Detective Ben*

1973. She sent money to them [a Swedish couple]
every month now. And when he asked why the
baby was never to know she was its mother, she
had answered, "What you never have, you cannot
lose." —Jacqueline Susann, *Once Is Not Enough*

**You can't make a silk purse out of a sow's
ear.** It is impossible to make something good of
what is bad by nature. The proverb is first found
in English in c.1514 in *Eclogues* by Alexander
Barclay (c.1476–1552), and is first attested in the
United States in *Modern Chivalry* (1816) by Hugh
Henry Brackenridge (1748–1816).

1922. *Stephen* (with exaggerated politeness): This
silken purse I made out of the sow's ear of the
public. —James Joyce, *Ulysses*

1946. "It is an election, all right."
"Can't you give it a little more?"
"When what you got to work with is Sam Mac-
Murfee," I said, "you haven't even got a sow's ear
to make a silk purse out of. I'm doing what I can."
—Robert Penn Warren, *All the King's Men*

1948. Bill, I wish you wouldn't talk that way.
Well, you can't change a sow's ear, Ina. —Norman Mailer, *The Naked and the Dead*

1957. He made silk purses from sow's ears. —*New
York Times Book Review*

1962. "It's rubbish," Hawke said. "I did my level
best, but there's a natural law about silk purses
and sow's ears. If it pays off it'll be luck." —Herman Wouk, *Youngblood Hawke*

1975. During the 1946 congressional campaign, he
[Harry Truman] had called union leader Al Whitney, "un-American" and "an enemy of the people,"
and Whitney shot back with a much-publicized

comment: "You can't make a President out of a ribbon clerk." —David Wallechinsky & Irving Wallace, *The People's Almanac*

1988. "Let the people who really want to teach come out," Mr. Jungkuntz said. "But remember, you can't make a silk purse out of a sow's ear. No methodology will make a good teacher out of someone who doesn't have the motivation." —*New York Times*

See also THE LEOPARD CAN'T CHANGE ITS SPOTS.

You can't make an omelet without breaking eggs. One cannot accomplish something worthwhile without some sacrifices. The proverb has been traced back to *Audi Alteram Partem* (1859) by T. P. Thompson. It is first attested in the United States in *Black Haiti* (1926) by B. Niles. The proverb is found in varying forms: *One cannot make an omelet without breaking eggs; Omelets are not made without breaking eggs; You can't cook an omelet without breaking eggs; You can't have an omelet unless you break the egg; You can make omelets without breaking eggs,* etc. The proverb has its counterpart in the French language: *On ne fait pas d'omelette sans casser des oeufs* or *On ne saurait faire une omelette sans casser des oeufs.*

1946. "He's a hard man," the Judge said. "He's played it hard and close. But there's one principle he's grasped: you don't make omelettes without breaking eggs. And precedents. He's broken plenty of eggs and he may make his omelettes." —Robert Penn Warren, *All the Kings Men*

1967. Bobby [Kennedy] would knock heads together when that was necessary. Then apologetic Jack would soothe feelings. But he was ready to defend Bobby's rudeness. "You can't make an omelet without breaking eggs," Jack argued. —Ralph de Toledano, *R.F.K.: The Man Who Would Be President*

1974. Some people must be hurt by progress. But that is unavoidable. "You can't make an omelet without breaking eggs." —Robert A. Caro, *The Power Broker*

1987. "His comment that one can't make an omelette without breaking eggs has often been cited as evidence of a callous disregard for little people," Mr. Volmer said. "But if anyone can tell me of a way of clearing a noxious slum without relocating the inhabitants, I'd be deeply grateful." —*New York Times*

1988. Mr. Gorbachev seems stuck with the official line, unable to acknowledge the impossibility of making an omelette without breaking eggs. But he may be able to buy time to allow the reforms to work. The key, Western economists argue, is to give consumers a taste of benefits to come. —*New York Times*

1994. Even before the backhoes were let loose on the north shore thoroughfare, the West Brighton Local Development Corp. put in place a process to keep merchants and contractors informed about the project.... "You have to break so many eggs to make an omelet," says Joyce Coward, the Staten Island borough chief for the city's Department of Business Services. —*Crain's New York Business*

See also LET THE CHIPS FALL WHERE THEY MAY; THERE ARE NO GAINS WITHOUT PAINS; YOU DON'T GET SOMETHING FOR NOTHING.

You can't make bricks without straw. One cannot make something properly without the necessary materials. The proverb is of Biblical origin (Old Testament). It has been traced back in English to *Heaven and Earth Reconciled* (1614) and *The Anatomy of Melancholy* (1624) by Robert Burton (1577–1640), and is first attested in the United States in about 1700.

Ye shall no more give the people straw to make brick, as heretofore; let them go and gather straw for themselves. —Exod. 5:7, *Authorized Version,* 1611

1934. "I never thought we had any chance," Heppenstall declared. "Can't make bricks without straw," Quilter pointed out cheerily.... "Can't make them without clay, at all events." —F. W. Crofts, *12:30 from Croydon*

1946. "And when you start out to do something ... you got to use what you've got. You got to use fellows like Byram, and Tiny Duffy, and that scum down in the Legislature. You can't make bricks without straw, and most of the time all the straw you got is secondhand straw from the cowpen." —Robert Penn Warren, *All the King's Men*

You can't mix business with pleasure. See NEVER MIX BUSINESS WITH PLEASURE.

You can't please everybody. No matter what you do, you'll never be able to make everyone happy. The proverb in English has been traced back to 1472, when it was used by E. Paston in a letter. It was first attested in the United States in the 1742 *Colonial Records of Georgia.* The proverb is of classical origin. It is found in varying forms: *It's hard to please everybody; You can't please everyone; You cannot please the whole world,* etc.

c.85–43 b.c.

It is a very hard undertaking to seek to please everybody. —Publilius Syrus, Maxim 675

1950. I cannot give you the formula for success, but I can give you the formula for failure—which is: Try to please everybody." —Speech by Herbert Bayard Swope

1992. YOU CAN'T PLEASE ALL OF THE PEOPLE ALL OF THE TIME —Headline, *New York Times*

1993. Once in office he [Clinton] began to waffle. He tried to please even more people than he had been obliged to please as a candidate. He tried, in fact, to please everyone. —*Times* (Trenton)

See also YOU CAN'T SERVE GOD AND MAMMON.

You can't put new wine in old bottles. See DON'T PUT NEW WINE IN OLD BOTTLES.

You can't serve God and mammon. You cannot commit yourself to two opposing people, ideas, etc. *Mammon* refers to material wealth. The proverb comes from the New Testament. It has been traced back in English to about 1330, and is first cited in the United States in Steere's *Daniel Catcher and Other Poems* (1713). The proverb is found in varying forms: *No man can serve two masters; No woman can serve two masters; It is difficult to serve two masters; it is even tougher to serve both a master and a mistress,* etc.

No man can serve two masters: for either he will hate the one, and love the other; or else he will hold to the one, and despise the other. Ye cannot serve God and mammon. —Matt. 6:24, *Authorized Version,* 1611

1922. —I am a servant of two masters, Stephen said, an English and an Italian. —James Joyce, *Ulysses*

1931. Those who set out to serve both God and Mammon soon discover that there isn't a God. —Logan Pearsall Smith, *Afterthoughts: Other People*

1992. "I think there's an intense amount of subtext in *Reservoir Dogs*," he says. "When I write, I'm serving two masters." —*New York Times Magazine*

You can't step twice into the same river. Nothing remains the same. The proverb has been traced back to Heraclitus (about 540–480 b.c.). *You can never step into the same river twice* is a variant of the proverb.

540–480 b.c.
You could not step twice into the same rivers; for other waters are ever flowing on to you. —Heraclitus, *On the Universe*

1993. "As a long-time newspaper person, I [Diane Dixon] lived my life by deadlines. But over the last few years, I've had to re-educate myself to take things one day at a time. You know, there's a saying: 'You can never step into the same river twice.' I believe that. Life is a series of changes; some are big, others are small. But if you want to keep going, you find a way to adjust to the changes so you can get on with the business of the rest of your life." —*U.S.1* (Princeton)

You can't take it with you. Material possessions will count for nothing when you're dead. The proverb has been traced back to *Masterman Ready* (1841) by Frederick Marryat (1792–1848), and is first attested in the United States in *Winkles* (1855). It was popularized by George S. Kaufman and Moss Hart's *You Can't Take It with You* (1936). The proverb is found in varying forms: *You can't take the dough with you; You can't take your money with you to spend in a grave; You can't take it with you when you go; You can take it with you,* etc.

1970. "Now all my life I've heard 'You can't take it with you.' Well, eight months ago when they tied me down with all this undignified plumbing and wiring, having nothing better to do I started thinking about that old saw. I decided that, if I couldn't take it with me, I wasn't going to go!" —Robert A. Heinlein, *I Will Fear No Evil*

1988. True, you can't take it with you, but then, that's not the place where it comes in handy. —quoted by Charles J. Givens in *Wealth Without Risk*

1989. Possibly Mr. Simplot had simply concluded that a foundation was not something that would add a glow to his family name well into the future. At any rate, he said, "Yeah, there's no way that you're going to take it with you or keep it for perpetuity after you're gone." —Vance Packard, *The Ultra Rich: How Much Is Too Much?*

1992. "As far as I'm concerned," she [Janine Turner] says, "the soul is what you've got to worry about when you die. You can't take a nice, trim, implanted body to heaven with you." —*People*

1993. OFTEN, YOU CAN TAKE IT WITH YOU —Headline, *New York Times*

See also EAT, DRINK, AND BE MERRY, FOR TOMORROW WE DIE; GATHER YE ROSEBUDS WHILE YE MAY.

You can't teach an old dog new tricks. As we age it's harder to learn new things. The proverb has been traced back to *Husbandry* (1523) by J. Fitzherbert, and in 1546, it was included in John Heywood's collection of proverbs. In 1672, it appeared in W. Walker's book of English and

Latin proverbs. It is first attested in the United States in the 1806 *Letters of John Randolph* (1834), and is found in varying forms: *An old dog will learn no new tricks; An old dog will learn no tricks; It's hard to teach old dogs new tricks,* etc.

1959. If you think you are going to teach your old dog new tricks—you are barking up the wrong tree. —*Bangor (Me.) Daily News*

1965. "I came to this country too late to learn all sorts of things. Slacks, for example, I push my legs, but they won't go in them. You can't teach an old bitch new tricks, no?" —George P. Elliott, *In the World*

1966. President Harding, well-intentioned but weak-willed, was a perfect "front" for the enterprising manufacturers and industrialists. The rigor mortis of reaction slowly set in, and critics raised feeble voices to lament, "You can't teach an Old Guard new tricks." —Thomas A. Bailey, *The American Pageant*

1974. "To the suggestion that he [Robert Moses] was independently wealthy and giving hard work and time to an unremunerative job, he smiled.

'... You can't teach an old dog new tricks and I'm 45 now. Ever since I was a kid I was interested in government.'" —Robert A. Caro, *The Power Broker*

1984. Nobody said it was easy to teach an old hound new tricks. But before you say it's impossible, take another look at Monsanto. —*Forbes*

1986. In fact, most of the time, the relationship between age and a decrement in performance is spurious. Age is not the determinant; the length of time someone has been in his job is. You *can* teach an old dog new tricks. —Judith M. Bardwick, *The Plateauing Trap*

1987. Since the release of the Tower report, Mr. Reagan has been trying to convey a more vigorous, "hands-on" image by making speeches, moving assistants and admitting past mistakes. But there is considerable doubt in the capital that, unlike the proverbial old dog, a 76-year-old man can learn new tricks. —*New York Times*

1989. Since I'm 95 years old, it may be that "you can't teach an old dog new tricks," but I'm just not comfortable with new appliances. They make me nervous and seem to know I'm a square. They never work for me. —*New York Times*

1993. Who says you can't teach an old salad new tricks. —Ad, *People*

1994. Can you teach an old propagandist new tricks? Zhu Muzhi is living proof of it. Assigned to craft a sophisticated international lobbying campaign to counter China's dismal human rights record, Mr. Zhu, 78 years old, is already a master of the sound bite—a quick study at the spin-control rules of Madison Avenue and Capitol Hill. —*New York Times*

You can't unscramble eggs. Once the damage is done, you can't undo it. The proverb originated in the United States about 1905 and is attributed to American financier, art collector, and philanthropist John Pierpont Morgan (1837–1913). *Scrambled eggs can't be unscrambled* is a variant of the proverb.

1928. Eggs cannot be unscrambled. —A. E. Apple, *Mr. Chang's Crime Ray*

1992. The owners argued today that if [Judge David] Doty granted the players' requests, competitive balance in the league would be destroyed. Even if the league should subsequently win an appeal of the McNeil case, said Frank Rothman, the league's lead attorney, too many players might have already changed teams and "you could never unscramble that egg." —*New York Times*

1994. "We believe that the reputations of innocent people could be damaged beyond retrieval," said William B. McGuire, president of the association.... "How do you go back and unscramble the egg?" said McGuire. "The potential damage to the attorney in some instances just can't be corrected." —*Times* (Trenton)

You can't win 'em all. Everyone loses sometimes. The proverb originated in the United States in the 1940s, probably among poker players.

1965. Kennedy looked exceedingly tired, but his mood was philosophical. He felt that he now knew certain soft spots in his administration, especially the CIA and the Joint Chiefs. He would never be overawed by professional military advice again. "We can't win them all," he said. —Arthur M. Schlesinger, Jr., *A Thousand Days*

1977. "Can't win 'em all," Fowler said in his soft voice. —William Safire, *Full Disclosure*

1991. But my children are comely and loving and self-possessed and walking over those parts of the world that interest them; and my daughter once kissed me and said, "You can't win them all, Daddy." And so I can't. —*John Cheever Journals* (Part II), *New Yorker*

See also YOU WIN SOME (A FEW), YOU LOSE SOME (A FEW).

You could have knocked me over with a feather. I was so surprised that the lightest touch would have felled me. The saying has been traced back to about 1821, and is found in varying forms: *You could have knocked me down without even a feather; You could have knocked me down with a leaf*, etc.

1936. "Well!" said Mrs. Merriwether showing the letter to Mrs. Elsing. "You can knock me down with a feather!" —Margaret Mitchell, *Gone With the Wind*

1984. I have not always been a perfect judge of human character, but I have never failed to recognize a golden opportunity when offered one on a silver platter or to go for the main chance when I found it close at hand. You could have knocked me over with a feather when I began to perceive how simple it was all going to be. —Joseph Heller, *God Knows*

1991. Compared with its previously released monthly estimate of the number of people on payrolls, the Labor Department's revised estimate for August shows that there were 79,200 fewer jobs held throughout the state at the end of that month, including 53,800 fewer in the city.... "You could have knocked us over with a feather," said Thomas A. Rodick, deputy director of the Labor Department's division of research and statistics. —*New York Times*

You could hear a pin drop. Said of a sudden, awkward silence. The phrase dates from the nineteenth century and is found in varying forms: *One might have heard a pin drop; One could have heard the proverbial pin or a straw falling in the silent room; So still you could hear a pin drop; So quiet you could hear a pin drop.*

1889. I stood and listened till my ears ached, but the night was so hollow about me like an empty church; not even a ripple stirred upon the shore; it seemed you might have heard a pin drop in the country. —Robert L. Stevenson, *The Master of Ballantrae*

1984. I think you could have heard a pin drop there on the road to Carmel as she hasted the final few yards on her animal, lighted off the ass, fell before me on her face at my feet, and bowed herself to the ground. —Joseph Heller, *God Knows*

1987. I knew Kirkpatrick meant business from the start.
I was sitting directly behind her the day she stood up and denounced UNESCO as a complete joke. You could have heard a pin drop in the chamber. —G. B. Trudeau, *Doonesbury Deluxe*

1991. "I looked at my parents, who hadn't spoken with each other for years, certain my marriage—only minutes old—was going to cause problems.... You could have heard a pin drop." —Kitty Kelley, *Nancy Reagan*

You don't get something for nothing. Nothing will come to you without effort on your part. The proverb has been traced back to *Sybil* (1845) by Benjamin Disraeli (1804–81), and is first attested in the United States in *Struggles and Triumphs* (1869) by Phineas Taylor Barnum (1810–91). "When people expect to get 'something for nothing,'" wrote P. T. Barnum, "they are sure to be cheated." The proverb is found in varying forms: *You can't get something for nothing; You can't expect something for nothing; You can't have anything for nothing; You can't beat something with nothing*, etc.

1845. To do nothing and get something, formed a boy's ideal of a manly career. —Benjamin Disraeli, *Sybil*

1985. "I want a scoop. You have to promise I'll be the first to know."
"We agreed all this was off the record."
"It *is* off the record. But you don't get something for nothing, Prince. What's in it for Polly? You owe me an exclusive." —Michael Korda, *Queenie*

1986. Who says you can't get something for nothing? We've got a new account that gives you free checking and a lot of other extras. Without asking you to add one penny more to the total balance of your bank accounts. —Ad, *New York Times*

1991. When you get something for nothing, you just haven't been billed for it yet. —Franklin P. Jones, quoted in *Reader's Digest*

1992. "Hey, I'm trying to do your guy a favor. Something for nothing."
"Nobody gets something for nothing." —Philip Friedman, *Inadmissible Evidence*

1993. There can't be any something for nothing, and we have to demonstrate that to people. This is not a free system. —Bill Clinton, *New York Times*

1994. Everybody can contribute something if we want to solve the health care crisis. There can't be any more something for nothing. —Bill Clinton, "State of the Union Address"

See also YOU GET NOTHING FOR NOTHING; YOU GET WHAT YOU PAY FOR.

You get nothing for nothing. You have to pay a price for everything you get. The proverb has been traced back to about 1380 (Chaucer). It is first attested in the United States in T. Walsh's

Dangerous Passenger (1959). The proverb is found in varying forms: *You never get anything for nothing; You can expect nothing for nothing; You get nowt for nowt; Nothing for nothing and not much for sixpence,* etc.

1988. "We *trade* notes. You don't get nothin' for nothin' in this business." —Nelson DeMille, *The Charm School*

1995. "The sooner the welfare reform is approved the better it is for the country. You don't work, you don't contribute, you get nothing for nothing." —Overheard at an employment office

See also YOU DON'T GET SOMETHING FOR NOTHING; YOU GET WHAT YOU PAY FOR.

You get what you pay for. What appears to be a bargain will probably turn out to be worthless.

1963. "She [Zinka] broke my heart. I didn't like that much. But that was the price. In this world, you get what you pay for." —Kurt Vonnegut, Jr., *Cat's Cradle*

1987. "I think they're just letting anyone on stage now," said Bonnie McKelvey, as "The Beer Barrel Polka" was sung. "You get what you pay for," she said. Admission was free. —*New York Times*

1988. "Just like any important part of life," said Middlebury's president, Olin Robison, "most Americans believe you get what you pay for." —*New York Times*

1991. "Without Edie, Loyal [Davis] would never have made it in Chicago. Without him, she wouldn't have been accepted. They [Nancy's parents] each got what they paid for." —Kitty Kelley, *Nancy Reagan*

1994. Everyone seemed outraged with Madonna's performance on Letterman. Yet she was on every wire service and the show's ratings soared. The shock schlocks contend they have a right to free speech. My mamma always said, "You get what you pay for." —*Times* (Trenton)

You have to learn to crawl before you can walk. Whatever the subject or skill, you have to learn the basic principles before going on to more advanced levels. The proverb has been traced back to *Douce* (c.1350), and is first cited in the United States in the 1737 *Jonathan Belcher Papers.* The saying is used in varying forms: *A child must learn to crawl before it can learn to walk; One must crawl before he walks; One must creep before he walks,* etc.

1993. Be patient; sometimes you have to crawl before you can walk. —Jeane Dixon, "Horoscope"

1994. "It's a little like having to remember how to crawl before I walk, before I jog, before I run," [Cris] Dickson said in an interview from New Zealand last week. —*New York Times*

See also YOU HAVE TO LEARN TO WALK BEFORE YOU CAN RUN.

You have to learn to walk before you can run. Learning the basics prepares you for more advanced tasks. The proverb has been traced back to *Douce* (c.1350), and in 1670, it was included in John Ray's book of English proverbs. It is first attested in the United States in a letter of George Washington's dated July 20, 1794. The saying occurs in varying forms: *You must learn to walk before you can run; You got to learn to walk before you can run; One mustn't be expected to fly before he is able to walk,* etc.

1794. We must walk as other countries have done before we can run. —George Washington, *Writings of George Washington*

1985. "Do you want me to take my clothes off in any special way?"

"Just take them off the way you normally do," Goldner said, puffing on his cigar. "Nothing fancy. We must learn to walk before we can run." —Michael Korda, *Queenie*

1991. Mr. Katoh doubts that ladling broth in soup kitchens is in the near future for I.B.C. "First, we have to get used to this," he said. "We have to walk before we run." —*New York Times*

See also YOU HAVE TO LEARN TO CRAWL BEFORE YOU CAN WALK.

You have to see it to believe it. It's so incredible you have to see it for yourself. *It has to be seen to be believed* is a variant of the saying.****

1922. Must be seen to be believed. —James Joyce, *Ulysses*

1951. "You ought to see him," he would tell them, as he locked the barred doors on the crowd gathered to hear the news. "He's terrific. You'd have to see it to believe it." —James Jones, *From Here to Eternity*

1983. ... the jewelry the two of them were wearing had to be seen to be believed. —Jackie Collins, *Hollywood Wives*

1985. "Aren't you willing to believe a person can change in three years?"

"I'd have to see it to believe it," she replied. —Erich Segal, *The Class*

1988. Lisa nodded. "You hear and read about this,

but you have to see it to believe it." —Nelson De-Mille, *The Charm School*

1991. The SCIF [Sensitive Compartmented Information Facility], as it was known, was a suite of offices that were protected by sophisticated monitoring and alarm systems, and shifts of armed squads around the clock…. The SCIF had to be seen to be believed. —Oliver L. North, *Under Fire*

1994. You have to see this place to believe it … —Ad, *U.S.1* (Princeton)

See also SEEING IS BELIEVING.

You have to take the bad with the good. One has to accept unpleasant things with the pleasant.

1962. Hawke said, "It's a wonderful show, every minute of it, and you were absolutely superb. They're all idiots."

Because he meant it, and spoke with his natural energy, the words struck home to the actor…. "I'm so glad. It is an amusing little thing, isn't it? In the theatre you take the good with the bad, and get on the next job." —Herman Wouk, *Youngblood Hawke*

1984. "You have got to learn to take the bad with the good," he advised me philosophically, scratching his pitted face with one hand and pausing to suck on a pomegranate he held in the other. —Joseph Heller, *God Knows*

1994. "This is New York, not Kansas. What do you expect? I have to take the good things with the bad. I can't let talk like that distract me." —*New York Times*

See also YOU HAVE TO TAKE THE BITTER WITH THE SWEET; YOU HAVE TO TAKE THE ROUGH WITH THE SMOOTH.

You have to take the bitter with the sweet. One has to accept unpleasant things along with the pleasant. The proverb has been traced back to John Heywood's collection of English proverbs (1546), and is first attested in the United States in the 1778 *Writings of George Washington*. The proverb is found in varying forms: *Always take the bitter with the sweet; One must take the bitter with the better; You've got to take the bitter with the sweet; You've got to learn to take the bitter with the sour,* etc.

1943. "I won't let him win all the time. If I did there wouldn't be any living in the house with him by the time he was a hundred. Besides I gotta raise him so he'll know how to face reality. To take the bitter with the sweet, the thorn with the rose, and the smell with the cheese. The old bugger!" —Robert Penn Warren, *At Heaven's Gate*

1987. "As the saying goes, from the bitter comes sometimes the sweet," Rabbi Spielman said. "I would hope that even though there might be a couple of negative events in the next couple of months, that from this would come open and complete cooperation." —*New York Times*

1993. "Life is hard … then you die!"

"Face it, Kudzu—you've got to learn to take the bitter with the sour!" —Doug Marlette, "Kudzu"

See also YOU HAVE TO TAKE THE BAD WITH THE GOOD; YOU HAVE TO TAKE THE ROUGH WITH THE SMOOTH.

You have to take the rough with the smooth. Your path will sometimes be rough, sometimes smooth. The proverb has been traced in English to *Tale of Beryn* (c.1400), and is first attested in the United States in 1775 in the *Life and Correspondence of Joseph Read* (1870). The proverb is found in varying forms: *One learns to take the rough with the smooth; Take the rough with the smooth.*

1400. Take your part as it comyth, of roughe and eke of smooth. —*Tale of Beryn*

1994. You take the rough with the smooth, the thick and the thin. It's called reality. —Ad, *New York Times Magazine*

1995. "A boot camp is not a bowl of cherries. One learns to take the rough with the smooth and the good with the bad. And that's exactly what boot camps are for." —Overheard at a bus stop

See also YOU HAVE TO TAKE THE BITTER WITH THE SWEET; YOU HAVE TO TAKE THE BAD WITH THE GOOD.

You know better than that. There's no excuse for your behavior. It is one of the most frequently used phrases in American English. The saying is found in varying forms: *You should have known better; You should have known better than to …,* etc.

1961. "What do you want here, Eth?"

"I want to help you."

"You know better than that." —John Steinbeck, *The Winter of Our Discontent*

1982. "You'll think I'm a hypochondriac …"

"I know you better than that, Alexandra." —Sidney Sheldon, *Master of the Game*

1983. She was a gay designer—rumor had it she was a dyke. Ross knew better than *that.* —Jackie Collins, *Hollywood Wives*

1985. "It's not any sillier than telling the child her father will send for her one day, Vicky."

"Well, he might."

"Vicky," Morgan said gently, "you know better

than that. Tiger had a family in Tasmania and another one in South Africa—and those are the ones we *know* about. By now he's probably in Hong Kong, or Australia. Or more likely in jail." —Michael Korda, *Queenie*

1986. "Are you drunk?" he shouted. "How *dare* you! How can *you*—of *all* people—accuse me of having homosexual tendencies? Surely you know me better than that?" —Jackie Collins, *Hollywood Husbands*

1988. "I've been told that I lack passion, but that doesn't affect me one way or the other," he said dryly. "Some people say I'm arrogant, but I know better than that." —*New York Times*

1991. "Don't play the frightened maiden with me, Scarlett. I know you better than that." —Alexandra Ripley, *Scarlett*

1994. Smith has been the Ward 1 council member since 1982. He said he was aware of the allegations and acknowledged that they could be partly motivated by political loyalties.... However, he said, "I would think somebody who has been as critical of other people about their campaign practices as Ms. Brizill has, should have known better than to violate the law." —*Washington Post*

You must cut your coat according to your cloth. One has to live within one's means and adapt oneself to circumstances. The proverb has been traced back to 1546: *Cut my coat after my cloth* (John Heywood) and is a translation of the Latin proverb: *Si non possis quod velis, velis id quod possis.* It is first attested in the United States in the 1720 *Letters of Robert Carter.* The proverb is found in varying forms: *Cut the coat according to the cloth; One cuts one's coat according to one's cloth; You've got to cut your coat according to your cloth,* etc.

> **1984.** We must cut our coat according to our cloth, and adapt ourselves to changing circumstances. —*Forbes*

> **1994.** "I try to stretch each dollar, you know. I never forget to cut my coat according to my cloth." —Overheard at a grocery store

You name it. Everyone or everything. There is nothing I can name that's not included. The phrase is part of the retailing locution *You name it, we have it* and has been used since the 1950s; it has been especially popular since 1970.

> **1984.** "Italy has been the aesthetic leader for centuries," says Palmer [chief of Chevrolet's Studio III and a rising star in General Motors Design]. "And the home base for design is still there, because

they set trends, the tone, in all European design, not just cars—jewelry, furniture, yachts, silver—you name it." —Quoted in *Metropolitan Home*

> **1985.** "Aaron, Charles is a prince, you know."
>
> "Yeah, yeah, an *Italian* prince. This town is full of princes, chrissake—Polish, Russian, Italian, you name it." —Michael Korda, *Queenie*

> **1986.** "Can you do me a favor?"
>
> By this time he was ready to do anything she asked. "Name it." —Jackie Collins, *Hollywood Husbands*

> **1987.** Who can be seen in that [hotel] lobby these days? "You name it," Mr. Klipstine said. —*New York Times*

> **1989.** "Five! Five times they put me on trial. The federal boys. The state boys. The city boys. Dope, gamblin', bribery, guns, racketeerin', whores. You name it, and they've tried me for it." —John Grisham, *A Time to Kill*

> **1993.** What kind of books?... "You name it," he said. Novels, children's books, coffee table books, large print and more. —*New York Times*

> **1994.** Stocks, bonds, arbitrage, international exchange rates, lines of credit, letters of marque, you name it. —*New York Times*

See also YOU NAME IT, WE HAVE IT.

You name it, we have it. You have only to name what you're looking for, and we can supply it. The saying comes from the retailing industry and has been used since the late 1940s. It is found in varying forms: *You name it, we got it; You name it—you could get it; You name it, we sell it; You name it, I have seen it; You name it, he knows something about it,* etc.

> **1946.** At each seat was a cheap cardboard fan bearing a garish Garden of Gethsemane, courtesy Tyndal's Hardware Co. (You-Name-It-We-Sell-It). —Harper Lee, *To Kill a Mockingbird*

> **1962.** "Hell, what kind a germs you want? You name it this island's got it." —James Jones, *The Thin Red Line*

> **1975.** Los Angeles was full. Pretty. Beautiful. Exotic. Erotic. Legs. Tits. Ass. You name it—you could get it. —Jackie Collins. *The World Is Full of Divorced Women*

> **1977.** "Sir, what kind of reports are resting here?"
>
> "It might be better to ask what kind of reports aren't buried here. We have reports on violence, studies on blacks, students, unemployment, the economy, the Communist threat, health care, law and order. You name it, and we've buried it."

—Art Buchwald, *Down the Seine and Up the Potomac*

1984. We enjoyed the finest fruits, no matter what season. Fancy chocolates, exotic flowers—you name it, we had it. —Lee Iacocca with William Novak, *Iacocca*

1989. "Staff, resources, expertise, experienced trial lawyers who do nothing but capital defense. Plus we have a number of highly competent doctors we use in these cases. You name it, we have it." —John Grisham, *A Time to Kill*

1991. Since April, Ms. [Jane] Cavalier had been searching for a home for what remained of Buckley DeCerchio. "I met with every single person who had their name on an agency in this country," she said. "You name it, I've seen it." —*New York Times*

1993. It would take half a page in this newspaper to list all the charges along the way: CAT scans and a host of other diagnostic tests, two hospital stays, biopsies, X-rays, drugs, transfusions, an ambulance, lab tests, chemotherapy … you name, I've had it. —*New York Times*

See also YOU NAME IT.

You never get anything for nothing. See YOU GET NOTHING FOR NOTHING.

You never had it so good. Your life is much better now than it used to be. The saying originated in the United States in the 1950s, and was used by Democratic leaders in their presidential bid in 1952. On July 20, 1957, the saying was employed by the then British prime minister Harold Macmillan.

1952. You never had it so good. —*Democratic Campaign* (Stevenson)

1966. In any case, Nixon's contention that "we never had it so good" was belied by the deepening business recession ("inventory readjustment" to the Republicans), which may well have proved decisive in the election. —Thomas A. Bailey, *The American Pageant*

1976. "No matter how bad things get, the politicians can always point to us and say that a majority of the people in this country really have never had it so good." —Art Buchwald, *Washington Is Leaking*

1989. He [Hubert Humphrey] asserted that the American people "have never had it so good," and warned that Nixon and the Republicans "will take it away." —Stephen E. Ambrose, *Nixon*

You never know a man until you live with him. It takes time to know a person inside out. The proverb is found in varying forms: *You never know a man until you bed with him a winter and summer; Eat a peck of salt with a man before you trust him,* etc. The Germans and the Russians use almost the same proverb: *Man muß erst einen Scheffel Salz mit ihm gegessen haben* (German) and Чтобы узнать человека, надо с ним пуд соли съесть (Russian)—"You never know a man until you've eaten a peck of salt with him."

1987. Evelyn said, "They say you never know a man until you live with him."

"That's right. Sipsey used to say, 'You never know what kind of fish you've got till you pull it out of the water"—so it's best that Stump never met his daddy. —Fannie Flagg, *Fried Green Tomatoes*

1993. "They have been going steady for some time now and they want to get married. He's a nice guy, but you never know a man until you live with him." —Overheard at a senior citizens center in Manhattan

See also YOU CAN'T LIVE WITH MEN; NEITHER CAN YOU LIVE WITHOUT THEM.

You never miss the water till the well runs dry. You don't realize how much you have until you lose it. The proverb is of Scottish origin and in about 1628 it was included in James Carmichael's *Collection of Scottish Proverbs*. In 1746, it appeared in Benjamin Franklin's *Poor Richard's Almanac*. The proverb is found in varying forms: *We only know the worth of water when the well is dry; You don't know what you've got till it's gone,* etc.

1746. When the well's dry, we know the worth of water. —Benjamin Franklin, *Poor Richard's Almanac*

1876. Do not let your chances like sunbeams pass you by,
For you never miss the water till the well runs dry.
            —Rowland Howard, *You Never Miss the Water*

1993. You know, Garfield … You don't know what you've got till it's gone. —Jim Davis, *Garfield*

1994. "It's a 'don't know what you got till it's gone' kind of thing," said Ms. Fair, alluding to the outpouring of feelings from Nirvana's fans. "Like when your granny dies and you realize what amazing peanut butter cookies she made." —*New York Times*

You pays your money, and you takes your choice. One has to take chances. The saying is of British origin and was first recorded in the British humor weekly magazine *Punch* in 1846. A customer in a cartoon, *The Ministerial Crisis*, is asking a showman, "Which *is* the Prime Minister?" … "Which ever you please, my little dear. You pays your money, and you takes your choice," answers the showman in broken English. In 1885, the saying was used in the United States by Mark Twain in his *Adventures of Huckleberry Finn*. The saying is found in varying forms: *You pay your money, and you take your choice; You pays your money, and you takes your chance; You pays your nickel, you takes your chances,* etc. The words *pays* and *takes* are colloquial forms.

1885. "Here's your opposition line! Here's your two sets o'heirs to old Peter Wilks—and you pays your money and you takes your choice!" —Mark Twain, *The Adventures of Huckleberry Finn*

1922. *Virag:* We can do you all brands, mild, medium and strong. Pay your money, take your choice. How happy could you be with either … —James Joyce, *Ulysses*

1982. Suddenly he turned to the projectionists and demanded, "How does it work? What makes it work? How do you get that moving picture up there on the wall?"

"Look, buster, it works. You pay your money and you take your choice. We're electricians. We ain't teachers." —Howard Fast, *Max*

1985. Richard R. Burt's [Assistant Secretary of State for European Affairs] favorite saying—"You pays your money, and you takes your choice." —*New York Times*

1988. You pays your money and you takes your chances. —Charles J. Givens, *Wealth Without Risk*
See also IF YOU DON'T LIKE IT, YOU CAN LUMP IT; TAKE IT OR LEAVE IT; YOU'VE MADE YOUR BED, NOW LIE IN IT.

You said it. I agree with you. You're absolutely right. The saying originated in the United States in the 1920s. *You said it, I didn't* is a variant.

1945. He looked over his shoulder, said aloud:—
"You've said it, Old Boss." —Emilie Loring, *Beyond the Sound of Guns*

1946. When he remarked to Baker: "These must be strenuous times in Washington," the heartfelt answer was: "You said it!" —Upton Sinclair, *A World to Win*

1961. "Do you want money enough so that even necromancy, thaumaturgy, juju, or any other dark practices are justified?"

"You said it!" —John Steinbeck, *The Winter of Our Discontent*

1987. "Boy, this course is really getting interesting."

"You said it. I didn't know half this stuff." —G. B. Trudeau, *Doonesbury Deluxe*

1987. *Q:* You weren't going to turn it over to the Democrats, then?

A: You said that, Senator. —"Iran-Contra Hearings," *New York Times*
See also YOU CAN SAY THAT AGAIN.

You scratch my back, I'll scratch yours. A favor should be reciprocated: you do a favor for me, I'll do one for you. The proverb has been traced back to Montaigne (1605), and is first attested in the United States in *Artemus Ward, His Book* (1865) by Artemus Ward, pen name of Charles Farrar Browne (1834–67). *You-scratch-my-back-I'll-scratch-yours* is used as an attribute to nouns. *You protect my ass, and I'll protect yours;* and *I'll kiss your ass if you kiss mine* are obscene variants of the proverb.

1961. "What difference does it make to anyone if I'm in the plane or not?"

"No difference."

"Sure, that's what I mean," Doc Daneeka said. "A little grease is what makes this world go round. One hand washes the other. Know what I mean? You scratch my back, I'll scratch yours." —Joseph Heller, *Catch-22*

1975. "Listen, kid, you don't want to be snapping pictures all your life. No offense—I know you're good, but I can steer you and the little lady right where the bread is. You stroke my balls, I stroke yours. You dig?" —Jackie Collins, *The World Is Full of Divorced Women*

1977. "Why did we do away with verandas?" she wondered.

"Bugs," the Floridian answered. "In olden times, people got bitten all the time, spent half their waking hours scratching. So then we had screened-in porches, which were teats on a bull in the winter. So then we made them glassed in patios. No more verandas, but no more bugs."

"I'll scratch your back if you'll scratch mine." —William Safire, *Full Disclosure*

1983. He recognized Josh Speed, an English rock star, and a couple of small-time I'll-kiss-your-ass-if-you-kiss-mine actors. —Jackie Collins, *Hollywood Wives*

1984. The connection between Lotus, one of the world's smallest can   kers, and Toyota, one of the largest, is a classic case of "You scratch my back,

I'll scratch yours ... and we'll all get rich." —*Forbes*

1988. The resourceful Sami, who could type as well as bank a nine-ball into a corner pocket, got a job as a secretary for Marian Rosen, the lawyer who had employed Kim to fly to Esalen. You scratch my back, I'll scratch yours. —Clifford Irving, *The Campbell Murder Case*

1989. There was an unspoken agreement within the Agency that went something like, "You protect my ass and I'll protect yours." —C. David Haymann, *A Woman Named Jackie*

1991. In the days of Iran's war with Iraq, he [a Hezbollah gunman] explains, the hostages "were a kind of 'you scratch my back and I'll scratch yours'" asset to Iran ..." —*Wall Street Journal*

1993. In their you-scratch-my-back-I-scratch-yours arrangement, Mr. Herd more than covers their crop losses if he gets paid for the work. —*New York Times*

See also ONE GOOD TURN DESERVES ANOTHER; ONE HAND WASHES THE OTHER.

You shall (will) reap what you sow. *See* AS YOU SOW SO (SHALL) YOU REAP.

You take my word for it. *See* TAKE MY WORD FOR IT.

You win some (a few), you lose some (a few). One can't win all the time. The saying has been traced back to *Captains Courageous* (1897) by Rudyard Kipling (1865–1936). It was originally used by gamblers who had lost a game. The saying is found in varying forms: *Somebody always wins, somebody always loses; Win some, lose some; You win one, you lose one*, etc.

1952. "You and Checker Charley are being beaten is all. Somebody always wins, and somebody always loses," said Finnerty. "That's the way it goes." —Kurt Vonnegut, Jr., *Player Piano*

1976. "I remember this quotation that Nathan had which always sounded so American. 'You win one and you lose one.' But I couldn't win anything." —William Styron, *Sophie's Choice*

1979. "What the hell. You win some, you lose some."
To which Barbara responded, "You certainly do." —Howard Fast, *The Establishment*

1984. Woman to postal clerk: "Is it all you can tell me about my lost package—'You win some, you lose some'?" —Quoted in *Reader's Digest*

1988. It's dispiriting to have a tin ear when you'd love to play the mandolin and sound like Cesare Siepi doing a Mozart serenade, but, as Kierkegaard observed, "That's life: you win some, you lose some." —*New York Times Magazine*

1991. As they say on the sidelines, you win some and you lose some. Last week, Wall Street's customers won the battle for more complete information about their brokers' past behavior, but were dealt a setback in a campaign for more time to sue over securities fraud complaints. —*New York Times*

1993. Win some, lose some. In November, New Jersey's voters will get a chance to decide if they want to change the State Constitution so that elected state officials can be recalled. —*Times* (Trenton)

1994. I'm not comparing myself. I'm saying that this is a metaphor for everybody's life, that it is in the living. It is in the campaigning, that you make your mark. Sometimes you win. Sometimes you lose. —Mario Cuomo, quoted in *New York Times*

See also YOU CAN'T WIN 'EM ALL.

You'll be damned if you do and damned if you don't. You can't win; no matter what you do someone will be unhappy. The saying originated in the United States in the 1830s in Lorenzo Dow's (1777–1834) *Reflections on the Love of God* (1836) in which he gives his definition of Calvinism, the belief in the absolute, divine sovereignty of God.

1836. You will and you won't—You'll be damned if you do—And you'll be damned if you don't. —Lorenzo Dow, *Reflections on the Love of God*

1978. "The President here will be damned if he'll be pushed out of office, and now that Arnold Nichols has grabbed his power for three weeks, the President will be damned if he'll ever resign if it means that Arnold becomes President." —William Safire, *Full Disclosure*

1991. They [the Democrats] might well be damned if they do defeat him [Judge Thomas], and damned if they don't, as the party that opposed a role-model, black, conservative opponent of quotas. Either way, George Bush wins. —*New York Times*

1993. In reality, Mr. Boutros-Ghali's embrace of the Clinton Administration seems merely a tactical maneuver. Scratch the surface and the unedited version spills forth.... "You're damned if you do and damned if you don't," he said. —*New York Times*

1994. "The toughest question I get is when people ask me what to do with policies of troubled companies," Mr. Daily said. "Usually there's a surrender charge involved to get out of the policy, so you're damned if you do and damned if you don't." —*New York Times*

You'll take the high road, and I'll take the low road. There's more than one way to reach a destination. The saying is a line from the Scottish folk song "Loch Lomond." *To take the high road* and *to take the low road* are commonly used expressions.

undated.

> Oh, you'll take the high road,
> And I'll take the low road,
> And I'll be in Scotland before you,
> But me and my true love will never meet again,
> On the bonnie, bonnie banks of Loch Lomond.
>
> —"Loch Lomond"

1986. He [Wingo] would say, "If you can't beat up an enemy at school, wait twenty years and beat up his wife and kid."

"Always take the high road, huh, Dad?" Savannah would answer, repeating one of my mother's oft-quoted clichés. —Pat Conroy, *The Prince of Tides*

1987. I warned you she might take the high road. —G. B. Trudeau, *Doonesbury Deluxe*

1992. When it comes to putting pressure on military contractors to stop making warplanes and guns and start making subway cars or electric autos, no group is more ambivalent than the nation's labor unions. "We take the high road," said Mark Roberts, an A.F.L.–C.I.O. official. "We are for shifting resources from weaponry to civilian goods." —*New York Times*

1993. Speaking directly across the TV airwaves to Bill Clinton, Sen. Kerrey said:

"Get back on the high road, Mr. President, where you were at your best." —*Times* (Trenton)

Your guess is as good as mine. You know as much as I do. The saying originated in the United States in the 1920s and is found in varying forms: *One guess is as good as another; One's guess is as good as another's,* etc.

1957. "You mean—the radioactivity?"

The naval officer nodded.

The scientist stood in thought. "Anybody's guess is as good as mine," he said at last. —Nevil Shute, *On the Beach*

1984. "And what do the Brits know?" Greer asked.

"Your guess is as good as mine, sir." —Tom Clancy, *The Hunt for Red October*

1987. "'... God, patriotism, and Reagan. That's the essence this campaign is trying hard to project.'"

No! Not trying, Sam. Succeeding. The only thing missing from this anecdote is a call from a White House aide saying "good piece."

Your guess is as good as Donaldson's or mine whether such techniques would have worked with a different candidate, or in a recession. —*New Republic*

1992. Would a second-term Bush, no longer needing to gamble on truckling to the far right, lead his Administration to the forefront of individual rights and personal freedom—and against the intrusion of Big Government and majoritarian morality? I have been a Bush watcher for lo these many years, and your guess is as good as mine. My guess is no. —*New York Times Magazine*

You're barking up the wrong tree. You're pursuing a wrong course of action. This saying originated in America in the early nineteenth century and alludes to a hunting dog pursuing raccoons. When a dog locates a raccoon at a tree, it stays at its foot and barks until its master comes. The saying appeared in the works of many American writers, such as James Hall, David Crockett, Albert Pike, and Thomas C. Haliburton. David Crockett wrote in his *Sketches and Eccentricities* (1833): "He reminded me of the meanest thing on God's earth, an old coon dog, barking up the wrong tree."

1982. Tim White worked for years with the Leakeys [anthropologists] in East Africa, but now he believes they are barking up the wrong tree. —*Christian Science Monitor*

1993. In the form of hunting, there is no such thing as barking up the wrong tree. When a squirrel dog locates a squirrel, a tree becomes a beehive of activity... both for the hunter and the hunted. —*Commercial Appeal* (Memphis, Tennessee)

1994. Federal researchers say they've collared some evidence about which kind of dogs are most likely to bite. Some animal experts say they're barking up the wrong tree. They say human ignorance of dog behavior, such as a child running up to hug a dog, often is to blame for dog bites. —*Hartford Courant*

1995. What about all the people who DON'T have kids who want the 850 turbo wagon? I think you're really barking up the wrong tree, as usual. —*Detroit News*

1997. Some pundits say families are paying more so professors can earn more doing less. As *Time* magazine put it, "Gone are the days of gentility." But if *Time* wants to blame faculty for higher tuition bills, it is barking up the wrong tree. —*Christian Science Monitor*

1998. Chase Manhattan Corp. may be barking up the wrong tree in its search for an acquisition to bolster its small but growing equity underwriting and research business. —*New York Post*

1998. A group of Oakland County commissioners is "barking up the wrong tree" if it hopes to eliminate the county executive position by switching to a charter form of government, Deputy County Executive Kenneth Rogers said. —*Detroit News*

You're never too old to learn. See IT'S NEVER TOO LATE TO LEARN.

Youth will be served. Young people should be treated well. The proverb has been traced back to *Lavengro* (1851) by George Borrow (1803–81), and is first attested in the United States in *Young Blood* (1930) by Stephen Vincent Benét. *Youth must be served* is a variant.

> **1851.** Youth will be served, every dog has his day, and mine has been a fine one. —George Borrow, *Lavengro*

> **1957.** Youth will be served, the saying goes. —*Time*

> **1987.** "You always whine and complain about our children's conduct, grades, latenesses, absences, and what not. Kids should be motivated, rewarded, and not bashed. Youth must be served, as my mother used to say." —Overheard at a PTA meeting

See also GATHER YE ROSEBUDS WHILE YE MAY; YOUTH WILL HAVE ITS FLING.

Youth will have its fling. Young people will have a time when they know only joy. The proverb has been traced back to *Accidence of Armoury* (1562), and is first attested in the United States in *House* (1921) by A. P. Herbert. The proverb is used as an excuse for the improper conduct of young people. *Youth must have its way* is a variant.

> **1921.** Youth'll 'ave its fling, they say. —A. P. Herbert, *House*

> **1989.** "There were rumors that after the assassination Jackie and Bobby became involved in a sexual relationship. Jackie, as we know from her marriage to JFK, had a history of going after unobtainable men. And Bobby, while nothing like JFK, enjoyed his share of flings." —C. David Heymann, *A Woman Named Jackie*

> **1992.** Even Mrs. Bush, who offset her carefully tended grandmotherly image with barbed comments all week, said in an interview with reporters before the Convention, "He [Bill Clinton] never denied having a fling, did he?" —*New Yorker*

See also GATHER YE ROSEBUDS WHILE YE MAY; YOUTH WILL BE SERVED.

You've come a long way, baby. In spite of all the resistance to your struggle for freedom, you've managed to make a lot of progress. This expression originated in the United States and was popularized as an advertising slogan to sell Virginia Slims cigarettes to women active in Women's Liberation in the 1970s.

> **1936.** "We've come a long way since those days, Ashley," she [Scarlett] said, trying to steady her voice, trying to fight the constriction in her throat. —Margaret Mitchell, *Gone With the Wind*

> **1985.** "You *have* come a long way, haven't you—Queenie?" —Michael Korda, *Queenie*

> **1988.** You've come a long way with me. —Harvey Mackay, *Swim with the Sharks without Being Eaten Alive*

> **1991.** Women state legislators sharing their stories at a San Diego conference sponsored by the Center for the American Woman and Politics contradicted the ubiquitous, brassy theme of Virginia Slims cigarette ads that proclaim, "You've come a long way, baby!" —*Times* (Trenton)

> **1993.** The National Rifle Association has come a long way, baby. For its latest ad campaign it has updated the kind of feminist slogans that Virginia Slims has used to sell cigarettes. Now the gun lobby is telling women "how to choose to refuse to be a victim." —*New York Times*

> **1994.** We've come a long way, baby, since songwriters waxed lyrical about cigarettes with lipstick traces and smoke getting in your eyes. —*New York Times Book Review*

You've got everything to lose and nothing to gain. See PROLETARIANS HAVE NOTHING TO LOSE BUT THEIR CHAINS.

You've got nothing to lose and a lot to gain. See PROLETARIANS HAVE NOTHING TO LOSE BUT THEIR CHAINS.

You've made your bed, now lie in it. You did exactly as you pleased, now you have to live with the consequences of your behavior and actions. The proverb has been traced back to about 1590 and is related to the fifteenth-century French proverb *Comme on faict son lict, on le treuve* ("As one makes one's bed, so one finds it"). It was included in George Herbert's collection of proverbs in 1640 and in James Kelly's collection in 1721. It is first attested in the United States in *Cy Whittaker's Place* (1908) by J. S. Lincoln, and is found in varying forms: *As one makes his bed, so must he lie; As you make your bed, so you must lie in it; As you made your apple-pie bed so you must lie on it; You have buttered your bed, and now you must lie on it; You buttered your bread—now lie in it,* etc.

1908. You've made your bed; now lay in it. —J. C. Lincoln, *Cy Whittaker's Place*

1922. You have made your second best bed and others must lie on it. —James Joyce, *Ulysses*

1957. This is my bed, as they say. I made it and I'll lie in it. —*New Yorker*

1979. "You know that her husband was mixed up in some gunrunning scheme for the State of Israel?"
"I've heard."
"Barbara is making her own bed. She has to sleep in it, Tom." —Howard Fast, *The Establishment*

1984. "Oh, hell, why am I crying on your shoulder? I made my own bed." —Howard Fast, *The Outsider*

See also AS YOU SOW SO (SHALL) YOU REAP; WHAT GOES AROUND, COMES AROUND.

BIBLIOGRAPHY

MAJOR COLLECTIONS OF PROVERBS AND SAYINGS:

Ammer, Christine. *The American Heritage Dictionary of Idioms.* Boston: Houghton Mifflin Company, 1997.

Ammer, Christine. *Have a Nice Day—No Problem!* New York: Dutton, 1992.

Andrews, Robert. *The Columbia Dictionary of Quotations.* New York: Columbia University Press, 1993.

Bartlett, John. *Familiar Quotations.* 16th edition. Edited by Justin Kaplan. Boston: Little Brown, 1992.

Baz, Patros D. *A Dictionary of Proverbs.* New York: Philosophical Library, 1963.

Bertram, Anne. *NTC's Dictionary of Proverbs and Clichés.* Lincolnwood, IL: National Textbook Co., 1993.

Boller, Paul F. and John George. *They Never Said It.* New York: Oxford, 1989.

Collis, Harry. *101 American English Proverbs.* Lincolnwood, IL: Passport Books, 1992.

Daintith, John, et al. *Who Said What When.* New York: Hippocrene, 1988.

Flavell, Linda & Roger. *Dictionary of Proverbs and their Origins.* New York: Hippocrene, 1997.

Funk, Charles Earle. *A Hog on Ice and Other Curious Expressions.* New York: Harper & Row, 1948.

_____. *Heavens to Betsy! and Other Curious Sayings.* New York: Harper & Row, 1955.

Hirsch, E.D, et al. *The Dictionary of Cultural Literacy.* Boston: Houghton Mifflin, 1988.

Keats, An. *A Little Book of Proverbs.* New York: Pyramid Books, 1970.

Keyes, Ralph. *Nice Guys Finish Seventh.* New York: HarperCollins, 1992.

The Macmillan Dictionary of Quotations. New York: Macmillan, 1989.

Mieder, Wolfgang, et al. *A Dictionary of American Proverbs.* New York: Oxford, 1992.

Ottenheimer, I. and M. *Familiar Quotations.* Baltimore: Ottenheimer, 1955.

Ottenheimer, *Proverbs and Epigrams.* Baltimore: Ottenheimer, 1954.

Palmatier, A. Robert and Harold L. Ray. *Dictionary of Sports Idioms.* Lincolnwood, IL.: National Textbook Company, 1993.

Partington, Angela. *The Oxford Dictionary of Quotations.* New York: Oxford, 1992.

Partridge, Eric. *A Dictionary of Catch Phrases.* New York: Scarborough, 1992.

Pickering, David. *Dictionary of Proverbs.* Cassel, 1958.

Rogers, James. *The Dictionary of Clichés.* New York: Facts on File, 1985.

Simpson, John. *The Concise Dictionary of Proverbs.* New York: Oxford, 1992.

Smith, Elmer L. *American Proverbs.* Lebanon,

PA: Applied Arts Publishers, 1968.

Spears, Richard A. *Common American Phrases.* Lincolnwood, IL: National Textbook Co., 1992.

_____. *NTC's American Idioms Dictionary.* Lincolnwood, IL: National Textbook Co., 1987.

_____. *NTC's Dictionary of American English Phrases.* Lincolnwood, IL: National Textbook Co., 1995.

_____. *NTC's Dictionary of American Slang and Colloquial Expressions.* Lincolnwood, IL: National Textbook Co., 1989.

Stevenson, Burton. *Macmillan (Home) Books of Proverbs, Maxims, and Familiar Phrases.* New York: Macmillan, 1948.

Whiting, Bartlett Jere. *Modern Proverbs and Proverbial Sayings.* Cambridge, MA: Harvard, 1989.

WORKS CITED IN THE DICTIONARY

Albee, Edward. *Who's Afraid of Virginia Woolf?* New York: Dramatists Play Service, 1962.

_____. *The Zoo Story and The Sandbox: Two Short Plays.* New York: Dramatists Play Service, 1961.

Alihan, Milla. *Corporate Etiquette.* New York: Mentor, 1979.

Ambrose, Stephen E. *Nixon.* Vol. 1. New York: Touchstone, 1988.

_____. *Nixon: The Triumph of a Politician, 1962–72.* New York: Simon & Schuster, 1989.

Andersen, Hans Christian. *Andersen's Fairy Tales.* New York: Grosset & Dunlap, 1945.

Anderson, Robert. *Tea and Sympathy.* New York: Random House, 1953.

Asprin, Robert. *Myth Directions.* New York: Ace Fantasy Books, 1982.

Bailey, Thomas A. *The American Pageant.* Boston: Heath, 1966.

Bain, Carl E., et al. *The Norton Introduction to Literature.* New York: Norton, 1973.

Bardwick, Judith. New York: Amacom, 1986.

Bellow, Saul. *Dangling Man.* New York: Vanguard, 1944.

_____. *Herzog.* New York: Viking, 1964.

_____. *Him with His Foot in His Mouth and Other Stories.* New York: Harper & Row, 1974.

_____. *Mr. Sammler's Planet.* New York: Viking, 1970.

Bernstein, Carl, and Bob Woodward. *All the President's Men.* New York: Simon & Schuster, 1974.

The Bible. King James Version, 1611.

Bliven, Bruce. "The Incomparable Ben Franklin." *Great Lives, Great Deeds.* Pleasantville, NY: Reader's Digest, 1964.

Bloom, Allan. *The Closing of the American Mind.* New York: Simon & Schuster, 1987.

Blume, Judy. *Just as Long as We're Together.* New York: Orchard, 1987.

Bolles, Richard Nelson. *What Color is Your Parachute?* New York: Ten Speed Press, 1972.

Boorstin, Daniel J., ed. *An American Primer: 1890–1910: Primary Sources in American History.* Chicago: University of Chicago, 1966.

Bradbury, Ray. *Fahrenheit 451.* New York: Simon and Schuster, 1953.

_____. *I Sing the Body Electric.* New York: Bantam, 1948.

Buchwald, Art. *Down the Seine and up the Potomac with Art Buchwald.* New York: Putnam, 1977.

_____. *Washington is Leaking.* New York: Putnam, 1976.

Bunch, Chris, and Allan Cole. *A Reckoning for Kings.* New York: Ballantine, 1987.

Burnham, David. *A Law unto Itself.* New York: Random House, 1990.

Burton, Robert. *Anatomy of Melancholy.* (1621) Edited by Holbrook Jackson. New York: Vintage, 1977.

Cabell, James Branch. *The Silver Stallion.* New York: McBride, 1926.

Capote, Truman. *In Cold Blood.* New York: Random House, 1965.

_____. *Other Voices, Other Rooms.* New York: Random House, 1948.

Care, Wayne. *Vietnam Spook Show.* New York: Ivy, 1989.

Caro, Robert A. *The Power Broker.* New York: Vintage, 1974.

Cervantes, Miguel. *Don Quixote.* (1605) Translated by J.M. Cohen. New York: Viking, 1970.

Chaucer, Geoffrey. *The Canterbury Tales.* (1393–1400) Translated by Nevill Coghill. New York: Penguin, 1951.

_____. *Troilus and Creseyde.* (1386–87) Translated by Nevill Coghill. New York: Penguin, 1971.

Cheever, John. *Falconer.* New York: Knopf, 1975.

_____. *The Wapshot Chronicle.* New York: Harper & Row, 1954.

_____. *The Wapshot Scandal.* New York: Harper & Row, 1964.

Clancy, Tom. *Clear and Present Danger.* New York: Berkley, 1989.

_____. *The Hunt for Red October.* New York: Berkley, 1984.

_____. *Red Storm Rising.* New York: Berkley, 1986.

Clinton, Hillary. *It Takes a Village and Other Lessons Children Teach Us.* New York: Simon & Schuster, 1996.

Chernow, Ron. *The House of Morgan.* New York: Atlantic Monthly, 1980.

Christopher, William and Barbara. *Mixed Blessings.* New York: Abingdon, 1989.

Cleaver, Eldridge. *Soul on Ice.* New York: Delta, 1968.

Cohen, Herb. *You Can Negotiate Anything.* New York: Citadel, 1980.

Collins, Jackie. *Hollywood Husbands.* New York: Pocket Books, 1986.

_____. *Hollywood Wives.* New York: Pocket Books, 1983.

_____. *The World is Full of Divorced Women.* New York: Warner, 1980.

Congreve, William. *The Complete Plays of William Congreve.* (1693–1700) Edited by Herbert Davis. Chicago: University of Chicago, 1967.

Conroy, Pat. *The Prince of Tides.* New York: Bantam, 1986.

Copeland, Lewis and Faye. *10,000 Jokes, Toasts and Stories.* Garden City, NY: Doubleday, 1939.

Cutler, John Henry. *Honey Fitz: Three Steps to the White House.* Indianapolis: Bobbs-Merrill, 1962.

DeMille, Nelson. *The Charm School.* New York: Warner, 1988.

De Toledano, Ralph. *R.F.K.* New York: Putnam, 1967.

Dickens, Charles. *David Copperfield.* (1850) New York: Oxford, 1981.

_____. *Oliver Twist.* (1837–39) New York: Penguin, 1966.

_____. *Our Mutual Friend.* (1865) New York: Oxford, 1989.

_____. *Pickwick Papers.* (1836–37) New York: Penguin, 1972.

_____. *A Tale of Two Cities.* (1859) New York: Bantam, 1989.

Dowling, Colette. *The Cinderella Complex.* New York: Summit, 1981.

Dreiser, Theodore. *The Financier.* (1912) New York: Penguin, 1995.

_____. *The Best Short Stories of Theodore Dreiser.* (1918) New York: Crowell, 1974.

_____. *The Titan.* New York: Lane, 1914.

Dye, Dale A. *Platoon.* New York: Charter, 1986.

Ehrlich, Judith, and Barry J. Rehfeld. *The New Crowd.* Boston: Little, Brown, 1989.

Eliot, Thomas Stearns. *The Cocktail Party.* (1950) In *The Complete Poems and Plays of T.S. Eliot.* New York: Harcourt Brace, 1971.

Elliot, George P. *In the World.* New York: Viking, 1965.

Fast, Howard. *The Establishment.* Boston: Houghton Mifflin, 1979.

_____. *The Immigrant's Daughter.* Boston: Houghton Mifflin, 1985.

_____. *Max.* Boston: Houghton Mifflin, 1982.

_____. *The Outsider.* Boston: Houghton Mifflin, 1984.

_____. *Second Generation.* New York: Dell, 1978.

Faulkner, William. *The Sound and the Fury.* New York: Vintage, 1929.

Feinsilber, Mike, and William B. Mead. *American Averages.* New York: Dolphin, 1980.

Fitzgerald, F. Scott. *The Great Gatsby.* New York: Scribner's, 1925.

_____. *Tender is the Night.* New York: Scribner's, 1934.

Flagg, Fannie. *Fried Green Tomatoes at the Whistle Stop Cafe.* New York: McGraw-Hill, 1987.

Flesch, Rudolf. *Lite English.* New York: Crown, 1983.

Franklin, Benjamin. *Poor Richard's Almanac.* (1735) New York: David McKay, 1973.

Friedman, Philip. *Inadmissible Evidence.* New York: Ivy, 1992.

Frost, Robert. *Robert Frost's Poems.* New York: Washington Square Books, 1965.

Fulghum, Robert. *All I Really Need to Know I Learned in Kindergarten.* New York: Villard, 1986.

Funk & Wagnalls New Encyclopedia. New York: Funk & Wagnalls, 1979–80.

Gazzo, Michael. *A Hatful of Rain.* New York: French, 1956.

Great American Folk Songs. New York: Dell, 1963.

Grisham, John. *The Firm.* New York: Doubleday, 1991.

_____. *The Pelican Brief.* New York: Doubleday, 1992.

_____. *A Time to Kill.* New York: Doubleday, 1989.

Gugliotta, Guy, and Jeff Leen. *Kings of Cocaine.* New York: Simon and Schuster, 1989.

Hamer, O. Stuart, et al. *Exploring the Old World.* Chicago: Follett, 1964.

Heller, Joseph. *Catch-22.* New York: Dell, 1955.

_____. *God Knows.* New York: Knopf, 1984.

Hellman, Lillian. *The Autumn Garden.* (1950) In *Six Plays by Lillian Hellman.* New York: Vintage, 1979.

Hemingway, Ernest. *For Whom the Bell Tolls.* New York: Scribner's, 1940.

_____. *Hemingway Reader.* New York: Scribner's, 1953.

_____. *The Old Man and the Sea.* New York: Scribner's 1952.

Hendrickson, Robert. *Business Talk.* New York: Stein and Day, 1984.

Heymann, C. David. *A Woman Named Jackie.* New York: Signet, 1989.

Hyatt, Carole, and Linda Gottlieb. *When Smart People Fail.* New York: Penguin, 1987.

Iacocca, Lee, with William Novak. *Iacocca: An Autobiography.* New York: Bantam, 1984.

Irving, Clifford. *Daddy's Girl: The Campbell Murder Case: A True Tale of Vengeance, Betrayal and Texas Justice.* New York: Summit, 1988.

Jessup, Claudia, and Genie Chipps. *The Women's Guide to Starting a Business.* New York: Holt, 1976.

Johnson, Paul. *Modern Times.* New York: Harper & Row, 1983.

Jones, James. *From Here to Eternity.* New York: Scribner's, 1951.

_____. *The Thin Red Line.* New York: Scribner's, 1962.

Joyce, James. *Ulysses.* (1934) New York: Vintage, 1986.

Kaufman, Bel. *Up the Down Staircase.* New York: Avon, 1964.

Kazan, Elia. *The Arrangement.* New York: Stein and Day, 1967.

Keen, Sam. *Fire in the Belly (On Being a Man).* New York: Bantam Doubleday Dell Publishers, 1992.

Kelley, Kitty. *Nancy Reagan.* New York: Simon & Schuster, 1991.

Keyes, Frances Parkinson. *All That Glitters.* New York: Avon, 1941.

King, Stephen. *It.* New York: Signet, 1986.

_____. *The Stand.* New York: Signet, 1978.

Kipling, Rudyard. *Complete Verse.* New York: Doubleday, 1939.

Koch, Edward I. *Mayor.* New York: Simon & Schuster, 1984.

Koontz, Dean R. *The House of Thunder.* New York: Berkley, 1982.

Korda, Michael. *The Fortune.* New York: Warner, 1989.

_____. *Queenie.* New York: Warner, 1985.

Landers, Ann. *Since You Ask Me.* New York: Prentice-Hall, 1961.

Lasky, Victor. *It Didn't Start with Watergate.* New York: Dell, 1977.

Lawrence, D.H. *Lady Chatterley's Lover.* (1928) New York: Signet, 1964.

Leamer, Laurence. *King of the Night.* New York: Morrow, 1989.

Lee, Harper. *To Kill a Mockingbird.* New York: Warner, 1960.

Levit, Mortimer. *The Executive Look.* New York: Atheneum, 1981.

Lewis, Michael. *Liar's Poker.* New York: Norton, 1989.

Lewis, Sinclair. *It Can't Happen Here.* New York:

Dell, 1935.

Longfellow, Henry Wadsworth. *Evangeline and Other Poems.* New York: Board of Education, 1946.

Loring, Emilie. *Beyond the Sound of Guns.* New York: Bantam, 1945.

Ludlum, Robert. *The Icarus Agenda.* New York: Bantam, 1988.

Mackay, Harvey. *Swim with the Sharks without Being Eaten Alive.* New York: Ivy, 1988.

Mailer, Norman. *The Executioner's Song.* New York: Ballantine, 1979.

_____. *The Naked and the Dead.* New York: Signet, 1948.

Malamud, Bernard. *The Natural.* New York: Pocket Books, 1961.

McBain, Ed. *Kiss.* New York: Morrow, 1992.

McPherson, James M. *Battle Cry of Freedom.* New York: Ballantine, 1989.

Melville, Herman. *Moby Dick.* (1851) New York: Signet, 1961.

Michener, James A. *Space.* New York: Fawcett Crest, 1982.

Millay, Edna St. Vincent. *A Few Figs from Thistles.* New York: Harper, 1918.

Miller, Arthur. *The Crucible.* New York: Bantam, 1952.

_____. *Death of a Salesman.* New York: Viking, 1949.

Mitchell, Margaret. *Gone with the Wind.* New York: Macmillan, 1936.

Moreau, Daniel. *Take Charge of Your Career.* Washington, DC: Kiplinger, 1990.

North, Oliver, with William Novak. *Under Fire.* New York: Harper, 1991.

Oates, Joyce Carol. *Do with Me What You Will.* New York: Vanguard, 1973.

_____. *Them.* New York: Fawcett Crest, 1969.

O'Neill, Eugene. *Desire under the Elms* (1924), *Strange Interlude* (1928), *Mourning Becomes Electra* (1931). In *Three Plays of Eugene O'Neill.* New York: Vintage, 1959.

Orwell, George. *Animal Farm.* New York: Harcourt, Brace, 1946.

_____. *1984.* New York: Harcourt, Brace, 1949.

Ostrovsky, Victor, and Claire Hoy. *By Way of Deception.* New York: St. Martin's, 1990.

Packard, Vance. *The Ultra Rich.* New York: Little,

Brown, 1989.

Payne, John Howard. "Home, Sweet Home." (1823) In *John Howard Payne: Dramatist, Poet, Actor: His Life and Writings.* Philadelphia: Lippincott, 1885.

Pearson, Carol S. *The Hero Within.* San Francisco: Harper & Row, 1989.

Peter, Laurence J. *Peter's Quotations.* New York: Bantam, 1980.

Peter, Laurence J., with Raymond Hull. *The Peter Principle.* New York: Bantam, 1966.

Platt, Nathaniel, and Muriel Jean Drummond. *Our World through the Ages.* Englewood Cliffs, NJ: Prentice-Hall, 1967.

Plumez, Jacqueline Hornor, with Karla Dougherty. *Divorcing a Corporation.* New York: Villard, 1985.

Puzo, Mario. *The Godfather.* New York: Putnam, 1969.

Reeves, Thomas. *A Question of Character: A Life of John F. Kennedy.* New York: Free Press, 1991.

Ripley, Alexandra. *Scarlett.* New York: Warner, 1991.

Ritti, R. Richard, and G. Ray Funkhouser. *The Ropes to Skip and the Ropes to Know.* New York: 1987.

Robbins, Harold. *Never Love a Stranger.* New York: Bantam, 1948.

Rogers, Henry C. *Rogers' Rules for Business Women.* New York: St. Martin's, 1988.

Safire, William. *Full Disclosure.* New York: Ballantine, 1977.

Salinger, J.D. *The Catcher in the Rye.* Boston: Little, Brown, 1951.

_____. *Nine Stories.* Boston: Little, Brown, 1953.

_____. *Raise High the Roof Beam, Carpenters.* Boston: Little, Brown, 1963.

Saturday Evening Post. *The Presidents.* Indianapolis: Curtis, 1980.

Schlesinger, Arthur M., Jr. *A Thousand Days: John F. Kennedy in the White House.* Boston: Houghton, Mifflin, 1965.

Schumacher, E.F. *Small is Beautiful.* Point Roberts, WA: Hartley & Marks Publishers, 1998.

Scott, John Anthony. *The Story of America.* Washington, D.C.: National Geographic

Society, 1984.

Segal, Erich. *The Class.* New York: Bantam, 1985.

_____. *Doctors.* New York: Bantam, 1988.

Shakespeare, William. *The Complete Works of Shakespeare.* New York: Oxford, 1929.

Sheldon, Sidney. *Master of the Game.* New York: Warner, 1981.

_____. *Rage of Angels.* New York: Warner, 1980.

Shute, Nevil. *On the Beach.* New York: Morrow, 1957.

Silberman, Charles E. *A Certain People.* New York: Summit, 1985.

Sinclair, Upton. *A World to Win.* New York: Viking, 1946.

Sondheim, Stephen, and Jule Styne. *Everything's Coming up Roses.* 1975.

Sper, Felix. *Favorite Modern Plays.* New York: Globe, 1956.

Steel, Danielle. *Mixed Blessings.* New York: Dell, 1992.

_____. *Palomino.* New York: Dell, 1981.

Steinbeck, John. *The Grapes of Wrath.* New York: Viking, 1939.

_____. *The Winter of Our Discontent.* New York: Bantam, 1961.

Stewart, James B. *Den of Thieves.* New York: Simon & Schuster, 1991.

Stone, Irving. *Adversary in the House.* New York: Signet, 1947.

Styron, William. *Sophie's Choice.* New York: Bantam, 1976.

Sullivan, Nancy. *The Treasury of American Short Stories.* Garden City, NY: International Collectors Library, 1965.

Susann, Jacqueline. *Once is Not Enough.* New York: Bantam, 1973.

Szep, Paul. *To a Different Drummer.* Brattleboro, VT: Lewis Pub. Co., 1983.

Thayer, Ernest Lawrence. "Casey at the Bat: A Ballad of the Republic Sung in the Year 1888." In *Story Poems.* New York: Washington Square Press, 1969.

Thomas, Dylan. "Do Not Go Gentle into That Good Night." (1952) In *Collected Poems.* New York: New Directions, 1953.

Thoreau, Henry David. *Walden.* (1854) New York: AMS Press, 1982.

Trudeau, Garry. *Doonesbury Deluxe.* New York: Holt, 1987.

Truman, Harry S. *Years of Trial and Hope.* Garden City, NY: Doubleday, 1956.

Twain, Mark. *Pudd'nhead Wilson.* (1894) New York: New American Library Penguin, 1964.

Updike, John. *The Music School.* New York: Fawcett Crest, 1962.

Van Buren, Abigail. *The Best of Dear Abby.* New York: Pocket Books, 1981.

Vidal, Gore. *The Judgement of Paris.* (1952) London: Heinemann, 1968.

Viorst, Judith. *Necessary Losses.* New York: Simon & Schuster, 1986.

Vonnegut, Kurt, Jr. *Breakfast of Champions.* New York: Dell, 1973.

_____. *Cat's Cradle.* New York: Dell, 1963.

_____. *The Eden Express.* New York: Bantam, 1975.

_____. *Galapagos.* New York: Dell, 1985.

_____. *Jailbird.* New York: Dell, 1979.

_____. *Player Piano.* New York: Bard, 1952.

Wallechinsky, David, and Irving Wallace. *The People's Almanac.* Garden City, NY: Doubleday, 1975.

Walton, Izzak. *The Compleat Angler.* (1653) New York: Modern Library, 1998.

Warren, Robert Penn. *All the King's Men.* New York: Bantam, 1946.

_____. *At Heaven's Gate.* New York: Signet, 1943.

Webster, Hutton. *History of Civilization.* Boston: Heath, 1940.

Williams, Tennessee. *Camino Real.* (1953) New York: New Directions, 1970.

_____. *A Streetcar Named Desire.* (1947) New York: New Directions, 1980.

Wolfe, Tom. *The Bonfire of the Vanities.* New York: Bantam, 1987.

Woodward, Bob. *The Commanders.* New York: Simon & Schuster, 1991.

Wordsworth, William. *The Poems.* (1793–1842) New York: Viking, 1990.

Wouk, Herman. *Inside, Outside.* Boston: Little, Brown, 1985.

_____. *Marjorie Morningstar.* Garden City, NY: Doubleday, 1955.

_____. *Youngblood Hawke.* Garden City, NY: Doubleday, 1962.

NEWSPAPERS CITED IN THE DICTIONARY:

Asbury Park Press
Arizona Republic
Amsterdam News (New York)
Boston Globe
Chicago Sun-Times
Chicago Tribune
Christian Science Monitor
Commerical Appeal (Memphis)
Crain's New York Business
Daily News (New York)
Daily Times (White Plains)
Detroit News
Fort Worth Star-Telegram
Hartford Courant

Jewish Press
Jewish Week (New York)
Knoxville News-Sentinel
Los Angeles Times
Manhattan Jewish Sentinel
Minneapolis Star-Tribune
MW Jewish News
New York City Tribune
New York Newsday
New York Observer
New York Post
New York Times
Packet/Ledger
Philadelphia Inquirer

Phoenix Gazette
Princeton Packet
St. Louis Post-Dispatch
Star-Ledger (Newark)
Sun-Sentinel (South Florida)
Time Off
Times (Trenton)
Trentonian
U.S. 1 (Princeton)
U.S.A. Today
Wall Street Journal
Washington Post
Washington Times

MAGAZINES CITED IN THE DICTIONARY:

AARP Bulletin
Allure
Atlantic
Athenaeum
Bits & Pieces
Business Week
Buzz
Car and Driver
Connoisseur
Entertainment Weekly
Esquire
Everybody's Magazine
Family Circle
Forbes
Fortune
Forward
GQ

Hadassah
Health
Houston Chronicle Magazine
Ladies' Home Journal
Lear's
Life
McCall's
Metropolitan Home
Modern Maturity
National Geographic
National Business Employment
    Weekly
Natural History
New Republic
New York
New York Times Book Review
New York Times Magazine

National Enquirer
New Yorker
Newsweek
Popular Science
Princeton Living
Reader's Digest
Redbook
(The) Sciences
Smithsonian
Star
Time
US
U.S. News & World Report
Vanity Fair
Vogue
Washingtonian
Weekly World News

INDEX

ABANDON
Abandon all hope, ye who enter here.

ABHOR
Nature abhors a vacuum.

ABILITY
From each according to his ability, to each according to his needs.

ABSENCE
Absence makes the heart grow fonder.

ABSOLUTE
Power corrupts, and absolute power corrupts absolutely.

ACCENTUATE
Accentuate the positive.

ACCIDENT
Accidents will happen in the best-regulated families.

ACCORDING
Cut the coat according to the cloth. *See* You must cut your coat according to your cloth.
From each according to his ability, to each according to his needs.
Judge not according to appearances.
You must cut your coat according to your cloth.

ACCOUNTING
There's no accounting for tastes.

ACHILLES
Achilles' heel.

ACORN
Even a blind pig occasionally picks up an acorn.
Great oaks from little acorns grow.

ACTION
Actions, not words. *See* Deeds, not words.
Actions speak louder than words.

ADAM
When Adam delved and Eve span, who was then the gentleman?

ADD
Don't add insult to injury.

ADO
Much ado about nothing.

ADVERSITY
Adversity makes strange bedfellows. *See* Misery makes strange bedfellows.

AFFAIR
There's a tide in the affairs of men.

AFTER
After a storm comes a calm.
After the feast comes the reckoning.
After us the deluge.
Don't close (bar, lock, shut) the barn (stable) door after the horse runs away (has fled, has been stolen).

The good that men do lives after them.

It is easy to be wise after the event.

AFTERWARDS

Keep your eyes wide open before marriage, half shut afterwards.

AGAIN

All the king's horses, and all the king's men, couldn't put Humpty together again.

The dog has returned to his vomit again. *See* The dog always returns to his vomit.

Everything old is new again.

Happy days are here again.

Here we go again.

If at first you don't succeed, try, try again.

It's déja vu all over again.

Let's get America moving again.

The Phoenix is rising again.

What has happened once can happen again.

You can say that again.

You can't go home again.

AGAINST

If you play both ends against the middle, the middle will soon fold up.

It goes against the grain.

Two strikes against someone (something). *See* Three strikes and you're out.

AGE

Age before beauty.

Age cannot wither her, nor custom stale her infinite variety.

AGREE

Birds in their little nests agree.

I couldn't agree (with you) more.

AID

Now is the time for all good men to come to the aid of their country.

AIN'T

If it ain't broke, don't fix it.

It ain't over till it's over. *See* It's not over till it's over.

The opera ain't over till the fat lady sings.

AIR

Don't air your dirty linen in public.

Don't build castles in the air.

ALBATROSS

It's an albatross around one's neck.

ALCOHOL

Alcohol (drinking) and driving don't mix. *See* Oil and water don't mix.

ALIEN

I am a man; and nothing human is alien to me.

ALIKE

All cats look alike in the dark. *See* All cats are gray in the dark.

Great minds think alike.

ALL

Abandon all hope, ye who enter here.

All animals are equal, but some animals are more equal than others.

All cats are gray in the dark.

All chiefs and no Indians.

All for one and one for all.

All good things come in threes.

All good things come to those who wait.

All good things must come to an end.

All hell broke loose.

All in a day's work. *See* It's all in a day's work.

All in the family. *See* It's all in the family.

All is for the best in the best of all possible worlds.

All is grist that comes to the mill. *See* It's all grist for the mill.

All is not gold that glitters. *See* All that glitters is not gold.

All men are created equal.

All or nothing.

All quiet along the Potomac.

All quiet on the Western Front.

All roads lead to Rome.

All systems go.

All that glitters is not gold.

All the king's horses, and all the king's men, couldn't put Humpty together again.

All the world's a stage.

All things to all men.

All work and no play makes Jack a dull boy.

Everything is not all peaches and cream.

If you've seen one, you've seen 'em all.

It all depends on whose ox is gored.

It is better to have loved and lost, than never to have loved at all.

It's all grist for the mill.

It's all in a day's work.

It's all in the family.

It's all over and done with.

It's all over but the shouting.

It's all systems go. *See* All systems go.

Let's all hang together or we shall surely hang separately. *See* We must indeed all hang together, or, most assuredly, we shall all hang separately.

Let's kill all the lawyers.

Life isn't all beer and skittles.

Love conquers all.

Now is the time for all good men to come to the aid of their country.

One nation under God, indivisible, with liberty and justice for all.

A rising tide will lift all boats.

That's all there is to it.

There's a time for all things. *See* There's a time and place for everything.

Vanity of vanities; all is vanity.

Warts and all.

We must indeed all hang together, or, most assuredly, we shall all hang separately.

With malice toward none, with charity for all.

The world is a stage and all the men and women merely players. *See* All the world's a stage.

You can't win 'em all.

ALONE

Laugh and the world laughs with you; weep and you weep alone.

Leave well enough alone.

Man does not live by bread alone.

ALWAYS

Always look on the bright side.

Always put your best foot forward.

A bad penny always turns up.

The bad workman always quarrels with his tools.

Cream always comes to the top.

The customer is always right.

The dog always returns to his vomit.

God is always on the side of the big battalions.

The grass is always greener on the other side of the fence.

The husband is always the last to find out.

It's always darkest before the dawn.

Once a crook, always a crook. *See* Once a thief,

always a thief.

Once a drunkard, always a drunkard. *See* Once a thief, always a thief.

Once a knave, always a knave. *See* Once a thief, always a thief.

Once a preacher, always a preacher. *See* Once a thief, always a thief.

Once a thief, always a thief.

Once a whore, always a whore. *See* Once a thief, always a thief.

Providence is always on the side of the big battalions. *See* God is always on the side of the big battalions.

There's always a first time for everything. *See* There must be a first time for everything.

There's always (a) tomorrow.

There's always room at the top.

The truth (always, often) hurts.

AMERICA, AMERICAN

The business of America is business.

Don't sell America short. *See* Never sell America short.

God bless America.

Let's get America moving again.

Never sell America short.

No one ever went broke underestimating the intelligence of the American people.

What's good for General Motors is good for America.

AMONG

There is honor (even) among thieves.

There's no honor among thieves. *See* There is honor (even) among thieves.

AMMUNITION

Praise the Lord and pass the ammunition.

ANGEL

Fools rush in where angels fear to tread.

ANIMAL

All animals are equal, but some animals are more equal than others.

ANOTHER

Another day, another dollar.

Another such victory, and we are undone.

He who fights and runs away, may live to fight
another day.

One good turn deserves another.

One man's loss is another man's gain.

One man's meat is another man's poison.

One man's trash is another man's treasure.

A rose by another name would smell as sweet.

Tomorrow is another day.

ANSWER

I won't take no for an answer.

A soft answer turns away wrath.

ANY

Any port in a storm.

A rose by any other name (color) would smell as sweet (the same). *See* A rose by another name would smell as sweet.

ANYBODY

Work never hurt anybody.

ANYONE

If anyone betrays you once, it's his fault; if he betrays you twice, it's your fault. *See* Fool me once, shame on you; fool me twice, shame on me.

ANYTHING

Anything for a quiet life.

Anything for (a little) peace and quiet. *See* Anything for a quiet life.

Anything goes!

Anything is possible.

Anything that can go wrong, will go wrong. *See* If anything can go wrong, it will.

Anything worth doing is worth doing well.

Don't believe anything (everything) you hear nor (and) half of what you read. *See* Believe only half of what you see and nothing you hear.

Don't start anything you can't finish.

He who never made a mistake never made anything.

If anything can go wrong, it will.

A man who makes no mistakes usually does not make anything. *See* He who never made a mistake never made anything.

You never get anything for nothing. *See* You get nothing for nothing.

ANYWHERE

If you can make it here, you can make it anywhere.

APPEAR

Talk of the devil, and he is bound to appear.

APPEARANCE

Appearances (looks) are deceiving (deceptive).

Judge not according to appearances.

Never judge from appearances. *See* Judge not according to appearances.

APPLE

An apple a day keeps the doctor away.

Comparing apples and oranges.

The apple doesn't fall far from the tree.

How do you like *them* apples?

One rotten apple spoils the barrel. *See* The rotten apple spoils the barrel.

The rotten apple spoils the barrel.

APRIL

April showers bring May flowers.

ARAB

He could sell sand to the Arabs. *See* He could sell ice to an Eskimo.

ARGUE

You can't argue with success.

ARM

A shot in the arm.

ARMY

An army marches on its stomach.

AROUND

An albatross around one's neck. *See* It's an albatross around one's neck.

It's an albatross around one's neck.

Prosperity is just around the corner.

What goes around, comes around.

ARRIVE

It is better to travel hopefully than to arrive.

ART

Art is long, life is short.

Life is short, art is long. *See* Art is long, life is short.

ASK

Ask, and it shall be given you; seek, and you shall find; knock, and it shall be opened unto you.

Ask me no questions and I'll tell you no lies.

Ask not what your country can do for you;
ask what
you can do for your country.

Shoot first and ask questions afterwards.

ASSUREDLY

We must indeed all hang together, or, most
assuredly, we shall all hang separately.

ATTACK

Attack is the best form of defense. *See* The
best
defense is a good offense.

ATTRACT

Honey catches (attracts) more flies than vinegar. *See* You can catch more flies with
honey than with vinegar.

Opposites attract.

AWAY

An apple a day keeps the doctor away.

Don't close (bar, lock, shut) the barn (stable)
door after the horse runs away (has fled,
has been stolen).

He who fights and runs away, may live to
fight another day.

Old soldiers never die; they just fade away.

A soft answer turns away wrath.

When the cat's away, the mice will play.

BABE, BABY

Don't throw out the baby with the bath water.

It's like taking candy from a baby.

Out of the mouths of babes and sucklings
come great truths.

You've come a long way, baby.

BACK

It's the last straw that breaks the camel's
back.

Step on a crack, break your mother's back.

You scratch my back, I'll scratch yours.

Back to the drawing board.

BAD

Bad money drives out good.

Bad news travels fast.

A bad penny always turns up.

The bad workman always quarrels with his
tools.

The good news is …; the bad news is …

Good news travels slowly; bad news travels
fast. *See* Bad news travels fast.

Good riddance to bad rubbish.

The good, the bad, and the ugly.

There's nothing good or bad but thinking
makes it so.

You have to take the bad with the good.

BAG

The cat is out of the bag.

To be left holding the bag.

BAIT

Fish or cut bait.

BALL

The ball is in your court.

It's a different (new) ball game (ballpark).

That's the way the ball bounces. *See* That's
the way the cookie crumbles.

BANG

Not with a bang but a whimper.

BAR

Don't close (bar, lock, shut) the barn (stable)
door after the horse runs away (has fled,
has been stolen).

BAREFOOT

The shoemaker's kids always go barefoot.

BARK

Barking dogs never bite.

The dogs bark, but the caravan goes on.

His bark is worse than his bite.

You're barking up the wrong tree.

BARN

Don't close (bar, lock, shut) the barn (stable)
door after the horse runs away (has fled,
has been stolen).

A jackass can kick a barn door down, but it
takes a carpenter to build one.

BARREL

The rotten apple spoils the barrel.

BASKET

Don't put all your eggs in one basket.

BATTALION

God is always on the side of the big battalions.

BATTLE

A good beginning is half the battle.

Half the battle. *See* A good beginning is half the battle.

It is better to lose the battle and win the war.

BE

Be careful what you wish for. You might get it. *See* Don't wish too hard: you might just get what you wished for.

Be it ever so humble, there's no place like home. *See* There's no place like home.

Be nice to people on your way up because you'll meet them ('em) on your way down.

Don't worry. Be happy.

To be, or not to be: that is the question.

What must be, must be. *See* What will be, will be.

What will be, will be.

BEARING

Beware of Greeks bearing gifts.

BEAST

It ain't a fit night out for man or beast.

BEAT

If you can't beat (lick) 'em, join 'em.

You can't beat a man at his own game.

You can't beat somebody with nobody.

BEAUTY

Age before beauty.

Beauty is in the eye of the beholder.

Beauty is only skin-deep.

Beauty is truth, truth beauty.

A thing of beauty is a joy for ever.

BED

As you make your bed, so you must lie in it. *See* You've made your bed, now lie in it.

Early to bed and early to rise, makes a man healthy, wealthy, and wise.

Life is no bed of roses.

You've made your bed, now lie in it.

BEDFELLOW

Misery makes strange bedfellows.

Politics makes strange bedfellows.

BEE

If a bee stings you once, it's the bee's fault; if a bee stings you twice, it's your own damn fault. *See* Fool me once, shame on you; fool me twice, shame on me.

BEEF

Where's the beef?

BEER

Life isn't all beer and skittles.

BEFORE

The calm before the storm. *See* After a storm comes a calm.

Cowards die many times before their death. *See* The coward dies many times.

The darkest hour is just before dawn. *See* It's always darkest before the dawn.

Death before dishonor. *See* Better death than dishonor.

Dig the well before you are thirsty.

Don't cast (throw) your pearls before swine.

Don't count your chickens before they are hatched.

Don't put the cart before the horse.

I have promises to keep, and miles to go before I sleep.

It's always darkest before the dawn.

Keep your eyes wide open before marriage, half shut afterwards.

The land was ours before we were the land's.

Look before you leap.

One must crawl before he walks. *See* You have to learn to crawl before you can walk.

Pride goes before a fall.

You have to learn to crawl before you can walk.

You have to learn to walk before you can run.

BEGET

Like begets like. *See* Like breeds like.

Money begets money.

BEGGAR

Beggars can't be choosers.

Give a beggar a horse and he will ride it to death.

If wishes were horses, beggars would ride.

BEGIN, BEGINNING

Charity begins at home.

A good beginning is half the battle.

I have not yet begun to fight.

In the beginning was the word.

A journey of a thousand miles begins with one step.

Life begins at forty.

BEHIND

Behind every great man there is a great
woman.

BEHOLDER

Beauty is in the eye of the beholder.

BELIEVE

Believe it or not.

Believe nothing you hear, and only half of
what you see. *See* Believe only half of what
you see and nothing you hear.

Believe only half of what you see and nothing
you hear.

Don't believe anything (everything) you hear
nor (and) half of what you read. *See*
Believe only half of what you see and nothing you hear.

If you believe that, there is a bridge in
Brooklyn I'd like to sell you.

A liar is not believed when he tells (speaks)
the truth.

Seeing is believing.

You better believe it.

You have to see it to believe it.

BELL

For whom the bell tolls.

That doesn't ring a bell.

BELONG

To the victor belong the spoils.

BEST

Accidents will happen in the best-regulated
families.

All is for the best in the best of all possible
worlds.

Always put your best foot forward.

The best defense is a good offense.

The best is yet to be.

The best-laid schemes of mice and men often
go (gang) a gley.

The best of friends must part.

The best things come in small packages.

The best things in life are free.

A dog is a man's best friend.

Father knows best.

He laughs best who laughs last.

Honesty is the best policy.

Hope for the best and prepare for the worst.

It was the best of times, it was the worst of
times.

Man's best friend is his dog. *See* A dog is a
man's best friend.

Mother knows best. *See* Father knows best.

That government is best which governs least.

BESTOW

Flowers leave fragrance in the hand that
bestows them.

BETRAY

If anyone betrays you once, it's his fault; if he
betrays you twice, it's your fault. *See* Fool me
once, shame on you; fool me twice, shame
on me.

BETTER

Better a big fish in a little pond than a little
fish in a big pond.

Better a live dog than a dead lion. *See* A living
dog is better than a dead lion.

Better death than dishonor.

Better late than never.

Better luck next time.

Better safe than sorry.

Better the devil you know than the devil you
don't know.

Better to give than to receive. *See* It is more
blessed to give than to receive.

Discretion is the better part of valor.

A good name is better than precious ointment.

Half a loaf is better than none (no bread).

It is better to be a big fish in a small pond
than a little fish in a big pond. *See* Better a
big fish in a little pond than a little fish in a
big pond.

It is better to be happy than wise.

It is better to be on the safe side.

It is better to be safe than sorry. *See* Better
safe than sorry.

It is better to die on your feet than live on
your

knees. *See* I would rather die on my feet than
live on my knees.

It is better to give than to receive. *See* It is
more blessed to give than to receive.

It is better to have loved and lost, than never
to have loved at all.

It is better to light one (little) candle than to

curse the darkness.

It is better to travel hopefully than to arrive.

A living dog is better than a dead lion.

Prevention is better than cure. *See* An ounce of prevention is worth a pound of cure.

The sooner the better.

Two heads are better than one.

Wisdom is better than rubies.

You better believe it.

You know better than that.

BETWEEN

Between a rock and a hard place.

Between Scylla and Charybdis.

Between the devil and the deep blue sea.

BEWARE

Beware of Greeks bearing gifts.

Let the buyer beware.

BIG, BIGGER

Better a big fish in a little pond than a little fish in a big pond.

Big Brother is watching you.

The bigger the better.

The bigger they are, the harder they fall.

The eyes are bigger than the stomach.

The further you go, the bigger the fall. *See* The bigger they are, the harder they fall.

If you can't run with the big dogs, stay under the porch.

If you're gonna run with the big dogs, you can't pee like a puppy. *See* If you can't run with the big dogs, stay under the porch.

It is better to be a big fish in a small pond than a little fish in a big pond. *See* Better a big fish in a little pond than a little fish in a big pond.

Speak softly and carry a big stick.

BILL

A clean bill of health.

BIRD

A bird in the hand is worth two in the bush.

Birds in their little nests agree.

Birds of a feather flock together.

The early bird catches the worm.

Fine feathers make fine birds.

It's not the early bird that catches the worm, but the smart one. *See* The early bird catches the worm.

It's the early bird that catches the worm. *See* The early bird catches the worm.

A little bird told (whispered to) me.

BITE, BITTEN

Barking dogs never bite.

Don't bite off more than you can chew.

His bark is worse than his bite.

Once bitten, twice shy. *See* Once burned, twice shy.

To bite the bullet.

When a dog bites a man, that is not news; but when a man bites a dog, that is news.

BITTER

You have to take the bitter with the sweet.

BLACK, BLACKER

The blacker the berry, the sweeter the juice.

The pot calling the kettle black.

There's a black sheep in every flock.

BLEED

Paper bleeds little.

BLESS, BLESSING

God bless America.

It is more blessed to give than to receive.

It's a blessing in disguise.

Blessed are they who expect nothing, for they shall not be disappointed.

BLIND

The blind leading the blind. *See* If the blind lead the blind, both shall fall into the ditch.

Even a blind pig occasionally picks up an acorn.

Friendship is blind. *See* Love is blind.

If the blind lead the blind, both shall fall into the ditch.

In the country of the blind, the one-eyed man is king.

Justice is blind.

Love is blind.

There are none so blind as those who will not see.

BLISS

Ignorance is bliss.

BLOOD

Blood is thicker than water.

Blood, toil, tears and sweat. *See* I have nothing to offer but blood, toil, tears, and sweat.

Blood will tell.

I have nothing to offer but blood, toil, tears, and sweat.

It's in the blood.

You can't get blood from a stone.

You can't get blood out of a turnip. *See* You can't get blood from a stone.

BLOW

It's an ill wind that blows no (nobody) good.

BLUE

Between the devil and the deep blue sea.

BOIL

A watched pot never boils.

BOND

A man's word is as good as his bond.

BONE

Sticks and stones may break my bones, but words (names) will never hurt me.

There's isn't a (specific) bone in one's body.

BOOK

Don't judge a book by its cover.

BOOT

Don't judge a man until you have walked a mile in his boots.

To die with one's boots on.

BOOTSTRAP

Don't try to pull yourself up by your own bootstraps.

BORN

Every man is not born with a silver spoon in his mouth.

A genius is born, not made. *See* Poets are born, not made.

Geniuses, like poets, are born, not taught. *See* Poets are born, not made.

He that is born to be hanged shall never be drowned.

I was not born yesterday.

Poets are born, not made.

There's a time to be born and a time to die. *See* There's a season and a time for every purpose under the heaven.

BOTH

Don't burn the (your) candle at both ends.

If you play both ends against the middle, the middle will soon fold up.

Never light your candle at both ends. *See* Don't burn the (your) candle at both ends.

A plague on both your houses.

BOTTLE

Don't put new wine in old bottles.

The genie is out of the bottle. *See* Let the genie out of the bottle.

Let the genie out of the bottle.

You can't put new wine in old bottles. *See* Don't put new wine in old bottles.

BOUNCE

That's the way the ball bounces. *See* That's the way the cookie crumbles.

BOWL

Life is just a bowl of cherries.

BOX

A Pandora's box.

BOY

All work and no play makes Jack a dull boy.

Boys will be boys.

You can take a boy out of the country, but you can't take the country out of the boy.

BRAVE

The coward dies a thousand deaths, the brave but one. *See* The coward dies many times.

Fortune favors the brave.

BREACH

Once more unto the breach, dear friends.

BREAD

Bread always falls buttered side down.

Cast your bread upon the waters.

Half a loaf is better than none (no bread).

It's the greatest thing since sliced bread.

Man does not live by bread alone.

Whose bread I eat, his song I sing.

BREAK, BROKE

All hell broke loose.

Give me a break!

If it ain't broke, don't fix it.

It's the last straw that breaks the camel's back.

Make or break.

Never give a sucker an even break.

No one ever went broke underestimating the intelligence of the American people.

Pandemonium broke loose. *See* All hell broke loose.

Promises are like piecrust: they are made to be broken.

Rules are made to be broken.

Sticks and stones may break my bones, but words (names) will never hurt me.

You can't make an omelet without breaking eggs.

BREAST

Hope springs eternal in the human breast.

Music hath charms to soothe the savage breast.

BREED

Familiarity breeds contempt.

Like breeds like.

Success breeds success.

BREVITY

Brevity is the soul of wit.

BRICK

You can't make bricks without straw.

BRIDGE

Don't burn your bridges behind you.

Don't cross the bridge till you come to it. *See* Let's cross that bridge when we come to it.

He would try to sell you the Brooklyn Bridge.

If you believe that, there is a bridge in Brooklyn I'd like to sell you.

Let's cross that bridge when we come to it.

Praise the bridge that carries you over.

That's water under the bridge (over the dam).

BRIGHT

Always look on the bright side.

BRING

April showers bring May flowers.

The mountain labored and brought forth a mouse.

BROOKLYN

He would try to sell you the Brooklyn Bridge.

If you believe that, there is a bridge in Brooklyn I'd like to sell you.

BROOM

A new broom sweeps clean.

BROTH

Too many cooks spoil the broth.

BROTHER

Am I my brother's keeper?

Big Brother is watching you.

Brother can you spare a dime?

I am not my brother's keeper. *See* Am I my brother's keeper?

BRUTE

Et tu, Brute?

BUBBLE

Double, double toil and trouble; fire burn, and cauldron bubble.

BUCK

The buck stops here.

BUCKET

It's a drop in the bucket.

BUDDY

Buddy can you spare a dime? *See* Brother can you spare a dime?

BUILD

Don't build castles in the air.

A jackass can kick a barn door down, but it takes a carpenter to build one.

Rome was not built in a day.

BULL

A bull in a china shop.

BUMP

If frogs had wings, they wouldn't bump their tails on rocks.

BUNK

History is bunk.

BURN

A burnt (burned) child fears (dreads) the fire.

Don't burn the (your) candle at both ends.

Don't burn your bridges behind you.

Double, double toil and trouble; fire burn, and cauldron bubble.

Money burns a hole in his pocket.

Nero fiddled while Rome burned.

Once burned, twice shy.

Put on the back burner.

Put on the front burner.

BURY

Let the dead bury the dead.

BUSH

A bird in the hand is worth two in the bush.

BUSHEL

Don't hide your light under a bushel.

BUSINESS

Business as usual.

Business before pleasure.

Business is business.

The business of America is business.

It's none of your business.

Never mix business with pleasure.

That's show business.

There's no business like show business.

BUT

But it does move!

But that's the way it is. *See* And that's the way it is.

Close but no cigar.

From the sublime to the ridiculous is but a step.

Gone but not forgotten.

I disapprove of what you say, but I will defend to the death your right to say it.

I have nothing to offer but blood, toil, tears, and sweat.

It never rains but it pours.

It's not what you know, but who you know.

It's not what you say, but how you say it.

It's not whether you win or lose but how you play the game.

A jackass can kick a barn door down, but it takes a carpenter to build one.

Life is but a dream.

Life is hard by the yard, but by the inch life's a cinch.

Many are called, but few are chosen.

No ifs, ands or buts

Nothing is certain but death and taxes.

The operation was successful—but the patient died.

Opportunity knocks but once.

Poverty is no sin.

The proletarians have nothing to lose but their chains.

The spirit is willing but the flesh is weak.

Thanks, but no thanks.

There's nothing good or bad but thinking makes it so.

Trust everyone, but cut the cards.

We have nothing to fear but fear itself. *See*

The only thing we have to fear is fear itself.

When a dog bites a man, that is not news; but when a man bites a dog, that is news.

You can run, but you can't hide.

You can take a boy out of the country, but you can't take the country out of the boy.

BUTTER

Butter wouldn't melt in his mouth.

BUY, BUYER

Don't buy a pig in a poke.

Let the buyer beware.

Money can't buy happiness.

Talk is cheap, but it takes money to buy land (liquor, whiskey). *See* Talk is cheap.

Would you buy a used car from this man?

BYGONE

Let bygones be bygones.

CAESAR

Caesar's wife must be above suspicion.

Render unto Caesar the things which are Caesar's and unto God the things that are God's.

CAKE

It's a piece of cake.

Let them eat cake.

You can't have your cake and eat it too.

CALL

Call a spade a spade.

Call me Ishmael.

Don't call us, we'll call you.

He who pays the piper calls the tune.

It's a close call.

Many are called, but few are chosen.

The pot calling the kettle black.

CALM

After a storm comes a calm.

CAMEL

It is easier for a camel to go (pass) through the eye of a needle than it is for a rich man to enter the kingdom of heaven.

It's the last straw that breaks the camel's back.

CAN

It's like opening a can of worms.

CANDLE

Better to light one candle than curse the darkness. *See* It is better to light one (little) candle than to curse the darkness.

Don't burn the (your) candle at both ends.

The game is not worth the candle.

The game is worth the candle. *See* The game is not worth the candle.

It is better to light one (little) candle than to curse the darkness.

Never light your candle at both ends. *See* Don't burn the (your) candle at both ends.

CANDY

It's like taking candy from a baby.

CANOE

Paddle your own canoe.

CAR

A car in every garage and a chicken in every pot. *See* A chicken in every pot.

Would you buy a used car from this man?

CARAVAN

The dogs bark, but the caravan goes on.

CARD

Trust everyone, but cut the cards.

CARE

I couldn't care less.

CAREFUL

Be careful what you wish for. You might get it. *See* Don't wish too hard: you might just get what you wished for.

CARPE DIEM.

See Seize the moment.

CARPENTER

A jackass can kick a barn door down, but it takes a carpenter to build one.

CARRY

Praise the bridge that carries you over.

Speak softly and carry a big stick.

CART

Don't put the cart before the horse.

CARTHAGE

Carthage must be destroyed.

CAST

The die is cast.

Don't cast (throw) your pearls before swine.

Let him who is without sin cast (throw) the first stone.

CASTLE

Don't build castles in Spain. *See* Don't build castles in the air.

Don't build castles in the air.

A man's home is his castle.

CAT

All cats are gray in the dark.

Cat got your tongue? *See* Has the cat got your tongue?

A cat has nine lives.

A/The cat in gloves catches no mice.

The cat is out of the bag.

Curiosity killed the cat.

Has the cat got your tongue?

There are more ways to kill a cat besides (without) choking (skinning) him to death. *See* There's more than one way to skin a cat.

There's more than one way to skin a cat.

When the cat's away, the mice will play.

CATCH

A cat in gloves catches no mice.

A drowning man will catch at a straw.

The early bird catches the worm.

Give a man a fish, and you feed him for a day; show (teach) him how to catch fish, and you feed him for a lifetime.

It takes a thief to catch a thief.

Set a thief to catch a thief. *See* It takes a thief to catch a thief.

You can catch more flies with honey than with vinegar.

CATCH-22

It's a Catch-22 situation.

CAULDRON

Double, double toil and trouble; fire burn, and cauldron bubble.

CAUTION

Don't throw caution to the wind.

CENT

What this country needs is a good five-cent cigar.

CERTAIN

Nothing is certain but death and taxes.

C'EST LA VIE.

See That's life.

CHAIN

A chain is no stronger than its weakest link.

The proletarians have nothing to lose but their chains.

CHANCE

Give peace a chance!

You pays your money, and you takes your chance. *See* You pays your money, and you takes your choice.

CHANGE

Don't change horses in midstream. *See* Don't swap horses in midstream.

Don't change the rules in the middle of the game.

The leopard can't change its spots.

The more things change, the more they stay the same.

Times change and we with time.

CHARACTER

Character is destiny.

CHARITY

Charity begins at home.

With malice toward none, with charity for all.

CHARM

Music hath charms to soothe the savage breast.

The third time is the charm.

CHARYBDIS

Between Scylla and Charybdis.

CHEAP

Prevention is cheaper than treatment. *See* An ounce of prevention is worth a pound of cure.

Talk is cheap.

CHECK

The check is in the mail.

CHERRY

Life is just a bowl of cherries.

CHEW

Don't bite off more than you can chew.

CHICKEN

A chicken in every pot.

The chickens have come home to roost.

Curses, like chickens, come home to roost. *See* The chickens have come to roost.

Don't count your chickens before they are hatched.

It's the fox guarding the chicken house. *See* Don't let the fox guard the henhouse.

Which came first, the chicken or the egg?

CHIEF

All chiefs and no Indians.

Hail to the Chief.

Too many chiefs and not enough Indians. *See* All chiefs and no Indians.

CHILD

The child is father of the man.

A cobbler's child is always the worst shod. *See* The shoemaker's kids always go barefoot.

Spare the rod and spoil the child.

It takes a village to raise a child.

CHIP

Let the chips fall where they may.

CHOICE

Hobson's choice.

You pays your money, and you takes your choice.

CHOKE

There are more ways to kill a cat besides (without) choking (skinning) him to death. *See* There's more than one way to skin a cat.

CHOOSE, CHOSEN, CHOOSER

Beggars can't be choosers.

Choose the lesser of two evils.

Many are called, but few are chosen.

Of two evils, choose the lesser. *See* Choose the lesser of two evils.

CIGAR

Close but no cigar.

What this country needs is a good five-cent cigar.

CINCH

Life is hard by the yard, but by the inch life's a cinch.

CIRCLE

The wheel comes full circle.

CITE

The devil can cite scripture for his purpose.

CITY HALL
You can't fight City Hall.

CLEAN, CLEANLINESS
A clean bill of health.

Cleanliness is next to godliness.

Keep your nose clean.

A new broom sweeps clean.

CLOSE
Close but no cigar.

Don't close (bar, lock, shut) the barn (stable) door after the horse runs away (has fled, has been stolen).

That's too close for comfort.

CLOSET
There's a skeleton in every closet.

CLOTH, CLOTHES, CLOTHING
Clothes don't make the man.

Clothes make the man.

The Emperor has no clothes on.

A/The wolf in sheep's clothing.

You must cut your coat according to your cloth.

CLOUD
Every cloud has a silver lining.

COAT
You must cut your coat according to your cloth.

COBBLER
A/The cobbler should stick to his last.

A cobbler's child is always the worst shod. *See* The shoemaker's kids always go barefoot.

COKE
He couldn't sell Coke in the Sahara. *See* He could sell ice to an Eskimo.

COLD
Cold hands, warm heart.

Feed a cold; starve a fever.

COLOR
That's a horse of a different color.

COMBINE
Combine business with pleasure. *See* Business before pleasure.

COME, CAME
After a storm comes a calm.

After the feast comes the reckoning.

All good things come in threes.

All good things come to those who wait.

All good things must come to an end.

All is grist that comes to the mill. *See* It's all grist for the mill

The best things come in small packages.

The British are coming.

The chickens have come home to roost.

Curses, like chickens, come home to roost. *See* The chickens have come home to roost.

Don't cross the bridge till you come to it. *See* Let's cross that bridge when we come to it.

Easy come, easy go.

Everything comes to an end. *See* All good things must come to an end.

Everything comes to those (the man, him) who (can, know how to) wait. *See* All good things come to those who wait.

Everything's coming up roses.

First come, first served.

From the mouths of babes come words of wisdom. *See* Out of the mouths of babes and sucklings come great truths.

I came, I saw, I conquered.

If the mountain will not come to Mohammed, Mohammed will go to the mountain.

It comes with the territory.

It will all come out in the wash.

It's a dream come true.

Let's cross that bridge when we come to it.

Nothing will come of nothing.

Now is the time for all good men to come to the aid of their country.

Out of the mouths of babes and sucklings come great truths.

The Russians are coming. *See* The British are coming.

Truth will (come) out.

What goes around, comes around.

What goes up must come down.

When you come to a fork in the road, take it.

Which came first, the chicken or the egg?

You've come a long way, baby.

COMFORT
That's too close for comfort.

COMPANY
A man is known (judged) by the company he keeps.

Misery loves company.

Money loves company. *See* Money begets money.

Two is company, three is a crowd.

COMPARISON
Comparisons are odious.

CONCENTRATE
I can't think when I concentrate.

CONDEMN
Those who cannot remember the past are condemned to repeat it.

CONQUER
Divide and conquer.

I came, I saw, I conquered.

CONSIDER
Consider the lilies of the field.

CONSISTENCY
A foolish consistency is the hobgoblin of little minds.

CONTEMPT
Familiarity breeds contempt.

COOK
Too many cooks spoil the broth.

COOKIE
That's the way the cookie crumbles.

CORRUPT
Power corrupts, and absolute power corrupts absolutely.

COST
It's the first step that costs. *See* The first step is the hardest.

COUNT
Don't count your chickens before they are hatched.

Stand up and be counted.

Who's counting?

COUNTENANCE
A merry heart makes a cheerful countenance.

COUNTRY, COUNTRYMEN
Ask not what your country can do for you; ask what you can do for your country.

First in war, first in peace, first in the hearts of his countrymen.

I only regret that I have but one life to lose for my country.

In the country of the blind, the one-eyed man is king.

My country, right or wrong. *See* Our country, right or wrong.

Now is the time for all good men to come to the aid of their country.

Our country, right or wrong.

A prophet is not without honor, save in his own country.

What this country needs is a good five-cent cigar.

You can take a boy out of the country, but you can't take the country out of the boy.

COURSE
The course of true love never did run smooth.

Let nature take its course.

Nature will take its course. *See* Let nature take its course.

COURT
The ball is in your court.

COVER
Don't judge a book by its cover.

COWARD
The coward dies many times.

CRACK
Step on a crack, break your mother's back.

CRAWL
You have to learn to crawl before you can walk.

CREAM
Cream always comes to the top.

CREDIT
Give credit where credit is due.

CRIME
Crime doesn't pay.

CROOK
I am not a crook.

Once a crook, always a crook. *See* Once a thief, always a thief.

CROSS
Crossing the Rubicon.

Don't cross the bridge till you come to it. *See* Let's cross that bridge when we come to it.

Keep your fingers crossed.

Let's cross that bridge when we come to it.

CROWD

Two is company, three is a crowd.

CROWN

Uneasy lies the head that wears the crown.

CRUMBLE

That's the way the cookie crumbles.

CRY

Cry (yell) uncle. *See* Say uncle.

Don't cry over spilled milk.

Laugh and the world laughs with you; cry and you cry alone. *See* Laugh and the world laughs with you; weep and you weep alone.

Never cry wolf.

CULTURE

When I hear the word culture, I reach for my gun.

CUP

The cup is either half empty or half full. *See* The glass is either half empty or half full.

It's not my cup of tea.

The last drop makes the cup run over.

There's many a slip between (the) cup and (the) lip.

CURE

Like cures like.

An ounce of prevention is worth a pound of cure.

What can't be cured must be endured.

CURIOSITY

Curiosity killed the cat.

CURSE

Curses, like chickens, come home to roost. *See* The chickens have come home to roost.

It is better to light one (small) candle than to curse the darkness.

CUSTOM

Age cannot wither her, nor custom stale her infinite variety.

CUSTOMER

The customer is always right.

CUT

Cut the coat according to the cloth. *See* You must cut your coat according to your cloth.

Don't cut off your nose to spite your face.

Fish or cut bait.

Trust everyone, but cut the cards.

You must cut your coat according to your cloth.

DAM

That's water under the bridge (over the dam).

DAMN

Damn the torpedoes! Full speed ahead!

If a bee stings you once, it's the bee's fault; if a bee stings you twice, it's your own damn fault. *See* Fool me once, shame on you; fool me twice, shame on me.

My dear, I don't give a damn.

You'll be damned if you do and damned if you don't.

DAMOCLES

The sword of Damocles hanging over one.

DANCE

He who dances must pay the fiddler.

DANGEROUS

A little knowledge (learning) is a dangerous thing.

DARK, DARKER, DARKEST, DARKNESS

All cats are gray in the dark.

Better to light one candle than curse the darkness. *See* It is better to light one (little) candle than to curse the darkness.

The darker the berry, the sweeter the juice. *See* The blacker the berry, the sweeter the juice.

The darkest hour is just before dawn. *See* It's always darkest before the dawn

I wouldn't like to meet him in the dark.

It is better to light one (little) candle than to curse the darkness.

It's always darkest before the dawn.

DATE

It's a date which will live in infamy.

DAUGHTER

Like mother, like daughter.

DAWN

It's always darkest before the dawn.

DAY

All in a day's work. *See* It's all in a day's work.

Another day, another dollar.

An apple a day keeps the doctor away.

Every dog has his day.

Give a man a fish, and you feed him for a day; show (teach) him how to catch fish, and you feed him for a lifetime.

Go ahead, make my day. *See* Make my day.

Happy days are here again.

He who fights and runs away, may live to fight another day.

I wouldn't give him the time of day.

It's all in a day's work.

Make my day.

One day at a time.

Rome was not built in a day.

Save for a rainy day.

Seize the day. *See* Seize the moment.

Tomorrow is another day.

DEAD

Better a live dog than a dead lion. *See* A living dog is better than a dead lion.

Dead in the water.

Dead men never bite.

Dead on arrival.

Dead men tell no tales.

Let the dead bury the dead.

A living dog is better than a dead lion.

Never speak ill of the dead.

Over my dead body.

DEAF

There are none so deaf as those who will not hear. *See* There are none so blind as those who will not see.

DEAR

Elementary, my dear Watson, elementary!

My dear, I don't give a damn.

Once more unto the breach, dear friends.

DEATH

Better death than dishonor.

The coward dies a thousand deaths, the brave but one. *See* The coward dies many times.

Cowards die many times before their death. *See* The coward dies many times.

Death is a great leveler.

Give me liberty or give me death!

I disapprove of what you say, but I will defend to the death your right to say it.

In this world nothing is certain but death and taxes. *See* Nothing is certain but death and taxes.

The reports of my death are greatly exaggerated.

There are more ways to kill a cat besides (without) choking (skinning) him to death. *See* There's more than one way to skin a cat.

Till death do us part.

DECEIVE, DECEPTIVE

Appearances (looks) are deceiving (deceptive).

What a tangled web we weave when first we practice to deceive.

DEED

Deeds, not words.

No good deed goes unpunished.

DEEP

Beauty is only skin-deep.

Between the devil and the deep blue sea.

Still waters run deep.

DEFEAT

Victory has a hundred fathers and defeat is an orphan.

DEFEND

Defend me from my friends. *See* Save us from our friends.

I disapprove of what you say, but I will defend to the death your right to say it.

DEFENSE

The best defense is good offense.

DÉJÀ VU.

It's déjà vu all over again.

DELUGE

After us the deluge.

DENMARK

Something is rotten in the state of Denmark.

DEPEND

It all depends on whose ox is gored.

DESERT

Rats desert a sinking ship.

DESERVE

One good turn deserves another.

DESIGN

Luck is the residue of design.

DESTROY

Carthage must be destroyed.

Whom the gods would destroy, they first make mad.

DETAILS

God is in the details.

DEVIL

Better the devil you know than the devil you don't know.

Between the devil and the deep blue sea.

The devil can cite scripture for his purpose.

The devil is in the details. *See* God is in the details.

The devil take the hindmost.

Every man for himself, and the devil take the hindmost. *See* The devil take the hindmost.

Give the devil his due.

Idle hands are the devil's tools.

Talk of the devil, and he is bound to appear.

Tell the truth and shame the devil.

DIE

The coward dies many times.

Do or die.

Eat, drink, and be merry, for tomorrow we die.

He who lives by the sword dies by the sword.

I would rather die on my feet than live on my knees.

Never say die.

Old habits die hard.

Old soldiers never die; they just fade away.

There's a time to be born and a time to die. *See*

There's a season and a time for every purpose under the heaven.

DIE (DICE)

The die is cast.

DIFFER

Tastes differ. *See* There's no accounting for tastes.

DIFFERENT

Different strokes for different folks.

It's a different (new) ball game (ballpark).

DIG

Dig the well before you are thirsty.

DIME

Brother can you spare a dime?

DIRTY

Don't air your dirty linen in public.

DISAPPROVE

I disapprove of what you say, but I will defend to the death your right to say it.

DISCONTENT

The winter of our discontent.

DISCRETION

Discretion is the better part of valor.

DISGRACE

Poverty is no disgrace. *See* Poverty is no sin.

DISGUISE

It's a blessing in disguise.

DISHONOR

Better death than dishonor.

DISPOSE

Man proposes, God disposes.

DITCH

If the blind lead the blind, both shall fall into the ditch.

DIVIDE

Divide and conquer.

United we stand, divided we fall.

DIVINE

To err is human, to forgive divine.

DO, DOES, DONE

Do as I say, not as I do.

Do as you would be done by. *See* Do unto others as you would have them do unto you.

Do not go gentle into that good night.

Do or die.

Do unto others as you would have them do unto you.

Easier said than done.

Easy does it.

Everybody talks about the weather, but nobody does anything about it.

Everybody's doin' it.

First, do no harm.

He who can, does; he who cannot, teaches. *See* Those who can, do. Those who cannot, teach.

Handsome (pretty) is as handsome (pretty)

does.

Here I stand. I can do no other.

If you want something done right, do it yourself.

The king can do no wrong.

A man's got to do what a man's got to do.

Never let your left hand know what your right hand is doing.

Watch what we do, not what we say.

What's done cannot be undone.

What's done is done.

When in doubt, do nothing.

When in Rome, do as the Romans do.

You'll be damned if you do and damned if you don't.

DOCTOR

An apple a day keeps the doctor away.

Doctor Livingstone, I presume.

Dr. Jekyll and Mr. Hyde.

It's just what the doctor ordered.

DOG

As a dog returns to his vomit, so a fool returns to his folly. *See* The dog always returns to his vomit.

Barking dogs never bite.

The dog always returns to his vomit.

Dog doesn't (won't) eat dog. *See* Dog eat dog.

Dog eat dog.

The dog has returned to his vomit again. *See* The dog always returns to his vomit.

A dog is a man's best friend.

The dogs bark, but the caravan goes on.

Every dog has his day.

He who lies down with dogs will rise up with fleas. *See* If you lie down with dogs, you'll get up with fleas.

If you can't run with the big dogs, stay under the porch.

If you lie down with dogs, you'll get up with fleas.

If you're gonna run with the big dogs, you can't pee like a puppy. *See* If you can't run with the big dogs, stay under the porch.

Let sleeping dogs lie.

Love me, love my dog.

A living dog is better than a dead lion.

The tail cannot shake the dog.

You can't teach an old dog new tricks.

DOLLAR

Another day, another dollar.

DOOR

Don't close (bar, lock, shut) the barn (stable) door after the horse runs away (has fled, has been stolen).

A jackass can kick a barn door down, but it takes a carpenter to build one.

Keep the wolf from the door. *See* The wolf is at the door.

Opportunity never knocks twice at any man's door. *See* Opportunity knocks but once.

When one door closes, another one opens.

The wolf is at the door.

DOUBLE

Double, double toil and trouble; fire burn, and cauldron bubble.

DOUBT

When in doubt, do nothing.

DOWN

A jackass can kick a barn door down, but it takes a carpenter to build one.

Sell down the river.

DOZEN

It's six of one and half a dozen of the other. *See* Six of one and half a dozen of the other.

DREAM

I have a dream.

It's a dream come true.

Life is but a dream.

DRINK

Alcohol (drinking) and driving don't mix. *See* Oil and water don't mix.

Eat, drink, and be merry, for tomorrow we die.

Water, water everywhere, nor any drop to drink.

DRIVE

Alcohol (drinking) and driving don't mix. *See* Oil and water don't mix.

Bad money drives out good.

What are you driving at?

DROP

It's a drop in the bucket.

Water, water everywhere, nor any drop to

drink.

You could hear a pin drop.

DROWNING

A drowning man will catch at a straw.

He could sell a drowning man a glass of water. *See* He could sell ice to an Eskimo.

DRUMMER

Marching to a different drummer.

DRUNKARD

Once a drunkard, always a drunkard. *See* Once a thief, always a thief.

DRY

Put your trust in God, and keep your powder dry.

You never miss the water till the well runs dry.

DUCK

Go hunting where the ducks are.

If it looks like a duck, walks like a duck, and quacks like a duck, it's a duck.

DUE

Give credit where credit is due.

Give the devil his due.

Pay the piper his due.

DULL

All work and no play makes Jack a dull boy.

DWARF

Dwarfs standing on the shoulders of giants. *See* If I have seen further it is by standing on the shoulders of giants.

EACH

From each according to his ability, to each according to his needs.

To each his own.

EAR

From your lips to God's ears.

It goes in one ear and out the other.

It's music to my ears.

Walls have ears.

You can't make a silk purse out of a sow's ear.

EARLY

The early bird catches the worm.

Early to bed and early to rise, makes a man healthy, wealthy, and wise.

EARN

A penny saved is a penny earned.

EARTH

Give me where to stand, and I will move the earth.

The meek shall inherit the earth.

EAST

East is East, and West is West, and never the twain shall meet.

EASY, EASIER

Easier said than done.

Easy come, easy go.

Easy does it.

It is easier for a camel to go (pass) through the eye of a needle than it is for a rich man to enter the kingdom of heaven.

It is easy to be wise after the event.

Take it easy.

EAT

Dog doesn't (won't) eat dog. *See* Dog eat dog.

Dog eat dog.

Eat, drink, and be merry, for tomorrow we die.

Eat to live; do not live to eat.

He who does not work, neither should he eat.

Let them eat cake.

The proof of the pudding is in the eating.

Whose bread I eat, his song I sing.

You are what you eat.

You can't have your cake and eat it too.

ECONOMY

It's the economy, Stupid!

EGG

Don't kill the goose that laid the golden egg.

Don't put all your eggs in one basket.

Don't (try to) teach your grandmother (how) to suck eggs.

Scrambled eggs can't be unscrambled. *See* You can't unscramble eggs.

Which came first, the chicken or the egg?

You can't make an omelet without breaking eggs.

You can't unscramble eggs.

ELEMENTARY

Elementary, my dear Watson, elementary!

ELEPHANT

An elephant never forgets.

EMPEROR

The Emperor has no clothes on.

EMPTY

The glass is either half empty or half full.

END

All good things must come to an end.

All's well that ends well

Don't burn the (your) candle at both ends.

The end justifies the means.

Everything comes to an end. *See* All good things must come to an end.

Everything has an end. *See* All good things must come to an end.

If you play both ends against the middle, the middle will soon fold up.

It's not the end of the world.

The light at the end of the tunnel. *See* There's always a light at the end of the tunnel.

Never light your candle at both ends. *See* Don't burn the (your) candle at both ends.

There's always a light at the end of the tunnel.

There's a pot of gold at the end of the rainbow.

You can't burn your candle at both ends. *See* Don't burn the (your) candle at both ends.

ENDURE

What can't be cured must be endured.

ENEMY

God save me from my friends—I can protect myself from my enemies. *See* Save us from our friends.

The enemy of my enemy is my friend.

Every man is his own worst enemy.

Save us from our enemies.

We have met the enemy, and they are ours.

With such friends, one hardly needs enemies.

ENOUGH

Enough is enough.

Give him enough rope and he'll hang himself.

Leave well enough alone.

Too many chiefs and not enough Indians. *See* All chiefs and no Indians.

A word to the wise is enough. *See* A word to the wise is sufficient.

ENTER

Abandon all hope, ye who enter here.

It is easier for a camel to go (pass) through the eye of a needle than it is for a rich man to enter the kingdom of heaven.

ENVELOPE

Pushing the envelope.

EQUAL

All animals are equal, but some animals are more equal than others.

All men are created equal.

ERR

To err is human, to forgive divine.

ESKIMO

He could sell ice to an Eskimo.

ET

Et tu, Brute?

ETERNAL

Hope springs eternal in the human breast.

EUREKA

Eureka!

EVEN

Don't get mad, get even.

Even a blind pig occasionally picks up an acorn.

Even a worm will turn.

Even Homer sometimes nods.

EVENT

It is easy to be wise after the event.

EVER

Be it ever so humble, there's no place like home. *See* There's no place like home.

A thing of beauty is a joy for ever.

EVERY

Behind every successful man there is a woman. *See* Behind every great man there is a great woman.

A car in every garage and a chicken in every pot. *See* A chicken in every pot.

A chicken in every pot.

Every cloud has a silver lining.

Every dog has his day.

Every employee tends to rise to his level of incompetence.

Every little bit helps.

Every man for himself.

Every man for himself, and the devil take the hindmost. *See* The devil take the hindmost.

Every man is his own worst enemy.

Every man is not born with a silver spoon in his mouth.

Every man is the architect of his own fortune.

Every man makes mistakes. *See* He who never made a mistake never made anything.

Every man to his own taste.

There are two sides to every story.

There's a season and a time for every purpose under the heaven.

There's a skeleton in every closet.

There's a sucker born every minute.

EVERYBODY

Everybody is wise after the event. *See* It is easier to be wise after the event.

Everybody talks about the weather, but nobody does anything about it.

Everybody's doin' it.

EVERYONE

Everyone has his fifteen minutes of fame.

Everyone to his own taste. *See* Every man to his own taste.

Everyone to whom much is given, of him will much be required.

Trust everyone, but cut the cards.

EVERYTHING

Don't believe anything (everything) you hear nor (and) half of what you read. *See* Believe only half of what you see and nothing you hear.

Everything but the kitchen sink.

Everything comes to an end. *See* All good things must come to an end.

Everything comes to those (the man, him) who (can, know how to) wait. *See* All good things come to those who wait.

Everything falls into place.

Everything has an end. *See* All good things must come to an end.

Everything is not all peaches and cream.

Everything old is new again.

Everything's coming up roses.

Everything's hunky-dory.

Everything's under control.

Money isn't everything.

A place for everything and everything in its place.

There's a time and place for everything.

There's always a first time for everything. *See* There must be a first time for everything.

There's a time for everything. *See* There's a time and place for everything.

There's good and bad in everything.

There must be a first time for everything.

Timing is everything.

Winning isn't everything, it's the only thing.

EVIL

Choose the lesser of two evils.

Evil to him who evil thinks.

Hear no evil, see no evil, speak no evil. *See* See no evil, hear no evil, speak no evil.

The love of money is the root of all evil. *See* Money is the root of all evil.

Money is the root of all evil.

Of two evils, choose the lesser. *See* Choose the lesser of two evils.

See no evil, hear no evil, speak no evil.

EXAGGERATE

The reports of my death are greatly exaggerated.

EXCEPTION

There is an exception to every rule.

EXCUSE

Ignorance of the law is no excuse.

EXPERIENCE

Experience is the best teacher.

EXTREME

Extremes meet. *See* Opposites meet.

EYE

Beauty is in the eye of the beholder.

An eye for an eye, a tooth for a tooth.

The eyes are bigger than the stomach.

The eyes are the mirror(s) of the soul (mind).

Don't fire until you see the whites of their eyes.

In the country of the blind, the one-eyed man is king.

It is easier for a camel to go (pass) through the eye of a needle than it is for a rich man to enter the kingdom of heaven.

Keep your eyes open and your mouth shut. *See* Keep your mouth shut and your eyes open.

Keep your eyes wide open before marriage, half shut afterwards.

Keep your mouth shut and your eyes open.

There's more to it than meets the eye.

FACE

Don't cut off your nose to spite your face.

Let's face it.

FACT

Fact is stranger than fiction. *See* Truth is stranger than fiction.

Facts are facts.

Facts are stubborn things.

FADE

Old soldiers never die; they just fade away.

FAILURE

Success is never final and failure is never fatal. *See* Success is never final.

FAINT

Faint heart never won fair lady.

FAIR

All's fair in love and war.

Faint heart never won fair lady.

Turnabout is fair play.

FALL

The apple doesn't fall far from the tree.

The bigger they are, the harder they fall.

Everything falls into place.

If the blind lead the blind, both shall fall into the ditch.

Let the chips fall where they may.

Pride goes before a fall.

The sky is not falling. *See* The sky is not going to fall.

The sky is not going to fall.

United we stand, divided we fall.

FAME

Everyone has his fifteen minutes of fame.

FAMILIARITY

Familiarity breeds contempt.

FAMILY

Accidents will happen in the best-regulated families.

All in the family. *See* It's all in the family.

As the family goes, so goes the nation. *See* As Maine goes, so goes the nation.

The family that prays together stays together.

It runs in the family.

It's all in the family.

There's a black sheep in every family. *See* There's a black sheep in every flock.

FAN

The shit hits the fan.

FANCY

In the spring a young man's fancy lightly turns to thoughts of love.

FAR

The apple doesn't fall far from the tree.

So far, so good.

FAST

Bad news travels fast.

FAT

The fat is in the fire.

It's not over till the fat lady sings. *See* The opera ain't over till the fat lady sings.

The opera ain't over till the fat lady sings.

FATAL

Success is never final and failure is never fatal. *See* Success is never final.

FATHER

The child is father of the man.

Father knows best.

Honor thy father and thy mother.

Like father, like son.

Victory has a hundred fathers and defeat is an orphan.

FAULT

If a bee stings you once, it's the bee's fault; if a bee stings you twice, it's your own damn fault. *See* Fool me once, shame on you; fool me twice, shame on me.

If anyone betrays you once, it's his fault; it he betrays you twice, it's your fault. *See* Fool me once, shame on you; fool me twice, shame on me.

FAVOR

Fortune favors the brave.

FEAR

Fear the Greeks bearing gifts. *See* Beware of Greeks bearing gifts.

Fools rush in where angels fear to tread.

I fear the Greeks, even when they are bearing gifts. *See* Beware of Greeks bearing gifts.

The only thing we have to fear is fear itself.

We have nothing to fear but fear itself. *See* The only thing we have to fear is fear itself.

FEAST

After the feast comes the reckoning.

FEATHER

Birds of a feather flock together.

Feather your own nest.

Fine feathers make fine birds.

FEED

Don't bite the hand that feeds you.

Feed a cold; starve a fever.

Give a man a fish, and you feed him for a day; show (teach) him how to catch fish, and you feed him for a lifetime.

FEEL

A man is as old as he feels.

FEET

I would rather die on my feet than live on my knees.

Keep your feet on the ground.

Stand on your own two feet.

FELL

Little strokes fell great oaks.

FENCE

Don't take (tear) down a fence (wall) unless you are sure why it was put up.

Good fences make good neighbors.

The grass is always greener on the other side of the fence.

FEVER

Feed a cold; starve a fever.

FEW

Many are called, but few are chosen.

You win some (a few), you lose some (a few).

FICTION

Truth is stranger than fiction.

FIDDLE, FIDDLER

He who dances must pay the fiddler.

Nero fiddled while Rome burned.

FIELD

Consider the lilies of the field.

FIFTEEN

Everyone has his fifteen minutes of fame.

FIGHT

Fight fire with fire.

He who fights and runs away, may live to fight another day.

I have not yet begun to fight.

You can't fight City Hall.

FIGURE

Figures don't lie.

It figures.

FINAL

Success is never final.

FIND, FINDER

Ask, and it shall be given you; seek, and you shall find; knock, and it shall be opened unto you.

Even a blind pig finds an acorn once in a while. *See* Even a blind pig occasionally picks up an acorn.

Finders keepers, losers weepers.

A good man is hard to find.

The husband is always the last to find out.

Seek and ye shall find. *See* Ask, and it shall be given you; seek, and you shall find; knock, and it shall be opened unto you.

FINE

Fine feathers make fine birds.

FINISH

Don't start anything you can't finish.

Nice guys finish last.

FIRE

Don't fire until you see the whites of their eyes.

Don't have too many irons in the fire.

Don't jump from the frying pan into the fire.

Don't play with fire.

Double, double toil and trouble; fire burn, and cauldron bubble.

The fat is in the fire.

Fight fire with fire.

Fire in the belly.

Fire is a good servant but a bad master.

He'll never set the world on fire.

No smoke without fire. *See* Where there's smoke, there's fire.

Out of the frying pan into the fire. *See* Don't jump from the frying pan into the fire.

Where there's smoke, there's fire.

FIRST

Do you want the good news or the bad first? *See* The good news is …; the bad news is …

First catch your rabbit and then make your stew.

First come, first served.

First, do no harm.

First impressions are the most lasting.

First in war, first in peace, first in the hearts of his countrymen.

The first one hundred years are the hardest.

The first step is the hardest.

First things first.

If at first you don't succeed, try, try again.

It's the first step that costs. *See* The first step is the hardest.

Let him who is without sin cast (throw) the first stone.

Put first things first. *See* First things first.

Safety first.

Shoot first and ask questions afterwards.

There must be a first time for everything.

What a tangled web we weave when first we practice to deceive.

Which came first, the chicken or the egg?

Whom the gods would destroy, they first make mad.

FISH

Better a big fish in a little pond than a little fish in a big pond.

Fish or cut bait.

A fish out of water.

A fish stinks from the head.

A fishing expedition.

Fish where the fish are.

Give a man a fish, and you feed him for a day; show (teach) him how to catch fish, and you feed him for a lifetime.

There are other fish in the sea.

FIT, FITTEST

It ain't a fit night out for man or beast.

If the shoe fits, wear it.

It's survival of the fittest.

You can't fit a round peg in a square hole.

FIVE

What this country needs is a good five-cent cigar.

FIX

If it ain't broke, don't fix it.

FLATTERY

Imitation is the sincerest form of flattery.

FLAUNT

If you've got it, flaunt it.

FLEA

If you lie down with dogs, you'll get up with fleas.

FLESH

The spirit is willing but the flesh is weak.

FLING

Youth will have its fling.

FLOCK

Birds of a feather flock together.

There's a black sheep in every flock.

FLOW

Go with the flow.

FLOWER

April showers bring May flowers.

Flowers leave fragrance in the hand that bestows them.

FLY

He wouldn't hurt a fly.

If a pig had wings, it could fly.

It takes two wings to fly.

Time flies.

You can catch more flies with honey than with vinegar.

You can't fly with one wing. *See* It takes two wings to fly.

FOLK

Different strokes for different folks.

FOLLY

As a dog returns to his vomit, so a fool returns to his folly. *See* A dog always returns to his vomit.

FONDER

Absence makes the heart grow fonder.

FOOL

A fool and his money are soon parted.

A fool can ask more questions in an hour than a wise man can answer in seven years.

Fool me once, shame on you; fool me twice, shame on me.

Fools rush in where angels fear to tread.

There's no fool like an old fool.

You can fool some of the people all the time, all the people some of the time, but you cannot fool all the people all the time.

FOOLISH

Don't be penny-wise and dollar-foolish. *See* Penny-wise and pound-foolish.

A foolish consistency is the hobgoblin of little minds.

Penny-wise and pound-foolish.

FOOT

Always put your best foot forward.

Give him an inch, and he will take a mile.

I wouldn't touch it (him) with a ten-foot pole.

The shoe is on the other foot.

FOOTPRINT

Footprints on the sands of time.

FORBIDDEN

Forbidden fruit is sweet.

FOREARMED

Forewarned is forearmed.

FOREWARNED

Forewarned is forearmed.

FORGET, FORGOTTEN

An elephant never forgets.

Forgive and forget.

Gone but not forgotten.

FORGIVE

Forgive and forget.

To err is human, to forgive divine.

FORK

When you come to a fork in the road, take it.

Fingers were made before forks.

FORM

Attack is the best form of defense. *See* The best defense is a good offense.

Imitation is the sincerest form of flattery.

FORTUNE

Fortune favors the brave.

FORWARD

Always put your best foot forward.

FOX

Don't let the fox guard the henhouse.

FRAGRANCE

Flowers leave fragrance in the hand that bestows them.

FRAILTY

Frailty, thy name is woman.

FREE

The best things in life are free.

The land of the free and the home of the brave.

There's no such thing as a free lunch.

There's no such thing as a free ride.

The truth shall make you free.

FREEZE

Till hell freezes over.

FRIDAY

Thank God It's Friday.

FRIEND, FRIENDSHIP

The best of friends must part.

Defend me from my friends. *See* Save us from our friends.

A dog is a man's best friend.

The enemy of my enemy is my friend.

A friend in need is a friend indeed.

Friendship is blind. *See* Love is blind.

God save me from my friends—I can protect myself from my enemies. *See* Save us from our friends.

Once more unto the breach, dear friends.

Save us from our friends.

Wealth makes many friends.

With such friends, one hardly needs enemies.

FROG

If frogs had wings, they wouldn't bump their tails on rocks.

FRUIT

Forbidden fruit is sweet.

A tree is known by its fruit.

FRYING PAN

Don't jump from the frying pan into the fire.

FULL

The cup is either half empty or half full. *See* The glass is either half empty or half full.

Damn the torpedoes! Full speed ahead!

Full speed (ahead)! *See* Damn the torpedoes! Full speed ahead!

The glass is either half empty or half full.

The wheel comes full circle.

FUNERAL

It's *your* funeral.

FURTHER

The further you go, the bigger the fall. *See* The bigger they are, the harder they fall.

If I have seen further it is by standing on the shoulders of giants.

Nothing could be further from the truth.

FURY

Hell hath no fury like a woman scorned.

FUTURE

The future ain't what it used to be.

I have seen the future, and it works.

GAIN

No pain, no gain. *See* There are no gains without pains.

Nothing ventured, nothing gained.

One man's loss is another man's gain.

There are no gains without pains.

GAME

Don't change the rules in the middle of the game.

The game is not worth the candle.

The game is worth the candle. *See* The game is not worth the candle.

It's a different (new) ball game (ballpark).

It's not whether you win or lose but how you play the game.

It's the only game in town.

That's the name of the game.

You can't beat a man at his own game.

GANDER

What's sauce for the goose is sauce for the gander.

GARAGE

A car in every garage and a chicken in every pot. *See* A chicken in every pot.

GATHER

Gather ye rosebuds while ye may.

A rolling stone gathers no moss.

GENERAL

War is too important to be left to the generals.

GENERATION

From shirtsleeves to shirtsleeves in three generations.

GENIE

Let the genie out of the bottle.

GENIUS

Genius is one percent inspiration and ninety-nine percent perspiration.

Genius is the capacity for taking infinite pains.

Geniuses, like poets, are born, not taught. *See* Poets are born, not made.

GENTLE

Do not go gentle into that good night.

GET, GOT

Cat got your tongue? *See* Has the cat got your tongue?

Don't get mad, get even.

Don't wish too hard: you might just get what you wished for.

Get your act together.

Has the cat got your tongue?

If you lie down with dogs, you'll get up with fleas.

If you've got it, flaunt it.

I'm from Missouri; you've got to show me.

It's getting out of hand.

Let's get America moving again.

Let's get it off the ground.

Let's get something off the ground. *See* Let's get it off the ground.

Let's get the show on the road.

Lie down with dogs, get up with fleas. *See* If you lie down with dogs, you'll get up with fleas.

Money gets money. *See* Money begets money.

The rich get richer and the poor get poorer.

Shit or get off the pot.

A/The squeaky wheel gets all the grease. *See* The wheel that does the squeaking is the one that gets the grease.

What you see is what you get.

The wheel that does the squeaking is the one

that gets the grease.

When the going gets tough, the tough get going.

When you got it, flaunt it. *See* If you've got it, flaunt it.

You can't get a quart into a pint pot.

You can't get blood from a stone.

You can't get blood out of a turnip. *See* You can't get blood from a stone.

You can't get something for nothing. *See* You don't get something for nothing.

You don't get something for nothing.

You get nothing for nothing.

You get what you pay for.

You never get anything for nothing. *See* You get nothing for nothing.

GIANT

If I have seen further it is by standing on the shoulders of giants.

GIFT

Beware of Greeks bearing gifts.

Never look a gift horse in the mouth.

GIPPER

Win this one for the Gipper.

GIRL

Girls will be girls. *See* Boys will be boys.

GIVE, GIVEN

Don't give up the ship.

Everyone to whom much is given, of him will much be required.

Give a man a fish, and you feed him for a day; show (teach) him how to catch fish, and you feed him for a lifetime.

Give credit where credit is due.

Give 'em hell, Harry!

Give him an inch, and he will take a mile.

Give him enough rope and he'll hang himself.

Give me a break!

Give me a place to stand, and I will move the earth. *See* Give me where to stand, and I will move the earth.

Give me liberty or give me death!

Give me where to stand, and I will move the earth.

Give me your tired, your poor.

Give peace a chance!

Give the devil his due.

I wouldn't give him the time of day.

It is more blessed to give than to receive.

It's better to give than to receive. *See* It is more blessed to give than to receive.

The Lord gives and the Lord takes always.

My dear, I don't give a damn.

Neither give nor take offense.

Never give a sucker an even break.

GLASS

The glass is either half empty or half full.

People who live in glass houses shouldn't throw stones.

GLITTER

All that glitters is not gold.

GLOVE

A/The cat in gloves catches no mice.

GO, GONE

Anything goes!

Anything that can go wrong, will go wrong. *See* If anything can go wrong, it will.

As go the cities, so goes the nation. *See* As Maine goes, so goes the nation.

As Maine goes, so goes the nation.

As Maine goes, so goes Vermont. *See* As Maine goes, so goes the nation.

As the family goes, so goes the nation. *See* As Maine goes, so goes the nation.

Do not go gentle into that good night.

The dogs bark, but the caravan goes on.

Easy come, easy go.

Go ahead, make my day. *See* Make my day.

Go for it!

Go west, young man.

Go with it. *See* Go with the flow.

Go with the flow.

Gone but not forgotten.

Gone with the wind.

Here goes!

Here today, gone tomorrow.

Here we go again.

I have promises to keep, and miles to go before I sleep.

If anything can go wrong, it will.

It goes against the grain.

It goes in one ear and out the other.

It goes with the territory. *See* It comes with the territory.

Love makes the world go round.

Money goes to money. *See* Money begets money.

Money makes the mare to go.

No good deed goes unpunished.

Pay as you go.

The shoemaker's kids always go barefoot.

The show must go on.

The sky is not going to fall.

So goes Maine, so goes the nation. *See* As Maine goes, so goes the nation.

What can go wrong, will go wrong. *See* If anything can go wrong, it will.

What goes around, comes around.

What goes up must come down.

When the going gets tough, the tough get going.

Where do we go from here?

GOD, GODLINESS

Cleanliness is next to godliness.

From your lips to God's ears.

God bless America.

God bless you.

God helps those who help themselves.

God is always on the side of the big battalions.

God is in the details.

God moves in a mysterious way.

God save me from my friends—I can protect myself from my enemies. *See* Save us from our friends.

God's in his heaven; all's right with the world.

If there were no God, it would be necessary to invent Him.

In God we trust.

It's in the lap of the gods.

Man proposes, God disposes.

The mills of the gods grind slowly, but they grind exceedingly fine.

One nation under God, indivisible, with liberty and justice for all.

Put your trust in God, and keep your powder dry.

So help me God.

Whom the gods would destroy, they first make mad.

You can't serve God and mammon.

GOLD, GOLDEN

All that glitters is not gold.

Don't kill the goose that laid the golden egg.

Silence is golden.

Speech is silver, silence is golden.

There's a pot of gold at the end of the rainbow.

GOOD

All good things come in threes.

All good things come to those who wait.

All good things must come to an end.

Bad money drives out good.

The best defense is a good offense.

Do not go gentle into that good night.

A good beginning is half the battle.

Good Americans, when they die, go to Paris.

Good fences make good neighbors.

A good man is hard to find.

A good name is better than precious ointment.

The good news is …; the bad news is …

Good news travels slowly; bad news travels fast. *See* Bad news travels fast.

A good reputation is more valuable than money.

Good riddance to bad rubbish.

The good that men do lives after them.

The good, the bad, and the ugly.

Good things come in small packages. *See* The best things come in small packages.

It's an ill wind that blows no (nobody) good.

It's too good to be true.

It's too much of a good thing.

A miss is as good as a mile.

Never had it so good. *See* You have never had it so good.

No good deed goes unpunished.

No news is good news.

Now is the time for all good men to come to the aid of their country.

One good turn deserves another.

The road to hell is paved with good intentions.

So far, so good.

There's good and bad in everything.

There's nothing good or bad but thinking makes it so.

What this country needs is a good five-cent cigar.

What's good for General Motors is good for America.

What's good for the goose is good for the gander. *See* What's sauce for the goose is sauce for the gander.

What's sauce for the goose is sauce for the gander.

You have never had it so good.

You have to take the bad with the good.

Your guess is as good as mine.

GOOSE

Don't kill the goose that laid the golden egg.

Kill the goose that laid the golden egg. *See* Don't kill the goose that laid the golden egg.

What's sauce for the goose is sauce for the gander.

GORE

It all depends on whose ox is gored.

GORILLA

It's an 800-pound gorilla.

GOVERN, GOVERNMENT

Government of the people, by the people, and for the people.

That government is best that governs least.

GRAB

How does that grab you?

GRAIN

It goes against the grain.

GRANDMOTHER

Don't (try to) teach your grandmother (how) to suck eggs.

GRASS

The grass is always greener on the other side of the fence.

Don't let the grass grow under your feet.

GRAVY

One man's gravy is another man's poison. *See* One man's meat is another man's poison.

GRAY

All cats are gray in the dark.

GREASE

The wheel that does the squeaking is the one that gets the grease.

GREAT, GREATLY

Behind every great man there is a great woman.

Great minds think alike.

Great oaks from little acorns grow.

Little strokes fell great oaks.

The reports of my death are greatly exaggerated.

Time is a great healer. *See* Time heals all wounds.

GREEK

Beware of Greeks bearing gifts.

Fear the Greeks bearing gifts. *See* Beware of Greeks bearing gifts.

It's Greek to me.

GRIND

The mills of the gods grind slowly, but they grind exceedingly fine.

GRINDSTONE

Keep your nose to the grindstone.

GRIST

It's all grist for the mill.

GROUND

Let's get it off the ground.

GROW

Absence makes the heart grow fonder.

Great oaks from little acorns grow.

It doesn't grow on trees. *See* Money doesn't grow on trees.

Money doesn't grow on trees.

GUARD

Don't let the fox guard the henhouse.

GUESS

Your guess is as good as mine.

GUILTY

A guilty conscience needs no accuser.

One is innocent until proven guilty.

GUN

Guns don't kill people. People do.

Stick to your guns.

When I hear the word culture, I reach for my gun.

GUY

Nice guys finish last.

HABIT

Old habits die hard.

HAIL

Hail to the Chief.

HALF

Believe nothing you hear, and only half of what you see. *See* Believe only half of what you see and nothing you hear.

Believe only half of what you see and nothing you hear.

The cup is either half empty or half full. *See* The glass is either half empty or half full.

The glass is either half empty or half full.

A good beginning is half the battle.

Half a loaf is better than none (no bread).

Six of one and half a dozen of the other.

HAND

A bird in the hand is worth two in the bush.

Cold hands, warm heart.

Don't bite the hand that feeds you.

Flowers leave fragrance in the hand that bestows them.

Idle hands are the devil's tools.

It's getting out of hand.

It's out of one's hands.

Let not your left hand know what your right hand does. *See* Never let your left hand know what your right hand is doing.

My hands are tied.

Never let your left hand know what your right hand is doing.

One hand washes the other.

HANDSOME

Handsome (pretty) is as handsome (pretty) does.

HANDWRITING

The handwriting is on the wall.

HANG

Give him enough rope and he'll hang himself.

Let's all hang together or we shall surely hang separately. *See* We must indeed all hang together, or, most assuredly, we shall all hang separately.

One might as well be hanged for a sheep as for a lamb.

The sword of Damocles hanging over one.

We must indeed all hang together, or, most assuredly, we shall all hang separately.

HAPPEN

Accidents will happen in the best-regulated families.

What has happened once can happen again.

HAPPINESS

Life, liberty, and the pursuit of happiness.

Money can't buy happiness.

HAPPY

Happy days are here again.

Happy is the country which has no history.

HARD, HARDLY

Between a rock and a hard place.

The bigger they are, the harder they fall.

Don't wish too hard: you might just get what you wished for.

The first hundred years are the hardest.

The first step is the hardest.

A good man is hard to find.

Life is hard by the yard, but by the inch life's a cinch.

Old habits die hard.

With such friends, one hardly needs enemies.

HARM

First, do no harm.

HARRY

Give 'em hell, Harry!

HASTE

Haste makes waste.

Make haste slowly.

Marry in haste, repent at leisure.

HATCH

Don't count your chickens before they are hatched.

HATE

He who spares his rod hates his son. *See* Spare the rod and spoil the child.

HAVE

Don't have too many irons in the fire.

Every dog has his day.

Everyone has his fifteen minutes of fame.

If a pig had wings, it could fly.

If frogs had wings, they wouldn't bump their tails on rocks.

Success has many parents. *See* Victory has a hundred fathers and defeat is an orphan.

Victory has a hundred fathers and defeat is an orphan.

You can't eat your cake and have it too. *See* You can't have your cake and eat it too.

You can't have your cake and eat it too.

You can't lose what you never had.

You never had it so good.

Youth will have its fling.

HAY

Make hay while the sun shines.

Work and pray, live on hay, you'll get pie in the sky when you die.

HAYSTACK

It's like looking for a needle in a haystack.

HEAD

A fish stinks from the head.

Heads I win, tails you lose.

Heads will roll.

I need that like I need a hole in my head.

Off with his (her) head!

An ostrich with its head in the sand.

Two heads are better than one.

Uneasy lies the head that wears the crown.

HEAL

Physician, heal thyself.

Time heals all wounds.

HEALTH, HEALTHY

A clean bill of health.

Early to bed and early to rise, makes a man healthy, wealthy, and wise.

HEAP

It takes a heap of living to make (a house) a home.

HEAR

Ask no questions and hear no lies. *See* Ask me no questions and I'll tell you no lies.

Believe only half of what you see and nothing you hear.

None so deaf as those who will not hear. *See* There are none so blind as those who will not see.

See no evil, hear no evil, speak no evil.

When I hear the word culture, I reach for my gun.

You could hear a pin drop.

HEART

Absence makes the heart grow fonder.

Cold hands, warm heart.

Don't wear your heart on your sleeve.

Faint heart never won fair lady.

First in war, first in peace, first in the hearts of his countrymen.

Home is where the heart is.

A merry heart makes a cheerful countenance.

The way to a man's heart is through his stomach.

What the eye doesn't see, the heart doesn't grieve for.

HEAT

If you can't stand the heat, get out of the kitchen.

HEAVEN

God's in his heaven; all's right with the world.

Heaven helps those who help themselves. *See* God helps those who help themselves.

It is easier for a camel to go (pass) through the eye of a needle than it is for a rich man to enter the kingdom of heaven.

Marriages are made in heaven.

There's a season and a time for every purpose under the heaven.

HEEL

Achilles' heel.

HELL

All hell broke loose.

Give 'em hell, Harry!

Hell hath no fury like a woman scorned.

The road to hell is paved with good intentions.

Till hell freezes over.

War is hell.

HELP

God helps those who help themselves.

Heaven helps those who help themselves. *See* God helps those who help themselves.

The Lord helps those who help themselves. *See* God helps those who help themselves.

So help me God.

HENHOUSE

Don't let the fox guard the henhouse.

HERE

Abandon all hope, ye who enter here.

The buck stops here.

Here goes!

Here I stand. I can do no other.

Here today, gone tomorrow.

Here we go again.

Kilroy was here.

Lafayette, we are here.

HERO

Heroes are made, not born. *See* Poets are born, not made.

No man is a hero to his valet.

HESITATE

He who hesitates is lost.

HIDE

Don't hide your light under a bushel.

You can run, but you can't hide.

HIGH

You'll take the high road, and I'll take the low road.

HINDMOST

The devil take the hindmost.

HISTORIAN

History doesn't repeat itself—historians do. *See* History repeats itself.

HISTORY

History is bunk.

History never repeats itself. *See* History repeats itself.

History repeats itself.

HIT

Don't hit a man when he's down.

The shit hits the fan.

HITCH

Hitch your wagon to a star.

HOBGOBLIN

A foolish consistency is the hobgoblin of little minds.

HOBSON

Hobson's choice.

HOLD

Hold your horses.

HOLE

I need that like I need a hole in my head.

Money burns a hole in his pocket.

You can't fit a round peg in a square hole.

HOMAGE

Hypocrisy is the homage that vice pays to virtue.

HOME

Charity begins at home.

The chickens have come home to roost.

Curses, like chickens, come home to roost. *See* The chickens have come home to roost.

A home away from home.

Home is where the heart is.

Home, sweet home.

It takes a heap of living to make (a house) a home.

The land of the free and the home of the brave.

A man's home is his castle.

Nothing to write home about.

There's no place like home.

You can't go home again.

HOMER

Even Homer sometimes nods.

HONESTY

Honesty is the best policy.

HONEY

You can catch more flies with honey than with vinegar.

HONOR

Honor thy father and thy mother.

A prophet is not without honor, save in his own country.

There is honor (even) among thieves.

There's no honor among thieves. *See* There is honor (even) among thieves.

HOPE, HOPEFULLY

Abandon all hope, ye who enter here.

Hope for the best and prepare for the worst.

Hope springs eternal in the human breast.

It is better to travel hopefully than to arrive.

Where there's life, there's hope.

HORN

Toot your own horn lest the same be never tooted.

HORSE

All the king's horses, and all the king's men,

couldn't put Humpty together again.

Don't change horses in midstream. *See* Don't swap horses in midstream.

Don't close (bar, lock, shut) the barn (stable) door after the horse runs away (has fled, has been stolen).

Don't look a gift horse in the mouth. *See* Never look a gift horse in the mouth.

Don't put the cart before the horse.

For want of a horse the rider was lost. *See* For want of a nail the kingdom was lost.

Hold your horses.

A horse of a different color. *See* That's a horse of a different color.

If wishes were horses, beggars would ride.

Never look a gift horse in the mouth.

That's a horse of a different color.

A Trojan horse.

You can lead a horse to water, but you cannot make him drink.

HOT

Strike while the iron is hot.

HOUR

A fool can ask more questions in an hour than a wise man can answer in seven years.

HOUSE

A house divided against itself cannot stand.

It takes a heap of living to make (a house) a home.

Never speak of rope in the house of a man who has been hanged.

People who live in glass houses shouldn't throw stones.

A plague on both your houses.

HOW

How do you like *them* apples?

How does that grab you?

It's not what you say, but how you say it.

It's not whether you win or lose but how you play the game.

HUMAN

Hope springs eternal in the human breast.

I am a man; and nothing human is alien to me.

To err is human, to forgive divine.

HUMBLE

Be it ever so humble, there's no place like

home. *See* There's no place like home.

HUMPTY (DUMPTY)

All the king's horses, and all the king's men, couldn't put Humpty together again.

HUNDRED

The first one hundred years are the hardest.

Victory has a hundred fathers and defeat is an orphan.

HURT

Nothing hurts like the truth. *See* The truth (always, often) hurts.

Sticks and stones may break my bones, but words (names) will never hurt me.

The truth (always, often) hurts.

What you don't know can't hurt you.

Work never hurt anybody.

HUSBAND

The husband is always the last to find out.

HYDE

Dr. Jekyll and Mr. Hyde.

HYPOCRISY

Hypocrisy is the homage that vice pays to virtue.

I

Am I my brother's keeper?

Do as I say, not as I do.

Doctor Livingstone, I presume?

Don't do as I do, but as I say. *See* Do as I say, not as I do.

Give me where to stand, and I will move the earth.

God save me from my friends—I can protect myself from my enemies. *See* Save us from our enemies.

I am a man; and nothing human is alien to me.

I am not my brother's keeper. *See* Am I my brother's keeper?

I am not a crook.

I am the state.

I am what I am and that's what I am.

I came, I saw, I conquered.

I cannot tell a lie.

I can't think when I concentrate.

I couldn't agree (with you) more.

I couldn't care less.

I disapprove of what you say, but I will defend to the death your right to say it.

I don't give a damn. *See* My dear, I don't give a damn.

I fear the Greeks, even when they are bearing gifts. *See* Beware of Greeks bearing gifts.

I have a dream.

I have news for you!

I have nothing to offer but blood, toil, tears, and sweat.

I have not yet begun to fight.

I have promises to keep, and miles to go before I sleep.

I have seen the future, and it works.

I need that like I need a hole in my head.

I never met a man I didn't like.

I only regret that I have but one life to lose for my country.

I shall return.

I think that I shall never see a poem lovely as a tree.

I think, therefore I am.

I told you so.

I was not born yesterday.

I won't take no for an answer.

I would rather die on my feet than live on my knees.

I wouldn't give him the time of day.

I wouldn't like to meet him in the dark.

I wouldn't touch it (him) with a ten-foot pole.

I wouldn't want to be in his shoes (place).

If I have seen further it is by standing on the shoulders of giants.

If I've told you once, I've told you a thousand times.

I'm from Missouri; you've got to show me.

On the whole, I'd rather be in Philadelphia.

When I hear the word culture, I reach for my gun.

Whose bread I eat, his song I sing.

You scratch my back, I'll scratch yours.

You'll take the high road, and I'll take the low road.

ICE
He could sell ice to an Eskimo.

ICEBERG
It's the tip of the iceberg.

IDLE
Idle hands are the devil's tools.

IF
If not us, who? If not now, when?

No ifs, ands or buts.

IGNORANCE
Ignorance is bliss.

Ignorance of the law is no excuse.

ILL
It's an ill wind that blows no (nobody) good.

Don't speak ill of the dead. *See* Never speak ill of the dead.

Never speak ill of the dead.

IMITATION
Imitation is the sincerest form of flattery.

IMPORTANT
War is too important to be left to the generals.

IMPRESSION
First impressions are the most lasting.

INCH
Give him an inch, and he will take a mile.

Life is hard by the yard, but by the inch life's a cinch.

INDEED
A friend in need is a friend indeed.

We must indeed all hang together, or, most assuredly, we shall all hang separately.

INDIAN
All chiefs and no Indians.

INDISPENSABLE
No person is indispensable.

INDIVISIBLE
One nation under God, indivisible, with liberty and justice for all.

INFALLIBLE
Nobody is infallible.

INFINITE
Age cannot wither her, nor custom stale her infinite variety.

INHERIT
The meek shall inherit the earth.

INJURY
Don't add insult to injury.

INNOCENT
One is innocent until proven guilty.

INSPIRATION
Genius is one percent inspiration and ninety-nine percent perspiration.

INSULT
Don't add insult to injury.

INTELLIGENCE
No one ever went broke underestimating the intelligence of the American people.

INTENTION
The road to hell is paved with good intentions.

INVENT, INVENTION
If there were no God, it would be necessary to invent Him.

Necessity is the mother of invention.

IRON
Don't have too many irons in the fire.

Strike while the iron is hot.

ISHMAEL
Call me Ishmael.

ISLAND
No man is an island.

JACK
All work and no play makes Jack a dull boy.

Jack of all trades and master of none.

JACKASS
A jackass can kick a barn door down, but it takes a carpenter to build one.

JEKYLL
Dr. Jekyll and Mr. Hyde.

JOIN
If you can't beat (lick) 'em, join 'em.

JONES
Keeping up with the Joneses.

JOSÉ
No way, José.

JOURNEY
A journey of a thousand miles begins with one step.

JOY
There's no joy in Mudville.

A thing of beauty is a joy for ever.

JUDGE, JUDGMENT
Don't judge a book by its cover.

Don't judge a man until you have walked a mile in his boots.

Don't pass judgment, that you may not be judged. *See* Judge not, that ye be not judged.

Judge not, that ye be not judged.

A man is known (judged) by the company he keeps.

Never judge a book by its cover. *See* Don't judge a book by its cover.

You can't judge a book by its cover. *See* Don't judge a book by its cover.

JUICE
The blacker the berry, the sweeter the juice.

The darker the berry, the sweeter the juice. *See* The blacker the berry, the sweeter the juice.

Let him stew in his own juice.

JUMP
Don't jump from the frying pan into the fire.

JUST
The darkest hour is just before the dawn. *See* It's always darkest before the dawn.

Don't wish too hard: you might just get what you wished for.

It's just what the doctor ordered.

Life is just a bowl of cherries.

Prosperity is just around the corner.

JUSTICE
Justice is blind.

One nation under God, indivisible, with liberty and justice for all.

JUSTIFY
The end justifies the means.

KEEP, KEEPER
Am I my brother's keeper?

An apple a day keeps the doctor away.

Finders keepers, losers weepers.

I am not my brother's keeper. *See* Am I my brother's keeper?

I have promises to keep, and miles to go before I sleep.

Keep a stiff upper lip.

Keep the wolf from the door. *See* The wolf is at the door.

Keep your chin up.

Keep your eyes open and your mouth shut. *See* Keep your mouth shut and your eyes open.

Keep your eyes wide open before marriage, half shut afterwards.

Keep your feet on the ground.

Keep your fingers crossed.

Keep your mouth shut and your eyes open.

Keep your nose clean.

Keep your nose to the grindstone.

Keep your powder dry. *See* Put your trust in God, and keep your powder dry.

Keeping up with the Joneses.

A man is known (judged) by the company he keeps.

Put your trust in God, and keep your powder dry.

KETTLE

The pot calling the kettle black.

KEY

Lock 'em up and throw away the key.

KICK

A jackass can kick a barn door down, but it takes a carpenter to build one.

KID

Kids will be kids. *See* Boys will be boys.

The shoemaker's kids always go barefoot.

KILL

Curiosity killed the cat.

Don't kill the goose that laid the golden egg.

Guns don't kill people. People do.

Kill the goose that laid the golden egg. *See* Don't kill the goose that laid the golden egg.

Let's kill all the lawyers.

There are more ways to kill a cat besides (without) choking (skinning) him to death. *See* There's more than one way to skin a cat.

KILROY

Kilroy was here.

KIND

It takes all kinds of people to make a world.

KING, KINGDOM

All the king's horses, and all the king's men, couldn't put Humpty together again.

For want of a nail the kingdom was lost.

In the country of the blind, the one-eyed man is king.

It is easier for a camel to go (pass) through the eye of a needle than it is for a rich man to enter the kingdom of heaven.

The king can do no wrong.

The king has no clothes on. *See* The Emperor has no clothes on.

The king is dead—long live the king.

Punctuality is the politeness of kings.

KITCHEN

Everything but the kitchen sink.

If you can't stand the heat, get out of the kitchen.

KNAVE

Once a knave always a knave. *See* Once a thief
always a thief.

KNEE

I would rather die on my feet than live on my knees.

KNOCK

Ask, and it shall be given you; seek, and you shall find; knock, and it shall be opened unto you.

Opportunity knocks but once.

Opportunity seldom knocks twice. *See* Opportunity knocks but once.

You could have knocked me over with a feather.

KNOW, KNOWLEDGE

Better the devil you know than the devil you don't know.

Everything comes to (the man, him) those who (can, know how to) wait. *See* All good things come to those who wait.

Father knows best.

The husband is always the last to know. *See* The husband is always the last to find out.

If you know what I mean.

It takes one to know one.

It's not what you know, it's who you know.

Knowledge is power.

Let not your left hand know what the right hand does. *See* Never let your left hand know what your right hand is doing.

A little knowledge (learning) is a dangerous thing.

A man is known (judged) by the company he keeps.

Mother knows best. *See* Father knows best.

Necessity knows no laws.

Never let your left hand know what your right hand is doing.

Not to know someone from Adam.

Those who know don't speak; those who speak don't know.

A tree is known by its fruit.

What did the President know, and when did he know it?

What you don't know can't hurt you.

You never know a man until you live with him.

LABOR

It's a labor of love.

The mountain labored and brought forth a mouse.

LACE

A lie can go around the world and back while the truth is lacing up its boots.

LADY

Faint heart never won fair lady.

The opera ain't over till the fat lady sings.

When a lady says no, she means perhaps; when she says perhaps, she means yes; when she says yes, she is no lady.

LAFAYETTE

Lafayette, we are here.

LAND

The land of the free and the home of the brave.

The land was ours before we were the land's.

This land is your land.

LAP

It's in the lap of the gods.

LAST

A/The cobbler should stick to his last.

First impressions are the most lasting.

He laughs best who laughs last.

He who laughs last, laughs longest. *See* He who laughs best laughs last.

The husband is always the last to find out.

It's the last straw that breaks the camel's back.

The last of the Mohicans.

Live every day as though it were your last.

Nice guys finish last.

LATE

Better late than never.

It's never too late to learn.

It's never too late to mend.

It's too little, too late.

LAUGH

He laughs best who laughs last.

He who laughs last, laughs longest. *See* He laughs best who laughs last.

Laugh and the world laughs with you; weep and you weep alone.

LAW, LAWYER

Ignorance of the law is no excuse.

Let's kill all the lawyers.

Murphy's law. *See* If anything can go wrong, it will.

Necessity knows no laws.

No one is above the law.

Possession is nine points of the law.

LAY

The best-laid schemes of mice and men often go (gang) a-gley.

Don't kill the goose that laid the golden egg.

LEAD

The blind leading the blind. *See* If the blind lead the blind, both shall fall into the ditch.

Don't lead with your chin.

If the blind lead the blind, both shall fall into the ditch.

Lead with the (one's) chin. *See* Don't lead with your chin.

One lie leads to another.

You can lead a horse to water, but you cannot make him drink.

LEAP

Look before you leap.

One small step for man, one giant leap for mankind. *See* That's one small step for [a] man, one giant leap for mankind.

That's one small step for ;oba;cb man, one giant leap for mankind.

LEARN, LEARNING

It's never too late to learn.

Learn from the mistakes of others.

A little knowledge (learning) is a dangerous thing.

Live and learn.

You have to learn to crawl before you can walk.

You have to learn to walk before you can run.

LEAVE, LEFT

Leave no stone unturned.

Leave well enough alone.

Take it or leave it.

War is too important to be left to the generals.

LEGION

Their name is legion.

LEISURE

Marry in haste, repent at leisure.

LEOPARD

The leopard can't change its spots.

LESS, LESSER, LEAST

Choose the lesser of two evils.

Least said, soonest mended.

Less is more.

That government is best which governs least.

LEST

Judge not, lest ye be judged. *See* Judge not, that ye be not judged.

Toot your own horn lest the same be never tooted.

LET

Let bygones be bygones.

Let him stew in his own juice.

Let him twist slowly, slowly in the wind.

Let him who is without sin cast (throw) the first stone.

Let nature take its course.

Let not your left hand know what your right hand is doing. *See* Never let your left hand know what your right hand is doing.

Let sleeping dogs lie.

Let the buyer beware.

Let the cat out of the bag. *See* The cat is out of the bag.

Let the chips fall where they may.

Let the cobbler (shoemaker) stick to his last.

See A/The cobbler should stick to his last.

Let the dead bury the dead.

Let the genie out of the bottle.

Let them eat cake.

Let there be light.

Let well enough alone. *See* Leave well enough alone.

Let's all hang together or we shall surely hang separately. *See* We must indeed all hang together, or, most assuredly, we shall all hang separately.

Let's cross that bridge when we come to it.

Let's face it.

Let's get America moving again.

Let's get it off the ground.

Let's get the show on the road.

Let's get to the bottom of it.

Let's kill all the lawyers.

Never let your left hand know what your right hand is doing.

LEVEL

Every employee tends to rise to his level of incompetence.

Water seeks it own level.

LIAR

A liar is not believed when he tells (speaks) the truth.

A liar should have a good memory.

LIBERTY

Give me liberty or give me death!

Life, liberty, and the pursuit of happiness.

One nation under God, indivisible, with liberty and justice for all.

LICK

If you can't beat (lick) 'em, join 'em.

LIE

Ask me no questions and I'll tell you no lies.

I cannot tell a lie.

A lie can go around the world and back while the truth is lacing its boots.

One lie leads to another.

There are lies, damned lies, and statistics.

LIE

As you make your bed, so you must lie in it. *See* You've made your bed, now lie in it.

If you lie down with dogs, you'll get up with fleas.

Let sleeping dogs lie.

Uneasy lies the head that wears the crown.

LIFE

Anything for a quiet life.

Art is long, life is short.

The best things in life are free.

A cat has nine lives.

I only regret that I have but one life to lose for my country.

Life begins at forty.

Life is but a dream.

Life is hard by the yard, but by the inch life's a cinch.

Life is just a bowl of cherries.

Life is no bed of roses.

Life is short and sweet.

Life is short, art is long. *See* Art is long, life is short.

Life is too short.

Life is what you make it.

Life isn't all beer and skittles.

Life, liberty, and the pursuit of happiness.

That's life.

Variety is the spice of life.

Where there's life there's hope.

LIFT

Lift yourself up by your own bootstraps. *See* Don't try to pull yourself up by your own bootstraps.

A rising tide will lift all boats.

LIGHT

Better to light one candle than curse the darkness.

See It is better to light one (little) candle than to curse the darkness.

Don't hide your light under a bushel.

It is better to light one (little) candle than to curse the darkness.

Let there be light.

Never light your candle at both ends. *See* Don't burn the (your) candle at both ends.

There's always a light at the end of the tunnel.

LIGHTLY

In the spring a young man's fancy lightly turns to thoughts of love.

LIGHTNING

Lightning never strikes in the same place twice.

LIKE

Be it ever so humble, there's no place like home. *See* There's no place like home.

Crime doesn't pay like it used to. *See* Crime doesn't pay.

Curses, like chickens, come home to roost. *See* The chickens have come home to roost.

How do you like *them* apples?

I need that like I need a hole in my head.

I never met a man I didn't like.

I wouldn't like to meet him in the dark.

If it looks like a duck, walks like a duck, and quacks like a duck, it's a duck.

If you believe that, there is a bridge in Brooklyn I'd like to sell you.

If you don't like it, you can lump it.

It's like looking for a needle in a haystack.

It's like opening a can of worms.

It's like taking candy from a baby.

Like attracts like.

Like begets like. *See* Like breeds like.

Like breeds like.

Like cures like.

Like father, like son.

Like mother, like daughter.

Promises are like piecrust: they are made to be broken.

There's no fool like an old fool.

There's no place like home.

LILY

Consider the lilies of the field.

LIMIT

The sky's the limit.

LINEN

Don't air your dirty linen in public.

LINING

Every cloud has a silver lining.

LINK

A chain is no stronger than its weakest link.

LION

A living dog is better than a dead lion.

March comes in like a lion and goes out like a lamb.

The lion shall lie down with the lamb.

LIP

From your lips to God's ears.

Keep a stiff upper lip.

Loose lips sink ships.

My lips are sealed.

Read my lips.

There's many a slip between (the) cup and (the) lip.

LITTLE

Anything for (a little) peace and quiet. *See* Anything for a quiet life.

Better a big fish in a little pond than a little fish in a big pond.

Birds in their little nests agree.

Consistency is the hobgoblin of little minds. *See* A foolish consistency is the hobgoblin of little minds.

A foolish consistency is the hobgoblin of little minds.

Great oaks from little acorns grow.

It is better to light one (little) candle than to curse the darkness.

It's too little, too late.

A little bird told (whispered to) me.

A little knowledge (learning) is a dangerous thing.

Little strokes fell great oaks.

Paper bleeds little.

LIVE

Better a live dog than a dead lion. *See* A living dog is better than a dead lion.

Eat to live; do not live to eat.

He who fights and runs away, may live to fight another day.

He who lives by the sword dies by the sword.

It takes a heap of living to make (a house) a home.

It's a date which will live in infamy.

The king is dead—long live the king.

Live and learn.

Live and let live.

Live every day as though it were your last.

A living dog is better than a dead lion.

Man does not live by bread alone.

People who live in glass houses shouldn't throw stones.

You can't live with men; neither can you live without them.

You never know a man until you live with him.

LIVINGSTONE

Doctor Livingstone, I presume.

LOAF

Half a loaf is better than none (no bread).

LOCK

Don't close (bar, lock, shut) the barn (stable) door after the horse runs away (has fled, has been stolen).

Lock 'em up and throw away the key.

LONG, LONGEST

Art is long, life is short.

He who laughs last, laughs longest. *See* He laughs best who laughs last.

You've come a long way, baby.

LOOK

Always look on the bright side.

Appearances (looks) are deceiving (deceptive).

Don't look a gift horse in the mouth. *See* Never look a gift horse in the mouth.

If it looks like a duck, walks like a duck, and quacks like a duck, it's a duck.

It's like looking for a needle in a haystack.

Look before you leap.

Never look a gift horse in the mouth.

LOOSE

All hell broke loose.

LORD

Don't take the name of the Lord in vain.

The Lord gives and the Lord takes away.

The Lord helps those who help themselves. *See* God helps those who help themselves.

The Lord moves in a mysterious way. *See* God moves in a mysterious way.

Praise the Lord and pass the ammunition.

LOSE, LOSER

Finders keepers, losers weepers.

Heads I win, tails you lose.

I only regret that I have but one life to lose for my country.

It is better to have loved and lost, than never to have loved at all.

The proletarians have nothing to lose but their chains.

You can't lose what you never had.

You win some (a few), you lose some (a few).

LOSS

One man's loss is another man's gain.

LOST

For want of a nail the kingdom was lost.

He who hesitates is lost.

LOUDER

Actions speak louder than words.

LOVE, LOVELY

All's fair in love and war.

The course of true love never did run smooth.

I think that I shall never see a poem lovely as a tree.

In the spring a young man's fancy lightly turns to thoughts of love.

It is better to have loved and lost, than never to have loved at all.

It's a labor of love.

Love conquers all.

Love is blind.

Love makes the world go round.

Love me, love my dog.

The love of money is the root of all evil. *See* Money is the root of all evil.

Love they neighbor as thyself. *See* Love your neighbor as yourself.

Love your neighbor as yourself.

Misery loves company.

Money loves company. *See* Money begets company.

The path of true love never runs smooth. *See* The course of true love never did run smooth.

True love never runs smooth. *See* The course of true love never did run smooth.

LUCK

Better luck next time.

Luck is the residue of design.

LUMP

If you don't like it, you can lump it.

LUNCH

There's no such thing as a free lunch.

MCCOY

It's the real McCoy.

MACHINE

A Rube Goldberg machine.

MAD

Don't get mad, get even.

Whom the gods would destroy, they first make mad.

MAGNANIMITY

In victory: magnanimity.

MAIL

The check is in the mail.

MAINE

As Maine goes, so goes the nation.

As Maine goes, so goes Vermont. *See* As Maine goes, so goes the nation.

So goes Maine, so goes the nation. *See* As Maine goes, so goes the nation.

MAKE, MADE

Absence makes the heart grow fonder.

Adversity makes strange bedfellows. *See* Misery makes strange bedfellows.

All work and no play makes Jack a dull boy.

As you make your bed, so you must lie in it. *See* You've made your bed, now lie in it.

Clothes don't make the man.

Clothes make the man.

Don't make a mountain out of a molehill.

Don't make the same mistake twice.

Early to bed and early to rise, makes a man healthy, wealthy, and wise.

Every man makes mistakes. *See* He who never made a mistake never made anything.

Fine feathers make fine birds.

Go ahead, make my day. *See* Make my day.

Haste makes waste.

He who never made a mistake never made anything.

If you can make it here, you can make it anywhere.

If you don't make mistakes you don't make anything.

See He who never made a mistake never made anything.

It takes a heap of living to make (a house) a home.

It takes all kinds of people to make a world.

446

It takes all sorts to make a world. *See* It takes all kinds of people to make a world.

It takes two to make a quarrel.

The last drop makes the cup run over.

Life is what you make it.

Make a virtue of necessity.

Make haste slowly.

Make hay while the sun shines.

Make it or break it. *See* Make or break.

Make my day.

Make or break.

Manners make the man.

Misery makes strange bedfellows.

Neither take offense nor make offense. *See* Neither give nor take offense.

One swallow does not make a summer.

Poets are born, not made.

Politics makes strange bedfellows.

Practice makes perfect.

Stone walls do not a prison make.

There's nothing good or bad but thinking makes it so.

Wealth makes many friends.

What makes someone tick?

You can lead a horse to water, but you cannot make him drink.

You can't make a silk purse out of a sow's ear.

You can't make an omelet without breaking eggs.

You can't make bricks without straw.

You've made your bed, now lie in it.

MALICE

With malice toward none, with charity for all.

MAMMON

You can't serve God and mammon.

MAN, MEN

All men are created equal.

All the king's horses, and all the king's men, couldn't put Humpty together again.

Behind every great man there is a great woman.

The best-laid schemes of mice and men often go (gang) a-gley.

The child is father of the man.

Clothes don't make the man.

Clothes make the man.

Dead men tell no tales.

A dog is a man's best friend.

Don't hit a man when he's down.

Don't judge a man until you have walked a mile in his boots.

Early to bed and early to rise, makes a man healthy, wealthy, and wise.

Every man for himself.

Every man for himself, and the devil take the hindmost. *See* The devil take the hindmost.

Every man is his own worst enemy.

Every man is not born with a silver spoon in his mouth.

Every man makes mistakes. *See* He who never made a mistake never made anything.

Every man to his own taste.

A fool can ask more questions in an hour than a wise man can answer in seven years.

A good man is hard to find.

The good that men do lives after them.

I am a man; and nothing human is alien to me.

I never met a man I didn't like.

In the country of the blind, the one-eyed man is king.

In the spring a young man's fancy lightly turns to thoughts of love.

It ain't a fit night out for man or beast.

Man does not live by bread alone.

A man is known (judged) by the company he keeps.

Man proposes, God disposes.

A man who makes no mistakes usually does not make anything. *See* He who never made a mistake never made anything.

A man's home is his castle.

A man's word is as good as his bond.

Manners make the man.

Never speak of rope in the house of a man who has been hanged.

No man can serve two masters. *See* You can't serve God and mammon.

No man is a hero to his valet.

No man is an island.

Now is the time for all good men to come to the aid of their country.

One man's gravy is another man's poison. *See* One man's meat is another man's poison.

One man's loss is another man's gain.

One man's meat is another man's poison.

One man's trash is another man's treasure.

One small step for man, one giant leap for mankind.
See That's one small step for ;oba;cb man, one giant leap for mankind.

That's one small step for ;oba;cb man, one giant leap for mankind.

There's a tide in the affairs of men.

Time and tide wait for no man.

The way to a man's heart is through his stomach.

When a dog bites a man, that is not news; but when a man bites a dog, that is news.

Would you buy a used car from this man?

You can't beat a man at his own game.

You can't live with men; neither can you live without them.

You never know a man until you bed with him a winter and summer. *See* You never know a man until you live with him.

You never know a man until you live with him.

MANNER
Manners make the man.

MANY
The coward dies many times.

Cowards die many times before their deaths. *See* The coward dies many times.

Don't have too many irons in the fire.

From many, one. *See* E pluribus unum.

Out of many, one. *See* E pluribus unum.

There's many a slip between (the) cup and (the) lip.

Wealth makes many friends.

MARINE
Tell that (it) to the marines.

MARRIAGE
Keep your eyes wide open before marriage, half shut afterwards.

Marriages are made in heaven.

MARRY
Marry in haste, repent at leisure.

MASTER
Jack of all trades and master of none.

No man can serve two masters. *See* You can't serve God and mammon.

MAY
April showers bring May flowers.

MAY
Don't pass judgment, that you may not be judged. *See* Judge not, that ye be not judged.

Gather ye rosebuds while ye may.

He who fights and runs away, may live to fight another day.

Let the chips fall where they may.

Sticks and stones may break my bones, but words (names) will never hurt me.

MEAN
If you know what I mean.

MEANS
The end justifies the means.

MEAT
One man's meat is another man's poison.

MEEK
The meek shall inherit the earth.

MEET, MET
Be nice to people on your way up because you'll meet them ('em) on your way down.

East is East, and West is West, and never the twain shall meet.

Extremes meet. *See* Opposites attract.

He met his Waterloo.

I never met a man I didn't like.

I wouldn't like to meet him in the dark.

There's more to it than meets the eye.

We have met the enemy, and they are ours.

MELT
Butter wouldn't melt in his mouth.

MEND
It's never too late to mend.

Least said, soonest mended.

MERRY, MERRIER
Eat, drink, and be merry, for tomorrow we die.

The more the merrier.

MESSENGER
Don't shoot the messenger.

MIDDLE
Don't change the rules in the middle of the game.

If you play both ends against the middle, the middle will soon fold up.

MIGHT, MIGHTIER

Might makes right.

The pen is mightier than the sword.

MILE

And miles to go before I sleep. *See* I have promises to keep, and miles to go before I sleep.

The first mile is always is the hardest. *See* The first step is the hardest.

Give him an inch, and he will take a mile.

I have promises to keep, and miles to go before I sleep.

A journey of a thousand miles begins with one step.

A miss is as good as a mile.

MILK

Don't cry over spilled milk.

MILL

All is grist that comes to the mill. *See* It's all grist for the mill.

It's all grist for the mill.

The mills of the gods grind slowly, but they grind exceedingly fine.

MIND

Consistency is the hobgoblin of little minds. *See* A foolish consistency is the hobgoblin of little minds.

The eyes are the mirror(s) of the soul (mind).

A foolish consistency is the hobgoblin of little minds.

Great minds think alike.

A mind is a terrible thing to waste.

Mind your p's and q's.

Out of sight, out of mind.

Who's minding the store?

MINUTE

Everyone has his fifteen minutes of fame.

There's a sucker born every minute.

MIRROR

The eyes are the mirror(s) of the soul (mind).

MISERY

Misery loves company.

Misery makes strange bedfellows.

MISS

A miss is as good as a mile.

They never miss an opportunity to miss an opportunity.

You never miss the water till the well runs dry.

MISSOURI

I'm from Missouri; you've got to show me.

MISTAKE

Don't make the same mistake twice.

He who never made a mistake never made anything.

If you don't make mistakes you don't make anything. *See* He who never made a mistake never made anything.

Learn from the mistakes of others.

MISTER

Dr. Jekyll and Mr. Hyde.

MIX

Alcohol (drinking) and driving don't mix. *See* Oil and water don't mix.

Don't mix business with pleasure. *See* Never mix business with pleasure.

Never mix business with pleasure.

Oil and water don't mix.

Smoking and sport don't mix. *See* Oil and water don't mix.

MOHAMMED

If the mountain will not come to Mohammed, then

Mohammed will go to the mountain.

MOHICAN

The last of the Mohicans.

MOLEHILL

Don't make a mountain out of a molehill.

MOMENT

Seize the moment.

MONDAY

Monday morning quarterbacking.

MONEY

Bad money drives out good.

A fool and his money are soon parted.

A good reputation is more valuable than money.

The love of money is the root of all evil. *See* Money is the root of all evil.

Money begets money.

Money burns a hole in his pocket.

Money can't buy happiness.

Money doesn't grow on trees.

Money doesn't stink. *See* Money has no smell.

Money gets to money. *See* Money begets money.

Money has no smell.

Money is no object.

Money is power.

Money is the root of all evil.

Money isn't everything.

Money loves company. *See* Money begets money.

Money makes money. *See* Money begets money.

Money makes the mare to go.

Money talks.

Put your money where your mouth is.

That's where the money is.

Time is money.

You pays your money, and you takes your choice.

MONKEY

Don't throw a monkey wrench in the works.

Monkey see, monkey do.

MORE

Don't bite off more than you can chew.

A fool can ask more questions in an hour than a wise man can answer in seven years.

A good reputation is more valuable than money.

It is more blessed to give than to receive.

The more the merrier.

The more things change, the more they stay the same.

Once more unto the breach, dear friends.

One more such victory and we are lost. *See* Another such victory, and we are lost.

There's more than one way to skin a cat.

There's more to it than meets the eye.

You can catch more flies with honey than with vinegar.

MORNING

Monday morning quarterbacking.

MOSS

A rolling stone gathers no moss.

MOST

First impressions are the most lasting.

MOTHER

Honor thy father and thy mother.

Like mother, like daughter.

A mother can take care of ten children, but sometimes ten children can't take care of one mother.

Mother knows best. *See* Father knows best.

The mother of all . . .

Necessity is the mother of invention.

Step on a crack, break your mother's back.

MOUNTAIN

Don't make a mountain out of a molehill.

If the mountain will not come to Mohammed, Mohammed will go to the mountain.

The mountain labored and brought forth a mouse.

MOUSE, MICE

The best-laid schemes of mice and men often go (gang) a-gley.

A/The cat in gloves catches no mice.

The mountain labored and brought forth a mouse.

When the cat's away, the mice will play.

MOUTH

Butter wouldn't melt in his mouth.

Don't look a gift horse in the mouth. *See* Never look a gift horse in the mouth.

From the mouths of babes come words of wisdom. *See* Out of the mouths of babes and sucklings come great truths.

Keep your mouth shut and your eyes open.

Never look a gift horse in the mouth.

Out of the mouths of babes and sucklings come great truths.

Put your money where your mouth is.

MOVE

But it does move!

Give me a place to stand, and I will move the earth. *See* Give me where to stand, and I will move the earth.

Give me where to stand, and I will move the earth.

God moves in a mysterious way.

Let's get America moving again.

The Lord moves in a mysterious way. *See* God

moves in a mysterious way.

Nevertheless, it does move! *See* But it does move!

MUCH

Everyone to whom much is given, of him will much be required.

It's too much of a good thing.

Much ado about nothing.

MUDVILLE

There's no joy in Mudville.

MUM

Mum's the word!

MURDER

Murder will out.

MURPHY

Murphy's law. *See* If anything can go wrong, it will.

MUSIC

It's music to my ears.

Music hath charms to soothe the savage breast.

MUST

All good things must come to an end.

As you make your bed, so you must lie in it. *See* You've made your bed, now lie in it.

The best of friends must part.

Carthage must be destroyed.

One must crawl before he walks. *See* You have to learn to crawl before you can walk.

The show must go on.

We must indeed all hang together, or, most assuredly, we shall all hang separately.

What goes up must come down.

What must be, must be. *See* What will be, will be.

MYSTERIOUS

God moves in a mysterious way.

NAIL

For want of a nail the kingdom was lost.

NAME

Don't take the name of the Lord in vain.

Frailty, thy name is woman!

A good name is better than precious ointment.

A rose by another name would smell as sweet.

Sticks and stones may break my bones, but

words (names) will never hurt me.

That's the name of the game.

Their name is legion.

What's in a name?

You name it.

You name it, we have it.

NATION

As go the cities, so goes the nation. *See* As Maine goes, so goes the nation.

As goes the family, so goes the nation. *See* As Maine goes, so goes the nation.

As Maine goes, so goes the nation.

One nation under God, indivisible, with liberty and justice for all.

NATURE

Let nature take its course.

Nature abhors a vacuum.

Nature will take its course. *See* Let nature take its course.

Self-preservation is the first law of nature.

NECESSARY

If there were no God, it would be necessary to invent Him.

NECESSITY

Make a virtue of necessity.

Necessity is the mother of invention.

Necessity knows no laws.

NECK

An albatross around one's neck. *See* It's an albatross around one's neck.

Don't stick your neck out.

It's an albatross around one's neck.

NEED

A friend in need is a friend indeed.

From each according to his ability, to each according to his needs.

I need that like I need a hole in my head.

What this country needs is a good five-cent cigar.

With such friends, one hardly needs enemies.

NEEDLE

It is easier for a camel to go (pass) through the eye of a needle than it is for a rich man to enter the kingdom of heaven.

It's like looking for a needle in a haystack.

NEIGHBOR

Good fences make good neighbors.

Love thy neighbor as thyself. *See* Love your neighbor as yourself.

Love your neighbor as yourself.

The rotten apple injures its neighbors. *See* The rotten apple spoils the barrel.

NERO

Nero fiddled while Rome burned.

NEST

Birds in their little nests agree.

Feather your own nest.

NEVER

Barking dogs never bite.

Better late than never.

The course of true love never did run smooth.

An elephant never forgets.

Faint heart never won fair lady.

He who never made a mistake never made anything.

I never met a man I didn't like.

I think that I shall never see a poem lovely as a tree.

It is better to have loved and lost, than never to have loved at all.

It never rains but it pours.

It's never too late to learn.

Lightning never strikes twice in the same place.

Never believe everything you hear. *See* Believe only half of what you see and nothing you hear.

Never cry wolf.

Never give a sucker an even break.

Never had it so good. *See* You never had it so good.

Never judge a book by its cover. *See* Don't judge a book by its cover.

Never let your left hand know what your right hand is doing.

Never light your candle at both ends. *See* Don't burn the (your) candle at both ends.

Never look a gift horse in the mouth.

Never make a mountain out of a molehill. *See* Don't make a mountain out of a molehill.

Never mix business with pleasure.

Never put off until tomorrow what you can do today.

Never say die.

Never say never.

Never sell America short.

Never speak ill of the dead.

Never speak of rope in the house of a man who has been hanged.

Never tell tales out of school.

Sticks and stones may break my bones, but words (names) will never hurt me.

Success is never final.

The sun never sets on the British Empire.

They never miss an opportunity to miss an opportunity.

Toot your own horn lest the same be never tooted.

A watched pot never boils.

A winner never quits, and a quitter never wins.

Words once spoken you can never recall.

Work never hurt anybody.

You never get anything for nothing. *See* You get nothing for nothing.

You never had it so good.

You never know a man until you live with him.

NEVERTHELESS

Nevertheless, it does move! *See* But it does move!

NEW

Don't put new wine in old bottles.

Everything old is new again.

A new broom sweeps clean.

There's nothing new under the sun.

You can't put new wine in old bottles. *See* Don't put new wine in old bottles.

You can't teach an old dog new tricks.

NEWS

Bad news travels fast.

The good news is ...; the bad news is ...

Good news travels slowly; bad news travels fast. *See* Bad news travels fast.

I have news for you!

No news is good news.

When a dog bites a man, that is not news; but when a man bites a dog, that is news.

NEXT

Better luck next time.

Cleanliness is next to godliness.

NICE

Nice guys finish last.

NICKEL

Don't take any wooden nickels.

NIGHT

Do not go gentle into that good night.

Ships that pass in the night.

NINE

A cat has nine lives.

Possession is nine points of the law.

A stitch in time saves nine.

NOBODY

Nobody is indispensable. *See* No person is indispensable.

Nobody is infallible.

Nobody is perfect.

You can't beat somebody with nobody.

NOD

Even Homer sometimes nods.

Homer sometimes nods. *See* Even Homer sometimes nods.

NONE

It's none of your business.

Jack of all trades and master of none.

There are none so blind as those who will not see.

There are none so deaf as those who will not hear. *See* There are none so blind as those who will not see.

With malice toward none, with charity for all.

NOSE

Don't cut off your nose to spite your face.

It's no skin off my nose.

Keep your nose clean.

Keep your nose to the grindstone.

NOTHING

All or nothing.

Believe only half of what you see and nothing you hear.

I am a man; and nothing human is alien to me.

If in doubt, do nothing. *See* When in doubt, do nothing.

In this world nothing is certain but death and taxes.

See Nothing is certain but death and taxes.

Nothing could be further from the truth.

Nothing human is alien to me. *See* I am a man; and nothing human is alien to me.

Nothing hurts like the truth. *See* The truth (always, often) hurts.

Nothing is certain but death and taxes.

Nothing new under the sun. *See* There's nothing new under the sun.

Nothing succeeds like success.

Nothing to write home about.

Nothing ventured, nothing gained.

Nothing will come of nothing.

There's nothing good or bad but thinking makes it so.

There's nothing new under the sun.

We have nothing to fear but fear itself. *See* The only thing we have to fear is fear itself.

When in doubt, do nothing.

You can't get something for nothing. *See* You don't get something for nothing.

You don't get something for nothing.

You get nothing for nothing.

You never get anything for nothing. *See* You get nothing for nothing.

NOW

If not us, who? If not now, when?

Now is the time for all good men to come to the aid of their country.

Now you see it, now you don't.

NUMBER

There's safety in numbers.

OAK

Great oaks from little acorns grow.

Little strokes fell great oaks.

OATS

Sow your wild oats.

OBJECT

Money is no object.

OCEAN

It's a drop in the ocean. *See* It's a drop in the bucket.

OFFENSE

The best defense is a good offense.

Neither give nor take offense.

Neither take offense nor make offense. *See* Neither give nor take offense.

Offense is the best defense. *See* The best defense is a good offense.

OFTEN

The best-laid schemes of mice and men often go (gang) a gley.

OIL

Oil and water don't mix.

OLD

Everything old is new again.

A man is as old as he feels.

Old habits die hard.

Old soldiers never die; they just fade away.

There's no fool like an old fool.

You can't put new wine in old bottles. *See* Don't put new wine in old bottles.

You can't teach an old dog new tricks.

OMELET

You can't make an omelet without breaking eggs.

ONCE

Fool me once, shame on you; fool me twice, shame on me.

If a bee stings you once, it's the bee's fault; if a bee stings you twice, it's your fault. *See* Fool me once, shame on you; fool me twice, shame on me.

If anyone betrays you once, it's his fault; if he betrays you twice, it's your fault. *See* Fool me once, shame on you; fool me twice, shame on me.

If I've told you once, I've told you a thousand times.

Once a crook, always a crook. *See* Once a thief, always a thief.

Once a drunkard, always a drunkard. *See* Once a thief, always a thief.

Once a knave, always a knave. *See* Once a thief, always a thief.

Once a preacher, always a preacher. *See* Once a thief, always a thief.

Once a thief, always a thief.

Once a whore, always a whore. *See* Once a thief, always a thief.

Once bitten, twice shy. *See* Once burned, twice shy.

Once burned, twice shy.

Once more unto the breach, dear friends.

One can't be in two places at once.

Opportunity knocks but once.

Words once spoken you can never recall.

ONE

All for one and one for all.

The coward dies a thousand deaths, the brave but one. *See* The coward dies many times.

Don't put all your eggs in one basket.

Genius is one percent inspiration and ninety-nine percent perspiration.

I wouldn't give him the time of day.

It's an albatross around one's neck.

It's not the early bird that catches the worm, but the smart one. *See* The early bird catches the worm.

It's out of one's hands.

It's six of one and half a dozen of the other. *See* Six of one and half a dozen of the other.

It takes one to know one.

A jackass can kick a barn door down, but it takes a carpenter to build one.

A journey with a thousand miles begins with one step.

Lead with one's chin. *See* Don't lead with your chin.

One can't be in two places at once.

One day at a time.

One for all and all for one. *See* All for one, and one for all.

One good turn deserves another.

One hand washes the other.

One is innocent until proven guilty.

One lie leads to another.

One man's gravy is another man's poison. *See* One man's meat is another man's poison.

One man's loss is another man's gain.

One man's meat is another man's poison.

One man's trash is another man's treasure.

One more such victory and we are lost. *See* Another such victory, and we are undone.

One must crawl before he walks. *See* You have to learn to crawl before you can walk.

One nation under God, indivisible, with liberty and justice for all.

One picture is worth a thousand words.

One rotten apple spoils the barrel. *See* The rotten apple spoils the barrel.

One small step for man, one giant leap for mankind. *See* That's one small step for [a] man, one giant leap for mankind.

One step at a time.

One swallow does not make a summer.

One thing at a time.

Out of many, one. *See* E pluribus unum.

Six of one and half a dozen of the other.

Sometimes one can't see the wood for the trees.

That's a small step for [a] man, one giant leap for mankind.

There's more than one way to skin a cat.

Two heads are better than one.

The wheel that does the squeaking is the one that gets the grease.

With such friends, one hardly needs enemies.

ONLY

Beauty is only skin-deep.

Believe nothing you hear, and only half of what you see. *See* Believe only half of what you see and nothing you hear.

Believe only half of what you see and nothing you hear.

I only regret that I have but one life to lose for my country.

The only thing we have to fear is fear itself.

OPEN

Ask, and it shall be given you; seek, and you shall find; knock, and it shall be opened unto you.

It's like opening a can of worms.

Keep your eyes open and your mouth shut. *See*

Keep your mouth shut and your eyes open.

Keep your eyes wide open before marriage and half shut afterwards.

Keep your mouth shut and your eyes open.

Knock, and it shall be opened unto you. *See* Ask, and it shall be given you; seek, and you shall find; knock, and it shall be opened unto you.

OPERA

The opera ain't over till the fat lady sings.

OPERATION

The operation was successful—but the patient died.

OPPORTUNITY

Opportunity knocks but once.

Opportunity never knocks twice at any man's door. *See* Opportunity knocks but once.

Opportunity seldom knocks twice. *See* Opportunity knocks but once.

They never miss an opportunity to miss an opportunity.

OPPOSITE

Opposites attract.

OPTIMIST

The optimist's cup is half full; the pessimist's cup is half empty. *See* The glass is either half empty or half full.

ORPHAN

Victory has a hundred fathers and defeat is an orphan.

OSTRICH

An ostrich with its head in the sand.

OTHER

Do unto others as you would have them do unto you.

The grass is always greener on the other side of the fence.

It goes in one ear and out the other.

Opposites attract each other. *See* Opposites attract.

The shoe is on the other foot.

Six of one and half a dozen of the other.

There are other fish in the sea.

OUNCE

An ounce of prevention is worth a pound of cure.

OVERCOME

We shall overcome.

OWN

Every man is his own worst enemy.

Every man to his own taste.

Feather your own nest.

If a bee stings you once, it's the bee's fault; if a bee stings you twice, it's your own damn fault. *See* Fool me once, shame on you; fool me twice, shame on me.

Paddle your own canoe.

A prophet is not without honor, save in his own country.

Stand on your own two feet.

To each his own.

Toot your own horn lest the same be never tooted.

Virtue is its own reward.

You can't beat a man at his own game.

OX

It all depends on whose ox is gored.

OYSTER

The world is an (one's) oyster.

PACKAGE

The best things come in small packages.

PADDLE

Paddle your own canoe.

PAIN

There are no gains without pains.

PAN

Don't jump from the frying pan into the fire.

PANDEMONIUM

Pandemonium broke loose. See All hell broke loose.

PANDORA

A Pandora's box.

PAPER

It's not worth the paper it is written on.

Paper bleeds little.

PART

The best of friends must part.

Discretion is the better part of valor.

A fool and his money are soon parted.

If you're not part of the solution, you're part of the problem.

Till death do us part.

PARTING

Parting is such sweet sorrow.

PARTY

The party's over!

PASS

Ships that pass in the night.

This, too, will (shall) pass.

PAST

Those who cannot remember the past are con-

demned to repeat it.

What's past is prologue.

PATIENCE

Patience is a virtue.

PATIENT

The operation was successful—but the patient died.

PAUL

Rob Peter to pay Paul.

PAVE

The road to hell is paved with good intentions.

PAY

Crime doesn't pay.

Crime doesn't pay like it used to. See Crime doesn't pay.

He who dances must pay the fiddler.

He who pays the piper calls the tune.

Pay as you go.

Pay the piper his due.

Rob Peter to pay Paul.

There'll be hell to pay.

There'll be the Devil to pay.

You get what you pay for.

You pays your money, and you takes your choice.

PEACE

Anything for (a little) peace and quiet. See Anything for a quiet life.

First in war, first in peace, first in the hearts of his countrymen.

Give peace a chance!

If you want peace, prepare for war.

PEARL

Don't cast (throw) your pearls before swine.

PEE

If you're gonna run with the big dogs, you can't pee like a puppy. See If you can't run with the big dogs, stay under the porch.

PEG

You can't fit a round peg in a square hole.

PEN

The pen is mightier than the sword.

PENNY

A bad penny always turns up.

A penny for your thoughts.

A penny saved is a penny earned.

Penny-wise and pound-foolish.

PEOPLE

Be nice to people on your way up because you'll meet them ('em) on your way down.

Don't step on other people's toes. *See* Don't tread on other people's toes.

Don't tread on other people's toes.

Government of the people, by the people, and for the people.

Guns don't kill people. People do.

It takes all kinds of people to make a world.

Let my people go.

No one ever went broke underestimating the intelligence of the American people.

People who live in glass houses shouldn't throw stones.

The voice of the people is the voice of God.

Where there's no vision, the people perish.

You can fool some of the people all the time, and all of the people some of the time, but you cannot fool all the people all the time.

PERCENT

Genius is one percent inspiration and ninety-nine percent perspiration.

PERFECT

No one is perfect. *See* Nobody is perfect.

Nobody is perfect.

Practice makes perfect.

PERISH

Where there's no vision, the people perish.

PERSON

No person is indispensable.

PERSPIRATION

Genius is one percent inspiration and ninety-nine percent perspiration.

PESSIMIST

The optimist's cup is half full; the pessimist's cup is half empty. *See* The glass is either half empty or half full.

PETER

The Peter Principle. *See* Every employee tends to rise to his level of incompetence.

Rob Peter to pay Paul.

PHILADELPHIA

On the whole, I'd rather be in Philadelphia.

PHOENIX

The phoenix is rising again.

PHYSICIAN

Physician, heal thyself.

PIANO-PLAYER

Don't shoot the piano-player: he's doing the best he can.

PICK

Even a blind pig occasionally picks up an acorn.

PICTURE

One picture is worth a thousand words.

PIE, PIECRUST

Pie in the sky. *See* Work and pray, live on hay, you'll get pie in the sky when you die.

Promises are like piecrust: they are made to be broken.

Work and pray, live on hay, you'll get pie in the sky when you die.

PIECE

It's a piece of cake.

Thirty pieces of silver.

PIG

Don't buy a pig in a poke.

Even a blind pig finds an acorn once in a while. *See*

Even a blind pig occasionally picks up an acorn.

Even a blind pig occasionally picks up an acorn.

If a pig had wings, it could fly.

A pig is a pig. *See* Pigs are pigs.

Pigs are pigs.

Pigs could fly if they had wings. *See* If a pig had wings, it could fly.

Pigs is pigs. *See* Pigs are pigs.

PIN

You could hear a pin drop.

PINT

You can't get a quart into a pint pot.

PIPE

Put that in your pipe and smoke it.

PIPER

He who calls the tune must pay the piper. *See* He who pays the piper calls the tune.

He who pays the piper calls the tune.

Pay the piper his due.

PLACE

Between a rock and a hard place.

Everything falls into place.

Lightning never strikes twice in the same place.

One can't be in two places at once.

A place for everything and everything in its place.

There's a time and place for everything.

There's no place like home.

PLAGUE

A plague on both your houses.

PLAY

All work and no play makes Jack a dull boy.

Don't play with fire.

If you play both ends against the middle, the middle will soon fold up.

It's not whether you win or lose but how you play the game.

Turnabout is fair play.

When the cat's away, the mice will play.

PLEASE

Take my wife—please!

PLEASURE

Business before pleasure.

Combine business with pleasure. *See* Business before pleasure.

Never mix business with pleasure.

PLURIBUS

E pluribus unum.

POCKET

Money burns a hole in his pocket.

POEM

I think that I shall never see a poem lovely as a tree.

POET

Poets are born, not made.

POINT

Possession is nine points of the law.

POISON

One man's meat is another man's poison.

POKE

Don't buy a pig in a poke.

POLE

I wouldn't touch it (him) with a ten-foot pole.

POLICY

Honesty is the best policy.

POLITENESS

Punctuality is the politeness of kings.

POLITICS

Politics as usual.

Politics makes strange bedfellows.

POND

Better a big fish in a little pond than a little fish in a big pond.

POOR

Give me your tired, your poor.

The rich get richer and the poor get poorer.

PORCH

If you can't run with the big dogs, stay under the porch.

PORT

Any port in a storm.

POSITIVE

Accentuate the positive.

POSSESSION

Possession is nine points of the law.

POSSIBLE

All is for the best in the best of all possible worlds.

Anything is possible.

POT

A chicken in every pot.

The pot calling the kettle black.

Shit or get off the pot.

There's a pot of gold at the end of the rainbow.

A watched pot never boils.

You can't get a quart into a pint pot.

POTOMAC

All quiet along the Potomac.

POUND

An ounce of prevention is worth a pound of

cure.

Penny-wise and pound-foolish.

POUR

Don't pour new wine in old bottles. *See* Don't put new wine in old bottles.

It never rains but it pours.

When it rains, it pours. *See* It never rains but it pours.

POVERTY

Poverty is no crime. *See* Poverty is no sin.

Poverty is no disgrace. *See* Poverty is no sin.

Poverty is no sin.

POWDER

Put your trust in God, and keep your powder dry.

POWER

Knowledge is power.

Money is power.

Power corrupts, and absolute power corrupts absolutely.

PRACTICE

Practice makes perfect.

Practice what you preach.

What a tangled web we weave when first we practice to deceive.

PRAISE

Praise the bridge that carries you over.

Praise the Lord and pass the ammunition.

PRAY

The family that prays together stays together.

On a wing and a prayer.

Sow your wild oats.

Work and pray, live on hay, you'll get pie in the sky when you die.

PREACH

Practice what you preach.

PRECIOUS

A good name is better than precious ointment.

PREPARE

Hope for the best and prepare for the worst.

If you want peace, prepare for war.

PRETTY

Handsome (pretty) is as handsome (pretty) does.

PREVENTION

An ounce of prevention is worth a pound of cure.

Prevention is better than cure. *See* An ounce of prevention is worth a pound of cure.

Prevention is cheaper than treatment. *See* An ounce of prevention is worth a pound of cure.

PRIDE

Pride goes before a fall.

PRISON

Stone walls do not a prison make.

PROBLEM

If you're not part of the solution, you're part of the problem.

No problem.

PROCRASTINATION

Procrastination is the thief of time.

PROLETARIANS

The proletarians have nothing to lose but their chains.

PROLOGUE

What's past is prologue.

PROMISE

I have promises to keep, and miles to go before I sleep.

A promise is a promise.

Promises are like piecrust: they are made to be broken.

Promises, promises!

PROOF

The proof of the pudding is in the eating.

PROPHET

A prophet is not without honor, save in his own country.

PROPOSE

Man proposes, God disposes.

PROSPERITY

Prosperity is just around the corner.

PROTECT

God save me from my friends—I can protect myself from my enemies. *See* Save us from our enemies.

PROVE

The exception proves the rule. *See* There is an

exception to every rule.

One is innocent until proven guilty.

PROVIDENCE

Providence is always on the side of the big battalions. *See* God is always on the side of the big battalions.

PUBLIC

Don't air your dirty linen in public.

PUDDING

The proof of the pudding is in the eating.

PULL

Don't try to pull yourself up by your own bootstraps.

PUNCTUALITY

Punctuality is the politeness of kings.

PUPPY

If you're gonna run with the big dogs, you can't pee like a puppy. *See* If you can't run with the big dogs, stay under the porch.

PURPOSE

The devil can cite scripture for his purpose.

There's a season and a time for every purpose under the heaven.

PURSE

You can't make a silk purse out of a sow's ear.

PURSUIT

Life, liberty, and the pursuit of happiness.

PUT

Always put your best foot forward.

Don't put all your eggs in one basket.

Don't put new wine in old bottles.

Don't put off until tomorrow what you can do today. *See* Never put off until tomorrow what you can do today.

Don't put the cart before the horse.

Never put off until tomorrow what you can do today.

Put first things first. *See* First things first.

Put that in your pipe and smoke it.

Put up or shut up.

Put your money where your mouth is.

Put your trust in God, and keep your powder dry.

You can't put new wine in old bottles. *See* Don't put new wine in old bottles.

PYRRHIC

Pyrrhic victory.

QUARREL

The bad workman always quarrels with his tools.

It takes two to make a quarrel.

QUART

You can't get a quart into a pint pot.

QUARTERBACKING

Monday morning quarterbacking.

QUESTION

Ask me no questions and I'll tell you no lies.

A fool can ask more questions in an hour than a wise man can answer in seven years.

That's the $64,000 question.

There are two sides to every question. *See* There are two sides to every story.

To be, or not to be: that is the question.

QUID

Quid pro quo.

QUIET

All quiet along the Potomac.

All quiet on the Western Front.

Anything for (a little) peace and quiet. *See* Anything for a quiet life.

Anything for a quiet life.

QUIT, QUITTER

A winner never quits, and a quitter never wins.

RACE

Slow and steady wins the race.

RAIN, RAINY

It never rains but it pours.

Save for a rainy day.

When it rains, it pours. *See* It never rains but it pours.

RAINBOW

There's a pot of gold at the end of the rainbow.

RASCAL

Turn the rascals out.

RAT

Rats desert a sinking ship.

RATHER

I would rather die on my feet than live on my

knees.

On the whole, I'd rather be in Philadelphia.

REACH

When I hear the word culture, I reach for my gun.

READ

Read my lips.

All I know is what I read in the papers.

REAL

It's the real McCoy.

It's the real thing.

REAP

As you sow, so (shall) you reap.

They that sow the wind shall reap the whirlwind.

You shall (will) reap what you sow. *See* As you sow, so (shall) you reap.

RECALL

Words once spoken you can never recall.

RECEIVE

It is more blessed to give than to receive.

RECKONING

After the feast comes the reckoning.

REGRET

I only regret that I have but one life to lose for my country.

REMEMBER

Remember the Alamo!

Those who cannot remember the past are condemned to repeat it.

RENDER

Render unto Caesar the things which are Caesar's and to God the things that are God's.

REPEAT

History doesn't repeat itself—historians do. *See*

History repeats itself.

History never repeats itself. *See* History repeats itself.

History repeats itself.

Those who cannot remember the past are condemned to repeat it.

REPENT

Marry in haste, repent at leisure.

REPORT

The reports of my death are greatly exaggerated.

REPUTATION

A good reputation is more valuable than money.

REQUIRE

Everyone to whom much is given, of him will much be required.

RESIDUE

Luck is the residue of design.

RETURN

The dog always returns to his vomit.

REVENGE

Revenge is sweet.

REWARD

Virtue is its own reward.

RICH, RICHER

It is easier for a camel to go (pass) through the eye of a needle than it is for a rich man to enter the kingdom of heaven.

The rich get richer and the poor get poorer.

RIDDANCE

Good riddance to bad rubbish!

RIDE

If wishes were horses, beggars would ride.

There's no such thing as a free ride.

RIDICULOUS

From the sublime to the ridiculous is but a step.

RIGHT

The customer is always right.

God's in his heaven; all's right with the world.

I disapprove of what you say, but I will defend to the death your right to say it.

Might makes right.

Never let your left hand know what your right hand is doing.

Our country, right or wrong.

Two wrongs don't make a right.

RISE

Early to bed and early to rise, makes a man healthy, wealthy, and wise.

A rising tide will lift all boats.

RIVER

Sell down the river.

You can't step twice into the same river.

ROAD

All roads lead to Rome.

It is a long road that has no turning.

Let's get the show on the road.

The road to hell is paved with good intentions.

When you come to a fork in the road, take it.

You'll take the high road, and I'll take the low road.

ROB

Rob Peter to pay Paul.

ROCK

Between a rock and a hard place.

If frogs had wings, they wouldn't bump their tails on rocks.

Don't rock the boat!

ROD

Spare the rod and spoil the child.

ROLL

Heads will roll.

A rolling stone gathers no moss.

ROME, ROMAN

All roads lead to Rome.

Nero fiddled while Rome burned.

Rome was not built in a day.

When in Rome do as the Romans do.

ROMEO

O Romeo, Romeo! wherefore art thou Romeo?

ROOM

There's always room at the top.

ROOST

The chickens have come home to roost.

ROOT

Money is the root of all evil.

ROPE

Give him enough rope and he'll hang himself.

Never speak of rope in the house of a man who has been hanged.

ROSE

Everything's coming up roses.

Life is no bed of roses.

A rose by another name would smell as sweet.

A rose is a rose is a rose is a rose.

ROSEBUD

Gather ye rosebuds while ye may.

ROTTEN

The rotten apple spoils the barrel.

Something is rotten in the state of Denmark.

ROUGH

You have to take the rough with the smooth.

ROUND

Love makes the world go round.

You can't fit a round peg in a square hole.

RUB

There's the rub.

RUBBISH

Good riddance to bad rubbish.

RUBE

A Rube Goldberg machine.

RUBICON

Crossing the Rubicon.

RUBIES

Wisdom is better than rubies.

RULE

Don't change the rules in the middle of the game.

The exception proves the rule. *See* There is an exception to every rule.

Rules are made to be broken.

There is an exception to every rule.

RUN

The course of true love never did run smooth.

Don't close (bar, lock, shut) the barn (stable) door after the horse runs away (has fled, has been stolen).

He who fights and runs away, may live to fight
another day.

If you can't run with the big dogs, stay under the porch.

If you're gonna run with the big dogs, you can't pee like a puppy. *See* If you can't run with the big dogs, stay under the porch.

It runs in the family.

Still waters run deep.

You can run, but you can't hide.

You have to learn to walk before you can run.

You never miss the water till the well runs dry.

RUSH

Fools rush in where angels fear to tread.

RUSSIAN

The Russians are coming. *See* The British are coming.

Scratch a Russian and you find a Tartar.

SAFE

Better safe than sorry.

The world must be made safe for democracy.

SAFETY

Safety first.

There's safety in numbers.

SAME

Don't make the same mistake twice.

Lightning never strikes twice in the same place.

Toot your own horn lest the same be never tooted.

You can't step twice into the same river.

SAND

Footprints on the sands of time.

He could sell sand to the Arabs. *See* He could sell ice to an Eskimo.

An ostrich with its head in the sand.

SANTA CLAUS

Yes, Virginia, there is a Santa Claus.

SAUCE

What's sauce for the goose is sauce for the gander.

SAVAGE

Music hath charms to soothe the savage breast.

SAVE

A prophet is not without honor, save in his own country.

Save for a rainy day.

Save us from our friends.

A stitch in time saves nine.

SAY, SAID

Do as I say, not as I do.

Don't do as I do, but as I say. *See* Do as I say, not as I do.

Easier said than done.

I disapprove of what you say, but I will defend to the death your right to say it.

It's not what you say, but how you say it.

Least said, soonest mended.

Never say die.

Never say never.

Say uncle.

Those who say don't know, and those who know don't say. *See* Those who know don't speak; those who speak don't know.

Watch what we do, not what we say.

When a lady says no, she means perhaps; when she says perhaps, she means yes; when she says yes, she is no lady.

You can say that again.

You said it.

SCHEME

The best-laid schemes of mice and men often go (gang) a-gley.

SCHOOL

Never tell tales out of school.

SCORN

Hell hath no fury like a woman scorned.

SCRAMBLE

Scrambled eggs can't be unscrambled. *See* You can't unscramble eggs.

SCRATCH

Scratch a Russian and you find a Tartar.

You scratch my back, I'll scratch yours.

SCRIPTURE

The devil can cite scripture for his purpose.

SEA

Between the devil and the deep blue sea.

There are other fish in the sea.

SEASON

There's a season and a time for every purpose under the heaven.

SEE

Believe nothing you hear, and only half of what you see. *See* Believe only half of what you see and nothing you hear.

Believe only half of what you see and nothing you hear.

I came, I saw, I conquered.

I have seen the future, and it works.

I think that I shall never see a poem lovely as a tree.

If I have seen further it is by standing on the shoulders of giants.

If you've seen one, you've seen 'em all.

None so blind as those who refuse to see. *See* There are none so blind as those who will not see.

Now you see it, now you don't.

See no evil, hear no evil, speak no evil.

Seeing is believing.

Sometimes one can't see the wood for the trees.

There are none so blind as those who will not see.

What you see is what you get.

You ain't seen nothin' yet.

SEEK

Seek and ye shall find. *See* Ask, and it shall be given you; seek, and you shall find; knock, and it shall be opened unto you.

Water seeks its own level.

SEIZE

Seize the moment.

SELDOM

Opportunity seldom knocks twice. *See* Opportunity knocks but once.

SELL

He could sell a drowning man a glass of water. *See* He could sell ice to an Eskimo.

He could sell ice to an Eskimo.

He could sell sand to the Arabs. *See* He could sell ice to an Eskimo.

Never sell America short.

Sell down the river.

SEPARATE

Separate the men from the boys.

Separate the sheep from the goats.

Separate the wheat from the chaff.

SEPARATELY

We must indeed all hang together, or, most assuredly, we shall all hang separately.

SERVE

First come, first served.

No man can serve two masters. *See* You can't serve God and mammon.

You can't serve God and mammon.

SET

Set a thief to catch a thief. *See* It takes a thief to catch a thief.

The sun never sets on the British Empire.

SEVEN

A fool can ask more questions in an hour than a wise man can answer in seven years.

SHAKE

The tail cannot shake the dog.

SHAME

Fool me once, shame on you; fool me twice, shame on me.

Tell the truth and shame the devil.

SHEEP

There's a black sheep in every flock.

A/The wolf in sheep's clothing.

SHINE

Make hay while the sun shines.

SHIP

Don't give up the ship.

Loose lips sink ships.

Rats desert a sinking ship.

Ships that pass in the night.

A slip of the lip can sink a ship. *See* Loose lips sink ships.

SHIRTSLEEVE

From shirtsleeves to shirtsleeves in three generations.

SHIT

The shit hits the fan.

Shit or get off the pot.

SHOE

For want of a nail, the shoe was lost; for want of a shoe, the horse was lost. *See* For want of a nail the kingdom was lost.

I wouldn't want to be in his shoes (place).

If the shoe fits, put it on. *See* If the shoe fits, wear it.

If the shoe fits, wear it.

The shoe is on the other foot.

SHOEMAKER

Let the cobbler (shoemaker) stick to his last. *See* A/The cobbler should stick to his last.

The shoemaker's kids always go barefoot.

SHOOT

Don't shoot the messenger.

Don't shoot the piano-player: he's doing the best he can.

Shoot first and ask questions afterwards.

SHORT

Art is long, life is short.

Life is short and sweet.

Life is too short.

Never sell America short.

SHOT

A shot in the arm.

SHOULDER

Dwarfs standing on the shoulders of giants. *See* If I have seen further it is by standing on the shoulders of giants.

If I have seen further it is by standing on the shoulders of giants.

On the shoulders of giants. *See* If I have seen further it is by standing on the shoulders of giants.

SHOUT

Don't shout until you are out of the woods.

It's all over but the shouting.

SHOW

Let's get the show on the road.

The show must go on.

SHOW BUSINESS

That's show business.

There's no business like show business.

SHOWER

April showers bring May flowers.

SHUT

It's no use to close (bar, lock, shut) the barn (stable) door after the horse has been stolen. *See* Don't close (bar, lock, shut) the barn (stable) door after the horse runs away (has fled, has been stolen).

SIDE

Always look on the bright side.

God is always on the side of the big battalions.

The grass is always greener on the other side of the fence.

It is better to be on the safe side.

Look on the bright side. *See* Always look on the bright side.

Providence is always on the side of the big battalions. *See* God is always on the side of the big battalions.

There are two sides to every story.

SIGHT

Out of sight, out of mind.

SIGN

It's a sign of the times.

SILENCE

Silence is golden.

Speech is silver, silence is golden.

SILK

You can't make a silk purse out of a sow's ear.

SILVER

Every cloud has a silver lining.

Every man is not born with a silver spoon in his mouth.

Speech is silver, silence is golden.

SIMPLE

It's as simple as that.

SIN

Let him who is without sin cast (throw) the first stone.

Poverty is no sin.

SINCEREST

Imitation is the sincerest form of flattery.

SING

The opera ain't over till the fat lady sings.

Whose bread I eat, his song I sing.

SINK

Everything but the kitchen sink.

Loose lips sink ships.

Rats desert a sinking ship.

Sink or swim.

A slip of the lip can sink a ship. *See* Loose lips sink ships.

SITUATION

It's a Catch-22 situation.

SIX

Six of one and half a dozen of the other.

SKELETON

There's a skeleton in every family closet.

SKIN

Beauty is only skin-deep.

It's no skin off my nose.

There's more than one way to skin a cat.

SKITTLE

Life isn't all beer and skittles.

SKY

Pie in the sky. *See* Work and pray, live on hay, you'll get pie in the sky when you die.

The sky is not falling. *See* The sky is not going to fall.

The sky is not going to fall.

The sky's the limit.

SLEEP

Let sleeping dogs lie.

SLEEVE

Don't wear your heart on your sleeve.

SLIP

There's many a slip between (the) cup and (the) lip.

SLOW, SLOWLY

Let him twist slowly, slowly in the wind.

Make haste slowly.

The mills of the gods grind slowly, but they grind exceedingly fine.

Slow and steady wins the race.

Slow but sure.

SMALL

The best things come in small packages.

It's a small world.

It's better to light one small candle than to curse the darkness. *See* It is better to light one (little) candle than to curse the darkness.

One small step for man, one giant leap for mankind. *See* That's one small step for [a] man, one giant leap for mankind.

Small world. *See* It's a small world.

That's one small step for [a] man, one giant leap for mankind.

SMART

It's not the early bird that catches the worm, but the smart one. *See* The early bird catches the worm.

SMELL

Money has no smell.

A rose by another name would smell as sweet.

SMOKE

No smoke without fire. *See* Where there's smoke, there's fire.

Put that in your pipe and smoke it.

Smoking and sports don't mix. *See* Oil and water don't mix.

Smoking gun.

Where there's smoke, there's fire.

SMOOTH

The course of true love never did run smooth.

You have to take the rough with the smooth.

SNOW

Where are the snows of yesteryear?

SO

As Maine goes, so goes the nation.

I told you so.

So far, so good.

So help me God.

SOFT

A soft answer turns away wrath.

SOLDIER

Old soldiers never die; they just fade away.

SOLOMON

The wisdom of Solomon.

SOLUTION

If you're not part of the solution, you're part of the problem.

SOME

All animals are equal, but some animals are more equal than others.

You can fool some of the people all the time, all the people some of the time, but you cannot fool all the people all the time.

You win some (a few), you lose some (a few).

SOMEBODY

You can't beat somebody with nobody.

SOMEONE

Two strikes against someone (something). *See* Three strikes and you're out.

What makes someone tick?

SOMETHING

If you want something done right, do it yourself.

Something is rotten in the state of Denmark.

Two strikes against someone (something). *See*

Three strikes and you're out.
You don't get something for nothing.

SOMETIMES
Even Homer sometimes nods.
A mother can take care of ten children, but sometimes ten children can't take care of one mother.
Sometimes one can't see the wood for the trees.

SON
Like father, like son.

SOON, SOONER, SOONEST
A fool and his money are soon parted.
Least said, soonest mended.
The sooner the better.

SOOTHE
Music hath charms to soothe the savage breast.

SORROW
Parting is such sweet sorrow.

SORRY
Better safe than sorry.
It is better to be safe than sorry. *See* Better safe than sorry.

SORT
It takes all sorts to make a world. *See* It takes all kinds of people to make a world.

SOUL
Brevity is the soul of wit.

SOW
As you sow, so (shall) you reap.
Sow your wild oats.
They that sow the wind shall reap the whirlwind.
You can't make a silk purse out of a sow's ear.

SPADE
Call a spade a spade.

SPAIN
Don't build castles in Spain. *See* Don't build castles in the air.

SPARE
Brother can you spare a dime?
Spare the rod and spoil the child.

SPEAK
Actions speak louder than words.

A liar is not believed when he tells (speaks) the truth.
Never speak ill of the dead.
Never speak of rope in the house of a man who has been hanged.
See no evil, hear no evil, speak no evil.
Speak of the devil! *See* Talk of the devil, and he is bound to appear.
Speak softly and carry a big stick.
Speak the truth and shame the devil. *See* Tell the truth and shame the devil.
Speak well of the dead. *See* Never speak ill of the dead.
Those who know don't speak; those who speak, don't know.
When X speaks, Y listens.

SPEECH
Speech is silver, silence is golden.

SPEED
Damn the torpedoes! Full speed ahead!

SPICE
Variety is the spice of life.

SPILL
Don't cry over spilled milk.

SPIRIT
The spirit is willing but the flesh is weak.

SPITE
Don't cut off your nose to spite your face.

SPOIL
Spare the rod and spoil the child.
The rotten apple spoils the barrel.
Too many cooks spoil the broth.

SPOILS
To the victor belong the spoils.

SPOON
Every man is not born with a silver spoon in his mouth.
He who sups with the Devil should have a long spoon.

SPOT
The leopard cannot change its spots.

SPRING
Hope springs eternal in the human breast.
In the spring a young man's fancy lightly turns to thoughts of love.

SQUARE

You can't fit a round peg in a square hole.

Back to square one.

SQUEAK

The wheel that does the squeaking is the one that gets the grease.

STABLE

Don't close (bar, lock, shut) the barn (stable) door after the horse runs away (has fled, has been stolen).

STAGE

All the world's a stage.

STAND

Dwarfs standing on the shoulders of giants. *See* If I have seen further it is by standing on the shoulders of giants.

An empty sack cannot stand upright.

Give me where to stand, and I will move the earth.

Here I stand. I can do no other.

If I have seen further it is by standing on the shoulders of giants.

If you can't stand the heat, get out of the kitchen.

Stand on your own two feet.

Stand up and be counted.

United we stand, divided we fall.

STAR

Hitch your wagon to a star.

START

Don't start anything you can't finish.

STARVE

Feed a cold; starve a fever.

STATE

I am the state.

Something is rotten in the state of Denmark.

STAY

The family that prays together stays together.

Stay tuned.

STEADY

Slow and steady wins the race.

STEP

Don't step on other people's toes. *See* Don't tread on other people's toes.

The first step is the hardest.

From the sublime to the ridiculous is but a step.

It's the first step that costs. *See* The first step is the hardest.

It's the first step that counts. *See* The first step is the hardest.

A journey of a thousand miles begins with one single step.

One small step for man, one giant leap for mankind. *See* That's one small step for [a] man, one giant leap for mankind.

One step at a time. *See* One thing at a time.

Step on a crack, break your mother's back.

Step up to the plate.

That's one small step for [a] man, one giant leap for mankind.

You can never step into the same river twice. *See* You can't step twice into the same river.

You can't step twice into the same river.

STEW

Let him stew in his own juice.

STICK

A/The cobbler should stick to his last.

Don't stick your neck out.

Let the cobbler (shoemaker) stick to his last. *See* A/The cobbler should stick to his last.

Speak softly and carry a big stick.

Stick to your guns.

Sticks and stones may break my bones, but words (names) will never hurt me.

STIFF

Keep a stiff upper lip.

STILL

Still waters run deep.

STING

If a bee stings you once, it's the bee's fault; if a bee stings you twice, it's your own damn fault. *See* Fool me once, shame on you; fool me twice, shame on me.

STINK

A fish stinks from the head.

Money doesn't stink. *See* Money has no smell.

STITCH

A stitch in time saves nine.

STOLEN

Don't close (bar, lock, shut) the barn (stable) door after the horse runs away (has fled, has been stolen).

Stolen waters are sweet.

STOMACH

An army marches on its stomach.

The eyes are bigger than the stomach.

The way to a man's heart is through his stomach.

STONE

Leave no stone unturned.

Let him who is without sin cast (throw) the first stone.

People who live in glass houses shouldn't throw stones.

A rolling stone gathers no moss.

Sticks and stones may break my bones, but words (names) will never hurt me.

Stone walls do not a prison make.

Those who live in glass houses shouldn't throw stones. *See* People who live in glass houses shouldn't throw stones.

You can't get blood from a stone.

STORM

After a storm comes a calm.

Any port in a storm.

The calm before the storm. *See* After a storm comes a calm.

STORY

There are two sides to every story.

STRANGE, STRANGER

Adversity makes strange bedfellows. *See* Misery makes strange bedfellows.

Fact is stranger than fiction. *See* Truth is stranger than fiction.

Misery makes strange bedfellows.

Politics makes strange bedfellows.

Truth is stranger than fiction.

STRAW

A drowning man will catch at a straw.

It's the last straw that breaks the camel's back.

You can't make bricks without straw.

STRENGTH

In unity there is strength.

STRIKE

Lightning never strikes twice in the same place.

Strike while the iron is hot.

Three strikes and you're in. *See* Three strikes and you're out.

Three strikes and you're out.

Two strikes against someone (something). *See* Three strikes and you're out.

STROKE

Different strokes for different folks.

Little strokes fell great oaks.

STRONGER

A chain is no stronger than its weakest link.

STUBBORN

Facts are stubborn things.

STUPID

It's the economy, Stupid!

SUBLIME

From the sublime to the ridiculous is but a step.

SUBSTITUTE

In war there is no substitute for victory.

SUCCEED, SUCCESS, SUCCESSFUL

Behind every successful man there is a woman. *See* Behind every great man there is a great woman.

If at first you don't succeed, try, try again.

Nothing succeeds like success.

Success breeds success.

Success has many parents. *See* Victory has a hundred fathers and defeat is an orphan.

Success is never final.

Success is never final and failure is never fatal. *See* Success is never final.

You can't argue with success.

SUCH

Another such victory, and we are undone.

Parting is such sweet sorrow.

There's no such thing as a free lunch.

There's no such thing as a free ride.

With such friends, one hardly needs enemies.

SUCK

Don't (try to) teach your grandmother (how) to suck eggs.

SUCKER

Never give a sucker an even break.

There's a sucker born every minute.

SUCKLING

Out of the mouths of babes and sucklings come great truths.

SUFFICIENT

A word to the wise is sufficient.

SUMMER

One swallow does not make a summer.

SUN

Make hay while the sun shines.

Nothing new under the sun. *See* There's nothing new under the sun.

The sun never sets on the British Empire.

There's nothing new under the sun.

SURE

Don't take (tear) down a fence (wall) unless you are sure why it was put up.

Slow but sure.

SURVIVAL

It's survival of the fittest.

SUSPICION

Caesar's wife must be above suspicion.

SWALLOW

One swallow does not make a summer.

SWEAT

Blood, toil, tears and sweat. *See* I have nothing to offer but blood, toil, tears, and sweat.

I have nothing to offer but blood, toil, tears, and sweat.

No sweat.

SWEEP

A new broom sweeps clean.

SWEET, SWEETER

The blacker the berry, the sweeter the juice.

The darker the berry, the sweeter the juice. *See* The blacker the berry, the sweeter the juice.

Forbidden fruit is sweet.

Parting is such sweet sorrow.

Revenge is sweet.

A rose by another name would smell as sweet.

Stolen waters are sweet.

You have to take the bitter with the sweet.

SWINE

Don't cast (throw) your pearls before swine.

SWORD

He who lives by the sword dies by the sword.

The pen is mightier than the sword.

The sword of Damocles hanging over one.

SYSTEM

All systems go.

TAIL

Heads I win, tails you lose.

He who has a tiger by the tail dare not let it go.

If frogs had wings, they wouldn't bump their tails on rocks.

The tail cannot shake the dog.

TAKE

The devil take the hindmost.

Don't take any wooden nickels.

Don't take (tear) down a fence (wall) unless you are sure why it was put up.

Don't take the name of the Lord in vain.

Give him an inch, and he will take a mile.

I won't take no for an answer.

It takes a heap of living to make (a house) a home.

It takes a thief to catch a thief.

It takes all kinds of people to make a world.

It takes all sorts to make a world. *See* It takes all kinds of people to make a world.

It takes one to know one.

It takes two to make a quarrel.

It takes two to tango.

It takes two wings to fly.

A jackass can kick a barn door down, but it takes a carpenter to build one.

Let nature take its course.

Nature will take its course. *See* Let nature take its course.

Neither give nor take offense.

Neither take offense nor make offense. *See* Neither give nor take offense.

Take it easy.

Take it from me.

Take it or leave it.

Take my wife—please!

470

Take my word for it.

Take the bitter with the sweet. *See* You have to take the bitter with the sweet.

When you come to a fork in the road, take it.

You can take a boy out of the country, but you can't take the country out of the boy.

You can't take it with you.

You have to take the bad with the good.

You have to take the bitter with the sweet.

You have to take the rough with the smooth.

You pays your money, and you takes your choice.

You take my word for it. *See* Take my word for it.

You'll take the high road, and I'll take the low road.

TALE

Dead men tell no tales.

Don't tell tales out of school. *See* Never tell tales out of school.

Never tell tales out of school.

TALK

Everybody talks about the weather, but nobody does anything about it.

Talk is cheap.

Talk of the devil, and he is bound to appear.

TANGLED

What a tangled web we weave when first we practice to deceive.

TANGO

It takes two to tango.

TASK

A task that's worth doing at all is worth doing well. *See* Anything worth doing is worth doing well.

TASTE

Every man to his own taste.

Tastes differ. *See* There's no accounting for tastes.

There's no accounting for tastes.

TAXES

Nothing is certain but death and taxes.

TEACH, TEACHER

Experience is the best teacher.

Give a man a fish, and you feed him for a day; show (teach) him how to catch fish, and you feed him for a lifetime.

He who can, does; he who cannot, teaches. *See* Those who can, do. Those who cannot, teach.

You can't teach an old dog new tricks.

TEAPOT

A tempest in a teapot.

TEARS

I have nothing to offer but blood, toil, tears, and sweat.

TELL, TOLD

Ask me no questions and I'll tell you no lies.

Blood will tell.

Dead men tell no tales.

I told you so.

If I've told you once, I've told you a thousand times.

A liar is not believed when he tells (speaks) the truth.

A little bird told (whispered to) me.

Tell that (it) to the marines.

Tell the truth and shame the devil.

Time will tell.

TEMPEST

A tempest in a teapot.

TEN

I wouldn't touch it (him) with a ten-foot pole.

TEND

Every employee tends to rise to his level of incompetence.

TERRIBLE

A mind is a terrible thing to waste.

TERRITORY

It comes with the territory.

TGIF.

See Thank God It's Friday.

THANK

Thank God It's Friday.

Thanks, but no thanks.

THAT

That's all there is to it.

That's that.

THEREFORE

I think, therefore I am.

THICKER

Blood is thicker than water.

THIEF

It takes a thief to catch a thief.

Procrastination is the thief of time.

Set a thief to catch a thief. *See* It takes a thief to catch a thief.

There is honor (even) among thieves.

There's no honor among thieves. *See* There is honor (even) among thieves.

THING

All good things come in threes.

All good things come to those who wait.

All good things must come to an end.

All things to all men.

The best things come in small packages.

The best things in life are free.

Facts are stubborn things.

First things first.

If a thing is worth doing, it's worth doing twice.

It's the greatest thing since sliced bread.

It's too much of a good thing.

A little knowledge (learning) is a dangerous thing.

A mind is a terrible thing to waste.

One step at a time.

One thing at a time.

The only thing we have to fear is fear itself.

Put first things first. *See* First things first.

Render unto Caesar the things which are Caesar's and unto God the things that are God's.

There's no such thing as a free lunch.

There's no such thing as a free ride.

A thing of beauty is a joy for ever.

A thing worth doing is worth doing well. *See* If a thing is worth doing, it's worth doing twice.

Winning isn't everything, it's the only thing.

THINK

Evil to him who evil thinks.

Great minds think alike.

I can't think when I concentrate.

I think that I shall never see a poem lovely as a tree.

I think, therefore I am.

There's nothing good or bad but thinking makes it so.

Think before you speak.

THOUGHTS

In the spring a young man's fancy lightly turns to thoughts of love.

A penny for your thoughts.

THIRD

The third time is the charm.

THIRSTY

Dig the well before you are thirsty.

THIRTY

Thirty pieces of silver.

THOUGH

Live every day as though it were your last.

THOUSAND

A coward dies a thousand deaths. *See* The coward dies many times.

The coward dies a thousand deaths, the brave but one. *See* The coward dies many times.

If I've told you once, I've told you a thousand times.

A journey of a thousand miles begins with one step.

A picture is worth a thousand words. *See* One picture is worth a thousand words.

One picture is worth a thousand words.

THREE

All good things come in threes.

Three strikes and you're in. *See* Three strikes and you're out.

Three strikes and you're out.

Two is company, three is a crowd.

THROW

Don't throw a monkey wrench in the works.

Don't throw caution to the wind.

Don't throw out the baby with the bath water.

Let him who is without sin cast (throw) the first stone.

People who live in glass houses shouldn't throw stones.

TICK

What makes someone tick?

TIDE

A rising tide will lift all boats.

There's a tide in the affairs of men.

Time and tide wait for no man.

TILL

It ain't over till it's over. *See* It's not over till it's over.

It ain't over till the fat lady sings. *See* The opera ain't over till the fat lady sings.

It's not over till it's over.

The opera ain't over till the fat lady sings.

Till death do us part.

Till hell freezes over.

You never miss the water till the well runs dry.

TIME

The coward dies many times.

Footprints on the sands of time.

I wouldn't give him the time of day.

If I've told you once, I've told you a thousand times.

It was the best of times, it was the worst of times.

It's a sign of the times.

Now is the time for all good men to come to the aid of their country.

One step at a time.

One thing at a time.

Procrastination is the thief of time.

A stitch in time saves nine.

There's a season and a time for every purpose under the heaven.

There's a time and place for everything.

There's a time for all things. *See* There's a time and place for everything.

There's a time for everything. *See* There's a time and place for everything.

There's a time to be born and a time to die. *See*

There's a season and a time for every purpose under heaven.

There's always a first time for everything. *See* There must be a first time for everything.

There's no time like the present.

The third time is the charm.

Time and tide wait for no man.

Time flies.

Time heals all wounds.

Time is money.

Time is of the essence.

A time to be born and a time to die. *See*

There's a season and a time for every purpose under heaven.

Time will tell.

Times change. *See* Times change and we with time.

Times change and we with time.

Timing is everything.

You can fool some of the people all the time, all the people some of the time, but you cannot fool all the people all the time.

TIP

It's the tip of the iceberg.

TIRED

Give me your tired, your poor.

TODAY

Don't put off until tomorrow what you can do today. *See* Never put off until tomorrow what you can do today.

Here today, gone tomorrow.

Never put off until tomorrow what you can do today.

TOE

Don't tread on other people's toes.

TOGETHER

All the king's horses, and all the king's men, couldn't put Humpty together again.

Birds of a feather flock together.

The family that prays together stays together.

If we don't hang together we will hang separately. *See* We must indeed all hang together, or, most assuredly, we shall all hang separately.

Let's all hang together or we shall surely hang separately. *See* We must indeed all hang together, or, most assuredly, we shall all hang separately.

We must indeed all hang together, or, most assuredly, we shall all hang separately.

TOIL

Blood, toil, tears and sweat. *See* I have nothing to offer but blood, toil, tears, and sweat.

Double, double toil and trouble; fire burn, and cauldron bubble.

I have nothing to offer but blood, toil, tears, and sweat.

TOMORROW

Don't put off until tomorrow what you can do today. *See* Never put off until tomorrow what you can do today.

Eat, drink, and be merry, for tomorrow we die.

Here today, gone tomorrow.

Never put off until tomorrow what you can do today.

There's always (a) tomorrow.

Tomorrow, and tomorrow, and tomorrow.

Tomorrow is another day.

TONGUE

Has the cat got your tongue?

TOO

Don't have too many irons in the fire.

It's never too late to learn.

It's never too late to mend.

It's too little, too late.

This, too, will (shall) pass.

Too little, too late. *See* It's too little, too late.

Too many chiefs and not enough Indians. *See* All chiefs and no Indians.

Too many cooks spoil the broth.

You can't have your cake and eat it too.

TOOL

The bad workman always quarrels with his tools.

TOOT

Toot your own horn lest the same be never tooted.

TOOTH

An eye for an eye, a tooth for a tooth.

TOP

Cream always comes to the top.

There's always room at the top.

TORPEDO

Damn the torpedoes! Full speed ahead!

TOUCH

I wouldn't touch it (him) with a ten-foot pole.

TOUGH

When the going gets tough, the tough get going.

TOWER

The Tower of Babel.

TRADE

Jack of all trades and master of none.

TRASH

One man's trash is another man's treasure.

TRAVEL

An army travels on its stomach. *See* An army marches on its stomach.

Bad news travels fast.

It is better to travel hopefully than to arrive.

TREAD

Don't tread on me.

Don't tread on other people's toes.

Fools rush in where angels fear to tread.

TREASURE

One man's trash is another man's treasure.

TREE

The apple doesn't fall far from the tree.

I think that I shall never see a poem lovely as a tree.

It doesn't grow on trees. *See* Money doesn't grow on trees.

Money doesn't grow on trees.

A tree is known by its fruit.

You're barking up the wrong tree.

TRICK

You can't teach an old dog new tricks.

TROJAN

A Trojan horse.

TROUBLE

Double, double toil and trouble; fire burn, and cauldron bubble.

TRUE

It's too good to be true.

The course of true love never did run smooth.

TRUST

Put your trust in God, and keep your powder dry.

TRUTH

Beauty is truth, truth beauty.

A liar is not believed even when he tells (speaks) the truth.

Nothing could be further from the truth.

Nothing hurts like the truth. *See* The truth (always, often) hurts.

Out of the mouths of babes and sucklings

come great truths.

Tell the truth and shame the devil.

The truth (always, often) hurts.

Truth is beauty. *See* Beauty is truth, truth beauty.

Truth is stranger than fiction.

Truth is truth to the end of reckoning.

Truth lies at the bottom of the well.

The truth shall make you free.

Truth will (come) out.

In wine there is truth.

TRY

Don't (try to) teach your grandmother (how) to suck eggs.

Don't try to pull yourself up by your own bootstraps.

He would try to sell you the Brooklyn Bridge.

If at first you don't succeed, try, try again.

TUNE

He who calls the tune must pay the piper. *See* He who pays the piper calls the tune.

He who pays the piper calls the tune.

Stay tuned.

TUNNEL

There's always a light at the end of the tunnel.

TURF

It comes (goes) with the turf. *See* It comes with the territory.

TURN

Even a worm will turn.

One good turn deserves another.

A soft answer turns away wrath.

Turn the rascals out.

The worm turns. *See* Even a worm will turn.

TURNABOUT

Turnabout is fair play.

TURNIP

You can't get blood out of a turnip. *See* You can't get blood from a stone.

TWAIN

East is East, and West is West, and never the twain shall meet.

TWICE

Lightning never strikes twice in the same place.

Once burned, twice shy.

You can't step twice into the same river.

TWIST

Let him twist slowly, slowly in the wind.

TWO

A bird in the hand is worth two in the bush.

Choose the lesser of two evils.

It takes two to make a quarrel.

It takes two to tango.

It takes two wings to fly.

No man can serve two masters. *See* You can't serve God and mammon.

Of two evils choose the lesser. *See* Choose the lesser of two evils.

One can't be in two places at once.

Stand on your own two feet.

There are two sides to every story.

Two heads are better than one.

Two is company, three is a crowd.

Two strikes against someone (something). *See* Three strikes and you're out.

Two wrongs don't make a right.

UNDERESTIMATE

No one ever went broke underestimating the intelligence of the American people.

UNDONE

Another such victory, and we are undone.

What's done cannot be undone.

UGLY

The good, the bad, and the ugly.

UNCLE

Say uncle.

UNEASY

Uneasy lies the head that wears the crown.

UNION

In union there is strength. *See* In unity there is strength.

UNITE, UNITED

United we stand, divided we fall.

Workers of the world, unite!

UNITY

In unity there is strength.

UNLESS

Don't take (tear) down a fence (wall) unless you are sure why it was put up.

UNPUNISHED

No good deed goes unpunished.

UNSCRAMBLE

You can't unscramble eggs.

UNTIL

Don't fire until you see the whites of their eyes.

Don't judge a man until you have walked a mile in his boots.

UNTURNED

Leave no stone unturned.

UNUM

E pluribus unum.

UPPER

Keep a stiff upper lip.

USE

There's no use crying over spilled (spilt) milk. *See* Don't cry over spilled milk.

Would you buy a used car from this man?

USUAL

Business as usual.

Politics as usual.

VACUUM

Nature abhors a vacuum.

VALET

No man is a hero to his valet.

VALOR

Discretion is the better part of valor.

VALUABLE

A good reputation is more valuable than money.

VANITY

Vanity of vanities; all is vanity.

VARIETY

Age cannot wither her, nor custom stale her infinite variety.

Variety is the spice of life.

VENGEANCE

Vengeance is sweet. *See* Revenge is sweet.

VENI

Veni, vidi, vici. *See* I came, I saw, I conquered.

VINO

In vino veritas. *See* In wine there is truth.

VENTURE

Nothing ventured, nothing gained.

VERMONT

As Maine goes, so goes Vermont. *See* As Maine goes, so goes the nation.

VICE

Hypocrisy is the homage that vice pays to virtue.

VICI

Veni, vidi, vici. *See* I came, I saw, I conquered.

VICTOR, VICTORY

Another such victory, and we are undone.

In victory: magnanimity.

In war there is no substitute for victory.

One more such victory and we are lost. *See* Another such victory, and we are undone.

Pyrrhic victory.

To the victor belong the spoils.

The victor get the spoils. *See* To the victor belong the spoils.

Victory has a hundred fathers and defeat is an orphan.

VIDI

Veni, vidi, vici, *See* I came, I saw, I conquered.

VINEGAR

You can catch more flies with honey than with vinegar.

VIRGINIA

Yes, Virginia, there is a Santa Claus.

VIRTUE

Hypocrisy is the homage that vice pays to virtue.

Make a virtue of necessity.

Patience is a virtue.

Virtue is its own reward.

VISION

Where there's no vision, the people perish.

VOMIT

The dog always returns to his vomit.

WAGON

Hitch your wagon to a star.

WAIT

All good things come to those who wait.

Everything comes to those (the man, him) who (can, know how to) wait. *See* All good things come to those who wait.

Time and tide wait for no man.

WALK

Don't judge a man until you have walked a mile in his boots.

If it looks like a duck, walks like a duck, and quacks like a duck, it's a duck.

You have to learn to crawl before you can walk.

You have to learn to walk before you can run.

WALL

Don't take (tear) down a fence (wall) unless you are sure why it was put up.

The handwriting is on the wall.

Humpty Dumpty sat on a wall. *See* All the king's horses, and all the king's men, couldn't put Humpty together again.

Stone walls do not a prison make.

Walls have ears.

WANT

For want of a nail the kingdom was lost.

If you want peace, prepare for war.

If you want something done right, do it yourself.

Waste not, want not.

WAR

All's fair in love and war.

First in war, first in peace, first in the hearts of his countrymen.

If you want peace, prepare for war.

In war there is no substitute for victory.

War is hell.

War is too important to be left to the generals.

WARM

Cold hands, warm heart.

WART

Warts and all.

WASH

Don't wash your dirty linen in public. *See* Don't air your dirty linen in public.

It will all come out in the wash.

It won't wash.

One hand washes the other.

WASTE

Haste makes waste.

A mind is a terrible thing to waste.

Waste not, want not.

WATCH

Big Brother is watching you.

Watch my lips. *See* Read my lips.

Watch what we do, not what we say.

A watched pot never boils.

WATER

Blood is thicker than water.

Don't throw out the baby with the bath water.

A fish out of water.

Oil and water don't mix.

Still waters run deep.

Stolen waters are sweet.

That's water under the bridge (over the dam).

Water seeks its own level.

Water, water everywhere, nor any drop to drink.

You can lead a horse to water, but you cannot make him drink.

You never miss the water till the well runs dry.

WATERLOO

He met his Waterloo.

WATSON

Elementary, my dear Watson, elementary!

WAY

And that's the way it is.

Be nice to people on your way up because you'll meet them ('em) on your way down.

But that's the way it is. *See* And that's the way it is.

God moves in a mysterious way.

No way, José.

That's the way the ball bounces. *See* That's the way the cookie crumbles.

That's the way to go! *See* Way to go!

There's more than one way to skin a cat.

The way to a man's heart is through his stomach.

Way to go!

Where there's a will, there's a way.

You can't have it both ways.

You've come a long way, baby.

WEAK, WEAKEST

A chain is no stronger than its weakest link.

The spirit is willing but the flesh is weak.

WEALTH, WEALTHY

Early to bed and early to rise, makes a man healthy, wealthy, and wise.

Wealth makes many friends.

WEAR

If the shoe fits, wear it.

Uneasy lies the head that wears the crown.

WEATHER

Everybody talks about the weather, but nobody does anything about it.

WEAVE

What a tangled web we weave when first we practice to deceive.

WEB

What a tangled web we weave when first we practice to deceive.

WEEP, WEEPER

Finders keepers, losers weepers.

Laugh and the world laughs with you; weep and you weep alone.

WELL

All's well that ends well.

Anything worth doing is worth doing well.

Doing well by doing good.

Leave well enough alone.

You never miss the water till the well runs dry.

WEST, WESTERN

All quiet on the Western Front.

East is East, and West is West, and never the twain shall meet.

Go west, young man.

WHEEL

A/The squeaky wheel gets all the grease. *See* The wheel that does the squeaking is the one that gets the grease.

The wheel comes full circle.

The wheel that does the squeaking is the one that gets the grease.

WHIRLWIND

They that sow the wind shall reap the whirlwind.

WHITE

Don't fire until you see the whites of their eyes.

WHOLE

On the whole, I'd rather be in Philadelphia.

WHORE

Once a whore, always a whore. *See* Once a thief, always a thief.

WIFE

Caesar's wife must be above suspicion.

Take my wife—please!

WILD

Sow your wild oats.

WILL

Where there's a will, there's a way.

WILLING

The spirit is willing but the flesh is weak.

WIN, WINNER

Faint heart never won fair lady.

Heads I win, tails you lose.

Slow and steady wins the race.

Win this one for the Gipper.

A winner never quits, and a quitter never wins.

Winning isn't everything; it's the only thing.

You can't win 'em all.

You win some (a few), you lose some (a few).

WIND

Don't throw caution to the wind.

Gone with the wind.

It's an ill wind that blows no (nobody) good.

Let him twist slowly, slowly in the wind.

They that sow the wind shall reap the whirlwind.

WINE

Don't put new wine in old bottles.

In wine there is truth.

WING

If a pig had wings, it could fly.

If frogs had wings, they would not bump their tails on rocks.

It takes two wings to fly.

Pigs could fly if they had wings. *See* If a pig had wings, it could fly.

You can't fly with one wing. *See* It takes two wings to fly.

WINTER

The winter of our discontent.

WISDOM

Wisdom is better than rubies.

The wisdom of Solomon.

WISE

As wise as Solomon. *See* The wisdom of Solomon.

Early to bed and early to rise, makes a man healthy, wealthy, and wise.

Everybody is wise after the event. *See* It is easy to be wise after the event.

It is easy to be wise after the event.

Penny-wise and pound-foolish.

A word to the wise is sufficient.

WISH

Don't wish too hard: you might just get what you wished for.

If wishes were horses, then beggars would ride.

WIT

Brevity is the soul of wit.

WITHOUT

Let him who is without sin cast (throw) the first stone.

No smoke without fire. *See* Where there's smoke, there's fire.

A prophet is not without honor, save in his own country.

There are no gains without pains.

There's no rule without an exception. *See* There is an exception to every rule.

You can't live with men; neither can you live without them.

You can't make an omelet without breaking eggs.

You can't make bricks without straw.

WOLF

A/The wolf in sheep's clothing.

The wolf is at the door.

WOMAN

Behind every great man there is a great woman.

Hell hath no fury like a woman scorned.

A woman's place is in the home.

A woman's work is never done.

WOOD

Don't shout until you are out of the woods.

Sometimes one can't see the wood for the trees.

WOODEN

Don't take any wooden nickels.

WORD

Actions, not words. *See* Deeds, not words.

Actions speak louder than words.

Deeds, not words.

In the beginning was the word.

A man's word is as good as his bond.

Mum's the word!

One picture is worth a thousand words.

Sticks and stones may break my bones, but words (names) will never hurt me.

Take my word for it.

When I hear the word culture, I reach for my gun.

A word to the wise is sufficient.

Words once spoken you can never recall.

WORK, WORKER, WORKMAN

All work and no play makes Jack a dull boy.

A bad workman always quarrels with his tools.

Don't throw a monkey wrench in the works.

He who does not work, neither should he eat.

I have seen the future, and it works.

It's all in a day's work.

Work and pray, live on hay, you'll get pie in the sky when you die.

Work never hurt anybody.

Workers of the world, unite!

WORLD

All is for the best in the best of all possible worlds.

All the world's a stage.

God's in his heaven; all's right with the world.

In this world nothing is certain but death and taxes. *See* Nothing is certain but death and taxes.

It takes all kinds of people to make a world.

It takes all sorts to make a world. *See* It takes all kinds of people to make a world.

It's a small world.

It's not the end of the world.

Laugh and the world laughs with you; weep and you weep alone.

Love makes the world go round.

Workers of the world, unite!

The world is a stage and all the men and women merely players. *See* All the world's a stage.

The world is an (one's) oyster.

WORM

The early bird catches the worm.

Even a worm will turn.

It's like opening a can of worms.

It's not the early bird that catches the worm, but the smart one. *See* The early bird catches the worm.

It's the early bird that catches the worm. *See* The early bird catches the worm.

The worm turns.

WORRY

Don't worry. Be happy.

WORSE

His bark is worse than his bite.

WORST

A cobbler's child is always the worst shod. *See* The shoemaker's kids always go barefoot.

Every man is his own worst enemy.

Hope for the best and prepare for the worst.

It was the best of times, it was the worst of times.

The worst is yet to come. *See* The best is yet to be.

WORTH

Anything worth doing is worth doing well.

A bird in the hand is worth two in the bush.

If a thing is worth doing, it's worth doing twice.

It's not worth the paper it is written on.

One picture is worth a thousand words.

An ounce of prevention is worth a pound of cure.

A thing worth doing is worth doing well. *See* If a thing is worth doing, it's worth doing twice.

WOUND

Time heals all wounds.

WRATH

A soft answer turns away wrath.

WRITE

It's not worth the paper it is written on.

Nothing to write home about.

WRONG

Fifty million Frenchmen can't be wrong.

If anything can go wrong, it will.

My country, right or wrong. *See* Our country, right or wrong.

Our country, right or wrong.

Two wrongs don't make a right.

YEAR

The first one hundred years are the hardest.

A fool can ask more questions in an hour than a wise man can answer in seven years.

YESTERDAY

I was not born yesterday.

YESTERYEAR

Where are the snows of yesteryear?

YET

The best is yet to be.

YOUNG

Go west, young man.

YOUTH

Youth will be served.

Youth will have its fling.